POLITICAL PHILOSOPHY

D1157470

POLITICAL PHILOSOPHY

~

The Essential Texts

FOURTH EDITION

Edited by

Steven M. Cahn
The City University of New York Graduate Center

New York   Oxford
OXFORD UNIVERSITY PRESS

Oxford University Press is a department of the University of Oxford.
It furthers the University's objective of excellence in research, scholarship,
and education by publishing worldwide. Oxford is a registered trade mark of
Oxford University Press in the UK and certain other countries.

Published in the United States of America by Oxford University Press
198 Madison Avenue, New York, NY 10016, United States of America.

Copyright © 2022, 2015, 2011, 2005 by Oxford University Press

For titles covered by Section 112 of the US Higher Education
Opportunity Act, please visit www.oup.com/us/he for the latest
information about pricing and alternate formats.

All rights reserved. No part of this publication may be reproduced, stored in
a retrieval system, or transmitted, in any form or by any means, without the
prior permission in writing of Oxford University Press, or as expressly permitted
by law, by license, or under terms agreed with the appropriate reproduction
rights organization. Inquiries concerning reproduction outside the scope of the
above should be sent to the Rights Department, Oxford University Press,
at the address above.

You must not circulate this work in any other form
and you must impose this same condition on any acquirer.

Library of Congress Cataloging-in-Publication Data
Names: Cahn, Steven M., editor.
Title: Political philosophy : the essential texts / edited by Steven Cahn.
Other titles: Political philosophy (Cahn)
Description: Fourth edition. | New York : Oxford University Press, 2022. |
  Includes bibliographical references. | Summary: "Political Philosophy:
  The Essential Texts, Fourth Edition, is ideal for survey courses in
  political philosophy. Offering extensive coverage from antiquity to the
  present, this historically organized collection presents the most
  significant works from nearly 2,500 years of political philosophy"—
  Provided by publisher.
Identifiers: LCCN 2021054128 (print) | LCCN 2021054129 (ebook) | ISBN
  9780197609170 | ISBN 9780197609187 (paperback) | ISBN 9780197609200
  (epub)
Subjects: LCSH: Political science—History—Sources. | Political
  science—Philosophy—Textbooks.
Classification: LCC JA71 .P6225 2022 (print) | LCC JA71 (ebook) | DDC
  320.01—dc23
LC record available at https://lccn.loc.gov/2021054128
LC ebook record available at https://lccn.loc.gov/2021054129

Printing number: 9 8 7 6 5 4 3 2 1
Printed by LSC Communications, Inc., United States of America

To my wife,
Marilyn Ross, M.D.

CONTENTS

~

DAVID HUME

ADAM SMITH

MARY WOLLSTONECRAFT

IMMANUEL KANT

EDMUND BURKE

G. W. F. HEGEL

JEREMY BENTHAM

CHARLES TAYLOR

JOHN RAWLS

ROBERT NOZICK

JÜRGEN HABERMAS

MICHEL FOUCAULT

MICHAEL J. SANDEL

VIRGINIA HELD

IRIS MARION YOUNG

*Complete works.

PREFACE

Political philosophy explores the nature and justification of government. The inquiry considers the strengths and weaknesses of different forms of polity, the relationship between the individual and the social order, and such ideals as rights, justice, liberty, equality, and community.

Those who embark on the study of the field soon become aware that a small number of historical and contemporary texts are widely regarded as central to the inquiry. This volume brings together in convenient form as many as feasible of these crucial works, either complete or in substantial excerpts. Unlike other collections in political philosophy that focus exclusively on either the history of the discipline or recent contributions to it, this reader contains both. Also unlike other anthologies, this collection includes significant materials concerning the growth of American democracy.

NEW TO THE FOURTH EDITION

- Readings have been added from Mary Wollstonecraft, W. E. B. Du Bois, Susan Moller Okin, Elizabeth S. Anderson, Gillian Brock, Sarah Song, Frederick Douglass, and Elizabeth Cady Stanton.
- Re-edited selections include Plato's *Republic*, Aristotle's *Politics*, Machiavelli's *The Prince* and *Discourses*, Hobbes's *Leviathan*, Locke's *Second Treatise*, Montesquieu's *The Spirit of the Laws*, Rousseau's *Discourse on the Origin of Equality* and *Of the Social Contract*, Adam Smith's *The Wealth of Nations*, *The Federalist Papers*, and John Stuart Mill's *On Liberty* and *The Subjection of Women*.
- Martha Nussbaum's essay "The Feminist Critique of Liberalism" has been replaced by her more recent essay "Capabilities and Social Justice."
- New introductions have been provided by Virginia Sapiro (Boston University) for Mary Wollstonecraft; Derrick Darby (Rutgers University) for W. E. B. Du Bois; Eva Feder Kittay (State University of New York at Stony Brook) for Martha Nussbaum; Rekha Nath (University of Alabama) for Elizabeth S. Anderson; Debra Satz (Stanford University) for Susan Moller Okin; Nicole Hassoun (State University of New York at Binghamton) for Gillian Brock; and Shelley Wilcox (San Francisco State University) for Sarah Song.

Acknowledgments

I am grateful to my editor, Andrew Blitzer, for his continuing support and advice, as well as to editorial assistants Rachel Boland and Lacey Harvey for their generous help, to project editor Marianne Paul for her conscientiousness, and to others on the staff of Oxford University Press for assistance throughout production.

I also appreciate suggestions from reviewers chosen by the Press: Abigail Aguilar (University of Nevada at Las Vegas), Carrie-Ann Biondi (Marymount Manhattan College), Chris Burdett (Virginia Commonwealth University), Harvey Cormier (Stony Brook University), Adam Cureton (University of Tennessee at Knoxville), Justin De-Plato (University of North Florida), David Estlund (Brown University), Brent Gilchrist (Brigham Young University), Loren Goldman (University of Pennsylvania), Jacob Held (University of Central Arkansas), Eric Manchester (Caldwell College), Joshua Miller (University of North Carolina at Charlotte), Zachary Simpson (University of Science and Arts of Oklahoma), James Skidmore (Idaho State University), James Sorens (State University of New York at Buffalo), Ernesto Verdeja (University of Notre Dame), and Matthew Weidenfeld (Elon University).

I relied often on the advice of my friend and thrice coeditor, Professor Robert B. Talisse, chair of the Department of Philosophy at Vanderbilt University. Our books *Political Philosophy in the Twenty-First Century*, containing the most recent influential work in political philosophy, and *Political Problems*, offering defenses of opposed positions regarding today's most controversial political issues, can be used to supplement this volume.

I owe special thanks to those who provided introductions: Cheshire Calhoun (Arizona State University), Thomas Christiano (University of Arizona), Joshua Cohen (Stanford University), Ann E. Cudd (University of Pittsburgh), Derrick Darby (Rutgers University), Charles L. Griswold Jr. (Boston University), Paul Guyer (Brown University), the late Jean Hampton, Nicole Hassoun (State University of New York at Binghamton), Mark Hulliung (Brandeis University), Eva Feder Kittay (State University of New York at Stony Brook), Richard Kraut (Northwestern University), Arthur Kuflik (University of Vermont), Michael McCarthy (Vassar College), Thomas A. McCarthy (Northwestern University), Richard Miller (Cornell University), Rehka Nath (University of Alabama), Virginia Sapiro (Boston University), Debra Satz (Stanford University), Richard Schacht (University of Illinois at Urbana-Champaign), Tommie Shelby (Harvard University), A. John Simmons (University of Virginia), Steven B. Smith (Yale University), Robert B. Talisse (Vanderbilt University), Jeremy Waldron (New York University), Paul J. Weithman (University of Notre Dame), Shelley Wilcox (San Francisco State University), and the late Burleigh T. Wilkins.

The list of contributors is a reminder that this work is a product of the learning and generosity of the community of scholars.

PLATO

~

INTRODUCTION

RICHARD KRAUT

Plato (427–347 BCE) was born into an aristocratic and wealthy Athenian family, and during his early years he experienced the intellectual and political ferment of his time and place. Many of the plays of Sophocles, Euripides, and Aristophanes were written during the last quarter of the fifth century, and the moral and political conflicts they dramatized for their fellow Athenians became Plato's problems as well. Plato's youth also roughly coincided with the Peloponnesian War (431–404), which ended in the defeat of democratic Athens at the hands of Sparta. At the close of the war, Sparta installed in Athens a government of thirty rulers (called "Thirty Tyrants" by later generations), who were selected for their antidemocratic sympathies. One of the most ruthless among them, Critias, was the cousin of Plato's mother; another, Charmides, was her brother. Both appear as interlocutors in some of Plato's dialogues.

Like many young people of his time, Plato fell under the spell of Socrates (469–399), an Athenian philosopher whose way of life is vividly preserved in Plato's *Apology*. Socrates wrote nothing and professed ignorance, but his suspicion that no one possesses moral knowledge, and his conviction that we must spend our lives searching for it, inspired many of his followers, Plato among them, to abandon their worldly ambitions and to live a philosophical life.

The Thirty who had been installed by Sparta were overthrown and democracy was restored in 403; but a few years later, in 399, Socrates was brought to trial and found guilty of not believing in the city's gods, of introducing new gods, and of corrupting the young. Some scholars believe that the prosecution of Socrates was motivated partly by the perception that he was a danger to the restored democracy. It is noteworthy that Plato's account of the speech Socrates gave in his own defense, the *Apology* (*apologia* means "defense"), contains both antipopulist elements (31–32) and a reminder that Socrates disobeyed the Thirty (32). Evidently, he could not easily be classified as a democrat or an antidemocrat. Similarly, in the *Crito*, Socrates is described as a man so satisfied with the Athenian legal system that he has hardly left the city's walls (52–53), and yet he insists that one should follow the commands of an expert and pay no attention to the opinions of the many (47). But were not the laws of democratic Athens an expression of the opinion of the many? Socrates does not explain the basis for his high regard for Athenian law.

Still more perplexing is an apparent inconsistency between the willingness Socrates expresses in the *Apology* to engage in various forms of disobedience and the arguments he accepts in the *Crito* for obeying one's city and its laws. He tells the jury that he will

1

obey the god who has commanded him to philosophize rather than any orders they give him (29), and yet in the *Crito* he refuses to escape from jail because he accepts the idea, proposed by the personified Laws of Athens, that he is subordinate to Athens as a child is to a parent or a slave to a master (50–51). If Socrates is willing to disobey his jurors, then why is he not equally willing to disregard their decision that he is to be punished by death?

It is unlikely that Plato means to portray Socrates as a muddled thinker. On the contrary, the impression he means to create is that Socrates is a man of penetrating insight and great argumentative skill. The apparent difficulties in Socrates's ideas are the devices Plato uses to provoke his readers into philosophical reflection. Just as his conversations with Socrates led him to philosophy, so he uses Socrates in his works to produce the same effect in us. Plato's dialogues create a sense of unfinished business: lines of thought are disrupted, and gaps in the argument remain unfilled. It is often difficult to know what Plato intends, because he never speaks in his own voice. He uses dramatic characters and portrays a clash of views because he regards the written word as a stimulus to philosophical insight rather than as the embodiment of wisdom.

We are told by ancient sources that after the death of Socrates in 399, Plato left Athens and spent time in Sicily, North Africa, and Egypt. Several of the thinkers he visited were associated with the Pythagorean school—a group of philosophers (named after the school's sixth-century founder, Pythagoras) who held that the human soul is reborn into other human and animal bodies after death. They were also intensely interested in the mathematical relationships (for example, in musical scales) that underlie many physical phenomena. As Plato moved beyond such early works as the *Apology* and *Crito*, both of these Pythagorean ideas—the transformation of the soul in its many lives and the mathematical nature of reality—came to the fore in his writings. When he returned to Athens in 387, he established a school (called the "Academy," after the grove beyond the city walls that was sacred to the hero Academos) devoted to the study of philosophical and scientific problems. Ancient writers describe two further visits of Plato to Sicily, in 367 and 361, undertaken to influence the course of Syracusan politics, both ending in failure. He remained the head of the Academy until his death in 347.

Although Socrates insists in the *Apology* that we cannot know what comes after death, in the *Phaedo* (a dialogue in which he holds his final conversation, before drinking a poison and dying) he presents a series of arguments for the immortality of the soul. One of the most striking components of this dialogue and others that were written during this period is their affirmation of the existence of a new kind of objective reality, which Socrates calls a "form" or "idea." (Capital letters—"Form," "Idea"—are sometimes used to name these objects, although this is not Plato's practice.) For example, the form of equality (Plato is thinking of the mathematical relationship) is not something that can be observed by the senses, but it exists nonetheless. It is an eternal and changeless object that can be known only by means of reason. The equal objects we observe are in some way defective copies of the perfect form; they are called equal because they somehow share in or participate in the form of equality. Plato does not attempt to give a complete list of the forms, but he believes that many of the words we use in mathematics ("triangle," "line," "two") and in evaluative discourse ("justice," "beauty," "good") are really names of these abstract objects. Whenever we speak, we are referring to forms, though most people assume that they are merely talking about a visible and perishable world. They are, Plato thinks, living in a dream world: they fail to realize that what they observe is a mere appearance and that a greater reality—the world of the forms—stands behind the appearances.

In *The Republic* (composed after the *Apology*, *Crito*, and *Phaedo*), Plato pursues a question that lies at the heart of Socrates's life and death. Although Socrates was a man of the highest moral integrity, he was thought to be so dangerous to his community that the majority of a jury of 501 fellow citizens condemned him to die. Since just action sometimes leads to death, since it can lie hidden from others and even be misinterpreted as injustice, does that not cast the most serious doubt on its value? Plato's guiding assumption, which he inherits from Socrates, is that no progress can be made in answering this question until we come to a fuller understanding of what justice is. (The Greek word is *dikaiosune*; in some contexts, its meaning is broader than that of our "justice" and encompasses any kind of right treatment of others.) Book I of *The Republic* portrays a series of unsuccessful attempts to define justice. Socrates here plays the role of someone who lacks knowledge and whose mission it is to reveal to others that they are equally ignorant. Although Thrasymachus, the most formidable interlocutor Socrates faces, is eventually defeated in argument, he plays a crucial role in the dialogue: any attempt to vindicate the life of a just person must address itself to the cynicism and immorality that Thrasymachus represents. Plato seems to be saying, in effect, that there is a Thrasymachus in all of us and that we can exorcise him only by means of a philosophical inquiry as wide-ranging as *The Republic*.

Starting with Book II, Socrates sheds his role as an ignorant inquirer who merely poses problems for others. For the remainder of the dialogue, he becomes a systematic philosopher who puts forward a grand theory about the nature of human beings, the ideal state, the soul, mathematics, knowledge, and the highest realities. His main interlocutors (Glaucon and Adeimantus, Plato's brothers) occasionally interact with him, but they play a role far different from the ones assigned to Cephalus, Polemarchus, and Thrasymachus in Book I. The strategy pursued throughout the remainder of *The Republic* is to exploit the fact that it is not merely individuals who can be characterized as just or unjust. We also use these terms to praise or discredit certain forms of government. Perhaps, then, we can grasp the nature of justice by asking what leads to the existence of a political community and what the justice of such a community consists in. This attempt to construe political and individual justice as the same property eventually leads to the proposal that justice consists in each part of a thing doing its own activity. In a just city or state, each position is filled by a person who is qualified to contribute to the good of the whole community. Similarly, in a just human being, each part of the soul operates in a way that best serves the whole human being.

By the end of Book IV, Socrates seems to be on the verge of completing his demonstration of the great value of justice—but, in a sense, his argument has only begun. The institutions of the ideal city—particularly abolition of the traditional family among rulers and eugenic sharing of sexual partners—have not yet been fully discussed. Plato's aim is to foster the greatest possible unity in the city, and he is willing to go to the greatest lengths to guarantee that his citizens owe their strongest allegiance to each other, rather than to blood relatives. But the topic that looms largest in Books V, VI, and VII is the proposal that the best political community is one that gives complete authority to rigorously trained and morally flawless philosophers. Strictly speaking, the only real philosophers are those whose understanding of value is based on their study of the forms, and in particular the form of the "good." Socrates refrains from saying how good is to be defined, and in this sense the entire project of *The Republic* is radically incomplete. But he seems to be suggesting that goodness has a mathematical nature: that is why it is so important that philosophers first be trained as mathematicians before they undertake the study of the highest form.

The dialogue reaches its culminating point with its depiction of the philosopher, for he or she is the human being of perfect justice. The search for the value of "justice" has led to the conclusion that this virtue is most fully present in those who understand the nature of the highest realities. Justice is the greatest good because the best sort of life is one in which the structure of one's soul is guided by one's love and understanding of the most valuable and real objects there are—the forms. Books VIII and IX round out Plato's argument by portraying the diseased political structures and fragmented psychologies that arise when worldly values—the love of honor, domination, wealth, and sexual pleasure—take priority over all others. In Book X, the peripheral and external rewards of justice, having been dismissed in Book II, are allowed to return and provide the finishing touches on Socrates's portrait of justice. Since the soul (or at least the rational part of it) does not perish, the good of justice does not come to an end when the body perishes. By postponing the question of posthumous existence to the end of *The Republic*, Socrates leads us to see that a life of justice would be worth living even if there were no afterlife.

Essays on many aspects of Plato's thought can be found in Richard Kraut, *The Cambridge Companion to Plato* (Cambridge: Cambridge University Press, 1992), and in Gail Fine's two volumes, *Plato 1* and *Plato 2* (Oxford: Oxford University Press, 1999). Full discussions of the *Apology* are provided by Thomas C. Brickhouse and Nicholas D. Smith, *Socrates on Trial* (Princeton, N.J.: Princeton University Press, 1989), and C. D. C. Reeve, *Socrates in the Apology* (Indianapolis: Hackett, 1989). Detailed analysis of the *Crito* is presented by Richard Kraut, *Socrates and the State* (Princeton, N.J.: Princeton University Press, 1989), and Roslyn Weiss, *Socrates Dissatisfied* (New York: Oxford University Press, 1998). For studies of *The Republic*, see Julia Annas, *An Introduction to Plato's Republic* (Oxford: Clarendon Press, 1981), Nicholas P. White, *A Companion to Plato's Republic* (Indianapolis: Hackett, 1979), C. D. C. Reeve, *Philosopher-Kings* (Princeton, N.J.: Princeton University Press, 1988), and Richard Kraut, *Plato's Republic: Critical Essays* (Lanham, Md.: Rowman & Littlefield, 1997). *The Cambridge History of Greek and Roman Political Thought*, edited by Christopher Rowe and Malcolm Schofield, in association with Simon Harrison and Melissa Lane (Cambridge: Cambridge University Press, 2000), contains seven chapters on Plato's politics.

Defence of Socrates

17a I don't know how you, fellow Athenians, have been affected by my accusers, but for my part I felt myself almost transported by them, so persuasively did they speak. And yet hardly a word they have said is true. Among their many falsehoods, one especially astonished me: their warning that you

b must be careful not to be taken in by me, because I am a clever speaker. It seemed to me the height of impudence on their part not to be embarrassed at being refuted straight away by the facts; once it became apparent that I was not a clever speaker at all—unless indeed they call a "clever" speaker one who speaks the truth. If that is what they mean, then I would admit to being an orator, although not on a par with them.

As I said, then, my accusers have said little or nothing true; whereas from me you shall hear the whole truth, though not, I assure

c you, fellow Athenians, in language adorned with fine words and phrases or dressed up, as theirs was: you shall hear my points made spontaneously in whatever words occur to me—persuaded as I am that my case is just. None of you should expect anything to be put differently, because it would not, of course, be at all fitting at my age, gentlemen, to come before you with artificial speeches, such as might be composed by a young lad.

One thing, moreover, I would earnestly beg of you, fellow Athenians. If you hear me defending myself with the same arguments I normally use at the bankers' tables in the market-place (where many of you have heard me) and elsewhere, please do not

d be surprised or protest on that account. You see, here is the reason: this is the first time I have ever appeared before a court of law, although I am over 70; so I am literally a stranger to the diction of this place. And if I really were a foreigner, you would naturally excuse me, were I to speak in the dialect and style in which I had been brought up; so in

18a the present case as well I ask you, in all fairness as I think, to disregard my manner of speaking—it may not be as good, or it may be better—but to consider and attend simply to the question whether or not my case is just; because that is the duty of a judge, as it is an orator's duty to speak the truth.

To begin with, fellow Athenians, it is fair that I should defend myself against the first set of charges falsely brought against me by my first accusers, and then turn to the later charges and the more recent ones. You see,

b I have been accused before you by many people for a long time now, for many years in fact, by people who spoke not a word of truth. It is those people I fear more than Anytus and his crowd, though they too are dangerous. But those others are more so, gentlemen: they have taken hold of most of you since childhood, and made persuasive accusations against me, yet without an ounce more truth in them. They say that there is one Socrates, a "wise man," who ponders what is above the earth and investigates everything beneath it, and turns the weaker argument into the stronger.

c

From *Defence of Socrates, Euthyphro,* and *Crito,* translated by David Gallop. Copyright © 1997 by Oxford University Press. Reprinted by permission of the publisher and translator. The notes and Index of Names are the translator's.

Those accusers who have spread such rumour about me, fellow Athenians, are the dangerous ones, because their audience believes that people who inquire into those matters also fail to acknowledge the gods. Moreover, those accusers are numerous, and have been denouncing me for a long time now, and they also spoke to you at an age at which you would be most likely to believe them, when some of you were children or young lads; and their accusations simply went by default for lack of any defence. But the most absurd thing of all is that one

d cannot even get to know their names or say who they were—except perhaps one who happens to be a comic playwright. The ones who have persuaded you by malicious slander, and also some who persuade others because they have been persuaded themselves, are all very hard to deal with: one cannot put any of them on the stand here in court, or cross-examine anybody, but one must literally engage in a sort of shadow-boxing to defend oneself, and cross-examine without anyone to answer. You too, then, should allow, as I just said, that I have two sets of accusers: one set who have accused me

e recently, and the other of long standing to whom I was just referring. And please grant that I need to defend myself against the latter first, since you too heard them accusing me earlier, and you heard far more from them than from these recent critics here.

Very well, then. I must defend myself,
19a fellow Athenians, and in so short a time must try to dispel the slander which you have had so long to absorb. That is the outcome I would wish for, should it be of any benefit to you and to me, and I should like to succeed in my defence—though I believe the task to be a difficult one, and am well aware of its nature. But let that turn out as God wills: I have to obey the law and present my defence.

Let us examine, from the beginning, the charge that has given rise to the slander against me—which was just what Meletus relied upon when he drew up this indictment. Very well then, what were my slanderers actually saying when they slandered me? Let me read out their deposition, as if they were my legal accusers:

"Socrates is guilty of being a busybody, in that he inquires into what is beneath the earth and in the sky, turns the weaker argument into the stronger, and teaches others to do the same."

The charges would run something like that. Indeed, you can see them for yourselves, enacted in *Aristophanes'* comedy: in that play, a character called "Socrates" swings around, claims to be walking on air, and talks a lot of other nonsense on subjects of which I have no understanding, great or small.

Not that I mean to belittle knowledge of that sort, if anyone really is learned in such matters—no matter how many of Meletus' lawsuits I might have to defend myself against—but the fact is, fellow Athenians, those subjects are not my concern at all. I call most of you to witness yourselves, and I ask you to make that quite clear to one another, if you have ever heard me in discussion (as many of you have). Tell one another, then, whether any of you has ever heard me discussing such subjects, either briefly or at length; and as a result you will realize that the other things said about me by the public are equally baseless.

In any event, there is no truth in those charges. Moreover, if you have heard from anyone that I undertake to educate people and charge fees, there is no truth in that either—though for that matter I do think it also a fine thing if anyone *is* able to educate people, as Gorgias of Leontini, Prodicus of Ceos, and Hippias of Elis profess to. Each of them can visit any city, gentlemen, and

20a persuade its young people, who may associate free of charge with any of their own citizens they wish, to leave those associations, and to join with them instead, paying fees and being grateful into the bargain.

On that topic, there is at present another expert here, a gentleman from Paros; I heard of his visit, because I happened to run into a man who has spent more money on sophists than everyone else put together—Callias, the son of Hipponicus. So I questioned him, since he has two sons himself.

b "Callias," I said, "if your two sons had been born as colts or calves, we could find and engage a tutor who could make them both excel superbly in the required qualities—and he'd be some sort of expert in horse-rearing or agriculture. But seeing that they are actually human, whom do you intend to engage as their tutor? Who has knowledge of the required human and civic qualities? I ask, because I assume you've given thought to the matter, having sons yourself. Is there such a person," I asked, "or not?"

"Certainly," he replied.

"Who is he?" I said; "Where does he come from, and what does he charge for tuition?"

"His name is Evenus, Socrates," he replied; "He comes from Paros, and he charges 5 minas."

c I thought Evenus was to be congratulated, if he really did possess that skill and imparted it for such a modest charge. I, at any rate, would certainly be giving myself fine airs and graces if I possessed that knowledge. But the fact is, fellow Athenians, I do not.

Now perhaps one of you will interject: "Well then, Socrates, what is the difficulty in your case? What is the source of these slanders against you? If you are not engaged in something out of the ordinary, why ever has so much rumour and talk arisen about you? It would surely never have arisen, unless you

d were up to something different from most people. Tell us what it is, then, so that we don't jump to conclusions about you."

That speaker makes a fair point, I think; and so I will try to show you just what it is that has earned me my reputation and notoriety. Please hear me out. Some of you will perhaps think I am joking, but I assure you that I shall be telling you the whole truth.

You see, fellow Athenians, I have gained this reputation on account of nothing but a certain sort of wisdom. And what sort of wisdom is that? It is a human kind of wisdom, perhaps, since it might just be true that I have wisdom of that sort. Maybe the people I just mentioned possess wisdom of a superhuman kind; otherwise I cannot explain it. For my part, I certainly do not possess that knowledge; and whoever says I do is lying and speaking with a view to slandering me—

Now please do not protest, fellow Athenians, even if I should sound to you rather boastful: I am not myself the source of the story I am about to tell you, but I shall refer you to a trustworthy authority. As evidence of my wisdom, if such it actually be, and of its nature, I shall call to witness before you the god at Delphi.

21a You remember Chaerephon, of course. He was a friend of mine from youth, and also a comrade in your party, who shared your recent exile and restoration. You recall too what sort of man Chaerephon was, how impetuous he was in any undertaking. Well, on one occasion he actually went to the Delphic oracle, and had the audacity to put the following question to it—as I said, please do not make a disturbance, gentlemen—he went and asked if there was anyone wiser than myself; to which the Pythia responded that there was no one. His brother here will testify to the court about that story, since Chaerephon himself is deceased.

Now keep in mind why I have been telling you this: it is because I am going to explain to you the origin of the slander against me. When I heard the story, I thought to myself: "What ever is the god saying? What can his riddle mean? Since I am all too conscious of not being wise in any matter, great or small, what ever can he mean by pronouncing me to be the wisest? Surely he cannot be lying: for him that would be out of the question."

So for a long time I was perplexed about what he could possibly mean. But then, with great reluctance, I proceeded to investigate the matter somewhat as follows. I went to one of the people who had a reputation for wisdom, thinking there, if anywhere, to disprove the oracle's utterance and declare to it: "Here is someone wiser than I am, and yet you said that I was the wisest."

So I interviewed this person—I need not mention his name, but he was someone in public life; and when I examined him, my experience went something like this, fellow Athenians: in conversing with him, I formed the opinion that, although the man was thought to be wise by many other people, and especially by himself, yet in reality he was not. So I then tried to show him that he thought himself wise without being so. I thereby earned his dislike, and that of many people present; but still, as I went away, I thought to myself: "I am wiser than that fellow, anyhow. Because neither of us, I dare say, knows anything of great value; but he thinks he knows a thing when he doesn't; whereas I neither know it in fact, nor think that I do. At any rate, it appears that I am wiser than he in just this one small respect: if I do not know something, I do not think that I do."

Next, I went to someone else, among people thought to be even wiser than the previous man, and I came to the same conclusion again; and so I was disliked by that man too, as well as by many others.

Well, after that I went on to visit one person after another. I realized, with dismay and alarm, that I was making enemies; but even so, I thought it my duty to attach the highest importance to the god's business; and therefore, in seeking the oracle's meaning, I had to go on to examine all those with any reputation for knowledge. And upon my word, fellow Athenians—because I am obliged to speak the truth before the court—I truly did experience something like this: as I pursued the god's inquiry, I found those held in the highest esteem were practically the most defective, whereas men who were supposed to be their inferiors were much better off in respect of understanding.

Let me, then, outline my wanderings for you, the various "labours" I kept undertaking, only to find that the oracle proved completely irrefutable. After I had done with the politicians, I turned to the poets—including tragedians, dithyrambic poets, and the rest—thinking that in their company I would be shown up as more ignorant than they were. So I picked up the poems over which I thought they had taken the most trouble, and questioned them about their meaning, so that I might also learn something from them in the process.

Now I'm embarrassed to tell you the truth, gentlemen, but it has to be said. Practically everyone else present could speak better than the poets themselves about their very own compositions. And so, once more, I soon realized this truth about them too: it was not from wisdom that they composed their works, but from a certain natural aptitude and inspiration, like that of seers and soothsayers—because those people too utter many fine words, yet know nothing of the matters on which they pronounce. It was obvious to me that the poets were in much the same situation; yet at the same time I realized that because of their compositions they thought themselves the wisest people in other matters as well, when they were not. So I left, believing that I was ahead of them in the same way as I was ahead of the politicians.

Then, finally, I went to the craftsmen, because I was conscious of knowing almost nothing myself, but felt sure that amongst them, at least, I would find much valuable knowledge. And in that expectation I was not disappointed: they did have knowledge in fields where I had none, and in that respect they were wiser than I. And yet, fellow Athenians, those able craftsmen seemed to me to suffer from the same failing as the poets: because of their excellence at their own trade, each claimed to be a great expert also on matters of the utmost importance; and this arrogance of theirs seemed to eclipse their wisdom. So I began to ask myself, on the oracle's behalf, whether I should prefer to be as I am, neither wise as they are wise, nor ignorant as they are ignorant, or to possess both their attributes; and in reply, I told myself and the oracle that I was better off as I was.

The effect of this questioning, fellow Athenians, was to earn me much hostility of a very vexing and trying sort, which has given rise to numerous slanders, including this reputation I have for being "wise"' because those present on each occasion imagine me to be wise regarding the matters on which I examine others. But in fact, gentlemen, it would appear that it is only the god who is truly wise; and that he is saying to us, through this oracle, that human wisdom is worth little or nothing. It seems that when he says "Socrates," he makes use of my name, merely taking me as an example—as if to say, "The wisest amongst you, human beings, is anyone like Socrates who has recognized that with respect to wisdom he is truly worthless."

That is why, even to this day, I still go about seeking out and searching into anyone I believe to be wise, citizen or foreigner, in obedience to the god. Then, as soon as I find that someone is not wise, I assist the god by proving that he is not. Because of this occupation, I have had no time at all for any activity to speak of, either in public affairs or in my family life; indeed, because of my service to the god, I live in extreme poverty.

In addition, the young people who follow me around of their own accord, the ones who have plenty of leisure because their parents are wealthiest, enjoy listening to people being cross-examined. Often, too, they copy my example themselves, and so attempt to cross-examine others. And I imagine that they find a great abundance of people who suppose themselves to possess some knowledge, but really know little or nothing. Consequently, the people they question are angry with me, though not with themselves, and say that there is a nasty pestilence abroad called "Socrates," who is corrupting the young.

Then, when asked just what he is doing or teaching, they have nothing to say, because they have no idea what he does; yet, rather than seem at a loss, they resort to the stock charges against all who pursue intellectual inquiry, trotting out "things in the sky and beneath the earth," "failing to acknowledge the gods," and "turning the weaker argument into the stronger." They would, I imagine, be loath to admit the truth, which is that their pretensions to knowledge have been exposed, and they are totally ignorant. So because these people have reputations to protect, I suppose, and are also both passionate and numerous, and have been speaking about me in a vigorous and persuasive style, they have long been filling your ears with vicious slander. It is on the strength of all this that Meletus, along with Anytus and Lycon, has proceeded against me: Meletus is aggrieved for the poets, Anytus for the craftsmen and politicians, and Lycon for the orators. And so, as I began by saying, I should be surprised if I could rid your minds of this slander in so short a time, when so much of it has accumulated.

There is the truth for you, fellow Athenians. I have spoken it without concealing anything from you, major or minor, and without glossing over anything. And yet I am virtually certain that it is my very candour that makes enemies for me—which goes to show that I am right: the slander against me is to that effect, and such is its

b explanation. And whether you look for one now or later, that is what you will find.

So much for my defence before you against the charges brought by my first group of accusers. Next, I shall try to defend myself against Meletus, good patriot that he claims to be, and against my more recent critics. So once again, as if they were a fresh set of accusers, let me in turn review their deposition. It runs something like this:

"Socrates is guilty of corrupting the young, and of failing to acknowledge the

c gods acknowledged by the city, but introducing new spiritual beings instead."

Such is the charge: let us examine each item within it.

Meletus says, then, that I am guilty of corrupting the young. Well I reply, fellow Athenians, that Meletus is guilty of trifling in a serious matter, in that he brings people to trial on frivolous grounds, and professes grave concern about matters for which he has never cared at all. I shall now try to prove to you too that that is so.

Step forward, Meletus, and answer me.

d It is your chief concern, is it not, that our younger people shall be as good as possible?
—It is.

Very well, will you please tell the judges who influences them for the better—because you must obviously know, seeing that you care? Having discovered me, as you allege, to be the one who is corrupting them, you bring me before the judges here and accuse me. So speak up, and tell the court who has an improving influence.

You see, Meletus, you remain silent, and have no answer. Yet doesn't that strike you as shameful, and as proof in itself of exactly what I say—that you have never cared about these matters at all? Come then, good fellow, tell us who influences them for the better.
—The laws.

Yes, but that is not what I'm asking, ex-   e
cellent fellow. I mean, which *person*, who already knows the laws to begin with?
—These gentlemen, the judges, Socrates.

What are you saying, Meletus? Can these people educate the young, and do they have an improving influence?
—Most certainly.

All of them, or some but not others?
—All of them.

My goodness, what welcome news, and what a generous supply of benefactors you speak of! And how about the audience here in court? Do they too have an improving influence, or not?   25a
—Yes, they do too.

And how about members of the Council?
—Yes, the Councillors too.

But in that case, how about people in the Assembly, its individual members, Meletus? They won't be corrupting their youngers, will they? Won't they all be good influences as well?
—Yes, they will too.

So every person in Athens, it would appear, has an excellent influence on them except for me, whereas I alone am corrupting them. Is that what you're saying?
—That is emphatically what I'm saying.

Then I find myself, if we are to believe you, in a most awkward predicament. Now answer me this. Do you think the same is true of horses? Is it everybody who improves   b
them, while a single person spoils them? Or isn't the opposite true: a single person, or at least very few people, namely the horse-trainers, can improve them; while lay people spoil them, don't they, if they have to do

with horses and make use of them? Isn't that true of horses as of all other animals, Meletus? Of course it is, whether you and Anytus deny it or not. In fact, I dare say our young people are extremely lucky if only c one person is corrupting them, while everyone else is doing them good.

All right, Meletus. Enough has been said to prove that you never were concerned about the young. You betray your irresponsibility plainly, because you have not cared at all about the charges on which you bring me before this court.

Furthermore, Meletus, tell us, in God's name, whether it is better to live among good fellow citizens or bad ones. Come sir, answer: I am not asking a hard question. Bad people have a harmful impact upon their closest companions at any given time, don't they, whereas good people have a good one?

—Yes.

d   Well, is there anyone who wants to be harmed by his companions rather than benefited?—Be a good fellow and keep on answering, as the law requires you to. Is there anyone who wants to be harmed?

—Of course not.

Now tell me this. In bringing me here, do you claim that I am corrupting and depraving the young intentionally or unintentionally?

—Intentionally, so I maintain.

Really, Meletus? Are you so much smarter at your age than I at mine as to realize that the bad have a harmful impact upon e   their closest companions at any given time, whereas the good have a beneficial effect? Am I, by contrast, so far gone in my stupidity as not to realize that if I make one of my companions vicious, I risk incurring harm at his hands? And am I, therefore, as you allege, doing so much damage intentionally?

That I cannot accept from you, Meletus, and neither could anyone else, I imagine.

Either I am not corrupting them—or if I 26a am, I am doing so unintentionally; so either way your charge is false. But if I am corrupting them unintentionally, the law does not require me to be brought to court for such mistakes, but rather to be taken aside for private instruction and admonition—since I shall obviously stop doing unintentional damage, if I learn better. But you avoided association with me and were unwilling to instruct me. Instead you bring me to court, where the law requires you to bring people who need punishment rather than enlightenment.

Very well, fellow Athenians. That part of my case is now proven: Meletus never cared   b about these matters, either a lot or a little. Nevertheless, Meletus, please tell us in what way you claim that I am corrupting our younger people. That is quite obvious, isn't it, from the indictment you drew up? It is by teaching them not to acknowledge the gods acknowledged by the city, but to accept new spiritual beings instead? You mean, don't you, that I am corrupting them by teaching them that?

—I most emphatically do.

Then, Meletus, in the name of those very gods we are now discussing, please clarify the matter further for me, and for the jury here. You see, I cannot make out   c what you mean. Is it that I am teaching people to acknowledge that some gods exist—in which case it follows that I do acknowledge their existence myself as well, and am not a complete atheist, hence am not guilty on that count—and yet that those gods are not the ones acknowledged by the city, but different ones? Is that your charge against me—namely, that they are different? Or are you saying that I acknowledge no gods at all myself, and teach the same to others?

—I am saying the latter: you acknowledge no gods at all.

d What ever makes you say that, Meletus, you strange fellow? Do I not even acknowledge, then, with the rest of mankind, that the sun and the moon are gods?

—By God, he does not, members of the jury, since he claims that the sun is made of rock, and the moon of earth!

My dear Meletus, do you imagine that it is Anaxagoras you are accusing? Do you have such contempt for the jury, and imagine them so illiterate as not to know that books by Anaxagoras of Clazomenae are crammed with such assertions? What's more, are the young learning those things
e from me when they can acquire them at the bookstalls, now and then, for a drachma at most, and so ridicule Socrates if he claims those ideas for his own, especially when they are so bizarre? In God's name, do you really think me as crazy as that? Do I acknowledge the existence of no god at all?

—By God no, none whatever.

I can't believe you, Meletus—nor, I think, can you believe yourself. To my mind, fellow Athenians, this fellow is an impudent scoundrel who has framed this indictment out of
27a sheer wanton impudence and insolence. He seems to have devised a sort of riddle in order to try me out: "Will Socrates the Wise tumble to my nice self-contradiction? Or shall I fool him along with my other listeners?" You see, he seems to me to be contradicting himself in the indictment. It's as if he were saying: "Socrates is guilty of not acknowledging gods, but of acknowledging gods"; and yet that is sheer tomfoolery.

I ask you to examine with me, gentlemen, just how that appears to be his mean-
b ing. Answer for us, Meletus; and the rest of you, please remember my initial request not to protest if I conduct the argument in my usual manner.

Is there anyone in the world, Meletus, who acknowledges that human phenomena exist, yet does not acknowledge human beings?—Require him to answer, gentlemen, and not to raise all kinds of confused objections. Is there anyone who does not acknowledge horses, yet does acknowledge equestrian phenomena? Or who does not acknowledge that musicians exist, yet does acknowledge musical phenomena?

There is no one, excellent fellow: if you don't wish to answer, I must answer for you, and for the jurors here. But at least   c
answer my next question yourself. Is there anyone who acknowledges that spiritual phenomena exist, yet does not acknowledge spirits?

—No.

How good of you to answer—albeit reluctantly and under compulsion from the jury. Well now, you say that I acknowledge spiritual beings and teach others to do so. Whether they actually be new or old is no matter: I do at any rate, by your account, acknowledge spiritual beings, which you have also mentioned in your sworn deposition. But if I acknowledge spiritual beings, then surely it follows quite inevitably that I must acknowledge spirits. Is that not so?—Yes, it is so: I assume your agreement, since you   d
don't answer. But we regard spirits, don't we, as either gods or children of gods? Yes or no?

—Yes.

Then given that I do believe in spirits, as you say, if spirits are gods of some sort, this is precisely what I claim when I say that you are presenting us with a riddle and making fun of us: you are saying that I do not believe in gods, and yet again that I do believe in gods, seeing that I believe in spirits.

On the other hand, if spirits are children of gods, some sort of bastard offspring from nymphs—or from whomever they are traditionally said, in each case, to be born—then who in the world could ever believe that there were children of gods, yet no gods? That would be just as absurd as accepting the existence of children of horses and asses—namely, mules—yet rejecting the existence of horses or asses!

In short, Meletus, you can only have drafted this either by way of trying us out, or because you were at a loss how to charge me with a genuine offence. How could you possibly persuade anyone with even the slightest intelligence that someone who accepts spiritual beings does not also accept 28a divine ones, and again that the same person also accepts neither spirits nor gods nor heroes? There is no conceivable way.

But enough, fellow Athenians. It needs no long defence, I think, to show that I am not guilty of the charges in Meletus' indictment; the foregoing will suffice. You may be sure, though, that what I was saying earlier is true: I have earned great hostility among many people. And that is what will convict me, if I am convicted: not Meletus or Anytus, but the slander and malice of the b crowd. They have certainly convicted many other good men as well, and I imagine they will do so again; there is no risk of their stopping with me.

Now someone may perhaps say: "Well then, are you not ashamed, Socrates, to have pursued a way of life which has now put you at risk of death?"

But it may be fair for me to answer him as follows: 'You are sadly mistaken, fellow, if you suppose that a man with even a grain of self-respect should reckon up the risks of living or dying, rather than simply consider, whenever he does something, whether c his actions are just or unjust, the deeds of a good man or a bad one. By your principles, presumably, all those demigods who died in the plain of Troy were inferior creatures— yes, even the son of Thetis, who showed so much scorn for danger, when the alternative was to endure dishonour. Thus, when he was eager to slay Hector, his mother, goddess

that she was, spoke to him—something like e this, I fancy:

> My child, if thou dost avenge the murder of
>   thy friend, Patroclus,
> And dost slay Hector, then straightway [so
>   runs the poem]
> Shalt thou die thyself, since doom is pre-
>   pared for thee
> Next after Hector's.

But though he heard that, he made light of death and danger, since he feared far d more to live as a base man, and to fail to avenge his dear ones. The poem goes on:

> Then straightway let me die, once I have
>   given the wrongdoer
> His deserts, lest I remain here by the beak-
>   prowed ships,
> An object of derision, and a burden upon the
>   earth.

Can you suppose that he gave any thought to death or danger?

You see, here is the truth of the matter, fellow Athenians. Wherever a man has taken up a position because he considers it best, or has been posted there by his commander, that is where I believe he should remain, steadfast in danger, taking no account at all of death or of anything else rather than dishonour. I would therefore have been acting e absurdly, fellow Athenians, if when assigned to a post at Potidaea, Amphipolis, or Delium by the superiors you had elected to command me, I remained where I was posted on those occasions at the risk of death, if ever any man did—whereas now that the god assigns me, as I became completely convinced, to the duty of leading the philosophical life 29a by examining myself and others, I desert that post from fear of death or anything else. Yes, that would be unthinkable; and then I truly should deserve to be brought to court for failing to acknowledge the gods' existence, in that I was disobedient to the oracle, was afraid of death, and thought I was wise when I was not.

After all, gentlemen, the fear of death amounts simply to thinking one is wise when one is not: it is thinking one knows something one does not know. No one knows, you see, whether death may not in fact prove the greatest of all blessings for mankind; but people fear it as if they knew it for certain to be the greatest of evils. And yet to think that one knows what one does not know must surely be the kind of folly which is reprehensible.

On this matter especially, gentlemen, that may be the nature of my own advantage over most people. If I really were to claim to be wiser than anyone in any respect, it would consist simply in this: just as I do not possess adequate knowledge of life in Hades, so I also realize that I do not possess it; whereas acting unjustly in disobedience to one's betters, whether god or human being, is something I *know* to be evil and shameful. Hence I shall never fear or flee from something which may indeed be a good for all I know, rather than from things I know to be evils.

Suppose, therefore, that you pay no heed to Anytus, but are prepared to let me go. He said I need never have been brought to court in the first place, but that once I had been, your only option was to put me to death. He declared before you that, if I got away from you this time, your sons would all be utterly corrupted by practising Socrates' teachings. Suppose, in the face of that, you were to say to me:

"Socrates, we will not listen to Anytus this time. We are prepared to let you go— but only on this condition: you are to pursue that quest of yours and practise philosophy no longer; and if you are caught doing it any more, you shall be put to death."

Well, as I just said, if you were prepared to let me go on those terms, I should reply to you as follows:

'I have the greatest fondness and affection for you, fellow Athenians, but I will obey my god rather than you; and so long as I draw breath and am able, I shall never give up practising philosophy, or exhorting and showing the way to any of you whom I ever encounter, by giving my usual sort of message. "Excellent friend," I shall say; "You are an Athenian. Your city is the most important and renowned for its wisdom and power; so are you not ashamed that, while you take care to acquire as much wealth as possible, with honour and glory as well, yet you take no care or thought for understanding or truth, or for the best possible state of your soul?"

"And should any of you dispute that, and claim that he does take such care, I will not let him go straight away nor leave him, but I will question and examine and put him to the test; and if I do not think he has acquired goodness, though he says he has, I shall say, 'Shame on you, for setting the lowest value upon the most precious things, and for rating inferior ones more highly!' That I shall do for anyone I encounter, young or old, alien or fellow citizen; but all the more for the latter, since your kinship with me is closer."

Those are my orders from my god, I do assure you. Indeed, I believe that no greater good has ever befallen you in our city than my service to my god; because all I do is to go about, persuading you, young and old alike, not to care for your bodies or for your wealth so intensely as for the greatest possible well-being of your souls. "It is not wealth," I tell you, "that produces goodness; rather, it is from goodness that wealth, and all other benefits for human beings, accrue to them in their private and public life."

If, in fact, I am corrupting the young by those assertions, you may call them harmful. But if anyone claims that I say anything different, he is talking nonsense. In the face of that I should like to say: "Fellow Athenians, you may listen to Anytus or not, as you please; and you may let me go or not, as

c   you please, because there is no chance of my acting otherwise, even if I have to die many times over—"

Stop protesting, fellow Athenians! Please abide by my request that you not protest against what I say, but hear me out; in fact, it will be in your interest, so I believe, to do so. You see, I am going to say some further things to you which may make you shout out—although I beg you not to.

You may be assured that if you put to death the sort of man I just said I was, you will not harm me more than you harm yourselves. Meletus or Anytus would not harm

d   me at all; nor, in fact, could they do so, since I believe it is out of the question for a better man to be harmed by his inferior. The latter may, of course, inflict death or banishment or disenfranchisement; and my accuser here, along with others no doubt, believes those to be great evils. But I do not. Rather, I believe it a far greater evil to try to kill a man unjustly, as he does now.

At this point, therefore, fellow Athenians, so far from pleading on my own behalf, as might be supposed, I am pleading on yours, in case by condemning me you should mistreat the gift which God has bestowed upon you—because if you put me to death, you

e   will not easily find another like me. The fact is, if I may put the point in a somewhat comical way, that I have been literally attached by God to our city, as if to a horse— a large thoroughbred, which is a bit sluggish because of its size, and needs to be aroused by some sort of gadfly. Yes, in me, I be-

31a lieve, God has attached to our city just such a creature—the kind which is constantly alighting everywhere on you, all day long, arousing, cajoling, or reproaching each and every one of you. You will not easily acquire another such gadfly, gentlemen; rather, if you take my advice, you will spare my life. I dare say, though, that you will get angry, like people who are awakened from their doze. Perhaps you will heed Anytus, and give me a swat: you could happily finish me off, and then spend the rest of your life asleep— unless God, in his compassion for you, were to send you someone else.

That I am, in fact, just the sort of gift that God would send to our city, you may   b recognize from this: it would not seem to be in human nature for me to have neglected all my own affairs, and put up with the neglect of my family for all these years, but constantly minded your interests, by visiting each of you in private like a father or an elder brother, urging you to be concerned about goodness. Of course, if I were gaining anything from that, or were being paid to urge that course upon you, my actions could be explained. But in fact you can see for yourselves that my accusers, who so shamelessly level all those other charges against me, could not muster the impudence to call evidence that I ever once obtained payment,   c or asked for any. It is I who can call evidence sufficient, I think, to show that I am speaking the truth—namely, my poverty.

Now it may perhaps seem peculiar that, as some say, I give this counsel by going around and dealing with others' concerns in private, yet do not venture to appear before the Assembly, and counsel the city about your business in public. But the reason for that is one you have frequently heard me give   d in many places: it is a certain divine or spiritual sign which comes to me, the very thing to which Meletus made mocking allusion in his indictment. It has been happening to me ever since childhood: a voice of some sort which comes, and which always—whenever it does come—restrains me from what I am about to do, yet never gives positive direction. That is what opposes my engaging in politics—and its opposition is an excellent thing, to my mind; because you may be quite sure, fellow Athenians, that if I had tried to engage in politics, I should have per-

e   ished long since, and should have been of no use either to you or to myself.

And please do not get angry if I tell you the truth. The fact is that there is no person on earth whose life will be spared by you or by any other majority, if he is genuinely opposed to many injustices and unlawful acts, and tries to prevent their occurrence in our

32a city. Rather, anyone who truly fights for what is just, if he is going to survive for even a short time, must act in a private capacity rather than a public one.

I will offer you conclusive evidence of that—not just words, but the sort of evidence that you respect, namely, actions. Just hear me tell my experiences, so that you may know that I would not submit to a single person for fear of death, contrary to what is just; nor would I do so, even if I were to lose my life on the spot. I shall mention things to you which are vulgar commonplaces of the courts; yet they are true.

Although I have never held any other

b   public office in our city, fellow Athenians, I have served on its Council. My own tribe, Antiochis, happened to be the presiding commission on the occasion when you wanted a collective trial for the ten generals who had failed to rescue the survivors from the naval battle. That was illegal, as you all later recognized. At the time I was the only commissioner opposed to your acting illegally, and I voted against the motion. And though its advocates were prepared to lay information against me and have me arrested, while you were urging them on by shouting, I believed

c   that I should face danger in siding with law and justice, rather than take your side for

fear of imprisonment or death, when your proposals were contrary to justice.

Those events took place while our city was still under democratic rule. But on a subsequent occasion, after the oligarchy had come to power, the Thirty summoned me and four others to the round chamber, with orders to arrest Leon the Salaminian, and fetch him from Salamis for execution; they were constantly issuing such orders, of course, to many others, in their wish to implicate as many as possible in their crimes. On that occasion, however, I showed, once   d again not just by words, but by my actions, that I couldn't care less about death—if that would not be putting it rather crudely—but that my one and only care was to avoid doing anything sinful or unjust. Thus, powerful as it was, that regime did not frighten me into unjust action: when we emerged from the round chamber, the other four went off to Salamis and arrested Leon, whereas I left them and went off home. For that I might easily have been put to death, had the regime   e not collapsed shortly afterwards. There are many witnesses who will testify before you about those events.

Do you imagine, then, that I would have survived all these years if I had been regularly active in public life, and had championed what was right in a manner worthy of a brave man, and valued that above all else, as was my duty? Far from it, fellow Athenians. I would not, and nor would any other   33a man. But in any public undertaking, that is the sort of person that I, for my part, shall prove to have been throughout my life; and likewise in my private life, because I have never been guilty of unjust association with anyone, including those whom my slanderers allege to have been my students.

I never, in fact, was anyone's instructor at any time. But if a person wanted to hear me talking, while I was engaging in my own business, I never grudged that to anyone, b young or old; nor do I hold conversation only when I receive payment, and not otherwise. Rather, I offer myself for questioning to wealthy and poor alike, and to anyone who may wish to answer in response to questions from me. Whether any of those people acquires a good character or not, I cannot fairly be held responsible, when I never at any time promised any of them that they would learn anything from me, nor gave them instruction. And if anyone claims that he ever learnt anything from me, or has heard privately something that everyone else did not hear as well, you may be sure that what he says is untrue.

c Why then, you may ask, do some people enjoy spending so much time in my company?— You have already heard, fellow Athenians: I have told you the whole truth—which is that my listeners enjoy the examination of those who think themselves wise but are not, since the process is not unamusing. But for me, I must tell you, it is a mission which I have been bidden to undertake by the god, through oracles and dreams, and through every means whereby a divine injunction to perform any task has ever been laid upon a human being.

d That is not only true, fellow Athenians, but is easily verified—because if I do corrupt any of our young people, or have corrupted others in the past, then presumably, when they grew older, should any of them have realized that I had at any time given them bad advice in their youth, they ought now to have appeared here themselves to accuse me and obtain redress. Or else, if they were unwilling to come in person, members of their families—fathers, brothers, or other relations—had their relatives suffered any harm at my hands, ought now to put it on record and obtain redress.

e In any case, many of those people are present, whom I can see: first there is Crito, my contemporary and fellow demesman, father of Critobulus here; then Lysanias of Sphettus, father of Aeschines here; next, Epigenes' father, Antiphon from Cephisia, is present; then again, there are others here whose brothers have spent time with me in these studies: Nicostratus, son of Theozotides, brother of Theodotus—Theodotus himself, incidentally, is deceased, so Nicostratus could not have come at his brother's 34a urging; and Paralius here, son of Demodocus, whose brother was Theages; also present is Ariston's son, Adimantus, whose brother is Plato here; and Aeantodorus, whose brother is Apollodorus here.

There are many others I could mention to you, from whom Meletus should surely have called some testimony during his own speech. However, if he forgot to do so then, let him call it now—I yield the floor to him—and if he has any such evidence, let him produce it. But quite the opposite is true, gentlemen: you will find that they are all prepared to support me, their corruptor, the one who is, according to Meletus b and Anytus, doing their relatives mischief. Support for me from the actual victims of corruption might perhaps be explained; but what of the uncorrupted—older men by now, and relatives of my victims? What reason would they have to support me, apart from the right and proper one, which is that they know very well that Meletus is lying, whereas I am telling the truth?

There it is, then, gentlemen. That, and perhaps more of the same, is about all I have to say in my defence. But perhaps, among your number, there may be someone who will c harbour resentment when he recalls a case of his own: he may have faced a less serious trial than this one, yet begged and implored the jury, weeping copiously, and producing his children here, along with many other relatives and loved ones, to gain as much sympathy as possible. By contrast, I shall do

none of those things, even though I am running what might be considered the ultimate risk. Perhaps someone with those thoughts will harden his heart against me; and enraged by those same thoughts, he may cast
d his vote against me in anger. Well, if any of you are so inclined—not that I expect it of you, but if anyone *should* be—I think it fair to answer him as follows:

"I naturally do have relatives, my excellent friend, because—in Homer's own words—I too was 'not born of oak nor of rock,' but of human parents; and so I do have relatives—including my sons, fellow Athenians. There are three of them: one is now a youth, while two are still children. Nevertheless, I shall not produce any of them here, and then entreat you to vote for my acquittal."

And why, you may ask, will I do no such thing? Not out of contempt or disrespect
e for you, fellow Athenians—whether or not I am facing death boldly is a different issue. The point is that with our reputations in mind—yours and our whole city's, as well as my own—I believe that any such behaviour would be ignominious, at my age and with the reputation I possess; that reputation may or may not, in fact, be deserved, but at least it is believed that Socrates stands out
35a in some way from the run of human beings. Well, if those of you who are believed to be pre-eminent in wisdom, courage, or any other form of goodness, are going to behave like that, it would be demeaning.

I have frequently seen such men when they face judgment: they have significant reputations, yet they put on astonishing performances, apparently in the belief that by dying they will suffer something unheard of—as if they would be immune from death, so long as you did not kill them! They seem to me to put our city to shame: they could
b give any foreigner the impression that men preeminent among Athenians in goodness, whom they select from their own number

to govern and hold other positions, are no better than women. I say this, fellow Athenians, because none of us who has even the slightest reputation should behave like that; nor should you put up with us if we try to do so. Rather, you should make one thing clear: you will be far more inclined to convict one who stages those pathetic charades and makes our city an object of derision, than one who keeps his composure.

But leaving reputation aside, gentlemen, I do not think it right to entreat the jury, nor to win acquittal in that way, instead of
c by informing and persuading them. A juror does not sit to dispense justice as a favour, but to determine where it lies. And he has sworn, not that he will favour whomever he pleases, but that he will try the case according to law. We should not, then, accustom you to transgress your oath, nor should you become accustomed to doing so: neither of us would be showing respect towards the gods. And therefore, fellow Athenians, do
d not require behaviour from me towards you which I consider neither proper nor right nor pious—more especially now, for God's sake, when I stand charged by Meletus here with impiety: because if I tried to persuade and coerce you with entreaties in spite of your oath, I clearly *would* be teaching you not to believe in gods; and I would stand literally self-convicted, by my defence, of failing to acknowledge them. But that is far from the truth: I do acknowledge them, fellow Athenians, as none of my accusers do; and I trust to you, and to God, to judge my case as shall be best for me and for yourselves.

For many reasons fellow Athenians, I am
e not dismayed by this outcome[1]—your con-
36a victing me, I mean—and especially because the outcome has come as no surprise to me. I wonder far more at the number of votes cast on each side, because I did not think the margin would be so narrow. Yet it seems, in

fact, that if a mere thirty votes had gone the other way, I should have been acquitted. Or rather, even as things stand, I consider that I have been cleared of Meletus' charges. Not only that, but one thing is obvious to every-

b   one: if Anytus had not come forward with Lycon to accuse me, Meletus would have forfeited 1,000 drachmas, since he would not have gained one-fifth of the votes cast.

But anyhow, this gentleman demands the death penalty for me. Very well, then: what alternative penalty shall I suggest to you, fellow Athenians? Clearly, it must be one I deserve. So what do I deserve to incur or to pay, for having taken it into my head not to lead an inactive life? Instead, I have neglected the things that concern most people—making money, managing an estate, gaining military or civic honours, or other positions of power, or joining political clubs and parties which have formed in our

c   city. I thought myself, in truth, too honest to survive if I engaged in those things. I did not pursue a course, therefore, in which I would be of no use to you or to myself. In-stead, by going to each individual privately, I tried to render a service for you which is— so I maintain—the highest service of all. Therefore that was the course I followed: I tried to persuade each of you not to care for any of his possessions rather than care for himself, striving for the utmost excellence and understanding; and not to care for our

d   city's possessions rather than for the city itself; and to care about other things in the same way.

So what treatment do I deserve for being such a benefactor? If I am to make a pro-posal truly in keeping with my deserts, fellow Athenians, it should be some ben-efit; and moreover, the sort of benefit that would be fitting for me. Well then, what *is* fitting for a poor man who is a benefac-tor, and who needs time free for exhorting you? Nothing could be more fitting, fellow

Athenians, than to give such a man regular free meals in the Prytaneum; indeed, that is far more fitting for him than for any of you who may have won an Olympic race with a pair or a team of horses: that victor brings you only the appearance of success, whereas I bring you the reality; besides, he is not in want of sustenance, whereas I am. So if, as justice demands, I am to make a proposal in   e keeping with my deserts, that is what I sug-   37a gest: free meals in the Prytaneum.

Now, in proposing this, I may seem to you, as when I talked about appeals for sym-pathy, to be speaking from sheer effrontery. But actually I have no such motive, fellow Athenians. My point is rather this: I am con-vinced that I do not treat any human being unjustly, at least intentionally—but I cannot make you share that conviction, because we have conversed together so briefly. I say this, because if it were the law here, as in other jurisdictions, that a capital case must not be tried in a single day, but over several, I   b think you could have been convinced; but as things stand, it is not easy to clear oneself of such grave allegations in a short time.

Since, therefore, I am persuaded, for my part, that I have treated no one unjustly, I have no intention whatever of so treating myself, nor of denouncing myself as deserv-ing ill, or proposing any such treatment for myself. Why should I do that? For fear of the penalty Meletus demands for me, when I say that I don't know if that is a good thing or a bad one? In preference to that, am I then to choose one of the things I know very well to be bad, and demand that instead? Imprisonment, for instance? Why should I   c live in prison, in servitude to the annually appointed prison commissioners? Well then, a fine, with imprisonment until I pay? That would amount to what I just mentioned, since I haven't the means to pay it.

Well then, should I propose banishment? Perhaps that is what you would propose for me. Yet I must surely be obsessed with survival, fellow Athenians, if I am so illogical as that. You, my fellow citizens, were

d unable to put up with my discourses and arguments, but they were so irksome and odious to you that you now seek to be rid of them. Could I not draw the inference, in that case, that others will hardly take kindly to them? Far from it, fellow Athenians. A fine life it would be for a person of my age to go into exile, and spend his days continually exchanging one city for another, and being repeatedly expelled—because I know very well that wherever I go, the young will come to hear me speaking, as they do here. And if

e I repel them, they will expel me themselves, by persuading their elders; while if I do not repel them, their fathers and relatives will expel me on their account.

Now, perhaps someone may say: "Socrates, could you not be so kind as to keep quiet and remain inactive, while living in exile?" This is the hardest point of all of which to convince some of you. Why? Because, if I tell you that that would mean disobeying my god, and that is why I cannot

38a remain inactive, you will disbelieve me and think that I am practising a sly evasion. Again, if I said that it really is the greatest benefit for a person to converse every day about goodness, and about the other subjects you have heard me discussing when examining myself and others—and that an unexamined life is no life for a human being to live—then you would believe me still less when I made those assertions. But the facts, gentlemen, are just as I claim them to be, though it is not easy to convince you of them. At the same time, I am not accustomed to think of myself as deserving anything bad. If I had money, I would

b have proposed a fine of as much as I could afford: that would have done me no harm at all. But the fact is that I have none—unless you wish to fix the penalty at a sum I could

pay. I could afford to pay you 1 mina, I suppose, so I suggest a fine of that amount—

One moment, fellow Athenians. Plato here, along with Crito, Critobulus, and Apollodorus, is urging me to propose 30 minas, and they are saying they will stand surety for that sum. So I propose a fine of that amount, and these people shall be your sufficient guarantors of its payment.

For the sake of a slight gain in time, fellow Athenians, you will incur infamy and blame c from those who would denigrate our city, for putting Socrates to death[2]—a "wise man" because those who wish to malign you will say I am wise, even if I am not; in any case, had you waited only a short time, you would have obtained that outcome automatically. You can see, of course, that I am now well advanced in life, and death is not far off. I d address that not to all of you, but to those who condemned me to death; and to those same people I would add something further.

Perhaps you imagine, gentlemen, that I have been convicted for lack of arguments of the sort I could have used to convince you, had I believed that I should do or say anything to gain acquittal. But that is far from true. I have been convicted, not for lack of arguments, but for lack of brazen impudence and willingness to address you in such terms as you would most like to be addressed in—that is to say, by weeping and wailing, and doing and saying much else that e I claim to be unworthy of me—the sorts of thing that you are so used to hearing from others. But just as I did not think during my defence that I should do anything unworthy of a free man because I was in danger, so now I have no regrets about defending myself as I did; I should far rather present such a defence and die, than live by defending myself in that other fashion.

In court, as in warfare, neither I nor anyone else should contrive to escape death 39a at any cost. On the battlefield too, it often becomes obvious that one could avoid death by throwing down one's arms and flinging oneself upon the mercy of one's pursuers. And in every sort of danger there are many other means of escaping death, if one is shameless enough to do or to say anything. I suggest that it is not death that is hard to

b avoid, gentlemen, but wicked- ness is far harder, since it is fleeter of foot than death. Thus, slow and elderly as I am, I have now been overtaken by the slower runner; while my accusers, adroit and quick-witted as they are, have been overtaken by the faster, which is wickedness. And so I take my leave, condemned to death by your judgment, whereas they stand for ever condemned to depravity and injustice as judged by Truth. And just as I accept my penalty, so must they. Things were bound to turn out this way, I suppose, and I imagine it is for the best.

In the next place, to those of you who

c voted against me, I wish to utter a prophecy. Indeed, I have now reached a point at which people are most given to prophesying—that is, when they are on the point of death. I warn you, my executioners, that as soon as I am dead retribution will come upon you— far more severe, I swear, than the sentence you have passed upon me. You have tried to kill me for now, in the belief that you will be relieved from giving an account of your

d lives. But in fact, I can tell you, you will face just the opposite outcome. There will be more critics to call you to account, people whom I have restrained for the time being though you were unaware of my doing so. They will be all the harder on you since they are younger, and you will rue it all the more—because if you imagine that by putting people to death you will prevent anyone from reviling you for not living rightly, you are badly mistaken. That way of escape is neither feasible nor honourable. Rather, the most honourable and easiest way is

not the silencing of others, but striving to make oneself as good a person as possible. So with that prophecy to those of you who voted against me, I take my leave.

As for those who voted for my acquittal, I should like to discuss the outcome of this   e case while the officials are occupied, and I am not yet on the way to the place where I must die. Please bear with me, gentlemen, just for this short time: there is no reason why we should not have a word with one another while that is still permitted.

Since I regard you as my friends, I am willing to show you the significance of what   40a has just befallen me. You see, gentlemen of the jury—and in applying that term to you, I probably use it correctly—something wonderful has just happened to me. Hitherto, the usual prophetic voice from my spiritual sign was continually active, and frequently opposed me even on trivial matters, if I was about to do anything amiss. But now something has befallen me, as you can see for yourselves, which one certainly might   b consider—and is generally held—to be the very worst of evils. Yet the sign from God did not oppose me, either when I left home this morning, or when I appeared here in court, or at any point when I was about to say anything during my speech; and yet in other discussions it has very often stopped me in mid-sentence. This time, though, it has not opposed me at any moment in anything I said or did in this whole business.

Now, what do I take to be the explanation for that? I will tell you: I suspect that what has befallen me is a blessing, and that those of us who suppose death to be an evil cannot be making a correct assumption. I   c have gained every ground for that suspicion, because my usual sign could not have failed to oppose me, unless I were going to incur some good result.

And let us also reflect upon how good a reason there is to hope that death is a b   good thing. It is, you see, one or other of two things: either to be dead is to be non-existent, as it were, and a dead person has no awareness whatever of anything at all; or else, as we are told, the soul undergoes some sort of transformation, or exchanging of this present world for another. Now

d   if there is, in fact, no awareness in death, but it is like sleep—the kind in which the sleeper does not even dream at all—then death would be a marvellous gain. Why, imagine that someone had to pick the night in which he slept so soundly that he did not even dream, and to compare all the other nights and days of his life with that one; suppose he had to say, upon consideration, how many days or nights in his life he had spent

e   better and more agreeably than that night; in that case, I think he would find them easy to count compared with his other days and nights—even if he were the Great King of Persia, let alone an ordinary person. Well, if death is like that, then for my part I call it a gain; because on that assumption the whole of time would seem no longer than a single night.

     On the other hand, if death is like taking a trip from here to another place, and if it is true, as we are told, that all of the dead do indeed exist in that other place, why then, gentlemen of the jury, what could be

41a a greater blessing than that? If upon arriving in Hades, and being rid of these people who profess to be "jurors," one is going to find those who are truly judges, and who are also said to sit in judgment there—Minos, Rhadamanthys, Aeacus, Triptolemus, and all other demigods who were righteous in their own lives—would that be a disappointing journey?

     Or again, what would any of you not give to share the company of Orpheus and Musaeus, of Hesiod and Homer? I say "you," since I personally would be willing to die many times over, if those tales are true.

Why? Because my own sojourn there would be wonderful, if I could meet Palamedes, or Ajax, son of Telamon, or anyone else of old who met their death through an unjust verdict. Whenever I met them, I could compare my own experiences with theirs—which would be not unamusing, I fancy—and best of all, I could spend time questioning and probing people there, just as I do here, to find out who among them is truly wise, and who thinks he is without being so.

     What would one not give, gentlemen of the jury, to be able to question the leader of the great expedition against Troy, or Odys-   c seus, or Sisyphus, or countless other men and women one could mention? Would it not be unspeakable good fortune to converse with them there, to mingle with them and question them? At least that isn't a reason, presumably, for people in that world to put you to death—because amongst other ways in which people there are more fortunate than those in our world, they have become immune from death for the rest of time, if what we are told is actually true.

     Moreover, you too, gentlemen of the jury, should be of good hope in the face of death, and fix your minds upon this single truth: nothing can harm a good man, either in life   d or in death; nor are his fortunes neglected by the gods. In fact, what has befallen me has come about by no mere accident; rather, it is clear to me that it was better I should die now and be rid of my troubles. That is also the reason why the divine sign at no point turned me back; and for my part, I bear those who condemned me, and my accusers, no ill will at all—though, to be   e sure, it was not with that intent that they were condemning and accusing me, but with intent to harm me—and they are culpable for that. Still, this much I ask of them. When my sons come of age, gentlemen, punish them: give them the same sort of trouble that I used to give you, if you think they care for money or anything else more than for goodness, and if they think highly of themselves when they are of no value. Reprove them, as I reproved you, for failing to care for the things they should, and for thinking highly of themselves when

42a they are worthless. If you will do that, then I shall have received my own just deserts from you, as will my sons.

But enough. It is now time to leave—for me to die, and for you to live—though

which of us has the better destiny is unclear to everyone, save only to God.

Notes

1. The verdict was "Guilty." Socrates here begins his second speech, proposing an alternative to the death penalty demanded by the prosecution.
2. The jury has now voted for the death penalty, and Socrates begins his final speech.

Crito

43a *Socrates*. Why have you come at this hour, Crito? It's still very early, isn't it?

Crito. Yes, very.

Socrates. About what time?

Crito. Just before daybreak.

Socrates. I'm surprised the prison-warder was willing to answer the door.

Crito. He knows me by now, Socrates, because I come and go here so often; and besides, I've done him a small favour.

Socrates. Have you just arrived, or have

b you been here for a while?

Crito. For quite a while.

Socrates. Then why didn't you wake me up right away instead of sitting by me in silence?

Crito. Well *of course* I didn't wake you, Socrates! I only wish I weren't so sleepless and wretched myself. I've been marvelling all this time as I saw how peacefully you were sleeping, and I deliberately kept from waking you, so that you could pass the time as peacefully as possible. I've often admired your disposition in the past, in fact all your

life; but more than ever in your present plight, you bear it so easily and patiently.

Socrates. Well, Crito, it really would be tiresome for a man of my age to get upset if the time has come when he must end his life.   c

Crito. And yet others of your age, Socrates, are over-taken by similar troubles, but their age brings them no relief from being upset at the fate which faces them.

Socrates. That's true. But tell me, why *have* you come so early?

Crito. I bring painful news, Socrates—not painful for you, I suppose, but painful and hard for me and all your friends—and hardest of all for me to bear, I think.   d

Socrates. What news is that? Is it that the ship has come back from Delos, the one on whose return I must die?

Crito. Well no, it hasn't arrived yet, but I think it will get here today, judging from reports of people who've come from Sunium, where they disembarked. That makes it obvious that it will get here today; and so tomorrow, Socrates, you will have to end your life.

From *Defence of Socrates, Euthyphro*, and *Crito*, translated by David Gallop. Copyright © 1997 by Oxford University Press. Reprinted by permission of the publisher and translator.

Socrates. Well, may that be for the best, Crito. If it so please the gods, so be it. All the same, I don't think it will get here today.

Crito. What makes you think that?

Socrates. I'll tell you. You see, I am to die on the day after the ship arrives, am I not?

Crito. At least that's what the authorities say.

Socrates. Then I don't think it will get here on the day that is just dawning, but on the next one. I infer that from a certain dream I had in the night—a short time ago, so it may be just as well that you didn't wake me.

Crito. And what was your dream?

Socrates. I dreamt that a lovely, handsome woman approached me, robed in white. She called me and said: 'Socrates,

> *Thou shalt reach fertile Phthia upon the*
> *third day.'*

Crito. What a curious dream, Socrates.

Socrates. Yet its meaning is clear, I think, Crito.

Crito. All too clear, it would seem. But please, Socrates, my dear friend, there is still time to take my advice, and make your escape—because if you die, I shall suffer more than one misfortune: not only shall I lose such a friend as I'll never find again, but it will look to many people, who hardly know you or me, as if I'd abandoned you—since I could have rescued you if I'd been willing to put up the money. And yet what could be more shameful than a reputation for valuing money more highly than friends? Most people won't believe that it was you who refused to leave this place yourself, despite our urging you to do so.

Socrates. But why should we care so much, my good Crito, about what most people believe? All the most capable people, whom we should take more seriously, will think the matter has been handled exactly as it has been.

Crito. Yet surely, Socrates, you can see that one must heed popular opinion too. Your present plight shows by itself that the populace can inflict not the least of evils, but just about the worst, if someone has been slandered in their presence.

Socrates. Ah Crito, if only the populace *could* inflict the worst of evils! Then they would also be capable of providing the greatest of goods, and a fine thing that would be. But the fact is that they can do neither: they are unable to give anyone understanding or lack of it, no matter what they do.

Crito. Well, if you say so. But tell me this, Socrates: can it be that you are worried for me and your other friends, in case the blackmailers give us trouble, if you escape, for having smuggled you out of here? Are you worried that we might be forced to forfeit all our property as well, or pay heavy fines, or even incur some further penalty? If you're afraid of anything like that, put it out of your mind. In rescuing you we are surely justified in taking that risk, or even worse if need be. Come on, listen to me and do as I say.

Socrates. Yes, those risks do worry me, Crito—amongst many others.

Crito. Then put those fears aside—because no great sum is needed to pay people who are willing to rescue you and get you out of here. Besides, you can surely see that those blackmailers are cheap, and it wouldn't take much to buy them off. My own means are available to you and would be ample, I'm sure. Then again, even if—out of concern on my behalf—you think you shouldn't be spending my money, there are visitors here who are ready to spend theirs. One of them, Simmias from Thebes, has actually brought enough money for this very purpose, while Cebes and quite a number of others are also prepared to contribute. So, as I say, you shouldn't hesitate to save yourself on account of those fears.

And don't let it trouble you, as you were saying in court, that you wouldn't know what to do with yourself if you went into

c   exile. There will be people to welcome you anywhere else you may go: if you want to go to Thessaly, I have friends there who will make much of you and give you safe refuge, so that no one from anywhere in Thessaly will trouble you.

Next, Socrates, I don't think that what you propose—giving yourself up, when you could be rescued—is even just. You are actually hastening to bring upon yourself just the sorts of thing which your enemies would hasten to bring upon you—indeed, they have done so—in their wish to destroy you.

What's more, I think you're betraying

d   those sons of yours. You will be deserting them, if you go off when you could be raising and educating them: as far as you're concerned, they will fare as best they may. In all likelihood, they'll meet the sort of fate which usually befalls orphans once they've lost their parents. Surely, one should either not have children at all, or else see the toil and trouble of their upbringing and education through to the end; yet you seem to me to prefer the easiest path. One should rather choose the path that a good and resolute man would choose, particularly

e   if one professes to cultivate goodness all one's life. Frankly, I'm ashamed for you and for us, your friends: it may appear that this whole predicament of yours has been handled with a certain feebleness on our part. What with the bringing of your case to court when that could have been avoided, the actual conduct of the trial, and now, to crown it all, this absurd outcome of the

46a   business, it may seem that the problem has eluded us through some fault or feebleness on our part—in that we failed to save you, and you failed to save yourself, when that was quite possible and feasible, if we had been any use at all.

Make sure, Socrates, that all this doesn't turn out badly, and a disgrace to you as well as us. Come now, form a plan—or rather, don't even plan, because the time for that is past, and only a single plan remains. Everything needs to be carried out during the coming night; and if we go on waiting around, it won't be possible or feasible any longer. Come on, Socrates, do all you can to take my advice, and do exactly what I say.

Socrates. My dear Crito, your zeal will be invaluable if it should have right on its side;   b but otherwise, the greater it is, the harder it makes matters. We must therefore consider whether or not the course you urge should be followed—because it is in my nature, not just now for the first time but always, to follow nothing within me but the principle which appears to me, upon reflection, to be best.

I cannot now reject the very principles that I previously adopted, just because this fate has overtaken me; rather, they appear to me much the same as ever, and I respect   c and honour the same ones that I did before. If we cannot find better ones to maintain in the present situation, you can be sure that I won't agree with you—not even if the power of the populace threatens us, like children, with more bogeymen than it does now, by visiting us with imprisonment, execution, or confiscation of property.

What, then, is the most reasonable way to consider the matter? Suppose we first take up the point you make about what people will think. Was it always an acceptable principle   d that one should pay heed to some opinions but not to others, or was it not? Or was it acceptable before I had to die, while now it is exposed as an idle assertion made for the sake of talk, when it is really childish nonsense? For my part, Crito, I'm eager to look into this together with you, to see whether the principle is to be viewed any differently, or in the same way, now that I'm in this position, and whether we should disregard or follow it.

As I recall, the following principle always used to be affirmed by people who thought they were talking sense: the principle, as I was just saying, that one should have a high regard for some opinions held by human beings, but not for others. Come now, Crito: don't you think that was a good principle? I ask because you are not, in all foreseeable likelihood, going to die tomorrow, and my present trouble shouldn't impair your judgment. Consider, then: don't you think it a good principle, that one shouldn't respect all human opinions, but only some and not others; or, again, that one shouldn't respect everyone's opinions, but those of some people, and not those of others? What do you say? Isn't that a good principle?

Crito. It is.

Socrates. And one should respect the good ones, but not the bad ones?

Crito. Yes.

Socrates. And good ones are those of people with understanding, whereas bad ones are those of people without it?

Crito. Of course.

Socrates. Now then, once again, how were such points established? When a man is in training, and concentrating upon that, does he pay heed to the praise or censure or opinion of each and every man, or only to those of the individual who happens to be his doctor or trainer?

Crito. Only to that individual's.

Socrates. Then he should fear the censures, and welcome the praises of that individual, but not those of most people.

Crito. Obviously.

Socrates. So he must base his actions and exercises, his eating and drinking, upon the opinion of the individual, the expert supervisor, rather than upon everyone else's.

Crito. True.

Socrates. Very well. If he disobeys that individual and disregards his opinion and his praises, but respects those of most people, who are ignorant, he'll suffer harm, won't he?

Crito. Of course.

Socrates. And what is that harm? What does it affect? What element within the disobedient man?

Crito. Obviously, it affects his body, because that's what it spoils.

Socrates. A good answer. And in other fields too, Crito—we needn't go through them all, but they surely include matters of just and unjust, honourable and dishonourable, good and bad, the subjects of our present deliberation—is it the opinion of most people that we should follow and fear, or is it that of the individual authority—assuming that some expert exists who should be respected and feared above all others? If we don't follow that person, won't we corrupt and impair the element which (as we agreed) is made better by what is just, but is spoilt by what is unjust? Or is there nothing in all that?

Crito. I accept it myself, Socrates.

Socrates. Well now, if we spoil the part of us that is improved by what is healthy but corrupted by what is unhealthy, because it is not expert opinion that we are following, are our lives worth living once it has been corrupted? The part in question is, of course, the body, isn't it?

Crito. Yes.

Socrates. And are our lives worth living with a poor or corrupted body?

Crito. Definitely not.

Socrates. Well then, are they worth living if the element which is impaired by what is unjust and benefited by what is just has been corrupted? Or do we consider the element to which justice or injustice belongs, whichever part of us it is, to be of less value than the body?

Crito. By no means.

Socrates. On the contrary, it is more precious?

Crito. Far more.

Socrates. Then, my good friend, we shouldn't care all that much about what the populace will say of us, but about what the expert on matters of justice and injustice will say, the individual authority, or Truth. In the first place, then, your proposal that we should care about popular opinion regarding just, honourable, or good actions, and their opposites, is mistaken.

"Even so," someone might say, "the populace has the power to put us to death."

b

Crito. *That's* certainly clear enough; one might say that, Socrates.

Socrates. You're right. But the principle we've rehearsed, my dear friend, still remains as true as it was before—for me at any rate. And now consider this further one, to see whether or not it still holds good for us. We should attach the highest value, shouldn't we, not to living, but to living well?

Crito. Why yes, that still holds.

Socrates. And living well is the same as living honourably or justly? Does that still hold or not?

Crito. Yes, it does.

Socrates. Then in the light of those admissions, we must ask the following question: is it just, or is it not, for me to try to get out of here, when Athenian authorities are unwilling to release me? Then, if it does seem just, let us attempt it; but if it doesn't, let us abandon the idea.

c

As for the questions you raise about expenses and reputation and bringing up children, I suspect they are the concerns of those who cheerfully put people to death, and would bring them back to life if they could, without any intelligence, namely, the populace. For us, however, because our principle so demands, there is no other question to ask except the one we just raised: shall we be acting justly—we who are rescued as well as the rescuers themselves—if we pay money and do favours to those who would get me out of here? Or shall we in truth be

d

acting unjustly if we do all those things? And if it is clear that we shall be acting unjustly in taking that course, then the question whether we shall have to die through standing firm and holding our peace, or suffer in any other way, ought not to weigh with us in comparison with acting unjustly.

Crito. I think that's finely *said*, Socrates; but do please consider what we should *do*.

Socrates. Let's examine that question together, dear friend; and if you have objections to anything I say, please raise them, and I'll listen to you—otherwise, good fellow, it's time to stop telling me, again and again, that I should leave here against the will of Athens. You see, I set great store upon persuading you as to my course of action, and not acting against your will. Come now, just consider whether you find the starting-point of our inquiry acceptable, and try to answer my questions according to your real beliefs.

e

49a

Crito. All right, I'll try.

Socrates. Do we maintain that people should on no account whatever do injustice willingly? Or may it be done in some circumstances but not in others? Is acting unjustly in no way good or honourable, as we frequently agreed in the past? Or have all those former agreements been jettisoned during these last few days? Can it be, Crito, that men of our age have long failed to notice, as we earnestly conversed with each other, that we ourselves were no better than children? Or is what we then used to say true above all else? Whether most people say so or not, and whether we must be treated more harshly or more leniently than at present, isn't it a fact, all the same, that acting unjustly is utterly bad and shameful for the agent? Yes or no?

b

Crito. Yes.

Socrates. So one must not act unjustly at all.

Crito. Absolutely not.

Socrates. Then, even if one is unjustly treated, one should not return injustice, as most people believe—given that one should act not unjustly at all.

Crito. Apparently not.

Socrates. Well now, Crito, should one ever ill-treat anybody or not?

Crito. Surely not, Socrates.

Socrates. And again, when one suffers illtreatment, is it just to return it, as most people maintain, or isn't it?

Crito. It is not just at all.

Socrates. Because there's no difference, I take it, between ill-treating people and treating them unjustly.

Crito. Correct.

Socrates. Then one shouldn't return injustice or ill-treatment to any human being, no matter how one may be treated by that person. And in making those admissions, Crito, watch out that you're not agreeing to anything contrary to your real beliefs. I say that, because I realize that the belief is held by few people, and always will be. Those who hold it share no common counsel with those who don't; but each group is bound to regard the other with contempt when they observe one another's decisions. You too, therefore, should consider very carefully whether you share that belief with me, and whether we may begin our deliberations from the following premiss: neither doing nor returning injustice is ever right, nor should one who is ill-treated defend himself by retaliation. Do you agree? Or do you dissent and not share my belief in that premiss? I've long been of that opinion myself, and I still am now; but if you've formed any different view, say so, and explain it. If you stand by our former view, however, then listen to my next point.

Crito. Well, I do stand by it and share that view, so go ahead.

Socrates. All right, I'll make my next point—or rather, ask a question. Should the things one agrees with someone else be done, provided they are just, or should one cheat?

Crito. They should be done.

Socrates. Then consider what follows. If we leave this place without having persuaded our city, are we or are we not ill-treating certain people, indeed people whom we ought least of all to be ill-treating? And would we be abiding by the things we agreed, those things being just, or not?

Crito. I can't answer your question, Socrates, because I don't understand it.

Socrates. Well, look at it this way. Suppose we were on the point of running away from here, or whatever else one should call it. Then the Laws, or the State of Athens, might come and confront us, and they might speak as follows:

"Please tell us, Socrates, what do you have in mind? With this action you are attempting, do you intend anything short of destroying us, the Laws and the city as a whole, to the best of your ability? Do you think that a city can still exist without being overturned, if the legal judgments rendered within it possess no force, but are nullified or invalidated by individuals?"

What shall we say, Crito, in answer to that and other such questions? Because somebody, particularly a legal advocate, might say a great deal on behalf of the law that is being invalidated here, the one requiring that judgments, once rendered, shall have authority. Shall we tell them: "Yes, that is our intention, because the city was treating us unjustly, by not judging our case correctly"? Is that to be our answer, or what?

Crito. Indeed it is, Socrates.

Socrates. And what if the Laws say: "And was that also part of the agreement between you and us, Socrates? Or did you agree to abide by whatever judgments the city rendered?"

Then, if we were surprised by their words, perhaps they might say: "Don't be surprised at what we are saying, Socrates, but answer us, seeing that you like to use question-and-answer. What complaint, pray, do you have d against the city and ourselves, that you should now attempt to destroy us? In the first place, was it not we who gave you birth? Did your father not marry your mother and beget you under our auspices? So will you inform those of us here who regulate marriages whether you have any criticism of them as poorly framed?"

"No, I have none," I should say.

"Well then, what of the laws dealing with children's upbringing and education, under which you were educated yourself? Did those of us Laws who are in charge of that

e area not give proper direction, when they required your father to educate you in the arts and physical training?"

"They did," I should say.

"Very good. In view of your birth, upbringing, and education, can you deny, first, that you belong to us as our offspring and slave, as your forebears also did? And if so, do you imagine that you are on equal terms with us in regard to what is just, and that whatever treatment we may accord to you, it is just for you to do the same thing back to us? You weren't on equal terms with your father, or your master (assuming you had one),

51a making it just for you to return the treatment you received—answering back when you were scolded, or striking back when you were struck, or doing many other things of the same sort. Will you then have licence against your fatherland and its Laws, if we try to destroy you, in the belief that that is just? Will you try to destroy us in return, to the best of your ability? And will you claim that in doing so you are acting justly, you who are genuinely exercised about goodness? Or are you, in your wisdom, unaware that, in comparison with your mother and father and all your other forebears, your fatherland

b is more precious and venerable, more sacred and held in higher esteem among gods, as well as among human beings who have any sense; and that you should revere your fatherland, deferring to it and appeasing it when

it is angry, more than your own father? You must either persuade it, or else do whatever it commands; and if it ordains that you must submit to certain treatment, then you must hold your peace and submit to it: whether that means being beaten or put in bonds, or whether it leads you into war to be wounded or killed, you must act accordingly, and that is what is just; you must neither give way nor retreat, nor leave your position; rather, in warfare, in court, and everywhere else, you

c must do whatever your city or fatherland commands, or else persuade it as to what is truly just; and if it is sinful to use violence against your mother or father, it is far more so to use it against your fatherland."

What shall we say to that, Crito? That the Laws are right or not?

Crito. I think they are.

Socrates. "Consider then, Socrates," the Laws might go on, 'whether the following is also true: in your present undertaking you are not proposing to treat us justly. We gave you birth, upbringing, and education, and a

d share in all the benefits we could provide for you along with all your fellow citizens. Nevertheless, we proclaim, by the formal granting of permission, that any Athenian who wishes, once he has been admitted to adult status, and has observed the conduct of city business and ourselves, the Laws, may—if he is dissatisfied with us—go wherever he pleases and take his property. Not one of us Laws hinders or forbids that: whether any of you wishes to emigrate to a colony, or to go and live as an alien elsewhere, he may go

e wherever he pleases and keep his property, if we and the city fail to satisfy him.

"We do say, however, that if any of you remains here after he has observed the system by which we dispense justice and otherwise manage our city, then he has agreed with us by his conduct to obey whatever orders we give him. And thus we claim that anyone who fails to obey is guilty on three counts: he disobeys us as his parents; he disobeys those who nurtured him; and after agreeing to obey us he neither obeys nor persuades us if we are 52a doing anything amiss, even though we offer him a choice, and do not harshly insist that he must do whatever we command. Instead, we give him two options: he must either persuade us or else do as we say; yet he does neither. Those are the charges, Socrates, to which we say you too will be liable if you carry out your intention; and among Athenians, you will be not the least liable, but one of the most."

And if I were to say, "How so?" perhaps they could fairly reproach me, observing that I am actually among those Athenians who have made that agreement with them most emphatically.

b "Socrates," they would say, 'we have every indication that you were content with us, as well as with our city, because you would never have stayed home here, more than is normal for all other Athenians, unless you were abnormally content. You never left our city for a festival—except once to go to the Isthmus—nor did you go elsewhere for other purposes, apart from military service. You never travelled abroad, as other people do; nor were you c eager for acquaintance with a different city or different laws: we and our city sufficed for you. Thus, you emphatically opted for us, and agreed to be a citizen on our terms. In particular, you fathered children in our city, which would suggest that you were content with it.

'Moreover, during your actual trial it was open to you, had you wished, to propose exile as your penalty; thus, what you are now attempting to do without the city's consent, you could then have done with it. On that occasion, you kept priding yourself that it would not trouble you if you had to die: you would choose death ahead of exile, so you said. Yet now you dishonour those d words, and show no regard for us, the Laws, in your effort to destroy us. You are acting as the meanest slave would act, by trying to run away in spite of those compacts and

agreements you made with us, whereby you agreed to be a citizen on our terms.

"First, then, answer us this question: are we right in claiming that you agreed, by your conduct if not verbally, that you would be a citizen on our terms? Or is that untrue?"

What shall we say in reply to that, Crito? Mustn't we agree?

Crito. We must, Socrates.

Socrates. "Then what does your action amount to," they would say, 'except breaking the compacts and agreements you made with us? By your own admission, you were not coerced or tricked into making them, or forced to reach a decision in a short time: you had seventy years in which it was open to you to leave if you were not happy with us, or if you thought those agreements unfair. Yet you preferred neither Lacedaemon nor Crete—places you often say are well governed—nor any 53a other Greek or foreign city: in fact, you went abroad less often than the lame and the blind or other cripples. Obviously, then, amongst Athenians you were exceptionally content with our city and with us, its Laws—because who would care for a city apart from its laws? Won't you, then, abide by your agreements now? Yes you will, if you listen to us, Socrates; and then at least you won't make yourself an object of derision by leaving the city.

'Just consider: if you break those agreements, and commit any of those offences, what good will you do yourself or those friends of yours? Your friends, pretty ob- b viously, will risk being exiled themselves, as well as being disenfranchised or losing their property. As for you, first of all, if you go to one of the nearest cities, Thebes or Megara—they are both well governed—you will arrive as an enemy of their political systems, Socrates: all who are concerned for their own cities will look askance at you, regarding you as a subverter of laws. You will also confirm your jurors in their judgment, making them think they decided your case c correctly: any subverter of laws, presumably, might well be thought to be a corrupter of young, unthinking people.

'Will you, then, avoid the best-governed cities and the most respectable of men? And if so, will your life be worth living? Or will you associate with those people, and be shameless enough to converse with them? And what will you say to them, Socrates? The things you used to say here, that goodness and justice are most precious to mankind, along with institutions and laws? Don't you

d   think that the predicament of Socrates will cut an ugly figure? Surely you must.

'Or will you take leave of those spots, and go to stay with those friends of Crito's up in Thessaly? That, of course, is a region of the utmost disorder and licence; so perhaps they would enjoy hearing from you about your comical escape from jail, when you dressed up in some outfit, wore a leather jerkin or some other runaway's garb, and altered your appearance. Will no one observe that you,

e   an old man with probably only a short time left to live, had the nerve to cling so greedily to life by violating the most important laws? Perhaps not, so long as you don't trouble anyone. Otherwise, Socrates, you will hear a great deal to your own discredit. You will live as every person's toady and lackey; and what will you be doing—apart from living it up in Thessaly, as if you had travelled all the way

54a to Thessaly to have dinner? As for those principles of yours about justice and goodness in general—tell us, where will they be then?

'Well then, is it for your children's sake that you wish to live, in order to bring them up and give them an education? How so? Will you bring them up and educate them by taking them off to Thessaly and making foreigners of them, so that they may gain that advantage too? Or if, instead of that, they are brought up here, will they be better brought up and educated just because you are alive, if you are not with them? Yes, you may say, because those friends of yours will take care of them. Then will they take care

of them if you travel to Thessaly, but not take care of them if you travel to Hades? Surely if those professing to be your friends are of any use at all, you must believe that   b they will.

"No, Socrates, listen to us, your own nurturers: do not place a higher value upon children, upon life, or upon anything else, than upon what is just, so that when you leave for Hades, this may be your whole defence before the authorities there: to take that course seems neither better nor more just or holy, for you or for any of your friends here in this world. Nor will it be better for you when you reach the next. As things stand, you will leave this world (if you do) as one   c who has been treated unjustly not by us Laws, but by human beings; whereas if you go into exile, thereby shamefully returning injustice for injustice and ill-treatment for ill-treatment, breaking the agreements and compacts you made with us, and inflicting harm upon the people you should least harm—yourself, your friends, your fatherland, and ourselves—then we shall be angry with you in your lifetime; and our brother Laws in Hades will not receive you kindly there, knowing that you tried, to the best of   d your ability, to destroy us too. Come then, do not let Crito persuade you to take his advice rather than ours."

That, Crito, my dear comrade, is what I seem to hear them saying, I do assure you. I am like the Corybantic revellers who think they are still hearing the music of pipes: the sound of those arguments is ringing loudly in my head, and makes me unable to hear the others. As far as these present thoughts of mine go, then, you may be sure that if you object to them, you will plead in vain. None the less, if you think you will do any good, speak up.

Crito. No, Socrates, I've nothing to say.

Socrates. Then let it be, Crito, and let us act accordingly, because that is the direction in which God is guiding us.   e

Republic

BOOK I

327 I went down yesterday to the Piraeus with Glaucon, the son of Ariston, to offer up prayer to the goddess, and also I wanted to see how the festival, then to be held for the first time, would be celebrated. I was very much pleased with the native Athenian procession; though that of the Thracians
b appeared to be no less brilliant. We had finished our prayers, and satisfied our curiosity, and were returning to the city, when Polemarchus, the son of Cephalus, caught sight of us at a distance, as we were on our way towards home, and told his servant to run and order us to wait for him. The servant came behind me, took hold of my cloak, and said, "Polemarchus asks you to wait."

I turned round and asked him where his master was. "There he is," he replied, "coming from behind. Wait for him."
c "We will wait," answered Glaucon. Soon afterwards Polemarchus came up, with Adeimantus the brother of Glaucon, and Niceratus the son of Nicias, and a few other persons, apparently coming away from the procession.

Polemarchus then said: Socrates, it looks to me as if you are rushing to leave for town.

You guess right, I replied.

Well, do you see how many we are?

Certainly I do.

Then either prove yourselves the stronger party, or else stay where you are.

No, I replied, there is still an alternative: suppose we persuade you that you ought to let us go.

Could you possibly persuade us, if we refused to listen?

Certainly not, replied Glaucon.

Get it through your head that we will not listen.

Then Adeimantus interjected and said, Are you not aware that towards evening 328 there will be a torch-race on horseback in honor of the goddess?

On horseback! I exclaimed. That is a novelty. Will they carry torches, and pass them on to one another, while the horses are racing? or how do you mean?

Just like that, replied Polemarchus. Besides, there will be a night-festival, which will be worth looking at. After dinner we will go out to see this festival, and there we will meet with many of our young men, with whom we can converse. Therefore stay, and do not refuse us. b

Upon this Glaucon said, It looks like we have to stay.

Well, said I, if you like, let us do so.

We went therefore home with Polemarchus, and found there his brothers Lysias and Euthydemus, and, along with them, Thrasymachus of Chalcedon, and Charmantides the Paeanian, and Cleitophon the son of Aristonymus. Polemarchus's father, Cephalus, was also in the house. He looked much older to me: for it was long since

From Plato, *The Republic*, translation by John Llewelyn Davies and David James Vaughan, revised by Andrea Tschemplik (Lanham, Md.: Rowman & Littlefield Publishers, 2005). Reprinted by permission of the publisher.

c   I had seen him. He was sitting on a cushioned chair, with a garland upon his head, as he happened to have been sacrificing in the court. We found seats placed round him, so we sat down there by his side. The moment Cephalus saw me, he greeted me, and said, It is seldom indeed, Socrates, that you pay us a visit at the Piraeus; you ought to come more often. If I were still strong enough to walk with ease to the city, there would be no occasion for your coming here, because d we should go to you. But as it is, you ought to come here more frequently. For I assure you that I find the decay of the mere bodily pleasures accompanied by a proportionate growth in my appetite for speeches and the pleasure I derive from it. Therefore do not refuse my request, but let these young men have the benefit of your company, and come often to see us as though you were visiting friends and relatives.

    To tell you the truth, Cephalus, I replied, e I delight in conversing with very old persons. For as they have gone before us on the road over which perhaps we also shall have to travel, I think we ought to try to learn from them what the nature of that road is—whether it be rough and difficult, or smooth and easy. And now that you have arrived at that period of life, which poets call "the threshold of Age," there is no one whose opinion I would more gladly ask. Is life painful at that age, or what report do you make of it?

329   I will certainly tell you, Socrates, what my own experience of it is. I and a few other people of my own age are in the habit of frequently meeting together, true to the old proverb. On these occasions, most of us give way to lamentations, and regret the pleasures of youth, and call up the memory of sex and drinking parties and banquets and similar proceedings. They are grievously discontent at the loss of what they consider great privileges, and describe themselves as living well in those days, whereas now, b by their own account, they cannot be said to live at all. Some also complain of the manner in which their relations insult their infirmities, and make this a ground for reproaching old age with the many miseries it brings upon them. But in my opinion, Socrates, these persons miss the true cause of their unhappiness. For if old age were the cause, the same discomforts would have been also felt by me, as an old man, and by every other person that has reached that period of life. But, as it is, I have before now met with several old men who expressed themselves in a quite different manner; and in particular I may mention Sophocles the poet, who was once asked in my presence, c "How do you feel about sex, Sophocles? are you still capable of it?" to which he replied, "Hush! if you please: to my great delight I have escaped from it, and feel as if I had escaped from a frantic and savage master." I thought then, as I do now, that he spoke wisely. For unquestionably old age brings us profound peace and freedom from this and other passions. When the appetites have abated, and their force is diminished, the description of Sophocles is perfectly real- d ized. It is like being delivered from a multitude of furious masters. But the complaints on this score, as well as the troubles with relatives, may all be referred to one cause, and that is, not the age, Socrates, but the character of the men. If they possess well-regulated souls and easy tempers, old age itself is no intolerable burden; but if they are differently constituted, why in that case, Socrates, they find even youth as difficult as old age.

    I admired these remarks of Cephalus and wishing him to go on talking, I endeavored to draw him out by saying: I think, Cephalus, that people do not generally welcome these e views of yours, because they think that it is not your character, but your great wealth that enables you to bear with old age. For the rich, it is said, have many consolations.

True, he said, they will not believe me; and they are partly right, though not so right as they suppose. There is great truth in the reply of Themistocles to the Seriphian who tauntingly told him that his reputation 330 was due not to himself, but to his country: "I should not have become famous if I had been a native of Seriphus; neither would you, if you had been an Athenian." And to those who, not being rich, are impatient with old age, it may be said with equal justice, that while on the one hand, a good man cannot be altogether cheerful with old age and poverty combined, so on the other, no wealth can ever make a bad man at peace with himself.

But has your property, Cephalus, been chiefly inherited or acquired?

b   You want to know how I have acquired it, Socrates? Why, in the conduct of money matters, I stand midway between my grandfather and my father. My grandfather, whose name I bear, inherited nearly as much property as I now possess, and increased it until it was many times as large; while my father Lysanias brought it down even below what it now is. For my part, I shall be content to leave it to these my sons not less, but if anything rather larger, than it was when it came into my hands.

I asked the question, I said, because you seemed to me to be not very fond of money— c   which is generally the case with those who have not made it themselves; whereas those who have made it, are attached to it twice as much as other people. For just as poets love their own works, and fathers their own children, in the same way those who have created a fortune value their money, not merely for its uses, like other persons, but because it is their own production. This makes them moreover disagreeable companions, because they will praise nothing but riches.

It is true, he replied.

Indeed it is, said I. But let me ask you   d one more question. What do you think is the greatest advantage that you have derived from being wealthy?

If I mention it, he replied, I shall perhaps get few persons to agree with me. Be assured, Socrates, that when a man is nearly persuaded that he is going to die, he feels alarmed and concerned about things which never affected him before. Until then he has laughed at the stories concerning those in Hades, which tell us that he who has done wrong here must suffer for it there; but now his mind is tormented with a fear that these   e stories may possibly be true. And either owing to the infirmity of old age, or because he is now nearer to what happens there, he has a clearer insight into those mysteries. However that may be, he becomes full of misgiving and apprehension, and sets himself to the task of calculating and reflecting whether he has done any wrong to anyone. Then, if he finds his life full of unjust deeds, he is apt to awaken from sleep in terror, chil-   331 dren do, and he lives haunted by gloomy anticipations. But for the man who is conscious of no unjust deeds sweet hope is always present, that "kind nurse of old age," as Pindar calls it. For indeed, Socrates, those are beautiful words of his, in which he says of the man who has lived a just and holy life,

Sweet Hope is his companion, cheering his heart,
The nurse of age; Hope, which, more than anything else,
Steers the capricious will of mortal men.

There is really a wonderful truth in this description. And it is this consideration, I think, that makes the possession of wealth most valuable, not for everybody, but for   b the decent and orderly person. Not to have cheated or lied to anyone against one's will, not to leave for the other world in fear, owing sacrifices to a god or money to a man, to this wealth contributes a great deal. There are many other uses as well. But after weighing them all separately, Socrates, I am inclined to consider this service as anything but the least important which riches can render to a sensible man.

You have spoken admirably, Cephalus. But are we to say that justice is this thing, namely to speak the truth and to give back what one has taken from another? Or is it possible for actions of this very nature to be sometimes just and sometimes unjust? For example, I suppose, everyone would admit that, if a man, while in the possession of his senses, were to place dangerous weapons in the hands of a friend, and afterwards in a fit of madness to demand them back, such a deposit ought not to be restored, and that his friend would not be a just man if he either returned the weapons, or consented to tell the whole truth to someone in such a condition.

You are right, he replied.

Then it does not provide a definition of justice to say that it consists in speaking the truth and restoring what one has received.

But it is indeed, Socrates, said Polemarchus, interrupting, at least if we are at all to believe Simonides.

Very well, said Cephalus, I will just leave the discussion to you. It is time for me to attend to the sacrifices.

Then Polemarchus inherits your share in it, does he not? I asked.

Certainly, he replied, with a smile; and immediately withdrew to the sacrifices.

Answer me then, I proceeded, you that are the heir to the discussion: What do you maintain to be the correct account of justice, as given by Simonides?

That to restore to each man what is his due, is just. To me it seems that Simonides is right in giving this account of the matter.

Well, certainly it is not an easy matter to disbelieve Simonides: for he is a wise and inspired man. But what he means by his words, you, Polemarchus, may perhaps understand, though I do not. It is clear that he does not mean what we were saying just now, namely, that property given by one person in trust to another, is to be returned to the donor, if he asks for it in a state of insanity. And yet I conclude that property given in trust is due to the truster. Is it not?

Yes, it is.

But, when the person who asks for it is not in his senses, it must not be returned on any account, must it?

True, it must not.

Then it would seem that Simonides means something different from this, when he says that it is just to restore what is due.

Most certainly he does, he replied. For he declares that the debt of friend to friend is to do good to one another, and not harm.

I understand. The person who returns money to a depositor does not restore what is due, if the repayment on the one side, and the receipt on the other, prove to be injurious, and if the two parties are friends. Is not this, according to you, the meaning of Simonides?

Certainly it is.

Well, must we restore to our enemies whatever happens to be due to them?

Yes, no doubt, what is due to them; and the debt of an enemy to an enemy is, I suppose, harm—because harm is what is fitting.

So then it would seem that Simonides, after the manner of poets, employed a riddle to describe the nature of justice: for apparently he thought that justice consisted in rendering to each man that which is appropriate to him, which he called his due. What do you think? Suppose that subsequently someone had asked him the following question: "That being the case, Simonides, what due and appropriate thing is rendered by the art called medicine, and what are the recipients?" What do you think he would have answered us?

Obviously he would have said that bodies are the recipients, and drugs, meats, and drinks, the things rendered.

And what due and appropriate thing is rendered by the art called cookery, and what are the recipients?

Seasoning is the thing rendered; meals are the recipients.

Good; then what is the thing rendered by the art that we are to call justice, and who are the recipients?

If we are to be at all guided by our previous statements, Socrates, assistance and harm are the things rendered, friends and enemies the recipients.

Then, by justice, Simonides means doing good to our friends and harm to our enemies, does he?

I think so.

Now, in cases of illness, who is best able to do good to friends and harm to enemies, with reference to health and disease?

A physician.

And, on a voyage, who is best able to do good to friends and harm to enemies, with reference to the perils of the sea?

A pilot.

Well, in what transaction, and with reference to what object, is the just man best able to help his friends and injure his enemies?

In the transactions of war, I imagine, as the ally of the former, and the antagonist of the latter.

Good. You will grant, my dear Polemarchus, that a physician is useless to persons in good health.

Certainly.

And a pilot to persons on shore.

Yes.

Is the just man, also, useless to those who are not at war?

I do not quite think that.

Then justice is useful in time of peace too, is it?

It is.

And so is farming, is it not?

Yes.

That is to say, as a means of acquiring the fruits of the earth.

Yes.

And further, the shoemaker's art is also useful, is it not?

Yes.

As a means of acquiring shoes, I suppose you will say.

Certainly.

Well then, of what do you think that justice promotes the use or acquisition in peacetime?

Of contracts, Socrates.

And by contracts do you understand partnerships, or something different?

Partnerships, certainly.

Then is it the just man, or the skillful checkers-player, that makes a good and useful partner in playing checkers?

The checkers-player.

Well, in bricklaying and stone masonry is the just man a more useful and a better partner than the regular builder?

By no means.

Well then, in what partnership is the just man superior to the harp-player, in the sense in which the harp-player is a better partner than the just man in playing music?

In a money-partnership, I think.

Except perhaps, Polemarchus, when the object is to lay out money—as when a horse is to be bought or sold by the partners—in which case, I imagine, the horse-dealer is better. Is he not?

Apparently he is.

And again, when a ship is to be bought or sold, the ship-builder or pilot is better.

It would seem so.

That being the case, when does the opportunity arrive for that joint use of silver or gold, in which the just man is more useful than anyone else?

When you want to place your money in trust and have it safe, Socrates.

That is to say, when it is to be deposited, and not to be put to any use?

Just so.

So that justice can only be usefully applied to money when the money is useless?

d

It looks like it.

In the same way, when you want to keep a pruning-knife, justice is useful whether you be in partnership or not; but when you want to use it, justice gives place to the art of those who tend grapevines.

Apparently.

Do you also maintain that, when you want to keep a shield or a lyre without using them, justice is useful; but when you want to use them, you require the art of the soldier or of the musician?

I must.

And so of everything else. Justice is useless when a thing is in use, but useful when it is out of use?

e

So it would seem.

Then, my friend, justice cannot be a very valuable thing if it is only useful as applied to things useless. But let us continue the inquiry thus. Is not the man who is most expert in dealing blows in an encounter, whether in boxing or otherwise, also most expert in deflecting blows?

Certainly.

Is it not also true that whoever is expert in repelling a disease, and evading its attack, is also extremely expert in producing it in others?

334

I think so.

And undoubtedly a man is well able to guard an army, when he has also a talent for stealing the enemy's plans and all his other operations.

Certainly.

That is to say, a man can guard expertly whatever he can thieve expertly.

So it would seem.

Hence, if the just man is expert in guarding money, he is also expert in stealing it.

I confess the argument points that way.

Then apparently it turns out that the just man is a kind of thief—something which   b
you have probably learnt from Homer, with whom Autolycus, the maternal grandfather of Odysseus, is a favorite, because, as the poet says, he outdid all men in thievishness and perjury. Justice therefore, according to you, Homer, and Simonides, appears to be a kind of art of stealing, whose object, however, is to help one's friends and injure one's enemies. Was not this your meaning?

Most certainly it was not, he replied; but I no longer know what I did mean. However, it is still my opinion that justice is helping one's friends, and hurting one's enemies.   c

Should you describe a man's friends as those who seem to him to be, or those who really are, honest men, though they may not seem so? And do you define a man's enemies on the same principle?

I should certainly expect a man to love all whom he thinks honest, and hate all whom he thinks wicked.

But do not people make mistakes in this matter, and imagine many persons to be honest who are not really honest, and many wicked who are not really wicked?

They do.

Then to such persons the good are enemies, and the bad are friends, are they not?

Certainly they are.

And, notwithstanding this, it is just   d
for such persons at such times to help the wicked, and to injure the good.

Apparently it is.

Yet surely the good are just, and injustice is foreign to their nature.

True.

Then, according to your argument, it is just to do harm to those who commit no injustice.

No way, Socrates, for that looks like a wicked speech.

Then it is just, said I, to injure the unjust and to assist the just.

That is evidently better than the former.

In that case, Polemarchus, the result will be that, in those numerous instances in which people have thoroughly mistaken their men, it is just for these mistaken persons to injure their friends, because in their eyes they are wicked; and to help their enemies, because they are good. And thus our statement will be in direct opposition to the meaning which we assigned to Simonides.

That consequence certainly follows, he replied. But let us change our positions: for very probably our definition of friend and enemy was incorrect.

What was our definition, Polemarchus?

That a friend is one who seems to be an honest man.

And what is to be our new definition?

That a friend is one who not only seems to be, but really is, an honest man; whereas the man who seems to be, but is not honest, is not really a friend, but only seems one. And I define an enemy on the same principle.

Then, by this way of speaking, the good man will, in all likelihood, be a friend, and the wicked an enemy.

Yes.

Then you would have us attach to the idea of justice more than that which we at first included in it, when we called it just to do good to our friend and bad to our enemy. We are now, if I understand you, to make an addition to this, and render it thus: It is just to do good to our friend if he is a good man, and to hurt our enemy if he is a bad man.

Precisely so, he replied; I think that this would be well said.

Now is it the act of a just man, I asked, to hurt anybody?

Certainly it is, he replied; that is to say, it is his duty to hurt those who are both wicked, and enemies of his.

Are horses made better, or worse, by being hurt?

Worse.

Worse with reference to the excellence of dogs, or that of horses?

That of horses.

Are dogs in the same way made worse by being hurt, with reference to the excellence of dogs, and not of horses?

Unquestionably they are.

And must we not, on the same principle, assert, my friend, that men, by being hurt, are lowered in the scale of virtue or human excellence?

Indeed we must.

But is not justice a virtue?

Undoubtedly it is.

And therefore, my friend, those men who are hurt necessarily become more unjust.

So it would seem.

Can musicians, by the art of music, make men unmusical?

They cannot.

Can riding-masters, by the art of riding, make men bad riders?

No.

But if so, can the just by justice make men unjust? In short, can the good by goodness make men bad?

No, it is impossible.

True; for, if I am not mistaken, it is the work, not of warmth, but of its opposite, to make things cold.

Yes.

And it is the work not of drought, but of its opposite, to make things wet.

Certainly.

Then it is the work not of good, but of its opposite, to hurt.

Apparently it is.

Well, is the just man good?

Certainly he is.

Then, Polemarchus, it is the work, not of the just man, but of his opposite, the unjust man, to hurt either friend or any other creature.

e You seem to me to be perfectly right, Socrates.

Hence if anyone asserts that it is just to render to every man his due, and if he understands by this, that what is due on the part of the just man is injury to his enemies, and assistance to his friends, the assertion is that of an unwise man. For what was said is untrue: because we have discovered that, in no instance, is it just to injure anybody.

I grant you are right.

Then you and I will make common cause against anyone who shall attribute this to Simonides, or Bias, or Pittacus, or any other wise and highly favored man.

Very good, said he; I, for one, am quite ready to take my share of the fighting.

336 Do you know who I think is the author of this saying, that it is just to help our friends, and hurt our enemies?

Who?

I attribute it to Periander, or Perdiccas, or Xerxes, or Ismenias the Theban, or some other rich man who thought himself very powerful.

You are perfectly right.

Well, but as we have again failed to dis-
b cover the true definition of justice and the just, what other definition can one propose?

While we were still in the middle of our discussion, Thrasymachus was, more than once, bent on interrupting the conversation with objections; but he was checked on each occasion by those who sat by, who wished to hear the argument out. However, when I had made this last remark and we had come to a pause, he could restrain himself no longer, but, gathering himself up like a wild beast, he sprang upon us, as if he would tear us in pieces. I and Polemarchus were terrified and startled; while Thrasymachus, raising his c voice to the company, said, What nonsense has possessed you and Polemarchus all this time, Socrates? And why do you play the fool together, submitting to one another? No, if you really wish to understand what justice is, do not confine yourself to asking questions, and making a display of refuting the answers that are returned—for you are aware that it is easier to ask questions than to answer them; but give us an answer also yourself, and tell us what you assert justice to be, and do not answer me by defining it as d the obligatory, or the advantageous, or the profitable, or the lucrative, or the expedient; but whatever your definition may be, let it be clear and precise: for I will not accept your answer, if you talk such trash as that.

When I heard this speech, I was astounded, and gazed at the speaker in terror; and I think if I had not set eyes on him before he eyed me, I should have been struck dumb. But, as it was, when he began to be exasperated by the conversation, I had looked him in the face first— so that I e was enabled to reply to him, and said with a slight tremble: Thrasymachus, do not be hard upon us. If I and Polemarchus are making mistakes in our examination of the subject, be assured that the error is involuntary. You do not suppose that, if we were looking for a piece of gold, we would ever willingly give way to one another in the search as to spoil the chance of finding it; and therefore, do not suppose that, in seeking for justice, which is a thing more precious than many pieces of gold, we should give way to one another so weakly as you describe, instead of doing our very best to bring it to light. You, my friend, may think so, if you choose; but I think we are unable 337 to do that. Surely then we might very reasonably expect to be pitied, not harshly treated, by such clever men as you.

When he had heard my reply, he burst out laughing very scornfully, and said: By Hercules! Here is an instance of that irony which Socrates affects. I knew how it would be, and warned the company that you would refuse to answer, and would be ironic, and do anything rather than reply, if anyone asked you a question.

Yes, you are a wise man, Thrasymachus, I replied; and therefore you were well aware b that, if you asked a person what factors make the number 12, and at the same time warned him thus: "Please do not tell me that 12 is twice 6, or 3 times 4, or 6 times 2, or 4 times 3. For I will not take such nonsense from you;" you were well aware, I dare say, that no one would give an answer to such an inquirer. But suppose the person replied to you thus: "Thrasymachus, explain yourself; am I to be precluded from all these answers which you have denounced? What, my good sir! even if one of these is the real answer, am I still to be precluded from giving it, and c am I to make a statement that is at variance with the truth? Or what is your meaning?" What reply should you make to this inquiry?

Oh, indeed! he exclaimed; as if the two cases were alike!

There is nothing to prevent their being so, I replied. However, suppose they are not alike; still if one of these answers seems the right one to the person questioned, do you think that our forbidding it, or not, will affect his determination to give the answer which he believes to be the correct one?

Do you not mean that this is what you are going to do? You will give one of the answers on which I have put a veto?

It would not surprise me if I did; sup-d posing I thought right to do so, after examination.

Then, what if I produce another answer on the subject of justice, unlike those I denounced, and superior to them all? What punishment do you think you deserve?

Simply the punishment which it is proper for the non-knower to submit to; and that is, I suppose, to be instructed by those who know. This, then, is the punishment which I, among others, deserve to suffer.

Really you are a pleasant person, he replied. But, besides being instructed, you must make me a payment.

I will, when I have any money, I replied.

But you have, said Glaucon. So, as far as money is a consideration, speak on, Thrasymachus. We will all contribute for Socrates.   e

Oh, to be sure! said he; in order that Socrates, I suppose, may pursue his usual plan of refusing to answer himself, while he criticizes and refutes the answers given by other people.

My excellent friend, said I, how can an answer be given by a person who, in the first place, does not, and confesses he does not, know what to answer; and who, in the next place, if he has any thoughts upon the subject, has been forbidden by a man who is not 338 afraid to say what he believes? No, it is more fitting that you should be the speaker; because you profess to know the subject, and to have something to say. Therefore do not decline; but gratify me by answering, and do not be reluctant to instruct Glaucon and the rest of the company as well.

When I had said this, Glaucon and the others begged him to comply. Now it was evident that Thrasymachus was eager to speak, in order that he might gain glory, because he thought himself in possession of a very fine answer. But he was still eager for me to be the one to answer. At last he gave in, and then said: This here then is   b the wisdom of Socrates! He will not give instruction himself, but he goes about and learns from others, without even showing gratitude for their lessons.

As for my learning from others, Thrasymachus, I replied, there you speak truly; but it is false of you to say that I pay no gratitude in return. I *do* pay all I can; and, as I have no money, I can only give praise. How readily I do this, if in my judgment a person speaks well, you will very soon find out, when you make your answer. For I expect *you* to speak well.

c Then listen, said he. I say that justice is simply the advantage of the stronger. Well, why do you not praise me? No, you refuse.

Not so, I replied; I am only waiting to understand your meaning, which at present I do not see. You say that the interest of the stronger is just. What in the world do you mean by this, Thrasymachus? You do not, I presume, mean anything like this, that, if Polydamas, the athlete, is stronger than we are, and it is for his interest to eat beef in order to strengthen his body, such food is d for the interest of us weaker men, and therefore is just.

You are disgusting, Socrates; you take up my speech in such a way as to damage it most easily.

No, no, my excellent friend; but state your meaning more clearly.

So you are not aware, he continued, that some cities are ruled by a tyrant, and others by a democracy, and others by an aristocracy?

Of course I am.

In every city does not superior strength reside in the ruling body?

Certainly it does.

And further, each regime has its laws e framed to suit its own interests. A democracy makes democratic laws, a tyrant tyrannical laws, and so on. Now by this procedure these regimes have pronounced that what is for the interest of themselves is just for their subjects; and whoever deviates from this, is chastised by them as guilty of ille-339 gality and injustice. Therefore, my good sir, my meaning is, that in all cities the same thing, namely, the interest of the established regime, is just. And superior strength, I presume, is to be found on the side of regime.

So that the conclusion of right reasoning is that the same thing, namely, the interest of the stronger, is everywhere just.

Now I understand your meaning, and I will endeavor to make out whether it is true or not. So then, Thrasymachus, you yourself in your answer have defined justice as interest, though you forbade my giving any such reply. To be sure, you have made an addition, and describe it as the interest of the stronger.

Yes, quite a trifling addition, perhaps.   b

It remains to be seen, whether it is an important one. We need to examine whether you spoke truly. I agree that justice is a matter of interest, but you expand this into the assertion that justice is the interest of the stronger—and I do not know about that. Therefore we must certainly examine it.

Please do so.

It shall be done. Be so good as to answer this question. You no doubt also maintain that it is just to obey the rulers?

I do.

Are the rulers infallible in every city, or   c are they liable to make a few mistakes?

No doubt they are liable to make mistakes.

And therefore, when they undertake to frame laws, is their work sometimes rightly, and sometimes wrongly done?

I should suppose so.

Do "rightly" and "wrongly" mean, respectively, legislating for, and against, their own interests? Or how do you state it?

Just as you do.

And do you maintain that whatever has been enacted by the rulers must be obeyed by their subjects, and that this is justice?

Unquestionably I do.   d

Then, according to your argument, it is not only just to do what makes for the interest of the stronger, but also to do what runs counter to his interest, in other words, the opposite of the former.

What are you saying?

What *you* say, I believe. But let us examine the point more thoroughly. Has it not been agreed that, when the rulers urge their subjects to do certain things, they are sometimes thoroughly mistaken as to what is best for themselves; and that, whatever is urged by them, it is just for their subjects to obey? Has not this been admitted?

Yes, I think so, he replied.

Then let me tell you, that you have also admitted that justice is doing what is disad-

e vantageous to the rulers and the stronger, namely whenever the rulers unintentionally order things that are bad for themselves and nevertheless insist that it is just to obey such things—that is what you said. In that case, O most wise Thrasymachus, must it not follow as a matter of course, that it is just to act in direct opposition to what you said? For, obviously, it is enjoined upon the weaker to do what is disadvantageous to the stronger.

340 Yes, indeed, Socrates, said Polemarchus; that is perfectly clear.

No doubt, retorted Cleitophon, if you appear as a witness in Socrates' behalf.

What do we want witnesses for? said Polemarchus. Thrasymachus himself admits that the rulers sometimes enjoin what is bad for themselves; and that it is just for their subjects to obey such injunctions.

No, Polemarchus; Thrasymachus laid it down that to do what the rulers command is just.

Yes, Cleitophon; and he also laid it down that the interest of the stronger is just. And having laid down these two positions, he

b further admitted that the stronger party sometimes orders its weaker subjects to do what is disadvantageous to its own interests. And the consequence of these admissions is, that what is for the interest of the stronger will be not a bit more just than what is not for his interest.

But, said Cleitophon, by the interest of the stronger he meant, what the stronger conceived to be for his own interest. His position was, that this must be done by the weaker, and that this is the notion of justice.

That was not what he said, replied Polemarchus.

It does not matter, Polemarchus, said I;   c if Thrasymachus chooses to speak this way now, let us make no objection to his doing so.

Tell me then, Thrasymachus, was this the definition you meant to give of justice, that it is what seems to the stronger to be to his advantage, whether it really be for his interest or not? Shall we take that as your account of it?

Certainly not, he replied; do you think I should call a man who is mistaken, at the time of his mistake, the stronger?

Why I thought that you said as much, when you admitted that rulers are not infallible, but do really commit some mistakes.   d

You are a self-seeking flatterer, Socrates. Do you now call that man a physician who is in error about the treatment of the sick, with strict reference to his error? Or do you call another an accountant, who makes a mistake in a calculation, at the time of his mistake, and with reference to that mistake? We say, to be sure, in so many words that the physician was in error, and the accoun-   e tant or the writer was in error; but in fact each of these, I imagine, in so far as he is what we call him, never falls into error. So that, to speak with precise accuracy, since you require such preciseness of language, no craftsman errs. For it is through a failure of knowledge that a man errs, and to that extent he is no craftsman; so that whether as craftsman, or wise man, or ruler, no one errs while he actually is what he professes to be; although everyone would say that such a physician was in error, or such a ruler was   341 in error. You should understand the answer

I just gave in this sense. But the statement, if expressed with perfect accuracy, would be that a ruler, in so far as he is a ruler, never errs, and so long as this is the case, he enacts what is best for himself, and this is what must be done by the one ruled. Therefore, as I began with saying, I call it just to do what is for the advantage of the stronger.

Very good, Thrasymachus; you think me a quibbler, do you?

Yes, a thorough-going quibbler.

Do you think that I ask you these questions with the mischievous intent of laying a trap for your argument?

b   I am quite sure of it. However you shall gain nothing by it; for you shall neither injure me by taking me unawares, nor will you be able to overpower me by argument.

I should not think of attempting it, my excellent friend! But that nothing of this kind may occur again, tell me whether you employ the words "ruler" and "stronger" in the popular sense of them, or with the precise meaning of which you were speaking just now, when you say that it is just for the weaker to do what is for the advantage of the ruler as being the stronger.

I mean a ruler in the strictest sense of the word. So now try your powers of quibbling and mischief; I ask for no mercy. But you

c   won't be able to succeed.

Why, do you suppose I should be so mad as to attempt to shave a lion, or play off quibbles on a Thrasymachus?

At any rate you tried it just now, though you failed utterly.

Enough of this banter, I replied. Tell me this: Is the physician of whom you spoke as being strictly a physician, a maker of money, or a healer of the sick? Take care you speak of the real physician.

A healer of the sick.

And what of a pilot? Is the true pilot a sailor or a commander of sailors?

d   A commander of sailors.

There is no need, I imagine, to take into account his being on board the ship, nor should he be called a sailor: for it is not in virtue of his being on board that he has the name of pilot, but in virtue of his art and of his rule over the sailors.

True.

Has not each of these persons an advantage of his own?

Certainly.

And is it not the proper end of their art to seek and procure what is for the advantage of each of them?

It is.

Has each of the arts any other advantage to pursue than its own highest perfection?   e

What does your question mean?

Why, if you were to ask me whether it is sufficient for a man's body to be a body, or whether it stands in need of something additional, I should say, Certainly it does. To this fact the discovery of the healing art is due, because the body is defective, and it is not enough for it to be a body. Therefore the art of medicine has been devised to provide the body with advantageous things. Should I be   342 right, do you think, in so expressing myself, or not?

You would be right.

Well then, is the art of medicine itself defective, or does every art need some additional virtue: just as the eyes need sight, and ears hearing, so that these organs need a certain art which investigates and provides what is conducive to their ends. Is there, I ask, any defective- ness in an art as such, so   b that every art should require another art to be concerned with its advantages, and this other provisional art would need a third, with a similar function, and so on, without any end? Or will each art investigate its own advantages? Or is it unnecessary either for itself, or for any other art, to inquire into the appropriate remedy for its own defects, because there are no defects or faults in any art, and because it is not the duty of an art to seek the interests of anything save that to which, as an art, it belongs, being itself free from hurt and blemish as a true art, so long as it continues to be what it is strictly and with integrity? View the question according to the strict meaning of terms, as we agreed.

c   Is it so or otherwise?

Apparently it is so, he replied.

Then the art of healing does not consider the interest of the art of healing, but the interest of the body.

Yes.

Nor horsemanship what is good for horsemanship, but for horses. Nor does any other art seek its own interest—for it has no wants—but the good of that to which as an art it belongs.

Apparently it is so.

Well, but you will grant, Thrasymachus, that an art rules and is stronger than that of which it is the art.

He assented, with great reluctance, to this proposition.

Then no science or knowledge investigates or orders the interest of the stronger,

d   but the interest of the weaker, its subject.

To this also he at last assented, though he attempted to be combative about it. After gaining his admission, I proceeded: Then is it not also true, that no physician, in so far as he is a physician, considers or orders what is for the physician's interest, but that all seek the good of their patients? For we have agreed that a physician strictly so called, is a ruler of bodies, and not a maker of money, have we not?

e   He allowed that we had.

And that a pilot strictly so called is a commander of sailors, and not a sailor?

We have.

Then this kind of pilot and commander will not seek and order the pilot's interest, but that of the sailor and the subordinate.

He reluctantly gave his assent.

And thus, Thrasymachus, all who are in any place of ruling, in so far as they are rulers, neither consider nor order their own interest, but that of the subjects for whom   343 they exercise their craft; and in all that they do or say, they act with an exclusive view to *them*, and to what is good and proper for *them*.

When we had arrived at this stage of the discussion, and it had become evident to all that the explanation of justice was completely reversed, Thrasymachus, instead of making any answer, said, Tell me, Socrates, do you have a wet-nurse?

Why? I rejoined; had you not better answer my questions than make inquiries of that sort?

Why because she leaves you to drivel, and omits to wipe your nose when you require it, so that in consequence of her neglect you cannot even distinguish between sheep and   b shepherd.

For what particular reason do you think so?

Because you think that shepherds and herdsmen regard the good of their sheep and of their oxen, and fatten them and take care of them with other views than to benefit their masters and themselves; and you actually imagine that the rulers in cities, those I mean who are really rulers, are otherwise minded towards their subjects than as one would feel towards sheep, or that they think of anything else by night   c and by day than how they may secure their own advantage. And you are so far wrong regarding justice and injustice, the just and the unjust, that you do not know that the just is really the good of another, that is to say the advantage of the stronger and of the ruler, but a disadvantage to those who are subordinates and servants; whereas injustice is the reverse, ruling those that are really simple-minded and just, so that they, as subjects, do what is for the interest of the unjust man who is stronger than they, and   d promote his happiness by their services, but not their own in the least degree. You may see by the following considerations, my most simple Socrates, that a just man everywhere has the worst of it, compared with an unjust man. In the first place, in their mutual dealings, wherever a just man enters into partnership with an unjust man, you will find that at the dissolution of the partnership the just man never has more than the unjust man, but always less. Then again in their dealings with the city, when there is a property-tax to pay, the just man will pay more and the unjust less, on the same amount of property; and when there is anything to receive, the one gets noth-

e ing, while the other makes great gains. And whenever either of them holds any ruling office, if the just man suffers no other loss, at least his private affairs fall into disorder through want of attention to them, while his principles forbid his deriving any benefit from the public money; and besides this, it is his fate to offend his friends and acquaintances every time that he refuses to serve them at the expense of justice. But with the unjust man everything is reversed. I am speaking of the case I mentioned just now, of an unjust man who has the power

344 to over-reach. To him you must direct your attention, if you wish to judge how much more profitable it is to a man's own self to be unjust than to be just. And you will learn this truth with the greatest ease, if you turn your attention to the most consummate form of injustice, which, while it makes the wrong-doer most happy, makes those who are wronged, and will not retaliate, most miserable. This form is a tyranny, which proceeds not by small degrees, but by wholesale, in its open or fraudulent appropriation of the property of others, whether it be sacred or profane, public or private; perpetrating offenses, if a person commits

b a part of the offense and is found out, he becomes liable to a penalty and incurs deep disgrace. For partial offenders in this class of crimes are called sacrilegious, kidnappers, burglars, thieves, and robbers. But when a man not only seizes the property of his fellow-citizens but captures and enslaves their persons also, instead of those dishonorable titles he is called happy and highly favored, not only by the men of his c own city, but also by all others who hear of the comprehensive injustice which he has wrought. For when people abuse injustice, they do so because they are afraid, not of committing it, but of suffering it. Thus it is, Socrates, that injustice, realized on an adequate scale, is a stronger, a freer, and a more lordly thing than justice; and as I said in the beginning, justice is the advantage of the stronger; injustice, a thing profitable d and advantageous to oneself.

When he had made this speech, Thrasymachus had it in mind to take his departure, after deluging our ears like a bath-man with this copious and unbroken flood of words. Our companions however would not let him go, but obliged him to stay and answer for his arguments. I myself also was especially urgent in my entreaties, exclaiming, Really, my good Thrasymachus, after flinging at us such a speech as this, do you have it in mind to take your leave, before you have satisfactorily taught us, or learned yourself, whether your argument is right or wrong? Do you e think you are undertaking to settle some insignificant question, and not the principles on which each of us must conduct his life in order to lead the most profitable existence?

What else am I supposed to think? said Thrasymachus.

So it seems, I said, or else that you are quite unconcerned about us, and feel no care whether we lead better or worse lives in our ignorance of what you profess to know. But please, my good sir, try to impart 345 your knowledge to us also—any benefit you confer on such a large party as we are will surely be no bad investment. For I tell you plainly for my own part that I am not convinced, and that I do not believe that injustice is more profitable than justice, even if it be let alone and go unhindered in doing what it wants. On the contrary, my good sir, let there be an unjust man, and let him have full power to practice injustice, either by evading detection or by fighting it out, still I am not convinced that such a course is more profitable than justice. This, perhaps, is the feeling of some others among us, as well as mine. Then do convince us satisfactorily, my highly-gifted friend, that we are not well advised in valuing justice above injustice.

But how, said he, can I persuade you? If you are not convinced by my recent statements, what more can I do for you? Must I take the speech and thrust it into your soul?

You should not do that, but in the first place stick to what you say, or if you change your ground, change it openly without deceiving us. As it is, Thrasymachus—for we must not yet take leave of our former investigations—you see that having first defined the meaning of the true physician, you did not think it necessary afterwards to adhere strictly to the true shepherd. On the contrary, you suppose him to feed his sheep, in so far as he is a shepherd, not with an eye to what is best for the flock, but, like a guest about to be feasted, with an eye to the feasting, or else to their sale, like a money-maker, and not like a shepherd. Whereas the only concern of the shepherd's art is, I presume, how it shall secure what is best for *that*, over which it is the appointed guardian. As far as concerns its own perfection, I suppose, sufficient provision is made for that, so long as it lives up to its name; and so I confess I thought we were obliged just now to admit that every regime, insofar as it is a regime, looks solely to the advantage of that which is ruled and tended by it,

whether that regime be of a public or a private nature. But what is your opinion? Do you think that the rulers in cities, who really rule, do so willingly?

No, I do not *think* it, I am sure of it.

But, Thrasymachus, what about other kinds of regime, do you not observe that no one is willing to rule, if he can help it, but that they all ask to be paid on the assumption that the advantages of their regime will not accrue to themselves, but to the governed? For answer me this question: Do we not say without hesitation, that every art is distinguished from other arts by having a distinctive capacity? Be so good, my dear sir, as not to answer contrary to your opinion, or we shall make no progress.

Yes, that is what distinguishes it.

And does not each of them provide us with some special and peculiar benefit? The art of healing, for example, giving us health, that of piloting safety at sea, and so on?

Certainly.

Then is there not an art of wages which provides us with wages, this being its proper power and ability? Or do you call the art of healing and that of piloting identical? Or, if you choose to employ strict definitions as you engaged to do, the fact of a man's regaining his health while acting as a pilot, through the beneficial effects of the sea-voyage, would not make you call the art of the pilot a healing art, would it?

Certainly not.

Nor would you so describe the art of wages, I think, assuming that a person remains healthy while earning his wages.

No.

Well then, would you call the physician's art a mercenary art, if fees be taken for medical attendance?

No.

Did we not allow that the benefit of each art was peculiar to itself?

Be it so.

Then whatever benefit accrues in common to all craftsmen is clearly derived from a common use of one and the same thing.

So it would seem.

And we further maintain, that if these craftsmen are benefited by earning wages, they owe it to their use of the wage-earning craft.

He reluctantly assented.

d Then this advantage, the receipt of pay, does not come to each from his own art, but, strictly considered, the art of healing produces health, and the art of wages produces pay; the art of house-building produces a house, while the art of wages follows it and produces pay; and so of all the rest: each works its own work, and benefits that which is its appointed subject. If, however, an art be practiced without pay, does the craftsman derive any benefit from his art?

Apparently not.

Does he also confer no benefit, when he e works for nothing?

I suppose he does confer benefit.

So far then, Thrasymachus, we see clearly, that an art or a regime never provides that which is profitable for itself, but as we said some time ago, it provides and orders what is profitable for the subject, looking to his interest who is the weaker, and not to the interest of the stronger. It was for these reasons that I said just now, my dear Thrasymachus, that no one will voluntarily take office, or assume the duty of correcting the disorders of others, but that all ask wages for the 347 work, because one who is to prosper in his art never practices or prescribes what is best for himself, but only what is best for the subject, so long as he acts within the limits of his art; and on these grounds, apparently, wages must be given to make men willing to hold office, in the shape of money or honor or, in case of refusal, in the form of punishment.

What do you mean, Socrates? asked Glaucon. I understand two out of the three

kinds of wages; but, what the punishment is, and how you could describe it as playing the part of wages, I do not understand.

Then, I said, you do not understand the wages of the best men, which induce the most virtuous to hold office, when in fact they consent to do so. Do you not know that b to be honor-loving and money-loving is considered a disgrace, and really is a disgrace?

I do.

For this reason, then, good men will not consent to rule, either for the sake of money or for that of honor. For they neither wish to get the name of hirelings by openly exacting pay for their duties, nor of thieves by using their power to obtain it secretly; nor yet will they take office for the sake of c honor, for they are not honor-loving. Therefore compulsion and the fear of a penalty must be brought to bear upon them, to make them consent to hold office—which is probably the reason why it is thought shameful to accept power willingly without waiting to be compelled. Now the heaviest of all penalties is to be ruled by a worse man, in case of one's own refusal to rule; and it is the fear of this, I believe, which induces the men most virtuous and fit to rule, and when they do so, they enter upon their rulership, not with any idea of coming into a good thing, but d as an unavoidable necessity, not expecting to enjoy themselves in it, but because they cannot find any person better or no worse than themselves, to whom they can commit it. For the probability is, that if there were a city composed of none but good men, it would be an object of competition to avoid the possession of power, just as now it is to obtain it; and then it would become clearly evident that it is not the nature of the genuine ruler to look to his own interest, but to that of the subject—so that every judicious man would choose to be the recipient of benefits, rather than to have the trouble of conferring them upon others. Therefore I

e will on no account concede to Thrasymachus that justice is the interest of the stronger. However, we will resume this inquiry
hereafter, for Thrasymachus now affirms
that the life of the unjust man is better than
the life of the just man; and this assertion
seems to me of much greater importance
than the other. Which side do you take,
Glaucon? And which do you think the truer
statement?

I for my part hold, he replied, that the life
of the just man is the more advantageous.

348 Did you hear, I asked, what a long list of
attractions Thrasymachus just now attributed to the life of the unjust man?

I did, but I am not convinced.

Should you then like us to convince him,
if we can find any means of doing so, that
what he says is not true?

Undoubtedly I should.

If then we adopt the plan of matching argument against argument, in which we enumerate all the advantages of being just, and
Thrasymachus replies, and we again put in
our rejoinder: it will be necessary to count
b and measure the advantages which are
claimed on both sides. And eventually we
shall want a jury to give a verdict between
us; but if we proceed in our inquiries, as we
lately did, by the method of mutual agreement, we ourselves shall be both judges and
advocates at the same time.

Precisely so.

Which plan, then, do you prefer?

The latter, he said.

Come then, Thrasymachus, said I, let
us start from the beginning, and oblige us
by answering: Do you assert that a perfect
injustice is more profitable than an equally
perfect justice?

Most decidedly I do; and I have said why.

Well then, how do you describe them
c under another aspect? Probably you call one
of them a virtue, and the other a vice?

Undoubtedly.

That is, justice a virtue, and injustice a vice?

A likely thing, my facetious friend, when
I assert that injustice is profitable, and justice the reverse.

Then what do you say?

Just the contrary.

Do you call justice a vice?

No, but I call it very noble or good-
natured simplicity.

Then do you call injustice ill nature?

No, I call it good judgment.   d

Do you think, Thrasymachus, that the
unjust are actually prudent and good?

Yes, those who are able to practice injustice on the complete scale, having the
power to reduce whole cities and nations of
men to slavery. You, perhaps, imagine that
I am speaking of petty criminals, and I certainly allow that even deeds like theirs are
profitable if they escape detection; but they
are not worthy to be considered in comparison with those I have just mentioned.

I quite understand what you mean; but I   e
did wonder at your ranking injustice under
the heads of virtue and wisdom, and justice
under the opposite.

Well, I do so rank them, without hesitation.

You have now taken up a more stubborn
position, my friend, and it is no longer easy
to know what to say. If after laying down the
position that injustice is profitable, you had
still admitted it to be a vice and a baseness,
as some others do, we should have had an
answer to give, speaking according to con-   349
ventionally received notions; but now it is
plain enough that you will maintain it to be
beautiful, and strong, and will ascribe to it
all the qualities which we have been in the
habit of ascribing to justice, seeing that you
have actually ventured to rank it as a portion of virtue and of wisdom.

You divine most correctly, he said.

Nevertheless, I must not shrink from pursuing the inquiry and the argument, so long
as I suppose that you are saying what you

think. If I am not mistaken, you are really not bantering now, Thrasymachus, but saying what you think to be the truth.

What difference does it make to you whether I think it true or not? You ought to refute the argument!

b   It makes none. But will you endeavor to answer me one more question? Do you think that a just man would wish to get the better of another just man in anything?

Certainly not, for then he would not be so charmingly simple as he is.

Would a just man outdo a just action?

No, he would not go beyond that either.

But would he get the better of an unjust man and think it just to do so, or would he not think it just?

He would think it just, and would have no scruples about doing it, but he would not be able to.

That was not my question, but whether a
c   just man both resolves and desires to outdo an unjust man, but not a just man?

Well, it is so.

But how is it with the unjust man? Would he undertake to get the better of a just man and a just action?

Undoubtedly, when he takes upon himself to outdo all and in every thing.

Then will not the unjust man also take advantage of another unjust man and an unjust action, and struggle that he may himself obtain more than anyone else?

He will.

Then let us put it in this form: The just man does not get the better of his like, but
d   his unlike; but the unjust man gets the better of both his like and his unlike?

Very well said.

And further, the unjust man is prudent and good, the just man is neither.

Well spoken again.

Does not the unjust man further resemble the wise and the good, whereas the just man does not resemble them?

Why, of course, similar people resemble others who are like them, whereas those who are different will not resemble them.

Very good; then the each is like those whom he resembles.

Why, what else would you have?

Very well, Thrasymachus; do you call one man musical, and another unmusical?

I do.

Which of them do you call sensible, and   e
which foolish?

The musical man, of course, I call sensible, and the unmusical, foolish.

Do you also say that wherein a man is sensible, in that he is good, and wherein foolish, bad?

Yes.

Do you speak in the same manner of a medical man?

I do.

Do you think then, my excellent friend, that a musician, when he is tuning a lyre, would wish to outdo a musician in the tightening or loosening of the strings, or would claim to get the better of him?

I do not.

Would he wish to get the better of an unmusical person?

Unquestionably he would.

How would a medical man act? Would he   350
wish to get the better of a medical man or medical practice in a question of diet?

Certainly not.

But he would try to get the better of an unprofessional man?

Yes.

Consider now, looking at every kind of knowledge and ignorance, whether you think that any knowledgeable man whatever would, by his own consent, choose to do or say more than another knowledgeable man, and not the same that one like himself would do in the same matter.

Well, perhaps the latter view is necessarily the true one.

But what do you say to the ignorant person? Would he not get the better of the knowledgeable and the unknowledgeable alike?

Perhaps.

And the knowledgeable person is wise?

Yes.

And the wise man is good.

Yes.

Then a good and a wise man will not wish to get the better of his like, but only of his unlike and opposite?

So it would seem.

But a bad and an ignorant man will take advantage of both his like and his opposite.

Apparently.

Well then, Thrasymachus, does not our unjust man get the better of both his like and his unlike? Was not that your statement?

It was.

But the just man will not go beyond his like, but only beyond his unlike?

Yes.

Consequently the just man resembles the wise and the good, whereas the unjust man resembles the bad and the ignorant.

So it would seem.

But we agreed, you know, that the character of each of them is identical with the character of those whom he resembles.

We did.

Consequently we have made the discovery, that the just man is wise and good, and the unjust man ignorant and bad.

Thrasymachus had made all these admissions, not in the easy manner in which I now relate them, but reluctantly and after much resistance, in the course of which he perspired profusely, as it was hot weather to boot. On that occasion also I saw what I had never seen before—Thrasymachus blushing. But when we had thus mutually agreed that justice was a part of virtue and of wisdom, and injustice of vice and ignorance, I proceeded thus: Very good, we will consider this point settled; but we said, you know, that injustice was also strong. Do you not remember it, Thrasymachus?

I do, he replied; but for my part I am not satisfied with your last conclusions, and I know what I could say on the subject. But if I were to express my thoughts, I am sure you would say that I was haranguing the people like a demagogue. Take your choice then; either allow me to say as much as I please, or if you prefer asking questions, do so; and I will do with you as we do with old women when they tell us stories: I will say "Good," and nod my head or shake it, as the occasion requires.

If so, do no violence to your own opinions.

Anything to please you, he said, as you will not allow me to speak. What else do you want?

Nothing, I assure you; but if you will do this, do so; and I will ask questions.

Proceed then.

Well then, I will repeat the question which I asked you just now, that our inquiry may be carried out continuously; namely, what sort of a thing justice is compared with injustice. It was said, I think, that injustice is more powerful and stronger than justice; but now, seeing that justice is both wisdom and virtue, and injustice is ignorance, it may easily be shown, I imagine, that justice is likewise stronger than injustice. No one can now fail to see this. But I do not wish to settle the question in such a simple way, Thrasymachus, but I would investigate it in the following manner: Would you admit that a city may be unjust, and that it may unjustly attempt to enslave other cities, and thus succeed in so doing, and hold many in such slavery to itself?

Undoubtedly; and this will be more frequently done by the best city, that is, the one that is most completely unjust, than by any other.

I understand, I said, that this is your position. But the question which I wish to consider is, whether the city that is stronger than another city, will have this power without the aid of justice, or whether justice will be indispensable to it.

c   If, as you said just now, justice is wisdom, justice must lend her aid; but if it is as I said, injustice must lend hers.

I am quite delighted to find, Thrasymachus, that you are not content merely to nod and shake your head, but give exceedingly good answers.

I do it to please you.

You are very good; but indulge me so far as to say, whether you think that either a city, or an army, or a band of thieves or robbers, or any other body of men, pursuing certain unjust ends in common, could succeed in any enterprise if they were to deal unjustly with one another?

d   Certainly not.

If they refrain from being unjust towards one another, will they not be more likely to succeed?

Yes, certainly.

Because, I presume, Thrasymachus, injustice breeds divisions and animosities and brawls between man and man, while justice creates unanimity and friendship; does it not?

So be it, he said; just so I don't quarrel with you.

Truly I am very much obliged to you, my excellent friend; but tell me this: If the working of injustice, wherever it exists, is to implant hatred, will not its presence, whether among freemen or slaves, cause them to hate one another, and to form parties, and dis-

e   able them from doing anything together?

Certainly.

Well, and if it exists in two persons, will they not quarrel and hate one another, and be enemies each to the other, and both of them hate the just?

They will.

And supposing, my admirable friend, that injustice has taken up its residence in a single individual, will it lose its proper power, or retain it just the same?

We will say it retains it.

And does not its power appear to be of such a nature, as to make any subject in which it resides, whether it be city, or family, or army, or anything else whatsoever, unable to act unitedly, because of the divisions and quarrels it excites; and moreover its makes   352 that thing hostile both to itself and to everything that opposes it, and to the just? Is it not so?

Certainly it is.

Then, if it appears in an individual also, it will produce all these its natural results. In the first place it will make him unable to act because of inward strife and division; in the next place, it will make him an enemy to himself and to the just, will it not?

It will.

And the gods, my friend, are just?

We will suppose they are.

Then to the gods also will the unjust man   b be an enemy, and the just a friend.

Feast on your argument, said he, to your heart's content: I will not oppose you, or I shall give offense to the company.

Be so good, said I, as to make my entertainment complete by continuing to answer as you have now been doing. I am aware, indeed, that the just are shown to be wiser, and better, and more able to act than the unjust, who are indeed incapable of any combined action. We do not speak with entire accuracy when we say that any party of unjust   c men ever acted vigorously in concert together. For, had they been thoroughly unjust, they could not have kept their hands off each other. But it is obvious that there was some justice at work in them, which made them refrain at any rate from injuring, at one and the same moment, both their comrades and

the objects of their attacks, and which enabled them to achieve what they did achieve;
and that their injustice partly disabled them,
even in the pursuit of their unjust ends, since
those who are complete villains, and thor-
d oughly unjust, are also thoroughly unable to
act. I understand that all this is true, and that
what you at first set down is not true. But
whether the just also live a better life, and are
happier than the unjust, is a question which
we proposed to consider next, and which we
now have to investigate. Now, I for my part,
think it is already apparent, from what we
have said, that they do; nevertheless, we must
examine the point still more carefully. For
we are debating no trivial question, but the
manner in which a man ought to live.

Please consider it.

I will. Tell me, do you think there is such
a thing as a horse's work.

c I do.

Would you, then, describe the work of a
horse, or of anything else whatever, as that
work, for the accomplishment of which it is
either the only instrument or the best one?

I do not understand.

Look at it this way. Can you see with anything besides eyes?

Certainly not.

Can you hear with anything besides ears?
No.

Then should we not justly say that seeing
and hearing are the functions of these
organs?

Yes, certainly.

Again, you might cut off a shoot of a
353 grape vine with a carving knife, or chisel, or
many other tools?

Undoubtedly.

But with no tool, I imagine, so well as
with the pruning knife made for the purpose.

True.

Then shall we not define pruning to be
the function of the pruning knife?

By all means.

Now then, I think, you will better understand what I wished to learn from you just
now, when I asked whether the function of
a thing is not that work for the accomplishment of which it is either the sole or the best
instrument?

I do understand, and I believe that this is
in every case the function of a thing.   b

Very well, do you not also think that everything which has an appointed function
has also a proper virtue? Let us go back to
the same instances—we say that the eyes
have a function?

They have.

Then have the eyes a virtue also?

They have.

And the ears—did we assign them a
function?

Yes.

Then have they a virtue also?

They have.

And is it the same with all other things?

The same.

Listen then. Do you suppose that the
eyes could accomplish their work well if   c
they had not their own proper virtue, that
virtue being replaced by a vice?

How could they? You mean, probably, if
sight is replaced by blindness.

I mean, whatever their virtue be, for
I have not come to that question yet. At
present I am asking whether it is through
their own peculiar virtue that things perform their proper functions well, and
through their own peculiar vice that they
perform them ill?

You cannot be wrong in that.

Then if the ears lose their own virtue, will
they execute their functions ill?

Certainly.   d

May we include all other things in the
same argument?

I think we may.

Come, then, consider this point next. Has
the soul any function which could not be

executed by means of anything else whatso-ever? For example, could we in justice assign managing and ruling, deliberation and the like, to anything but the soul, or should we pronounce them to be peculiar to it?

We could ascribe them to nothing else.

Again, shall we declare life to be a func-tion of the soul?

Decidedly.

Do we not also maintain that the soul has a virtue?

e   We do.

Then can it ever so happen, Thrasyma-chus, that the soul will perform its func-tions well when destitute of its own peculiar virtue, or is that impossible?

Impossible.

Then a bad soul necessarily manages and rules badly, and a good soul must do all these things well.

Unquestionably.

Now did we not grant that justice was a virtue of the soul, and injustice a vice?

We did.

Consequently the just soul and the just 354   man will live well, and the unjust man ill?

Apparently, according to your argument.

And you will allow that he who lives well is blessed and happy, and that he who lives otherwise is the reverse.

Unquestionably.

Consequently the just man is happy, and the unjust man miserable.

Let us suppose them to be so.

But surely it is not misery, but happiness, that is advantageous.

Undoubtedly.

Never then, my excellent Thrasymachus, is injustice more advantageous than justice.

Well, Socrates, let this be your entertain-ment for the feast of Bendis.

I have to thank *you* for it, Thrasymachus, because you recovered your temper, and left off being angry with me. Nevertheless, I b   have not been well entertained; but that was

my own fault, and not yours. For as glut-tons seize upon every new dish as it goes round, and taste its contents before they have had a reasonable enjoyment of its pre-decessor, so I seem to myself to have left the question which we were at first examining, concerning what the just is, before we had found out the answer to it, in order to rush to the inquiry whether this unknown thing is a vice and an ignorance, or a virtue and a wisdom; and again, when a new argument, that injustice is more profitable than jus-tice, was subsequently started, I could not refrain from passing from the other to this, so that at present the result of our conversa-tion is that I know nothing. For while I do not know what justice is, I am little likely to   c know whether it is in fact a virtue or not, or whether its owner is happy or unhappy.

BOOK II

When I had made these remarks I thought I was to be freed from the discussion; whereas   357 it seems it was only a prelude. For Glaucon, with that eminent courage which he displays on all occasions, would not accept the re-treat of Thrasymachus, and began thus: Socrates, do you wish really to convince us that it is on every account better to be just than to be unjust, or only to seem to have   b convinced us?

If it were up to me, I replied, I should prefer convincing you really.

Then, he proceeded, you are not doing what you wish. Let me ask you, Is there, in your opinion, a class of good things of such a kind that we are glad to possess them, not because we desire their consequences, but simply welcoming them for their own sake? Take, for example, the feelings of enjoyment and all those pleasures that are harmless, and that are followed by no con-sequences, beyond simple enjoyment in their possession.

Yes, I certainly think there is a class of this description.

c   Well, is there another class, do you think, of those which we value, both for their own sake and for their results? Such as intelligence, and sight, and health—all of which we surely welcome on both accounts.

Yes.

And do you further recognize a third class of good things, which would include gymnastics training, and submission to medical treatment in illness, as well as the practice of medicine, and all other means of making money? Things like these we should describe as irksome, and yet beneficial to us; and while we should reject them viewed

d   simply in themselves, we accept them for the sake of the rewards, and of the other consequences which result from them.

Yes, undoubtedly there is such a third class also; but what then?

In which of these classes do you place justice?

358   I should say in the highest—that is, among the good things which will be valued by one who is in the pursuit of true happiness, alike for their own sake and for their consequences. . . .

365   When views like these, he continued, my dear Socrates, are proclaimed and repeated with so much variety, concerning the honors in which virtue and vice are respectively held by gods and men, what can we suppose is the effect produced on the minds of all those good-natured young men, who are able, after skimming like birds, as it were, over all that they hear, to draw conclusions from it, as to what sort of man one must be, and

b   the path in which he must walk, in order to live the best possible life? In all probability a young man would say to himself in the words of Pindar, "Shall I by justice or by crooked wiles climb to a loftier stronghold, and, having thus fenced myself in, live my life?" For common opinion declares that to

be just without being also thought just, is no advantage to me, but only entails manifest trouble and loss; whereas if I am unjust and get myself a name for justice, an unspeakably marvelous life is promised me. Very well then, since the appearance, as the wise   c
inform me, overpowers the truth, and is the sovereign dispenser of happiness, to this I must of course wholly devote myself; I must draw round about me a picture of virtue to serve as an exterior front, but behind me I must keep the fox with its cunning and shiftiness—of which that most clever Archilochus tells us. Yes but, it will be objected, it is not an easy matter always to conceal one's wickedness. No, we shall reply, nor yet is anything else easy that is great; nevertheless, if happiness is to be our goal, this must   d
be our path, as the steps of the argument indicate. To assist in keeping up the deception, we will form secret societies and clubs. There are, moreover, teachers of persuasion, who impart skill in popular and court oratory; and so by persuasion or by force, we shall gain our ends, and carry on our dishonest proceedings with impunity. But, it is urged, neither evasion nor violence can succeed with the gods. Well, but if they either do not exist, or do not concern themselves with the affairs of men, why need we concern ourselves to evade their observation? But if they do exist, and do pay attention to us, we know nothing and have heard nothing of them from any other quarter than the   e
current traditions and the genealogies of poets; and these very authorities state that the gods are beings who may be persuaded and diverted from their purpose by sacrifices and meek supplications and votive offerings. Therefore we must believe them in both statements or in neither. If we are to believe them, we will act unjustly, and offer sacrifices from the proceeds of our crimes. For if we are just, we shall, it is true, escape   366
punishment at the hands of the gods, but

we renounce the profits which accrue from injustice; but if we are unjust, we shall not only make these gains, but also by putting up prayers when we overstep and make mistakes, we shall prevail upon the gods to let us go unscathed. But then, it is again objected, in Hades we shall pay the just penalty for the crimes committed here, either in our own persons or in those of our children's children. But my friend, the champion of the argument will continue, the mystic rites, again, are very powerful, and the absolving

b gods, as we are told by the mightiest cities, and by the sons of the gods who have appeared as poets and inspired prophets, who inform us that these things are so.

What consideration, therefore, remains which should induce us to prefer justice to the greatest injustice? Since if we combine injustice with a spurious decorum, we shall fare to our liking with the gods and with men, in this life and the next, according to the most numerous and the highest authori-

c ties. Considering all that has been said, by what device, Socrates, can a man who has any advantages, either of high talent, or wealth, or personal appearance, or birth, bring himself to honor justice, instead of smiling when he hears it praised? Indeed, if there is any one who is able to show the falsity of what we have said, and who is fully convinced that justice is best, far from being angry with the unjust, he doubtless makes great allowance for them, knowing that, with the exception of those who may possibly refrain from injustice through the disgust of a godlike nature or from the ac-

d quisition of knowledge, there is certainly no one else who is willingly just; but it is from cowardice, or age, or some other infirmity, that men condemn injustice, simply because they lack the power to commit it. And the truth of this is proved by the fact, that the first of these people who comes to power is the first to commit injustice, to the extent

of his ability. And the cause of all this is simply that fact, which my brother and I both stated at the very beginning of this whole argument, Socrates, saying: With all e due respect, to you who profess to be admirers of justice—beginning with the heroes of old, of whom accounts have descended to the present generation—have every one of you, without exception, made the praise of justice and condemnation of injustice turn solely upon the reputation and honor and gifts resulting from them; but what each is in itself, by its own peculiar force as it resides in the soul of its possessor, unseen either by gods or men, has never, in poetry or in prose, been adequately discussed, so as to show that injustice is the greatest curse that a soul can receive into itself, and justice the greatest blessing. Had this been the language used by all of you from the start, and had you tried to persuade us of this from our childhood, we should not be on the watch to check one another in the commis- 367 sion of injustice, because everyone would be his own watchman, fearful lest by committing injustice he might attach to himself the greatest of evils.

All this, Socrates, and perhaps still more than this, would be put forward respecting justice and injustice, by Thrasymachus, and I dare say by others also; thus vulgarly, in my opinion, turning around the power of each. For my own part, I confess—for I do not want to hide anything from you—that b I have a great desire to hear you defend the opposite view, and therefore I have exerted myself to speak as forcefully as I can. So do not limit your argument to the proposition that justice is stronger than injustice, but show us what is that influence exerted by each of them on its possessor, whereby the one is in itself a blessing, and the other a curse; and take away the estimation in which the two are held, as Glaucon urged you to do. For if you omit to withdraw from each quality its true reputation and to add the false, we shall declare that you are praising, not the reality, but the appearance of justice, and blaming, not the reality, but the semblance of injustice; that your advice, in fact, is to be unjust without being found out, and that you hold with Thrasymachus, that justice is another man's good, being for the advantage of the stronger; injustice a man's own interest and advantage, but against the interest of the weaker. Since then you have allowed that justice is one of the greatest goods, the possession of which is valuable, both for the sake of their results, and also in a higher degree for their own sake, such as sight, hearing, understanding, health, and everything else which is genuinely good in its own nature and not merely reputed to be good. Select for commendation this particular feature of justice, I mean the benefit which in itself it confers on its possessor, in contrast with the harm which injustice inflicts. The rewards and reputations leave to others to praise; because in others I can tolerate this mode of praising justice and condemning injustice, which consists in eulogizing or reviling the reputations and the rewards which are connected with them; but in you I cannot, unless you require it, because you have spent your whole life in investigating such questions, and such only. Therefore do not content yourself with proving to us that justice is better than injustice; but show us what is that influence exerted by each on its possessor, by which, whether gods and men see it or not, the one is in itself a good, and the other a detriment.

Much as I had always admired the nature of both Glaucon and Adeimantus, I confess that on this occasion I was quite charmed with what I had heard; so I said: Aptly indeed did Glaucon's admirer address you, sons of the man there named, in the first line of his elegiac poem, after you had distinguished yourselves in the battle of Megara, saying:

Race of a famous man, ye godlike sons of Ariston.

This seems to me well said, my friends, for there is something truly godlike in the state of your minds, if you are not convinced that injustice is better than justice, when you can plead its cause so well. I do believe that you really are not convinced of it. But I infer it from your general character; for judging merely from your statements I should have distrusted you. But the more I place confidence in you, the more I am perplexed how to deal with the case; for though I do not know how I am to render assistance, having learnt how unequal I am to the task from your rejection of my answer to Thrasymachus, wherein I imagined that I had demonstrated that justice is better than injustice; yet, on the other hand, I dare not refuse my assistance, because I am afraid that it might be unholy, when I hear justice disparaged in my presence, to lose heart and desert her, so long as breath and utterance are left in me. My best plan, therefore, is to come to her aid insofar as I can.

Thereupon Glaucon, and all the rest with him, requested me by all means to give my assistance, and not to let the conversation drop, but thoroughly to investigate what each of them is, and the truth with regard to their respective advantages. So I said what seemed to me to be the case. The inquiry we are undertaking is no trivial one, but demands a keen sight, as it appears to me. Therefore, since we are not all that clever, I think we had better adopt a mode of inquiry which may be thus illustrated. Suppose we had been ordered to read small writing at a distance, not having very good eyesight, and that one of us discovered that the same writing was to be found somewhere else in larger letters, and upon a larger space, we should have looked upon it as a piece of luck, I imagine, that we could read the latter first, and then examine the smaller, and observe whether the two were same.

Undoubtedly we should, said Adeimantus; but what parallel can you see to this, e Socrates, in our inquiry after justice?

I will tell you, I replied. We speak of justice as residing in an individual man, and also as residing in an entire city, do we not?

Certainly we do, he said.

Well, a city is larger than one man.

It is.

Perhaps, then, justice may exist in larger proportions in the greater subject, and thus be easier to discover; so, if you please, let 369 us first investigate what justice is like in cities; afterwards let us apply the same inquiry to the individual, looking for the counterpart of the greater as it exists in the form of the less.

Indeed, he said, I think your plan is a good one.

If then we were to trace in speech the gradual formation of a city, should we also see the growth of its justice or of its injustice?

Perhaps we should.

b   Then, if this were done, might we not hope to see more easily the object of our search?

Yes, much more easily.

Is it your advice, then, that we should attempt to carry out our plan? It is no trifling task, I imagine; therefore consider it well.

We have considered it, said Adeimantus; yes, do so by all means.

Well then, I proceeded, the formation of a city is due, as I imagine, to this fact, that we are not individually self-sufficient, but have many wants. Or would you assign any other principle for the founding of cities?

No I agree with you, he replied.

Thus it is, then, that owing to our many c wants, and because each seeks the aid of others to supply his various requirements, we gather many associates and helpers into one dwelling-place, and give to this joint dwelling the name of city. Is it so?

Undoubtedly.

And every one who gives or takes in exchange, whatever it be that he exchanges, does so from a belief that it is better of himself.

Certainly.

Now then, let us construe our city in speech from the beginning. It will owe its construction, it appears, to our needs.

Unquestionably.

Well, but the first and most pressing of d all wants is that of sustenance to enable us to exist as living creatures.

Most decidedly.

Our second want would be that of a house, and our third that of clothing and the like.

True.

Then let us know what will render our city adequate to the supply of so many things. Must we not begin with a farmer for one, and a house-builder, and besides these a weaver? Will these suffice, or shall we add to them a shoemaker, and perhaps some other person who ministers to our bodily wants?

By all means.

Then the smallest possible city will consist of four or five men.

So it seems.

To proceed then, ought each of these to place his own work at the disposal of the e community, so that the single farmer, for example, shall provide food for four, spending four times the amount of time and labor upon the preparation of food, and sharing it with others; or must he neglect of them, and produce for his own consumption alone 370 the fourth part of this quantity of food, in a fourth part of the time, spending the other three parts, one in making his house, another in procuring himself clothes, and the third in providing himself with shoes, saving himself the trouble of sharing with others, and doing his own business by himself, and for himself?

To this Adeimantus replied, Well, Socrates, perhaps the former plan is the easier of the two.

Really, I said, by Zeus, it is not improbable; for I recollect myself, after your answer, that, in the first place, no two persons are born exactly alike, but each differs in his nature, one being suited for one occupation, and another b for another. Do you not think so?

I do.

Well, when is a man likely to succeed best? When he divides his exertions among many skills, or when he devotes himself exclusively to one?

When he devotes himself to one.

Again, it is also clear, I imagine, that if a person lets the right moment for any work go by, it never returns.

It is quite clear.

For the thing to be done does not choose, I imagine, to await the leisure of the doer, but the doer must be at the call of the thing c to be done, and not treat it as a secondary affair.

He must.

From these considerations it follows that all things will be produced in superior quantity and quality, and with greater ease, when each man, being freed from other tasks, works at a single occupation, in accordance with his nature and at the right moment.

Unquestionably.

More than four citizens, then, Adeimantus, are needed to provide the requisites which we named. For the farmer, it appears, will not make his own plough, if it is to be a d good one, nor his hoe, nor any of the other tools employed in agriculture. No more will the builder make the numerous tools which

he also requires; and so of the weaver and the shoemaker.

True.

Then we shall have carpenters and smiths, and many other artisans of the kind, who will become members of our little city, and create a population.

Certainly.

Still it will not yet be very large, supposing we add to them cowherds and shepherds, and the rest of that class, in order that the farmers may have oxen for plowing, and the e house-builders, as well as the farmers, beasts of burden for hauling, and the weavers and shoe-makers wool and leather.

It will not be a small city, either, if it contains all these.

Moreover, it is scarcely possible to plant the actual city in a place where it will have no need of imports.

No, it is impossible.

Then it will further require a new class of persons to bring from other cities all that it requires.

It will.

Well, but if the agent goes empty-handed, carrying with him none of the products in-demand among those people from whom 371 our city is to procure what it requires, he will also come empty-handed away, will he not?

I think so.

Then it must produce at home not only enough for itself, but also articles of the right kind and quantity to accommodate those whose services it needs.

It must.

Then our city requires larger numbers both of farmers and other craftsmen.

Yes, it does.

And among the rest it will need more of those agents also, who are to export and import the several products, and these are merchants, are they not?

Yes.

Then we shall require merchants also.

Certainly.

And if the commerce is carried on by sea, there will be a further demand for a considerable number of other persons, who are skilled in the practice of navigation.

A considerable number, undoubtedly.

But now tell me, In the city itself how are they to exchange their several productions? For it was to promote this exchange, you know, that we formed the community, and so founded our city.

Clearly, by buying and selling.

Then this will give rise to a market and a currency, for the sake of exchange.

Undoubtedly.

Suppose then that the farmer, or one of the other craftsmen, should come with some of his produce into the market, at a time when none of those who wish to make an exchange with him are there, is he to leave his occupation and sit idle in the market-place?

By no means, there are persons who, with an eye to this contingency, undertake the service required; and these in well-regulated cities are, generally speaking, persons of excessive physical weakness, who are of no use in other kinds of labor. Their business is to remain on the spot in the market, and give money for goods to those who want to sell, and goods for money to those who want to buy.

This demand, then, causes a class of tradesmen to spring up in our city. For do we not give the name of trademen to those who station themselves in the market, to minister to buying and selling, applying the term merchants to those who go about from city to city?

Exactly so.

In addition to these, I imagine, there is also another class of servants, consisting of those whose reasoning capacities do not recommend them as associates, but whose bodily strength is equal to hard labor. These, selling the use of their strength and calling the price of it wage, are thus named, I believe, wage-earners. Is it not so?

Precisely.

Then wage-earners also form, as it seems, a complementary portion of a city.

I think so.

Shall we say then, Adeimantus, that our city has at length grown to its full stature?

Perhaps so.

Where then, shall we find justice and injustice in it? With which of these elements that we have contemplated, has it simultaneously made its entrance?

I have no notion, Socrates, unless perhaps it be discoverable somewhere in the mutual relations of these same persons.

Well, perhaps you are right. We must investigate the matter, and not flinch from the task. Let us consider then, in the first place, what kind of life will be led by persons thus provided. I presume they will produce bread and wine, and clothes and shoes, and build themselves houses; and in summer, no doubt, they will generally work naked and without shoes, while in winter they will be suitably clothed and shod. And they will live, I suppose, on barley and wheat, baking cakes of the meal, and kneading loaves of the flour. And spreading these excellent cakes and loaves upon mats of straw or on clean leaves, and themselves reclining on rude beds of yew or myrtle-boughs, they will make merry, themselves and their children, drinking their wine, wearing garlands, and singing the praises of the gods, enjoying one another's society, and not begetting children beyond their means, through a prudent fear of poverty or war.

Glaucon here interrupted me, remarking, Apparently you describe your men as feasting without any seasonings.

True, I said, I had forgotten. Of course they will have something to season their food—salt, no doubt, and olives and cheese, together with the country fare of boiled onions and cabbage. We shall also set before them a dessert, I imagine, of figs and chick-peas and beans; and they may roast myrtle-berries and beech-nuts at the fire, taking wine with their fruit in moderation. And thus passing their days in peace and sound health, they will, in all probability, live to an advanced age, and dying, bequeath to their children a life in which their own will be reproduced.

Upon this Glaucon exclaimed, Why Socrates, if you were founding a community of swine, this is just the style in which you would fatten them up!

How then, said I, would you have them live, Glaucon?

In the customary manner, he replied. They ought to recline on couches, I should think, if they are not to have a hard life of it, and dine off tables, and have the usual dishes and dessert in the way we do now.

Very good. I understand. Apparently we are considering the growth not of a city merely, but of a luxurious city. I dare say it is not a bad plan, for by this extension of our inquiry we shall perhaps discover how it is that justice and injustice take root in cities. Now it appears to me that the city which we have described is the true and, so to speak, healthy city. But if you wish us to contemplate a city that is suffering from in-flammation, there is nothing to hinder us. Some people will not be satisfied, it seems, with the fare or the mode of life which we have described, but must have, in addition, couches and tables and every other article of furniture, as well as seasonings and fragrant oils, and perfumes, and courtesans, and con-fectionery; and all these in plentiful variety. Moreover, we must not limit ourselves now to essentials in those articles which we speci-fied at first, I mean houses and clothes and shoes, but we must set painting and embroi-dery to work, and acquire gold and ivory, and all similar valuables, must we not?

Yes.

Then we shall also have to enlarge our city, for our first or healthy city will not now be of sufficient size, but requires to be in-creased in bulk, and needs to be filled with a multitude of callings, which do not exist in cities to satisfy any natural want. For exam-ple, the whole class of hunters, and all who practice the art of imitation, including many who use forms and colors, and many who use music; and poets also—and their helpers, the rhapsodes, actors, dancers, contractors; and lastly, the craftsmen of all sorts of articles, and among others those who make parts of feminine adornments. We shall similarly re-quire more personal servants, shall we not? That is to say, teachers, wetnurses, dry-nurses, beauticians, barbers, and cooks moreover and butchers? Swineherds again are among the additions we shall require, a class of per-sons not to be found, because not needed, in our former city, but needed among the rest in this. We shall also need great quantities of all kinds of cattle, for those who may wish to eat them, shall we not?

Of course we shall.

Then shall we not experience the need of medical men also, to a much greater extent under this than under the former life-style?

Yes, indeed.

The land too, I presume, which was for-merly sufficient for the support of its then inhabitants will be now too small, and ad-equate no longer. Shall we say so?

Certainly.

Then must we not cut ourselves a slice of our neighbor's territory, if we are to have land enough both for pasture and tillage, while they will do the same to ours, if they, like us, permit themselves to overstep the limit of necessities, and plunge into the un-bounded acquisition of wealth?

It must inevitably be so, Socrates.

Will our next step be to go to war, Glau-con, or how will it be?

As you say.

At this stage of our inquiry let us avoid asserting either that war does good or that it does harm, confining ourselves to this statement, that we have further traced the origin of war to causes which bring about whatever ills befall a city, either in its public capacity, or in its individual members.

Exactly so.

Once more then, my friend, our city must be larger and not just by a small extent, but 374 by a whole army, which must go forth and do battle with all invaders in defense of its entire property, and of the things we were just now describing.

How so? he asked. Are not those persons sufficient of themselves?

They are not, if you and all the rest of us were right in the admissions which we made, when we were modeling our city. We admitted, I think, if you remember, that it was impossible for one man to work well at many crafts.

True.

Well then, is not the business of war
b looked upon as a craft in itself?

Undoubtedly.

And have we not as much reason to concern ourselves about the craft of war as the craft of shoemaking?

Quite as much.

But we cautioned the shoemaker, you know, against attempting to be a farmer or a weaver or a builder besides, with a view to our shoemaking work being well done; and to every other artisan we assigned in like manner one occupation, namely, that for which he was naturally fitted, and in which, if he let other things alone, and worked at
c it all his time without neglecting his opportunities, he was likely to prove a successful workman. Now is it not of the greatest moment that the work of war should be well done? Or is it so easy, that anyone can succeed in it and be at the same time a farmer or

a shoemaker or a laborer at any other craft whatever, although there is no one in the world who could become a good checkers-player or dice-player by merely taking up the game at unoccupied moments, instead of pursuing it as his special study from his childhood? And will it be enough for a man merely to handle a shield or the other arms d and implements of war? Will that make him competent to play his part well on that very day in an engagement of heavy troops or in any other military service—although the mere handling of any other instrument will never make anyone a true craftsman or athlete, nor will such instrument be even useful to one who has neither learnt its capabilities nor exercised himself sufficiently in its practical applications?

If it were so, these implements of war would be very valuable, he said.

In proportion, then, to the importance of the work which these guardians have to do, it will require more leisure than most, as well as extraordinary skill and attention. I e quite think so.

Will it not also require natural endowments suited to this particular occupation?

Undoubtedly.

Then, apparently, it will be up to us to choose, if we can, the kind of nature which qualifies its possessors for the guardianship of a city.

Certainly; it belongs to us.

Then, by Zeus, we have taken upon ourselves no trifling task; nevertheless, there must be no flinching, so long as our strength holds out.

No, there must not.

Do you think then, I asked, that there is 375 any difference, in the qualities required for keeping guard, between a well-bred puppy and a gallant young man?

I do not quite understand you.

Why, I suppose, for instance, they both must be quick to see things and swift to overtake what they perceive, and strong also, in case they have to fight what they have caught.

Certainly, all these qualities are required.

Moreover, they must be brave if they are to fight well.

Undoubtedly.

But will either a horse, or a dog, or any other animal, be likely to be brave if it is not spirited? Or have you failed to observe what an irresistible and unconquerable thing is the spirit so that under its influence every creature will be fearless and unconquerable in the face of any danger?

I have observed it.

We know then what bodily qualities are required in our guardian.

We do.

And also what qualities of the soul, namely, that he must be spirited.

Yes.

How then, Glaucon, if such be their natural disposition, are they to be kept from behaving fiercely to one another, and to the rest of the citizens?

It will not be easy, by Zeus.

Nevertheless, they certainly ought to be gentle to their friends, and dangerous only to their enemies—else they will not wait for others to destroy them, but will be the first to do it for themselves.

True.

What then shall we do? Where shall we find a character at once gentle and high-spirited? For I suppose a gentle nature is the opposite of a spirited one?

Apparently it is.

Nevertheless a man who is devoid of either gentleness or spirit cannot possibly make a good guardian. And as they seem to be incompatible, the result is, that a good guardian is an impossibility.

It looks like it, he said.

Here then I was perplexed, but having reconsidered our conversation, I said, We deserve, my friend, to be puzzled, for we have deserted the image which we set before us.

How so?

It never struck us, that after all there are natures, though we fancied there were none, which combine these opposite qualities.

And where is such a combination to be found?

You may see it in several animals, but particularly in the one which we ourselves compared to our guardian. For I suppose you know that it is the natural disposition of well-bred dogs to be perfectly gentle to their friends and acquaintance, but the reverse to strangers.

Certainly I do.

Therefore the thing is possible; and we are not contradicting nature in our endeavor to give such a character to our guardian.

So it would seem.

Then is it your opinion, that in one who is to make a good guardian it is further required that he be a philosopher as well as high-spirited?

How so? I do not understand you.

You will notice in dogs this other trait, which is really marvelous in the creature.

What is that?

Whenever they see someone they don't know they are irritated before they have been provoked by any ill treatment, but when they see someone they are acquainted with they welcome him, though they may never have experienced any kindness at his hands. Has this never excited your wonder?

I never paid attention to this before, but no doubt they do behave so.

Well, but this affection is a very clever thing in the dog, and truly philosophical.

How so?

Why, because the only mark by which he distinguishes between the appearance of a friend and that of an enemy is, that he knows the former and is ignorant of the latter. How, I ask, can the creature be other than fond of learning when it makes knowledge and ignorance the criteria of the familiar and the strange?

Beyond a question, it must be fond of learning.

Well, is not the love of learning the same thing as a philosophical disposition?

It is, he said.

c Shall we not then assert with confidence in the case of a man also, that if he is to show a gentle disposition towards his relatives and acquaintances, he must have a turn for learning and philosophy?

Be it so, he said.

Then in our judgment the man who is a fine and good guardian of the city will be in his nature philosophical, high-spirited, swift-footed, and strong.

Undoubtedly he will.

This then will be the original character of our guardians. But in what way shall we rear and educate them? And will the investigation of this point help us on towards discovering that which is the object of all our speculations, namely, the manner in which justice and injustice grow up in a city? For I wish us neither to omit anything useful, nor to occupy ourselves with anything redundant, in our inquiry.

d

Hereupon Glaucon's brother observed, Well, for my part, I fully anticipate that this inquiry will be useful.

If so, by Zeus, I said, we must certainly not give it up, my dear Adeimantus, even though it should prove somewhat long.

Indeed we must not.

Come then, like leisurely story-tellers in a story, let us describe the education of our men.

Yes, let us do so.

e What then is the education to be? Perhaps we could hardly find a better than that which the experience of the past has already discovered, which consists, I believe, in gymnastics for the body, and music for the soul.

It does.

Shall we not then begin our course of education with music rather than with gymnastics?

Undoubtedly we shall.

Under the term music, do you include speeches or not?

I do.

And of speeches there are two kinds, the true and the false.

Yes.

And must we instruct our pupils in both   377 but in the false first?

I do not understand what you mean.

Do you not understand that we begin with children by telling them stories? And these, I suppose, to speak generally, are false, though they contain some truths; and we employ such stories in the treatment of children at an earlier period than gymnastic exercises.

True.

That is what I meant when I said that music ought to be taken up before gymnastics.

You are right.

Then are you aware, that in every work the beginning is the most important part,   b especially in dealing with anything young and tender? That is the time when any impression one desires is most readily stamped upon it.

Precisely so.

Shall we then permit our children without scruple to hear any stories composed by any authors whatever, and so to receive into their souls opinions generally the reverse of those which *we* think they ought to entertain, when they are grown up to manhood?

No, we shall not permit it on any account. . . .

Then apparently it will be our first duty to be in charge over the story-makers, selecting their good productions, and rejecting the bad. And the selected stories we shall advise   c our nurses and mothers to repeat to their children, that they may shape their bodies with their hands. But we shall have to throw out the greater part of those which are now in vogue.

Which do you mean? he asked.

In the greater stories, I answered, we shall also be able to make out the lesser ones. For the general character and tendency of both the greater and the lesser must doubtless be

d identical. Do you not think so?

I do; but I am equally uncertain which you mean by the greater.

I mean the stories which Hesiod, and Homer, and the other poets, tell us. For they, I imagine, have composed false stories which they told, and still tell, to men.

What kind of stories do you mean, and what is the fault that you find with them?

A fault, I replied, which deserved the earliest and gravest condemnation, especially if the lie has no beauty.

What is this fault?

It is whenever an author gives a poor rep-

e resentation of the characters of gods and heroes, like a painter, whose picture bears no resemblance to the objects he wishes to paint.

Yes, it is quite right to condemn such faults; but explain further what we mean, and give some examples.

In the first place, the poet who conceived the greatest lie on the greatest subjects invented an ugly story when he told how Uranus acted as Hesiod declares he did,

378 and also how Cronus had his revenge upon him. And again, even if the deeds of Cronus and his son's treatment of him were true, it would not have been right, I should have thought, to tell them so casually to young and thoughtless persons; on the contrary, it would be best to keep quiet; or, if for some reason they must be told, they should be imparted under the seal of secrecy to as few hearers as possible, and that after the

sacrifice, not of a pig, but of some rare and costly victim, for the purpose of restricting their number as far as possible.

Certainly, these are offensive stories.

They are; and therefore, Ademantus,   b they must not be repeated in our city. No; we must not tell a youthful listener that he will be doing nothing extraordinary if he commit the most extreme injustice, nor if he should chastise the unjust acts of a father in the most unscrupulous manner, but will simply be doing what the first and greatest of the gods have done before him.

I assure you, he said, I quite agree with you as to the impropriety of such stories.

Nor yet, I continued, is it proper to say in any case—what is indeed untrue—that   c gods wage war against gods, and intrigue and fight among themselves; that is, if the future guardians of our city are to deem it a most disgraceful thing to quarrel lightly with one another. Far less ought we to select as subjects for fiction and embroidery the battles of the giants and the various other feuds in which gods and heroes fight against their own family and kin. But if there is any possibility of persuading them that to quarrel with one's fellow is an impiety of which no member of a city was ever guilty, such ought rather to be the language told to our children from the first, by old   d men and old women, and when they grow older, our poets must be compelled to write in such a strain. But stories like the chaining of Hera by her son, and the flinging of Hephaestus out of heaven for trying to take his mother's part when his father was beating her, and all those battles of the gods which are to be found in Homer, must be refused admittance into our city, whether the meaning is hidden or not. For a child cannot discriminate between what is supposition and what is not; and whatever at that age is adopted as a matter of belief has   e a tendency to become fixed and indelible, and therefore, perhaps, we ought to esteem it of the greatest important that the stories children first hear should be adapted in the most perfect manner to the promotion of virtue.

There is certainly reason in this. But if anyone were to proceed to ask us which these are, and which stories convey them, how should we answer him?

379 To which I replied, My dear Adeimantus, you and I are not poets, on the present condition, but founders of a city. And founders ought certainly to know the molds in which their poets are to cast their stories, and from which they are not permitted to deviate; but they are not bound to compose stories themselves. . . .

BOOK III

412b . . . Very good; then what will be the next point for us to settle? Is it not this, which of the persons so educated are to be the rulers, and which the ruled?

c   Unquestionably it is.

There can be no doubt that the rulers must be the elderly men, and the subjects would be the younger.

True.

And also that the rulers must be the best men among them.

True again.

Are not the best farmers those who are most skilled in farming?

Yes.

In the present case, as we require the best guardians, shall we not find them in those who are most capable of guarding a city?

Yes.

Then for this purpose must they not be prudent and powerful, and, moreover, care for the city?

They must.

d   And a man will care most for that which he loves?

Of course.

And assuredly he will love that most whose interests he regards as identical with his own, and in whose prosperity or adversity he believes his own fortunes to be involved.

Just so.

Then we must select from the whole body of guardians those men who appear to us, after due observation, to be remarkable above others for the zeal with which, through their whole life, they have done what they have thought advantageous to the   e city, and inflexibly refused to do what they thought the reverse.

Yes, these are the suitable persons, he said.

Then I think we must watch them at every stage of their life, to see if they are tenacious guardians of this conviction, and never bewitched or forced into a forgetful banishment of the opinion that they ought to do what is best for the city. . . .

. . . I shall try, I say, to persuade first the rulers themselves and the military class, and 414d after them the rest of the city, that when we were training and instructing them, they only thought, as in dreams, that all this was happening to them and about them, while in truth they were in course of formation and training in the bowels of the earth, where they themselves, their armor, and the rest of their equipments were manufactured. As soon as they were finished, the earth,   e their real mother, sent them up to its surface; and, consequently, that they ought now to take thought for the land in which they dwell, as their mother and nurse, and repel all attacks upon it, and to feel towards their fellow-citizens as brothers born of the earth.

It was not without reason that you were so long ashamed to tell us your lie.

I dare say; nevertheless, hear the rest of the story. We shall tell our people, in mythical 415 language: You are doubtless all brothers, as many as inhabit the city, but the god who created you mixed gold in the composition of such of you as are qualified to rule, which is why they are most honored, while in the auxiliaries he made silver an ingredient, assigning iron and bronze to the farmers and the other workmen. Therefore, inasmuch as you are all related to one another, although your children will generally resemble their parents, yet sometimes a golden parent will produce a silver child, and a silver parent a golden

b child, and so on, each producing any. The rulers therefore have received this charge first and above all from the gods, to observe nothing more closely, as good guardians, than the children that are born, to see which of these metals is mixed in their souls. And if a child be born in their class with an alloy of bronze or iron, they are to have no manner of pity upon it, but giving it the value that belongs to its nature, they are to thrust it among artisans or farmers; and if again among these latter a child be born with any admixture of

c gold or silver, they will honour it, and they are to raise it either to the class of guardians, or to that of auxiliaries, because there is an oracle which declares that the city shall then perish when it is guarded by iron or bronze. Can you suggest any device by which we can make them believe this story?

None at all by which we could persuade the men with whom we begin our new city; but I think there could be such a device for

d their sons, and the next generation, and all subsequent generations. . . .

BOOK IV

428d . . . Tell me, then, does our newly-organized city contain any kind of knowledge, residing in any section of the citizens, which takes measures, not in behalf of anything in the city, but in behalf of the city as a whole, devising in what manner its internal and foreign relations may best be regulated?

Certainly it does.

What is this knowledge, and in whom does it reside?

It is the science of guardianship, and it resides in that ruling part, whom we just now called our perfect guardians.

Then in virtue of this knowledge what do you call the city?

I call it prudent in counsel and truly wise.

Which do you suppose will be the more numerous class in our city, the smiths, or   e these genuine guardians?

The smiths will far outnumber the others.

Then will the guardians be the smallest of all the classes possessing this or that branch of knowledge, and bearing this or that name in consequence?

Yes, much the smallest.

Then it is the knowledge residing in its smallest part or section, that is to say, in the predominant and ruling body, which entitles a city, organized agreeably to nature, to be called wise as a whole; and that part appropriately is to partake of the knowledge which alone of all kinds of   429 knowledge is properly called wisdom, is naturally, as it appears, the least numerous body in the city.

Most true.

Here then we have made out—I do not know how—in some way or other, one of the four qualities, and the part of the city in which it is seated.

To my mind, said he, it has been made out satisfactorily.

Again, there can assuredly be no great difficulty in discerning courage itself, and the part in which it resides, and which entitles the city to be called brave.

How so?

In pronouncing a city to be cowardly or brave, who would look to any but that por   b tion of it which fights in its defense and takes the field in its behalf?

No one would look to anything else.

No; and for this reason, I imagine, that the cowardice or courage of the city itself is not necessarily implied in that of the other parts.

No, it is not.

Then a city is brave as well as wise, in virtue of a certain portion of itself, because c it has in that portion a power which can always keep safe the right opinion concerning things to be feared, which teaches that they are such as the legislator has declared in the prescribed education. Is not this what you call courage?

I did not quite understand what you said; be so good as to repeat it.

I say that courage is a kind of safekeeping.

What kind of safekeeping?

The safekeeping of the opinion created by law through education, which teaches what things and what kind of things are to be feared. And when I spoke of keeping it safe throughout everything, I meant d that opinion was to be thoroughly preserved alike in moments of pain and of pleasure, of desire and of fear, and never to be cast away. And if you like, I will illustrate it by a comparison which seems to me an apt one.

I should like it.

Well then, you know that dyers, when they wish to dye wool so as to give it the true sea-purple, first select from the numerous colors one variety, that of white wool, and then subject it to much careful preparatory dressing, that it may take the color as brilliantly as possible; after which they e proceed to dye it. And when the wool has been dyed on this system, its color is indelible, and no washing either with or without soap can rob it of its brilliancy. But when this course has not been pursued, you know the results, whether this or any other color be dyed without previous preparation.

I know that the dye washes out in a ridiculous way.

You may understand from this what we were laboring, to the best of our ability, to 430 bring about, when we were selecting our soldiers and training them in music and gymnastics. Imagine that we were only contriving how they might be best persuaded to accept, as it were, the color of the laws, in order that their opinion concerning things to be feared, and on all other subjects, might be indelible, owing to their congenial nature and appropriate training, and that their color might not be washed out by such terribly efficacious detergents as pleasure, which b works more powerfully than soda or lye, and pain, and fear, and desire, which are more potent than any other solvent in the world. This power, therefore, to hold fast continually the right and lawful opinion concerning things to be feared and things not to be feared, I define to be courage, and call it by that name, if you do not object.

No, I do not; for when the right opinion on these matters is held without education, as by beasts and slaves, you would not, I think, regard it as altogether legitimate, and you would give it some other name than courage. c

Most true.

Then I accept this account of courage.

Do so, at least as an account of the political courage, and you will be right. On a future occasion, if you like, we will go into this question more fully; at present it is beside our inquiry, the object of which is justice. We have done enough therefore, I imagine, for the investigation of courage.

You are right.

Two things, I proceeded, now remain, that we must look for in the city, moderation, and that which is the cause of all these d investigations, justice.

Exactly so.

Well, not to trouble ourselves any further about moderation, is there any way by which we can discover justice?

For my part, said he, I do not know, nor do I wish justice to be brought to light first, if we are to make no further inquiry after moderation, so, if you wish to gratify me, examine into the latter, before you proceed to the former.

Indeed, I do wish it, for I am not unjust.

e   Proceed then with the examination.

I will; and from our present point of view, moderation has more the appearance of a concord or harmony, than the former qualities had.

How so?

Moderation is, I imagine, a kind of order and a mastery, as men say, over certain pleasures and desires. Thus we plainly hear people talking of a man's being stronger than himself, in some sense or other; and other similar expressions are used, in which we may find a clue. Is it not so?

Most certainly it is.

But is not the expression "stronger than himself" a ridiculous one? For the man who
431 is stronger than himself will also, I presume, be weaker than himself, and the weaker will be the stronger. For the subject of all these phrases is the same person.

Undoubtedly.

Well, I continued, it appears to me that the meaning of the expression is, that in the person himself, that is, in his soul, there resides a better principle and a weaker, and when the naturally better principle is master over the worse, this state of things is described by the term "stronger than himself." Certainly it is a term of praise; but when in consequence of poor training, or the influence of associates, the smaller force of the better principle is overpowered by the greater
b numbers of the worse, the person so situated is described in terms of reproach and condemnation, as weaker than himself, and a dissolute person.

Yes, this seems a likely account of it.

Now turn your eyes towards our new city, and you will find one of these conditions realized in it. You will allow that it may fairly be called "Stronger than itself," if moderation and self-mastery may be ascribed to that in which the better principle governs the worse.

I am looking as you direct, and I acknowledge the truth of what you say.

It will further be admitted that those desires, and pleasures, and pains, which are   c many and various, will be chiefly found in children, and women, and servants; and those who are called free among the common many.

Precisely so.

On the other hand, those simple and moderate desires, which go hand in hand with intelligence and right opinion, under the guidance of reasoning, will be found in a small number of men, that is, in those of the best natures and the best education.

True.

Do you not see that the parallel to this   d exists in your city—in other words, that the desires of the many common people are there controlled by the desires and the prudence of the more decent few?

I do.

If any city then may be described as stronger than itself, its pleasures, and its desires, then ours may be so characterized.

Most certainly.

May we not then also call it moderate, on all these accounts?

Surely we may.

And again, if there is any city in which the rulers and the ruled are unanimous on   e the question who ought to govern, such unanimity will exist in ours. Do you not think so?

Most assuredly I do.

In which of the two classes of citizens will you say that moderation resides, when they are in this condition? In the rulers or in the ruled?

In both, I suppose.

Do you see, then, that we were not bad prophets when we divined just now that moderation resembled a kind of harmony?

How do you mean?

Because it does not operate like courage and wisdom, which, by residing in par-432 ticular sections of the city, make it brave and wise respectively; but simply spreads throughout the whole, producing an accord between the weakest and the strongest and the middle part, whether you measure by the standard of prudence, or bodily strength, or numbers, or wealth, or anything else of the kind. We shall be fully justified in pronouncing moderation to be that unanimity, which we described as a concord between the naturally better element and the naturally worse, whether in a city or in a single person, as to which of the two has the right to rule.

b   I fully agree with you.

Very well, I continued; we have discerned in our city three out of the four principles, as far as our opinion goes. Now what will that remaining form be through which the city will further participate in virtue? This, we may be sure, is justice.

Evidently it is.

Now then, Glaucon, we must be like hunters surrounding a bush, and must take care that justice nowhere escape us and dis-c   appear from our view, for it is manifest that she is somewhere here; so look for her, and strive to gain a sight of her, for perhaps you may discover her first, and give the alarm to me.

I wish I might, replied he; but you will use me quite well enough, if, instead of that, you will treat me as one who is following your steps, and is able to see what is pointed out to him.

Follow me then, after joining your prayers with mine.

I will do so; just you lead the way.

Truly, said I, the place seems to be shady and inaccessible, dark and hard to traverse; but still we must go on.

Yes, that we must.   d

Here I caught a glimpse, and exclaimed, Aha! Glaucon, here is something that looks like a track, and I believe the game will not altogether escape us.

That is good news.

Upon my word, said I, we are in a most foolish predicament.

How so?

Why, my blessed man, it appears that what we were looking for has been rolling before our feet from the beginning, and we never saw it, but did the most ridiculous thing. Just as people at times go about looking for something which they hold in their   e hands, so we, instead of fixing our eyes upon the thing itself, kept gazing at some point in the distance, and this was probably the reason why it eluded our search.

What do you mean?

This—that I believe we ourselves were just now saying and hearing it, without understanding that we were in a way describing it ourselves.

Your preface seems long to one who is anxious for the explanation.

Well then, listen, and judge whether I am   433 right or not. What at the beginning we laid down as a universal rule of action, when we were founding our city, this, if I am not mistaken, or some modification of it, is justice. I think we affirmed, if you recollect, and frequently repeated, that every individual ought to have some one occupation in the city, which should be that to which his natural capacity was best adapted.

We did say so.

And again, we have often heard people say, that to mind one's own business, and not be meddlesome, is justice; and we have often said the same thing ourselves.

We have said so.   b

Then it would seem, my friend, that to do one's own business, in some shape or other, is justice. Do you know from what I infer this?

No; be so good as to tell me.

I think that the remainder left in the city, after eliminating the things we have already considered, I mean moderation, and courage, and wisdom, must be what brought them into being, and which preserves them there so long as they exist in it. Now we affirmed that the remainder, when three out

c   of the four were found, would be justice.

Yes, unquestionably it would.

If, however, it were required to decide which of these qualities will by virtue of its presence in the city do the greatest good, it would be difficult to determine; whether it will be the harmony of opinion between the rulers and the ruled, or the faithful adherence on the part of the soldiers to the lawful belief concerning the things which are, and the things which are not, to be feared; or the existence of prudence and guardianship in the rulers; or whether the virtue of the city

d   may not be chiefly traced to the presence of that fourth principle in every child and woman, in every slave, freeman, and artisan, in the ruler and in the ruled, requiring each to do his own work, and not meddle with many things.

It would be a difficult point to settle, unquestionably.

Thus it appears that, in promoting the virtue of a city, the power that makes each member of it do his own work, may compete with its wisdom, and its moderation, and its courage.

Decidedly it may.

But if there is a principle which rivals

e   these qualities in promoting the virtue of a city, will you not determine it to be justice?

Most assuredly.

Consider the question in another light, and see whether you will come to the same

conclusion. Will you assign to the rulers of the city the judging of law-suits?

Certainly.

Will not their judgments be guided, above everything, by the desire that no one may appropriate what belongs to others, nor be deprived of what is his own?

Yes, that will be their main study.

Because that is just?

Yes.

Thus, according to this view also, it will be granted that to have and do what belongs   434 to us and is our own, is justice.

True.

Now observe whether you hold the same opinion that I do. If a carpenter should undertake to execute the work of a shoemaker, or a shoemaker that of a carpenter, either by interchanging their tools and honors, or by the same person undertaking both trades, with all the changes involved in it, do you think it would greatly damage the city?

Not very greatly.

But when one whom nature has made an craftsman, or a producer of any other kind, is so elated by wealth, or a large con-   b nection, or bodily strength, or any similar advantages, as to intrude himself into the class of the warriors; or when a warrior intrudes himself into the class of the counselors and guardians, of which he is unworthy, and when these interchange their tools and their distinctions, or when one and the same person attempts to discharge all these duties at once, then, I imagine, you will agree with me, that such change and meddling among these will be ruinous to the city.

Most assuredly they will.

Then any intermeddling in the three parts, or change from one to another, would   c inflict great damage on the city, and may properly be described, as doing the most extreme harm.

Quite so.

And will you not admit that the greatest harm towards one's own city is injustice?

Unquestionably.

This then is injustice. On the other hand, let us state that, conversely, adherence to their own business on the part of the moneymakers, the military, and the guardians, each of these doing its own work in the city, is justice, and will render the city just.

d   I fully agree, he said.

Let us not state it yet quite positively; but if we find, on applying this form to the individual man, that there too it is recognized as constituting justice, we will then give our assent—for what more can we say?—But if not, in that case we will begin a new inquiry. At present, however, let us complete the investigation which we undertook in the belief that, if we first endeavored to contemplate justice in some larger subject which contains it, we should find it easier to discern its nature in the individual man. Such a subject we recognized in a city, and accordingly we organized the best we

e   could, being sure that justice must reside in a good city. The view, therefore, which presented itself to us there, let us now apply to the individual; and if it be admitted, we shall be satisfied; but if we should find something different in the case of the individual, we will again go back to our city,

435 and put our theory to the test. And perhaps by considering the two cases side by side, and rubbing them together, we may cause justice to flash out from the contact, like fire from dry bits of wood, and when it has become visible to us, may settle it firmly in our own minds.

There is method in your proposal, he replied, and so let us do.

And I said, When two things, a greater and a less, are called by a common name, are they, in so far as the common name applies, unlike or like?

Like.

Then a just man will not differ from a just city, so far as the form of justice is involved,   b
but the two will be like.

They will.

Well, but we resolved that a city was just, when the three natural kinds present in it were severally occupied in doing their proper work; and that it was moderate, and brave, and wise, in consequence of certain affections and customs of these same classes.

True.

Then, my friend, we shall make the same cclaim in the case of the single individual, and, supposing him to have the same forms in his soul, on account of having the same affections as those in the city, we shall judge that he can be deemed worthy of the same names as the city.

It must inevitably be so. . . .

BOOK V

. . . I must return, then, to a portion of our 451c
subject which perhaps I ought to have discussed before in its proper place. But after all, the present order may be the best; the male drama having been played out; we proceed then with the performance of the women; especially since this is the order of your challenge.

For people born and educated as we have described, the only right method, in my opinion, of acquiring and using children and women will be found in following the path we first embarked on. The aim of our argument was, I believe, to make our men as it were guardians of a herd.

Yes.

Let us keep on the same track, and give   d
corresponding rules for the propagation of the species, and for rearing the young; and let us observe whether we find them suitable or not.

How do you mean?

Like this. Do we think that the females of watch-dogs ought to guard the flock along with the males, and hunt with them, and share in all their other duties; or that the females ought to stay at home, because they are disabled by having to breed and rear the puppies, while the males are to labor and be charged with all the care of the flocks?

e   We expect them to share in whatever is to be done; only we treat the females as the weaker, and the males as the stronger.

Is it possible to use animals for the same work, if you do not give them the same training and education?

It is not.

452   If then we are to employ the women in the same duties as the men, we must give them the same instructions.

Yes.

To the men we gave music and gymnastic.

Yes.

Then we must train the women also in the same two arts, giving them besides a military education, and treating them in the same way as the men.

It follows naturally from what you say.

Perhaps many of the details of the question before us might appear unusually ridiculous, if carried out in the manner proposed.

No doubt they would.

Which of them do you find the most ridiculous?

b   Is it not obviously the notion of the women exercising naked in the palaestrae with the men, and not only the young women, but even those of an advanced age, just like those old men in the gymnasia, who, in spite of wrinkles and ugliness, still keep up their fondness for active exercises?

Yes, by Zeus; at the present day that would appear truly ridiculous.

Well then, as we have started the subject, we must not be afraid of the numerous jokes which witty men may make upon the notion

c   of carrying out such a change in reference

to the gymnasia and music; and above all, in the wearing of armor and riding on horseback.

You are right.

On the contrary, as we have begun the discussion, we must travel on to the rougher ground of our law, entreating these witty men to leave off their usual practice, and try to be serious; and reminding them that not long ago it was thought shameful and ridiculous among the Greeks, as it is now among most barbarians, for men to be seen naked. And when the Cretans first, and after them the Spartans began the practice of gymnastic exercises, the wits of the time had it in their power to make a comedy out of it. Do   d you not think so?

I do.

But when it became clear that it was better to strip than to cover up the body, and when the ridiculous effect of this plan on the eye had given way before the arguments establishing its superiority, it was at the same time demonstrated, I imagine, that he is a fool who thinks anything ridiculous but that which is bad, and who attempts to   e get a laugh by assuming any object to be ridiculous other than that which is bad; or who does not seriously lay down any other mark of beauty than that which is good.

Most assuredly.

Must we not then first come to an agreement as to whether the regulations proposed   453 are possible or not, and give to any one, whether of a playful or serious turn, an opportunity of raising the question, whether the nature of the human female is such as to enable her to share in all the deeds of the male, or whether she is wholly unequal to any, or equal to some and not to others; and in particular how that is with respect to war? Will not this be the way to make the best beginning, and, in all probability, the best ending also?

Yes, quite so.

Would you like, then, that we should argue against ourselves in behalf of an objector, that the opposition may not be attacked without a defense?

b   There is no reason why we should not.

Then let us say in his behalf: "Socrates and Glaucon, there is no need for others to advance anything against you; for you yourselves, at the beginning of your scheme for constructing a city, admitted that every individual therein ought, in accordance with nature, to do the one work which belongs

c   to him." "We did admit this, I imagine; how could we do otherwise?"

"Can you deny that there is a very marked difference between the nature of woman and that of man?"

"Of course there is a difference."

"Then is it not fitting to assign to each sex a different work, appropriate to its peculiar nature?"

"Undoubtedly."

"Then if so, you must be in error now, and be contradicting yourselves when you go on to say, that men and women ought to engage in the same occupations, when their natures are so widely diverse?" Do you have any answer to that objection, my clever friend?

It is not so very easy to find one at a moment's notice; but I shall beg you, and I do so now, to state what the arguments on our

d   side are, and to interpret them for us.

These objections, Glaucon, and many others like them, are what I anticipated all along; and that is why I was afraid and reluctant to meddle with the law that regulates the possession of the women and children, and the rearing of the latter.

By Zeus, it seems no easy task.

Why no; but the fact is, that whether you fall into a small swimming pool, or into the middle of the great ocean, you have to swim all the same.

Exactly so.

Then is it not best for us, in the present instance, to swim out and endeavor to emerge in safety from the discussion, in the hope that either a dolphin may take us on his back, or some other improbable rescue present itself?

It would seem so.   e

Come then, I continued, let us see if we can find the way out. We admitted, you say, that different natures ought to have different occupations, and that the natures of men and women are different; but now we maintain that these different natures ought to engage in the same occupations. Is this your charge against us?

Precisely.

Truly, Glaucon, the power of the art of   454
contradiction is very extraordinary.

How so?

Because it seems to me that many fall into it even against their will, and think they are discussing, when they are merely debating, because they cannot distinguish the various forms of what is said, but carry on their opposition to what is stated, by attacking the mere words, employing the art of eristical debate, and not that of dialectical discussion.

This is no doubt the case with many; does it apply to us at the present moment?

Most assuredly it does; at any rate there   b
is every appearance of our having fallen unintentionally into a verbal contradiction.

How so?

Following only the name, we say, in the boldest style of eristical debate, that different natures ought not to engage in the same pursuits. But we did not in any way consider what form of sameness and difference of nature and what that referred to, and what we were distinguishing when we assigned different pursuits to different natures, and the same pursuits to the same natures.

It is true we have not considered that.

c   That being the case, it is open to us apparently to ask ourselves whether bald men and long-haired men are of the same or of opposite natures, and after admitting the latter to be the case, we may say that if bald men make shoes, long-haired men must not be allowed to make them, or if the long-haired men make them, the others must be forbidden to do so.

No, that would be ridiculous.

It is ridiculous for any other reason that that we did not agree on "the same" and "different nature" in every respect, being engaged only with that form of likeness

d   and difference which applied directly to the pursuits in question? For example, we said that a male and female physician have the same nature and soul. Or do you not think so?

I do.

And that a man who would make a good physician had a different nature from one who would make a good carpenter.

Of course he has.

If, then, the class of men and women appear to differ in reference to any art, or other occupation, we shall say that such occupation must be assigned to the one or the

e   other. But if we find the difference to consist simply in the fact that the female bears and the male mounts, we shall assert that it has not yet been by any means demonstrated that the difference between man and woman touches our purpose; on the contrary, we shall still think it proper for our guardians and their wives to engage in the same pursuits.

And rightly.

455   Shall we not proceed to call upon our opponents to inform us what is that particular art or occupation connected with the organization of a city, in reference to which the nature of a man and a woman are not the same, but different?

We certainly are entitled to do so.

Well, perhaps it might be pleaded by others, as it was a little while ago by you, that it is not easy to give a satisfactory answer at a moment's notice; but that, with time for consideration, it would not be difficult to do so.

True, it might.

Would you, then, like us to beg the man who voices such objections to accompany   b us, to see if we can show him that no occupation which belongs to the ordering of a city is peculiar to women?

By all means.

Well then, we will address him thus: "Tell us whether, when you say that one man is well-suited for a particular study, and that another is not, you mean that the former learns it easily, the latter with difficulty; and that the one with little instruction can find out much for himself in the subject he has studied, whereas the other after much teaching and practice cannot even retain what he has learned; and that the reasoning of the one is duly aided, that of the other thwarted,   c by the bodily powers? Are not these the only marks by which you define the possession and the want of natural talents for any pursuit?"

Every one will say yes.

Well then, do you know of any branch of human industry in which the female sex is not inferior in these respects to the male? Or need we go the length of specifying the art of weaving, and the manufacture of pastry and preserves, in which women are thought   d to excel, and in which their defeat is most laughed at?

You are perfectly right, that in almost every employment the one class is vastly superior to the other. There are many women, no doubt, who are better in many things than many men; but, speaking generally, it is as you say.

I conclude then, my friend, that none of the occupations concerned with ordering a city belong to woman as woman, nor yet to man as man; but natural gifts are to be found here and there, in both animals alike; and, so far as her nature is concerned, the woman is admissible to all pursuits as well as the man; though in all of them the woman is weaker than the man.

Precisely so.

Shall we then appropriate all duties to men, and none to women?

How can we?

On the contrary, we shall hold, I imagine, that one woman may have talents for medicine, and another be without them; and that one may be musical, and another unmusical.

Undoubtedly.

And shall we not also say, that one woman may have qualifications for gymnastic exercises, and for war, and another be unwarlike, and without a taste for gymnastics?

I think we shall.

Again, may there not be a lover of wisdom in one, and a hatred of it in another? And may not one be spirited, and another without spirit?

True again.

If that be so, there are some women who are fit, and others who are unfit, for the office of guardians. For were not those the qualities that we selected, in the case of the men, as marking their fitness for that office?

Yes, they were.

Then as far as the guardianship of a city is concerned, there is no difference between the natures of the man and of the woman, but only various degrees of weakness and strength.

Apparently there is none.

Then we shall have to select duly qualified women also, to share in the life and guardianship with the duly qualified men; since we find that they are competent, and of kindred nature with the men.

Just so.

And must we not assign the same pursuit to the same natures?

We must.

Then we have come full circle to our former position, and we admit that it is no violation of nature to assign music and gymnastics to the wives of our guardians.

Precisely so.

Then our intended legislation was not impossible, or visionary, since the proposed law was in accordance with nature. But rather it is the contrary way of doing things nowadays, that most likely is what is against nature.

So it appears.

Our inquiry was, whether the proposed arrangement would be possible, and whether it was the best one, was it not?

It was.

Are we quite agreed that it is possible?

Yes.

Then the next point to be settled is, that it is also the best arrangement?

Yes, obviously.

Very well; if the question is how to render a woman fit for the office of guardian, we shall not have one education for men, and another for women, especially as the nature affected is the same in both cases.

No, the education will be the same.

Well then, I should like to have your opinion on the following question.

And what is it?

On what principle do you in your own mind estimate one man as better than another? Or do you look upon all as equal?

Certainly I do not.

Then in the city we were founding, which of the two classes have, in your opinion, been made the better men, the guardians educated as we have described, or the shoemakers brought up to shoemaking?

It is ridiculous to ask.

I understand you; but tell me, are not these the best of all the citizens?

e   Yes, by far.

And will not these women be better than all the other women?

Yes, by far, again.

Can there be anything better for a city than that it should contain the best possible men and women?

There cannot.

And this result will be brought about by music and gymnastics employed as we described?

457   Undoubtedly.

Then our intended regulation is not only possible, but also the best one for the city.

It is.

Then the women of our guardians must strip for their exercises, inasmuch as they will put on virtue instead of robes, and must bear their part in war and the other duties comprised in the guardianship of the city, and must engage in no other occupations; though of these tasks the lighter parts must be given to the women rather than to the men, in consideration of the weakness of their sex. But as for the man who laughs at the idea of undressed women going

b   through gymnastic exercises, as a means of realizing what is most perfect, his ridicule is but "unripe fruit plucked from the tree of wisdom," and he knows not, to all appearance, what he is laughing at or what he is doing. For it is and ever will be a most excellent maxim, that the useful is beautiful, and the harmful ugly.

Most assuredly it is.

Here then is one wave, as I may call it, which we may perhaps consider ourselves to have surmounted, in our discussion of the law relating to women; so that, instead of our being altogether swamped by our assertion that it is the duty of our male and female guardians to have all their pursuits in common, our argument is found to be in a manner at one with itself, stating what is

c   both possible and beneficial.

Yes indeed, he replied, it is no insignificant wave that you have surmounted.

You will not call it a large one, I continued, when you see the next.

Just go on, and let me see it.

The last law and those which preceded it involve, as I conceive, another to this effect.

What is it?

That these women shall be, without exception, the common wives of these men, and that no one shall have a wife of his own.   d
Likewise that the children shall be common, and that the parent shall not know his child, nor the child his parent.

This law, he replied, is much more likely than the former to excite distrust both as to its possibility and usefulness.

As to whether it is beneficial, I said, I think no one could deny that it would be the greatest good for the women and children to be common to all, if it were possible; but I expect that the most controversy would be about whether it is possible.

Both points might very well be disputed.   e

Then there will be a conflict of argument. I thought I should run away and get off from one of them, if you agreed to the benefit of the plan, so that I should only have to discuss its possibility.

But you were found out in your attempt to escape; so please give an account of both.

I must pay the penalty. Grant me however this one favor: Permit me to take a holiday, like lazy-minded men, who are   458
used to feasting themselves on their own thoughts, whenever they walk alone. Such persons, you know, before they have found in what manner their wishes could become reality, pass that by, to avoid the fatigue of thinking whether such wishes are possible or not, and assume that what they desire is already theirs. And after that they proceed to arrange the remainder of the business, and please themselves with running over what they mean to do under the assumed   b

circumstances, thus aggravating the laziness of an already lazy soul. So at this moment I too am yielding to laziness. I want to postpone considering the question. And assuming its possibility for the moment, I shall inquire, if you will permit me, what arrangements the rulers will make when our rule is carried out, trying also to show that in practice it would be the most advantageous of all things, both to the city and to its guardians. These points I will first try to examine thoroughly in company with you, and take the others afterwards, if you permit me.

You have my permission, he replied. So proceed with the inquiry.

I think then, I proceeded, that if our rulers shall prove worthy of the name, and their auxiliaries likewise, the latter will be willing to execute the orders they receive, and the former, in issuing those orders, will obey our laws; and in whatever cases we have left the details to them, they will imitate the laws.

So we may expect.

It will be your duty, therefore, as their lawgiver, to select the women just as you selected the men, and to place them together, taking care, as far as possible, that they shall be of similar nature. Now inasmuch as the dwellings and mess-tables are all common, and no one possesses anything in the shape of private property, both sexes will live together, and as a consequence of their mingling in the gymnasium in active exercises, and in the rest of their daily life, they will be led, I imagine, by an inborn necessity, through which they will sexually mix with one another. Do you not think this will be inevitable?

The necessity surely will not be a geometrical necessity, but that of love, which perhaps is more constraining than the other in its power to persuade and draw after it the mass of men.

Quite so. But in the next place, Glaucon, disorderly mixing, or indeed irregularity of any kind, would not be holy among the members of a happy city, and will not be permitted by the rulers.

And rightly so.

Manifestly, then, our next care will be to make the marriage-union as sacred a thing as we possibly can. And this sanctity will attach to the marriages which are most beneficial.

Precisely so.

Then tell me, Glaucon, how this end is to be attained, for I know you keep in your house both sporting dogs, and a great number of game birds. I ask you in the name of Zeus, therefore, to inform me whether you have paid any attention to marriages and the breeding of these animals.

In what respect?

In the first place, though all are well-bred, are there not some which are, or grow to be, superior to the rest?

There are.

Do you then breed from all alike, or are you anxious to breed as much as possible from the best?

From the best.

And at what age? When they are very young, or very old, or when they are in their prime?

When they are in their prime.

And if you were to pursue a different course, do you think your breed of birds and dogs would be much worse for you?

I do.

Do you think it would be different with horses, or any other animals?

Certainly not; it would be absurd to suppose it.

Good heavens! my dear friend, I exclaimed, what very first-rate men our rulers ought to be, if the analogy hold with regard to the human species.

Well, it certainly does. But why first-rate?

Because they will be obliged to use medicine to a great extent. Now you know when bodies do not require medicine, but are willing to submit to a regimen, we think an ordinary doctor good enough for them; but when it is necessary to administer medicines, we know that a more courageous physician must be called in.

True; but how does this apply?

Thus. It is probable that our rulers will
d   be compelled to have recourse to a good deal of falsehood and deceit for the benefit of their subjects. And, if you recollect, we said that all such practices were useful in the form of medicine.

Yes, and we were right.

Well then, it appears that this is right and applies particularly to the questions of marriage and procreation.

How so?

It follows from what has been already granted, that the best men and women ought to be brought together as often as possible, and the worst as seldom as possible, and that the offspring of the former
e   unions ought to be reared, and that of the latter abandoned, if the flock is to attain to first-rate excellence; and these proceedings ought to be kept a secret from all but the rulers themselves, if the herd of guardians is also to be as free as possible from internal strife.

You are perfectly right.

Then we shall have to ordain certain festivals, at which we shall bring together the brides and the bridegrooms, and we must
460 have sacrifices performed, and hymns composed by our poets in strains appropriate to the occasion; but the number of marriages we shall place under the control of the rulers, in order that they may, as far as they can, keep the population at the same point, taking into consideration the effects of war and disease, and all such agents, that our city may, to the best of our power, be

prevented from becoming either too great or too small.

You are right.

We must therefore contrive an ingenious system of lots, I imagine, in order that those ordinary persons may blame chance and not the rulers for the union.

Certainly.

And those of our young men who distinguish themselves in the war or elsewhere,
will receive, along with other privileges and   b
rewards, more plentiful intercourse with the women, in order that, under this pretext, the greatest number of children may be the offspring of such parents.

You are right.

And, as fast as the children are born, they will be received by the officers appointed for the purpose, whether men or women, or both. I presume that the city-offices also will be held in common both by men and women.

They will.

Well, these officers, I suppose, will take
the children of good parents, and place   c
them in the general nursery under the charge of certain nurses, living apart in a particular quarter of the city; while those of inferior parents, and all deformed children that are born to the others, will be concealed, as is fitting, in some unspoken and unseen hiding-place.

Yes, if the species of the guardians is to be kept pure.

And will not these same officers have to care for the rearing of the children, bringing the mothers to the nursery when their breasts are full, but taking every precaution
that no mother shall know her own child,   d
and providing other women that have milk, if the mothers have not enough? And must they not take care to limit the time during which the mothers are to suckle the children, committing the task of sitting up at night, and the other troubles that go with infancy, to nurses and attendants?

You make child-bearing a very easy business for the wives of the guardians.

Yes, and so it ought to be. Now let us proceed to the next object of our interest. We said, you remember, that the children ought to be the offspring of parents who are still in their prime.

True.

e   And do you agree with me that the prime of life may be reasonably reckoned at a period of twenty years for a woman, and thirty for a man?

Which years?

I should make it the rule for a woman to bear children to the city from her twentieth to her fortieth year; and for a man, after he is past his prime at running, and from then on to beget children to the city until he is fifty-five years old.

461   Doubtless, he said, in both sexes, this is the period of their prime, both of body and in terms of prudence.

If, then, a man who is either above or under this age shall meddle with the business of begetting children for the regime, we shall declare his act to be an offense which is unholy and unjust. After all, he is raising up a child for the city who, should detection be avoided, will have been conceived under cover of darkness by the aid of dire incontinence, instead of having been begotten under the sanction of those sacrifices and prayers which are to be offered up at every
b   marriage ceremonial by priests and priestesses and the whole city, to the effect that the children to be born may ever be better and more beneficent than their good and beneficent parents.

You are right.

The same law will hold if a man who is still of an age to be a father touches a woman, who is also of the proper age, without the introduction of the rule, for we shall accuse him of raising up to the city an illegitimate, unsponsored, and unholy child.

You are perfectly right.

But as soon as the women and the men are past the prescribed age, we shall allow the latter, I imagine, to associate freely with whomsoever they please, except a daughter,   c
or mother, or daughter's child, or grandmother; and in like manner we shall permit the women to associate with any man, except a son or a father, or one of their relations in the direct line, ascending or descending; but only after giving them strict orders to do their best, if possible, to prevent any child, if one should be so conceived, from seeing the light, but if that cannot sometimes be helped, to dispose of the infant on the understanding that the fruit of such a union is not to be reared.

That too is a reasonable plan; but how are they to distinguish fathers, and daughters, and the relations you described just now?   d

Not at all, I replied; only, all the children that are born between the seventh and tenth month from the day on which one of their number was married, are to be called by him, if male, his sons, if female, his daughters; and they shall call him father, and their children he shall call his grandchildren; these again shall call him and his fellow-bridegrooms and brides, grandfathers and grandmothers; likewise all shall regard as brothers and sisters those that were born in the period during which their own fathers and mothers were bringing them into the world. And as we said just now, all these shall refrain from   e
touching one another. But the law will allow intercourse between brothers and sisters, if the lot chances to fall that way, and if the Delphic priestess also gives it her sanction.

That is quite right, said he.

Such will be the character, Glaucon, of the community of women and children that is to prevail among the guardians of your city. The argument must now go on to establish that the plan is in keeping with the rest of our regime, and by far the best arrangement. Or can you propose any other course?

462 Do as you say, by Zeus.

Will not the first principle for an agreement on this point between us be to ask ourselves what we can name as the greatest good in the constitution of a city, at which the legislator ought to aim in making his laws, and what as the greatest harm? And the next, to inquire whether the plan we described just now harmonizes with the traces of the good, but not with the bad?

Most decidedly.

Do we know then of any greater harm to the city, than that which should tear it asunder, and make it into a multitude of b cities instead of one? Or of any higher good than that which should bind it together, and make it one?

We do not.

Well, then, does not a community of feeling in pleasure and pain bind the citizens together, when they all, so far as is possible, rejoice and grieve alike, at the same births and the same deaths?

Most assuredly it does.

And does not isolation in these feelings produce disunion, when some are much pleased and others equally grieved, at the same events affecting the city and its inmates?

c Of course it does.

And does not this state of things arise when the words "mine" and "not mine" are not pronounced by all simultaneously in the city? And when there is the same discrepancy in the use of the word "another's"?

Precisely so.

That city then is best managed in which the largest proportion of citizens apply the words "mine" and "not mine" similarly to the same objects.

Yes, much the best.

Or, in other words, that city which comes nearest to the condition of a single human being. Thus, when one of our fingers is hurt, the whole fellowship that spreads through the body up to the soul, and there forms an organized unity under the ruling principle, is sensible of the hurt, and there is a universal and simultaneous feeling of pain in sympathy with the wounded part; and therefore we say that the human being has a pain in his finger. And in speaking of any other part whatso-   d ever, the same account may be given of the pain felt when it suffers, and the pleasure felt when it is eased.

The same, no doubt; and to return to your question, there is a very close analogy between such a case and the condition of the best-governed city.

Then I think that, when any good or harm comes to one of the citizens, a city such as we are describing will be more likely than another to regard the affected member   e as a part of itself; and to share as a whole with his pleasure or his pain. . . .

The more you talk in this strain, he said, the less likely shall we be to let you off from   472 explaining how this regime is possible. So proceed with your explanation, and let us have no more delay. . . .

Do you think any the worse of the merits of an artist, who has painted a paradigm of the most beautiful human being, and has left nothing lacking in the picture, because he cannot prove that such a man as he has painted might possibly exist?

No, indeed, I do not.

Well, were not we likewise professing to   e make in speech the paradigm of a good city?

Yes, certainly.

Then will our argument suffer at all, do you think, if we cannot prove that it is possible for a city to be organized in the way we have said?

Certainly not.

This then is the truth of it; but if for your gratification I must also exert myself and demonstrate in what way and under what conditions it is most possible, I must ask you to agree again to the same points for the sake of this demonstration.

Which do you mean?

473 Can anything be accomplished in the city as it is said? Or is it the case that practice by nature attains less to the truth than does speech? Never mind if some think otherwise; tell me whether you admit this fact or not.

I do admit it.

Then do not force me to exhibit the details in every way in deed as we went through them in speech; but if we find out how a city may be organized and gets very close to our b description, you must admit that we have discovered the possibility of realizing the plan which you require me to consider. Shall you not be content if you gain this much? For my own part I shall be.

So shall I.

Then our next step apparently must be, to try to search out and demonstrate what there is now amiss in the working of our cities, preventing their being governed in the manner described, and what is the smallest change that would enable a city to assume this form of regime, confining ourselves, if possible, to a single change; if not, to two; or else, to such as are fewest in number and least important in their influence.

c Let us by all means endeavor to do so.

Well, I proceeded, there is one change by which, as I think we might show, the required transformation would be secured; but it is certainly neither a small nor an easy change, though it is a possible one.

What is it? . . .

Unless it happen either than philosophers acquire the kingly power in cities, or that those who are now called kings and rulers d be genuinely and adequately philosophical,

that is to say, unless political power and philosophy be united in the same place, most of those who at present pursue one to the exclusion of the other being necessarily excluded from either, there will be no deliverance, my dear Glaucon, for cities, nor yet, I believe, for the human race; neither can the regime, which we have now sketched in speech, ever grow into a possibility until then, and see the light of the sun. But my awareness of how entirely paradoxical this was made me all along so reluctant to give expression to it. It is difficult to see any other way by which happiness can be attained, by the city or by the individual. . . .

BOOK VI

Here Adeimantus interposed and said; It 487b is true, Socrates, that no one can dispute these conclusions; but still, every time you say such things, the hearers feel certain misgivings of the following kind. They imagine that, from inexperience in questioning and answering, at each question they are led a little astray by the argument, until, at the close of the discussion, these little divergences are found to amount to a serious false step, which makes them contradict their original statements. And, as unskillful checkers-players are in the end hemmed into c a corner by the skillful, until they cannot make a move, just in the same way your hearers conceive themselves to be at last hemmed in and reduced to silence by this novel kind of checkers, played with words instead of counters. But that doesn't make it any more true. And, in saying this, I have the present occasion before my eye. For at this moment a person will tell you, that though at each question he cannot oppose you with words, yet in practice he sees that all the students of philosophy, who have devoted themselves to it for any length of time, instead of taking it up for educational d purposes and dropping it while still young, in most cases become exceedingly eccentric, quite depraved in fact, while even those who appear the most respectable are nonetheless far worse off for the pursuit which you commend, they become useless to their cities.

When he had said this, I replied: Then do you think that what has been said is deceptive?

I am not sure, he answered; but I should be glad to hear what you think of it.

Let me tell you, that I think we were speaking the truth.

e How then can it be right to assert that the miseries of our cities will find no relief, until those philosophers who, on our own admission, are useless to them, become their rulers?

You are asking a question, I replied, which I must answer by the help of an image.

And you, I suppose, have not been in the habit of using images.

Ah! Are you making fun of me, now that you have got me upon a subject in which 488 demonstration is so difficult? However, listen to the illustration, that you may see still better how greedy I am for images. So cruel is the position in which those respectable men are placed, in reference to their cities, that there is no single thing whose position is analogous to theirs. Consequently I have to collect materials from several quarters for the image which I am to use in their defense, like painters when they paint goat-stags and similar monsters. Think of a fleet, or a single ship, in which the state of affairs on board is as follows. The owner, you are to suppose, is taller and stronger b than any of the crew, but rather deaf, and rather nearsighted, and correspondingly deficient in nautical skill; and the sailors are quarreling together about piloting, each of them thinking he has a right to steer the vessel, although up to that moment he has never studied the art, and cannot name his

instructor, or the time when he served his apprenticeship. More than this, they assert that it is a thing which positively cannot be taught, and are even ready to tear in pieces the person who affirms that it can. c Meanwhile they crowd incessantly round the person of the ship-owner, begging and beseeching him with every importunity to entrust the helm to them; and occasionally, failing to persuade him, while others succeed better, these disappointed candidates kill their successful rivals, or fling them overboard, and, after binding the noble ship-owner hand and foot with drugs or strong drink, or disabling him by some other contrivance, they rule the ship, and apply its contents to their own purposes, and pass their time at sea in drinking and feasting, as you might expect with such a crew. And besides all this, they compliment d with the title of "able seaman," "pilot," "skillful navigator," any sailor that can second them cleverly in either persuading or forcing the ship-owner into installing them in command of the ship, while they condemn as useless everyone whose talents are of a different order, they don't know that the true pilot must devote his attention to the year and its seasons, to the sky, and the stars, and the winds, and all that concerns his art, if he intends to be really e fit to command a ship; and thinking it impossible to acquire and practice, along with the pilot's art, the art of maintaining the pilot's authority whether some of the crew like it or not. Such being the state of things on board, do you not think that the pilot who is really master of his craft is sure to be called a useless, stargazing babbler by those 489 who form the crews of ships run like this?

Yes, that he will, replied Adeimantus.

Well, said I, I suppose you do not need to scrutinize my image, to remind you that it is a true picture of our cities insofar as their disposition towards philosophers is concerned; on the contrary, I think you understand my meaning.

Yes, quite.

That being the case, when a person expresses his astonishment that philosophers are not respected in our cities, begin by telling him our illustration, and try to persuade him that it would be far more astonishing if they were respected.

Well, I will.

And go on to tell him that he is right in saying that those most suitable for philosophy are considered most useless by the many; only recommend him to lay the blame for it not on these good people themselves, but upon those who decline their services. For it is not in the nature of things that a pilot should petition the sailors to submit to his authority, or that the wise should wait at the rich man's door. No, the author of that bit of cleverness was wrong. For the real truth is, that, just as a sick man, whether he be rich or poor, must attend at the physician's door, so all who require to be ruled must attend at the gate of him who is able to rule, it being against nature that the ruler, supposing him to be really good for anything, should have to beg his subjects to submit to his rule. In fact, you will not be wrong, if you compare the statesmen of our time to the sailors whom we were just now describing, and the useless visionary talkers, as they are called by our politicians, you can compare to those who are truly pilots.

You are perfectly right.

Under these circumstances, and among men like these, it is not easy for that best of occupations to be in good repute with those to whose pursuits it is directly opposed. But far the most grievous and most obstinate slander, under which philosophy labors, is due to her professed followers—who are doubtless the persons meant by the accuser of philosophy, when he declares, as you tell us, that most of those who approach her are utterly depraved, while even her best pupils are useless—to the truth of which remark I assented, did I not?

Yes, you did.

We have explained the reason why the good are useless, have we not?

Certainly we have. . . .

Well then, I continued, the causes of the 497slander against philosophy, and the injustice of it, have in my opinion been satisfactorily disposed of, unless you have anything to add.

No, I have nothing more to say on this topic. . . .

BOOK VII

Now then, I proceeded to say, compare our natural condition, as far as education and the lack of education are concerned, to a state of things like the following. Imagine a number of human beings living in an underground cave-like chamber, with an entrance open to the light, extending along the entire length of the cave, in which they have been confined, from their childhood, with their legs and necks so shackled, that they are obliged to sit still and look straight forward, because their chains make it impossible for them to turn their heads round. And imagine a bright fire burning some way off, above and behind them, and a kind of roadway above which passes between the fire and the prisoners, with a low wall built along it, like the screens which puppeteers put up in front of their audience, and above which they exhibit their puppets.

I see, he replied.

Also picture to yourself a number of persons walking behind this wall, and carrying with them statues of men, and images of other animals, fashioned in wood and stone and all kinds of materials, together with various other articles, which are above the wall. And, as you might expect, let some of the passers-by be talking, and others silent.

You are describing a strange scene, and strange prisoners.

They resemble us, I replied. For let me ask you, in the first place, whether persons so confined could have seen anything of themselves or of each other, beyond the shadows thrown by the fire upon the part of the cave facing them?

Certainly not, if you suppose them to have been compelled all their lifetime to keep their heads unmoved.

b

And what about the things carried past them? Is not the same true with regard to them?

Unquestionably it is.

And if they were able to converse with one another, do you not think that they would be in the habit of giving names to the things which they saw before them?

Doubtless they would.

Again, if their prison-house returned an echo from the part facing them, whenever one of the passers-by opened his lips, to what, let me ask you, could they refer the voice, if not to the shadow which was passing?

They would refer it to that, by Zeus.

Then surely such persons would hold the shadows of those manufactured articles to be the only truth.

c

Without a doubt they would.

Now consider what would happen if the course of nature brought them a release from their fetters, and a remedy for their foolishness, in the following manner. Let us suppose that one of them has been released, and compelled suddenly to stand up, and turn his head around and walk with open eyes towards the light—and let us suppose that he goes through all these actions with pain, and that the dazzling splendor renders him incapable of perceiving those things of which he formerly used to see only the shadows. What answer should you expect him to give, if someone were to tell him that

d

in those days he was watching foolery, but that now he is somewhat nearer to reality, and is turned towards things more real, and sees more correctly? Above all, what would you expect if he were to point out to him the several objects that are passing by, and question him, and compel him to answer what they are? Should you not expect him to be puzzled, and to regard his old visions as truer than the things now shown his shown?

Yes, much truer.

And if he were further compelled to gaze at the light itself, would not his eyes be distressed, do you think, and would he not shrink and turn away to the things which he could see distinctly, and consider them to be really clearer than the things pointed out to him?

e

Just so.

And if some one were to drag him violently up the rough and steep ascent from the cave, and refuse to let him go until he had drawn him out into the light of the sun, do you not think that he would be vexed and indignant at such treatment, and on reaching the light, would he not find his eyes so dazzled by the glare as to be incapable of making out so much as one of the objects that are now called true?

516

Yes, he would find it so at first.

Hence, I suppose, it will be necessary for him to become accustomed before he is able to see the things above. At first he will be most successful in distinguishing shadows, then he will discern the images of men and other things in water, and afterwards the things themselves? And after this he will raise his eyes to encounter the light of the moon and stars, finding it less difficult to study the heavenly bodies and the heaven itself by night, than the sun and the sun's light by day.

b

Doubtless.

Last of all, I imagine, he will be able to observe and contemplate the nature of the sun, not as it appears in water or on alien ground, but as it is in itself in its own region.

Of course.

His next step will be to draw the conclusion, that the sun is the provider of the seasons and the years, and the guardian of all things in the visible world, and in a manner the cause of all those things which he and his companions used to see.

Obviously, this will be his next step.

What then? When he recalls to mind his first home, and the wisdom of the place, and his old fellow-prisoners, do you not think he will think himself happy on account of the change, and pity them?

Assuredly he will.

And if it was their practice in those days to receive honor and praise one from another, and to give prizes to him who had the keenest eye for the things passing by, and who remembered best all that used to precede and follow and accompany it, and from these divined most ably what was going to come next, do you imagine that he will desire these prizes, and envy those who receive honor and exercise authority among them? Do you not rather imagine that he will feel what Homer describes, to "drudge on the lands of a master, serving a man of no great estate," and be ready to go through anything, rather than entertain those opinions, and live in that fashion?

For my own part, he replied, I am quite of that opinion. I believe he would consent to go through anything rather than live in that way.

And now consider what would happen if such a man were to descend again and seat himself on his old seat? Coming so suddenly out of the sun, would he not find his eyes blinded with the darkness of the place?

Certainly, he would.

And if he were forced to form a judgment again, about those previously mentioned shadows, and to compete earnestly against those who had always been prisoners, while his sight continued dim, and his eyes unsteady, and if he needed quite some time to get adjusted—would he not be made a laughingstock, and would it not be said of him, that he had gone up only to come back again with his eyesight destroyed, and that it was not worthwhile even to attempt the ascent? And if anyone endeavored to set them free and carry them to the light, would they not go so far as to put him to death, if they could only manage to get their hands on him?

Yes, that they would.

Now this imaginary case, my dear Glaucon, you must apply in all its parts to our former statements, by comparing the region which the eye reveals to the prison-house, and the light of the fire to the power of the sun. And if, by the upward ascent and the contemplation of the things above, you understand the journeying of the soul into the intelligible region, you will not disappoint my hopes, since you desire to be told what they are; though, indeed, god only knows whether they are true. But, be that as it may, the view which I take of the phenomena is the following. In the world of knowledge, the idea of the good is the limit of what can be seen, and it can barely be seen; but, when seen, we cannot help concluding that it is in every case the source of all that is right and beautiful, in the visible world giving birth to light and its master, and in the intelligible world, as master, providing truth and mind—and that whoever would act prudently, either in private or in public, must see it.

To the best of my power, said he, I quite agree with you.

That being the case, I continued, agree with me on another point, and do not be surprised, that those who have climbed so high are unwilling to mind the business of human beings, because their souls are eager d to spend all their time in that upper region. For how could it be otherwise, if in turn it follows from the image we've discussed before?

True, it could scarcely be otherwise.

Well, do you think it amazing that a person who has turned from the contemplation of the divine to the study of human things, should betray awkwardness, and appear very ridiculous, when with his sight still dazed, and before he has become sufficiently accustomed to the surrounding darkness, he finds himself compelled to contend in courts of law, or elsewhere, about the shadows of justice, or images which cast the shadows, and to take up in what way e these things are to be grasped by those who have never yet had a glimpse of justice itself?

No, it is anything but amazing.

But an intelligent person will remember 518 that the eyes may be confused in two distinct ways and from two distinct causes, that is to say, by sudden transitions either from light to darkness, or from darkness to light. And, believing that these same things hold for the soul, whenever such a person sees a case in which the soul is perplexed and unable to distinguish objects, he will not laugh unintelligently, but will rather examine whether it has just come from a brighter life, and has been blinded by the novelty of darkness, or whether it has come from the depths of igb norance into a more brilliant life, and has been dazzled by the unusual splendor; and not until then will he consider the first soul happy in its life and condition, or have pity on the second. And if he chooses to laugh at the second soul, such laughter will be less ridiculous than that which is raised at the expense of the soul that has descended from the light of a higher region.

You are speaking in a sensible manner.

Hence, if this is true, we must consider the following about these matters, that educ cation is not what certain men proclaim.

They say, I think, that they can infuse the soul with knowledge, when it was not in there, just as sight might be instilled in blinded eyes.

True, they do indeed assert that.

Whereas, our present argument shows us that there is a faculty residing in the soul of each person, and an instrument enabling each of us to learn; and that, just as we might suppose it to be impossible to turn the eye round from darkness to light without turning the whole body, so must this faculty, or this instrument, be wheeled round, in company with the entire soul, from the world of becoming, until it be enabled to endure the contemplation of the world of being and the d brightest part thereof, which, according to us, is the idea of the good. Am I not right?

You are.

Hence, I continued, there should be an art of this turning around, involving the way that the change will most easily and most effectually be brought about. Its object will not be to produce in the person the power of seeing. On the contrary, it assumes that he possesses it, though he is turned in a wrong direction, and does not look towards the right quarter—and its aim is to remedy this defect.

So it would appear.

Hence, on the one hand, the other so-called virtues of the soul seem to resemble those of the body, inasmuch as they really do not preexist in the soul, but are formed e in it in the course of time by habit and exercise; while the virtue of prudence, on the other hand, does, above everything else, appear to be more divine, which never loses its energy, but depending on which way it is turned, becomes useful and serviceable, or else remains useless and harmful. For you 519 must have noticed how keen-sighted are the puny souls of those who have the reputation of being wise but vicious, and how sharply they distinguish the things to which they are directed, thus proving that their powers of vision are by no means feeble, though they have been compelled to become the servants of wickedness, so that the more sharply they see, the more numerous are the harms which they work.

Yes, indeed it is the case.

But, I proceeded, if from earliest childhood this part of their nature had been hammered out and its ties of becoming
b knocked off— those leaden, earth-born weights, which grow and cling to the pleasures of eating and gluttonous enjoyments of a similar nature, and which keep the eye of the soul turned upon the things below— if, I repeat, they had been released from these snares, and turned round to look at true things, then these very same souls of these very same men would have had as keen an eye for such pursuits as they actually have for those in which they are now engaged.

Yes, probably it would be so.

Once more, is it not also probable, or rather does it not follow our previous remarks, that neither those who are uneducated and inexperienced in truth, nor those who spend their time continuously on their education all their life, can ever be adequate guardians of the city, the
c former, because they have no single goal in life, to which they are to constitute the end and aim of all their conduct both in private and in public? And the latter, because they will not act without compulsion, believing that, while yet alive, they have emigrated to the islands of the blest?

That is true.

It is, therefore, our task as founders of the city, I continued, to constrain the best
d natures to arrive at that learning which we formerly pronounced the highest, and to set eyes upon the good, and to mount that ascent we spoke of; and, when they have mounted and looked long enough, we must

take care to refuse to permit them that which is at present allowed.

And what is that?

Staying where they are, and refusing to descend again to those prisoners, or partake of their toils and honors, be they mean or more serious.

Then are we to do them an injustice, and make them live a life that is worse than the one within their reach?   e

You have again forgotten, my friend, that law does not ask itself how some one part of a city is to live extraordinarily well. On the contrary, it tries to bring about this result in the entire city—for which purpose it links the citizens together by persuasion and by 520 constraint, makes them share with one another the benefit which each individual can contribute to the commonwealth, and does actually create men of this sort in the city, not with the intention of letting them go each on his own way, but by using them to make a beginning towards binding the city together.

True, he replied, I had forgotten.

Therefore reflect, Glaucon, that far from wronging the future philosophers of our city, we shall only be treating them justly, if we put them under the additional obligation of guarding and caring for the   b others. We shall say with good reason that when men of this type come to be in other cities, it is likely that they will not partake in the labor of the city. For they take root in a city spontaneously, against the will of the prevailing regime. And it is but just that a self-sown plant, which is indebted to no one for support, should have no inclination to pay to anybody wages for attendance. But in your case, it is we that have begotten you for the city as well as for yourselves, to be like leaders and kings of a hive, better and more perfectly educated than the rest, and more capable of playing a part in both lives. You must therefore descend by turns,   c and associate with the rest of the community, and you must accustom yourselves to the contemplation of these dark things. For, when accustomed, you will see ten thousand times better than the residents, and you will recognize what each image is, and what is its original, because you have seen the truth of beautiful and just and good things. And in this way, for you and for us, the city is ruled in a waking state and not in a dream like so many of our present cities, which are mostly composed of men who fight among themselves for shadows, and are feuding to gain rulership, which they regard as a great good. Whereas I conceive the truth is this. That city in which those who are going to rule are least eager to rule will inevitably be ruled in the best and least factious manner, and a contrary result will ensue if the rulers are of a contrary disposition.

You are perfectly right.

And do you imagine that our pupils, when addressed in this way, will disobey our commands, and refuse to toil with us in the city by turns, while they spend most of their time together in that pure region?

Impossible, he replied, for certainly it is a just command and those who are to obey it are just men. No, doubtless each of them will undertake ruling as a necessary thing—the opposite of what is pursued by the present rulers in each city.

True, my friend, the case stands thus. If you can find a life better than ruling for those who are going to rule, you may possibly realize a well-governed city. For only in such a city will the rulers be those who are really rich, not in gold, but in a good and prudent life, which is the wealth necessary for a happy man. But if beggars, and persons who hunger after private goods, take the reins of the city, supposing that they are privileged to snatch good from their power, all goes wrong. For then ruling is made an object of strife, both civil war and family

feuds, and conflicts of this nature, ruin not only these men themselves, but also the rest of the city.

That is most true.

And can you mention any life which despises political offices, except the life of true philosophy?

No by Zeus, I cannot.

Well, but the task of ruling must be undertaken by persons who aren't lovers of it; otherwise, their rival lovers will fight.

Unquestionably it must.

Then what persons will you compel to become guardians of the city other than the ones who are most prudent about how best to rule the city and who have other honors and a life better than the political life?

None other, he said. . . .

BOOK VIII

. . . And now we must proceed, I should suppose, to examine in what way democracy arises, and what is its character when it has arisen, in order that once again we may discover the character of the corresponding man, and place him by our side for judgment.

Yes, if we would act consistently, we must take that course.

Is not the transition from oligarchy to democracy brought about by an intemperate craving for what it has set down as good, the necessity to become as wealthy as possible?

Describe it.

Since the power of the rulers in an oligarchic city is, I believe, wholly due to their great wealth, they are unwilling to put the licentious young men of their time under restraint, to the extent of rendering it illegal for them to spend and waste their property. They hope, by purchasing the possessions of such persons, and by lending money to them, to make themselves still richer and more honored.

Most unquestionably.

And is it not manifest by this time, that it is impossible for the citizens of a city to honor wealth, and at the same time acquire a proper amount of moderation, because they cannot avoid neglecting either the one or the other?

d It is pretty well manifest, he replied.

Hence the rulers in such cities, by their reckless admission of unrestrained license, not unfrequently compel men of noble birth to become poor.

Yes, that they do.

And the persons thus impoverished lurk, I should suppose, in the city, harnessed and armed with stings—some owing debts, and others disfranchised, and others laboring under both misfortunes—hating and plotting against the new owners of their property, and against all who are better off than themselves, and longing for change.

True.

These money-makers, on the other hand,
e keep prying after their own interests, and apparently do not see their enemies; and, whenever one of the remainder yields them opportunity, they wound him by infusing their silver, and then recover interest many
556 times as great as the parent sum, and thus make the drone and the beggar multiply in the city.

Yes, that they do.

And they cannot make up their minds to extinguish this great ill, as it is bursting into flames, either by prohibiting people from disposing of their property at their own pleasure, or by employing another method, which provides by a different law for the removal of such dangers.

What law do you mean?

I mean one which is next best to the former, and which constrains the citizens to apply themselves to virtue. For if it be enacted that voluntary contracts be as a general rule entered into at the proper risk of the contractor, people will be less shameless b in their money-dealings in the city, and such ills as we have just now described will be less common.

Yes, much less common.

But as it is, the various inducements I have mentioned encourage the rulers in the city to handle their subjects in this way. On the other hand, if we look at the rulers themselves and their children, do we not see that the young men are made luxurious and lazy both in body and soul, and so idle and soft that they cannot resist pleasure and c encounter pain?

Unquestionably they are.

And that their seniors are indifferent to everything except making money, and as careless about virtue as the poor themselves?

Certainly they are.

In this state of things, when the rulers and their subjects encounter one another either in traveling or in some other common occupation, whether it be a pilgrimage or a military expedition, in which they are fellow-sailors or fellow-soldiers; or when they are witnesses of one another's behavior in moments of danger, in which the poor can by no possibility be despised by the rich, because it often happens that a rich man, reared in the shade and with excess fat, finds d himself posted in battle by the side of some lean and sunburned poor man, who sees his labored breathing and perplexity. When, I repeat, all this takes place, do you imagine that these poor men can avoid thinking, that it is through their own cowardice that such incapable people are wealthy, or that they can refrain from repeating to one another, when they meet in private, "These men are ours, for they are nothing"?

I am quite sure that they do so.

Now just as a sickly body requires but a small additional impulse from without to bring on an attack of illness, and sometimes even without any external provocation e is divided against itself, so, in the same way, does not this city, whose condition is identical with that of a diseased body, require only the slight excuse of an external alliance introduced by the one party from an oligarchic city, or by the other from a democratic, to bring on an acute disease and an inward battle? And is it not sometimes, even without such external 557 influences, distracted by factions?

Most decidedly it is.

Democracy, then, I think, arises, whenever the poor win the day, killing some of the opposite party, expelling others, and admitting the remainder to an equal participation in regime and ruling, and most commonly the offices in such a city are given by lot.

Yes, you have correctly described the establishment of democracy, whether it be brought about by resorting to arms, or by the terrified withdrawal of the other party.

And now tell me, I continued, in what style these persons administer the city, and b what is the character of this third regime. For obviously we shall find the corresponding man marked, to a certain extent, with the same features.

True, said he.

First of all, are they not free, and does not liberty of act and speech abound in the city, and has not a man license therein to do what he wants?

Yes, so we are told.

And clearly, where such license is permitted, every citizen will arrange his own manner of life as suits his pleasure.

Clearly he will.

c   Hence I should suppose, that in this regime there will be the greatest diversity of human beings.

Unquestionably there will.

Possibly, I proceeded, this regime may be the prettiest of all. Embroidered as it is with every kind of character, it may be thought as beautiful as a colored dress embroidered with every kind of flower. And perhaps,

I added, as children and women admire dresses of many colors, so many persons will judge it to be the most beautiful.

No doubt many will.

Yes, my excellent friend, and it would   d be a good plan to explore it, if we were in search of a regime.

Why so?

Because it contains within it every kind of regime in consequence of that license of which I spoke; and perhaps a person wishing to found a city, as we were just now doing, ought to go into a democratic city, as a bazaar of regimes, and pick out whatever sort pleases him, and then found his regime according to the choice he has made.

We may safely say that he is not likely to   e be at a loss for patterns.

Again, consider that, in this city, you are not obliged to rule, though your talents may be equal to the task; and that you need not submit to being ruled, if you dislike it, or go to war when your fellow-citizens are at war, or keep peace when they are doing so, if you do not want peace; and again, consider that, though a law forbids your holding office or sitting on a jury, you may nevertheless do both the one and the other, should it occur   558 to you to do so. And now tell me, is not such a course of life divinely pleasant for the moment?

Yes perhaps it is, he replied, for the moment.

Once more. Is not the leniency regarding some who have been tried in a court of law exquisite? Or have you failed to notice in such a regime how men who have been condemned to death or exile, stay all the same, and walk about the streets, and parade like heroes, as if no one saw or cared?

I have seen many instances of it, he replied.

And is there not something splendid in the sympathy of such a regime, lacking pettiness?

b   It positively scorns what we were saying when we were founding our city, to the effect that no one who is not endowed with a transcendent nature, can ever become a good man, unless from his earliest childhood he plays among beautiful objects and studies all beautiful things. How magnificently it tramples all this underfoot, without troubling itself in the least about the previous pursuits of those who enter on a political course, whom it raises to honor, if they only

c   assert to the multitude that they wish well.

Yes, he said, it behaves very grandly.

These, then, will be some of the features of democracy, to which we might add others of the same family; and it will be, in all likelihood, an agreeable, anarchic, many-colored regime, dealing with all alike on a footing of equality, whether they be really equal or not.

The facts you mention are well known.

And now let me ask you to examine the character of the corresponding individual. Or must we begin, as in the case of the regime, by investigating his origin?

Yes, he replied.

Then am I not right in supposing that he will be the son of the miserly and oligarchic

d   man, bred up under his father's eye, and in his father's character?

Doubtless he will.

And this son, like the father, will put a violent constraint upon those pleasures within him that tend to extravagance and not to money-getting—which, you know, are called unnecessary pleasures.

Clearly he will.

Now, that we may not talk in the dark, would you like us first to define the necessary and unnecessary appetites?

I should.

May we not justly apply the term "necessary" to those appetites which we cannot get

e   rid of, and to those whose satisfaction benefits us? For our nature cannot help feeling both these classes of desires, can it?

Certainly it cannot.

Then we shall be justified in applying   559 necessity to them.

We shall.

Again, shall we not be right to assert that all those appetites are unnecessary, which we can get rid of from youth—and anyway their presence never does us any good, and in some cases does positive harm?

Yes, we shall be right.

Would it not be as well to select an example of the existing appetites of each kind, in order that we may gain a general type?

Decidedly it would.

Will not the appetite for food—that is to say, simple bread and meat—within the bounds of health and good condition, be a   b necessary appetite?

I think so.

The appetite for bread at least is surely necessary by a double claim, being not only beneficial, but also indispensable to the support of life.

Yes.

On the other hand, the appetite for meat is necessary, so far as it may contribute advantageously to a good condition.

Certainly.

Again, the appetite for other meats of a less simple kind, of which most people can rid themselves by early education and training, and which is hurtful to the body, and harmful to the soul, in its endeavors after prudence and moderation, may be rightly styled an unnecessary appetite, may it not?   c

Yes, most rightly.

And must we not assert that the appetites of this second class are also expensive, whereas the others contribute to money-making, because they are a help for our work?

Undoubtedly.

Can we say the same of sex and the other appetites?

Yes.

Now did we not describe the man, to whom we lately gave the name of drone, as one burdened with those expensive pleasures and desires, and governed by the unnecessary appetites; while we described the man, who is ruled by the necessary, as miserly and oligarchic?

Undoubtedly we did.

Let us now return, I continued, and explain how the oligarchic man is transformed into the democratic. It looks to me like it mostly happens in the following way.

How?

I would have you suppose that a young man's transition from inward oligarchy to democracy begins the moment when, after being brought up as we were saying just now, without education and in a miserly way, he has tasted the honey of the drones, and made acquaintance with fiery and terrible wild beasts, who are able to procure him all kinds of pleasures, of a varied and manifold nature.

It cannot be otherwise.

And may we say that, just as the city was transformed by the assistance given by a foreign alliance to one of the two parties, like to like; so, in the same way, the young man is transformed by the analogous assistance from without, afforded by a form of appetites kindred and similar to one of the two parties within him?

Assuredly we may.

And should the oligarchic element within him be supported by some counter-alliance, derived perhaps from his father, or perhaps from his other relations, who rebuke and reproach him, then, I imagine, there follows discord and resistance and an inward battling with himself.

Undoubtedly.

And occasionally, I imagine, the democratic interest yields to the oligarchic, and certain of the appetites are either destroyed or expelled, owing to the presence of a sense of shame in the young man's soul—and order is once more restored.

Yes, this does take place sometimes.

But some new appetites, I suppose, akin to those expelled, are secretly nurtured, and, owing to the lack of knowledge in his father's training, become numerous and strong.

Yes, this is generally the case.

And these appetites, of course, draw him to his old associates, and by their secret intercourse engender in him a multitude of others.

Undoubtedly.

And finally, I imagine, they seize upon the acropolis of the young man's soul, because they perceive it to be destitute of beautiful studies and practices and true speeches, which are the very ones to keep the best watch and guard over the thought of men who are loved by the gods.

Yes, quite the best.

And in their absence, I think, false and pretentious speeches and opinions rise up in the man, and seize that place.

That they do.

Does he not, in consequence, return to those Lotus-eaters, and dwell with them without disguise? And if his relatives send any assistance to the miserly element of his soul, do not those pretensions close the gates of the royal fortress within him, and not only refuse an entrance to the actual auxiliary force, but even decline to admit an embassy of individuals in the shape of admonitions from elder persons? And do they not fight in person and gain the day, giving shame a dishonorable discharge in the name of folly, and expelling moderation with insults under the name of cowardice? And do they not prove, by the aid of many useless appetites, that moderation and orderly expenditure are boorish and illiberal, and banish them as such beyond the border?

Most certainly they do.

And no doubt, when, by emptying out these virtues they have purified the soul of him who is now in their power, and is being initiated by them into the great mysteries, they proceed at once to restore insolence, anarchy, wastefulness, and shamelessness, in great splendor, accompanied by a numerous chorus, and with crowns on their heads, extolling them, and calling them by soft names, describing insolence as a good education, anarchy as freedom, wastefulness as magnificence, and shamelessness as courage. Is not this, I asked, pretty much the way in which the man who is brought up in the gratification only of necessary appetites changes, already in his youth, liberating from servitude and control the unnecessary and useless pleasures?

Yes, very evidently it is, he replied.

From that day forward a man of this description spends, I should suppose, just as much money and labor and time on unnecessary as upon necessary pleasures. But, should he be so fortunate as to set a limit to his wildness, and, as he grows older, when the tumult of passion has mostly gone by, should he go so far as to readmit to a certain extent portions of the banished, and not surrender himself wholly to the invaders, in that case, it is the habit of his life to make no distinction between his pleasures, but to hand over the rule to passing pleasures, as if chosen by lot, and to turn to another, when the first is satisfied—scorning none, but fostering equality.

Exactly so.

Yes, I proceeded, and whenever he is told that though some pleasures belong to the appetites which are good and honorable, others belong to the bad appetites; and that the former ought to be practiced and respected, but the latter chastised and enslaved, he does not receive this true speech, or admit it into his watchpost. On the contrary, at all these assertions he shakes his head, and maintains that all appetites are alike, and ought to be equally respected.

Yes, this is precisely his condition, and his behavior.

Hence, I continued, he lives from day to day to the end, in the gratification of the casual appetites—now drinking himself drunk while listening to the flute, and soon putting himself on a diet—and then idling and neglecting everything, and then living like a student of philosophy. And often he takes a part in public affairs, and starting up, speaks and acts according to the impulse of the moment. Now he follows eagerly in the steps of certain soldiers he admires; and soon he takes to trade, because he envies the successful trader. And there is no order or constraining rule in his life; but he calls this life of his sweet, free, and blessed and follows it out to the end.

Well, said he, you have certainly described the life of a man who believes in the law of equality.

Yes, I replied, and I conceive it to be also a manifold life, replete with very many characters. And I imagine that this is the man who, by the beautiful variety of his nature, answers to the city which we described—a man whose life many men and many women would envy, and who contains within him very many paradigms of regimes and characters.

True.

What then? May we place this man opposite democracy, in the belief that he may be rightly addressed as democratic?

Be it so, he replied.

It only remains for us, I continued, to describe the most beautiful of all regimes, and the most beautiful of all men, that is to say, tyranny and the tyrant.

You are quite right.

Come then, my dear friend, tell me in what way tyranny arises. That it is a transformation of democracy, is all but obvious.

It is. . . .

565   And is it not always the practice of the people to select a special leader of their cause, whom they maintain and exalt to greatness?

Yes, it is their practice.

d   Then, obviously, whenever a tyrant grows up naturally, his origin may be traced wholly to this leadership, which is the root from which he shoots.

That is quite obvious.

And what are the first steps in the transformation of the leader into a tyrant? Can we doubt that the change dates from the time when the leader has begun to act like the man in that legend which is told in reference to the temple of Lycaean Zeus in Arcadia?

What legend?

e   According to it, the man who tasted one piece of human entrails, which was minced up with the other entrails of other victims, was inevitably turned into a wolf. Have you never heard the story?

Yes, I have.

In like manner, should the people's leader find the populace so very compliant that he need make no scruple of shedding kindred blood; should he bring unjust charges against a man, as such persons love to do, prosecute his victim, and murder him, making away with human life, and tasting the blood of his fellows with unholy tongue and lips; should he banish, and kill, and give the signal for canceling debts and redistributing the land; is it not the inevitable destiny of such a man either to be destroyed by his enemies, or to become a tyrant, and be turned from a man into a wolf?

There is no escape from it—necessarily so.

Such is the fate of the man who stirs up faction against the propertied class.

It is.

And if he is banished, and afterwards restored in despite of his enemies, does he not return a complete tyrant?

Obviously he does.

And if his enemies find themselves unable   b
to expel him, or to put him to death, by accusing him before the city, in that case they take measures to remove him secretly by a violent end.

Yes, that is what usually happens.

In order to prevent this, those who have gone so far always adopt that notorious device of the tyrant, which consists in asking the people for a body-guard, in order that the people's friend may not be lost to them.

Just so.   c

And the people, I imagine, grant the request, for they are alarmed on his account, while they are confident on their own.

Just so.

Consequently, when this is observed by a man who has wealth, and with his wealth the character of being a hater of people, forthwith, in accordance with the oracle given to Croesus,

By the pebbly bed of the Hermus,
He flees and stays no more, nor shuns the
reproach for being a coward.

He would not have the chance of shunning it a second time.

And those that are arrested are given up   566
to death, I imagine.

Of course they are.

But as for that leader himself, it is quite clear that far from being laid "great in his greatness," he has overthrown many others,   d
and stands in the chariot of the city, turned from a leader into a perfected tyrant.

Yes, there is no help for it.

Well, I continued, are we to discuss the happiness both of the man himself, and of the city in which such a mortal resides?

By all means let us do so, he replied.

Well, in his early days, and at the beginning of his tyranny, has he not a smile and a greeting for everybody that he meets, and does he not repudiate the idea of his being a tyrant, and promise largely both in public and in private; and is it not his practice to forgive debts, and make grants of land to the people and to all those around him, while he pretends to be gentle and gracious to all?

It cannot be otherwise.

But as soon as he has relieved himself of his exiled enemies, by becoming reconciled to some, and by destroying others, his first measure is, I imagine, to be constantly inciting wars, in order that the people may stand in need of a leader.

That's likely.

Is it not further his intention so to impoverish his subjects by war-taxes, as to constrain them to devote themselves to the requirements of the day, and thus render them less likely to plot against himself?

Manifestly it is.

And am I not right in supposing that, should he suspect any persons of harboring a spirit of freedom such as would not put up with his ruling, it is his intention to throw them in the way of the enemy, and so get rid of them without suspicion? For all these reasons must not a tyrant be always stirring up war?

He must.

Then is it not the obvious result of such a course, that he gets more and more detested by the citizens?

Of course it is.

And does it not follow that the bravest of those who helped to establish him and who are in power speak their mind fearlessly to him and to one another, and criticize his policies?

So one would expect.

Now, if the tyrant is to keep up his authority, he must put all these people quietly out of the way, until he has left himself not a friend nor an enemy who is worth anything.

Certainly he must.

Then he must keenly notice who is manly, who high-minded, who prudent, who wealthy. And in such a happy condition is he, that, whether he wishes it or not, he is compelled to be the enemy of all these, and to plot against them, until he has purged them out of the city.

What a glorious purification!

Yes, said I, it runs directly counter to the process by which the physician purges the body. For the physician removes what is bad, and leaves what is good; but the tyrant removes the good, and leaves the bad.

Why, apparently, it is his only course, if he wishes to reign.

In fact he is bound in the chains of a delightful necessity, which orders him either to live with a crowd of ordinary men and be hated by them, or else to cease to exist.

That is the alternative.

Hence, in proportion as he grows more and more detested by the citizens for such conduct, he will require a more numerous and a more trusty bodyguard, will he not?

Of course he will.

And tell me what people can he trust, and where will he get them from?

Oh, they will come in flocks spontaneously, if he pays them their wages.

By the dog, I believe you are thinking of another miscellaneous swarm of foreign drones.

You are not mistaken.

But would he hesitate to enlist recruits on the spot?

By what process?

By taking their slaves from the citizens, freeing them, and enrolling them in his own bodyguard.

Most decidedly he would not hesitate, for such persons are really his most trusty adherents.

A tyrant is, indeed, a blessed thing, according to your account, if he adopts such
568   men as friends and faithful adherents, after he has destroyed those former ones.

Well, he certainly does take this course.

And do not these comrades of his admire him highly, and do not the new citizens associate with him, while the decent hate and shun him?

How can it be otherwise? . . .

d   . . . Let us return to the inquiry, how that army of the tyrant, that beautiful, large, many-colored and ever-changing army, is to be supported.

It is clear, he replied, that, if there be sacred money in the city, the tyrant will spend it as long as it lasts, along with the property of those whom he has destroyed, so that the war-taxes, which the people are compelled to pay, will be proportionally diminished.

But what is he to do when this resource
e   fails?

Evidently he will draw on his father's property for the maintenance of himself and his drinking buddies, his comrades both male and female.

I understand you. You mean that the people that begat the tyrant, will maintain him and his companions.

It cannot avoid doing so.

But do explain yourself, I proceeded. Suppose the people are annoyed, and assert that it is unjust for a father to have to maintain a grown-up son, since, on the contrary, the son ought to maintain the father; and that they had begotten and installed him not with the intent, that, when he was grown big, they should be made the slaves of their own slaves, and maintain
569   contrary, the son ought to maintain the

him and them with a mob of others, but with the intent that, under his leadership, they should be freed from the rich men of the city, and the gentlemen, as they are called; and suppose they now bid him depart out of the city, together with his friends, like a father expelling a son from home along with some riotous drinking buddies? What then?

The people will finally, by Zeus, most certainly discover how weak they are in comparison with the beast which they have   b
begotten and cherished and exalted, and that, in ejecting him, they are the weaker expelling the stronger.

What! I exclaimed. Will the tyrant venture to lay violent hands on his father, and beat him if he refuses to comply with his wishes?

Yes, that he will, once he has taken away his father's weapons.

You call the tyrant a parricide, and a hardhearted nurse of old age; and, apparently, the regime will henceforth be an open and avowed tyranny; and, according to the proverb, the people, trying to avoid the frying-pan of the enslavement to free men,   c
will have fallen into the fire of a tyranny exercised by slaves—in other words, they will have exchanged that vast and unseasonable freedom for the new dress of the harshest and bitterest enslavement to slaves.

No doubt that is the course of events.

Well then, will any one be disposed to disagree with us, if we assert that we have discussed satisfactorily the transition from democracy to tyranny, and the character of the latter when established?

We have done so quite satisfactorily, he replied.

ARISTOTLE

~

INTRODUCTION

RICHARD KRAUT

Aristotle (384–322 BCE) was born in Stagira, a town near the Aegean Sea in the north of Greece, and was raised in the royal residence of Macedon, where his father, Nicomachus, was a doctor attached to the court of King Amyntas III. In 367, at the age of seventeen, Aristotle was sent to Athens to study at the Academy, a school established by Plato for inquiry into philosophical, scientific, and political questions. Aristotle remained as one of its members for twenty years and departed at Plato's death in 347. He subsequently took up residence in several locations where he could pursue his research—Assos (in Asia Minor) and Lesbos (in the eastern Aegean)—and then in 343 returned to Macedon, where he remained until 336. Ancient sources tell us that during this time he was a tutor to the son of Philip II, Alexander (familiar to us as Alexander the Great), who was thirteen when Aristotle arrived. Philip had taken over the throne of Macedon in 359, at the end of a power struggle caused by the death of Amyntas some ten years earlier. During his reign Macedon's military power increased greatly, and in 338, having defeated Athens and Corinth in the battle of Chaeronea, it held sway over the Greek world. Philip was assassinated in 336 (a fact noted without comment by Aristotle at *Politics* V.10 1311b1–2). The following year Aristotle returned to Athens and established his own center of research and teaching in the Lyceum. During that period his wife, Pythias, whom he had married during his stay in Assos, died, and he formed a relationship with Herpyllis, who bore him a son, named Nicomachus (after his grandfather). Aristotle departed once again in 323 when Alexander died and several cities, including Athens, unsuccessfully tried to escape from the control of Macedon. There is little doubt that this second departure (one year before his death in 322) was motivated by the Athenian revolt against Macedon. Although Aristotle spent a considerable part of his adult life in Athens, he was never an Athenian citizen, and his relationship with the city was, at times, evidently strained.

Ancient testimony about Aristotle's works indicates that many of them were lost during the centuries that followed his death. Some were written in dialogue form—the genre favored by Plato—and were intended for a broad audience. The works that survive, some in an unfinished and roughly organized form, are highly concentrated in expression and are intended for a more specialized group of students. Some of them formed the basis for lectures that Aristotle gave at the Lyceum. They occupy almost 2,500 pages of small print in modern editions and cover nearly all of the branches of knowledge that existed in Aristotle's time or that he helped invent.

Aristotle was the founder of the formal study of inferential relationships (logic), and he developed a conception of knowledge and reality that gives a larger role to perception, material composition, and empirical research than had been allowed by Plato. A large proportion of his writings are devoted to the exploration of scientific matters (particularly biology) and to questions about the concepts (for example, cause, essence, change) that must be employed in our understanding of nature. He champions the idea that we must pursue knowledge by different methods, each appropriate to the subject matter under investigation. Practical questions, for example, must be explored in order to improve human life and not simply for the sake of knowledge. By contrast, the celestial world and biological species (both of which Aristotle took to be eternal and unchanging) are to be studied because theoretical understanding is by itself a precious thing. Aristotle holds that the proper pursuit of scientific understanding will lead to the realization that there must be a single divine cause of the universe. His god is a perfect being that causes all change without itself being changed; this god should inspire our love and admiration, but does not have moral qualities or a concern for human life.

Although Aristotle believes that one aspect of the human soul survives the destruction of the body, he does not follow Plato in regarding our mortal existence as a time of preparation for a future life, or as a punishment for mistakes we made in a previous life—for he holds that we have no such past or future lives. To talk about the soul (and Aristotle believes that all living things have souls, even plants and animals) is not to refer to a self-standing entity that can inhabit different bodies, but rather to the various powers that an embodied thing has: such processes as growth, reproduction, perception, and locomotion. Since humans are a kind of animal, we of course have the powers of the soul that all animals have, but we differ from the rest of nature in that we also have the capacity to make choices, experience emotions that are susceptible to rational control, learn a language, and look for and find reasons for what we believe. All of these capacities are comprehended by Aristotle's word for reason (*logos*). We are unique in that the matter of which we are composed is arranged in a way that makes us capable of all of these activities of reason.

Because Aristotle takes human beings to be essentially enmattered, he assumes that death is an event that brings our well-being to a close, and the whole of his practical philosophy is therefore devoted to the question of what it is for mortal beings like ourselves to fare well. His principal work devoted to this question is the *Nicomachean Ethics*. The word "Nicomachean" is not used by Aristotle himself; presumably it was added by a later editor and is a reference to Aristotle's son or father. (An earlier treatise, similar in content and structure to the *Nicomachean Ethics*, is called the *Eudemian Ethics*. Eudemus was a student and friend of Aristotle's and shared many of his research interests.) But the word *ethos*, from which our "ethics" is derived, is ubiquitous in Aristotle's practical writings, and he refers to some of these as ethical discourses. *Ethos* means "character," and the *Nicomachean Ethics* therefore announces in its title that it is a study of character and the many forms it takes.

But the starting point of Aristotle's practical thought is not character but *eudaimonia* (often translated "happiness"). He points out that our desires and actions are not all at the same level: some goals and activities are pursued for the sake of something else, and those further goals are in turn subordinate to others. What lies at the top of this hierarchy is of the utmost importance, and it is therefore the foremost task of ethical theory to arrive at a better understanding of what it is. Aristotle holds that the best conception of our highest end will identify it not with some distant goal that we achieve only at the end of our lives, or with some extrinsic reward that can easily be lost, but with the day-by-day excellent use we can make of our powers as rational beings. Happiness, in other words, consists in the excellent or virtuous activity of the rational soul, and all lower goods (honors, pleasures, power, wealth) are to be pursued because they in some way accompany excellent activity or provide us with the resources we need to engage in virtuous activity over the course of our lives. Character is of central importance to human life because in order to excel in all of its many important spheres, we must learn how to become a certain sort of person. We must train our judgment and emotions so that we know which pleasures to pursue, how to control our fear and make effective decisions in the face of great danger, how to spend money wisely and avoid both excessive disdain for or attraction to it, how to make fair allocations of goods to others, and so on. In each of these areas of life, success involves skill at finding the act that best avoids excess or deficiency, and therefore each of the ethical virtues is a state that lies between a vice of excess and a vice of deficiency.

Aristotle holds that the life that most fully develops the practical virtues is one of active engagement in the most important deliberative matters that face one's city—a political life, in other words. Although he believes that political activity should not be valued as highly as philosophy (which includes the study of science and culminates in reverence for the divine), he realizes that a life of theoretical study will be of interest only to a small number of his contemporaries. Most members of his audience, he assumes, plan to lead a political life, and so he takes his principal task as a practical philosopher to be the examination of the various ways in which civic life can be improved. He conceives of the *Nicomachean Ethics* as a political treatise, because the political leaders he is training must be guided by a full understanding of the proper goal of all legislation: human well-being.

The treatise he refers to as *Politics* was written during his final period of residence in Athens, as were his ethical works. Book I provides a preliminary discussion of the origin of the *polis* (often translated "city," or "state," or "city-state"), and the elements out of which it is made (households). The growth of the city out of smaller social units provides evidence that it is the sort of thing that exists by nature rather than convention. There is nothing arbitrary about leading a life devoted to the well-being of the political community, because the *polis* is the inevitable outgrowth of our natural psychological dispositions. Just as a seed naturally tends to develop in ways that serve its good, so human beings, over many generations, will come to participate in complex social organizations governed by collective deliberation. That is what Aristotle means when he says that human beings are political animals. But he also holds that some human beings (most women and most inhabitants of lands to the north or east of Greece) do not possess the capacity to engage in political deliberation and must play subordinate roles in civic life—marriage partners (in the case of Greek women) and slaves (in the case of non-Greek men and women).

The rest of the *Politics* serves a double purpose: it investigates the question, "What is the best constitution we can achieve, when we are at our best?" and it also examines the various ways in which any regime—even a tyranny—can be improved. (The project of constitutional amelioration was pursued in the Lyceum through empirical research: it produced studies of the constitutions of 158 cities. Only one—that of Athens—survives; it was discovered in the late nineteenth century.) Aristotle's ideal city is one in which all citizens are educated to be virtuous. Unlike the utopian scheme Plato depicts in *The Republic*, it is a community in which all citizens participate as equals, each having received from the city the same education and all sharing a single conception of well-being. Although Aristotle claims in Book I that the city is naturally prior to each of its citizens, he does not take this to mean that the city is the only community to which we should form an allegiance. Against *The Republic*, which proposes the abolition of the family and private property within the ruling class, Aristotle holds, in Book II of the *Politics*, that young children are best cared for by their own parents and that property will best serve the common good if each citizen has control over the allocation of his resources.

Books III through VI examine a wide variety of political systems, ranging from such correct forms as kingship, aristocracy, and *politeia* (often translated "polity," or "republic") to the defective regimes that correspond to them—tyranny, oligarchy, and democracy. Aristotle has a deep awareness of the ways in which the mutual hatred of rich and poor corrodes public life. His assumption that democracy is inherently corrupt rests on his allegation that in cities like Athens the poor develop a class consciousness that undermines their capacity to treat the wealthy in a fair way. But he believes that the rich are no less prone to class bias than the poor and argues that the poor can achieve a wisdom of sorts when they meet collectively—provided that they have a minimal degree of decency. The best sort of political system that requires only an ordinary level of character development is one in which most citizens have a middling level of wealth and thereby avoid the corrupting effects that are likely when resources are excessive or deficient. That middling kind of constitution, Aristotle thinks, would not be as desirable as a kingship or aristocracy, because the latter are regimes governed by individuals so outstanding that the collective wisdom of the many is no match for theirs. But he is pessimistic about the chances of achieving any of the three correct political systems. For the most part, political leaders must make the best of bad materials. They must learn how to make oligarchies and democracies—the rule of the rich or of the poor—less uniformly oligarchical or democratic. Elites and masses must learn how to work with each other, each party using its mistrust of the other to ensure that the injustices so common in political life do not get out of hand. Evidently, Aristotle is fully aware that politics must usually settle for modest accomplishments, but that does not undermine his conviction that, for most of us, a life devoted to the public good is the best we can achieve.

Brief and accessible accounts of Aristotle's approach to philosophy are presented by J. L. Ackrill, *Aristotle the Philosopher* (New York: Oxford University Press, 1981), Jonathan Lear, *Aristotle: The Desire to Understand* (Cambridge: Cambridge University Press, 1988), and Jonathan Barnes (ed.), *The Cambridge Companion to Aristotle* (Cambridge: Cambridge University Press, 1995). A comprehensive discussion of his epistemology, metaphysics, ethics, and politics can be found in Terence Irwin, *Aristotle's First Principles* (Oxford: Clarendon Press, 1988). Full analyses of nearly all of the topics in the *Nicomachean Ethics* are available in W. F. R. Hardie, *Aristotle's Ethical Theory*, 2d ed. (Oxford: Clarendon Press, 1980), and Sarah Broadie, *Ethics with Aristotle* (New York: Oxford University Press, 1991).

Aristotle's moral psychology is discussed by John M. Cooper in *Reason and Emotion* (Princeton, N.J.: Princeton University Press, 1998), chs. 8–19. The relation between contemplative and practical activity is examined in Richard Kraut, *Aristotle on the Human Good* (Princeton, N.J.: Princeton University Press, 1989), and C. D. C. Reeve, *Practices of Reason* (Oxford: Clarendon Press, 1992). Helpful collections of essays are Amelie Rorty, *Essays on Aristotle's Ethics* (Berkeley: University of California Press, 1980), Nancy Sherman, *Aristotle's Ethics: Critical Essays* (Lanham, Md.: Rowman & Littlefield, 1999), and David Keyt and Fred Miller Jr., *A Companion to Aristotle's Politics* (Oxford: Blackwell, 1991). Wide-ranging studies of Aristotle as a political philosopher are Steven Salkever, *Finding the Mean* (Princeton, N.J.: Princeton University Press, 1990), Bernard Yack, *The Problems of a Political Animal* (Berkeley: University of California Press, 1993), and Fred Miller Jr., *Nature, Justice and Rights in Aristotle's Politics* (Oxford: Clarendon Press, 1995). Aristotle's conception of value is contrasted with that of Plato in Martha C. Nussbaum's *The Fragility of Goodness* (Cambridge: Cambridge University Press, 1986). *The Cambridge History of Greek and Roman Political Thought*, edited by Christopher Rowe and Malcolm Schofield, in association with Simon Harrison and Melissa Lane (Cambridge: Cambridge University Press, 2000), contains five chapters on Aristotle's *Politics*.

Nicomachean Ethics

BOOK I • THE GOOD FOR MAN

Subject of Our Inquiry

All human activities aim at some good: some goods subordinate to others

1. Every art and every inquiry, and similarly every action and pursuit, is thought to aim at some good; and for this reason the good has rightly been declared to be that at which all things aim . . .
2. If, then, there is some end of the things we do, which we desire for its own sake (everything else being desired for the sake of this) . . . clearly this must be the chief good . . .
7. Now such a thing happiness, above all else, is held to be; for this we choose always for itself and never for the sake of something else . . .

Presumably, however, to say that happiness is the chief good seems a platitude, and a clearer account of what is still desired. This might perhaps be given, if we could first ascertain the function of man. For just as for a flute-player, a sculptor, or any artist, and, in general, for all things that have a function or activity, the good and the "well" is thought to reside in the function, so would it seem to be for man, if he has a function. Have the carpenter, then, and the tanner certain functions or activities, and has man none? Is he born without a function? Or as eye, hand, foot, and in general each of the parts evidently has a function, may one lay it down that man similarly has a function apart from all these? What then can this be? Life seems to belong even to plants, but we are seeking what is peculiar to man. Let us exclude, therefore, the life of nutrition and growth. Next there would be a life of perception, but *it* also seems

From Aristotle, *Nicomachean Ethics*, revised edition; edited and translated by David Ross. Copyright © 1998. Reprinted by permission of Oxford University Press.

to be shared even by the horse, the ox, and every animal. There remains then, an active life of the element that has a rational principle. . . . Now if the function of man is an activity of soul which follows or implies a rational principle, and if . . . any action is well performed when it is performed in accordance with the appropriate excellence . . . human good turns out to be activity of soul exhibiting excellence. . . .

But we must add "in a complete life." For one swallow does not make a summer, nor does one day; and so too one day, or a short time, does not make a man blessed and happy. . . .

BOOK II • MORAL VIRTUE

Moral Virtue, How Produced, in What Medium and in What Manner Exhibited

Moral virtue, like the arts, is acquired by repetition of the corresponding acts

1. Virtue, then, being of two kinds, intellectual and moral, intellectual virtue in the main owes both its birth, and its growth to teaching (for which reason it requires experience and time), while moral virtue comes about as a result of habit. . . . From this it is also plain that none of the moral virtues arises in us by nature; for nothing that exists by nature can form a habit contrary to its nature. For instance the stone which by nature moves downwards cannot be habituated to move upwards, not even if one tries to train it by throwing it up ten thousand times; nor can fire be habituated to move downwards, nor can anything else that by nature behaves in one way be trained to behave in another. Neither by nature, then, nor contrary to nature do the virtues arise in us; rather we are adapted by nature to receive them, and are made perfect by habit.

Again, of all the things that come to us by nature we first acquire the potentiality and later exhibit the activity (this is plain in the case of the senses; for it was not by often seeing or often hearing that we got these senses, but on the contrary we had them before we used them, and did not come to have them by using them); but the virtues we get by first exercising them, as also happens in the case of the arts as well. For the things we have to learn before we can do them, we learn by doing them, e.g. men become builders by building and lyre-players by playing the lyre; so too we become just by doing just acts, temperate by doing temperate acts, brave by doing brave acts. . . .

It makes no small difference, then, whether we form habits of one kind or of another from our very youth; it makes a very great difference, or rather *all* the difference.

2. Since, then, the present inquiry does not aim at theoretical knowledge like the others (for we are inquiring not in order to know what virtue is, but in order to become good, since otherwise our inquiry would have been of no use), we must examine the nature of actions, namely how we ought to do them; for these determine also the nature of the states of character that are produced, as we have said. . . .

First, then, let us consider this, that it is the nature of such things to be destroyed by defect and excess, as we see in the case of strength and of health (for to gain light on things imperceptible we must use the evidence of sensible things); exercise either excessive or defective destroys the strength, and similarly drink or food which is above or below a certain amount destroys the health, while that which is proportionate both produces and increases and preserves it. So too is it, then, in the case of temperance and courage and the other virtues. For the man who flies from and fears everything and does not stand his ground against anything becomes a coward, and the man who fears nothing at all but goes to meet every danger becomes rash; and similarly the man who indulges in every pleasure and abstains from none becomes self-indulgent, while the man who shuns every pleasure, as boors do, becomes in a way insensible; temperance and courage, then, are destroyed by excess and defect, and preserved by the mean.

But not only are the sources and causes of their origination and growth the same as those of their destruction, but also the sphere of their actualization will be the same; for this is also true of the things which are more evident to sense, e.g. of strength; it is produced by taking much food and undergoing much exertion, and it is the strong man that will be most able to do these things. So too is it with the virtues; by abstaining from pleasures we become temperate, and it is when we have become so that we are most able to abstain from them; and similarly too in the case of courage; for by being habituated to despise things that are fearful and to stand our ground against them we become brave, and it is when we have become so that we shall be most able to stand our ground against them. . . .

4. The question might be asked, what we mean by saying that we must become just by doing just acts, and temperate by doing temperate acts; for if men do just and temperate acts, they are already just and temperate, exactly as, if they do what is in accordance with the laws of grammar and of music, they are grammarians and musicians.

Or is this not true even of the arts? It is possible to do something that is in accordance with the laws of grammar, either by chance or under the guidance of another. A man will be a grammarian, then, only when he has both said something grammatical and said it grammatically; and this means doing it in accordance with the grammatical knowledge in himself.

Again, the case of the arts and that of the virtues are not similar; for the products of the arts have their goodness in themselves, so that it is enough that they should have a certain character, but if the arts that are in accordance with the virtues have themselves a certain character it does not follow that they are done justly or temperately. The agent also must be in a certain condition when he does them; in the first place he must have knowledge, secondly he must choose the acts, and choose them for their own sakes, and thirdly his action must proceed from a firm and unchangeable character. These are not reckoned in as conditions of the possession of the arts, except the bare knowledge; but as a condition of the possession of the virtues knowledge has little or no weight, while the other conditions count not for a little but for everything, i.e. the very conditions which result from often doing just and temperate acts.

Actions, then, are called just and temperate when they are such as the just or the temperate man would do; but it is not the man who does those that is just and temperate, but the man who also does them as just and temperate men do them. It is well said, then, that it is by doing just acts that the just man is produced, and by doing temperate acts the temperate man; without doing these no one would have even a prospect of becoming good.

But most people do not do these, but take refuge in theory and think they are being philosophers and will become good in this way, behaving somewhat like patients who listen attentively to their doctors, but do none of the things they are ordered to do. As the latter will not be made well in body by such a course of treatment, the former will not be made well in soul by such a course of philosophy. . . .

6. Every virtue or excellence both brings into good condition the thing of which it is the excellence and makes the work of that thing be done well; e.g. the excellence of the eye makes both the eye and its work good; for it is by the excellence of the eye that we see well. Similarly the excellence of the horse makes a horse both good in itself and good at running and at carrying its rider and at awaiting the attack of the enemy. Therefore, if this is true in every case, the virtue of man also will be the state of character which makes a man good and which makes him do his own work well.

How this is to happen we have stated already, but it will be made plain also by the following consideration of the specific nature of virtue. In everything that is continuous and divisible it is possible to take more, less, or an equal amount, and that either in terms of the thing itself or relatively to us; and the equal is an intermediate between excess and defect. By the intermediate in the object I mean that which is equidistant from each of the extremes, which is one and the same for all men; by the intermediate relatively to us that which is neither too much nor too little—and this is not one, nor the same for all. For instance, if ten is many and two is few, six is the intermediate, taken in terms of the object; for it exceeds and is exceeded by an equal amount; this is intermediate according to arithmetical proportion. But the intermediate relatively to us is not to be taken so; if ten pounds are too much for a particular person to eat and two too little, it does not follow that the trainer will order six pounds; for this also is perhaps too much for the person who is to take it, or too little—too little for Milo, too much for the beginner in athletic exercises. The same is true of running and wrestling. Thus a master of any art avoids excess and defect, but seeks the intermediate and chooses this—the intermediate not in the object but relatively to us.

If it is thus, then, that every art does its work well—by looking to the intermediate and judging its works by this standard (so that we often say of good works of art that it is not possible either to take away or to add anything, implying that excess and defect destroy the goodness of works of art, while the mean preserves it; and good artists, as we say, look to this in their work), and if, further, virtue is more exact and better than any art, as nature also is, then virtue must have the quality of aiming at the intermediate. I mean moral virtue; for it is this that is concerned with passions and actions, and in these there is excess, defect, and the intermediate. For instance, both fear and confidence and appetite and anger and pity and in general pleasure and pain may be felt both too much and too little, and in both cases not well; but to feel them at the right times, with reference to the right objects, towards the right people, with the right motive, and in the right way, is what is both intermediate and best, and this is characteristic of virtue. Similarly with regard to actions also there is excess, defect, and the intermediate. Now virtue is concerned with passions and actions, in which excess is a form of failure, and so is defect, while the intermediate is praised and is a form of

success; and being praised and being successful are both characteristics of virtue. Therefore virtue is a kind of mean, since, as we have seen, it aims at what is intermediate. . . .

But not every action nor every passion admits of a mean; for some have names that already imply badness, e.g. spite, shamelessness, envy, and in the case of actions adultery, theft, murder; for all of these and suchlike things imply by their names that they are themselves bad, and not the excesses or deficiencies of them. It is not possible, then, ever to be right with regard to them; one must always be wrong. Nor does goodness or badness with regard to such things depend on committing adultery with the right woman, at the right time, and in the right way, but simply to do any of them is to go wrong. . . .

9. The moral virtue is a mean, then, and in what sense it is so, and that it is a mean between two vices, the one involving excess, the other deficiency, and that it is such because its character is to aim at what is intermediate in passions and in actions, has been sufficiently stated. Hence also it is no easy task to be good. For in everything it is no easy task to find the middle, e.g., to find the middle of a circle is not for everyone but for him who knows; so, too, anyone can get angry—that is easy—or give or spend money; but to do this to the right person, to the right extent, at the right time, with the right motive, and in the right way, *that* is not for everyone, nor is it easy; wherefore goodness is both rare and laudable and noble. . . .

But we must consider the things towards which we ourselves also are easily carried away; for some of us tend to one thing, some to another; and this will be recognizable from the pleasure and the pain we feel. We must drag ourselves away to the contrary extreme; for we shall get into the intermediate state by drawing well away from error. . . .

So much, then, is plain, that the intermediate state is in all things to be praised, but that we must incline sometimes towards the excess, sometimes towards the deficiency; for so shall we most easily hit the mean and what is right.

Politics

BOOK I

The Household and the City

A: The Political Association and Its Relation to Other Associations

CHAPTER 1

1252ª1 Observation shows us, first, that every city [polis] is a species of association, and, secondly, that all associations come into being for the sake of some good—for all men do all their acts with a view to achieving something which is, in their view, a good. It is clear therefore that all associations aim at some good, and that the particular association which is the most sovereign of all, and includes all the rest, will pursue this aim most, and will thus be directed to the most sovereign of all goods. This most sovereign and inclusive association is the city [or polis], as it is called, or the political association.

1252ª7 It is a mistake to believe that the statesman is the same as the monarch of a kingdom, or the manager of a household, or the master of a number of slaves. Those who hold this view consider that each one of these differs from the others not with a difference of kind, but according to the number, large or small, of those with whom he deals. On this view someone who is concerned with few people is a master, someone who is concerned with more is the manager of a household, and someone who is concerned with still more is a statesman, or a monarch. This view abolishes any real difference between a large household and a small city; and it also reduces the difference between the "statesman" and the monarch to the one fact that the latter has an uncontrolled and sole authority, while the former exercises his authority in conformity with the rules imposed by the art of statesmanship and as one who rules and is ruled in turn. But this is a view which cannot be accepted as correct.

1252ª18 Our point will be made clear if we proceed to consider the matter according to our normal method of analysis. Just as, in all other fields, a compound should be analysed until we reach its simple elements (or, in other words, the smallest parts of the whole which it constitutes), so we must also consider analytically the elements of which a city is composed. We shall then gain a better insight into the way in which these differ from one another; and we shall also be in a position to discover whether there is any kind of expertise to be acquired in connection with the matters under discussion.

CHAPTER 2

1252ª24 In this, as in other fields, we shall be able to study our subject best if we begin at the beginning and consider things in the process of their growth. First of all, there must necessarily be a union or pairing of those who cannot exist without one another. Male and female must unite for the reproduction of the species—not from deliberate intention, but from the natural impulse, which exists in animals generally as it also exists in plants, to leave behind them something of the same nature as themselves. Next, there must

From *Politics*, translated by Ernest Barker, revised by R. F. Stalley. Reprinted by permission of Oxford University Press.

necessarily be a union of the naturally ruling element with the element which is naturally ruled, for the preservation of both. The element which is able, by virtue of its intelligence, to exercise forethought, is naturally a ruling and master element; the element which is able, by virtue of its bodily power, to do the physical work, is a ruled element, which is naturally in a state of slavery; and master and slave have accordingly a common interest.

1252ᵇ2 The female and the slave are naturally distinguished from one another. Nature makes nothing in a miserly spirit, as smiths do when they make the Delphic knife to serve a number of purposes: she makes each separate thing for a separate end; and she does so because the instrument is most perfectly made when it serves a single purpose and not a variety of purposes. Among barbarians, however, the female and the slave occupy the same position—the reason being that no naturally ruling element exists among them, and conjugal union thus comes to be a union of a female who is a slave with a male who is also a slave. . . . The first form of association naturally instituted for the satisfaction of daily recurrent needs is thus the family. . . .

1252ᵇ17 The next form of association—which is also the first to be formed from more households than one, and for the satisfaction of something more than daily recurrent needs—is the village. The most natural form of the village appears to be that of a colony [or offshoot] from a family; and some have thus called the members of the village by the name of "sucklings of the same milk," or, again, of "sons and the sons of sons." This, it may be noted, is the reason why cities were originally ruled, as the peoples of the barbarian world still are, by kings. They were formed of people who were already monarchically governed, for every household is monarchically governed by the eldest of the kin, just as villages, when they are offshoots from the household, are similarly governed in virtue of the kinship between their members. This is what Homer describes:

Each of them ruleth
Over his children and wives,

a passage which shows that they lived in scattered groups, as indeed men generally did in ancient times. The fact that men generally were governed by kings in ancient times, and that some still continue to be governed in that way, is the reason that leads everyone to say that the gods are also governed by a king. People make the lives of the gods in the likeness of their own—as they also make their shapes.

1252ᵇ27 When we come to the final and perfect association, formed from a number of villages, we have already reached the city [or *polis*]. This may be said to have reached the height of full self-sufficiency; or rather we may say that while it comes into existence for the sake of mere life, it exists for the sake of a good life. For this reason every city exists by nature, just as did the earlier associations [from which it grew]. It is the end or consummation to which those associations move, and the "nature" of things consists in their end or consummation; for what each thing is when its growth is completed we call the nature of that thing, whether it be a man or a horse or a family. Again the end, or final cause, is the best and self-sufficiency is both the end, and the best.

1253ᵃ2 From these considerations it is evident that the city belongs to the class of things that exist by nature, and that man is by nature a political animal. He who is without a city, by reason of his own nature and not of some accident, is either a poor sort of being, or a being higher than man: he is like the man of whom Homer wrote in denunciation:

Clanless and lawless and hearthless is he.

The man who is such by nature at once plunges into a passion of war; he is in the position of a solitary advanced piece in a game of draughts.

1253ᵃ7 It is thus clear that man is a political animal, in a higher degree than bees or other gregarious animals. Nature, according to our theory, makes nothing in vain; and man alone of the animals is furnished with the faculty of language. The mere making of sounds serves to indicate pleasure and pain, and is thus a faculty that belongs to animals in general: their nature enables them to attain the point at which they have perceptions of pleasure and pain, and can signify those perceptions to one another. But language serves to declare what is advantageous and what is the reverse, and it is the peculiarity of man, in comparison with other animals, that he alone possesses a perception of good and evil, of the just and the unjust, and other similar qualities; and it is association in these things which makes a family and a city.

1253ª18 We may now proceed to add that the city is prior in the order of nature to the family and the individual. The reason for this is that the whole is necessarily prior to the part. If the whole body is destroyed, there will not be a foot or a hand, except in that ambiguous sense in which one uses the same word to indicate a different thing, as when one speaks of a "hand" made of stone; for a hand, when destroyed [by the destruction of the whole body], will be no better than a stone "hand." All things derive their essential character from their function and their capacity; and it follows that if they are no longer fit to discharge their function, we ought not to say that they are still the same things, but only that, by an ambiguity, they still have the same names.

1253ª25 We thus see that the city exists by nature and that it is prior to the individual. For if the individual is not self-sufficient when he is isolated he will stand in the same relation to the whole as other parts do to their wholes. The man who is isolated, who is unable to share in the benefits of political association, or has no need to share because he is already self-sufficient, is no part of the city, and must therefore be either a beast or a god. There is therefore a natural impulse in all men towards an association of this sort. But the man who first constructed such an association was none the less the greatest of benefactors. Man, when perfected, is the best of animals; but if he be isolated from law and justice he is the worst of all. Injustice is all the graver when it is armed injustice; and man is furnished from birth with weapons which are intended to serve the purposes of wisdom and goodness, but which may be used in preference for opposite ends. That is why, if he be without goodness [of mind and character], he is a most unholy and savage being, and worse than all others in the indulgence of lust and gluttony. The virtue of justice belongs to the city; for justice is an ordering of the political association, and the virtue of justice consists in the determination of what is just.

B: The Association of the Household and Its Different Factors

CHAPTER 4

1253ᵇ23 Property is part of the household and the art of acquiring property is part of household management, for it is impossible to live well, or indeed at all, unless the necessary conditions are present. Thus the same holds true in the sphere of household management as in the specialized arts: each must be furnished with its appropriate instruments if its function is to be fulfilled. Instruments are partly inanimate and partly animate: the steersman of a ship, for instance, has an inanimate instrument in the rudder, and an animate instrument in the look-out man (for in the arts a subordinate is of the nature of an instrument). Each article of property is thus an instrument for the purpose of life, property in general is a quantity of such instruments, the slave is an animate article of property, and subordinates, or servants, in general may be described as instruments which are prior to other instruments. We can imagine a situation in which each instrument could do its own work, at the word of command or by intelligent anticipation, like the statues of Daedalus or the tripods made by Hephaestus, of which the poet relates that

Of their own motion they entered the conclave of Gods on Olympus.

A shuttle would then weave of itself, and a plectrum would do its own harp-playing. In this situation managers would not need subordinates and masters would not need slaves.

1254ᵃ1 The instruments of which we have just been speaking are instruments of production; but property is an instrument of action. From the shuttle there issues something which is different, and exists apart, from the immediate act of its use; but from garments or beds there comes only the one fact of their use. We may add that, since production and action are different in kind, and both of them need instruments, those instruments must also show a corresponding difference. Life is action and not production; and therefore the slave is a servant in the sphere of action.

1254ᵃ8 The term "article of property" is used in the same way in which the term "part" is also used. A part is not only a part of something other than itself: it also belongs entirely to that other thing. It is the same with an article of property. Accordingly, while the master is merely the master of the slave, and does not belong to him, the slave is not only the slave of his master; he also belongs entirely to him.

1254ᵃ13 From these considerations we can see clearly what is the nature of the slave and what is his capacity: anybody who by his nature is not his own man, but another's, is by his nature a slave; anybody who, being a man, is an article of property is another's man; an article of property is an instrument intended for the purpose of action and separable from its possessor.

CHAPTER 5

1254ᵃ17 . . . In all cases where there is a compound, constituted of more than one part but forming one common entity, whether the parts be continuous or discrete, a ruling element and a ruled can always be traced. This characteristic is present in animate beings by virtue of the whole constitution of nature; for even in things which are inanimate there is a sort of ruling principle, such as is to be found, for example, in a musical harmony. But such considerations perhaps belong to a more popular method of inquiry; and we may

content ourselves here with saying that animate beings are composed, in the first place, of soul and body, with the former naturally ruling and the latter naturally ruled. When investigating the natural state of things, we must fix our attention, not on those which are in a corrupt, but on those which are in a natural condition. It follows that we must consider the man who is in the best state both of body and soul, and in whom the rule of soul over body is accordingly evident; for with vicious people or those in a vicious condition, the reverse would often appear to be true—the body ruling the soul as the result of their evil and unnatural condition.

1254ᵇ2 It is possible, as we have said, to observe first in animate beings the presence of a ruling authority, both of the sort exercised by a master over slaves and of the sort exercised by a statesman over fellow citizens. The soul rules the body with the authority of a master: reason rules the appetite with the authority of a statesman or a monarch. In this sphere it is clearly natural and beneficial to the body that it should be ruled by the soul, and again it is natural and beneficial to the affective part of the soul that it should be ruled by the reason and the rational part; whereas the equality of the two elements, or their reverse relation, is always detrimental. The same principle is true of the relation of man to other animals. Tame animals have a better nature than wild, and it is better for all such animals that they should be ruled by man because they then get the benefit of preservation. Again, the relation of male to female is naturally that of the superior to the inferior, of the ruling to the ruled. This general principle must similarly hold good of all human beings generally.

1254ᵇ16 We may thus conclude that all men who differ from others as much as the body differs from the soul, or an animal from a man (and this is the case with all whose function is bodily service, and who produce their best when they supply such service)—all such are by nature slaves. In their case, as in the other cases just mentioned, it is better to be ruled by a master. Someone is thus a slave by nature if he is capable of becoming the property of another (and for this reason does actually become another's property) and if he participates in reason to the extent of apprehending it in another, though destitute of it himself. Other animals do not apprehend reason but obey their instincts. Even so there is little divergence in the way they are used; both of them (slaves and tame animals) provide bodily assistance in satisfying essential needs.

1254ᵇ27 It is nature's intention also to erect a physical difference between the bodies of freemen and those of the slaves, giving the latter strength for the menial duties of life, but making the former upright in carriage and (though useless for physical labour) useful for the various purposes of civic life—a life which tends, as it develops, to be divided into military service and the occupations of peace. The contrary of nature's intention, however, often happens: there are some slaves who have the bodies of freemen, as there are others who have a freeman's soul. But, if there were men who were as distinguished in their bodies alone as are the statues of the gods, all would agree that the others should be their slaves. And if this is true when the difference is one of the body, it may be affirmed with still greater justice when the difference is one of the soul; though it is not as easy to see the beauty of the soul as it is to see that of the body.

1254ᵇ39 It is thus clear that, just as some are by nature free, so others are by nature slaves, and for these latter the condition of slavery is both beneficial and just.

BOOK II

Review of Constitutions

A: Constitutions in Theory

CHAPTER 1

1260ᵇ36 Our starting-point must be the one that is natural for such a discussion. It is necessary either that the citizens have all things in common, or that they have nothing in common, or that they have some things in common, and others not. It is clearly impossible that they should have nothing in common: the constitution of a city involves in itself some sort of association, and its members must in the first place share a common locality. Just as a single city [*polis*] must have a single locality, so citizens are those who share in a single city. But is it better that a city which is to be well conducted should share in all the things in which it is possible for it to share, or that it should share in some things and not in others? It is certainly possible that the citizens should share children and women and property with one another. This is the plan proposed in the *Republic* of Plato, where "Socrates" argues that children and women and property should be held in common. We are thus faced by the question whether it is better to remain in our present condition or to follow the rule of life laid down in the *Republic*.

CHAPTER 2

1261ᵃ10 A system in which women are common to all involves, among many others, the following difficulties. The object for which Socrates states that it ought to be instituted is evidently not established by the arguments which he uses. Moreover, the end which he states as necessary for the city [*polis*] is impracticable; and yet he gives no account of the lines on which it ought to be interpreted. I have in mind here the idea, which Socrates takes as his premiss, that the greatest possible unity of the whole city is the supreme good. Yet it is obvious that a city which goes on becoming more and more of a unit, will eventually cease to be a city at all. A city, by its nature, is some sort of plurality. If it becomes more of a unit, it will first become a household instead of a city, and then an individual instead of a household; for we should all call the household more of a unit than the city, and the individual more of a unit than the household. It follows that, even if we could, we ought not to achieve this object: it would be the destruction of the city.

1261ᵃ22 Not only is the city composed of a *number* of people: it is also composed of different *kinds* of people, for a city cannot be composed of those who are like one another. There is a difference between a city and a military alliance. An alliance, formed by its very nature for the sake of the mutual help which its members can render to one another, possesses utility purely in virtue of its quantity, even if there is no difference of kind among its members. It is like a weight which depresses the scales more heavily in the balance. In this respect a *city* will also differ from a tribe, assuming that the members of the tribe are not scattered in separate villages, but [are united in a confederacy] like the Arcadians. A real unity must be made up of elements which differ in kind. It follows that the stability of every city depends on each of its elements rendering to the others an amount equivalent to what it receives from them—a principle already laid down in the *Ethics*. This has to be the case even among free and equal citizens. They cannot all rule simultaneously; they must therefore each hold office for a year, unless they adopt some other arrangement or some other period of time. In this way it comes about that all are rulers, just as it would if shoemakers and carpenters changed their occupations so that the same people were not always following these professions. Since the arrangement [followed in the arts and crafts] is also better when applied to the affairs of the political association, it would clearly be better for the same people always to be rulers wherever possible. But where this is impossible, through the natural equality of all the citizens—and also because justice requires the participation of all in office (whether office be a good thing or a bad)—there is an imitation of it, if equals retire from office in turn and are all, apart from their period of office, in the same position. This means that some rule, and others are ruled, in turn, as if they had become, for the time being, different people. We may add that even those who are rulers differ from one another, some holding one kind of office and some another.

1261ᵇ6 These considerations are sufficient to show, first, that it is not the nature of the city to be a unit in the sense in which some thinkers say that it is, and secondly, that what is said to be the supreme good of a city is really its ruin. But surely the "good" of each thing is what preserves it in being.

1261ᵇ10 There is still another consideration which may be used to prove that the policy of attempting an extreme unification of the city is not a good policy. A household is something which attains a greater degree of self-sufficiency than an individual; and a city, in turn, is something which attains self-sufficiency to a greater degree than a household. But it becomes fully a city, only when the association which forms it is large enough to be self-sufficing. On the assumption, therefore, that the higher degree of self-sufficiency is the more desirable thing, the lesser degree of unity is more desirable than the greater.

CHAPTER 3

1261ᵇ16 Even if it were the supreme good of a political association that it should have the greatest possible unity, this unity does not appear to follow from the formula of "All men saying 'Mine' and 'Not mine' at the same time," which, in the view of "Socrates," is the index of the perfect unity of a city. The word "all" has a double sense: if it means "each separately," the object which "Socrates" desires to realize may perhaps be realized in a greater degree: each and all separately will then say "My wife" (or "My son") of one and the same person; and each and all separately will speak in the same way of property, and of every other concern. But it is not in the sense of "each separately" that all who have children and women in common will actually speak of them. They will all call them "Mine"; but they will do so collectively, and not individually. The same is true of property also; [all will call it "Mine"] but they will do so in the sense of "all collectively," and not in the sense of "each separately." It is therefore clear that there is a certain fallacy in the use of the term "all." "All" and "both" and "odd" and "even" are liable by their ambiguity to produce captious arguments even in reasoned discussions. We may therefore conclude that the formula of "all men saying 'Mine' of the same object" is in one sense something fine but impracticable, and in another sense does nothing to promote harmony.

1261ᵇ32 In addition to these problems the formula also involves another disadvantage. What is common to the greatest number gets the least amount of care. People pay most attention to what is their own: they care less for what is common; or, at any rate, they care for it only to the extent to which each is individually concerned. Even where there is no other cause for inattention, people are more prone to neglect their duty when they think that another is attending to it: this is what happens in domestic service, where many attendants are sometimes of less assistance than a few. [The scheme proposed in the *Republic* means that] each citizen will have a thousand sons: they will not be the sons of each citizen individually: any son whatever will be equally the son of any father whatever. The result will be that all will equally neglect them.

1262ᵃ1 Furthermore each person, when he says "Mine" of any citizen who is prosperous or the reverse, is speaking fractionally. He means only that he is "Mine" to the extent of a fraction determined by the total number of citizens. When he says "He is mine" or "He is so-and-so's," the term "Mine" or "So-and-so's" is used with reference to the whole body concerned—the whole thousand, or whatever may be the total number of citizens. Even so he cannot be sure; for there is no evidence who had a child born to him, or whether, if one was born, it managed to survive. Which is the better system—that each of two thousand, or ten thousand, people should say "Mine" of a child in this fractional sense, or that each should say "Mine" in the sense in which the word is now used in ordinary cities? As things are, one man calls by the name of "*My* son" the same person whom a second man calls by the name of "*My* brother": a third calls him "*My* cousin" or

"*My* relative," because he is somehow related to him, either by blood or by connection through marriage; while besides these different modes of address someone else may use still another, and call him "*My* clansman" or "*My* tribesman." It is better to be someone's own cousin than to be his son after this fashion. Even on Plato's system it is impossible to avoid the chance that some of the citizens might guess who are their brothers, or children, or fathers, or mothers. The resemblances between children and parents must inevitably lead to their drawing conclusions about one another. That this actually happens in real life is stated as fact by some of the writers on descriptive geography. They tell us that some of the inhabitants of upper Libya have their women in common; but the children born of such unions can still be distinguished by their resemblance to their fathers. Indeed there are some women, and some females in the animal world (mares, for instance, and cows), that show a strong natural tendency to produce offspring resembling the male parent: the Pharsalian mare which was called the "Just Return" is a good example.

CHAPTER 4

1262ᵃ25 There are also other difficulties which those who construct such a community will not find it easy to avoid. We may take as examples cases of assault, homicide, whether unintentional or intentional, fighting, and slander. All these offences, when they are committed against father or mother or a near relative, differ from offences against people who are not so related, in being breaches of natural piety. Such offences must happen more frequently when men are ignorant of their relatives than when they know who they are; and when they do happen, the customary penance can be made if people know their relatives, but none can be made if they are ignorant of them. It is also surprising that, after having made sons common to all, he should simply forbid lovers from engaging in carnal intercourse. Nor does he forbid other familiarities which, if practised between son and father, or brother and brother, are the very height of indecency, all the more as this form of love [even if it is not expressed] is in itself indecent. It is surprising, too, that he should debar male lovers from carnal intercourse on the one ground of the excessive violence of the pleasure, and that he should think it a matter of indifference that the lovers may be father and son, or again that they may be brothers.

1262ª40 Community of women and children would seem to be more useful if it were practised among the farmers rather than among the guardians. The spirit of friendship is likely to exist to a lesser degree where women and children are common; and the governed class ought to have little of that spirit if it is to obey and not to attempt revolution. Generally, such a system must produce results directly opposed to those which a system of properly constituted laws should produce, and equally opposed to the very object for which, in the view of "Socrates," this community of women and children ought to be instituted. Friendship, we believe, is the chief good of cities, because it is the best safeguard against the danger of factional disputes. "Socrates" himself particularly commends the ideal of the unity of the city; and that unity is commonly held, and expressly stated by him, to be the result of friendship. We may cite the argument of the discourses on love, where "Aristophanes," as we know, speaks of lovers desiring out of friendship to grow together into a unity, and to be one instead of two. Now in that case it would be inevitable that both or at least one of them should cease to exist. But in the case of the political association there would be merely a watery sort of friendship: a father would be very little disposed to say "Mine" of a son, and a son would be as little disposed to say "Mine" of a father. Just as a little sweet wine, mixed with a great deal of water, produces a tasteless mixture, so family feeling is diluted and tasteless when family names have as little meaning as they have in a constitution of this sort, and when there is so little reason for a father treating his sons as sons, or a son treating his father as a father, or brothers one another as brothers. There are two

things which particularly move people to care for and love an object. One of these is that the object should belong to yourself: the other is that you should like it. Neither of these motives can exist among those who live under a constitution such as this.

1262ᵇ24 There is still a further difficulty. It concerns the way in which children born among the farmers and craftsmen are to be transferred to the guardian class, and vice versa. How such transposition is actually to be effected is a matter of great perplexity; and in any case those who transfer such children, and assign them their new place, will be bound to know who are the children so placed and with whom they are being placed. In addition, those problems of assault, unnatural affection, and homicide, which have already been mentioned, will occur even more in the case of these people. Those transferred from the guardian class to that of the other citizens will cease for the future to address the guardians as brothers, or children, or fathers, or mothers, as the case may be; and it will have the same effect for those who have been transferred from among the other citizens to the guardians. Such people will no longer avoid committing these offences on account of their kinship.

1262ᵇ35 This may serve as a determination of the issues raised by the idea of community of women and children.

CHAPTER 5

1262ᵇ39 The next subject for consideration is property. What is the proper system of property for citizens who are to live under the best form of constitution? Should property be held in common or not? This is an issue which may be considered in itself, and apart from any proposals for community of women and children. Even if women and children are held separately, as is now universally the case, questions relating to property still remain for discussion. Should use and ownership both be common? For example, there may be a system under which plots of land are owned separately, but the crops (as actually happens among some tribal peoples) are brought into a common stock for the purpose of consumption. Secondly, and conversely, the land may be held in common ownership, and may also be cultivated in common, but the crops may be divided among individuals for their private use: some of the barbarian peoples are also said to practise this second method of sharing. Thirdly, the plots and the crops may both be common.

1263ª8 When the cultivators of the soil are a different body from the citizens who own it, the position will be different and easier to handle; but when the citizens who own the soil do the work themselves, the problems of property will cause a good deal of trouble. If they do not share equally in the work and in the enjoyment of the produce, those who do more work and get less of the produce will be bound to raise complaints against those who get a large reward and do little work. In general it is a difficult business to live together and to share in any form of human activity, but it is specially difficult in such matters. Fellow-travellers who merely share in a journey furnish an illustration: they generally quarrel about ordinary matters and take offence on petty occasions. So, again, the servants with whom we are most prone to take offence are those who are particularly employed in ordinary everyday services.

1263ª21 Difficulties such as these, and many others, are involved in a system of community of property. The present system would be far preferable, if it were embellished with social customs and the enactment of proper laws. It would possess the advantages of both systems, and would combine the merits of a system of community of property with those of the system of private property. For, although there is a sense in which property *ought* to be common, it should in general be private. When everyone has his own separate sphere of interest, there will not be the same ground for quarrels; and they will make more effort, because each man will feel that he is applying himself to what is his own.

1263ª30 On such a scheme, too, moral goodness will ensure that the property of each is made to serve the use of all, in the spirit of the proverb which says "Friends' goods are goods in common." Even now there are some cities in which the outlines of such a scheme are so far apparent, as to suggest that it is not impossible; in well-ordered cities, more particularly, there are some elements of it already existing, and others which might be added. [In these cities] each citizen has his own property; part of which he makes available to his friends, and part of which he uses as though it was common property. In Sparta, for example, men use one another's slaves, and one another's horses and dogs, as if they were their own; and they take provisions on a journey, if they happen to be in need, from the farms in the countryside. It is clear from what has been said that the better system is that under which property is privately owned but is put to common use; and the function proper to the legislator is to make men so disposed that they will treat property in this way.

1263ª40 In addition, to think of a thing as your own makes an inexpressible difference, so far as pleasure is concerned. It may well be that regard for oneself is a feeling implanted by nature, and not a mere random impulse. Self-love is rightly censured, but that is not so much loving oneself as loving one-self in excess. It is the same with one who loves money; after all, virtually everyone loves things of this kind. We may add that a very great pleasure is to be found in doing a kindness and giving some help to friends, or guests, or comrades; and such kindness and help become possible only when property is privately owned. But not only are these pleasures impossible under a system in which the city is excessively unified; the activities of two forms of goodness are also obviously destroyed. The first of these is temperance in the matter of sexual relations (it is an act of moral value to keep away from the wife of another through temperance): the second is generosity in the use of property. In a city which is excessively unified no man can show himself generous, or indeed do a generous act; for the function of generosity consists in the proper use which is made of property.

1263ᵇ15 This kind of legislation may appear to wear an attractive face and to demonstrate benevolence. The hearer receives it gladly, thinking that everybody will feel towards everybody else some marvellous sense of friendship—all the more as the evils now existing under ordinary forms of government (lawsuits about contracts, convictions for perjury, and obsequious flatteries of the rich) are denounced as due to the absence of a system of common property. None of these, however, is due to property not being held in common. They all arise from wickedness. Indeed it is a fact of observation that those who own common property, and share in its management, are far more often at variance with one another than those who have property separately—though those who are at variance in consequence of sharing in property look to us few in number when we compare them with the mass of those who own their property privately.

1263ᵇ27 What is more, justice demands that we should take into account not only the evils which people will be spared when they have begun to hold their property in common, but also the benefits of which they will be deprived. Their life can be seen to be utterly impossible.

1263ᵇ29 The cause of the fallacy into which "Socrates" falls must be held to be his incorrect premiss. It is true that unity in some respects is necessary both for the household and for the city, but unity in all respects is not. There is a point at which a city, by advancing in unity, will cease to be a city: there is another point at which it will still be a city, but a worse one because it has come close to ceasing altogether to be a city. It is as if you were to turn harmony into mere unison, or to reduce a theme to a single beat. The truth is that the city, as has already been said, is a plurality; and education is therefore *the* means of making it a community and giving it unity. It is therefore surprising that one who intends to introduce a system of education, and who believes that the city can achieve goodness by means of this system, should none the less think that he is setting it on the right track by such methods as he actually proposes, rather than by the method of social customs, of mental culture, and of legislation. An example of such legislation may be found in Sparta and Crete, where the legislator has made the institution of property serve a common use by the system of common meals.

1264ᵃ1 There is another matter which must not be ignored: we are bound to pay some regard to the long past and the passage of the years, in which these things would not have gone unnoticed if they had been really good. Almost, everything has been discovered already; though some things have not been combined with one another, and others are not put into practice. It would shed a great deal of light on these matters, if we could watch the actual construction of such a constitution. The foundation of any city will always involve the division and distribution of its members into classes, partly in the form of associations for common meals, and partly in that of clans and tribes. It follows that the only peculiar feature of the legislation is the rule that the guardians are not to farm the land; and even that is a rule which the Spartans are already attempting to follow.

1264ᵃ11 "Socrates" does not explain the character of the whole constitution so far as concerns those who share in it, nor indeed is it easy to explain. The mass of the citizens who are not guardians will be, in effect, nearly the whole of the citizen body. But their position is left undefined. We are not told whether the fanners are also to have property in common, or to own it individually; nor do we learn whether their women and children are to be common to them all, or to belong to each separately.

1264ᵃ17 The first alternative is that all things should belong to them all in common. In that case, what will be the difference between them and the guardians? What advantage will they gain by accepting the government of the guardians? What convinces them actually to accept it?—unless it be some device such as is used in Crete, where the serfs are allowed to enjoy the same general privileges as their masters, and are excluded only from athletic exercises and the possession of arms.

1264ª22 The second alternative is that these institutions should be the same for the farmers as they are in most cities today. In that case, we may inquire, what the character of their association will be? There will inevitably be two cities in one, and those cities will be opposed to one another—the guardians being made into something of the nature of an army of occupation, and the farmers, artisans, and others being given the position of ordinary civilians. Again, legal complaints, and actions at law, and all the other evils which he describes as existing in cities as they are, will equally exist among them. Certainly "Socrates" says that, in virtue of their education, they will not need a number of regulations (such as city ordinances, market by-laws, and the like); but it is also true that he provides education only for the guardians. A further difficulty is that he has the farmers control their holdings on condition that they pay a quota of their produce to the guardians. This is likely to make them far more difficult to handle, and much more filled with high ideas of their own importance, than other people's helots, penestae, or serfs.

1264ª36 In any case there is no indication whether it is necessary for these arrangements to be the same [for the farmers as for the guardians] or not, nor are other matters connected with this made clear—matters such as the position of the farmers in the political system, the nature of their education, and the character of the law they are to observe. We thus find it difficult to discover what the farming class will be like, and yet this is a matter of the highest importance if the common life of the guardians is to be preserved. The third and last alternative is that the farmers should have a system of community of women, combined with a system of private property. In that case, who will see to the house while the men are seeing to the business of the fields? And, for that matter, who will see to the house, when the farmers have property as well as women in common? It is strange, too, that Plato should draw an analogy from the animal world in order to prove that women should follow the same pursuits as men. Animals do not have households to manage.

1264ᵇ6 There is also an element of danger in the method of government which "Socrates" proposes to institute. He makes the same people be rulers all the time. This is a system which must cause factional conflict even among the elements which have no particular standing, and all the more, therefore, among the high-spirited and martial elements. It is obviously necessary for him to make the same people rulers all the time. The "divine gold" cannot be sometimes mixed in the souls of one group and sometimes in those of another, but must always be in the same people. This is why he says that when they were first created "the god mixed gold in the composition" of some, silver in that of others, and brass and iron in that of the rest, who were to be craftsmen and farmers. It is a further objection that he deprives his guardians even of happiness, maintaining that the object of the legislator should be for the whole city to be happy. It is impossible for the whole city to be happy unless all, or most, or at least some of its parts are happy. The quality of being happy is not of the same order as the quality of being even. That may exist in a whole without existing in either of its parts: the quality of being happy cannot. Furthermore, if the guardians are not happy, who else is? Certainly not the craftsmen, or the mass of the common people.

1264ᵇ24 We may thus conclude that the constitution which "Socrates" describes raises all the difficulties we have mentioned, and others which are no less serious.

BOOK III

The Theory of Citizenship and Constitutions

A: Citizenship

CHAPTER 1

1274ᵇ32 When we are dealing with constitutions, and seeking to discover the essence and the attributes of each form, our first investigation may well be directed to the city [the *polis*] itself; and we may begin by asking, "What is the city?" This is at present a disputed question—while some say, "It was the city that did such and such an act," others say, "It was not the city, but the oligarchy or the tyrant." All the activity of the statesman and the lawgiver is obviously concerned with the city, and a constitution is a way of organizing the inhabitants of a city.

1274ᵇ38 A city belongs to the order of "compounds," just like any other thing which forms a single "whole," while being composed, none the less, of a number of different parts. This being the case, it clearly follows that we must inquire first about the citizen. In other words, a city is a certain number of citizens; and so we must consider who should properly be called a citizen and what a citizen really is. The definition of a citizen is a question which is often disputed: there is no general agreement on who is a citizen. It may be that someone who is a citizen in a democracy is not one in an oligarchy. We may leave out of consideration those who enjoy the title of "citizen" in some special sense, for example, naturalized citizens. A citizen proper is not one by virtue of residence in a given place: for even aliens and slaves may share the common place of residence. Nor [can the title of "citizen" be given to] those who share in legal processes only to the extent of being entitled to sue and be sued in the courts. This is something which belongs also to aliens who share it by virtue of a treaty; though it is to be noted that there are many places where resident aliens are obliged to choose a legal protector, so that they only share to a limited extent in this form of association. They are like children who are still too young to be entered on the roll of citizens, or men who are old enough to have been excused from civic duties. There is a sense in which these may be called citizens, but it is not altogether an unqualified sense: we must add the reservation that the young are undeveloped, and the old superannuated citizens, or we must use some other qualification; the exact term we apply does not matter, for the meaning is clear.

1275ᵃ19 We are seeking to discover the citizen in the strict sense, who has no such defect to be

made good. Similar questions may also be raised and answered about those who are exiled or disenfranchised. The citizen in this strict sense is best defined by the one criterion that he shares in the administration of justice and in the holding of office. . . .

1275ᵇ13 . . . We say that one who is entitled to share in deliberative or judicial office is thereby a citizen of that city, and a city, in its simplest terms, is a body of such people adequate in number for achieving a self-sufficient existence.

CHAPTER 3

1276ᵃ34 Assuming a single population inhabiting a single territory, shall we say that the city retains its identity as long as the stock of its inhabitants continues to be the same (although the old members are always dying and new members are always being born), and shall we thus apply to the city the analogy of rivers and fountains, to which we ascribe a constant identity in spite of the fact that part of their water is always flowing in and part always flowing out? Or must we take a different view, and say that even though the population remains the same, the city, for the reason already mentioned, may none the less change?

1276ᵇ1 If a city is a form of association, and if this form of association is an association of citizens in a constitution, it would seem to follow inevitably that when the constitution undergoes a change in form, and becomes a different constitution, the city will likewise cease to be the same city. We say that a chorus which appears at one time as a comic and at another as a tragic chorus is not the same—and this in spite of the fact that the members often remain the same. What is true of the chorus is also true of every other kind of association, and of all other compounds generally. If the form of its composition is different, the compound becomes a different compound. A scale composed of the same notes will be a different scale depending on whether it is in the Dorian or the Phrygian mode. If this is the case, it is obvious that in determining the identity of the city we must look to the constitution. Whether the same group of people inhabits a city, or a totally different group, we are free to call it the same city, or a different city. It is a different question whether it is right to pay debts or to repudiate them when a city changes its constitution into another form.

CHAPTER 4

1276ᵇ16 A question connected with those which have just been discussed is the question whether the excellence of a good man and that of a good citizen are identical or different. If this question is to be investigated, we must first describe the excellence of the citizen in some sort of outline. Just as a sailor is a member of an association, so too is a citizen. Sailors differ from one another in virtue of the different capacities in which they act: one is a rower, another a steersman, another a look-out man; and others will have still other such titles. It is, nevertheless, clear that, while the most accurate definition of the excellence of each sailor will be special to the man concerned, a common definition of excellence will apply to all, inasmuch as safety in navigation is the common task of all and the object at which each of the sailors aims. The same is also true of citizens. Though they differ, the end which they all serve is the safety of their association; and this association consists in the constitution. The conclusion to which we are thus led is that the excellence of the citizen must be an excellence relative to the constitution. It follows that if there are several different kinds of constitution there cannot be a single absolute excellence of the good citizen. But the good man is a man so called in virtue of a single absolute excellence.

1276ᵇ34 It is thus clear that it is possible to be a good citizen without possessing the excellence by which one is a good man. But we may reach the same conclusion in another way, by discussing the question with particular reference to the best constitution. Although it is impossible for a city to be composed entirely of good men, each citizen must, none the less, perform well his particular function and this requires [the appropriate

kind of] excellence. But, since it is impossible for all the citizens to be alike, the excellence of a citizen cannot be identical with that of a good man. The excellence of a good citizen must belong to all citizens, because that is the condition necessary for the city being the best city; but the excellence of a good man cannot possibly belong to all—unless, indeed, we hold that every citizen of a good city must also be a good man. Furthermore, the city is composed of unlike elements. Just as a living being is composed of soul and body, or the soul of the different elements of reason and appetite, or the household of man and wife, or property of master and slave, so the city too is composed of different and unlike elements, among them not only the various elements already mentioned, but also others in addition. It follows that there cannot be a single excellence common to all the citizens, any more than there can be a single excellence common to the leader of a dramatic chorus and his assistants.

1277ᵃ12 Although it is clear from these considerations why they are not in all cases identical, the question may still be raised whether there are not some cases in which the excellence of the good man and that of the good citizen are the same. We say that a good ruler is a good man and possesses practical wisdom, while the citizen does not need to have practical wisdom. Indeed there are some who hold that the very training of the ruler should be, from the first, of a different kind; and it is a matter of observation that the sons of kings are specially trained in riding and the art of war. Thus Euripides says

> *No subtleties for me,*
> *But what the city most needs,*

which implies a special training for the ruler. We may thus assume that the excellence of the good ruler is identical with that of the good man. But subjects too are citizens. It follows that the excellence of the good citizen cannot be identical with that of the good man in all cases, though it may be so in a particular case. The excellence of the ordinary citizen is different from that of the ruler;

and this may well be the reason why Jason [the tyrant of Pherae] said that he was "a hungry man except when he was tyrant," meaning that he did not know how to live as an ordinary person.

1277ᵃ25 On the other hand, people hold in esteem the capacity both to rule and to obey, and they regard the excellence of a good citizen as being a matter of ruling and obeying well. Now if the excellence of the good man is in ruling, while that of the good citizen is in both ruling and obeying, these two excellences cannot be held in the same esteem.

1277ᵃ29 Since it thus seems that ruler and ruled should acquire different kinds of knowledge, rather than the same kind, while the citizen should have both sorts of knowledge, and share in both, we can now see the next step which our argument has to take. There is rule of the sort which is exercised by a master; and by this we mean the sort of rule connected with the necessary functions of life. Here it is not necessary for the ruler to know how to do the task himself, but only to know how to use those who do: indeed the former kind of knowledge (by which we mean an ability to do menial services personally) has a servile character. There are a number of kinds of servant, because there are a number of kinds of menial service which have to be rendered. One of these forms of service is that which is rendered by manual labourers. These, as their very name signifies, are those who live by the work of their hands; and the menial craftsman [or mechanic] belongs to this class. This is the reason why in some cities the manual workers were once upon a time excluded from office, in the days before the institution of the extreme form of democracy. The occupations pursued by those who are subject to rule of the sort just mentioned need never be studied by the good man, or by the statesman, or by the good citizen—except occasionally and in order to satisfy some personal need, in which case there ceases to be any question of the relation of master and slave.

1277ᵇ7 But there is also rule of the sort which is exercised over those who are similar in birth to the ruler, and are similarly free. Rule of this sort is

what we call political rule; and this is the sort of rule which the ruler must begin to learn by being ruled—just as one learns to be a commander of cavalry by serving under another commander, or to be a general of infantry by serving under another general and by acting first as colonel and, even before that, as captain. This is why it is a good saying that "you cannot be ruler unless you have first been ruled." Ruler and ruled have indeed different excellences; but the fact remains that the good citizen must possess the knowledge and the capacity requisite for ruling as well as for being ruled, and the excellence of a citizen may be defined as consisting in "a knowledge of rule over free men from both points of view."

1277ᵇ16 A good man, also, will need both, even though the temperance and justice required for ruling have a different character. Equally, the excellence (justice, for example) of a good man who is a subject in a free city will not be of a single kind. It will include different sorts: one sort which fits him to act as a ruler, and one which fits him to act as a subject. The temperance and the courage of a man differ from those of a woman in much the same sort of way. A man would be thought cowardly if his courage were only the same as that of a courageous woman; and conversely a woman would be thought a gossip if she showed no more decorum than that which befits a good man. The function of the man in the household is different from that of the woman: it is the function of the one to acquire, and of the other to keep.

1277ᵇ25 Practical wisdom is the only form of excellence which is peculiar to the ruler. The other forms must, it would seem, belong equally to rulers and subjects. The excellence of subjects cannot be practical wisdom, and may be defined as "right opinion." The ruled may be compared to a flute-maker: the ruler is like a flute-player who uses what the flute-maker makes.

1277ᵇ30 These considerations will show whether the excellence of the good man and that of the good citizen are identical or different—or in what sense they are identical and in what sense they are different.

B:Constitutions and Their Classification

CHAPTER 6

1278ᵇ6 Having determined these matters we have next to consider whether there is a single type of constitution, or whether there are a number of types. If there are a number of types, what are these types; how many of them are there; and how do they differ? A constitution [or *politeia*] may be defined as "the organization of a city [or *polis*], in respect of its offices generally, but especially in respect of that particular office which is sovereign in all issues." The civic body is everywhere the sovereign of the city; in fact the civic body is the constitution itself. In democratic cities, for example, the people [*demos*] is sovereign: in oligarchies, on the other hand, the few [or *oligoi*] have that position; and this difference in the sovereign bodies is the reason why we say that the two types of constitution differ—as we may equally apply the same reasoning to other types besides these.

1278ᵇ15 We must first ascertain two things: the nature of the end for which a city exists, and the various kinds of rule to which mankind and its associations are subject. It has already been stated, in our first book (where we were concerned with the management of the household and the control of slaves), that "man is a political animal." For this reason people desire to live a social life even when they stand in no need of mutual succour; but they are also drawn together by a common interest, in proportion as each attains a share in the good life. The good life is the chief end, both for the community as a whole and for each of us individually. But people also come together, and form and maintain political associations, merely for the sake of life; for perhaps there is some element of the good even in the simple fact of living, so long as the evils of existence do not preponderate too heavily. It is an evident fact that most people cling hard enough to life to be willing to endure a good deal of suffering, which implies that life has in it a sort of healthy happiness and a natural quality of pleasure.

1278ᵇ30 It is easy enough to distinguish the various kinds of rule of which people commonly speak; and indeed we have often had occasion to define them ourselves in works intended for the general public. The rule of a master is one kind; and here, though there is really a common interest which unites the natural master and the natural slave, the fact remains that the rule is primarily exercised with a view to the master's interest, and only incidentally with a view to that of the slave, who must be preserved in existence if the rule is to remain. Rule over wife and children, and over the household generally, is a second kind of rule, which we have called by the name of household management. Here the rule is either exercised in the interest of the ruled or for the attainment of some advantage common to both ruler and ruled. Essentially it is exercised in the interest of the ruled, as is also plainly the case with other arts besides that of ruling, such as medicine and gymnastics—though an art may incidentally be exercised for the benefit of its practitioner, and there is nothing to prevent (say) a trainer from becoming occasionally a member of the class he instructs, in the same sort of way as a steersman is always one of the crew. Thus a trainer or steersman primarily considers the good of those who are subject to his authority; but when he becomes one of them personally, he incidentally shares in the benefit of that good—the steersman thus being also a member of the crew, and the trainer (though still a trainer) becoming also a member of the class which he instructs.

1279ᵃ8 For this reason, when the constitution of a city is constructed on the principle that its members are equals and peers, the citizens think it proper that they should hold office by turns. At any rate this is the natural system, and the system which used to be followed in the days when people believed that they ought to serve by turns, and each assumed that others would take over the duty of considering his benefit, just as he himself, during his term of office, had considered their interest. Today because of the profits to be derived from office and the handling of public property, people want to hold office continuously. It is as if they were invalids, who got the benefit of being healthy by being permanently in office: at any rate their ardour for office is just what it would be if that were the case. The conclusion which follows is clear: those constitutions which consider the common interest are right constitutions, judged by the standard of absolute justice. Those constitutions which consider only the personal interest of the rulers are all wrong constitutions, or perversions of the right forms. Such perverted forms are despotic; whereas the city is an association of freemen.

CHAPTER 7

1279ᵃ22 Now that these matters have been determined, the next subject for consideration is the number and nature of the different constitutions. We may first examine those constitutions that are rightly formed, since, when these have been determined, the different perversions will at once be apparent.

1279ᵃ25 The term "constitution" [*politeia*] signifies the same thing as the term "civic body" [*politeuma*]. The civic body in every city [*polis*] is the sovereign [*to kurion*]; and the sovereign must necessarily be either One, or Few, or Many. On this basis we may say that when the One, or the Few, or the Many rule with a view to the common interest, the constitutions under which they do so must necessarily be right constitutions. On the other hand, the constitutions directed to the personal interest of the One, or the Few, or the Masses, must necessarily be perversions. Either we should say that those who do not share in the constitution are not citizens, or they ought to have their share of the benefits. According to customary usage, among monarchical forms of government the type which looks to the common interest is called Kingship; among forms of government by a few people (but more than one) it is called Aristocracy—that name being given to this species either because the best [*aristoi*] are

the rulers, or because its object is what is best [*ariston*] for the city and its members. Finally, when the masses govern the city with a view to the common interest, the form of government is called by the generic name common to all constitutions (or polities)—the name of "Constitutional Government." There is a good reason for this usage: it is possible for one man, or a few, to be of outstanding excellence; but when it comes to a large number, we can hardly expect precision in all the varieties of excellence. What we can expect particularly is the military kind of excellence, which is the kind that shows itself in a mass. This is the reason why the defence forces are the most sovereign body under this constitution, and those who possess arms are the ones who participate in it.

1279ᵇ4 The perversions that correspond to the constitutions just mentioned are: Tyranny, [the perversion of] Kingship; Oligarchy [the perversion of] Aristocracy; and Democracy [the perversion of] "Constitutional Government" [or polity]. Tyranny is a government by a single person directed to the interest of that person; Oligarchy is directed to the interest of the well-to-do; Democracy is directed to the interest of the poor. None of these benefits the common interest.

CHAPTER 8

1279ᵇ16 Tyranny, as has just been said, is single-person government of the political association on the lines of despotism; oligarchy exists where those who have property are the sovereign authority of the constitution; and, conversely, democracy exists where the sovereign authority is composed of the poorer classes, who are without much property.

1279ᵇ20 The first difficulty which arises is a matter of definition. It could be that the majority are well-to-do and that these hold the sovereignty in a city; but when the majority is sovereign there is [said to be] democracy. Similarly it could happen that the poorer classes were fewer in number than the well-to-do, and yet were stronger and had sovereign authority in the constitution; but where a small number has sovereignty there is said to be oligarchy. Thus it may seem that the definitions we have given of these constitutions cannot be correct.

1279ᵇ26 We might attempt to overcome the difficulty by combining both of the factors: wealth with paucity of numbers, and poverty with mass. On this basis oligarchy might be defined as the constitution under which the rich, being also few in number, hold the public offices; and similarly democracy might be defined as the constitution under which the poor, being also many in number, are in control. But this involves us in another difficulty. If there are no forms of oligarchy and democracy other than those enumerated, what names are we to give to the constitutions just suggested as conceivable—those where the wealthy form a majority and the poor a minority, and where the wealthy majority in the one case, and the poor minority in the other, are the sovereign authority of the constitution? The course of the argument thus appears to show that whether the sovereign body is small or large in number (as it is respectively in oligarchies or in democracies) is an accidental attribute, due to the simple fact that the wealthy are generally few and the poor are generally numerous. Therefore the causes originally mentioned are not in fact the real causes of the difference between oligarchies and democracies. The real ground of the difference between oligarchy and democracy is poverty and riches. It is inevitable that there should be an oligarchy where the rulers, whether they are few or many, owe their position to riches; and it is equally inevitable that there should be democracy where the poor rule.

1280ᵃ2 It happens, however, as we have just remarked, that the former [i.e. the wealthy] are few and the latter [i.e. the poor] are numerous. It is only a few who have riches, but all alike share in free status; and it is on these grounds that the two parties dispute the control of the constitution.

BOOK IV

Actual Constitutions and Their Varieties

C: The Type of Constitution Which Is Most Generally Practicable

CHAPTER 11

1295ᵃ25 We have now to consider what is the best constitution and the best way of life for the majority of cities and the majority of mankind. In doing so, we shall not employ a standard of excellence above the reach of ordinary people, or a standard of education requiring exceptional natural endowments and equipment, or the standard of a constitution which attains an ideal level. We shall be concerned only with the sort of life which most people are able to share and the sort of constitution which it is possible for most cities to enjoy. The "aristocracies," so called, of which we have just been treating, either lie at one extreme, beyond the reach of most cities, or they approach so closely to what is called "constitutional government" [polity] that the two can be considered as a single form.

1295ᵃ34 The issues we have just raised can all be decided in the light of one body of fundamental principles. If we were right when, in the *Ethics*, we stated that the truly happy life is one of goodness lived in freedom from impediments and that goodness consists in a mean, it follows that the best way of life is one which consists in a mean, and a mean of the kind attainable by each individual. Further, the same criteria should determine the goodness or badness of the city and that of the constitution; for a constitution is the way in which a city lives. In all cities there are three parts: the very rich, the very poor, and the third class which forms the mean between these two. Now, since it is admitted that moderation and the mean are always best it is clear that in the ownership of all gifts of fortune a middle condition will be the best. Those who are in this condition are the most ready to listen to reason. Those who are over-handsome, over-strong, over-noble, or over-wealthy, and, at the opposite extreme, those who are over-poor, overweak, or utterly ignoble, find it hard to follow the lead of reason. Those in the first class tend more to arrogance and serious offences: those in the second tend too much to criminality and petty offences; and most wrongdoing arises either from arrogance or criminality. [It is a further characteristic of those in the middle that] they are least prone either to refuse office or to seek it, both of which tendencies are dangerous to cities.

1295^b13 It must also be added that those who enjoy too many advantages—strength, wealth, friends, and so forth—are both unwilling to obey and ignorant how to obey. This [defect] appears in them from the first, during childhood and in homelife: nurtured in luxury, they never acquire a habit of obedience, even in school. But those who suffer from a lack of such things are far too mean and poor-spirited. Thus there are those who are ignorant how to rule and only know how to obey, as if they were slaves, and, on the other hand, there are those who are ignorant how to obey any sort of authority and only know how to rule as if they were masters [of slaves]. The result is a city, not of freemen, but only of slaves and masters: a state of envy on the one side and of contempt on the other. Nothing could be further removed from the spirit of friendship or of a political association. An association depends on friendship—after all, people will not even take a journey in common with their enemies. A city aims at being, as far as possible, composed of equals and peers, which is the condition of those in the middle, more than any group. It follows that this kind of city is bound to have the best constitution since it is composed of the elements which, on our view, naturally go to make up a city. The middle classes enjoy a greater security themselves than any other class. They do not, like the poor, desire the goods of others; nor do others desire their possessions, as the poor desire those of the rich, and since they neither plot against others, nor are plotted against themselves, they

live free from danger. Phocylides was therefore right when he prayed:

> *Many things are best for those in the middle;*
> *I want to be at the middle of the city.*

1295^b34 It is clear from our argument, first, that the best form of political association is one where power is vested in the middle class, and, secondly, that good government is attainable in those cities where there is a large middle class—large enough, if possible, to be stronger than both of the other classes, but at any rate large enough to be stronger than either of them singly; for in that case its addition to either will suffice to turn the scale, and will prevent either of the opposing extremes from becoming dominant. It is therefore the greatest of blessings for a city that its members should possess a moderate and adequate property. Where some have great possessions, and others have nothing at all, the result is either an extreme democracy or an unmixed oligarchy; or it may even be, as a result of the excesses of both sides, a tyranny. Tyranny grows out of the most immature type of democracy, or out of oligarchy, but much less frequently out of constitutions of the middle order, or those which approximate to them. We shall explain the reason for this later, when we come to treat of the ways in which constitutions change.

1296^a7 Meanwhile, it is clear that the middle type of constitution is best. It is the one type free from faction; where the middle class is large, there is less likelihood of faction and dissension than in any other constitution. Large cities are generally more free from faction just because they have a large middle class. In small cities, on the other hand, it is easy for the whole population to be divided into only two classes; nothing is left in the middle, and all, or almost all, are either poor or rich. Democracies are generally more secure and more permanent than oligarchies because of their middle class. This is more numerous, and has a larger share of [offices and] honours, than it does in oligarchies. Where democracies have no middle class, and the poor are greatly superior in number, trouble ensues, and they are speedily ruined. It must also be considered a proof of its value that the best legislators have come from the middle class. Solon was one, as he makes clear in his poems: Lycurgus was another (after all he was not a king); and the same is true of Charondas and most of the other legislators.

1296ᵃ22 What has just been said also serves to explain why most constitutions are either democratic or oligarchical. The middle class in these cities is often small; and the result is that as happens whenever one class—be it the owners of property or the masses—gains the advantage, it oversteps the mean, and draws the constitution in its own direction so that either a democracy or an oligarchy comes into being. In addition, factious disputes and struggles readily arise between the masses and the rich; and the side, whichever it is, that wins the day, instead of establishing a constitution based on the common interest and the principle of equality, exacts as the prize of victory a greater share in the constitution. It then institutes either a democracy or an oligarchy. Furthermore, those who have gained ascendancy in Greece have paid an exclusive regard to their own types of constitution; one has instituted democracies in the cities [under its control], while the other has set up oligarchies: each has looked to its own advantage, and neither to that of the cities it controlled. These reasons explain why a middle or mixed type of constitution has never been established—or, at the most, has only been established on a few occasions and in a few cities. One man, and one only, of all who have hitherto been in a position of ascendancy, has allowed himself to be persuaded to allow this sort of system to be established. And now it has also become the habit for cities not even to want a system of equality. Instead they seek to dominate or, if beaten, to submit.

1296ᵇ2 It is clear, from these arguments, which is the best constitution, and what are the reasons why it is so and it is easy to see which of the others (given that we distinguish several varieties of democracy and several varieties of oligarchy) should be placed first, which second, and so on in turn, according as their quality is better or worse. The nearest to the

best must always be better, and the one farthest removed from the mean must always be worse, unless we are judging on the basis of a particular assumption. I use the words "on the basis of a particular assumption" because it often turns out that, although one sort of constitution may be preferable, there is nothing to prevent another sort from being better suited to certain peoples.

D: What Sort of Constitution is Desirable for What Sort of Civic Body? (Chapters 12–13)

CHAPTER 12

1296ᵇ13 The next topic to consider, after what we have said, is: "What particular constitution is suited to what particular people and what sort of constitution is suited to what sort of population?" Now, we must first grasp a general principle which holds for all constitutions—that the part of a city which wishes a constitution to continue must be stronger than the part which does not.

1296ᵇ17 Quality and quantity both go to the making of every city. By "quality" we mean free birth, wealth, culture, and nobility of descent; by "quantity" we mean superiority in numbers. Now quality may belong to one of the parts which compose a city, and quantity to another. For example, those who are low-born may be more numerous than the highborn, or the poor than the rich; but the superiority of one side in quantity may not be as great as their inferiority in quality. Quantity and quality must thus be placed in the balance against one another. Where the number of the poor exceeds the proportion just described, there will naturally be a democracy; and the particular variety of democracy will depend on the form of superiority which is shown, in each particular case, by the mass of the people. If, for example, the farmers exceed the others in number, we shall have the first form of democracy: if the mechanics and day-labourers are most numerous, we shall have the "extreme" form, and the same will be true of the intermediate forms between these. Where the superiority of the rich and the notables in point of quality is greater than their inferiority in point of quantity, there will be an oligarchy; and the particular variety of oligarchy will similarly depend on the particular form of superiority which is shown by the oligarchical body.

1296ᵇ34 A legislator should always make the members of the middle class partners in the constitution. If the laws he makes are oligarchical, he should direct his attention to the middle class, and, if they are democratic, he should seek to attach that same class to those laws. Where the middle class outweighs in numbers both the other classes, or even one of them, it is possible for a constitution to be permanent. There is no risk, in such a case, of the rich uniting with the poor to oppose the middle class: neither will ever be willing to be subject to the other; and if they try to find a constitution which is more in their common interest than this, they will fail to find one. Neither class would tolerate a system of ruling in turns: they have too little confidence in one another. A [neutral] arbitrator always gives the best ground for confidence; and the "man in the middle" is such an arbitrator. The better, and the more equitable, the mixture in a constitution, the more durable it will be. An error often made by those who desire to establish aristocratic constitutions is that they not only give more power to the well-to-do, but they also deceive the people. Illusory benefits must always produce real evils in the long run; and the encroachments made by the rich are more destructive to a constitution than those of the people.

BOOK V

Causes of Factional Conflict and Constitutional Change

A: The General Causes of Factional Conflict and Change in All Types of Constitution

CHAPTER 2

1302ᵃ16 Since we have to consider the various reasons which lead to the rise of factions and changes in constitutions, we had better begin with a general view of their origins and causes. They may be said to be three in number; and we must begin by giving a brief outline of each of them separately. We have to investigate (1) the state of mind which leads to faction; (2) the objects which are at stake; and (3) the causes which give rise to political disturbance and factional disputes.

1302ᵃ22 The principle and general cause of an attitude of mind which disposes people towards change is the cause of which we have just spoken. There are some who engage in factional disputes because their minds are filled by a passion for equality, which arises from their thinking that they have less in spite of being the equals of those who have more. There are others who do it because their minds are filled with a passion for inequality (i.e. superiority), which arises from their conceiving that they get no advantage over others (but only an equal amount, or even a smaller amount) although they are really more than equal to others. (Either of these passions may have some justification; and either may be without any.) Thus inferiors form factions in order to be equals, and equals in order to be superiors.

1302ᵃ31 This is the state of mind which creates faction. The objects which are at stake are profit and honour and their opposites, for people start factional disputes in cities with the object of avoiding some disgrace, or a fine, on themselves or on their friends.

1302ᵃ34 The causes and origins of disturbances—i.e. the factors which encourage the attitude of mind and lead to the pursuit of the objects which have just been mentioned—may be counted, from one point of view, as seven, but from another as more than that number. Two of these causes [profit and honour] are identical with two of the objects which have just been mentioned; but act in a different way. People get angry on account of profit and honour, not because they want to get them themselves: but because they see other people getting a larger share—some justly and some unjustly—than they themselves get. Other causes are: arrogant behaviour, fear, superiority, contempt, or a disproportionate increase.

Others, which act in a different way, are election intrigues; wilful negligence; trifling changes; and dissimilarity.

C:Methods of Ensuring Constitutional Stability in the Three Previous Types of Constitution and More Generally

CHAPTER 8

1308ᵇ31 The most important rule of all, in all types of constitution, is that provision should be made—not only by law, but also by the general system of economy—to prevent the officials from being able to use their office for their own gain. This is a matter which demands attention in oligarchical constitutions, above all others. The masses are not so greatly offended at being excluded from office (they may even be glad to be given the leisure for attending to their own business); what really annoys them is to think that those who have the enjoyment of office are embezzling public funds. That makes them feel a double annoyance at a double loss—the loss of profit as well as office. If an arrangement could be made to stop people from using office as a means of private gain, it would provide a way—the only possible way—for combining democracy with aristocracy. Both the notables and the masses could then get what they desire. All would be able to hold office, as befits a democracy: the notables would actually be in office, as befits an aristocracy. Both results could be achieved simultaneously if the use of office as a means of profit were made impossible. The poor would no longer desire to hold office (because they would derive no advantage from doing so), and they would prefer to attend to their own affairs. The rich would be able to afford to take office, as they would need no subvention from public funds to meet its expenses. The poor would thus have the advantage of becoming wealthy by diligent attention to work; the notables would enjoy the consolation of not being governed by any chance comer.

1309ᵃ10 To prevent the embezzling of public money, the outgoing officers should hand over the funds [under their charge] in the presence of the whole civic body; and inventories of them should be deposited with each clan, ward, and tribe. To ensure that no profit should be made by any official in other ways, the law should provide for the award of honours to those who earn a good reputation.

1309ᵃ14 In democracies, the rich should be spared. Not only should their estates be safe from the threat of redistribution: the produce of the estates should be equally secure; and the practice of sharing it out, which has insensibly developed under some constitutions, should not be allowed. It is good policy, too, to prevent the rich, even if they are willing, from undertaking expensive, and yet useless, public services, such as the equipping of choruses for dramatic festivals, or the provision of the expenses of torch-races, or other services of that sort. In oligarchies, on the other hand, a good deal of attention should be paid to the poor. They should be assigned those offices from which profits can be made; and if a rich man does violence against them the penalties should be heavier than if he had been guilty of violence against members of his own class. Nor should inheritances pass by title of bequest; they should go by descent, and not more than one inheritance should ever go to one person. On this system estates would be more evenly distributed, and more of the poor might rise to a position of affluence.

1309ᵃ27 In matters other than property it is beneficial both for oligarchies and for democracies to give a position of equality, or even of precedence, to those who have a smaller share in the constitution—in a democracy to the rich; in an oligarchy to the poor. An exception must, however, be made for the sovereign offices of the constitution. These should be entrusted only, or at any rate entrusted mainly, to those who have [full] membership in the constitution.

CHAPTER 9

1309ᵃ33 Three qualifications are necessary in those who have to fill the sovereign offices.

The first is loyalty to the established constitution. The second is a high degree of capacity for the duties of the office. The third is goodness of character and justice, in the particular form which suits the nature of each constitution. (If what is just varies from constitution to constitution, the quality of justice must also have its corresponding varieties.) Where these three qualifications are not united in a single person, a problem obviously arises: [how is the choice to be made?] For instance, A may possess military capacity, but be neither good in character nor loyal to the constitution. B may be just in character and loyal to the constitution, [but deficient in capacity]. How are we to choose? It would seem that we ought to consider two points—which quality do people on the whole have more of and which less. Thus, for a military office, we must have regard to military experience rather than character: people in general have less military capacity and more honesty. For the post of custodian of property, or that of treasurer, we must follow the opposite rule: such posts require a standard of character above the average, but the knowledge which they demand is such as we all possess. A further problem may also be raised: if someone possesses the two qualifications of capacity and loyalty to the constitution, is there any need for him to have the third qualification (a good character), and will not the first two, by themselves, secure the public interest? We may answer that those who possess these two first qualifications may lack self-control, and just as such people fail to serve their own interests— even though they possess self-knowledge and self-loyalty—so nothing prevents some people from being in the same position with regard to the public interest.

1309ᵇ14 Generally, we may add, a constitution will tend to be preserved by the observance of all the legal rules already suggested, in the course of our argument, as making for constitutional stability. Here we may note, as of paramount importance, the elementary principle which has been again and again suggested—the principle of ensuring that the number of those who wish a constitution to continue shall be greater than the number of those who do not.

1309ᵇ18 In addition to all these things, there is another which ought to be remembered, but which, in fact, is forgotten in perverted forms of government. This is the value of the mean. Many of the measures which are reckoned democratic really undermine democracies: many which are reckoned oligarchical actually undermine oligarchies. Those who think that theirs is the only form of goodness, push matters to an extreme. They fail to see that proportion is as necessary to a constitution as it is (let us say) to a nose. A nose may deviate in some degree from the ideal of straightness, and incline towards the hooked or the snub, without ceasing to be well shaped and agreeable to the eye. But push the deviation still further towards either of these extremes, and the nose will begin to be out of proportion with the rest of the face: carry it further still, and it will cease to look like a nose at all, because it will go too far towards one, and too far away from the other, of these two opposite extremes. What is true of the nose, and of other parts of the body, is true also of constitutions. Both oligarchy and democracy may be tolerable forms of government, even though they deviate from the ideal. But if you push either of them further still [in the direction to which it tends], you will begin by making it a worse constitution, and you may end by turning it into something which is not a constitution at all.

1309ᵇ35 It is thus the duty of legislators and statesmen to know which democratic measures preserve, and which destroy, a democracy; similarly, it is their duty to know which oligarchical measures will save, and which will ruin, an oligarchy. Neither of these constitutions can exist, or continue in existence, unless it includes both the rich and the poor. If, therefore, a system of equal ownership is introduced into either, the result will inevitably be a new and different form of constitution; and the radical legislation which abolishes riches and poverty will thus abolish along with them the constitutions [based on their presence]. Errors are made alike in democracies and oligarchies. They are made, for instance, by demagogues, in those democracies where the will of the people is superior to the law. Demagogues are always dividing the city into two, and waging war against the rich. Their proper policy is the very reverse: they should always profess to be speaking in defence of the rich. A similar policy should be followed in oligarchies: the oligarchs should profess to speak on behalf of the poor; and the oaths they take should be the opposite of those which they now take. There are cities in which their oath runs, "I will bear ill will to the people, and I will plan against them all the evil I can." The opinion which they ought to hold and exhibit is the very opposite; and their oaths should contain the declaration, "I will not do wrong to the people."

1310ª12 The greatest, however, of all the means we have mentioned for ensuring the stability of constitutions—but one which is nowadays generally neglected—is the education of citizens in the spirit of their constitution. There is no advantage in the best of laws, even when they are sanctioned by general civic consent, if the citizens themselves have not been attuned, by the force of habit and the influence of teaching, to the right constitutional temper—which will be the temper of democracy where the laws are democratic, and where they are oligarchical will be that of oligarchy. If an individual can lack self-control, so can a city. The education of a citizen in the spirit of his constitution does not consist in his doing the actions in which the partisans of oligarchy, or the adherents of democracy, delight. It consists in his doing the actions which make it possible to have an oligarchy, or a democracy. Actual practice, today, is on very different lines. In oligarchies the sons of those in office live lives of luxury, and this at a time when the sons of the poor are being hardened by exercise, and by their daily work, and are thus acquiring the will and the power to create a revolution. In democracies of the type which is regarded as being peculiarly democratic the policy followed is the very reverse of their real interest. The reason for this is a false conception of liberty. There are two features which are generally held to define democracy. One of them is the sovereignty of the majority; the other is the liberty of individuals. Justice is assumed to consist in equality and equality in regarding the will of the masses as sovereign; liberty is assumed to consist in "doing what one likes." The result of such a view is that, in these extreme democracies, each individual lives as he likes—or, as Euripides says,

For any end he chances to desire.

This is a mean conception [of liberty]. To live by the rule of the constitution ought not to be regarded as slavery, but rather as salvation.

Such, in general, are the causes which lead to the change and destruction of constitutions, and such are the means of ensuring their preservation and stability.

CICERO

~

INTRODUCTION

RICHARD KRAUT

Marcus Tullius Cicero (106–43 BCE) was born in Arpinum, about seventy miles south-east of Rome, to a family that had powerful connections and was active in local politics. After several years of military service, he studied law and oratory in Rome, and became acquainted with the ideas of Stoicism and Academic Skepticism. He came under the influence of Philo of Larissa, the head of Plato's Academy in Athens, who had fled to Rome in 88 to escape the invasion of hostile forces. Philo advocated a mild form of Skepticism: although certainty is never achievable, the best strategy for forming one's beliefs is to examine both sides of every question and accept whichever seems, at the time, more persuasive. That principle was to form the basis of Cicero's approach to philosophy.

He began his legal career while in his twenties, but interrupted it for several years to travel and to continue his studies in Athens. During this period he became more fully acquainted with the wide range of philosophical options being debated by rival schools of thought: Stoicism, Epicureanism, and updated versions of Platonism and Aristotelianism. He returned to Rome in the mid-70s and resumed his career in law and politics, which culminated in his election to the office of consul, the supreme Roman magistracy, at the age of forty-three (the minimal age required for this office). He exposed and thwarted a revolutionary conspiracy (headed by Cataline), and championed the execution of the conspirators without trial—an action that won him powerful enemies. His influence began to decline when, in the year 60, Caesar, Pompey, and Crassus formed a triumvirate.

Cicero turned increasingly to a career as a writer in the 50s, and composed *On the Republic* and *On the Laws* during this period. Civil war between Caesar and Pompey broke out in 49. As the war continued, Cicero withdrew entirely from public life for the first time. His output during this period was remarkable: over a dozen substantial works between 46 and 44. It was also during this time that he divorced his wife, remarried and divorced again, and suffered the loss of his daughter. Caesar, whom Cicero regarded as a villain, was named perpetual dictator in 44, and was killed by conspirators on March 15 of the same year—an event that forms the center of Shakespeare's *Julius Caesar*. The following year, Antony (also the subject of one of Shakespeare's plays), Lepidus, and Octavian formed a second triumvirate—an event that led to Cicero's assassination on December 7.

Cicero's principal contributions to moral and political philosophy are contained in four works: *On the Republic*, *On the Laws*, *On Ends*, and *On Duties*. *On Ends* examines the conflict between Epicureans and Stoics regarding the final end of human life: should it be pleasure (the Epicurean view) or virtue (as Stoics think)? *On Duties* contains an examination of the principal virtues: wisdom, social virtue (subdivided into justice and liberality), greatness of spirit, and seemliness (*decorum*); followed by an examination of two questions inspired by Plato's *Republic:* What is beneficial? Is it possible for the paths of virtue and benefits to diverge? In both of these treatises, Cicero writes as a defender of Stoic ideas—an option that the Skepticism he learned from Philo left open to him. On balance, he finds unpersuasive the Epicurean argument that makes pleasure the end of life. And although he rejects the view, widely accepted among Stoics, that virtue is the sole good, he finds no cases in which there is a genuine conflict between virtue and other goods.

It is not merely in the field of ethics that Cicero finds the Stoics have better arguments than do the Epicureans. He is repelled by the Epicurean thesis that a wise person will refrain from a life of active political participation. The Stoic principle that virtue is the sole good is one that has considerable appeal to him, because it provides a grounding for one of his strongest convictions: that the highest calling for a human being is to devote himself to the political community of which he is a part. Another work of Cicero's, *On the Nature of the Gods*, also features a debate between the Epicureans and the Stoics. The former portray the gods as beings so self-sufficient and happy that they take no interest in creating worlds or guiding human life. By contrast, the Stoics regard the cosmos as a single connected substance permeated by divine and rational guidance. At the end of the dialogue, Cicero indicates his preference for the Stoic conception of the world, which provides a far better basis for a moral order among human beings.

Cicero's earlier political works—*On the Republic* and *On the Laws*—take their inspiration from the Platonic dialogues after which they are named. They are linked works: *On the Republic* proposes a conception of the ideal constitution, and *On the Laws* fills out the details by proposing a system of laws for such a state. (By contrast, the two Platonic dialogues that Cicero took as his models portray quite different cities: the first is ruled exclusively by philosophers, the second almost exclusively by nonphilosophers.) We possess only about one-quarter of the text of *On the Republic* (a work divided into six books); even that much was lost between 600 and 1819, and its contents were known only through the references and citations of authors (particularly Augustine) who had read Cicero before 600. (Its final section, "Scipio's Dream," discusses the immortality of the soul and the final rewards of the statesman. It was well known in the medieval period.) *On the Laws* was left incomplete; we have much of Books I and II, and less of III, but there are indications that Cicero planned and perhaps wrote portions of at least two more books. Despite the fragmentary availability of these texts, their influence on moral and political thought from the medieval through the modern periods was enormous. Cicero's stature as a judicious thinker and prose stylist, a philosopher whose balanced judgments took on added credibility because they were informed by years of political experience, reached its height in the eighteenth century, when he won the admiration of Charles de Secondat Montesquieu, David Hume, Adam Smith, Edmund Burke, John Adams, and Thomas Jefferson.

Cicero opens *On the Republic* with an introduction in praise of the political life, but the rest of the work contains a conversation, which he says had been reported to him, between Scipio (more fully: Publius Cornelius Scipio Aemilianus Africanus), a great general and orator of the second century, and several of his associates. The conversation takes place during a political crisis in 129; Cicero's contemporary readers would have known that Scipio was overtaken by events and murdered several days later. Scipio therefore plays for Cicero a role similar to the one Socrates had played for Plato: he was a hero whose ideas did not prevail, and whose country suffered his loss. *On the Republic* holds up Roman institutions as precisely the ones that an ideal state must have—but Cicero places a discussion of those institutions in the past, because he thinks that, since the time of Scipio, they have been corrupted by such men as Caesar. There is a striking contrast here between Cicero's work and Plato's: the Greek philosopher is eager to show how radically different an ideal city would be from the one in which he is a citizen, whereas the Roman thinker believes that the Rome that had existed only a few generations ago had already reached an ideal form.

The starting point the interlocutors use for their discussion of the best form of government is the division of forms of rule into three kinds: rule by one (monarchy), by few (aristocracy), or by many (popular rule). This typology dates back to the Greeks: it can be found in Herodotus and was more fully developed by Plato in the *Statesman* and Aristotle in the *Politics*. Scipio says that any of these three systems can, under the right conditions, be tolerable; and he rehearses the arguments that can be given for and against each. He concludes, however, that although monarchy is the best of the three simple forms, a still better arrangement—in fact, the best possible—is not to give exclusive power to one, or few, or many, but rather to balance each of these three factors, giving each its appropriate weight.

In effect, Cicero, using Scipio as his mouthpiece, is arguing that the structure of the Roman Republic, which gives to its two elected consuls regal power and to the senate aristocratic power, with the tribunes and popular assemblies wielding democratic power, has achieved the ideal political balance. In designating a mixed government as ideal, Scipio is following the lead of Polybius, the Greek historian of the second century BCE, who, in Book 6 of his *Histories*, attributed the remarkable rise and military success of Rome to the fact that it had a mixed constitution. Scipio does not claim that each of the three elements that need to be mixed should have equal power. But it is significant that he regards popular participation as one necessary element in an ideal constitution. That popular element is present in his theory from the start, for the opening move he makes in his conversation is to define the *res publica* as a *res populi*: "a commonwealth is the property of a people."

Like Plato's *Laws*, Cicero's *On the Laws* consists of a dialogue among three people on a long summer day. The principal speaker is Cicero himself, and his interlocutors are his younger brother, Quintus, and his close friend, Atticus. Most of the work is devoted to a detailed description of an ideal law code, but as a preliminary step Cicero puts forward a conception of law as "the highest reason implanted in nature." Here Cicero is relying, once again, on Stoic ideas, for the Stoics see the whole cosmos as infused with divine and rational planning. Although the written laws devised by imperfect human beings may vary from one place to another, and may be abolished, the true laws upon which our human laws should be modeled exist at all times and are to be obeyed by all human beings. Their basis lies in the nature of human beings, who exhibit the same sociability and tendencies toward good and bad ends alike. Once we acknowledge that tyrants must be resisted, and that the popularity of a decree does not make it just, we must recognize the validity of eternal and universal law. Cicero's ideas on this subject played an important role in Aquinas's analysis of law in the *Summa Theologiae*.

For an overview of Cicero's political thought, see E. M. Atkins's contribution to *The Cambridge History of Greek and Roman Political Thought*, edited by Christopher Rowe and Malcolm Schofield, in association with Simon Harrison and Melissa Lane (Cambridge: Cambridge University Press, 2000), pp. 477–516. A recent translation of *On the Republic* and *On the Laws*, together with helpful notes, is provided by James G. Zetzel (Cambridge: Cambridge University Press, 1999). For the background to Cicero's writings, see Elizabeth Rawson, *Intellectual Life in the Late Roman Republic* (Baltimore: Johns Hopkins University Press, 1985). See too her brief biography, *Cicero: A Portrait* (London: Allen Lane, 1975). Various aspects of Cicero's thought are explored in J. G. F. Powell (ed.), *Cicero the Philosopher* (Oxford: Clarendon Press, 1995). A brief introduction to the Hellenistic schools is provided by R. W. Sharples, *Stoics, Epicureans, and Skeptics* (London: Routledge, 1996). For a comprehensive study that stresses Cicero's conservatism, see Neal Wood, *Cicero's Social and Political Thought* (Berkeley: University of California Press, 1988).

On the Republic

BOOK I

[IV. Few may have imagined, in view of all I had suffered, that when,] as I retired from the consulship, I took my oath before an assembly of the people, and the Roman people took the same oath, that the republic was safe [as a result of my efforts alone.] I was amply repaid thereby for all the anxiety and vexation that resulted from the injustice done to me. And yet my sufferings brought me more honour than trouble, more glory than vexation, and the joy I found in the affectionate longing felt for me by good citizens was greater than my grief at the exultation of the wicked. But, as I said before, if it had happened otherwise, how could I complain? For none of the misfortunes

that fell to my lot in consequence of my great services was unexpected by me or more serious than I had foreseen. For such was my nature that, although, on account of the manifold pleasures I found in the studies which had engaged me from boyhood, it would have been possible for me, on the one hand, to reap greater profit from a quiet life than other men, or, on the other hand, if any disaster should happen to us all, to suffer no more than my fair share of the common misfortune, yet I could not hesitate to expose myself to the severest storms, and, I might almost say, even to thunderbolts, for the sake of the safety of my fellow-citizens, and to secure, at the cost of my own personal danger, a quiet life for all the rest. For, in truth, our country has not given us birth

Reprinted by permission of the publisher from *De Re Publica* by Cicero, translated by Clinton Walker Keyes, Cambridge, Mass.: Harvard University Press. Copyright © 1928 by the President and Fellows of Harvard College.

and education without expecting to receive some sustenance, as it were, from us in return; nor has it been merely to serve our convenience that she has granted to our leisure a safe refuge and for our moments of repose a calm retreat; on the contrary, she has given us these advantages so that she may appropriate to her own use the greater and more important part of our courage, our talents, and our wisdom, leaving to us for our own private uses only so much as may be left after her needs have been satisfied.

V. Moreover we ought certainly not to listen to the other excuses to which these men resort, that they may be more free to enjoy the quiet life. They say, for example, that it is mostly worthless men who take part in politics, men with whom it is degrading to be compared, while to have conflict with them, especially when the mob is aroused, is a wretched and dangerous task. Therefore, they maintain, a wise man should not attempt to take the reins, as he cannot restrain the insane and untamed fury of the common herd; nor is it proper for a freeman, by contending with vile and wicked opponents, to submit to the scourgings of abuse or expose himself to wrongs which are intolerable to the wise—as if, in the view of good, brave, and high-minded men, there could be any nobler motive for entering public life than the resolution not to be ruled by wicked men and not to allow the republic to be destroyed by them, seeing that the philosophers themselves, even if they should desire to help, would be impotent.

VI. And who in the world can approve of the single exception they make, when they say that no wise man will take any part in public affairs unless some emergency compels him to do so? As if any greater emergency could come upon anyone than that with which I was confronted; and what could I have done in that crisis unless I had been consul at the time? And how could I have been consul unless I had held to a manner of life from my boyhood which led me to the highest office of State in spite of my equestrian birth? Hence it is clear that the opportunity of serving the State, however great be the dangers with which it is threatened,

does not come suddenly, or when we wish it, unless we are in such a position that it is possible for us to take action. It has always seemed to me that the most amazing of the teachings of learned men is that they deny their own ability to steer when the sea is calm, having never learned the art nor cared to know it, while at the same time they assure us that, when the waves dash highest, they will take the helm. For it is their habit to proclaim openly, and even to make it their great boast, that they have neither learned nor do they teach anything about the principles of the State, either to establish it or to safeguard it, and that they consider the knowledge of such things unsuited to learned or wise men, but better to be left to those who have trained themselves in that business. How can it be reasonable, therefore, for them to promise to aid the State in case they are compelled by an emergency to do so, when they do not know how to rule the State when no emergency threatens it, though this is a much easier task than the other? Indeed, if it be true that the wise man does not, as a general thing, willingly descend from his lofty heights to statecraft, but does not decline the duty if conditions force him to assume it, yet I should think he ought by no means to neglect this science of politics, because it is his duty to acquire in advance all the knowledge that, for aught he knows, it may be necessary for him to use at some future time.

VII. I have treated these matters at considerable length because I have planned and undertaken in this work a discussion of the State; hence, in order that this discussion might not be valueless, I had, in the first place, to remove all grounds for hesitation about taking part in public affairs. Yet if there be any who are influenced by the authority of philosophers, let them for a few moments listen and attend to those whose authority and reputation stand highest among learned men; for even if these have not governed the State themselves, nevertheless, since they have dealt with the State in many investigations and treatises, I consider that they have performed a certain function of their own in the State. And in fact I note that nearly every one of those Seven whom the Greeks called "wise" took an important part in the affairs of government. For there is really no other occupation in which human virtue approaches more closely the august function of the gods than that of founding new States or preserving those already in existence.

VIII. Wherefore, since it is my good fortune to have accomplished, in the actual government of the republic, something worthy to live in men's memories, and also to have acquired some skill in setting forth political principles through practice and also by reason of my enthusiasm for learning and teaching, [I consider myself not unsuited to the task I have now undertaken; for, as a matter of fact, this combination of accomplishments is rare among those who are considered] authorities [on statecraft], since while certain men in former times have shown great skill in theoretical discussion, they are discovered to have accomplished nothing practical, and there have been others who have been efficient in action, but clumsy in exposition. Indeed the principles I am about to state are not at all new or original to myself, but it is my intention to recall a discussion carried on by men who were at a certain period the most eminent and wisest in our republic. This discussion was once reported to you, in your youth, and to me by Publius Rutilius Rufus, when we were spending several days together at Smyrna; in it, I believe, very little is omitted that would contribute greatly to a logical exposition of the whole subject.

XXIV. *Scipio.* I will . . . at once begin my discussion, following the rule which, I think, ought always to be observed in the exposition of a subject if one wishes to avoid confusion; that is, that if the name of a subject is agreed upon, the meaning of this name should first be explained. Not until this meaning is agreed upon should the actual discussion be begun; for the qualities of the thing to be discussed can never be understood unless one understands first exactly what the thing itself is. Therefore, since the commonwealth is the subject of our investigation, let us first consider exactly what it is that we are investigating. . . .

XXV. *Scipio.* Well, then, a commonwealth is the property of a people. But a people is not any collection of human beings brought together in any sort of way, but an assemblage of people in large numbers associated in an agreement with respect to justice and a partnership for the common good. The first cause of such an association is not so much the weakness of the individual as a certain social spirit which nature has implanted in man. . . .

XXVI. Such an assemblage of men . . . established itself in a definite place, at first in order to provide dwellings; and this place being fortified by its natural situation and by their labours, they called such a collection of dwellings a town or city, and provided it with shrines and gathering places which were common property. Therefore every people, which is such a gathering of large numbers as I have described, every city, which is an orderly settlement of a people, every commonwealth, which, as I said, is "the property of a people," must be governed by some deliberative body if it is to be permanent. And this deliberative body must, in the first place, always owe its beginning to the same cause as that which produced the State itself. In the second place, this function must either be granted to one man, or to certain selected citizens, or must be assumed by the whole body of citizens. And so when the supreme authority is in the hands of one man, we call him a king, and the form of this State a kingship. When selected citizens hold this power, we say that the State is ruled by an aristocracy. But a popular government (for so it is called) exists when all the power is in the hands of the people. And any one of these three forms of government (if only the bond which originally joined the citizens together in the partnership of the State holds fast), though not perfect or in my opinion the best, is tolerable, though one of them may be superior to another. For either a just and wise king, or a select number of leading citizens, or even the people itself, though this is the least commendable type, can nevertheless, as it seems, form a government that is not unstable, provided that no elements of injustice or greed are mingled with it.

XXVII. But in kingships the subjects have too small a share in the administration of justice and in deliberation; and in aristocracies the masses can hardly have their share of liberty, since they are entirely excluded from deliberation for the common weal and from power; and when all the power is in the people's hands, even though they exercise it with justice and moderation, yet the resulting equality itself is inequitable, since it allows no distinctions in rank. Therefore, even though the Persian Cyrus was the most just and wisest of kings, that form of government does not seem to me the most desirable, since "the property of the people" (for that is what a commonwealth is, as I have said) is administered at the nod and caprice of one man; even though the Massilians, now under our protection, are ruled with the greatest justice by a select number of their leading citizens, such a situation is nevertheless to some extent like slavery for a people; and even though the Athenians at certain periods, after they had deprived the Areopagus of its power, succeeded in carrying on all their public business by the resolutions and decrees of the people, their State, because it had no definite distinctions in rank, could not maintain its fair renown.

XXVIII. I am now speaking of these three forms of government, not when they are confused and mingled with one another, but when they retain their appropriate character. All of them are, in the first place, subject each to the faults I have mentioned, and they suffer from other dangerous faults in addition: for before every one of them lies a slippery and precipitous path leading to a certain depraved form that is a close neighbour to it. For underneath the tolerable, or, if you like, the lovable King Cyrus (to cite him as a pre-eminent example) lies the utterly cruel Phalaris, impelling him to an arbitrary change of character; for the absolute rule of one man will easily and quickly degenerate into a tyranny like his. And a close neighbour to the excellent Massilian government, conducted by a few leading citizens, is such a partisan combination of thirty men as once ruled Athens. And as for the absolute power

of the Athenian people—not to seek other examples of popular government— . . . it changed into the fury and licence of a mob. . . .

XXIX. . . . A wise man should be acquainted with these changes, but it calls for great citizens and for a man of almost divine powers to foresee them when they threaten, and, while holding the reins of government, to direct their courses and keep them under his control. Therefore I consider a fourth form of government the most commendable—that form which is a well-regulated mixture of the three which I mentioned at first.

XXX. *Laelius.* I know that is your opinion, Africanus, for I have often heard you say so. Nevertheless, if it will not give you too much trouble, I should like to know which you consider the best of the three forms of government of which you have been speaking. . . .

XXXI. *Scipio.* Every State is such as its ruler's character and will make it. Hence liberty has no dwelling-place in any State except that in which the people's power is the greatest, and surely nothing can be sweeter than liberty; but if it is not the same for all, it does not deserve the name of liberty. And how can it be the same for all, I will not say in a kingdom, where there is no obscurity or doubt about the slavery of the subject, but even in States where everyone is ostensibly free? I mean States in which the people vote, elect commanders and officials, are canvassed for their votes, and have bills proposed to them, but really grant only what they would have to grant even if they were unwilling to do so, and are asked to give to others what they do not possess themselves. For they have no share in the governing power, in the deliberative function, or in the courts, over which selected judges preside, for those privileges are granted on the basis of birth or wealth. But in a free nation, such as the Rhodians or the Athenians, there is not one of the citizens who [may not hold the offices of State and take an active part in the government.] . . .

XXXII. [Our authorities] say [that] when one person or a few stand out from the crowd as richer and more prosperous, then, as a result of the haughty and arrogant behaviour of these, there arises [a government of one or a few], the cowardly and weak giving way and bowing down to the pride of wealth. But if the people would maintain their rights, they say that no form of government would be superior, either in liberty or happiness, for they themselves would be masters of the laws and the courts, of war and peace, of international agreements, and of every citizen's life and property; this government alone, they believe, can rightly be called a commonwealth, that is, "the property of the people." And it is for that reason, they say, that "the property of the people" is often liberated from the domination of kings or senators, while free peoples do not seek kings or the power and wealth of aristocracies. And indeed they claim that this free popular government ought not to be entirely rejected on account of the excesses of an unbridled mob, for, according to them, when a sovereign people is pervaded by a spirit of harmony and tests every measure by the standard of their own safety and liberty, no form of government is less subject to change or more stable. And they insist that harmony is very easily obtainable in a State where the interests of all are the same, for discord arises from conflicting interests, where different measures are advantageous to different citizens. Therefore they maintain that when a senate has been supreme, the State has never had a stable government, and that such stability is less attainable by far in kingdoms, in which, as Ennius says,

No sacred partnership or honour is.

Therefore, since law is the bond which unites the civic association, and the justice enforced by law is the same for all, by what justice can an association of citizens be held together when there is no equality among the citizens? For if we cannot agree to equalize men's wealth, and equality of innate ability is impossible, the legal rights at least of those who are citizens of the same commonwealth ought to be equal. For what is a State except an association or partnership in justice? . . .

XXXIII. Indeed they think that States of the other kinds have no right at all to the names which they arrogate to themselves. For why should I give the name of king the title of Jupiter the Best, to a man who is greedy for personal power and absolute authority, a man who lords it over an oppressed people? Should I not rather call him tyrant? For tyrants may be merciful as well as oppressive; so that the only difference between the nations governed by these rulers is that between the slaves of a kind and those of a cruel master; for in any case the subjects must be slaves. And how could Sparta, at the time when the mode of life inculcated by her constitution was considered so excellent, be assured of always having good and just kings, when a person of any sort, if he was born of the royal family, had to be accepted as king? As to aristocrats, who could tolerate men that have claimed the title without the people's acquiescence, but merely by their own will? For how is a man adjudged to be "the best"? On the basis of knowledge, skill, learning, [and similar qualities surely, not because of his own desire to possess the title!] . . .

XXXIV. If [the State] leaves [the selection of its rulers] to chance, it will be as quickly overturned as a ship whose pilot should be chosen by lot from among the passengers. But if a free people chooses the men to whom it is to entrust its fortunes, and, since it desires its own safety, chooses the best men, then certainly the safety of the State depends upon the wisdom of its best men, especially since Nature has provided not only that those men who are superior in virtue and in spirit should rule the weaker, but also that the weaker should be willing to obey the stronger.

But they claim that this ideal form of State has been rejected on account of the false notions of men, who, through their ignorance of virtue—for just as virtue is possessed by only a few, so it can be distinguished and perceived by only a few—think that the best men are those who are rich, prosperous, or born of famous families. For when, on account of this mistaken notion of the common people, the State begins to be ruled by the riches, instead of the virtue, of a few men, these rulers tenaciously retain the title, though they do not possess the character, of the "best." For riches, names, and power, when they lack wisdom and the knowledge of how to live and to rule over others, are full of dishonour and insolent pride, nor is there any more depraved type of State than that in which the richest are accounted the best. But what can be nobler than the government of the State by virtue? For then the man who rules others is not himself a slave to any passion, but has already acquired for himself all those qualities to which he is training and summoning his fellows. Such a man imposes no laws upon the people that he does not obey himself, but puts his own life before his fellow-citizens as their law. If a single individual of this character could order all things properly in a State, there would be no need of more than one ruler; or if the citizens as a body could see what was best and agree upon it, no one would desire a selected group of rulers. It has been the difficulty of formulating policies that has transferred the power from a king to a larger number; and the perversity and rashness of popular assemblies that have transferred it from the many to the few. Thus, between the weakness of a single ruler and the rashness of the many, aristocracies have occupied that intermediate position which represents the utmost moderation; and in a State ruled by its best men, the citizens must necessarily enjoy the greatest happiness, being freed from all cares and worries, when once they have entrusted the preservation of their tranquillity to others, whose duty it is to guard it vigilantly and never to allow the people to think that their interests are being neglected by their rulers. For that equality of legal rights of which free peoples are so fond cannot be maintained (for the people themselves, though free and un-restrained, give very many special powers to many individuals, and create great distinctions among men and the honours granted to them), and what is called equality is really most inequitable. For when equal honour is given to the highest and the lowest—for men of both types must exist in every nation—then this very "fairness" is most

unfair; but this cannot happen in States ruled by their best citizens. These arguments and others like them, Laelius, are approximately those which are advanced by men who consider this form of government the best.

XXXV. *Laelius.* But what about yourself, Scipio? Which of these three forms do you consider the best?

Scipio. You are right to ask which I consider the best of the three, for I do not approve of any of them when employed by itself, and consider the form which is a combination of all of them superior to any single one of them. But if I were compelled to approve one single unmixed form, [I might choose] the kingship . . . the name of king seems like that of father to us, since the king provides for the citizens as if they were his own children, and is more eager to protect them than . . . to be sustained by the care of one man who is the most virtuous and most eminent. But here are the aristocrats, with the claim that they can do this more effectively, and that there will be more wisdom in the counsels of several than in those of one man, and an equal amount of fairness and scrupulousness. And here also are the people, shouting with a loud voice that they are willing to obey neither one nor a few, that nothing is sweeter than liberty even to wild beasts, and that all who are slaves, whether to a king or to an aristocracy, are deprived of liberty. Thus kings attract us by our affection for them, aristocracies by their wisdom, and popular governments by their freedom, so that in comparing them it is difficult to say which one prefers. . . .

XLII. *Scipio.* When I have set forth my ideas in regard to the form of State which I consider the best, I shall have to take up in greater detail those changes to which States are liable, though I think it will not be at all easy for any such changes to take place in the State which I have in mind. But the first and most certain of these changes is the one that takes place in kingships: when the king begins to be unjust, that form of government is immediately at an end, and the king has become a tyrant. This is the worst sort of government, though closely related to the best. If the best men overthrow it, as usually happens, then the State is in the second of its three stages; for this form is similar to a kingship, being one in which a paternal council of leading men makes good provision for the people's welfare. But if the people themselves have killed or driven out the tyrant, they govern rather moderately, as long as they are wise and prudent, and, delighting in their exploit, they endeavour to maintain the government they have themselves set up. But if the people ever rebel against a just king and deprive him of his kingdom, or, as happens more frequently, taste the blood of the aristocracy and subject the whole State to their own caprices (and do not dream, Laelius, that any sea or any conflagration is so powerful that it cannot be more easily subdued than an unbridled multitude enjoying unwonted power), then we have a condition which is splendidly described by Plato, if only I can reproduce his description in Latin; it is difficult, but I will attempt it.

XLIII. He says: "When the insatiable throats of the people have become dry with the thirst for liberty, and, served by evil ministers, they have drained in their thirst a draught of liberty which, instead of being moderately tempered, is too strong for them, then, unless the magistrates and men of high rank are very mild and indulgent, serving them with liberty in generous quantities, the people persecute them, charge them with crime and impeach them, calling them despots, kings, and tyrants." I think you are acquainted with this passage.

Laelius. It is very familiar to me.

Scipio. He continues thus: "Those who follow the lead of prominent citizens are persecuted by such a people and called willing slaves; but those who, though in office, try to act like private citizens, and those private citizens who try to destroy all distinction between a private citizen and a magistrate are praised to the skies and loaded with honours. It necessarily follows in such a State that liberty prevails everywhere, to such an extent that not only are homes one and all without a

master, but the vice of anarchy extends even to the domestic animals, until finally the father fears his son, the son flouts his father, all sense of shame disappears, and all is so absolutely free that there is no distinction between citizen and alien; the schoolmaster fears and flatters his pupils, and pupils despise their masters; youths take on the gravity of age, and old men stoop to the games of youth, for fear they may be disliked by their juniors and seem to them too serious. Under such conditions even the slaves come to behave with unseemly freedom, wives have the same rights as their husbands, and in the abundance of liberty even the dogs, the horses, and the asses are so free in their running about that men must make way for them in the streets. Therefore," he concludes, "the final result of this boundless licence is that the minds of the citizens become so squeamish and sensitive that, if the authority of government is exercised in the smallest degree, they become angry and cannot bear it. On this account they begin to neglect the laws as well, and so finally are utterly without a master of any kind."

XLIV. *Laelius.* You have given us his description with great exactness.

Scipio. Well, to return now to my own style of discourse, he also says that from this exaggerated licence, which is the only thing such people call liberty, tyrants spring up as from a root, and are, as it were, engendered. For just as an excess of power in the hands of the aristocrats results in the overthrow of an aristocracy, so liberty itself reduces a people who possess it in too great degree to servitude. Thus everything which is in excess—when, for instance, either in the weather, or in the fields, or in men's bodies, conditions have been too favourable—is usually changed into its opposite; and this is especially true in States, where such excess of liberty either in nations or in individuals turns into an excess of servitude. This extreme liberty gives birth to a tyrant and the utterly unjust and cruel servitude of the tyranny. For out of such an ungoverned, or rather, untamed, populace someone is usually chosen as leader against those leading citizens who have already been subjected to persecution and cast down from their leadership—some bold and depraved man, who shamelessly harasses oftentimes even those who have deserved well of the State, and curries favour with the people by bestowing upon them the property of others as well as his own. To such a man, because he has much reason to be afraid if he remains a private citizen, official power is given and continually renewed; he is also surrounded by armed guards, as was Pisistratus at Athens; and finally he emerges as a tyrant over the very people who have raised him to power. If the better citizens overthrow such a tyrant, as often happens, then the State is re-established; but if it is the bolder sort who do so, then we have that oligarchy which is only a tyranny of another kind. This same form of government also arises from the excellent rule of an aristocracy, when some bad influence turns the leading citizens themselves from the right path. Thus the ruling power of the State, like a ball, is snatched from kings by tyrants, from tyrants by aristocrats or the people, and from them again by an oligarchical faction or a tyrant, so that no single form of government ever maintains itself very long.

XLV. Since this is true, the kingship, in my opinion, is by far the best of the three primary forms, but a moderate and balanced form of government which is a combination of the three good simple forms is preferable even to the kingship. For there should be a supreme and royal element in the State, some power also ought to be granted to the leading citizens, and certain matters should be left to the judgment and desires of the masses. Such a constitution, in the first place, offers in a high degree a sort of equality, which is a thing free men can hardly do without for any considerable length of time, and, secondly, it has stability. For the primary forms already mentioned degenerate easily into the corresponding perverted forms, the king being replaced by a despot, the aristocracy by an oligarchical faction, and the people by a mob and anarchy; but whereas these forms are frequently changed into new ones, this does not usually happen in the case of the mixed and evenly balanced constitution, except through great faults in the governing class. For there is no reason for a change when every citizen is firmly established in his own station, and there underlies it no perverted form into which it can plunge and sink.

On the Laws

BOOK I

V. *Atticus.* I consider it a logical thing that, since you have already written a treatise on the constitution of the ideal State, you should also write one on its laws. For I note that this was done by your beloved Plato, whom you admire, revere above all others, and love above all others.

Marcus. Is it your wish, then, that, as he discussed the institutions of States and the ideal laws with Clinias and the Spartan Megillus in Crete on a summer day amid the cypress groves and forest paths of Cnossus, sometimes walking about, sometimes resting—you recall his description—we, in like manner, strolling or taking our ease among these stately poplars on the green and shady river bank, shall discuss the same subjects along somewhat broader lines than the practice of the courts calls for?

A. I should certainly like to hear such a conversation.

M. What does Quintus say?

Reprinted by permission of the publisher from *De Legibus* by Cicero, translated by Clinton Walker Keyes, Cambridge, Mass.: Harvard University Press. Copyright © 1928 by the President and Fellows of Harvard College.

Q. No other subject would suit me better.

M. And you are wise, for you must understand that in no other kind of discussion can one bring out so clearly what Nature's gifts to man are, what a wealth of most excellent possessions the human mind enjoys, what the purpose is, to strive after and accomplish which we have been born and placed in this world, what it is that unites men, and what natural fellowship there is among them. For it is only after all these things have been made clear that the origin of Law and Justice can be discovered.

A. Then you do not think that the science of law is to be derived from the praetor's edict, as the majority do now, or from the Twelve Tables, as people used to think, but from the deepest mysteries of philosophy?

M. Quite right; for in our present conversation, Pomponius, we are not trying to learn how to protect ourselves legally, or how to answer clients' questions. Such problems may be important, and in fact they are; for in former times many eminent men made a specialty of their solution, and at present one person performs this duty with the greatest authority and skill. But in our present investigation we intend to cover the whole range of universal Justice and Law in such a way that our own civil law, as it is called, will be confined to a small and narrow corner. For we must explain the nature of Justice, and this must be sought for in the nature of man; we must also consider the laws by which States ought to be governed; then we must deal with the enactments and decrees of nations which are already formulated and put in writing; and among these the civil law, as it is called, of the Roman people will not fail to find a place.

VI. *Q.* You probe deep, and seek, as you should, the very fountain-head, to find what we are after, brother. And those who teach the civil law in any other way are teaching not so much the path of justice as of litigation.

M. There you are mistaken, Quintus, for it is rather ignorance of the law than knowledge of it that leads to litigation. But that will come later; now let us investigate the origins of Justice.

Well then, the most learned men have determined to begin with Law, and it would seem that they are right, if, according to their definition, Law is the highest reason, implanted in Nature, which commands what ought to be done and forbids the opposite. This reason, when firmly fixed and fully developed in the human mind, is Law. And so they believe that Law is intelligence, whose natural function it is to command right conduct and forbid wrongdoing. They think that this quality has derived its name in Greek from the idea of granting to every man his own, and in our language I believe it has been named from the idea of choosing. For as they have attributed the idea of fairness to the word law, so we have given it that of selection, though both ideas properly belong to Law. Now if this is correct, as I think it to be in general, then the origin of Justice is to be found in Law, for Law is a natural force; it is the mind and reason of the intelligent man, the standard by which Justice and Injustice are measured. But since our whole discussion has to do with the reasoning of the populace, it will sometimes be necessary to speak in the popular manner, and give the name of law to that which in written form decrees whatever it wishes, either by command or prohibition. For such is the crowd's definition of law. But in determining what Justice is, let us begin with that supreme Law which had its origin ages before any written law existed or any State had been established.

Q. Indeed that will be preferable and more suitable to the character of the conversation we have begun.

M. Well, then, shall we seek the origin of Justice itself at its fountain-head? For when that is discovered we shall undoubtedly have a standard by which the things we are seeking may be tested.

Q. I think that is certainly what we must do.

A. Put me down also as agreeing with your brother's opinion.

M. Since, then, we must retain and preserve that constitution of the State which Scipio proved to be the best in the six books devoted to the subject, and all our laws must be fitted to that type of State, and since we must also inculcate good morals, and not prescribe everything in writing, I shall seek the root of Justice in Nature, under whose guidance our whole discussion must be conducted.

A. Quite right. Surely with her as our guide, it will be impossible for us to go astray.

VII. *M.* Do you grant us, then, Pomponius (for I am aware of what Quintus thinks), that it is by the might of the immortal gods, or by their nature, reason, power, mind, will, or any other term which may make my meaning clearer, that all Nature is governed? For if you do not admit it, we must begin our argument with this problem before taking up anything else.

A. Surely I will grant it, if you insist upon it, for the singing of the birds about us and the babbling of the streams relieve me from all fear that I may be overheard by any of my comrades in the School.

M. Yet you must be careful; for it is their way to become very angry at times, as virtuous men will; and they will not tolerate your treason, if they hear of it, to the opening passage of that excellent book, in which the author has written, "God troubles himself about nothing, neither his own concerns nor those of others."

A. Continue, if you please, for I am eager to learn what my admission will lead to.

M. I will not make the argument long. Your admission leads us to this: that animal which we call man, endowed with foresight and quick intelligence, complex, keen, possessing memory, full of reason and prudence, has been given a certain distinguished status by the supreme God who created him; for he is the only one among so many different kinds and varieties of living beings who has a share in reason and thought, while all the rest are deprived of it. But what is more divine, I will not say in man only, but in all heaven and earth, than reason? And reason, when it is full grown and perfected, is rightly called wisdom. Therefore, since there is nothing better than reason, and since it exists both in man and God, the first common possession of man and God is reason. But those who have reason in common must also have right reason in common. And since right reason is Law, we must believe that men have Law also in common with the gods. Further, those who share Law must also share Justice; and those who share these are to be regarded as members of the same commonwealth. If indeed they obey the same authorities and powers, this is true in a far greater degree; but as a matter of fact they do obey this celestial system, the divine mind, and the God of transcendent power. Hence we must now conceive of this whole universe as one commonwealth of which both gods and men are members. . . .

X. *A.* Ye immortal gods, how far back you go to find the origins of Justice! And you discourse so eloquently that I not only have no desire to hasten on to the consideration of the civil law, concerning which I was expecting you to speak, but I should have no objection to your spending even the entire day on your present topic; for the matters which you have taken up, no doubt, merely as preparatory to another subject, are of greater import than the subject itself to which they form an introduction.

M. The points which are now being briefly touched upon are certainly important; but out of all the material of the philosophers' discussions, surely there comes nothing more valuable than the full realization that we are born for Justice, and that right is based, not upon men's opinions, but upon Nature. This fact will immediately be plain if you once get a clear conception of man's fellowship and union with his fellowmen. For no single thing is so like another, so exactly its counterpart, as all of us are to one another. Nay, if bad habits and false beliefs did not twist the weaker minds and turn them in whatever direction they are inclined, no one would be so like his own self as all men would be like all others. And so, however we may define man, a single definition will apply to all. This is a sufficient proof that there is no difference in kind between man and man; for if there were, one definition could not be applicable to all men; and indeed reason, which alone raises us above the level of the beasts and enables us to draw inferences, to prove and disprove, to discuss and solve problems, and to come to conclusions, is certainly common to us all, and, though varying in what it learns, at least in the capacity to learn it is invariable. For the same things are invariably perceived by the senses, and those things which stimulate the senses, stimulate them in the same way in all men; and those rudimentary beginnings of intelligence to which I have referred, which are imprinted on our minds, are imprinted on all minds alike; and speech, the mind's interpreter, though differing in the choice of words, agrees in the sentiments expressed. In fact, there is no human being of any race who, if he finds a guide, cannot attain to virtue.

XI. The similarity of the human race is clearly marked in its evil tendencies as well as in its goodness. For pleasure also attracts all men; and even though it is an enticement to vice, yet it has some likeness to what is naturally good. For it delights us by its lightness and agreeableness; and for this reason, by an error of thought, it is embraced as something wholesome. It is through a similar misconception that we shun death as though it were a dissolution of nature, and cling to life because it keeps us in the sphere in which we were born; and that we look upon pain as one of the greatest of evils, not only because of its cruelty, but also because it seems to lead to the destruction of nature. In the same way, on account of the similarity between moral worth and renown, those who are publicly honoured are considered happy, while those who do not attain fame are thought miserable. Troubles, joys, desires, and fears haunt the minds of all men without distinction, and even if different men have different beliefs, that does not prove, for example, that it is not the same quality of superstition that besets those races which worship dogs and cats as gods, as that which torments other races. But what nation does not love courtesy, kindliness, gratitude, and remembrance of favours bestowed? What people does not hate and despise the haughty, the wicked, the cruel, and the ungrateful? Inasmuch as these considerations prove to us that the whole human race is

bound together in unity, it follows, finally, that knowledge of the principles of right living is what makes men better. . . .

XV. But the most foolish notion of all is the belief that everything is just which is found in the customs or laws of nations. Would that be true, even if these laws had been enacted by tyrants? If the well-known Thirty had desired to enact a set of laws at Athens, or if the Athenians without exception were delighted by the tyrants' laws, that would not entitle such laws to be regarded as just, would it? No more, in my opinion, should that law be considered just which a Roman interrex proposed, to the effect that a dictator might put to death with impunity any citizen he wished, even without a trial. For Justice is one; it binds all human society, and is based on one Law, which is right reason applied to command and prohibition. Whoever knows not this Law, whether it has been recorded in writing anywhere or not, is without Justice.

But if Justice is conformity to written laws and national customs, and if, as the same persons claim, everything is to be tested by the standard of utility, then anyone who thinks it will be profitable to him will, if he is able, disregard and violate the laws. It follows that Justice does not exist at all, if it does not exist in Nature, and if that form of it which is based on utility can be overthrown by that very utility itself. And if Nature is not to be considered the foundation of Justice, that will mean the destruction [of the virtues on which human society depends]. For where then will there be a place for generosity, or love of country, or loyalty, or the inclination to be of service to others or to show gratitude for favours received? For these virtues originate in our natural inclination to love our fellow-men, and this is the foundation of Justice. Otherwise not merely consideration for men but also rites and pious observances in honour of the gods are done away with; for I think that these ought to be maintained, not through fear, but on account of the close relationship which exists between man and God.

XVI. But if the principles of Justice were founded on the decrees of peoples, the edicts of princes, or the decisions of judges, then Justice would sanction robbery and adultery and forgery of wills, in case these acts were approved by the votes or decrees of the populace. But if so great a power belongs to the decisions and decrees of fools that the laws of Nature can be changed by their votes, then why do they not ordain that what is bad and baneful shall be considered good and salutary? Or, if a law can make Justice out of In-justice, can it not also make good out of bad? But in fact we can perceive the difference between good laws and bad by referring them to no other stan-dard than Nature; indeed, it is not merely Justice and Injustice which are distinguished by Nature, but also and without exception things which are honourable and dishonourable. For since an in-telligence common to us all makes things known to us and formulates them in our minds, honour-able actions are ascribed by us to virtue, and dis-honourable actions to vice; and only a madman would conclude that these judgments are matters of opinion, and not fixed by Nature. For even what we, by a misuse of the term, call the virtue of a tree or of a horse, is not a matter of opinion, but is based on Nature. And if that is true, honourable and dishonourable actions must also be distin-guished by Nature. For if virtue in general is to be tested by opinion, then its several parts must also be so tested; who, therefore, would judge a man of prudence and, if I may say so, hard common sense, not by his own character but by some exter-nal circumstance? For virtue is reason completely developed; and this certainly is natural; therefore everything honourable is likewise natural.

XVII. For just as truth and falsehood, the logical and illogical, are judged by themselves and not by anything else, so the steadfast and continu-ous use of reason in the conduct of life, which is virtue, and also inconstancy, which is vice, [are judged] by their own nature.

[Or, when a farmer judges the quality of a tree by nature,] shall we not use the same standard in regard to the characters of young men? Then shall we judge character by Nature, and judge virtue and vice, which result from character, by

some other standard? But if we adopt the same standard for them, must we not refer the hon-ourable and the base to Nature also? Whatever good thing is praiseworthy must have within itself something which deserves praise, for goodness itself is good by reason not of opinion but of Nature. For, if this were not true, men would also be happy by reason of opinion; and what state-ment could be more absurd than that? Wherefore since both good and evil are judged by Nature and are natural principles, surely honourable and base actions must also be distinguished in a simi-lar way and referred to the standard of Nature. But we are confused by the variety of men's be-liefs and by their disagreements, and because this same variation is not found in the senses, we think that Nature has made these accurate, and say that those things about which different people have different opinions and the same people not always identical opinions are unreal. However, this is far from being the case. For our senses are not per-verted by parent, nurse, teacher, poet, or the stage, nor led astray by popular feeling; but against our minds all sorts of plots are constantly being laid, either by those whom I have just mentioned, who, taking possession of them while still tender and unformed, colour and bend them as they wish, or else by that enemy which lurks deep within us, entwined in our every sense—that counterfeit of good, which is, however, the mother of all evils—pleasure. Corrupted by her allurements, we fail to discern clearly what things are by Nature good, because the same seductiveness and itching does not attend them.

XVIII. To close now our discussion of this whole subject, the conclusion, which stands clearly before our eyes from what has already been said, is this: Justice and all things honourable are to be sought for their own sake. And indeed all good men love fairness in itself and Justice in itself, and it is unnatural for a good man to make such a mistake as to love what does not deserve love for itself alone. Therefore Justice must be sought and cultivated for her own sake; and if this is true of Justice, it is also true of equity; and if this is the case with equity, then all the other virtues are also to be cherished for their own sake. What of generosity? Is it disinterested or does it look to a recompense? If a man is kind without any reward, then it is disinterested; but if he receives payment, then it is hired. It cannot be doubted that he who is called generous or kind answers the call of duty, not of gain. Therefore equity also demands no reward or price; consequently it is sought for its own sake. And the same motive and purpose characterize all the virtues.

In addition, if it be true that virtue is sought for the sake of other benefits and not for its own sake, there will be only one virtue, which will most properly be called a vice. For in proportion as anyone makes his own advantage absolutely the sole standard of all his actions, to that extent he is absolutely not a good man; therefore those who measure virtue by the reward it brings believe in the existence of no virtue except vice. For where shall we find a kindly man, if no one does a kindness for the sake of anyone else than himself? Who can be considered grateful, if even those who repay favours have no real consideration for those to whom they repay them? What becomes of that sacred thing, friendship, if even the friend himself is not loved for his own sake, "with the whole heart," as people say? Why, according to this theory, a friend should even be deserted and cast aside as soon as there is no longer hope of benefit and profit from his friendship! But what could be more inhuman than that? If, on the other hand, friendship is to be sought for its own sake, then the society of our fellow-men, fairness, and Justice, are also to be sought for their own sake. If this is not the case then there is no such thing as Justice at all, for the very height of injustice is to seek pay for Justice.

AUGUSTINE

~

INTRODUCTION

PAUL J. WEITHMAN

Augustine (354–430 CE) was born in Thagaste in a part of northern Africa that is included in present-day Algeria but was then one of the backwaters of the Roman Empire. He was a promising young man who received the education typical of a well-schooled provincial. His education, first in Thagaste and then in Carthage, emphasized the Latin classics. A gifted writer and speaker, he became a teacher of rhetoric in Thagaste. Augustine's early successes sparked his aspirations for achievement in the larger world. In 383 he left North Africa for Italy and in 384 settled in Milan to teach rhetoric. He soon became disillusioned with his early careerism and retired to study philosophy in 386. In 387, after a dramatic conversion, Augustine was baptized a Christian. He returned to North Africa in 388 and was ordained a priest in 391. Intending to lead a quiet life, he was instead consecrated bishop of Hippo in 395.

Augustine was to live and serve in Hippo for the remaining thirty-five years of his life. He produced a vast literary corpus of sermons, commentaries, treatises, and letters while attending to the daily administrative duties of an important church official. But the events of Augustine's professional life are merely visible peaks pushed upward by great subterranean movements. The real drama of Augustine's life was interior. His was a riveting spiritual and intellectual journey that led him from the ambitions of a young rhetorician to the monastic life, from there to the episcopacy of Hippo, and thence to accomplishments that make him one of the greatest theologians of Latin Christianity. Augustine chronicles the first thirty-three years of this journey in his *Confessions*, a classic of Western literature.

Augustine's interior drama was played out against the backdrop of the late Roman Empire. It is hard to overstate Rome's importance for his life and thought. He was educated in Latin, the lingua franca of the empire and a language he spoke and wrote with consummate skill. For a time, he aspired to prominence within Rome and gravitated toward its center. He imbibed Rome's literature and its history. He absorbed and then reacted against its culture and mores. It was the most powerful empire the world had ever known. He thought its evident decline in his own adulthood signaled what he called the "old age of the world." The invasion of Rome by the Goths provided the occasion for his greatest work, *The City of God*, a work in which Rome's accomplishments typify the glories sought and achieved by human societies. In his old age Augustine saw Rome's grip on North Africa being broken. When he died in 430, the Vandals were besieging Hippo. Augustine's political thought was profoundly conditioned by his reflections on the moral and political rise and decay of Rome.

Claims about Augustine's political philosophy must be made with care. Augustine never wrote a book or a treatise devoted to such philosophy. Discussions of politics and political philosophy crop up often in his work, but Augustine is primarily a theologian rather than a philosopher. It is questionable whether he thought political philosophy has a subject matter that can be cleanly marked off from that of theology. His own discussions of politics draw heavily on theology, as well as on psychology, history, and social theory. Even so, it is possible to assemble a coherent body of political thought from remarks and discussions scattered throughout Augustine's many writings, especially from his monumental *The City of God*.

Augustine began writing *The City of God* after Rome was sacked in 410. The sack caused many wealthy and cultured Romans to flee the city. In due course some found their way to Augustine's part of North Africa. Trying to comprehend what had happened, many of them blamed the sack on Rome's abandonment of the traditional deities who had long protected it in favor of a Christian god whose impotence left them vulnerable. Thus the tragedy that befell Rome was, they alleged, the consequence of the conversion of the empire under Constantine nearly a century before. Augustine took up his pen to answer the charge and defend Christianity. When he finally put it down fourteen years later, he had completed a massive work of theology, polemical history, philosophy of culture, and social psychology.

In *The City of God* Augustine argued that despite the surface diversity of language, nations, and ways of life, human beings are most fundamentally divided by a single cleavage: that between those who belong to the City of God and those who belong to the Earthly City. This is not a divide between citizens of two different political entities, like Rome and Carthage, nor is it a divide between the institutional church and the world. Augustine is emphatic that members of both the City of God and the Earthly City can be found in any political society. Members of both cities can also be found both inside and outside the church. The difference between the members of the two cities is a difference in their most fundamental orientations to what is good. It is a difference, Augustine would say, in their most fundamental loves.

Augustine distinguishes two ways of loving that are especially important. One is what he calls "use"; the other is what he calls "enjoyment." We enjoy things when we love them for their own sake. We use them when we love them for the sake of something else. Only God is worthy of being loved entirely for His own sake, Augustine thinks, and only the enjoyment of God can quiet all our desires. Other things and persons, including ourselves, ought to be loved in relation to God. Human sinfulness is a turn away from God. It is a tendency to love oneself and to love other things in relation to self. This elevation of the self and the self's desires Augustine associates with the sin of pride. Augustine thinks that all human beings are sinful to some extent. All, he thinks, are at least somewhat tainted by the sin of pride. At the same time, Augustine thinks all human beings retain a desire for God. This shows itself in a desire for true peace, for the quiescence of desire that only love of God can bring. Because all human beings are prone to love of self while they retain at least a confused love of God, all human beings, Augustine thinks, have divided wills. This tension within each person is responsible for the tensions that mar even the most intimate of human relationships and are a salient feature of political life.

Despite the fact that all human beings have divided wills, Augustine thinks some are fundamentally oriented toward God while others love themselves. Those whose fundamental orientation is toward God constitute the City of God. This is a city dispersed in time and space and includes the angels and the saints as well as some of those in earthly life. Those whose fundamental orientation is toward the self constitute the Earthly City. The latter enjoy the world and are at home in it. Those of the former who are in this world are, Augustine says, merely "on pilgrimage" in it. Citizens of both cities live side by side in every political society and in the church, to be sorted out only at the last judgment.

In Book XIX of *The City of God*, Augustine says that earthly peace—peace within an earthly society and peace between societies—is a compromise between members of the two cities. This suggests that politics is driven by conflicts among members of the two groups. In fact, Augustine's analysis of politics is considerably more subtle. Augustine does think that those who most fundamentally love themselves also love glory, fame, and domination. In *The City of God* Augustine seizes on the love of domination as one of the driving forces of political history. It accounts for why human beings build empires. It accounts for the pride that citizens of an empire take in its power and for the patriotism that makes them willing to die for it. The Romans' love of domination helps to account for the hegemony of the Roman Empire over Augustine's world. It also accounts for the conflict, tension, and disorder that erupt within groups. But Augustine would be quick to point out that because all human beings are divided, even those who love God can be moved by pride, love of domination, and undue attachment to material goods. They too need to be humbled and disciplined.

Humility and discipline are exactly what Augustine thinks political authority exists to provide. Augustine thinks of political power as the power to control adults through coercion and the threat of coercion. If human beings had remained sinless, this form of authority would not be needed. Human groups could have been directed by forms of authority more like paternal authority than political. That is why Augustine says at the beginning of Book XIX, chapter 15, that according to the order of nature, human beings have dominion over animals but not over other human beings. Political authority is the divinely ordained response to human sinfulness and the disordered loves that result from sinfulness.

The proper aims of political authority must be limited because the means at its disposal are of limited efficacy. One of Augustine's constant themes is the opacity of the human heart. Human beings cannot fully know their own or others' motives. It follows that those in political authority cannot know the hearts and minds of their subjects, still less restore their hearts and minds to order by the use of force. Since perfect peace, Augustine says, is perfect tranquility and order within and among human beings, political authority can hope only to bring about a partial and imperfect peace. The most it can hope to do is restrain people so that they are not too harmful to one another. By doing so, it establishes the limited peace that all need in order to live. Members of the Earthly City enjoy this peace and try to establish it on their own terms. Members of the City of God use it in the course of their pilgrimage, but they do not enjoy it.

By claiming that political authority cannot make human beings good but can only restrain their wickedness, Augustine takes a firm stand against a tradition of republican political thought known to him through the writings of Cicero. One of the best known of Cicero's works is *De Re Publica*, a dialogue that Augustine knew well. The main character in the dialogue is Scipio Africanus the younger, the Roman general who defeated Carthage in 136 BCE. In a passage to which Augustine refers in Book XIX of *The City of God*, Cicero attributes to Scipio the view that political societies like Rome are partnerships of justice and that their strength depends upon the virtue of their citizens. Augustine notes that justice requires giving to each his due. He continues that it therefore requires worshipping the true God. Since the true God was not worshipped in Rome at the time of Cicero, Augustine thinks it follows that Rome was unjust. If Scipio's definition is correct, then Rome was not a society. Furthermore, since Augustine insists that human beings can be truly virtuous only when they worship the true God, it follows that the Romans whose virtue Scipio credits with preserving their city were not really virtuous at all.

This conclusion is one Augustine repeats throughout his writings, but most forcefully in *The City of God*. Some of the most rhetorically powerful passages in that work are those in which he recalls episodes of injustice and brutality from Roman history that apologist historians of the empire prefer to overlook. Again and again he insists that those who built and sustained Rome were moved by an idolatrous pride in their city and by desires for its fame and domination. Because these vices required some self-restraint, they were able to masquerade as the virtues for which Augustine thinks Scipio mistook them. The republican view of politics, according to which political life develops the virtues that are needed to sustain political society, is one Augustine thinks he has undercut by the time he arrives at Book XIX.

But if a society like Rome does not depend upon or develop the virtues of citizens, what does sustain it? In Book XIX of *The City of God*, Augustine famously offers an alternative definition of society. According to his definition, a society is a group united by a common object of love. To assess the moral quality of a society, it is necessary to look at what it loves. Because earthly societies contain both those who love God and those who exalt themselves, both members of the City of God and members of the Earthly City, Augustine thinks that what holds societies together is simply their citizens' common desire for peace. The peace the Romans tried to establish was a peace on their own terms, one that gave them dominion over others. The peace of this most powerful of empires, and the peace of all other earthly societies as well, therefore pales beside the true peace of the City of God. Thus in Book XIX Augustine realizes the aim of *The City of God*, which he says in Book I is to glorify the City of God by comparing it with "cities of other allegiance."

The best biography of Augustine in any language is Peter Brown's *Augustine of Hippo* (Berkeley: University of California Press, 1967). Relatively few works on Augustine's political thought are available in English. Herbert Deane's *The Political and Social Ideas of St. Augustine* (New York: Columbia University Press, 1963) is the most useful; J. N. Figgis's *The Political Aspects of St. Augustine's "City of God"* (London: Longman's, 1921) is dated but should not be overlooked. R. A. Markus's *Saeculum* (Cambridge: Cambridge University Press, 1970) is a classic work that bears on Augustine's political thought.

The City of God

BOOK XIX

12.

Anyone who joins me in an examination, however slight, of human affairs, and the human nature we all share, recognizes that just as there is no man who does not wish for joy, so there is no man who does not wish for peace. Indeed, even when men choose war, their only wish is for victory; which shows that their desire in fighting is for peace with glory. For what is victory but the conquest of the opposing side? And when this is achieved, there will be peace. Even wars, then are waged with peace as their object, even when they are waged by those who are concerned to exercise their warlike prowess, either in command or in the actual fighting. Hence it is an established fact that peace is the desired end of war. For every man is in quest of peace, even in waging war, whereas no one is in quest of war when making peace. In fact, even when men wish a present state of peace to be disturbed they do so not because they hate peace, but because they desire the present peace to be exchanged for one that suits their wishes. Thus their desire is not that there should not be peace but that it should be the kind of peace they wish for. Even in the extreme case when they have separated themselves from others by sedition, they cannot achieve their aim unless they maintain some sort of semblance of peace with their confederates in conspiracy. Moreover, even robbers, to ensure greater efficiency and security in their assaults on the peace of the rest of mankind, desire to preserve peace with their associates.

Indeed, one robber may be so unequalled in strength and so wary of having anyone to share his plans that he does not trust any associate, but plots his crimes and achieves his successes by himself, carrying off his booty after overcoming and dispatching such as he can; yet even so he maintains some kind of shadow of peace, at least with those whom he cannot kill, and from whom he wishes to conceal his activities. At the same time, he is anxious, of course, to be at peace in his own home, with his wife and children and any other members of his household; without doubt he is delighted to have them obedient to his beck and call. For if this does not happen, he is indignant; he scolds and punishes; and, if need be, he employs savage measures to impose on his household a peace which, he feels, cannot exist unless all the other elements in the same domestic society are subject to one head; and this head, in his own home, is himself. Thus, if he were offered the servitude of a larger number, of a city, maybe, or a whole nation, on the condition that they should all show the same subservience he had demanded from his household, then he would no longer lurk like a brigand in his hide-out; he would raise himself on high as a king for all to see—although the same greed and malignity would persist in him.

We see, then, that all men desire to be at peace with their own people while wishing to impose their will upon those people's lives. For even when they wage war on others, their wish is to make those opponents their own people, if they can—to subject them, and to impose on them their own conditions of peace.

Let us, however, suppose such a man as is described in the verse of epic legends, a creature so unsociable and savage that they perhaps preferred to call him a semi-human rather than a human being. Now although his kingdom was the solitude of a dreadful cavern, and although he was so

From Saint Augustine, *Concerning the City of God Against the Pagans*, translated by Henry Bettenson (London: Penguin Books, 2003).

unequalled in wickedness that a name was found for him derived from that quality (he was called Cacus, and *kakos* is the Greek word for "wicked"); although he had no wife with whom to exchange endearments, no children to play with when little or to give orders to when they were a little bigger, no friends with whom to enjoy a chat, not even his father, Vulcan (he was happier than his father only in this important respect—that he did not beget another such monster as himself); although he never gave anything to anyone, but took what he wanted from anyone he could and removed, when he could, anyone he wished to remove; despite all this, in the very solitude of his cave, the floor of which, in Vergil's description, reeked ever with the blood of recent slaughter his only desire was for a peace in which no one should disturb him, and no man's violence, or the dread of it, should trouble his repose. Above all, he desired to be at peace with his own body; and in so far as he achieved this, all was well with him. He gave the orders and his limbs obeyed. But his mortal nature rebelled against him because of its insatiable desires, and stirred up the civil strife of hunger, intending to dissociate the soul from the body and to exclude it; and then he sought with all possible haste to pacify that mortal nature, and to that end he ravished, murdered, and devoured. And thus, for all his monstrous savagery, his aim was still to ensure peace, for the preservation of his life, by these monstrous and savage methods. Accordingly, if he had been willing to maintain, in relation to others also, the peace he was so busily concerned to preserve in his own case and in himself, he would not have been called wicked, or a monster, or semi-human. Or if it was his outward appearance and his belching of murky flames that frightened away human companions, it may be that it was not lust for inflicting injury but the necessity of preserving his life that made him so savage. Perhaps, after all, he never existed or, more probably, he was not like the description given by poetic fantasy; for if Cacus had not been excessively blamed, Hercules would have received inadequate praise. And therefore the existence of such a man, or rather semi-human, is discredited, as are many similar poetical fictions.

We observe, then, that even the most savage beasts, from whom Cacus derived the wild-beast side of his nature (he was in fact also called a semi-beast), safeguard their own species by a kind of peace, by coition, by begetting and bearing young, by cherishing them and rearing them; even though most of them are not gregarious but solitary—not, that is, like sheep, deer, doves, starlings, and bees, but like lions, wolves, foxes, eagles and owls. What tigress does not gently purr over her cubs, and subdue her fierceness to caress them? What kite, however solitary as he hovers over his prey, does not find a mate, build a nest, help to hatch the eggs, rear the young birds, and, as we may say, preserve with the mother of his family a domestic society as peaceful as he can make it? How much more strongly is a human being drawn by the laws of his nature, so to speak, to enter upon a fellowship with all his fellowmen and to keep peace with them, as far as lies in him. For even the wicked when they go to war do so to defend the peace of their own people, and desire to make all men their own people, if they can, so that all men and all things might together be subservient to one master. And how could that happen, unless they should consent to a peace of his dictation either through love or through fear? Thus pride is a perverted imitation of God. For pride hates a fellowship of equality under God, and seeks to impose its own dominion on fellow men, in place of God's rule. This means that it hates the just peace of God, and loves its own peace of injustice. And yet it cannot help loving peace of some kind or other. For no creature's perversion is so contrary to nature as to destroy the very last vestiges of its nature.

It comes to this, then; a man who has learnt to prefer right to wrong and the rightly ordered to the perverted, sees that the peace of the unjust, compared with the peace of the just, is not worthy even of the name of peace. Yet even what is perverted must of necessity be in, or derived from, or associated with—that is, in a sense, at peace with—some part of the order of things among which it has its being or of which it consists. Otherwise it would not exist at all. For instance if anyone were to hang upside-down, this position of the body and arrangement of the limbs is undoubtedly perverted, because what should be on top, according to the dictates of nature, is underneath, and what nature intends to be underneath is on top. This perverted attitude disturbs the peace of the flesh and causes distress for that reason. For all that, the breath is at peace with its body and is busily engaged for its preservation; that is why there is something to endure the pain. And even if the breath is finally driven from the body by its distresses, still, as long as the framework of the limbs holds together, what remains retains a kind of peace among the bodily parts; hence there is still something to hang there. And in that the earthly body pulls towards the earth, and pulls against the binding rope that holds it suspended, it tends towards the position of its own peace, and by what might be called the appeal of its weight, it demands a place where it may rest. And so even when it is by now lifeless and devoid of all sensation it does not depart from the peace of its natural position, either while possessed of it or while tending towards it. Again, if treatment with embalming fluids is applied to prevent the dissolution and disintegration of the corpse in its present shape, a kind of peace still connects the parts with one another and keeps the whole mass fixed in its earthly condition, an appropriate, and therefore a peaceable state.

On the other hand, if no preservative treatment is given, and the body is left for nature to take its course, there is for a time a kind of tumult in the corpse of exhalations disagreeable and offensive to our senses (for that is what we smell in putrefaction), which lasts until the body unites with the elements of the world as, little by little, and particle by particle, it vanishes into their peace. Nevertheless, nothing is in any way removed, in this process, from the control of the laws of the supreme Creator and Ruler who directs the peace of the whole scheme of things. For although minute animals are produced in the corpse of a larger animal, those little bodies, each and all of them, by the same law of their Creator, are subservient to their

little souls in the peace that preserves their lives. And even if the flesh of dead animals is devoured by other animals, in whatever direction it is taken, with whatever substances it is united, into whatever substances it is converted and transformed, it still finds itself subject to the same laws which are diffused throughout the whole of matter for the preservation of every mortal species, establishing peace by a harmony of congruous elements.

13.

The peace of the body, we conclude, is a tempering of the component parts in duly ordered proportion; the peace of the irrational soul is a duly ordered repose of the appetites; the peace of the rational soul is the duly ordered agreement of cognition and action. The peace of body and soul is the duly ordered life and health of a living creature; peace between mortal man and God is an ordered obedience, in faith, in subjection to an everlasting law; peace between men is an ordered agreement of mind with mind; the peace of a home is the ordered agreement among those who live together about giving and obeying orders; the peace of the Heavenly City is a perfectly ordered and perfectly harmonious fellowship in the enjoyment of God, and a mutual fellowship in God; the peace of the whole universe is the tranquillity of order—and order is the arrangement of things equal and unequal in a pattern which assigns to each its proper position.

It follows that the wretched, since, in so far as they are wretched, they are obviously not in a state of peace, lack the tranquillity of order, a state in which there is no disturbance of mind. In spite of that, because their wretchedness is deserved and just, they cannot be outside the scope of order. They are not, indeed, united with the blessed; yet it is by the law of order that they are sundered from them. And when they are free from disturbance of mind, they are adjusted to their situation, with however small a degree of harmony. Thus they have amongst them some tranquillity of order, and therefore some peace. But they are still wretched just because, although they enjoy some degree of serenity and freedom from suffering, they are not in a condition where they have the right to be serene and free from pain. They are yet more wretched, however, if they are not at peace with the law by which the natural order is governed. Now when they suffer, their peace is disturbed in the part where they suffer; and yet peace still continues in the part which feels no burning pain, and where the natural frame is not broken up. Just as there is life, then, without pain, whereas there can be no pain when there is no life, so there is peace without any war, but no war without some degree of peace. This is not a consequence of war as such, but of the fact that war is waged by or within persons who are in some sense natural beings—for they could have no kind of existence without some kind of peace as the condition of their being.

There exists, then, a nature in which there is no evil, in which, indeed, no evil can exist; but there cannot exist a nature in which there is no good. Hence not even the nature of the Devil himself is evil, in so far as it is a nature; it is perversion that makes it evil. And so the Devil did not stand firm in the truth, and yet he did not escape the judgement of the truth. He did not continue in the tranquillity of order; but that did not mean that he escaped from the power of the imposer of order. The good that God imparts, which the Devil has in his nature, does not withdraw him from God's justice by which his punishment is ordained. But God, in punishing, does not chastise the good which he created, but the evil which the Devil has committed. And God does not take away all that he gave to that nature; he takes something, and yet he leaves something, so that there may be some being left to feel pain at the deprivation.

Now this pain is in itself evidence of the good that was taken away and the good that was left. In fact, if no good had been left there could have been no grief for lost good. For a sinner is in a worse state if he rejoices in the loss of righteousness; but a sinner who feels anguish, though he may gain no good from his anguish, is at least grieving at the loss of salvation. And since righteousness and salvation are both good, and the loss of any good calls for grief rather than for joy (assuming that there is no compensation for the loss in the shape of a higher good—for example, righteousness of character is a higher good than health of body), the unrighteous man's grief in his punishment is more appropriate than his rejoicing in sin. Hence, just as delight in the abandonment of good, when a man sins, is evidence of a bad will, so grief at the loss of good, when a man is punished, is evidence of a good nature. For when a man grieves at the loss of the peace of his nature, his grief arises from some remnants of that peace, which ensure that his nature is still on friendly terms with itself. Moreover, it is entirely right that in the last punishment the wicked and ungodly should bewail in their agonies the loss of their "natural" goods, and realize that he who divested them of these goods with perfect justice is God, whom they despised when with supreme generosity he bestowed them.

God then, created all things in supreme wisdom and ordered them in perfect justice; and in establishing the mortal race of mankind as the greatest ornament of earthly things, he has given to mankind certain good things suitable to this life. These are: temporal peace, in proportion to the short span of a mortal life—the peace that consists in bodily health and soundness, and in fellowship with one's kind; and everything necessary to safeguard or recover this peace—those things, for example, which are appropriate and accessible to our senses: light, speech, air to breathe, water to drink, and whatever is suitable for the feeding and clothing of the body, for the care of the body and the adornment of the person. And all this is granted under the most equitable condition: that every mortal who uses aright such goods, goods designed to serve the peace of mortal men, shall receive goods greater in degree and superior in kind, namely, the peace of immortality, and the glory and honour appropriate to it in a life which is eternal for the enjoyment of God and of one's neighbour in God, whereas he who wrongly uses those mortal goods shall lose them, and shall not receive the blessings of eternal life.

15.

This relationship is prescribed by the order of nature, and it is in this situation that God created man. For he says, "Let him have lordship over the fish of the sea, the birds of the sky . . . and all the reptiles that crawl on the earth." He did not wish the rational being, made in his own image, to have dominion over any but irrational creatures, not man over man, but man over the beasts. Hence the first just men were set up as shepherds of flocks, rather than as kings of men, so that in this way also God might convey the message of what was required by the order of nature, and what was demanded by the deserts of sinners—for it is understood, of course, that the condition of slavery is justly imposed on the sinner. That is why we do not hear of a slave anywhere in the Scriptures until Noah, the just man, punished his son's sin with this word; and so that son deserved this name because of his misdeed, not because of his nature. The origin of the Latin word for slave, *servus*, is believed to be derived from the fact that those who by the laws of war could rightly be put to death by the conquerors, became *servi*, slaves, when they were preserved, receiving this name from their preservation. But even this enslavement could not have happened, if it were not for the deserts of sin. For even when a just war is fought it is in defence of his sin that the other side is contending; and victory, even when the victory falls to the wicked, is a humiliation visited on the conquered by divine judgement, either to correct or to punish their sins. We have a witness to this in Daniel, a man of God, who in captivity confesses to God his own sins and the sins of his people, and in devout grief testifies that they are the cause of that captivity. The first cause of slavery, then, is sin, whereby man was subjected to man in the condition of bondage; and this can only happen by the judgement of God, with whom there is no injustice, and who knows how to allot different punishments according to the deserts of the offenders.

Now, as our Lord above says, "Everyone who commits sin is sin's slave," and that is why, though many devout men are slaves to unrighteous masters, yet the masters they serve are not themselves free men; "for when a man is conquered by another he is also bound as a slave to his conqueror." And obviously it is a happier lot to be slave to a human being than to a lust; and, in fact, the most pitiless domination that devastates the hearts of men, is that exercised by this very lust for domination, to mention no others. However, in that order of peace in which men are subordinate to other men, humility is as salutary for the servants as pride is harmful to the masters. And yet by nature, in the condition in which God created man, no man is the slave either of man or of sin. But it remains true that slavery as a punishment is also ordained by that law which enjoins the preservation of the order of nature, and forbids its disturbance; in fact, if nothing had been done to contravene that law, there would have been nothing to require the discipline of slavery as a punishment. That explains also the Apostle's admonition to slaves, that they should be subject to their masters, and serve them loyally and willingly. What he means is that if they cannot be set free by their masters, they themselves may thus make their slavery, in a sense, free, by serving not with the slyness of fear, but with the fidelity of affection, until all injustice disappears and all human lordship and power is annihilated, and God is all in all.

16.

. . . Those who are genuine "fathers of their household" are concerned for the welfare of all in their households in respect of the worship and service of God, as if they were all their children, longing and praying that they may come to the heavenly home, where it will not be a necessary duty to give orders to men, because it will no longer be a necessary duty to be concerned for the welfare of those who are already in the felicity of that immortal state. But until that home is reached, the fathers have an obligation to exercise the authority of masters greater than the duty of slaves to put up with their condition as servants.

However, if anyone in the household is, through his disobedience, an enemy to the domestic peace, he is reproved by a word, or by a blow, or any other kind of punishment that is just and legitimate, to the extent allowed by human society; but this is for the benefit of the offender, intended to readjust him to the domestic peace from which he had broken away. For just as it is not an act of kindness to help a man, when the effect of the help is to make him lose a greater good, so it is not a blameless act to spare a man, when by so doing you let him fall into a greater sin. Hence the duty of anyone who would be blameless includes not only doing no harm to anyone but also restraining a man from sin or punishing his sin, so that either the man who is chastised may be corrected by his experience, or others may be deterred by his example. Now a man's house ought to be the beginning, or rather a small component part of the city, and every beginning is directed to some end of its own kind, and every component part contributes to the completeness of the whole of which it forms a part. The implication is quite apparent, that domestic peace contributes to the peace of the city—that is, the ordered harmony of those who live together in a house in the matter of giving and obeying orders, contributes to the ordered harmony concerning authority and obedience obtaining among the citizens. Consequently it is fitting that the father of a household should take his rules from the law of the city, and govern his household in such a way that it fits in with the peace of the city.

17.

But a household of human beings whose life is not based on faith is in pursuit of an earthly peace based on the things belonging to this temporal life, and on its advantages, whereas a household of human beings whose life is based on faith looks forward to the blessings which are promised as eternal in the future, making use of earthly and temporal things like a pilgrim in a foreign land, who does not let himself be taken in by them or distracted from his course towards God, but rather treats them as supports which help him more easily to bear the burdens of "the corruptible body which weighs heavy on the soul"; they must on no account be allowed to increase the load. Thus both kinds of men and both kinds of households alike make use of the things essential for this mortal life; but each has its own very different end in making use of them. So also the earthly city, whose life is not based on faith, aims at an earthly peace, and it limits the harmonious agreement of citizens concerning the giving and obeying of orders to the establishment of a kind of compromise between human wills about the things relevant to mortal life. In contrast, the Heavenly City—or rather that part of it which is on pilgrimage in this condition of mortality, and which lives on the basis of faith—must needs make use of this peace also, until this mortal state, for which this kind of peace is essential, passes away. And therefore, it leads what we may call a life of captivity in this earthly city as in a foreign land, although it has already received the promise of redemption, and the gift of the Spirit as a kind of pledge of it; and yet it does not hesitate to obey the laws of the earthly city by which those things which are designed for the support of this mortal life are regulated; and the purpose of this obedience is that, since this mortal condition is shared by both cities, a harmony may be preserved between them in things that are relevant to this condition.

But this earthly city has had some philosophers belonging to it whose theories are rejected by the teaching inspired by God. Either led astray by their own speculation or deluded by demons, these thinkers reached the belief that there are many gods who must be won over to serve human ends, and also that they have, as it were, different departments with different responsibilities attached. Thus the body is the department of one god, the mind that of another; and within the body itself, one god is in charge of the head, another of the neck and so on with each of the separate members.

Similarly, within the mind, one is responsible for natural ability, another for learning, another for anger, another for lust; and in the accessories of life there are separate gods over the departments of flocks, grain, wine, oil, forests, coinage, navigation, war and victory, marriage, birth, fertility, and so on. The Heavenly City, in contrast, knows only one God as the object of worship, and decrees, with faithful devotion, that he only is to be served with that service which the Greeks call *latreia*, which is due to God alone. And the result of this difference has been that the Heavenly City could not have laws of religion common with the earthly city, and in defence of her religious laws she was bound to dissent from those who thought differently and to prove a burdensome nuisance to them. Thus she had to endure their anger and hatred, and the assaults of persecution; until at length that City shattered the morale of her adversaries by the terror inspired by her numbers, and by the help she continually received from God.

While this Heavenly City, therefore, is on pilgrimage in this world, she calls out citizens from all nations and so collects a society of aliens, speaking all languages. She takes no account of any difference in customs, laws, and institutions, by which earthly peace is achieved and preserved—not that she annuls or abolishes any of those, rather, she maintains them and follows them (for whatever divergences there are among the diverse nations, those institutions have one single aim—earthly peace), provided that no hindrance is presented thereby to the religion which teaches that the one supreme and true God is to be worshipped. Thus even the Heavenly City in her pilgrimage here on earth makes use of the earthly peace and defends and seeks the compromise between human wills in respect of the provisions relevant to the mortal nature of man, so far as may be permitted without detriment to true religion and piety. In fact, that City relates the earthly peace to the heavenly peace, which is so truly peaceful that it should be regarded as the only peace deserving the name, at least in respect of the rational creation; for this peace is the perfectly ordered and completely harmonious fellowship in the enjoyment of God, and of each other in God. When we arrive at that state of peace, there will be no longer a life that ends in death, but a life that is life in sure and sober truth; there will be no animal body to "weigh down the soul" in its process of corruption; there will be a spiritual body with no cravings, a body subdued in every part to the will. This peace the Heavenly City possesses in faith while on its pilgrimage, and it lives a life of righteousness, based on this faith, having the attainment of that peace in view in every good action it performs in relation to God, and in relation to a neighbour, since the life of a city is inevitably a social life.

21.

This brings me to the place where I must fulfil, as briefly and clearly as I may, the promise I gave in the second book. I there promised that I would show that there never was a Roman commonwealth answering to the definitions advanced by Scipio in Cicero's *On the Republic*. For Scipio gives a brief definition of the state, or commonwealth, as the "weal of the people." Now if this is a true definition there never was a Roman commonwealth, because the Roman state was never the "weal of the people," according to Scipio's definition. For he defined a "people" as a multitude "united in association by a common sense of right and a community of interest." He explains in the discussion what he means by "a common sense of right," showing that a state cannot be maintained without justice, and where there is no true justice there can be no right. For any action according to right is inevitably a just action, while no unjust action can possibly be according to right. For unjust human institutions are not to be called or supposed to be institutions of right, since even they themselves say that right is what has flowed from the fount of justice; as for the notion of justice commonly put forward by some misguided thinkers, that it is "the interest of the strongest," they hold this to be a false conception.

Therefore, where there is no true justice there can be no "association of men united by a common sense of right," and therefore no people answering to the definition of Scipio, or Cicero. And if there is no people then there is no "weal of the people," but some kind of a mob, not deserving the name of a people. If, therefore, a commonwealth is the "weal of the people," and if a people does not exist where there is no "association by a common sense of right," and there is no right where there is no justice, the irresistible conclusion is that where there is no justice there is no commonwealth. Moreover, justice is that virtue which assigns to everyone his due. Then what kind of justice is it that takes a man away from the true God and subjects him to unclean demons? Is this to assign to every man his due? Or are we to say that a man is unjust when he takes an estate from a man who has bought it and hands it over to someone who has no right to it, while we give the name of just to a man who takes himself away from the Lord God who made him, and becomes the servant of malignant spirits?

There is, to be sure, in the same work, *On the Republic*, a most vigorous and powerful argument on behalf of justice against injustice. Earlier in the discussion a plea was put forward for injustice against justice, and it was alleged that a state cannot stand or be governed except by injustice, and it was posited as the strongest point in this case that it was unjust that men should be servants to other men as their masters; and yet an imperial city, the head of a great commonwealth, cannot rule its provinces except by adopting this injustice. Now it was urged in reply on the side of justice, that this situation is just, on the ground that servitude is in the interest of such men as the provincials, and that it is established for their benefit. when rightly established—that is, when unprincipled men are deprived of the freedom to do wrong with impunity. It was also asserted that the subjugated will be better off, because they were worse off before subjugation. In confirmation of this line of reasoning a notable illustration was adduced, ostensibly taken from nature. It was

stated thus: "How is it then that God rules man, the soul rules the body, the reason rules lust and the other perverted elements in the soul?" By this analogy it is shown plainly enough that servitude is beneficial for some men, and that servitude to God, at least, is beneficial to all.

Now in serving God the soul rightly commands the body, and in the soul itself the reason which is subject to its Lord God rightly commands the lusts and the other perverted elements. That being so, when a man does not serve God, what amount of justice are we to suppose to exist in his being? For if a soul does not serve God it cannot with any kind of justice command the body, nor can a man's reason control the vicious elements in the soul. And if there is no justice in such a man, there can be no sort of doubt that there is no justice in a gathering which consists of such men. Here, then, there is not that "consent to the law" which makes a mob into a people, and it is "the weal of the people" that is said to make a "commonwealth." As for the "community of interest" in virtue of which, according to our definition, a gathering of men is called a "people," is there any need for me to talk about this? Although, to be sure, if you give the matter careful thought, there are no advantages for men who live ungodly lives, the lives of all those who do not serve God, but serve demons—demons all the more blasphemous in that they desire that sacrifice be offered to them as to gods, though in fact they are most unclean spirits. However, I consider that what I have said about "a common sense of right" is enough to make it apparent that by this definition people amongst whom there is no justice can never be said to have a commonwealth.

Now if it is said that the Romans in their commonwealth did not serve unclean spirits but good and holy gods, do we have to repeat, time and time again, the same things that we have already said often enough—in fact, more than often enough? Surely no one who has read the earlier books of this work and has reached this point can doubt that the Romans served evil and impure demons? If he can, he is either excessively dense, or unscrupulously argumentative! But, to say no more of the character of the gods the Romans worshipped with sacrifice, it is written in the Law of the true God, "Anyone who sacrifices to gods instead of to the Lord only, will be extirpated." This shows that sacrifice to gods, whether good or bad, was against the will of him who uttered this command with so heavy a threat.

23.

. . . And yet it is we ourselves—we, his City—who are his best, his most glorious sacrifice. The mystic symbol of this sacrifice we celebrate in our oblations, familiar to the faithful, as we have maintained in previous books. For the sacrificial victims offered by the Jews, as a foreshadowing of what was to come, were destined to come to an end. This was declared by divine oracles through the lips of the holy prophets, in resounding tones, saying that the nations from the furthest East to the furthest West would offer one sacrifice, as we now see happening. I have extracted as many of those oracles as seemed sufficient, and have already scattered them throughout this work. It follows that justice is found where God, the one supreme God, rules an obedient City according to his grace, forbidding sacrifice to any being save himself alone; and where in consequence the soul rules the body in all men who belong to this City and obey God, and the reason faithfully rules the vices in a lawful system of subordination; so that just as the individual righteous man lives on the basis of faith which is active in love, so the association, or people, of righteous men lives on the same basis of faith, active in love, the love with which a man loves God as God ought to be loved, and loves his neighbour as himself. But where this justice does not exist, there is certainly no "association of men united by a common sense of right and by a community of interest." Therefore there is no commonwealth; for where there is no "people," there is no "weal of the people."

24.

If, on the other hand, another definition than this is found for a "people," for example, if one should say, "A people is the association of a multitude of rational beings united by a common agreement on the objects of their love," then it follows that to observe the character of a particular people we must examine the objects of its love. And yet, whatever those objects, if it is the association of a multitude not of animals but of rational beings, and is united by a common agreement about the objects of its love, then there is no absurdity in applying to it the title of a "people." And, obviously, the better the objects of this agreement, the better the people; the worse the objects of this love, the worse the people. By this definition of ours, the Roman people is a people and its estate is indubitably a commonwealth. But as for the objects of that people's love—both in the earliest times and in subsequent periods—and the morality of that people as it proceeded to bloody strife of parties and then to the social and civil wars, and corrupted and disrupted that very unity which is, as it were, the health of a people—for all this we have the witness of history; and I have had a great deal to say about it in my preceding books. And yet I shall not make that a reason for asserting that a people is not really a people or that a state is not a commonwealth, so long as there remains an association of some kind or other between a multitude of rational beings united by a common agreement on the objects of its love.

THOMAS AQUINAS

~

INTRODUCTION

PAUL J. WEITHMAN

Thomas Aquinas (1224–1274) was born to a family of minor nobility in southern Italy. The part of Italy in which he was born was then part of the Kingdom of Sicily, which was itself part of the Holy Roman Empire. His family estate was close to the frontier between Sicily and the papal states. Because of the ongoing struggle between the emperor and the pope for control of Italy, the estate's location required Aquinas's family to shift their political allegiances with the changing fortunes of the two sides. Despite the facts that Thomas's father and brother were active participants in the struggle and that his brother apparently tried to attract him to the emperor's court, Thomas took no part. Aquinas was attached to the papal court for some time during his adulthood, but in an academic rather than a political capacity. Though he made important contributions to political philosophy, his work does not bear the imprint of his own or his family's political experiences.

Aquinas spent most of his life as a member of the Order of Friars Preachers, also known as the "Dominicans" after their founder St. Dominic. In Aquinas's time the Dominicans lived in the cities of Europe rather than in rural monasteries. They were poor corporately as well as individually and their communities were supported by alms begged by some of their members.

Aquinas began his higher education by studying the liberal arts in Paris. There he first encountered the texts of Aristotle, which were to exercise a powerful hold on his philosophical work. He continued his study of philosophy under Albertus Magnus (1206–1280) in Cologne and began the advanced study of theology under him. Aquinas returned to Paris in 1252 and became a professor of theology at the university there in 1256. He held the chair of theology for a three-year term, then spent two years in both Paris and Italy. From 1268 until 1272 he held a chair in Paris for a second time, after which he went to Naples for the last two years of his teaching career.

A few weeks before Christmas of 1273 Aquinas had what he subsequently described as a profoundly moving mystical experience, one that led him to believe that the works on which he had spent his life were intellectually worthless. Overcome by the memory of this experience, weakened by chronic obesity and habitual overwork, he produced virtually nothing more. While on a journey early in February of 1274 he suffered a seizure, quite probably brought on by a subdural hematoma resulting from an accidental blow to the head. Aquinas died on March 7, 1274.

Throughout his life and after his death Aquinas had a reputation for great piety and personal sanctity. He was declared a saint in 1323.

Aquinas achieved a staggering literary output during his seventeen years as a teacher and scholar. He commented on all four gospels, on many of the Pauline epistles, and on several books of the Hebrew bible. He wrote commentaries on much of Aristotle. He left behind homilies, a few letters, a number of short treatises on philosophical subjects and lengthy treatises on a variety of topics in philosophy and theology. He also left a number of "Quodlibetal Questions," long answers to theological and philosophical questions posed during open debates held at the University of Paris. Aquinas's two most substantial and best-known works are the *Summa Contra Gentiles* and the much longer *Summa Theologiae*. In them Aquinas attempted to present and defend the teachings of Catholicism in a systematic way that provided them a rigorous philosophical basis. In doing so he confronted his views, not only with counterarguments that were in the air during his own time, but also with arguments drawn from Maimonides, from Arabic philosophers, and from classical and patristic sources. The most important influence on this work, however, was the philosophy of Aristotle.

The works of Aristotle had been lost to the West and largely unknown to it for centuries before Aquinas, though they were known to and commented on in the Islamic world. Aristotle's texts made their way into Europe in the early part of the thirteenth century through contacts between Christian and Arab scholars. His philosophical works seemed to present a systematic view of the world, of human inquiry, and of the good human life that was at odds with the central tenets of European Christianity. The god of Aristotle's *Metaphysics*, for example, was detached and self-absorbed, and took no active part in human history. The good life as Aristotle envisioned it seemed that of a cultured Athenian gentleman rather than that of the Christian saint. The study and teaching of Aristotle was therefore not only novel but also highly controversial in Aquinas's time. It was Aquinas's great achievement to show Aristotle's thought to be consistent with Christianity by building his own vast philosophical and theological system upon it. Much of the difficult technical vocabulary that permeates Aquinas's work is drawn from Aristotle. The influence of Aristotle is evident in virtually every element of his thought.

Aquinas's views on the central questions of political philosophy are not easy to discern. Despite his huge output, he never completed a free-standing work of political philosophy. His commentary on Aristotle's *Politics* was unfinished at his death. He began a work called *On Kingship* for a king of Cyprus who was also a Dominican benefactor. When the king died before its completion, Aquinas stopped work on the treatise and it was later finished by his student Ptolemy of Lucca. Aquinas paid very little attention to questions about political institutions. There are places where he suggests a preference for a mixed constitution if the people are sufficiently virtuous to participate in governing themselves either directly or through representatives. Like Aristotle, he is also attracted to unmixed monarchy if someone worthy of the office can be found. The political situation of his day should have interested him in the relationship between the papacy and secular rulers. His remarks on the subject are cautious rather than groundbreaking. He considers the authority of non-Christian rulers and the permissibility of non-Christian religious practices: on both subjects he is cautiously tolerant.

The substance of Aquinas's political thought must and can be culled from passages scattered throughout his work, especially from the *Summa Theologiae*. There he wrote much that has implications for politics and political philosophy, but he almost always did so in the course of discussing something else. His treatment of peace occurs in a long discussion of charity, where it is followed closely by a discussion of mercy and more distantly by treatments of war and schism. His discussion of property comes early in a long treatment of justice, a discussion in which he gives a good deal more attention to various forms of verbal injustice like slander than he does to theft.

While Aristotle explicitly treats political questions at much greater length than does Aquinas, Aquinas's location of political questions in his discussion of moral ones is Aristotelian in spirit. This is because Aristotle's treatment of political questions was highly moralized. Aristotle thought of political life as an arena in which the good human life is lived. In it, he thought, citizens develop and exercise the virtues. It is natural that a follower of Aristotle like Aquinas should take up political questions in the course of discussing virtues like charity and justice and vices like injustice, quarrelsomeness, and avarice.

The central notion in Aquinas's political thought is one that he found in Aristotle: the common good of political society, sometimes called the "political common good." This is a good shared in by, and hence common to, the members of a given political society. It consists, Aquinas says, in a society's justice and peace. These are goods of which all members partake. The prevalence of justice and peace makes it possible for members of society to enjoy other goods Aquinas thinks part of a good life, like family life and religion. Family life and religious life, in turn, reach their fullest expression or are "perfected" when enjoyed in a just and peaceful society. The fact that these ingredients of the good life are perfected in a well-ordered political community explains why Aquinas, like Aristotle, thinks of such a community as the self-sufficient arena in which the good life can be lived.

The most influential part of Aquinas's political thought, interestingly, is also the part of it that is least Aristotelian. That is his discussion of law. His treatment of law, like his treatment of other political questions, is located in a much larger discussion of other moral issues. Thus he takes up human and natural law, as well as divine and eternal law, in the course of a very long discussion of the various causes of human action; in this discussion law takes its place alongside a general discussion of passions, habits, virtues, vices, and grace.

The eternal law, Aquinas says, is the divine plan by which God created and rules the universe. God intended all created things to flourish. The eternal law or divine plan indicates the activities in which they do so. Given the complexity of the created world, Aquinas thinks that much of the eternal law is known only to God. The natural law is that part of the divine law which is accessible to human reason and which indicates how human beings flourish. It includes the basic provisions of morality that must be observed if human beings are to live well. These, Aquinas thinks, are invariant across time and place. Human law, sometimes called "positive law," is the law made or posited by human legislators; to be authoritative, that law must be consistent with the natural law. It cannot enjoin things that the fundamental principles of morality forbid. If it does, Aquinas insists that no one is bound to obey it. Latter-day advocates of civil disobedience have often turned to Aquinas's discussion of unjust laws to defend their actions. Aquinas thinks that human law must also foster religion. It cannot justly enjoin heretical practices; if circumstances permit, it should encourage orthodox ones. Finally, it must promote the common good rather than the legislator's own benefit.

Aquinas's discussion of law is drawn from the *Summa Theologiae*, each article of which has a complicated internal structure. After posing the subquestion with which a given article is concerned, Aquinas will raise several objections to the position he is about to defend. Sometimes these will be cited without attribution. Since scholastic writers never cite living authors by name, these may have been objections propounded by his contemporaries. Other objections will be drawn from scripture or from patristic or classical sources. Aquinas will then adduce an authoritative statement, prefaced by, "On the contrary," which supports his own position. Only then does he proceed to defend his own view, beginning with, "I answer that." Finally, he will answer the objections with which he began, thus showing how his own position can be reconciled with arguments to the contrary that have some authority behind them.

Aquinas's style, which seems unusual to us, would have been quite familiar to the university students for whom Aquinas wrote the *Summa*. "Disputations" were common events in medieval universities. In them a professor posed a question or was asked one from the audience. Graduate students would be assigned one or the other side of the question and would have to produce arguments and authorities in support of the thesis they were assigned. After the arguments for both sides had been heard, the master would "determine" the question by giving arguments supporting his own position and showing where those on the contrary had gone wrong. Many of Aquinas's students would have participated in these ego-bruising events, and all would have seen them. They would have thought the *Summa* was organized in a natural way, though Aquinas seems to be the first actually to have organized his writings in the disputational format. Modern readers find it easiest to begin with Aquinas's own answer to a question and only then to work through his objections and replies.

The best biographies of Aquinas in English are James A. Weisheipl, OP, *Friar Thomas D'Aquino* (Washington, D.C.: Catholic University of America Press, 1983), and J.-P. Torrell, OP, *Saint Thomas Aquinas: The Man and His Work*, translated by Robert Royal (Washington, D.C.: Catholic University of America Press, 1996). The best discussion of Aquinas's political thought is John Finnis, *Aquinas: Moral, Political and Legal Theory* (Oxford: Oxford University Press, 1998). A useful introduction to Aquinas's natural law ethics is Ralph McInery, *Ethica Thomistica* (Washington, D.C.: Catholic University of America Press, 1997).

Summa Theologiae

QUESTION 90: OF THE ESSENCE OF LAW

[In Four Articles]

We have now to consider the extrinsic principles of acts. Now the extrinsic principle inclining to evil is the devil, of whose temptations we have spoken in the First Part. But the extrinsic principle moving to good is God, Who both instructs us by means of His law and assists us by His grace; wherefore, in the first place, we must speak of law; in the second place, of grace.

Concerning law, we must consider (1) law itself in general; (2) its parts. Concerning law in general, three points offer themselves for our consideration: (1) its essence; (2) the different kinds of law; (3) the effects of law.

Under the first head, there are four points of inquiry: (1) Whether law is something pertaining to reason? (2) concerning the end of law; (3) its cause; (4) the promulgation of law.

First Article: Is Law Something Pertaining to Reason?

We proceed thus to the First Article:

Objection. 1. It would seem that law is not something pertaining to reason. For the Apostle says: "I see another law in my members," etc. But nothing pertaining to reason is in the members, since the reason does not make use of a bodily organ. Therefore, law is not something pertaining to reason.

Obj. 2. Further, in the reason there is nothing else but power, habit, and act. But law is not the power itself of reason. In like manner, neither is it a habit of reason, because the habits of reason are the intellectual virtues of which we have spoken above. Nor, again, is it an act of reason because then law would cease when the act of reason ceases, for instance, while we are asleep. Therefore, law is nothing pertaining to reason.

Obj. 3. Further, the law moves those who are subject to it to act aright. But it belongs properly to the will to move to act, as is evident from what has been said above. Therefore, law pertains not to the reason but to the will, according to the words of the Jurist: "Whatever pleases the ruler has the force of law."

On the contrary, It belongs to the law to command and to forbid. But it belongs to reason to command, as stated above. Therefore, law is something pertaining to reason.

I answer that Law is a certain rule and measure of acts whereby man is induced to act or is restrained from acting; for *lex* (law) is derived from *ligare* (to bind) because it binds one to act. Now the rule and measure of human acts is reason, which is the first principle of human acts, as is evident from what has been stated above, since it belongs to reason to direct to the end, which is the first principle in all matters of action, according to the Philosopher. Now, that which is the principle in any genus is the rule and measure of that genus, for instance, unity in the genus of numbers, and the first movement in the genus of movements. Consequently, it follows that law is something pertaining to reason.

Reply Obj. 1. Since law is a kind of rule and measure, it may be in something in two ways. First, as in that which measures and rules; and since this is proper to reason, it follows that, in this way, law is in reason alone. Second, as in that which is measured and ruled. In this way, law is in all those things that

Reprinted from Aquinas, *On Law, Morality, and Politics,* edited, with introduction, by William P. Baumgarth and Richard J. Regan, S.J. (Cambridge, Mass.: Avatar Books of Cambridge, 1988) by permission of the publisher.

are inclined to something by reason of some law, so that any inclination arising from a law may be called a law, not essentially but by participation as it were. And thus the inclination of the members to concupiscence is called "the law of the members."

Reply Obj. 2. Just as, in external action, we may consider the work and the work done—for instance, the work of building and the house built, so in the acts of reason we may consider the act itself of reason, i.e., to understand and to reason, and something produced by this act. With regard to the speculative reason, this is first of all the definition; secondly, the proposition; thirdly, the syllogism or argument. And since also the practical reason makes use of a kind of syllogism in respect to the work to be done, as stated above and as the Philosopher teaches, hence we find in the practical reason something that holds the same position in regard to operations as, in the speculative intellect, the proposition holds in regard to conclusions. Suchlike universal propositions of the practical intellect that are directed to actions have the nature of law. And these propositions are sometimes under our actual consideration, while sometimes they are retained in the reason by means of a habit.

Reply Obj. 3. Reason has its power of moving from the will, as stated above, for it is due to the fact that one wills the end that the reason issues its commands as regards things ordained to the end. But in order that the volition of what is commanded may have the nature of law, it needs to be in accord with some rule of reason. And in this sense is to be understood the saying that the will of the ruler has the force of law; otherwise, the ruler's will would savor of lawlessness rather than of law.

Second Article: Is the Law Always Directed to the Common Good?

We proceed thus to the Second Article:

Obj. 1. It would seem that the law is not always directed to the common good as to its end. For it belongs to law to command and to forbid. But commands are directed to certain individual goods. Therefore, the end of the law is not always the common good.

Obj. 2. Further, the law directs man in his actions. But human actions are concerned with particular matters. Therefore, the law is directed to some particular good.

Obj. 3. Further, Isidore says, "If the law is based on reason, whatever is based on reason will be a law." But reason is the foundation not only of what is ordained to the common good but also of that which is directed to private good. Therefore, the law is not only directed to the common good but also to the private good of an individual.

On the contrary, Isidore says that "Laws are enacted for no private profit but for the common benefit of the citizens."

I answer that, As stated above, the law belongs to that which is a principle of human acts because it is their rule and measure. Now, as reason is a principle of human acts, so in reason itself there is something which is the principle in respect of all the rest; wherefore to this principle chiefly and mainly law must needs be referred. Now the first principle in practical matters, which are the object of the practical reason, is the last end, and the last end of human life is bliss or happiness, as stated above. Consequently, the law must needs regard principally the relationship to happiness. Moreover, since every part is ordained to the whole as imperfect to perfect, and since a single man is a part of the perfect community, the law must needs regard properly the relationship to universal happiness. Wherefore the Philosopher, in the above definition of legal matters, mentions both happiness and the body politic, for he says that we call those legal matters just "which are adapted to produce and preserve happiness and its parts for the body politic" since the political community is a perfect community, as he says in *Politics* I, 1.

Now, in every genus, that which belongs to it most of all is the principle of the others, and the others belong to that genus in subordination to that thing; thus fire, which is chief among hot things, is the cause of heat in mixed bodies, and these are said to be hot insofar as they have a share of fire. Consequently, since the law is chiefly ordained to the common good, any other precept in regard to some individual work must needs be devoid of the nature of a law, save insofar as it is ordered to the common good. Therefore, every law is ordained to the common good.

Reply Obj. 1. A command denotes an application of a law to matters regulated by the law. Now the order to the common good, at which the law aims, is applicable to particular ends. And in this way, commands are given even concerning particular matters.

Reply Obj. 2. Actions are indeed concerned with particular matters, but those particular matters are referable to the common good, not as to a common genus or species, but as to a common final cause, according as the common good is said to be the common end.

Reply Obj. 3. Just as nothing stands firm with regard to the speculative reason except that which is traced back to the first indemonstrable principles, so nothing stands firm with regard to the practical reason unless it be directed to the last end which is the common good, and whatever stands to reason in this sense has the nature of a law.

Third Article: Is the Reason of Any Person Competent to Make Laws?

We proceed thus to the Third Article:

Obj 1. It would seem that the reason of any person is competent to make laws. For the Apostle says that "when the Gentiles, who have not the law, do by nature those things that are of the law, . . . they are a law to themselves." Now he says this of all in general. Therefore, anyone can make a law for himself.

Obj. 2. Further, as the Philosopher says, "The intention of the lawgiver is to lead men to virtue." But every man can lead another to virtue. Therefore, the reason of any man is competent to make laws.

Obj. 3. Further, just as the ruler of a political community governs the political community, so every father of a family governs his household. But the ruler of a political community can make laws for the political community. Therefore, every father of a family can make laws for his household.

On the contrary, Isidore says, "A law is an ordinance of the people, whereby something is sanctioned by nobles together with commoners." Not everyone, therefore, is competent to make law.

I answer that Law, properly speaking, regards first and chiefly an ordering to the common good. Now to order anything to the common good belongs either to the whole people or to someone who is the vicegerent of the whole people. And, therefore, the making of law belongs either to the whole people or to a public personage who has care of the whole people, since, in all other matters, the directing of anything to the end concerns him to whom the end belongs.

Reply Obj. 1. As stated above, law is in a person not only as in one that rules but also by participation as in one that is ruled. In the latter way, each one is a law to himself, insofar as he shares the direction that he receives from one who rules him. Hence the same text goes on, "who show the work of the law written in their hearts."

Reply Obj. 2. A private person cannot lead another to virtue efficaciously, for he can only advise, and if his advice be not taken, it has no coercive power, such as the law should have in order to prove an efficacious inducement to virtue, as the Philosopher says. But this coercive power is vested in the whole people or in some public personage to whom it belongs to inflict penalties, as we shall state further on. Wherefore, the framing of laws belongs to him alone.

Reply Obj. 3. As one man is a part of the household, so a household is a part of the political community, and the political community is a perfect community, according to *Politics* I, 1. And, therefore, as the good of one man is not the last end but is ordained to the common good, so too the good of one household is ordained to the good of a single political community, which is a perfect community. Consequently, he that governs a family can indeed make certain commands or ordinances but not such as to have properly the nature of law.

Fourth Article: Is Promulgation Essential to a Law?

We proceed thus to the Fourth Article:

Obj. 1. It would seem that promulgation is not essential to a law. For the natural law above all has the nature of law. But the natural law needs no promulgation. Therefore, it is not essential to a law that it be promulgated.

Obj. 2. Further, it belongs properly to a law to bind one to do or not to do something. But the obligation of fulfilling a law touches not only those in whose presence it is promulgated but also others. Therefore, promulgation is not essential to a law.

Obj. 3. Further, the obligation of a law extends even to the future since "laws are binding in matters of the future," as the jurists say. But promulgation is made to those who are present. Therefore, it is not essential to a law.

On the contrary, It is laid down in the *Decretum,* dist. 4, that "Laws are established when they are promulgated."

I answer that, As stated above, a law is imposed on others by way of a rule and measure. Now a rule or measure is imposed by being applied to those who are to be ruled and measured by it. Wherefore, in order that a law obtain the binding force which is proper to a law, it must needs be applied to the men who have to be ruled by it. Such application is made by its being notified to them by promulgation. Wherefore promulgation is necessary for the law to obtain its force.

Thus, from the four preceding articles, the definition of law may be gathered, and it is nothing else than a certain ordinance of reason for the common good, made by him who has care of the community, and promulgated.

Reply Obj. 1. The natural law is promulgated by the very fact that God instilled it into men's minds so as to be known by them naturally.

Reply Obj. 2. Those who are not present when a law is promulgated are bound to observe the law, insofar as it is notified or can be notified to them by others after it has been promulgated.

Reply Obj. 3. The promulgation that takes place now extends to future time by reason of the durability of written characters, by which means it is continually promulgated. Hence Isidore says that *"lex* (law) is derived from *legere* (to read) because it is written."

QUESTION 91: OF THE VARIOUS KINDS OF LAW

[In Six Articles]

We must now consider the various kinds of law, under which head there are six points of inquiry: (1) Whether there is an eternal law? (2) Whether there is a natural law? (3) Whether there is a human law? (4) Whether there is a divine law? (5) Whether there is one divine law or several? (6) Whether there is a law of sin?

First Article: Is There an Eternal Law?

We proceed thus to the First Article:

Obj. 1. It would seem that there is no eternal law because every law is imposed on someone. But there was not someone from eternity on whom a law could be imposed since God alone was from eternity. Therefore, no law is eternal.

Obj. 2. Further, promulgation is essential to law. But promulgation could not be from eternity because there was no one to whom it could be promulgated from eternity. Therefore, no law can be eternal.

Obj. 3. Further, a law implies order to an end. But nothing ordained to an end is eternal, for the last end alone is eternal. Therefore, no law is eternal.

On the contrary, Augustine says, "That law which is the supreme reason cannot be understood to be otherwise than unchangeable and eternal."

I answer that, As stated above, a law is nothing else but a dictate of practical reason in the ruler who governs a perfect community. Now it is evident, granted that the world is ruled by divine providence, as was stated in the First Part, that the whole community of the universe is governed by divine reason. Wherefore, the very idea of the government of things in God the Ruler of the universe has the nature of a law. And since the divine reason's conception of things is not subject to time but is eternal, according to Pr. 8:23, therefore it is that this kind of law must be called eternal.

Reply Obj. 1. Those things that are not in themselves exist with God inasmuch as they are foreknown and preordained by Him, according to Rom. 4:17, "Who calls those things that are not, as those that are." Accordingly, the eternal concept of the divine law bears the nature of an eternal law insofar as it is ordained by God to the government of things foreknown by Him.

Reply Obj. 2. Promulgation is made by word of mouth or in writing, and in both ways the eternal law is promulgated, because both the divine word and the writing of the Book of Life are eternal. But the promulgation cannot be from eternity on the part of the creature that hears or reads.

Reply Obj. 3. The law implies order to an end actively, insofar as it directs certain things to an end, but not passively—that is to say, the law itself is not ordained to an end—except accidentally, in a governor whose end is extrinsic to him, and to which end his law must needs be ordained. But the end of the divine government is God Himself, and His law is not distinct from Himself. Wherefore the eternal law is not ordained to another end.

Second Article: Is There a Natural Law in Us?

We proceed thus to the Second Article:

Obj. 1. It would seem that there is no natural law in us because man is governed sufficiently by the eternal law; for Augustine says that "the eternal law is that by which it is right that all things should be most orderly." But nature does not abound in superfluities, as neither does it fail in necessaries. Therefore, there is no natural law in man.

Obj. 2. Further, by the law man is directed in his acts to the end, as stated above. But the directing of human acts to their end is not by nature, as is the case in irrational creatures, which act for an end solely by their natural appetite, whereas man acts for an end by his reason and will. Therefore, there is no natural law for man.

Obj. 3. Further, the more a man is free, the less is he under the law. But man is freer than all other animals on account of his free will, with which he is endowed above all other animals. Since,

therefore, other animals are not subject to a natural law, neither is man subject to a natural law.

On the contrary, A gloss on Rom. 2:14 ("When the Gentiles, who have not the law, do by nature those things that are of the law") comments as follows: "Although they have no written law, yet they have the natural law, whereby each one knows, and is conscious of, what is good and what is evil."

I answer that, As stated above, law, being a rule and measure, can be in a person in two ways: in one way, as in him that rules and measures; in another way, as in that which is ruled and measured, since a thing is ruled and measured insofar as it partakes of the rule or measure. Wherefore, since all things subject to divine providence are ruled and measured by the eternal law, as was stated above, it is evident that all things partake somewhat of the eternal law insofar as, namely, from its being imprinted on them, they derive their respective inclinations to their proper acts and ends. Now among all others, the rational creature is subject to divine providence in a more excellent way, insofar as it partakes of a share of providence, by being provident both for itself and for others. Wherefore it has a share of the eternal reason, whereby it has a natural inclination to its proper act and end, and this participation of the eternal law in the rational creature is called the natural law. Hence the Psalmist, after saying "offer up the sacrifice of justice," as though someone asked what the works of justice are, adds: "Many say, 'Who shows us good things?'," in answer to which question he says: "The light of Your countenance, O lord, is signed upon us"; thus implying that the light of natural reason, whereby we discern what is good and what is evil, which pertains to the natural law, is nothing else than an imprint on us of the divine light. It is therefore evident that the natural law is nothing else than the rational creature's participation of the eternal law.

Reply Obj. 1. This argument would hold if the natural law were something different from the eternal law, whereas it is nothing but a participation thereof, as stated above.

Reply Obj. 2. Every act of reason and will in us is derived from that which is according to nature, as stated above; for every act of reasoning is based on principles that are known naturally, and every act of appetite in respect of the means is derived from the natural appetite in respect of the last end. Accordingly, the first direction of our acts to their end must needs be in virtue of the natural law.

Reply Obj. 3. Even irrational animals partake in their own way of the eternal reason, just as the rational creature does. But because the rational creature partakes thereof in an intellectual and rational manner, therefore the participation of the eternal law in the rational creature is properly called a law, since a law is something pertaining to reason, as stated above. Irrational creatures, however, do not partake thereof in a rational manner, wherefore, there is no participation of the eternal law in them, except by way of similitude.

Third Article: Is There a Human Law?

We proceed thus to the Third Article:

Obj. 1. It would seem that there is not a human law. For the natural law is a participation of the eternal law, as stated above. Now, through the eternal law, "all things are most orderly," as Augustine states. Therefore, the natural law suffices for the ordering of all human affairs. Consequently, there is no need for a human law.

Obj. 2. Further, a law has the nature of a measure, as stated above. But human reason is not a measure of things, but vice versa, as stated in *Metaphysics* IX, 1. Therefore, no law can emanate from human reason.

Obj. 3. Further, a measure should be most certain, as stated in *Metaphysics* 10. But the dictates of human reason in matters of conduct are uncertain, according to Wisdom 9:14: "The thoughts of mortal men are fearful, and our counsels uncertain." Therefore, no law can emanate from human reason.

On the contrary, Augustine distinguishes two kinds of law: the one eternal; the other temporal, which he calls human.

I answer that, As stated above, a law is a certain dictate of practical reason. Now it is to be observed that the same procedure takes place in the practical and in the speculative reason, for

each proceeds from principles to conclusions, as stated above (ibid.). Accordingly, we conclude that just as, in the speculative reason, from naturally known indemonstrable principles we draw the conclusions of the various sciences, the knowledge of which is not imparted to us by nature but acquired by the efforts of reason, so too it is from the precepts of the natural law, as from general and indemonstrable principles, that the human reason needs to proceed to certain particular determinations of the laws. These particular determinations, devised by human reason, are called human laws, provided the other essential conditions of law be observed as stated above. Wherefore, Tully says in his *Rhetoric* that "justice has its source in nature; thence certain things came into custom by reason of their utility; afterward these things which emanated from nature and were approved by custom were sanctioned by fear and reverence for the law."

Reply Obj. 1. The human reason cannot have a full participation of the dictate of the divine reason but according to its own mode and imperfectly. Consequently, as on the part of the speculative reason, by a natural participation of divine wisdom, there is in us the knowledge of certain general principles but not proper knowledge of each single truth, such as that contained in the divine wisdom, so too on the part of the practical reason, man has a natural participation of the eternal law according to certain general principles but not as regards the particular determinations of individual cases, which are, however, contained in the eternal law. Hence the need for human reason to proceed further to particular legal sanctions.

Reply Obj. 2. Human reason is not of itself the rule of things, but the principles impressed on it by nature are general rules and measures of all things relating to human conduct, whereof the natural reason is the rule and measure, although it is not the measure of things that are from nature.

Reply Obj. 3. The practical reason is concerned with practical matters, which are singular and contingent, but not with necessary things, with which the speculative reason is concerned. Wherefore human laws cannot have that inerrancy that belongs to the demonstrated conclusions of sciences. Nor is it necessary for every measure to be altogether unerring and certain but according as it is possible in its own particular genus.

QUESTION 94: OF THE NATURAL LAW

[In Six Articles]

We must now consider the natural law, concerning which there are six points of inquiry: (1) What is the natural law? (2) What are the precepts of the natural law? (3) Whether all acts of virtue are prescribed by the natural law? (4) Whether the natural law is the same in all? (5) Whether it is changeable? (6) Whether it can be abolished from the heart of man?

First Article: Is the Natural Law a Habit?

We proceed thus to the First Article:

Obj. 1. It would seem that the natural law is a habit because, as the Philosopher says, "there are three things in the soul: power, habit, and passion." But the natural law is not one of the soul's powers, nor is it one of the passions, as we may see by going through them one by one. Therefore, the natural law is a habit.

Obj. 2. Further, Basil says that the conscience or "*synderesis* is the law of our mind," which can only apply to the natural law. But *synderesis* is a habit, as was shown in the First Part. Therefore, the natural law is a habit.

Obj. 3. Further, the natural law abides in man always, as will be shown further on. But man's reason, to which the law pertains, does not always think about the natural law. Therefore, the natural law is not an act but a habit.

On the contrary, Augustine says that "a habit is that whereby something is done when necessary." But such is not the natural law since it is in infants and in the damned who cannot act by it. Therefore, the natural law is not a habit.

I answer that, A thing may be called a habit in two ways. First, properly and essentially, and thus the natural law is not a habit. For it has been stated above that the natural law is something appointed by reason, just as a proposition is a work of reason. Now, that which a man does is not the same as that whereby he does it, for he makes a becoming speech by the habit of grammar. Since, then, a habit is that by which we act, a law cannot be a habit properly and essentially.

Secondly, the term "habit" may be applied to that which we hold by a habit; thus faith may mean that which we hold by faith. And accordingly, since the precepts of the natural law are sometimes considered by reason actually, while sometimes they are in the reason only habitually, in this way the natural law may be called a habit. Thus, in speculative matters, the indemonstrable principles are not the habit itself whereby we hold those principles but are the principles the habit of which we possess.

Reply Obj. 1. The Philosopher proposes there to discover the genus of virtue, and since it is evident that virtue is a principle of action, he mentions only those things which are principles of human acts, viz., powers, habits, and passions. But there are other things in the soul besides these three: there are acts; thus to will is in the one that wills; again, things known are in the knower. Moreover, its own natural properties are in the soul, such as immortality and the like.

Reply Obj. 2. Synderesis is said to be the law of our mind because it is a habit containing the precepts of the natural law, which are the first principles of human actions.

Reply Obj. 3. This argument proves that the natural law is held habitually, and this is granted.

To the argument advanced in the contrary sense we reply that sometimes a man is unable to make use of that which is in him habitually on account of some impediment; thus, on account of sleep, a man is unable to use the habit of reasoning. In like manner, through the deficiency of his age, a child cannot use the habit of understanding principles, or the natural law, which is in him habitually.

Second Article: Does the Natural Law Contain Several Precepts or One Only?

We proceed thus to the Second Article:

Obj. 1. It would seem that the natural law contains, not several precepts, but one only. For law is a kind of precept, as stated above. If, therefore, there were many precepts of the natural law, it would follow that there are also many natural laws.

Obj. 2. Further, the natural law is consequent to human nature. But human nature as a whole is one, though, as to its parts, it is manifold. Therefore, either there is but one precept of the law of nature, on account of the unity of nature as a whole, or there are many by reason of the number of parts of human nature. The result would be that even things relating to the inclination of the concupiscible faculty belong to the natural law.

Obj. 3. Further, law is something pertaining to reason, as stated above. Now, reason is but one in man. Therefore, there is only one precept of the natural law.

On the contrary, The precepts of the natural law in man stand in relation to practical matters as the first principles to matters of demonstration. But there are several first indemonstrable principles. Therefore, there are also several precepts of the natural law.

I answer that, As stated above, the precepts of the natural law are to the practical reason what the first principles of demonstrations are to the speculative reason because both are self-evident principles. Now a thing is said to be self-evident in two ways: first, in itself; secondly, in relation to us. Any proposition is said to be self-evident in itself if its predicate is contained in the notion of the subject, although, to one who knows not the definition of the subject, it happens that such a proposition is not self-evident. For instance, this proposition, "Man is a rational being," is in its very nature self-evident, since who says "man" says "a rational being," and yet to one who knows not what a man is, this proposition is not self-evident. Hence it is that, as Boethius says, certain axioms or propositions are universally self-evident to all, and such are those propositions whose terms are known to all, as "Every whole is greater than its part," and, "Things equal to one and the same are equal to one another." But some propositions are self-evident only to the wise who understand the meaning of the terms of such propositions; thus to one who understands that an angel is not a body, it is self-evident that an angel is not circumspectively

in a place, but this is not evident to the unlearned, for they cannot grasp it.

Now, a certain order is to be found in those things that are apprehended universally. For that which, before aught else, falls under apprehension, is "being," the notion of which is included in all things whatsoever a man apprehends. Wherefore the first indemonstrable principle is that the same thing cannot be affirmed and denied at the same time, which is based on the nature of "being" and "not-being," and on this principle all others are based, as it is stated in *Metaphysics* IV. Now, as "being" is the first thing that falls under the apprehension simply, so "good" is the first thing that falls under the apprehension of the practical reason, which is directed to action, since every agent acts for an end under the aspect of good. Consequently, the first principle in the practical reason is one founded on the notion of good, viz., that good is that which all things seek after. Hence this is the first precept of law, that good is to be done and pursued, and evil is to be avoided. All other precepts of the natural law are based upon this, so that whatever the practical reason naturally apprehends as man's good (or evil) belongs to the precepts of the natural law as something to be done or avoided.

Since, however, good has the nature of an end, and evil the nature of a contrary, hence it is that all those things to which man has a natural inclination are naturally apprehended by reason as being good and, consequently, as objects of pursuit, and their contraries as evil and objects of avoidance. Wherefore the order of the precepts of the natural law is according to the order of natural inclinations. Because in man there is first of all an inclination to good in accordance with the nature which he has in common with all substances, inasmuch as every substance seeks the preservation of its own being according to its nature, and by reason of this inclination, whatever is a means of preserving human life and of warding off its obstacles to the natural law. Secondly, there is in man an inclination to things that pertain to him more specially according to that nature which he has in common with other animals, and in virtue of this inclination, those things are said to belong to the natural law "which nature has taught to all animals," such as sexual intercourse, education of offspring, and so forth. Thirdly, there is in man an inclination to good according to the nature of his reason, which nature is proper to him; thus man has a natural inclination to know the truth about God and to live in society, and in this respect, whatever pertains to this inclination belongs to the natural law, for instance, to shun ignorance, to avoid offending those among whom one has to live, and other such things regarding the above inclination.

Reply Obj. 1. All these precepts of the law of nature have the character of one natural law inasmuch as they flow from one first precept.

Reply Obj. 2. All the inclinations of any parts whatsoever of human nature, e.g., of the concupiscible and irascible parts, insofar as they are ruled by reason, belong to the natural law and are reduced to one first precept, as stated above, so that the precepts of the natural law are many in themselves but are based on one common foundation.

Reply Obj. 3. Although reason is one in itself, yet it directs all things regarding man, so that whatever can be ruled by reason is contained under the law of reason.

Third Article: Are All Acts of Virtue Prescribed by the Natural Law?

We proceed thus to the Third Article:

Obj. 1. It would seem that not all acts of virtue are prescribed by the natural law because, as stated above, it is essential to a law that it be ordained to the common good. But some acts of virtue are ordained to the private good of the individual, as is evident especially in regard to acts of temperance. Therefore, not all acts of virtue are the subject of natural law.

Obj. 2. Further, every sin is opposed to some virtuous act. If, therefore, all acts of virtue are prescribed by the natural law, it seems to follow that all sins are against nature, whereas this applies to certain special sins.

Obj. 3. Further, those things which are according to nature are common to all. But acts of virtue are not common to all, since a thing is virtuous in one and vicious in another. Therefore, not all acts of virtue are prescribed by the natural law.

On the contrary, Damascene says that "virtues are natural." Therefore, virtuous acts also are a subject of the natural law.

I answer that We may speak of virtuous acts in two ways: first, under the aspect of virtuous; secondly, as such and such acts considered in their proper species. If, then, we speak of acts of virtue considered as virtuous, thus all virtuous acts belong to the natural law. For it has been stated that to the natural law belongs everything to which a man is inclined according to his nature. Now each thing is inclined naturally to an operation that is suitable to it according to its form; thus fire is inclined to give heat. Wherefore, since the rational soul is the proper form of man, there is in every man a natural inclination to act according to reason, and this is to act according to virtue. Consequently, considered thus, all acts of virtue are prescribed by the natural law, since each one's reason naturally dictates to him to act virtuously. But if we speak of virtuous acts considered in themselves, i.e., in their proper species, thus not all virtuous acts are prescribed by the natural law; the many things are done virtuously to which nature does not incline at first, but which, through the inquiry of reason, have been found by men to be conducive to well-living.

Reply Obj. 1. Temperance is about the natural concupiscences of food, drink, and sexual matters, which are indeed ordained to the natural common good, just as other matters of law are ordained to the moral common good.

Reply Obj. 2. By human nature we may mean either that which is proper to man—and in this sense all sins, as being against reason, are also against nature, as Damascene states—or we may mean that nature which is common to man and other animals, and in this sense certain special sins are said to be against nature; thus, contrary to heterosexual intercourse, which is natural to all animals, is male homosexual union, which has received the special name of the unnatural vice.

Reply Obj. 3. This argument considers acts in themselves. For it is owing to the various conditions of men that certain acts are virtuous for some as being proportionate and becoming to them, while they are vicious for others as being out of proportion to them.

Fourth Article: Is the Natural Law the Same in All Men?

We proceed thus to the Fourth Article:

Obj. 1. It would seem that the natural law is not the same in all. For it is stated in the *Decretum* that "the natural law is that which is contained in the Law and the Gospel." But this is not common to all men because, as it is written, "all do not obey the gospel." Therefore, the natural law is not the same in all men.

Obj. 2. Further, "Things which are according to the law are said to be just," as stated in *Ethics* V. But it is stated in the same book that nothing is so universally just as not to be subject to change in regard to some men. Therefore, even the natural law is not the same in all men.

Obj. 3. Further, as stated above, to the natural law belongs everything to which a man is inclined according to his nature. Now, different men are naturally inclined to different things, some to the desire of pleasures, others to the desire of honors, and other men to other things. Therefore, there is not one natural law for all.

On the contrary, Isidore says, "The natural law is common to all nations."

I answer that, As stated above, to the natural law belong those things to which a man is inclined naturally, and among these, it is proper to man to be inclined to act according to reason. Now the process of reason is from the common to the proper, as stated in *Phys.* I. The speculative reason, however, is differently situated in this matter from the practical reason. For, since the speculative reason is concerned chiefly with necessary things, which cannot be otherwise than they are, its proper conclusions, like the universal principles, contain the truth without fail. The practical reason, on the other hand, is concerned with contingent matters, about which human actions are concerned, and consequently, although there is necessity in the general principles, the more we descend to matters of detail, the more frequently we encounter deviations. Accordingly, then, in speculative matters, truth is the same for all men both as to principles and as to conclusions, although the truth is not known to all as regards the conclusions but only as regards the principles which are called common notions. But in matters of action, truth or practical rectitude is not the same for all as to matters of detail but only as to the general principles, and where there is the same rectitude in matters of detail, it is not equally known to all.

It is, therefore, evident that, as regards the general principles, whether of speculative or practical reason, truth or rectitude is the same for all and is equally known by all. As to the proper conclusions of the speculative reason, the truth is the same for all but is not equally known to all; thus it is true for all that the three angles of a triangle are together equal to two right angles, although it is not known to all. But as to the proper conclusions of the practical reason, neither is the truth or rectitude the same for all, nor, where it is the same, is it equally known by all. Thus it is right and true for all to act according to reason, and from this principle, it follows as a proper conclusion that goods entrusted to another should be restored to their owner. Now this is true for the majority of cases, but it may happen in a particular case that it would be injurious, and therefore unreasonable, to restore goods held in trust, for instance, if they are claimed for the purpose of fighting against one's country. And this principle will be found to fail the more according as we descend further into detail, e.g., if one were to say that goods held in trust should be restored with such and such a guarantee or in such and such a way, because the greater the number of conditions added, the greater the number of ways in which the principle may fail, so that it be not right to restore or not to restore.

Consequently, we must say that the natural law as to general principles is the same for all both as to rectitude and as to knowledge. But as to certain matters of detail, which are conclusions, as it were, of those general principles, it is the same for all in the majority of cases both as to rectitude and as to knowledge, and yet, in some few cases, it may fail both as to rectitude by reason of certain obstacles (just as natures subject to generation and corruption fail in some few cases on account of some obstacle) and as to knowledge, since, in some, the reason is perverted by passion or evil habit or an evil disposition of nature; thus, formerly, theft, although it is expressly contrary to the natural law, was not considered wrong among the Germans, as Julius Caesar relates.

Reply Obj. 1. The meaning of the sentence quoted is not that whatever is contained in the Law and the Gospel belongs to the natural law, since they contain many things that are above nature, but that whatever belongs to the natural law is fully contained in them. Wherefore Gratian, after saying that "the natural law is what is contained in the Law and the Gospel," adds at once, by way of example, "by which everyone is commanded to do to others as he would be done by."

Reply Obj. 2. The saying of the Philosopher is to be understood of things that are naturally just, not as general principles but as conclusions drawn from them, having rectitude in the majority of cases but failing in a few.

Reply Obj. 3. As, in man, reason rules and commands the other powers, so all the natural inclinations belonging to the other powers must needs be directed according to reason. Wherefore it is universally right for all men that all their inclinations should be directed according to reason.

Fifth Article: Can the Natural Law Be Changed?

We proceed thus to the Fifth Article:

Obj. 1. It would seem that the natural law can be changed because, on Sir. 17:9, "He gave them instructions, and the law of life," a gloss says: "He wished the law of the letter to be written in order to correct the law of nature." But that which is corrected is changed. Therefore, the natural law can be changed.

Obj. 2. Further, the slaying of the innocent, adultery, and theft are against the natural law. But we find these things changed by God, as when God commanded Abraham to slay his innocent son, and when He ordered the Jews to borrow and purloin the vessels of the Egyptians, and when He commanded Hosea to take to himself "a wife of fornications." Therefore, the natural law can be changed.

Obj. 3. Further, Isidore says that "the possession of all things in common and universal freedom are matters of natural law." But these things are seen to be changed by human laws. Therefore, it seems that the natural law is subject to change.

On the contrary, It is said in the *Decretum:* "The natural law dates from the creation of the rational creature. It does not vary according to time but remains unchangeable."

I answer that A change in the natural law may be understood in two ways. First, by way of addition. In this sense, nothing hinders the natural law from being changed, since many things, for the benefit of human life, have been added over and above the natural law both by the divine law and by human laws.

Secondly, a change in the natural law may be understood by way of subtraction, so that what previously was according to the natural law ceases to be so. In this sense, the natural law is altogether unchangeable in its first principles, but in its secondary principles, which, as we have said, are like certain proper conclusions closely related to the first principles, the natural law is not changed so that what it prescribes be not right in most cases. But it may be changed in some particular cases of rare occurrence through some special causes hindering the observance of such precepts, as stated above.

Reply Obj. 1. The written law is said to be given for the correction of the natural law, either because it supplies what was wanting to the natural law or because the natural law was perverted in the hearts of some men as to certain matters, so that they esteemed those things good which are naturally evil, which perversion stood in need of correction.

Reply Obj. 2. All men alike, both guilty and innocent, die the death of nature, which death of nature is inflicted by the power of God on account of original sin, according to 1 Kings: "The Lord kills and makes alive." Consequently, by the command of God, death can be inflicted on any man, guilty or innocent, without any injustice whatever. In like manner, adultery is intercourse with another's wife, who is allotted to him by the law handed down by God. Consequently, intercourse with any woman, by the command of God, is neither adultery nor fornication. The same applies to theft, which is the taking of another's property. For whatever is taken by the command of God, to Whom all things belong, is not taken against the will of its owner, whereas it is in this that theft consists. Nor is it only in human things that whatever is commanded by God is right but also in natural things—whatever is done by God is, in some way, natural, as stated in the First Part.

Reply Obj. 3. A thing is said to belong to the natural law in two ways. First, because nature inclines thereto, e.g., that one should not do harm to another. Secondly, because nature did not bring in the contrary; thus we might say that for man to be naked is of the natural law because nature did not give him clothes, but art invented them. In this sense, "the possession of all things in common and universal freedom" are said to be of the natural law because, to wit, the distinction of possessions and slavery were not brought in by nature but devised by human reason for the benefit of human life. Accordingly, the law of nature was not changed in this respect except by addition.

Sixth Article: Can the Law of Nature Be Abolished from the Heart of Man?

We proceed thus to the Sixth Article:

Obj. 1. It would seem that the natural law can be abolished from the heart of man because, on Rom. 2:14, "When the Gentiles who have not the law," etc., a gloss says that "the law of righteousness, which sin had blotted out, is graven on the heart of man when he is restored by grace." But the law of righteousness is the law of nature. Therefore, the law of nature can be blotted out.

Obj. 2. Further, the law of grace is more efficacious than the law of nature. But the law of grace is blotted out by sin. Much more, therefore, can the law of nature be blotted out.

Obj. 3. Further, that which is established by law is made just. But many things are legally established which are contrary to the law of nature. Therefore, the law of nature can be abolished from the heart of man.

On the contrary, Augustine says, "Thy law is written in the hearts of men, which iniquity itself effaces not." But the law which is written in men's hearts is the natural law. Therefore, the natural law cannot be blotted out.

I answer that, As stated above, there belong to the natural law, first, certain most general precepts that are known to all; and secondly, certain secondary and more detailed precepts which are, as it were, conclusions following closely from first principles. As to those general principles, the natural law, in the abstract, can nowise be blotted out from men's hearts. But it is blotted out in the case of particular action insofar as reason is hindered from applying the general principles to a particular point of practice on account of concupiscence or some other passion, as stated above. But as to the other, i.e., the secondary precepts, the natural law can be blotted out from the human heart either by evil persuasions, just as in speculative matters errors occur in respect of necessary conclusions, or by vicious customs and corrupt habits, as among some men theft and even unnatural vices, as the Apostle states, were not esteemed sinful.

Reply Obj. 1. Sin blots out the law of nature in particular cases, not universally, except perchance in regard to the secondary precepts of the natural law, in the way stated above.

Reply Obj. 2. Although grace is more efficacious than nature, yet nature is more essential to man and therefore more enduring.

Reply Obj. 3. The argument is true of the secondary precepts of the natural law, against which some legislators have framed certain enactments which are unjust.

NICCOLÒ MACHIAVELLI

~

INTRODUCTION

STEVEN B. SMITH

Niccolò Machiavelli (1469–1527) was born in Florence at the height of its cultural fame under the rule of the Medici family. As a young man he saw the Medicis overthrown by a charismatic Dominican friar named Girolamo Savonarola who sought to impose a kind of theocracy on the Florentines. Savonarola's experiment with a republic of Christian virtue proved short-lived, and in its place a new government was established by Piero Soderini under which Machiavelli occupied the office of the secretary of the Second Chancery—a diplomatic post—for fourteen years from 1498 to 1512. After the fall of Soderini and the return of the Medicis, Machiavelli was briefly tortured and then exiled from Florence to a small estate that he owned on the outskirts of the city. It was from here—from this life of political exile—that he wrote voluminous letters to friends seeking knowledge of political happenings and where in one letter to Francesco Vettori dated from December 1513, he mentions that he was writing a short book titled *The Prince*.

The Prince is doubtless the most famous (or infamous) book on politics ever written. Machiavelli's fame rests on the claim—universally acknowledged—to have introduced the language of realism into political theory. While he certainly had his predecessors—one need only think of Thucydides or Tacitus—it is Machiavelli who is best remembered as an advocate of pure *Realpolitik* that would find expression in the works of the great political realists from Hobbes to Bismarck, Max Weber, and Henry Kissinger. Machiavelli's realism is asserted in the fifteenth chapter of *The Prince*, where we read:

> But since my intention is to write something useful for anyone who understands it, it seemed more suitable to me to search after the effectual truth of the matter rather than its imagined one. And many writers have imagined for themselves republics and principalities that have never been seen nor known to exist in reality; for there is such a gap between how one lives and how one ought to live that anyone who abandons what is done for what ought to be done learns his ruin rather than his preservation.

Machiavelli's claim here is to put politics on a new foundation, to give it a realism that it had not previously possessed, to free it from the illusions of the imagination, and to provide a "lower" conception of human nature that would be more in accord with actual human behavior. On his telling of the story, the ancients were utopians who believed in an orderly cosmos and tried to figure out what was the appropriate human place within it, whereas the proper task was to make nature serve our ends. He presents himself as the bearer of a new truth—"the effectual truth of the matter"—that is concerned not with how things ought to be but with how things are. It is knowledge of the "is" rather than the "ought." Machiavelli's realism is often associated with a related claim that he is the founder of a new "science" of politics. By *science* is meant here the causal analysis of facts and their relations where causes are understood to be not the Aristotelian focus on final causes or the study of ends, but on efficient causes or the study of means. It would be based on a new appreciation for empiricism, an inductive spirit that limits itself to what can be seen, observed, measured, and quantified. The new Machiavellian political science would be a science of power.

Yet while the picture of Machiavelli as a scientific realist is no doubt true in part, it does less than justice to the Florentine's innovations. Machiavelli approached politics with the sense of possibility and adventure that we typically associate with the high-water mark of Renaissance Florence. Although the term *Renaissance* actually means "rebirth," it was a time of extraordinary innovation. The Renaissance was not just a recovery of the old; it was a harbinger of the new. Machiavelli was a contemporary of Leonardo da Vinci and Michelangelo and he thought of politics as a work of art, as a product of the human will and certain newfound powers of creativity and human agency. The historian Jacob Burckhardt remains the most perceptive analyst of this new disposition that assumed the proportions of a new image of human nature, not Adam or Prometheus, but Proteus—a character distinguished on account of limitless powers of self-transformation without self-destruction. This Protean quality of individuality and self-expression came alive in fifteenth century Italy initially with Boccaccio and Pico della Mirandola, who both explored it with unequaled gusto.

These features of Protean individualism all fit Machiavelli like a glove. *The Prince* is replete with the language of greatness and nobility that scarcely fits the standard realist model. The image of Machiavelli as a cautious pragmatist carefully calculating means to ends fails to account for his continual appeals to *spirito* and *anima*, the love of glory, fame, and high ambition. He speaks of imitating "the greatest examples," men like Moses, Romulus, and Cyrus. And as if this were not enough, his work is replete with the messianic imagery of enslavement, liberation, and future redemption. Machiavelli makes frequent use of the language of prophecy and the religious imagination, but turns it in the direction of some future emancipation. This is especially true in the last chapter of *The Prince* where Machiavelli makes clear that the ideal kingdom to come will occur in Italy only after it has succeeded in subduing its foreign conquerors, including the Church. Machiavelli did not so much reflect his age as create it.

In perhaps the most important book on Machiavelli ever written, Leo Strauss declared Machiavelli to be a "teacher of evil." What else can you say of a man whose name has become virtually synonymous with cruelty, deceit, and betrayal? Whether or not he is a teacher of evil, it is clear that questions of good and bad appear on virtually every page of *The Prince*. He is not simply a teacher of cautious pragmatism, of how to adjust the means to fit the ends; he is offering nothing short of a comprehensive reevaluation of our basic moral vocabulary of good and bad. In his famous formula he sets out to teach the prince "how not to be good."

Machiavelli does not so much reject the idea of the good as he redefines it. He is continually speaking the language of virtue—actually *virtù*—a word that retains the Latin root for the word "man" and which translates into something like our term for manliness. What most distinguishes Machiavelli's use of this term is that he seeks to locate it in certain extreme situations such as political foundings, changes of regimes, wars, and revolutions. What distinguishes Machiavelli from his predecessors is his attempt to take the extraordinary situation—the extreme—as the normal situation and then make morality fit the extreme. His examples are typically drawn from situations *in extremis* where the very survival or independence of society is at stake. We might call these existential moments in politics. In such situations—and only in such situations— is it permissible to violate the precepts of ordinary morality and for Machiavelli every situation is potentially an existential situation.

The model of Machiavellian *virtù* is the Renaissance statesman and condottieri Cesare Borgia, the son of Pope Alexander VI. In chapter VII of *The Prince* he gives a powerful example of Cesare's virtue in practice. Here Machiavelli tells the story of how Cesare appointed one of his lieutenants, Remirro di Orco, "a cruel and able man" to help organize a territory not far from the outskirts of Florence. Remirro was an efficient officer and soon established order, but in order to show that he was in charge Cesare ordered Remirro to be murdered and the body and bloody knife to be displayed in the town square. "The ferocity of such a spectacle," Machiavelli concludes, "left those people satisfied and amazed at the same time."

No one can read Machiavelli's descriptions of political assassination, conquest, and usurpation without sensing his deep admiration, even celebration, of acts of creative violence. Thus can he heap praise on Hannibal whose "inhuman cruelty, which along with his many other abilities, made him always respected and terrifying in the eyes of his soldiers." He treated violence not as an unfortunate byproduct of political necessity, but as a supreme political virtue from which form is imposed on matter. But Machiavelli was not a sadist. He did not celebrate cruelty for its own sake. In a deeply revealing passage he deplored Ferdinand of Aragon for his acts of "pious cruelty" in expelling the Jews from Spain.

Machiavelli's ethic of violence is connected to the belief that the great civilizations in history—the Persian, the Hebrew, the Roman—all grew out of acts of cruelty, domination, and conquest. The great political leaders past and present were not monks or moral philosophers calibrating finely tuned theories of justice but men with "dirty hands" who were prepared to use instruments of deceit, cruelty, and even murder to achieve conspicuous greatness. Machiavelli takes a perverse delight in bringing out the dependence of flourishing and successful civilizations on initial acts of fratricide, murder, and civil war.

Machiavelli's ethics are avowedly immoralist. What he wants the prince to value above all else is glory, fame, and honor. This is what has been sought by the most "excellent men," Moses, Theseus, Cyrus, and maybe Borgia, but which others, like Agathocles, lacked. The ethic of glory is a distinctively nonmoral good. It aims not at justice, fairness, or friendship, but at fostering those qualities that bring with them memorable greatness and lasting fame. The question that animates *The Prince* is how to recapture some of the pagan spirit of worldly power and greatness that contributed to the flourishing of the ancient states. It is this ethic of worldly glory that Machiavelli believes has been most reviled by the moralists of the Christian period and that has directly contributed to the decadence, weakness, and disunity of the states of his time.

Machiavelli's question of how to achieve lasting fame is answered not in *The Prince* but in his longest and arguably greatest work the *Discourses on Livy*. The *Discourses* were written between 1513 and 1517 but not published until after Machiavelli's death. *The Prince* follows the traditional genre of the mirror of princes. It is a manual on how to achieve and maintain princely power. The *Discourses* is commonly regarded as Machiavelli's book on republics. It takes the form of a historical and political commentary on the first ten books of Titus Livy's history of Rome. Livy told the history of Rome from its founding to the establishment of the republic and its height of power. In choosing to present his teaching by means of a commentary on the greatest Roman historian, Machiavelli calls the reader's attention to the greatness, the unsurpassable greatness, of republican Rome. For anyone who wants to understand greatness he seems to say, you must study Rome.

Machiavelli hopes to whet his readers' appetite for Rome in the preface to the *Discourses*. This is where he famously announces his discovery of "new methods and institutions" and compares himself to Christopher Columbus in entering into "unknown oceans and lands." The paradox at the heart of the *Discourses* is that Machiavelli's claim to novelty—his nautical image of the discovery of new lands—is actually a recovery of a forgotten land, the land of republican Rome. How does Machiavelli make something very old appear to be new and unprecedented? One answer is that he uses Livy—a respected and respectable authority—as a means to advocate for his own views on what constitutes a well-ordered republic.

Machiavelli encourages his readers not just to idly and eclectically reflect on antiquity, but to actively imitate the great deeds of their ancient ancestors. It is this, he says, that has led him to write a commentary on Livy. Indeed, to do full justice to the *Discourses* one would need to read it with constant reference to Livy and to Machiavelli's many other classical sources. To be sure, the *Discourses* is no ordinary commentary. He uses Livy promiscuously, and at times Livy disappears altogether from Machiavelli's text. He hopes to improve upon Livy and therefore to improve upon Rome. Machiavelli was not content to confine himself to the study of ancient sources alone, but was constantly comparing "ancient with modern affairs" in order to draw "practical knowledge" from them.

Most importantly, Machiavelli sought to inspire a taste for political liberty that could only come about through his rehabilitation of Rome. Rome was the model of what a republic could be. But Machiavelli was not a slavish admirer of the past for its own sake. The great defect of Rome, he tells us, is that it achieved its greatness not through planning but through fortune or luck. We cannot afford to rely on *fortuna*. Armed with the right science, we can free ourselves from dependence on fortune; we will be able to take affairs into our own hands and to achieve through our own unaided efforts what in the past had been consigned to the province of wish, prayer, or the cycle of history. What Rome had done haphazardly, can be done again, but this time consciously or through design. We can imitate Rome and improve upon it. We can learn to conquer chance and in so doing create, perhaps for the first time, a new immortal republic.

Machiavelli was not simply an idle dreamer. He was a prophet of the modern world. His work proved remarkably successful and he wrote in a way that he hoped would ensure success. He was one of those "unarmed prophets" who conquered not through the sword but through the pen. His writings attracted imitators and followers.

Just over a century after Machiavelli's death, his work inspired those English republicans during the English Civil War to overthrow their king and establish a republic in its place. A century later, revolutionaries in America and France overthrew their monarchies to establish their own experiments with republican government. Is Machiavelli the founder—the true founder—of the American republic? Would it be too humiliating to our national pride to see in our immaculate conception the hand of the wily Florentine? This is a subject worthy of consideration.

Isaiah Berlin, "The Originality of Machiavelli," *Against the Current: Essays in the History of Ideas*, edited by Henry Hardy (New York: Viking Press, 1980), is a brilliant interpretation of Machiavelli as one of sources of the modern theory of value pluralism. Victoria Kahn, *Machiavellian Rhetoric: From the Counter-Reformation to Milton* (Princeton, N.J.: Princeton University Press, 1994), is a study of the influence of Machiavelli on English Renaissance literature. John McCormick, *Machiavellian Democracy* (New York: Cambridge University Press, 2011), is an unconventional interpretation and defense of Machiavelli as a theorist of radical democracy. J. G. A. Pocock, *The Machiavellian Moment: Florentine Political Thought and the Republican Tradition* (Princeton, N.J.: Princeton University Press, 1975), is a highly influential study of the role of Machiavelli's ideas in the creation of a republican political tradition in England and North America. Leo Strauss, *Thoughts on Machiavelli* (Chicago: University of Chicago Press, 1978), is a masterful study of Machiavelli as the founder of modern political philosophy.

The Prince

CHAPTER I

How Many Kinds of Principalities There Are and the Way They Are Acquired

All states, all dominions that have had and continue to have power over men were and still are either republics or principalities. Principalities are either hereditary, in which instance the family of the prince has ruled for generations, or they are new. The new ones are either completely new, as was Milan for Francesco Sforza, or they are like members added to the hereditary state of the prince who acquires them, as is the Kingdom of Naples for the King of Spain. Dominions taken in this way are either used to living under a prince or are accustomed to being free; and they are gained either by the arms of others or by one's own, either through fortune or through ingenuity.

CHAPTER II

On Hereditary Principalities

I shall set aside any discussion of republics, because I treated them elsewhere at length. I shall consider solely the principality, developing as I go the topics mentioned above; and I shall discuss how these principalities can be governed and maintained.

Copyright © by Peter Bondanella and Mark Musa, 1984. Reprinted from *The Prince* by Niccolò Machiavelli, translated by Peter Bondanella and Mark Musa (World Classics, 1984) by permission of Oxford University Press.

I say, then, that in hereditary states accustomed to the rule of their prince's family there are far fewer difficulties in maintaining them than in new states; for it suffices simply not to break ancient customs, and then to suit one's actions to unexpected events; in this manner, if such a prince is of ordinary ability, he will always maintain his state, unless some extraordinary and inordinate force deprive him of it; and although it may be taken away from him, he will regain it with the slightest mistake of the usurper. . . .

CHAPTER III

On Mixed Principalities

But it is the new principality that causes difficulties. In the first place, if it is not completely new but is instead an acquisition (so that the two parts together may be called mixed), its difficulties derive from one natural problem inherent in all new principalities: men gladly change their masters, thinking to better themselves; and this belief causes them to take arms against their ruler; but they fool themselves in this, since with experience they see that things have become worse. This stems from another natural and ordinary necessity, which is that a new prince must always offend his new subjects both through his soldiers and other countless injuries that are involved in his new conquest; thus, you have made enemies of all those you injured in occupying the principality and you are unable to maintain as friends those who helped you to rise to power, since you cannot satisfy them in the way that they had supposed, nor can you use strong measures against them, for you are in their debt; because, although one may have the most powerful of armies, he always needs the support of the inhabitants to seize a province. For these reasons, Louis XII, King of France, quickly occupied Milan and just as quickly lost it; and the first time, the troops of Ludovico alone were needed to retake it from him, because those citizens who had opened the gates of the city to the king, finding themselves deceived in their

beliefs and in that future improvement they had anticipated, could not support the offences of the new prince.

It is indeed true that when lands which have rebelled once are taken a second time, it is more difficult to lose them; for the lord, taking advantage of the revolt, is less reticent about punishing offenders, ferreting out suspects, and shoring up weak positions. So that, if only a Duke Ludovico threatening the borders was sufficient for France to lose Milan the first time, the whole world had to oppose her and destroy her armies or chase them from Italy to cause her to lose it the second time; and this happened for the reasons mentioned above. Nevertheless, it was taken from her both the first and the second time.

The general explanations for the first loss have been discussed; now there remains to specify those for the second, and to see what remedies the King of France had, and those that one in the same situation might have, so that he might be able to maintain a stronger grip on his conquest than did France. Therefore, I say that those dominions which, upon being conquered, are added to the long-established state of him who acquires them are either of the same province and language or they are not. When they are, it is easier to hold them, especially when they are unaccustomed to freedom; and to possess them securely, it is only necessary to have extinguished the family line of the prince who ruled them, because in so far as other things are concerned, men live peacefully as long as their old way of life is maintained and there is no change in customs: thus, we have seen what happened in the case of Burgundy, Brittany, Gascony, and Normandy, which have been part of France for such a long time; and although there are some linguistic differences, nevertheless the customs are similar and they have been able to get along together easily. And anyone who acquires these lands and wishes to maintain them must bear two things in mind: first, that the family line of the old prince must be extinguished; second, that neither their laws nor their taxes be altered;

as a result they will become in a very brief time one body with the old principality.

But when dominions are acquired in a province that is not similar in language, customs, and laws, it is here that difficulties arise; and it is here that one needs much good fortune and much diligence to hold on to them. And one of the best and most efficacious remedies would be for the person who has taken possession of them to go and live there. This would make that possession more secure and durable, as the Turks did with Greece; for despite all the other precautions they took to retain that dominion, if they had not gone there to live, it would have been impossible for them to hold on to it. Because, by being on the spot, one sees trouble at its birth and one can quickly remedy it; not being there, one hears about it after it has grown and there is no longer any remedy. Moreover, the province would not be plundered by one's own officers; the subjects would be pleased to have direct recourse to their prince; thus, wishing to be good subjects, they have more reason to love him and, wanting to be otherwise, more reason to fear him. Anyone who might wish to invade that dominion from abroad would be more hesitant; so that, living right there, the prince can only with the greatest of difficulties lose it.

The other and better solution is to send colonies into one or two places that will act as supports for your own state; for it is necessary that the prince either do this or maintain a large number of infantry and cavalry. Colonies do not cost much, and with little or no expense a prince can send and maintain them; and in so doing he hurts only those whose fields and houses have been taken and given to the new inhabitants, who are only a small part of that state; and those that he hurts, being dispersed and poor, can never be a threat to him, and all others remain on the one hand unharmed (and because of this, they should remain silent), and on the other afraid of making a mistake, for fear that what happened to those who were dispossessed might happen to them. I conclude that these colonies are not expensive, they are more faithful, and they create fewer

difficulties; and those who are hurt cannot pose a threat, since they are poor and scattered, as I have already said. Concerning this, it should be noted that one must either pamper or do away with men, because they will avenge themselves for minor offences while for more serious ones they cannot; so that any harm done to a man must be the kind that removes any fear of revenge. But by maintaining soldiers there instead of colonies, one spends much more, being obliged to consume all the revenues of the state in guarding its borders, so that the profit becomes a loss; and far greater injury is committed, since the entire state is harmed by the army changing quarters from one place to another; everybody resents this inconvenience, and everyone becomes an enemy; and these are enemies that can be harmful, since they remain, although conquered, in their own home. And so, in every respect, this kind of defence is as useless as the other kind, colonization, is useful. . . .

CHAPTER V

How Cities or Principalities Should Be Governed That Lived by Their Own Laws Before They Were Occupied

As I have said, when those states that are acquired are used to living by their own laws and in freedom, there are three methods of holding on to them: the first is to destroy them; the second is to go there in person to live; the third is to allow them to live with their own laws, forcing them to pay a tribute and creating therein a government made up of a few people who will keep the state friendly toward you. For such a government, having been created by that prince, knows it cannot last without his friendship and his power, and it must do everything possible to maintain them; and a city used to living in freedom is more easily maintained through the means of its own citizens than in any other way, if you decide to preserve it.

As examples, there are the Spartans and the Romans. The Spartans held Athens and Thebes by building therein a government consisting of a few people; eventually they lost them both. The Romans, in order to hold Capua, Carthage, and Numantia, destroyed them and did not lose them; they wished to hold Greece in almost the same manner as the Spartans held it, making it free and leaving it under its own laws, and they did not succeed; thus, they were obliged to destroy many of the cities in that province in order to retain it. For, in fact, there is no secure means of holding on to them except by destroying them. And anyone who becomes lord of a city used to living in liberty and does not destroy it may expect to be destroyed by it, because such a city always has as a refuge, in any rebellion, the spirit of liberty and its ancient institutions, neither of which is ever forgotten either because of the passing of time or because of the bestowal of benefits. And it matters little what one does or foresees, since if one does not separate or scatter the inhabitants, they will not forget that spirit or those institutions; and immediately, in every case, they will return to them just as Pisa did after one hundred years of being held in servitude by the Florentines. But when cities or provinces are accustomed to living under a prince and the family of that prince has been extinguished, they, being on the one hand used to obedience and, on the other, not having their old prince and not being able to agree on choosing another from amongst themselves, yet not knowing how to live as free men, are as a result hesitant in taking up arms, and a prince can win them over and assure himself of their support with greater ease. But in republics there is greater vitality, greater hatred, greater desire for revenge; the memory of ancient liberty does not and cannot allow them to submit, so that the most secure course is either to destroy them or to go there to live.

CHAPTER VI

On New Principalities Acquired by One's Own Arms and Skill

No one should marvel if, in speaking of principalities that are totally new as to their prince and organization, I use the most illustrious examples;

since men almost always tread the paths made by others and proceed in their affairs by imitation, although they are not completely able to stay on the path of others nor attain the skill of those they imitate, a prudent man should always enter those paths taken by great men and imitate those who have been most excellent, so that if one's own skill does not match theirs, at least it will have the smell of it; and he should proceed like those prudent archers who, aware of the strength of their bow when the target they are aiming at seems too distant, set their sights much higher than the designated target, not in order to reach to such a height with their arrow but rather to be able, with the aid of such a high aim, to strike the target.

I say, therefore, that in completely new principalities, where there is a new prince, one finds in maintaining them more or less difficulty according to the greater or lesser skill of the one who acquires them. And because this act of transition from private citizen to prince presupposes either ingenuity or fortune, it appears that either the one or the other of these two things should, in part, mitigate many of the problems; nevertheless, he who relies upon fortune less maintains his position best. Things are also facilitated when the prince, having no other dominions to govern, is constrained to come to live there in person. But to come to those who, by means of their own skill and not because of fortune, have become princes, I say that the most admirable are Moses, Cyrus, Romulus, Theseus, and the like. And although we should not discuss Moses, since he was a mere executor of things ordered by God, nevertheless he must be admired, if for nothing but that grace which made him worthy of talking with God. But let us consider Cyrus and the others who have acquired or founded kingdoms; you will find them all admirable; and if their deeds and their particular institutions are considered, they will not appear different from those of Moses, who had so great a guide. And examining their deeds and their lives, one can see that they received nothing from fortune except the opportunity, which gave them the material they could mould into whatever form they desired; and without that opportunity the strength of their spirit would have been extinguished, and without that strength the opportunity would have come in vain.

It was therefore necessary for Moses to find the people of Israel in Egypt slaves and oppressed by the Egyptians in order that they might be disposed to follow him to escape this servitude. It was necessary for Romulus not to stay in Alba and to be exposed at birth so that he might become King of Rome and founder of that nation. It was necessary for Cyrus to find the Persians discontented with the empire of the Medes, and the Medes soft and effeminate after a lengthy peace. Theseus could not have shown his skill if he had not found the Athenians scattered. These opportunities, therefore, made these men successful, and their outstanding ingenuity made that opportunity known to them, whereby their nations were ennobled and became prosperous.

Like these men, those who become princes through their skill acquire the principality with difficulty, but they hold on to it easily; and the difficulties they encounter in acquiring the principality grow, in part, out of the new institutions and methods they are obliged to introduce in order to found their state and their security. And one should bear in mind that there is nothing more difficult to execute, nor more dubious of success, nor more dangerous to administer than to introduce a new order of things; for he who introduces it has all those who profit from the old order as his enemies, and he has only lukewarm allies in all those who might profit from the new. This lukewarmness partly stems from fear of their adversaries, who have the law on their side, and partly from the scepticism of men, who do not truly believe in new things unless they have actually had personal experience of them. Therefore, it happens that whenever those who are enemies have the chance to attack, they do so enthusiastically, whereas those others defend hesitantly, so that they, together with the prince, are in danger.

It is necessary, however, if we desire to examine this subject thoroughly, to observe whether these innovators act on their own or are dependent on others: that is, if they are forced to beg or are able to use power in conducting their affairs. In the first case, they always come to a bad end and never accomplish anything; but when they depend on their own resources and can use power, then only seldom do they find themselves in peril. From this comes the fact that all armed prophets were victorious and the unarmed came to ruin. Besides what has been said, people are fickle by nature; and it is simple to convince them of something but difficult to hold them in that conviction; and, therefore, affairs should be managed in such a way that when they no longer believe, they can be made to believe by force. Moses, Cyrus, Theseus, and Romulus could not have made their institutions long respected if they had been unarmed; as in our times happened to Brother Girolamo Savonarola, who was ruined by his new institutions when the populace began no longer to believe in them, since he had no way of holding steady those who had believed nor of making the disbelievers believe. Therefore, such men have great problems in getting ahead, and they meet all their dangers as they proceed, and they must overcome them with their skill; but once they have overcome them and have begun to be respected, having removed those who were envious of their merits, they remain powerful, secure, honoured, and happy. . . .

CHAPTER VII

On New Principalities Acquired with the Arms of Others and by Fortune

Those private citizens who become princes through fortune alone do so with little effort, but they maintain their position only with a great deal; they meet no obstacles along their way since they fly to success, but all their problems arise when they have arrived. And these are the men who are granted a state either because they have money or because they enjoy the favour of him who grants it: this occurred to many in Greece in the cities of Ionia and the Hellespont, where Darius created princes in order that he might hold these cities for his security and glory; in like manner were set up those emperors who from private citizens came to power by bribing the soldiers. Such men depend solely upon two very uncertain and unstable things; the will and the fortune of him who granted them the state; they do not know how and are not able to maintain their position. They do not know how, since if men are not of great intelligence and ingenuity, it is not reasonable that they know how to rule, having always lived as private citizens; they are not able to, since they do not have forces that are friendly and faithful. Besides, states that rise quickly, just as all the other things of nature that are born and grow rapidly, cannot have roots and ramifications; the first bad weather kills them, unless these men who have suddenly become princes, as I have noted, are of such ability that they know how to prepare themselves quickly and to preserve what fortune has put in their laps, and to construct afterwards those foundations that others have built before becoming princes. . . .

CHAPTER VIII

On Those Who Have Become Princes Through Wickedness

But because there are yet two more ways one can from an ordinary citizen become prince, which cannot completely be attributed to either fortune or skill, I believe they should not be left unmentioned, although one of them will be discussed at greater length in a treatise on republics. These two are: when one becomes prince through some wicked and nefarious means or when a private citizen becomes prince of his native city through the favour of his fellow citizens. And in discussing the first way, I shall cite two examples, one from classical times and the other from recent days, without otherwise entering into the merits of this method, since I consider them sufficient for anyone forced to imitate them.

Agathocles the Sicilian, not only from being an ordinary citizen but from being of low and abject status, became King of Syracuse. This

man, a potter's son, lived a wicked life at every stage of his career; yet he joined to his wickedness such strength of mind and of body that, when he entered upon a military career, he rose through the ranks to become commander of Syracuse. Once placed in such a position, having decided to become prince and to hold with violence and without any obligations to others what had been granted to him by universal consent, and having made an agreement with Hamilcar the Carthaginian, who was waging war with his armies in Sicily, he called together one morning the people and the senate of Syracuse as if he were going to discuss things concerning the state; and with a prearranged signal, he had his troops kill all the senators and the richest citizens; and when they were dead, he seized and held the rule of the city without any opposition from the citizenry. And although he was twice defeated by the Carthaginians and eventually besieged, not only was he able to defend his city but, leaving part of his troops for the defence of the siege, with his other men he attacked Africa, and in a short time he freed Syracuse from the siege and forced the Carthaginians into dire straits: they were obliged to make peace with him and to be content with possession of Africa and to leave Sicily to Agathocles.

Anyone, therefore, who examines the deeds and the life of this man will observe nothing or very little that can be attributed to fortune; since, as was said earlier, not with the aid of others but by rising through the ranks, which involved a thousand hardships and dangers, did he come to rule the principality which he then maintained by many brave and dangerous actions. Still, it cannot be called ingenuity to kill one's fellow citizens, to betray friends, to be without faith, without mercy, without religion; by these means one can acquire power but not glory. For if one were to consider Agathocles's ability in getting into and out of dangers, and his greatness of spirit in supporting and in overcoming adversaries, one can see no reason why he should be judged inferior to any most excellent commander; nevertheless, his vicious cruelty and inhumanity, along with numerous wicked deeds, do not permit us to honour him among the most excellent of men. One cannot, therefore, attribute to either fortune or skill what he accomplished without either the one or the other. . . .

One might wonder how Agathocles and others like him, after so many betrayals and cruelties, could live for such a long time secure in their cities and defend themselves from outside enemies without being plotted against by their own citizens; many others, using cruel means, were unable even in peaceful times to hold on to their state, not to speak of the uncertain times of war. I believe that this depends on whether cruelty be well or badly used. Well used are those cruelties (if it is permitted to speak well of evil) that are carried out in a single stroke, done out of necessity to protect oneself, and are not continued but are instead converted into the greatest possible benefits for the subjects. Badly used are those cruelties which, although being few at the outset, grow with the passing of time instead of disappearing. Those who follow the first method can remedy their condition with God and with men as Agathocles did; the others cannot possibly survive.

Wherefore it is to be noted that in taking a state its conqueror should weigh all the harmful things he must do and do them all at once so as not to have to repeat them every day, and in not repeating them to be able to make men feel secure and win them over with the benefits he bestows upon them. Anyone who does otherwise, either out of timidity or because of poor advice, is always obliged to keep his knife in his hand; nor can he ever count upon his subjects, who, because of their fresh and continual injuries, cannot feel secure with him. Injuries, therefore, should be inflicted all at the same time, for the less they are tasted, the less they offend; and benefits should be distributed a bit at a time in order that they may be savoured fully. And a prince should, above all, live with his subjects in such a way that no unforeseen event, either good or bad, may make him alter his course; for when emergencies arise in adverse conditions, you are not in time to resort to cruelty, and the good you do will help you little, since it will be judged a forced measure and you will earn from it no thanks whatsoever.

CHAPTER IX

On the Civil Principality

But coming to the second instance, when a private citizen, not through wickedness or any other intolerable violence, but with the favour of his fellow citizens, becomes prince of his native city (this can be called a civil principality, the acquisition of which neither depends completely upon skill nor upon fortune, but instead upon a mixture of shrewdness and luck), I maintain that one reaches this princedom either with the favour of the common people or with that of the nobility. For these two different humours are found in every body politic; and they arise from the fact that the people do not wish to be commanded or oppressed by the nobles, and the nobles desire to command and to oppress the people; and from these two opposed appetites there arises one of three effects: either a principality or liberty or anarchy.

A principality is brought about either by the common people or by the nobility, depending on which of the two parties has the opportunity. For when the nobles see that they cannot resist the populace, they begin to support one among them and make him prince in order to be able, under his protection, to satisfy their appetites. The common people as well, seeing that they cannot resist the nobility, give their support to one man and make him prince in order to have the protection of his authority. He who attains the principality with the aid of the nobility maintains it with more difficulty than he who becomes prince with the assistance of the common people, for he finds himself a prince amidst many who feel themselves to be his equals, and because of this he can neither govern nor manage them as he wishes. But he who attains the principality through popular favour finds himself alone and has around him either no one or very few who are not ready to obey him.

Moreover, one cannot honestly satisfy the nobles without harming others, but the common people can certainly be satisfied: their desire is more just than that of the nobles—the former want not to be oppressed and the latter want to oppress. Moreover, a prince can never make himself secure when the people are his enemy because they are so many; he can make himself secure against the nobles because they are so few. The worst that a prince can expect from a hostile people is to be abandoned by them; but with a hostile nobility not only does he have to fear being abandoned but also that they will unite against him; for, being more perceptive and shrewder, they always have time to save themselves, to seek the favours of the side they believe will win. Furthermore, a prince must always live with the same common people; but he can easily do without the same nobles, having the power to create them and to destroy them from day to day and to take away and give back their prestige as he sees fit.

And in order to clarify this point better, I say that the nobles should be considered chiefly in two ways: either they conduct themselves in such a way that they commit themselves completely to your cause or they do not. Those who commit themselves and are not greedy should be honoured and loved; those who do not commit themselves can be analysed in two ways. They act in this manner out of fear and a natural lack of courage, in which case you should make use of them, especially those who are wise advisers, since in prosperous times they will gain you honour and in adverse times you need not fear them. But when, cunningly and influenced by ambition, they refrain from committing themselves to you, this is a sign that they think more of themselves than of you; and the prince should be wary of such men and fear them as if they were open enemies, because they will always, in adverse times, help to bring about his downfall.

However, one who becomes prince with the support of the common people must keep them as his friends; this is easy for him, since the only thing they ask of him is not to be oppressed.

But one who, against the will of the common people, becomes prince with the assistance of the nobility should, before all else, seek to win the people's support, which should be easy if he takes them under his protection. And because men, when they are well treated by those from whom they expected harm, are more obliged to their benefactor, the common people quickly become better disposed toward him than if he had become prince with their support. And a prince can gain their favour in various ways, but because they vary according to the situation no fixed rules can be given for them, and therefore I shall not talk about them. I shall conclude by saying only that a prince must have the friendship of the common people; otherwise he will have no support in times of adversity.

Nabis, prince of the Spartans, withstood the attacks of all of Greece and of one of Rome's most victorious armies, and he defended his city and his own rule against them, and when danger was near he needed only to protect himself from a few of his subjects; but if he had had the common people against him, this would not have been sufficient. And let no one dispute my opinion by citing that trite proverb, "He who builds upon the people builds upon the mud," because that is true when a private citizen lays his foundations and allows himself to believe that the common people will free him if he is oppressed by enemies or by the public officials (in this case a man might often find himself deceived, like the Gracchi of Rome or like Messer Giorgio Scali of Florence); but when the prince who builds his foundations on the people is one who is able to command and is a man of spirit, not bewildered by adversities, and does not lack other necessities, and through his courage and his institutions keeps up the spirits of the populace, he will never find himself deceived by the common people, and he will discover that he has laid sound foundations.

Principalities of this type are usually endangered when they are about to change from a proper civil society to an absolute form of government. For these princes either rule by themselves or by means of public officials; in the latter case their position is weaker and more dangerous since they depend entirely upon the will of those citizens who are appointed to hold the offices; these men, especially in adverse times, can very easily seize the state either by open opposition or by disobedience. And in such times of danger the prince has no time for taking absolute control, for the citizens and subjects who are used to receiving their orders from public officials are, in these crises, not willing to obey his orders; and in doubtful times he will always find a scarcity of men he can trust. Such a prince cannot rely upon what he sees during periods of calm, when the citizens need his rule, because then everyone comes running, makes promises, and each one is willing to die for him—since death is unlikely; but in times of adversity, when the state needs its citizens, then few are to be found. And this experiment is all the more dangerous in that it can be made but once. And, therefore, a wise prince should think of a method by which his citizens, at all times and in every circumstance, will need the assistance of the state and of himself; and then they will always be loyal to him.

CHAPTER XV

On Those Things for Which Men, and Particularly Princes, Are Praised or Blamed

Now there remains to be examined what should be the methods and procedures of a prince in dealing with his subjects and friends. And because I know that many have written about this, I am afraid that by writing about it again I shall be thought of as presumptuous, since in discussing this material I depart radically from the procedures of others. But since my intention is to write something useful for anyone who understands it, it seemed more suitable to me to search after the effectual truth of the matter rather than its imagined one. And many writers have imagined for themselves republics and principalities that have never been seen nor known to exist in reality; for there is such a gap between how one lives and how one ought to live that anyone who abandons what is done for

what ought to be done learns his ruin rather than his preservation: for a man who wishes to profess goodness at all times will come to ruin among so many who are not good. Hence it is necessary for a prince who wishes to maintain his position to learn how not to be good, and to use this knowledge or not to use it according to necessity.

Leaving aside, therefore, the imagined things concerning a prince, and taking into account those that are true, I say that all men, when they are spoken of, and particularly princes, since they are placed on a higher level, are judged by some of these qualities which bring them either blame or praise. And this is why one is considered generous, another miserly (to use a Tuscan word, since "avaricious" in our language is still used to mean one who wishes to acquire by means of theft; we call "miserly" one who excessively avoids using what he has); one is considered a giver, the other rapacious; one cruel, another merciful; one treacherous, another faithful; one effeminate and cowardly, another bold and courageous; one humane, another haughty; one lascivious, another chaste; one trustworthy, another frivolous; one religious, another unbelieving; and the like. And I know that everyone will admit that it would be a very praiseworthy thing to find in a prince, of the qualities mentioned above, those that are held to be good; but since it is neither possible to have them nor to observe them all completely, because the human condition does not permit it, a prince must be prudent enough to know how to escape the bad reputation of those vices that would lose the state for him, and must protect himself from those that will not lose it for him, if this is possible; but if he cannot, he need not concern himself unduly if he ignores these less serious vices. And, moreover, he need not worry about incurring the bad reputation of those vices without which it would be difficult to hold his state; since, carefully taking everything into account, he will discover that something which appears to be a virtue, if pursued, will end in his destruction; while some other thing which seems to be a vice, if pursued, will result in his safety and his well-being.

CHAPTER XVII

On Cruelty and Mercy, and Whether It Is Better to Be Loved Than to Be Feared or the Contrary

Proceeding to the other qualities mentioned above, I say that every prince must desire to be considered merciful and not cruel; nevertheless, he must take care not to misuse this mercy. Cesare Borgia was considered cruel; none the less, his cruelty had brought order to Romagna, united it, restored it to peace and obedience. If we examine this carefully, we shall see that he was more merciful than the Florentine people, who, in order to avoid being considered cruel, allowed the destruction of Pistoia. Therefore, a prince must not worry about the reproach of cruelty when it is a matter of keeping his subjects united and loyal; for with a very few examples of cruelty he will be more compassionate than those who, out of excessive mercy, permit disorders to continue, from which arise murders and plundering; for these usually harm the community at large, while the executions that come from the prince harm particular individuals. And the new prince, above all other princes, cannot escape the reputation of being called cruel, since new states are full of dangers. And Virgil, through Dido, states: "My difficult condition and the newness of my rule make me act in such a manner, and to set guards over my land on all sides."

Nevertheless, a prince must be cautious in believing and in acting; nor should he be afraid of his own shadow; and he should proceed in such a manner, tempered by prudence and humanity, so that too much trust may not render him imprudent nor too much distrust render him intolerable.

From this arises an argument: whether it is better to be loved than to be feared, or the contrary. I reply that one should like to be both one and the other; but since it is difficult to join them together, it is much safer to be feared than to be loved when one of the two must be lacking. For one can generally say this about men: that they are ungrateful, fickle, simulators and deceivers, avoiders of danger, greedy for gain; and while you work for their good they are completely yours, offering you their blood, their property, their lives, and their sons, as I said earlier, when danger is far away; but when it comes nearer to you they turn away. And that prince who bases his power entirely on their words, finding himself completely without other preparations, comes to ruin; for friendships that are acquired by a price and not by greatness and nobility of character are purchased but are not owned, and at the proper moment they cannot be spent. And men are less hesitant about harming someone who makes himself loved than one who makes himself feared because love is held together by a chain of obligation which, since men are wretched creatures, is broken on every occasion in which their own interests are concerned; but fear is sustained by a dread of punishment which will never abandon you.

A prince must nevertheless make himself feared in such a manner that he will avoid hatred, even if he does not acquire love; since to be feared and not be hated can very well be combined; and this will always be so when he keeps his hands off the property and the women of his citizens and his subjects. And if he must take someone's life, he should do so when there is proper justification and manifest cause; but, above all, he should avoid seizing the property of others; for men forget more quickly the death of their father than the loss of their patrimony. Moreover, reasons for seizing their property are never lacking; and he who begins to live by stealing always finds a reason for taking what belongs to others; on the contrary, reasons for taking a life are rarer and disappear sooner.

But when the prince is with his armies and has under his command a multitude of troops, then it is absolutely necessary that he not worry about being considered cruel; for without that reputation he will never keep an army united or prepared for any combat. Among the praiseworthy deeds of Hannibal is counted this: that, having a very large army, made up of all kinds of men, which he commanded in foreign lands, there never arose the slightest dissension, neither among themselves nor against their leader, both during his good and his bad fortune. This could not have arisen from anything other than his inhuman cruelty, which along with his many other qualities, made him always respected and terrifying in the eyes of his soldiers; and without that, to attain the same effect, his other qualities would not have sufficed. And the writers of history, having considered this matter very little, on the one hand admire these deeds of his and on the other condemn the main cause of them. . . .

I conclude, therefore, returning to the problem of being feared and loved, that since men love at their own pleasure and fear at the pleasure of the prince, a wise prince should build his foundation upon that which belongs to him, not upon that which belongs to others: he must strive only to avoid hatred, as has been said.

CHAPTER XVIII

How a Prince Should Keep His Word

How praiseworthy it is for a prince to keep his word and to live by integrity and not by deceit everyone knows; nevertheless, one sees from the experience of our times that the princes who have accomplished great deeds are those who have known how to manipulate the minds of men by shrewdness; and in the end they have surpassed those who laid their foundations upon loyalty.

You must, therefore, know that there are two means of fighting: one according to the laws, the other with force; the first way is proper to man, the second to beasts; but because the first, in many cases is not sufficient, it becomes necessary to have recourse to the second. Therefore, a prince must know how to use wisely the natures of the beast and the man. This policy was taught to princes allegorically by the ancient writers, who described how Achilles and many other ancient princes were given to Chiron the Centaur to be raised and taught under his discipline. This can

only mean that, having a half-beast and half-man as a teacher, a prince must know how to employ the nature of the one and the other; and the one without the other cannot endure.

Since, then, a prince must know how to make good use of the nature of the beast, he should choose from among the beasts the fox and the lion; for the lion cannot defend itself from traps and the fox cannot protect itself from wolves. It is therefore necessary to be a fox in order to recognize the traps and a lion in order to frighten the wolves. Those who play only the part of the lion do not understand matters. A wise ruler, therefore, cannot and should not keep his word when such an observance of faith would be to his disadvantage and when the reasons which made him promise are removed. And if men were all good, this rule would not be good; but since men are a contemptible lot and will not keep their promises to you, you likewise need not keep yours to them. A prince never lacks legitimate reasons to break his promise. Of this one could cite an endless number of modern examples to show how many pacts, how many promises have been made null and void because of the infidelity of princes; and he who has known best how to use the fox has come to a better end. But it is necessary to know how to disguise this nature well and to be a great hypocrite and a liar: and men are so simple-minded and so controlled by their present needs that one who deceives will always find another who will allow himself to be deceived. . . .

Therefore, it is not necessary for a prince to have all of the above-mentioned qualities, but it is very necessary for him to appear to have them. Furthermore, I shall be so bold as to assert this: that having them and practising them at all times is harmful; and appearing to have them is useful; for instance, to seem merciful, faithful, humane, trustworthy, religious, and to be so; but his mind should be disposed in such a way that should it become necessary not to be so, he will be able and know how to change to the contrary. And it is essential to understand this: that a prince, and especially a new prince, cannot observe all those things for which men are considered good, for in order to maintain the state he is often obliged to act against his promise, against charity, against humanity, and against religion. And therefore, it is necessary that he have a mind ready to turn itself according to the way the winds of fortune and the changeability of affairs require him; and, as I said above, as long as it is possible, he should not stray from the good, but he should know how to enter into evil when necessity commands.

A prince, therefore, must be very careful never to let anything slip from his lips which is not full of the five qualities mentioned above: he should appear, upon seeing and hearing him, to be all mercy, all faithfulness, all integrity, all kindness, all religion. And there is nothing more necessary than to seem to possess this last quality. And men in general judge more by the eyes than their hands; for everyone can see but few can feel. Everyone sees what you seem to be, few touch upon what you are, and those few who do not dare to contradict the opinion of the many who have the majesty of the state to defend them; and in the actions of all men, and especially of princes, where there is no impartial arbiter, one must consider the final result. Let a prince therefore act to conquer and to maintain the state; his methods will always be judged honourable and will be praised by all; for ordinary people are always deceived by appearances and by the outcome of a thing; and in the world there is nothing but ordinary people; and there is no room for the few, while the many have a place to lean on. A certain prince of the present day, whom I shall refrain from naming, preaches nothing but peace and faith, and to both one and the other he is entirely opposed; and both, if he had put them into practice, would have cost him many times over either his reputation or his state.

CHAPTER XIX

On Avoiding Being Despised and Hated

But now that I have talked about the most important of the qualities mentioned above, I would like to discuss the others briefly in this general manner: that the prince, as was noted above, should concentrate upon avoiding those things which make him hated and despised; and when he has avoided this, he will have carried out his duties and will find no danger whatsoever in other vices. As I have said, what makes him hated above all else is being rapacious and a usurper of the property and the women of his subjects; he must refrain from this; and in most cases, so long as you do not deprive them of either their property or their honour, the majority of men live happily; and you have only to deal with the ambition of a few, who can be restrained without difficulty and by many means. What makes him despised is being considered changeable, frivolous, effeminate, cowardly, irresolute; from these qualities a prince must guard himself as if from a reef, and he must strive to make everyone recognize in his actions greatness, spirit, dignity, and strength; and concerning the private affairs of his subjects, he must insist that his decision be irrevocable; and he should maintain himself in such a way that no man could imagine that he can deceive or cheat him.

That prince who projects such an opinion of himself is greatly esteemed; and it is difficult to conspire against a man with such a reputation and difficult to attack him, provided that he is understood to be of great merit and revered by his subjects. For a prince should have two fears: one, internal, concerning his subjects; the other, external, concerning foreign powers. From the latter he can defend himself by his good troops and friends; and he will always have good friends if he has good troops; and internal affairs will always be stable when external affairs are stable, provided that they are not already disturbed by a conspiracy; and even if external conditions change, if he is properly organized and lives as I have said and does not lose control of himself, he will always be able to withstand every attack, just as I said that Nabis the Spartan did. But concerning his subjects, when external affairs do not change, he has to fear that they may conspire secretly: the prince secures himself from this by avoiding being hated or despised and by keeping the people satis-fied with him; this is a necessary accomplishment, as was treated above at length. And one of the most powerful remedies a prince has against con-spiracies is not to be hated by the masses; for a man who plans a conspiracy always believes that he will satisfy the people by killing the prince; but when he thinks he might anger them, he cannot work up the courage to undertake such a deed; for the problems on the side of the conspirators are countless. And experience demonstrates that there have been many conspiracies but few have been concluded successfully; for anyone who conspires cannot be alone, nor can he find companions except from amongst those whom he believes to be dissatisfied; and as soon as you have revealed your intention to one malcontent, you give him the means to make himself content, since he can have everything he desires by uncovering the plot; so much is this so that, seeing a sure gain on the one hand and one doubtful and full of danger on the other, if he is to maintain faith with you he has to be either an unusually good friend or a completely determined enemy of the prince. And to repeat the matter briefly, I say that on the part of the con-spirator there is nothing but fear, jealousy, and the thought of punishment that terrifies him; but on the part of the prince there is the majesty of the principality, the laws, the defences of friends and the state to protect him; so that, with the good will of the people added to these things, it is impossible for anyone to be so rash as to plot against him. For, where usually a conspirator has to be afraid before he executes his evil deed, in this case he must be afraid even after the crime is performed, having the people as an enemy, nor can he hope to find any refuge because of this. . . .

I conclude, therefore, that a prince should not be too concerned with conspiracies when the people are well disposed toward him; but when the populace is hostile and regards him with hatred, he must fear everything and everyone. And well-organized states and wise princes have, with great diligence, taken care not to anger the nobles and to satisfy the common people and keep them contented; for this is one of the most important concerns that a prince has.

CHAPTER XXV

On Fortune's Role in Human Affairs and How She Can Be Dealt With

It is not unknown to me that many have held, and still hold, the opinion that the things of this world are, in a manner, controlled by fortune and by God, that men with their wisdom cannot control them, and, on the contrary, that men can have no remedy whatsoever for them; and for this reason they might judge that they need not sweat much over such matters but let them be governed by fate. This opinion has been more strongly held in our own times because of the great variation of affairs that has been observed and that is being observed every day which is beyond human con-jecture. Sometimes, as I think about these things, I am inclined to their opinion to a certain extent. Nevertheless, in order that our free will be not ex-tinguished, I judge it to be true that fortune is the arbiter of one half of our actions, but that she still leaves the control of the other half, or almost that, to us. And I compare her to one of those ruinous rivers that, when they become enraged, flood the plains, tear down the trees and buildings, taking up earth from one spot and placing it upon an-other; everyone flees from them, everyone yields to their onslaught, unable to oppose them in any way. But although they are of such a nature, it does not follow that when the weather is calm we cannot take precautions with embankments and dikes, so that when they rise up again either the waters will be channelled off or their impetus will not be either so unchecked or so damaging. The same things happen where fortune is concerned: she shows her force where there is no organized strength to resist her; and she directs her impact there where she knows that dikes and embank-ments are not constructed to hold her. . . .

I conclude, therefore, that since fortune changes and men remain set in their ways, men will succeed when the two are in harmony and fail when they are not in accord. I am certainly convinced of this: that it is better to be impetuous than cautious, because fortune is a woman, and it is necessary, in order to keep her down, to beat her and to struggle with her. And it is seen that she more often allows herself to be taken over by men who are impetuous than by those who make cold advances; and then, being a woman, she is always the friend of young men, for they are less cautious, more aggressive, and they command her with more audacity.

CHAPTER XXVI

An Exhortation to Liberate Italy From the Barbarians

Considering, therefore, all of the things mentioned above, and reflecting as to whether the times are suitable, at present, to honour a new prince in Italy, and if there is the material that might give a skilful and prudent prince the opportunity to introduce a form of government that would bring him honour and good to the people of Italy, it seems to me that so many circumstances are favourable to such a new prince that I know of no other time more appropriate. And if, as I said, it was necessary that the people of Israel be slaves in Egypt in order to recognize Moses' ability, and it was necessary that the Persians be oppressed by the Medes to recognize the greatness of spirit in

Cyrus, and it was necessary that the Athenians be dispersed to realize the excellence of Theseus, then, likewise, at the present time, in order to recognize the ability of an Italian spirit, it was necessary that Italy be reduced to her present condition and that she be more enslaved than the Hebrews, more servile than the Persians, more scattered than the Athenians; without a leader, without organization, beaten, despoiled, ripped apart, overrun, and prey to every sort of catastrophe. . . .

This opportunity, therefore, must not be permitted to pass by so that Italy, after so long a time, may behold its redeemer. Nor can I express with what love he will be received in all those provinces that have suffered through these foreign floods; with what thirst for revenge, with what obstinate loyalty, with what compassion, with what tears! What doors will be closed to him? Which people will deny him obedience? What jealousy could oppose him? What Italian would deny him homage? For everyone, this barbarian dominion stinks! Therefore, may your illustrious house take up this mission with the spirit and with that hope in which just undertakings are begun; so that under your banner this country may be ennobled and, under your guidance, those words of Petrarch may come true:

> *Ingenuity over rage*
> *Will take up arms; and the battle will be short.*
> *For ancient valour*
> *In Italian hearts is not yet dead.*

Discourses

BOOK ONE

2. How Many Kinds of State There Are and of What Kind Was That of Rome

I propose to dispense with a discussion of cities which from the outset have been subject to another power, and shall speak only of those which have

from the outset been far removed from any kind of external servitude, but, instead, have from the start been governed in accordance with their wishes, whether as republics or principalities. As such cities have had diverse origins, so too they have had diverse laws and institutions. For either at the outset, or before very long, to some of them laws have been given by some one person at some one time, as laws were given to the Spartans by Lycurgus; whereas others have acquired them by chance and at different times as occasion arose. This was the case in Rome.

Happy indeed should we call that state which produces a man so prudent that men can live securely under the laws which he prescribes without having to emend them. Sparta, for instance, observed its laws for more than eight hundred years without corrupting them and without any dangerous disturbance. Unhappy, on the other hand, in some degree is that city to be deemed which, not having chanced to meet with a prudent organizer, has to reorganize itself. And, of such, that is the more unhappy which is the more remote from order; and that is the more remote from order whose institutions have missed altogether the straight road which leads it to its perfect and true destiny. For it is almost impossible that states of this type should by any eventuality be set on the right road again; whereas those which, if their order is not perfect, have made a good beginning and are capable of improvement, may become perfect should something happen which provides the opportunity. It should, however, be noted that they will never introduce order without incurring danger, because few men ever welcome new laws setting up a new order in the state unless necessity makes it clear to them that there is need for such laws; and since such a necessity cannot arise without danger, the state may easily be ruined before the new order has been brought to completion. The republic of Florence bears this out, for owing to what happened at Arezzo in '02 it was reconstituted, and owing to what happened at Prato in '12 its constitution was destroyed.

It being now my intention to discuss what were the institutions of the city of Rome and what events conduced to its perfection, I would remark that those who have written about states say that there are to be found in them one of three forms of government, called by them *Principality, Aristocracy* and *Democracy*, and that those who set up a government in any particular state must adopt one of them, as best suits their purpose.

Others—and with better judgement many think—say that there are six types of government, of which three are very bad, and three are good in themselves but easily become corrupt, so that they too must be classed as pernicious. Those that are good are the three above mentioned. Those that are bad are the other three, which depend on them, and each of them is so like the one associated with it that it easily passes from one form to the other. For *Principality* easily becomes *Tyranny*. From *Aristocracy* the transition to *Oligarchy* is an easy one. *Democracy* is without difficulty converted into *Anarchy*. So that if anyone who is organizing a commonwealth sets up one of the three first forms of government, he sets up what will last but for a while, since there are no means whereby to prevent it passing into its contrary, on account of the likeness which in such a case virtue has to vice.

These variations of government among men are due to chance. For in the beginning of the world, when its inhabitants were few, they lived for a time scattered like the beasts. Then, with the multiplication of their offspring, they drew together and, in order the better to be able to defend themselves, began to look about for a man stronger and more courageous than the rest, made him their head, and obeyed him.

It was thus that men learned how to distinguish what is honest and good from what is pernicious and wicked, for the sight of someone injuring his benefactor evoked in them hatred and sympathy and they blamed the ungrateful and respected those who showed gratitude, well aware that the same injuries might have been done to themselves. Hence to prevent evil of this kind they took to making laws and to assigning punishments to those who contravened them. The notion of justice thus came into being.

In this way it came about that, when later on they had to choose a prince, they did not have recourse to the boldest as formerly, but to one who excelled in prudence and justice.

Translated by Leslie J. Walker, S.J., revised by Brian Richardson.

But when at a yet later stage they began to make the prince hereditary instead of electing him, his heirs soon began to degenerate as compared with their ancestors, and, forsaking virtuous deeds, considered that princes have nought else to do but to surpass other men in extravagance, lasciviousness, and every other form of licentiousness. With the result that the prince came to be hated, and, since he was hated, came to be afraid, and from fear soon passed to offensive action, which quickly brought about a tyranny.

From which, before long, was begotten the source of their downhill; for tyranny gave rise to conspiracies and plots against princes, organized not by timid and weak men, but by men conspicuous for their liberality, magnanimity, wealth and ability, for such men could not stand the dishonourable life the prince was leading. The masses, therefore, at the instigation of these powerful leaders, took up arms against the prince, and, when he had been liquidated, submitted to the authority of those whom they looked upon as their liberators. Hence the latter, to whom the very term "sole head" had become odious, formed themselves into a government. Moreover, in the beginning, mindful of what they had suffered under a tyranny, they ruled in accordance with the laws which they had made, subordinated their own convenience to the common advantage, and, both in private matters and public affairs, governed and preserved order with the utmost diligence.

But when the administration passed to their descendants who had no experience of the changeability of fortune, had not been through bad times, and instead of remaining content with the civic equality then prevailing, reverted to avarice, ambition and to seizing other men's womenfolk, they caused government by an aristocracy to become government by an oligarchy in which civic rights were entirely disregarded; so that in a short time there came to pass in their case the same thing as happened to the tyrant, for the masses, sick of their government, were ready to help anyone who had any sort of plan for attacking their rulers; and so there soon arose someone who with the aid of the masses liquidated them.

Then, since the memory of the prince and of the injuries inflicted by him was still fresh, and since, having got rid of government by the few, they had no desire to return to that of a prince, they turned to a democratic form of government, which they organized in such a way that no sort of authority was vested either in a few powerful men or in a prince.

And, since all forms of government are to some extent respected at the outset, this democratic form of government maintained itself for a while but not for long, especially when the generation that had organized it had passed away. For anarchy quickly supervened, in which no respect was shown either for the individual or for the official, and which was such that, as everyone did what he liked, all sorts of outrages were constantly committed. The outcome was inevitable. Either at the suggestion of some good man or because this anarchy had to be got rid of somehow, principality was once again restored. And from this there was, stage by stage, a return to anarchy, by way of the transitions and for the reasons assigned.

This, then, is the cycle through which all commonwealths pass, whether they govern themselves or are governed. But rarely do they return to the same form of government, for there can scarce be a state of such vitality that it can undergo often such changes and yet remain in being. What usually happens is that, while in a state of commotion in which it lacks both counsel and strength, a state becomes subject to a neighbouring and better organized state. Were it not so, a commonwealth might go on for ever passing through these governmental transitions.

I maintain then, that all the forms of government mentioned above are far from satisfactory, the three good ones because their life is so short, the three bad ones because of their inherent malignity. Hence prudent legislators, aware of their defects, refrained from adopting as such any one of these forms, and chose instead one that shared in them all, since they thought such a government would be stronger and more stable, for if in one and the same state there was principality, aristocracy and democracy each would keep watch over the other.

Lycurgus is one of those who have earned no small measure of praise for constitutions of this kind. For in the laws which he gave to Sparta, he assigned to the kings, to the aristocracy and to the populace each its own function, and thus introduced a form of government which lasted for more than eight hundred years to his every great credit and to the tranquillity of that city.

It was not so in the case of Solon, who drew up laws for Athens, for he set up merely a democratic form of government, which was so short-lived that he saw before his death the birth of a tyranny under Pisistratus; and though, forty years later, Pisistratus' heirs were expelled, and Athens returned to liberty because it again adopted a democratic form of government in accordance with Solon's laws, it did not retain its liberty for more than a hundred years. For, in spite of the fact that many constitutions were made whereby to restrain the arrogance of the upper class and the licentiousness of the general public, for which Solon had made no provision, none the less Athens had a very short life as compared with that of Sparta because with democracy Solon had not blended either princely power or that of the aristocracy.

But let us come to Rome. In spite of the fact that Rome had no Lycurgus to give it at the outset such a constitution as would ensure to it a long life of freedom, yet, owing to friction between the plebs and the senate, so many things happened that chance effected what had not been provided by a law giver. So that, if Rome did not get fortune's first gift, it got its second. For her early institutions, though defective, were not on wrong lines and so might pave the way to perfection. For Romulus and the rest of the kings made many good laws quite compatible with freedom; but, because their aim was to found a kingdom, not a republic, when the city became free, it lacked many institutions essential to the preservation of liberty, which had to be provided, since they had not been provided by the kings. So, when it came to pass that its kings lost their sovereignty, for reasons and in the manner described earlier in this discourse, those who had expelled them

at once appointed two consuls to take the place of the king, so that what they expelled was the title of king, not the royal power. In the republic, then, at this stage there were the consuls and the senate, so that as yet it comprised but two of the aforesaid estates, namely, Principality and Aristocracy. It remained to find a place for Democracy. This came about when the Roman nobility became so overbearing for reasons which will be given later—that the populace rose against them, and they were constrained by the fear that they might lose all, to grant the populace a share in the government; the senate and the consuls retaining, however, sufficient authority for them to be able to maintain their position in the republic.

It was in this way that tribunes of the plebs came to be appointed, and their appointment did much to stabilize the form of government in this republic, for in its government all three estates now had a share. And so favoured was it by fortune that, though the transition from Monarchy to Aristocracy and thence to Democracy, took place by the very stages and for the very reasons laid down earlier in this discourse, none the less the granting of authority to the aristocracy did not abolish altogether the royal estate, nor was the authority of the aristocracy wholly removed when the populace was granted a share in it. On the contrary, the blending of these estates made a perfect commonwealth; and since it was friction between the plebs and the senate that brought this perfection about, in the next two chapters we shall show more fully how this came to be.

10. Those Who Set Up a Tyranny Are No Less Blameworthy Than Are the Founders of a Republic or a Kingdom Praiseworthy

Of all men that are praised, those are praised most who have played the chief part in founding a religion. Next come those who have founded either republics or kingdoms. After them in the order of celebratees are ranked army commanders who have added to the extent of their own dominions or to that of their country's. With whom may be conjoined men of letters of many different kinds who are each celebrated according to their status. Some modicum of praise is also ascribed to any man who excels in some art and in the practice of it, and of these the number is legion. On the other hand, those are held to be infamous and detestable who extirpate religion, subvert kingdoms and republics, make war on virtue, on letters, and on any art that brings advantage and honour to the human race, i.e. the profane, the violent, the ignorant, the worthless, the idle, the coward. Nor will there ever be anyone, be he foolish or wise, wicked or good, who, if called upon to choose between these two classes of men, will not praise the one that calls for praise and blame the one that calls for blame.

And yet, notwithstanding this, almost all men, deceived by the false semblance of good and the false semblance of renown, allow themselves either wilfully or ignorantly to slip into the ranks of those who deserve blame rather than praise; and, when they might have founded a republic or a kingdom to their immortal honour, turn their thoughts to tyranny, and fail to see what fame, what glory, security, tranquillity, conjoined with peace of mind, they are missing by adopting this course, and what infamy, scorn, abhorrence, danger and disquiet they are incurring.

Nor is it possible for anybody, whether he be but a private citizen living in some republic, or has been fortunate enough or virtuous enough to have become a prince, to read history and to make use of the records of ancient deeds, without preferring, if he be a private citizen, to conduct himself in his fatherland rather as Scipio did than as Caesar did, or, if he be a prince, as did Agesilaus, Timoleon and Dion, rather than as did Nabis, Phalaris and Dionysius, for he could not but see how strongly the latter are dismissed with scorn, and how highly the former are praised. He would also notice that Timoleon and the like had no less authority in their respective countries than had Dionysius or Phalaris in theirs, and would observe that they enjoyed far greater security.

Nor should anyone be deceived by Caesar's renown when he finds writers extolling him before others, for those who praise him have either been corrupted by his fortune or overawed by the long continuance of the empire which, since it was ruled under that name, did not permit writers to speak freely of him. If, however, anyone desires to know what writers would have said, had they been free, he has but to look at what they say of Catiline. For Caesar is the more blameworthy of the two, in that he who has done wrong is more blameworthy than he who has but desired to do wrong. Or, again, let him look at the praise bestowed on Brutus: Caesar they could not find fault with on account of his power, so they cry up his enemy.

Let he who has become a prince in a republic consider, after Rome became an Empire, how much more praise is due to those emperors who acted, like good princes, in accordance with the laws, than to those who acted otherwise. It will be found that Titus, Nerva, Trajan, Hadrian, Antoninus and Marcus, had no need of soldiers to form a praetorian guard, nor of a multitude of legions to protect them, for their defence lay in their habits, the goodwill of the people, and the affection of the senate. It will be seen, too, in the case of Caligula, Nero, Vitellius and other bad emperors, how it availed them little to have armies from the East and from the West to save them from the enemies they had made by their bad habits and their evil life.

If the history of these emperors be pondered well, it should serve as a striking lesson to any prince, and should teach him to distinguish between the ways of renown and of infamy, the ways of security and of fear. For of the twenty-six emperors from Caesar to Maximinus, sixteen were assassinated and only ten died a natural death. And, if some of those who were killed were good men, as Galba and Pertinax were, their death was due to the corruption which their predecessors had introduced among the troops. While, if among those who died ordinary death, there was a wicked man, like Severus, it must be put down to his great good luck and to his "virtue," two things of which few men enjoy both. It will be seen, too, from a perusal of their history on what principle a good kingdom should rest; for all the emperors who acquired imperial power by inheritance were bad men, with the exception of Titus; those who acquired it through adoption, were all good, like the five counting from Nerva to Marcus; and when it fell to their heirs a period of decadence again ensued.

Let a prince put before himself the period from Nerva to Marcus, and let him compare it with the preceding period and with that which came after, and then let him decide in which he would rather have been born, and during which he would have chosen to be emperor. What he will find when good princes were ruling, is a prince securely reigning among subjects no less secure, a world replete with peace and justice. He will see the senate's authority respected, the magistrates honoured, rich citizens enjoying their wealth, nobility and virtue held in the highest esteem, and everything working smoothly and going well. He will notice, on the other hand, the absence of any rancour, any licentiousness, corruption or ambition, and that in this golden age everyone is free to hold and to defend his own opinion. He will behold, in short, the world triumphant, its prince glorious and respected by all, the people fond of him and secure under his rule.

If he then looks attentively at the times of the other emperors, he will find them distraught with wars, torn by seditions, brutal alike in peace and in war, princes frequently killed by assassins, civil wars and foreign wars constantly occurring, Italy in travail and ever a prey to fresh misfortunes, its cities demolished and pillaged. He will see Rome burnt, its Capitol demolished by its own citizens, ancient temples lying desolate, religious rites grown corrupt, adultery rampant throughout the city. He will find the sea covered with exiles and the rocks stained with blood. In Rome he will see countless atrocities perpetrated; rank, riches, the honours men have won, and, above all, virtue, looked upon as a capital crime. He will find calumniators rewarded, servants suborned to turn against their masters, freed men to turn against their patrons, and those who lack enemies attacked by their friends. He will thus happily learn how much Rome, Italy, and the world owed to Caesar.

There can be no question but that every human being will be afraid to imitate the bad times, and will be imbued with an ardent desire to emulate the good. And, should a good prince seek worldly renown, he should most certainly covet possession of a city that has become corrupt, not, with Caesar, to complete its spoliation, but, with Romulus, to reform it. Nor in very truth can the heavens afford men a better opportunity of acquiring renown; nor can men desire anything better than this. And if in order to reform a city one were obliged to give up the principate, someone who did not reform it in order not to fall from that rank would have some excuse. There is, however, no excuse if one can both keep the principate and reform the city.

In conclusion, then, let those to whom the heavens grant such opportunities reflect that two courses are open to them: either so to behave that in life they rest secure and in death become renowned, or so to behave that in life they are in continual straits, and in death leave behind all imperishable record of their infamy.

THOMAS HOBBES

~

INTRODUCTION

JEAN HAMPTON

Thomas Hobbes (1588–1679) was born in Malmesbury, England, arriving prematurely because, he claimed, rumors that the Spanish armada was off the coast of England ready to invade scared his mother: "She brought twins to birth, myself and fear at the same time." Ironically, fear of death was the central psychological assumption of his moral and political theorizing as an adult. Hobbes's father was a clergyman, whom some reports describe as prone to drink and violence, and who eventually deserted his family to avoid a charge of assault. Educated at the expense of his uncle, Hobbes attended Oxford from 1603 to 1608. Because he was not from a wealthy family, on graduation he got a job as the tutor and companion of William Cavendish, who eventually became the Earl of Devonshire. Thus began Hobbes's long association with that family; except for a few brief periods, he remained in service to them for nearly seventy years. He also worked briefly for Sir Francis Bacon, serving as his amanuensis and translator.

According to his friend and biographer John Aubrey, Hobbes's philosophical interests owed much to the geometer Euclid, whose proofs he loved because of the way they relied on logical reasoning to derive surprising and sometimes seemingly implausible conclusions from highly plausible and seemingly innocuous premises. However, Hobbes's first full-scale philosophical manuscript was not circulated until 1640. This work, called *The Elements of Laws, Natural and Politic*, advocated the creation of an absolute sovereign in order to secure the peace and stability of the community. Because of the antiroyalist sentiment at this time (which eventually resulted in full-scale civil war and the beheading of King Charles I), many people, including members of Parliament, were outraged by the manuscript, and Hobbes believed he had to flee for his life to Europe (he used to boast that he was one of the "first to flee" from England). Like many prominent royalist sympathizers he spent the rest of the civil war in Paris, where he enjoyed philosophical conversations with French intellectuals (such as Gassendi and Mersenne) and exiled British thinkers. During that time he wrote *De Cive* (*The Citizen*) (1642), a reworked version of his argument in *The Elements of Laws* (written in Latin but later published in English in 1651 under the title *The Philosophical Rudiments of Government*). In 1651 he published his masterpiece *Leviathan*, which contains his mature argument for absolute sovereignty.

Oliver Cromwell was in power when *Leviathan* was completed, and Cromwell supposedly welcomed the book because of the way its arguments could be used to justify any de facto political authority even if it was installed through rebellion. Accordingly, Hobbes was allowed to come home, unlike other royalist exiles (who resented Hobbes's return and considered him to have sold out to the new Puritan regime). On his return, he continued philosophizing in areas other than political philosophy, producing works in philosophy of law, history, metaphysics, and epistemology (including ontology, scientific method, and free will), and topics in science and mathematics (including optics, geometry, and human physiology). After the restoration of King Charles II, Hobbes enjoyed access to the king because of his wit and intelligence. However, he remained a highly controversial figure throughout the country, both because of his political absolutism and because of his materialistic metaphysics and his views on free will and religion, which were viewed by many of the larger population as "atheistic" and heretical. Hobbes died at the ripe old age of ninety-one.

Hobbes's argument for absolute sovereignty in all his political writings makes use of the idea of a "social contract," an idea also used by other political thinkers of his day but which Hobbes revolutionized in ways that powerfully influenced the political thinking of subsequent philosophers such as Locke, Rousseau, and Kant. Imagine, says Hobbes, a "state of nature" prior to the creation of all governments. In this state human behavior would be unchecked by law, and since Hobbes believed that human beings are predominantly self-interested (concerned above all else with their own preservation), he argues that they would inevitably come into conflict with one another, while having little or no other-regarding sentiments or psychological resources to resolve those conflicts. So before long, he says, there would be a "war of every one against every one," so that every person's life in this natural state would be "solitary, poor, nasty, brutish and short" (*Leviathan*, ch. 13). To remedy such war and satisfy their desire for self-preservation, people, Hobbes argues, would be rational to contract with one another to create a government run by a sovereign holding absolute power, because only absolute power is sufficient to resolve disputes that otherwise would precipitate conflict dissolving the commonwealth and threatening the lives of all. Such an argument is meant to show the kind of government we contemporary human beings would be rational to create and sustain, lest we descend into a state of war analogous to the one that would exist in the state of nature. Note that Hobbes doesn't require that sovereignty be held only by an absolute monarchy; he also recognizes that sovereignty can be invested in a small number of people, constituting an oligarchy, or in all the people, constituting a democracy. Hobbes explicitly prefers the absolute monarchy but believes the other two forms of government are also viable. What is not viable, in his view, is some form of "mixed" government with different branches of government holding different components of political authority, or governments in which power is supposed to be limited by a constitution or by a contract made between the government and the people. Such limits or divisions, says Hobbes, will only lead to conflicts that cannot be resolved by self-interested people, who require for peace a unified sovereignty with the power to decide any issue that might lead to conflict in the regime.

Hobbes's use of this social contract argument was occasioned in large part by his rejection of the scholastic philosophizing of many of his contemporaries and his forebears, who he thought were too inclined to appeal to authority rather than reason, and too inclined to use nonsensical or empty terms (such as "immaterial substance" or "consubstantiation"). Accordingly, Hobbes turned to science, and particularly to geometry, as a guide to constructing a theory of our moral and political life. Starting with what he took to be sound premises, Hobbes sought to construct a social contract argument so as to derive, in geometric fashion, valid conclusions about morals and politics in a way that would command assent even from those reluctant to endorse such conclusions. Hobbes's faith in the power of reason to provide truth in moral and political matters makes him an Enlightenment thinker, although, ironically, it is partly because he thinks there will be persistent failures of rationality in any human community that peace must be secured by giving the ruler absolute power.

Does Hobbes's argument work? To create an absolute sovereign, Hobbes says that each person must agree with every other person to "give up" his or her "right to all things" to the sovereign, thereby "authorizing" the sovereign to rule in this community. But can people who are committed to securing their self-preservation above all else rationally risk giving up *all* their rights to another? Hobbes explicitly compares subjects to servants and sovereigns to masters. But is such voluntary political "enslavement" even psychologically possible for people as Hobbes describes them? Observant readers will note qualifications to the alienation of all power to the sovereign in chapter 21. For example, Hobbes writes: "The obligation of subjects to the sovereign, is understood to last as long as, and no longer, than the power lasteth, by which he is able to protect them. For the right men have by nature to protect themselves, when none else can protect them, can by no covenant be relinquished."

But is such a qualification consistent with the idea that the sovereign has absolute power over his subjects? The ultimate validity of Hobbes's argument has been questioned by generations of readers, who have tended to be both intrigued by its power and alarmed by its conclusions.

For an overview of Hobbes's work, see Tom Sorell, *Hobbes* (London: Routledge & Kegan Paul, 1986). For a view of Hobbes's life by one of his contemporaries, see the discussion of Hobbes in John Aubrey's *Brief Lives*, edited by Oliver Lawson Dick (Ann Arbor: University of Michigan Press, 1975). For three detailed examinations of the validity of Hobbes's social contract argument, see David Gauthier, *The Logic of Leviathan* (Oxford: Oxford University Press, 1969), Jean Hampton, *Hobbes and the Social Contract Tradition* (Cambridge: Cambridge University Press, 1986), and Gregory Kavka, *Hobbesian Moral and Political Theory* (Princeton, N.J.: Princeton University Press, 1986). Many of the nonpolitical aspects of Hobbes's thinking are discussed in J. W. N. Watkins, *Hobbes's System of Ideas* (London: Hutchison, 1965). For a discussion of Hobbes's religious arguments in *Leviathan*, see A. P. Martinich, *The Two Gods of Leviathan* (Cambridge: Cambridge University Press, 1992), and S. A. Lloyd, *Ideals as Interest in Hobbes's Leviathan* (Cambridge: Cambridge University Press, 1992). Finally, for a collection of classic interpretive essays on Hobbes's work, see K. C. Brown, *Hobbes Studies* (Oxford: Blackwell, 1965).

Leviathan

THE INTRODUCTION

Nature (the art whereby God hath made and governs the world) is by the *art* of man, as in many other things, so in this also imitated, that it can make an artificial animal. For seeing life is but a motion of limbs, the beginning whereof is in some principal part within; why may we not say that all *automata* (engines that move themselves by springs and wheels as doth a watch) have an artificial life? For what is the *heart*, but a *spring;* and the *nerves*, but so many *strings;* and the *joints*, but so many *wheels*, giving motion to the whole body, such as was intended by the artificer? *Art* goes yet further, imitating that rational and most excellent work of nature, *man.* For by art is created that great LEVIATHAN called a COMMONWEALTH, or STATE, (in Latin CIVITAS) which is but an artificial man; though of greater stature and strength than the natural, for whose protection and defence it was intended; and in which, the *sovereignty* is an artificial *soul*, as giving life and motion to the whole body; the *magistrates*, and other *officers* of judicature and execution, artificial *joints; reward* and *punishment* (by which fastened to the seat of the sovereignty every joint and member is moved to perform his duty) are the *nerves*, that do the same in the body natural; the *wealth* and *riches* of all the particular members, are the *strength; salus populi* (the *people's safety*) its *business; counsellors*, by whom all things needful for it to know are suggested unto it, are the *memory; equity*, and *laws*, an artificial *reason* and *will; concord, health; sedition, sickness;* and *civil war, death.* Lastly, the *pacts* and *covenants*, by which the parts of this body politic were at first made, set together, and united, resemble that *fiat*, or the *let us make man*, pronounced by God in the creation. . . .

PART 1

Of Man

Chapter 6

OF THE INTERIOR BEGINNINGS OF VOLUNTARY MOTIONS: COMMONLY CALLED THE PASSIONS; AND THE SPEECHES BY WHICH THEY ARE EXPRESSED

There be in animals, two sorts of *motions* peculiar to them: one called *vital;* begun in generation, and continued without interruption through their whole life; such as are the *course* of the *blood*, the *pulse*, the *breathing*, the *concoction, nutrition, excretion,* &c.; to which motions there needs no help of imagination: the other is *animal motion*, otherwise called *voluntary motion;* as to *go*, to *speak*, to *move* any of our limbs, in such manner as is first fancied in our minds. That sense is motion in the organs and interior parts of man's body, caused by the action of the things we see, hear, &c.; and that fancy is but the relics of the same motion, remaining after sense, has been already said in the first and second chapters. And because *going, speaking*, and the like voluntary motions, depend always upon a precedent thought of *whither, which way*, and *what;* it is evident, that the imagination is the first internal beginning of all voluntary motion. And although unstudied men do not conceive any motion at all to be there, where the thing moved is invisible; or the space it is moved in, is (for the shortness of it) insensible; yet that doth not hinder, but that such motions are. For let a space be never so little, that which is moved over a greater space, whereof that little one is part, must first be moved over that. These small beginnings of motion, within the body of man, before they appear in walking, speaking, striking, and other visible actions, are commonly called ENDEAVOUR.

This endeavour, when it is toward something which causes it, is called APPETITE, or DESIRE; the latter, being the general name; and the other, oftentimes restrained to signify the desire of food, namely *hunger* and *thirst*. And when the endeavour is fromward something, it is generally called AVERSION. These words, *appetite* and *aversion*, we have from the *Latins;* and they both of them signify the motions, one of approaching, the other of retiring. So also do the Greek words for the same, which are όρμή and α'φορμή. For nature itself does often press upon men those truths, which afterwards, when they look for somewhat beyond nature, they stumble at. For the Schools find in mere appetite to go, or move, no actual motion at all: but because some motion they must acknowledge, they call it metaphorical motion; which is but an absurd speech: for though words may be called metaphorical; bodies and motions cannot.

That which men desire, they are also said to LOVE: and to HATE those things for which they have aversion. So that desire and love are the same thing; save that by desire, we always signify the absence of the object; by love, most commonly the presence of the same. So also by aversion, we signify the absence; and by hate, the presence of the object.

Of appetites and aversions, some are born with men; as appetite of food, appetite of excretion and exoneration, (which may also and more properly be called aversions, from somewhat they feel in their bodies;) and some other appetites, not many. The rest, which are appetites of particular things, proceed from experience, and trial of their effects upon themselves or other men. For of things we know not at all, or believe not to be, we can have no further desire, than to taste and try. But aversion we have for things, not only which we know have hurt us, but also that we do not know whether they will hurt us, or not.

Those things which we neither desire, nor hate, we are said to *contemn;* CONTEMPT being

nothing else but an immobility, or contumacy of the heart, in resisting the action of certain things; and proceeding from that the heart is already moved otherwise, by other more potent objects; or from want of experience of them.

And because the constitution of a man's body is in continual mutation, it is impossible that all the same things should always cause in him the same appetites, and aversions: much less can all men consent, in the desire of almost any one and the same object.

But whatsoever is the object of any man's appetite or desire, that is it which he for his part calleth *good:* and the object of his hate and aversion, *evil;* and of his contempt, *vile* and *inconsiderable.* For these words of good, evil, and contemptible, are ever used with relation to the person that useth them: there being nothing simply and absolutely so; nor any common rule of good and evil, to be taken from the nature of the objects themselves; but from the person of the man (where there is no commonwealth;) or, (in a commonwealth,) from the person that representeth it; or from an arbitrator or judge, whom men disagreeing shall by consent set up, and make his sentence the rule thereof. . . .

Continual success in obtaining those things which a man from time to time desireth, that is to say, continual prospering, is that men call FELICITY; I mean the felicity of this life. For there is no such thing as perpetual tranquillity of mind, while we live here; because life itself is but motion, and can never be without desire, nor without fear, no more than without sense. What kind of felicity God hath ordained to them that devoutly honour Him, a man shall no sooner know, than enjoy; being joys, that now are as incomprehensible, as the word of schoolmen *beatifical vision* is unintelligible.

The form of speech whereby men signify their opinion of the goodness of any thing, is PRAISE. That whereby they signify the power and greatness of any thing, is MAGNIFYING. And that whereby they signify the opinion they have of a man's felicity, is by the Greeks called μακαρισμός for which we have no name in our tongue. And thus much is sufficient for the present purpose, to have been said of the PASSIONS.

Chapter 10

OF POWER, WORTH, DIGNITY, HONOUR, AND WORTHINESS

The power *of a man*, (to take it universally), is his present means, to obtain some future apparent good; and is either *original* or *instrumental*.

Natural power, is the eminence of the faculties of body, or mind: as extraordinary strength, form, prudence, arts, eloquence, liberality, nobility. *Instrumental* are those powers, which acquired by these, or by fortune, are means and instruments to acquire more: as riches, reputation, friends, and the secret working of God, which men call good luck. For the nature of power, is in this point, like to fame, increasing as it proceeds; or like the motion of heavy bodies, which the further they go, make still the more haste.

The greatest of human powers, is that which is compounded of the powers of most men, united by consent, in one person, natural, or civil, that has the use of all their powers depending on his will; such as is the power of a common-wealth: or depending on the wills of each particular; such as is the power of a faction or of divers factions leagued. Therefore to have servants, is power; to have friends, is power: for they are strengths united.

Also riches joined with liberality, is power; because it procureth friends, and servants: without liberality, not so; because in this case they defend not; but expose men to envy, as a prey.

Reputation of power, is power; because it draweth with it the adherence of those that need protection.

So is reputation of love of a man's country, (called popularity,) for the same reason.

Also, what quality soever maketh a man beloved, or feared of many; of the reputation of such quality, is power; because it is a means to have the assistance, and service of many.

Good success is power; because it maketh reputation of wisdom, or good fortune; which makes men either fear him, or rely on him.

Affability of men already in power, is increase of power; because it gaineth love.

Reputation of prudence in the conduct of peace or war, is power; because to prudent men, we commit the government of ourselves, more willingly than to others.

Nobility is power, not in all places, but only in those commonwealths, where it has privileges: for in such privileges consisteth their power.

Eloquence is power, because it is seeming prudence.

Form is power; because being a promise of good, it recommendeth men to the favour of women and strangers.

The sciences, are small power; because not eminent; and therefore, not acknowledged in any man; nor are at all, but in a few, and in them, but of a few things. For science is of that nature, as none can understand it to be, but such as in a good measure have attained it.

Arts of public use, as fortification, making of engines, and other instruments of war; because they confer to defence, and victory, are power: and though the true mother of them, be science, namely the mathematics; yet, because they are brought into the light, by the hand of the artificer, they be esteemed (the midwife passing with the vulgar for the mother,) as his issue.

The *value*, or WORTH of a man, is as of all other things, his price; that is to say, so much as would be given for the use of his power: and therefore is not absolute; but a thing dependant on the need and judgment of another. An able conductor of soldiers, is of great price in time of war present, or imminent; but in peace not so. A learned and uncorrupt judge, is much worth in time of peace; but not so much in war. And as in other things, so in men, not the seller, but the buyer determines the price. For let a man (as most men do,) rate themselves at the highest value they can; yet their true value is no more than it is esteemed by others. . . .

Chapter 13

OF THE NATURAL CONDITION OF MANKIND AS CONCERNING THEIR FELICITY, AND MISERY

Nature hath made men so equal, in the faculties of body, and mind; as that though there be found one man sometimes manifestly stronger in body, or of quicker mind than another; yet when all is reckoned together, the difference between man, and man, is not so considerable, as that one man can thereupon claim to himself any benefit, to which another may not pretend, as well as he. For as to the strength of body, the weakest has strength enough to kill the strongest, either by secret machination, or by confederacy with others, that are in the same danger as himself.

And as to the faculties of the mind, (setting aside the arts grounded upon words, and especially that skill of proceeding upon general, and infallible rules, called science; which very few have, and but in few things; as being not a native faculty, born with us; nor attained, (as prudence,) while we look after someone else,) I find yet a greater equality amongst men, than that of strength. For prudence, is but experience; which equal time, equally bestows on all men, in those things they equally apply themselves unto. That which may perhaps make such equality incredible, is but a vain conceit of one's own wisdom, which almost all men think they have in a greater degree, than the vulgar; that is, than all men but themselves, and a few others, whom by fame, or for concurring with themselves, they approve. For such is the nature of men, that howsoever they may acknowledge many others to be more witty, or more eloquent, or more learned; yet they will hardly believe there be many so wise as themselves: For they see their own wit at hand, and other men's at a distance. But this proveth rather that men are in that point equal, than unequal. For there is not ordinarily a greater sign of the equal distribution of any thing, than that every man is contented with his share.

From this equality of ability, ariseth equality of hope in the attaining of our ends. And

therefore if any two men desire the same thing, which nevertheless they cannot both enjoy, they become enemies; and in the way to their end, (which is principally their own conservation, and sometimes their delectation only,) endeavour to destroy, or subdue one another. And from hence it comes to pass, that where an invader hath no more to fear, than another man's single power; if one plant, sow, build, or possess a convenient seat, others may probably be expected to come prepared with forces united, to dispossess, and deprive him, not only of the fruit of his labour, but also of his life, or liberty. And the invader again is in the like danger of another.

And from this diffidence of one another, there is no way for any man to secure himself, so reasonable, as anticipation; that is, by force, or wiles, to master the persons of all men he can, so long, till he see no other power great enough to endanger him: and this is no more than his own conservation requireth, and is generally allowed. Also because there be some, that taking pleasure in contemplating their own power in the acts of conquest, which they pursue farther than their security requires; if others, that otherwise would be glad to be at ease within modest bounds, should not by invasion increase their power, they would not be able, long time, by standing only on their defence, to subsist. And by consequence, such augmentation of dominion over men, being necessary to a man's conservation, it ought to be allowed him.

Again, men have no pleasure, (but on the contrary a great deal of grief) in keeping company, where there is no power able to over-awe them all. For every man looketh that his companion should value him, at the same rate he sets upon himself: and upon all signs of contempt, or undervaluing, naturally endeavours, as far as he dares (which amongst them that have no common power to keep them in quiet, is far enough to make them destroy each other,) to extort a greater value from his contemners, by damage; and from others, by the example.

So that in the nature of man, we find three principal causes of quarrel. First, competition; secondly, diffidence; thirdly, glory.

The first, maketh man invade for gain; the second, for safety; and the third, for reputation. The first use violence, to make themselves masters of other men's persons, wives, children, and cattle; the second, to defend them; the third, for trifles, as a word, a smile, a different opinion, and any other sign of undervalue, either direct in their persons, or by reflection in their kindred, their friends, their nation, their profession, or their name.

Hereby it is manifest, that during the time men live without a common power to keep them all in awe, they are in that condition which is called war; and such a war, as is of every man, against every man. For WAR, consisteth not in battle only, or the act of fighting; but in a tract of time, wherein the will to contend by battle is sufficiently known: and therefore the notion of *time*, is to be considered in the nature of war; as it is in the nature of weather. For as the nature of foul weather, lieth not in a shower or two of rain; but in an inclination thereto of many days together: so the nature of war, consisteth not in actual fighting; but in the known disposition thereto, during all the time there is no assurance to the contrary. All other time is PEACE.

Whatsoever therefore is consequent to a time of war, where every man is enemy to every man; the same is consequent to the time, wherein men live without other security, than what their own strength, and their own invention shall furnish them withal. In such condition, there is no place for industry; because the fruit thereof is uncertain: and consequently no culture of the earth; no navigation, nor use of the commodities that may be imported by sea; no commodious building; no instruments of moving, and removing such things as require much force; no knowledge of the face of the earth; no account of time; no arts; no letters; no society; and which is worst of all, continual fear, and danger of violent death; and the life of man, solitary, poor, nasty, brutish, and short.

It may seem strange to some man, that has not well weighed these things; that nature should thus dissociate, and render men apt to invade, and destroy one another: and he may therefore, not trusting to this inference, made from the passions, desire perhaps to have the same confirmed by experience. Let him therefore consider with himself, when taking a journey, he arms himself, and seeks to go well accompanied; when going to sleep, he locks his doors; when even in his house he locks his chests; and this when he knows there be laws, and public officers, armed, to revenge all injuries shall be done him; what opinion he has of his fellow subjects, when he rides armed; of his fellow citizens, when he locks his doors; and of his children, and servants, when he locks his chests. Does he not there as much accuse mankind by his actions, as I do by my words? But neither of us accuse man's nature in it. The desires, and other passions of man, are in themselves no sin. No more are the actions, that proceed from those passions, till they know a law that forbids them: which till laws be made they cannot know: nor can any law be made, till they have agreed upon the person that shall make it.

It may peradventure be thought, there was never such a time, nor condition of war as this; and I believe it was never generally so, over all the world: but there are many places, where they live so now. For the savage people in many places of *America*, except the government of small families, the concord whereof dependeth on natural lust, have no government at all; and live at this day in that brutish manner, as I said before. Howsoever, it may be perceived what manner of life there would be, where there were no common power to fear; by the manner of life, which men that have formerly lived under a peacefull government, use to degenerate into, in a civil war.

But though there had never been any time, wherein particular men were in a condition of war one against another; yet in all times, kings, and persons of sovereign authority, because of their independency, are in continual jealousies, and in the state and posture of gladiators; having their weapons pointing, and their eyes fixed on one another; that is, their forts, garrisons, and guns upon the frontiers of their kingdoms; and continual spies upon their neighbours; which is a posture of war. But because they uphold thereby, the industry of their subjects; there does not follow from it, that misery, which accompanies the liberty of particular men.

To this war of every man against every man, this also is consequent; that nothing can be unjust. The notions of right and wrong, justice and injustice have there no place. Where there is no common power, there is no law: where no law, no injustice. Force, and fraud, are in war the two cardinal virtues. Justice, and injustice are none of the faculties neither of the body, nor mind. If they were, they might be in a man that were alone in the world, as well as his senses, and passions. They are qualities, that relate to men in society, not in solitude. It is consequent also to the same condition, that there be no propriety, no dominion, no *mine* and *thine* distinct; but only that to be every man's, that he can get; and for so long, as he can keep it. And thus much for the ill condition, which many by mere nature is actually placed in; though with a possibility to come out of it, consisting partly in the passions, partly in his reason.

The passions that incline men to peace, are fear of death; desire of such things as are necessary to commodious living; and a hope by their industry to obtain them. And reason suggesteth convenient articles of peace, upon which men may be drawn to agreement. These articles, are they, which otherwise are called the Laws of Nature; whereof I shall speak more particularly, in the two following chapters.

Chapter 14

OF THE FIRST AND SECOND NATU-RAL LAWS, AND OF CONTRACTS

The RIGHT OF NATURE, which writers commonly call *jus naturale*, is the liberty each man hath, to use his own power, as he will himself, for the preservation of his own nature; that is to say, of his own life; and consequently, of doing any thing, which in his own judgment, and reason, he shall conceive to be the aptest means thereunto.

By LIBERTY, is understood, according to the proper signification of the word, the absence of external impediments: which impediments, may

oft take away part of a man's power to do what he would; but cannot hinder him from using the power left him, according as his judgment, and reason shall dictate to him.

A LAW OF NATURE, (*lex naturalis*,) is a precept, or general rule, found out by reason, by which a man is forbidden to do that, which is destructive of his life, or taketh away the means of preserving the same; and to omit that, by which he thinketh it may be best preserved. For though they that speak of this subject, use to confound *jus*, and *lex, right* and *law;* yet they ought to be distinguished; because RIGHT, consisteth in liberty to do, or to forbear; whereas LAW, determineth, and bindeth to one of them: so that law, and right, differ as much, as obligation, and liberty; which in one and the same matter are inconsistent.

And because the condition of man, (as hath been declared in the precedent chapter) is a condition of war of every one against every one; in which case every one is governed by his own reason; and there is nothing he can make use of, that may not be a help unto him, in preserving his life against his enemies; it followeth, that in such a condition, every man has a right to every thing: even to one another's body. And therefore, as long as this natural right of every man to every thing endureth, there can be no security to any man, (how strong or wise soever he be,) of living out the time, which nature ordinarily alloweth men to live. And consequently it is a precept, or general rule of reason, *that every man, ought to endeavour peace, as far as he has hope of obtaining it; and when he cannot obtain it, that he may seek, and use, all helps, and advantages of war.* The first branch of which rule, containeth the first, and fundamental law of nature; which is, *to seek peace, and follow it.* The second, the sum of the right of nature; which is, *by all means we can, to defend ourselves.*

From this fundamental law of nature, by which men are commanded to endeavor peace, is derived this second law; *that a man be willing, when others are so too, as farforth, as for peace, and defence of himself he shall think it necessary, to lay down this right to all things; and be contented with so much liberty against other men, as he would allow other men against himself.* For as long as every man holdeth this right, of doing any thing he liketh; so long are all men in the condition of war. But if other men will not lay down their right, as well as he; then there is no reason for any one, to divest himself of his: for that were to expose himself to prey, (which no man is bound to) rather than to dispose himself to peace. This is that law of the Gospel; *whatsoever you require that others should do for you, that do ye to them.* And that law of all men, *quod tibi fieri non vis, alteri ne feceris.* [Do not unto others what you would not have done unto you.—S.M.C.]

To *lay down* a man's *right* to any thing, is to *divest* himself of the *liberty,* of hindering another of the benefit of his own right to the same. For he that renounceth, or passeth away his right, giveth not to any other man a right which he had not before; because there is nothing to which every man had not right by nature: but only standeth out of his way, that he may enjoy his own original right, without hindrance from him; not without hindrance from another. So that the effect which redoundeth to one man, by another man's defect of right, is but so much diminution of impediments to the use of his own right original.

Right is laid aside, either by simply renouncing it; or by transferring it to another. By *simply* RENOUNCING; when he cares not to whom the benefit thereof redoundeth. By TRANSFER-RING; when he intendeth the benefit thereof to some certain person, or persons. And when a man hath in either manner abandoned, or granted away his right; then is he said to be OBLIGED, or BOUND, not to hinder those, to whom such right is granted, or abandoned, from the benefit of it: and that he *ought,* and it is his DUTY, not to make void that voluntary act of his own: and that such hindrance is INJUSTICE, and INJURY, as being *sine jure;* the right being before renounced, or transferred. So that *injury,* or *injustice,* in the controversies of the world, is somewhat like to that, which in the disputations of scholars is called *absurdity.* For as it is there called an absurdity, to contradict what one maintained in the beginning: so in the world, it is called injustice, and injury, voluntarily to undo that, which from the beginning he had voluntarily done. The way by which a man either simply renounceth, or transferreth his right, is a declaration, or signification, by some voluntary and sufficient sign, or signs, that he doth so renounce, or transfer; or hath so renounced, or transferred the same, to him that accepteth it. And these signs are either words only, or actions only; or (as it happeneth most often) both words, and actions. And the same are the BONDS, by which men are bound, and obliged: bonds, that have their strength, not from their own nature, (for nothing is more easily broken than a man's word,) but from fear of some evil consequence upon the rupture.

Whensoever a man transferreth his right, or renounceth it; it is either in consideration of some right reciprocally transferred to himself; or for some other good he hopeth for thereby. For it is a voluntary act: and of the voluntary acts of every man, the object is some *good to himself.* And therefore there be some rights, which no man can be understood by any words, or other signs, to have abandoned, or transferred. As first a man cannot lay down the right of resisting them, that assault him by force, to take away his life; because he cannot be understood to aim thereby, at any good to himself. The same may be said of wounds, and chains, and imprisonment; both because there is no benefit consequent to such patience; as there is to the patience of suffering another to be wounded, or imprisoned: as also because a man cannot tell, when he seeth men proceed against him by violence, whether they intend his death or not. And lastly the motive, and end for which this renouncing, and transferring of right is introduced, is nothing else but the security of a man's person, in his life, and in the means of so preserving life, as not to be weary of it. And therefore if a man by words, or other signs, seem to despoil himself of the end, for which those signs were intended; he is not to be understood as if he meant it, or that it was his will; but that he was ignorant of how such words and actions were to be interpreted.

The mutual transferring of right, is that which men call CONTRACT. . . .

There is difference between transferring of right to the thing; and transferring, or tradition, that is delivery of the thing itself. For the thing may be delivered together with the translation of the right; as in buying and selling with ready-money; or exchange of goods, or lands: and it may be delivered some time after.

Again, one of the contractors, may deliver the thing contracted for on his part, and leave the other to perform his part at some determinate time after, and in the mean time be trusted; and then the contract on his part, is called Pact, or Covenant: or both parts may contract now, to perform hereafter: in which cases, he that is to perform in time to come, being trusted, his performance is called *keeping of promise*, or faith; and he failing of performance, if it be voluntary, *violation of faith*.

When the transferring of right, is not mutual: but one of the parties transferreth, in hope to gain thereby friendship, or service from another, or from his friends; or in hope to gain the reputation of charity, or magnanimity; or to deliver his mind from the pain of compassion; or in hope of reward in heaven; this is not contract, but Gift, Free-Gift, Grace: which words signify one and the same thing. . . .

Words alone, if they be of the time to come, and contain a bare promise, are an insufficient sign of a free gift, and therefore not obligatory. For if they be of the time to come, as *to-morrow I will give*, they are a sign I have not given yet, and consequently that my right is not transferred, but remaineth till I transfer it by some other act. But if the words be of the time present, or past, as, *I have given*, or, *do give to be delivered to-morrow*, then is my tomorrow's right given away to-day; and that by the virtue of the words, though there were no other argument of my will. . . .

If a covenant be made, wherein neither of the parties perform presently, but trust one another; in

the condition of mere nature, which is a condition of war of every man against every man, upon any reasonable suspicion, it is void: but if there be a common power set over them both, with right and force sufficient to compel performance, it is not void. For he that performeth first, has no assurance the other will perform after; because the bonds of words are too weak to bridle men's ambition, avarice, anger, and other passions, without the fear of some coercive power; which in the condition of mere nature, where all men are equal, and judges of the justness of their own fears, cannot possibly be supposed. And therefore he which performeth first, does but betray himself to his enemy; contrary to the right, he can never abandon, of defending his life, and means of living.

But in a civil estate, where there is a power set up to constrain those that would otherwise violate their faith, that fear is no more reasonable; and for that cause, he which by the covenant is to perform first, is obliged so to do.

The cause of fear, which maketh such a covenant invalid, must be always something arising after the covenant made; as some new fact, or other sign of the will not to perform: else it cannot make the covenant void. For that which could not hinder a man from promising, ought not to be admitted as a hindrance of performing.

He that transferreth any right, transferreth the means of enjoying it, as far as lieth in his power. As he that selleth land, is understood to transfer the herbage, and whatsoever grows upon it: nor can he that sells a mill turn away the stream that drives it. And they that give to a man the right of government in sovereignty, are understood to give him the right of levying money to maintain soldiers; and of appointing magistrates for the administration of justice.

To make covenants with brute beasts, is impossible; because not understanding our speech, they understand not, nor accept of any translation of right; nor can translate any right to another: and without mutual acceptation, there is no covenant.

To make covenant with God, is impossible, but by mediation of such as God speaketh to, either by revelation supernatural, or by his lieutenants that govern under him, and in his name: for otherwise we know now whether our covenants be accepted, or not. And therefore they that vow anything contrary to any law of nature, vow in vain; as being a thing unjust to pay such vow. And if it be a thing commanded by the law of nature, it is not the vow, but the law that binds them.

The matter, or subject of a covenant, is always something that falleth under deliberation; for to covenant, is an act of the will; that is to say, an act, and the last act of deliberation; and is therefore always understood to be something to come; and which is judged possible for him that covenanteth, to perform.

And therefore, to promise that which is known to be impossible, is no covenant. But if that prove impossible afterwards, which before was thought possible, the covenant is valid, and bindeth, though not to the thing itself, yet to the value; or, if that also be impossible, to the unfeigned endeavour of performing as much as is possible: for to more no man can be obliged.

Men are freed of their covenants two ways; by performing; or by being forgiven. For performance, is the natural end of obligation; and forgiveness, the restitution of liberty; as being a retransferring of that right, in which the obligation consisted.

Covenants entered into by fear, in the condition of mere nature, are obligatory. For example, if I covenant to pay a ransom, or service, for my life, to an enemy; I am bound by it: for it is a contract, wherein one receiveth the benefit of life; the other is to receive money, or service for it; and consequently, where no other law, as in the condition of mere nature, forbiddeth the performance, the covenant is valid. Therefore prisoners of war, if trusted with the payment of their ransom, are obliged to pay it: and if a weaker prince, make a disadvantageous peace with a stronger, for fear; he is bound to keep it; unless, as hath been said before, there ariseth some new, and just cause of fear, to renew the war. And even in commonwealths, if I be forced to redeem myself from a thief by promising

him money, I am bound to pay it, till the civil law discharge me. For whatsoever I may lawfully do without obligation, the same I may lawfully covenant to do through fear: and what I lawfully covenant, I cannot lawfully break.

A former covenant, makes void a later. For a man that hath passed away his right to one man to-day, hath it not to pass to-morrow to another: and therefore the later promise passeth no right, but is null.

A covenant not to defend myself from force, by force, is always void. For, as I have showed before, no man can transfer, or lay down his right to save himself from death, wounds, imprisonment, the avoiding whereof is the only end of laying down any right; and therefore the promise of not resisting force, in no covenant transferreth any right; nor is obliging. For though a man may covenant thus, *unless I do so, or so, kill me;* he cannot covenant thus, *unless I do so, or so, I will not resist you, when you come to kill me.* For man by nature chooseth the lesser evil, which is danger of death in resisting; rather than the greater, which is certain and present death in not resisting. And this is granted to be true by all men, in that they lead criminals to execution, and prison, with armed men, notwithstanding that such criminals have consented to the law, by which they are condemned. . . .

The force of words, being, as I have formerly noted, too weak to hold men to the performance of their covenants; there are in man's nature, but two imaginable helps to strengthen it. And those are either a fear of the consequence of breaking their word; or a glory, or pride in appearing not to need to break it. This latter is a generosity too rarely found to be presumed on, especially in the pursuers of wealth, command, or sensual pleasure; which are the greatest part of mankind. The passion to be reckoned upon, is fear; whereof there be two very general objects; one, the power of spirits invisible; the other, the power of those men they shall therein offend. Of these two, though the former be the greatest power, yet the fear of the latter is commonly the greater fear. The fear of the former is in every man, his own religion: which hath place in the nature of man before civil society. The latter hath not so; at least not place enough, to keep men to their promises; because in the condition of mere nature, the inequality of power is not discerned, but by the event of battle. So that before the time of civil society, or in the interruption thereof by war, there is nothing can strengthen a *covenant of peace agreed on, against the temptations of avarice, ambition, lust, or other strong desire, but the fear of that invisible power, which they every one worship as God;* and fear as a revenger of their perfidy. All therefore that can be done between two men not subject to civil power, is to put one another to swear by the God he feareth. . . .

Chapter 15

OF OTHER LAWS OF NATURE

From that law of nature, by which we are obliged to transfer to another, such rights, as being retained, hinder the peace of mankind, there followeth a third; which is this, *that men perform their covenants made:* without which, covenants are in vain, and but empty words; and the right of all men to all things remaining, we are still in the condition of war.

And in this law of nature, consisteth the fountain and original of JUSTICE. For where no covenant hath preceded, there hath no right been transferred, and every man has right to every thing; and consequently, no action can be unjust. But when a covenant is made, then to break it is *unjust;* and the definition of INJUSTICE, is no other than *the not performance of covenant.* And whatsoever is not unjust, is *just.*

But because covenants of mutual trust, where there is fear of not performance on either part, (as hath been said in the former chapter,) are invalid; though the original of justice be the making of covenants; yet injustice actually there can be none, till the cause of such fear be taken away; which while men are in the natural condition of war, cannot be done. Therefore before the names

of just, and unjust can have place, there must be some coercive power, to compel men equally to the performance of their covenants, by the terror of some punishment, greater than the benefit they expect by the breach of their covenant; and to make good that propriety, which by mutual contract men acquire, in recompense of the universal right they abandon: and such power there is none before the erection of a commonwealth. And this is also to be gathered out of the ordinary definition of justice in the Schools: for they say, that *justice is the constant will of giving to every man his own.* And therefore where there is no *own,* that is, no propriety, there is no injustice; and where there is no coercive power erected, that is, where there is no commonwealth, there is no propriety; all men having right to all things: therefore where there is no commonwealth, there nothing is unjust. So that the nature of justice, consisteth in keeping of valid covenants: but the validity of covenants begins not but with the constitution of a civil power, sufficient to compel men to keep them: and then it is also that propriety begins.

The fool hath said in his heart, there is no such thing as justice; and sometimes also with his tongue; seriously alleging, that every man's conservation, and contentment, being committed to his own care, there could be no reason, why every man might not do what he thought conduced thereunto: and therefore also to make, or not make; keep, or not keep covenants, was not against reason, when it conduced to one's benefit. He does not therein deny, that there be covenants; and that they are sometimes broken, sometimes kept; and that such breach of them may be called injustice, and the observance of them justice: but he questioneth, whether injustice, taking away the fear of God, (for the same fool hath said in his heart there is no God,) may not sometimes stand with that reason, which dictateth to every man his own good; and particularly then, when it conduceth to such a benefit, as shall put a man in a condition, to neglect not only the dispraise, and revilings, but also the power of other men. The kingdom of God is gotten by violence: but what if it could be gotten by unjust violence? were it against reason so to get it, when it is impossible to receive hurt by it? and if it be not against reason, it is not against justice; or else justice is not to be approved for good. From such reasoning as this, successful wickedness hath obtained the name of virtue: and some that in all other things have disallowed the violation of faith; yet have allowed it, when it is for the getting of a kingdom. And the heathen that believed, that *Saturn* was deposed by his son *Jupiter*, believed nevertheless the same *Jupiter* to be the avenger of injustice: somewhat like to a piece of law in *Coke's Commentaries on Littleton;* where he says, if the right heir of the crown be attainted of treason; yet the crown shall descend to him, and *eo instante* the attainder be void: from which instances a man will be very prone to infer; that when the heir apparent of a kingdom, shall kill him that is in possession, though his father; you may call it injustice, or by what other name you will; yet it can never be against reason, seeing all the voluntary actions of men tend to the benefit of themselves; and those actions are most reasonable, that conduce most to their ends. This specious reasoning is nevertheless false.

For the question is not of promises mutual, where there is no security of performance on either side; as when there is no civil power erected over the parties promising; for such promises are no covenants: but either where one of the parties has performed already; or where there is a power to make him perform; there is the question whether it be against reason, that is, against the benefit of the other to perform, or not. And I say it is not against reason. For the manifestation whereof, we are to consider; first, that when a man doth a thing, which notwithstanding any thing can be foreseen, and reckoned on, tendeth to his own destruction, howsoever some accident which he could not expect, arriving may turn it to his benefit; yet such events do not make it reasonably or wisely done. Secondly, that in a condition of war, wherein every man to every man, for want of a common power to keep them all in awe, is an enemy, there is no man can hope by his

own strength, or wit, to defend himself from destruction, without the help of confederates; where every one expects the same defence by the confederation, that any one else does: and therefore he which declares he thinks it reason to deceive those that help him, can in reason expect no other means of safety, than what can be had from his own single power. He therefore that breaketh his covenant, and consequently declareth that he thinks he may with reason do so, cannot be received into any society, that unite themselves for peace and defence, but by the error of them that receive him; nor when he is received, be retained in it, without seeing the danger of their error; which errors a man cannot reasonably reckon upon as the means of his security: and therefore if he be left, or cast out of society, he perisheth; and if he live in society, it is by the errors of other men, which he could not foresee, nor reckon upon; and consequently against the reason of his preservation; and so, as all men that contribute not to his destruction, forbear him only out of ignorance of what is good for themselves.

As for the instance of gaining the secure and perpetual felicity of heaven, by any way; it is frivolous: there being but one way imaginable; and that is not breaking, but keeping of covenant.

And for the other instances of attaining sovereignty by rebellion; it is manifest, that though the event follow, yet because it cannot reasonably be expected, but rather the contrary; and because by gaining it so, others are taught to gain the same in like manner, the attempt thereof is against reason. Justice therefore, that is to say, keeping of covenant, is a rule of reason, by which we are forbidden to do any thing destructive to our life; and consequently a law of nature.

There be some that proceed further; and will not have the law of nature, to be those rules which conduce to the preservation of man's life on earth; but to the attaining of an eternal felicity after death; to which they think the breach of covenant may conduce; and consequently be just and reasonable; (such are they that think it a work of merit to kill, or depose, or rebel against, the sovereign power constituted over them by their own consent.) But because there is no natural knowledge of man's estate after death; much less of the reward that is then to be given to breach of faith; but only a belief grounded upon other men's saying, that they know it supernaturally, or that they know those, that knew them, that knew others, that knew it supernaturally; breach of faith cannot be called a precept of reason, or nature.

Others, that allow for a law of nature, the keeping of faith, do nevertheless make exception of certain persons; as heretics, and such as use not to perform their covenant to others: and this also is against reason. For if any fault of a man, be sufficient to discharge our covenant made; the same ought in reason to have been sufficient to have hindered the making of it. . . .

As justice dependeth on antecedent covenant; so does GRATITUDE depend on antecedent grace; that is to say, antecedent free-gift: and is the fourth law of nature: which may be conceived in this form, *that a man which receiveth benefit from another of mere grace, endeavour that he which giveth it, have no reasonable cause to repent him of his good will.* For no man giveth, but with intention of good to himself; because gift is voluntary; and of all voluntary acts, the object is to every man his own good; of which if men see they shall be frustrated, there will be no beginning of benevolence, or trust; nor consequently of mutual help; nor of reconciliation of one man to another; and therefore they are to remain still in the condition of *war;* which is contrary to the first and fundamental law of nature, which commandeth men to *seek peace.* The breach of this law, is called *ingratitude;* and hath the same relation to grace, that injustice hath to obligation by covenant.

A fifth law of nature, is COMPLAISANCE; that is to say, *that every man strive to accommodate himself to the rest.* For the understanding whereof, we may consider, that there is in men's aptness to society, a diversity of nature, rising from their diversity of affections; not unlike to that we see in stones brought together for the building of an edifice. For as that stone which

by the asperity, and irregularity of figure, takes more room from others, than itself fills; and for the hardness, cannot be easily made plain, and thereby hindereth the building, is by the builders cast away as unprofitable, and troublesome: so also, a man that by asperity of nature, will strive to retain those things which to himself are superfluous, and to others necessary; and for the stubbornness of his passions, cannot be corrected, is to be left, or cast out of society, as cumbersome thereunto. For seeing every man, not only by right, but also by necessity of nature, is supposed to endeavour all he can, to obtain that which is necessary for his conservation; he that shall oppose himself against it, for things superfluous, is guilty of the war that thereupon is to follow; and therefore doth that, which is contrary to the fundamental law of nature, which commandeth *to seek peace.* The observers of this law, may be called SOCIABLE, (the Latins call them *commodi;*) the contrary, *stubborn, insociable, froward, intractable.*

A sixth law of nature, is that, *that upon caution of the future time, a man ought to pardon the offences past of them that repenting, desire it.* For PARDON, is nothing but granting of peace; which though granted to them that persevere in their hostility, be not peace, but fear; yet not granted to them that give caution of the future time, is sign of an aversion to peace; and therefore contrary to the law of nature.

A seventh is, *that in revenges,* (that is retribution of evil for evil,) *men look not at the greatness of the evil past, but the greatness of the good to follow.* Whereby we are forbidden to inflict punishment with any other design, than for correction of the offender, or direction to others. For this law is consequent to the next before it, that commandeth pardon, upon security of the future time. Besides, revenge without respect to the example, and profit to come, is a triumph, or glorying in the hurt of another, tending to no end; (for the end is always somewhat to come;) and glorying to no end, is vain-glory, and contrary to reason; and to hurt without reason, tendeth to the introduction of war; which is against the law of nature; and is commonly styled by the name of *cruelty*.

And because all signs of hatred, or contempt, provoke to fight, insomuch as most men choose rather to hazard their life, than not to be revenged; we may in the eighth place, for a law of nature, set down this precept, *that no man by deed, word, countenance, or gesture, declare hatred, or contempt of another*. The breach of which law, is commonly called *contumely*.

The question who is the better man, has no place in the condition of mere nature; where, (as has been shewn before,) all men are equal. The inequality that now is, has been introduced by the laws civil. I know that *Aristotle* in the first book of his *Politics*, for a foundation of his doctrine, maketh men by nature, some more worthy to command, meaning the wiser sort, (such as he thought himself to be for his philosophy;) others to serve, (meaning those that had strong bodies, but were not philosophers as he;) as if master and servant were not introduced by consent of men, but by difference of wit: which is not only against reason; but also against experience. For there are very few so foolish, that had not rather govern themselves, than be governed by others; nor when the wise in their own conceit, contend by force, with them who distrust their own wisdom, do they always, or often, or almost at any time, get the victory. If nature therefore have made men equal, that equality is to be acknowledged: or if nature have made men unequal; yet because men that think themselves equal, will not enter into conditions of peace, but upon equal terms, such equality must be admitted. And therefore for the ninth law of nature, I put this, *that every man acknowledge other for his equal by nature*. The breach of this precept is *pride*.

On this law, dependeth another, *that at the entrance into conditions of peace, no man require to reserve to himself any right, which he is not content should be reserved to every one of the rest*. As it is necessary for all men that seek peace, to lay down certain rights of nature; that is to say, not to have liberty to do all they list: so is it necessary for man's life, to retain some; as right to govern their own bodies; enjoy air, water, motion, ways to go from place to place; and all things else without which a man cannot live, or not live well. If in this case, at the making of peace, men require for themselves, that which they would not have to be granted to others, they do contrary to the precedent law, that commandeth the acknowledgment of natural equality, and therefore also against the law of nature. The observers of this law, are those we call *modest*, and the breakers *arrogant* men. . . .

And because, though men be never so willing to observe these laws, there may nevertheless arise questions concerning a man's action; first, whether it were done, or not done; secondly, (if done,) whether against the law, or not against the law; the former whereof, is called a question *of fact;* the latter a question *of right;* therefore unless the parties to the question, covenant mutually to stand to the sentence of another, they are as far from peace as ever. This other, to whose sentence they submit, is called an ARBITRATOR. And therefore it is of the law of nature, *that they that are at controversy, submit their right to the judgment of an arbitrator*.

And seeing every man is presumed to do all things in order to his own benefit, no man is a fit arbitrator in his cause: and if he were never so fit; yet equity allowing to each party equal benefit, if one be admitted to be judge, the other is to be admitted also; and so the controversy, that is, the cause of war, remains, against the law of nature.

For the same reason no man in any cause ought to be received for arbitrator, to whom greater profit, or honour, or pleasure apparently ariseth out of the victory of one party, than of the other: for he hath taken (though an unavoidable bribe, yet) a bribe; and no man can be obliged to trust him. And thus also the controversy, and the condition of war remaineth, contrary to the law of nature.

And in a controversy of *fact*, the judge being to give no more credit to one, than to the other, (if there be no other arguments,) must give credit to a third; or to a third and fourth; or more: for else the question is undecided, and left to force, contrary to the law of nature.

These are the laws of nature, dictating peace, for a means of the conservation of men in multitudes; and which only concern the doctrine of civil society. There be other things tending to the destruction of particular men; as drunkenness, and all other parts of intemperance; which may therefore also be reckoned amongst those things which the law of nature hath forbidden; but are not necessary to be mentioned, nor are pertinent enough to this place.

And though this may seem too subtle a deduction of the laws of nature, to be taken notice of by all men; whereof the most part are too busy in getting food, and the rest too negligent to understand; yet to leave all men inexcusable, they have been contracted into one easy sum, intelligible, even to the meanest capacity; and that is, *Do not that to another, which thou wouldest not have done to thyself;* which sheweth him, that he has no more to do in learning the laws of nature, but, when weighing the actions of other men with his own, they seem too heavy, to put them into the other part of the balance, and his own into their place, that his own passions, and self-love, may add nothing to the weight; and then there is none of these laws of nature that will not appear unto him very reasonable.

The laws of nature oblige *in foro interno;* that is to say, they bind to a desire they should take place: but *in foro externo;* that is, to the putting them in act, not always. For he that should be modest, and tractable, and perform all he promises, in such time, and place, where no man else should do so, should but make himself a prey to others, and procure his own certain ruin, contrary to the ground of all laws of nature, which tend to nature's preservation. And again, he that having sufficient security, that others shall observe the same laws towards him, observes them not himself, seeketh not peace, but war; and consequently the destruction of his nature by violence.

And whatsoever laws bind *in foro interno*, may be broken, not only by a fact contrary to the law, but also by a fact according to it, in case a man think it contrary. For though his action in this case, be according to the law; yet his purpose was against the law; which, where the obligation is *in foro interno*, is a breach.

The laws of nature are immutable and eternal; for injustice, ingratitude, arrogance, pride, iniquity, acception of persons, and the rest, can never be made lawful. For it can never be that war shall preserve life, and peace destroy it.

The same laws, because they oblige only to a desire, and endeavour, I mean an unfeigned and constant endeavour, are easy to be observed. For in that they require nothing but endeavour; he that endeavoureth their performance, fulfilleth them; and he that fulfilleth the law, is just.

And the science of them, is the true and only moral philosophy. For moral philosophy is nothing else but the science of what is *good*, and *evil*, in the conversation, and society of mankind. *Good*, and *evil*, are names that signify our appetites, and aversions; which in different tempers, customs, and doctrines of man, are different: and divers men, differ not only in their judgment, on the senses of what is pleasant, and unpleasant to the taste, smell, hearing, touch, and sight; but also of what is comfortable, or disagreeable to reason, in the actions of common life. Nay, the same man, in divers times, differs from himself; and one time praiseth, that is, calleth good, what another time he dispraiseth, and calleth evil: from whence arise disputes, controversies, and at last war. And therefore so long a man is in the condition of mere nature, (which is a condition of war,) as private appetite is the measure of good, and evil: and consequently all men agree on this, that peace is good, and therefore also the way, or means of peace, which, (as I have shewed before) are *justice, gratitude, modesty, equity, mercy*, and the rest of the laws of nature, are good; that is to say, *moral virtues;* and their contrary *vices;* evil. Now the science of virtue and vice, is moral philosophy; and therefore the true doctrine of the laws of nature, is the true moral philosophy. But the writers of moral philosopy, though they acknowledge the same virtues and vices; yet not seeing wherein consisted their goodness; nor that they come to be praised, as the means of peaceable, sociable, and comfortable living; place them in a mediocrity of passions: as if not the cause, but the degree of daring, made fortitude; or not the cause, but the quantity of a gift, made liberality.

These dictates of reason, men use to call by the name of laws; but improperly: for they are but conclusions, or theorems concerning what conduceth to the conservation and defence of themselves; whereas law, properly, is the word of him, that by right hath command over others. But yet if we consider the same theorems, as delivered in the word of God, that by right commandeth all things; then are they properly called laws.

PART 2

Of Commonwealth

Chapter 17

OF THE CAUSES, GENERATION, AND DEFINITION OF A COMMONWEALTH

The final cause, end, or design of men, (who naturally love liberty, and dominion over others,) in the introduction of that restraint upon themselves, (in which we see them live in commonwealths,) is the foresight of their own preservation, and of a more contented life thereby; that is to say, of getting themselves out from that miserable condition of war, which is necessarily consequent (as hath been shown), to, the natural passions of men, when there is no visible power to keep them in awe, and tie them by fear of punishment to the performance of their covenants, and observation of those laws of nature set down in the fourteenth and fifteenth chapters.

For the laws of nature (as *justice, equity, modesty, mercy,* and (in sum) *doing to others, as we would be done to,*) of themselves, without the terror of some power, to cause them to be observed, are contrary to our natural passions, that carry us to partiality, pride, revenge, and the like.

And covenants, without the sword, are but words, and of no strength to secure a man at all. Therefore notwithstanding the laws of nature, (which every one hath then kept, when he has the will to keep them, when he can do it safely,) if there be no power erected, or not great enough for our security; every man will, and may lawfully rely on his own strength and art, for caution against all other men. And in all places, where men have lived by small families, to rob and spoil one another, has been a trade, and so far from being reputed against the law of nature, that the greater spoils they gained, the greater was their honour; and men observed no other laws therein, but the laws of honour; that is, to abstain from cruelty, leaving to men their lives, and instruments of husbandry. And as small families did then; so now do cities and kingdoms which are but greater families (for their own security) enlarge their dominions, upon all pretences of danger, and fear of invasion, or assistance that may be given to invaders, endeavour as much as they can, to subdue, or weaken their neighbours, by open force, and secret arts, for want of other caution, justly; and are remembered for it in after ages with honour.

Nor is it the joining together of a small number of men, that gives them this security; because in small numbers, small additions on the one side or the other, make the advantage of strength so great, as is sufficient to carry the victory; and therefore gives encouragement to an invasion. The multitude sufficient to confide in for our security, is not determined by any certain number, but by comparison with the enemy we fear; and is then sufficient, when the odds of the enemy is not of so visible and conspicuous moment, to determine the event of war, as to move him to attempt.

And be there never so great a multitude; yet if their actions be directed according to their particular judgments, and particular appetites, they can expect thereby no defence, nor protection, neither against a common enemy, nor against the injuries of one another. For being distracted in opinions concerning the best use and application of their strength, they do not help, but hinder one another;

and reduce their strength by mutual opposition to nothing: whereby they are easily, not only subdued by a very few that agree together; but also when there is no common enemy, they make war upon each other, for their particular interests. For if we could suppose a great multitude of men to consent in the observation of justice, and other laws of nature, without a common power to keep them all in awe; we might as well suppose all mankind to do the same; and then there neither would be, nor need to be any civil government, or commonwealth at all; because there would be peace without subjection.

Nor is it enough for the security, which men desire should last all the time of their life, that they be governed, and directed by one judgment, for a limited time; as in one battle, or one war. For though they obtain a victory by their unanimous endeavour against a foreign enemy; yet afterwards, when either they have no common enemy, or he that by one part is held for an enemy, is by another part held for a friend, they must needs by the difference of their interests dissolve, and fall again into a war amongst themselves.

It is true, that certain living creatures, as bees, and ants, live sociably one with another, (which are therefore by *Aristotle* numbered amongst political creatures;) and yet have no other direction, than their particular judgments and appetites; nor speech, whereby one of them can signify to another, what he thinks expedient for the common benefit: and therefore some man may perhaps desire to know, why mankind cannot do the same. To which I answer,

First, that men are continually in competition for honour and dignity, which these creatures are not; and consequently amongst men there ariseth on that ground, envy and hatred, and finally war; but amongst these not so.

Secondly, that amongst these creatures, the common good differeth not from the private; and being by nature inclined to their private, they procure thereby the common benefit. But man, whose joy consisteth in comparing himself with other men, can relish nothing but what is eminent.

Thirdly, that these creatures, having not, (as man) the use of reason, do not see, nor think they see any fault, in the administration of their common business; whereas amongst men, there are very many, that think themselves wiser, and abler to govern the public, better than the rest; and these strive to reform and innovate, one this way, another that way; and thereby bring it into distraction and civil war.

Fourthly, that these creatures, though they have some use of voice, in making known to one another their desires, and other affections; yet they want that art of words, by which some men can represent to others, that which is good, in the likeness of evil; and evil, in the likeness of good; and augment, or diminish the apparent greatness of good and evil; discontenting men, and troubling their peace at their pleasure.

Fifthly, irrational creatures cannot distinguish between *injury*, and *damage*; and therefore as long as they be at ease, they are not offended with their fellows: whereas man is then most troublesome, when he is most at ease: for then it is that he loves to shew his wisdom, and control the actions of them that govern the commonwealth.

Lastly, the agreement of these creatures is natural; that of men, is by covenant only, which is artificial: and therefore it is no wonder if there be somewhat else required (besides covenant) to make their agreement constant and lasting; which is a common power, to keep them in awe, and to direct their actions to the common benefit.

The only way to erect such a common power, as may be able to defend them from the invasion of foreigners, and the injuries of one another, and thereby to secure them in such sort, as that by their own industry, and by the fruits of the earth, they may nourish themselves and live contentedly; is, to confer all their power and strength upon one man, or upon one assembly of men, that may reduce all their wills, by plurality of voices, unto one will: which is as much as to say, to appoint one man, or assembly of men, to bear their person; and even one to own, and acknowledge himself to be author of whatsoever he that so beareth their person, shall act, or cause to be acted, in those things which concern the common peace and safety; and therein to submit their wills, every one to his will, and their judgments, to his judgment. This is more than consent, or concord; it is a real unity of them all, in one and the same person, made by covenant of every man with every man, in such manner, as if every man should say to every man, *I authorise and give up my right of governing myself, to this man, or to this assembly of men, on this condition, that thou give up thy right to him, and authorize all his actions in like manner.* This done, the multitude so united in one person, is called a COMMONWEALTH, in Latin CIVITAS. This is the generation of that great LEVIATHAN, or rather (to speak more reverently) of that *mortal god*, to which we owe under the *immortal God*, our peace and defence. For by this authority, given him by every particular man in the commonwealth, he hath the use of so much power and strength conferred on him, that by terror thereof, he is enabled to form the wills of them all, to peace at home, and mutual aid against their enemies abroad. And in him consisteth the essence of the commonwealth; which (to define it,) *is one person, of whose acts a great multitude, by mutual covenants one with another, have made themselves every one the author, to the end he may use the strength and means of them all, as he shall think expedient, for their peace and common defence.*

And he that carrieth this person, is called SOVEREIGN, and said to have sovereign power; and every one besides, his SUBJECT.

The attaining to this sovereign power, is by two ways. One, by natural force; as when a man maketh his children, to submit themselves, and their children to his government, as being able to destroy them if they refuse; or by war subdueth his enemies to his will, giving them their lives on that condition. The other, is when men agree amongst themselves, to submit to some man, or assembly of men, voluntarily, on confidence to be protected by him against all others. This latter, may be called a political commonwealth, or commonwealth by *institution;* and the former, a commonwealth by *acquisition.* And first, I shall speak of a commonwealth by institution.

Chapter 18

OF THE RIGHTS OF SOVEREIGNS BY INSTITUTION

A *commonwealth* is said to be *instituted*, when a *multitude* of men do agree, and *covenant, every one, with every one,* that to whatsoever *man*, or *assembly of men*, shall be given by the major part, the *right to present* the person of them all, (that is to say, to be their *representative;*) every one, as well he that *voted for it*, as he that *voted against it*, shall *authorize* all the actions and judgments, of that man, or assembly of men, in the same manner, as if they were his own, to the end, to live peaceably amongst themselves, and be protected against other men.

From this institution of a commonwealth are derived all the *rights*, and *faculties* of him, or them, on whom the sovereign power is conferred by the consent of the people assembled.

First, because they covenant, it is to be understood, they are not obliged by former covenant to any thing repugnant hereunto. And consequently they that have already instituted a commonwealth, being thereby bound by covenant, to own the actions, and judgments of one, cannot lawfully make a new covenant, amongst themselves, to be obedient to any other, in any thing whatsoever, without his permission. And therefore, they that are subjects to a monarch, cannot without his leave cast off monarchy, and return to the confusion of a disunited multitude; nor transfer their person from him that beareth it, to another man, or other assembly of men: for they are bound, every man to every man, to own, and be reputed author of all, that he that already is their sovereign, shall do, and judge fit to be done: so that any one man dissenting, all the rest should break their covenant made to that man, which is injustice: and they have also every man given the sovereignty to him that beareth their person;

and therefore if they depose him, they take from him that which is his own, and so again it is injustice. Besides, if he that attempteth to depose his sovereign, be killed, or punished by him for such attempt, he is author of his own punishment, as being by the institution, author of all his sovereign shall do: and because it is injustice for a man to do any thing, for which he may be punished by his own authority, he is also upon that title, unjust. And whereas some men have pretended for their disobedience to their sovereign, a new covenant, made, not with men, but with God; this also is unjust: for there is no covenant with God, but by mediation of somebody that representeth God's person; which none doth but God's lieutenant, who hath the sovereignty under God. But this pretence of covenant with God, is so evident a lie, even in the pretender's own consciences, that it is not only an act of an unjust, but also of a vile, and unmanly disposition.

Secondly, because the right of bearing the person of them all, is given to him they make sovereign, by covenant only of one to another, and not of him to any of them; there can happen no breach of covenant on the part of the sovereign; and consequently none of his subjects, by any pretence of forfeiture, can be freed from his subjection. That he which is made sovereign maketh no covenant with his subjects beforehand, is manifest; because either he must make it with the whole multitude, as one party to the covenant; or he must make a several covenant with every man. With the whole, as one party, it is impossible; because as yet they are not one person: and if he make so many several covenants as there be men, those covenants after he hath the sovereignty are void, because what act soever can be pretended by any one of them for breach thereof, is the act both of himself, and of all the rest, because done in the person, and by the right of every one of them in particular. Besides, if any one, or more of them, pretend a breach of the covenant made by the sovereign at his institution; and others, or one other of his subjects, or himself alone, pretend there was no such breach, there is in this

case, no judge to decide the controversy; it returns therefore to the sword again; and every man recovereth the right of protecting himself by his own strength, contrary to the design they had in the institution. It is therefore in vain to grant sovereignty by way of precedent covenant. The opinion that any monarch receiveth his power by covenant, that is to say, on condition, proceedeth from want of understanding this easy truth, that covenants being but words and breath, have no force to oblige, contain, constrain, or protect any man, but what it has from the public sword; that is, from the untied hands of that man, or assembly of men that hath the sovereignty, and whose actions are avouched by them all, and performed by the strength of them all, in him united. But when an assembly of men is made sovereign; then no man imagineth any such covenant to have passed in the institution; for no man is so dull as to say, for example, the people of Rome made a covenant with the Romans, to hold the sovereignty on such or such conditions; which not performed, the Romans might lawfully depose the Roman people. That men see not the reason to be alike in a monarchy, and in a popular government, proceedeth from the ambition of some, that are kinder to the government of an assembly, whereof they may hope to participate, than of monarchy, which they despair to enjoy.

Thirdly, because the major part hath by consenting voices declared a sovereign; he that dissented must now consent with the rest; that is, be contented to avow all the actions he shall do, or else justly be destroyed by the rest. For if he voluntarily entered into the congregation of them that were assembled, he sufficiently declared thereby his will, (and therefore tacitly covenanted) to stand to what the major part should ordain: and therefore if he refuse to stand thereto, or make protestation against any of their decrees, he does contrary to his covenant, and therefore unjustly. And whether he be of the congregation, or not; and whether his consent be asked, or not, he must either submit to their decrees, or be left in the condition of war he was in before; wherein he might without injustice be destroyed by any man whatsoever.

Fourthly, because every subject is by this institution author of all the actions, and judgments of the sovereign instituted; it follows, that whatsoever he doth, it can be no injury to any of his subjects; nor ought he to be by any of them accused of injustice. For he that doth any thing by authority from another, doth therein no injury to him by whose authority he acteth; but by this institution of a commonwealth, every particular man is author of all the sovereign doth; and consequently he that complaineth of injury from his sovereign, complaineth of that whereof he himself is author; and therefore ought not to accuse any man but himself; no nor himself of injury; because to do injury to one's self, is impossible. It is true that they that have sovereign power, may commit iniquity; but not injustice, or injury in the proper signification.

Fifthly, and consequently to that which was said last, no man that hath sovereign power can justly be put to death, or otherwise in any manner by his subjects punished. For seeing every subject is author of the actions of his sovereign; he punisheth another, for the actions committed by himself.

And because the end of this institution, is the peace and defence of them all; and whosoever has right to the end, has right to the means; it belongeth of right, to whatsoever man, or assembly that hath the sovereignty, to be judge both of the means of peace and defence; and also of the hindrances, and disturbances of the same; and to do whatsoever he shall think necessary to be done, both beforehand, for the preserving of peace and security, by prevention of discord at home, and hostility from abroad; and, when peace and security are lost, for the recovery of the same. And therefore,

Sixthly, it is annexed to the sovereignty, to be judge of what opinions and doctrines are averse, and what conducting to peace; and consequently, on what occasions, how far, and what, men are to be trusted withal, in speaking to multitudes of people; and who shall examine the doctrines of all books before they be published. For the actions of men proceed from their opinions; and in the well-governing of opinions, consisteth the well-governing of men's actions, in order to their peace, and concord. And though in matter of doctrine, nothing ought to be regarded but the truth; yet this is not repugnant to regulating of the same by peace. For doctrine repugnant to peace, can no more be true, than peace and concord can be against the law of nature. It is true, that in a commonwealth, where by the negligence, or unskillfulness of governors, and teachers, false doctrines are by time generally received; the contrary truths may be generally offensive: Yet the most sudden, and rough busling in of a new truth, that can be, does never break the peace, but only sometimes awake the war. For those men that are so remissly governed, that they dare take up arms, to defend, or introduce an opinion, are still in war; and their condition not peace, but only a cessation of arms for fear of one another; and they live as it were, in the precincts of battle continually. It belongeth therefore to him that hath the sovereign power, to be judge, or constitute all judges of opinions and doctrines, as a thing necessary to peace; thereby to prevent discord and civil war.

Seventhly, is annexed to the sovereignty, the whole power of prescribing the rules, whereby every man may know, what goods he may enjoy, and what actions he may do, without being molested by any of his fellow-subjects; and this is it men call *propriety*. For before constitution of sovereign power (as hath already been shown) all men had right to all things; which necessarily causeth war: and therefore this propriety, being necessary to peace, and depending on sovereign power, is the act of that power, in order to the public peace. These rules of propriety (or *meum* and *tuum*) and of *good, evil, lawful,* and *unlawful* in the actions of subjects, are the civil laws; that is to say, the laws of each commonwealth in particular; though the name of civil law be now restrained to the ancient civil laws of the city of *Rome;* which being the head of a great part of the world, her laws at that time were in these parts the civil law.

Eighthly, is annexed to the sovereignty, the right of judicature; that is to say, of hearing and deciding all controversies, which may arise concerning law, either civil, or natural; or concerning fact. For without the decision of controversies, there is no protection of one subject, against the injuries of another; the laws concerning *meum* and *tuum* are in vain; and to every man remaineth, from the natural and necessary appetite of his own conservation, the right of protecting himself by his private strength, which is the condition of war; and contrary to the end for which every commonwealth is instituted.

Ninthly, is annexed to the sovereignty, the right of making war and peace with other nations, and commonwealths; that is to say, of judging when it is for the public good, and how great forces are to be assembled, armed, and paid for that end; and to levy money upon the subjects, to defray the expenses thereof. For the power by which the people are to be defended, consisteth in their armies; and the strength of an army, in the union of their strength under one command; which command the sovereign instituted, therefore hath; because the command of the *militia*, without other institution, maketh him that hath it sovereign. And therefore whosoever is made general of an army, he that hath the sovereign power is always generalissimo.

Tenthly, is annexed to the sovereignty, the choosing of all counsellors, ministers, magistrates, and officers, both in peace, and war. For seeing the sovereign is charged with the end, which is the common peace and defence, he is understood to have power to use such means, as he shall think most fit for his discharge.

Eleventhly, to the sovereign is committed the power of rewarding with riches, or honour; and of punishing with corporal, or pecuniary punishment, or with ignominy every subject according to the law he hath formerly made; or if there be no law made, according as he shall judge most to conduce to the encouraging of men to serve the commonwealth, or deterring of them from doing disservice to the same.

Lastly, considering what values men are naturally apt to set upon themselves; what respect they look for from others; and how little they value other men; from whence continually arise amongst them, emulation, quarrels, factions, and at last war, to the destroying of one another, and diminution of their strength against a common enemy; it is necessary that there be laws of honour, and a public rate of the worth of such men as have deserved, or are able to deserve well of the commonwealth; and that there be force in the hands of some or other, to put those laws in execution. But it hath already been shown, that not only the whole *militia*, or forces of the commonwealth; but also the judicature of all controversies, is annexed to the sovereignty. To the sovereign therefore it belongeth also to give titles of honour; and to appoint what order of place, and dignity, each man shall hold; and what signs of respect, in public or private meetings, they shall give to one another. . . .

But a man may here object, that the condition of subjects is very miserable; as being obnoxious to the lusts, and other irregular passions of him, or them that have so unlimited a power in their hands. And commonly that they live under a monarch, think it the fault of monarchy; and they that live under the government of democracy, or other sovereign assembly, attribute all the inconvenience to that form of commonwealth; whereas the power in all forms, if they be perfect enough to protect them, is the same; not considering that the estate of man can never be without some incommodity or other; and that the greatest, that in any form of government can possibly happen to the people in general, is scarce sensible, in respect to the miseries, and horrible calamities, that accompany a civil war, or that dissolute condition of masterless men, without subjection to laws, and a coercive power to tie their hands from rapine and revenge: nor considering that the greatest pressure of sovereign governors, proceedeth not from any delight, or profit they can expect in the damage or weakening of their subjects, in whose vigour, consisteth their own strength and glory; but in the restiveness of themselves, that unwillingly contributing to their own defence, make it necessary for their governors to draw from them what they can in time of peace, that they may have means on any emergent occasion, or sudden need, to resist, or take advantage on their enemies. For all men are by nature provided of notable multiplying glasses, (that is their passions and self-love,) through which, every little payment appeareth a great grievance; but are destitute of those prospective glasses, (namely moral and civil science,) to see afar off the miseries that hang over them, and cannot without such payments be avoided.

Chapter 19

OF THE SEVERAL KINDS OF COMMONWEALTH BY INSTITUTION, AND OF SUCCESSION TO THE SOVEREIGN POWER

The difference of commonwealths, consisteth in the difference of the sovereign, or the person representative of all and every one of the multitude. And because the sovereignty is either in one man, or in an assembly of more than one; and into that assembly either every man hath right to enter, or not every one, but certain men distinguished from the rest; it is manifest, there can be but three kinds of commonwealth. For the representative must needs be one man, or more: and if more, then it is the assembly of all, or but of a part. When the representative is one man, then is the commonwealth a MONARCHY: when an assembly of all that will come together, then it is a DEMOCRACY, or popular commonwealth: when an assembly of a part only, then it is called an ARISTOCRACY. Other kind of commonwealth there can be none: for either one, or more, or all, must have the sovereign power (which I have shown to be indivisible) entire.

There be other names of government, in the histories, and books of policy; as *tyranny*, and *oligarchy:* But they are not the names of other forms of government, but of the same forms misliked.

For they that are discontented under *monarchy*, call it *tyranny;* and they that are displeased with *aristocracy*, call it *oligarchy:* so also, they which find themselves grieved under a *democracy*, call it *anarchy*, (which signifies want of government); and yet I think no man believes, that want of government, is any new kind of government: nor by the same reason ought they to believe, that the government is of one kind, when they like it, and another, when they mislike it, or are oppressed by the governors.

It is manifest, that men who are in absolute liberty, may, if they please, give authority to one man, to represent them every one; as well as give such authority to any assembly of men whatsoever; and consequently may subject themselves, if they think good, to a monarch, as absolutely, as to any other representative. Therefore, where there is already erected a sovereign power, there can be no other representative of the same people, but only to certain particular ends, by the sovereign limited. For that were to erect two sovereigns; and every man to have his person represented by two actors, that by opposing one another, must needs divide that power, which (if men will live in peace) is indivisible; and thereby reduce the multitude into the condition of war, contrary to the end for which all sovereignty is instituted. And therefore as it is absurd, to think that a sovereign assembly, inviting the people of their dominion, to send up their deputies, with power to make known their advice, or desires, should therefore hold such deputies, rather than themselves, for the absolute representative of the people: so it is absurd also, to think the same in a monarchy. And I know not how this so manifest a truth, should of late be so little observed; that in a monarchy, he that had the sovereignty from a descent of 600 years, was alone called sovereign, had the title of Majesty from every one of his subjects, and was unquestionably taken by them for their king, was notwithstanding never considered as their representative; that name without contradiction passing for the title of those men, which at his command were sent up by the people to carry their petitions, and give him (if he permitted it) their advice. Which may serve as an admonition, for those that are the true, and absolute representative of a people, to instruct men in the nature of that office, and to take heed how they admit of any other general representation upon any occasion whatsoever, if they mean to discharge the trust committed to them.

The difference between these three kinds of commonwealth, consisteth not in the difference of power; but in the difference of convenience, or aptitude to produce the peace, and security of the people; for which end they were instituted. And to compare monarchy with the other two, we may observe; first, that whosoever beareth the person of the people, or is one of that assembly that bears it, beareth also his own natural person. And though he be careful in his politic person to procure the common interest; yet he is more, or no less careful to procure the private good of himself, his family, kindred and friends; and for the most part, if the public interest chance to cross the private, he prefers the private: for the passions of men, are commonly more potent than their reason. From whence it follows, that where the public and private interest are most closely united, there is the public most advanced. Now in monarchy, the private interest is the same with the public. The riches, power, and honour of a monarch arise only from the riches, strength and reputation of his subjects. For no king can be rich, nor glorious, nor secure, whose subjects are either poor, or contemptible, or too weak through want, or dissention, to maintain a war against their enemies: whereas in a democracy, or aristocracy, the public prosperity confers not so much to the private fortune of one that is corrupt, or ambitious, as doth many times a perfidious advice, a treacherous action, or a civil war.

Secondly, that a monarch receiveth counsel of whom, when, and where he pleaseth; and consequently may hear the opinion of men versed in the matter about which he deliberates, of what rank or quality soever, and as long before the time of action, and with as much secrecy, as he will. But when a sovereign assembly has need of counsel, none are admitted but such as have a right thereto from the beginning; which for the most part are of those who have been versed more in the acquisition of wealth than of knowledge; and are to give their advice in long discourses, which may, and do commonly excite men to action, but not govern them in it. For the *understanding* is by the flame of the passions, never enlightened, but dazzled: Nor is there any place, or time, wherein an assembly can receive counsel with secrecy, because of their own multitude.

Thirdly, that the resolutions of a monarch, are subject to no other inconstancy, than that of human nature; but in assemblies, besides that of nature, there ariseth an inconstancy from the number. For the absence of a few, that would have the resolution once taken, continue firm (which may happen by security, negligence, or private impediments) or the diligent appearance of a few of the contrary opinion, undoes to day, all that was concluded yesterday.

Fourthly, that a monarch cannot disagree with himself, out of envy, or interest; but an assembly may; and that to such a height, as may produce a civil war.

Fifthly, that in monarchy there is this inconvenience; that any subject, by the power of one man, for the enriching of a favourite or flatterer, may be deprived of all he possesseth; which I confess is a great and inevitable inconvenience. But the same may as well happen, where the sovereign power is in an assembly: for their power is the same; and they are as subject to evil counsel, and to be seduced by orators, as a monarch by flatterers; and becoming one another's flatterers, serve one another's covetousness and ambition by turns. And whereas the favourites of monarchs, are few, and they have none else to advance but their own kindred; the favourites of an assembly, are many; and the kindred much more numerous, than of any monarch. Besides, there is no favourite of a monarch, which cannot as well succour his friends, as hurt his enemies: but orators, that is to say, favourites of sovereign assemblies, though they have great power to hurt, have little to save.

For to accuse, requires less eloquence (such is man's nature) than to excuse; and condemnation, than absolution more resembles justice. . . .

Chapter 21

OF THE LIBERTY OF SUBJECTS

Liberty, or freedom, signifieth, properly, the absence of opposition; by opposition, I mean external impediments of motion; and may be applied no less to irrational, and inanimate creatures, than to rational. For whatsoever is so tied, or environed, as it cannot move, but within a certain space, which space is determined by the opposition of some external body, we say it hath not liberty to go further. And so of all living creatures, whilst they are imprisoned, or restrained, with walls, or chains; and of the water whilst it is kept in by banks, or vessels, that otherwise would spread itself into a larger space, we use to say, they are not at liberty, to move in such manner, as without those external impediments they would. But when the impediment of motion, is in the constitution of the thing itself, we use not to say, it wants the liberty; but the power to move; as when a stone lieth still, or a man is fastened to his bed by sickness.

And according to this proper, and generally received meaning of the word, a Freeman, *is he, that in those things, which by his strength and wit he is able to do, is not hindered to do what he has a will to.* But when the words *free* and *liberty*, are applied to any thing but *bodies*, they are abused; for that which is not subject to motion, is not subject to impediment: and therefore, when it is said, for example, the way is free, no liberty of the way is signified, but of those that walk in it without stop. And when we say a gift is free, there is not meant any liberty of the gift, but of the giver, that was not bound by any law, or covenant to give it. So when we *speak freely*, it is not the liberty of voice, or pronunciation, but of the man, whom no law hath obliged to speak otherwise than he did. Lastly, from the use of the word *freewill*, no liberty can be inferred of the will, desire, or inclination, but the liberty of the man; which consisteth in this, that he finds no stop, in doing what he has the will, desire, or inclination to do.

Fear and liberty are consistent; as when a man throweth his goods into the sea for *fear* the ship should sink, he doth it nevertheless very willingly, and may refuse to do it if he will: it is therefore the action of one that was *free:* so a man sometimes pays his debt, only for *fear* of imprisonment, which because nobody hindered him from detaining, was the action of a man at *liberty*. And generally all actions which men do in commonwealths, for *fear* of the law, are actions, which the doers had *liberty* to omit.

Liberty, and *necessity* are consistent: as in the water, that hath not only *liberty*, but a *necessity* of descending by the channel; so likewise in the actions which men voluntarily do: which, because they proceed from their will, proceed from *liberty;* and yet, because every act of man's will, and every desire, and inclination proceedeth from some cause, and that from another cause, in a continual chain, whose first link is in the hand of God the first of all causes, they proceed from *necessity*. So that to him that could see the connexion of those causes, the *necessity* of all men's voluntary actions, would appear manifest. And therefore God, that seeth, and disposeth all things, seeth also that the *liberty* of man in doing what he will, is accompanied with the *necessity* of doing that which God will, and no more, nor less. For though men may do many things, which God does not command, nor is therefore author of them; yet they can have no passion, nor appetite to any thing, of which appetite God's will is not the cause. And did not his will assure the *necessity* of man's will, and consequently of all that on man's will dependeth, the *liberty* of men would be a contradiction, and impediment to the omnipotence and *liberty* of God. And this shall suffice, (as to the matter in hand) of that natural *liberty*, which only is properly called *liberty*.

But as men, for the attaining of peace, and conservation of themselves thereby, have made an artificial man, which we call a commonwealth; so also have they made artificial chains, called *civil laws*, which they themselves, by mutual covenants, have fastened at one end, to the lips of that man, or assembly, to whom they have given the sovereign power; and at the other end to their own ears. These bonds, in their own nature but weak, may nevertheless be made to hold, by the danger, though not by the difficulty of breaking them.

In relation to these bonds only it is, that I am to speak now, of the *liberty* of *subjects*. For seeing there is no commonwealth in the world, wherein there be rules enough set down, for the regulating of all the actions, and words of men; as being a thing impossible: it followeth necessarily, that in all kinds of actions by the laws prætermitted, men have the liberty, of doing what their own reasons shall suggest, for the most profitable to themselves. For if we take liberty in the proper sense, for corporal liberty; that is to say, freedom from chains and prison; it were very absurd for men to clamour as they do, for the liberty they so manifestly enjoy. Again, if we take liberty, for an exemption from laws, it is no less absurd, for men to demand as they do, that liberty, by which all other men may be masters of their lives. And yet, as absurd as it is, this is it they demand; not knowing that the laws are of no power to protect them, without a sword in the hands of a man, or men, to cause those laws to be put in execution. The liberty of a subject, lieth therefore only in those things, which in regulating their actions, the sovereign hath prætermitted: such as is the liberty to buy, and sell, and otherwise contract with one another; to choose their own abode, their own diet, their own trade of life, and institute their children as they themselves think fit; and the like.

Nevertheless we are not to understand, that by such liberty, the sovereign power of life and death, is either abolished, or limited. For it has been already shown, that nothing the sovereign representative can do to a subject, on what pretence soever, can properly be called injustice, or injury; because every subject is author of every act the sovereign doth; so that he never wanteth right to any thing, otherwise, than as he himself is

the subject of God, and bound thereby to observe the laws of nature. And therefore it may, and doth often happen in commonwealths, that a subject may be put to death, by the command of the sovereign power; and yet neither do the other wrong; as when Jephtha caused his daughter to be sacrificed: in which, and the like cases, he that so dieth, had liberty to do the action, for which he is nevertheless, without injury put to death. And the same holdeth also in a sovereign prince, that putteth to death an innocent subject. For though the action be against the law of nature, as being contrary to equity, as was the killing of Uriah, by David; yet it was not an injury to Uriah, but to God. Not to Uriah, because the right to do what he pleased was given him by Uriah himself: and yet to God, because David was God's subject, and prohibited all iniquity by the law of nature. . . .

The liberty, whereof there is so frequent and honourable mention, in the histories, and philosophy of the ancient Greeks, and Romans, and in the writings, and discourse of those that from them have received all their learning in the politics, is not the liberty of particular men; but the liberty of the commonwealth: which is the same with that which every man then should have, if there were no civil laws, nor commonwealth at all. And the effects of it also be the same. For as amongst masterless men, there is perpetual war, of every man against his neighbor; no inheritance, to transmit to the son, nor to expect from the father; no propriety of goods, or lands; no security; but a full and absolute liberty in every particular man: so in states, and commonwealths not dependent on one another, every commonwealth, not every man, has an absolute liberty, to do what it shall judge, that is to say, what that man, or assembly that representeth it, shall judge most conducing to their benefit. But withal, they live in the condition of a perpetual war, and upon the confines of battle, with their frontiers armed, and cannons planted against their neighbors round about. The Athenians, and Romans were free; that is, free commonwealths: not that any particular men had the liberty to resist their own representative; but that their representative had the liberty to resist, or invade other people. There is written on the turrets of the city of Lucca in great characters at this day, the word Libertas; yet no man can thence infer, that a particular man has more liberty, or immunity from the service of the commonwealth there, than in Constantinople. Whether a commonwealth be monarchical, or popular, the freedom is still the same.

But it is an easy thing, for men to be deceived, by the specious name of liberty; and for want of judgment to distinguish, mistake that for their private inheritance, and birth-right, which is the right of the public only. And when the same error is confirmed by the authority of men in reputation for their writings on this subject, it is no wonder if it produce sedition, and change of government. In these western parts of the world, we are made to receive our opinions concerning the institution, and rights of commonwealths, from Aristotle, Cicero, and other men, Greeks and Romans, that living under popular states, derived those rights, not from the principles of nature, but transcribed them into their books, out of the practice of their own commonwealths, which were popular; as the grammarians describe the rules of language, out of the practice of the time; or the rules of poetry, out of the poems of Homer and Virgil. And because the Athenians were taught, to keep them from desire of changing their government, that they were freemen, and all that lived under monarchy were slaves; therefore Aristotle puts it down in his *Politics, In democracy*, Liberty *is to be supposed: for it is commonly held, that no man is Free in any other government*. And as Aristotle; so Cicero, and other writers have grounded their civil doctrine, on the opinions of the Romans, who were taught to hate monarchy, at first, by them that having deposed their sovereign; shared amongst them the sovereignty of Rome; and afterwards by their successors. And by reading of these Greek, and Latin authors, men from their childhood have gotten a habit, under a false show of liberty, of favouring tumults, and of licentious controlling the actions of their sovereigns, and

again of controlling those controllers; with the effusion of so much blood, as I think I may truly say, there was never any thing so dearly bought, as these western parts have bought the learning of the Greek and Latin tongues.

To come now to the particulars of the true liberty of a subject; that is to say, what are the things, which though commanded by the sovereign, he may nevertheless, without injustice, refuse to do; we are to consider, what rights we pass away, when we make a commonwealth; or (which is all one,) what liberty we deny ourselves, by owning all the actions (without exception) of the man, or assembly we make our sovereign. For in the act of our *submission*, consisteth both our *obligation*, and our *liberty;* which must therefore be inferred by arguments taken from thence; there being no obligation on any man, which ariseth not from some act of his own; for all men equally, are by nature free. And because such arguments, must either be drawn from the express words, *I authorise all his actions*, or from the intention of him that submitteth himself to his power, (which intention is to be understood by the end for which he so submitteth;) the obligation, and liberty of the subject, is to be derived, either from those words, (or others equivalent;) or else from the end of the institution of sovereignty, namely, the peace of the subjects within themselves, and their defence against a common enemy.

First therefore, seeing sovereignty by institution, is by covenant of every one to every one; and sovereignty by acquisition, by covenants of the vanquished to the victor, or child to the parent; it is manifest, that every subject has liberty in all those things, the right whereof cannot by covenant be transferred. I have shewn before in the 14th chapter, that covenants, not to defend a man's own body, are void. Therefore,

If the sovereign command a man (though justly condemned,) to kill, wound, or maim himself; or not to resist those that assault him; or to abstain from the use of food, air, medicine, or any other thing, without which he cannot live; yet hath that man the liberty to disobey.

If a man be interrogated by the sovereign, or his authority, concerning a crime done by himself, he is not bound (without assurance of pardon) to confess it; because no man (as I have shown in the same chapter) can be obliged by covenant to accuse himself.

Again, the consent of a subject to sovereign power, is contained in these words, *I authorize, or take upon me, all his actions;* in which there is no restriction at all, of his own former natural liberty: for by allowing him to *kill me,* I am not bound to kill myself when he commands me. It is one thing to say, *kill me, or my fellow, if you please;* another thing to say, *I will kill myself, or my fellow.* It followeth therefore, that

No man is bound by the words themselves, either to kill himself, or any other man; and consequently, that the obligation a man may sometimes have, upon the command of the sovereign to execute any dangerous, or dishonourable office, dependeth not on the words of our submission; but on the intention, which is to be understood by the end thereof. When therefore our refusal to obey, frustrates the end for which the sovereignty was ordained; then there is no liberty to refuse: otherwise there is.

Upon this ground, a man that is commanded as a soldier to fight against the enemy, though his sovereign have right enough to punish his refusal with death, may nevertheless in many cases refuse, without injustice; as when he substituteth a sufficient soldier in his place: for in this case he deserteth not the service of the commonwealth. And there is allowance to be made for natural timorousness; not only to women, (of whom no such dangerous duty is expected,) but also to men of feminine courage. When armies fight, there is on one side, or both, a running away; yet when they do it not out of treachery, but fear, they are not esteemed to do it unjustly, but dishonourably. For the same reason, to avoid battle, is not injustice, but cowardice. But he that inrolleth himself a soldier, or taketh imprest money, taketh away the excuse of a timorous nature; and is obliged, not only to go to the battle, but also not to run from

it, without his captain's leave. And when the defence of the commonwealth, requireth at once the help of all that are able to bear arms, every one is obliged; because otherwise the institution of the commonwealth, which they have not the purpose, or courage to preserve, was in vain.

To resist the sword of the commonwealth, in defence of another man, guilty, or innocent, no man hath liberty; because such liberty, takes away from the sovereign, the means of protecting us; and is therefore destructive of the very essence of government. But in case a great many men together, have already resisted the sovereign power unjustly, or committed some capital crime, for which every one of them expecteth death, whether have they not the liberty then to join together, and assist, and defend one another? Certainly they have: for they but defend their lives, which the guilty man may as well do, as the innocent. There was indeed injustice in the first breach of their duty; their bearing of arms subsequent to it, though it be to maintain what they have done, is no new unjust act. And if it be only to defend their persons, it is not unjust at all. But the offer of pardon taketh from them, to whom it is offered, the plea of self-defence, and maketh their perserverance in assisting, or defending the rest, unlawful.

As for other liberties, they depend on the silence of the law. In cases where the sovereign has prescribed no rule, there the subject hath the liberty to do, or forbear, according to his own discretion. And therefore such liberty is in some places more, and in some less; and in some times more, in other times less, according as they that have the sovereignty shall think most convenient. As for example, there was a time, when in England a man might enter into his own land, and dispossess such as wrongfully possessed it, by force. But in aftertimes, that liberty of forcible entry, was taken away by a statute made (by the king,) in parliament. And in some places of the world, men have the liberty of many wives: in other places, such liberty is not allowed.

If a subject have a controversy with his sovereign, of debt, or of right of possession of lands or goods, or concerning any service required at his hands, or concerning any penalty, corporal, or pecuniary, grounded on a precedent law; he hath the same liberty to sue for his right, as if it were against a subject; and before such judges, as are appointed by the sovereign. For seeing the sovereign demandeth by force of a former law, and not by virtue of his power; he declareth thereby, that he requireth no more, than shall appear to be due by that law. The suit therefore is not contrary to the will of the sovereign; and consequently the subject hath the liberty to demand the hearing of his cause; and sentence, according to that law. But if he demand, or take anything by pretence of his power; there lieth, in that case, no action of law; for all that is done by him in virtue of his power, is done by the authority of every subject, and consequently he that brings an action against the sovereign, brings it against himself.

If a monarch, or sovereign assembly, grant a liberty to all, or any of his subjects, which grant standing, he is disabled to provide for their safety, the grant is void; unless he directly renounce, or transfer the sovereignty to another. For in that he might openly, if it had been his will, and in plain terms, have renounced, or transferred it, and did not; it is to be understood it was not his will, but that the grant proceeded from ignorance of the repugnancy between such a liberty and the sovereign power; and therefore the sovereignty is still retained; and consequently all those powers, which are necessary to the exercising thereof; such as are the power of war, and peace, of judicature, of appointing officers, and councillors, of levying money, and the rest named in the 18th chapter.

The obligation of subjects to the sovereign, is understood to last as long, and no longer, than the power lasteth, by which he is able to protect them. For the right men have by nature to protect themselves, when none else can protect them, can by no covenant be relinquished. The sovereignty is the soul of the commonwealth; which once departed from the body, the members do no more receive their motion from it. The end of obedience is protection; which, wheresoever a man seeth it,

either in his own, or in another's sword, nature applieth his obedience to it, and his endeavour to maintain it. And though sovereignty, in the intention of them that make it, be immortal; yet is it in its own nature, not only subject to violent death, by foreign war; but also through the ignorance, and passions of men, it hath in it, from the very institution, many seeds of a natural mortality, by intestine discord.

If a subject be taken prisoner in war; or his person or his means of life be within the guards of the enemy, and hath his life and corporal liberty given him, on condition to be subject to the victor, he hath liberty to accept the condition; and having accepted it, is the subject of him that took him; because he had no other way to preserve himself. The case is the same, if he detained on the same terms, in a foreign country. But if a man be held in prison, or bonds, or is not trusted with the liberty of his body; he cannot be understood to be bound by covenant to subjection; and therefore may, if he can, make his escape by any means whatsoever.

If a monarch shall relinquish the sovereignty, both for himself, and his heirs; his subjects return to the absolute liberty of nature; because, though nature may declare who are his sons, and who are the nearest of his kin; yet it dependeth on his own will, as hath been said in the precedent chapter, who shall be his heir. If therefore he will have no heir, there is no sovereignty, nor subjection. The case is the same, if he die without known kindred, and without declaration of his heir. For then there can no heir be known, and consequently no subjection be due.

If the sovereign banish his subject; during the banishment, he is not subject. But he that is sent on a message, or hath leave to travel, is still subject; but it is, by contract between sovereigns, not by virtue of the covenant of subjection. For whosoever entereth into another's dominion, is subject to all the laws thereof; unless he have a privilege of the amity of the sovereigns, or by special licence.

If a monarch subdued by war, render himself subject to the victor; his subjects are delivered from their former obligation, and become obliged to the victor. If he be held prisoner, or have not the liberty of his own body; he is not understood to have given away the right of sovereignty; and therefore his subjects are obliged to yield obedience to the magistrates formerly placed, governing not in their own name, but in his. For, his right remaining, the question is only of the administration; that is to say, of the magistrates and officers; which, if he have not means to name, he is supposed to approve those, which he himself had formerly appointed.

Chapter 29

OF THOSE THINGS THAT WEAKEN, OR TEND TO THE DISSOLUTION OF A COMMONWEALTH

Though nothing can be immortal, which mortals make; yet, if men had the use of reason they pretend to, their commonwealths might be secured, at least, from perishing by internal diseases. For by the nature of their institution, they are designed to live, as long as mankind, or as the laws of nature, or as justice itself, which gives them life. Therefore when they come to be dissolved, not by external violence, but intestine disorder, the fault is not in men, as they are the *matter;* but as they are the *makers,* and orderers of them. For men, as they become at last weary of irregular jostling, and hewing one another, and desire with all their hearts, to conform themselves into one firm and lasting edifice; so for want, both of the art of making fit laws, to square their actions by, and also of humility, and patience, to suffer the rude and cumbersome points of their present greatness to be taken off, they cannot without the help of a very able architect, be compiled, into any other than a crazy building, such as hardly lasting out their own time, must assuredly fall upon the heads of their posterity.

Amongst the *infirmities* therefore of a commonwealth, I will reckon in the first place, those that arise from an imperfect institution, and

resemble the diseases of a natural body, which proceed from a defectuous procreation.

Of which, this is one, *that a man to obtain a kingdom, is sometimes content with less power, than to the peace, and defence of the commonwealth is necessarily required.* From whence it cometh to pass, that when the exercise of the power laid by, is for the public safety to be resumed, it hath the resemblance of an unjust act; which disposeth great numbers of men (when occasion is presented) to rebel; in the same manner as the bodies of children, gotten by diseased parents, are subject either to untimely death, or to purge the ill quality, derived from their vicious conception, by breaking out into biles and scabs. And when kings deny themselves some such necessary power, it is not always (though sometimes), out of ignorance of what is necessary to the office they undertake; but many times out of a hope to recover the same again at their pleasure: Wherein they reason not well; because such as will hold them to their promises, shall be maintained against them by foreign commonwealths; who in order to the good of their own subjects let slip few occasions to *weaken* the estate of their neighbours. So was *Thomas Becket,* archbishop of *Canterbury,* supported against *Henry* the Second, by the Pope; the subjection of ecclesiastics to the commonwealth, having been dispensed with by *William the Conqueror* at his reception, when he took an oath, not to infringe the liberty of the church. And so were the *barons,* whose power was by *William Rufus* (to have their help in transferring the succession from his elder brother, to himself,) increased to a degree, inconsistent with the sovereign power, maintained in their rebellion against *King John,* by the French. . . .

In the second place, I observe the *diseases* of a commonwealth, that proceed from the poison of seditious doctrines, whereof one is, *That every private man is judge of good and evil actions.* This is true in the condition of mere nature, where there are no civil laws; and also under civil government, in such cases as are not determined by the law. But otherwise it is manifest, that the measure of good and evil actions, is the civil law; and the judge the legislator, who is always representative of the commonwealth. From this false doctrine, men are disposed to debate with themselves, and dispute the commands of the commonwealth; and afterwards to obey, or disobey them, as in their private judgments they shall think fit. Whereby the commonwealth is distracted and *weakened*.

Another doctrine repugnant to civil society, is, that *whatsoever a man does against his conscience, is sin;* and it dependeth on the presumption of making himself judge of good and evil. For a man's conscience, and his judgment is the same thing; and as the judgment, so also the conscience may be erroneous. Therefore, though he that is subject to no civil law, sinneth in all he does against his conscience, because he has no other rule to follow but his own reason; yet it is not so with him that lives in a commonwealth; because the law is the public conscience, by which he hath already undertaken to be guided. Otherwise in such diversity, as there is of private consciences, which are but private opinions, the commonwealth must needs be distracted, and no man dare to obey the sovereign power, farther than it shall seem good in his own eyes.

It hath been also commonly taught, *that faith and sanctity, are not to be attained by study and reason, but by supernatural inspiration, or infusion,* which granted, I see not why any man should render a reason of his faith; or why every Christian should not be also a prophet; or why any man should take the law of his country, rather than his own inspiration, for the rule of his action. And thus we fall again into the fault of taking upon us to judge of good and evil; or to make judges of it, such private men as pretend to be supernaturally inspired, to the dissolution of all civil government. Faith comes by hearing, and hearing by those accidents, which guide us into the presence of them that speak to us; which accidents are all contrived by God Almighty; and yet are not supernatural, but only, for the great number of them that concur to every effect, unobservable. Faith and sanctity, are indeed not very frequent; but yet they are not miracles, but brought to pass by education, discipline, correction, and other natural ways, by which God worketh them in his elect, at such time as he thinketh fit. And these three opinions, pernicious to peace and government, have in this part of the world, proceeded chiefly from the tongues, and pens of unlearned divines; who joining the words of Holy Scripture together, otherwise than is agreeable to reason, do what they can, to make men think, that sanctity and natural reason, cannot stand together.

A fourth opinion, repugnant to the nature of a commonwealth, is this, *that he that hath the sovereign power, is subject to the civil laws.* It is true, that sovereigns are all subject to the laws of nature; because such laws be divine, and cannot by any man, or commonwealth be abrogated. But to those laws which the sovereign himself, that is, which the commonwealth maketh, he is not subject. For to be subject to laws, is to be subject to the commonwealth, that is to the sovereign representative, that is to himself; which is not subjection, but freedom from the laws. Which error, because it setteth the laws above the sovereign, setteth also a judge above him, and a power to punish him; which is to make a new sovereign; and again for the same reason a third, to punish the second; and so continually without end, to the confusion, and dissolution of the commonwealth.

A fifth doctrine, that tendeth to the dissolution of a commonwealth, is, *that every private man has an absolute propriety in his goods; such, as excludeth the right of the sovereign.* Every man has indeed a propriety that excludes the right of every other subject: and he has it only from the sovereign power; without the protection whereof, every other man should have equal right to the same. But if the right of the sovereign also be excluded, he cannot perform the office they have put him into; which is, to defend them both from foreign enemies, and from the injuries of one another; and consequently there is no longer a commonwealth.

And if the propriety of subjects, exclude not the right of the sovereign representative to their goods; much less to their offices of judicature, or execution, in which they represent the sovereign himself.

There is a sixth doctrine, plainly, and directly against the essence of a commonwealth; and it is this, *that the sovereign power may be divided*. For what is it to divide the power of a commonwealth, but to dissolve it; for powers divided mutually destroy each other. And for these doctrines, men are chiefly beholding to some of those, that making profession of the laws, endeavour to make them depend upon their own learning, and not upon the legislative power. . . .

As there have been doctors, that hold there be three souls in a man; so there be also that think there may be more souls, (that is, more sovereigns,) than one, in a commonwealth; and set up a *supremacy* against the *sovereignty; canons* against *laws;* and a *ghostly authority* against the *civil;* working on men's minds, with words and distinctions, that of themselves signify nothing, but bewray (by their obscurity) that there walketh (as some think invisibly) another kingdom, as it were a kingdom of fairies, in the dark. Now seeing it is manifest, that the civil power, and the power of the commonwealth is the same thing; and that supremacy, and the power of making canons, and granting faculties, implieth a commonwealth; it followeth, that where one is sovereign, another supreme; where one can make laws, and another make canons; there must needs be two commonwealths, of one and the same subjects; which is a kingdom divided in itself, and cannot stand. For notwithstanding the insignificant distinction of *temporal*, and *ghostly*, they are still two kingdoms, and every subject is subject to two masters. For seeing the *ghostly* power challengeth the right to declare what is sin it challengeth by consequence to declare what is law, (sin being nothing but the transgression of the law;) and again, the civil power challenging to declare what is law, every subject must obey two masters, who both will have their commands be observed as law; which is impossible. Or, if it be but one kingdom, either the *civil*, which is the *power* of the commonwealth, must be subordinate to the *ghostly*, and then there is no sovereignty but the *ghostly;* or the

ghostly, must be subordinate to the *temporal*, and then there is no *supremacy*, but the *temporal*. When therefore these two powers oppose one another, the commonwealth cannot but be in great danger of civil war, and dissolution. For the *civil* authority being more visible, and standing in the clearer light of natural reason, cannot choose but draw to it in all times a very considerable part of the people: and the *spiritual*, though it stand in the darkness of School distinctions, and hard words; yet because the fear of darkness, and ghosts, is greater than other fears, cannot want a party sufficient to trouble, and sometimes to destroy a commonwealth, and this is a disease which not unfitly may be compared to the epilepsy, or falling sickness (which the Jews took to be one kind of possession by spirits) in the body natural. For as in this disease, there is an unnatural spirit, or wind in the head that obstructeth the roots of the nerves, and moving them violently, taketh away the motion which naturally they should have from the power of the soul in the brain, and thereby causeth violent, and irregular motions (which men call convulsions) in the parts; insomuch as he that is seized therewith, falleth down sometimes into the water, and sometimes into the fire, as a man deprived of his senses; so also in the body politic, when the spiritual power, moveth the members of a commonwealth, by the terror of punishments, and hope of rewards (which are the nerves of it,) otherwise than by the civil power (which is the soul of the commonwealth), they ought to be moved; and by strange, and hard words suffocates their understanding, it must needs thereby distract the people, and either overwhelm the commonwealth with oppression, or cast it into the fire of a civil war.

Sometimes also in the merely civil government, there be more than one soul: as when the power of levying money, (which is the nutritive faculty,) has depended on a general assembly; the power of conduct and command, (which is the motive faculty,) on one man; and the power of making laws, (which is the rational faculty,) on the accidental consent, not only of those two, but also of a third; this endangereth the commonwealth, sometimes for want of consent to good laws; but most often for want of such nourishment, as is necessary to life, and motion. For although few perceive, that such government, is not government, but division of the commonwealth into three factions, and call it mixed monarchy; yet the truth is, that it is not one independent commonwealth, but three independent factions; nor one representative person, but three. In the kingdom of God, there may be three persons independent, without breach of unity in God that reigneth; but where men reign, that be subject to diversity of opinions, it cannot be so. And therefore if the king bear the person of the people, and the general assembly bear also the person of the people, and another assembly bear the person of a part of the people, they are not one person, nor one sovereign, but three persons, and three sovereigns.

To what disease in the natural body of man I may exactly compare this irregularity of a commonwealth, I know not. But I have seen a man, that had another man growing out of his side, with an head, arms, breast, and stomach, of his own: if he had had another man growing out of his other side, the comparison might then have been exact.

Hitherto I have named such diseases of a commonwealth, as are of the greatest, and most present danger. There be other not so great; which nevertheless are not unfit to be observed. At first, the difficulty of raising money, for the necessary uses of the commonwealth; especially in the approach of war. This difficulty ariseth from the opinion, that every subject hath a propriety in his lands and goods, exclusive of the sovereign's right to the use of the same. From whence it cometh to pass, that the sovereign power, which foreseeth the necessities and dangers of the commonwealth, finding the passage of money to the public treasury obstructed, by the tenacity of the people, whereas it ought to extend itself, to encounter, and prevent such dangers in their beginnings, contracteth itself as long as it can, and when it cannot longer, struggles with the people by stratagems of law, to obtain little sums, which not sufficing, he is fain at last violently to open the way for present

supply, or perish; and being put often to these extremities, at last reduceth the people to their due temper; or else the commonwealth must perish. Insomuch as we may compare this distemper very aptly to an ague; wherein, the fleshly parts being congealed, or by venomous matter obstructed, the veins which by their natural course empty themselves into the heart, are not, as they ought to be, supplied from the arteries, whereby there succeedeth at first a cold contraction, and trembling of the limbs; and afterward a hot, and strong endeavour of the heart, to force a passage for the blood; and before it can do that, contenteth itself with the small refreshments of such things as cool for a time, till, if nature be strong enough, it break at last the contumacy of the parts obstructed, and dissipateth the venom into sweat; or, if nature be too weak, the patient dieth.

Again, there is sometimes in a commonwealth, a disease, which resembleth the pleurisy; and that is, when the treasure of the commonwealth, flowing out of its due course, is gathered together in too much abundance, in one, or a few private men, by monopolies, or by farms of the public revenues; in the same manner as the blood in a pleurisy, getting into the membrane of the breast, breedeth there an inflammation, accompanied with a fever, and painful stitches.

Also, the popularity of a potent subject, unless the commonwealth have very good caution of his fidelity, is a dangerous disease; because the people, which should receive their motion from the authority of the sovereign, by the flattery and by the reputation of an ambitious man are drawn away from their obedience to the laws, to follow a man, of whose virtues, and designs they have no knowledge. And this is commonly of more danger in a popular government, than in a monarchy; because an army is of so great force, and multitude, as it may easily be made believe, they are the people. By this means it was, that Julius Caesar, who was set up by the people against the senate, having won to himself the affections of his army, made himself master both of senate and people. And this proceeding of popular, and ambitious men, is plain rebellion; and may be resembled to the effects of witchcraft.

Another infirmity of a commonwealth, is the immoderate greatness of a town, when it is able to furnish out of its own circuit, the number, and expense of a great army; as also the great number of corporations; which are as it were many lesser commonwealths in the bowels of a greater, like worms in the entrails of a natural man. To which may be added, the liberty of disputing against absolute power, by pretenders to political prudence; which though bred for the most part in the lees of the people, yet animated by false doctrines, are perpetually meddling with the fundamental laws, to the molestation of the commonwealth; like the little worms, which physicians call *ascarides*.

We may further add, the insatiable appetite of enlarging dominion; with the incurable *wounds* thereby many times received from the enemy; and the *wens*, of ununited conquests, which are many times a burthen, and with less danger lost, than kept; as also the *lethargy* of ease, and *consumption* of riot and vain expense.

Lastly, when in a war, foreign or intestine, the enemies get a final victory; so as, the forces of the commonwealth keeping the field no longer, there is no further protection of subjects in their loyalty; then is the commonwealth Dissolved, and every man at liberty to protect himself by such courses as his own discretion shall suggest unto him. For the sovereign is the public soul, giving life and motion to the commonwealth; which expiring, the members are governed by it no more, than the carcase of a man, by his departed, though immortal, soul. For though the right of a sovereign monarch cannot be extinguished by the act of another; yet the obligation of the members may. For he that wants protection, may seek it anywhere; and when he hath it, is obliged, without fraudulent pretence of having submitted himself out of fear, to protect his protection as long as he is able. But when the power of an assembly is once suppressed, the right of the same perisheth utterly; because the assembly itself is extinct; and consequently, there is no possibility for the sovereignty to re-enter.

BARUCH SPINOZA

~

INTRODUCTION

STEVEN B. SMITH

Baruch (Benedict) Spinoza (1632–1677) was born in Amsterdam, a descendent of Portuguese Marranos, that is, Jews who had fled the Inquisition for the relative safety of Holland. Virtually nothing is known of Spinoza's early life. He was educated at a traditional Jewish yeshiva where he studied Hebrew and Talmud. Spinoza was a polymath who spoke Spanish, Portuguese, and Dutch, and wrote his major philosophical works in Latin. At the age of twenty-four, he was put under the *herem*, or edict of excommunication expelling him from the synagogue. The reasons for the ban on Spinoza are not fully known, although they are almost certainly connected to the increasingly heterodox opinions on religion that he had come to espouse.

Spinoza left Amsterdam in 1660, settling first in Rijnsburg, a suburb of Leiden, and later moving to Voorsburg outside The Hague. He earned his living as a lens grinder and famously turned down an offer of a professorship at Heidelberg on the grounds that it would interfere with his independence of mind. Spinoza lived a life of uncommon detachment and isolation. He was befriended by members of some of the more liberal Protestant sects of the time, but Spinoza was not an apostate and refused to convert to Christianity. Although he lived alone and aloof, he was sought out by the leading scientists and philosophers of the day, including Leibniz and Henry Oldenburg, the secretary of the Royal Academy in London. Spinoza died of consumption in The Hague at the age of forty-four.

Spinoza was a writer who combined an unusual degree of boldness and secrecy. As an excommunicated Jew living on the margins of Dutch society, he knew at first hand the sting of religious persecution and the dangers of speaking one's mind openly. His signet ring bore the Latin inscription *caute*, or caution. He took pains to conceal his opinions even from those most intimate with him. With the exception of an early commentary on the philosophy of Descartes (1663), none of the other works published by Spinoza bore his name. His major work of political philosophy, the *Theologico-Political Treatise* (*TPT*) was published anonymously in 1670 and carried the imprimatur of a fictitious Hamburg publishing house. The work for which he is best known, the *Ethics*, was published posthumously for reasons of prudence and safety. A shorter work, *The Political Treatise*, was left unfinished at the time of his death.

At the same time that he expressed a prudent fear of the power of the multitude, Spinoza took an active stand on the major political struggles of his time. Like Machiavelli's *The Prince*, which Spinoza greatly admired, the *TPT* was a passionate and partisan tract written to advance the fortunes of a political cause. This cause was the republican faction in Dutch politics championed by Jan de Witt against the monarchist faction led by the House of Orange and supported by the Calvinist clergy. Like the Collegiants and Mennonites with whom he associated, Spinoza was a republican in politics and an advocate of toleration in theology. The best state, he declared, is one where "everyone's judgment is free and unshackled" and where "each may worship God as his conscience dictates." Two years after the publication of the *TPT*, De Witt and his brother were savagely murdered by an angry mob, an action that signaled Spinoza's withdrawal from political involvement. *Ultimi barbarorum* was his final judgment on the De Witt affair.

As the title of the *TPT* implies, it is a work divided into two distinguishable, yet hardly equal, parts. The first fifteen chapters are devoted to a lengthy and painstaking critique of biblical theology. Taking up the traditional themes of prophecy, law, and miracles, Spinoza submits each in turn to withering criticism. The Bible is on his account an imaginative, but ultimately primitive, record of the mentality of an ancient culture. Its teachings were intended to instill habits of obedience and justice in superstitious and fear-driven people. The aim of the first part of the *TPT* was to liberate human reason (or philosophy) from the authority of Scripture.

Having completed the critique of theology in the first fifteen chapters of the *TPT*, Spinoza devotes the remainder of the book to the critique of politics. The *TPT* is notable as the first work of modern political philosophy to endorse democracy as the best regime (*optima Republica*). Spinoza derives the legitimacy of democratic government at least in part from premises borrowed from his most important contemporary, Thomas Hobbes. Like Hobbes, Spinoza begins with a perfectly realistic, hard-boiled picture of human nature. There is in every living being an impulse (*conatus*) toward self-preservation. It follows that in the state of nature every being has the natural right to preserve itself by whatever means are at its disposal. Like Hobbes also, Spinoza invokes the metaphor of a social contract as the means by which individuals agree with one another to reduce the state of war to a condition of peace.

Spinoza departs from Hobbes, however, in two interesting and important ways. First, because the natural right of every being is identical to its power, Spinoza draws the conclusion that the majority in any community has by definition the preponderance of right on its side. Unlike the Hobbesian contract that displays a marked preference for monarchy, for Spinoza only a democratic sovereign can ensure against the dangers of arbitrary rule stemming from the investiture of power in the hands of one person. Second, unlike Hobbes who maintained that the avoidance of war is the greatest political good, Spinoza endorses democracy for its enhancement of human freedom. Democracy is desirable because it fosters the conditions for reason and the expression of our individual faculties. To a degree developed later by Rousseau and Kant, not peace and security but freedom becomes the true end of political life. Democracy is the form of government most consistent with the modern treatment of natural right and in agreement with human liberty.

The kind of democracy advocated by Spinoza is what today would be called a *liberal democracy*. A central feature of this democracy is its incorporation of the widest possible freedom of thought and opinion. The *TPT* provides several, not necessarily consistent, justifications for toleration. In the first place, toleration is said to follow from the doctrine of natural right strictly understood. If the right of nature means the liberty to do whatever our power permits, then by nature the sovereign's power must be limited to the control of external behavior. Because "no man's mind can possibly lie wholly at the disposition of another," the sovereign must leave the contents of the mind entirely to the individual's private discretion.

The *TPT* also argues historically and pragmatically that attempts to control the content of thought have invariably backfired. Rather than producing consensus and harmony, policies of intolerance and persecution have unwittingly bred conflict and opposition. The effort to criminalize opinions has led even honorable men to don the mantle of revolution. Note that unlike later defenders of toleration, Spinoza does not say that the effort to control thought violates some sacred or privileged sphere of individual privacy. Persecution is wrong, not because it is immoral, but because it is inherently self-defeating.

Most importantly, Spinoza defends freedom of speech because it fosters a certain kind of human being with certain distinctive traits of character and mind. Like John Stuart Mill in the midnineteenth century, Spinoza defends toleration, not as an end in itself but because it encourages the development of individual judgment and personal autonomy. The kind of human being envisaged by Spinoza is one who prizes individual liberty "before all things dear and precious." In the *Ethics*, Spinoza provides a particularly vivid portrait of the autonomous individual as one who strives to be independent of tradition and external sources of authority, who acts rather than being acted upon, and whose thoughts and actions stem not from envy and fear but from feelings of love and friendship. Above all, this person thinks of nothing so much as life itself and the means necessary to its enhancement. While Spinoza's idea of freedom has certain classical precedents in the works of Plato and the Stoics, it remains to a considerable degree a modern creation. To a greater extent than in the past, freedom is based on notions of individual autonomy, self-mastery, and courage.

Spinoza is one of the first thinkers to argue that the fruits of toleration are beneficial, not merely for the individual, but for society as a whole. The *TPT* draws an explicit connection between freedom of speech and the progress of the liberal arts. Like Descartes, Spinoza saw the tremendous potential locked inside the emergent sciences of nature, especially medicine, as a tool for increasing the ease and comfort of life. But Spinoza also recognized that intellectual and material progress does not take place in a vacuum. The progress of the arts and sciences is linked by him to issues of trade and commerce. Intellectual freedom is only possible in an environment that encourages commercial freedom. Spinoza's democracy is, then, necessarily a commercial republic where one finds a combination of economic, political, and religious liberty.

Spinoza's preference for the modern commercial republic is based on an emphatic rejection of the older classical republic theorized in the writings of Plato and Aristotle. For the ancients, the republic was a small, polis-like body characterized by a high degree of moral and religious homogeneity. Spinoza's defense of commercial and intellectual freedom indicates a preference for large, cosmopolitan, or "open societies" marked by a diversity of opinions and lifestyles. Furthermore, the classical republics displayed a severity and moral austerity demanding from its citizens a self-sacrificing devotion to the common good. Conversely, Spinoza's commercial republic is characterized less by virtue than by liberty in its many dimensions. Liberty is said to bring not only the progress of the arts and sciences but also the refinement and improvement of behavior. The

TPT concludes with a ringing praise of the commercial republic of Amsterdam, where the effects of liberty are on display for all to see.

Only in the following century would Spinoza's arguments in favor of the commercial republic bear fruit in the works of Montesquieu, Hume, and Adam Smith. Everywhere the commercial republic was proposed as a more humane alternative to the theologico-political regimes that had previously dominated European thought and practice. Such a regime would favor commercial over rural interests, the city over the country, and the rule of interest and utility over the devotion to lofty but intangible goals. The enjoyment of life rather than its mortification, a disposition to cultivate freedom rather than regret it, the celebration of the urbane pleasures of good food, companionship, the appreciation of beauty and music—such were the goals of Spinoza's *optima Republica*.

The number of studies of Spinoza's political thought available in English is sparse. Leo Strauss, *Spinoza's Critique of Religion*, trans. E. M. Sinclair (New York: Schocken, 1965), puts Spinoza's political theory within the context of his critique of theology; Yirmiyahu Yovel, *Spinoza and Other Heretics*, 2 vols. (Princeton, N.J.: Princeton University Press, 1991), examines Spinoza's excommunication against the background of the Marrano community and its influence on his manner of writing; Lewis Feuer, *Spinoza and the Rise of Liberalism* (Boston: Beacon, 1958), remains a useful guide to Spinoza's relation to radical currents within Dutch politics of his time; and Steven B. Smith, "Spinoza's Democratic Turn: Chapter 16 of the 'Theologico-Political Treatise,'" *Review of Metaphysics*, Vol. 48, No. 2 (1994), attempts to understand Spinoza's neglected role within the history of democratic theory.

Theologico-Political Treatise

CHAPTER XVI

Of the Foundations of a State; Of the Natural and Civil Rights of Individuals; and Of the Rights of the Sovereign Power

Hitherto our care has been to separate philosophy from theology, and to show the freedom of thought which such separation insures to both. It is now time to determine the limits to which such freedom of thought and discussion may extend itself in the ideal state. For the due consideration of this question we must examine the foundations of a state, first turning our attention to the natural rights of individuals, and afterwards to religion and the state as a whole.

By the right and ordinance of nature, I merely mean those natural laws wherewith we conceive every individual to be conditioned by nature, so as to live and act in a given way. For instance, fishes are naturally conditioned for swimming, and the greater for devouring the less; therefore fishes enjoy the water, and the greater devour the less by sovereign natural right. For it is certain that nature, taken in the abstract, has sovereign right to do anything she can; in other words, her right is co-extensive with her power. The power of nature is the power of God, which has sovereign

The Chief Works of Benedict de Spinoza, Vol. 1. Translated by R. H. M. Elwes, New York: Dover, 1951.

right over all things; and, inasmuch as the power of nature is simply the aggregate of the powers of all her individual components, it follows that every individual has sovereign right to do all that he can; in other words, the rights of an individual extend to the utmost limits of his power as it has been conditioned. Now it is the sovereign law and right of nature that each individual should endeavour to preserve itself as it is, without regard to anything but itself; therefore this sovereign law and right belongs to every individual, namely, to exist and act according to its natural conditions. We do not here acknowledge any difference between mankind and other individual natural entities, nor between men endowed with reason and those to whom reason is unknown; nor between fools, madmen, and sane men. Whatsoever an individual does by the laws of its nature it has a sovereign right to do, inasmuch as it acts as it was conditioned by nature, and cannot act otherwise. Wherefore among men, so long as they are considered as living under the sway of nature, he who does not yet know reason, or who has not yet acquired the habit of virtue, acts solely according to the laws of his desire with as sovereign a right as he who orders his life entirely by the laws of reason.

That is, as the wise man has sovereign right to do all that reason dictates, or to live according to the Laws of reason, as also the ignorant and foolish man has sovereign right to do all that desire dictates, or to live according to the laws of desire. This is identical with the teaching of Paul, who acknowledges that previous to the law—that is, as long as men are considered of as living under the sway of nature, there is no sin.

The natural right of the individual man is thus determined, not by sound reason, but by desire and power. All are not naturally conditioned so as to act according to the laws and rules of reason; nay, on the contrary, all men are born ignorant, and before they can learn the right way of life and acquire the habit of virtue, the greater part of their life, even if they have been well brought up, has passed away. Nevertheless, they are in the meanwhile bound to live and preserve themselves as far as they can by the unaided impulses of desire. Nature has given them no other guide, and has denied them the present power of living according to sound reason; so that they are no more bound to live by the dictates of an enlightened mind, than a cat is bound to live by the laws of the nature of a lion.

Whatsoever, therefore, an individual (considered as under the sway of nature) thinks useful for himself, whether led by sound reason or impelled by the passions, that he has a sovereign right to seek and to take for himself as he best can, whether by force, cunning, entreaty, or any other means; consequently he may regard as an enemy anyone who hinders the accomplishment of his purpose.

It follows from what we have said that the right and ordinance of nature, under which all men are born, and under which they mostly live, only prohibits such things as no one desires, and no one can attain: it does not forbid strife, nor hatred, nor anger, nor deceit, nor, indeed, any of the means suggested by desire.

This we need not wonder at, for nature is not bounded by the laws of human reason, which aims only at man's true benefit and preservation; her limits are infinitely wider, and have reference to the eternal order of nature, wherein man is but a speck; it is by the necessity of this alone that all individuals are conditioned for living and acting in a particular way. If anything, therefore, in nature seems to us ridiculous, absurd, or evil, it is because we only know in part, and are almost entirely ignorant of the order and interdependence of nature as a whole, and also because we want everything to be arranged according to the dictates of our human reason; in reality that which reason considers evil, is not evil in respect to the order and laws of nature as a whole, but only in respect to the laws of our reason.

Nevertheless, no one can doubt that it is much better for us to live according to the laws and assured dictates of reason, for, as we said, they have men's true good for their object. Moreover, everyone wishes to live as far as possible securely beyond the reach of fear, and this would be quite impossible so long as everyone did everything he liked, and reason's claim was lowered to a par with those of hatred and anger; there is no one who is not ill at ease in the midst of enmity, hatred, anger, and deceit, and who does not seek to avoid them as much as he can. When we reflect that men without mutual help, or the aid of reason, must needs live most miserably, as we clearly proved in Chap. V, we shall plainly see that men must necessarily come to an agreement to live together as securely and well as possible if they are to enjoy as a whole the rights which naturally belong to them as individuals, and their life should be no more conditioned by the force and desire of individuals, but by the power and will of the whole body. This end they will be unable to attain if desire be their only guide (for by the laws of desire each man is drawn in a different direction); they must, therefore, most firmly decree and establish that they will be guided in everything by reason (which nobody will dare openly to repudiate lest he should be taken for a madman), and will restrain any desire which is injurious to a man's fellows, that they will do to all as they would be done by, and that they will defend their neighbour's rights as their own.

How such a compact as this should be entered into, how ratified and established, we will now inquire.

Now it is a universal law of human nature that no one ever neglects anything which he judges to be good, except with the hope of gaining a greater good, or from the fear of a greater evil; nor does anyone endure an evil except for the sake of avoiding a greater evil, or gaining a greater good. That is, everyone will, of two goods, choose that which he thinks the greatest; and, of two evils, that which he thinks the least. I say advisedly that which he thinks the greatest or the least, for it does not necessarily follow that he judges right. This law is so deeply implanted in the human mind that it ought to be counted among eternal truths and axioms.

As a necessary consequence of the principle just enunciated, no one can honestly promise to forego the right which he has over all things,

and in general no one will abide by his promises, unless under the fear of a greater evil, or the hope of a greater good. An example will make the matter clearer. Suppose that a robber forces me to promise that I will give him my goods at his will and pleasure. It is plain (inasmuch as my natural right is, as I have shown, co-extensive with my power) that if I can free myself from this robber by stratagem, by assenting to his demands, I have the natural right to do so, and to pretend to accept his conditions. Or again, suppose I have genuinely promised someone that for the space of twenty days I will not taste food or any nourishment; and suppose I afterwards find that my promise was foolish, and cannot be kept without very great injury to myself; as I am bound by natural law and right to choose the least of two evils, I have complete right to break my compact, and act as if my promise had never been uttered. I say that I should have perfect natural right to do so, whether I was actuated by true and evident reason, or whether I was actuated by mere opinion in thinking I had promised rashly; whether my reasons were true or false, I should be in fear of a greater evil, which, by the ordinance of nature, I should strive to avoid by every means in my power.

We may, therefore, conclude that a compact is only made valid by its utility, without which it becomes null and void. It is, therefore, foolish to ask a man to keep his faith with us for ever, unless we also endeavour that the violation of the compact we enter into shall involve for the violator more harm than good. This consideration should have very great weight in forming a state. However, if all men could be easily led by reason alone, and could recognize what is best and most useful for a state, there would be no one who would not forswear deceit, for every one would keep most religiously to their compact in their desire for the chief good, namely, the preservation of the state, and would cherish good faith above all things as the shield and buckler of the commonwealth. However, it is far from being the case that all men can always be easily led by reason alone; everyone is drawn away by his pleasure, While avarice, ambition, envy, hatred, and the like so engross the mind that reason has no place therein. Hence, though men make promises with all the appearances of good faith, and agree that they will keep to their engagement, no one can absolutely rely on another man's promise unless there is something behind it. Everyone has by nature a right to act deceitfully, and to break his compacts, unless he be restrained by the hope of some greater good, or the fear of some greater evil.

However, as we have shown that the natural right of the individual is only limited by his power, it is clear that by transferring, either willingly or under compulsion, this power into the hands of another, he in so doing necessarily cedes also a part of his right; and further, that the sovereign right over all men belongs to him who has sovereign power, wherewith he can compel men by force, or restrain them by threats of the universally feared punishment of death; such sovereign right he will retain only so long as he can maintain his power of enforcing his will; otherwise he will totter on his throne, and no one who is stronger than he will be bound unwillingly to obey him.

In this manner a society can be formed without any violation of natural right, and the covenant can always be strictly kept—that is, if each individual hands over the whole of his power to the body politic, the latter will then possess sovereign natural right over all things; that is, it will have sole and unquestioned dominion, and everyone will be bound to obey, under pain of the severest punishment. A body politic of this kind is called a Democracy, which may be defined as a society which wields all its power as a whole. The sovereign power is not restrained by any laws, but everyone is bound to obey it in all things; such is the state of things implied when men either tacitly or expressly handed over to it all their power of self-defence, or in other words, all their right. For if they had wished to retain any right for themselves, they ought to have taken precautions for its defence and preservation; as they have not done so, and indeed could not have done so without dividing and consequently ruining the state,

they placed themselves absolutely at the mercy of the sovereign power; and, therefore, having acted (as we have shown) as reason and necessity demanded, they are obliged to fulfil the commands of the sovereign power, however absurd these may be, else they will be public enemies, and will act against reason, which urges the preservation of the state as a primary duty. For reason bids us choose the least of two evils.

Furthermore, this danger of submitting absolutely to the dominion and will of another, is one which may be incurred with a light heart: for we have shown that sovereigns only possess this right of imposing their will, so long as they have the full power to enforce it: if such power be lost their right to command is lost also, or lapses to those who have assumed it and can keep it. Thus it is very rare for sovereigns to impose thoroughly irrational commands, for they are bound to consult their own interests, and retain their power by consulting the public good and acting according to the dictates of reason, as Seneca says, "violenta imperia nemo continuit diu." No one can long retain a tyrant's sway.

In a democracy, irrational commands are still less to be feared: for it is almost impossible that the majority of a people, especially if it be a large one, should agree in an irrational design: and, moreover, the basis and aim of a democracy is to avoid the desires as irrational, and to bring men as far as possible under the control of reason, so that they may live in peace and harmony: if this basis be removed the whole fabric falls to ruin.

Such being the ends in view for the sovereign power, the duty of subjects is, as I have said, to obey its commands, and to recognize no right save that which it sanctions.

It will, perhaps, be thought that we are turning subjects into slaves: for slaves obey commands and free men live as they like; but this idea is based on a misconception, for the true slave is he who is led away by his pleasures and can neither see what is good for him nor act accordingly: he alone is free who lives with free consent under the entire guidance of reason.

Action in obedience to orders does take away freedom in a certain sense, but it does not, therefore, make a man a slave, all depends on the object of the action. If the object of the action be the good of the state, and not the good of the agent, the latter is a slave and does himself no good. But in a state or kingdom where the weal of the whole people, and not that of the ruler, is the supreme law, obedience to the sovereign power does not make a man a slave, of no use to himself, but a subject. Therefore, that state is the freest whose laws are founded on sound reason, so that every member of it may, if he will, be free; that is, live with full consent under the entire guidance of reason.

Children, though they are bound to obey all the commands of their parents, are yet not slaves: for the commands of parents look generally to the children's benefit.

We must, therefore, acknowledge a great difference between a slave, a son, and a subject; their positions may be thus defined. A slave is one who is bound to obey his master's orders, though they are given solely in the master's interest: a son is one who obeys his father's orders, given in his own interest; a subject obeys the orders of the sovereign power, given for the common interest, wherein he is included.

I think I have now shown sufficiently clearly the basis of a democracy: I have especially desired to do so, for I believe it to be of all forms of government the most natural, and the most consonant with individual liberty. In it no one transfers his natural right so absolutely that he has no further voice in affairs, he only hands it over to the majority of a society, whereof he is a unit. Thus all men remain, as they were in the state of nature, equals.

This is the only form of government which I have treated of at length, for it is the one most akin to my purpose of showing the benefits of freedom in a state.

I may pass over the fundamental principles of other forms of government, for we may gather from what has been said whence their right arises without going into its origin. The possessor of sovereign power, whether he be one, or many, or the whole body politic, has the sovereign right of imposing any commands he pleases: and he who has either voluntarily, or under compulsion, transferred the right to defend him to another, has, in so doing, renounced his natural right and is therefore bound to obey, in all things, the commands of the sovereign power; and will be bound so to do so long as the king, or nobles, or the people preserve the sovereign power which formed the basis of the original transfer. I need add no more.

The bases and rights of dominion being thus displayed, we shall readily be able to define private civil right, wrong, justice, and injustice, with their relations to the state; and also to determine what constitutes an ally, or an enemy, or the crime of treason.

By private civil right we can only mean the liberty every man possesses to preserve his existence, a liberty limited by the edicts of the sovereign power, and preserved only by its authority: for when a man has transferred to another his right of living as he likes, which was only limited by his power, that is, has transferred his liberty and power of self-defence, he is bound to live as that other dictates, and to trust to him entirely for his defence. Wrong takes place when a citizen, or subject, is forced by another to undergo some loss or pain in contradiction to the authority of the law, or the edict of the sovereign power.

Wrong is conceivable only in an organized community: nor can it ever accrue to subjects from any act of the sovereign, who has the right to do what he likes. It can only arise, therefore, between private persons, who are bound by law and right not to injure one another. Justice consists in the habitual rendering to every man his lawful due: injustice consists in depriving a man, under the pretence of legality, of what the laws, rightly interpreted, would allow him. These last are also called equity and iniquity, because those who administer the laws are bound to show no respect of persons, but to account all men equal, and to defend every man's right equally, neither envying the rich nor despising the poor.

The men of two states become allies, when for the sake of avoiding war, or for some other advantage, they covenant to do each other no hurt, but on the contrary, to assist each other if necessity arises, each retaining his independence. Such a covenant is valid so long as its basis of danger or advantage is in force: no one enters into an engagement, or is bound to stand by his compacts unless there be a hope of some accruing good, or the fear of some evil: if this basis be removed the compact thereby becomes void: this has been abundantly shown by experience. For although different states make treaties not to harm one another, they always take every possible precaution against such treaties being broken by the stronger party, and do not rely on the compact, unless there is a sufficiently obvious object and advantage to both parties in observing it. Otherwise they would fear a breach of faith, nor would there be any wrong done thereby: for who in his proper senses, and aware of the right of the sovereign power, would trust in the promises of one who has the will and the power to do what he likes, and who aims solely at the safety and advantage of his dominion? Moreover, if we consult loyalty and religion, we shall see that no one in possession of power ought to abide by his promises to the injury of his dominion; for he cannot keep such promises without breaking the engagement he made with his subjects, by which both he and they are most solemnly bound.

An enemy is one who lives apart from the state, and does not recognize its authority either as a subject or as an ally. It is not hatred which makes a man an enemy, but the rights of the state. The rights of the state are the same in regard to him who does not recognize by any compact the state authority, as they are against him who has done the state an injury: it has the right to force him as best it can, either to submit, or to contract an alliance.

Lastly, treason can only be committed by subjects, who by compact, either tacit or expressed, have transferred all their rights to the state: a subject is said to have committed this crime when he has attempted, for whatever reason, to seize the sovereign power, or to place it in different hands. I say, *has attempted*, for if punishment were not to overtake him till he had succeeded, it would often come too late, the sovereign rights would have been acquired or transferred already.

I also say, *has attempted, for whatever reason, to seize the sovereign power*, and I recognize no difference whether such an attempt should be followed by public loss or public gain. Whatever be his reason for acting, the crime is treason, and he is rightly condemned: in war, everyone would admit the justice of his sentence. If a man does not keep to his post, but approaches the enemy without the knowledge of his commander, whatever may be his motive, so long as he acts on his own motion, even if he advances with the design of defeating the enemy, he is rightly put to death, because he has violated his oath, and infringed the rights of his commander. That all citizens are equally bound by these rights in time of peace, is not so generally recognized, but the reasons for obedience are in both cases, identical. The state must be preserved and directed by the sole authority of the sovereign, and such authority and right have been accorded by universal consent to him alone: if, therefore, anyone else attempts, without his consent, to execute any public enterprise, even though the state might (as we said) reap benefit therefrom, such person has none the less infringed the sovereign's right, and would be rightly punished for treason.

In order that every scruple may be removed, we may now answer the inquiry, whether our former assertion that everyone who has not the practice of reason, may, in the state of nature, live by sovereign natural right, according to the laws of his desires, is not in direct opposition to the law and right of God as revealed. For as all men absolutely (whether they be less endowed with reason or more) are equally bound by the Divine command to love their neighbour as themselves, it may be said that they cannot, without wrong, do injury to anyone, or live according to their desires.

This objection, so far as the state of nature is concerned, can be easily answered, for the state of nature is, both in nature and in time, prior to religion. No one knows by nature that he owes any obedience to God, nor can he attain thereto by any exercise of his reason, but solely by revelation confirmed by signs. Therefore, previous to revelation, no one is bound by a Divine law and right of which he is necessarily in ignorance. The state of nature must by no means be confounded with a state of religion, but must be conceived as without either religion or law, and consequently without sin or wrong: this is how we have described it, and we are confirmed by the authority of Paul. It is not only in respect of ignorance that we conceive the state of nature as prior to, and lacking the Divine revealed law and right; but in respect of freedom also, wherewith all men are born endowed.

If men were naturally bound by the Divine law and right, or if the Divine law and right were a natural necessity, there would have been no need for God to make a covenant with mankind, and to bind them thereto with an oath and agreement.

We must, then, fully grant that the Divine law and right originated at the time when men by express covenant agreed to obey God in all things, and ceded, as it were, their natural freedom, transferring their rights to God in the manner described in speaking of the formation of a state.

However, I will treat of these matters more at length presently.

It may be insisted that sovereigns are as much bound by the Divine law as subjects: whereas we have asserted that they retain their natural rights, and may do whatever they like.

In order to clear up the whole difficulty, which arises rather concerning the natural right than the natural state, I maintain that everyone is bound, in the state of nature, to live according to Divine law, in the same way as he is bound to fire according to the dictates of sound reason; namely, inasmuch as it is to his advantage, and necessary for his salvation; but, if he will not so live, he may do otherwise at his own risk. He is thus bound to live according to his own laws, not according to anyone else's, and to recognize no man as a judge, or as a superior in religion. Such, in my opinion, is the position of a

sovereign, for he may take advice from his fellow-men, but he is not bound to recognize any as a judge, nor anyone besides himself as an arbitrator on any question of right, unless it be a prophet sent expressly by God and attesting his mission by indisputable signs. Even then he does not recognize a man, but God Himself as His judge.

If a sovereign refuses to obey God as revealed in His law, he does so at his own risk and loss, but without violating any civil or natural right. For the civil right is dependent on his own decree; and natural right is dependent on the laws of nature, which latter are not adapted to religion, whose sole aim is the good of humanity, but to the order of nature—that is, to God's eternal decree unknown to us.

This truth seems to be adumbrated in a somewhat obscurer form by those who maintain that men can sin against God's revelation, but not against the eternal decree by which He has ordained all things.

We may be asked, what should we do if the sovereign commands anything contrary to religion, and the obedience which we have expressly vowed to God? should we obey the Divine law or the human law? I shall treat of this question at length hereafter, and will therefore merely say now, that God should be obeyed before all else, when we have a certain and indisputable revelation of His will: but men are very prone to error on religious subjects, and, according to the diversity of their dispositions, are wont with considerable stir to put forward their own inventions, as experience more than sufficiently attests, so that if no one were bound to obey the state in matters which, in his own opinion concern religion, the rights of the state would be dependent on every man's judgment and passions. No one would consider himself bound to obey laws framed against his faith or superstition; and on this pretext he might assume unbounded license. In this way, the rights of the civil authorities would be utterly set at nought, so that we must conclude that the sovereign power, which alone is bound both by Divine and natural right to preserve and guard the laws of the state, should have supreme authority for making any laws about religion which it thinks fit; all are bound to obey its behests on the subject in accordance with their promise which God bids them to keep.

However, if the sovereign power be heathen, we should either enter into no engagements therewith, and yield up our lives sooner than transfer to it any of our rights; or, if the engagement be made, and our rights transferred, we should (inasmuch as we should have ourselves transferred the right of defending ourselves and our religion) be bound to obey them, and to keep our word: we might even rightly be bound so to do, except in those cases where God, by indisputable revelation, has promised His special aid against tyranny, or given us special exemption from obedience. Thus we see that, of all the Jews in Babylon, there were only three youths who were certain of the help of God, and, therefore, refused to obey Nebuchadnezzar. All the rest, with the sole exception of Daniel, who was beloved by the king, were doubtless compelled by right to obey, perhaps thinking that they had been delivered up by God into the hands of the king, and that the king had obtained and preserved his dominion by God's design. On the other hand, Eleazar, before his country had utterly fallen, wished to give a proof of his constancy to his compatriots, in order that they might follow in his footsteps, and go to any lengths, rather than allow their right and power to be transferred to the Greeks, or brave any torture rather than swear allegiance to the heathen. Instances are occurring every day in confirmation of what I here advance. The rulers of Christian kingdoms do not hesitate, with a view to strengthening their dominion, to make treaties with Turks and heathen, and to give orders to their subjects who settle among such peoples not to assume more freedom, either in things secular or religious, than is set down in the treaty, or allowed by the foreign government. We may see this exemplified in the Dutch treaty with the Japanese, which I have already mentioned.

CHAPTER XX

That in a Free State Every Man May Think What He Likes, and Say What He Thinks.

If men's minds were as easily controlled as their tongues, every king would sit safely on his throne, and government by compulsion would cease; for every subject would shape his life according to the intentions of his rulers, and would esteem a thing true or false, good or evil, just or unjust, in obedience to their dictates. However, we have shown already (Chapter XVII) that no man's mind can possibly lie wholly at the disposition of another, for no one can willingly transfer his natural right of free reason and judgment, or be compelled so to do. For this reason government which attempts to control minds is accounted tyrannical, and it is considered an abuse of sovereignty and a usurpation of the rights of subjects, to seek to prescribe what shall be accepted as true, or rejected as false, or what opinions should actuate men in their worship of God. All these questions fall within a man's natural right, which he cannot abdicate even with his own consent.

I admit that the judgment can be biased in many ways, and to an almost incredible degree, so that while exempt from direct external control it may be so dependent on another man's words, that it may fitly be said to be ruled by him; but although this influence is carried to great lengths, it has never gone so far as to invalidate the statement, that every man's understanding is his own, and that brains are as diverse as palates.

Moses, not by fraud, but by Divine virtue, gained such a hold over the popular judgment that he was accounted superhuman, and believed to speak and act through the inspiration of the Deity; nevertheless, even he could not escape murmurs and evil interpretations. How much less then can other monarchs avoid them! Yet such unlimited power, if it exists at all, must belong to a monarch, and least of all to a democracy, where the whole or a great part of the people wield authority collectively. This is a fact which I think everyone can explain for himself.

However unlimited, therefore, the power of a sovereign may be, however implicitly it is trusted as the exponent of law and religion, it can never prevent men from forming judgments according to their intellect, or being influenced by any given emotion. It is true that it has the right to treat as enemies all men whose opinions do not, on all subjects, entirely coincide with its own; but we are not discussing its strict rights, but its proper course of action. I grant that it has the right to rule in the most violent manner, and to put citizens to death for very trivial causes, but no one supposes it can do this with the approval of sound judgment. Nay, inasmuch as such things cannot be done without extreme peril to itself, we may even deny that it has the absolute power to do them, or, consequently, the absolute right; for the rights of the sovereign are limited by his power.

Since, therefore, no one can abdicate his freedom of judgment and feeling; since every man is by indefeasible natural right the master of his own thoughts, it follows that men thinking in diverse and contradictory fashions, cannot, without disastrous results, be compelled to speak only according to the dictates of the supreme power. Not even the most experienced, to say nothing of the multitude, know how to keep silence. Men's common failing is to confide their plans to others, though there be need for secrecy, so that a government would be most harsh which deprived the individual of his freedom of saying and teaching what he thought; and would be moderate if such freedom were granted. Still we cannot deny that authority may be as much injured by words as by actions; hence, although the freedom we are discussing cannot be entirely denied to subjects, its unlimited concession would be most baneful; we must, therefore, now inquire, how far such freedom can and ought to be conceded without danger to the peace of the state, or the power of the rulers; and this, as I said at the beginning of Chapter XVI, is my principal object.

It follows, plainly, from the explanation given above, of the foundations of a state, that the ultimate aim of government is not to rule, or restrain, by fear, nor to exact obedience, but contrariwise, to free every man from fear, that he may live in all possible security; in other words, to strengthen his natural right to exist and work without injury to himself or others.

No, the object of government is not to change men from rational beings into beasts or puppets, but to enable them to develop their minds and bodies in security, and to employ their reason unshackled; neither showing hatred, anger, or deceit, nor watched with the eyes of jealousy and injustice. In fact, the true aim of government is liberty.

Now we have seen that in forming a state the power of making laws must either be vested in the body of the citizens, or in a portion of them, or in one man. For, although men's free judgments are very diverse, each one thinking that he alone knows everything, and although complete unanimity of feeling and speech is out of the question, it is impossible to preserve peace, unless individuals abdicate their right of acting entirely on their own judgment. Therefore, the individual justly cedes the right of free action, though not of free reason and judgment; no one can act against the authorities without danger to the state, though his feelings and judgment may be at varience therewith; he may even speak against them, provided that he does so from rational conviction, not from fraud, anger, or hatred, and provided that he does not attempt to introduce any change on his private authority.

For instance, supposing a man shows that a law is repugnant to sound reason, and should therefore be repealed; if he submits his opinion to the judgment of the authorities (who, alone, have the right of making and repealing laws), and meanwhile acts in nowise contrary to that law, he has deserved well of the state, and has behaved as a good citizen should; but if he accuses the authorities of injustice, and stirs up the people against them, or if he seditiously strives to abrogate the law without their consent, he is a mere agitator and rebel.

Thus we see how an individual may declare and teach what he believes, without injury to the authority of his rulers, or to the public peace; namely, by leaving in their hands the entire power of legislation as it affects action, and by doing nothing against their laws, though he be compelled often to act in contradiction to what he believes, and openly feels, to be best.

Such a course can be taken without detriment to justice and dutifulness, nay, it is the one which a just and dutiful man would adopt. We have shown that justice is dependent on the laws of the authorities, so that no one who contravenes their accepted decrees can be just, while the highest regard for duty, as we have pointed out in the preceding chapter, is exercised in maintaining public peace and tranquillity; these could not be preserved if every man were to live as he pleased; therefore it is no less than undutiful for a man to act contrary to his country's laws, for if the practice became universal the ruin of states would necessarily follow.

Hence, so long as a man acts in obedience to the laws of his rulers, he in nowise contravenes his reason, for in obedience to reason he transferred the right of controlling his actions from his own hands to theirs. This doctrine we can confirm from actual custom, for in a conference of great and small powers, schemes are seldom carried unanimously, yet all unite in carrying out what is decided on, whether they voted for or against. But I return to my proposition.

From the fundamental notions of a state, we have discovered how a man may exercise free judgment without detriment to the supreme power: from the same premises we can no less easily determine what opinions would be seditious. Evidently those which by their very nature nullify the compact by which the right of free action was ceded. For instance, a man who holds that the supreme power has no rights over him, or that promises ought not to be kept, or that everyone should live as he pleases, or other doctrines of this nature in direct opposition to the above-mentioned

contract, is seditious, not so much from his actual opinions and judgment, as from the deeds which they involve; for he who maintains such theories abrogates the contract which tacitly, or openly, he made with his rulers. Other opinions which do not involve acts violating the contract, such as revenge, anger, and the like, are not seditious, unless it be in some corrupt state, where superstitious and ambitious persons, unable to endure men of learning, are so popular with the multitude that their word is more valued than the law.

However, I do not deny that there are some doctrines which, while they are apparently only concerned with abstract truths and falsehoods, are yet propounded and published with unworthy motives. This question we have discussed in Chapter XV, and shown that reason should nevertheless remain unshackled. If we hold to the principle that a man's loyalty to the state should be judged, like his loyalty to God, from his actions only—namely, from his charity towards his neighbours; we cannot doubt that the best government will allow freedom of philosophical speculation no less than of religious belief. I confess that from such freedom inconveniences may sometimes arise, but what question was ever settled so wisely that no abuses could possibly spring therefrom? He who seeks to regulate everything by law, is more likely to arouse vices than to reform them. It is best to grant what cannot be abolished, even though it be in itself harmful. How many evils spring from luxury, envy, avarice, drunkenness, and the like, yet these are tolerated—vices as they are—because they cannot be prevented by legal enactments. How much more then should free thought be granted, seeing that it is in itself a virtue and that it cannot be crushed! Besides, the evil results can easily be checked, as I will show, by the secular authorities, not to mention that such freedom is absolutely necessary for progress in science and the liberal arts: for no man follows such pursuits to advantage unless his judgment be entirely free and unhampered.

But let it be granted that freedom may be crushed, and men be so bound down, that they do not dare to utter a whisper, save at the bidding of their rulers; nevertheless this can never be carried to the pitch of making them think according to authority, so that the necessary consequences would be that men would daily be thinking one thing and saying another, to the corruption of good faith, that mainstay of government, and to the fostering of hateful flattery and perfidy, whence spring stratagems, and the corruption of every good art.

It is far from possible to impose uniformity of speech, for the more rulers strive to curtail freedom of speech, the more obstinately are they resisted; not indeed by the avaricious, the flatterers, and other numskulls, who think supreme salvation consists in filling their stomachs and gloating over their moneybags, but by those whom good education, sound morality, and virtue have rendered more free. Men, as generally constituted, are most prone to resent the branding as criminal of opinions which they believe to be true, and the prescription as wicked of that which inspires them with piety towards God and man; hence they are ready to forswear the laws and conspire against the authorities, thinking it not shameful but honourable to stir up seditions and perpetuate any sort of crime with this end in view. Such being the constitution of human nature, we see that laws directed against opinions affect the generous-minded rather than the wicked, and are adapted less for coercing criminals than for irritating the upright; so that they cannot be maintained without great peril to the state.

Moreover, such laws are almost always useless, for those who hold that the opinions proscribed are sound, cannot possibly obey the law; whereas those who already reject them as false, accept the law as a kind of privilege, and make such boast of it, that authority is powerless to repeal it, even if such a course be subsequently desired.

To these considerations may be added what we said in Chapter XVIII in treating of the history of the Hebrews. And, lastly, how many schisms have arisen in the Church from the attempt of the authorities to decide by law the intricacies of theological controversy! If men were not allured by the hope of getting the law and the authorities on their side, of triumphing over their adversaries in the sight of an applauding multitude, and of acquiring honourable distinctions, they would not strive so maliciously, nor would such fury sway their minds. This is taught not only by reason but by daily examples, for laws of this kind prescribing what every man shall believe and forbidding anyone to speak or write to the contrary, have often been passed, as sops or concessions to the anger of those who cannot tolerate men of enlightenment, and who, by such harsh and crooked enactments, can easily turn the devotion of the masses into fury and direct it against whom they will.

How much better would it be to restrain popular anger and fury, instead of passing useless laws, which can only be broken by those who love virtue and the liberal arts, thus paring down the state till it is too small to harbour men of talent. What greater misfortune for a state can be conceived than that honourable men should be sent like criminals into exile, because they hold diverse opinions which they cannot disguise? What, I say, can be more hurtful than that men who have committed no crime or wickedness should, simply because they are enlightened, be treated as enemies and put to death, and that the scaffold, the terror of evil-doers, should become the arena where the highest examples of tolerance and virtue are displayed to the people with all the marks of ignominy that authority can devise?

He that knows himself to be upright does not fear the death of a criminal, and shrinks from no punishment; his mind is not wrung with remorse for any disgraceful deed: he holds that death in a good cause is no punishment, but an honour, and that death for freedom is glory.

What purpose then is served by the death of such men, what example is proclaimed? The cause for which they die is unknown to the idle and the foolish, hateful to the turbulent, loved by the upright. The only lesson we can draw from such scenes is to flatter the persecutor, or else to imitate the victim.

If formal assent is not to be esteemed above conviction, and if governments are to retain a firm hold of authority and not be compelled to yield to agitators, it is imperative that freedom of judgment should be granted, so that men may live together in harmony, however diverse, or even openly contradictory their opinions may be. We cannot doubt that such is the best system of government and open to the fewest objections, since it is the one most in harmony with human nature. In a democracy (the most natural form of government, as we have shown in Chapter XVI) everyone submits to the control of authority over his actions, but not over his judgment and reason; that is, seeing that all cannot think alike, the voice of the majority has the force of law, subject to repeal if circumstances bring about a change of opinion. In proportion as the power of free judgment is withheld we depart from the natural condition of mankind, and consequently the government becomes more tyrannical.

In order to prove that from such freedom no inconvenience arises, which cannot easily be checked by the exercise of the sovereign power, and that men's actions can easily be kept in bounds, though their opinions be at open varience, it will be well to cite an example. Such an one is not very far to seek. The city of Amsterdam reaps the fruit of this freedom in its own great prosperity and in the admiration of all other people. For in this most flourishing state, and most splendid city, men of every nation and religion live together in the greatest harmony, and ask no questions before trusting their goods to a fellow-citizen, save whether he be rich or poor, and whether he generally acts honestly, or the reverse. His religion and sect is considered of no importance: for it has no effect before the judges in gaining or losing a cause, and there is no sect so despised that its followers, provided that they harm no one, pay every man his due, and live uprightly, are deprived of the protection of the magisterial authority.

On the other hand, when the religious controversy between Remonstrants and Counter-Remonstrants began to be taken up by politicians and the States, it grew into a schism, and abundantly showed that laws dealing with religion and seeking to settle its controversies are much more calculated to irritate than to reform, and that they give rise to extreme licence: further, it was seen that schisms do not originate in a love of truth, which is a source of courtesy and gentleness, but rather in an inordinate desire for supremacy. From all these considerations it is clearer than the sun at noonday, that the true schismatics are those who condemn other men's writings, and seditiously stir up the quarrelsome masses against their authors, rather than those authors themselves, who generally write only for the learned, and appeal solely to reason. In fact, the real disturbers of the peace are those who, in a free state, seek to curtail the liberty of judgment which they are unable to tyrannize over.

I have thus shown:—I. That it is impossible to deprive men of the liberty of saying what they think. II. That such liberty can be conceded to every man without injury to the rights and authority of the sovereign power, and that every man may retain it without injury to such rights, provided that he does not presume upon it to the extent of introducing any new rights into the state, or acting in any way contrary to the existing laws. III. That every man may enjoy this liberty without detriment to the public peace, and that no inconveniences arise therefrom which cannot easily be checked. IV. That every man may enjoy it without injury to his allegiance. V. That laws dealing with speculative problems are entirely useless. VI. Lastly, that not only may such liberty be granted without prejudice to the public peace, to loyalty, and to the rights of rulers, but that it is even necessary for their preservation. For when people try to take it away, and bring to trial not only the acts which alone are capable of offending, but also the opinions of mankind, they only succeed in surrounding their victims with an appearance of martyrdom, and raise feelings of pity and revenge rather than of terror. Uprightness and good faith are thus corrupted, flatterers and traitors are encouraged, and sectarians triumph, inasmuch as concessions have been made to their animosity, and they have gained the state sanction for the doctrines of which they are the interpreters. Hence they arrogate to themselves the state authority and rights, and do not scruple to assert that they have been directly chosen by God, and that their laws are Divine, whereas the laws of the state are human, and should therefore yield obedience to the laws of God—in other words, to their own laws. Everyone must see that this is not a state of affairs conducive to public welfare. Wherefore, as we have shown in Chapter XVIII, the safest way for a state is to lay down the rule that religion is comprised solely in the exercise of charity and justice, and that the rights of rulers in sacred, no less than in secular matters, should merely have to do with actions, but that every man should think what he likes and say what he thinks.

I have thus fulfilled the task I set myself in this treatise. It remains only to call attention to the fact that I have written nothing which I do not most willingly submit to the examination and approval of my country's rulers; and that I am willing to retract anything which they shall decide to be repugnant to the laws, or prejudicial to the public good. I know that I am a man, and as a man liable to error, but against error I have taken scrupulous care, and have striven to keep in entire accordance with the laws of my country, with loyalty, and with morality.

JOHN LOCKE

~

INTRODUCTION

A. JOHN SIMMONS

John Locke (1632–1704) was born in Somerset, England, the son of an attorney and small landowner. Locke's family had Puritan leanings, and his father served during Locke's youth in one of the parliamentary armies fighting the forces of Charles I during the civil war. Thanks to his father's connections, Locke received an excellent education of the sort generally reserved for the more privileged, concluding at Christ Church, Oxford, with which Locke remained associated in various capacities until 1684. Locke's (unpublished) writings from his time at Christ Church (in the early 1660s) were surprisingly illiberal, arguing against many of the positions we would today identify as paradigmatically Lockean (such as religious toleration and popular consent as the basis of political authority). Locke's turn toward more liberal views seems to have been a product of his close association with Lord Ashley, later the first Earl of Shaftesbury, for whom Locke served in various positions beginning in 1667. Shaftesbury was a leading Whig politician of the period, and through him Locke gained both intimate knowledge of English political life and an appreciation of the Whig principles that are given philosophical expression and defense in Locke's mature writings.

It was also through Shaftesbury that Locke became involved in the revolutionary political plotting of the early 1680s, in which the opposition Whigs attempted to prevent the Catholic Duke of York (later James II) from succeeding his brother Charles II on the English throne. The full extent of Locke's involvement in the radical Whig plans for assassination and insurrection is not known, but the clear danger of arrest forced Locke to follow Shaftesbury into exile in Holland in 1683. Locke did not return to England until 1689, after the Glorious Revolution and Settlement had removed James and initiated the reign of William and Mary. It was 1689 as well that saw Locke's first publications (at the age of fifty-seven), which included all of Locke's best-known philosophical works—*An Essay Concerning Human Understanding*, *Two Treatises of Government*, and *A Letter Concerning Toleration* (though all of these were largely completed considerably earlier and the latter two were published anonymously). Locke spent his remaining years actively, enjoying his new role as a revered intellectual, holding a number of minor political offices, and writing extensively on religion, education, and finance. Locke lived during this period, and eventually died in 1704, at the home of his longtime friend Lady Masham, daughter of the philosopher Ralph Cudworth. Locke's influence on both political philosophy and political practice was considerable; his work inspired later socialists (like the young Marx), liberals, and conservatives alike, and many revolutionaries of the eighteenth century knew and were guided by Locke's work.

Locke is generally characterized as one of the first great liberal political philosophers. While he was certainly not as much of an egalitarian as are most contemporary liberals, this characterization still seems fair; for Locke's entire philosophy (including his epistemology and philosophy of language) sides with individual freedom against the forces of authoritarian repression and inculcation, and Locke was one of the first noteworthy philosophers of whom this was true. Locke straightforwardly embraces the moral and political individualism of liberalism, according to which individual persons are the proper primary subjects of moral judgments and polities must be viewed as artificial constructions for the purpose of serving individuals' interests. Similarly, the hard distinction between the private and public realms, so central to liberal thought, is prominently displayed in Locke's philosophy. According to Locke, my religion is my own business, like my finances, my health, and my family life. What I labor to produce is private to me, an extension of my person. Provided only that I observe the requirements of natural law, these private matters are beyond society's rightful reach.

The public realm, by contrast, is to be thought of as simply a just framework of institutions, designed solely to secure our basic rights and provide what is necessary for a stable, peaceful society, within the limited constraints of which each person may freely choose his or her private lifestyle. The proper end of society, Locke claims, is what people aim at in entering it, which is no more than peace and security for their private endeavors. From this view flows naturally the liberal emphases on limited government and toleration of diverse views and lifestyles. Society should refuse to tolerate only that which endangers others or society (though Locke, notoriously, believed that Catholicism and atheism could be rightly suppressed on these grounds).

The general structure of Locke's moral and political philosophy can be helpfully characterized if we view it as attempting to reveal the nature and limits of the political relationship—that is, of the relationship between persons that makes them members of the same political society (what Locke calls a civil society or commonwealth). This relationship, as Locke understands it, is a moral relationship that can hold only between free persons and that can be based only on freely given consent. The argument of the *Second Treatise* can then be seen as having the following structure: the first six chapters concern *non*political relations; chapters 7 through 9 concern the source or ground of the political relationship; and chapters 10 through 19 concern the forms and limits of the political relationship.

Chapters 1 through 6 are devoted to explaining those relations that are conceptually prepolitical, in the sense that they are relations whose moral bases can hold independent of civil society; this is Locke's way of attempting to define the boundaries of the political. Thus, we are offered in these chapters accounts of the state of nature (that relation in which stand any two persons who are not members of the same civil society), the state of war (into which people can enter without civil societies), the right to freedom from subjection (that all who are under the law of nature naturally enjoy), and the natural duties (also imposed by natural law) that stand as moral constraints even in the absence of legal and political institutions. Just punishment, private property, and marital and family rights and responsibilities are all explained in nonlegal, nonpolitical terms; all are possible in the state of nature, without civil laws or states.

This understanding of the natural moral condition of persons then sets the terms for understanding the political relationship, as requiring certain kinds of departures from the natural condition. The right to punish (according to our own conception of what natural law permits), which each possesses naturally, must be surrendered by each to society; a genuine civil society enjoys a moral monopoly on the use of force (except for rightful self-defense) within its territories. Similarly, private property (and particularly property in land) must be subjected to society's jurisdiction; civil societies have the right to enforce their laws throughout (and control the boundaries of) their incorporated territories. The political relationship, then, is defined in terms of transitions from our natural condition, with the rights of civil societies being understood as simply composed from those surrendered by individuals in their transitions from natural to political conditions.

Chapters 7 through 9 of the *Second Treatise* argue for this understanding of the political, maintaining as well that the sole possible source of the transition from natural to political is the voluntary consent of each individual who becomes a member of a civil society. This consent can be either tacit or expressed, but it is not binding if given under duress. Civil societies originate, Locke maintains, in a contract between all of their members, which transfers rights to the society and which binds the members together into one society committed to mutual security. That society may then entrust the rights it holds to a government, which must exercise those entrusted rights for the common good. Societies or governments that obtain their power in other ways are simply illegitimate (i.e., not genuine civil societies at all).

The remainder of the *Second Treatise* is devoted to elaboration of the limits on and possible forms of the political relationship (and, consequently, of the moral limits on governments), as well as the consequences of societies or governments exceeding those limits. We can only give binding consent, Locke argues, to participate in arrangements that satisfy the demands of natural law and that improve our condition over that which we would enjoy in a state of nature. These limits on our power to bind ourselves set as well the limits on societal and governmental authority famously elaborated by Locke in Chapter 11 of the *Second Treatise*; societies or governments that exceed those limits count as attempting to make war upon or to enslave their subjects, and binding consent to such efforts cannot be given.

Thus, governments that obtain their power by force, rather than by trust from their subjects, or those once-legitimate governments that exceed the limits of authority to which we can give binding consent (as Locke supposed the government of the Stuart monarchs had done), simply fail to possess any de jure authority at all. Such illegitimate powers can be rightfully resisted (by any wronged individual), removed from power, and forced to make reparations for harms done in their wrongful uses of coercion, just as a highwayman or a pirate can rightfully be treated. Locke's language even suggests his approval of tyrannicide (a quite radical position for Locke's day), since those who make unjust war upon (or attempt to enslave) others can, according to the argument of chapters 3 and 4, be justifiably killed at will by those they have wronged.

The most central and most influential theses of the *Second Treatise* seem to be these: (a) that all persons are naturally free, born to (and enjoying fully on achieving mature rationality) a set of natural rights to freely govern their own lives within the bounds of natural law; (b) that labor is the sole source of original property, grounding for the laborer private property rights in the products of that labor (provided that enough and as good of what nature provides is left for others to claim through their labor); (c) that free consent is the sole source of legitimate political authority and of the correlative political obligations of citizens in a civil society; (d) that political authority is limited in its legitimate scope to securing by legal coercion persons' natural rights to life, liberty, health, and estate; and (e) that popular resistance to government, including resistance by force, is justified wherever governments cause serious harm to persons by operating beyond these limits on political authority.

The relations between the arguments of the *Second Treatise* and those of *A Letter Concerning Toleration* are not entirely clear, for nowhere in the *Treatises* does Locke discuss (or even mention) religious toleration (nor does he directly mention or closely reproduce any of the arguments of the *Treatises* in the *Letter*). The explanation for this is certainly not that Locke regarded questions of religious toleration as of secondary importance in his political philosophy, for he had written extensively on them through-out his adult life (and he added three more letters on the subject after the first, the last of which he was writing at the time of his death). Perhaps their omission from the *Trea-tises* was due to Locke's fear that his views on toleration would lack wide appeal, thus diluting the influence of a text (the *Treatises*) that was designed to encourage popular resistance to the government.

Nonetheless, it is easy to read the *Letter* as simply an unincorporated part of the argument of the *Second Treatise*. For Locke uses in the *Letter* the same kinds of arguments used in the *Second Treatise* to establish the limits on the authority of societies and governments. Here, however, they are used to establish the conclusion that tolera-tion of diverse (harmless) religious practices is required within a legitimate civil society. The argument from the limits on binding consent again appears, though in a different form: the people cannot consent to (hence, render legitimate) policies of religious intol-erance, Locke argues, because they cannot conform their wills in matters of religious belief to an authority's commands. And Locke again argues that the civil magistrate's (or government's) authority is limited to that which is necessary to the end of civil society, which is again characterized in terms of securing individuals' possession and pursuit of their civil interests (in life, liberty, health, and property). Since control over people's (harmless) religious practices is not necessary to this end, religious toleration is required, as part of respecting the rights the people must be understood to retain in any consensual creation of civil society.

The magistrate's monopoly on the use of force, essential for securing the people's property (i.e., their rights), can have no role in securing for them salvation. Our po-litical authorities are no more likely than we to know, are far less interested in our progress on than are we, and can in any event do with coercion nothing to advance us down the road to knowledge and sincere practice of the true religion. Locke's views on these issues changed considerably during the course of his writings on toleration. In his (unpublished) 1660 *First Tract on Government*, Locke argued that because the magis-trate requires the power to legislate on "indifferent" matters (i.e., concerning behavior neither commanded nor forbidden by God), he must have the right to legislate on indif-ferent religious matters (and so to control his subjects' religious practices). By the time of his 1689 *Letter*, however, Locke had distinguished between those indifferent matters that are and those that are not the magistrate's proper business; and religious indifferent matters (such as the details of religious observances), having no real impact on the process of securing our rights, are no longer thought by Locke to fall within the proper scope of governmental authority.

The *Second Treatise* and the *Letter* were not, of course Locke's only works in political and moral philosophy. Locke's *Essay Concerning Human Understanding* includes discussions of the nature of moral knowledge, as well as hints of the justifications Locke intends for the natural law morality he employs in the *Treatises*. Further, in addition to Locke's subsequent letters on toleration and his *First Treatises of Government* (which is principally a polemic against, and a duel of scriptural interpretation with, the works of Robert Filmer), Locke produced many unpublished essays on these subjects, including his early, substantial *Two Tracts on Government* and *Essays on the Law of Nature*.

All of the most important of Locke's unpublished essays are included in M. Goldie (ed.), *Locke: Political Essays* (Cambridge: Cambridge University Press, 1997). A few of the many noteworthy secondary works on Locke's moral and political philosophy are J. Dunn, *The Political Thought of John Locke* (Cambridge: Cambridge University Press, 1969); J. Tully, *A Discourse on Property* (Cambridge: Cambridge University Press, 1980); J. Colman, *John Locke's Moral Philosophy* (Edinburgh: Edinburgh University Press, 1983); R. Ashcraft, *Locke's Two Treatises of Government* (Boston: Allen & Unwin, 1987); A. J. Simmons, *The Lockean Theory of Rights* (Princeton, N.J.: Princeton University Press, 1992), and *On the Edge of Anarchy* (Princeton, N.J.: Princeton University Press, 1993); J. Marshall, *John Locke* (Cambridge: Cambridge University Press, 1994); and D. A. Lloyd Thomas, *Locke on Government* (London: Routledge, 1995).

Second Treatise of Government

CHAPTER I

2. . . . I think it may not be amiss, to set down what I take to be political power; that the power of a magistrate over a subject may be distinguished from that of a father over his children, a master over his servant, a husband over his wife, and a lord over his slave. All which distinct powers happening sometimes together in the same man, if he be considered under these different relations, it may help us to distinguish these powers one from another, and show the difference between a ruler of a commonwealth, a father of a family, and a captain of a galley.

3. Political power, then, I take to be a right of making laws and penalties of death, and consequently all less penalties for the regulating and preserving of property, and of employing the force of the community, in the execution of such laws, and in the defence of the commonwealth from foreign injury; and all this only for the public good.

CHAPTER II

Of the State of Nature

4. To understand political power, right, and derive it from its original, we must consider what state all men are naturally in, and that is, a state of perfect freedom to order their actions, and dispose of their possessions and persons, as they think fit, within the bounds of the law of nature; without

asking leave, or depending upon the will of any other man.

A state also of equality, wherein all the power and jurisdiction is reciprocal, no one having more than another; there being nothing more evident, than that creatures of the same species and rank, promiscuously born to all the same advantages of nature, and the use of the same faculties, should also be equal one amongst another without subordination or subjection; unless the lord and master of them all should, by any manifest declaration of his will, set one above another, and confer on him, by an evident and clear appointment, an undoubted right to dominion and sovereignty.

6. But though this be a state of liberty, yet it is not a state of licence: though man in that state have an uncontrollable liberty to dispose of his person or possessions, yet he has not liberty to destroy himself, or so much as any creature in his possession, but where some nobler use than its bare preservation calls for it. The state of nature has a law of nature to govern it, which obliges every one: And reason, which is that law, teaches all mankind, who will but consult it, that being all equal and independent, no one ought to harm another in his life, health, liberty, or possessions. For men being all the workmanship of one omnipotent and infinitely wise Maker; all the servants of one sovereign master, sent into the world by his order, and about his business; they are his property, whose workmanship they are, made to last during his, not another's pleasure. And being furnished with like faculties, sharing all in one community of nature, there cannot be supposed any such subordination among us, that may authorize us to destroy another, as if we were made for one another's uses, as the inferior ranks of creatures are for ours. Everyone, as he is bound to preserve himself, and not to quit his station willfully, so by the like reason, when his own preservation comes not in competition, ought he, as much as he can, to preserve the rest of mankind, and may not, unless it be to do justice to an offender, take away or impair the life, or what tends to the preservation of life, the liberty, health, limb, or goods of another.

7. And that all men may be restrained from invading others rights, and from doing hurt to one another, and the law of nature be observed, which willeth the peace and preservation of all mankind, the execution of the law of nature is, in that state, put into every man's hands, whereby everyone has a right to punish the transgressors of that law to such a degree as may hinder its violation. For the law of nature would, as all other laws that concern men in this world, be in vain, if there were nobody that in the state of nature had a power to execute that law, and thereby preserve the innocent and restrain offenders. And if anyone in the state of nature may punish another for any evil he has done, everyone may do so. For in that state of perfect equality, where naturally there is no superiority or jurisdiction of one over another, what any may do in prosecution of that law, everyone must needs have a right to do.

8. And thus, in the state of nature, one man comes by a power over another; but yet no absolute or arbitrary power, to use a criminal, when he has got him in his hands, according to the passionate heats, or boundless extravagancy of his own will; but only to retribute to him, so far as calm reason and conscience dictate, what is proportionate to his transgression; which is so much as may serve for reparation and restraint. For these two are the only reasons, why one man may lawfully do harm to another, which is that we call punishment. In transgressing the law of nature, the offender declares himself to live by another rule than that of reason and common equity, which is that measure God has set to the actions of men, for their mutual security; and so he becomes dangerous to mankind, the tie, which is to secure them from injury and violence, being slighted and broken by him. Which being a trespass against the whole species, and the peace and safety of it, provided for by the law of nature; every man upon this score, by the right he hath to preserve mankind in general, may restrain, or, where it is necessary, destroy things noxious to them, and so may bring such evil on anyone, who hath transgressed that law, as may make him repent the doing of it, and thereby deter him, and by his

example others, from doing the like mischief. And in this case, and upon this ground, every man hath a right to punish the offender, and be executioner of the law of nature.

9. I doubt not but this will seem a very strange doctrine to some men: but before they condemn it, I desire them to resolve me, by what right any prince or state can put to death, or punish an alien, for any crime he commits in their country. It is certain their laws, by virtue of any sanction they receive from the promulgated will of the legislative, reach not a stranger. They speak not to him, nor, if they did, is he bound to hearken to them. The legislative authority, by which they are in force over the subjects of that commonwealth, hath no power over him. Those who have the supreme power of making laws in England, France, or Holland, are to an Indian but like the rest of the world, men without authority: And therefore, if by the law of nature every man has not a power to punish offences against it, as he soberly judges the case to require, I see not how the magistrates of any community can punish an alien of another country; since in reference to him, they can have no more power, than what every man naturally may have over another.

10. Besides the crime which consists in violating the law, and varying from the right rule of reason, whereby a man so far becomes degenerate, and declares himself to quit the principles of human nature, and to be a noxious creature, there is commonly injury done to some person or other, and some other man receives damage by his transgression, in which case he who has received any damage, has besides the right of punishment common to him with other men, a particular right to seek reparation from him that has done it. And any other person who finds it just, may also join with him that is injured, and assist him in recovering from the offender so much as may make satisfaction for the harm he has suffered.

11. From these two distinct rights, the one of punishing the crime for restraint, and preventing the like offence, which right of punishing is in everybody; the other of taking reparation, which belongs only to the injured party; comes it to pass that the magistrate, who by being magistrate, has the common right of punishing put into his hands, can often, where the public good demands not the execution of the law, remit the punishment of criminal offences by his own authority, but yet cannot remit the satisfaction due to any private man, for the damage he has received. That, he who has suffered the damage has a right to demand in his own name, and he alone can remit: The damnified person has this power of appropriating to himself the goods or service of the offender, by right of self-preservation, as every man has a power to punish the crime, to prevent its being committed again, by the right he has of preserving all mankind; and doing all reasonable things he can in order to that end: And thus it is, that every man, in the state of nature, has a power to kill a murderer, both to deter others from doing the like injury, which no reparation can compensate, by the example of the punishment that attends it from everybody, and also to secure men from the attempts of a criminal, who having renounced reason, the common rule and measure, God has given to mankind, has by the unjust violence and slaughter he has committed upon one, declared war against all mankind; and therefore may be destroyed as a lion or a tiger, one of those wild savage beasts, with whom men can have no society nor security: And upon this is grounded the great law of nature, "Whoso sheddeth man's blood, by man shall his blood be shed." And Cain was so fully convinced, that everyone had a right to destroy such a criminal, that after the murder of his brother, he cries out, "Every one that findeth me, shall slay me;" so plain was it writ in the hearts of all mankind.

12. By the same reason may a man in the state of nature punish the lesser breaches of that law. It will perhaps be demanded, with death? I answer, each transgression may be punished to that degree, and with so much severity, as will suffice to make it an ill bargain to the offender, give him cause to repent, and terrify others from doing the like. Every offence that can be committed in the

state of nature, may in the state of nature be also punished equally, and as far forth as it may, in a commonwealth: for though it would be besides my present purpose, to enter here into the particulars of the law of nature, or its measures of punishment; yet it is certain there is such a law, and that too, as intelligible and plain to a rational creature, and a studier of that law, as the positive laws of commonwealths, nay possibly plainer; as much as reason is easier to be understood, than the fancies and intricate contrivances of men, following contrary and hidden interests put into words; for so truly are a great part of the municipal laws of countries, which are only so far right, as they are founded on the law of nature, by which they are to be regulated and interpreted.

13. To this strange doctrine, viz. That in the state of nature every one has the executive power of the law of nature, I doubt not but it will be objected, that it is unreasonable for men to be judges in their own cases, that self-love will make men partial to themselves and their friends: And on the other side, that ill nature, passion and revenge will carry them too far in punishing others; and hence nothing but confusion and disorder will follow, and that therefore God has certainly appointed government to restrain the partiality and violence of men. I easily grant, that civil government is the proper remedy for the inconveniencies of the state of nature, which must certainly be great, where men may be judges in their own case, since it is easy to be imagined, that he who was so unjust as to do his brother an injury, will scarce be so just as to condemn himself for it: But I shall desire those who make this objection to remember, that absolute monarchs are but men, and if government is to be the remedy of those evils, which necessarily follow from men's being judges in their own cases, and the state of nature is therefore not to be endured, I desire to know what kind of government that is, and how much better it is than the state of nature, where one man commanding a multitude, has the liberty to be judge in his own case, and may do to all his subjects whatever he pleases, without

the least liberty to anyone to question or control those who execute his pleasure? and in whatsoever he doth, whether led by reason, mistake or passion, must be submitted to? Much better it is in the state of nature, wherein men are not bound to submit to the unjust will of another: And if he that judges, judges amiss in his own, or any other case, he is answerable for it to the rest of mankind.

14. It is often asked as a mighty objection, where are, or ever were, there any men in such a state of nature? To which it may suffice as an answer at present: That since all princes and rulers of independent governments, all through the world, are in a state of nature, it is plain the world never was, nor ever will be, without numbers of men in that state. I have named all governors of independent communities, whether they are, or are not, in league with others. For it is not every compact that puts an end to the state of nature between men, but only this one of agreeing together mutually to enter into one community, and make one body politic; other promises and compacts men may make one with another, and yet still be in the state of nature. The promises and bargains for truck, &c. between the two men in the desert island, mentioned by Garcilasso de la Vega, in his history of Peru; or between a Swiss and an Indian, in the woods of America, are binding to them, though they are perfectly in a state of nature, in reference to one another. For truth and keeping of faith belongs to men as men, and not as members of society.

CHAPTER III

Of the State of War

16. The state of war is a state of enmity and destruction: And therefore declaring by word or action, not a passionate and hasty, but a sedate settled design upon another man's life, puts him in a state of war with him against whom he has declared such an intention, and so has exposed his life to the other's power to be taken away by him,

or anyone that joins with him in his defence, and espouses his quarrel: it being reasonable and just I should have a right to destroy that which threatens me with destruction. For by the fundamental law of nature, man being to be preserved as much as possible, when all cannot be preserved, the safety of the innocent is to be preferred: And one may destroy a man who makes war upon him, or has discovered an enmity to his being, for the same reason that he may kill a wolf or a lion; because such men are not under the ties of the common law of reason, have no other rule, but that of force and violence, and so may be treated as beasts of prey, those dangerous and noxious creatures, that will be sure to destroy him whenever he falls into their power.

17. And hence it is, that he who attempts to get another man into his absolute power, does thereby put himself into a state of war with him; it being to be understood as a declaration of a design upon his life. For I have reason to conclude, that he who would get me into his power without my consent, would use me as he pleased when he got me there, and destroy me too when he had a fancy to it; for nobody can desire to have me in his absolute power unless it be to compel me by force to that which is against the right of my freedom, i.e. make me a slave. To be free from such force is the only security of my preservation; and reason bids me look on him, as an enemy to my preservation, who would take away that freedom which is the fence to it; so that he who makes an attempt to enslave me, thereby puts himself into a state of war with me. He that, in the state of nature, would take away the freedom that belongs to anyone in that state, must necessarily be supposed to have a design to take away everything else, that freedom being the foundation of all the rest: As he that, in the state of society, would take away the freedom belonging to those of that society or commonwealth, must be supposed to design to take away from them everything else, and so be looked on as in a state of war.

18. This makes it lawful for a man to kill a thief, who has not in the least hurt him, nor declared any design upon his life, any farther, than by the use of force, so to get him in his power, as to take away his money, or what he pleases, from him; because using force, where he has no right, to get me into his power, let his pretence be what it will, I have no reason to suppose, that he, who would take away my liberty, would not, when he had me in his power, take away everything else. And therefore it is lawful for me to treat him as one who has put himself into a state of war with me, i.e. kill him if I can; for to that hazard does he justly expose himself, whoever introduces a state of war, and is aggressor in it.

19. And here we have the plain difference between the state of nature and the state of war; which however some men have confounded, are as far distant, as a state of peace, good will, mutual assistance and preservation, and a state of enmity, malice, violence and mutual destruction, are one from another. Men living together according to reason, without a common superior on earth, with authority to judge between them, is properly the state of nature. But force, or a declared design of force, upon the person of another, where there is no common superior on earth to appeal to for relief, is the state of war: And it is the want of such an appeal gives a man the right of war even against an aggressor, though he be in society and a fellow subject. Thus a thief, whom I cannot harm, but by appeal to the law, for having stolen all that I am worth, I may kill, when he sets on me to rob me but of my horse or coat; because the law, which was made for my preservation, where it cannot interpose to secure my life from present force, which, if lost, is capable of no reparation, permits me my own defence, and the right of war, a liberty to kill the aggressor, because the aggressor allows not time to appeal to our common judge, nor the decision of the law, for remedy in a case where the mischief may be irreparable. Want of a common judge with authority, puts all men in a state of

nature: Force without right, upon a man's person, makes a state of war, both where there is, and is not, a common judge.

20. But when the actual force is over, the state of war ceases between those that are in society, and are equally on both sides subjected to the fair determination of the law; because then there lies open the remedy of appeal for the past injury, and to prevent future harm: but where no such appeal is, as in the state of nature, for want of positive laws, and judges with authority to appeal to, the state of war once begun, continues with a right to the innocent party to destroy the other whenever he can, until the aggressor offers peace, and desires reconciliation on such terms as may repair any wrongs he has already done, and secure the innocent for the future: nay, where an appeal to the law, and constituted judges, lies open, but the remedy is denied by a manifest perverting of justice, and a barefaced wresting of the laws to protect or indemnify the violence or injuries of some men, or party of men, there it is hard to imagine any thing but a state of war. For wherever violence is used, and injury done, though by hands appointed to administer justice, it is still violence and injury, however coloured with the name, pretences, or forms of law, the end whereof being to protect and redress the innocent, by an unbiassed application of it, to all who are under it; wherever that is not bona fide done, war is made upon the sufferers, who having no appeal on earth to right them, they are left to the only remedy in such cases, an appeal to heaven.

21. To avoid this *state of war* (wherein there is no appeal but to heaven, and wherein every the least difference is apt to end, where there is no authority to decide between the contenders) is one great reason of men's putting themselves into society, and quitting the state of nature: for where there is an authority, a power on earth, from which relief can be had by *appeal*, there the continuance of the *state of war* is excluded, and the controversy is decided by that power. Had there been any such court, any superior jurisdiction on earth, to determine the right between

Jephtha and the *Ammonites*, they had never come to a *state of war*: but we see he was forced to appeal to heaven. . . .

CHAPTER IV

Of Slavery

22. The natural liberty of man is to be free from any superior power on earth, and not to be under the will or legislative authority of man, but to have only the law of nature for his rule. The liberty of man, in society, is to be under no other legislative power; but that established, by consent, in the commonwealth; nor under the dominion of any will, or restraint of any law, but what that legislative shall enact, according to the trust put in it. Freedom then is not what Sir Robert Filmer tells us, O, A. 55. "a liberty for every one to do what he lists, to live as he pleases, and not to be tied by any laws:" But freedom of men under government, is, to have a standing rule to live by, common to every one of that society, and made by the legislative power erected in it; a liberty to follow my own will in all things, where the rule prescribes not; and not to be subject to the inconstant, uncertain, unknown, arbitrary will of another man: As freedom of nature is, to be under no other restraint but the law of nature.

23. This freedom from absolute, arbitrary power, is so necessary to, and closely joined with a man's preservation, that he cannot part with it, but by what forfeits his preservation and life together. For a man, not having the power of his own life, cannot, by compact, or his own consent, enslave himself to any one, nor put himself under the absolute, arbitrary power of another, to take away his life, when he pleases. Nobody can give more power than he has himself; and he that cannot take away his own life, cannot give another power over it. Indeed, having by his fault forfeited his own life, by some act that deserves death; he, to whom he has forfeited it, may (when he has him in his power) delay to take it, and make use of him to his own service, and he does him no injury by it.

For, whenever he finds the hardship of his slavery outweigh the value of his life, it is in his power, by resisting the will of his master, to draw on himself the death he desires.

24. This is the perfect condition of slavery, which is nothing else, but the state of war continued, between a lawful conqueror and a captive. For, if once compact enter between them, and make an agreement for a limited power on the one side, and obedience on the other, the state of war and slavery ceases, as long as the compact endures. For, as has been said, no man can, by agreement, pass over to another that which he hath not in himself, a power over his own life. . . .

CHAPTER V

Of Property

25. Whether we consider natural reason, which tells us, that men, being once born, have a right to their preservation, and consequently to meat and drink, and such other things as nature affords for their subsistence: or revelation, which gives us an account of those grants God made of the world to Adam, and to Noah, and his sons, it is very clear, that God, as King David says, Psal. cxv. 16, "has given the earth to the children of men," given it to mankind in common. But this being supposed, it seems to some a very great difficulty how anyone should ever come to have a property in anything: I will not content myself to answer, that if it be difficult to make out property, upon a supposition, that God gave the world to Adam, and his posterity in common; it is impossible that any man, but one universal monarch, should have any property upon a supposition, that God gave the world to Adam, and his heirs in succession, exclusive of all the rest of his posterity. But I shall endeavour to show, how men might come to have a property in several parts of that which God gave to mankind in common, and that without any express compact of all the commoners.

26. God, who has given the world to men in common, has also given them reason to make use of it to the best advantage of life, and convenience. The earth, and all that is therein, is given to men for the support and comfort of their being. And though all the fruits it naturally produces, and beasts it feeds, belong to mankind in common, as they are produced by the spontaneous hand of nature; and nobody has originally a private dominion, exclusive of the rest of mankind, in any of them, as they are thus in their natural state: yet being given for the use of men, there must of necessity be a means to appropriate them some way or other, before they can be of any use, or at all beneficial to any particular man. The fruit, or venison, which nourishes the wild Indian, who knows no enclosure, and is still a tenant in common, must be his, and so his, i.e. a part of him, that another can no longer have any right to it, before it can do him any good for the support of his life.

27. Though the earth, and all inferior creatures, be common to all men, yet every man has a property in his own person: this nobody has any right to but himself. The labour of his body, and the work of his hands, we may say, are properly his. Whatsoever then he removes out of the state that nature has provided, and left it in, he has mixed his labour with, and joined to it something that is his own, and thereby makes it his property. It being by him removed from the common state nature has placed it in, it has by this labour something annexed to it, that excludes the common right of other men. For this labour being the unquestionable property of the labourer, no man but he can have a right to what that is once joined to, at least where there is enough, and as good, left in common for others.

28. He that is nourished by the acorns he picked up under an oak, or the apples he gathered from the trees in the wood, has certainly appropriated them to himself. Nobody can deny but the nourishment is his. I ask then, when did they begin to be his? When he digested? Or when he eat? Or when he boiled? Or when he brought them home? Or when he picked them up? And it is plain, if the first gathering made them not his,

nothing else could. That labour put a distinction between them and common: that added something to them more than nature, the common mother of all, had done; and so they became his private right. And will anyone say he had no right to those acorns or apples he thus appropriated, because he had not the consent of all mankind to make them his? Was it a robbery thus to assume to himself what belonged to all in common? If such a consent as that was necessary, man had starved, notwithstanding the plenty God had given him. We see in commons, which remain so by compact, that it is the taking any part of what is common, and removing it out of the state nature leaves it in, which begins the property; without which the common is of no use. And the taking of this or that part does not depend on the express consent of all the commoners. Thus the grass my horse has bit; the turfs my servant has cut; and the ore I have digged in any place, where I have a right to them in common with others, become my property, without the assignation or consent of anybody. The labour that was mine, removing them out of that common state they were in, has fixed my property in them.

29. By making an explicit consent of every commoner, necessary to any one's appropriating to himself any part of what is given in common, children or servants could not cut the meat, which their father or master had provided for them in common, without assigning to every one his peculiar part. Though the water running in the fountain be every one's, yet who can doubt, but that in the pitcher is his only who drew it out? His *labour* hath taken it out of the hands of nature, where it was common, and belonged equally to all her children, and *hath* thereby *appropriated* it to himself. . . .

31. It will perhaps be objected to this, that "if gathering the acorns, or other fruits of the earth, &c. makes a right to them, then anyone may engross as much as he will." To which I answer, Not so. The same law of nature, that does by this means give us property, does also bound that property too. "God has given us all things richly,"

1 Tim; vi. 17, is the voice of reason confirmed by inspiration. But how far has he given it us? To enjoy. As much as anyone can make use of to any advantage of life before it spoils, so much he may by his labour fix a property in: whatever is beyond this, is more than his share, and belongs to others. Nothing was made by God for man to spoil or destroy. And thus, considering the plenty of natural provisions there was a long time in the world, and the few spenders; and to how small a part of that provision the industry of one man could extend itself, and engross it to the prejudice of others; especially keeping within the bounds, set by reason, of what might serve for his use; there could be then little room for quarrels or contentions about property so established.

32. But the chief matter of property being now not the fruits of the earth, and the beasts that subsist on it, but the earth it self; as that which takes in, and carries with it all the rest: I think it is plain, that property in that too is acquired as the former. As much land as a man tills, plants, improves, cultivates, and can use the product of, so much is his property. He by his labour does, as it were, enclose it from the common. Nor will it invalidate his right, to say everybody else has an equal title to it; and therefore he cannot appropriate, he cannot enclose, without the consent of all his fellow commoners, all mankind. God, when he gave the world in common to all mankind, commanded man also to labour, and the penury of his condition required it of him. God and his reason commanded him to subdue the earth, i.e. improve it for the benefit of life, and therein lay out something upon it that was his own, his labour. He that, in obedience to this command of God, subdued, tilled, and sowed any part of it, thereby annexed to it something that was his property, which another had no title to, nor could without injury take from him.

33. Nor was this appropriation of any parcel of land, by improving it, any prejudice to any other man, since there was still enough, and as good left; and more than the yet unprovided could use. So that, in effect, there was never the less left for

others because of his enclosure for himself. For he that leaves as much as another can make use of, does as good as take nothing at all. Nobody could think himself injured by the drinking of another man, though he took a good draught, who had a whole river of the same water left him to quench his thirst: And the case of land and water, where there is enough of both, is perfectly the same.

34. God gave the world to men in common; but since he gave it them for their benefit, and the greatest conveniences of life they were capable to draw from it, it cannot be supposed he meant it should always remain common and uncultivated. He gave it to the use of the industrious and rational (and *labour* was to be *his title* to it) not to the fancy or covetousness of the quarrelsome and contentious. He that had as good left for his improvement, as was already taken up, needed not complain, ought not to meddle with what was already improved by another's labour: If he did, it is plain he desired the benefit of another's pains, which he had no right to, and not the ground which God had given him in common with others to labour on, and whereof there was as good left, as that already possessed, and more than he knew what to do with, or his industry could reach to.

36. The *measure of property* nature has well set by the extent of men's *labour and the conveniencies of life*: no man's labour could subdue, or appropriate all; nor could his enjoyment consume more than a small part; so that it was impossible for any man, this way, to intrench upon the right of another, or acquire to himself a property, to the prejudice of his neighbour, who would still have room for as good, and as large a possession (after the other had taken out his) as before it was appropriated. This *measure* did confine every man's *possession* to a very moderate proportion, and such as he might appropriate to himself, without injury to any body, in the first ages of the world, when men were more in danger to be lost, by wandering from their company, in the then vast wilderness of the earth, than to be straitened for want of room to plant in. And the same *measure* may be allowed still without prejudice to any body, as full as the

world seems: for supposing a man, or family, in the state they were at first peopling of the world by the children of *Adam*, or *Noah*; let him plant in some in-land, vacant places of *America*, we shall find that the *possessions* he could make himself, upon the *measures* we have given, would not be very large, nor, even to this day, prejudice the rest of mankind, or give them reason to complain, or think themselves injured by this man's incroachment, though the race of men have now spread themselves to all the corners of the world, and do infinitely exceed the small number was at the beginning. Nay, the extent of *ground* is of so little value, *without labour*, that I have heard it affirmed, that in *Spain* itself a man may be permitted to plough, sow and reap, without being disturbed, upon land he has no other title to, but only his making use of it. But, on the contrary, the inhabitants think themselves beholden to him, who, by his industry on neglected, and consequently waste land, has increased the stock of corn, which they wanted. But be this as it will, which I lay no stress on; this I dare boldly affirm, that the same *rule of propriety*, (*viz.*) that every man should have as much as he could make use of, would hold still in the world, without straitening any body; since there is land enough in the world to suffice double the inhabitants, had not the *invention of money*, and the tacit agreement *of* men to put a value on it, introduced (by consent) larger possessions, and a right to them; *which, how* it has done, I shall by and by shew more at large.

37. This is certain, that in the beginning, before the desire of having more than man needed had altered the intrinsic value of things, which depends only on their usefulness to the life of man; or had *agreed, that a little piece of yellow metal*, which would keep without wasting or decay, should be worth a great piece of flesh, or a whole heap of corn; though men had a right to appropriate, by their labour, each one to himself as much of the things of nature as he could use: yet this could not be much, nor to the prejudice of others, where the same plenty was still left to those who would use the same industry. To which let me add, that he

who appropriates land to himself by his labour, does not lessen, but increase the common stock of mankind. For the provisions serving to the support of human life, produced by one acre of enclosed and cultivated land, are (to speak much within compass) ten times more than those which are yielded by an acre of land of an equal richness lying waste in common. And therefore he that encloses land, and has a greater plenty of the conveniencies of life from ten acres, than he could have from an hundred left to nature, may truly be said to give ninety acres to mankind. For his labour now supplies him with provisions out of ten acres, which were by the product of an hundred lying in common. I have here rated the improved land very low, in making its product but as ten to one, when it is much nearer an hundred to one. For I ask, whether in the wild woods and uncultivated waste of America, left to nature, without any improvement, tillage, or husbandry, a thousand acres yield the needy and wretched inhabitants as many conveniencies of life, as ten acres equally fertile land do in Devonshire, where they are well cultivated?

Before the appropriation of land, he who gathered as much of the wild fruit, killed, caught, or tamed, as many of the beasts as he could; he that so employed his pains about any of the spontaneous products of nature, as any way to alter them from the state which nature put them in, *by* placing any of his *labour* on them, did thereby *acquire a propriety in them*: but if they perished, in his possession, without their due use; if the fruits rotted, or the venison putrified, before he could spend it, he offended against the common law of nature, and was liable to be punished; he invaded his neighbour's share, for he had *no right, farther than his use* called for any of them, and they might serve to afford him conveniencies of life.

38. The same *measures* governed the *possession of land* too: whatsoever he tilled and reaped, laid up and made use of, before it spoiled, that was his peculiar right; whatsoever he enclosed, and could feed, and make use of, the cattle and product was also his. But if either the grass of his inclosure rotted on the ground, or the fruit of his planting perished without gathering, and laying up, this part of the earth, notwithstanding his inclosure, was still to be looked on as waste, and might be the possession of any other. Thus, at the beginning, *Cain* might take as much ground as he could till, and make it his own land, and yet leave enough to *Abel's* sheep to feed on; a few acres would serve for both their possessions. But as families increased, and industry inlarged their stocks, their *possessions inlarged* with the need of them; but yet it was commonly *without any fixed property in the ground* they made use of, till they incorporated, settled themselves together, and built cities; and then, by consent, they came in time, to set out the *bounds of their distinct territories*, and agree on limits between them and their neighbours; and by laws within themselves, settled the *properties* of those of the same society: for we see, that in that part of the world which was first inhabited, and therefore like to be best peopled, even as low down as *Abrahams* time, they wandered with their flocks, and their herds, which was their substance, freely up and down; and this *Abraham* did, in a country where he was a stranger. Whence it is plain, that at least a great part of the *land lay in common;* that the inhabitants valued it not, nor claimed property in any more than they made use of. But when there was not room enough in the same place, for their herds to feed together, they by consent, as *Abraham* and *Lot* did, *Gen.* xiii. 5. separated and inlarged their pasture, where it best liked them. . . .

40. Nor is it so strange, as perhaps before consideration it may appear, that the *property of labour* should be able to over-balance the community of land. For it is *labour* indeed that *puts the difference of value* on every thing; and let any one consider what the difference is between an acre of land planted with tobacco or sugar, sown with wheat or barley, and an acre of the same land lying in common, without any husbandry upon it, and he will find, that the improvement of *labour makes* the far greater part of the value. I think it will be but a very modest computation to say, that of the *products* of the earth useful to the life

of man, nine tenths are the *effects of labour*: nay, if we will rightly estimate things as they come to our use, and cast up the several expences about them, what in them is purely owing to *nature*, and what to *labour*, we shall find, that in most of them ninety-nine hundredths are wholly to be put on the account of *labour*.

43 . . . It is *labour* then which *puts the greatest part of value upon land*, without which it would scarcely be worth any thing: it is to that we owe the greatest part of all its useful products; for all that the straw, bran, bread, of that acre of wheat, is more worth than the product of an acre of as good land, which lies waste, is all the effect of labour: for it is not barely the plough-man's pains, the reaper's and threshers toil, and the baker's sweat, is to be counted into the *bread* we eat; the labour of those who broke the oxen, who digged and wrought the iron and stones, who felled and framed the timber employed about the plough, mill, oven, or any other utensils, which are a vast number, requisite to this corn, from its being feed to be sown to its being made bread, must all be *charged on* the account of labour, and received as an effect *of* that: nature and the earth furnished only the almost worthless materials, as in themselves. It would be a strange *catalogue of things, that industry provided and made use of, about every loaf of bread*, before it came to our use, if we could trace them; iron, wood, leather, bark, timber, stone, bricks, coals, lime, cloth, dying drugs, pitch, tar, masts, ropes, and all the materials made use of in the ship, that brought any of the commodities made use of by any of the workmen, to any part of the work; all which it would be almost impossible, at least too long, to reckon up.

44. From all which it is evident, that though the things of nature are given in common, yet man, by being master of himself, and *proprietor of his own person, and the actions or labour of it, had still in himself the great foundation of property*; and that, which made up the great part of what he applied to the support or comfort of his being, when invention and arts had improved the conveniences of life, was perfectly his own, and did not belong in common to others.

45. Thus *labour*, in the beginning, *gave a right of property*, wherever any one was pleased to employ it upon what was common, which remained a long while the far greater part, and is yet more than mankind makes use of. Men, at first, for the most part, contented themselves with what unassisted nature offered to their necessities: and though afterwards, in some parts of the world, (where the increase of people and stock, with the *use of money*, had made land scarce, and so of some value) the several *communities* settled the bounds of their distinct territories, and by laws within themselves regulated the properties of the private men of their society, and so, by *compact* and agreement, *settled the property* which labour and industry began; and the leagues that have been made between several states and kingdoms, either expressly or tacitly disowning all claim and right to the land in the other's possession, have, by common consent, given up their pretences to their natural common right, which originally they had to those countries, and so have, by *positive agreement, settled a property* amongst themselves, in distinct parts and parcels of the earth; yet there are still *great tracts of ground* to be found, which (the inhabitants thereof not having joined with the rest of mankind, in the consent of the use of their common money) *lie waste*, and are more than the people who dwell on it do, or can make use of, and so still lie in common. Though this can scarce happen amongst that part of mankind that have consented to the use of money.

46. The greatest part of *things really useful* to the life of man, and such as the necessity of subsisting made the first commoners of the world look after, as it doth the Americans now, *are* generally things of *short duration*; such as, if they are not consumed by use, will decay and perish of themselves: gold, silver, and diamonds, are things that fancy or agreement hath put the value on, more than real use, and the necessary support of life. Now of those good things which nature hath provided in common, every one had a right,

(as hath been said) to as much as he could use, and property in all that he could affect with his labour; all that his industry could extend to, to alter from the state nature had put it in, was his. He that *gathered* a hundred bushels of acorns or apples, had thereby a *property* in them, they were his goods as soon as gathered. He was only to look, that he used them before they spoiled, else he took more than his share, and robbed others. And indeed it was a foolish thing, as well as dishonest, to hoard up more than he could make use of. If he gave away a part to any body else, so that it perished not uselessly in his possession, these he also made use of. And if he also bartered away plums, that would have rotted in a week, for nuts that would last good for his eating a whole year, he did no injury; he wasted not the common stock; destroyed no part of the portion of goods that belonged to others, so long as nothing perished uselessly in his hands. Again, if he would give his nuts for a piece of metal, pleased with its colour; or exchange his sheep for shells, or wool for a sparkling pebble or a diamond, and keep those by him all his life, he invaded not the right of others, he might heap up as much of these durable things as he pleased; the *exceeding of the bounds of* his *just property* not lying in the largeness of his possession, but the perishing of any thing uselessly in it.

47. And thus *came in the use of money*, some lasting thing that men might keep without spoiling, and that by mutual consent men would take in exchange for the truly useful, but perishable supports of life.

48. And as different degrees of industry were apt to give men possessions in different proportions, so this *invention of money* gave them the opportunity to continue and enlarge them. For supposing an island, separate from all possible commerce with the rest of the world, wherein there were but an hundred families, but there were sheep, horses, and cows, with other useful animals, wholesome fruits, and land enough for corn for a hundred thousand times as many, but nothing in the island, either because of its commonness, or perishableness, fit to supply the place of *money*: What reason could any one have there to enlarge

his possessions beyond the use of his family and a plentiful supply to its *consumption*, either in what their own industry produced, or they could barter for like perishable, useful commodities with others? Where there is not something, both lasting and scarce, and so valuable to be hoarded up, there men will not be apt to enlarge their *possessions of land*, were it never so rich, never so free for them to take. For I ask, what would a man value ten thousand, or an hundred thousand acres of excellent *land*, ready cultivated and well stocked too with cattle, in the middle of the inland parts of America, where he had no hopes of commerce with other parts of the world, to draw *money* to him by the sale of the product? It would not be worth the enclosing, and we should see him give up again to the wild common of nature, whatever was more than would supply the conveniences of life to be had there for him and his family.

50. But since gold and silver, being little useful to the life of man in proportion to food, raiment, and carriage, has its *value* only from the consent of men, whereof *labour* yet *makes*, in great part, the *measure*, it is plain, that men have agreed to a disproportionate and unequal *possession of the earth*, they having, by a tacit and voluntary consent, found out a way how a man may fairly possess more land than he himself can use the product of, by receiving in exchange for the overplus, gold and silver, which may be hoarded up without injury to any one; these metals not spoiling or decaying in the hands of the possessor. This partage of things in an inequality of private possessions, men have made practicable out of the bounds of society, and without compact, only by putting a value on gold and silver, and tacitly agreeing in the use of money. For in governments, the laws regulate the right of property, and the possession of land is determined by positive constitutions.

51. And thus, I think, it is very easy to conceive, without any difficulty *how labour could at first begin a title of property* in the common things of nature, and how the spending it upon our uses bounded it. So that there could then be no reason of quarrelling about title, nor any doubt about the largeness of possession it gave. Right

and conveniency went together; for as a man had a right to all he could employ his labour upon, so he had no temptation to labour for more than he could make use of. This left no room for controversy about the title, nor for encroachment on the right of others; what portion a man carved to himself, was easily seen; and it was useless, as well as dishonest, to carve himself too much, or take more than he needed.

CHAPTER VII

Of Political or Civil Society

77. God having made man such a creature, that in his own judgment, it was not good for him to be alone, put him under strong obligations of necessity, convenience, and inclination, to drive him into society, as well as fitted him with understanding and language to continue and enjoy it. The first society was between man and wife, which gave beginning to that between parents and children; to which, in time, that between master and servant came to be added; and though all these might, and commonly did meet together, and make up but one family, wherein the master or mistress of it had some sort of rule proper to a family; each of these, or all together, came short of political society, as we shall see, if we consider the different ends, ties, and bounds of each of these.

87. Man being born, as has been proved, with a title to perfect freedom, and an uncontrolled enjoyment of all the rights and privileges of the law of nature, equally with any other man, or number of men in the world, has by nature a power, not only to preserve his property, that is, his life, liberty, and estate, against the injuries and attempts of other men; but to judge of and punish the breaches of that law in others, as he is persuaded the offence deserves, even with death itself, in crimes where the heinousness of the fact, in his opinion, requires it. But because no political society can be, nor subsist, without having in itself the power to preserve the property, and, in order thereunto, punish the offences of all those of that society; there and there only is political

society, where every one of the members hath quitted his natural power, resigned it up into the hands of the community in all cases that excludes him not from appealing for protection to the law established by it. And thus all private judgment of every particular member being excluded, the community comes to be umpire by settled standing rules, indifferent, and the same to all parties; and by men having authority from the community, for the execution of those rules, decides all the differences that may happen between any members of that society concerning any matter of right; and punishes those offences which any member has committed against the society, with such penalties as the law has established, whereby it is easy to discern, who are, and who are not, in political society together. Those who are united into one body, and have a common established law and judicature to appeal to, with authority to decide controversies between them, and punish offenders, are in civil society one with another: but those who have no such common appeal, I mean on earth, are still in the state of nature, each being, where there is no other, judge for himself, and executioner: which is, as I have before showed, the perfect state of nature.

88. And thus the commonwealth comes by a power to set down what punishment shall belong to the several transgressions which they think worthy of it, committed amongst the members of that society, (which is the power of making laws) as well as it has the power to punish any injury done unto any of its members, by anyone that is not of it, (which is the power of war and peace,) and all this for the preservation of the property of all the members of that society, as far as is possible. But though every man who has entered into civil society, and is become a member of any commonwealth, has thereby quitted his power to punish offences against the law of nature, in prosecution of his own private judgment; yet with the judgment of offences, which he has given up to the legislative in all cases, where he can appeal to the magistrate, he has given a right to the commonwealth to employ his force, for the execution of the judgments of the commonwealth whenever he shall be

called to it; which indeed are his own judgments, they being made by himself, or his representative. And herein we have the original of the legislative and executive power of civil society, which is to judge by standing laws, how far offences are to be punished, when committed within the commonwealth; and also to determine, by occasional judgments founded on the present circumstances of the fact, how far injuries from without are to be vindicated; and in both these to employ all the force of all the members, when there shall be need.

89. Whenever therefore any number of men are so united into one society, as to quit everyone his executive power of the law of nature, and to resign it to the public, there and there only is a political, or civil society. And this is done, wherever any number of men, in the state of nature, enter into society to make one people, one body politic, under one supreme government; or else when any one joins himself to, and incorporates with any government already made. For hereby he authorizes the society, or, which is all one, the legislative thereof, to make laws for him, as the public good of the society shall require; to the execution whereof, his own assistance (as to his own degrees) is due. And this puts men out of a state of nature into that of a commonwealth, by setting up a judge on earth, with authority to determine all the controversies, and redress the injuries that may happen to any member of the commonwealth: which judge is the legislative, or magistrate appointed by it. And wherever there are any number of men, however associated, that have no such decisive power to appeal to, there they are still in the state of nature.

90. Hence it is evident, that absolute monarchy, which by some men is counted the only government in the world, is indeed inconsistent with civil society, and so can be no form of civil government at all; for the end of civil society being to avoid and remedy these inconveniencies of the state of nature, which necessarily follow from every man's being judge in his own case, by setting up a known authority, to which everyone of that society may appeal upon any injury received, or controversy that may arise, and which everyone of the society ought to obey; wherever any persons are, who have not such an authority to appeal to for the decision of any difference between them, there those persons are still in the state of nature. And so is every absolute prince, in respect of those who are under his dominion.

91. For he being supposed to have all, both legislative and executive power in himself alone, there is no judge to be found, no appeal lies open to any one, who may fairly, and indifferently, and with authority decide, and from whose decision relief and redress may be expected of any injury or inconveniency that may be suffered from the prince, or by his order: so that such a man, however entitled, czar, or grand seignior, or how you please, is as much in the state of nature, with all under his dominion, as he is with the rest of mankind. For wherever any two men are, who have no standing rule, and common judge to appeal to on earth, for the determination of controversies of right between them, there they are still in the state of nature, and under all the inconveniencies of it, with only this woeful difference to the subject, or rather slave of an absolute prince; that whereas in the ordinary state of nature he has a liberty to judge of his right, and, according to the best of his power, to maintain it; now, whenever his property is invaded by the will and order of his monarch, he has not only no appeal, as those in society ought to have, but, as if he were degraded from the common state of rational creatures, is denied a liberty to judge of, or to defend his right; and so is exposed to all the misery and inconveniencies that a man can fear from one, who being in the unrestrained state of nature, is yet corrupted with flattery, and armed with power.

CHAPTER VIII

Of the Beginning of Political Societies

95. Men being, as has been said, by nature, all free, equal, and independent, no one can be put out of this estate, and subjected to the political power of another, without his own consent. The only way,

whereby any one divests himself of his natural liberty, and puts on the bonds of civil society, is by agreeing with other men to join and unite into a community, for their comfortable, safe, and peaceable living one amongst another, in a secure enjoyment of their properties, and a greater security against any, that are not of it. This any number of men may do, because it injures not the freedom of the rest; they are left as they were in the liberty of the state of nature. When any number of men have so consented to make one community or government, they are thereby presently incorporated, and make one body politic, wherein the majority have a right to act and conclude the rest.

96. For when any number of men have, by the consent of every individual, made a community, they have thereby made that community one body, with a power to act as one body, which is only by the will and determination of the majority. For that which acts any community, being only the consent of the individuals of it, and it being necessary to that which greater force carries it, which is the consent of the majority: or else it is impossible it should act or continue one body, one community, which the consent of every individual that united into it, agreed that it should; and so everyone is bound by that consent to be concluded by the majority. And therefore we see, that in assemblies, empowered to act by positive laws, where no number is set by that positive law which empowers them, the act of the majority passes for the act of the whole, and of course determines, as having, by the law of nature and reason, the power of the whole.

97. And thus every man, by consenting with others to make one body politic under one government, puts himself under an obligation, to everyone of that society, to submit to the determination of the majority, and to be concluded by it; or else this original compact, whereby he with others incorporate into one society, would signify nothing, and be no compact, if he be left free, and under no other ties than he was in before in the state of nature. For what appearance would there be of any compact? What new engagement if he were no farther tied by any decrees of the society, than he himself thought fit, and did actually consent to? This would be still as great a liberty, as he himself had before his compact, or anyone else in the state of nature has, who may submit himself, and consent to any acts of it if he thinks fit.

98. For if the consent of the majority shall not, in reason, be received as the act of the whole, and conclude every individual; nothing but the consent of every individual can make anything to be the act of the whole: But such a consent is next to impossible ever to be had, if we consider the infirmities of health, and avocations of business, which in a number, though much less than that of a commonwealth, will necessarily keep many away from the public assembly. To which if we add the variety of opinions, and contrariety of interests, which unavoidably happen in all collections of men, the coming into society upon such terms would be only like Cato's coming into the theatre, only to go out again. Such a constitution as this would make the mighty leviathan of a shorter duration than the feeblest creatures, and not let it outlast the day it was born in: which cannot be supposed, till we can think, that rational creatures should desire and constitute societies only to be dissolved. For where the majority cannot conclude the rest, there they cannot act as one body, and consequently will be immediately dissolved again.

99. Whosoever therefore out of a state of nature unite into a community, must be understood to give up all the power, necessary to the ends for which they unite into society, to the majority of the community, unless they expressly agreed in any number greater than the majority. And this is done by barely agreeing to unite into one political society, which is all the compact that is, or needs be, between the individuals, that enter into, or make up a commonwealth. And thus, that which begins and actually constitutes any political society, is nothing, but the consent of any number of freemen capable of a majority, to unite and incorporate into such a society. And this is that, and that only, which did, or could give beginning to any lawful government in the world.

119. Every man being, as has been shown, naturally free, and nothing being able to put him into subjection to any earthly power, but only his own consent; it is to be considered, what shall be understood to be a sufficient declaration of a man's consent, to make him subject to the laws of any government. There is a common distinction of an express and a tacit consent, which will concern our present case. Nobody doubts but an express consent, of any man entering into any society, makes him a perfect member of that society, a subject of that government. The difficulty is, what ought to be looked upon as a tacit consent, and how far it binds, i.e. how far anyone shall be looked on to have consented, and thereby submitted to any government, where he has made no expressions of it at all. And to this I say, that every man, that has any possessions, or enjoyment of any part of the dominions of any government, doth thereby give his tacit consent, and is as far forth obliged to obedience to the laws of that government, during such enjoyment, as anyone under it; whether this his possession be of land, to him and his heirs for ever, or a lodging only for a week; or whether it be barely travelling freely on the highway: and, in effect, it reaches as far as the very being of anyone within the territories of that government.

120. To understand this the better, it is fit to consider, that every man, when he at first incorporates himself into any commonwealth, he, by his uniting himself thereunto, annexed also, and submits to the community, those possessions which he has, or shall acquire, that do not already belong to any other government. For it would be a direct contradiction, for anyone to enter into society with others for the securing and regulating of property, and yet to suppose, his land, whose property is to be regulated by the laws of the society, should be exempt from the jurisdiction of that government, to which he himself, the proprietor of the land, is a subject. By the same act therefore, whereby anyone unites his person, which was before free, to any commonwealth; by the same he unites his possessions, which were before free, to it also: and they become, both of them, person

and possession, subject to the government and dominion of that commonwealth, as long as it has a being. Whoever therefore, from thenceforth, by inheritance, purchase, permission, or otherways, enjoys any part of the land so annexed to, and under the government of that commonwealth, must take it with the condition it is under; that is, of submitting to the government of the commonwealth, under whose jurisdiction it is, as far forth as any subject of it.

121. But since the government has a direct jurisdiction only over the land, and reaches the possessor of it, (before he has actually incorporated himself in the society) only as he dwells upon, and enjoys that; the obligation anyone is under, by virtue of such enjoyment, to submit to the government, begins and ends with the enjoyment: so that whenever the owner, who has given nothing but such a tacit consent to the government, will, by donation, sale, or otherwise, quit the said possession, he is at liberty to go and incorporate himself into any other commonwealth; or to agree with others to begin a new one, in vacuis locis, in any part of the world they can find free and unpossessed: whereas he, that has once, by actual agreement, and any express declaration, given his consent to be of any commonwealth, is perpetually and indispensably obliged to be, and remain unalterably a subject to it, and can never be again in the liberty of the state of nature; unless, by any calamity, the government he was under comes to be dissolved, or else by some public act cuts him off from being any longer a member of it.

122. But submitting to the laws of any country, living quietly, and enjoying privileges and protection under them, makes not a man a member of that society: this is only a local protection and homage due to and from all those, who, not being in a state of war, come within the territories belonging to any government, to all parts whereof the force of its laws extends. But this no more makes a man a member of that society, a perpetual subject of that commonwealth, than it would make a man a subject to another, in whose family he found it convenient to abide for some

time, though, whilst he continued in it, he were obliged to comply with the laws, and submit to the government he found there. And thus we see, that foreigners, by living all their lives under another government, and enjoying the privileges and protection of it, though they are bound, even in conscience, to submit to its administration, as far forth as any denison; yet do not thereby come to be subjects or members of that commonwealth. Nothing can make any man so, but his actually entering into it by positive engagement, and express promise and compact. This is that, which I think, concerning the beginning of political societies, and that consent which makes anyone a member of any commonwealth.

CHAPTER IX

Of the Ends of Political Society and Government

123. If man in the state of nature be so free, as has been said; if he be absolute lord of his own person and possessions, equal to the greatest, and subject to nobody, why will he part with his freedom? why will he give up his empire, and subject himself to the dominion and control of any other power? To which it is obvious to answer, that though in the state of nature he has such a right, yet the enjoyment of it is very uncertain, and constantly exposed to the invasion of others. For all being kings as much as he, every man his equal, and the greater part no strict observers of equity and justice, the enjoyment of the property he has in this state is very unsafe, very unsecure. This makes him willing to quit this condition, which, however free, is full of fears and continual dangers: and it is not without reason, that he seeks out, and is willing to join in society with others, who are already united, or have a mind to unite, for the mutual preservation of their lives, liberties, and estates, which I call by the general name, property.

124. The great and chief end, therefore, of men's uniting into commonwealths, and putting themselves under government, is the preservation of their property. To which in the state of nature there are many things wanting.

First, There wants an established, settled, known law, received and allowed by common consent to be the standard of right and wrong, and the common measure to decide all controversies between them. For though the law of nature be plain and intelligible to all rational creatures; yet men being biassed by their interest, as well as ignorant for want of studying it, are not apt to allow of it as a law binding to them in the application of it to their particular cases.

125. Secondly, In the state of nature there wants a known and indifferent judge, with authority to determine all differences according to the established law. For everyone in that state being both judge and executioner of the law of nature, men being partial to themselves, passion and revenge is very apt to carry them too far, and with too much heat, in their own cases; as well as negligence, and unconcernedness, to make them too remiss in other men's.

126. Thirdly, In the state of nature, there often wants power to back and support the sentence when right, and to give it due execution. They who by any injustice offended, will seldom fail, where they are able, by force to make good their injustice; such resistance many times makes the punishment dangerous, and frequently destructive, to those who attempt it.

127. Thus mankind, notwithstanding all the privileges of the state of nature, being but in an ill condition, while they remain in it, are quickly driven into society. Hence it comes to pass that we seldom find any number of men live any time together in this state. The inconveniencies that they are therein exposed to, by the irregular and uncertain exercise of the power every man has of punishing the transgressions of others, make them take sanctuary under the established laws of government, and therein seek the preservation of their property. It is this makes them so willingly give up every one his single power of punishing, to be exercised by such alone, as shall be

appointed to it amongst them; and by such rules as the community, or those authorized by them to that purpose, shall agree on. And in this we have the original right and rise of both the legislative and executive power, as well as of the governments and societies themselves.

128. For in the state of nature, to omit the liberty he has of innocent delights, a man has two powers.

The first is to do whatsoever he thinks fit for the preservation of himself and others within the permission of the law of nature: by which law, common to them all, he and all the rest of mankind are one community, make up one society, distinct from all other creatures. And, were it not for the corruption and viciousness of degenerate men, there would be no need of any other; no necessity that men should separate from this great and natural community, and by positive agreements combine into smaller and divided associations.

The other power a man has in the state of nature, is the power to punish the crimes committed against that law. Both these he gives up, when he joins in a private, if I may so call it, or particular politic society, and incorporates into any commonwealth, separate from the rest of mankind.

129. The first power, viz. of doing whatsoever he thought fit for the preservation of himself, and the rest of mankind, he gives up to be regulated by laws made by the society, so far forth as the preservation of himself and the rest of that society shall require; which laws of the society in many things confine the liberty he had by the law of nature.

130. Secondly, The power of punishing he wholly gives up, and engages his natural force, (which he might before employ in the execution of the law of nature, by his own single authority, as he thought fit) to assist the executive power of the society, as the law thereof shall require. For being now in a new state, wherein he is to enjoy many conveniencies, from the labour, assistance, and society of others in the same community, as well as protection from its whole strength; he is to

part also, with as much of his natural liberty, in providing for himself, as the good, prosperity, and safety of the society shall require; which is not only necessary, but just, since the other members of the society do the like.

131. But though men, when they enter into society, give up the equality, liberty, and executive power they had in the state of nature, into the hands of the society, to be so far disposed of by the legislative, as the good of the society shall require; yet it being only with an intention in everyone the better to preserve himself, his liberty and property; (for no rational creature can be supposed to change his condition with an intention to be worse) the power of the society, or legislative constituted by them, can never be supposed to extend farther, than the common good; but is obliged to secure everyone's property, by providing against those three defects above mentioned, that made the state of nature so unsafe and uneasy. And so whoever has the legislative or supreme power of any commonwealth, is bound to govern by established standing laws, promulgated and known to the people, and not by extemporary decrees; by indifferent and upright judges, who are to decide controversies by those laws; and to employ the force of the community at home, only in the execution of such laws; or abroad to prevent or redress foreign injuries, and secure the community from inroads and invasion. And all this to be directed to no other end, but the peace, safety, and public good of the people.

CHAPTER XI

Of the Extent of the Legislative Power

134. The great end of men's entering into society being the enjoyment of their properties in peace and safety, and the great instrument and means of that being the laws established in that society; the first and fundamental positive law of all commonwealths is the establishing of the legislative power; as the first and fundamental natural law, which is to govern even the legislative itself, is

the preservation of the society, and (as far as will consist with the public good) of every person in it. This legislative is not only the supreme power of the commonwealth, but sacred and unalterable in the hands where the community have once placed it; nor can any edict of anybody else, in what form soever conceived, or by what power soever backed, have the force and obligation of a law, which has not its sanction from that legislative which the public has chosen and appointed; for without this the law could not have that, which is absolutely necessary to its being a law, the consent of the society; over whom nobody can have a power to make laws, but by their own consent, and by authority received from them; and therefore all the obedience, which by the most solemn ties any one can be obliged to pay, ultimately terminates in this supreme power, and is directed by those laws which it enacts; nor can any oaths to any foreign power whatsoever, or any domestic subordinate power, discharge any member of the society from his obedience to the legislative, acting pursuant to their trust; nor oblige him to any obedience contrary to the laws so enacted, or farther than they do allow; it being ridiculous to imagine one can be tied ultimately to obey any power in the society, which is not the supreme.

135. Though the legislative, whether placed in one or more, whether it be always in being, or only by intervals, though it be the supreme power in every commonwealth; yet,

First, It is not, nor can possibly be absolutely arbitrary over the lives and fortunes of the people. For it being but the joint power of every member of the society given up to that person, or assembly, which is legislator, it can be no more than those persons had in a state of nature before they entered into society, and gave up to the community. For nobody can transfer to another more power than he has in himself; and nobody has an absolute arbitrary power over himself, or over any other, to destroy his own life, or take away the life or property of another. A man, as has been proved, cannot subject himself to the arbitrary power of another; and having in the state

of nature no arbitrary power over the life, liberty, or possession of another, but only so much as the law of nature gave him for the preservation of himself and the rest of mankind; this is all he doth, or can give up to the commonwealth, and by it to the legislative power, so that the legislative can have no more than this. Their power, in the utmost bounds of it, is limited to the public good of the society. It is a power, that has no other end but preservation, and therefore can never have a right to destroy, enslave, or designedly to impoverish the subjects. The obligations of the law of nature cease not in society, but only in many cases are drawn closer, and have by human laws known penalties annexed to them, to enforce their observation. Thus the law of nature stands as an eternal rule to all men, legislators as well as others. The rules that they make for other men's actions, must, as well as their own and other men's actions, be conformable to the law of nature, i.e. to the will of God, of which that is a declaration; and the fundamental law of nature being the preservation of mankind, no human sanction can be good or valid against it.

136. Secondly, The legislative or supreme authority cannot assume to itself a power to rule, by extemporary, arbitrary decrees, but is bound to dispense justice, and decide the rights of the subject, by promulgated, standing laws, and known authorised judges. For the law of nature being unwritten, and so nowhere to be found, but in the minds of men; they who through passion, or interest, shall miscite, or misapply it, cannot so easily be convinced of their mistake, where there is no established judge: and so it serves not, as it ought, to determine the rights, and fence the properties of those that live under it; especially where everyone is judge, interpreter, and executioner of it too, and that in his own case: and he that has right on his side having ordinarily but his own single strength, has not force enough to defend himself from injuries, or to punish delinquents. To avoid these inconveniencies, which disorder men's properties in the state of nature, men unite into societies, that they may have the united strength of the

whole society to secure and defend their properties, and may have standing rules to bound it, by which everyone may know what is his. To this end it is that men give up all their natural power to the society which they enter into, and the community put the legislative power into such hands as they think fit: with this trust, that they shall be governed by declared laws, or else their peace, quiet, and property will still be at the same uncertainty, as it was in the state of nature.

137. Absolute arbitrary power, or governing without settled standing laws, can neither of them consist with the ends of society and government, which men would not quit the freedom of the state of nature for, and tie themselves up under, were it not to preserve their lives, liberties, and fortunes, and by stated rules of right and property to secure their peace and quiet. It cannot be supposed that they should intend, had they a power so to do, to give to anyone, or more, an absolute arbitrary power over their persons and estates, and put a force into the magistrate's hand to execute his unlimited will arbitrarily upon them. This were to put themselves into a worse condition than the state of nature, wherein they had a liberty to defend their right against the injuries of others, and were upon equal terms of force to maintain it, whether invaded by a single man, or many in combination. Whereas by supposing they have given up themselves to the absolute arbitrary power and will of a legislator, they have disarmed themselves, and armed him, to make a prey of them when he pleases. He being in a much worse condition, who is exposed to the arbitrary power of one man, who has the command of 100,000, than he that is exposed to the arbitrary power of 100,000 single men; nobody being secure, that his will, who has such a command, is better than that of other men, though his force be 100,000 times stronger. And therefore, whatever form the commonwealth is under, the ruling power ought to govern by declared and received laws, and not by extemporary dictates and undetermined resolutions. For then mankind will be in a far worse condition than in the state of nature, if they shall have armed one or

a few men with the joint power of a multitude, to force them to obey at pleasure the exorbitant and unlimited decrees of their sudden thoughts, or unrestrained, and till that moment unknown wills, without having any measures set down which may guide and justify their actions; for all the power the government has, being only for the good of the society, as it ought not to be arbitrary and at pleasure, so it ought to be exercised by established and promulgated laws; that both the people may know their duty, and be safe and secure within the limits of the law, and the rulers too kept within their bounds, and not to be tempted, by the power they have in their hands, to employ it to such purposes, and by such measures, as they would not have known, and own not willingly.

138. Thirdly, The supreme power cannot take from any man part of his property without his own consent. For the preservation of property being the end of government, and that for which men enter into society, it necessarily supposes and requires, that the people should have property, without which they must be supposed to lose that, by entering into society, which was the end for which they entered into it; too gross an absurdity for any man to own. Men therefore in society having property, they have such right to the goods, which by the law of the community are theirs, that nobody has a right to take their substance or any part of it from them, without their own consent; without this they have no property at all. For I have truly no property in that, which another can by right take from me, when he pleases, against my consent. Hence it is a mistake to think, that the supreme or legislative power of any commonwealth can do what it will, and dispose of the estates of the subject arbitrarily, or take any part of them at pleasure. This is not much to be feared in governments where the legislative consists, wholly or in part, in assemblies which are variable, whose members, upon the dissolution of the assembly, are subjects under the common laws of their country, equally with the rest. But in governments, where the legislative is in one lasting assembly always in being, or in one man, as

in absolute monarchies, there is danger still, that they will think themselves to have a distinct interest from the rest of the community; and so will be apt to increase their own riches and power by taking what they think fit from the people. For a man's property is not at all secure, though there be good and equitable laws to set the bounds of it between him and his fellow subjects, if he who commands those subjects, have power to take from any private man, what part he pleases of his property, and use and dispose of it as he thinks good. . . .

140. It is true, governments cannot be supported without great charge, and it is fit everyone who enjoys his share of the protection, should pay out of his estate his proportion for the maintenance of it. But still it must be with his own consent, i.e. the consent of the majority, giving it either by themselves, or their representatives chosen by them. For if anyone shall claim a power to lay and levy taxes on the people, by his own authority, and without such consent of the people, he thereby invades the fundamental law of property, and subverts the end of government. For what property have I in that, which another may by right take when he pleases, to himself?

141. Fourthly, The legislative cannot transfer the power of making laws to any other hands. For it being but a delegated power from the people, they who have it cannot pass it over to others. The people alone can appoint the form of the commonwealth, which is by constituting the legislative, and appointing in whose hands that shall be. And when the people have said, we will submit to rules, and be governed by laws made by such men, and in such forms, nobody else can say other men shall make laws for them; nor can the people be bound by any laws, but such as are enacted by those whom they have chosen, and authorized to make laws for them. The power of the legislative being derived from the people by a positive voluntary grant and institution, can be no other than what that positive grant conveyed, which being only to make laws, and not to make legislators, the legislative can have no power to transfer their

authority of making laws and place it in other hands.

142. These are the bounds which the trust, that is put in them by the society and the law of God and nature, have *set to the legislative* power of every commonwealth, in all forms of government.

First, They are to govern by *promulgated established laws*, not to be varied in particular cases, but to have one rule for rich and poor, for the favourite at court, and the countryman at plough.

Secondly, These laws also ought to be designed for no other end ultimately, but *the good of the people*.

Thirdly, They must *not raise taxes* on the *property of the people, without the consent of the people*, given by themselves or their deputies. And this properly concerns only such governments where the legislative is always in being, or at least where the people have not reserved any part of the legislative to deputies, to be from time to time chosen by themselves.

Fourthly, The legislative neither must *nor can transfer the power of making laws* to any body else, or place it any where, but where the people have.

CHAPTER XII

Of the Legislative, Executive, and Federative Power of the Commonwealth

143. The legislative power is that, which has a right to direct how the force of the commonwealth shall be employed for preserving the community and the members of it. But because those laws which are constantly to be executed, and whose force is always to continue, may be made in a little time; therefore there is no need, that the legislative should be always in being, not having always business to do. And because it may be too great a temptation to human frailty, apt to grasp at power, for the same persons, who have the power of making laws, to have also in their hands the power to execute them, whereby they may exempt themselves from obedience to the laws they make, and suit the law, both in its making and execution,

to their own private advantage, and thereby come to have a distinct interest from the rest of the community, contrary to the end of society and government: therefore in well ordered commonwealths, where the good of the whole is so considered, as it ought, the legislative power is put into the hands of diverse persons, who, duly assembled, have by themselves, or jointly with others, a power to make laws; which when they have done, being separated again, they are themselves subject to the laws they have made; which is a new and near tie upon them, to take care that they make them for the public good.

144. But because the laws, that are at once, and in a short time made, have a constant and lasting force, and need a perpetual execution, or an attendance thereunto: therefore it is necessary there should be a power always in being, which should see to the execution of the laws that are made, and remain in force. And thus the legislative and executive power come often to be separated.

145. There is another power in every commonwealth, which one may call natural, because it is that which answers to the power every man naturally had before he entered into society. For though in a commonwealth, the members of it are distinct persons still in reference to one another, and as such are governed by the laws of the society; yet in reference to the rest of mankind, they make one body, which is, as every member of it before was, still in the state of nature with the rest of mankind. Hence it is, that the controversies that happen between any man of the society with those that are out of it, are managed by the public; and an injury done to a member of their body engages the whole in the reparation of it. So that, under this consideration, the whole community is one body in the state of nature, in respect of all other states or persons out of its community.

146. This therefore contains the power of war and peace, leagues and alliances, and all the transactions, with all persons and communities without the commonwealth; and may be called federative,

if anyone pleases. So the thing be understood, I am indifferent as to the name.

147. These two powers, executive and federative, though they be really distinct in themselves, yet one comprehending the execution of the municipal laws of the society within itself, upon all that are parts of it; the other the management of the security and interest of the public without, with all those that it may receive benefit or damage from; yet they are always almost united. And though this federative power in the well or ill management of it be of great moment to the commonwealth, yet it is much less capable to be directed by antecedent, standing, positive laws, than the executive; and so must necessarily be left to the prudence and wisdom of those whose hands it is in, to be managed for the public good. For the laws that concern subjects one amongst another, being to direct their actions, may well enough precede them. But what is to be done in reference to foreigners, depending much upon their actions, and the variation of designs, and interests, must be left in great part to the prudence of those who have this power committed to them, to be managed by the best of their skill, for the advantage of the commonwealth.

CHAPTER XIII

Of the Subordination of the Powers of the Commonwealth

149. Though in a constituted commonwealth, standing upon its own basis, and acting according to its own nature, that is, acting for the preservation of the community, there can be but *one supreme power*, which is the *legislative*, to which all the rest are and must be subordinate; yet the legislative being only a fiduciary power to act for certain ends, there remains still *in the people a supreme power to remove or alter the legislative*, when they find the legislative act contrary to the trust reposed in them. For all *power given with trust* for the attaining an end, being limited by that end; whenever that end is manifestly neglected or

opposed, the trust must necessarily be forfeited, and the power devolve into the hands of those that gave it, who may place it anew where they shall think best for their safety and security. And thus the *community* perpetually *retains a supreme power* of saving themselves from the attempts and designs of any body, even of their legislators, whenever they shall be so foolish, or so wicked, as to lay and carry on designs against the liberties and properties of the subject. For no man, or society of men, having a power to deliver up their preservation, or consequently the means of it, to the absolute will and arbitrary dominion of another; whenever any one shall go about to bring them into such a slavish condition, they will always have a right to preserve what they have not a power to part with; and to rid themselves of those who invade this fundamental, sacred, and unalterable law of self-preservation, for which they entered into society. And thus the community may be said in this respect to be *always the supreme power*, but not as considered under any form of government, because this power of the people can never take place till the government be dissolved.

150. In all cases, whilst the government subsists, the *legislative is the supreme power*. For what can give laws to another, must needs be superior to him; and since the legislative is no otherwise legislative of the society, but by the right it has to make laws for all the parts, and for every member of the society, prescribing rules to their actions, and giving power of execution, where they are transgressed; the legislative must needs be the supreme, and all other powers, in any members or parts of the society, derived from and subordinate to it.

151. In some commonwealths, where the legislative is not always in being, and the executive is vested in a single person, who has also a share in the legislative; there that single person in a very tolerable sense may also be called supreme; not that he has in himself all the supreme power, which is that of law-making; but because he has in him the supreme execution, from whom all inferiour magistrates derive all their several subordinate powers, or at least the greatest part of them: having also no legislative superiour to him, there being no law to be made without his consent, which cannot be expected should ever subject him to the other part of the legislative, he is properly enough in this sense *supreme*. But yet it is to be observed, that though *oaths of allegiance* and fealty are taken to him, it is not to him as supreme legislator, but as *supreme executor* of the law, made by a joint power of him with others: allegiance being nothing but an *obedience according to law*, which when he violates, he has no right to obedience, nor can claim it otherwise, than as the public person invested with the power of the law; and so is to be considered as the image, phantom, or representative of the commonwealth, acted by the will of the society, declared in its laws; and thus he has no will, no power, but that of the law. But when he quits this representation, this public will, and acts by his own private will, he degrades himself, and is but a single private person without power, and without will, that has no right to obedience; the members owing no obedience but to the public will of the society.

152. The *executive power*, placed any where but in a person that has also a share in the legislative, is visibly subordinate and accountable to it, and may be at pleasure changed and displaced; so that it is not the *supreme executive power* that is exempt from subordination, but the *supreme executive power* vested in one, who having a share in the legislative, has no distinct superiour legislative to be subordinate and accountable to, farther than he himself shall join and consent; so that he is no more subordinate than he himself shall think fit, which one may certainly conclude will be but very little. Of other ministerial and subordinate powers in a commonwealth, we need not speak, they being so multiplied with infinite variety in the different customs and constitutions of distinct commonwealths, that it is impossible to give a particular account of them all. Only thus much, which is necessary to our present purpose, we may take notice of concerning them, that they have no

manner of authority, any of them, beyond what is by positive grant and commission delegated to them, and are all of them accountable to some other power in the commonwealth.

CHAPTER XVIII

Of Tyranny

199. As usurpation is the exercise of power, which another has a right to, so tyranny is the exercise of power beyond right, which nobody can have a right to. And this is making use of the power anyone has in his hands, not for the good of those who are under it, but for his own private separate advantage. When the governor, however entitled, makes not the law, but his will, the rule; and his commands and actions are not directed to the preservation of the properties of his people, but the satisfaction of his own ambition, revenge, covetousness, or any other irregular passion.

201. It is a mistake to think this fault is proper only to monarchies; other forms of government are liable to it, as well as that. For wherever the power, that is put in any hands for the government of the people, and the preservation of their properties, is applied to other ends, and made use of to impoverish, harass, or subdue them to the arbitrary and irregular commands of those that have it; there it presently becomes tyranny, whether those that thus use it are one or many. . . .

202. Wherever law ends, tyranny begins, if the law be transgressed to another's harm; and whosoever in authority exceeds the power given him by the law, and makes use of the force he has under his command, to compass that upon the subject, which the law allows not, ceases in that to be a magistrate; and, acting without authority, may be opposed as any other man, who by force invades the right of another. This is acknowledged in subordinate magistrates. He that has authority to seize my person in the street, may be opposed as a thief and a robber if he endeavours to break into my house to execute a writ, notwithstanding that I know he has such a warrant, and such

a legal authority, as will empower him to arrest me abroad. And why this should not hold in the highest, as well as in the most inferior magistrate, I would gladly be informed. Is it reasonable that the eldest brother, because he has the greatest part of his father's estate, should thereby have a right to take away any of his younger brother's portions? Or, that a rich man, who possessed a whole country, should from thence have a right to seize, when he pleased, the cottage and garden of his poor neighbour? The being rightfully possessed of great power and riches, exceedingly beyond the greatest part of the sons of Adam, is so far from being an excuse, much less a reason for rapine and oppression, which the endamaging another without authority is, that it is a great aggravation of it. For the exceeding the bounds of authority is no more a right in a great, than in a petty officer; no more justifiable in a king than a constable; but is so much the worse in him, in that he has more trust put in him, has already a much greater share than the rest of his brethren, and is supposed, from the advantages of his education, employment, and counsellors, to be more knowing in the measures of right or wrong.

203. May the commands then of a prince be opposed? may he be resisted as often as anyone shall find himself aggrieved, and but imagine he has not right done him? This will unhinge and overturn all polities, and, instead of government and order, leave nothing but anarchy and confusion.

204. To this I answer, that force is to be opposed to nothing but to unjust and unlawful force; whoever makes any opposition in any other case, draws on himself a just condemnation both from God and man; and so no such danger or confusion will follow, as is often suggested. . . .

CHAPTER XIX

Of the Dissolution of Government

211. He that will with any clearness speak of the dissolution of government, ought in the first place to distinguish between the dissolution of the

society and the dissolution of the government. That which makes the community, and brings men out of the loose state of nature into one politic society, is the agreement which everyone has with the rest to incorporate, and act as one body, and so be one distinct commonwealth. The usual, and almost only way whereby this union is dissolved, is the inroad of foreign force making a conquest upon them. For in that case, (not being able to maintain and support themselves, as one entire and independent body) the union belonging to that body which consisted therein, must necessarily cease, and so everyone return to the state he was in before, with a liberty to shift for himself, and provide for his own safety, as he thinks fit, in some other society. Whenever the society is dissolved, it is certain the government of that society cannot remain. Thus conquerors' swords often cut up governments by the roots, and mangle societies to pieces, separating the subdued or scattered multitude from the protection of, and dependence on, that society which ought to have preserved them from violence. The world is too well instructed in, and too forward to allow of, this way of dissolving of governments, to need any more to be said of it; and there wants not much argument to prove, that where the society is dissolved, the government cannot remain; that being as impossible, as for the frame of a house to subsist when the materials of it are scattered and dissipated by a whirlwind, or jumbled into a confused heap by an earthquake.

212. Besides this overturning from without, governments are dissolved from within.

First, When the legislative is altered. Civil society being a state of peace, amongst those who are of it, from whom the state of war is excluded by the umpirage, which they have provided in their legislative, for the ending all differences that may arise amongst any of them; it is in their legislative, that the members of a commonwealth are united, and combined together into one coherent living body. This is the soul that gives form, life, and unity to the commonwealth: from hence the several members have their mutual influence, sympathy, and connection; and therefore, when the legislative is broken, or dissolved, dissolution and death follows. For, the essence and union of the society consisting in having one will, the legislative, when once established by the majority, has the declaring, and as it were keeping of that will. The constitution of the legislative is the first and fundamental act of society, whereby provision is made for the continuation of their union, under the direction of persons, and bonds of laws, made by persons authorized thereunto, by the consent and appointment of the people; without which no one man, or number of men, amongst them, can have authority of making laws that shall be binding to the rest. When anyone, or more, shall take upon them to make laws, whom the people have not appointed so to do, they make laws without authority, which the people are not therefore bound to obey; by which means they come again to be out of subjection, and may constitute to themselves a new legislative, as they think best, being in full liberty to resist the force of those, who without authority would impose anything upon them. Every one is at the disposure of his own will, when those who had, by the delegation of the society, the declaring of the public will, are excluded from it, and others usurp the place, who have no such authority or delegation.

220. In these and the like cases, *when the government is dissolved*, the people are at liberty to provide for themselves, by erecting a new legislative, differing from the other, by the change of persons, or form, or both, as they shall find it most for their safety and good. For the *society* can never, by the fault of another, lose the native and original right it has to preserve itself; which can only be done by a settled legislative, and a fair and impartial execution of the laws made by it. But the state of mankind is not so miserable that they are not capable of using this remedy, till it be too late to look for any. To tell *people* they *may provide for themselves*, by erecting a new legislative, when by oppression, artifice, or being delivered over to a foreign power, their old one is gone, is only to tell them, they may expect relief when it

is too late, and the evil is past cure. This is in effect no more, than to bid them first be slaves, and then to take care of their liberty; and when their chains are on, tell them, they may act like freemen. This, if barely so, is rather mockery than relief; and men can never be secure from tyranny, if there be no means to escape it, till they are perfectly under it: And therefore it is, that they have not only a right to get out of it, but to prevent it.

221. There is, therefore, secondly, another way whereby governments are dissolved, and that is, when the legislative, or the prince either of them, act contrary to their trust.

First, The legislative acts against the trust reposed in them, when they endeavour to invade the property of the subject, and to make themselves, or any part of the community, masters, or arbitrary disposers of the lives, liberties, or fortunes of the people.

222. The reason why men enter into society, is the preservation of their property; and the end why they choose and authorize a legislative, is, that there may be laws made, and rules set, as guards and fences to the properties of all the members of the society: to limit the power, and moderate the dominion, of every part and member of the society. For since it can never be supposed to be the will of the society, that the legislative should have a power to destroy that, which everyone designs to secure, by entering into society, and for which the people submitted themselves to legislators of their own making, whenever the legislators endeavour to take away and destroy the property of the people, or to reduce them to slavery under arbitrary power, they put themselves into a state of war with the people, who are thereupon absolved from any farther obedience, and are left to the common refuge, which God hath provided for all men, against force and violence. Whensoever therefore the legislative shall transgress this fundamental rule of society; and either by ambition, fear, folly or corruption, endeavour to grasp themselves, or put into the hands of any other an absolute power over the lives, liberties, and estates of the people; by this breach of trust they forfeit

the power, the people had put into their hands, for quite contrary ends, and it devolves to the people, who have a right to resume their original liberty, and, by the establishment of a new legislative, (such as they shall think fit) provide for their own safety and security, which is the end for which they are in society. What I have said here, concerning the legislative in general, holds true also concerning the supreme executor, who having a double trust put in him, both to have a part in the legislative, and the supreme execution of the law, acts against both, when he goes about to set up his own arbitrary will, as the law of the society. He acts also contrary to his trust, when he either employs the force, treasure, and offices of the society to corrupt the representatives, and gain them to his purposes; or openly pre-engages the electors, and prescribes to their choice, such, whom he has by solicitations, threats, promises, or otherwise, won to his designs: and employs them to bring in such, who have promised before-hand, what to vote, and what to enact. Thus to regulate candidates and electors, and new model the ways of election, what is it but to cut up the government by the roots, and poison the very fountain of public security? for the people having reserved to themselves the choice of their representatives, as the fence to their properties, could do it for no other end, but that they might always be freely chosen, and so chosen, freely act, and advise, as the necessity of the commonwealth, and the public good should, upon examination and mature debate, be judged to require. This, those who give their votes before they hear the debate, and have weighed the reasons on all sides, are not capable of doing. To prepare such an assembly as this, and endeavour to set up the declared abettors of his own will, for the true representatives of the people, and the lawmakers of the society, is certainly as great a breach of trust, and as perfect a declaration of a design to subvert the government, as is possible to be met with. To which if one shall add rewards and punishments visibly employed to the same end, and all the arts of perverted law made use of, to take off and destroy all that stand in the way of such a design, and will not comply and consent to betray the liberties of their country, it will be past doubt what is doing. What power they ought to have in the society, who thus employ it contrary to the trust that went along with it in its first institution, is easy to determine; and one cannot but see, that he, who has once attempted any such thing as this, cannot any longer be trusted.

223. To this perhaps it will be said, that the people being ignorant, and always discontented, to lay the foundation of government in the unsteady opinion and uncertain humour of the people, is to expose it to certain ruin; and no government will be able long to subsist, if the people may set up a new legislative, whenever they take offence at the old one. To this I answer, quite the contrary. People are not so easily got out of their old forms as some are apt to suggest. They are hardly to be prevailed with to amend the acknowledged faults in the frame they have been accustomed to. And if there be any original defects, or adventitious ones introduced by time, or corruption: it is not an easy thing to get them changed, even when all the world sees there is an opportunity for it. This slowness and aversion in the people to quit their old constitutions, has in the many revolutions which have been seen in this kingdom, in this and former ages, still kept us to, or, after some interval of fruitless attempts, still brought us back again to, our old legislative of king, lords, and commons: and whatever provocations have made the crown be taken from some of our princes heads, they never carried the people so far as to place it in another line.

224. But it will be said, this hypothesis lays a ferment for frequent rebellion. To which I answer,

First, No more than any other hypothesis: for when the people are made miserable, and find themselves exposed to the ill usage of arbitrary power, cry up their governors as much as you will, for sons of Jupiter; let them be sacred or divine, descended, or authorized from heaven; give them out for whom or what you please, the same will happen. The people generally ill treated, and contrary to right, will be ready upon any occasion to ease themselves of a burden that sits heavy upon them. They will wish, and seek for the opportunity, which in the change, weakness, and accidents of human affairs, seldom delays long to offer itself. He must have lived but a little while in the world, who has not seen examples of this in his time; and he must have read very little, who cannot produce examples of it in all sorts of governments in the world.

225. Secondly, I answer, such revolutions happen not upon every little mismanagement in public affairs. Great mistakes in the ruling part, many wrong and inconvenient laws, and all the slips of human frailty, will be borne by the people without mutiny or murmur. But if a long train of abuses, prevarications and artifices, all tending the same way, make the design visible to the people, and they cannot but feel what they lie under, and see whither they are going; it is not to be wondered, that they should then rouse themselves, and endeavour to put the rule into such hands which may secure to them the ends for which government was at first erected; and without which, ancient names, and specious forms, are so far from being better, that they are much worse, than the state of nature, or pure anarchy; the inconveniencies being all as great and as near, but the remedy farther off and more difficult.

226. Thirdly, I answer, that this doctrine of a power in the people of providing for their safety anew, by a new legislative, when their legislators have acted contrary to their trust, by invading their property, is the best fence against rebellion, and the probablest means to hinder it. For rebellion being an opposition, not to persons, but authority, which is founded only in the constitutions and laws of the government; those, whoever they be, who by force break through, and by force justify their violation of them, are truly and properly rebels. For when men, by entering into society and civil government, have excluded force, and introduced laws for the preservation of property, peace, and unity amongst themselves; those who set up force again in opposition to the laws, do *rebellare*, that is, bring back again the state of war, and are

properly rebels: Which they who are in power, (by the pretence they have to authority, the temptation of force they have in their hands, and the flattery of those about them) being likeliest to do; the properest way to prevent the evil, is to show them the danger and injustice of it, who are under the greatest temptation to run into it.

227. In both the forementioned cases, when either the legislative is changed, or the legislators act contrary to the end for which they were constituted, those who are guilty are guilty of rebellion; for if anyone by force takes away the established legislative of any society, and the laws by them made pursuant to their trust, he thereby takes away the umpirage, which everyone had consented to, for a peaceable decision of all their controversies, and a bar to the state of war amongst them. They who remove, or change the legislative, take away this decisive power, which nobody can have but by the appointment and consent of the people; and so destroying the authority which the people did, and nobody else can set up, and introducing a power which the people have not authorized, they actually introduce a state of war, which is that of force without authority; and thus by removing the legislative established by the society, (in whose decisions the people acquiesced and united, as to that of their own will) they untie the knot, and expose the people anew to the state of war. And if those, who by force take away the legislative, are rebels, the legislators themselves, as has been shown, can be no less esteemed so; when they, who were set up for the protection and preservation of the people, their liberties and properties, shall by force invade and endeavour to take them away; and so they putting themselves into a state of war with those who made them the protectors and guardians of their peace, are properly, and with the greatest aggravation, *rebellantes*, rebels.

228. But if they, who say, "it lays a foundation for rebellion," mean that it may occasion civil wars, or intestine broils, to tell the people they are absolved from obedience when, illegal attempts are made upon their liberties or properties, and

may oppose the unlawful violence of those who were their magistrates, when they invade their properties contrary to the trust put in them; and that therefore this doctrine is not to be allowed, being so destructive to the peace of the world: they may as well say, upon the same ground, that honest men may not oppose robbers or pirates, because this may occasion disorder or bloodshed. If any *mischief* come in such cases, it is not to be charged upon him who defends his own right, but on *him that invades* his neighbour's. If the innocent honest man must quietly quit all he has, for peace sake, to him who will lay violent hands upon it, I desire it may be considered, what a kind of peace there will be in the world, which consists only in violence and rapine; and which is to be maintained only for the benefit of robbers and oppressors. Who would not think it an admirable peace betwixt the mighty and the mean, when the lamb, without resistance, yielded his throat to be torn by the imperious wolf? Polyphemus's den gives us a perfect pattern of such a peace, and such a government, wherein Ulysses and his companions had nothing to do, but quietly to suffer themselves to be devoured. And no doubt Ulysses, who was a prudent man, preached up *passive obedience*, and exhorted them to a quiet submission, by representing to them of what concernment peace was to mankind; and by shewing the inconveniencies might happen, if they should offer to resist Polyphemus, who had now the power over them.

229. The end of government is the good of mankind: and which is *best for mankind*, that the people should be always exposed to the boundless will of tyranny; or that the rulers should be sometimes liable to be opposed, when they grow exorbitant in the use of their power, and employ it for the destruction, and not the preservation of the properties of their people?

230. Nor let any one say, that mischief can arise from hence, as often as it shall please a busy head, or turbulent spirit, to desire the alteration of the government. It is true, such men may stir, whenever they please; but it will be only to their own just ruin and perdition. For till the mischief

be grown general, and the ill designs of the rulers become visible, or their attempts sensible to the greater part, the people, who are more disposed to suffer than right themselves by resistance, are not apt to stir. The examples of particular injustice or oppression, of here and there an unfortunate man, moves them not. But if they universally have a persuasion, grounded upon manifest evidence, that designs are carrying on against their liberties, and the general course and tendency of things cannot but give them strong suspicions of the evil intention of their governors, who is to be blamed for it? Who can help it, if they, who might avoid it, bring themselves into this suspicion? Are the people to be blamed, if they have the sense of rational creatures, and can think of things no otherwise than as they find and feel them? And is it not rather *their fault*, who put things into such a posture, that they would not have them thought to be as they are? I grant, that the pride, ambition, and turbulency of private men, have sometimes caused great disorders in commonwealths, and factions have been fatal to states and kingdoms. But whether *the mischief* hath *oftener* begun *in the peoples wantonness*, and a desire to cast off the lawful authority of their rulers, or in *the rulers insolence*, and endeavours to get and exercise an arbitrary power over their people; whether oppression, or disobedience, gave the first rise to the disorder; I leave it to impartial history to determine. This I am sure, whoever, either ruler or subject, by force goes about to invade the rights of either prince or people, and lays the foundation for *overturning* the constitution and frame of *any just government;* is highly guilty of the greatest crime, I think, a man is capable of; being to answer for all those mischiefs of blood, rapine, and desolation, which the breaking to pieces of governments bring on a country. And he who does it, is justly to be esteemed the common enemy and pest of mankind, and is to be treated accordingly. . . .

243. To conclude, The power that every individual gave the society, when he entered into it, can never revert to the individuals again, as long as the society lasts, but will always remain in the community; because without this there can be no community, no commonwealth, which is contrary to the original agreement: so also when the society has placed the legislative in any assembly of men, to continue in them and their successors, with direction and authority for providing such successors, the legislative can never revert to the people whilst that government lasts: Because, having provided a legislative with power to continue forever, they have given up their political power to the legislative, and cannot resume it. But if they have set limits to the duration of their legislative, and made this supreme power in any person, or assembly, only temporary; or else, when by the miscarriages of those in authority, it is forfeited; upon the forfeiture, or at the determination of the time set, it reverts to the society, and the people have a right to act as supreme, and continue the legislative in themselves; or erect a new form, or under the old form place it in new hands, as they think good.

Letter Concerning Toleration

HONORED SIR,

Since you are pleased to inquire what are my thoughts about the mutual toleration of Christians in their different professions of religion, I must needs answer you freely that I esteem that toleration to be the chief characteristic mark of the true church. For whatsoever some people boast of the antiquity of places and names, or of the pomp of their outward worship; others, of the reformation of their discipline; all, of the orthodoxy of their faith—for everyone is orthodox to himself—these things, and all others of this nature, are much rather marks of men striving for power and empire over one another than of the church of Christ. Let anyone have never so true a claim to all these things, yet if he be destitute of charity, meekness, and goodwill in general toward all mankind, even to those that are not Christians, he is certainly yet short of being a true Christian himself. "The kings of the Gentiles exercise lordship over them," said our Saviour to His disciples, "but ye shall not be so" [Luke 22:25]. The business of true religion is quite another thing. It is not instituted in order to the erecting of an external pomp, nor to the obtaining of ecclesiastical dominion, nor to the exercising of compulsive force, but to the regulating of men's lives, according to the rules of virtue and piety. Whosoever will list himself under the banner of Christ must in the first place, and above all things, make war upon his own lusts and vices. It is in vain for any man to usurp the name of Christian without holiness of life, purity of manners, benignity and meekness of spirit. "Let everyone that nameth the name of Christ, depart from iniquity" [2 Tim. 2:19]. "Thou, when thou art converted, strengthen thy brethren," said our Lord to Peter [Luke 22:32]. It would, indeed, be very hard for one that appears careless about his salvation to persuade me that he were extremely concerned for mine. For it is impossible that those should sincerely and heartily apply themselves to make other people Christians who have not really embraced the Christian religion in their own hearts. If the Gospel and the apostles may be credited, no man can be a Christian without charity, and without that faith which works, not by force, but by love. Now I appeal to the consciences of those that persecute, torment, destroy, and kill other men upon pretense of religion, whether they do it out of friendship and kindness toward them or no? And I shall then indeed, and not until then, believe they do so, when I shall see those fiery zealots correcting, in the same manner, their friends and familiar acquaintance for the manifest sins they commit against the precepts of the Gospel; when I shall see them persecute with fire and sword the members of their own communion that are tainted with enormous vices, and without amendment are in danger of eternal perdition;

and when I shall see them thus express their love and desire of the salvation of their souls by the infliction of torments and exercise of all manner of cruelties. For if it be out of a principle of charity, as they pretend, and love to men's souls, that they deprive them of their estates, maim them with corporal punishments, starve and torment them in noisome prisons, and in the end even take away their lives—I say, if all this be done merely to make men Christians and procure their salvation, why then do they suffer whoredom, fraud, malice, and suchlike enormities, which (according to the apostle [Rom. 1]) manifestly relish of heathenish corruption, to predominate so much and abound amongst their flocks and people? These, and suchlike things, are certainly more contrary to the glory of God, to the purity of the church, and to the salvation of souls, than any conscientious dissent from ecclesiastical decisions, or separation from public worship, whilst accompanied with innocence of life. Why then does this burning zeal for God, for the church, and for the salvation of souls—burning I say, literally, with fire and faggot—moral vices and wickednesses, without any chastisement, which are acknowledged by all men to be diametrically opposite to the profession of Christianity, and bend all its nerves either to the introducing of ceremonies, or to the establishment of opinions, which for the most part are about nice and intricate matters that exceed the capacity of ordinary understandings? Which of the parties contending about these things is in the right, which of them is guilty of schism or heresy, whether those that domineer or those that suffer, will then at last be manifest when the causes of their separation comes to be judged of. He, certainly, that follows Christ embraces His doctrine and bears His yoke, though he forsake both father and mother, separate from the public assemblies and ceremonies of his country, or whomsoever or whatsoever else he relinquishes, will not then be judged a heretic.

Now, though the divisions that are amongst sects should be allowed to be never so obstructive of the salvation of souls; yet, nevertheless, adultery, fornication, uncleanliness, lasciviousness, idolatry, and suchlike things, cannot be denied to be works of the flesh, concerning which the apostle has expressly declared [Gal. 5] that "they who do them shall not inherit the kingdom of God." Whosoever, therefore, is sincerely solicitous about the kingdom of God, and thinks it his duty to endeavor the enlargement of it amongst men, ought to apply himself with no less care and industry to the rooting out of these immoralities than to the extirpation of sects. But if anyone do otherwise, and whilst he is cruel and implacable toward those that differ from him in opinion, he be indulgent to such iniquities and immoralities as are unbecoming the name of a Christian, let such a one talk never so much of the church, he plainly demonstrates by his actions that it is another kingdom he aims at, and not the advancement of the kingdom of God.

That any man should think fit to cause another man—whose salvation he heartily desires—to expire in torments, and that even in an unconverted state, would, I confess, seem very strange to me and I think to any other also. But nobody, surely, will ever believe that such a carriage can proceed from charity, love, or goodwill. If anyone maintain that men ought to be compelled by fire and sword to profess certain doctrines, and conform to this or that exterior worship, without any regard had unto their morals; if anyone endeavor to convert those that are erroneous unto the faith, by forcing them to profess things that they do not believe and allowing them to practice things that the Gospel does not permit, it cannot be doubted indeed but such a one is desirous to have a numerous assembly joined in the same profession with himself; but that he principally intends by those means to compose a truly Christian church is altogether incredible. It is not, therefore, to be wondered at if those who do not really contend for the advancement of the true religion, and of the church of Christ, make use of arms that do not belong to the Christian warfare. If, like the Captain of our salvation, they sincerely desired the good of souls, they would tread in the steps and follow the perfect example of that Prince of Peace, who sent out His soldiers to the subduing of nations, and gathering them into His church, not armed with the sword or other instruments of force, but prepared with the Gospel of peace and with the exemplary holiness of their conversation. This was His method. Though if infidels were to be converted by force, if those that are either blind or obstinate were to be drawn off from their errors by armed soldiers, we know very well that it was much more easy for Him to do it with armies of heavenly legions than for any son of the church, how potent soever, with all his dragoons.

The toleration of those that differ from others in matters of religion is so agreeable to the Gospel of Jesus Christ, and to the genuine reason of mankind, that it seems monstrous for men to be so blind as not to perceive the necessity and advantage of it in so clear a light. I will not here tax the pride and ambition of some, the passion and uncharitable zeal of others. These are faults from which human affairs can perhaps scarce ever be perfectly freed; but yet such as nobody will bear the plain imputation of, without covering them with some specious color; and so pretend to commendation, whilst they are carried away by their own irregular passions. But, however, that some may not color their spirit of persecution and un-Christian cruelty with a pretense of care of the public weal and observation of the laws; and that others, under pretense of religion, may not seek impunity for their libertinism and licentiousness—in a word, that none may impose either upon himself or others by the pretenses of loyalty and obedience to the prince, or of tenderness and sincerity in the worship of God; I esteem it above all things necessary to distinguish exactly the business of civil government from that of religion, and to settle the just bounds that lie between the one and the other. If this be not done, there can be no end put to the controversies that will be always arising between those that have, or at least pretend to have, on the one side, a concernment for the interest of men's souls, and, on the other side, a care of the commonwealth.

The commonwealth seems to me to be a society of men constituted only for the procuring, preserving, and advancing their own civil interests.

Civil interests I call life, liberty, health, and indolency of body; and the possession of outward things, such as money, lands, houses, furniture, and the like.

It is the duty of the civil magistrate, by the impartial execution of equal laws, to secure unto all the people in general, and to every one of his subjects in particular, the just possession of these things belonging to this life. If anyone presume to violate the laws of public justice and equity, established for the preservation of those things, his presumption is to be checked by the fear of punishment consisting of the deprivation or diminution of those civil interests or goods which otherwise he might and ought to enjoy. But seeing no man does willingly suffer himself to be punished by the deprivation of any part of his goods, and much less of his liberty or life, therefore is the magistrate armed with the force and strength of all his subjects, in order to the punishment of those that violate any other man's rights.

Now that the whole jurisdiction of the magistrate reaches only to these civil concernments; and that all civil power, right and dominion is bounded and confined to the only care of promoting these things; and that it neither can nor ought in any manner to be extended to the salvation of souls, these following considerations seem unto me abundantly to demonstrate.

First, because the care of souls is not committed to the civil magistrate any more than to other men. It is not committed unto him, I say, by God; because it appears not that God has ever given any such authority to one man over another, as to compel anyone to his religion. Nor can any such power be vested in the magistrate by the consent of the people, because no man can so far abandon the care of his own salvation as blindly to leave to the choice of any other, whether prince or subject, to prescribe to him what faith or worship he shall embrace. For no man can, if he would, conform his faith to the dictates of another. All the life and power of true religion consist in the inward and full persuasion of the mind; and faith is not faith without believing. Whatever profession we make, to whatever outward worship we conform, if we are not fully satisfied in our own mind that the one is true, and the other well pleasing unto God, such profession and such practice, far from being any furtherance, are indeed great obstacles to our salvation. For in this manner, instead of expiating other sins by the exercise of religion, I say, in offering thus unto God Almighty such a worship as we esteem to be displeasing unto Him, we add unto the number of our other sins those also of hypocrisy and contempt of His Divine Majesty.

In the second place, the care of souls cannot belong to the civil magistrate because his power consists only in outward force; but true and saving religion consists in the inward persuasion of the mind, without which nothing can be acceptable to God. And such is the nature of the understanding that it cannot be compelled to the belief of anything by outward force. Confiscation of estate, imprisonment, torments, nothing of that nature can have any such efficacy as to make men change the inward judgment that they have framed of things.

It may indeed be alleged that the magistrate may make use of arguments, and thereby draw the heterodox into the way of truth and procure their salvation. I grant it; but this is common to him with other men. In teaching, instructing, and redressing the erroneous by reason, he may certainly do what becomes any good man to do. Magistracy does not oblige him to put off either humanity or Christianity; but it is one thing to persuade, another to command; one thing to press with arguments, another with penalties. This civil power alone has a right to do; to the other, goodwill is authority enough. Every man has commission to admonish, exhort, convince another of error, and, by reasoning, to draw him into truth; but to give laws, receive obedience, and compel with the sword, belongs to none but the magistrate. And upon this ground I affirm that the magistrate's power extends not to the establishing of any articles of faith or forms of worship by the force of his laws. For laws are of no force at all without penalties, and penalties in this case are absolutely impertinent, because they are not proper to convince the mind. Neither the profession of any articles of faith, nor the conformity to any outward form of worship (as has been already said), can be available to the salvation of souls unless the truth of the one, and the acceptableness of the other unto God, be thoroughly believed by those that so profess and practice. But penalties are no way capable to produce such belief. It is only light and evidence that can work a change in men's opinions; which light can in no manner proceed from corporal sufferings or any other outward penalties.

In the third place, the care of the salvation of men's souls cannot belong to the magistrate; because, though the rigor of laws and the force of penalties were capable to convince and change men's minds, yet would not that help at all to the salvation of their souls. For there being but one truth, one way to heaven, what hope is there that more men would be led into it if they had no rule but the religion of the court, and were put under the necessity to quit the light of their own reason, and oppose the dictates of their own consciences, and blindly to resign themselves up to the will of their governors and to the religion which either ignorance, ambition, or superstition had chanced to establish in the countries where they were born? In the variety and contradiction of opinions in religion, wherein the princes of the world are as much divided as in their secular interests, the narrow way would be much straitened; one country alone would be in the right, and all the rest of the world put under an obligation of following their princes in the ways that lead to destruction; and that which heightens the absurdity, and very ill suits the notion of a Deity, men would owe their eternal happiness or misery to the places of their nativity.

These considerations, to omit many others that might have been urged to the same purpose, seem unto me sufficient to conclude that all the power of civil government relates only to men's civil interests, is confined to the care of the things of this world, and hath nothing to do with the world to come.

Let us now consider what a church is. A church, then, I take to be a voluntary society of men, joining themselves together of their own accord in order to the public worshiping of God in such manner as they judge acceptable to Him, and effectual to the salvation of their souls.

I say it is a free and voluntary society. Nobody is born a member of any church; otherwise the religion of parents would descend unto children by the same right of inheritance as their temporal estates, and everyone would hold his faith by the same tenure he does his lands, than which nothing can be imagined more absurd. Thus, therefore, that matter stands. No man by nature is bound unto any particular church or sect, but everyone joins himself voluntarily to that society in which he believes he has found that profession and worship which is truly acceptable to God. The hope of salvation, as it was the only cause of his entrance into that communion, so it can be the only reason of his stay there. For if afterwards he discover anything either erroneous in the doctrine or incongruous in the worship of that society to which he has joined himself, why should it not be as free for him to go out as it was to enter? No member of a religious society can be tied with any other bonds but what proceed from the certain expectation of eternal life. A church, then, is a society of members voluntarily uniting to that end.

It follows now that we consider what is the power of this church, and unto what laws it is subject.

Forasmuch as no society, how free soever, or upon whatsoever slight occasion instituted, whether of philosophers for learning, of merchants for commerce, or of men of leisure for mutual conversation and discourse, no church or company, I say, can in the least subsist and hold together, but will presently dissolve and break into pieces, unless it be regulated by some order. Place and time of meeting must be agreed on;

rules for admitting and excluding members must be established; distinction of officers, and putting things into a regular course, and suchlike, cannot be omitted. But since the joining together of several members into this church society, as has already been demonstrated, is absolutely free and spontaneous, it necessarily follows that the right of making its laws can belong to none but the society itself; or, at least (which is the same thing), to those whom the society by common consent has authorized thereunto.

Some, perhaps, may object that no such society can be said to be a true church unless it have in it a bishop or presbyter, with ruling authority derived from the very apostles, and continued down to the present times by an uninterrupted succession.

To these I answer: In the first place, let them show me the edict by which Christ has imposed that law upon His church. And let not any man think me impertinent if in a thing of this consequence I require that the terms of that edict be very express and positive; for the promise He has made us [Matt. 18:20], that wheresoever two or three are gathered together in His name He will be in the midst of them, seems to imply the contrary. Whether such an assembly want anything necessary to a true church, pray do you consider. Certain I am that nothing can be there wanting unto the salvation of souls, which is sufficient to our purpose.

Next, pray observe how great have always been the divisions amongst even those who lay so much stress upon the divine institution and continued succession of a certain order of rulers in the church. Now their very dissension unavoidably puts us upon a necessity of deliberating and, consequently, allows a liberty of choosing that which upon consideration we prefer.

And, in the last place, I consent that these men have a ruler in their church, established by such a long series of succession as they judge necessary, provided I may have liberty at the same time to join myself to that society in which I am persuaded those things are to be found which are necessary to the salvation of my soul. In this manner

ecclesiastical liberty will be preserved on all sides, and no man will have a legislator imposed upon him but whom himself has chosen.

But since men are so solicitous about the true church, I would only ask them here, by the way, if it be not more agreeable to the church of Christ to make the conditions of her communion consist in such things, and such things only, as the Holy Spirit has in the Holy Scriptures declared, in express words, to be necessary to salvation; I ask, I say, whether this be not more agreeable to the church of Christ than for men to impose their own inventions and interpretations upon others as if they were of Divine authority, and to establish by ecclesiastical laws, as absolutely necessary to the profession of Christianity, such things as the Holy Scriptures do either not mention or at least not expressly command? Whosoever requires those things in order to ecclesiastical communion, which Christ does not require in order to life eternal, he may, perhaps, indeed constitute a society accommodated to his own opinion and his own advantage; but how that can be called the church of Christ which is established upon laws that are not His, and which excludes such persons from its communion as He will one day receive into the Kingdom of Heaven, I understand not. But this being not a proper place to inquire into the marks of the true church, I will only mind those that contend so earnestly for the decrees of their own society and that cry out continually, The Church! the Church! with as much noise, and perhaps upon the same principle, as the Ephesian silversmiths did for their Diana; this, I say, I desire to mind them of, that the Gospel frequently declares that the true disciples of Christ must suffer persecution; but that the church of Christ should persecute others, and force others by fire and sword to embrace her faith and doctrine, I could never yet find in any of the books of the New Testament.

The end of a religious society (as has already been said) is the public worship of God and, by means thereof, the acquisition of eternal life. All discipline ought therefore to tend to that end, and all ecclesiastical laws to be thereunto confined.

Nothing ought nor can be transacted in this society relating to the possession of civil and worldly goods. No force is here to be made use of upon any occasion whatsoever. For force belongs wholly to the civil magistrate, and the possession of all outward goods is subject to his jurisdiction.

But, it may be asked, by what means then shall ecclesiastical laws be established if they must be thus destitute of all compulsive power? I answer: They must be established by means suitable to the nature of such things, whereof the external profession and observation—if not proceeding from a thorough conviction and approbation of the mind—is altogether useless and unprofitable. The arms by which the members of this society are to be kept within their duty are exhortations, admonitions, and advices. If by these means the offenders will not be reclaimed and the erroneous convinced, there remains nothing further to be done but that such stubborn and obstinate persons who give no ground to hope for their reformation, should be cast out and separated from the society. This is the last and utmost force of ecclesiastical authority. No other punishment can thereby be inflicted than that, the relation ceasing between the body and the member which is cut off. The person so condemned ceases to be a part of that church.

These things being thus determined, let us inquire, in the next place, how far the duty of toleration extends, and what is required from everyone by it?

And, first, I hold that no church is bound, by the duty of toleration, to retain any such person in her bosom as, after admonition, continues obstinately to offend against the laws of the society. For these being the condition of communion and the bond of the society, if the breach of them were permitted without any animadversion the society would immediately be thereby dissolved. But, nevertheless, in all such cases care is to be taken that the sentence of excommunication, and the execution thereof, carry with it no rough usage of word or action whereby the ejected person may any wise be damnified in body or estate. For all force (as has

often been said) belongs only to the magistrate, nor ought any private persons at any time to use force unless it be in self-defense against unjust violence. Excommunication neither does nor can, deprive the excommunicated person of any of those civil goods that he formerly possessed. All those things belong to the civil government and are under the magistrate's protection. The whole force of excommunication consists only in this: that the resolution of the society in that respect being declared, the union that was between the body and some member comes thereby to be dissolved; and that relation ceasing, the participation of some certain things which the society communicated to its members, and unto which no man has any civil right, comes also to cease. For there is no civil injury done unto the excommunicated person by the church minister's refusing him that bread and wine, in the celebration of the Lord's Supper, which was not bought with his but other men's money.

Secondly, no private person has any right in any manner to prejudice another person in his civil enjoyments because he is of another church or religion. All the rights and franchises that belong to him as a man or as a denizen are inviolably to be preserved to him. These are not the business of religion. No violence nor injury is to be offered him, whether he be Christian or pagan. Nay, we must not content ourselves with the narrow measures of bare justice; charity, bounty, and liberality must be added to it. This the Gospel enjoins, this reason directs, and this that natural fellowship we are born into requires of us. If any man err from the right way, it is his own misfortune, no injury to thee; nor therefore art thou to punish him in the things of this life because thou supposes! he will be miserable in that which is to come.

What I say concerning the mutual toleration of private persons differing from one another in religion, I understand also of particular churches which stand, as it were, in the same relation to each other as private persons among themselves: nor has any one of them any manner of jurisdiction over any other; no, not even when the civil magistrate (as it sometimes happens) comes to be of this or the other communion. For the civil government can give no new right to the church, nor the church to the civil government. So that whether the magistrate join himself to any church, or separate from it, the church remains always as it was before—a free and voluntary society. It neither requires the power of the sword by the magistrate's coming to it, nor does it lose the right of instruction and excommunication by his going from it. This is the fundamental and immutable right of a spontaneous society—that it has power to remove any of its members who transgress the rules of its institution; but it cannot, by the accession of any new members, acquire any right of jurisdiction over those that are not joined with it. And therefore peace, equity, and friendship are always mutually to be observed by particular churches, in the same manner as by private persons, without any pretense of superiority or jurisdiction over one another.

That the thing may be made clearer by an example, let us suppose two churches—the one of Arminians, the other of Calvinists—residing in the city of Constantinople. Will anyone say that either of these churches has right to deprive the members of the other of their estates and liberty (as we see practiced elsewhere), because of their differing from it in some doctrines and ceremonies, whilst the Turks in the meanwhile silently stand by and laugh to see with what inhuman cruelty Christians thus rage against Christians? But if one of these churches hath this power of treating the other ill, I ask which of them it is to whom that power belongs, and by what right? It will be answered, undoubtedly, that it is the orthodox church which has the right of authority over the erroneous or heretical. This is, in great and specious words, to say just nothing at all. For every church is orthodox to itself; to others, erroneous or heretical. For whatsoever any church believes it believes to be true; and the contrary unto those things it pronounces to be error. So that the controversy between these churches about the truth of their doctrines and the purity of their worship is on both sides equal; nor is there any judge,

either at Constantinople or elsewhere upon earth, by whose sentence it can be determined. The decision of that question belongs only to the Supreme Judge of all men, to whom also alone belongs the punishment of the erroneous. In the meanwhile, let those men consider how heinously they sin, who, adding injustice, if not to their error, yet certainly to their pride, do rashly and arrogantly take upon them to misuse the servants of another master, who are not at all accountable to them.

Nay, further: if it could be manifest which of these two dissenting churches were in the right, there would not accrue thereby unto the orthodox any right of destroying the other. For churches have neither any jurisdiction in worldly matters, nor are fire and sword any proper instruments wherewith to convince men's minds of error, and inform them of the truth. Let us suppose, nevertheless, that the civil magistrate inclined to favor one of them and to put his sword into their hands, that (by his consent) they might chastise the dissenters as they pleased. Will any man say that any right can be derived unto a Christian church over its brethren from a Turkish emperor? An infidel, who has himself no authority to punish Christians for the articles of their faith, cannot confer such an authority upon any society of Christians, nor give unto them a right which he has not himself. This would be the case at Constantinople; and the reason of the thing is the same in any Christian kingdom. The civil power is the same in every place. Nor can that power, in the hands of a Christian prince, confer any greater authority upon the church than in the hands of a heathen; which is to say, just none at all.

Nevertheless, it is worthy to be observed and lamented that the most violent of these defenders of the truth, the opposers of errors, the exclaimers against schism, do hardly ever let loose this their zeal for God, with which they are so warmed and inflamed, unless where they have the civil magistrate on their side. But so soon as ever court favor has given them the better end of the staff, and they begin to feel themselves the stronger, then presently peace and charity are to be laid aside. Otherwise they are religiously to be observed. Where they have not the power to carry on persecution and to become masters, there they desire to live upon fair terms and preach up toleration. When they are not strengthened with the civil power, then they can bear most patiently and unmovedly the contagion of idolatry, superstition, and heresy in their neighborhood; of which on other occasions the interest of religion makes them to be extremely apprehensive. They do not forwardly attack those errors which are in fashion at court or are countenanced by the government. Here they can be content to spare their arguments; which yet (with their leave) is the only right method of propagating truth, which has no such way of prevailing as when strong arguments and good reason are joined with the softness of civility and good usage.

Nobody, therefore, in fine, neither single persons nor churches, nay, nor even commonwealths, have any just title to invade the civil rights and worldly goods of each other upon pretense of religion. Those that are of another opinion would do well to consider with themselves how pernicious a seed of discord and war, how powerful a provocation to endless hatreds, rapines, and slaughters they thereby furnish unto mankind. No peace and security, no, not so much as common friendship, can ever be established or preserved amongst men so long as this opinion prevails that dominion is founded in grace and that religion is to be propagated by force of arms.

MONTESQUIEU

~

INTRODUCTION

MARK HULLIUNG

Charles-Louis de Secondat, Baron de Montesquieu, was born on January 19, 1689, at the château of La Brède, located near the city of Bordeaux in southwestern France. While in Paris during 1755, he contracted a fever on January 29 and died on February 10 amidst the usual eighteenth-century tug of war between priests eager to announce a deathbed profession of orthodoxy and the equally vehement denials of the avant-garde thinkers, the *philosophes*, that he had wavered at the final moment in his commitment to the cause of the Enlightenment.

Whatever the circumstances of his death, the undeniable truth of Montesquieu's life is that he was a great and pioneering figure of the French Enlightenment, and that his sphere of intellectual influence spanned many foreign lands, reaching as far west as the American colonies and as far east as the Russia of Catherine the Great. All the *philosophes*—Diderot, d'Alembert, Helvétius, among others—accepted and built on certain of his themes. His efforts to reform the cruel laws that treated crimes as sins became theirs, and the same holds for his plea on behalf of religious tolerance of Protestants and Jews, his corresponding outcry against the Revocation of the Edict of Nantes and the Spanish Inquisition, and his denunciation of the bloody conquests of the Spaniards in the Americas.

Although Paris was the center of French culture, there was no need for Montesquieu to travel to the capital to gain his initial intellectual inspiration when in his own Gasçon backyard he could learn so much from the great Montaigne (1533–1592), author of the *Essays*. Nauseated by the brutality of the wars of religion, disgusted by the murderous actions of the Spaniards searching for gold in the New World, Montaigne found more humanity among cannibals than in the ranks of the European conquerors. Cannibals kill humans only when hungry; Europeans kill sometimes for aristocratic sport, at other times to accumulate pieces of a shiny metal, or to plant their flag and crucifix on foreign soil. Who, then, is the savage? Montesquieu seconded Montaigne's opinion and added that the slave trade in his century proved Europeans were far from enlightened during the age of the Enlightenment.

Montesquieu also shared with Montaigne a philosophical skepticism, a denial that absolute truth is accessible to the human mind. How intolerable is intolerance when certainty is beyond our grasp, all knowledge deriving from the senses and hence relative to our persons. In his notebook, Montesquieu commented that the mistake of most philosophers had been to ignore that the terms *beautiful, good, noble, grand*, and *perfect* are "relative to the beings who use them." One and only one absolute existed for Montesquieu, the absolute evil of despotism. To ward off the worst possibilities was in consequence his primary concern, and to that end he, unlike Montaigne, gave a great deal of thought to political institutions—and to the social, economic, and cultural prerequisites of limited rule. In general, he discovered that Protestant, commercial, and constitutionalist Holland and England represented the best Europe had to offer, just as Catholic, economically retarded, and politically absolutist Spain and Portugal represented the worst. Above all, Montesquieu believed, France must avoid following in the historical footsteps of reactionary and regressive Spain.

Although the *philosophes* reiterated his specific findings, Montesquieu remained a unique figure among his kind in his method of reasoning. In contrast to his Parisian compatriots who espoused philosophies of natural rights and utilitarianism, he conducted his studies through the comparative method. The "more than/less than" judgments of comparative analysis suited his skeptical outlook and assisted him in anchoring his aspirations, not in the utopian speculation for which he had no use, but in concrete historical possibilities. Bored though he was with his legal duties at the *parlement* of Bordeaux, Montesquieu made effective use of his training in the law while writing his masterpiece, *The Spirit of the Laws* (1748), a pathbreaking adventure in what is now known as the *sociology of law*.

As early as 1721, Montesquieu established his reputation as a writer with the publication of his *Persian Letters*. Then, as now, the first of his major writings was received by his readers as a witty, sly, satirical work, poking fun at the pretence of Europeans, the French in particular. His audience was titillated, it is true, by the sometimes sexually frank letters passed back and forth between the traveler, Usbek, and his wives sequestered in the Persian harem. No one, however, paid much attention to the underlying significance of Montesquieu's portrait of the battle of the sexes in Persia. Hence, a year before his death, Montesquieu found it necessary to write a new preface to the *Persian Letters*, in which he pointed out that the book was a novel, not a series of disjointed letters. In effect, Montesquieu implied that the story of the eventual rebellion of Roxane against her despotic husband was the chief meaning of the work. Usbek is an enlightened man, a kind of Persian *philosophe*, but he is also a good Persian male and as such has been inured from birth to regard women as property. Persia is a despotic country, and the family, in consequence, is a miniature despotism.

It was always Montesquieu's position that despotic power benefits no one, not even the despot. And so it is that Usbek acknowledges how completely jealousy consumes him. We can well imagine his devastation on learning that Roxane has taken her life rather than lie again in his arms.

Montesquieu's first major publication presents a depiction of what he will call "Oriental despotism" in *The Spirit of the Laws*. His second book, *Considerations on the Greatness of the Romans and the Cause of Their Decline* (1734), concerns the model of the ancient civic republic, which likewise reappears in his magnum opus. Athenians, Spartans, and Romans were as politically free as Persians were enslaved, yet Montesquieu's monograph on the Roman republic reprises the theme of despotism in its account of war and aggrandizement. Having accepted Machiavelli's claim that the Romans were the most ruthless and conniving power politicians of all times, Montesquieu adds that the despotism they perpetrated abroad caused the decline of their civic virtue at home. Expansion of the Roman city-state steadily undermined the civic ethos, in that it fostered a yearning for privacy and personal wealth; the time had arrived when the Romans would conclude that the life of citizenship takes up too many evenings.

In *The Spirit of the Laws*, Montesquieu posited that each type of political regime was reinforced by a characteristic social ethos, despotism by "fear," the ancient republic by (civic) "virtue," and he added a newly conceptualized model of a monarchical regime, complemented by the social principle of "honor." By *monarchy*, Montesquieu understood the social and political structure that had evolved from the chaos of feudalism to the divine-right absolutism of the Old Regime. What prevented this government from doing its worst were the "intermediary bodies," the First and Second Estates, and the massive and tangled world of privileges and exemptions that were to be struck down during the French Revolution. If the society of the Old Regime revolved around a code of aristocratic honor, that was because the prerevolutionary bourgeoisie wanted to join rather than displace the nobility. Molière's *Bourgeois Gentleman* is the classic statement of middle-class aspirations to buy a noble title and put on aristocratic airs.

The key term in Montesquieu's use of the comparative method is *feudalism*. When comparing the Western world to the Eastern, he held that it was the presence of royal absolutism on both sides of the globe that made regimes comparable; it was the presence of feudal social structures in countries such as France and their absence in Persia or China that differentiated Oriental despotism from Western kingship. Take away the structure of feudal privileges and inequalities, keep the absolute monarch, and France will become a despotic state. No sooner did Voltaire read the chapters devoted to the study of "intermediary bodies," their prominence in Europe and nonexistence elsewhere, than he concluded that Montesquieu had written *The Spirit of the Laws* to apologize for the vested interests of the nobility to which he was born.

Had Voltaire read *The Spirit of the Laws* more carefully, he would have noted that, to Montesquieu, the feudal factor did more than differentiate West from East. It also permitted him to compare one Western country with another, because each of the various European societies had evolved from a common feudal embryo. Poland and Hungary, with their weak monarchs, unruly nobility, downtrodden peasantry, and anemic urban centers were in the eighteenth century as France had been during the Middle Ages. Montesquieu's depiction of the Middle Ages as a time when a multitude of local despots dominated the countryside proves how little love he had for the First and Second Estates when they did not serve as "intermediary bodies" blocking the arbitrary will of an absolute monarch.

How reluctant Montesquieu was to count on intermediary bodies under any circumstances is evident in his frequent remarks on Spain. Supposedly an absolute monarchy modified by clergy and nobles, the Spanish regime was in truth, and with disastrous consequences, the captive of the intermediary powers. As it turns out, a divine-right monarch all too frequently is dictated to by the Church, which in Spain led to the Inquisition and in France led to the Revocation of the Edict of Nantes, a measure depriving the French monarch of his most economically productive subjects, the Protestant Huguenots. Not reasons of state but hatreds of the clergy are what motivates public policy in Europe, which hardly needs to import Oriental despotism by abolishing the intermediary bodies when the retention of the feudal social structure so effectively produces a homegrown variety of despotic government. What damage the Church does not do, the nobility inflicts upon the Spanish nation: aristocratic "honor," envied even by the middle class, disdains commerce, such that all nobles and would-be nobles prefer a life of leisure and conspicuous consumption to one of entrepreneurship. A work ethic has no chance to take root in Spain where both the clergy and the nobility remove the lands from productivity. Once the leading power of Europe, Spain (like Portugal) has become the village idiot of the Western world.

If the retention of intermediary bodies (Spain) was no guarantee against despotism, neither did their demise automatically entail the advent of a despotic regime. "Abolish the privileges of the lords, the clergy, and cities in a monarchy," wrote Montesquieu, "and you will soon have a popular state, or else a despotic government." Across the Channel, he spied a "popular state." "The English, to favor their liberty, have abolished all the intermediate powers of which their monarchy was composed." Having consumed its Old Regime during the upheavals of the seventeenth century, England had emerged as a postfeudal society, and was freer than ever before because it held fast to its constitutional politics at the same time that it discarded its social past.

England was the freest country on the face of the earth, Holland the second freest. Both nations were commercial republics, Holland explicitly so, whereas England was a "republic hiding under the form of a monarchy." Although he admired civic virtue, Montesquieu feared the suppression of private life in the ancient republics. His was a modern notion of freedom that would be safeguarded by the checks and balances, the separation of powers, he spelled out in the famous Book XI, Chapter 6, of *The Spirit of the Laws*.

Montesquieu was, in short, a champion of what today is known as liberalism. All his writings were devoted to combating prejudice, inhumanity, and arbitrary government. His message was one of tolerance, acceptance of diversity, and moderation. "Political liberty is found only in moderate governments. . . . Who dares say it? Virtue itself has need of limits." Mutual forebearance, not religious or ideological righteousness, is what makes for a sociopolitical order in which common human decency is indeed common.

Robert Shackleton, *Montesquieu* (Oxford: Oxford University Press, 1961) is the standard biography. Jean Starobinski, *Montesquieu par lui-même* (Paris: Seuil, 1953), offers autobiographical jottings and commentary. Judith Shklar, *Montesquieu* (Oxford: Oxford University Press, 1987), is the best brief study. Mark Hulliung, *Montesquieu and the Old Regime* (Berkeley: University of California Press, 1976), provides a comprehensive interpretation.

The Spirit of the Laws

BOOK I

LAWS IN GENERAL

Chapter I

The Relationship of Laws to Beings of Different Kinds

Laws, in the broadest meaning of the term, are the necessary relations that derive from the nature of things. In this sense all beings have their laws. The Supreme Being has his laws, the material world has its laws, those beings superior in intelligence to man have their laws, the animals their laws, man has his laws.

Some have argued that a blind fatality has produced everything we perceive in the world. But what is more absurd than the contention that a blind fatality could produce intelligent beings?

There is, then, a primitive reason; and laws are the relations between it and different sorts of being, as well as the relations of these beings to one another.

God's relationship to the universe is both that of Creator and Preserver; the laws He has followed in creation are those He follows in preservation. He acts according to these rules because He knows them; He knows them because He has made them; He has made them because they are related to His wisdom and power.

Since we see that the world, formed by the movement of matter, and lacking intelligence, continues to exist, its motion must be governed by invariable laws. Could another world than this be imagined, it too would have have constant rules, or else it would be destroyed. . . .

As a physical being, man is, like all other bodies, governed by invariable laws. As an intelligent being, he never ceases violating those laws established by God and changing the others he has himself made. He must guide himself; yet he is a limited being. He is subject to ignorance and error, like all finite intelligences; even the little he knows slips from him. As a creature dominated by sensation, he is subject to a thousand passions. Such a being might at any moment forget his creator; God has reminded man by the laws of religion. Such a being at any moment forget himself; philosophers have reminded him by the laws of morality. Made to live in society, he might forget his fellows; legislators have recalled him to his duties by political and civil laws.

Chapter III

Positive Laws

The common power may be in the hands of a single person, or of many. Some have thought that because nature has established the power of the parent, the most natural government is that of a single person. But the example of paternal power proves nothing. For if the power of the father is an argument for rule by a single man, then, in the event of the father's death, the power inherited by his brothers, or after the death of the brothers, the power inherited by their children, is an argument for government by the many. Political power necessarily involves the union of several families.

There is a better way of deciding the extent to which a government is natural, and that is its conformity to the genius of the people for which it was established.

Translated by Thomas Nugent, London: G. Bell and Sons, 1902, spelling updated, footnotes omitted.

The power of individuals cannot be united without the conjunction of all their wills. . . .

Law in general is human reason, to the extent that it governs all the peoples of the earth. The political and civil laws of each nation ought to be only particular cases of the application of human reason.

Laws ought to be so appropriate to the people for whom they were made that it would be highly unlikely that the laws of one nation could suit another.

Laws should be relative to the nature and principle of the government that is established, or that one would like to establish. Such a relationship ought to be present, whether they constitute a government as do public laws, or maintain a government, as do civil laws.

Laws should be relative to the physical characteristics of the country, to the climate, whether freezing, burning, or temperate; to the quality of its terrain, to its location and extent; to the style of life of its inhabitants, whether farmers, hunters, or shepherds; the laws should be relative to the degree of liberty permitted by the constitution; to the inhabitants' religion, inclinations, riches, number, commerce, mores, and customs. Finally, the laws are related to one another; their origins are related, as is the intent of the legislator, and the order of things on which they were established. They must be considered from all these points of view.

This is what I shall undertake to do in this following work. I shall examine all these relationships. Taken together they comprise what is called *The Spirit of the Laws.*

BOOK II

LAWS THAT DERIVE DIRECTLY FROM THE NATURE OF THE GOVERNMENT

Chapter I

The Three Types of Government and Their Respective Natures

The three species of government are republican, monarchial, and despotic. To discover their nature, nothing more is necessary than to inspect the ideas of them held by the uneducated. I presuppose three such definitions, ot rather, facts: "in a republican government either the people as a body or else only a part of the people hold the supreme power"; "in a monarchical government a single person governs, but by fixed and established laws"; "in a despotic government, on the contrary, a single man, unrestrained by law or other rules, dominates everything by his will and caprices."

This is what I call the nature of each type of government. . . .

Chapter II

Republican Government and the Laws That Follow from Democracy

Whenever the people as a body hold supreme power in a republic, this is a democracy. Whenever the supreme power is in the hands of one part of the people, this is called an aristocracy.

The people in a democracy is in some respects the monarch; in others, the subject.

It can be the monarch only by casting those votes that are the wills of its members. Then the will of the sovereign is the sovereign himself. Thus the laws fundamental to this type of government are those that establish who is eligible to vote. In a democracy it is crucial to have fixed rules determining how the right to vote is to be given, who is to exercise this power, who is to receive it, and what matters are to be decided by vote. This is just as important as it is to know in a monarchy who is the monarch and how he ought to rule. . . .

The people, which holds the sovereign power, ought itself to do everything it can do well; that which it cannot do well must be done by its ministers.

The people may be said to have only when they have been named by the people itself. Thus it is a maxim fundamental to this type of government that the people must name its ministers, that is, its magistrates. . . .

Just as most citizens who have enough ability to choose others lack enough to be elected themselves, so the people, although capable of calling others to account for their administration, cannot by itself administer the state's business. . . .

Likewise fundamental to a democracy is the law determining the conditions for casting ballots. It is of the utmost importance whether balloting is public or secret. In one of the later phases of the Roman Republic laws were enacted that made balloting secret. Cicero wrote that these laws were among the most important causes of the republic's fall. Yet since various republics follow quite different practices, I ought to state here my assessment of them.

There can be no doubt that when the people votes, it should do so in public; this ought to be regarded as another law fundamental to democracy. For it is necessary that the lower classes (*le petit peuple*) be enlightened by those of higher rank, that the precipitous qualities of the lower classes be held in check by the grave example of certain notables. Hence, by making the ballot secret in the Roman Republic, all was lost; it was no longer possible to enlighten the populace when it took the wrong track. The contrary is true when the body of nobles votes in an aristocracy, or when the senate votes in a democracy. Since in both cases it is most important to prevent the rise of intrigues (*les brigues*), there cannot be too much secrecy.

Intrigue in a senate is dangerous; it is no less so in a body composed of nobles. But intrigue is quite another thing for the people, whose nature is to act by passion. . . .

Still another law fundamental to democracy is that the people alone enacts laws. . . .

CHAPTER III

Laws that Follow from the Nature of Aristocracy

In an aristocracy, sovereign power is lodged in the hands of a certain number of persons. These both make laws and carry them out. The rest of the people has no more power in regard to them than do the subjects of a monarchy in regard to their ruler. . . .

In a republic the sudden rise of a citizen to extraordinary power produces monarchy, or

more than monarchy. Under monarchical government, the laws have provided for, or been accommodated to the constitution; the very principle of the government checks the ruler. But when a citizen of a republic gains extraordinary power, the damage done is greater, because being unanticipated by the law, there exists no way of checking it. . . .

The best aristocracy is that in which the part or the people which does not share political power is so poor and few in number. that those who do dominate have no interest in oppressing the rest. . . .

Aristocratic families, therefore, ought to be, as much as possible, members of the people. The more an aristocracy resembles a democracy, the more perfect it is; the more it resembles a monarchy, the more imperfect.

The most imperfect of all is when that part of the people which obeys is in a state of civil slavery to that part which commands. This is the case with the aristocracy of Poland, where the peasants are slaves to the nobility.

CHAPTER IV

Laws that Follow from the Nature of Monarchical Government

Intermediary powers, although subordinate to and dependent upon the ruler, constitute the nature of monarchical government, that is, one in which a single person governs by fundamental laws. . . .

The most natural of such subordinate intermediary powers is that of the nobility. In a sense, the nobility is one part of the essence of monarchy, whose fundamental maxim is: "without a monarchy, no nobility; without a nobility, no monarchy." There are, of course, despots, but these are something else.

In certain European states, there are those who contemplate the abolition of all judicial functions exercised by those who are lords by feudal tenures. The authors of this proposal have failed to notice that this has already been done by the Parliament of England. Abolish in a monarchy the privileges of the feudal lords, of the clergy, of the nobility, and the cities, and you will soon have either a democratic state or a despotism. . . .

The power of the clergy is as dangerous in a republic, as it is appropriate to a monarchy, especially one verging on despotism. Now that Spain and Portugal have been deprived of their laws, what would become of them, if it were not for the church, which alone checks arbitrary power. The power of the church is good as a barrier when no other is available. Since despotism inflicts the most dreadful evils upon human nature, anything that limits despotism is good. Even an evil may thus be transformed into a benefit.

Just as the ocean, which threatens to inundate the earth, is checked by weeds and the smallest pebbles on its shore, so monarchs, whose power seems unbounded, are checked by the smallest obstacles, and allow their natural pride to be modified by protests and petitions.

In order to increase their liberty, the English have abolished all the intermediary powers that constituted their monarchy. They have good reason to guard their liberty, for were they to lose it, they would become one of the most enslaved peoples on earth.

CHAPTER V

Laws that Follow from the Nature of the Despotic State

From the nature of despotic power, it follows that the single person who holds it should pass it over to another individual who puts it to use. Anyone whom his five senses inform continually that he is everything, and others, nothing, is naturally lazy, voluptuous, and ignorant. Hence he neglects public affairs. But were he to entrust his power to many others, there would be disputes among them. Each contender would form a cabal to support his claim to be the despot's first slave; the ruler would then have to return to administering the state. . . .

BOOK III

THE PRINCIPLES OF THE THREE GOVERNMENTS

Chapter I

What Distinguishes the Nature of a Government from Its Principle

. . . There is this difference between the nature of government and its principle: its nature is what makes it what it is; its principle is what makes it act. The first is its peculiar structure; the second, the human passions that set it in motion.

For laws ought to relate to the principle of each type of government just as much as they do to its nature. . . .

Chapter II

The Principle of Each Government

I have already stated that the nature of a republican government consists in supreme power being held by either the people as a collective body, or by certain families. The nature of monarchical government is that sovereign power is in the hands of the prince, who, however, exercises it according to established laws. The nature of a despotic government is that a single person rules by his own will and caprice. Nothing more is needed to determine the respective principles of these three types of government; they follow naturally from what has already been said. . . .

Chapter III

The Principle of Democracy

No great probity is required for the support or maintenance of either a monarchical or despotic government. The force of laws in monarchy and threat of the prince's power in despotism direct or repress everyone. But in a popular government, still another spring is necessary and that is virtue.

What I have stated here is confirmed by all history and conforms closely to the nature of things. For it is clear that in a monarchy, where he who executes the laws judges himself to be above them, there is less need of virtue than in a democratic government, where the person who executes the laws perceives himself as subject to them, and feels their weight.

It is no less clear that a monarch who, through bad advice or negligence, ceases to execute the laws, may easily remedy this evil; he has only to change his council or himself correct any such negligence. But the state is ruined if the laws are no longer being executed in a democratic government. For this can happen only after the republic has been corrupted. . . .

When virtue no longer exists, ambition enters those hearts capable of it, and avarice becomes universal. The objects of desire are changed. What was once loved is loved no more: citizens who formerly considered themselves as free because of their laws now wish to be free from them. Every citizen is like a slave in flight from from the house of his master. What used to be accepted as a maxim of equity is now is called rigor; what was once considered a rule is now called constraint; what was once considered the attention [of the law-abiding] now is called fear. Avarice, which used to mean acquisitiveness now connotes frugality. Formerly, private wealth was the source of public funds; now public funds are treated as the inheritance of private persons. The republic is turned into an empty shell, and its former force is transformed into nothing more than the power of a few citizens and the license of all. . . .

Chapter IV

The Principle of Aristocracy

An aristocratic government requires virtue, as is the case in a democracy. But it is true that virtue is not so much an absolute prerequisite of aristocracy as of democracy.

In an aristocracy the people, who bear the same relation to the nobility as do subjects to a monarch, is kept in order by laws made by the nobles. The people in an aristocracy, therefore, needs virtue less than the people in a democracy.

But how is the nobility to be kept in order? They who are meant to execute the laws against their colleagues, will immediately perceive that they are acting against themselves. From the very nature of the aristocratic constitution, it follows that virtue is necessary in the nobles as a body.

Inherent in an aristocratic government is a certain force unknown to democracy. In an aristocracy, nobles form a body which by exercising its privilege to serve its own special interest, restrains the people. Thus the mere existence of such laws provides sufficient motivation for the nobles to carry them out. . . .

Moderation is, therefore, the very soul of this government, and by this I mean a moderation which derives from virtue, not what which has its origin in the cowardice and indolence of the soul.

Chapter V

Virtue Is Not the Principle of Monarchical Government

In monarchies, when great things are to be done, they are made to depend as little as possible upon virtue. As in the best machines, skill consists of using the smallest possible number of movement, springs, and wheels.

The existence of the monarchical state does not depend upon love of country, desire for true glory, self-denial, the sacrifice of those interests dear to us, or upon any of the heroic virtues displayed by the ancients, but known to us only by the accounts of them we have heard.

In monarchy, laws replace all the virtues, which are here superfluous. The state excuses you from any obligation to be virtuous; in its eyes an action committed without anyone noticing it, in a sense has no legal consequences.

Although by their nature all crimes are public, nevertheless a distinction is generally made between those crimes which are truly public and those crimes which are private, and are so called because they damage an individual more than the whole of society.

For in republics, private crimes are more public; that is, they violate the constitution of the state more than the interests of individuals. In monarchies, public crimes are more private; that is, they violate the interests of individuals more than the constitution of the state itself. . . .

Chapter VII

The Principle of Monarchy

. . . In a republic, ambition is pernicious. In a monarchy it has good effects; it gives life to that type of government. Its advantage lies in that it is not dangerous, because a monarchy can continue to restrain it.

This form of government may be said to resemble the system of the universe itself, in which there is a force that constantly pushes all bodies away from the center, and a power of gravitation that attracts these bodies to it. Honor sets all the parts of the body politic in motion, and by its very action connects them; thus every individual moves towards the public good, while he has been thinking only of promoting his own interests.

It is true that, philosophically speaking, it is a false honor that links all the parts of the state. But even this false honor is as useful to the public as true honor could possibly be to private persons. . . .

Chapter VIII

Honor Is Not the Principle of Despotic States

Honor is in no way the principle of despotic states. Since in them all men are equal, no one may be preferred to any other. Since all men are slaves, no distinction may be made among them.

Besides, honor has its own laws and rules, which it cannot compromise; it is determined by its own caprice and cannot accept the caprice of another. Hence honor is found only in those states where the constitution is fixed, and which has known laws.

How could a despot permit honor? Honor depends upon scorning life; the despot has power only because he can deprive men of life. How could honor tolerate the despot? Honor has fixed rules and even its caprices are regularized; the despot has no rule, and his caprices destroy all others. . . .

Chapter IX

The Principle of Despotic Government

A republic requires virtue; a monarchy, honor; a despotic government, fear. There, virtue is not at all necessary; honor, dangerous. . . .

BOOK V

THE LAWS PROVIDED BY THE LEGISLATOR OUGHT TO BE RELATIVE TO THE PRINCIPLE OF GOVERNMENT

Chapter II

What Is Meant by Virtue in a Political State

Virtue in a republic is a very simple thing: it is love of the republic, it is a feeling, and not a consequence of knowledge. Thus in such a state, virtue may inspire the lowliest man as much as the highest. Once the people have acquired good maxims [to guide their conduct], they hold to them longer than those regarded as men of honor. Corruption rarely begins with the people. It is often the case that their limited knowledge attaches them all the more strongly to what is already established.

Love of country leads to good mores; good mores, to love of country. The less we are able to satisfy our private passions, the more we can devote ourselves to those passions connected with the public good. . . .

Chapter III

What Love of the Republic Means in a Democracy

In a democracy, to love the republic is to love democracy; to love democracy is to love equality.

Again, to love democracy is to love frugality. Democracy ought to provide everyone with the same happiness and the same advantages, the same pleasures and the same expectations. This can be done only by frugality on the part of all.

In a democracy, love for equality so limits ambition that the only desire, the only happiness permissible is that of rendering greater services to one's country than do all its other citizens. They cannot render the same service, but they all have an equal obligation to render what they can. From birth on, one contracts so immense a debt to one's country, that it can never be discharged. . . .

Well-ordered democracies, by establishing frugality within private families, have made possible expenditures. This was the case with Athens and Rome, where the means for magnificence and excess were created by this very frugality. Just as religion requires purity of those making offerings to the gods, so the laws require frugal mores of citizens so that they may make their contribution to their native land.

The good sense and happiness of individuals depend to a considerable extent upon their talents and wealth being neither too great nor too small. . . .

Chapter IV

How Love of Equality and Frugality Is Inspired

. . . Thus the maxim is true which holds that if equality and frugality are to be loved in a republic, those virtues must previously have been established by law.

Chapter V

How Laws Establish Equality in a Democracy

Some ancient legislators such as Lycurgus and Romulus, divided up the land equally. This can take place only when a new republic is established, or else when an ancient republic becomes so corrupted that a state of mind develops in which the poor believe themselves obligated to seek, and rich to accept, such a remedy.

If a legislator, when making a division of this kind, does not at the same time enact laws to support it, then the constitution he has established will be short lived. Inequality will return through the opening left by the law, and the republic will be ruined. . . .

In a democracy, although real equality is the soult of the state, it is nevertheless so difficult to

establish that exactitude on this point ought not to be carried to the extreme. It is enough to place citizens by a census within catagories that reduce differences or fix them at a given level. After that is must be by specific laws that inequalities are compensated for by taxes imposed upon the rich, and by relief given to the poor. Only moderate wealth can give or suffer such adjustments. Men of great walth regard as an insult everything not assigned them on the basis of their claims to superiority in power and honor.

Every inequality in democracy ought to be derived from the very nature of democracy and from the principle of equality itself. For example, it may be feared that in a democracy those who need regular work in order to live may be impoverished by serving as a magistrate, or that they might neglect its functions; that artisans might be made too proud, that an excessive number of freed slaves might become more powerful than the original citizens. In such cases, equality among citizens may be denied by democracy for the utility of democracy. But this equality which is denied is only apparent. For a man ruined by his tenure of office will be in a worse condition than other citizens; such a man, obliged to neglect his own functions, will reduce other citizens to a condition worse than his own, and so on.

Chapter VI

How Laws Ought to Maintain Frugality in Democracies

In a well-ordered democracy, it is not enough that the shares of land be equal; they must also be small, as was the case with the Romans. . . .

It is true that when a democracy is based upon commerce, it may well happen that individuals may have great wealth without corrupting mores. For the spirit of commerce is accompanied by frugality, economy, moderation, labor, wisdom, tranquility, order and restraint. It follows that as long as this spirit lasts, the riches produced by it can have no bad effects. But trouble begins when excessive wealth destroys this spirit of commerce. It is then that all at once are created those disorders due to inequality, which up to this time had not been felt.

If the spirit of commerce is to be maintained, the principal citizens themselves must be involved in it; this spirit must exist in pure form, without any compromise with any other; all laws must favor it; and this by the provision that wealth be divided in proportion to increases in commerce. Thus every poor citizen will be taken care of so that he can work on the same basis as all others, while every rich citizen will be reduced to circumstances so moderate that he will have to work if he wishes either to conserve what he has or to add to it.

In a commercial republic, it is wise to have a law of inheritance that provides all children with an equal share in their father's estate. . . .

Chapter VIII

How, in an Aristocracy, the Laws Ought to Be Relative to the Principle of Government

In an aristocracy, if the people is virtuous, the state will enjoy a prosperity much like that produced by popular government; in this way it will become powerful. But rarely is there much virtue where men's fortunes are as unequal as they are likely to be in aristocracies. Hence the laws must encourage, to the greatest extent possible, a spirit of moderation, and seek to restore that equality which the constitution necessarily removes.

The spirit of moderation is what is called virtue in an aristocracy, where it holds the place of equality in a democratic state. . . .

In aristocratic states, there are two main sources of disorders: excessive inequality between those who govern and those who are governed, and the same degree of inequality among the different members of the ruling group. From these two types of inequality arise those hatreds and jealousies which the laws ought to prevent or terminate. . . .

Chapter IX

How, in a Monarchy, Laws Ought to Be Relative to Its Principle

Since honor is the principle of this type of government, the laws ought to be related to it.

They must operate in such a way as to support that nobility, of which honor is, so to speak, both the child and father.

They must make the nobility hereditary, not to serve as the boundary between the power of the ruler and the weakness of the people, but as the tie that binds them together. . . .

Chapter X

Prompt Action in Monarchies

Monarchical government has one great advantage over republican: since public business is guided by a single person, the executive power can operate more speedily. But since speed can degenerate into haste, the laws ought to impose some delay. Laws not only ought to support the nature of each constitution, but also to provide remedies for those disadvantages which may result from that same nature.

Cardinal Richelieu would have monarchies eliminate those thornlike bodies (*les épines des compagnies*) which make endless difficulties about everything. Even if despotism had not ruled that man's heart, it still would have dominated his thought.

Those bodies which serve as the depositaries of the law never obey better than when they move slowly. It is in this way that they bring to the ruler's affairs that sort of reflection which can scarcely be expected either from courtiers ignorant of the state's laws, or from royal councils which always move too hastily.

What would have become of the finest monarchy in the world if its magistrates had not, by their delays, their complaints and entreaties, limited the exercise of its kings' powers, even when applied to the most virtuous of their causes? For these monarchs, had they consulted only their own generous souls, would have without calculating bestowed excessive rewards upon those who had served them with a similarly uncalculating courage and fidelity.

Chapter XI

The Excellence of Monarchical Government

Monarchical government has one great advantage over the despotic. By its very nature, the monarchy requires that below the ruler there be several orders which uphold the constitution. Thus the state is made more permanent; the constitution, more stable; and the safety of those who govern, more assured. . . .

Just as a people living under a good civil government are happier than those who wander lawless and leaderless through the forests, so the monarchs who live under the fundamental laws of their state are happier than despots who have nothing of this kind to moderate either the passions of their people or those of their own heart.

Chapter XII

The Same Subject Continued

There is no point in looking for magnanimity in despotic states, for the ruler cannot display a greatness he does not himself possess. Glory is here absent.

It is in monarchies that subjects gather around a king to receive light from him; each of them has, so to speak, more space, and can exercise those virtues which impart to the soul not independence, but grandeur.

Chapter XIII

The Idea of Despotism

When the savages of Louisiana want fruit, they cut down the tree at its base and gather the fruit. Despotic government operates in the same way.

Chapter XIV

How, in a Despotic Government, the Laws Are Relative to Its Principle

The principle of despotic government is fear. A timid, ignorant, cowed people does not need many laws.

In such a state, everything ought to revolve around two or three ideas. Hence there is no need to add any new ones. When you teach an animal, you take great pains not to let him change his trainer, his task, or his pace. You make an impression upon his brain by two or three movements, and no more. . . .

Since the principle of despotic government is fear, its goal is tranquility. But this is not peace;

but the silence which falls upon cities about to be occupied by the enemy.

Since strength lies, not in the state, but in the army that founded it, the state cannot defend itself without the army. But this poses a formidable threat to the ruler. How, then, is the security of the state to be reconciled with that of the ruler's person? . . .

After everything that has been said here, it might appear that human nature would never cease rebelling against despotic government. But despite the love men have for liberty, despite their hatred of violence, most of the world's people are subject to despotic rule. That is easily understood. To construct a moderate government requires that powers be combined, regulated, moderated, and set in motion. Ballast must be placed in one power to make it capable of resisting another. This can be done only by a masterpiece of legislation which rarely occurs by chance, and which prudence is seldom given the opportunity to attain. By contrast, [the simplicity] of despotic government is striking and obvious; it is uniform throughout, and since only the passions are required for its establishment, anyone is capable of that.

BOOK VIII

CORRUPTION OF PRINCIPLE IN THE THREE GOVERNMENTS

Chapter I

General Idea of This Book

The corruption of every type of government almost always begins with the corruption of its principles.

Chapter II

Corruption of the Principle of Democracy

The principle of democracy is corrupted in two ways: when a democracy loses the spirit of equality; when the spirit of equality becomes extreme, that is, when everyone wishes to be the equal of those he has chosen to command him. Then the people, no longer capable of enduring the power it has itself delegated, wishes to do everything itself: to replace the senate in deliberation, the magistrates in execution, and the judges in their function.

When this is the case, there can no longer be any virtue in a republic. . . .

Thus democracy has to avoid two types of excess: the spirit of inequality, which leads to aristocracy, or to the rule of a single person; and the spirit of extreme inequality, which leads to despotism under one ruler, since such rule always ends with conquest. . . .

Chapter II

The Spirit of Extreme Equality

The spirit of true equality is as far removed from that of extreme equality, as is heaven from earth. The spirit of true equality consists, not in creating a situation in which everyone commands, or in which no one is commanded, but rather in our obeying or commanding only our equals. It does not seek to avoid having a master, but rather to have only its equals as its masters.

It is indeed true that in the state of nature, men were born equal, but they could not remain so. Society makes them lose this equality, and it can be regained only by resort to the use of the laws.

There is this difference between a democracy which is well ordered, and one which is not: in the first, men are equal only as citizens; in the second, they are also equal as magistrates, senators, judges, fathers, husbands, or as masters.

Virtue by its nature is closely allied to liberty, but virtue is no nearer to extreme liberty than it is to servitude.

Chapter V

Corruption of the Principle of Aristocracy

Corruption occurs in aristocracy when the power of the nobles becomes arbitrary. In this case, there can no longer be any virtue either in governors or in the governed.

When the ruling families observe the laws, this is a monarchy ruled by many monarchs. This arrangement is by its nature very good indeed, for almost all these rulers are linked by the laws. But when the ruling families do not observe the laws, this becomes a despotic state ruled by too many despots. . . .

Corruption reaches its extreme point when the power of the nobles is made hereditary, for then it becomes almost impossible for them to be moderate. If the nobles are few, their power increases, but their security increases. When power increases while security diminishes, a point is reached resembling that of the despot, whose power is as excessive as his danger is great.

If there is a large number of nobles in a hereditary aristocracy, the government will be less violent. But since this creates a situation in which little virtue is likely to be found, the nobles will fall into a spirit of nonchalance, idleness, abandon. And this means that the state no longer will have strength or its spring. . . .

Chapter VI

Corruption of the Principle of Monarchy

As democracies are subverted when the people usurps the functions of the senate, the magistrates, and the judges, so monarchies become corrupted when constituted bodies (*corps*) are gradually deprived of their prerogatives, or towns of their privileges. In such cases, democracies move toward the despotism of all; monarchies, toward the despotism of a single person. . . .

Monarchy is lost when a king believes that he better displays his power in transforming the order of things than in conforming to them; when he deprives some of their natural functions and bestows them upon others; when he cares more for his fantasies than for his judgment.

Monarchy is lost when a king, centering everything upon himself, summons the state to his capital, the capital to his court, and the court to his own person. . . .

Chapter X

Corruption of the Principle of Despotic Government

The principle of despotic government is in the process of being corrupted because it is corrupt by nature. Other governments perish because accidents occur which violate their respective principles; despotic government is ruined by its own inherent defect when accidents fail to keep its principle from corrupting itself. . . .

BOOK XI

LAWS THAT COMPRISE POLITICAL LIBERTY: THEIR RELATION TO THE CONSTITUTION

Chapter VI

The English Constitution

In every government, there are three sorts of powers: the legislative; the executive, in regard to those matters determined by the laws of nations; and the executive, in regard to those matters determined by the civil law.

By virtue of the first, the ruler or magistrate makes laws, either temporarily, or for all time, as well as correcting or abrogating those already in existence. By virtue of the second, he makes war or peace, sends or receives ambassadors, ensures security, and makes provision against invasion. By virtue of the third power, he punishes crimes, or passes judgment upon disputes arising among individuals. This is called the judicial power; the second, simply the executive power of the state.

For a citizen, the political liberty is that tranquillity of mind which derives from his sense of security. Liberty of this kind presupposes a government so ordered that no citizen need fear another.

When both the legislative and executive powers are united in the same person or body of magistrates, there is no liberty. For then it may be feared that the same monarch or senate has made tyrannical laws in order to execute them in a tyrannical way.

Again, there is no liberty, if the power to judge is not separated from the legislative and executive powers. Were the judicial power joined to the legislative, the life and liberty of the citizens would be subject to arbitrary power. For the judge would then be the legislator. Were the judicial power joined to the executive, the judge could acquire enough strength to become an oppressor.

All would be lost if the same man, or the same body, whether composed of notables, nobles, or the people, were to exercise these three powers: that of making laws, that of executing public decisions, and that of judging crimes or disputes arising among individuals. . . .

In a free state, every man who is considered a free citizen ought to be governed by himself. Hence the people as an estate ought to have the legislative power. However, since this is impossible in large states and subject to many disadvantages in small ones, the people must do by its representatives everything it cannot itself do.

Everyone knows much better the needs of his city than those of other cities; he is a better judge of his neighbors' capacities than those possessed by their other compatriots. Members of the legislative body should not be drawn, therefore, from the nation in the general. What is more appropriate is that the inhabitants of every place of importance elect a representative.

The great advantage of representatives is their capacity to discussing public business. For this the people [as a body] are quite unfitted, and this is among the greatest disadvantages of democracy.

It is not at all necessary that representatives, whose constituents have given them general directions, await as well specific directions on each issue. . . . It is true that this way of proceeding would turn the words of deputies into something closer to the voice of the nation. But this would occasion infinite delays and turn every deputy into the master of every other. Thus, in the most urgent circumstances, all the nation's force might be arrested by the caprice of a single person. . . .

Most the ancient republics suffered from this great defect: the people had the right to take decisions involving action of a kind that required participating in the subsequent execution of such decisions. And of this they are quite incapable. They should enter into government only to the extent of choosing of representatives, something very much within their reach. Although few men can assess precisely the qualifications of candidates for office, nevertheless everyone can know in general whether or not the person he chooses is better informed than other candidates.

Nor ought the representative body be chosen to take some decision involving executive action by itself, for which it is not fit. Rather it ought to be chosen to make laws, or to see whether the laws it has already made have been well executed, both matters for which it is very well fitted, and indeed, can be done by no other body. . . .

BOOK XIX

LAWS: THEIR RELATION TO THOSE PRINCIPLES THAT FORM THE GENERAL SPIRIT, MORES, AND MANNERS OF A NATION

Chapter III

On Tyranny

There are two sorts of tyranny: that which is real and consists of the violence of government; and another which is a tyranny of opinion and makes itself felt when those who govern institute things contrary to a nation's mode of thought. . . .

Chapter IV

What is Meant by the General Spirit

Men are ruled by many causes: climate, religion, laws, maxims of government, examples drawn from the past, mores, manners. Out of them is formed the general spirit of a nation.

To the extent that any one of these causes acquires greater force in nation, the other causes are weakened. Nature and climate virtually dominate savages, manners govern the Chinese, laws are the tyrants in Japan, mores once set the tone of life in Sparta, as did their maxims of government and ancient mores for the Romans.

Chapter V

How Important It Is Not to Change the General Spirit of a Nation

. . . The legislator ought to follow the spirit of the nation whenever to do so is not contrary to the principles of its government. For we do best what we do freely while following our natural genius.

Were pedantry to be imposed upon a nation, which is naturally gay, the state would gain nothing either at home or abroad. Let it then do frivolous things seriously, and serious things gaily.

JEAN-JACQUES ROUSSEAU

~

INTRODUCTION

JOSHUA COHEN

Jean-Jacques Rousseau (1712–1778) was born in Geneva. His mother died two days after his birth, and his father—a watchmaker—fled when Rousseau was ten. Raised by his uncle, Rousseau left Geneva at age sixteen and eventually settled in Paris in the early 1740s. Despite the geographic separation, Rousseau maintained a strong public identification with Geneva throughout much of his life. He came to intellectual maturity in absolutist France, in debate with the leading thinkers of the French Enlightenment, but the image of Geneva as a small, self-governing republic, in which the people are sovereign and all citizens are subject to law, continued to provide political bearings.

Whereas Rousseau's early experience in Geneva inspired his political thought, his theory of human nature came to him later, and in a flash, as he walked from Paris to Vincennes in 1749 (he was on his way to visit Diderot, then imprisoned in the château of Vincennes). Reflecting on a question set by the Academy of Dijon—"Has the restoration of the sciences and the arts contributed to the purification of morals?"—Rousseau was overtaken, he says, by a flood of ideas, "a thousand lights." Lying at the heart of this "sudden inspiration" was the thought that dominated his subsequent writing: "that man is naturally good, and that it is solely by [our] institutions that men become wicked." This conception of natural goodness—an alternative to the Augustinian doctrine of original sin and the Hobbesian theory of human nature—is, as Rousseau explained to Archbishop Beaumont of Paris, the "fundamental principle of all morals" and the basis of "all my writings."

Unified by this fundamental idea, Rousseau's principal writings on human nature and politics fall into three groups. In his early, "critical" essays—the *Discourse on the Arts and Sciences* (1750), *Discourse on the Origins of Inequality* (1755), and *Letter to M. d'Alembert on the Theater* (1758)—he challenges the Enlightenment view that the advance of science and understanding has improved the human condition, making human life freer, happier, and more virtuous. Rousseau rejects this complacent view and reveals a darker side to intellectual progress. Connecting enlightenment with the evolution of constraint, unhappiness, and vice, he explains how human beings, though naturally good, have been corrupted. His more positive writings—*Of the Social Contract, Emile,* the best-selling novel *New Heloise* (1761), *Letters from the Mountain* (1764), and constitutional proposals for Corsica (1765) and Poland (1772)—present a scheme of political institutions and a program of education that would cure our corrupt condition, restoring freedom through virtue and providing us with a life suited to our nature. In his autobiographical, confessional writings—including his *Confessions, Reveries of the Solitary*

Walker, and *Rousseau, Judge of Jean-Jacques*, all published after Rousseau's death—he testifies to his own authenticity, insisting that he has not been caught up in the web of deception, hypocrisy, and manipulation that defines conventional society. These writings, though intensely personal and self-revealing, also present a universal message: Rousseau's own uncorrupted sincerity is evidence of humanity's natural goodness and illustrates the possibility of extricating ourselves from self-imposed misery and vice.

Rousseau's political philosophy describes the terms of that extrication. The fundamental political problem, he says, is "to find a form of association that defends and protects the person and goods of each associate with all the common force, and by means of which each one uniting with all, nevertheless obeys only himself and remains as free as before." The importance of this problem reflects the central role in our nature of self-love and freedom. Because we love ourselves, we cannot be indifferent to the security of our person and goods. But not just any form of protection will do. We are "born free," with a capacity to choose and to regulate our own conduct. This capacity is the source of humanity's special worth, of our standing as moral agents who can make claims on others and take responsibility for our conduct. Freedom is so fundamental that "renouncing one's liberty is renouncing one's dignity as a man, the rights of humanity and even its duties." So we must find a form of security that does not demand such renunciation.

Of the Social Contract presents Rousseau's solution: a political society that achieves a "harmony of obedience and freedom." In this society, obedience to authority does not require a subordination of will that denies our freedom and corrupts our sensibilities. The proposed harmony is puzzling. How *could* each person accept political authority, thus uniting with all for common security, while obeying only himself or herself, achieving the "moral freedom" that consists in giving the law to oneself, and so remaining "as free as before"?

Rousseau's explanation has two components, corresponding to two kinds of doubt about the possibility of such a political society—doubts about *content* and *motivation*.

The problem of content arises because accepting authority, which is required for security, appears to involve letting oneself be ruled by the decisions of others (perhaps the majority). To show that self-government can be reconciled with the chains of social connection and bonds of political authority, we need some way to dispel this appearance—to show that the idea of such reconciliation is even coherent.

Rousseau's conception of a society guided by a *general will* addresses this problem. In such a society, the political obligations of citizens are fixed by laws; those laws reflect a shared understanding of the common good; and that understanding expresses an equal concern for the good of each citizen. Because the content of the conception of the common good reflects an equal concern with the well-being of each citizen, the society provides security for the person and goods of each. Because citizens share the conception, and it is embodied in law, each citizen remains free in fulfilling legal obligations. Those obligations are acceptable to citizens as free agents because each can regard the obligations to the common good as self-imposed.

Rousseau's solution to the fundamental problem requires, then, that the parties to the social compact treat each other as equals, both in the institution of equal citizenship and in regulating conduct by reference to reasons of the common good.

To institutionalize and sustain the supremacy of the general will, Rousseau proposes a system of nonrepresentative, direct democracy. Citizens themselves are to assemble regularly to reaffirm their social bonds, evaluate the performance of the executive, and choose the fundamental laws that will best advance their common good.

Even if we grant, however, that the society of the general will solves the content problem, we may still wonder whether such an ideal society is a human possibility. It requires, after all, a shared conception of, and allegiance to, the common good. But widespread vice—selfishness, pride, jealousy, envy—naturally prompts the thought that this ideal is inconsistent with human motivations.

Hobbes would certainly have rejected Rousseau's view for this reason. Surveying what he called the "known natural inclinations of mankind," Hobbes found desires for individual preservation and happiness; he noted the strength of human fears about violent death; he observed (in at least some people) passions of pride, jealousy, and envy rooted in a sense of natural differences of worth and a concern that relative social standing mirror those presumptively natural differences. And he found that people are often blinded by passion into acting for near-term advantages and against their own longer term interests. Departing from these observations, he concluded that we need a sovereign with unconditional authority, whose power is sufficient to overawe subjects, tame their pride with fear, and ensure the social peace required to protect human life and happiness.

Hobbes's defense of political submission is driven, in short, by his general pessimism about human capacities for self-regulation. More particularly, he was skeptical about the motivational power of reason of the common good because he did not see human beings as moved by a concern to treat others as equals. Concerned with preservation and happiness, we have at most an instrumental concern with equality; insofar as we are prone to pride, we will reject equality as inconsistent with our naturally superior worth and an insult to our dignity.

Rousseau's case for the motivational possibility of a general will and the political autonomy it makes possible would have been simpler had he rejected Hobbes's psychological observations. But Rousseau found little basis for disagreeing with Hobbes's dismal description: "Men are wicked," he says in the *Discourse on the Origins of Inequality*, adding that "a sad and constant experience makes proof unnecessary." We observe widespread vice, and underlying that vice can discern a "frenzy to distinguish ourselves," an "ardent desire to raise one's relative fortune less out of genuine need than in order to place oneself above others." This frenzy and desire, in turn, have roots in an inflated, false sense of self-worth; struck by differences of social station, we fail to see that "man is the same in all stations."

This description naturally prompts the pessimistic thought that the society of the general will is incompatible with human motivations, that human nature has no place for the commitment to equality and the common good required for political autonomy. And if we could directly infer intrinsic properties of human nature from observed motivations—if, for example, the "ardent desire" for advantage over others were an original predisposition, or the inflated sense of self-worth an original sentiment—that pessimistic thought would be true, and we would be compelled to reject the possibility of a political society in which citizens give the law to themselves. But we are not required to accept that direct inference, and therefore not required to draw the pessimistic implications. That is the point of Rousseau's *Second Discourse*. It presents, as Rousseau describes it, a "genealogy of vice." The point of that genealogy is to turn back an argument that begins with the "sad and constant experience" of human vice, that attributes such vice to a natural desire for advantage, or a naturally exaggerated sense of our own worth, and that ends by rejecting as unrealistic an ideal of free association among equals. Rousseau's strategy is to explain all human vice in terms of social circumstance, without postulating any original predisposition to it: although human beings are *naturally good*, the experience of social inequality encourages the desire for advantage and inflamed sense of self-worth that produce constraint, vice, and misery.

Rousseau's explanation, then, constitutes a defense of human nature. And that defense permits us to hope, with reason, for a society whose members respect one another as equals, and in so doing respond to the demands of self-love and freedom.

On the unity of Rousseau's writings, see Ernst Cassirer, *The Question of Jean-Jacques Rousseau*, translated and edited by Peter Gay (Bloomington: University of Indiana Press, 1963). For an integrated account of Rousseau's view of human nature and his political ideas, see Joshua Cohen, *Rousseau: A Free Community of Equals* (Oxford: Oxford University Press, 2010). Jean Starobinski provides a psychological interpretation of Rousseau's work, underscoring Rousseau's concern for transparency in human relations, in *Jean-Jacques Rousseau: Transparency and Obstruction*, translated by Arthur Goldhammer (Chicago: University of Chicago Press, 1988). On the theory of natural goodness, see Arthur Melzer, *The Natural Goodness of Man: The System of Rousseau's Thought* (Chicago: University of Chicago Press, 1990), and Frederick Neuhouser, *Rousseau's Theodicy of Self-Love: Evil, Rationality, and the Drive for Recognition* (Oxford: Oxford University Press, 2008). For a discussion of Rousseau's political thought against the background of early modern political theory, see Robert Derathe, *Jean-Jacques Rousseau et la Science Politique de son Temps* (Paris: Presses Universitaire de France, 1950). For a discussion of Rousseau's views in connection with Genevan culture and politics, see John Stephenson Spink, *Jean-Jacques Rousseau et Gèneve: essai sur les idées politiques et religieuses dé Rousseau dans leur relation avec la pensée genevoise au XVIIIe* (Paris: Boívin, 1934). On Rousseau's conception of democracy, in relation to traditional debate about democracy and political conflict in eighteenth-century Geneva, see James Miller, *Rousseau: Dreamer of Democracy* (New Haven, Conn.: Yale University Press, 1984). On Rousseau's critique of representative government, see Richard Fralin, *Rousseau and Representation* (New York: Columbia University Press, 1978). The best discussion of Rousseau's psychological views is N. J. Dent's *Rousseau* (Oxford: Blackwell, 1988). For Rousseau's views on women, see Susan Moller Okin, *Women and Political Thought* (Princeton, N.J.: Princeton University Press, 1979), Part 3, and Joel Schwartz, *The Sexual Politics of Jean-Jacques Rousseau* (Chicago: University of Chicago Press, 1984). Patrick Riley provides an illuminating account of the theological background to Rosseau's conception of the general will in *The General Will Before Rousseau: The Transformation of the Divine into the Civic* (Princeton, N.J.: Princeton University Press, 1986).

A Discourse on the Origin of Inequality

THE FIRST PART

Important as it may be, in order to judge rightly of the natural state of man, to consider him from his origin, and to examine him, as it were, in the embryo of his species, I shall not follow his organization through its successive developments, nor shall I stay to inquire what his animal system must have been at the beginning, in order to become at length what it actually is. . . . I shall suppose his conformation to have been at all times what it appears to us at this day; that he always walked on two legs, made use of his hands as we do, directed his looks over all nature, and measured with his eyes the vast expanse of the heavens.

If we strip this being, thus constituted, of all the supernatural gifts he may have received, and all the artificial faculties he can have acquired only by a long process; if we consider him, in a word, just as he must have come from the hands of nature, we behold in him an animal weaker than some, and less agile than others; but, taking him all round, the most advantageously organized of any. I see him satisfying his hunger at the first oak, and slaking his thirst at the first brook: finding his bed at the foot of the tree which afforded him a repast; and, with that, all his wants supplied.

While the earth was left to its natural fertility and covered with immense forests, whose trees were never mutilated by the axe, it would present on every side both sustenance and shelter for every species of animal. Men, dispersed up and down among the rest, would observe and imitate their industry, and thus attain even to the instinct of the beasts, with the advantage that, whereas every species of brutes was confined to one particular instinct, man, who perhaps has not any one peculiar to himself, would appropriate them all, and live upon most of those different foods, which other animals shared among themselves; and thus would find his subsistence much more easily than any of the rest.

Accustomed from their infancy to the inclemencies of the weather and the rigour of the seasons, inured to fatigue, and forced, naked and unarmed, to defend themselves and their prey from other ferocious animals, or to escape them by flight, men would acquire a robust and almost unalterable constitution. The children, bringing with them into the world the excellent constitution of their parents, and fortifying it by the very exercises which first produced it, would thus acquire all the vigour of which the human frame is capable. Nature in this case treats them exactly as Sparta treated the children of her citizens: those who come well formed into the world she renders strong and robust, and all the rest she destroys . . . .

The body of a savage man being the only instrument he understands, he uses it for various purposes, of which ours, for want of practice, are incapable: for our industry deprives us of that force and agility which necessity obliges him to acquire. If he had had an axe, would he have been able with his naked arm to break so large a branch from a tree? If he had had a sling, would he have been able to throw a stone with so great velocity? If he had had a ladder, would he have been so nimble in climbing a tree? If he had had a horse, would he have been himself so swift of foot? Give civilized man time to gather all his

Translated by G. D. H. Cole. Everyman's Library, David Campbell Publishers Ltd. The notes in brackets are the translator's.

machines about him, and he will no doubt easily beat the savage; but if you would see a still more unequal contest, set them together naked and unarmed, and you will soon see the advantage of having all our forces constantly at our disposal, of being always prepared for every event, and of carrying one's self, as it were, perpetually whole and entire about one. . . .

Hitherto I have considered merely the physical man; let us now take a view of him on his metaphysical and moral side.

I see nothing in any animal but an ingenious machine, to which nature hath given senses to wind itself up, and to guard itself, to a certain degree, against anything that might tend to disorder or destroy it. I perceive exactly the same things in the human machine, with this difference, that in the operations of the brute, nature is the sole agent, whereas man has some share in his own operations, in his character as a free agent. The one chooses and refuses by instinct, the other from an act of free will: hence the brute cannot deviate from the rule prescribed to it, even when it would be advantageous for it to do so; and, on the contrary, man frequently deviates from such rules to his own prejudice Thus a pigeon would be starved to death by the side of a dish of the choicest meats, and a cat on a heap of fruit or grain; though it is certain that either might find nourishment in the foods which it thus rejects with disdain, did it think of trying them. Hence it is that dissolute men run into excesses which bring on fevers and death; because the mind depraves the senses, and the will continues to speak when nature is silent.

Every animal has ideas, since it has senses; it even combines those ideas in a certain degree; and it is only in degree that man differs in this respect, from the brute. Some philosophers have even maintained that there is a greater difference between one man and another than between some men and some beasts. It is not, therefore, so much the understanding that constitutes the specific difference between the man and the brute, as the human quality of free agency. Nature lays her

commands on every animal, and the brute obeys her voice. Man receives the same impulsion, but at the same time knows himself at liberty to acquiesce or resist: and it is particularly in his consciousness of this liberty that the spirituality of his soul is displayed. For physics may explain, in some measure, the mechanism of the senses and the formation of ideas; but in the power of willing or rather of choosing, and in the feeling of this power, nothing is to be found but acts which are purely spiritual and wholly inexplicable by the laws of mechanism.

Yet, if the difficulties attending all these questions should still leave room for dispute about this difference between men and brutes, there is another very specific quality which distinguishes them, and which will admit of no dispute. This is the faculty of self-improvement, which, by the help of circumstances, gradually develops all the rest of our faculties, and is inherent in the species as in the individual: whereas a brute is, at the end of a few months, all he will ever be during his whole life, and his species, at the end of a thousand years, exactly what it was the first year of that thousand. Why is man alone liable to grow into a dotard? Is it not because he returns, in this, to his primitive state; and that, while the brute, which has acquired nothing and has therefore nothing to lose, still retains the force of instinct, man, who loses, by age or accident, all that his *perfectibility* had enabled him to gain, falls by this means lower than the brutes themselves? It would be melancholy, were we forced to admit that this distinctive and almost unlimited faculty is the source of all human misfortunes; that it is this which, in time, draws man out of his original state, in which he would have spent his days insensibly in peace and innocence; that it is this faculty, which, successively producing m different ages his discoveries and his errors, his vices and his virtues, makes him at length a tyrant both over himself and over nature. It would be shocking to be obliged to regard as a benefactor the man who first suggested to the Oroonoko Indians the use of the boards they apply to the temples of their children, which secure to them some part at least of their imbecility and original happiness.

Savage man, left by nature solely to the direction of instinct, or rather indemnified for what he may lack by faculties capable at first of supplying its place, and afterwards of raising him much above it, must accordingly begin with purely animal functions: thus seeing and feeling must be his first condition, which would be common to him and all other animals. To will, and not to will, to desire and to fear, must be the first, and almost the only operations of his soul, till new circumstances occasion new developments of his faculties.

Whatever moralists may hold, the human understanding is greatly indebted to the passions, which, it is universally allowed, are also much indebted to the understanding. It is by the activity of the passions that our reason is improved; for we desire knowledge only because we wish to enjoy; and it is impossible to conceive any reason why a person who has neither fears nor desires should give himself the trouble of reasoning. The passions, again, originate in our wants, and their progress depends on that of our knowledge; for we cannot desire or fear anything, except from the idea we have of it, or from the simple impulse of nature. Now savage man, being destitute of every species of enlightenment, can have no passions save those of the latter kind: his desires never go beyond his physical wants. The only goods he recognizes in the universe are food, a female, and sleep: the only evils he fears are pain and hunger. I say pain, and not death: for no animal can know what it is to die; the knowledge of death and its terrors being one of the first acquisitions made by man in departing from an animal state. . . .

For myself, I am so aghast at the increasing difficulties which present themselves, and so well convinced of the almost demonstrable impossibility that languages should owe their original institution to merely human means, that I leave, to any one who will undertake it, the discussion of the difficult problem: which was the more necessary, the existence of society to the invention

of language, or the invention of language to the establishment of society. But be the origins of language and society what they may, it may be at least inferred, from the little care which nature has taken to unite mankind by mutual wants, and to facilitate the use of speech, that she has contributed little to make them sociable, and has put little of her own into all they have done to create such bonds of union. It is in fact impossible to conceive why, in a state of nature, one man should stand more in need of the assistance of another, than a monkey or a wolf of the assistance of another of its kind: or, granting that he did, what motives could induce that other to assist him; or, even then, by what means they could agree about the conditions. I know it is incessantly repeated that man would in such a state have been the most miserable of creatures; and indeed, if it be true, as I think I have proved, that he must have lived many ages, before he could have either desire or an opportunity of emerging from it, this would only be an accusation against nature, and not against the being which she had thus unhappily constituted. But as I understand the word "miserable," it either has no meaning at all, or else signifies only a painful privation of something, or a state of suffering either in body or soul. I should be glad to have explained to me, what kind of misery a free being, whose heart is at ease and whose body is in health, can possibly suffer. I would like to know which is the more likely to become insupportable to those who take part in it: the life of society or the life of nature. We hardly see anyone around us except people who are complaining of their existence; many even deprive themselves of it if they can and all divine and human laws put together can hardly put a stop to this disorder. I would like to know if anyone has heard of a savage who took it into his head, when he was free, to complain of life and to kill himself. Let us be less arrogant, then, when we judge on which side real misery is found. Nothing, on the other hand, could be more miserable than a savage exposed to the dazzling light of our "civilization," tormented by our passions and reasoning about a state different from his own. It appears that providence most wisely determined that the faculties, which he potentially possessed, should develop themselves only as occasion offered to exercise them, in order that they might not be superfluous or perplexing to him, by appearing before their time, nor slow and useless when the need for them arose. In instinct alone, he had all he required for living in the state of nature; and with a developed understanding he has only just enough to support life in society.

It appears, at first view, that men in a state of nature, having no moral relations or determinate obligations one with another, could not be either good or bad, virtuous or vicious; unless we take these terms in a physical sense, and call, in an individual, those qualities vices which may be injurious to his preservation, and those virtues which contribute to it; in which case, he would have to be accounted most virtuous, who put least check on the pure impulses of nature. But without deviating from the ordinary sense of the words, it will be proper to suspend the judgment we might be led to form on such a state, and be on our guard against our prejudices, till we have weighed the matter in the scales of impartiality, and seen whether virtues or vices preponderate among civilized men: and whether their virtues do them more good than their vices do harm; till we have discovered whether the progress of the sciences sufficiently indemnifies them for the mischiefs they do one another, in proportion as they are better informed of the good they ought to do; or whether they would not be, on the whole, in a much happier condition if they had nothing to fear or to hope from any one, than as they are, subjected to universal dependence, and obliged to take everything from those who engage to give them nothing in return.

Above all, let us not conclude, with Hobbes, that because man has no idea of goodness, he must be naturally wicked; that he is vicious because he does not know virtue; that he always refuses to do his fellow-creatures services which he does not think they have a right to demand; or that by virtue of the right he justly claims to all he

needs, he foolishly imagines himself the sole proprietor of the whole universe. Hobbes had seen clearly the defects of all the modern definitions of natural right: but the consequences which he deduces from his own show that he understands it in an equally false sense. In reasoning on the principles he lays down, he ought to have said that the state of nature, being that in which the care for our own preservation is the least prejudicial to that of others, was consequently the best calculated to promote peace, and the most suitable for mankind. He does say the exact opposite, in consequence of having improperly admitted, as a part of savage man's care for self-preservation, the gratification of a multitude of passions which are the work of society, and have made laws necessary. A bad man, he says, is a robust child. But it remains to be proved whether man in a state of nature is this robust child: and, should we grant that he is, what would he infer? Why truly, that if this man, when robust and strong, were dependent on others as he is when feeble, there is no extravagance he would not be guilty of; that he would beat his mother when she was too slow in giving him her breast; that he would strangle one of his younger brothers, if he should be troublesome to him, or bite the leg of another, if he put him to any inconvenience. But that man in the state of nature is both strong and dependent involves two contrary suppositions. Man is weak when he is dependent, and is his own master before he comes to be strong. Hobbes did not reflect that the same cause, which prevents a savage from making use of his reason, as our jurists hold, prevents him also from abusing his faculties, as Hobbes himself allows: so that it may be justly said that savages are not bad merely because they do not know what it is to be good: for it is neither the development of the understanding nor the restraint of law that hinders them from doing ill; but the peacefulness of their passions, and their ignorance of vice: *tanto plus in illis proficit vitiorum ignoratio, quam in his cognitio virtutis.* There is another principle which has escaped Hobbes; which, having been bestowed on mankind, to moderate, on certain occasions, the impetuosity of *amour-propre*, or, before its birth, the desire of self-preservation, tempers the ardour with which he pursues his own welfare, by an innate repugnance at seeing a fellow-creature suffer. I think I need not fear contradiction in holding man to be possessed of the only natural virtue, which could not be denied him by the most violent detractor of human virtue. I am speaking of compassion, which is a disposition suitable to creatures so weak and subject to so many evils as we certainly are: by so much the more universal and useful to mankind, as it comes before any kind of reflection; and at the same time so natural, that the very brutes themselves sometimes give evident proofs of it. Not to mention the tenderness of mothers for their offspring and the perils they encounter to save them from danger, it is well known that horses show a reluctance to trample on living bodies. One animal never passes by the dead body of another of its species without disquiet: some even give their fellows a sort of burial; while the mournful lowings of the cattle when they enter the slaughter-house show the impressions made on them by the horrible spectacle which meets them. We find, with pleasure, the author of *The Fable of the Bees* obliged to own that man is a compassionate and sensible being, and laying aside his cold subtlety of style, in the example he gives, to present us with the pathetic description of a man who, from a place of confinement, is compelled to behold a wild beast tear a child from the arms of its mother, grinding its tender limbs with its murderous teeth, and tearing its palpitating entrails with its claws. What horrid agitation must not the eyewitness of such a scene experience, although he would not be personally concerned! What anguish would he not suffer at not being able to give any assistance to the fainting mother and the dying infant!

Such is the pure emotion of nature, prior to all kinds of reflection! Such is the force of natural compassion, which the greatest depravity of morals has as yet hardly been able to destroy! for we daily find at our theatres men affected,

nay, shedding tears at the sufferings of a wretch who, were he in the tyrant's place, would probably even add to the torments of his enemies; like the bloodthirsty Sulla, who was so sensitive to ills he had not caused, or that Alexander of Pheros who did not dare to go and see any tragedy acted, for fear of being seen weeping with Andromache and Priam, though he could listen without emotion to the cries of all the citizens who were daily strangled at his command. . . .

Mandeville well knew that, in spite of all their morality, men would have never been better than monsters, had not nature bestowed on them a sense of compassion, to aid their reason: but he did not see that from this quality alone flow all those social virtues, of which he denied man the possession. But what is generosity, clemency, or humanity but compassion applied to the weak, to the guilty, or to mankind in general? Even benevolence and friendship are, if we judge rightly, only the effects of compassion, constantly set upon a particular object: for how is it different to wish that another person may not suffer pain and uneasiness and to wish him happy? Were it even true that pity is no more than a feeling which puts us in the place of the sufferer, a feeling obscure yet lively in a savage, developed yet feeble in civilized man; this truth would have no other consequence than to confirm my argument. Compassion must, in fact, be the stronger, the more the animal beholding any kind of distress identifies himself with the animal that suffers. Now, it is plain that such identification must have been much more perfect in a state of nature than it is in a state of reason. It is reason that engenders *amour-propre*, and reflection that confirms it: it is reason which turns man's mind back upon itself, and divides him from everything that could disturb or afflict him. It is philosophy that isolates him, and bids him say, at sight of the misfortunes of others: "Perish if you will, I am secure." Nothing but such general evils as threaten the whole community can disturb the tranquil sleep of the philosopher, or tear him from his bed. A murder may with impunity be committed under his window;

he has only to put his hands to his ears and argue a little with himself, to prevent nature, which is shocked within him, from identifying itself with the unfortunate sufferer. Uncivilized man has not this admirable talent; and for want of reason and wisdom, is always foolishly ready to obey the first promptings of humanity. It is the populace that flocks together at riots and street brawls, while the wise man prudently makes off. It is the mob and the market-women, who part the combatants, and stop decent people from cutting one another's throats.

It is then certain that compassion is a natural feeling, which, by moderating the activity of love of self in each individual, contributes to the preservation of the whole species. It is this compassion that hurries us without reflection to the relief of those who are in distress: it is this which in a state of nature supplies the place of laws, morals, and virtues, with the advantage that none are tempted to disobey its gentle voice: it is this which will always prevent a sturdy savage from robbing a weak child or a feeble old man of the sustenance they may have with pain and difficulty acquired, if he sees a possibility of providing for himself by other means: it is this which, instead of inculcating that sublime maxim of rational justice, *Do to others as you would have them do unto you*, inspires all men with that other maxim of natural goodness, much less perfect indeed, but perhaps more useful; *Do good to yourself with as little evil as possible to others*. In a word, it is rather in this natural feeling than in any subtle arguments that we must look for the cause of that repugnance, which every man would experience in doing evil, even independently of the maxims of education. Although it might belong to Socrates and other minds of the like craft to acquire virtue by reason, the human race would long since have ceased to be, had its preservation depended only on the reasonings of the individuals composing it.

With passions so little active, and so good a curb, men, being rather wild than wicked, and more intent to guard themselves against the mischief that might be done them, than to do mischief to others,

were by no means subject to very perilous dissensions. They maintained no kind of intercourse with one another, and were consequently strangers to vanity, deference, esteem, and contempt; they had not the least idea of "mine" and "thine," and no true conception of justice; they looked upon every violence to which they were subjected, rather as an injury that might easily be repaired than as a crime that ought to be punished; and they never thought of taking revenge, unless perhaps mechanically and on the spot, as a dog will sometimes bite the stone which is thrown at him. Their quarrels therefore would seldom have very bloody consequences; for the subject of them would be merely the question of subsistence. But I am aware of one greater danger, which remains to be noticed.

Let us conclude then that man in a state of nature, wandering up and down the forests, without industry, without speech, and without home, an equal stranger to war and to all ties, neither standing in need of his fellow-creatures nor having any desire to hurt them, and perhaps even not distinguishing them one from another; let us conclude that, being self-sufficient and subject to so few passions, he could have no feelings or knowledge but such as befitted his situation; that he felt only his actual necessities, and disregarded everything he did not think himself immediately concerned to notice, and that his understanding made no greater progress than his vanity. If by accident he made any discovery, he was the less able to communicate it to others, as he did not know even his own children. Every art would necessarily perish with its inventor, where there was no kind of education among men, and generations succeeded generations without the least advance; when, all setting out from the same point, centuries must have elapsed in the barbarism of the first ages; when the race was already old, and man remained a child. . . .

Having proved that the inequality of mankind is hardly felt, and that its influence is next to nothing in a state of nature, I must next show its origin and trace its progress in the successive developments of the human mind. Having shown that human *perfectibility*, the social virtues, and the other faculties which natural man potentially possessed, could never develop of themselves, but must require the fortuitous concurrence of many foreign causes that might never arise, and without which he would have remained for ever in his primitive conditions, I must now collect and consider the different accidents which may have improved the human understanding while depraving the species, and made man wicked while making him sociable; so as to bring him and the world from that distant period to the point at which we now behold them. . . .

THE SECOND PART

The first man who, having enclosed a piece of ground, bethought himself of saying "This is mine," and found people simple enough to believe him, was the real founder of civil society. From how many crimes, wars, and murders, from how many horrors and misfortunes might not any one have saved mankind, by pulling up the stakes, or filling up the ditch, and crying to his fellows: "Beware of listening to this impostor; you are undone if you once forget that the fruits of the earth belong to us all, and the earth itself to nobody." But there is great probability that things had then already come to such a pitch, that they could no longer continue as they were; for the idea of property depends on many prior ideas, which could only be acquired successively, and cannot have been formed all at once in the human mind. Mankind must have made very considerable progress, and acquired considerable knowledge and industry which they must also have transmitted and increased from age to age, before they arrived at this last point of the state of nature. Let us then go farther back, and endeavour to unify under a single point of view that slow succession of events and discoveries in the most natural order.

Man's first feeling was that of his own existence, and his first care that of self-preservation. The produce of the earth furnished him with all he needed, and instinct told him how to use it.

Hunger and other appetites made him at various times experience various modes of existence; and among these was one which urged him to propagate his species—a blind propensity that, having nothing to do with the heart, produced a merely animal act. The want once gratified, the two sexes knew each other no more; and even the offspring was nothing to its mother, as soon as it could do without her.

Such was the condition of infant man; the life of an animal limited at first to mere sensations, and hardly profiting by the gifts nature bestowed on him, much less capable of entertaining a thought of forcing anything from her. But difficulties soon presented themselves, and it became necessary to learn how to surmount them: the height of the trees, which prevented him from gathering their fruits, the competition of other animals desirous of the same fruits, and the ferocity of those who sought to deprive man himself of life, all obliged him to apply himself to bodily exercises. He had to be active, swift of foot, and vigorous in fight. Natural weapons, stones, and sticks, were easily found: he learnt to surmount the obstacles of nature, to contend in case of necessity with other animals, and to dispute for the means of subsistence even with other men, or to indemnify himself for what he was forced to give up to a stronger.

In proportion as the human race grew more numerous, men's cares increased. The difference of soils, climates, and seasons, must have introduced some differences into their manner of living. Barren years, long and sharp winters, scorching summers which parched the fruits of the earth, must have demanded a new industry. On the seashore and the banks of rivers, they invented the hook and line, and became fishermen and eaters of fish. In the forests they made bows and arrows, and became huntsmen and warriors. In cold countries they clothed themselves with the skins of the beasts they had slain. The lightning, a volcano, or some lucky chance acquainted them with fire, a new resource against the rigours of winter: they next learned how to preserve this element, then how to reproduce it, and finally how to prepare with it the flesh of animals which before they had eaten raw.

The way these different beings and phenomena impinged on him and on each other must naturally have engendered in man's mind the awareness of certain relationships. Thus the relationships which we denote by the terms great, small, strong, weak, swift, slow, fearful, bold, and the like, almost insensibly compared at need, must have at length produced in him a kind of reflection, or rather a mechanical prudence, which would indicate to him the precautions most necessary to his security.

The new intelligence which resulted from this development increased his superiority over other animals, by making him sensible of it. He would now endeavour, therefore, to ensnare them, would play them a thousand tricks, and though many of them might surpass him in swiftness or in strength, would in time become the master of some and the scourge of others. Thus, the first time he looked into himself, he felt the first emotion of pride; and, at a time when he scarce knew how to distinguish the different orders of beings, by looking upon his species as of the highest order, he prepared the way for assuming pre-eminence as an individual.

Other men, it is true, were not then to him what they now are to us, and he had no greater intercourse with them than with other animals; yet they were not neglected in his observations. The conformities, which he would in time discover between them, and between himself and his female, led him to judge of others which were not then perceptible; and finding that they all behaved as he himself would have done in like circumstances, he naturally inferred that their manner of thinking and acting was altogether in conformity with his own. This important truth, once deeply impressed on his mind, must have induced him, from an intuitive feeling more certain and much more rapid than any kind of reasoning, to pursue the rules of conduct, which he had best observe towards them, for his own security and advantage.

Taught by experience that the love of well-being is the sole motive of human actions, he found himself in a position to distinguish the few cases, in which mutual interest might justify him in relying upon the assistance of his fellows; and also the still fewer cases in which a conflict of interests might give cause to suspect them. In the former case, he joined in the same herd with them, or at most in some kind of loose association, that laid no restraint on its members, and lasted no longer than the transitory occasion that formed it. In the latter case, every one sought his own private advantage, either by open force, if he thought himself strong enough, or by address and cunning, if he felt himself the weaker.

In this manner, men may have insensibly acquired some gross ideas of mutual undertakings, and of the advantages of fulfilling them: that is, just so far as their present and apparent interest was concerned; for they were perfect strangers to foresight, and were so far from troubling themselves about the distant future, that they hardly thought of the morrow. If a deer was to be taken, every one saw that, in order to succeed, he must abide faithfully by his post: but if a hare happened to come within the reach of any one of them, it is not to be doubted that he pursued it without scruple, and, having seized his prey, cared very little, if by so doing he caused his companions to miss theirs.

It is easy to understand that such intercourse would not require a language much more refined than that of rooks or monkeys, who associate together for much the same purpose. Inarticulate cries, plenty of gestures, and some imitative sounds, must have been for a long time the universal language; and by the addition, in every country, of some conventional articulate sounds (of which, as I have already intimated, the first institution is not too easy to explain) particular languages were produced; but these were rude and imperfect, and nearly such as are now to be found among some savage nations.

Hurried on by the rapidity of time, by the abundance of things I have to say, and by the almost insensible progress of things in their beginnings, I pass over in an instant a multitude of ages; for the slower the events were in their succession, the more rapidly may they be described.

These first advances enabled men to make others with greater rapidity. In proportion as they grew enlightened, they grew industrious. They ceased to fall asleep under the first tree, or in the first cave that afforded them shelter; they invented several kinds of implements of hard and sharp stones, which they used to dig up the earth, and to cut wood; then they made huts out of branches, and afterwards learnt to plaster them over with mud and clay. This was the epoch of a first revolution, which established and distinguished families, and introduced a kind of property, in itself the source of a thousand quarrels and conflicts. As, however, the strongest were probably the first to build themselves huts which they felt themselves able to defend, it may be concluded that the weak found it much easier and safer to imitate, than to attempt to dislodge them: and of those who were once provided with huts, none could have any inducement to appropriate that of his neighbour; not indeed so much because it did not belong to him, as because it could be of no use, and he could not make himself master of it without exposing himself to a desperate battle with the family which occupied it.

The first expansions of the human heart were the effects of a novel situation, which united husbands and wives, fathers and children, under one roof. The habit of living together soon gave rise to the finest feelings known to humanity, conjugal love and paternal affection. Every family became a little society, the more united because liberty and reciprocal attachment were the only bonds of its union. The sexes, whose manner of life had been hitherto the same, began now to adopt different ways of living. The women became more sedentary, and accustomed themselves to mind the hut and their children, while the men went abroad in search of their common subsistence. From living a softer life, both sexes also began to lose something of their strength and ferocity: but,

if individuals became to some extent less able to encounter wild beasts separately, they found it, on the other hand, easier to assemble and resist in common.

The simplicity and solitude of man's life in this new condition, the paucity of his wants, and the implements he had invented to satisfy them, left him a great deal of leisure, which he employed to furnish himself with many conveniences unknown to his fathers: and this was the first yoke he inadvertently imposed on himself, and the first source of the evils he prepared for his descendants. For, besides continuing thus to enervate both body and mind, these conveniences lost with use almost all their power to please, and even degenerated into real needs, till the want of them became far more disagreeable than the possession of them had been pleasant. Men would have been unhappy at the loss of them, though the possession did not make them happy.

We can here see a little better how the use of speech became established, and insensibly improved in each family, and we may form a conjecture also concerning the manner in which various causes may have extended and accelerated the progress of language, by making it more and more necessary. Floods or earthquakes surrounded inhabited districts with precipices or waters: revolutions of the globe tore off portions from the continent, and made them islands. It is readily seen that among men thus collected and compelled to live together, a common idiom must have arisen much more easily than among those who still wandered through the forests of the continent. Thus it is very possible that after their first essays in navigation the islanders brought over the use of speech to the continent: and it is at least very probable that communities and languages were first established in islands, and even came to perfection there before they were known on the mainland.

Everything now begins to change its aspect. Men, who have up to now been roving in the woods, by taking to a more settled manner of life, come gradually together, form separate bodies, and at length in every country arises a distinct nation, united in character and manners, not by regulations or laws, but by uniformity of life and food, and the common influence of climate. Permanent neighbourhood could not fail to produce, in time, some connection between different families. Young people of opposite sexes lived in neighbouring huts and the casual unions between them which resulted from the call of nature soon led, as they came to know each other better, to another kind which was no less pleasant and more permanent. They became accustomed to looking more closely at the different objects of their desires and to making comparisons; imperceptibly they acquired ideas of beauty and merit which led to feelings of preference. In consequence of seeing each other often, they could not do without seeing each other constantly. A tender and pleasant feeling insinuated itself into their souls, and the least opposition turned it into an impetuous fury: with love arose jealousy; discord triumphed, and human blood was sacrificed to the gentlest of all passions.

As ideas and feelings succeeded one another, and heart and head were brought into play, men continued to lay aside their original wildness; their private connections became every day more intimate as their limits extended. They accustomed themselves to assemble before their huts round a large tree; singing and dancing, the true offspring of love and leisure, became the amusement, or rather the occupation, of men and women thus assembled together with nothing else to do. Each one began to consider the rest, and to wish to be considered in turn; and thus a value came to be attached to public esteem. Whoever sang or danced best, whoever was the handsomest, the strongest, the most dexterous, or the most eloquent, came to be of most consideration; and this was the first step towards inequality, and at the same time towards vice. From these first distinctions arose on the one side vanity and contempt and on the other shame and envy: and the fermentation caused by these new leavens ended by producing combinations fatal to innocence and happiness.

As soon as men began to value one another, and the idea of consideration had got a footing in the mind, every one put in his claim to it, and it became impossible to refuse it to any with impunity. Hence arose the first obligations of civility even among savages; and every intended injury became an affront; because, besides the hurt which might result from it, the party injured was certain to find in it a contempt for his person, which was often more insupportable than the hurt itself.

Thus, as every man punished the contempt shown him by others, in proportion to his opinion of himself, revenge became terrible, and men bloody and cruel. This is precisely the state reached by most of the savage nations known to us: and it is for want of having made a proper distinction in our ideas, and seen how very far they already are from the state of nature, that so many writers have hastily concluded that man is naturally cruel, and requires civil institutions to make him more mild; whereas nothing is more gentle than man in his primitive state, as he is placed by nature at an equal distance from the stupidity of brutes, and the fatal ingenuity of civilized man. Equally confined by instinct and reason to the sole care of guarding himself against the mischiefs which threaten him, he is restrained by natural compassion from doing any injury to others, and is not led to do such a thing even in return for injuries received. For, according to the axiom of the wise Locke, "There can be no injury, where there is no property."

But it must be remarked that the society thus formed, and the relations thus established among men, required of them qualities different from those which they possessed from their primitive constitution. Morality began to appear in human actions, and every one, before the institution of law, was the only judge and avenger of the injuries done him, so that the goodness which was suitable in the pure state of nature was no longer proper in the newborn state of society. Punishments had to be made more severe, as opportunities of offending became more frequent, and the dread of vengeance had to take the place of the rigour of the law. Thus, though men had become less patient, and their natural compassion had already suffered some diminution, this period of expansion of the human faculties, keeping a just mean between the indolence of the primitive state and the petulant activity of our *amour-propre*, must have been the happiest and most stable of epochs. The more we reflect on it, the more we shall find that this state was the least subject to revolutions, and altogether the very best man could experience; so that he can have departed from it only through some fatal accident, which, for the public good, should never have happened. The example of savages, most of whom have been found in this state, seems to prove that men were meant to remain in it, that it is the real youth of the world, and that all subsequent advances have been apparently so many steps towards the perfection of the individual, but in reality towards the decrepitude of the species.

So long as men remained content with their rustic huts, so long as they were satisfied with clothes made of the skins of animals and sewn together with thorns and fish-bones, adorned themselves only with feathers and shells, and continued to paint their bodies different colours, to improve and beautify their bows and arrows, and to make with sharp-edged stones fishing boats or clumsy musical instruments; in a word, so long as they undertook only what a single person could accomplish, and confined themselves to such arts as did not require the joint labour of several hands, they lived free, healthy, honest, and happy lives, in so far as their nature allowed, and they continued to enjoy the pleasures of mutual and independent intercourse. But from the moment one man began to stand in need of the help of another; from the moment it appeared advantageous to any one man to have enough provisions for two, equality disappeared, property was introduced, work became indispensable, and vast forests became smiling fields, which man had to water with the sweat of his brow, and where slavery and misery were soon seen to germinate and grow up with the crops.

Metallurgy and agriculture were the two arts which produced this great revolution. The poets tell us it was gold and silver, but, for the philosophers, it was iron and corn, which first civilized men, and ruined humanity. Thus both were unknown to the savages of America, who for that reason are still savage: the other nations also seem to have continued in a state of barbarism while they praised only one of these arts. One of the best reasons, perhaps, why Europe has been, if not longer, at least more constantly and highly civilized than the rest of the world, is that it is at once the most abundant in iron and the most fertile in corn.

It is difficult to conjecture how men first came to know and use iron; for it is impossible to suppose they would of themselves think of digging the ore out of the mine, and preparing it for smelting, before they knew what would be the result. On the other hand, we have the less reason to suppose this discovery the effect of any accidental fire, as mines are only formed in barren places, bare of trees and plants; so that it looks as if nature had taken pains to keep the fatal secret from us. There remains, therefore, only the extraordinary accident of some volcano which, by ejecting metallic substances already in fusion, suggested to the spectators the idea of imitating the natural operation. And we must further conceive them as possessed of uncommon courage and foresight, to undertake so laborious a work, with so distant a prospect of drawing advantage from it; yet these qualities are united only in minds more advanced than we can suppose those of these first discoverers to have been.

With regard to agriculture, the principles of it were known long before they were put in practice; and it is indeed hardly possible that men, constantly employed in drawing their subsistence from plants and trees, should not readily acquire a knowledge of the means made use of by nature for the propagation of plant life. It was in all probability very long, however, before their industry took that turn, either because trees, which together with hunting and fishing afforded them food, did not require their attention; or because they were ignorant of the use of corn, or without instruments to cultivate it; or because they lacked foresight to future needs; or lastly, because they were without means of preventing others from robbing them of the fruit of their labour.

When they grew more industrious, it is natural to believe that they began, with the help of sharp stones and pointed sticks, to cultivate a few vegetables or roots around their huts; though it was long before they knew how to prepare corn, or were provided with the implements necessary for raising it in any large quantity; not to mention how essential it is, for husbandry, to consent to immediate loss, in order to reap a future gain—a precaution very foreign to the turn of a savage's mind; for, as I have said, he hardly foresees in the morning what he will need at night.

The invention of the other arts must therefore have been necessary to compel mankind to apply themselves to agriculture. No sooner were artificers wanted to smelt and forge iron, than others were required to maintain them; the more hands that were employed in manufactures, the fewer were left to provide for the common subsistence, though the number of mouths to be furnished with food remained the same: and as some required commodities in exchange for their iron, the rest at length discovered the method of making iron serve for the multiplication of commodities. By this means the arts of husbandry and agriculture were established on the one hand, and the art of working metals and multiplying their uses on the other.

The cultivation of the earth necessarily brought about its distribution; and property, once recognized, gave rise to the first rules of justice; for, to secure each man his own, it had to be possible for each to have something. Besides, as men began to look forward to the future, and all had something to lose, every one had reason to apprehend that reprisals would follow any injury he might do to another. This origin is so much the more natural, as it is impossible to conceive how property can come from anything but manual labour: for what else can a man add to things which he does not originally create, so as to make them his own property? It is the husbandman's labour alone that, giving him a title to the produce of the ground he has tilled, gives him a claim also to the land itself, at least till harvest; and so, from year to year, a constant possession which is easily transformed into property. When the ancients, says Grotius, gave to Ceres the title of Legislatrix, and to a festival celebrated in her honour the name of Thesmophoria, they meant by that that the distribution of lands had produced a new kind of right: that is to say, the right of property, which is different from the right deducible from the law of nature.

In this state of affairs, equality might have been sustained, had the talents of individuals been equal, and had, for example, the use of iron and the consumption of commodities always exactly balanced each other; but, as there was nothing to preserve this balance, it was soon distributed; the strongest did most work; the most skilful turned his labour to best account; the most ingenious devised methods of diminishing his labour: the husbandman wanted more iron, or the smith more corn, and, while both laboured equally, the one gained a great deal by his work, while the other could hardly support himself. Thus natural inequality unfolds itself insensibly with that of combination, and the difference between men, developed by their different circumstances, becomes more sensible and permanent in its effects, and begins to have an influence, in the same proportion, over the lot of individuals.

Matters once at this pitch, it is easy to imagine the rest. I shall not detain the reader with a description of the successive invention of other arts, the development of language, the trial and utilization of talents, the inequality of fortunes, the use and abuse of riches, and all the details connected with them which the reader can easily supply for himself. I shall confine myself to a glance at mankind in this new situation.

Behold then all human faculties developed, memory and imagination in full play, *amour-propre* interested, reason active, and the mind almost at the highest point of its perfection. Behold all the natural qualities in action, the rank and condition of every man assigned him; not merely his share of property and his power to serve or injure others, but also his wit, beauty, strength or skill, merit or talents: and these being the only qualities capable of commanding respect, it soon became necessary to possess or to affect them.

It now became the interest of men to appear what they really were not. To be and to seem became two totally different things; and from this distinction sprang insolent pomp and cheating trickery, with all the numerous vices that go in their train. On the other hand, free and independent as men were before, they were now, in consequence of a multiplicity of new wants, brought into subjection, as it were, to all nature, and particularly to one another; and each became in some degree a slave even in becoming the master of other men: if rich, they stood in need of the services of others; if poor, of their assistance; and even a middle condition did not enable them to do without one another. Man must now, therefore, have been perpetually employed in getting others to interest themselves in his lot, and in making them, apparently at least, if not really, find their advantage in promoting his own. Thus he must have been sly and artful in his behaviour to some, and imperious and cruel to others; being under a kind of necessity to ill-use all the persons of whom he stood in need, when he could not frighten them into compliance, and did not judge it his interest to be useful to them. Insatiable ambition, the thirst of raising their respective fortunes, not so much from real want as from the desire to surpass others, inspired all men with a vile propensity to injure one another, and with a secret jealousy, which is the more dangerous, as it puts on the mask of benevolence, to carry its point with greater security. In a word, there arose rivalry and competition on the one hand, and conflicting interests on the other, together with a secret desire on both of profiting at the expense of others. All these evils were the first effects of property, and the inseparable attendants of growing inequality.

Before the invention of signs to represent riches, wealth could hardly consist in anything but lands and cattle, the only real possessions men can have. But, when inheritances so increased in number and extent as to occupy the whole of the land, and to border on one another, one man could aggrandize himself only at the expense of another; at the same time the supernumeraries, who had been too weak or too indolent to make such acquisitions, and had grown poor without sustaining any loss, because, while they saw everything change around them, they remained still the same, were obliged to receive their subsistence, or steal it, from the rich; and this soon bred, according to their different characters, dominion and slavery, or violence and rapine. The wealthy, on their part, had no sooner begun to taste the pleasure of command, than they disdained all others, and, using their old slaves to acquire new, thought of nothing but subduing and enslaving their neighbours; like ravenous wolves, which, having once tasted human flesh, despise every other food and thenceforth seek only men to devour.

Thus, as the most powerful or the most miserable considered their might or misery as a kind of right to the possessions of others, equivalent, in their opinion, to that of property, the destruction of equality was attended by the most terrible disorders. Usurpations by the rich, robbery by the poor, and the unbridled passions of both, suppressed the cries of natural compassion and the still feeble voice of justice, and filled men with avarice, ambition, and vice. Between the tide of the strongest and that of the first occupier, there arose perpetual conflicts, which never ended but in battles and bloodshed. The newborn state of society thus gave rise to a horrible state of war; men thus harassed and depraved were no longer capable of retracing their steps or renouncing the fatal acquisitions they had made, but, labouring by the abuse of the faculties which do them honour, merely to their own confusion, brought themselves to the brink of ruin. . . .

It is impossible that men should not at length have reflected on so wretched a situation, and on the calamities that overwhelmed them. The rich, in particular, must have felt how much they suffered by a constant state of war, of which they bore all the expense; and in which, though all risked their lives, they alone risked their property. Besides, however speciously they might disguise their usurpations, they knew that they were founded on precarious and false titles; so that, if others took from them by force what they themselves had gained by force, they would have no reason to complain. Even those who had been enriched by their own industry, could hardly base their proprietorship on better claims. It was in vain to repeat: "I built this well; I gained this spot by my industry." Who gave you your standing, it might be answered, and what right have you to demand payment of us for doing what we never asked you to do? Do you not know that numbers of your fellow-creatures are starving, for want of what you have too much of? You ought to have had the express and universal consent of mankind, before appropriating more of the common subsistence than you needed for your own maintenance. Destitute of valid reasons to justify and sufficient strength to defend himself, able to crush individuals with ease, but easily crushed himself by a troop of bandits, one against all, and incapable, on account of mutual jealousy, of joining with his equals against numerous enemies united by the common hope of plunder, the rich man, thus urged by necessity, conceived at length the profoundest plan that ever entered the mind of man: this was to employ in his favour the forces of those who attacked him, to make allies of his adversaries, to inspire them with different maxims, and to give them other institutions as favourable to himself as the law of nature was unfavourable.

With this view, after having represented to his neighbours the horror of a situation which armed every man against the rest, and made their possessions as burdensome to them as their wants, and in which no safety could be expected either in riches or in poverty, he readily devised plausible arguments to make them close with his design. "Let us join," said he, "to guard the weak from oppression, to restrain the ambitious, and secure to every man the possession of what belongs to him: let us institute rules of justice and peace, to which all without exception may be obliged to conform; rules that may in some measure make amends for the caprices of fortune, by subjecting equally the powerful and the weak to the observance of reciprocal obligations. Let us, in a word, instead of turning our forces against ourselves, collect them in a supreme power which may govern us by wise laws, protect and defend all the members of the association, repulse their common enemies, and maintain eternal harmony among us."

Far fewer words to this purpose would have been enough to impose on men so barbarous and easily seduced; especially as they had too many disputes among themselves to do without arbitrators, and too much ambition and avarice to go long without masters. All ran headlong to their chains, in hopes of securing their liberty; for they had just wit enough to perceive the advantages of political institutions, without experience enough to enable them to foresee the dangers. The most capable of foreseeing the dangers were the very persons who expected to benefit by them; and even the most prudent judged it not inexpedient to sacrifice one part of their freedom to ensure the rest; as a wounded man has his arm cut off to save the rest of his body.

Such was, or may well have been, the origin of society and law, which bound new fetters on the poor, and gave new powers to the rich; which irretrievably destroyed natural liberty, eternally fixed the law of property and inequality, converted clever usurpation into unalterable right, and, for the advantage of a few ambitious individuals, subjected all mankind to perpetual labour, slavery, and wretchedness. It is easy to see how the establishment of one community made that of all the rest necessary, and how, in order to make head against united forces, the rest of mankind had to unite in turn. Societies soon multiplied and spread over the face of the earth, till hardly a corner of the world was left in which a man could escape the yoke, and withdraw his head from beneath the sword which he saw perpetually hanging over him by a thread. Civil right having thus become the common rule among the members of each community, the law of nature maintained its place only between different communities, where, under the name of the right of nations, it was qualified by certain tacit conventions, in order to make commerce practicable, and serve as a substitute for natural compassion, which lost, when applied to societies, almost all the influence it had over individuals, and survived no longer except in some great cosmopolitan spirits, who, breaking down the imaginary barriers that separate different peoples, follow the example of our Sovereign Creator, and include the whole human race in their benevolence.

But bodies politic, remaining thus in a state of nature among themselves, presently experienced the inconveniences which had obliged individuals to forsake it; for this state became still more fatal to these great bodies than it had been to the individuals of whom they were composed. Hence arose national wars, battles, murders, and reprisals, which shock nature and outrage reason; together with all those horrible prejudices which class among the virtues the honour of shedding human blood. The most distinguished men hence learned to consider cutting each other's throats a duty; at length men massacred their fellow-creatures by thousands without so much as knowing why, and committed more murders in a single day's fighting, and more violent outrages in the sack of a single town, than were committed in the state of nature during whole ages over the whole earth. Such were the first effects which we can see to have followed the division of mankind into different communities. . . .

If the reader thus discovers and retraces the lost and forgotten road, by which man must have passed from the state of nature to the state of society; if he carefully restores, along with the intermediate situations which I have just described, those which want of time has compelled me to suppress, or my imagination has failed to suggest,

he cannot fail to be struck by the vast distance which separates the two states. It is in tracing this slow succession that he will find the solution of a number of problems of politics and morals, which philosophers cannot settle. He will feel that, men being different in different ages, the reason why Diogenes could not find a man was that he sought among his contemporaries a man of an earlier period. He will see that Cato died with Rome and liberty, because he did not fit the age in which he lived; the greatest of men served only to astonish a world which he would certainly have ruled, had he lived five hundred years sooner. In a word, he will explain how the soul and the passions of men insensibly change their very nature; why our wants and pleasures in the end seek new objects; and why, the original man having vanished by degrees, society offers to us only an assembly of artificial men and factitious passions, which are the work of all these new relations, and without any real foundation in nature. We are taught nothing on this subject, by reflection, that is not entirely confirmed by observation. The savage and the civilized man differ so much in the bottom of their hearts and in their inclinations, that what constitutes the supreme happiness of one would reduce the other to despair. The former breathes only peace and liberty; he desires only to live and be free from labour; even the *ataraxia* of the Stoic falls far short of his profound indifference to every other object. Civilized man, on the other hand, is always moving, sweating, toiling, and racking his brains to find still more laborious occupations: he goes on in drudgery to his last moment, and even seeks death to put himself in a position to live, or renounces life to acquire immortality. He pays his court to men in power, whom he hates, and to the wealthy, whom he despises; he stops at nothing to have the honour of serving them; he is not ashamed to value himself on his own meanness and their protection; and, proud of his slavery, he speaks with disdain of those, who have not the honour of sharing it. What a sight would the perplexing and envied labours of a European minister of State present to the eyes of a Caribbean!

How many cruel deaths would not this indolent savage prefer to the horrors of such a life, which is seldom even sweetened by the pleasure of doing good! But, for him to see into the motives of all this solicitude the words power and "reputation" would have to bear some meaning in his mind; he would have to know that there are men who set a value on the opinion of the rest of the world; who can be made happy and satisfied with themselves rather on the testimony of other people than on their own. In reality, the source of all these differences is, that the savage lives within himself, while social man lives constantly outside himself, and only knows how to live in the opinion of others, so that he seems to receive the consciousness of his own existence merely from the judgment of others concerning him. It is not to my present purpose to insist on the indifference to good and evil which arises from this disposition, in spite of our many fine works on morality, or to show how, everything being reduced to appearances, there is but art and mummery in even honour, friendship, virtue, and often vice itself, of which we at length learn the secret of boasting; to show, in short, how, always asking others what we are, and never daring to ask ourselves, in the midst of so much philosophy, humanity, and civilization, and of such sublime codes of morality, we have nothing to show for ourselves but a frivolous and deceitful appearance, honour without virtue, reason without wisdom, and pleasure without happiness. It

is sufficient that I have proved that this is not by any means the original state of man, but that it is merely the spirit of society, and the inequality which society produces, that thus transform and alter all our natural inclinations.

I have endeavoured to trace the origin and progress of inequality, and the institution and abuse of political societies, as far as these are capable of being deduced from the nature of man merely by the light of reason, and independently of those sacred dogmas which give the sanction of divine right to sovereign authority. It follows from this survey that, as there is hardly any inequality in the state of nature, all the inequality which now prevails owes its strength and growth to the development of our faculties and the advance of the human mind, and becomes at last permanent an legitimate by the establishment of property and laws. Secondly, it follows that moral inequality, authorized by positive right alone, clashes with natural right, whenever it is not proportionate to physical inequality— a distinction which sufficiently determines what we ought to think of that species of inequality which prevails in all civilized countries; since it is plainly contrary to the law of nature, however defined, that children should command old men, fools wise men, and that the privileged few should gorge themselves with superfluities, while the starving multitude are in want of the bare necessities of life.

Of the Social Contract

BOOK I

I want to inquire whether, taking men as they are and laws as they can be, it is possible to have some legitimate and certain rule of administration in civil affairs. In this investigation I shall always strive to

ally what right permits with what interest prescribes, so that justice and utility may not be divided.

I enter upon this inquiry without proving the importance of my subject. I shall be asked whether I am a prince or a legislator that I write on Politics. I reply that I am not, and that it is

Translated by Charles M. Sherover; reprinted with his permission.

for this reason that I write on Politics. If I were a prince or a legislator, I should not waste my time in saying what ought to be done; I should do it or remain silent.

Having been born a citizen of a free State, and a member of the sovereign, however feeble an influence my voice may have in public affairs, the right to vote upon them is sufficient to impose on me the duty of informing myself about them. I feel happy, whenever I meditate on governments, always to find in my researches new reasons for loving that of my own country!

I. Subject of this First Book

Man is born free, and everywhere he is in chains. One believes himself the master of others, and yet he is a greater slave than they. How has this change come about? I do not know. What can render it legitimate? I believe that I can settle this question.

If I considered only force and the results that proceed from it, I should say that so long as a People is compelled to obey and does obey, it does well; but that, so soon as it can shake off the yoke and does shake it off, it does better; for, recovering its liberty by the same right by which it was taken away, either it is justified in resuming it, or there was no justification for depriving them of it. But the social order is a sacred right which serves as a basis for all others. Yet this right does not come from nature; it is therefore based on conventions. The question is to know what these conventions are. Before coming to that, I must establish what I have just laid down.

II. Of the First Societies

The most ancient of all societies, and the only natural one, is the family. Nevertheless children remain bound to their father only as long as they have need of him for their own preservation. As soon as this need ceases, the natural bond is dissolved. The children freed from the obedience which they owe to their father, and the father from the cares which he owes to his children, become equally independent. If they remain united, it is no longer naturally but voluntarily, and the family itself is kept together only by convention.

This common liberty is a consequence of man's nature. His first law is to attend to his own preservation, his first cares are those which he owes to himself, and as soon as he comes to years of discretion, being sole judge of the means adapted for his own preservation, he becomes thereby his own master.

III. Of the Right of the Strongest

The strongest man is never strong enough to be always master, unless he transforms his force into right, and obedience into duty. Hence the right of the strongest—a right assumed ironically in appearance, and really established in principle. But will this word never be explained to us? Force is a physical power; I do not see what morality can result from its effects. To yield to force is an act of necessity, not of will; it is at most an act of prudence. In what sense could it be a duty?

Let us suppose for a moment this pretended right. I say that nothing results from it but an inexplicable muddle. For as soon as force constitutes right, the effect changes with the cause; every force which overcomes the first succeeds to its right (privilege). As soon as one can disobey with impunity, he may do so legitimately; and since the strongest is always in the right, it remains merely to act in such a way that one may be the strongest. But what sort of a right perishes when force ceases? If it is necessary to obey by compulsion, there is no need to obey by duty; and if men are no longer forced to obey, obligation is at an end. Obviously, then, this word "right" adds nothing to force; it means nothing here at all.

Obey the powers that be. If that means yield to force, the precept is good but superfluous; I warrant that it will never be violated. All power comes from God, I admit; but every disease does also. Does it follow that we are prohibited from calling in a physician? If a brigand should surprise me in the recesses of a wood: not only am I bound to give up my purse when forced, but am I also in conscience bound to do so when I might conceal it? For after all, the pistol which he holds is also a power.

Let us agree, then, that might does not make right, and that we are obligated to obey only legitimate powers. Thus my original questions ever recur.

IV. Of Slavery

Since no man has a natural authority over his fellow men, and since force is not the source of right, conventions remain as the basis of all legitimate authority among men.

If an individual, says Grotius, can alienate his liberty and become the slave of a master, why should a whole people not be able to alienate theirs, and subject themselves to a king? In this there are a good many equivocal words that require explanation; but let us confine ourselves to the word *alienate*. To alienate is to give or sell. Now a man who becomes another's slave does not give himself; he sells himself at the very least for his subsistence; but why does a people sell itself? Far from a king supplying to his subjects their subsistence, he draws his from them; and according to Rabelais, a king does not live on little. Do subjects, then, give up their persons on condition that their goods also shall be taken? I do not see what is left for them to keep.

It will be said that the despot secures to his subjects civil peace. Just so; but what do they gain by that, if the wars which his ambition brings upon them, together with his insatiable greed and the vexations of his administration, dishearten them more than their own dissensions would? What do they gain if this peace itself is one of their miseries? One lives peacefully also in dungeons; is this enough to find them good? The Greeks confined in the cave of the Cyclops lived peacefully until their turn came to be devoured.

To say that a man gives himself for nothing is to say something absurd and inconceivable; such an act is illegitimate and worthless, for the simple reason that he who performs it is not in his right mind. To say the same thing of a whole people is to suppose a people of madmen; and madness does not make right.

Even if each person could alienate himself, he could not alienate his children; they are born men and free; their liberty belongs to them, and no one has a right to dispose of it except themselves. Before they have come to an age of discretion, the father can, in their name, stipulate conditions for their preservation and welfare, but not surrender them irrevocably and unconditionally; for such a bequest is contrary to the ends of nature, and exceeds the rights of paternity. It would be necessary, therefore, to ensure that an arbitrary government might be legitimate, that with each generation the people have the option of accepting it or rejecting it; but in that case this government would no longer be arbitrary.

To renounce one's liberty is to renounce one's quality as a man, the rights of humanity and even its duties. For whoever renounces everything there is no possible compensation. Such renunciation is incompatible with man's nature; and to deprive his actions of all morality is tantamount to depriving his will of all freedom. Finally, a convention which stipulates absolute authority on the one side and unlimited obedience on the other is vain and contradictory. Is it not clear that one is under no obligations whatsoever toward a man from whom one has a right to demand everything? And does not this single condition, without equivalent, without exchange, entail the nullity of the act? For what right would my slave have against me, since all that he has belongs to me? His right being mine, this right of me against myself is a meaningless phrase.

V. That It Is Always Necessary to Go Back to a First Convention

Even if I were in accord with all that I have so far refuted, those who favor despotism would be no farther advanced. There will always be a great difference between subduing a multitude and ruling a society. If scattered men, however numerous they may be, are subjected successively to a single person, this seems to me only a case of master and slaves, not of a people and its chief: they form, if you will, an aggregation, but not an association, for they have neither public property nor a body politic. Such a man, had he enslaved half the world, is always only one individual; his interest, separated from that of the rest, is always only a private interest. If he dies, his empire after him is left scattered and disunited, as an oak dissolves and becomes a heap of ashes after the fire has consumed it.

A people, says Grotius, can give itself to a king. According to Grotius, a people, then, is a people before it gives itself to a king. This gift itself is a civil act, and presupposes a public deliberation. Hence, before examining the act by which a people elects a king, it would be good to examine the act by which a people is a people. For this act being necessarily anterior to the other, is the real foundation of the society.

In fact, if there were no anterior convention, where, unless the election were unanimous, would be the obligation upon the minority to submit to the decision of the majority? And whence do the hundred who desire a master derive the right to vote on behalf of ten who do not desire one? The law of the plurality of votes is itself established by convention, and presupposes unanimity at least once.

VI. Of the Social Pact

I suppose that men have reached a point at which the obstacles that endanger their preservation in the state of nature prevail by their resistance over the forces which each individual can exert in order to maintain himself in that state. Then this primitive condition can no longer subsist, and the human race would perish unless it changed its manner of being.

Now as men cannot create any new forces, but only unite and direct those that exist, they have no other means of self-preservation than to form by aggregation a sum of forces which may overcome the resistance, to put them in action by a single motive power, and to make them work in concert.

This sum of forces can be produced only by the combination of many; but the strength and freedom of each man being the primary instruments of his preservation, how can he pledge them without injuring himself, and without neglecting the care which he owes to himself? This difficulty, applied to my subject, may be stated in these terms:

"To find a form of association which defends and protects with the whole force of the community the person and goods of every associate, and by means of which each, uniting with all, nevertheless obeys only himself, and remains as free as before." Such is the fundamental problem to which the social contract gives the solution.

The clauses of this contract are so determined by the nature of the act that the slightest modification would render them vain and ineffectual; so that, although perhaps they have never been formally enunciated, they are everywhere the same, everywhere tacitly admitted and recognized; until, the social pact being violated, each man regains his initial rights and recovers his natural liberty, while losing the conventional liberty for which he renounced it.

These clauses, rightly understood, are all reducible to one only, namely the total alienation of each associate, with all of his rights, to the whole community: For, in the first place, as each gives himself up entirely, the condition is equal for all, and, the condition being equal for all, no one has any interest in making it burdensome to others.

Further, the alienation being made without reserve, the union is as perfect as it can be, and no associate has anything more to claim. For if some rights were left to individuals, since there would be no common superior who could judge between them and the public, each, being on some point his own judge, would soon claim to be so on all; the state of nature would still subsist, and the association would necessarily become tyrannical or useless.

Finally, each, in giving himself to all, gives himself to nobody; and as there is not one associate over whom we do not acquire the same rights which we concede to him over ourselves, we gain the equivalent of all that we lose, and more power to preserve what we have.

If, then, everything which is not of the essence of the social pact is set aside, one finds that it reduces itself to the following terms: *Each of us puts in common his person and his whole power under the supreme direction of the general will; and in return we receive in a body every member as an indivisible part of the whole.*

Forthwith, instead of the particular person of each contracting part, this act of association produces a moral and collective body, which is composed of as many members as the assembly has voices, and which receives from this same act its unity, its common *self* [*moi*], its life, and its will. This public person, which is thus formed by the union of all the individual members, formerly took the name of *City* and now takes that of *Republic* or *body politic*, which is called by its members *State* when it is passive, *Sovereign* when it is active, *Power* when it is compared to similar bodies. With regard to the associates, they take collectively the name of *people*, and are called individually *Citizens*, as participating in the sovereign authority, and *Subjects*, as subjected to the laws of the State. But these terms are often confused and are mistaken one for another; it is sufficient to know how to distinguish them when they are used with complete precision.

VII. Of the Sovereign

One sees by this formula that the act of association includes a reciprocal engagement between the public and the individual, and that each individual, contracting so to speak with himself, is engaged in a double relation: namely, as a member of the Sovereign toward individuals, and as a member of the State toward the Sovereign. But we cannot apply here the maxim of civil right that no one is bound by engagements made with himself; for there is a great difference between being obligated to oneself and to a whole of which one forms a part.

It is necessary to note further that the public deliberation which can obligate all subjects to the Sovereign in consequence of the two different relations under which each of them is regarded cannot, for a contrary reason, bind the Sovereign to itself; and that accordingly it is contrary to the nature of the body politic for the Sovereign to impose on itself a law which it cannot transgress. As it can only be considered under one and the same relation, it is in the position of an individual contracting with himself; thus we see that there is not, nor can there be, any kind of fundamental law obligatory for the body of the people, not even the social contract. This does not imply that such a body cannot perfectly well enter into engagements with others in what does not derogate from this contract; for, with regard to foreigners, it becomes a simple being, an individual.

But the body politic or Sovereign, deriving its existence only from the sanctity of the contract, can never bind itself, even to others, in anything that derogates from the original act, such as to alienate some portion of itself, or submission to another Sovereign. To violate the act by which it exists would be to annihilate itself; and what is nothing produces nothing.

As soon as this multitude is thus united into one body, it is impossible to injure one of the members without attacking the body; still less to injure the body without the members feeling the effects. Thus duty and interest equally obligate the two contracting parties to give mutual assistance; and the same men should seek to combine in this twofold relationship all the advantages which are attendant on it.

Now the Sovereign, being formed only of the individuals who compose it, neither has nor can have any interest contrary to theirs; consequently the Sovereign power needs no guarantee toward its subjects, because it is impossible that the body should wish to injure all its members; and we shall see hereafter that it can injure no one in particular. The Sovereign, for the simple reason that it is, is always everything that it ought to be.

But this is not the case with respect to the relation of subjects to the Sovereign, which, notwithstanding the common interest, would have no security for the performance of their engagements, unless it found means to ensure their fidelity.

Indeed, each individual may, as a man, have a particular will contrary to, or divergent from, the general will which he has as a Citizen. His private interest may speak to him quite differently from the common interest; his absolute and naturally independent existence may make him regard what he owes to the common cause as a gratuitous contribution, the loss of which will be less harmful to others than will the payment of it be onerous to him; and viewing the moral person that constitutes the State as a being of reason because it is not a man, he would be willing to enjoy the rights of a citizen without being willing to fulfill the duties of a subject: an injustice, the progress of which would bring about the ruin of the body politic.

In order, then, that the social pact may not be a vain formula, it tacitly includes this engagement, which can alone give force to the others— that whoever refuses to obey the general will shall be constrained to do so by the whole body; which means nothing else than that he shall be forced to be free; for such is the condition which, giving each Citizen to his Fatherland, guarantees him from all personal dependence, a condition that makes up the spark and interplay of the political mechanism, and alone renders legitimate civil engagements, which, without it, would be absurd and tyrannical, and subject to the most enormous abuse.

VIII. Of the Civil State

This passage from the state of nature to the civil state produces in man a very remarkable change, by substituting in his conduct justice for instinct, and by giving his actions the morality that they previously lacked. It is only when the voice of duty succeeds physical impulsion, and right succeeds appetite, that man, who till then had only looked after himself, sees that he is forced to act on other principles, and to consult his reason before listening to his inclinations. Although, in this state, he is deprived of many advantages he holds from nature, he gains such great ones in return, that his faculties are exercised and developed; his ideas are expanded; his feelings are ennobled; his whole soul is exalted to such a degree that, if the abuses of this new condition did not often degrade him below that from which he has emerged, he should ceaselessly bless the happy moment that removed him from it forever, and transformed him from a stupid and ignorant animal into an intelligent being and a man.

Let us reduce this whole balance to terms easy to compare. What man loses by the social contract is his natural liberty and an unlimited right to anything which tempts him and which he is able to attain; what he gains is civil liberty and the ownership of all that he possesses. In order not to be mistaken about these compensations, we must clearly distinguish natural liberty, which is limited only by the force of the individual, from civil liberty, which is limited by the general will; and possession, which is only the result of force or the right of the first occupant, from ownership, which can only be based on a positive title.

Besides the preceding, one can add to the acquisitions of the civil state the moral freedom which alone renders man truly master of himself; for the impulsion of mere appetite is slavery, and obedience to the law one prescribes to oneself is freedom. But I have already said too much on this subject, and the philosophical meaning of the term *liberty* does not belong to my subject here.

IX. Of Real Property

Each member of the community gives himself up to it at the moment of its formation, just as he actually is, himself and all his force, of which the goods he possesses form a part. It is not that by this act possession changes its nature in changing hands and becomes property in those of the Sovereign; but, as the powers of the City are incomparably greater than those of an individual, public possession is also, in fact, more secure and more irrevocable, without being more legitimate, at least for foreigners. For the State, with regard to its members, is master of all their property by the social contract, which in the State serves as the basis of all rights; but with regard to other powers it is master only by right of first occupant which it holds from private individuals.

The right of first occupant, although more real than that of the strongest, becomes a true right only after the establishment of property [ownership]. Every man has by nature a right to all that is necessary to him; but the positive act which makes him owner of certain goods excludes him from the rest. His portion having been allotted, he ought to confine himself to it, and he has no further right against the community. That is why the right of first occupant, so weak in the state of nature, is respected by every member of a civil society. In this right one respects not so much what belongs to others as what does not belong to oneself.

Generally, in order to authorize the right of first occupant over any land whatsoever, the following conditions are needed. First, the land must not yet be inhabited by anyone; second, a man must occupy only the area required for his subsistence; third, he must take possession of it not by an empty ceremony but by labor and cultivation, the only mark of ownership which, in the absence of legal title, ought to be respected by others.

Indeed, to grant the right of first occupant according to necessity and labor, is it not to extend this right as far as it can go? Can one assign limits to this right? Will the mere setting foot on common ground be sufficient to presume an immediate claim to the ownership of it? Will the power of driving away other men from it for a moment suffice to deprive them of the right of ever returning to it? How can a man or a people take possession of an immense territory and rob the whole human race of it except by a punishable usurpation, since henceforth other men are deprived of the place of residence and sustenance which nature gives to them in common? When

Núñez de Balboa on the seashore took possession of the Pacific Ocean and of the whole of South America in the name of the crown of Castile, was this sufficient to dispossess all the inhabitants, and exclude from it all the Princes in the world? On this stand, such ceremonies might have been multiplied vainly enough; and the Catholic King in his cabinet might, by a single stroke, have taken possession of the whole universe; only cutting off afterward from his empire what was previously occupied by other Princes.

It can be understood how the lands of individuals, united and contiguous, become public territory, and how the right of sovereignty, extending itself from the subjects to the land which they occupy, becomes at once real and personal; this places the possessors in greater dependence, and makes their own powers a guarantee for their fidelity. An advantage which ancient monarchs do not appear to have clearly sensed, for, calling themselves only Kings of the Persians or Scythians or Macedonians, they seem to have viewed themselves as chiefs of men rather than as owners of countries. Those of today call themselves more cleverly Kings of France, Spain, England, etc. In thus holding the land they are quite sure of holding its inhabitants.

What is remarkable about this alienation is that the community, in receiving the property of individuals, far from robbing them of it, only assures them lawful possession, and changes usurpation into true right, enjoyment into ownership. Then the possessors, being considered as depositaries of the public property, and their rights being respected by all members of the State, and maintained with all its power against the foreign intruder, have, as it were, by a transfer advantageous to the public and still more to themselves, acquired all that they have given up. This is a paradox which is easily explained by distinguishing between the rights which the Sovereign and the owner have over the same property, as shall be seen later.

It may also happen that men begin to unite before they possess anything, and that afterward taking over territory sufficient for all, they enjoy it in common, or share it among themselves, either equally or in proportions fixed by the Sovereign. In whatever manner this acquisition is made, the right which every individual has over his own property is always subordinate to the right which the community has over all; otherwise there would be neither solidity in the social union, nor real force in the exercise of Sovereignty.

I shall close this chapter and this book with a remark which ought to serve as a basis for the whole social system; it is that instead of destroying natural equality, the fundamental pact, on the contrary, substitutes a moral and legitimate equality for the physical inequality which nature imposed upon men, so that, although unequal in strength or talent, they all become equal by convention and legal right.

BOOK II

I. That Sovereignty Is Inalienable

The first and most important consequence of the principles established above is that the general will can only direct the forces of the State in keeping with the end for which it was instituted, which is the common good; for if the opposition of private interests has made the establishment of societies necessary, the harmony of these same interests has made it possible. That which is common to these different interests forms the social bond; and if there were not some point in which all interests agree, no society could exist. Now it is only on this common interest that the society should be governed.

I say, then, that sovereignty, being only the exercise of the general will, can never be alienated, and that the Sovereign, which is only a collective being, can be represented only by itself; power can well be transmitted, but will cannot.

In fact, if it is not impossible that a private will agree on some point with the general will, it is at least impossible that this agreement should be lasting and constant, for the private will naturally tends to preferences, and the general will to equality. It is still more impossible to have a guarantee for this agreement; even though it should always exist, it would be an effect not of art but of chance. The Sovereign may indeed say: I now will what a certain man wills, or at least what he says that he wills; but it cannot say: what that man wills tomorrow, I shall also will; since it is absurd that the will should bind itself for the future and since it is not incumbent on any will to consent to anything contrary to the good of the being that wills. If, then, the people promises simply to obey, it dissolves itself by that act, it loses its quality as a people; at the instant that there is a master, there is no longer a Sovereign, and forthwith the body politic is destroyed.

This is not to say that the orders of the chiefs cannot pass for expressions of the general will, so long as the Sovereign, free to oppose them, does not do so. In such case, from the universal silence one should presume the consent of the people. This will be explained at greater length.

II. That Sovereignty Is Indivisible

For the same reason that sovereignty is inalienable, it is indivisible. For either the will is general or it is not; it is the will either of the body of the people, or only of a part. In the first case, this declared will is an act of sovereignty and constitutes law. In the second case, it is only a private will, or an act of magistracy; it is at most a decree. . . .

III. Whether the General Will Can Err

It follows from what precedes that the general will is always upright and always tends toward the public utility; but it does not follow that the deliberations of the people always have the same rectitude. One wishes always his own good, but does not always discern it. The people is never corrupted, though often deceived, and then only does it seem to will that which is bad.

There is often a great difference between the will of all and the general will; the latter regards only the common interest, the other regards private interests and is only the sum of particular wills: but remove from these wills the pluses and minuses which cancel each other out and the general will remains as the sum of the differences.

If, when an adequately informed people deliberates, the Citizens having no communication among themselves, from the large number of small differences the general will would always result, and the deliberation would always be good. But when factions are formed, partial associations at the expense of the whole, the will of each of these associations becomes general with regard to its members, and particular with regard to the State: one is then able to say that there are no longer as many voters as there are men, but only as many as there are associations. The differences become less numerous and yield a less general result. Finally, when one of these associations is so large that it overcomes the rest, you no longer have a sum of small differences as the result, but a unique difference; then there no longer is a general will, and the opinion which dominates is only a private opinion.

It matters, then, in order to have the general will expressed well, that there be no partial societies in the State, and that each Citizen speak only his own opinions. Such was the unique and sublime institution of the great Lycurgus. But if there are partial associations, it is necessary to multiply their number and so prevent inequality, as was done by Solon, Numa, and Servius. These precautions are the only valid ones, in order that the general will always be enlightened and that the people are not deceived.

IV. Of the Limits of the Sovereign Power

If the State or the City is only a moral person whose life consists in the union of its members, and if the most important of its cares is that of its own conservation, it needs a universal and compulsive force to move and dispose every part in the manner most appropriate for the whole. As nature gives each man an absolute power over all his limbs, the social pact gives the body politic an absolute power over all its members, and it is the same power which, directed by the general will, bears, as I have said, the name of sovereignty.

But beyond the public person, we have to consider the private persons who compose it, and whose life and liberty are naturally independent of it. It is then necessary to distinguish clearly the respective rights of the Citizens and of the Sovereign as well as between the duties which the former have to fulfill as subjects and the natural right which they ought to enjoy in their quality as men.

Granted that whatever part of his power, his goods, and his liberty each alienates by the social pact is only that part whose use is important to the community; we must also agree that the Sovereign alone is judge of that importance.

All the services that a citizen can render to the State, he owes to it as soon as the Sovereign demands them; but the Sovereign, on its side, cannot impose any burden on its subjects that is useless to the community; it cannot even wish to do so; because under the law of reason nothing happens without cause, just as under the law of nature.

The engagements which bind us to the social body are obligatory only because they are mutual, and their nature is such that in fulfilling them one cannot work for others without also working for oneself. Why is the general will always upright, and why do all constantly desire the well-being of each, if not because no one appropriates this word *each* to himself without thinking of himself as voting on behalf of all? This proves that equality of right and the notion of justice it produces derive from the preference which each gives to himself, and consequently from the nature of man; that the general will, to be truly such, must be just in its object as in its essence; that it ought to proceed from all in order to be applicable to all; and that it loses its natural rectitude when it is directed to some individual and determinate object, because in that case, judging from what is foreign to us, we have no true principle of equity to guide us.

In effect, so soon as a matter of fact or particular right is in question on a point which has not been regulated by a previous general convention, the affair becomes contentious. It is a lawsuit in which the interested individuals are one of the parties and the public the other, but in which I perceive neither the law which must be followed, nor the judge who should decide. It would be ridiculous to wish to refer the matter for an express decision of the general will, which can only be the decision of one of the parties, and which, consequently, is for the other party only a will that is foreign, partial, and inclined on such an occasion to injustice as well as it is subject to error. Thus, just as a particular will cannot represent the general will, the general will in turn changes its nature when it has a particular object and cannot, as general, decide about either a man or a fact. When the people of Athens, for example, named or deposed their chiefs, decreed honor to one, imposed penalties on another, and by multitudes of particular decrees exercised indiscriminately all the functions of government, the people no longer had any general will properly so called; it no longer acted as Sovereign but as Magistrate. This will appear contrary to common ideas, but I must be allowed time to set forth my own.

What generalizes the will, one must see from this, is not so much the number of voices as the common interest that unites them; for, in this institution, each necessarily submits to the conditions that he imposes on others: an admirable accord of interest and justice which gives to common deliberations a spirit of equity that seems to disappear in the discussion of any particular affair, for want of a common interest to unite and identify the ruling principle of the judge with that of the party.

By whatever path we return to our principle, we always arrive at the same conclusion: the social pact establishes among citizens such an equality that they all engage themselves under the same conditions and ought to enjoy the same rights. Thus, by the nature of the pact, every act of sovereignty, that is to say every authentic act

of the general will, obligates or favors all the citizens equally; so that the Sovereign knows only the body of the nation, and distinguishes none of those who compose it. What then is properly an act of sovereignty? It is not a convention of the superior with an inferior, but a convention of the body with each of its members. A legitimate convention, because it has the social contract for its base; equitable, because it is common to all; useful, because it can have no object other than the general welfare; and firm, because it has for its guarantee the public force and supreme power. So long as the subjects submit only to such conventions, they obey no one, but only their own will; and to ask how far the respective rights of the Sovereign and the Citizens extend is to ask up to which point the latter can engage themselves, each toward all and all toward each.

One sees thereby that the Sovereign power, wholly absolute, wholly sacred, wholly inviolable as it is, neither passes nor can pass the limits of general conventions, and that every man can fully dispose of what is left to him of his goods and his liberty by these conventions; so that the Sovereign never has a right to burden one subject more than another, because then the matter becomes individual, and its power is no longer competent.

These distinctions once admitted, it is so false that in the social contract there is, on the part of individuals, any real renunciation, that their situation, as a result of this contract, is in reality preferable to what it was before: instead of an alienation they have only made an advantageous exchange of an uncertain and precarious mode of existence for a better and more assured one, of natural independence for liberty, of the power to injure others for their own safety, and of their strength, which others might overcome, for a right which the social union renders invincible. Their life itself, which they have dedicated to the State, is continually protected by it; and when they expose their lives for its defense, what do they do but restore what they have received from it? What do they do but what they would do more frequently and with more risk in the state of nature, when, engaging in inevitable struggles, they would defend at the peril of their lives their means of preserving it? All have to fight, if need be, for the fatherland, it is true; but then no one ever has to fight for himself. Do we not gain, still, to run this risk for that which assures our safety, a part of the risks we would have to run for ourselves as soon as our security was taken away?

VI. Of the Law

By the social pact we have given existence and life to the body politic; it is now a matter of giving it movement and will through legislation. For the original act by which this body is formed and united still determines nothing with respect to what it should do to preserve itself.

What is good and conforming to order is such by the nature of things and independent of human conventions. All justice comes from God, he alone is the source; but if we knew how to receive it from so high, we would need neither government nor laws. Without doubt there is a universal justice emanating from reason alone; but this justice, in order to be admitted among us, must be reciprocal. Considering things from a human viewpoint, the laws of justice, lacking a natural sanction, are ineffectual among men; they only bring good to the wicked and evil to the just man when he observes them with everyone else and no one observes them with him. Conventions and laws are then needed in order to unite rights with duties and to bring justice to its object. In the state of nature, where everything is common, I owe nothing to those to whom I have promised nothing, and I recognize as belonging to others only what is useless to me. It is not so in the civil state, where all the rights are fixed by the law.

But what then is a law? As long as one continues to attach to this word only metaphysical ideas, one will continue to reason without understanding, and when one will have said what a law of nature is, one will not have a better idea of what is a law of the State.

I have already said that there is no general will concerning a particular object. In effect, this particular object is either in the State or outside the State. If it is outside the State, a will that is foreign to it is not general in relation to it; and if within the State, that object is part of it; then there is formed between the whole and its part a relation which makes the whole two separate entities, of which the part is one, and the whole less this same part is the other. But the whole less one part is not the whole, and so long as the relation subsists, there is no longer any whole but two unequal parts: from which it follows that the will of one of them is no longer general in relation to the other.

But when the whole people decrees for the whole people, it considers only itself; and if a relation is then formed, it is between the entire object from one point of view and the whole object from another point of view, without any division of the whole. It is this act that I call a law.

When I say that the object of the laws is always general, I mean that the law considers the subjects in a body and the actions as abstract, never a man as an individual nor a particular action. Thus the law can very well decree that there will be privileges, but it cannot confer them on anyone by name; the law can create several Classes of Citizens, even assign the characteristics that confer a right to membership in these Classes, but it cannot name specific persons to be admitted to them; it can establish a royal Government and a hereditary succession, but it cannot elect a king or appoint a royal family; in a word, no function that relates to an individual object belongs to the legislative power.

On this idea one sees instantly that it is no longer necessary to ask who is responsible for making the laws, since they are acts of the general will; nor whether the Prince is above the laws, since he is a member of the State; nor if the law can be unjust, since no one is unjust to himself; nor how one is free and subject to the laws, since they are only registers of our wills.

One sees further that the law uniting the universality of the will with that of the object, what any man, whoever he may be, orders on his own, is not a law; what is ordered even by the Sovereign regarding a particular object is not a law, but a decree, not an act of sovereignty, but of magistracy.

I therefore call every State ruled by laws a Republic, under whatever form of administration it could have; for then only the public interest governs and the public entity [Latin: *res publica*] is real. Every legitimate Government is republican; I will explain later what Government is.

Laws are properly only the conditions of the civil association. The People, submitting to the laws, ought to be their author; it concerns only those who are associating together to regulate the conditions of the society. But how will they regulate them? Will it be in a common accord by sudden inspiration? Does the body politic have an organ to announce its will? Who will give it the foresight necessary to frame its acts and publish them in advance, or how will it pronounce them at the moment of need? How will a blind multitude, which often does not know what it wants because it rarely knows what is good for it, carry out an enterprise so great and also difficult as a system of legislation? By itself the people always wants the good, but by itself does not always discern it. The general will is always upright, but the judgment which guides it is not always enlightened. It is necessary to make it see objects as they are, sometimes as they ought to appear, to point out the good road it seeks, to guard it from the seduction of private wills, to bring before its eyes considerations of places and times, to balance the attraction of present and tangible advantages against the danger of distant and hidden evils. Private individuals see the good they reject; the public wants the good it does not see. All have equal need of guides. It is necessary to obligate the former to conform their wishes to their reason; it is necessary to teach the latter to know what it wants. Then from public enlightenment results the union of the understanding and the will in the social body, hence the precise concourse of the parts, and finally the maximum force of the whole. From this arises the necessity of a Legislator.

VII. Of the Legislator

In order to discover the best rules of society which are suitable to nations, there would be needed a superior intelligence who saw all the passions of men and who had not experienced any of them; who would have no relation to our nature and yet knew it thoroughly; whose happiness would not depend on us and who would be quite willing to occupy himself with ours; finally, one who, preparing for himself a distant glory in the progress of time, could work in one age and find satisfaction in another. Gods would be needed to give laws to men.

The same reasoning that Caligula used as to fact, Plato used with regard to right in order to define the civil or royal person whom he seeks in his book on ruling [i.e., the *Statesman*]. But if it is true that a great Prince is a rare man, what will a great Legislator be? The first has only to follow the model which the other has to propose. The latter is the engineer who invents the machine, the former is only the workman who puts it in readiness and makes it work. In the birth of societies, says Montesquieu, it is the chiefs of republics who make the institutions, and afterward it is the institutions which form the chiefs of republics.

He who dares to undertake the instituting of a people ought to feel himself capable, as it were, of changing human nature; of transforming each individual, who in himself is a perfect and solitary whole, into part of a greater whole from which this individual receives in some way his life and his being; of altering the constitution of man so as to reinforce it; of substituting a partial and moral existence for the physical and independent existence we have all received from nature. It is necessary, in a word, to remove man's own forces in order to give him some that are strange and which he is not able to use without the help of others. The more these natural forces are dead and annihilated, the greater and more durable are those acquired, the more too is the institution solid and perfect: so that if each Citizen is nothing, and can be nothing, except in combination with all others, and if the force acquired by the whole be equal or superior to the sum of the natural forces of all individuals, one can say that legislation has attained the highest possible point of perfection.

The Legislator is in all respects an extraordinary man in the State. If he ought to be so by his genius, he is not less so by his function. It is not magistracy, it is not sovereignty. This office, which constitutes the republic, does not enter into its constitution; it is a particular and superior function which has nothing in common with human dominion; for if he who controls men should not have control over the laws, he who has control over the laws should not control men; otherwise, the laws, as ministers of his passions, would often serve only to perpetuate his acts of injustice; he would never be able to prevent his private views from corrupting the sacredness of his work....

He who drafts the laws, then, does not have or should not have any legislative right, and even the people cannot, if it wishes, divest itself of this incommunicable right, because according to the fundamental pact, only the general will obligates individuals and one cannot be assured that a particular will has conformed to the general will until after it has been submitted to the free votes of the people; I have already said that, but it is not useless to repeat it.

Thus one finds at the same time in the work of legislation two things which seem incompatible: an enterprise above human force, and to execute it an authority that is nothing.

Another difficulty merits attention. Wise men who wish to speak their own language to the people instead of using the common speech will not be understood. Besides, there are a thousand kinds of ideas that it is impossible to translate into the language of the people. Very general views and very remote objects are equally beyond their grasp: each individual, appreciating no other plan of government than that which relates to his private interest, appreciates with difficulty the advantages he should receive from the continual privations which good laws impose. For a newly formed people to be able to appreciate the sane maxims of politics and to follow the fundamental rules of statecraft, it would be necessary that the effect could become the cause; that the social spirit, which ought to be the accomplishment of the institution, would preside over the institution itself; and that men be already, prior to the laws, that which they should become by means of them. Since the Legislator is able to employ neither force nor reasoning, he must have recourse to an authority of a different order, which can win without violence and persuade with convincing.

This is what in all times has forced the fathers of nations to have recourse to the intervention of heaven, and to give the Gods credit for their own wisdom, to the end that the peoples, brought under the laws of the State as to those of nature, and recognizing the same power in the formation of man and in that of the city, obey with liberty and bear with docility the yoke of public felicity.

This sublime reason which rises above the reach of common men the Legislator places in the mouth of the immortals in order to win over by divine authority those unable to be moved by human prudence. But not every man can make the Gods speak or be believed when he announces himself as their interpreter. The great soul of the Legislator is the true miracle which should prove his mission. Any man can engrave stone tablets, or buy an oracle, or feign a secret relationship with some divinity, or train a bird to speak in his ear, or find some other crude means of imposing on the people. He who knows only this could even assemble by chance a crowd of madmen, but he will never found an empire and his extravagant work will soon perish with him. Vain delusions form a transient bond; only wisdom renders it durable. The Judaic law which still subsists, and that of the child of Ishmael, which has ruled half the world for ten centuries, still proclaim today the great men who enunciated them; and while proud philosophy or blind party spirit sees in them only lucky impostors, the true student of politics admires in their institutions this great and powerful genius who presides over durable institutions.

It is not necessary to conclude from this with Warburton that politics and religions have among us a common object, but rather that in the origin of nations, one serves as instrument of the other.

XI. Of the Diverse Systems of Legislation

If one seeks to find precisely what constitutes the greatest good of all, which ought to be the goal of every system of legislation, one will find that it reduces itself to two principal objects, *liberty* and *equality*. Liberty, because all self-dependence is so much force taken away from the body of the State; equality because liberty cannot subsist without it.

I have already said what civil liberty is; with regard to equality, it is necessary not to understand by this word that every degree of power and of wealth should be absolutely the same, but that, as to power, it should be above all violence and never exercised except in virtue of position and the laws; and as to wealth, no citizen should be so opulent as to be able to buy another, and none so poor as to be constrained to sell himself. This presumes on the side of the mighty moderation, of goods and influence, and on the side of the lowly, moderation of avarice and of covetousness.

This equality is said to be a chimerical fantasy which cannot exist in practice. But if abuse is inevitable, does it follow that abuse should not be at least regulated? It is precisely because the force of things always tends to destroy equality that the force of legislation should always tend to maintain it. . . .

BOOK III

Before speaking of the diverse forms of Government, let us try to fix the precise meaning of that word, which has not yet been very well explained.

I. Of Government in General

I warn the reader that this chapter should be read with care, and that I do not know the art of being clear to those who do not wish to be attentive.

Every free action has two causes which concur to produce it, the one moral, namely the will that determines the act; the other physical, namely the power that executes it. When I walk toward an object, it is first necessary that I want to go there; in the second place, that my feet carry me there. Should a paralytic wish to run, should an agile man not wish to do so, both will remain where they are. The body politic has the same motive power: in it one likewise distinguishes force and will. The latter is under the name of *legislative power*, the former under the name of *executive power*. Nothing is or should be done there [in the body politic] without their concurrence.

We have seen that the legislative power belongs to the people, and can belong to it alone. It is easy to see, on the contrary, by the principles already established, that the executive power cannot belong to the general public as Legislative or Sovereign; because this power consists only in particular acts which are not the province of the law, nor consequently of the Sovereign, all of whose acts can only be laws.

It is then necessary for the public force to have an appropriate agent that unifies it and puts it to work according to the directions of the general will, which serves as the means of communication between the State and the Sovereign, which in some way accomplishes in the public person what the union of soul and body does in man. This is in the State the reason for Government, improperly confused with the Sovereign, of which it is only the Minister.

What then is the Government? An intermediate body established between the subjects and the Sovereign for their mutual correspondence, charged with the execution of the laws, and to the maintenance of liberty, both civil and political.

The members of this body are called Magistrates or *Kings*, that is to say *Governors;* and the body as a whole bears the name of *Prince*. Thus those who claim that the act by which a people submits to its chiefs is not a contract are quite correct. It is absolutely only a commission, an employment in which simple officers of the

Sovereign exercise in its name the power which it has entrusted to them, and which it can limit, modify, and take back when it pleases to do so, since the alienation of such a right is incompatible with the nature of the social body, and contrary to the goal of the association.

I then call *Government* or supreme administration the legitimate exercise of the executive power, and Prince or Magistrate, the man or the body charged with that administration.

In the Government are found the intermediary forces, whose relationship composes the relation of the whole to the whole or of the Sovereign to the State. One can represent this last relation by that of the extremes of a continuous proportion, of which the proportional mean is the Government. The Government receives from the Sovereign the orders it gives to the people, and so that the State may be in good equilibrium it is necessary, all things considered that there be equality between the product or power of the Government taken in itself and the product or power of the citizens, who are sovereigns on one side and subjects on the other.

Further, one could not alter any of these three terms without instantly destroying the proportion. If the Sovereign wishes to govern, or if the Magistrate wishes to provide laws, or if the subjects refuse to obey, disorder takes the place of regularity, force and will no longer act in concert, and the State falls into despotism or anarchy. Finally, as there is only one proportional mean in each relationship, only one good government is possible in a State. But, as a thousand events can change the relationships of a people, different Governments are able to be good not only for diverse peoples, but for the same people at different times.

To try to give an idea of the diverse relations which reign between the two extremes, I will take as an example the number of people, as an easy relationship to express.

Suppose the State is composed of ten thousand citizens. The Sovereign can only be considered collectively and as a body. But each private person in his quality as subject is considered as an individual. Thus the Sovereign is to the subject as ten thousand to one; this is to say that each member of the State is only one ten thousandth of the sovereign authority, even he is entirely subjected to it. Should the people be composed of one hundred thousand men, the condition of the subjects does not change, and each bears equally the entire dominion of the laws, while his vote, reduced to one hundred thousandth, has ten times less influence in their forming. The subject, then, always remains one, the ratio of the Sovereign to the subject always increases in proportion to the number of Citizens. Whence it follows that the larger the State grows, the more liberty diminishes.

When I say that the ratio increases, I understand that it is farther removed from equality. Thus the larger the ratio in the geometric sense, the lesser the relation in the everyday sense; in the first, the relation is considered according to the quantity measured by the quotient, and in the latter, considered according to identity, estimated by similarity.

Now the less the individual wills relate to the general will, that is to say customary conduct to the laws, the more repressive force has to be increased. The Government, then, in order to be good, should be relatively stronger as the people becomes more numerous.

On the other hand, the growth of the State giving the trustees of public authority more temptations and means to abuse their power, the more the Government has to have force to contain the people, the more force the Sovereign should have in turn in order to contain the Government. I speak here not of an absolute force, but of the relative force of the diverse parts of the State.

It follows from this double ratio that the continued proportion between the Sovereign, the Prince, and the people is hardly an arbitrary idea, but a necessary consequence of the nature of the political body. It follows further that one of the extremes, namely the people as subject, being fixed and represented by unity, whenever the double ratio increases or diminishes, the single ratio increases or diminishes similarly, and consequently the middle term is changed. This serves to show that there is no one constitution of Government unique and absolute, but that it is possible to have as many Governments of different natures as there are States of different sizes.

If, in reducing this system to ridicule, one would say that in order to find this proportional mean, and form the body of Government, it is only necessary, according to me, to take the square root of the number of the people, I would respond that I take that number here only as an example, that the relations of which I speak are measured not solely by the number of men, but in general by the amount of action, which results from combining a multitude of causes; that, moreover, if to express myself in fewer words I borrow geometric terms for a moment, I am aware of the fact that geometric precision has no place in moral quantities.

The Government is on a small scale what the body politic which contains it is on the large scale. It is a moral person endowed with certain faculties, active as the Sovereign, passive as the State, and one can break it down into other, similar relations, from which consequently arise a new proportion, and still another within this, similar to the order of tribunals, until one arrives at an indivisible middle term, that is to say one sole chief or supreme magistrate, who is able to be represented, in the middle of this progression, much as the unifying element between the series of fractions and that of whole numbers.

Without embarrassing ourselves with this multiplication of terms, let us be content to consider the Government as a new body within the State, distinct from the people and the Sovereign, and intermediate between the two.

The essential difference between these two bodies is that the State exists by itself, and the Government exists only through the Sovereign. Thus only the dominant will of the Prince is or ought to be the general will or the law; its force is only the public force concentrated in itself: as soon as it wishes to derive from itself some absolute and independent act, the bond tying the whole together begins to loosen. Finally, if it should happen that

the Prince have a particular will more active than that of the Sovereign, and if, in order to obey this private will, he use some of the public force which is in its hands, so that there would be, so to speak, two Sovereigns, one of right and the other of fact: at that instant the social union would vanish and the body politic be dissolved.

However, for the body of the Government to have an existence, a real life that distinguishes it from the body of the State, for all its members to be able to act in concert and fulfill the purpose for which it has been instituted, it needs a particular *self*, a sensibility common to its members, a force, a will of its own that tends toward its own conservation. This particular existence presumes assemblies, councils, a power to deliberate, to resolve, rights, titles, privileges which belong exclusively to the Prince, and which render the condition of the magistrate more honorable, in proportion to which it is more arduous. The difficulties lie in the method of disposing, within the whole, this subordinate whole, in such a way that it may not weaken the general constitution while strengthening its own; that it always distinguish its particular force directed to its own conservation from the public force directed to the conservation of the State, and that, in a word, it always be ready to sacrifice the Government to the people and not the people to the Government.

Besides, although the artificial body of the Government is the product of another artificial body, and has in some respects only a borrowed and subordinate life, that does not prevent it from being able to act with more or less vigor or speed, to enjoy, so to speak, more or less robust health. Finally, without directly departing from the goal for which it was instituted, it can deviate more or less from it according to the manner in which it is constituted.

From all these differences arise the diverse relations that the Government ought to have with the body of the State, according to the accidental and particular relationships by which that same State is modified. For often the Government that is best in itself will become the most vicious, if its relations are not altered according to the defects of the body politic to which it belongs.

II. Of the Principle Which Constitutes the Diverse Forms of Government

In order to expose the general cause of these differences, it is necessary to distinguish here the Prince and the Government, as I have already distinguished the State from the Sovereign.

The body of the magistracy can be composed of a greater or lesser number of members. We have said that the relation of the Sovereign to the subjects was greater as the number of people was greater, and by an evident analogy we can say the same of the Government with regard to the Magistrates.

Now the total force of the Government, being always that of the State, does not vary: from which it follows that the more of that force it uses on its own members, the less remains for it to act on the whole people.

Thus the more numerous are the Magistrates, the weaker the Government. As that maxim is fundamental, let us apply it to clarify it better.

We can distinguish in the person of the magistrate three essentially different wills. First, the individual's own will, which tends only to his private advantage; second, the common will of the magistrates, which relates itself uniquely to the advantage of the Prince, and which can be called the corporate will, being general in relation to the Government, and particular in relation to the State, of which the Government is a part; third, the will of the people, or the sovereign will, which is general as much in relation to the State considered as the whole, as in relation to the Government considered as part of the whole.

In a perfect system of legislation, the particular or individual will ought to be null, the corporate will proper to the Government very subordinate, and consequently the general or sovereign will always dominant and the sole rule of all the others.

According to the natural order, on the contrary, these different wills become more active as they become more concentrated. Thus the general will is always the weakest, the corporate will has the second rank, and the private will is first of all; so that in the Government each member is first himself, then Magistrate, and then citizen, a gradation directly opposed to what the social order requires.

Granting this, suppose that the whole Government is in the hands of one man. The particular will and the corporate will are then perfectly united, and consequently the latter is in the highest possible degree of intensity. Further, as it is the degree of will on which the use of force depends, and the absolute force of the Government does not vary, it follows that the most active of Governments is that of one man.

On the contrary, suppose we unite the Government with the legislative authority; let us make the Sovereign into the Prince and all of the Citizens into as many Magistrates. Then the corporate will, confounded with the general will, will be no more active than it and will leave to the particular will its full force. Thus the Government, always with the same absolute force, will have attained its *minimum* relative force or activity.

These relations are incontestable, and other considerations also serve to confirm them. One sees, for example, that each magistrate is more active in his group than each citizen is in his, and consequently the particular will has much more influence in the acts of the Government than in those of the Sovereign; for each magistrate is nearly always charged with some function of Government, while each citizen, taken separately, exercises no function of sovereignty. Besides, the more a State is extended, the more its real force is increased even though not by reason of its size: but if the State remains the same, the magistrates may well be multiplied without the Government acquiring any more real force, because that force is the force of the State, whose measure remains unchanged. Thus the relative force or activity of the Government diminishes, without its absolute or real force being able to increase.

It is also certain that public matters are expedited more slowly as more people are charged with them, that in giving too much importance to prudence one does not give enough to fortune, that one lets opportunity escape, and that owing to excessive deliberation the fruits of deliberation are often lost.

I have just proved that the Government is weakened as the magistrates are multiplied, and I have already proved that the larger the population, the more the repressive force should be increased. From this it follows that the ratio of the magistrates to the Government ought to be the inverse ratio of subjects to Sovereign; this is to say that the more the State grows, the more the Government should shrink; so that the number of chiefs diminishes as the number of people is increased.

But I speak here only of the relative force of Government, not of its rectitude: for, on the contrary, the more numerous the magistracy, the more the corporate will approaches the general will; whereas under a single magistrate, this same corporate will is, I have said, only a particular will. Thus one loses on one side what one gains on the other, and the art of the Legislator is to know how to fix the point where the force and the will of the Government are always combined in the reciprocal proportion most advantageous to the State.

III. Division of Governments

We have seen in the preceding chapter why one distinguishes the diverse species or forms of Governments by the number of members who compose them; it remains to see here how this division is made.

The Sovereign can, in the first place, commit the charge of Government to all the people or the majority of the people, in such a way that more citizens are magistrates than simply individual citizens. One gives to this form of government the name of *Democracy*.

Or it can confine the Government to the hands of a small number, so that there are more simple Citizens than magistrates; this form bears the name of *Aristocracy*.

Finally, it can concentrate the whole Government in the hands of one sole magistrate from whom all the others derive their power. This third form is the most common and is called *Monarchy* or royal Government.

One should note that all these forms or at least the first two are more or less variable and may indeed have a considerable range; for Democracy can embrace all the people or be restricted to half. Aristocracy, in its turn, can confine itself to half the number down to the smallest, indeterminately. Royalty itself is susceptible to some division. Sparta always had two Kings by its constitution; and one has seen in the Roman Empire as many as eight Emperors at one time without being able to say that the Empire was divided. Thus there is a point where each form of Government blends with the next, and one sees that, under three sole types, Government can really be divided into as many diverse forms as the State has Citizens.

There is more: this same Government being in some respects able to subdivide itself into other parts, one part administered in one manner and the other part in another, from these three combined forms there can emerge a multitude of mixed forms, each of which is multipliable by all the simple forms.

In all times, there has been much dispute about the best form of Government, without considering that each of them is the best in certain cases, and the worst in others.

If in different States the number of supreme magistrates should be in an inverse ratio to that of the Citizens, it follows that generally Democratic Government suits small states, Aristocratic medium-sized, and Monarchical large ones. This rule is immediately derived from the principle, but how count the multitude of circumstances which can furnish exceptions?

IV. Of Democracy

He who makes the law knows better than anyone how it ought to be executed and interpreted. It seems then that there could be no better constitution than the one in which the executive power is joined to the legislative. But it is just that which renders this Government insufficient in certain regards, because things that ought to be distinguished are not, and the prince and the Sovereign, being the same person, only form as it were a Government without a Government.

It is not good that he who makes the laws execute them, nor that the body of the people turn their attention away from general considerations in order to give it to particular objects. Nothing is more dangerous than the influence of private interests in public affairs, and the abuse of laws by the Government is a lesser evil than the corruption of the Legislator, the inevitable result of private considerations. Then, the State having been corrupted in its substance, all reform becomes impossible. A people who would never abuse the Government would not abuse independence either; a people who would always govern well would have no need of being governed.

To take the term in a rigorous sense, there has never existed a true Democracy, and it will never exist. It is contrary to the natural order that the greater number should govern and that the lesser number should be governed. One cannot imagine the people remaining constantly assembled in order to attend to public affairs, and one readily sees that it would not know how to establish commissions for this purpose without the form of the administration changing.

In fact, I think it possible to lay down as a principle that when the functions of the government are divided among several tribunals, sooner or later those with the fewest members acquire the greatest authority, if only because of the facility in expediting the public business which naturally brings this about.

Besides, how many things difficult to unite does this Government presume! First, a very small State where the people are easily assembled and where each citizen can easily know all the others; second, a great simplicity of moral customs, which prevents a multitude of public matters and thorny discussions; next, a great equality of rank and fortune, without which equality in rights and

authority would not long subsist; finally, little or no luxury because luxury either is the result of wealth or renders it necessary; it corrupts both the rich and the poor, the one by possession, the other by covetousness; it sells the fatherland to indolence and vanity; it deprives the State of all its citizens in order to enslave some to others, and all to opinion.

That is why a celebrated author has named virtue as the principle of the Republic, for all these conditions could not subsist without virtue; but failing to make the necessary distinctions, this great genius often lacked accuracy and sometimes clarity, and did not see that the Sovereign authority being everywhere the same, the same principle ought to function in every well-constituted State, more or less, it is true, according to the form of Government.

Let us add that there is no Government so subject to civil wars and internal agitations as the Democratic or popular, because there is none which tends so strongly and continually to change its form, nor demands more vigilance and courage in order to be maintained in its own form. It is especially in this constitution that the Citizen ought to arm himself with force and steadfastness and to say each day of his life from his heart what a virtuous Palatine said in the Diet of Poland: "Malo periculosam libertatem quam quietum servitium." [I prefer liberty with danger to peace with slavery.]

If there were a people of Gods, it would govern itself democratically. A Government so perfect is not suited to men.

V. Of Aristocracy

We have here two very distinct moral persons, namely the Government and the Sovereign, and consequently two general wills, the one in relation to all the citizens, the other solely for the members of the administration. Thus, although the Government is able to regulate its internal policy as it pleases, it is never able to speak to the people in the name of the Sovereign, that is to say in the name of the people itself; this must never be forgotten.

The first societies governed themselves aristocratically. The family heads deliberated among themselves about public affairs. The young people deferred without distress to the authority of experience. Hence the names of *Priests, Ancients, Senate, Elders*. The savages of North America still govern themselves this way in our day, and are very well governed.

But, as the inequality due to institutions prevailed over natural inequality, wealth or power was preferred to age, and Aristocracy became elective. Finally, the power transmitted with the father's goods to the children created patrician families, rendering the Government hereditary, and one witnessed Senators twenty years of age.

There are then three kinds of Aristocracy: natural, elective, hereditary. The first is suited only for simple peoples; the third is the worst of all governments. The second is the best: it is Aristocracy properly named.

Beyond the advantage of the distinction between the two powers, aristocracy has that of the choice of its members; for in popular Government all the Citizens are born magistrates; but this one limits them to a small number, and they only become so by election: a means by which probity, insight, experience, and all the other reasons for public preference and esteem are so many new guarantees of being wisely governed.

Additionally, assemblies are more conveniently held, public affairs are better discussed, expedited with more order and diligence, the repute of the State is better sustained abroad by venerable Senators than by an unknown or scorned multitude.

In a word, it is the best and most natural order that the wisest should govern the multitude, when it is certain that they will govern it for its profit and not for their own; there being no need to uselessly multiply devices, nor to do with twenty thousand men what one hundred well-chosen men can do still better. But it need be remarked that the corporate interest begins here to direct the public force less under the rule of the general will, and

that another inevitable propensity removes from the laws a part of the executive power.

With regard to particular proprieties, a State should not be so small, nor a people so simple and righteous, that the execution of the laws immediately ensues from the public will, as in a good Democracy. Nor again must a nation be so large that the chiefs, dispersed in order to govern, are able to determine the Sovereign each in his own department, and begin by making themselves independent in order to finally become the masters.

But if Aristocracy requires some fewer virtues than popular Government, it requires others which are properly its own; as moderation among the wealthy and contentment among the poor; for it seems that a rigorous equality would be out of place there; it was not even observed in Sparta.

Further, if this form permits a certain inequality of fortune, it is indeed so that generally the administration of public affairs should be entrusted to those who are better able to give their time to it, but not, as Aristotle claims, so that the wealthy always be preferred. On the contrary, it is important that an opposite choice should sometimes inform the people that there are more important reasons for preference in the merits of men than in their wealth.

VI. Of Monarchy

Up to this point we have considered the Prince as a moral and collective person, united by the force of the laws, and entrusted with the executive power in the State. We now have to consider this power united in the hands of one natural person, a real man, who alone has the right to dispose of it according to the laws. He is what one calls a Monarch or a King.

Completely contrary to other administrations where a collective entity represents an individual, in this one an individual represents a collective entity; so that the moral unity which constitutes the Prince is at the same time a physical unity, in which all the faculties which the law combines in the other with such effort are found naturally combined.

Thus the will of the people, and the will of the Prince, and the public force of the State, and the private force of the Government, all respond to the same motive, all the mechanisms of the machine are in the same hand, everything works to the same end; there are no opposing movements that cancel each other, and one can imagine no kind of constitution in which a lesser effort produces more notable an action. Archimedes tranquilly seated on the shore and effortlessly pulling along a large Vessel represents to me a skillful monarch governing his vast States from his private study, and making everything move while appearing to be motionless.

But if there is no Government that has more vigor, there is none where the private will has greater sway and more easily dominates others; everything works to the same end, it is true, but this end is not the goal of public happiness, and the very force of the Administration ceaselessly operates to the detriment of the State.

Kings want to be absolute, and from afar one calls out to them that the best means for being so is to make themselves loved by their peoples. This maxim is very fine and even very true in some respects. Unfortunately, it will always be jeered at in the Courts. Power which comes from the love of the peoples is without doubt the greater; but it is precarious and conditional, and never will satisfy Princes. The best Kings wish to be able to be wicked if it pleases them, without ceasing to be the masters. A political sermonizer will tell them in vain that the power of the people being their own, their greatest interest is that the people should be flourishing, numerous, formidable. They know very well that is not true. Their personal interest is first that the People be weak, miserable, and never able to resist them. I admit that, supposing the subjects always perfectly submissive, the interest of the Prince should then be that the people are powerful, to the end that this power, being his own, would make him formidable to his neighbors; but this interest is only secondary and subordinate, and as the two suppositions are incompatible, it is natural that Princes

always give preference to the maxim which is most immediately useful to them. It is this that Samuel strongly represented to the Hebrews; it is this that Machiavelli made evident. While feigning to give lessons to the Kings he has given great ones to the peoples. *The Prince* of Machiavelli is the book of republicans.

We have found, by general relationships, that monarchy is suitable only to large States, and we find this again by examining it itself. The more numerous the public administration, the more the ratio of the Prince to the subjects diminishes and approaches equality, so that this relation is one of equality even as in Democracy. This same ratio increases as the Government shrinks, and it is at its *maximum* when the Government is in the hands of a single man. Then there is found too great a distance between the Prince and the People, and the State lacks cohesiveness. In order to create this, intermediary orders are needed. Princes, Grandees, and the nobility are necessary to fill them. Now none of this is suited to a small State, which is ruined by all these distinctions.

But if it is difficult that a large State be well governed, it is much more difficult that it be well governed by one man alone, and everyone knows what happens when the King appoints deputies.

An essential and inevitable defect which will always place monarchical government beneath the republican is that in the latter the public voice hardly ever raises to the highest positions any but enlightened and capable men, who fill them with honor; whereas those who attain rank in monarchies are most often merely petty bunglers, petty rascals, petty intriguers, whose petty talents, which enable them to attain high posts in the Courts, only serve to show the public their ineptitude as soon as they have attained these posts. The people is mistaken in its choice much less than the Prince, and a man of true merit is almost as rare in the ministry as a fool at the head of a republican government. Also, when by some lucky chance one of those men born to govern takes control of public business in a monarchy almost wrecked by this crowd of fine managers, one is totally surprised by the resources that he finds, and it is an epoch-making event in a country.

For a monarchical State to be well governed, it would be necessary that its size or extent be proportionate to the capabilities of he who governs. It is easier to conquer than to rule. With a sufficient lever, the world can be moved by a finger, but to sustain it requires the shoulders of Hercules. Should the State be the least bit large, the Prince is nearly always too small for it. When on the contrary it happens that the State is too small for its chief, which is very rare, it is still badly governed, because the chief, always following the grandeur of his views, forgets the people's interest, and makes them no less discontent by the abuse of his overabundant talents than does a chief limited by those which he lacks. It would require, so to speak, that a kingdom enlarge or contract itself in every reign according to the capacity of the Prince; rather, as the talents of a Senate are more stable, the State is able to have permanent boundaries and the administration would not go on any less well.

The most perceptible inconvenience of the Government of a single person is the lack of that continual succession which forms in the other two an uninterrupted bond. One King dies, another is needed; elections leave dangerous intervals, they are stormy, and unless the Citizens have a disinterestedness and integrity which this Government hardly manages to permit, intrigue and corruption intermingle throughout. It is difficult for one to whom the State has been sold not to sell it in turn, and recoup for himself from the helpless the money that the powerful have extorted from him. Sooner or later everything becomes venal under such an administration, and the peace which is enjoyed under kings is worse than the disorder of these interregnums.

What has been done to prevent these ills? Crowns have been made hereditary in certain families, and an order of succession has been established which prevents any dispute at the death of Kings. That is to say, substituting the inconvenience of regencies for that of elections, an apparent tranquillity has been preferred to a wise administration, and it is preferred to risk having infants, monsters, or imbeciles for chiefs than having to argue over the choice of good Kings; it has not been considered that in thus exposing oneself to the risk of this alternative, one sets nearly all the odds against himself. It was a very sensible reply that Dionysius the Younger gave to his father, who, reproaching him for a dishonorable action, said: "Have I given you such an example?" "Ah," replied the son, "your father was not king."

Everything conspires to deprive a man elevated to command others of justice and reason. Much trouble is taken, it is said, to teach young Princes the art of ruling: it does not seem that this education profits them. One would do better to begin by teaching them the art of obeying. The greatest kings celebrated by history were not brought up to rule; it is a science that one has never mastered less than after having studied it too much, and that one acquires better by obeying than by commanding. *Nam ultissimus idem ac brevissimus bonarum malarumque rerum delectus, cogitare quid aut nolueris sub alio principe, aut volueris.* [Because the best and shortest way to discover what is good and what is bad is to ask what you would have wished to happen or not to happen, if another than you had been king.]

One consequence of this lack of coherence is the instability of royal government, which, being regulated alternatively on one level and then on another, according to the character of the ruling Prince or of the people ruling for him, cannot long maintain a fixed aim or a consistent course of conduct: this variation, which always makes the state drift from maxim to maxim, from project to project, does not take place in other Governments, where the prince is always the same. Thus one sees that in general if there is more cunning in a Court, there is more wisdom in a Senate, and that Republics go to their goals by more constant and better-followed policies; whereas each revolution in the [royal] Ministry produces one in the State; the maxim common to all Ministers, and nearly all Kings, being to take up the reverse of their predecessors in everything.

From this same incoherence is found the solution of a sophism very familiar to all defenders of royalty; not only is civil Government compared to the Government of the household and the prince to the father of the family, an error already refuted, but all the virtues of which he will have need are liberally ascribed to this magistrate, while always supposing that the Prince is what he ought to be; with the aid of this supposition royal Government is evidently preferable to any other, because it is incontestably the strongest, and in order to also be the best, it lacks only a corporate will more conformable to the general will.

But if, according to Plato the king by nature is such a rare person, how many times will nature and fortune converge to crown him? And if royal education necessarily corrupts those who receive it, what should one hope from a succession of men trained to rule? It is surely deliberate self-deception to confound royal Government with that of a good King. To see what this Government is in itself, it is necessary to consider it under stupid or wicked Princes; for they will come to the Throne as such, or the Throne will make them such.

These difficulties have not escaped our Authors, but they are not embarrassed by them. The remedy is, they say, to obey without a murmur. God gives bad Kings in his anger, and one must endure them as chastisements from Heaven. This discourse is edifying, without doubt; but I do not know if it is not more appropriate to the pulpit than in a book about politics. What is to be said of a doctor who promises miracles and whose entire art is to exhort his sick charge to have patience? One knows well that it is necessary to suffer a bad Government when one has one: the question should be how to find a good one.

VII. Of Mixed Governments

Properly speaking, there is no simple Government. A single Chief must have subordinate magistrates; a popular Government must have a Chief. Thus, in the partition of the executive power, there is always a gradation from the greater number to the less, with this difference, that sometimes the greater number depends on the lesser number, and sometimes the lesser number on the greater number.

Sometimes there is an equal division, either when the constituent parts are in mutual dependence, as in the Government of England; or when the authority of each part is independent but imperfect, as in Poland. This latter form is bad, because there is no unity in the government, and the State lacks cohesion.

Which is better, a simple Government or a mixed Government? This question is much debated among political thinkers, and it requires the same response I have already given concerning every form of Government.

Simple Government is best in itself, solely because it is simple. But when the executive power does not depend enough on the legislative, that is to say when there is a greater ratio between the Prince and the Sovereign than between the people and the Prince, this defect of proportion must be remedied by dividing the Government; for then all its parts have no less authority over the subjects, and their division renders all of them together less strong against the Sovereign.

The same disadvantage is also prevented by establishing intermediate magistrates who, leaving the Government in its entirety, only serve to balance the two powers and to maintain their respective rights. Then the Government is not mixed, it is tempered.

One can remedy the opposite disadvantage by similar means, and when the Government is too loose, Tribunals can be established to concentrate it: this is practiced in all Democracies. In the first case one divides the Government to weaken it, and in the second, in order to reinforce it; for the *maximum* force and weakness are found equally in simple Governments, whereas the mixed forms provide a medium force.

BOOK IV

I. That the General Will Is Indestructible

As long as several men together consider themselves as a single body, they have only one will which relates to the common preservation and to the general well-being. Then all the activities of the State are vigorous and simple, its maxims are clear and luminous, it has no entangled and conflicting interests, the common good is clearly apparent everywhere and only good sense is needed to perceive it. Peace, union, equality, are enemies of political subtleties. Upright and simple men are hard to deceive because of their simplicity; snares and refined pretexts do not impose upon them; they are not even clever enough to be duped. When one sees among the happiest people in the world groups of peasants regulating the affairs of State under an oak tree and always conducting themselves wisely, can one keep from scorning the refinement of other nations, who render themselves illustrious and miserable with so much art and mystery?

A State thus governed has need of very few Laws, and to the extent that it becomes necessary to promulgate new ones, this necessity is universally seen. The first man who proposes them does no more than say what all have already felt, and there is no question of intrigues or eloquence in order to pass into law what each has already resolved to do, as soon as he is sure that the others will do likewise.

What deceives those who reason is that seeing only States badly constituted from their origin, they are impressed by the impossibility of maintaining a similar polity in such States. They laugh on imagining all the follies to which a cunning knave, an insinuating speaker, could persuade the people of Paris or London. They do not know that Cromwell would have been put to hard labor by the people of Berne, and the Duke of Beaufort imprisoned by the Genevans.

But when the social bond begins to loosen and the State to weaken; when private interests begin to make themselves felt and the small societies to influence the great one, the common interest degenerates and finds opponents: unanimity reigns no more in the votes, the general will is no longer the will of all, contradictions, debates arise, and the best advice does not pass without disputes.

Finally, when the State, near its ruin, subsists only as a vain and illusory form, when the social bond is broken in all hearts, when the vilest interest impudently takes on the sacred name of the public good, then the general will becomes mute; all, guided by secret motives, no longer express their opinions as Citizens, as if the State had never existed; and they falsely pass under the name of Laws iniquitous decrees which have only private interest as their goal.

Does it follow from this that the general will is annihilated or corrupted? No, it is always constant, unalterable, and pure; but it is subordinated to others that prevail over it. Each, detaching his own interest from the common interest, sees clearly that he cannot completely separate himself from it, but his part in the public evil does not seem anything to him compared with the exclusive good he intends to appropriate. This private good excepted, he wishes the general good for his own interest as strongly as anyone else. Even in selling his vote for money he does not extinguish the general will in himself; he eludes it. The fault he commits is to change the status of the question and to answer another than what he has been asked; so that instead of saying by his vote, "It is advantageous to the State," he says, "It is advantageous to a certain man or a certain party that such or such a motion passes." Thus the law of public order in the assemblies is not so much to maintain the general will as to make sure that it always is questioned and that it always responds.

I could here present many reflections on the simple right of voting in every act of sovereignty; a right which nothing is able to take away from the Citizens; and on the right to state opinions, to propose, divide, to discuss, that the Government has always great care to leave only to its members; but this important matter would require a separate treatise, and I cannot say everything in this one.

II. Of Voting

From the preceding chapter one sees that the manner in which general affairs are managed gives a sufficiently accurate indication of the actual state of the habitual conduct, and the health of the body politic. The more harmony reigns in the assemblies, that is to say the closer opinions approach unanimity, the more dominant is the general will; but long debates, dissensions, tumult, indicate the ascendancy of private interests and the decline of the State.

This seems less evident when two or more orders enter into its constitution, as in Rome the Patricians and the Plebeians, whose quarrels often troubled the *comitia*, even in the finest times of the republic; but this exception is more apparent than real, for then, by the vice inherent in the body politic, there are, so to speak, two States in one: what is not true of the two together is true of each separately. And in fact, even in the stormiest times the plebiscites of the people, when the Senate did not interfere with them, always passed tranquilly and by a large majority of votes: the Citizens having only one interest, the people only one will.

At the other extremity of the circle unanimity returns. It is when the citizens, having fallen into slavery, no longer have either liberty or will. Then fright and flattery change votes into acclamations; one no longer deliberates, but adores or curses. Such was the vile manner of expressing opinions in the Senate under the Emperors. Sometimes it was done with ridiculous precautions. Tacitus observed that under Otho, the Senators, in overwhelming Vitellius with execrations, arranged to make a frightening noise at the same time so that if, by chance, he became the master, he would not know what each of them had said.

From these diverse considerations arise the maxims by which one ought to regulate the manner of counting the votes and comparing opinions, according to whether the general will is more or less easy to know, and the State more or less declining.

There is only one single law which by its nature requires unanimous consent. It is the social pact: for civil association is the most voluntary act in the world; every man being born free and master of himself, no one can, under any pretext whatever, subjugate him without his assent. To decide that the son of a slave is born a slave is to decide that he is not born a man.

If, then, at the time of the social pact, there are found some opponents of it, their opposition does not invalidate the contract, it only prevents them from being included in it: they are foreigners among citizens. When the State is instituted, consent is in residence; to live in a territory is to submit oneself to sovereignty.

Outside of this basic contract, the voice of the greater number always obliges all the others; it is a consequence of the contract itself. But one asks how a man can be free and forced to conform to wills that are not his own. How are opponents free and yet subject to laws to which they have not consented?

I respond that the question is poorly posed. The citizen consents to all the laws, even those which are passed despite him, and even to those that punish him when he dares to violate any of them. The constant will of all the members of the State is the general will: by it they are citizens and free. When a law is proposed in the assembly of the People, what is asked of them is not precisely whether they approve the proposition or reject it, but whether or not it conforms to the general will which is their own: each in giving his vote states his opinion on that question, and from the counting of the votes is taken the declaration of the general will. When the opinion contrary to mine prevails, that only proves that I was mistaken, and that what I had considered to be the general will was not. If my private opinion had prevailed, I would have done something other than I had wanted to do, and then I would not have been free.

This supposes, it is true, that all the characteristics of the general will are still in the majority; when they cease to be there, whichever side one takes, there is no longer any liberty.

In showing earlier how private wills have been substituted for the general will in public deliberations, I have sufficiently indicated the practicable means for preventing this abuse; I will speak of it again later on. With regard to the proportional number of the votes required to declare this will, I have also stated the principles by which one can determine it. The difference of a single vote breaks a tie, only one opposed breaks unanimity; but between unanimity and a tie vote there are many unequal divisions, at each of which one can fix this number according to the condition and needs of the body politic.

Two general maxims can serve to regulate these ratios: the one, that the more important and serious the deliberations, the closer the prevailing opinion should approach unanimity; the other, that the more the matter requires speed of decision, the more one can reduce the prescribed difference in the division of opinions: in deliberations that must be resolved immediately, a majority by one vote should suffice. The first of these maxims seems more suitable to laws, and the second to business matters. Be that as it may, it is by their combination that the best ratios are established by which a majority can decide.

DAVID HUME

~

INTRODUCTION

ARTHUR KUFLIK

The most far-ranging of early modern British philosophers, David Hume (1711–1776) was born in Edinburgh, Scotland, to a modestly prosperous, small landholding family. When David was two years old, his father died. By the age of twelve, Hume was studying at Edinburgh University. Between 1734 and 1737, he drafted what was to become his first, and now widely regarded as his greatest, work: *A Treatise of Human Nature*. Two volumes ("Of the Understanding" and "Of the Passions") appeared in 1739 when Hume was twenty-eight, and the final volume ("Of Morals") in 1740. But Hume was greatly disappointed in the lack of attention to the work, later claiming it "fell deadborn from the press." His *Essays, Moral, Political, and Literary*, including "Of Parties in General," was published in 1741 to 1742. Over the years, Hume revised these essays and added others such as "Of the Original Contract" (1748).

Eventually, Hume reworked the ideas he had first propounded in the *Treatise* in the form of shorter, and he believed, better written, pieces, including *An Enquiry Concerning the Principles of Morals* (1751), which by Hume's estimation was his "incomparably" finest work. Hume published his six-volume *The History of England* between 1754 and 1762, and it became the standard reference for nearly a century. The autobiographical *My Own Life*, and other essays, including "Of the Origin of Government," were published posthumously in 1777. The controversial *Dialogues Concerning Natural Religion* finally appeared in 1779.

Between 1763 and 1766, Hume lived in Paris, where he became a celebrated intellectual companion to famous French Enlightenment figures. In 1766, he brought Rousseau back with him to England. Having tried to help the emotionally unstable Rousseau flee from persecution in Switzerland, Hume was stunned when Rousseau accused him of treachery.

For the last two years of his life, Hume endured illness. In late summer of 1776, he received a visit from Adam Smith, one of his closest friends. Encouraged to see Hume in good spirits, Smith "could not help entertaining some faint hopes" of a recovery. "Your hopes are groundless," the older philosopher replied. Hume "then diverted himself" by depicting an imaginary dialogue with the mythological boatman who conveys people to the netherworld. Asking for more time to correct his works and to see how the public would then receive them, Hume envisioned himself bluntly rebuffed: "There will be no end to such excuses. . . . Get into the boat this instant, you lazy, loitering rogue." Hume died soon thereafter.

For Hume, it would be a myth to suppose that people were originally "savage" loners, devoid of trust, in desperate need of government to save them from ceaseless strife. Human beings are naturally motivated, not only by self-concern but by various benevolent inclinations as well: self-sacrificing devotion to their children, pity for the unfortunate, and a measure of genuine kindness toward friends and immediate neighbors. Indeed, the basic unit of human life is the family, and individuals "are trained up by their parents to some rule of conduct and behavior" (*Enquiry Concerning the Principles of Morals [EPM]*, III, I). Moreover, families can live in society with one another even without government, so long as they are few in number and have comparatively modest material aspirations. Society enables people to combine their powers, benefit from division of labor and specialization of tasks, and reduce one another's exposure to "fortune and accidents" (*Treatise*, III, II, II).

But as naturally sociable as people are, society is not immune to serious destabilizing influences. In Hume's view, conflict over "external" goods is especially threatening to the peace and stability of society. This is because of their "easy and loose transition." To secure social peace, Hume urges that there be "stability of possessions" and transference only by "consent" (rather than by force and fraud). But these lofty ideas need to be filled in by more specific guidelines. Such norms—regulating the allocation and use of external goods (property) and fixing the conditions under which people can regard one another as obligated (contract)—are the rules of what Hume calls "justice."

If people were wholly and unlimitedly benevolent, *or* if resources were infinitely abundant, there would be no need for justice. But benevolence, though real, is limited. Moreover, material resources, though generally sufficient for everyone's survival, are not so abundant as to permit everyone to take as much as might seem desirable. So in the circumstances that normally prevail, a scheme of justice is socially necessary.

But which rules of justice can best serve the purpose of securing social peace? Hume had earlier rejected the proposal that each particular good be assigned to whichever individual would make the best personal, or public, use of it. In the *Enquiry*, he considers, and rejects for much the same reasons, a different proposal: Distribute material goods in proportion to each person's moral merit. Because different people can so easily interpret such rules in such different (and typically self-serving) ways, their adoption is more likely to exacerbate than to resolve conflict. The rule "to each equally" seems more promising but suffers from at least two fatal defects: (1) Without differential rewards, society will become far less productive; so strict equality causes more poverty than it alleviates. (2) In the face of inevitable differences in talent, industry, and care, people will wind up with unequal possessions, no matter how equal the initial distribution. To identify and correct such departures from equality, there will have to be frequent interference in people's lives; authority so extensive "must soon degenerate into tyranny."

How then *should* "stability of possession" be achieved? For Hume, appropriate rules of property must be clear and relatively easy to apply. Familiar property rules (e.g., title belongs to the current possessor, or the first possessor, or the longest possessor) are useful, if somewhat conventional, stipulations. In the *Enquiry*, Hume suggests that some considerations are less arbitrarily connected to the support of society. "Who cannot see," he asks, that "whatever is produced or improved by a man's art or industry ought, for ever, to be secured to him"? This rule is evidently not a mere product of the "finer turns of the imagination"; but in contrast with Locke, neither is it grounded in some natural right to the products of one's own labor. The point is simply to encourage productive work.

In the *Treatise*, Hume had described schemes of justice as a "remedy" that "is not deriv'd from nature, but from artifice." That justice is an "artificial" virtue might mislead someone into thinking that it is not really a virtue at all, or not to be taken as seriously as other virtues. In an appendix to the *Enquiry*, Hume clarified himself with the aid of a brilliant metaphor: Acts of benevolence may be compared to stones placed one by one on a wall—*each* stone makes a positive difference. While acts of justice are like stones in a vaulted arch—there must be an overall scheme or design to which *most* of the stones conform if the structure is to stand at all.

Granted the social need for rules of justice, is it also necessary to have government enforce the rules? If human beings were perfectly just, government might be unnecessary. But people are typically led astray by the tendency to prefer what is "near" to what is "remote." Thus, self-love typically favors present satisfaction over long-term wellbeing; and benevolent concern is liable to confine itself to a small circle of friends and neighbors without regard to the larger public interest. Hume argues that although we cannot change our natures, we can "change our circumstances" by setting up appropriate forms of government. Under a wisely arranged political system, the protection of the public interest is made to be in the *personal* interest of those individuals who hold positions of public authority.

From the discussion thus far one might suppose that government's role is limited to keeping the peace, upholding property rights, and enforcing contracts. But in the *Treatise*, Hume clearly associates government with more ambitious public policies as well. As society grows bigger, Hume sees government playing an essential role in coordinating large-scale cooperative endeavors and punishing individuals who try to free-ride on the efforts of others. "Thus bridges are built; harbours open'd; ramparts rais'd; canals form'd; fleets equip'd; and armies disciplin'd; every where by the care of government, which tho' compos'd of men subject to all human infirmities, becomes, by one of the finest and most subtle inventions imaginable . . . in some measure, exempte from all these infirmities" (*Treatise*, III, II, VII).

Hume's initial enthusiasm about this "finest" invention would be tempered in his later writings as he came to recognize more fully the sources of conflict among citizens, and the potential for negligence and corruption in public officials. Thus in "Of Parties in General," Hume laments the ways in which division along theological, ideological, and even racial lines can be at least as destabilizing as conflicts of economic interest. And in such essays as "Of the Origin of Government," Hume grapples with the objection that even "the magistrate himself may often be negligent, or partial, or unjust in his administration." He then indicates two ways of modifying the design of political institutions that could help keep public officials in the service of public, not merely private, interests. Echoing Montesquieu and anticipating Madison, he suggests that there must be "a partition of powers among several members." In addition, those who have a share of the power, thus divided, "must act by general and equal laws, that are previously known." Thus the "invention" of government is actually "finest" when power is so distributed as to create checks and balances against abuse and corruption, and when it is exercised not in an arbitrary or highly discretionary way but according to the principles of rule by law.

Even if we grant that government is a good idea, when is a particular claim to governmental authority legitimate? And when, if ever, is resistance to putative authority justifiable? Hume argues against the claim that a government is legitimate *only* if originally formed by an agreement between itself and the people. For one thing, if we try to ground the duty of allegiance to government in the duty to do what we have given our word to do, there is still the problem of explaining how and why we are bound to keep our word, And it would be circular to respond "because we have given our word to do so." In the end, we can only justify the duty of keeping our word by appealing to what is necessary to the support of society. But this same consideration will *directly* ground our duty of allegiance to government as well. So appealing to contract is an inadequately roundabout way of getting to the ultimate source of political legitimacy and dutiful allegiance.

In opposition to the doctrine of absolute monarchy, Hume recognizes that legitimate authority is not unconditional. To be sure, the "total dissolution" of government is one of the most "terrible" things that can happen. Yet there have been rulers whose tyranny was so contrary to fundamental human interests that it would be a "perversion of common sense" to condemn those who took up arms against them. Hence, "Where a civil law is so perverse as to cross all the interests of society, it loses all its authority, and men judge by the ideas of natural justice, which are conformable to those interests" (*EPM*, III, II, n. 3). Hume obviously believes that such circumstances are rare, but hardly impossible; and that while violent revolution is not to be contemplated lightly, it is sometimes the only viable remaining course. The philosophical point is that disobedience is not to be based on an appeal either to natural rights or to some fictitious original contract, whose terms one alleges to have been violated. Rather, if the justification for having and obeying government is the "general interests and necessities of society," then disobedience can be justified on the same ground. But is there some precise way to know when it is right to resist authority? No. For "'tis certainly impossible for the laws, or even for philosophy, to establish any *particular* rules, by which we may know when resistance is lawful; and decide all controversies which may arise on that subject" (*Treatise*, III, II, X).

Such reluctance to produce an exact formula for political life is characteristic of Hume's approach. In his last political essay, "Of the Origin of Government," for example, we are told that in the contest "between Authority and Liberty . . . neither of them can absolutely prevail," but we are not told very much more about the exact scope of either. When doing political theory, why paint with so broad a brush? For Hume there is a deeper reason, reflecting his own empiricist temperament: "I am apt . . . to entertain a suspicion, that the world is still too young to fix many general truths in politics" ("Of Civil Liberty"). Though we must try to find a sensible middle ground between unacceptable extremes, there is a limit to the precision we can sensibly expect to achieve without greater historical experience and deeper understanding of human nature.

For excellent general studies of Hume's thought, see Norman Kemp Smith, *The Philosophy of David Hume* (London: Macmillan, 1964); Barry Stroud, *Hume* (London: Routledge & Kegan Paul, 1977); and Annette C. Baier, *A Progress of Sentiments: Reflections on Hume's Treatise* (Cambridge, Mass.: Harvard University Press, 1991).

A lucid introduction to Hume's ethical thought, helpfully placing it in the context of the British moral tradition from which it evolved, is *Hume's Moral Theory* (London: Routledge & Kegan Paul, 1980) by J. L. Mackie. Hume's ideas about value, virtue, and justice are carefully examined in light of their psychological underpinnings by Pall S. Ardal in *Passion and Value in Hume's Treatise* (Edinburgh: Edinburgh University Press, 1989).

Looking at Hume from the perspective of contemporary political philosophy, Brian Barry provides a searching analysis in *Theories of Justice* (Berkeley: University of California Press, 1989, Vol. 1, Chap. 4). In *Hume's Philosophy of Common Life* (Chicago: University of Chicago Press, 1984), Donald W. Livingston interprets Hume as a political conservative. The opposite case for regarding Hume as a would-be reformer of established political practices is ably argued by John B. Stewart in *Opinion and Reform in Hume's Political Philosophy* (Princeton, N.J.: Princeton University Press, 1992). Frederick G. Whelan, *Order and Artifice in Hume's Political Philosophy* (Princeton, N.J.: Princeton University Press, 1985) shows how Hume treats history and experience as sources of political value.

An Enquiry Concerning the Principles of Morals

SECTION III

Part I

Of Justice

That Justice is useful to society, and consequently that *part* of its merit, at least, must arise from that consideration, it would be a superfluous undertaking to prove. That public utility is the *sole* origin of justice, and that reflections on the beneficial consequences of this virtue are the *sole* foundation of its merit; this proposition, being more curious and important, will better deserve our examination and enquiry.

Let us suppose, that nature has bestowed on the human race such profuse *abundance* of all *external* conveniences, that, without any uncertainty in the event, without any care or industry on our part, every individual finds himself fully provided with whatever his most voracious appetites can want, or luxurious imagination wish or desire. His natural beauty, we shall suppose, surpasses all acquired ornaments: The perpetual clemency of the seasons renders useless all cloaths or covering: The raw herbage affords him the most delicious fare; the clear fountain, the richest beverage. No laborious occupation required: No tillage: No navigation. Music, poetry, and contemplation, form his sole business: Conversation, mirth, and friendship his sole amusement.

It seems evident, that, in such a happy state, every other social virtue would flourish, and receive tenfold encrease; but the cautious, jealous virtue of justice would never once have been dreamed of. For what purpose make a partition of goods, where every one has already more than enough? Why give rise to property, where there cannot possibly be any injury? Why call this object *mine*, when, upon the seizing of it by another, I need but stretch out my hand to possess myself of what is equally valuable? Justice, in that case, being totally USELESS, would be an idle ceremonial, and could never possibly have place in the catalogue of virtues.

We see, even in the present necessitous condition of mankind, that, wherever any benefit is bestowed by nature in an unlimited abundance, we leave it always in common among the whole human race, and make no subdivisions of right and property. Water and air, though the most necessary of all objects, are not challenged as the property of individuals; nor can any man commit injustice by the most lavish use and enjoyment of these blessings. In fertile extensive countries, with few inhabitants, land is regarded on the same footing. And no topic is so much insisted on by those, who defend the liberty of the seas, as the unexhausted use of them in navigation. Were the advantages, procured by navigation, as inexhaustible, these reasoners had never had any adversaries to refute; nor had any claims ever been advanced of a separate, exclusive dominion over the ocean.

It may happen, in some countries, at some periods, that there be established a property in water, none in land; If the latter be in greater abundance than can be used by the inhabitants, and the former be found, with difficulty, and in very small quantities.

Again; suppose, that, though the necessities of human race continue the same as at present, yet the mind is so enlarged, and so replete with friendship and generosity, that every man has the utmost tenderness for every man, and feels no more concern for his own interest than for that of his fellows: It seems evident, that the USE of justice would, in this case, be suspended by such an extensive benevolence; nor would the divisions and barriers of property and obligation have ever been thought of. Why should I bind another, by a deed or promise, to do me any good office, when I know that he is already prompted, by the strongest inclination, to seek my happiness, and would, of himself, perform the desired service; except the hurt, he thereby receives, be greater than the benefit accruing to me? in which case, he knows, that, from my innate humanity and friendship, I should be the first to oppose myself to his imprudent generosity. Why raise land-marks between my neighbour's field and mine, when my heart has made no division between our interests; but shares all his joys and sorrows with the same force and vivacity as if originally my own? Every man, upon this supposition, being a second self to another, would trust all his interests to the discretion

of every man; without jealousy, without partition, without distinction. And the whole human race would form only one family; where all would lie in common, and be used freely, without regard to property; but cautiously too, with as entire regard to the necessities of each individual, as if our own interests were most intimately concerned.

In the present disposition of the human heart, it would, perhaps, be difficult to find compleat instances of such enlarged affections; but still we may observe, that the case of families approaches towards it; and the stronger the mutual benevolence is among the individuals, the nearer it approaches; till all distinction of property be, in a great measure, lost and confounded among them. Between married persons, the cement of friendship is by the laws supposed so strong as to abolish all division of possessions: and has often, in reality, the force ascribed to it. And it is observable, that, during the ardour of new enthusiasms, when every principle is inflamed into extravagance, the community of goods has frequently been attempted: and nothing but experience of its inconveniencies, from the returning or disguised selfishness of men, could make the imprudent fanatics adopt anew the ideas of justice and of separate property. So true is it, that this virtue derives its existence entirely from its necessary *use* to the intercourse and social state of mankind.

To make this truth more evident, let us reverse the foregoing suppositions; and carrying every thing to the opposite extreme, consider what would be the effect of these new situations. Suppose a society to fall into such want of all common necessaries, that the utmost frugality and industry cannot preserve the greater number from perishing, and the whole from extreme misery: It will readily, I believe, be admitted, that the strict laws of justice are suspended, in such a pressing emergence, and give place to the stronger motives of necessity and self-preservation. Is it any crime, after a shipwreck, to seize whatever means or instrument of safety one can lay hold of, without regard to former limitations of property? Or if a city besieged were perishing with hunger; can we imagine, that men will see any means of preservation before them, and lose their lives, from a scrupulous regard to what, in other situations, would be the rules of equity and justice? The USE and TENDENCY of that virtue is to procure happiness and security, by preserving order in society: But where the society is ready to perish from extreme necessity, no greater evil can be dreaded from violence and injustice; and every man may now provide for himself by all the means, which prudence can dictate, or humanity permit. The public, even in less urgent necessities, opens granaries, without the consent of proprietors; as justly supposing, that the authority of magistracy may, consistent with equity, extend so far: But were any number of men to assemble, without the tye of laws or civil jurisdiction; would an equal partition of bread in a famine, though effected by power and even violence, be regarded as criminal or injurious?

Suppose likewise, that it should be a virtuous man's fate to fall into the society of ruffians, remote from the protection of laws and government; what conduct must he embrace in that melancholy situation? He sees such a desperate rapaciousness prevail; such a disregard to equity, such contempt of order, such stupid blindness to future consequences, as must immediately have the most tragical conclusion, and must terminate in destruction to the greater number, and in a total dissolution of society to the rest. He, mean while, can have no other expedient than to arm himself, to whomever the sword he seizes, or the buckler, may belong: To make provision of all means of defence and security: And his particular regard to justice being no longer of USE to his own safety or that of others, he must consult the dictates of self preservation alone, without concern for those who no longer merit his care and attention.

When any man, even in political society, renders himself, by his crimes, obnoxious to the public, he is punished by the laws in his goods and person; that is, the ordinary rules of justice are, with regard to him, suspended for a moment, and it becomes equitable to inflict on him, for the *benefit* of society, what, otherwise, he could not suffer without wrong or injury.

The rage and violence of public war; what is it but a suspension of justice among the warring parties, who perceive, that this virtue is now no longer of any *use* or advantage to them? The laws of war, which then succeed to those of equity and justice, are rules calculated for the *advantage* and *utility* of that particular state, in which men are now placed. And were a civilized nation engaged with barbarians, who observed no rules even of war; the former must also suspend their observance of them, where they no longer serve to any purpose; and must render every action or rencounter as bloody and pernicious as possible to the first aggressors.

Thus, the rules of equity or justice depend entirely on the particular state and condition, in which men are placed, and owe their origin and existence to that UTILITY, which results to the public from their strict and regular observance. Reverse, in any considerable circumstance, the condition of men: Produce extreme abundance or extreme necessity: Implant in the human breast perfect moderation and humanity, or perfect rapaciousness and malice: By rendering justice totally *useless*, you thereby totally destroy its essence, and suspend its obligation upon mankind.

The common situation of society is a medium amidst all these extremes. We are naturally partial to ourselves, and to our friends; but are capable of learning the advantage resulting from a more equitable conduct. Few enjoyments are given us from the open and liberal hand of nature; but by art, labour, and industry, we can extract them in great abundance. Hence the ideas of property become necessary in all civil society: Hence justice derives its usefulness to the public: And hence alone arises its merit and moral obligation.

These conclusions are so natural and obvious, that they have not escaped even the poets, in their descriptions of the felicity, attending the golden age or the reign of Saturn. The seasons, in that first period of nature, were so temperate, if we credit these agreeable fictions, that there was no necessity for men to provide themselves with cloaths and houses, as a security against the violence of heat and cold: The rivers flowed with wine and milk: The oaks yielded honey; and nature spontaneously produced her greatest delicacies. Nor were these the chief advantages of that happy age. Tempests were not alone removed from nature; but those more furious tempests were unknown to human breasts, which now cause such uproar, and engender such confusion. Avarice, ambition, cruelty, selfishness, were never heard of: Cordial affection, compassion, sympathy, were the only movements with which the mind was yet acquainted. Even the punctilious distinction of *mine* and *thine* was banished from among that happy race of mortals, and carried with it the very notion of property and obligation, justice and injustice.

This *poetical* fiction of the *golden age* is, in some respects, of a piece with the *philosophical* fiction of the *state of nature*; only that the former is represented as the most charming and most peaceable condition, which can possibly be imagined; whereas the latter is painted out as a state of mutual war and violence, attended with the most extreme necessity. On the first origin of mankind, we are told, their ignorance and savage nature were so prevalent, that they could give no mutual trust, but must each depend upon himself, and his own force or cunning for protection and security. No law was heard of: No rule of justice known: No distinction of property regarded: Power was the only measure of right; and a perpetual war of all against all was the result of men's untamed selfishness and barbarity.[1]

Whether such a condition of human nature could ever exist, or if it did, could continue so long as to merit the appellation of a *state*, may justly be doubted. Men are necessarily born in a family-society, at least; and are trained up by their parents to some rule of conduct and behaviour. But this must be admitted, that, if such

a state of mutual war and violence was ever real, the suspension of all laws of justice, from their absolute inutility, is a necessary and infallible consequence. . . .

Part II

. . . The dilemma seems obvious: As justice evidently tends to promote public utility and to support civil society, the sentiment of justice is either derived from our reflecting on that tendency, or like hunger, thirst, and other appetites, resentment, love of life, attachment to offspring, and other passions, arises from a simple original instinct in the human breast, which nature has implanted for like salutary purposes. If the latter be the case, it follows, that property, which is the object of justice, is also distinguished by a simple, original instinct, and is not ascertained by any argument or reflection. But who is there that ever heard of such an instinct? Or is this a subject, in which new discoveries can be made? We may as well attempt to discover, in the body, new senses, which had before escaped the observation of all mankind.

But farther, though it seems a very simple proposition to say, that nature, by an instinctive sentiment, distinguishes property, yet in reality we shall find, that there are required for that purpose ten thousand different instincts, and these employed about objects of the greatest intricacy and nicest discernment. For when a definition of *property* is required, that relation is found to resolve itself into any possession acquired by occupation, by industry, by prescription, by inheritance, by contract, &c. Can we think, that nature, by an original instinct, instructs us in all these methods of acquisition?

These words too, inheritance and contract, stand for ideas infinitely complicated; and to define them exactly, a hundred volumes of laws, and a thousand volumes of commentators, have not been found sufficient. Does nature, whose instincts in men are simple, embrace such complicated and artificial objects, and create a rational creature, without trusting any thing to the operation of his reason?

But even though all this were admitted, it would not be satisfactory. Positive laws can certainly transfer property. Is it by another original instinct, that we recognize the authority of kings and senates, and mark all the boundaries of their jurisdiction? Judges too, even though their sentence be erroneous and illegal, must be allowed, for the sake of peace and order, to have decisive authority, and ultimately to determine property. Have we original, innate ideas of praetors and chancellors and juries? Who sees not, that all these institutions arise merely from the necessities of human society?

All birds of the same species, in every age and country, build their nests alike: In this we see the force of instinct. Men, in different times and places, frame their houses differently: Here we perceive the influence of reason and custom. A like inference may be drawn from comparing the instinct of generation and the institution of property.

How great soever the variety of municipal laws, it must be confessed, that their chief out-lines pretty regularly concur; because the purposes, to which they tend, are every where exactly similar. In like manner, all houses have a roof and walls, windows and chimneys; though diversified in their shape, figure, and materials. The purposes of the latter, directed to the conveniences of human life, discover not more plainly their origin from reason and reflection, than do those of the former, which point all to a like end.

I need not mention the variations, which all the rules of property receive from the finer turns and connexions of the imagination, and from the subtilties and abstractions of law-topics and reasonings. There is no possibility of reconciling this observation to the notion of original instincts.

What alone will beget a doubt concerning the theory, on which I insist, is the influence of education and acquired habits, by which we are so accustomed to blame injustice, that we are not, in every instance, conscious of any immediate reflection on the pernicious consequences of it. The views the most familiar to us are apt, for that very reason, to escape us; and what we have very frequently performed from certain motives, we are apt likewise to continue mechanically, without recalling, on every occasion, the reflections, which first determined us. The convenience, or rather necessity, which leads to justice, is so universal, and every where points so much to the same rules, that the habit takes place in all societies: and it is not without some scrutiny, that we are able to ascertain its true origin. The matter, however, is not so obscure, but that, even in common life, we have, every moment, recourse to the principle of public utility, and ask, *What must become of the world. if such practices prevail? How could society subsist under such disorders?* Were the distinction or separation of possessions entirely useless, can any one conceive, that it ever should have obtained in society?

Thus we seem, upon the whole, to have attained a knowledge of the force of that principle here insisted on, and can determine what degree of esteem or moral approbation may result from reflections on public interest and utility. The necessity of justice to the support of society is the SOLE foundation of that virtue; and since no moral excellence is more highly esteemed, we may conclude, that this circumstance of usefulness has, in general, the strongest energy, and most entire command over our sentiments. It must, therefore, be the source of a considerable part of the merit ascribed to humanity, benevolence, friendship, public spirit, and other social virtues of that stamp; as it is the SOLE source of the moral approbation paid to fidelity, justice, veracity, integrity, and those other estimable and useful qualities and principles. It is entirely agreeable to the rules of philosophy, and even of common reason; where any principle has been found to have a great force and energy in one instance, to ascribe to it a like energy in all similar instances. This indeed is Newton's chief rule of philosophizing.

Note

1. This fiction of a state of nature, as a state of war, was not first started by Mr. Hobbes, as is commonly imagined. Plato endeavours to refute an hypothesis very like it in the second, third, and fourth books *de republica*. Cicero on the contrary, supposes it certain and universally acknowledged in the following passage. ... "Can there be anyone among you, jurors, who does not know that nature had brought things about so that, at one time, before natural or civil law was discerned, scattered and landless men roamed the countryside, men who had just as much as they had been able to snatch by force and defend by bloodshed and violence? Then those men who first stood out for their exceptional virtue and judgment, having recognized men's natural talent for training and ingenuity, brought the nomads together and led them from savagery into justice and mildness. And after human and divine law were discovered, then matters were arranged for the general good, which we call public affairs, then common meeting places, which were later called communities, and eventually homes were brought within walls, which we call cities. And so there is no more difference between this orderly civilized life, and that former savagery, than there is between Law and Violence. If we prefer not to use one of these, we must use the other. Do we want violence eradicated? Then law must prevail, i.e., the verdicts in which all law is contained. Are the verdicts disliked or ignored? Then violence must prevail. Everyone understands this."

Of Parties in General

Of all men, that distinguish themselves by memorable *achievements*, the first place of honour seems due to Legislators and founders of states, who transmit a system of laws and institutions to secure the peace, happiness, and liberty of future generations. The influence of useful inventions in the arts and sciences may, perhaps, extend farther than that of wise laws, whose effects are limited both in time and place; but the benefit arising from the former, is not so sensible as that which results from the latter. Speculative sciences do, indeed, improve the mind; but this advantage reaches only to a few persons, who have leisure to apply themselves to them. And as to practical arts, which increase the commodities and enjoyments of life, it is well known, that men's happiness consists not so much in an abundance of these, as in the peace and security with which they possess them; and those blessings can only be derived from good government. Not to mention, that general virtue and good morals in a state, which are so requisite to happiness, can never arise from the most refined precepts of philosophy, or even the severest injunctions of religion; but must proceed entirely from the virtuous education of youth, the effect of wise laws and institutions. I must, therefore, presume to differ from Lord Bacon in this particular, and must regard antiquity as somewhat unjust in its distribution of honours, when it made gods of all the inventors of useful arts, such as Ceres Bacchus Aesculapius; and dignify legislators, such as Romulus and Theseus, only with the appellation of demigods and heroes.

As much as legislators and founders of states ought to be honoured and respected among men, as much ought the founders of sects and factions to be detested and hated; because the influence of faction is directly contrary to that of laws. Factions subvert government, render laws impotent, and beget the fiercest animosities among men of the same nation, who ought to give mutual assistance and protection to each other. And what should render the founders of parties more odious is, the difficulty of extirpating these weeds, when once they have taken root in any state. They naturally propagate themselves for many centuries, and seldom end but by the total dissolution of that government, in which they are sown. They are, besides, plants which grow most plentifully in the richest soil; and though absolute governments be not wholly free from them, it must be confessed, that they rise more easily, and propagate themselves faster in free governments, where they always infect the legislature itself, which alone could be able, by the steady application of rewards and punishments, to eradicate them.

Factions may be divided into Personal and Real that is, into factions, founded on personal friendship or animosity among such as compose the contending parties, and into those founded on some real difference of sentiment or interest. The reason of this distinction is obvious; though I must acknowledge, that parties are seldom found pure and unmixed, either of the one kind or the other. It is not often seen, that a government divides into factions, where there is no difference in the views of the constituent members, either real or apparent, trivial or material: And in those factions, which are founded on the most real and most material difference, there is always observed a great deal of personal animosity or affection. But notwithstanding this mixture, a party may be denominated either personal or real, according to that principle which is predominant, and is found to have the greatest influence.

Personal factions arise most easily in small republics. Every domestic quarrel, there, becomes an affair of state. Love, vanity, emulation, any passion, as well as ambition and resentment, begets public division. . . .

Men have such a propensity to divide into personal factions, that the smallest appearance of real difference will produce them. What can be imagined more trivial than the difference between one colour of livery and another in horse races? Yet this difference begat two most inveterate factions in the Greek empire, the Prasini and Veneti who never suspended their animosities, till they ruined that unhappy government.

We find in the Roman history a remarkable dissension between two tribes, the Pollia and Papiria, which continued for the space of near three hundred years, and discovered itself in their suffrages at every election of magistrates.

This faction was the more remarkable, as it could continue for so long a tract of time; even though it did not spread itself, nor draw any of the other tribes into a share of the quarrel. If mankind had not a strong propensity to such divisions, the indifference of the rest of the community must have suppressed this foolish animosity, that had not any aliment of new benefits and injuries, of general sympathy and antipathy, which never fail to take place, when the whole state is rent into two equal factions.

Nothing is more usual than to see parties, which have begun upon a real difference, continue even after that difference is lost. When men are once inlisted on opposite sides, they contract an affection to the persons with whom they are united, and an animosity against their antagonists: And these passions they often transmit to their posterity. . . .

The civil wars which arose some few years ago in Morocco, between the *blacks* and *whites*, merely on account of their complexion, are founded on a pleasant difference. We laugh at them; but I believe, were things rightly examined, we afford much more occasion of ridicule to the Moors. For, what are all the wars of religion, which have prevailed in this polite and knowing part of the world? They are certainly more absurd than the Moorish civil wars. The difference of complexion is a sensible and a real difference: But the controversy about an article of faith, which is utterly absurd and unintelligible, is not a difference in sentiment, but in a few phrases and expressions, which one party accepts of, without understanding them; and the other refuses in the same manner.

Real factions may be divided into those from *interest*, from *principle* and from *affection*. Of all factions, the first are the most reasonable, and the most excusable. Where two orders of men, such as the nobles and people, have a distinct authority in a government, not very accurately balanced and modelled, they naturally follow a distinct interest; nor can we reasonably expect a different conduct, considering that degree of selfishness implanted in human nature. It requires great skill in a legislator to prevent such parties; and many philosophers are of opinion, that this secret, like the *grand elixir*, or *perpetual motion*, may amuse men in theory, but can never possibly be reduced to practice. In despotic governments, indeed, factions often do not appear; but they are not the less real; or rather, they are more real and more pernicious, upon that very account. The distinct orders of men, nobles and people, soldiers and merchants, have all a distinct interest; but the more powerful oppresses the weaker with impunity, and without resistance; which begets a seeming tranquillity in such governments.

There has been an attempt in England to divide the *landed* and *trading* part of the nation; but without success. The interests of these two bodies are not really distinct, and never will be so, till our public debts increase to such a degree, as to become altogether oppressive and intolerable.

Parties from *principle*, especially abstract speculative principle, are known only to modern times, and are, perhaps, the most extraordinary and unaccountable *phoenomenon*, that has yet appeared in human affairs. Where different principles beget a contrariety of conduct, which is the case with all different political principles, the matter may be more easily explained. A man, who esteems the true right of government to lie in one man, or one family, cannot easily agree with his fellow-citizen, who thinks that another man or family is possessed of this right. Each naturally wishes that right may take place, according to his own notions of it. But where the difference of principle is attended with no contrariety of action, but every one may follow his own way, without interfering with his neighbour, as happens in all religious controversies; what madness, what fury can beget such unhappy and such fatal divisions?

Two men travelling on the highway, the one east, the other west, can easily pass each other, if the way be broad enough: But two men, reasoning upon opposite principles of religion, cannot so easily pass, without shocking; though one should think, that the way were also, in that case, sufficiently broad, and that each might proceed, without interruption, in his own course. But such is the nature of the human mind, that it always lays hold on every mind that approaches it; and as it is wonderfully fortified by an unanimity of sentiments, so is it shocked and disturbed by any contrariety. Hence the eagerness, which most people discover in a dispute; and hence their impatience of opposition, even in the most speculative and indifferent opinions.

This principle, however frivolous it may appear, seems to have been the origin of all religious wars and divisions. But as this principle is universal in human nature, its effects would not have been confined to one age, and to one sect of religion, did it not there concur with other more accidental causes, which raise it to such a height, as to produce the greatest misery and devastation. Most religions of the ancient world arose in the unknown ages of government, when men were as yet barbarous and uninstructed, and the prince, as well as peasant, was disposed to receive, with implicit faith, every pious tale or fiction, which was offered him. The magistrate embraced the religion of the people, and entering cordially into the care of sacred matters, naturally acquired an authority in them, and united the ecclesiastical with the civil power. But the *Christian* religion arising, while principles directly opposite to it were firmly established in the polite part of the world, who despised the nation that first broached this novelty; no wonder, that, in such circumstances, it was but little countenanced by the civil magistrate, and that the priesthood was allowed to engross all the authority in the new sect. So bad a use did they make of this power, even in those early times, that the primitive persecutions may, perhaps, *in part*, be ascribed to the violence instilled by them into their followers. And the same principles of priestly government continuing, after Christianity became the established religion, they have engendered a spirit of persecution, which has ever since been the poison of human society, and the source of the most inveterate factions in every government. Such divisions, therefore, on the part of the people, may justly be esteemed factions of *principle;* but, on the part of the priests, who are the prime movers, they are really factions of *interest*.

There is another cause (beside the authority of the priests, and the separation of the ecclesiastical and civil powers) which has contributed to render Christendom the scene of religious wars and divisions. Religions, that arise in ages totally ignorant and barbarous, consist mostly of traditional tales and fictions, which may be different in every sect, without being contrary to each other; and even when they are contrary, every one adheres to the tradition of his own sect, without much reasoning or disputation. But as philosophy was widely spread over the world, at the time when Christianity arose, the teachers of the new sect were obliged to form a system of speculative opinions; to divide, with some accuracy, their articles of faith; and to explain, comment, confute, and defend with all the subtilty of argument and science. Hence naturally arose keenness in dispute, when the Christian religion came to be split into new divisions and heresies: And this keenness assisted the priests in their policy, of begetting a mutual hatred and antipathy among their deluded followers. Sects of philosophy, in the ancient world, were more zealous than parties of religion; but in modern times, parties of religion are more furious and enraged than the most cruel factions that ever arose from interest and ambition.

I have mentioned parties from *affection* as a kind of *real* parties, beside those from *interest* and *principle*. By parties from affection, I understand those which are founded on the different attachments of men towards particular families and persons, whom they desire to rule over them. These factions are often very violent; though, I must own, it may seem unaccountable, that men should attach themselves so strongly to persons, with whom they are no wise acquainted, whom perhaps they never saw, and from whom they never received, nor can ever hope for any favour. Yet this we often find to be the case, and even with men, who, on other occasions, discover no great generosity of spirit, nor are found to be easily transported by friendship beyond their own interest. We are apt to think the relation between us and our sovereign very close and intimate. The splendour of majesty and power bestows an importance on the fortunes even of a single person. And when a man's good-nature does not give him this imaginary interest, his ill-nature will, from spite and opposition to persons whose sentiments are different from his own.

Of the Original Contract

As no party, in the present age, can well support itself, without a philosophical or speculative system of principles, annexed to its political or practical one; we accordingly find, that each of the factions, into which this nation is divided, has reared up a fabric of the former kind, in order to protect and cover that scheme of actions, which it pursues.

The people being commonly very rude builders, especially in this speculative way, and more especially still, when actuated by party-zeal; it is natural to imagine, that their workmanship must be a little unshapely, and discover evident marks of that violence and hurry, in which it was raised. The one party, by tracing up government to the Deity, endeavour to render it so sacred and inviolate, that it must be little less than sacrilege, however tyrannical it may become, to touch or invade it, in the smallest article. The other party, by founding government altogether on the consent of the People, suppose that there is a kind of *original contract*, by which the subjects have tacitly reserved the power of resisting their sovereign, whenever they find themselves aggrieved by that authority, with which they have, for certain purposes, voluntarily entrusted him. These are the speculative principles of the two parties; and these too are the practical consequences deduced from them.

I shall venture to affirm, *That both these* systems *of speculative principles are just; though not in the sense, intended by the parties*: And, *That both the* schemes *of practical consequences are prudent; though not in the extremes, to which each party, in opposition to the other, has commonly endeavoured to carry them.*

That the Deity is the ultimate author of all government will never be denied by any, who admit a general providence, and allow, that all events in the universe are conducted by an uniform plan, and directed to wise purposes. As it is impossible for the human race to subsist, at least in any comfortable or secure state, without the protection of government; this institution must certainly have been intended by that beneficent Being, who means the good of all his creatures: And as it has universally, in fact, taken place, in all countries, and all ages; we may conclude, with still greater certainty, that it was intended by that omniscient Being, who can never be deceived by any event or operation. But since he gave rise to it, not by any particular or miraculous interposition, but by his concealed and universal efficacy; a sovereign cannot, properly speaking, be called his vice-gerent, in any other sense than every power or force, being derived from him, may be said to act by his commission. Whatever actually happens is comprehended in the general plan or intention of providence; nor has the greatest and most lawful prince any more reason, upon that account, to plead a peculiar sacredness or inviolable authority, than an inferior magistrate, or even an usurper, or even a robber and a pirate. The same divine superintendent, who, for wise purposes, invested a Titus or a Trajan with authority, did also, for purposes, no doubt, equally wise, though unknown, bestow power on a Borgia or an Angria. The same causes, which gave rise to the sovereign power in every state, established likewise every petty jurisdiction in it, and every limited authority. A constable, therefore, no less than a king, acts by a divine commission, and possesses an indefeasible right.

When we consider how nearly equal all men are in their bodily force, and even in their mental powers and faculties, till cultivated by education; we must necessarily allow, that nothing but their own consent could, at first, associate them together, and subject them to any authority. The people, if we trace government to its first origin in the woods and deserts, are the source of all power and jurisdiction, and voluntarily, for the sake of peace and order, abandoned their native liberty, and received laws from their equal and companion. The conditions, upon which they were willing to submit, were either expressed, or were so clear and obvious, that it might well be esteemed superfluous to express them. If this, then, be meant by the *original contract*, it cannot be denied, that all government is, at first, founded on a contract, and that the most ancient rude combinations of mankind were formed chiefly by that principle. In vain, are we asked in what records this charter of our liberties is registered. It was not written on parchment, nor yet on leaves or barks of trees. It preceded the use of writing and all the other civilized arts of life. But we trace it plainly in the nature of man, and in the equality, or something approaching equality, which we find in all the individuals of that species. The force, which now prevails, and which is founded on fleets and armies, is plainly political, and derived from authority, the effect of established government. A man's natural force consists only in the vigour of his limbs, and the firmness of his courage; which could never subject multitudes to the command of one. Nothing but their own consent, and their sense of the advantages resulting from peace and order, could have had that influence.

Yet even this consent was long very imperfect, and could not be the basis of a regular administration. The chieftain, who had probably acquired his influence during the continuance of war, ruled more by persuasion than command; and till he could employ force to reduce the refractory and disobedient, the society could scarcely be said to have attained a state of civil government. No compact or agreement, it is evident, was expressly formed for general submission; an idea far beyond the comprehension of savages: Each exertion of authority in the chieftain must have been particular, and called forth by the present exigencies of the case: The sensible utility, resulting from his interposition, made these exertions become daily more frequent; and their frequency gradually produced an habitual, and, if you please to call it so, a voluntary, and therefore precarious, acquiescence in the people.

But philosophers, who have embraced a party (if that be not a contradiction in terms) are not contented with these concessions. They assert, not only that government in its earliest infancy arose from consent or rather the voluntary acquiescence of the people; but also, that, even at present, when it has attained full maturity, it rests on no other foundation. They affirm, that all men are still born equal, and owe allegiance to no prince or government, unless bound by the obligation and sanction of a *promise*. And as no man, without some equivalent, would forego the advantages of his native liberty, and subject himself to the will of another; this promise is always understood to be conditional, and imposes on him no obligation, unless he meet with justice and protection from his sovereign. These advantages the sovereign promises him in return; and if he fail in the execution, he has broken, on his part, the articles of engagement, and has thereby freed his subject from all obligations to allegiance. Such, according to these philosophers, is the foundation of authority in every government; and such the right of resistance, possessed by every subject.

But would these reasoners look abroad into the world, they would meet with nothing that, in the least, corresponds to their ideas, or can warrant so refined and philosophical a system. On the contrary, we find, everywhere, princes, who claim their subjects as their property, and assert their independent right of sovereignty, from conquest or succession. We find also, everywhere, subjects, who acknowledge this right in their prince, and suppose themselves born under obligations of obedience to a certain sovereign, as much as under the ties of reverence and duty to certain parents. These connexions are always conceived to be equally independent of our consent, in Persia and China; in France and Spain; and even in Holland and England, wherever the doctrines above-mentioned have not been carefully inculcated. Obedience or subjection becomes so familiar, that most men never make any enquiry about its origin or cause, more than about the principle of gravity, resistance, or the most universal laws of nature. Or if curiosity ever move them; as soon as they learn, that they themselves and their ancestors have, for several ages, or from time immemorial, been subject to such a form of government or such a family; they immediately acquiesce, and acknowledge their obligation to allegiance. Were you to preach, in most parts of the world, that political connexions are founded altogether on voluntary consent or a mutual promise, the magistrate would soon imprison you, as seditious, for loosening the ties of obedience; if your friends did not before shut you up as delirious, for advancing such absurdities. It is strange, that an act of the mind, which every individual is supposed to have formed, and after he came to the use of reason too, otherwise it could have no authority; that this act, I say, should be so much unknown to all of them, that, over the face of the whole earth, there scarcely remain any traces or memory of it.

But the contract, on which government is founded, is said to be the *original contract;* and consequently may be supposed too old to fall under the knowledge of the present generation. If the agreement, by which savage men first associated and conjoined their force, be here meant, this is acknowledged to be real; but being so ancient, and being obliterated by a thousand changes of government and princes, it cannot now be supposed to retain any authority. If we would say any thing to the purpose, we must assert, that every particular government, which is lawful, and which imposes any duty of allegiance on the subject, was, at first, founded on consent and a voluntary compact. But besides that this supposes the consent of the fathers to bind the children, even to the most remote generations, (which republican writers will never allow) besides this, I say, it is not justified by history or experience, in any age or country of the world.

Almost all the governments, which exist at present, or of which there remains any record in story, have been founded originally, either on usurpation or conquest, or both, without any presence of a fair consent, or voluntary subjection of the people. When an artful and bold man is placed at the head of an army or faction, it is often easy for him, by employing, sometimes violence, sometimes false pretences, to establish his dominion over a people a hundred times more numerous than his partizans. He allows no such open communication, that his enemies can know, with certainty, their number or force. He gives them no leisure to assemble together in a body to oppose him. Even all those, who are the instruments of his usurpation, may wish his fall; but their ignorance of each other's intention keeps them in awe, and is the sole cause of his security. By such arts as these, many governments have been established; and this is all the *original contract*, which they have to boast of.

The face of the earth is continually changing, by the increase of small kingdoms into great empires, by the dissolution of great empires into smaller kingdoms, by the planting of colonies, by the migration of tribes. Is there any thing discoverable in all these events, but force and violence? Where is the mutual agreement or voluntary association so much talked of?

Even the smoothest way, by which a nation may receive a foreign master, by marriage or a will, is not extremely honourable for the people; but supposes them to be disposed of, like a dowry or a legacy, according to the pleasure or interest of their rulers.

But where no force interposes, and election takes place; what is this election so highly vaunted? It is either the combination of a few great men, who decide for the whole, and will allow of no opposition: Or it is the fury of a multitude, that follow a seditious ringleader, who is not known, perhaps, to a dozen among them, and who owes his advancement merely to his own impudence, or to the momentary caprice of his fellows.

Are these disorderly elections, which are rare too, of such mighty authority, as to be the only lawful foundation of all government and allegiance?

In reality, there is not a more terrible event, than a total dissolution of government, which gives liberty to the multitude, and makes the determination or choice of a new establishment depend upon a number, which nearly approaches to that of the body of the people: For it never comes entirely to the whole body of them. Every wise man, then, wishes to see, at the head of a powerful and obedient army, a general, who may speedily seize the prize, and give to the people a master, which they are so unfit to choose for themselves. So little correspondent is fact and reality to those philosophical notions. . . .

The republic of Athens was, I believe, the most extensive democracy, that we read of in history: Yet if we make the requisite allowances for the women, the slaves, and the strangers, we shall find, that that establishment was not, at first, made, not any law ever voted, by a tenth part of those who were bound to pay obedience to it: Not to mention the islands and foreign dominions, which the Athenians claimed as theirs by right of conquest. And as it is well known, that popular assemblies in that city were always full of licence and disorder, notwithstanding the institutions and laws by which they were checked: How much more disorderly must they prove, where they form not the established constitution, but meet tumultuously on the dissolution of the ancient government, in order to give rise to a new one? How chimerical must it be to talk of a choice in such circumstances? . . .

It is in vain to say, that all governments are or should be, at first, founded on popular consent, as much as the necessity of human affairs will admit. This favours entirely my pretension. I maintain, that human affairs will never admit of this consent; seldom of the appearance of it.

But that conquest or usurpation, that is, in plain terms, force, by dissolving the ancient governments, is the origin of almost all the new ones, which were ever established in the world. And that in the few cases, where consent may seem to have taken place, it was commonly so irregular, so confined, or so much intermixed either with fraud or violence, that it cannot have any great authority.

My intention here is not to exclude the consent of the people from being one just foundation of government where it has place. It is surely the best and most sacred of any. I only pretend, that it has very seldom had place in any degree, and never almost in its full extent. And that therefore some other foundation of government must also be admitted.

Were all men possessed of so inflexible a regard to justice, that, of themselves, they would totally abstain from the properties of others; they had for ever remained in a state of absolute liberty, without subjection to any magistrate or political society: But this is a state of perfection, of which human nature is justly deemed incapable. Again; were all men possessed of so perfect an understanding, as always to know their own interests, no form of government had ever been submitted to, but what was established on consent, and was fully canvassed by every member of the society: But this state of perfection is likewise much superior to human nature. Reason, history, and experience show us, that all political societies have had an origin much less accurate and regular; and were one to choose a period of time, when the people's consent was the least regarded in public transactions, it would be precisely on the establishment of a new government. In a settled constitution, their inclinations are often consulted; but during the fury of revolutions, conquests, and public convulsions, military force or political craft usually decides the controversy.

When a new government is established, by whatever means, the people are commonly dissatisfied with it, and pay obedience more from fear and necessity, than from any idea of allegiance or of moral obligation. The prince is watchful and jealous, and must carefully guard against every beginning or appearance of insurrection. Time, by degrees, removes all these difficulties, and accustoms the nation to regard, as their lawful or native princes, that family, which, at first, they considered as usurpers or foreign conquerors. In order to found this opinion, they have no recourse to any notion of voluntary consent or promise, which, they know, never was, in this case, either expected or demanded. The original establishment was formed by violence, and submitted to from necessity. The subsequent administration is also supported by power, and acquiesced in by the people, not as a matter of choice, but of obligation. They imagine not, that their consent gives their prince a title: But they willingly consent, because they think, that, from long possession, he has acquired a title, independent of their choice or inclination.

Should it be said, that, by living under the dominion of a prince, which one might leave, every individual has given a *tacit* consent to his authority, and promised him obedience; it may be answered, that such an implied consent can only have place, where a man imagines, that the matter depends on his choice. But where he thinks (as all mankind do who are born under established governments) that by his birth he owes allegiance to a certain prince or certain form of government; it would be absurd to infer a consent or choice, which he expressly, in this case, renounces and disclaims.

Can we seriously say, that a poor peasant or artizan has a free choice to leave his country, when he knows no foreign language or manners, and lives from day to day, by the small wages which he acquires? We may as well assert, that a man, by remaining in a vessel, freely consents to the dominion of the master; though he was carried on board while asleep, and must leap into the ocean, and perish, the moment he leaves her. . . .

A company of men, who should leave their native country, in order to people some uninhabited region, might dream of recovering their native freedom; but they would soon find, that their prince still laid claim to them, and called them his subjects, even in their new settlement. And in this he would but act conformably to the common ideas of mankind.

The truest *tacit* consent of this kind, that is ever observed, is when a foreigner settles in any country, and is beforehand acquainted with the prince, and government, and laws, to which he must submit: Yet is his allegiance, though more voluntary, much less expected or depended on, than that of a natural born subject. On the contrary, his native prince still asserts a claim to him. And if he punish not the renegade, when he seizes him in war with his new prince's commission; this clemency is not founded on the municipal law, which in all countries condemns the prisoner; but on the consent of princes, who have agreed to this indulgence, in order to prevent reprisals.

Did one generation of men go off the stage at once, and another succeed, as is the case with silk-worms and butterflies, the new race, if they had sense enough to choose their government, which surely is never the case with men, might voluntarily, and by general consent, establish their own form of civil polity, without any regard to the laws or precedents, which prevailed among their ancestors. But as human society is in perpetual flux, one man every hour going out of the world, another coming into it, it is necessary, in order to preserve stability in government, that the new brood should conform themselves to the established constitution, and nearly follow the path which their fathers, treading in the footsteps of theirs, had marked out to them. Some innovations must necessarily have place in every human institution, and it is happy where the enlightened genius of the age give these a direction to the side of reason, liberty, and justice: but violent innovations no individual is entitled to make: they are even dangerous to be attempted by the legislature: more ill than good is ever to be expected from them: and if history affords examples to the contrary, they are not to be drawn into precedent, and are only to be regarded as

proofs, that the science of politics affords few rules, which will not admit of some exception, and which may not sometimes be controuled by fortune and accident. The violent innovations in the reign of Henry VIII proceeded from an imperious monarch, seconded by the appearance of legislative authority: Those in the reign of Charles I were derived from faction and fanaticism; and both of them have proved happy in the issue: But even the former were long the source of many disorders, and still more dangers; and if the measures of allegiance were to be taken from the latter, a total anarchy must have place in human society, and a final period at once be put to every government.

Suppose, that an usurper, after having banished his lawful prince and royal family, should establish his dominion for ten or a dozen years in any country, and should preserve so exact a discipline in his troops, and so regular a disposition in his garrisons, that no insurrection had ever been raised, or even murmur heard, against his administration: Can it be asserted, that the people, who in their hearts abhor his treason, have tacitly consented to his authority, and promised him allegiance, merely because, from necessity, they live under his dominion? Suppose again their native prince restored, by means of an army, which he levies in foreign countries: They receive him with joy and exultation, and show plainly with what reluctance they had submitted to any other yoke. I may now ask, upon what foundation the prince's title stands? Not on popular consent surely: For though the people willingly acquiesce in his authority, they never imagine, that their consent made him sovereign. They consent; because they apprehend him to be already, by birth, their lawful sovereign. And as to that tacit consent, which may now be inferred from their living under his dominion, this is no more than what they formerly gave to the tyrant and usurper.

When we assert, that all lawful government arises from the consent of the people, we certainly do them a great deal more honour than they deserve, or even expect and desire from us. After the Roman dominions became too unwieldly for the republic to govern them, the people, over the whole known world, were extremely grateful to Augustus for that authority, which, by violence, he had established over them; and they showed an equal disposition to submit to the successor, whom he left them, by his last will and testament. It was afterwards their misfortune, that there never was, in one family, any long regular succession; but that their line of princes was continually broken, either by private assassinations or public rebellions. The *praetorian* bands, on the failure of every family, set up one emperor; the legions in the East a second; those in Germany, perhaps, a third: And the sword alone could decide the controversy. The condition of the people, in that mighty monarchy, was to be lamented, not because the choice of the emperor was never left to them; for that was impracticable: But because they never fell under any succession of masters, who might regularly follow each other. As to the violence and wars and bloodshed, occasioned by every new settlement; these were not blameable, because they were inevitable. . . .

All *moral* duties may be divided into two kinds. The *first* are those, to which men are impelled by a natural instinct or immediate propensity, which operates on them, independent of all ideas of obligation, and of all views, either to public or private utility. Of this nature are, love of children, gratitude to benefactors, pity to the unfortunate. When we reflect on the advantage, which results to society from such humane instincts, we pay them the just tribute of moral approbation and esteem: But the person, actuated by them, feels their power and influence, antecedent to any such reflection.

The *second* kind of moral duties are such as are not supported by any original instinct of nature, but are performed entirely from a sense of obligation, when we consider the necessities of human society, and the impossibility of supporting it, if these duties were neglected. It is thus *justice* or a regard to the property of others, *fidelity* or the observance of promises, become obligatory, and

acquire an authority over mankind. For as it is evident, that every man loves himself better than any other person, he is naturally impelled to extend his acquisitions as much as possible; and nothing can restrain him in this propensity, but reflection and experience, by which he learns the pernicious effects of that licence, and the total dissolution of society which must ensue from it. His original inclination, therefore, or instinct, is here checked and restrained by a subsequent judgment or observation.

The case is precisely the same with the political or civil duty of *allegiance* as with the natural duties of justice and fidelity. Our primary instincts lead us, either to indulge ourselves in unlimited freedom, or to seek dominion over others: And it is reflection only which engages us to sacrifice such strong passions to the interests of peace and public order. A small degree of experience and observation suffices to teach us, that society cannot possibly be maintained without the authority of magistrates, and that this authority must soon fall into contempt, where exact obedience is not paid to it. The observation of these general and obvious interests is the source of all allegiance, and of that moral obligation, which we attribute to it.

What necessity, therefore, is there to found the duty of *allegiance* or obedience to magistrates on that of *fidelity* or a regard to promises, and to suppose, that it is the consent of each individual, which subjects him to government; when it appears, that both allegiance and fidelity stand precisely on the same foundation, and are both submitted to by mankind, on account of the apparent interests and necessities of human society? We are bound to obey our sovereign, it is said; because we have given a tacit promise to that purpose. But why are we bound to observe our promise? It must here be asserted, that the commerce and intercourse of mankind, which are of such mighty advantage, can have no security where men pay no regard to their engagements. In like manner, may it be said, that men could not live at all in society, at least in a civilized society, without laws and magistrates and judges, to prevent the encroachments of the strong upon the weak, of the violent upon the just and equitable. The obligation to allegiance being of like force and authority with the obligation to fidelity, we gain nothing by resolving the one into the other. The general interests or necessities of society are sufficient to establish both.

If the reason be asked of that obedience, which we are bound to pay to government, I readily answer, *because society could not otherwise subsist*: And this answer is clear and intelligible to all mankind. Your answer is, *because we should keep our word*. But besides, that no body, till trained in a philosophical system, can either comprehend or relish this answer: Besides this, I say, you find yourself embarrassed, when it is asked, *why we are bound to keep our word?* Nor can you give any answer, but what would, immediately, without any circuit, have accounted for our obligation to allegiance.

But *to whom is allegiance due? And who is our lawful sovereign?* This question is often the most difficult of any, and liable to infinite discussions. When people are so happy, that they can answer, *Our present sovereign, who inherits, in a direct line, from ancestors, that have governed us for many ages;* this answer admits of no reply; even though historians, in tracing up to the remotest antiquity, the origin of that royal family, may find, as commonly happens, that its first authority was derived from usurpation and violence. It is confessed, that private justice, or the abstinence from the properties of others, is a most cardinal virtue: Yet reason tells us, that there is no property in durable objects, such as lands or houses, when carefully examined in passing from hand to hand, but must, in some period, have been founded on fraud and injustice. The necessities of human society, neither in private nor public life, will allow of such an accurate enquiry: And there is no virtue or moral duty, but what may, with facility, be refined away, if we indulge a false philosophy, in sifting and scrutinizing it, by every captious rule of logic, in every light or position, in which it may be placed. . . .

. . . The general obligation, which binds us to government, is the interest and necessities of society; and this obligation is very strong. The determination of it to this or that particular prince or form of government is frequently more uncertain and dubious. Present possession has considerable authority in these cases, and greater than in private property; because of the disorders which attend all revolutions and changes of government.

We shall only observe, before we conclude, that, though an appeal to general opinion may justly, in the speculative sciences of metaphysics, natural philosophy, or astronomy, be deemed unfair and inconclusive, yet in all questions with regard to morals, as well as criticism, there is really no other standard, by which any controversy can ever be decided. And nothing is a clearer proof, that a theory of this kind is erroneous, than to find, that it leads to paradoxes, repugnant to the common sentiments of mankind, and to the practice and opinion of all nations and all ages. The doctrine, which founds all lawful government on an *original contract*, or consent of the people, is plainly of this kind; nor has the most noted of its partisans, in prosecution of it, scrupled to affirm, *that absolute monarchy is inconsistent with civil society, and so can be no form of civil government at all; and that the supreme power in a state cannot take from any man, by taxes and impositions, any part of his property, without his own consent or that of his representatives.* What authority any moral reasoning can have, which leads into opinions so wide of the general practice of mankind, in every place but this single kingdom, it is easy to determine.

The only passage I meet with in antiquity, where the obligation of obedience to government is ascribed to a promise, is in Plato's *Crito*: where Socrates refuses to escape from prison, because he had tacitly promised to obey the laws. Thus he builds a *tory* consequence of passive obedience, on a *whig* foundation of the original contract.

New discoveries are not to be expected in these matters. If scarce any man, till very lately, ever imagined that government was founded on compact, it is certain, that it cannot, in general, have any such foundation.

Of the Origin of Government

Man, born in a family, is compelled to maintain society, from necessity, from natural inclination, and from habit. The same creature, in his farther progress, is engaged to establish political society, in order to administer justice; without which there can be no peace among them, nor safety, nor mutual intercourse. We are, therefore, to look upon all the vast apparatus of our government, as having ultimately no other object or purpose but the distribution of justice, or, in other words, the support of the twelve judges. Kings and parliaments, fleets and armies, officers of the court and revenue, ambassadors, ministers, and privy-counsellors, are all subordinate in their end to this part of administration. Even the clergy, as their duty leads them to inculcate morality, may justly be thought, so far as regards this world, to have no other useful object of their institution.

All men are sensible of the necessity of justice to maintain peace and order; and all men are sensible of the necessity of peace and order for the maintenance of society. Yet, notwithstanding this strong and obvious necessity, such is the frailty or perverseness of our nature! it is impossible to keep men, faithfully and unerringly, in the paths of justice. Some extraordinary circumstances may happen, in which a man finds his interests to be more promoted by fraud or rapine, than hurt by the breach which his injustice makes in the social union. But much more frequently, he is seduced from his great and important, but distant interests, by the allurement of present, though often very frivolous temptations. This great weakness is incurable in human nature.

Men must, therefore, endeavour to palliate what they cannot cure. They must institute some persons, under the appellation of magistrates, whose peculiar office it is, to point out the decrees of equity, to punish transgressors, to correct fraud and violence, and to oblige men, however reluctant, to consult their own real and permanent interests. In a word, Obedience is a new duty which must be invented to support that of Justice; and the ties of equity must be corroborated by those of allegiance.

But still, viewing matters in an abstract light, it may be thought, that nothing is gained by this alliance, and that the factitious duty of obedience, from its very nature, lays as feeble a hold of the human mind, as the primitive and natural duty of justice. Peculiar interests and present temptations may overcome the one as well as the other. They are equally exposed to the same inconvenience. And the man, who is inclined to be a bad neighbour, must be led by the same motives, well or ill understood, to be a bad citizen and subject. Not to mention, that the magistrate himself may often be negligent, or partial, or unjust in his administration.

Experience, however, proves, that there is a great difference between the cases. Order in society, we find, is much better maintained by means of government; and our duty to the magistrate is more strictly guarded by the principles of human nature, than our duty to our fellow-citizens. The love of dominion is so strong in the breast of man, that many, not only submit to, but court all the dangers, and fatigues, and cares of government; and men, once raised to that station, though often led astray by private passions, find, in ordinary cases, a visible interest in the impartial administration of justice. The persons, who first attain this distinction by the consent, tacit or express, of the people, must be endowed with superior personal qualities of valour, force, integrity, or prudence, which command respect and confidence: and after government is established, a regard to birth, rank, and station has a mighty influence over men, and enforces the decrees of the magistrate. The prince or leader exclaims against every disorder, which disturbs his society. He summons all his partisans and all men of probity to aid him in correcting and redressing it: and he is readily followed by all indifferent persons in the execution of his office.

He soon acquires the power of rewarding these services; and in the progress of society, he establishes subordinate ministers and often a military force, who find an immediate and a visible interest, in supporting his authority. Habit soon consolidates what other principles of human nature had imperfectly founded; and men, once accustomed to obedience, never think of departing from that path, in which they and their ancestors have constantly trod, and to which they are confined by so many urgent and visible motives.

But though this progress of human affairs may appear certain and inevitable, and though the support which allegiance brings to justice, be founded on obvious principles of human nature, it cannot be expected that men should beforehand be able to discover them, or foresee their operation. Government commences more casually and more imperfectly. It is probable, that the first ascendant of one man over multitudes begun during a state of war; where the superiority of courage and of genius discovers itself most visibly, where unanimity and concert are most requisite, and where the pernicious effects of disorder are most sensibly felt. The long continuance of that state, an incident common among savage tribes, enured the people to submission; and if the chieftain possessed as much equity as prudence and valour, he became, even during peace, the arbiter of all differences, and could gradually, by a mixture of force and consent, establish his authority. The benefit sensibly felt from his influence, made it be cherished by the people, at least by the peaceable and well disposed among them; and if his son enjoyed the same good qualities, government advanced the sooner to maturity and perfection; but was still in a feeble state, till the farther progress of improvement procured the magistrate a revenue, and enabled him to bestow rewards on the several instruments of his administration, and to inflict punishments on the refractory and disobedient. Before that period, each exertion of his influence must have been particular, and founded on the peculiar circumstances of the case. After it, submission was no longer a matter of choice in the bulk of the community, but was rigorously exacted by the authority of the supreme magistrate.

In all governments, there is a perpetual intestine struggle, open or secret, between Authority and Liberty; and neither of them can ever absolutely prevail in the contest. A great sacrifice of liberty must necessarily be made in every government; yet even the authority, which confines liberty, can never, and perhaps ought never, in any constitution, to become quite entire and uncontroulable. The sultan is master of the life and fortune of any individual; but will not be permitted to impose new taxes on his subjects: a French monarch can impose taxes at pleasure; but would find it dangerous to attempt the lives and fortunes of individuals. Religion also, in most countries, is commonly found to be a very intractable principle; and other principles or prejudices frequently resist all the authority of the civil magistrate; whose power, being founded on opinion, can never subvert other opinions, equally rooted with that of his title to dominion. The government, which, in common appellation, receives the appellation of free, is that which admits of a partition of power among several members, whose united authority is no less, or is commonly greater than that of any monarch; but who, in the usual course of administration, must act by general and equal laws, that are previously known to all the members and to all their subjects. In this sense, it must be owned, that liberty is the perfection of civil society; but still authority must be acknowledged essential to its very existence: and in those contests, which so often take place between the one and the other, the latter may, on that account, challenge the preference. Unless perhaps one may say (and it may be said with some reason) that a circumstance, which is essential to the existence of civil society, must always support itself, and needs be guarded with less jealousy, than one that contributes only to its perfection, which the indolence of men is so apt to neglect, or their ignorance to overlook.

ADAM SMITH

~

INTRODUCTION

CHARLES L. GRISWOLD JR.

Adam Smith (1723–1790) was a luminary in what is now called "the Scottish Enlightenment." Relatively little is known about his private life; he did not write an autobiography, and in spite of his fame as well as his friendship with leading figures of the day (such as Hume and Voltaire), his correspondence reveals surprisingly little about him as a man. He was clearly of stern character, strict discipline, skeptical disposition (and thus much opposed to extravagant religious or political claims), and complete trustworthiness. In many ways he appears to have been the perfect Stoic, needing little, independent, self-directed, and with emotions under watchful supervision. He did not live a monastic life, however; he had a wide circle of friends from many walks of life and regularly participated in meetings of literary, scientific, and business circles.

Smith attended Glasgow University, where he studied with Francis Hutcheson, and then Oxford, on the educational quality of which he subsequently commented caustically in the *Wealth of Nations*. In 1751, Smith was named professor of logic at Glasgow University; he taught logic (which he rapidly transformed into a course on rhetoric), jurisprudence, and political theory. The next year, he became professor of moral philosophy at Glasgow, and his subject expanded to include ethics. After rising to the position of vice-rector of the university, Smith resigned his chair in 1764 to serve as traveling tutor to the third Duke of Buccleuch. Smith spent the next several years in France, where he met many of the leading *philosophes*, as well as French political economists. By 1767, he had returned to his native Kirkcaldy, where he lived with his mother (Smith never married) and worked on further revision of his books, as well as on drafts of others. In 1778, he was named commissioner of customs for Scotland and of salt duties, and he relocated to Edinburgh. A decade later, he also served as rector of Glasgow University. As appropriate to his international reputation and position, Smith was consulted about various issues of the day, including about relations with the American colonies.

Smith published just two books, *The Theory of Moral Sentiments* (first edition 1759) and *An Inquiry into the Nature and Causes of the Wealth of Nations* (first edition 1776), each in a series of emended and expanded editions. From the first editions on, these two books were remarkably successful, and with impressive speed elevated Smith to the stature of an international celebrity. His work was rapidly translated into several languages and taken seriously by thinkers of the order of Burke, Hume, Bentham, Kant, and Hegel. Smith conceived of these books as parts of a much more extended corpus that was to have included a "Philosophical History of the Liberal and Elegant Arts";

a treatment of "natural jurisprudence" (an analysis of the "natural rules of justice" or "general principles of law and government"); and a detailed account of the evolution of these rules of natural justice. Unfortunately, Smith instructed that almost all of his unpublished manuscripts were to be destroyed on his death. Two sets of student notes of his lectures on jurisprudence were discovered long after, and they help us understand what part of the missing system might have looked like. A number of posthumously published essays (now available in a volume entitled *Essays on Philosophical Subjects*), along with the student notes of his lectures on rhetoric, give us a reasonable picture of his "philosophical history" of rhetoric, the imitative arts, and both philosophy and science. These essays demonstrate Smith's vast and imaginative grasp of those areas and outline a philosophy of science that seeks to account for theory acceptance in broadly "aesthetic" terms. The "psychology" of inquiry, and the connection between knowledge, rhetoric, and aesthetics, clearly fascinated Smith, as is evident in the *Theory of Moral Sentiments* as well.

The *Wealth of Nations* attempts to explain why free economic, political, and religious markets are not only more efficient (when properly regulated) in increasing the wealth of nations but also more in keeping with nature, more likely to win the approval of an impartial spectator than would monopolistic alternatives, and of course praiseworthy because supportive of liberty. The book thus makes a broad-gauged case for a modern commercial society. Taken together, Smith's two books attempt to show how virtue, liberty, and material welfare can complement each other. He shows full awareness of the potentially dehumanizing force of what was later called "capitalism," and sought remedies for it in schemes for liberal education and properly organized religion. He harshly criticized colonialism, slavery, and racism. Book V of the *Wealth of Nations* offers an ingenious "free market" solution to the problem of religious faction, one that depends on the assumptions in the *Theory of Moral Sentiments* about the psychology of moderation and fanaticism, a solution that strikingly foreshadows James Madison's famous proposals in the tenth and fifty-first *Federalist Papers* for controlling civil strife. Smith hopes that the result of fair competition among religions will be to "reduce the doctrine of the greater part of them to that pure and rational religion, free from every mixture of absurdity, imposture, or fanaticism, such as wise men have in all ages of the world wished to see established." Unlike Marx, Smith did not take religion to be the opium of the people, nor did he think that the religious impulse can, or should, be extirpated. He thought that it can have a constructive role, but under conditions of liberty of religious belief. The argument in the *Wealth of Nations* in favor of liberty is not only based on its utility in the service of wealth but also on its connection with justice and the flourishing of virtues such as moderation and prudence. The relationship between liberal institutional arrangements (such as the separation between church and state) and virtue is a circular one for Smith. The wrong arrangements elicit fanaticism and corruption, which in turn further illiberal institutions.

In the "obvious and simple system of natural liberty," Smith writes, "every man, as long as he does not violate the laws of justice, is left perfectly free to pursue his own interest his own way, and to bring both his industry and capital into competition with those of any other man, or order of men." The government is left with the duties of promoting public works, protecting society from invasion, and protecting its citizens from one other. These are areas in which the efforts of individuals are insufficient. In Smith's hands, these supply a wide entrance for government intervention in society, and he is never dogmatic in defining precisely what government may or may not do. Smith does not advocate mere laissez-faire, and he sees a role for the state in regulating, or encouraging, or even supporting the arts, education, commerce, and many other areas.

In complex ways, Smith's work self-consciously synthesizes ancient and modern thought; it is both of the Enlightenment and the counter-Enlightenment, as is clear in Smith's subtle discussions of the relationship between commerce and virtue. Smith provides a fascinating window on the old "quarrel between ancients and moderns." He does so with marked self-consciousness about his approach, showing a sophisticated awareness of his own methodology and rhetoric.

The combination of the incompleteness of Smith's corpus, his decision in the two published books not to comment on the unity of the moral philosophy and political economy, the dialectical quality of his writing, the intrinsic difficulty of the issues, and the eclecticism of his thinking, have made it a challenge to articulate the unity of his project. The problem of the unity of Smith's books became a cause célèbre in nineteenth-century German scholarship, where it gained the impressive technical designation of "das Adam-Smith Problem." The alleged problem consisted in part in the unity of the doctrine of sympathy and benevolence of the one work, with that of selfishness and acquisitiveness of the other. While stated thus, the problem is based on a misunderstanding of the terms "sympathy" and "self-interest." At a deeper level, the questions of the relationship between self-interest and duty toward others, between socially derived morals and independent moral norms, remains. But these are general philosophical problems, and to Smith's credit he thought them through with integrity and an open mind. His general argument in favor of a modern commercial republic is nuanced and qualified as appropriate, and is all the more powerful for it.

The secondary literature on Smith is vast. A small sample of the widely divergent but fine work on Smith includes V. Brown's *Adam Smith's Discourse: Canonicity, Commerce and Conscience* (London: Routledge, 1994), a book that deploys recent literary theory in a novel interpretation of Smith; J. Cropsey's classic *Polity and Economy: An Interpretation of the Principles of Adam Smith* (Westport, Conn.: Greenwood Press, 1977), in which Smith is placed in the decisively "modern" tradition of political philosophy stemming from Machiavelli and Hobbes; and K. Haakonssen's *The Science of a Legislator: The Natural Jurisprudence of David Hume & Adam Smith* (Cambridge: Cambridge University Press, 1981), a work exploring Smith's theory of justice and arguing for the centrality of "natural jurisprudence" to Smith's philosophy. *Wealth and Virtue* (Cambridge: Cambridge University Press, 1983), edited by I. Hont and M. Ignatieff, contains useful essays about Smith's seemingly paradoxical arguments on this classical theme. D. D. Raphael's *Adam Smith* (Oxford: Oxford University Press, 1985) supplies a useful and precise overview of Smith and his thought. A. S. Skinner's *A System of Social Science: Paper Relating to Adam Smith* (Oxford: Clarendon Press, 1979) brings together a number of Skinner's seminal papers on Smith, while D. Winch's *Adam Smith's Politics: An Essay in Historiographic Revision* (Cambridge: Cambridge University Press, 1978) counters the view that Smith assimilated "politics" to "economics," and with attention to the historical context it reconstructs the substance of Smith's political theory. For an overview of the secondary literature, see M. B. Lightwood's *A Selected Bibliography of Significant Works About Adam Smith* (Philadelphia: University of Pennsylvania Press, 1984) and F. Cordasco and B. Franklin's *Adam Smith: A Bibliographical Checklist* (New York: B. Franklin, 1950).

For a recent comprehensive discussion of Smith's philosophy (one that places particular emphasis on connections between Smith and contemporary moral and political philosophy, as well as on Smith's contribution to and criticisms of the Enlightenment), see C. L. Griswold, *Adam Smith and the Virtues of Enlightenment* (Cambridge: Cambridge University Press, 1999). Another recent philosophical work of relevance is S. Fleischacker's *A Third Concept of Liberty: Judgment and Freedom in Kant and Adam Smith* (Princeton, N.J.: Princeton University Press, 1999).

The Wealth of Nations

INTRODUCTION AND PLAN OF THE WORK

The annual labour of every nation is the fund which originally supplies it with all the necessaries and conveniencies of life which it annually consumes, and which consist always, either in the immediate produce of that labour, or in what is purchased with that produce from other nations.

According therefore, as this produce, or what is purchased with it, bears a greater or smaller proportion to the number of those who are to consume it, the nation will be better or worse supplied with all the necessaries and conveniencies for which it has occasion.

But this proportion must in every nation be regulated by two different circumstances; first, by the skill, dexterity, and judgment with which its labour is generally applied; and, secondly, by the proportion between the number of those who are employed in useful labour, and that of those who are not so employed. Whatever be the soil, climate, or extent of territory of any particular nation, the abundance or scantiness of its annual supply must, in that particular situation, depend upon those two circumstances.

The abundance or scantiness of this supply too seems to depend more upon the former of those two circumstances than upon the latter.

Among the savage nations of hunters and fishers, every individual who is able to work, is more or less employed in useful labour, and endeavours to provide, as well as he can, the necessaries and conveniencies of life, for himself, or such of his family or tribe as are either too old, or too young, or too infirm to go a hunting and fishing. Such nations, however, are so miserably poor, that, from mere want, they are frequently reduced, or, at least, think themselves reduced, to the necessity sometimes of directly destroying, and sometimes of abandoning their infants, their old people, and those afflicted with lingering diseases, to perish with hunger, or to be devoured by wild beasts. Among civilized and thriving nations, on the contrary, though a great number of people do not labour at all, many of whom consume the produce of ten times, frequently of a hundred times more labour than the greater part of those who work; yet the produce of the whole labour of the society is so great, that all are often abundantly supplied, and a workman, even of the lowest and poorest order, if he is frugal and industrious, may enjoy a greater share of the necessaries and conveniencies of life than it is possible for any savage to acquire. . . .

Whatever be the actual state of the skill, dexterity, and judgment with which labour is applied in any nation, the abundance or scantiness of its annual supply must depend, during the continuance of that state, upon the proportion between the number of those who are annually employed in useful labour, and that of those who are not so employed. . . .

Nations tolerably well advanced as to skill, dexterity, and judgment, in the application of labour, have followed very different plans in the general conduct or direction of it; and those plans have not all been equally favourable to the greatness of its produce. The policy of some nations has given extraordinary encouragement to the industry of the country. . . .

Though those different plans were, perhaps, first introduced by the private interests and prejudices of particular orders of men, without any regard to, or foresight of, their consequences upon the general welfare of the society; yet they have given occasion to very different theories of political economy; of which some magnify the importance of that industry which is carried on in towns, others of that which is carried on in the country. Those theories have had a considerable influence, not only upon the opinions of men of learning, but upon the public conduct of princes and sovereign states. . . .

BOOK I

Of the Causes of Improvement in the Productive Powers of Labour, and of the Order According to Which Its Produce Is Naturally Distributed Among the Different Ranks of the People

Chapter I

OF THE DIVISION OF LABOUR

The greatest improvement in the productive powers of labour, and the greater part of the skill, dexterity, and judgment with which it is any where directed, or applied, seem to have been the effects of the division of labour.

The effects of the division of labour, in the general business of society, will be more easily understood, by considering in what manner it operates in some particular manufactures. It is commonly supposed to be carried further in some very trifling ones; not perhaps that it really is carried further in them than in others of more importance: but in those trifling manufactures which are destined to supply the small wants of but a small number of people, the whole number of workmen must necessarily be small; and those employed in every different branch of the work can often be collected into the same workhouse, and placed at once under the view of the spectator. In those great manufactures, on the contrary, which are destined to supply the great wants of the great body of the people, every different branch of the work employs so great a number of workmen, that it is impossible to collect them all into the same workhouse. We can seldom see more, at one time, than those employed in one single branch. Though in such manufactures, therefore, the work may really be divided into a much greater number of parts, than in those of a more trifling nature, the division is not near so obvious, and has accordingly been much less observed.

To take an example, therefore, from a very trifling manufacture; but one in which the division of labour has been very often taken notice of, the trade of the pin-maker; a workman not educated to this business (which the division of labour has rendered a distinct trade), nor acquainted with the use of the machinery employed in it (to the invention of which the same division of labour has probably given occasion), could scarce, perhaps, with his utmost industry, make one pin in a day, and certainly could not make twenty. But in the way in which this business is now carried on, not only the whole work is a peculiar trade, but it is divided into a number of branches, of which the greater part are likewise peculiar trades. One man draws out the wire, another straights it, a third cuts it, a fourth points it, a fifth grinds it at the top for receiving the head; to make the head requires two or three distinct operations; to put it on, is a peculiar business, to whiten the pins is another;

it is even a trade by itself to put them into the paper; and the important business of making a pin is, in this manner, divided into about eighteen distinct operations, which, in some manufactories, are all performed by distinct hands, though in others the same man will sometimes perform two or three of them. I have seen a small manufactory of this kind where ten men only were employed, and where some of them consequently performed two or three distinct operations. But though they were very poor, and therefore but indifferently accommodated with the necessary machinery, they could, when they exerted themselves, make among them about twelve pounds of pins in a day. There are in a pound upwards of four thousand pins of a middling size. Those ten persons, therefore, could make among them upwards of forty-eight thousand pins in a day. Each person, therefore, making a tenth part of forty-eight thousand pins, might be considered as making four thousand eight hundred pins in a day. But if they had all wrought separately and independently, and without any of them having been educated to this peculiar business, they certainly could not each of them have made twenty, perhaps not one pin in a day; that is, certainly, not the two hundred and fortieth, perhaps not the four thousand eight hundredth part of what they are at present capable of performing, in consequence of a proper division and combination of their different operations. . . .

In every other art and manufacture, the effects of the division of labour are similar to what they are in this very trifling one; though in many of them, the labour can neither be so much subdivided, nor reduced to so great a simplicity of operation. The division of labour, however, so far as it can be introduced, occasions, in every art, a proportionable increase of the productive powers of labour. The separation of different trades and employments from one another seems to have taken place in consequence of this advantage. This separation too is generally carried furthest in those countries which enjoy the highest degree of industry and improvement; what is the work of

one man in a rude state of society being generally that of several in an improved one. . . .

It is the great multiplication of the productions of all the different arts, in consequence of the division of labour, which occasions, in a well-governed society, that universal opulence which extends itself to the lowest ranks of the people. Every workman has a great quantity of his own work to dispose of beyond what he himself has occasion for; and every other workman being exactly in the same situation, he is enabled to exchange a great quantity of his own goods for a great quantity, or, what comes to the same thing, for the price of a great quantity of theirs. He supplies them abundantly with what they have occasion for, and they accommodate him as amply with what he has occasion for, and a general plenty diffuses itself through all the different ranks of the society. . . .

Chapter II

OF THE PRINCIPLE WHICH GIVES OCCASION TO THE DIVISION OF LABOUR

This division of labour, from which so many advantages are derived, is not originally the effect of any human wisdom, which foresees and intends that general opulence to which it gives occasion. It is the necessary, though very slow and gradual consequence of a certain propensity in human nature which has in view no such extensive utility; the propensity to truck, barter, and exchange one thing for another.

Whether this propensity be one of those original principles in human nature, of which no further account can be given; or whether, as seems more probable, it be the necessary consequence of the faculties of reason and speech, it belongs not to our present subject to inquire. It is common to all men, and to be found in no other race of animals, which seem to know neither this nor any other species of contracts. Two greyhounds, in running down the same hare, have sometimes the appearance of acting in some sort of concert. Each turns her towards his companion, or endeavours to intercept her when his companion turns her towards himself. This, however, is not the effect of any contract, but of the accidental concurrence of their passions in the same object at that particular time. Nobody ever saw a dog make a fair and deliberate exchange of one bone for another with another dog. Nobody ever saw one animal by its gestures, and natural cries signify to another, this is mine, that yours; I am willing to give this for that. When an animal wants to obtain something either of a man or of another animal, it has no other means of persuasion but to gain the favour of those whose service it requires. A puppy fawns upon its dam, and a spaniel endeavours by a thousand attractions to engage the attention of its master who is at dinner, when it wants to be fed by him. Man sometimes uses the same arts with his brethren, and when he has no other means of engaging them to act according to his inclinations, endeavours by every servile and fawning attention to obtain their good will. He has not time, however, to do this upon every occasion. In civilized society he stands at all times in need of the co-operation and assistance of great multitudes, while his whole life is scarce sufficient to gain the friendship of a few persons. In almost every other race of animals each individual, when it is grown up to maturity, is entirely independent, and in its natural state has occasion for the assistance of no other living creature. But man has almost constant occasion for the help of his brethren, and it is in vain for him to expect it from their benevolence only. He will be more likely to prevail if he can interest their self-love in his favour, and show them that it is for their own advantage to do for him what he requires of them. Whoever offers to another a bargain of any kind, proposes to do this. Give me that which I want, and you shall have this which you want, is the meaning of every such offer; and it is in this manner that we obtain from one another the far greater part of those good offices which we stand in need of. It is not from the benevolence of the butcher, the brewer, or the baker, that we expect our dinner, but from their regard to their own interest. We address ourselves, not to their humanity but to their self-love, and never talk to them of our own necessities but of their advantages. Nobody but a beggar chooses to depend chiefly upon the benevolence of his fellow-citizens. Even a beggar does not depend upon it entirely. The charity of well-disposed people, indeed, supplies him with the whole fund of his subsistence. But though this principle ultimately provides him with all the necessaries of life which he has occasion for, it neither does nor can provide him with them as he has occasion for them. The greater part of his occasional wants are supplied in the same manner as those of other people, by treaty, by barter, and by purchase. With the money which one man gives him he purchases food. The old clothes which another bestows upon him he exchanges for other old clothes which suit him better, or for lodging, or for food, or for money, with which he can buy either food, clothes, or lodging, as he has occasion.

As it is by treaty, by barter, and by purchase, that we obtain from one another the greater part of those mutual good offices which we stand in need of, so it is this same trucking disposition which originally gives occasion to the division of labour. In a tribe of hunters or shepherds a particular person makes bows and arrows, for example, with more readiness and dexterity than any other. He frequently exchanges them for cattle or for venison with his companions; and he finds at last that he can in this manner get more cattle and venison, than if he himself went to the field to catch them. From a regard to his own interest, therefore, the making of bows and arrows grows to be his chief business, and he becomes a sort of armourer. Another excels in making the frames and covers of their little huts or moveable houses. He is accustomed to be of use in this way to his neighbours, who reward him in the same manner with cattle and with venison, till at last he finds it his interest to dedicate himself entirely to this employment, and to become a sort of house-carpenter. In the same manner a third becomes a smith or a brazier, a fourth a tanner or dresser of hides or skins, the principal part of the clothing of savages. And thus the certainty of being able to exchange all that surplus part of the produce of his own labour, which is over and above his own consumption, for such parts of the produce of other men's labour as he may have occasion for, encourages every man to apply himself to a particular occupation, and to cultivate and bring to perfection whatever talent or genius he may possess for that particular species of business.

The difference of natural talents in different men is, in reality, much less than we are aware of; and the very different genius which appears to distinguish men of different professions, when grown up to maturity, is not upon many occasions so much the cause, as the effect of the division of labour. The difference between the most dissimilar characters, between a philosopher and a common street porter, for example, seems to arise not so much from nature, as from habit, custom, and education. . . .

Chapter V

OF THE REAL AND NOMINAL PRICE OF COMMODITIES, OR OF THEIR PRICE IN LABOUR, AND THEIR PRICE IN MONEY

Every man is rich or poor according to the degree in which he can afford to enjoy the necessaries, conveniencies, and amusements of human life. But after the division of labour has once thoroughly taken place, it is but a very small part of these with which a man's own labour can supply him. The far greater part of them he must derive from the labour of other people, and he must be rich or poor according to the quantity of that labour which he can command, or which he can afford to purchase. The value of any commodity, therefore, to the person who possesses it, and who means not to use or consume it himself, but to exchange it for other commodities, is equal to the quantity of labour which it enables him to purchase or command. Labour, therefore, is the real measure of the exchangeable value of all commodities.

The real price of every thing, what every thing really costs to the man who wants to acquire it, is the toil and trouble of acquiring it. What every thing is really worth to the man who has acquired it, and who wants to dispose of it or exchange it

for something *else, is the toil and trouble which it can save to himself,* and which it can impose upon other people. What is bought with money or with goods is purchased by labour as much as what we acquire by the toil of our own body. That money or those goods indeed save us this toil. They contain the value of a certain quantity of labour which we exchange for what is supposed at the time to contain the value of an equal quantity. Labour was the first price, the original purchase money that was paid for all things. It was not by gold or by silver, but by labour, that all the wealth of the world was originally purchased; and its value, to those who possess it and who want to exchange it for some new productions, is precisely equal to the quantity of labour which it can enable them to purchase or command.

Wealth, as Mr. Hobbes says, is power. But the person who either acquires, or succeeds to a great fortune, does not necessarily acquire or succeed to any political power, either civil or military. His fortune may, perhaps, afford him the means of acquiring both, but the mere possession of that fortune does not necessarily convey to him either. The power which that possession immediately and directly conveys to him, is the power of purchasing; a certain command over all the labour, or over all the produce of labour which is then in the market. His fortune is greater or less, precisely in proportion to the extent of this power; or to the quantity either of other men's labour, or, what is the same thing, of the produce of other men's labour, which it enables him to purchase or command. The exchangeable value of every thing must always be precisely equal to the extent of this power which it conveys to its owner.

But though labour be the real measure of the exchangeable value of all commodities, it is not that by which their value is commonly estimated. It is often difficult to ascertain the proportion between two different quantities of labour. The time spent in two different sorts of work will not always alone determine this proportion. The different degrees of hardship endured, and of ingenuity exercised, must likewise be taken into account. There may be more labour in an hour's hard work than in two hours easy business; or in an hour's application to a trade which it cost ten years labour to learn, than in a month's *industry at an ordinary and obvious employment*. But it is not easy to find any accurate measure either of hardship or ingenuity. In exchanging indeed the different productions of different sorts of labour for one another, some allowance is commonly made for both. It is adjusted, however, not by any accurate measure, but by the higgling and bargaining of the market, according to that sort of rough equality which, though not exact, is sufficient for carrying on the business of common life.

Every commodity besides, is more frequently exchanged for, and thereby compared with, other commodities than with labour. It is more natural, therefore, to estimate its exchangeable value by the quantity of some other commodity than by that of the labour which it can purchase. The greater part of people too understand better what is meant by a quantity of a particular commodity, than by a quantity of labour. The one is a plain palpable object; the other an abstract notion, which, though it can be made sufficiently intelligible, is not altogether so natural and obvious.

But when barter ceases, and money has become the common instrument of commerce, every particular commodity is more frequently exchanged for money than for any other commodity. The butcher seldom carries his beef or his mutton to the baker, or the brewer, in order to exchange them for bread or for beer, but he carries them to the market, where he exchanges them for money, and afterwards exchanges that money for bread and for beer. The quantity of money which he gets for them regulates too the quantity of bread and beer which he can afterwards purchase. It is more natural and obvious to him, therefore, to estimate their value by the quantity of money, the commodity for which he immediately exchanges them, than by that of bread and beer, the commodities for which he can exchange them only by the intervention of another commodity; and rather to say that his butcher's meat is worth threepence or

fourpence a pound, than that it is worth three or four pounds of bread, or three or four quarts of small beer. Hence it comes to pass, that the exchangeable value of every commodity is more frequently estimated by the quantity of money, than by the quantity either of labour or of any other commodity which can be had in exchange for it.

Gold and silver, however, like every other commodity, vary in their value, are sometimes cheaper and sometimes dearer, sometimes of easier and sometimes of more difficult purchase. The quantity of labour which any particular quantity of them can purchase or command, or the quantity of other goods which it will exchange for, depends always upon the fertility or barrenness of the mines which happen to be known about the time when such exchanges are made. The discovery of the abundant mines of America reduced, in the sixteenth century, the value of gold and silver in Europe to about a third of what it had been before. As it cost less labour to bring those metals from the mine to the market, so when they were brought thither they could purchase or command less labour; and this revolution in their value, though perhaps the greatest, is by no means the only one of which history gives some account. But as a measure of quantity, such as the natural foot, fathom, or handful, which is continually varying in its own quantity, can never be an accurate measure of the quantity of other things; so a commodity which is itself continually varying in its own value, can never be an accurate measure of the value of other commodities. Equal quantities of labour, at all times and places, may be said to be of equal value to the labourer. In his ordinary state of health, strength and spirits; in the ordinary degree of his skill and dexterity, he must always lay down the same portion of his ease, his liberty, and his happiness. The price which he pays must always be the same, whatever may be the quantity of goods which he receives in return for it. Of these, indeed, it may sometimes purchase a greater and sometimes a smaller quantity; but it is their value which varies, not that of the labour which purchases them. At all times and places that is dear which it is difficult to come at, or which it costs much labour to acquire; and that cheap which is to be had easily, or with very little labour. Labour alone, therefore, never varying in its own value, is alone the ultimate arid real standard by which the value of all commodities can at all times and places be estimated and compared. It is their real price; money is their nominal price only.

But though equal quantities of labour are always of equal value to the labourer, yet to the person who employs him they appear sometimes to be of greater and sometimes of smaller value. He purchases them sometimes with a greater and sometimes with a smaller quantity of goods, and to him the price of labour seems to vary like that of all other things. It appears to him dear in the one case, and cheap in the other. In reality, however, it is the goods which are cheap in the one case, and dear in the other.

In this popular sense, therefore, labour, like commodities, may be said to have a real and a nominal price. Its real price may be said to consist in the quantity of the necessaries and conveniencies of life which are given for it; its nominal price, in the quantity of money. The labourer is rich or poor, is well or ill rewarded, in proportion to the real, not to the nominal price of his labour. . . .

Chapter VIII

OF THE WAGES OF LABOUR

The produce of labour constitutes the natural recompense or wages of labour.

In that original state of things, which precedes both the appropriation of land and the accumulation of stock, the whole produce of labour belongs to the labourer. He has neither landlord nor master to share with him.

Had this state continued, the wages of labour would have augmented with all those improvements in its productive powers to which the division of labour gives occasion. All things would gradually have become cheaper. They would have been produced by a smaller quantity of labour,

and as the commodities produced by equal quantities of labour would naturally in this state of things be exchanged for one another, they would have been purchased likewise with the produce of a smaller quantity.

But though all things would have become cheaper in reality, in appearance many things might have become dearer than before, or have been exchanged for a greater quantity of other goods. Let us suppose, for example, that in the greater part of employments the productive powers of labour had been improved to tenfold, or that a day's labour could produce ten times the quantity of work which it had done originally; but that in a particular employment they had been improved only to double, or that a day's labour could produce only twice the quantity of work which it had done before. In exchanging the produce of a day's labour in the greater part of employments for that of a day's labour in this particular one, ten times the original quantity of work in them would purchase only twice the original quantity in it. Any particular quantity in it, therefore, a pound weight, for example, would appear to be five times dearer than before. In reality, however, it would be twice as cheap. Though it required five times the quantity of other goods to purchase it, it would require only half the quantity of labour either to purchase or to produce it. The acquisition, therefore, would be twice as easy as before.

But this original state of things, in which the labourer enjoyed the whole produce of his own labour, could not last beyond the first introduction of the appropriation of land and the accumulation of stock. It was at an end, therefore, long before the most considerable improvements were made in the productive powers of labour, and it would be to no purpose to trace further what might have been its effects upon the recompense or wages of labour.

As soon as land becomes private property, the landlord demands a share of almost all the produce which the labourer can either raise, or collect from it. His rent makes the first deduction from the produce of the labour which is employed upon land.

It seldom happens that the person who tills the ground has wherewithal to maintain himself till he reaps the harvest. His maintenance is generally advanced to him from the stock of a master, the farmer who employs him, and who would have no interest to employ him, unless he was to share in the produce of his labour, or unless his stock was to be replaced to him with a profit. This profit makes a second deduction from the produce of the labour which is employed upon land.

The produce of almost all other labour is liable to the like deduction of profit. In all arts and manufactures the greater part of the workmen stand in need of a master to advance them the materials of their work, and their wages and maintenance till it be completed. He shares in the produce of their labour, or in the value which it adds to the materials upon which it is bestowed; and in this share consists his profit.

It sometimes happens, indeed, that a single independent workman has stock sufficient both to purchase the materials of his work, and to maintain himself till it be completed. He is both master and workman, and enjoys the whole produce of his own labour, or the whole value which it adds to the materials upon which it is bestowed. It includes what are usually two distinct revenues, belonging to two distinct persons, the profits of stock, and the wages of labour.

Such cases, however, are not very frequent, and in every part of Europe, twenty workmen serve under a master for one that is independent; and the wages of labour are everywhere understood to be, what they usually are, when the labourer is one person, and the owner of the stock which employs him another.

What are the common wages of labour depends everywhere upon the contract usually made between those two parties, whose interests are by no means the same. The workmen desire to get as much, the masters to give as little as possible. The former are disposed to combine in order to raise, the latter in order to lower the wages of labour.

It is not, however, difficult to foresee which of the two parties must, upon all ordinary occasions, have the advantage in the dispute, and force the other into a compliance with their terms. The masters, being fewer in number, can combine much more easily; and the law, besides, authorizes, or at least does not prohibit their combinations, while it prohibits those of the workmen. We have no acts of parliament against combining to lower the price of work; but many against combining to raise it. In all such disputes the masters can hold out much longer. A landlord, a farmer, a master manufacturer, or merchant, though they did not employ a single workman, could generally live a year or two upon the stocks which they have already acquired. Many workmen could not subsist a week, few could subsist a month, and scarce any a year without employment. In the long run the workman may be as necessary to his master as his master is to him; but the necessity is not so immediate.

We rarely hear, it has been said, of the combinations of masters; though frequently of those of workmen. But whoever imagines, upon this account, that masters rarely combine, is as ignorant of the world as of the subject. Masters are always and everywhere in a sort of tacit, but constant and uniform combination, not to raise the wages of labour above their actual rate. To violate this combination is everywhere a most unpopular action, and a sort of reproach to a master among his neighbours and equals. We seldom, indeed, hear of this combination, because it is the usual, and one may say, the natural state of things which nobody ever hears of. Masters too sometimes enter into particular combinations to sink the wages of labour even below this rate. These are always conducted with the utmost silence and secrecy, till the moment of execution, and when the workmen yield, as they sometimes do, without resistance, though severely felt by them, they are never heard of by other people. Such combinations, however, are frequently resisted by a contrary defensive combination of the workmen; who sometimes too, without any provocation of this kind, combine of their own accord to raise the price of their labour. Their usual pretences are, sometimes the high price of provisions; sometimes the great profit which their masters make by their work. But whether their combinations be offensive or defensive, they are always abundantly heard of. In order to bring the point to a speedy decision, they have always recourse to the loudest clamour, and sometimes to the most shocking violence and outrage. They are desperate, and act with the folly and extravagance of desperate men, who must either starve, or frighten their masters into an immediate compliance with their demands. The masters upon these occasions are just as clamorous upon the other side, and never cease to call aloud for the assistance of the civil magistrate, and the rigorous execution of those laws which have been enacted with so much severity against the combinations of servants, labourers, and journeymen. The workmen, accordingly, very seldom derive any advantage from the violence of those tumultuous combinations, which, partly from the interposition of the civil magistrate, partly from the superior steadiness of the masters, partly from the necessity which the greater part of the workmen are under of submitting for the sake of present subsistence, generally end in nothing, but the punishment or ruin of the ring-leaders.

But though in disputes with their workmen, masters must generally have the advantage, there is however a certain rate below which it seems impossible to reduce, for any considerable time, the ordinary wages even of the lowest species of labour.

A man must always live by his work, and his wages must at least be sufficient to maintain him . . .

BOOK IV

Of Systems of Political Economy

Chapter II

OF RESTRAINTS UPON THE IMPORTATION
FROM FOREIGN COUNTRIES OF SUCH GOODS
AS CAN BE PRODUCED AT HOME

By restraining, either by high duties, or by absolute prohibitions, the importation of such goods from foreign countries as can be produced at home, the monopoly of the home market is more or less secured to the domestic industry employed in producing them. Thus the prohibition of importing either live cattle or salt provisions from foreign countries secures to the graziers of Great Britain the monopoly of the home market for butcher's meat. The high duties upon the importation of corn, which in times of moderate plenty amount to a prohibition, give a like advantage to the growers of that commodity. The prohibition of the importation of foreign woolens is equally favourable to the woolen manufacturers. The silk manufacture, though altogether employed upon foreign materials, has lately obtained the same advantage. The linen manufacture has not yet obtained it, but is making great strides toward it. Many other sorts of manufacturers have, in the same manner, obtained in Great Britain, either altogether, or very nearly, a monopoly against their countrymen. The variety of goods of which the importation into Great Britain is prohibited, either absolutely, or under certain circumstances, greatly exceeds what can easily be suspected by those who are not well acquainted with the laws of the customs.

That this monopoly of the home market frequently gives great encouragement to that particular species of industry which enjoys it, and frequently turns toward that employment a greater share of both the labour and stock of the society than would otherwise have gone to it, cannot be doubted. But whether it tends either to increase the general industry of the society, or to give it the most advantageous direction, is not, perhaps, altogether so evident.

The general industry of the society never can exceed what the capital of the society can employ. As the number of workmen that can be kept in employment by any particular person must bear a certain proportion to his capital, so the number of those that can be continually employed by all the members of a great society must bear a certain proportion to the whole capital of that society and never can exceed that proportion. No regulation of commerce can increase the quantity of industry in any society beyond what its capital can maintain. It can only divert a part of it into a direction into which it might not otherwise have gone; and it is by no means certain that this artificial direction is likely to be more advantageous to the society than that into which it would have gone of its own accord.

Every individual is continually exerting himself to find out the most advantageous employment for whatever capital he can command. It is his own advantage, indeed, and not that of the society, which he has in view. But the study of his own advantage naturally, or rather necessarily leads him to prefer that employment which is most advantageous to the society.

First, every individual endeavours to employ his capital as near home as he can, and consequently as much as he can in the support of domestic industry; provided always that he can thereby obtain the ordinary, or not a great deal less than the ordinary profits of stock. . . .

Thus, upon equal or nearly equal profits, every wholesale merchant naturally prefers the home trade to the foreign trade of consumption, and the foreign trade of consumption to the carrying trade. In the home trade his capital is never so long out of his sight as it frequently is in the foreign trade of consumption. He can know better the character and situation of the persons whom he trusts, and if he should happen to be deceived, he knows better the laws of the country from which he must seek redress. In the carrying trade, the capital of the merchant is, as it were, divided between two foreign countries, and no part of it is ever necessarily brought home or placed under his own immediate view and command. The capital which an Amsterdam merchant employs in carrying corn from Königsberg to Lisbon, and fruit and wine from Lisbon to Königsberg, must generally be the one half of it at Königsberg and the other half of Lisbon. No part of it need ever come to Amsterdam. The natural residence of such a merchant should either be at Königsberg or Lisbon, and it can only be some very particular circumstances which can make him prefer the residence of Amsterdam. The uneasiness, however, which he feels at being separated so far from his capital generally determines him to bring part both of

the Königsberg goods which he destines for the market of Lisbon, and of the Lisbon goods which he destines for that of Königsberg, to Amsterdam; and though this necessarily subjects him to a double charge of loading and unloading, as well as to the payment of some duties and customs, yet for the sake of having some part of his capital always under his own view and command, he willingly submits to this extraordinary charge; and it is in this manner that every country which has any considerable share of the carrying trade becomes always the emporium, or general market, for the goods of all the different countries whose trade it carries on. The merchant, in order to save a second loading and unloading, endeavors always to sell in the home market as much of the goods of all those different countries as he can, and thus, so far as he can, to convert his carrying trade into a foreign trade of consumption. A merchant, in the same manner, who is engaged in the foreign trade of consumption, when he collects goods for foreign markets, will always be glad, upon equal or nearly equal profits, to sell as great a part of them at home as he can. He saves himself the risk and trouble of exportation, when, so far as he can, he thus converts his foreign trade of consumption into a home trade. Home is in this manner the center, if I may say so, around which the capitals of the inhabitants of every country are continually circulating, and toward which they are always tending, though by particular causes they may sometimes be driven off and repelled from it toward more distant employments. But a capital employed in the home trade, it has already been shown, necessarily puts into motion a greater quantity of domestic industry and gives revenue and employment to a greater number of the inhabitants of the country than an equal capital employed in the foreign trade of consumption; and one employed in the foreign trade of consumption has the same advantage over an equal capital employed in the carrying trade. Upon equal, or only nearly equal, profits, therefore, every individual naturally inclines to employ his capital in the manner in which it is likely to afford the greatest support to domestic industry, and to give revenue and employment to the greatest number of people of his own country.

Secondly, every individual who employs his capital in the support of domestic industry necessarily endeavors so to direct that industry that its produce may be of the greatest possible value.

The produce of industry is what it adds to the subject or materials upon which it is employed. In proportion as the value of this produce is great or small, so will likewise be the profits of the employer. But it is only for the sake of profit that any man employs a capital in the support of industry; and he will always, therefore, endeavor to employ it in the support of that industry of which the produce is likely to be of the greatest value, or to exchange for the greatest quantity either of money or of other goods.

But the annual revenue of every society is always precisely equal to the exchangeable value of the whole annual produce of its industry, or rather is precisely the same thing with that exchangeable value. As every individual, therefore, endeavors as much as he can both to employ his capital in the support of domestic industry and so to direct that industry that its produce may be of the greatest value; every individual necessarily labours to render the annual revenue of the society as great as he can. He generally, indeed, neither intends to promote the public interest, nor knows how much he is promoting it. By preferring the support of domestic to that of foreign industry, he intends only his own security; and by directing that industry in such a manner as its produce may be of the greatest value, he intends only his own gain, and he is in this, as in many other cases, led by an invisible hand to promote an end which was no part of his intention. Nor is it always the worse for the society that it was no part of it. By pursuing his own interest he frequently promotes that of the society more effectually than when he really intends to promote it. I have never known much good done by those who affected trade for the public good. It is an affectation, indeed, not very common

among merchants, and very few words need be employed in dissuading them from it. . . .

As every individual, therefore, endeavours as much as he can both to employ his capital in the support of domestic industry, and so to direct that industry that its produce may be of the greatest value; every individual necessarily labours to render the annual revenue of the society as great as he can. He generally, indeed, neither intends to promote the public interest, nor knows how much he is promoting it. By preferring the support of domestic to that of foreign industry, he intends only his own security; and by directing that industry in such a manner as its produce may be of the greatest value, he intends only his own gain, and he is in this, as in many other cases, led by an invisible hand to promote an end which was no part of his intention. Nor is it always the worse for the society that it was no part of it. By pursuing his own interest he frequently promotes that of the society more effectually than when he really intends to promote it. I have never known much good done by those who affected to trade for the public good. It is an affectation, indeed, not very common among merchants, and very few words need be employed in dissuading them from it . . .

Chapter IX

OF THE AGRICULTURAL SYSTEMS . . .

. . . All systems either of preference or of restraint, therefore, being thus completely taken away, the obvious and simple system of natural liberty establishes itself of its own accord. Every man, as long as he does not violate the laws of justice, is left perfectly free to pursue his own interest his own way, and to bring both his industry and capital into competition with those of any other man, or order of men. The sovereign is completely discharged from a duty, in the attempting to perform which he must always be exposed to innumerable delusions, and for the proper performance of which no human wisdom or knowledge could ever be sufficient; the duty of superintending the industry of private people, and of directing it towards the employments most suitable to the interest of the society. According to the system of natural liberty, the sovereign has only three duties to attend to; three duties of great importance, indeed, but plain and intelligible to common understandings: first, the duty of protecting the society from the violence and invasion of other independent societies; secondly, the duty of protecting, as far as possible, every member of the society from the injustice or oppression of every other member of it, or the duty of establishing an exact administration of justice; and, thirdly, the duty of erecting and maintaining certain public works and certain public institutions, which it can never be for the interest of any individual, or small number of individuals, to erect and maintain; because the profit could never repay the expense to any individual or small number of individuals, though it may frequently do much more than repay it to a great society.

The proper performance of those several duties of the sovereign necessarily supposes a certain expense; and this expense again necessarily requires a certain revenue to support it. . . .

BOOK V

Of the Revenue of the Sovereign or Commonwealth

Chapter I

OF THE EXPENSES OF THE SOVEREIGN OR COMMONWEALTH

Part I

Of the Expense of Defense

The first duty of the sovereign, that of protecting the society from the violence and invasion of other independent societies, can be performed only by means of a military force. But the expense both of preparing this military force in time of peace, and of employing it in time of war, is very different in the different states of society, in the different periods of improvement. . . .

In a more advanced state of society, two different causes contribute to render it altogether impossible that they who take the field should maintain themselves at their own expense. Those two causes are the progress of manufactures, and the improvement in the art of war.

Though a husbandman should be employed in an expedition, provided it begins after seedtime and ends before harvest, the interruption of his business will not always occasion any considerable diminution of his revenue. Without the intervention of his labour, nature does herself the greater part of the work which remains to be done. But the moment that an artificer, a smith, a carpenter, or a weaver, for example, quits his workhouse, the sole source of his revenue is completely dried up. Nature does nothing for him, he does all for himself. When he takes the field, therefore, in defence of the public, as he has no revenue to maintain himself, he must necessarily be maintained by the public. But in a country of which a greater part of the inhabitants are artificers and manufacturers, a great part of the people who go to war must be drawn from those classes, and must therefore be maintained by the public as long as they are employed in its service.

When the art of war too has gradually grown up to be a very intricate and complicated science, when the event of war ceases to be determined, as in the first ages of society, by a single irregular skirmish or battle, but when the contest is generally spun out through several different campaigns, each of which lasts during the greater part of the year; it becomes universally necessary that the public should maintain those who serve the public in war, at least while they are employed in that service. Whatever in time of peace might be the ordinary occupation of those who go to war, so very tedious and expensive a service would otherwise be by far too heavy a burden upon them. . . .

Part II

Of the Expense of Justice

The second duty of the sovereign, that of protecting, as far as possible, every member of the society from the injustice or oppression of every other member of it, or the duty of establishing an exact administration of justice, requires two very different degrees of expense in the different periods of society.

Among nations of hunters, as there is scarce any property, or at least none that exceeds the value of two or three days labour; so there is seldom any established magistrate or any regular administration of justice. Men who have no property can injure one another only in their persons or reputations. But when one man kills, wounds, beats, or defames another, though he to whom the injury is done suffers, he who does it receives no benefit. It is otherwise with the injuries to property. The benefit of the person who does the injury is often equal to the loss of him who suffers it. Envy, malice, or resentment are the only passions which can prompt one man to injure another in his person or reputation. But the greater part of men are not very frequently under the influence of those passions; and the very worst men are so only occasionally. As their gratification too, how agreeable soever it may be to certain characters, is not attended with any real or permanent advantage, it is in the greater part of men commonly restrained by prudential considerations. Men may live together in society with some tolerable degree of security, though there is no civil magistrate to protect them from the injustice of those passions. But avarice and ambition in the rich, in the poor the hatred of labour and the love of present ease and enjoyment, are the passions which prompt to invade property, passions much more steady in their operation, and much more universal in their influence. Wherever there is great property, there is great inequality. For one very rich man, there must be at least five hundred poor, and the affluence of the few supposes the indigence of the many. The affluence of the rich excites the indignation of the poor, who are often both driven by want, and prompted by envy, to invade his possessions. It is only under the shelter of the civil magistrate that the owner of the valuable property, which is acquired by the labour of many years, or perhaps of many successive generations, can sleep a single night in security. He is at all times surrounded by unknown enemies, whom, though he never provoked, he can never appease, and from whose injustice he can be protected only by the powerful arm of the civil magistrate continually held up to chastise it. The acquisition of valuable and extensive property, therefore, necessarily requires the establishment of civil government. Where there is no property, or at least none that exceeds the value of two or three days labour, civil government is not so necessary.

Civil government supposed a certain subordination. But as the necessity of civil government gradually grows up with the acquisition of valuable property, so the principal causes which naturally introduce subordination gradually grow up with the growth of that valuable property.

The causes or circumstances which naturally introduce subordination, or which naturally, and antecedent to any civil institution, give some men some superiority over the greater part of their brethren, seem to be four in number.

The first of those causes or circumstances is the superiority of personal qualifications, of strength, beauty, and agility of body; of wisdom, and virtue, of prudence, justice, fortitude, and moderation of mind. The qualifications of the body, unless supported by those of the mind, can give little authority in any period of society. He is a very strong man who, by mere strength of body, can force two weak ones to obey him. The qualifications of the mind can alone give very great authority. They are, however, invisible qualities; always disputable, and generally disputed. No society, whether barbarous or civilized, has ever found it convenient to settle the rules of precedency of rank and subordination according to those invisible qualities; but according to something that is more plain and palpable.

The second of those causes or circumstances is the superiority of age. An old man, provided his age is not so far advanced as to give suspicion of dotage, is everywhere more respected than a young man of equal rank, fortune, and abilities. Among nations of hunters, such as the native tribes of North America, age is the sole foundation of rank and precedency. Among them, father is the appellation of a superior; brother, of an equal; and son, of an inferior. In the most opulent and civilized nations, age regulates rank among those who are in every other respect equal, and among whom, therefore, there is nothing else to regulate it. Among brothers and among sisters, the eldest always take place; and in the succession of the paternal estate every thing which cannot be divided, but must go entire to one person, such as a title of honour, is in most cases given to the eldest. Age is a plain and palpable quality which admits of no dispute.

The third of those causes or circumstances is the superiority of fortune. The authority of riches, however, though great in every age of society, is perhaps greatest in the rudest age of society which admits of any considerable inequality of fortune. A Tartar chief, the increase of whose herds and flocks is sufficient to maintain a thousand men, cannot well employ that increase in any other way than in maintaining a thousand men. The rude state of his society does not afford him any manufactured produce, any trinkets or baubles of any kind, for which he can exchange that part of his rude produce which is over and above his own consumption. The thousand men whom he thus maintains, depending entirely upon him for their subsistence, must both obey his orders in war, and submit to his jurisdiction in peace. He is necessarily both their general and their judge, and his chieftainship is the necessary effect of the superiority of his fortune. In an opulent and civilized society a man may possess a much greater fortune, and yet not be able to command a dozen of people. Though the produce of his estate may be sufficient to maintain, and may perhaps actually maintain, more than a thousand people, yet as those people pay for every thing which they get from him, as he gives scarce anything to anybody but in exchange for an equivalent, there is scarce anybody who considers himself as entirely dependent upon him, and his authority extends only over a few menial servants. The authority of fortune, however, is very great even in an opulent and civilized society. That it is much greater than that either of age or of personal qualities has been the constant complaint of every period of society which admitted of any considerable inequality of fortune. The first period of society that of hunters, admits of no such inequality. Universal poverty establishes there universal equality, and the superiority either of age or of personal qualities are the feeble, but the sole foundations of authority and subordination. There is therefore little or no authority or subordination in this period of society. The second period of society, that of shepherds, admits of very great inequalities of fortune, and there is no period in which the superiority of fortune gives so great authority to those who possess it. There is no period accordingly in which authority and subordination are more perfectly established. The authority of an Arabian sherif is very great; that of a Tartar khan altogether despotical.

The fourth of those causes or circumstances is the superiority of birth. Superiority of birth supposes an ancient superiority of fortune in the family of the person who claims it. All families are equally ancient; and the ancestors of the prince, though they may be better known, cannot well be more numerous than those of the beggar. Antiquity of family means everywhere the antiquity either of wealth, or of that greatness which is commonly either founded upon wealth, or accompanied with it. Upstart greatness is everywhere less respected than ancient greatness. The hatred of usurpers, the love of the family of an ancient monarch, are, in a great measure, founded upon the contempt which men naturally have for the former, and upon their veneration for the latter. As a military officer submits without reluctance to the authority of a superior by whom he has always been commanded, but cannot bear that his inferior should be set over his head; so men easily submit to a family to whom they and their ancestors have always submitted; but are fired with indignation when another family, in whom they had never acknowledged any such superiority, assumes a dominion over them.

The distinction of birth, being subsequent to the inequality of fortune, can have no place in nations of hunters, among whom all men, being equal in fortune, must likewise be very nearly equal in birth. The son of a wise and brave man may, indeed, even among them, be somewhat more respected than a man of equal merit who has the misfortune to be the son of a fool or a coward. The difference, however, will not be very great; and there never was, I believe, a great family in the world whose illustration was entirely derived from the inheritance of wisdom and virtue.

The distinction of birth not only may but always does take place among nations of shepherds. Such nations are always strangers to every sort of luxury, and great wealth can scarce ever be dissipated among them by improvident profusion. There are no nations accordingly who abound more in families revered and honoured on account of their descent from a long race of great and illustrious ancestors; because there are no nations among whom wealth is likely to continue longer in the same families.

Birth and fortune are evidently the two circumstances which principally set one man above another. They are the two great sources of personal distinction, and are therefore the principal causes which naturally establish authority and subordination among men. Among nations of shepherds both those causes operate with their full force. The great shepherd or herdsman, respected on account of his great wealth, and of the great number of those who depend upon him for subsistence, and revered on account of the nobleness of his birth, and of the immemorial antiquity of his illustrious family, has a natural authority over all the inferior shepherds or herdsmen of his horde or clan. He can command the united force of a greater number of people than any of them. His military power is greater than that of any of them. In time of war they are all of them naturally disposed to muster themselves under his banner, rather than under that of any other person, and his birth and fortune thus naturally procure to him some sort of executive power. By commanding too the united force of a greater number of people than any of them, he is best able to compel any one of them who may have injured another to compensate the wrong. He is the person, therefore, to whom all those who are too weak to defend themselves naturally look up for protection. It is to him that they naturally complain of the injuries which they imagine have been done to them, and his interposition in such cases is more easily submitted to, even by the person complained of, than that of any other person would be. His birth and fortune thus naturally procure him some sort of judicial authority.

It is in the age of shepherds, in the second period of society, that the inequality of fortune first begins to take place, and introduces among men a degree of authority and subordination which could not possibly exist before. It thereby introduces some degree of that civil government which is indispensably necessary for its own preservation: and it seems to do this naturally, and even independent of the consideration of that necessity. The consideration of that necessity comes no doubt afterwards to contribute very much to maintain and secure that authority and subordination. The rich, in particular, are necessarily interested to support that order of things, which can alone secure them in the possession of their own advantages. Men of inferior wealth combine to defend those of superior wealth in the possession of their property, in order that men of superior wealth may combine to defend them in the possession of theirs. All the inferior shepherds and herdsmen feel that the security of their own herds and flocks depends upon the security of those of the great shepherd or herdsman; that the maintenance of their lesser authority depends upon that of his greater authority, and that upon their subordination to him depends his power of keeping their inferiors in subordination to them. They constitute a sort of little nobility, who feel themselves interested to defend the property and to support the authority of their own little sovereign, in order that he may be able to defend their property and to support their authority. Civil government, so far as it is instituted for the security of property, is in reality instituted for the defense of the rich against the poor, or of those who have some property against those who have none at all.

The judicial authority of such a sovereign, however, far from being a cause of expense, was for a long time a source of revenue to him. The persons who applied to him for justice were always willing to pay for it, and a present never failed to accompany a petition. After the authority of the sovereign too was thoroughly established, the person found guilty, over and above the satisfaction which he was obliged to make to the party, was likewise forced to pay an amercement to the sovereign. He had given trouble, he had disturbed, he had broke the peace of his lord the king, and for those offenses an amercement was thought due. In the Tartar governments of Asia, in the governments of Europe which were founded by the German and Scythian nations who overturned the Roman empire, the administration of justice was a considerable source of revenue, both to the sovereign and to all the lesser chiefs or lords who exercised under him any particular jurisdiction, either over some particular tribe or clan, or over some particular territory or district. Originally both the sovereign and the inferior chiefs used to exercise this jurisdiction in their own persons. Afterwards they universally found it convenient to delegate it to some substitute, bailiff, or judge. This substitute, however, was still obliged to account to his principal or constituent for the profits of the jurisdiction. Whoever reads the instructions which were given to the judges of the circuit in the time of Henry II will see clearly that those judges were a sort of itinerant factors, sent round the country for the purpose of levying certain branches of the king's revenue. In those days the administration of justice not only afforded a certain revenue to the sovereign, but to procure this revenue seems to have been one of the principal advantages which he proposed to obtain by the administration of justice.

This scheme of making the administration of justice subservient to the purposes of revenue could scarce fail to be productive of several very gross abuses. The person who applied for justice with a large present in his hand was likely to get something more than justice; while he who applied for it with a small one was likely to get something less. Justice too might frequently be delayed, in order that this present might be repeated. The amercement, besides, of the person complained of, might frequently suggest a very strong reason for finding him in the wrong, even when he had not really been so. That such abuses were far from being uncommon, the ancient history of every country in Europe bears witness.

When the sovereign or chief exercised his judicial authority in his own person, how much soever he might abuse it, it must have been scarce possible to get any redress; because there could seldom be anybody powerful enough to call him to account. When he exercised it by a bailiff, indeed, redress might sometimes be had. If it was for his own benefit only that the bailiff had been guilty of any act of injustice, the sovereign himself might not always be unwilling to punish him, or to oblige him to repair the wrong. But if it was for the benefit of his sovereign, if it was in order to make court to the person who appointed him and who might prefer him, that he had committed any act of oppression, redress would upon most occasions be as impossible as if the sovereign had committed it himself. In all barbarous governments, accordingly, in all those ancient governments of Europe in particular, which were founded upon the ruins of the Roman empire, the administration of justice appears for a long time to have been extremely corrupt; far from being quite equal and impartial even under the best monarchs, and altogether profligate under the worst. . . .

Part III

Of the Expense of Public Works and Public Institutions

The third and last duty of the sovereign or commonwealth is that of erecting and maintaining those public institutions and those public works, which, though they may be in the highest degree advantageous to a great society, are, however, of such a nature that the profit could never repay the expense to any individual or small number of individuals and which it therefore cannot be expected that any individual or small number of individuals should erect or maintain. The performance of this duty requires too very different degrees of expense in the different periods of society.

After the public institutions and public works necessary for the defense of the society, and for the administration of justice, both of which have already been mentioned, the other works and institutions of this kind are chiefly those for facilitating the commerce of the society, and those for promoting the instruction of the people. The institutions for instruction are of two kinds: those for the education of the youth, and those for the instruction of people of all ages. . . .

ARTICLE I

Of the Public Works and Institutions for Facilitating the Commerce of the Society

That the erection and maintenance of the public works which facilitate the commerce of any country, such as good roads, bridges, navigable canals, harbors, &c. must require very different degrees of expense in the different periods of society, is evident without any proof. The expense of making and maintaining the public roads of any country must evidently increase with the annual produce of the land and labour of that country, or with the quantity and weight of the goods which it becomes necessary to fetch and carry upon those roads. The strength of a bridge must be suited to the number and weight of the carriages which are

likely to pass over it. The depth and the supply of water for a navigable canal must be proportioned to the number and tonnage of the lighters which are likely to carry goods upon it; the extent of a harbor to the number of the shipping which are likely to take shelter in it.

It does not seem necessary that the expense of those public works should be defrayed from that public revenue, as it is commonly called, of which the collection and application are in most countries assigned to the executive power. The greater part of such public works may easily be so managed as to afford a particular revenue sufficient for defraying their own expense, without bringing any burden upon the general revenue of the society.

A highway, a bridge, a navigable canal, for example, may in most cases be both made and maintained by a small toll upon the carriages which make use of them: a harbor, by a moderate port-duty upon the tonnage of the shipping which load or unload in it. The coinage, another institution for facilitating commerce, in many countries not only defrays its own expense, but affords a small revenue or seignorage to the sovereign. The post office, another institution for the same purpose, over and above defraying its own expense, affords in almost all countries a very considerable revenue to the sovereign. . . .

CONCLUSION

The expense of defending the society, and that of supporting the dignity of the chief magistrate, are both laid out for the general benefit of the whole society. It is reasonable, therefore, that they should be defrayed by the general contribution of the whole society, all the different members contributing, as nearly as possible, in proportion to their respective abilities.

The expense of the administration of justice too, may, no doubt, be considered as laid out for the benefit of the whole society. There is no impropriety, therefore, in its being defrayed by the general contribution of the whole society. The persons, however, who give occasion to this expense are those who, by their injustice in one way or another, make it necessary to seek redress or protection from the courts of justice. The persons again most immediately benefited by this expense, are those whom the courts of justice either restore to their rights, or maintain in their rights. The expense of the administration of justice, therefore, may very properly be defrayed by the particular contribution of one or other, or both of those two different sets of persons, according as different occasions may require, that is, by the fees of court. It cannot be necessary to have recourse to the general contribution of the whole society, except for the conviction of those criminals who have not themselves any estate or fund sufficient for paying those fees.

Those local or provincial expenses of which the benefit is local or provincial (what is laid out, for example, upon the police of a particular town or district) ought to be defrayed by a local or provincial revenue, and ought to be no burden upon the general revenue of the society. It is unjust that the whole society should contribute towards an expence of which the benefit is confined to a part of the society.

The expense of maintaining good roads and communications is, no doubt, beneficial to the whole society, and may, therefore, without any injustice, be defrayed by the general contribution of the whole society. This expense, however, is most immediately and directly beneficial to those who travel or carry goods from one place to another, and to those who consume such goods. . . .

The expense of the institutions for education and religious instruction, is likewise, no doubt, beneficial to the whole society, and may, therefore, without injustice, be defrayed by the general contribution of the whole society. This expense, however, might perhaps with equal propriety, and even with some advantage, be defrayed altogether by those who receive the immediate benefit of such education and instruction, or by the voluntary contribution of those who think they have occasion for either the one or the other.

When the institutions or public works which are beneficial to the whole society, either cannot be maintained altogether, or are not maintained altogether by the contribution of such particular members of the society as are most immediately benefited by them, the deficiency must in most cases be made up by the general contribution of the whole society. The general revenue of the society, over and above defraying the expense of defending the society, and of supporting the dignity of the chief magistrate, must make up for the deficiency of many particular branches of revenue. The sources of this general or public revenue, I shall endeavour to explain in the following chapter.

Chapter II

OF THE SOURCES OF THE GENERAL OR PUBLIC REVENUE OF THE SOCIETY

The revenue which must defray, not only the expense of defending the society and of supporting the dignity of the chief magistrate, but all the other necessary expenses of government, for which the constitution of the state has not provided any particular revenue, may be drawn, either, first, from some fund which peculiarly belongs to the sovereign or commonwealth, and which is independent of the revenue of the people; or, secondly, from the revenue of the people. . . .

Part II

Of Taxes

Before I enter upon the examination of particular taxes, it is necessary to premise the four following maxims with regard to taxes in general.

I. The subjects of every state ought to contribute towards the support of the government, as nearly as possible, in proportion to their respective abilities; that is, in proportion to the revenue which they respectively enjoy under the protection of the state. The expense of government to the individuals of a great nation, is like the expense of management to the joint tenants of a great estate who are all obliged to contribute in proportion to their respective interests in the estate. In the observation or neglect of this maxim consists, what is called the equality or inequality of taxation. Every tax, it must be observed once for all, which falls finally upon one only of the three sorts of revenue above-mentioned, is necessarily unequal, in so far as it does not affect the other two. In the following examination of different taxes I shall seldom take much further notice of this sort of inequality, but shall, in most cases, confine my observations to that inequality which is occasioned by a particular tax falling unequally even upon that particular sort of private revenue which is affected by it.

II. The tax which each individual is bound to pay ought to be certain, and not arbitrary. The time of payment, the manner of payment, the quantity to be paid, ought all to be clear and plain to the contributor, and to every other person. Where it is otherwise, every person subject to the tax is put more or less in the power of the tax-gatherer, who can either aggravate the tax upon any obnoxious contributor, or extort, by the terror of such aggravation, some present or perquisite to himself. The uncertainty of taxation encourages the insolence and favours the corruption of an order of men who are naturally unpopular, even where they are neither insolent nor corrupt. The certainty of what each individual ought to pay is, in taxation, a matter of so great importance, that a very considerable degree of inequality, it appears, I believe, from the experience of all nations, is not near so great an evil as a very small degree of uncertainty.

III. Every tax ought to be levied at the time, or in the manner in which it is most likely to be convenient for the contributor to pay it. A tax upon the rent of land or of houses, payable at the same term at which such rents are usually paid, is levied at the time when it is most likely to be convenient for the contributor to pay; or, when he is most likely to have wherewithal to pay. Taxes upon such consumable goods as are articles of luxury, are all finally paid by the consumer, and generally in a manner that is very convenient for him. He pays them by, little and little, as he has occasion to buy the goods. As he is at liberty too, either to buy, or not to buy as he pleases, it must be his own fault if he ever suffers any considerable inconveniency from such taxes.

IV. Every tax ought to be so contrived as both to take out and to keep out of the pockets of the people as little as possible, over and above what it brings into the public treasury of the state. A tax may either take out or keep out of the pockets of the people a great deal more than it brings into the public treasury, in the four following ways. First, the levying of it may require a great number of officers, whose salaries may eat up the greater part of the produce of the tax, and whose perquisites may impose another additional tax upon the people. Secondly, it may obstruct the industry of the people, and discourage them from applying to certain branches of business which might give maintenance and employment to great multitudes. While it obliges the people to pay, it may thus diminish, or perhaps destroy some of the funds, which might enable them more easily to do so. Thirdly, by the forfeitures and other penalties which those unfortunate individuals incur who attempt unsuccessfully to evade the tax, it may frequently ruin them, and thereby put an end to the benefit which the community might have received from the employment of their capitals. An injudicious tax offers a great temptation to smuggling. But the penalties of smuggling must rise in proportion to the temptation. The law, contrary to all the ordinary principles of justice, first creates the temptation, and then punishes those who yield to it; and it commonly enhances the punishment too in proportion to the very circumstance which ought certainly to alleviate it, the temptation to commit the crime. Fourthly, by subjecting the people to the frequent visits, and the odious examination of the tax-gatherers, it may expose them to much unnecessary trouble, vexation, and oppression; and though vexation is not, strictly speaking, expense, it is certainly equivalent to the expense at which every man would be willing to redeem himself from it. It is in some one or other of these four different ways that taxes are frequently so much more burdensome to the people than they are beneficial to the sovereign. . . .

Chapter III

OF PUBLIC DEBTS

. . . A country abounding with merchants and manufacturers, necessarily abounds with a set of people through whose hands not only their own capitals, but the capitals of all those who either lend them money, or trust them with goods, pass as frequently, or more frequently, than the revenue of a private man, who, without trade or business, lives upon his income, passes through his hands. The revenue of such a man can regularly pass through his hands only once in a year. But the whole amount of the capital and credit of a merchant, who deals in a trade of which the returns are very quick, may sometimes pass through his hands two, three, or four times in a year. A country abounding with merchants and manufacturers, therefore, necessarily abounds with a set of people who have it at all times in their power to advance, if they choose to do so, a very large sum of money to government. Hence the ability in the subjects of a commercial state to lend.

Commerce and manufactures can seldom flourish long in any state which does not enjoy a regular administration of justice, in which the people do not feel themselves secure in the possession of their property, in which the faith of contracts is not supported by law, and in which the authority of the state is not supposed to be regularly employed in enforcing the payment of debts from all those who are able to pay. Commerce and manufactures, in short, can seldom flourish in any state in which there is not a certain degree of confidence in the justice of government. The same confidence which disposes great merchants and manufacturers, upon ordinary occasions, to trust their property to the protection of a particular government; disposes them, upon extraordinary occasions, to trust that government with the use of their property. By lending money to government, they do not even for a moment diminish their ability to carry on their trade and manufactures. On the contrary, they commonly augment it. The necessities of the state render government upon most occasions willing to borrow upon terms extremely advantageous to the lender. The security which it grants to the original creditor, is made transferable to any other creditor, and, from the universal confidence in the justice of the state, generally sells in the market for more than was originally paid for it. The merchant or monied man makes money by lending money to government, and instead of diminishing, increases his trading capital. He generally considers it as a favor, therefore, when the administration admits him to share in the first subscription for a new loan. Hence the inclination or willingness in the subjects of a commercial state to lend.

The government of such a state is very apt to repose itself upon this ability and willingness of its subjects to lend it their money on extraordinary occasions. It foresees the facility of borrowing, and therefore dispenses itself from the duty of saving.

In a rude state of society there are no great mercantile or manufacturing capitals. The individuals who hoard whatever money they can save, and who conceal their hoard, do so from a distrust of the justice of government, from a fear that if it was known that they had a hoard, and where that hoard was to be found, they would quickly be plundered. In such a state of things few people would be able, and nobody would be willing, to lend their money to government on extraordinary exigencies. The sovereign feels that he must provide for such exigencies by saving, because he foresees the absolute impossibility of borrowing. This foresight increases still further his natural disposition to save.

The progress of the enormous debts which at present oppress, and will in the long-run probably ruin, all the great nations of Europe, has been pretty uniform. Nations, like private men, have generally begun to borrow upon what may be called personal credit, without assigning or mortgaging any particular fund for the payment of the debt; and when this resource has failed them, they have gone on to borrow upon assignments or mortgages of particular funds. . . .

It is not contrary to justice that . . . America should contribute towards the discharge of the public debt of Great Britain. . . .

The expense of the peace establishment of the colonies was, before the commencement of the present disturbances, very considerable, and is an expense which may, and if no revenue can be drawn from them, ought certainly to be saved altogether. This constant expense in time of peace, though very great, is insignificant in comparison with what the defence of the colonies has cost us in time of war. The last war, which was undertaken altogether on account of the colonies, cost Great Britain, it has already been observed, upwards of ninety millions. The Spanish war of 1739 was principally undertaken on their account; in which, and in the French war that was the consequence of it, Great Britain spent upwards of forty millions, a great part of which ought justly to be charged to the colonies. In those two wars the colonies cost Great Britain much more than double the sum which the national debt amounted to before the commencement of the first of them. Had it not been for those wars that debt might, and probably would by this time, have been completely paid; and had it not been for the colonies, the former of those wars might not, and the latter certainly would not have been undertaken. It was because the colonies were supposed to be provinces of the British empire, that this expense was laid out upon them. But countries which contribute neither revenue nor military force towards the support of the empire, cannot be considered as provinces. They may perhaps be considered as appendages,

as a sort of splendid and showy equipage of the empire. But if the empire can no longer support the expense of keeping up this equipage, it ought certainly to lay it down; and if it cannot raise its revenue in proportion to its expense, it ought, at least, to accommodate its expense to its revenue. If the colonies, notwithstanding their refusal to submit to British taxes, are still to be considered as provinces of the British empire, their defence in some future war may cost Great Britain as great an expense as it ever has done in any former war. The rulers of Great Britain have, for more than a century past, amused the people with the imagination that they possessed a great empire on the west side of the Atlantic. This empire, however, has hitherto existed in imagination only. It has hitherto been, not an empire, but the project of an empire; not a gold mine, but the project of a gold mine; a project which has cost, which continues to cost, and which, if pursued in the same way as it has been hitherto, is likely to cost immense expense, without being likely to bring any profit: for the effects of the monopoly of the colony trade, it has been shown, are, to the great body of the people, mere loss instead of profit. It is surely now time that our rulers should either realize this golden dream, in which they have been indulging themselves, perhaps, as well as the people; or, that they should awake from it themselves and endeavour to awaken the people. If the project cannot be completed, it ought to be given up. If any of the provinces of the British empire cannot be made to contribute towards the support of the whole empire, it is surely time that Great Britain should free herself from the expense of defending those provinces in time of war, and of supporting any part of their civil or military establishments in time of peace, and endeavour to accommodate her future views and designs to the real mediocrity of her circumstances.

MARY WOLLSTONECRAFT

~

INTRODUCTION

VIRGINIA SAPIRO

Mary Wollstonecraft was born in London in 1759, one of seven children in a family that experienced significant hardship. Her father tried many different lines of work without success, moved his family often, and, when drunk, was violent to his wife and probably to his daughter. Wollstonecraft remembered her mother as submissive, seeking to avoid trouble.

Nothing about Wollstonecraft's early years suggested that she would become one of the most influential modern writers. After all, she was a woman, and in her era women were rarely given an academic education beyond learning how to read and do a little arithmetic. They were generally regarded as incapable of rational thought, and if needing to earn a living, had few options, including teaching young children, making clothing, or prostituting themselves.

Women had no legal rights. Without a husband's permission, married women could not own property (other than the clothes on their back), make contracts, or seek employment without a husband's permission. The husband "owned" their children. When a woman married she was assumed to have consented to sexual relations upon demand of her husband, and little recourse was available if he assaulted her. Women writers were a rarity, and no "women's movement" or feminism existed.

Wollstonecraft had little formal education. She did various jobs open to a woman: she was a mother's helper, she sewed, and with her sisters she started a school. Fortunately the North London town where she lived and taught had a community of important radical intellectuals from whom she learned much about contemporary philosophy and politics. These people led to her most important professional connection—Joseph Johnson, a radical publisher and journal editor for whom she wrote scores of book reviews (this activity became her main source of education) and translations (she taught herself other languages). She thus became a professional writer.

Her first works were on education, including *Thoughts on the Education of Daughters: with Reflections on Female Conduct, in the More Important Duties of Life* (1787); *Original Stories from Real Life: with Conversations Calculated to Regulate the Affections and Form the Mind to Truth and Goodness* (1788); and *The Female Reader: or Miscellaneous Pieces, in Prose and verse: Selected form the Best Writers, and Disposed under Proper Heads: for the Improvement of Young Women* (1789). She also wrote fiction based loosely on her life: *Mary, A Fiction* (1788).

In 1790 Wollstonecraft published her first major book in political philosophy: *A Vindication of the Rights of Men*. Her friend Richard Price, a moral philosopher, minister, and mathematician had written a defense of the French Revolution, an event that was wildly unpopular in England, and in reply Edmund Burke wrote an expanded attack on Price and other intellectual defenders of the Revolution titled *Reflections on the Revolution in France*. Many writers jumped into the fray to criticize Burke's work, most famously Thomas Paine in his *Rights of Man*. But the first work published in this stream was Wollstonecraft's *A Vindication of the Rights of Men*. Its themes included the evils of "unnatural distinctions," or social inequality based on birth (including sex) and wealth; the terrible impact of this inequality on all society; the importance of reason, independent thinking, and liberty rather than mere adherence to tradition and convention; and the centrality for citizenship of virtue, or principle-based reason.

Her masterwork was *A Vindication of the Rights of Woman* (1792), a portion of which is reprinted here. In many ways this work is an extension of the ideas of *A Vindication of the Rights of Men*. Wollstonecraft analyzed the condition of women in the same way she analyzed other cases of unjust inequalities—that is, inequalities based not on actual merit but on birth, domination, and oppression. She argued that the guiding principle of both a good society and a good individual is *virtue*, by which she meant our actions and feelings as guided by principled reason and conscience. She rejected gendered notions of virtue, which for women usually referred just to sexual chastity and the appearance of chastity (because for women the appearance of chastity was more important than its actuality), and for men usually referred to "honor" based on violence.

Without well-developed reason, she insisted, people cannot be virtuous. *Reason*, for Wollstonecraft, was principled thinking that required independent strength of mind rather than reliance on faith, tradition, social convention, or prejudice. The chief goal of education should be the development of reason. Virtue was expressed through *morals*, or principled actions, and not *manners*, the codes of conduct expected of people depending on their social situation.

She believed that most people are not virtuous, and that they rely overly on *sensibility*, feelings, and emotions not governed by reason. For Wollstonecraft, a society structured by deep inequalities cannot foster reason or virtue, because no one can develop the independence of mind required for reason. People in a position of subservience to others must act and think as their superiors require. But neither are people in the dominant position able to acquire reason and virtue, because they live in a false world in which others are subject to their will. They actually become *dependent* on their domination of others. People come to see both these inequalities and the resulting impact on people's character as natural and right. Society is the grand educator of us all, and if it is designed around *unnatural distinctions*, people learn to benefit from and strive for a lack of virtue.

In *The Rights of Woman*. Wollstonecraft applies these ideas to gender inequality and domination. She discusses their impact on women (especially) as well as men, demonstrating how differences of character and actions come to appear natural. She dedicated her book to Charles-Maurice de Talleyrand-Perigord, whom she had met because he was designing a new system of education for post-Revolutionary France. She imagined that the Revolution would open up the possibility for a new era of virtue.

Soon after she completed *The Rights of Woman*, Wollstonecraft departed for Paris to see the French Revolution up close. Her admiration disappeared as she witnessed the

Reign of Terror (1792–1793), when the Revolutionary leadership oversaw massacres and imprisonment that led to the death of more than 25,000 people, some of whom were Wollstonecraft's friends.

Nevertheless, she remained in France for some time and wrote a book of her reflections on the Revolution: *An Historical and Moral View of the Origin and Progress of the French Revolution; and the Effect it has produced in Europe* (1794), in which she further developed what could be described as a political psychology of oppression and change. She argued that the French Revolution, despite originally being based on rational, virtuous principles, went awry because of the difficulty for people raised in an unjust society to be just, a pessimistic view of the possibility of virtuous transformations of society.

Her sojourn in France transformed her life in more personal ways. She met an American adventurer and entrepreneur, Gilbert Imlay, who became her lover and, in 1794, the father of her daughter, Fanny. Despite Wollstonecraft's increasing desperation—including two suicide attempts—in seeking to get Imlay to pay attention to his child and to her, he displayed little interest except in one respect.

When a ship and valuable cargo belonging to Imlay was stolen and taken to Scandinavia, Imlay asked Wollstonecraft to find the ship and negotiate to retrieve it, so she set out with her baby and traveled through Sweden, Norway, and Denmark on her mission. One cannot overemphasize how unusual and dangerous it was for this woman at a time of war to travel on her own with a baby. We do not know whether she accomplished the task, but her journey resulted in one of her most successful and influential books.

She had sent letters to Imlay filled with reflections on the lands, people, and societies she observed, and she created a masterpiece from them: *Letters Written in Sweden, Norway, and Denmark* (1796). It is not merely a travel narrative but is clearly influenced both by Jean-Jacques Rousseau's *Reveries of a Solitary Walker* (1782), which from a solitary perspective intermingled personal reflections, political philosophy, and observations of the world, as well as Edmund Burke's theories of the sublime. This book inspired a young generation of Romantic writers such as William Wordsworth, Samuel Taylor Coleridge, and Percy Bysshe Shelley. One of the original parts of the book is its point of view—that of a woman, traveling with her baby, offering a distinctive feminist perspective.

Wollstonecraft was back in London in early 1796, having resigned herself to the end of her relationship with Imlay. She soon became involved with a man she had known since before her travels: the philosopher and novelist William Godwin (1756–1836), famous for being one of the intellectual founders of anarchist thought. She became pregnant again, and although the lovers chose to live near each other rather than share a household, they married early in 1797. She gave birth to a daughter in September, but died ten days later of septicemia, a lethal infection. She was thirty-eight years old.

Wollstonecraft left various partial manuscripts when she died, the most complete of which was the novel *Maria, Or the Wrongs of Woman*. We cannot know exactly what it would have looked like had she lived to complete it, but it was her most radical work, interweaving a story of gender, race, and class violence and oppression. William Godwin completed the book and published it in 1798.

Wollstonecraft's second daughter became one of the most influential writers of her era: Mary Godwin, who upon her marriage to Percy Bysshe Shelley, came to be known to history as Mary Wollstonecraft Shelley, the author among other works of *Franken-stein; or the Modern Prometheus* (1818).

A portion of *A Vindication of the Rights of Woman* is reprinted here. In the dedica-tion she writes, "My main argument is built on this simple principle, that if [woman] be not prepared by education to become the companion of man, she will stop the progress of knowledge and virtue; for truth must be common to all, or it will be inefficacious with respect to its influence on general practice." She does not mean *companion* in the sense of individual marriages but a broader partnership in advancing enlightenment and the quality of society.

The dedication also focuses on men's unjust treatment of women. She notes she is writing in a revolutionary period when men are fighting to be free and to be allowed "to judge for themselves respecting their own happiness, [is it] not inconsistent and unjust to subjugate women, even though you firmly believe that you are acting in the manner best calculated to promote their happiness? Who made man the exclusive judge, if woman partake with him the gift of reason?" She says that all tyrants of every sort, from the king to the slave master to the husband, act similarly.

Wollstonecraft's introduction notes that women everywhere are in a deplorable state, for which she blames men who treat women in terms of their gender rather than as "human beings." Women are given a "false system of education" aimed at making them "alluring" rather than rational, and therefore they cannot be virtuous. Once again, when she says women are educated away from virtue, she insists that she is not using that word in the conventional sense when associated with women, referring to sexual abstinence, but virtue in the sense of a human being devoted to self-improvement and fulfilling one's duties as a member of society.

The end of the introduction raises a paradox of political psychology to which Woll-stonecraft returns repeatedly: Women are subordinated by men to become objects of desire, things of beauty, weak and child-like, not rational and independent. Men thus act as tyrants over women *because* they cannot respect women as they have encouraged women to be.

But women's subordination also teaches women themselves to become tyrants. Like all human beings, women seek to put themselves in the most advantageous position to survive and flourish. If all they are left with is the tools of sexual attraction to men, then those are the assets they will use to support themselves. Being in a subordinate position, they know they have to use these assets cleverly to protect themselves. This is a brilliant theory of the political psychology of domination and subordination, arguing that it places everyone in the relationship of inequality, keeping all, and therefore their society, from becoming virtuous.

The rest of this excerpt is Chapter 4, devoted to an elaboration of all these important points about rationality, virtue, subordination, and the political psychology of domina-tion and subordination. Wollstonecraft emphasizes the need for women to develop the strength of mind to take control over themselves. She admired both the American and French Revolutions for the people's demand for more self-governance. She also believed in a revolution that gives individual citizens, including women, the power to govern themselves and their behavior through the powers of reason and strength of mind that are the basis for virtue. Her retort to Rousseau, who feared that women would become too powerful over men, was that women should seek to gain power over themselves.

What is her vision for a better society for women? This chapter offers some of the answer; the rest lies elsewhere in *The Rights of Woman*. She wants both women and men to take up their family duties with principled rationality that will support virtue. She wants women and men alike to attend to their duties more responsibly. She believed that women are responsible for the youngest children (only they have the capacity to feed babies, after all), but that they must be able to support themselves if they have no husband, so that they are not forced to marry. She imagines various kinds of work women can do, including serving in government.

Wollstonecraft's major proposals for change involve establishing a system of public education that would teach boys and girls of all classes together when they are very young, leaving plenty of time for active games to strengthen their bodies. Because no public school systems existed at that time, this proposal was radical. After a few years the school would be divided into different groups of children depending on their ultimate life destination, likely corresponding to both class and gender. Much of this book is an argument against *Emile*, Rousseau's work on education and child-rearing, in which he structured his educational ideas around the principle that men should dominate women.

Wollstonecraft knew what she wanted society to look like, and part of it was raising children differently and creating a new system of schooling. But she repeatedly displayed her belief that people learn from their environment, so becoming more rational and virtuous is difficult unless society is structured rationally and virtuously. People, however, are unlikely to create a more just society without first becoming more rational and virtuous. How, then, will change happen? That conundrum of politics is one we still face.

Godwin published *Memoirs of the Author of A Vindication of the Rights of Woman* (1798), a biography of Wollstonecraft, which emphasized the lurid more than it ought to have done and solidified her reputation in many people's minds as a dangerous radical whose works were to be read only among advocates of women's rights.

Yet Wollstonecraft has been an inspiration to generations of feminists. Her portrait hung on the wall of the National Woman Suffrage Association office, and feminists searching for serious writing to help them understand the plight of women have often found their way to her. Although until recently, mainstream scholars have not given her writings their due, in recent decades as the contributions of women to political thought have been more widely recognized, excellent scholarship on Wollstonecraft has grown, and the neglect of her work has begun to be rectified.

An absorbing biography is Lyndall Gordon, *Vindication: A Life of Mary Wollstonecraft* (New York: Harper Perennial, 2006). The first major treatment of Mary Wollstonecraft's complete work as political theory is Virginia Sapiro, *A Vindication of Political Virtue: The Political Theory of Mary Wollstonecraft* (Chicago: University of Chicago Press, 1992). *The Wollstonecraftian Mind*, edited by Sandrine Bergès, Eileen Hunt Botting, and Alan Coffee (New York: Routledge, 2010), is a collection of thirty-eight articles by international scholars on all aspects of Wollstonecraft's work.

A Vindication of the Rights of Woman

To

M. Talleyrand-Périgord,

Late Bishop Of Autun

Sɪʀ,—Having read with great pleasure a pamphlet which you have lately published, I dedicate this volume to you; to induce you to reconsider the subject, and maturely weigh what I have advanced respecting the rights of woman and national education: and I call with the firm tone of humanity; for my arguments, Sir, are dictated by a disinterested spirit—I plead for my sex—not for myself. Independence I have long considered as the grand blessing of life, the basis of every virtue—and independence I will ever secure by contracting my wants, though I were to live on a barren heath.

It is then an affection for the whole human race that makes my pen dart rapidly along to support what I believe to be the cause of virtue: and the same motive leads me earnestly to wish to see woman placed in a station in which she would advance, instead of retarding, the progress of those glorious principles that give a substance to morality. My opinion, indeed, respecting the rights and duties of woman, seems to flow so naturally from these simple principles, that I think it scarcely possible, but that some of the enlarged minds who formed your admirable constitution, will coincide with me.

In France there is undoubtedly a more general diffusion of knowledge than in any part of the European world, and I attribute it, in a great measure, to the social intercourse which has long subsisted between the sexes. It is true, I utter my sentiments with freedom, that in France the very essence of sensuality has been extracted to regale the voluptuary, and a kind of sentimental lust has prevailed, which, together with the system of duplicity that the whole tenour of their political and civil government taught, have given a sinister sort of sagacity to the French character properly termed finesse; from which naturally flow a polish of manners that injures the substance, by hunting sincerity out of society.—And, modesty, the fairest garb of virtue! has been more grossly insulted in France than even in England, till their women have treated as *prudish* that attention to decency, which brutes instinctively observe.

Manners and morals are so nearly allied that they have often been confounded; but, though the former should only be the natural reflection of the latter, yet, when various causes have produced factitious and corrupt manners, which are very early caught, morality becomes an empty name. The personal reserve, and sacred respect for cleanliness and delicacy in domestic life, which French women almost despise, are the graceful pillars of modesty; but, far from despising them, it the pure flame of patriotism have reached their bosoms, they should labour to improve the morals of their fellow-citizens, by teaching men, not only to respect modesty in women, but to acquire it themselves, as the only way to merit their esteem.

Contending for the rights of woman, my main argument is built on this simple principle, that if she be not prepared by education to become the companion of man, she will stop the progress of knowledge and virtue; for truth must be common to all, or it will be inefficacious with respect to its influence on general practice. And how can woman be expected to co-operate unless she know why she ought to be virtuous, unless freedom strengthen her reason till she comprehend her duty, and see in what manner it is connected with her real good? If children are be educated to understand the true principle of patriotism, their mother must be a patriot; and the love of mankind, from which an orderly tram of virtues spring, can only be produced by considering the moral and civil interest of mankind; but the education and situation of woman, at present, shuts her out from such investigations.

In this work I have produced many arguments, which to me were conclusive, to prove that the prevailing notion respecting a sexual character was subversive of morality, and I have contended, that to render the human body and mind more perfect, chastity must more universally prevail and that chastity will never be respected in the male world till the person of a woman is not, as it were, idolized, when little virtue or sense embellish it with the grand traces of mental beauty, or the interesting simplicity of affection.

Consider, Sir, dispassionately, these observations—for a glimpse of this truth seemed to open before you when you observed, "that to see one half of the human race excluded by the other from all participation of government, was a political phænomenon that, according to abstract principles, it was impossible to explain." If so, on what does your constitution rest? If the abstract rights of man will bear discussion and explanation, those of woman, by a parity of reasoning, will not shrink from the same test: though a different opinion prevails in this country, built on the very arguments which you use to justify the oppression of woman—prescription.

Consider, I address you as a legislator, whether, when men contend for their freedom, and to be allowed to judge for themselves respecting their own happiness, it be not inconsistent and unjust to subjugate women, even though you firmly believe that you are acting in the manner best calculated to promote their happiness? Who made man the exclusive judge, if woman partake with him the gift of reason?

In this style, argue tyrants of every denomination, from the weak king to the weak father of a family; they are all eager to crush reason; yet always assert that they usurp its throne only to be useful. Do you not act a similar part, when you *force* all women, by denying them civil and political rights, to remain immured in their families groping in the dark? for surely, Sir, you will not assert, that a duty can be binding which is not founded on reason? If indeed this be their destination, arguments may be drawn from reason: and thus augustly supported, the more understanding women acquire, the more they will be attached to their duty—comprehending it—for unless they comprehend it, unless their morals be fixed on the same immutable principle as those of man, no authority can make them discharge it in a virtuous manner. They may be convenient slaves, but slavery will have its constant effect, degrading the master and the abject dependent.

But, if women are to be excluded, without having a voice, from a participation of the natural rights of mankind, prove first, to ward off the charge of injustice and inconsistency, that they want reason—else this flaw in your NEW CONSTITUTION will ever shew that man must, in some shape, act like a tyrant, and tyranny, in whatever part of society it rears its brazen front, will ever undermine morality.

I have repeatedly asserted, and produced what appeared to me irrefragable arguments drawn from matters of fact, to prove my assertion, that women cannot, by force, be confined to domestic concerns; for they will, however ignorant, intermeddle with more weighty affairs, neglecting private duties only to disturb, by cunning tricks, the orderly plans of reason which rise above their comprehension.

Besides, whilst they are only made to acquire personal accomplishments, men will seek for pleasure in variety, and faithless husbands will make faithless wives; such ignorant beings, indeed, will be very excusable when, not taught to respect public good, nor allowed any civil rights, they attempt to do themselves justice by retaliation.

The box of mischief thus opened in society, what is to preserve private virtue, the only security of public freedom and universal happiness?

Let there be then no coercion *established* in society, and the common law of gravity prevailing, the sexes will fall into their proper places. And, now that more equitable laws are forming your citizens, marriage may become more sacred: your young men may choose wives from motives of affection, and your maidens allow love to root out vanity.

The father of a family will not then weaken his constitution and debase his sentiments, by visiting the harlot, nor forget, in obeying the call of appetite, the purpose for which it was implanted. And, the mother will not neglect her children to practise the arts of coquetry, when sense and modesty secure her the friendship of her husband.

But; till men become attentive to the duty of a father, it is vain to expect women to spend that time in their nursery which they, "wise in their generation," choose to spend at their glass; for this exertion of cunning is only an instinct of nature to enable them to obtain indirectly a little of that power of which they are unjustly denied a share: for, if women are not permitted to enjoy legitimate rights, they will render both men and themselves vicious, to obtain illicit privileges.

I wish, Sir, to set some investigations of this kind afloat in France; and should they lead to a confirmation of my principles, when your constitution is revised the Rights of Woman may be respected, if it be fully proved that reason calls for this respect, and loudly demands JUSTICE for one half of the human race.

I am, SIR,
Your's respectfully,
M. W.

INTRODUCTION

After considering the historic page, and viewing the living world with anxious solicitude, the most melancholy emotions of sorrowful indignation have depressed my spirits, and I have sighed when obliged to confess, that either nature has made a great difference between man and man, or that the civilization which has hitherto taken place in the world has been very partial. I have turned over various books written on the subject of education, and patiently observed the conduct of parents and the management of schools; but what has been the result?—a profound conviction that the neglected education of my fellow-creatures is the grand source of the misery I deplore; and that women, in particular, are rendered weak and wretched by a variety of concurring causes, originating from one hasty conclusion. The conduct and manners of women, in fact, evidently prove that their minds are not in a healthy state; for, like the flowers which are planted in too rich a soil, strength and usefulness are sacrificed to beauty; and the flaunting leaves, after having pleased a fastidious eye, fade, disregarded on the stalk, long before the season when they ought to have arrived at maturity.—One cause of this barren blooming I attribute to a false system of education, gathered from the books written on this subject by men who, considering females rather as women than human creatures, have been more anxious to make them alluring mistresses than affectionate wives and rational mothers; and the understanding of the sex has been so bubbled by this specious homage, that the civilized women of the present century, with a few exceptions, are only anxious to inspire love, when they ought to cherish a nobler ambition, and by their abilities and virtues exact respect.

In a treatise, therefore, on female rights and manners, the works which have been particularly written for their improvement must not be overlooked; especially when it is asserted, in direct terms, that the minds of women are enfeebled by false refinement; that the books of instruction, written by men of genius, have had the same tendency as more frivolous productions; and that, in the true style of Mahometanism, they are treated as a kind of subordinate beings, and not as a part of the human species, when improveable reason is allowed to be the dignified distinction which raises men above the brute creation, and puts a natural sceptre in a feeble hand.

Yet, because I am a woman, I would not lead my readers to suppose that I mean violently to agitate the contested question respecting the equality or inferiority of the sex; but as the subject lies in my way, and I cannot pass it over without subjecting the main tendency of my reasoning to misconstruction, I shall stop a moment to deliver, in a few words, my opinion.—In the government of the physical world it is observable that the female in point of strength is, in general, inferior to the male. This is the law of nature; and it does not appear to be suspended or abrogated in favour of woman. A degree of physical superiority cannot, therefore, be denied—and it is a noble prerogative! But not content with this natural pre-eminence, men endeavour to sink us still lower, mere y to render us alluring objects for a moment; and women, intoxicated by the adoration which men, under the influence of their senses, pay them, do not seek to obtain a durable interest in their hearts, or to become the friends of the fellow creatures who find amusement in their society.

I am aware of an obvious inference:—from every quarter have I heard exclamations against masculine women; but where are they to be found? If by this appellation men mean to inveigh against their ardour in hunting, shooting, and gaming, I shall most cordially join in the cry; but if it be against the imitation of manly virtues, or, more properly speaking, the attainment of those talents and virtues, the exercise of which ennobles the human character, and which raise females in the scale of animal being when they are comprehensively termed mankind;—all those who view them with a philosophic eye must, I should think, wish with me, that they may every day grow more and more masculine.

This discussion naturally divides the subject. I shall first consider women in the grand light of human creatures, who, in common with men, are placed on this earth to unfold their faculties; and afterwards I shall more particularly point out their peculiar designation.

I wish also to steer clear of an error which many respectable writers have fallen into; for the instruction which has hitherto been addressed to women, has rather been applicable to *ladies* . . .

but, addressing my sex in a firmer tone, I pay particular attention to those in the middle class, because they appear to be in the most natural state. Perhaps the seeds of false refinement, immorality, and vanity, have ever been shed by the great. Weak, artificial beings, raised above the common wants and affections of their race, in a premature unnatural manner, undermine the very foundation of virtue, and spread corruption through the whole mass of society! As a class of mankind they have the strongest claim to pity; the education of the rich tends to render them vain and helpless, and the unfolding mind is not strengthened by the practice of those duties which dignify the human character.—They only live to amuse themselves, and by the same law which in nature invariably produces certain effects, they soon only afford barren amusement.

But as I purpose taking a separate view of the different ranks of society, and of the moral character of women, in each, this hint is, for the present, sufficient; and I have only alluded to the subject, because it appears to me to be the very essence of an introduction to give a cursory account of the contents of the work it introduces.

My own sex, I hope, will excuse me, if I treat them like rational creatures, instead of flattering their *fascinating* graces, and viewing them as if they were in a state of perpetual childhood, unable to stand alone. I earnestly wish to point out in what true dignity and human happiness consists—I wish to persuade women to endeavour to acquire strength, both of mind and body, and to convince them that the soft phrases, susceptibility of heart, delicacy of sentiment, and refinement of taste, are almost synonymous with epithets of weakness, and that those beings who are only the objects of pity and that kind of love, which has been termed its sister, will soon become objects of contempt.

Dismissing then those pretty feminine phrases, which the men condescendingly use to soften our slavish dependence, and despising that weak elegancy of mind, exquisite sensibility, and sweet docility of manners, supposed to be the sexual characteristics of the weaker vessel, I wish to shew that elegance is inferior to virtue, that the first object of laudable ambition is to obtain a character as a human being, regardless of the distinction of sex; and that secondary views should be brought to this simple touchstone.

This is a rough sketch of my plan; and should I express my conviction with the energetic emotions that I feel whenever I think of the subject, the dictates of experience and reflection will be felt by some of my readers. Animated by this important object, I shall disdain to cull my phrases or polish my style;—I aim at being useful, and sincerity will render me unaffected; for, wishing rather to persuade by the force of my arguments, than dazzle by the elegance of my language, I shall not waste my time in rounding periods, or in fabricating the turgid bombast of artificial feelings, which, coming from the head, never reach the heart.—I shall be employed about things, not words!—and, anxious to render my sex more respectable members of society, I shall try to avoid that flowery diction which has slided from essays into novels, and from novels into familiar letters and conversation.

These pretty superlatives, dropping glibly from the tongue, vitiate the taste, and create a kind of sickly delicacy that turns away from simple unadorned truth; and a deluge of false sentiments and overstretched feelings, stifling the natural emotions of the heart, render the domestic pleasures insipid, that ought to sweeten the exercise of those severe duties, which educate a rational and immortal being for a nobler field of action.

The education of women has, of late, been more attended to than formerly; yet they are still reckoned a frivolous sex, and ridiculed or pitied by the writers who endeavour by satire or instruction to improve them. It is acknowledged that they spend many of the first years of their lives in acquiring a smattering of accomplishments; meanwhile strength of body and mind are sacrificed to libertine notions of beauty, to the desire of establishing themselves,—the only way women can rise in the world,—by marriage. And this

desire making mere animals of them, when they marry they act as such children may be expected to act:—they dress; they paint, and nickname God's creatures.—Surely these weak beings are only fit for a seraglio!—Can they be expected to govern a family with judgment, or take care of the poor babes whom they bring into the world?

If then it can be fairly deduced from the present conduct of the sex, from the prevalent fondness for pleasure which takes place of ambition and those nobler passions that open and enlarge the soul; that the instruction which women have hitherto received has only tended, with the constitution of civil society, to render them insignificant objects of desire—mere propagators of fools!—if it can be proved that in aiming to accomplish them, without cultivating their understandings, they are taken out of their sphere of duties, and made ridiculous and useless when the short-lived bloom of beauty is over, I presume that *rational* men will excuse me for endeavouring to persuade them to become more masculine and respectable.

Indeed the word masculine is only a bugbear: there is little reason to fear that women will acquire too much courage or fortitude; for their apparent inferiority with respect to bodily strength, must render them, in some degree, dependent on men in the various relations of life; but why should it be increased by prejudices that give a sex to virtue, and confound simple truths with sensual reveries?

Women are, in fact, so much degraded by mistaken notions of female excellence, that I do not mean to add a paradox when I assert, that this artificial weakness produces a propensity to tyrannize, and gives birth to cunning, the natural opponent of strength, which leads them to play off those contemptible infantine airs that undermine esteem even whilst they excite desire. Let men become more chaste and modest, and if women do not grow wiser in the same ratio, it will be clear that they have weaker understandings. It seems scarcely necessary to say, that I now speak of the sex in general. Many individuals have more sense than their male relatives; and, as nothing preponderates where there is a constant struggle for an equilibrium, without it has naturally more gravity, some women govern their husbands without degrading themselves, because intellect will always govern.

CHAPTER IV

Observations on the State of Degradation to Which Woman Is Reduced by Various Causes

That woman is naturally weak, or degraded by a concurrence of circumstances, is, I think, clear. But this position I shall simply contrast with a conclusion, which I have frequently heard fall from sensible men in favour of an aristocracy: that the mass of mankind cannot be anything, or the obsequious slaves, who patiently allow themselves to be driven forward, would feel their own consequence, and spurn their chains. Men, they further observe, submit every where to oppression, when they have only to lift up their heads to throw off the yoke; yet, instead of asserting their birthright, they quietly lick the dust, and say, let us eat and drink, for to-morrow we die. Women, I argue from analogy, are degraded by the same propensity to enjoy the present moment; and, at last, despise the freedom which they have not sufficient virtue to struggle to attain. But I must be more explicit. . . .

The stamen of immortality, if I may be allowed the phrase, is the perfectibility of human reason; for, were man created perfect, or did a flood of knowledge break in upon him, when he arrived at maturity, that precluded error, I should doubt whether his existence would be continued after the dissolution of the body. But, in the present state of things, every difficulty in morals that escapes from human discussion, and equally baffles the investigation of profound thinking, and the lightning glance of genius, is an argument on which I build my belief of the immortality of the soul. Reason is, consequentially, the simple power of improvement; or, more properly speaking, of discerning truth. Every individual is in this respect a world in itself. More or less may be conspicuous in one being than another; but the nature of reason must be the same in all, if it be an emanation of divinity, the tie that connects the creature with the Creator; for, can that soul be stamped with the heavenly image, that is not perfected by the exercise of its own reason? Yet outwardly ornamented with elaborate care, and so adorned to delight man, "that with honour he may love," the soul of woman is not allowed to have this distinction, and man, ever placed between her and reason, she is always represented as only created to see through a gross medium, and to take things on trust. But dismissing these fanciful theories, and considering woman as a whole, let it be what it will, instead of a part of man, the inquiry is whether she have reason or not. If she have, which, for a moment, I will take for granted, she was not created merely to be the solace of man, and the sexual should not destroy the human character.

Into this error men have, probably, been led by viewing education in a false light; not considering it as the first step to form a being advancing gradually towards perfection; but only as a preparation for life. . . . been denied to woman; and instinct, sublimated into wit and cunning, for the purposes of life, has been substituted in its stead.

The power of generalizing ideas, of drawing comprehensive conclusions from individual observations, is the only acquirement, for an immortal being, that really deserves the name of knowledge. Merely to observe, without endeavouring to account for any thing, may (in a very incomplete manner) serve as the common sense of life; but where is the store laid up that is to clothe the soul when it leaves the body?

This power has not only been denied to women; but writers have insisted that it is inconsistent, with a few exceptions, with their sexual character. Let men prove this, and I shall grant that woman only exists for man. I must, however, previously remark, that the power of generalizing ideas, to any great extent, is not very common amongst men or women. But this exercise is the true cultivation of the understanding; and every thing conspires to render the cultivation of the understanding more difficult in the female than the male world. . . .

Necessity has been proverbially termed the mother of invention—the aphorism may be extended to virtue. It is an acquirement, and an acquirement to which pleasure must be sacrificed—and who sacrifices pleasure when it is within the grasp, whose mind has not been opened and strengthened by adversity, or the pursuit of knowledge goaded on by necessity?—Happy is it when people have the cares of life to struggle with; for these struggles prevent their becoming a prey to enervating vices, merely from idleness! But, if from their birth men and women be placed in a torrid zone, with the meridian sun of pleasure darting directly upon them, how can they suffi-ciently brace their minds to discharge the duties of life, or even to relish the affections that carry them out of themselves?

Pleasure is the business of woman's life, ac-cording to the present modification of society, and while it continues to be so, little can be expected from such weak beings. Inheriting, in a lineal descent from the first fair defect in nature, the sovereignty of beauty, they have, to maintain their power, resigned the natural rights, which the exercise of reason might have procured them, and chosen rather to be short-lived queens than labour to obtain the sober pleasures that arise from equality. . . .

Lewis the XIVth, in particular, spread facti-tious manners, and caught, in a specious way, the whole nation in his toils; for, establishing an artful chain of despotism, he made it the interest of the people at large, individually to respect his station and support his power. And women, whom he flattered by a puerile attention to the whole sex, obtained in his reign that prince-like distinction so fatal to reason and virtue.

A king is always a king—and a woman always a woman: his authority and her sex, ever stand be-tween them and rational converse. . . .

For if, excepting warriors, no great men, of any denomination, have ever appeared amongst the nobility, may it not be fairly inferred that their local situation swallowed up the man, and produced a character similar to that of women, who are *localized*, if I may be allowed the word, by the rank they are placed in, by *courtesy*? Women, commonly called Ladies, are not to be contradicted in company, are not allowed to exert any manual strength; and from them the negative virtues only are expected, when any virtues are expected, patience, docility, good-hu-mour, and flexibility; virtues incompatible with any vigorous exertion of intellect. Besides, by living more with each other, and being seldom absolutely alone, they are more under the influ-ence of sentiments than passions. Solitude and reflection are necessary to give to wishes the force of passions, and to enable the imagination to enlarge the object, and make it the most desir-able. The same may be said of the rich; they do not sufficiently deal in general ideas, collected by impassioned thinking, or calm investigation, to acquire that strength of character on which great resolves are built. . . .

In the middle rank of life, to continue the comparison, men, in their youth, are prepared for professions, and marriage is not considered as the grand feature in their lives; whilst women, on the contrary, have no other scheme to sharpen their faculties. It is not business, extensive plans, or any of the excursive flights of ambition, that engross their attention; no, their thoughts are not employed in rearing such noble structures. To rise in the world, and have the liberty of running from pleasure to pleasure, they must marry ad-vantageously, and to this object their time is sacri-ficed, and their persons often legally prostituted. A man when he enters any profession has his eye steadily fixed on some future advantage (and the mind gains great strength by having all its efforts directed to one point), and, full of his business, pleasure is considered as mere relaxation; whilst women seek for pleasure as the main purpose of existence. In fact, from the education, which they receive from society, the love of pleasure may be said to govern them all; but does this prove that there is a sex in souls? It would be just as rational to declare that the courtiers in France, when a destructive system of despotism had formed their character, were not men, because liberty, virtue, and humanity, were sacrificed to pleasure and vanity.—Fatal passions, which have ever domineered over the *whole* race!

The same love of pleasure, fostered by the whole tendency of their education, gives a trifling turn to the conduct of women in most circumstances . . .

In short, women, in general, as well as the rich of both sexes, have acquired all the follies and vices of civilization, and missed the useful fruit. It is not necessary for me always to premise, that I speak of the condition of the whole sex, leaving exceptions out of the question. Their senses are inflamed, and their understandings neglected, consequently they become the prey of their senses, delicately termed sensibility, and are blown about by every momentary gust of feeling. Civilized women are, therefore, so weakened by false refinement, that, respecting morals, their condition is much below what it would be were they left in a state nearer to nature. . . .

Riches and honours prevent a man from enlarging his understanding, and enervate all his powers by reversing the order of nature, which has ever made true pleasure the reward of labour. Pleasure—enervating pleasure is, likewise, within women's reach without earning it. . . .

CHAPTER XII

On National Education

Let an enlightened nation then try what effect reason would have to bring them back to nature, and their duty; and allowing them to share advantages of education and government with man see whether they will become better, as they grow wiser and become free. They cannot be injured by the experiment; for it is not in the power of man to render them more insignificant than they are at present.

To render this practicable, day schools, for particular ages, should be established by government, in which boys and girls might be educated together. The school for the younger children, from five to nine years of age, ought to be absolutely free and open to all classes. A sufficient number of masters should also be chosen by a select committee, in each parish, to whom any complaint of negligence, &c. might be made, if signed by six of the children's parents.

Ushers would then be unnecessary; for I believe experience will ever prove that this kind of subordinate authority is particularly injurious to the morals of youth. What, indeed, can tend to deprave the character more than outward submission and inward contempt? Yet how can boys be expected to treat an usher with respect, when the master seems to consider him in the light of a servant, and almost to countenance the ridicule which becomes the chief amusement of the boys during the play hours?

But nothing of this kind could occur in an elementary day-school, where boys and girls, the rich and poor, should meet together. And to prevent any of the distinctions of vanity, they should be dressed alike, and all obliged to submit to the same discipline, or leave the school. The schoolroom ought to be surrounded by a large piece of ground, in which the children might be usefully exercised, for at this age they should not be confined to any sedentary employment for more than an hour at a time. But these relaxations might all be rendered a part of elementary education, for many things improve and amuse the senses, when introduced as a kind of show, to the principles of which, dryly laid down, children would turn a deaf ear. For instance, botany, mechanics, and astronomy. Reading, writing, arithmetic, natural history, and some simple experiments in natural philosophy, might fill up the day; but these pursuits should never encroach on gymnastic plays in the open air. The elements of religion, history, the history of man, and politics, might also be taught by conversations, in the Socratic form.

After the age of nine, girls and boys, intended for domestic employments, or mechanical trades, ought to be removed to other schools, and receive instruction, in some measure appropriated to the destination of each individual, the two sexes being still together in the morning; but in the afternoon, the girls should attend a school, where plain-work, mantua-making, millinery, &c. would be their employment.

The young people of superior abilities, or fortune, might now be taught, in another school, the dead and living languages, the elements of science, and continue the study of history and politics, on a more extensive scale, which would not exclude polite literature.

Girls and boys still together? I hear some readers ask: yes. And I should not fear any other consequence than that some early attachment might take place; which, whilst it had the best effect on the moral character of the young people, might not perfectly agree with the views of the parents, for it will be a long time, I fear, before the world will be so far enlightened that parents, only anxious to render their children virtuous, shall allow them to choose companions for life themselves.

Besides, this would be a sure way to promote early marriages, and from early marriages the most salutary physical and moral effects naturally flow. What a different character does a married citizen assume from the selfish coxcomb, who lives, but for himself, and who is often afraid to marry lest he should not be able to live in a certain style. Great emergencies excepted, which would rarely occur in a society of which equality was the basis, a man can only be prepared to discharge the duties of public life, by the habitual practice of those inferiour ones which form the man.

In this plan of education the constitution of boys would not be ruined by the early debaucheries, which now make men so selfish, or girls rendered weak and vain, by indolence, and frivolous pursuits. But, I presuppose, that such a degree of equality should be established between the sexes as would shut out gallantry and coquetry, yet allow friendship and love to temper the heart for the discharge of higher duties.

These would be schools of morality—and the happiness of man, allowed to flow from the pure springs of duty and affection, what advances might not the human mind make? Society can only be happy and free in proportion as it is virtuous; but the present distinctions, established in society, corrode all private, and blast all public virtue.

IMMANUEL KANT

INTRODUCTION

PAUL GUYER

Immanuel Kant (1724–1804), who lived his entire life in the remote East Prussian capital of Königsberg, nevertheless became the most important philosopher of the European Enlightenment. He devoted his life to reconciling the certitude of Newtonian science with the certitude of human freedom, which he conceived as our deepest moral and political value. He argued for both the certainty and the limits of scientific determinism in his magnum opus, the *Critique of Pure Reason* of 1781. He followed that with his three key works in moral and political philosophy, the *Groundwork for the Metaphysics of Morals* (1785), the *Critique of Practical Reason* (1788), and the *Metaphysics of Morals* (1797), which included his political and legal philosophy in the "Doctrine of Right" and his ethics in the "Doctrine of Virtue." He also presented his political philosophy in essays and pamphlets, including "What Is Enlightenment?" (1784), "On the Old Saw: That May Be Right in Theory But It Won't Work in Practice" (1793), and *Perpetual Peace* (1795). The *Critique of the Power of Judgment* (1790), which deals with both aesthetic and teleological judgments, that is, with judgments about beauty and sublimity in both nature and art and judgments about the purposiveness of nature, shows how we can combine our scientific knowledge and moral principles into a coherent view of our place in the world, and *Religion Within the Boundaries of Reason Alone* (1793) argues that religious faith must be grounded in moral reasoning and argues that our freedom of the will implies both the possibility of sin ("radical evil") and the possibility of our own moral conversion without the need for divine assistance.

In the *Lectures on Ethics* that he gave for many years, Kant maintained that "the inner worth of the world, the *summum bonum*, is freedom according to a choice that is not necessitated to act." Yet he also recognized that "if freedom is not restricted by objective rules, the result is much savage disorder." Kant's challenge in moral theory was to establish the unconditional value of human freedom and to explain how human beings can regulate their freedom without sacrificing it. The challenge for Kant's political philosophy was to reconcile the possibility of the organized use of coercion in the state with the maintenance of that freedom that is supposed to be advanced by the state, thus both justifying and limiting the organized use of coercion.

The role of freedom itself as our most fundamental value emerges gradually over the course of the *Groundwork for the Metaphysics of Morals* and then becomes clearer in Kant's works of the 1790s. Kant starts the *Groundwork* by arguing that the common-sense conceptions of good will and duty show that morally worthy actions are motivated not by personal desire for the ends that might result from them but only by respect for the moral law itself. This argument means that the moral law cannot concern the desirability of actions or the happiness that would result from them and can instead require nothing but the conformity of the principles or, as Kant calls them, the "maxims" of the moral agent to the form of rationality itself, that is, universality. Thus Kant arrives at the first formulation of the categorical imperative—his name for the fundamental principle of morality valid for any rational being as it presents itself to human beings, who in virtue of their dual nature, animal as well as rational, do not always want to obey it—as "*I ought never to act except in such a way that I could also will that my maxim should become a universal law.*"

In the second section of the *Groundwork*, Kant arrives at the same formulation of the moral law by means of a more complicated philosophical argument and also develops several further formulations of the categorical imperative that reveal that it is a formula for the preservation and promotion of human freedom. Kant begins this argument, as he also does in the *Critique of Practical Reason*, with the assumption that a moral law must be necessary and universal, thus knowable a priori, in contrast to any recommendations or counsels for happiness, which are inevitably contingent and particular; moral imperatives must thus be categorical rather than merely hypothetical, that is, valid only on particular assumptions true for some agents but not all. He then argues that the very concept of a categorical imperative implies the same principle he had reached in the first section from his common-sense arguments about good will and duty, because the only thing that an imperative that is to be categorical can require is that whatever maxims of action an agent acts on be universalizable. But now Kant argues not that the categorical imperative can have nothing to do with the ends or goals of action at all, but rather that it must be a rule for realizing an *objective* and *necessary* end rather than merely *subjective* and *contingent* ends. And this is where the fundamental value of freedom first appears in the *Groundwork*, for now Kant argues that this objective and necessary end can be nothing other than the free and rational agency of human beings, our power to determine our particular ends freely but consistently with others doing the same. This leads to the second main formulation of the categorical imperative, that we "so act that [we] use humanity, whether in [our] own person or the person of any other, always at the same time as an end, never merely as a means." As Kant's illustrations of this principle show, what it requires is that we always treat human beings as agents whose freedom is unconditionally valuable: our duties are first to preserve the existence of free agents, then to preserve the possibility of their exercise of free choice (or the possibility of their own consent to our actions), then to promote the conditions under which their free choice can be successfully exercised (by the cultivation of talents), and finally, when consistent with all the previous obligations, to assist in the successful pursuit of freely chosen ends (the duty of beneficence).

Kant's second formulation of the categorical imperative thus both grounds and reveals the full import of the first, but it also leads to a third formulation, the requirement to act so that "all maxims from one's own lawgiving are to harmonize with a possible realm of ends." A realm of ends is precisely what would arise if everyone were treated as an end and never merely as a means. That is, in a kingdom of ends, each person would be treated as an unconditionally valuable free agent, whose existence and capacity for free choice must be preserved, and whose particular objectives are valuable precisely because they have been freely chosen. The realization of freely chosen ends is what produces happiness, so Kant makes it clear in the *Critique of Practical Reason* that even if happiness cannot be the *ground* of morally worthy motivation, the happiness of all consistent with the universal observation of the moral law should be the *outcome* of moral conduct (this is what Kant calls the "highest good"), and thus that moral conduct can be rational only if we believe that the union of universal virtue and universal happiness is possible; for this reason Kant argues in his famous "postulates of pure practical reason" that the rationality of moral conduct requires belief in a common Author of the laws of both nature and morality, or God. The project of determining what part of the laws for the preservation and promotion of freedom or the realization of a realm of ends must and can be coercively enforced without undermining freedom is the project of Kant's political philosophy, which he begins in the second and third sections of the essay on "Theory and Practice" after a first section in which he refines his treatment of the highest good, especially his contrast between the motive and the object of morality.

In the second section of "Theory and Practice," Kant erects a theory of the limited scope of government that is one of the classical statements of liberalism, aimed against the Hobbesian theory of absolute and undivided rule and the absolutist practice of his own Prussian government. Like John Stuart Mill in *On Liberty* half a century later, although in terms that are less familiar to those in the Anglo-American tradition, Kant argues that just government must be nonpaternalistic, or that state intervention in the exercise of individual liberty is both permissible and necessary only to prevent one person's exercise of liberty from restricting others' exercise of their liberty, not whenever the rulers of a state think they know better than their subjects what would make them happy. Kant's theory of the proper role of government is only developed fully in the "Doctrine of Right" of the *Metaphysics of Morals*, not presented here, where he argues that the exercise of human freedom inevitably involves the use of external objects, and thus the first role of government is the regulation of property rights. For Kant property rights cannot be understood as a unilateral relation between a person and an object, but can only be understood as an omnilateral relation among wills, an agreement among all the persons who could control an object, in the first instance a plot of land, about who will get to control it. But if everyone involved is to be able to agree to such a division of rights *freely*, the moral condition for a just system of rights, then the division of rights must be basically fair. Such an agreement can only be made determinate and secure by the collective agency of a state, thus the state has an inevitable role in maintaining a fair system of property rights. However, there is no requirement for fairness in the expression of beliefs: one person's expression of beliefs, whether others like them, is not an imposition on others, for they do not have to believe what another tells them. Thus the state has neither a need nor a right to control belief—another profoundly anti-Hobbesian point in Kant's political philosophy.

So Kant argues for the need for the state to regulate property rights, but for the obligation of the state to defend only a fair system of such rights, and for an extensive right to freedom of conscience and expression. However, Kant's version of liberalism includes only a limited right to political participation, excluding those who are economically dependent on others—servants, laborers for wages, and women—from the right to vote for political representation. This restriction now seems unfair, although it was commonly advocated in the eighteenth century as a way to avoid the multiplication of the votes of those who did hold power over others on the assumption that dependents would always vote in the interest of their masters. Another issue on which Kant seems to differ with modern liberalism and for a change to agree with Hobbes is the denial of a right to rebellion. Kant argues that the only just form of government is a republic in which citizens are free and equal before the law, but he argues that citizens do not have a right to use force to reform or overthrow even an unjust government. But here Kant's argument is actually carefully crafted. He argues that in order to claim property rights, humans have an obligation to enter into a state and that the overthrow of a state produces anarchy and thus violates this basic obligation. But he also argues that it is the *legislature* of a state which represents the general will of its populace, or embodies its freedom, not the *executive*, and that the legislature, thus the people *through* their parliament, have every right to attempt to reform or depose an unjust executive. However, the legislature does not have the right to exercise coercion against him because the coercive enforcement of the laws is the assigned role of the executive, and a state that allowed for two or more centers of coercion would be anarchy, not a state at all. At the same time, Kant argues that a just state must allow freedom of the pen or the press so that the people can make their criticisms known to both their legislature and their executive, and in one of his very last works, the *Conflict of the Faculties* of 1798, he went so far as to argue that even in a system where all universities are state institutions and all professors state employees, the members of the philosophical faculty (the equivalent of the modern faculty of arts and sciences), whose public role is simply to search for truth, have an obligation to make their criticisms of the state known, and the state has the obligation to allow them to do so and even to listen to them.

The third section of "Theory and Practice" begins the argument that Kant completes in *Perpetual Peace*, namely that justice requires fairness and security of property rights not only within national boundaries but also, because we all live on the finite surface of a globe no part of which is completely inaccessible from any other, fairness and security across the entire globe, or world peace. Kant argues that this peace can be realized only through a world federation of republics. Kant argues that republics not only maximize internal justice but also that republics would be far less likely to make war on each other than monarchies are because the republics' citizens who would have to fight wars could get to vote on going to war. But he also argues that the goal of world peace would be better served by a federation of republics than by a single world government because any government that is too large tends to degenerate into tyranny. Kant thus argues that it is a good thing that natural divisions of language and religion tend to lead to a system of independent nations, as long as they all ultimately develop into genuine republics. This view represents the complex mix of idealism and realism present throughout Kant's political philosophy. *Toward Perpetual Peace* itself is a complex mix of irony and sincerity, humorously written in the form of a treaty with preliminary and definitive articles. The preliminary articles argue that even when nations make war on each other, a future peace will be possible only if they make war in a way that does not create permanent hatreds; the definitive articles argue that peace will become actual only when governments led by "moral politicians" turn themselves into republics, although each government must do this on its own and not be forced to become a republic by external intervention. This was a radical argument for Kant to make in 1795, when the autocratic governments of Europe were gathering their forces to resist the spread of the republican principles of the French Revolution, but it would also be an argument that would cut against France as well a few years later when France transformed itself from a republic into an empire and tried to spread its version of liberalism to the rest of Europe by force rather than by example.

The literature on Kant's moral and political philosophy is vast. An overview of Kant's philosophy is Paul Guyer, *Kant* (London: Routledge, 2006). Two multi-authored introductions to Kant are Paul Guyer (ed.), *The Cambridge Companion to Kant* (Cambridge: Cambridge University Press, 1992), and Paul Guyer (ed.), *The Cambridge Companion to Kant and Modern Philosophy* (Cambridge: Cambridge University Press, 2006). The latter has increased coverage of Kant's moral and political philosophy. Another is Graham Bird (ed.), *A Companion to Kant* (Oxford: Blackwell, 2006). A lucid survey of Kant's moral philosophy is contained in John Rawls, *Lectures on the History of Moral Philosophy* (Cambridge, Mass.: Harvard University Press, 2000); a multi-authored survey of Kant's moral philosophy is Thomas E. Hill Jr. (ed.), *The Blackwell Guide to Kant's Ethics* (Chichester: Wiley-Blackwell, 2009); and an engaging survey of both Kant's moral and political philosophy is Allen W. Wood, *Kantian Ethics* (Cambridge: Cambridge University Press, 2008). In discussion of the *Groundwork*, Herbert James Paton, *The Categorical Imperative: A Study in Kant's Moral Philosophy* (London: Hutchinson, 1947), remains valuable; recent commentaries on the *Groundwork* include Paul Guyer, *Kant's Groundwork for the Metaphysics of Morals: A Reader's Guide* (London: Continuum, 2007), Jens Timmermann, *Kant's Groundwork of the Metaphysics of Morals: A Commentary* (Cambridge: Cambridge University Press, 2007), and Sally Sedgwick, *Kant's Groundwork of the Metaphysics of Morals: An Introduction* (Cambridge: Cambridge University Press, 2008). A multi-authored collection of papers on the *Groundwork* is Paul Guyer (ed.), *Kant's Groundwork of the Metaphysics of Morals: Critical Essays* (Lanham, Md.: Rowman & Littlefield, 1998).

Among recent books on Kant's political philosophy, some of the most useful are Howard Williams, *Kant's Political Philosophy* (New York: St. Martin's Press, 1983); Leslie A. Mulholland, *Kant's System of Rights* (New York: Columbia University Press, 1990); Allen D. Rosen, *Kant's Theory of Justice* (Ithaca, N.Y.: Cornell University Press, 1993); and most recently Katrin Flikschuh, *Kant and Modern Political Philosophy* (Cambridge: Cambridge University Press, 2000), which disputes Rawls's reconstruction of Kant's political philosophy. An interesting collection of essays on Kant's political philosophy by diverse authors is Jane Kneller and Sidney Axinn (eds.), *Autonomy and Community: Readings in Contemporary Kantian Social Philosophy* (Albany: State University of New York Press, 1998). A collection of essays on Kant's program for world peace is James Bohman and Matthias Lutz-Bachmann (eds.), *Perpetual Peace: Essays on Kant's Cosmopolitan Ideal* (Cambridge, Mass.: MIT Press, 1997).

Finally, three collections of their authors' essays covering both Kant's moral and his political philosophy are Paul Guyer, *Kant on Freedom, Law, and Happiness* (Cambridge: Cambridge University Press, 2000); Thomas E. Hill Jr., *Respect, Pluralism, and Justice: Kantian Perspectives* (Oxford: Oxford University Press, 2000); and Onora O'Neill, *Bounds of Justice* (Cambridge: Cambridge University Press, 2000).

Groundwork for the Metaphysics of Morals

CHAPTER I

Passage from the Common Rational Knowledge of Morality to the Philosophical

It is impossible to imagine anything at all in the world, or even beyond it, that can be called good without qualification—except a *good will*. Intelligence, wit, judgement, and the other mental talents, whatever we may call them, or courage, decisiveness, and perseverance, are, as qualities of *temperament* certainly good and desirable in many respects; but they can also be extremely bad and harmful when the will which makes use of these *gifts of nature* and whose specific quality we refer to as *character* is not good. It is exactly the same with *gifts of fortune*. Power, wealth, honour, even health and that total well-being and contentment with one's condition which we call *"happiness,"* can make a person bold but consequently often reckless as well, unless a good will is present to correct their influence on the mind, thus adjusting the whole principle of one's action to render it conformable to universal ends. It goes without saying that the sight of a creature enjoying uninterrupted prosperity, but never feeling the slightest pull of a pure and good will, cannot excite approval in a rational and impartial spectator. Consequently, a good will seems to constitute the indispensable condition even of our worthiness to be happy. . . .

A good will is not good because of its effects or accomplishments, and not because of its adequacy to achieve any proposed end: it is good only by virtue of its willing—that is, it is good in itself. Considered in itself it is to be treasured as incomparably higher than anything it could ever bring about merely in order to satisfy some inclination or, if you like, the sum total of all inclinations. Even if it were to happen that, because of some particularly unfortunate fate or the miserly bequest of a step-motherly nature, this will were completely powerless to carry out its aims; if with even its utmost effort it still accomplished nothing, so that only good will itself remained (not, of course, as a mere wish, but as the summoning of every means in our power), even then it would still, like a jewel, glisten in its own right, as something that has its full worth in itself. Its utility or ineffectuality can neither add to nor subtract from this worth. Utility would be merely, as it were, its setting, enabling us to handle it better in our ordinary dealings or to attract to it the attention of those who are not yet experts, but not why we recommend it to experts and determine its worth. . . .

We must thus develop the concept of a will estimable in itself and good apart from any further aim. This concept is already present in the natural, healthy mind, which requires not so much instruction as merely clarification. It is this concept that always holds the highest place in estimating the total worth of our actions and it constitutes the condition of all the rest. Let us then take up the concept of *duty*, which includes that of a good will, the latter however being here under certain subjective limitations and obstacles. These, so far from hiding a good will or disguising it, rather bring it out by contrast and make it shine forth more brightly. . . .

It is a duty to help others where one can, and besides this many souls are so compassionately

From Immanuel Kant, *Groundwork for the Metaphysics of Morals,* translated by Arnulf Zweig. Copyright © 2002. Reprinted by permission of Oxford University Press.

disposed that, without any further motive of vanity or self-interest, they find an inner pleasure in spreading joy around them, taking delight in the contentment of others, so far as they have brought it about. Yet I maintain that, however dutiful and kind an action of this sort may be, it still has no genuinely moral worth. It is on a level with other inclinations—for example, the inclination to pursue honour, which if fortunate enough to aim at something generally useful and consistent with duty, something consequently honourable, deserves praise and encouragement but not esteem. For its maxim lacks the moral merit of such actions done not out of inclination but out of *duty*. Suppose then that the mind of this humanitarian were overclouded by sorrows of his own which extinguished all compassion for the fate of others, but that he still had the power to assist others in distress; suppose though that their adversity no longer stirred him, because he is preoccupied with his own; and now imagine that, though no longer moved by any inclination, he nevertheless tears himself out of this deadly apathy and does the action without any inclination, solely out of duty. Then for the first time his action has its genuine moral worth. Furthermore, if nature had put little sympathy into this or that person's heart; if he, though an honest man, were cold in temperament and indifferent to the sufferings of others—perhaps because he has the special gifts of patience and fortitude in his own sufferings and he assumes or even demands the same of others; if such a man (who would in truth not be the worst product of nature) were not exactly fashioned by nature to be a humanitarian, would he not still find in himself a source from which he might give himself a worth far higher than that of a good-natured temperament? Assuredly he would. It is precisely in this that the worth of character begins to show—a moral worth, and incomparably the highest—namely, that he does good, not out of inclination, but out of duty. . . .

The second proposition is this: The moral worth of an action done out of duty has its moral worth, not *in the objective* to be reached by that action, but in the maxim in accordance with which the action is decided upon; it depends, therefore, not on actualizing the object of the action, but solely on the *principle of volition* in accordance with which the action was done, without any regard for objects of the faculty of desire. . . .

The third proposition, which follows from the two preceding, I would express in this way: *Duty is the necessity of an act done out of respect for the law*. While I can certainly have an *inclination* for an object that results from my proposed action, I can never *respect it*, precisely because it is nothing but an effect of a will and not its activity. Similarly I cannot respect any inclination whatsoever, whether it be my own inclination or that of another. At most I can approve of that towards which I feel an inclination, and occasionally I can like the object of somebody else's inclination myself—that is, see it as conducive to my own advantage. But the only thing that could be an object of respect (and thus a commandment) for me is something that is conjoined with my will purely as a ground and never as a consequence, something that does not serve my inclination but overpowers it or at least excludes it entirely from my decision-making—consequently, nothing but the law itself. Now if an action done out of duty is supposed to exclude totally the influence of inclination, and, along with inclination, every object of volition, then nothing remains that could determine the will except objectively *the law* and subjectively *pure respect* for this practical law. What is left therefore is the maxim, to obey this sort of law even when doing so is prejudicial to all my inclinations.

Thus the moral worth of an action depends neither on the result expected from that action nor on any principle of action that has to borrow its motive from this expected result. For all these results (such as one's own pleasurable condition or even the promotion of the happiness of others) could have been brought about by other causes as well. It would not require the will of a rational being to produce them, but it is only in such a will that the highest and unconditional good can be found. That pre-eminent good which we call "moral" consists therefore in nothing but *the* idea *of the law* in itself, which certainly *is present only in a rational being*—so far as that idea, and not an expected result, is the determining ground of the will. And this pre-eminent good is already present in the person who acts in accordance with this idea; we need not await the result of the action in order to find it. . . .

CHAPTER II

Transition from Popular Moral Philosophy to a Metaphysics of Morals

There is, however, *one* end that we may presuppose as actual in all rational beings (so far as they are dependent beings to whom imperatives apply); and thus there is one aim which they not only *might* have, but which we can assume with certainty that they all *do* have by a necessity of nature and that aim is *perfect happiness*. The hypothetical imperative which affrms the practical necessity of an action as a means to the promotion of perfect happiness is an assertoric imperative. We must not characterize it as necessary merely for some uncertain, merely possible purpose, but as necessary for a purpose that we can presuppose a priori and with certainty to be present in everyone because it belongs to the essence of human beings. Now we can call skill in the choice of the means to one's own greatest well-being "prudence" in the narrowest sense of the word. So the imperative concerning the choice of means to one's own happiness—that is, the precept of prudence—still remains hypothetical; the action is commanded not absolutely but only as a means to a further end.

Finally, there is one imperative which commands a certain line of conduct directly, without assuming or being conditional on any further goal to be reached by that conduct. This imperative is categorical. It is concerned not with the material of the action and its anticipated result, but with its form and with the principle from which the action itself results. And what is essentially good

in the action consists in the [agent's] disposition, whatever the result may be. This imperative may be called the imperative of morality. . . .

. . . Everything in nature works in accordance with laws. Only a rational being has the power to act in accordance with the idea of laws—that is, in accordance with principles—and thus has a will. . . .

All imperatives command either hypothetically or categorically. Hypothetical imperatives declare a possible action to be practically necessary as a means to the attainment of something else that one wants (or that one may want). A categorical imperative would be one that represented an action as itself objectively necessary, without regard to any further end.

Since every practical law presents a possible action as good and therefore as necessary for a subject whose actions are determined by reason, all imperatives are therefore formulae for determining an action which is necessary according to the principle of a will in some way good. If the action would be good only as a means to something else, the imperative is hypothetical; if the action is thought of as good in itself and therefore as necessary for a will which of itself conforms to reason as its principle, then the imperative is categorical. . . .

The question now arises "How are all these imperatives possible?" This question does not ask how an action commanded by the imperative can be performed, but merely how we can understand the constraining of the will, which imperatives express in setting us a task. How an imperative of skill is possible requires no special discussion. Whoever wills the end also wills (so far as reason has decisive influence on his actions) the means which are indispensably necessary and in his power. . . .

By contrast, "How is the imperative of morality possible?" is beyond all doubt the one question in need of solution. For the moral imperative is in no way hypothetical, and consequently the objective necessity, which it affirms, cannot be supported by any presupposition, as was the case with hypothetical imperatives. But we must never forget that it is impossible to settle by any example, i.e., empirically, whether there is any imperative of this kind at all; we should rather worry that all imperatives that seem to be categorical may yet be hypothetical in some hidden way. For example, when it is said, "You must abstain from making deceitful promises," one assumes that the necessity for this abstention is not mere advice so as to avoid some further evil—as though the meaning of what was said was, You ought not to make a deceitful promise lest, when it comes to light, you destroy your credit. On the contrary, an action of this kind would have to be considered as bad in itself, and the imperative of the prohibition would be therefore categorical. Even so, no example can show with certainty that the will would be determined here solely by the law without any further motivation, although it may appear to be so; for it is always possible that fear of disgrace, perhaps also hidden dread of other risks, may unconsciously influence the will. Who can prove by experience the non-existence of a cause? For experience shows only that we do not perceive it. In such a case, however, the so-called moral imperative, which as such appears to be categorical and unconditional, would in fact be only a pragmatic prescription calling attention to our own advantage and merely instructing us to take this into account. . . .

If I think of a *hypothetical* imperative as such, I do not know before hand what it will contain—not until I am given its condition. But if I think of a *categorical imperative*, I know right away what it contains. For since this imperative contains, besides the law, only the necessity that the maxim conform to this law, while the law, as we have seen, contains no condition limiting it, there is nothing left over to which the maxim of action should conform except the universality of a law as such; and it is only this conformity that the imperative asserts to be necessary. There is therefore only one categorical imperative and it is this: "Act only on that maxim by which you can at the same time will that it should become a universal law." . . .

We shall now enumerate some duties, dividing them in the usual way into duties towards ourselves and duties towards others and into perfect and imperfect duties.

1. A man feels sick of life as the result of a mounting series of misfortunes that has reduced him to hopelessness, but he still possesses enough of his reason to ask himself whether it would not be contrary to his duty to himself to take his own life. Now he tests whether the maxim of his action could really become a universal law of nature. His maxim, however, is: "I make it my principle out of self-love to shorten my life if its continuance threatens more evil than it promises advantage." The only further question is whether this principle of self-love can become a universal law of nature. But one sees at once that a nature whose law was that the very same feeling meant to promote life should actually destroy life would contradict itself, and hence would not endure as nature. The maxim therefore could not possibly be a general law of nature and thus it wholly contradicts the supreme principle of all duty.

2. Another finds himself driven by need to borrow money. He knows very well that he will not be able to pay it back, but he sees too that nobody will lend him anything unless he firmly promises to pay it back within a fixed time. He wants to make such a promise, but he still has enough conscience to ask himself, "Isn't it impermissible and contrary to duty to get out of one's difficulties this way?" Suppose, however, that he did decide to do it. The maxim of his action would run thus: "When I believe myself short of money, I will borrow money and promise to pay it back, even though I know that this will never be done." Now this principle of self-love or personal advantage is perhaps quite compatible with my own entire future welfare; only there remains the question "Is it right?" I therefore transform the unfair demand of self-love into a universal law and frame my question thus: "How would things stand if my maxim became a universal law?" I then see immediately that this maxim can never qualify as a

self-consistent universal law of nature, but must necessarily contradict itself. For the universality of a law that permits anyone who believes himself to be in need to make any promise he pleases with the intention of not keeping it would make promising, and the very purpose one has in promising, itself impossible. For no one would believe he was being promised anything, but would laugh at any such utterance as hollow pretence.

3. A third finds in himself a talent that, with a certain amount of cultivation, could make him a useful man for all sorts of purposes. But he sees himself in comfortable circumstances, and he prefers to give himself up to pleasure rather than to bother about increasing and improving his fortunate natural aptitudes. Yet he asks himself further "Does my maxim of neglecting my natural gifts, besides agreeing with my taste for amusement, agree also with what is called duty?" He then sees that a nature could indeed endure under such a universal law, even if (like the South Sea Islanders) every man should let his talents rust and should be bent on devoting his life solely to idleness, amusement, procreation—in a word, to enjoyment. Only he cannot possibly *will* that this should become a universal law of nature or should be implanted in us as such a law by a natural instinct. For as a rational being he necessarily wills that all his powers should be developed, since they are after all useful to him and given to him for all sorts of possible purposes.

4. A fourth man, who is himself flourishing but sees others who have to struggle with great hardships (and whom he could easily help) thinks to himself: "What do I care? Let every one be as happy as Heaven intends or as he can make himself; I won't deprive him of anything; I won't even envy him; but I don't feel like contributing anything to his well-being or to helping him in his distress!" Now admittedly if such an attitude were a universal law of nature, the human race could survive perfectly well and doubtless even better than when everybody chatters about sympathy and good will, and even makes an effort, now and then, to practise them, but, when one can get away with it, swindles, traffics

in human rights, or violates them in other ways. But although it is possible that a universal law of nature in accord with this maxim could exist, it is impossible to *will* that such a principle should hold everywhere as a law of nature. For a will that intended this would be in conflict with itself, since many situations might arise in which the man needs love and sympathy from others, and in which, by such a law of nature generated by his own will, he would rob himself of all hope of the help he wants.

These are some of the many actual duties—or at least of what we take to be actual—whose derivation from the single principle cited above is perspicuous. We must be able to will that a maxim of our action should become a universal law—this is the authoritative model for moral judging of action generally. Some actions are so constituted that we cannot even *conceive* without contradiction that their maxim be a universal law of nature, let alone that we could *will* that it *ought* to become one. In the case of other actions, we do not find this inner impossibility, but it is still impossible to *will* that their maxim should be raised to the universality of a law of nature, because such a will would contradict itself. . . .

If we now look at ourselves whenever we transgress a duty, we find that we in fact do not intend that our maxim should become a universal law. For this is impossible for us. What we really intend is rather that its opposite should remain a law generally; we only take the liberty of making an *exception* to it, for ourselves or (of course just this once) to satisfy our inclination. Consequently if we weighed it all up from one and the same perspective—that of reason—we should find a contradiction in our own will, the contradiction that a certain principle should be objectively necessary as a universal law and yet subjectively should not hold universally but should admit of exceptions. . . .

Suppose, however, there were something *whose existence in itself* had an absolute worth, something that, as an end *in itself*, could be a ground of definite laws. Then in it and in it alone, would the ground of a possible categorical imperative, that is, of a practical law, reside.

Now, I say, a human being, and in general every rational being, *does exist* as an end in himself, *not merely as a means* to be used by this or that will as it pleases. In all his actions, whether they are directed to himself or to other rational beings, a human being must always be viewed *at the same time as an end.* All the objects of inclination have only a conditional worth; for if these inclinations and the needs based on them did not exist, their object would be worthless. But inclinations themselves, as sources of needs, are so far from having absolute value to make them desirable for their own sake that it must rather be the universal wish of every rational being to be wholly free of them. Thus the value of any object *that is to be acquired* by our action is always conditional. Beings whose existence depends not on our will but on nature still have only a relative value as means and are therefore called *things*, if they lack reason. Rational beings, on the other hand, are called *persons* because, their nature already marks them out as ends in themselves—that is, as something which ought not to be used *merely* as a means—and consequently imposes restrictions on all choice making (and is an object of respect). Persons, therefore, are not merely subjective ends whose existence as an effect of our actions has a value *for us.* They are *objective ends*—that is, things whose existence is in itself an end, and indeed an end such that no other end can be substituted for it, no end to which they should serve *merely* as a means. For if this were not so, there would be nothing at all having *absolute value* anywhere. But if all value were conditional, and thus contingent, then no supreme principle could be found for reason at all.

If then there is to be a supreme practical principle and a categorical imperative for the human will, it must be such that it forms an objective principle of the will from the idea of something which is necessarily an end for everyone because *it is an end in itself*, a principle that can therefore serve as a universal practical law. The ground of this principle is: *Rational nature exists as an end in itself.* This is the way in which a human being necessarily conceives his own existence, and it is therefore a *subjective* principle of human actions. But it is also the way in which every other rational being conceives his existence, on the same rational ground which holds also for me; hence it is at the same time an *objective* principle from which, since it is a supreme practical ground, it must be possible to derive all laws of the will. The practical imperative will therefore be the following: *Act in such a way that you treat humanity, whether in your own person or in any other person, always at the same time as an end, never merely as a means.* We will now see whether this can be carried out in practice.

Let us keep to our previous examples.

First, . . . the man who contemplates suicide will ask himself whether his action could be compatible with the Idea of humanity as *an end in itself.* If he damages himself in order to escape from a painful situation, he is making use of a person *merely as a means* to maintain a tolerable state of affairs till the end of his life. But a human being is not a thing—not something to be used *merely* as a means: he must always in all his actions be regarded as an end in himself. Hence I cannot dispose of a human being in my own person, by maiming, corrupting, or killing him. (I must here forego a more precise definition of this principle that would forestall any misunderstanding—for example, as to having limbs amputated to save myself or exposing my life to danger in order to preserve it, and so on—this discussion belongs to ethics proper.)

Secondly, . . . the man who has in mind making a false promise to others will see at once that he is intending to make use of another person *merely as a means* to an end which that person does not share. For the person whom I seek to use for my own purposes by such a promise cannot possibly agree with my way of treating him, and so cannot himself share the end of the action. This incompatibility with the principle of duty to others can be seen more distinctly when we bring in examples of attacks on the freedom and property of others. For then it is manifest that a violator of the rights of human beings intends to use the person of others merely as a means without taking into consideration that, as rational beings, they must always at the same time be valued as ends—that is, treated only as beings who must themselves be able to share in the end of the very same action.

Thirdly, . . . it is not enough that an action not conflict with humanity in our own person as an end in itself: it must also *harmonize with this end.* Now there are in humanity capacities for greater perfection that form part of nature's purpose for humanity in our own person. To neglect these can perhaps be compatible with the *survival* of humanity as an end in itself, but not with the *promotion* of that end.

Fourthly, . . . the natural end that all human beings seek is their own perfect happiness. Now the human race might indeed exist if everybody contributed nothing to the happiness of others but at the same time refrained from deliberately impairing it. This harmonizing with humanity *as an end in itself* would, however, be merely negative and not positive, unless everyone also endeavours, as far as he can, to further the ends of others. For the ends of any person who is an end in himself must, if this idea is to have its full effect in me, be also, as far as possible, *my* ends. . . .

If we look back on all the previous efforts to discover the principle of morality, it is no wonder that they have all had to fail. One saw that human beings are bound to laws by their duty, but it never occurred to anyone that they are subject only to *laws which they themselves have given* but which are nevertheless *universal,* and that people are bound only to act in conformity with a will that is their own but that is, according to nature's purpose, a will that gives universal law. For when one thought of human beings merely as subject to a law (whatever it might be), the law had to carry with it some interest, as stimulus or compulsion to obedience, because it did not spring as law from their *own* will: in order to conform to the law, their will had to be compelled by *something else* to act in a certain way. But this strictly

necessary consequence meant that all the labour spent in trying to find a supreme foundation for duty was irrevocably lost. For what one discovered was never duty, but only the necessity of acting from a certain interest. This interest might be one's own or another's. But the resulting imperative was bound to be always a conditional one and could not at all serve as a moral commandment. I therefore want to call my principle the principle of the *Autonomy* of the will in contrast with all others, which I therefore count as *Heteronomy.*

The concept of every rational being as a being who must regard itself as making universal law by all the maxims of its will, and must seek to judge itself and its actions from this standpoint, leads to a closely connected and very fruitful concept—namely, that of *a kingdom of ends.*

I understand by a "kingdom" the systematic union of different rational beings under common laws. Now since laws determine ends as regards their universal validity, we can—if we abstract from the personal differences between rational beings, and also from the content of their private ends—conceive a whole of all ends systematically united (a whole composed of rational beings as ends in themselves and also of the personal ends which each may set for himself); that is, we can conceive of a kingdom of ends which is possible in accordance with the aforesaid principles.

For rational beings all stand under the *law* that each of them should treat himself and all others *never merely as a means* but always *at the same time as an end in himself.* But from this there arises a systematic union of rational beings through shared objective laws—that is, a kingdom. Since these laws aim precisely at the relation of such beings to one another as ends and means, this kingdom may be called a kingdom of ends (admittedly only an ideal).

A rational being, however, belongs to the kingdom of ends as a *member,* if, while legislating its universal laws, he is also subject to these laws. He belongs to the kingdom as its *head,* if, as legislating, he is not subject to the will of any other being.

A rational being must always regard himself as lawgiving in a kingdom of ends made possible through freedom of the will—whether as member or as head. But he cannot maintain the position of head merely through the maxim of his will, but only if he is a completely independent being, without needs and with an unlimited power adequate to his will.

Thus morality consists in the relation of all action to just that lawgiving through which a kingdom of ends is made possible. But this law-giving must be found in every rational being itself and must be capable of arising from the will of that being. The principle of its will is therefore this: never to perform any action except one whose maxim could also be a universal law, and thus to act only on a maxim *through which the will could regard itself at the same time as enacting universal law*. If maxims are not already by their very nature in harmony with this objective principle of rational beings as legislating universal law, the necessity of acting on this principle is called a constraint on the choice of actions, i.e., *duty*. Duty does not apply to the head in a kingdom of ends, but it does apply to every member and to all of them in equal measure.

The practical necessity of acting on this principle—that is, duty—is not based at all on feelings, impulses, and inclinations, but only on the relation of rational beings to one another, a relation in which the will of a rational being must always be regarded as *lawgiving*, because otherwise it could not be thought of as *an end in itself*. Reason thus relates every maxim of a universally legislating will to every other will and also to every action towards oneself: it does so, not because of any further motive or future advantage, but from the Idea of the *dignity* of a rational being who obeys no law other than one which he himself also enacts.

In the kingdom of ends everything has either a *price* or a *dignity*. Whatever has a price can be replaced by something else as *equivalent*.

Whatever by contrast is exalted above all price and so admits of no equivalent has a dignity.

Whatever is relative to universal human inclinations and needs has a *market price*. Whatever, even without presupposing a need, accords with a certain taste—that is, with satisfaction in the mere random play of our mental powers—has an *attachment price*. But that which constitutes the sole condition under which anything can be an end in itself has not mere relative worth, i.e., a price, but an inner worth—i.e., *dignity*.

Now morality is the only condition under which a rational being can be an end in itself; for only through this is it possible to be a lawgiving member in the kingdom of ends. Therefore morality, and humanity so far as it is capable of morality, is the only thing that has dignity. Skill and diligence in work have a market price; wit, lively imagination, and humour have an attachment price but fidelity to promises and benevolence out of basic principles (not out of instinct) have an inner worth. Nature and art alike offer nothing that could replace their lack; for their worth consists not in the effects which result from them, not in the advantage or profit they produce, but in the intentions—that is, in the maxims of the will—which are ready in this way to reveal themselves in action even if they are not favoured by success. Such actions too need no recommendation from any subjective disposition or taste in order to be regarded with immediate favour and approval; they need no direct predilection or feeling for them. They exhibit as an object of immediate respect the will that performs them; since nothing but reason is required in order to *impose* them on the will. Nor is the will to be *coaxed* into them, which would anyhow be a contradiction in the case of duties. This assessment lets us recognize the value of such a mental attitude as dignity and puts it infinitely above all price, with which it cannot be brought into comparison or computation without, as it were, violating its holiness.

And what is it then that justifies a morally good disposition, or virtue, in making such lofty claims?

It is nothing less than the *sharing* which it allows to a rational being in *giving universal laws*, which therefore renders him fit to be a member in a possible kingdom of ends. His own nature as an end in himself already marked out this fitness and therefore his status as lawgiver in a kingdom of ends and as free from all laws of nature, obedient only to those laws which he himself prescribes, laws according to which his maxims can participate in the making of universal law (to which he at the same time subjects himself). For nothing can have worth other than that determined for it by the law. But the lawgiving that determines all worth must therefore have a dignity, i.e., an unconditional and incomparable worth. The word *"respect"* is the only suitable expression for the esteem that a rational being must necessarily feel for such lawgiving. *Autonomy* is thus the basis of the dignity of human nature and of every rational nature.

Our three ways of presenting the principle of morality are basically only so many formulations of precisely the same law, each one of them by itself uniting the other two within it. There is nevertheless a difference among them, which, however, is more subjectively than objectively practical: that is to say, the different formulations aim to bring an Idea of reason closer to intuition (by means of a certain analogy) and thus nearer to feeling. All maxims have:

1. A *form*, which consists in universality; and in this respect the formula of the moral imperative is expressed thus: "Maxims must be chosen as if they were to hold as universal laws of nature."
2. A *matter*—that is, an end; and in this respect the formula says: "A rational being, as by its very nature an end and thus an end in itself, must serve every maxim as the limiting condition restricting the pursuit of all merely relative and arbitrary ends."
3. A *complete determination* of all maxims by means of the following formula: "All maxims which stem from autonomous lawgiving are to harmonize with a possible kingdom of ends and with a kingdom of nature." Progression that takes place here as elsewhere is through the categories of unity, plurality, and totality: *unity* of the form of the will (its universality); *plurality* of its matter (its objects—that is, its ends); and the totality or *all-comprehensiveness* of its system of ends. It is, however, better if in moral *judgement* one proceeds always in accordance with the strict method and takes as one's basic principle the universal formula of the categorical imperative: *"Act on that maxim that can at the same time make itself into a universal law."* If, however, we wish also to *gain a hearing* for the moral law, it is very useful to bring one and the same action under the three stated formulae and thereby, as far as possible, bring the moral law closer to intuition.

We can now end at the point from which we began—namely, with the concept of an unconditionally good will. A *will* is *absolutely good* if it cannot be evil—that is, if its maxim, when made into a universal law, can never be in conflict with itself. This principle is therefore also its supreme law: "Act always on that maxim whose universality as a law you can at the same time will." This is the one principle on which a will can never be in conflict with itself, and such an imperative is categorical. Since the validity of the will, as a universal law for possible actions, is analogous to the universal connection of the existence of things under universal laws, which is the formal aspect of nature in general, we can also express the categorical imperative as follows: *"Act on maxims which can at the same time have as their object [making] themselves into universal laws of nature."* This then gives us the formula for an absolutely good will.

On the Old Saw: That May Be Right in Theory But It Won't Work in Practice

II. ON THE RELATION OF THEORY TO PRACTICE IN CONSTITUTIONAL LAW

(*contra* Hobbes)

Among the contracts that enable groups of people to unite in a society (*pactum sociale*), the one to be found a civil constitution between them (*pactum unionis civilis*) is a special kind. As far as *execution* is concerned, it has much in common with any other contract aimed at the joint promotion of some purpose; it is essentially different from the rest, however, in the principle of what it founds (*constitutionis civilis*). The union of many people for some common end which they all *have* is found in all social contracts. But their union as an end in itself—as the end that everyone *ought to have*, and thus as the first and unconditioned duty in each external relationship of human beings who cannot avoid influencing one another—does not occur in a society unless it has attained to the civil state, i.e., unless it constitutes a community. The end, now, which in such an external relation is in itself a duty, and itself the supreme formal condition of all other external duties (*conditio sine qua non*), is the legal order (the right) of people *under public coercive laws*, by which each can be assigned his own, and each protected against the incursions of all others.

Yet the concept of external law as such derives completely from the concept of *freedom* in the external relations of men to one another. It has nothing whatever to do with the pursuit of happiness, the end which all men have by nature, or with the prescription of means to that end. There simply must not be any mingling of that law as such with the end of happiness posing as its determining ground. *Law* is the limitation of each man's freedom to the condition of its consistency with everyone's freedom to the extent possible in accordance with a universal law. And *public law* is the totality of the *external laws* that serve to make such thoroughgoing consistency possible. Since every limitation of freedom by another's arbitrary will is termed coercion, it follows that a civil constitution is a relationship of *free* men who are nonetheless subject to coercive laws, their overall freedom in relation to others notwithstanding. They are subject to those laws because reason itself wills it so, pure reason which legislates a priori and irrespective of the empirical ends that have been summed up under the general name happiness. For human ideas regarding those ends differ greatly, and each man seeks them in a different place, so that their will cannot be brought under a common principle nor, consequently, under an external law consistent with everyone's freedom.

The civil state, viewed purely as a legal state, is thus based a priori upon the following principles:

1. The *freedom* of each member of society as a *human being;*
2. The *equality* of each member with every other member as a *subject of the state;*
3. The *independence* of each member of the community as a *citizen.*

Translated by E. B. Ashton. Reprinted by permission of the University of Pennsylvania Press.

These principles are not laws given by a state already established, but they are the only laws that make it possible to found a state in accordance with pure rational principles of external human law as such. Therefore:

1. Human *freedom* as a principle for the constitution of a community I express in this formula: No man can compel me to be happy after his fashion, according to his conception of the wellbeing of someone else. Instead, everybody may pursue his happiness in the manner that seems best to him, provided he does not infringe on other people's freedom to pursue similar ends, i.e., on another's right to do whatever can coexist with every man's freedom under a possible universal law.

If a government were founded on the principle of benevolence toward the people, as a *father's* toward his children—in other words, if it were a *paternalistic government (imperium paternale)* with the subjects, as minors, unable to tell what is truly beneficial or detrimental to them, obliged to wait for the head of state to judge what should constitute their happiness and be kind enough to desire it also—such a government would be the worst conceivable *despotism*. It would be a constitution that cancels every freedom of the subjects, who retain no rights at all. A *patriotic* rather than *paternalistic* government *(imperium, non paternale, sed patrioticum)* is the only one conceivable for people capable of having rights, and also the only one conceivable for a benevolent ruler. For the *patriotic* way of thinking is that which makes everyone in the state, including the ruler, look upon the community as his mother's womb, or on the country as his father's land where he himself came into being, and which he must leave behind as a cherished pledge, in order to protect the rights of the community by laws issuing from the common will, not deeming himself entitled to subject it to the uses of his unconditional discretion.

This right to freedom belongs to every member of the community as a human being, provided he is a being capable of having rights at all.

2. The *equality* of subjects may be phrased as follows: Each member of the community has rights that entitle him to coerce every other member. Only the community's head is excepted from that coercion. Not being a member of the community but its creator or preserver, he also is authorized to coerce without being subject to legal coercion himself. Whoever is *subject* to laws in a state is a subject; that is to say, coercion by laws applies to him as to all other members of the community, with the sole exception of one single (physical or moral) person, the head of state, who is the only one capable of exerting all legal coercion. For if he too could be coerced he would not be the head of the state, and the sequence of subordination would continue upwards ad infinitum. And if there were two persons free from coercion, neither of them would be subject to coercive laws and neither one could wrong the other—which is impossible.

But this thorough equality of persons as the subjects of a state is quite consistent with the greatest inequality in the quantity and degree of their possessions, whether these be physical or mental superiority, external gifts of fortune, or simply rights (of which there can be many) with respects to others. One man's welfare, therefore, is greatly dependent on another's will, as the poor man's on the will of the rich; one must obey, as a child its parents or a wife her husband, when the other commands; or, one will serve as a day-laborer while the other pays wages, and so forth. And yet, as subjects all of them are equal *before the law* which, as the expression of the general will, can only be singular, and concerns the form of the right, not the matter or the object to which I have a right. For it is only by means of the public law and its executor, the head of state, that a man can coerce anyone else, but by the same means everyone else will resist him in like measure; and no one can lose this capacity to coerce—i.e., to have rights against others—except in consequence of his own crime. Nor can a man give it up of his own accord; there is no contract, no legal act, by which he can put himself in the position of having no rights any more, only duties. For if he were to do so, he would be depriving himself of the right to make a contract, and so the contract would cancel itself.

This idea of the human equality of men as subjects in a community results in the following formula: Each member of the community must be permitted to rise in it to any status or class (appropriate to a subject) to which his talent, industry, and luck may take him. And his fellow subjects may not block his way by any *hereditary* prerogative, as members of some specific privileged class, to keep him and his heirs beneath that class forever.

For right consists merely in limiting everybody else's freedom to the point where it can coexist with my freedom according to a universal law, and the public law in a community is no more than a state of actual legislation in accordance with this principle and combined with power. Due to this legislation, consequently, all members of a people live as subjects in a state of law *(status iuridicus)*, namely, in a state of equilibrium between the effect and counter-effect of wills that limit each other in accordance with the universal law of freedom. This is what we call the civil state; and in that state the *innate right* of everyone is the *same* (i.e., until he takes an action affecting that right), entitling him to compel all others to observe the bounds within which their use of their freedom is compatible with mine. Since a man's birth is not an *action* of his and thus does not bring upon him unequal legal status, nor subject him to any coercive laws other than those which he, as a subject of the sole supreme lawmaking power, shares with all the rest, there can be no one member of the community, no fellow subject, who is innately privileged over another. No man can leave to his descendants any prerogative of the *status* he holds in the community; nor can he forcibly keep them, who are qualified by birth to be masters, so to speak, from rising by their own merits to higher levels in the order of ranks—where one is superior, another inferior, though neither is *imperans* while the other is *subjectus*. A man may leave his heirs everything else; and in a sequence of descendants, considerable inequality of financial circumstances may result between the members of a community, between wage earners, tenants, landowners and the laborers who till the land, and so on. Only one thing he cannot prevent: the right of the less favored to rise to the same favored circumstances if enabled to do so by their talent, industry, and luck. For otherwise the testator would be allowed to coerce without being coercible in turn by the reaction of others, and would exceed the level of a fellow subject.

Nor can a man living in the legal framework of a community be stripped of this quality by anything save his own crime. He can never lose it, neither by contract nor by acts of war *(occupatio bellica)*, for no legal act, neither his own nor another's, can terminate his proprietary rights in himself. No such act can put him into the class of domestic animals which we use at will for any kind of service and keep in that state without their consent for as long as we please, albeit with the restriction—sometimes religiously sanctioned, as among the Hindus—that they not be maimed or killed. No matter what his circumstances, a man may be deemed happy as long as he knows that the law does not discriminate in favor of his fellow subjects, that if he fails to rise to their level it is not due to the irresistible will of others but solely to himself, to his own faculties or resolve, or to circumstances for which he can hold no one else responsible.[1]

3. *Independence (sibisufficientia)* of a member of a community as a *citizen*, that is to say, a co-legislator. With regard to legislation all men are free and equal *under* public law as already enacted, though they are not equal with respect to the right to *enact* that law. Those who are not able to have this right are still, as members of the community, required to obey its law, and share in its protection, though not as *citizens* but only as *partakers* in the law's protection.

For all rights depend upon laws. But a public law that determines what all men are to be legally permitted or forbidden is the act of a public will from which all rights issue, and which must therefore be incapable of wronging anyone. There is but one will for which this is possible: the will of the people as a whole (when all decide about all, and each, accordingly, decides about himself)—because the one man to whom each person can do no legal wrong is himself. If it is otherwise, any decision made for all by a will other than the will of all might be an injustice, and a further law would still be required to limit such a will's enactments. Thus no particular will can serve as lawmaker for a community. (In fact, the very concept of a community is made up of the coinciding concepts of the external freedom, the equality, and the *unity* of the will of *all* and, since the combination of the first two requires voting, independence is the premise of the last.) This basic law, which can emerge only from the general, united popular will, is called the *original contract*.

Every man who has the right to vote on this legislation is termed a *citizen (citoyen,* i.e., a *citizen* of the *state*, not of a city or borough, a *bourgeois).* The only necessary qualification, aside from the *natural* one of not being a child or a woman, is that he be *his own master (sui iuris):* that he own some sort of property—among which may be counted any skill, craft, fine art, or science that supports him. This is to say that whenever he needs to acquire things from others in order to live, he will acquire them only by *disposing* of what is *his own,*[2] not by allowing others to use his services, so that he will not, in the proper sense of the word, be anyone's servant but the community's. Here, then, craftsmen and large (or small) landowners are all equal, each entitled to cast one vote only. We may disregard the question how one man can rightly come to own more land than his own hands can put to use (for acquisition by armed conquest is not original acquisition), and how so many who otherwise would have been capable of acquiring permanent property happen to be reduced to serving that landowner for their livelihood. In any event it would conflict with the previous principle, equality, if the large landowning class were so privileged by law that either its descendants would always remain large landowners (of the feudal type, whose estates could not

be divided by sale or inheritance so as to benefit more of the people), or that in case of such division none but members of a certain, arbitrarily chosen class could acquire any part of the estates. The large landed proprietor eliminates the votes of as many smaller proprietors as could occupy his place; thus he is not voting in their name and, consequently, has only one vote.

It is necessary, then, to rely exclusively on the ability, industry, and luck of each community member, that these will enable each of them in time to acquire a part of the community, and enable all to acquire the whole. But these differences cannot be taken into account in the making of the general laws. The number of eligible voters on legislation must be set one per capital of property owners, and not according to the size of their possessions.

Yet *all* of those who have this right to vote must agree that the public law is just. Otherwise there would be a legal conflict between those who agree and those who disagree, and the resolution of that conflict would require an additional, higher principle of law. Since we cannot expect unanimity of a whole people, however, the only attainable outcome to be foreseen is a majority of votes—and not a majority of direct voters, in a large nation, but only a majority of those delegated as representatives of the people. The acceptance by general consent, hence by *contract,* of the principle that this majority suffices must be the supreme ground on which to establish a civil constitution. Here we have an original contract on which alone a civil and thus consistently legal constitution among men can be based and a community established.

Yet this contract, which we call *contractus originarius* or *pactum sociale,* as the coalition of every particular and private will within a people into a common public will for purposes of purely legal legislation, need by no means to be presupposed as a fact. It is not necessary first to demonstrate historically, so to speak, that a people, whose rights and duties we have inherited, must really have performed such an act *at some time* and must have left us, by word of mouth or in writing, some reliable news or instrument of it, before we are to consider ourselves bound by an existing civil constitution. It is rather a *mere idea* of reason, albeit one with indubitable practical reality, obligating every lawmaker to frame his laws so that they *might* have come from the united will of an entire people, and to regard any subject who would be a citizen as if he had joined in voting for such a will. For this is the touchstone of the legitimacy of all public law. If a law is so framed that all the people *could not possibly* give it their consent—as, for example, a law granting the hereditary *privilege* of *master status* to a certain class of *subjects*—the law is unjust; but if it is *at all possible* that a people might agree on it, then the people's duty is to look upon the law as just, even assuming that their present situation or the tenor of their present way of thinking were such that, if consulted, they would probably refuse to agree.[3]

But this restriction obviously applies to the lawmaker's judgment only, not to the subject's. If a people were to judge that a certain actual legislation will with the utmost probability deprive them of their happiness—what can such a people do? Should they not resist? The answer can be only: they can do nothing but obey. For the question is not what happiness the subject may expect from the establishment of a community or from its administration. Rather, the issue is first of all the legal order which is thereby to be secured for all. This is the supreme principle from which all maxims concerning a community must start, and which is not limited by any other principle. Regarding happiness no universally valid principle of legislation can be given. For both the circumstances of the time and the high contradictory and constantly changing delusions in which each man seeks his happiness (and no one can prescribe for him where he should seek it) render all fixed principles impossible and unfit by themselves to serve as principles of legislation. The proposition *salus publica suprema civitatis lex est*—the public welfare is the community's highest law—remains undiminished in validity and public esteem; but

the common weal to be considered *first of all* is precisely that legal constitution which secures the freedom of everyone by means of laws, leaving him to pursue his happiness by whichever way seems best to him as long as he does not infringe upon that universal freedom under the law and thus upon the rights of other fellow subjects.

When the supreme power makes laws that are initially aimed at happiness—at the prosperity of citizens, at population, and the like—this is not done for the purpose of establishing a civil constitution. It is done simply as a means to *secure the state of law*, chiefly against the people's foreign enemies. The head of state must have the authority to judge by himself alone whether such laws are needed for the community to flourish as it must in order to safeguard its strength and stability, internally as well as against foreign foes. But the purpose is not to make the people happy, against their will as it were; the only purpose is to make them exist as a community.[4] The lawmaker may err in judging whether or not those measures are *prudently* taken; but there can be no error of judgment when he asks himself whether or not the law is in accord with the legal principle. For here he possesses that infallible yardstick (and a priori at that)—the idea of the original contract. (He need not wait for experience, as he must in following the principle of happiness, to instruct him first about the suitability of his means.) Just as long as it is not self-contradictory to assume that all the people consent to such a law, however distasteful they may find it, the law is in accord with justice. But if a public law is in accord with justice, if it is unimpeachable, irreprehensible from the point of view of the right, it carries with it the authority to coerce and, conversely, a ban on any active resistance to the lawmaker's will. In other words, the power in the state that lends effect to the law is irresistible, and there is no legally existing community that does not have such power to crush all inner resistance, since this resistance would be following a maxim whose general application would destroy all civil constitutions in which alone men can have rights.

It follows that any resistance to the supreme lawmaking power, any incitement of dissatisfied subjects to action, any uprising that bursts into rebellion—that all this is the worst, most punishable crime in a community. For it shatters the community's foundations. And this ban is *absolute*, so unconditional that even though that supreme power or its agent, the head of state, may have broken the original contract, even though in the subject's eyes he may have forfeited the right to legislate by empowering the government to rule tyrannically by sheer violence, even then the subject is allowed no resistance, no violent counteraction. The reason is that once a civil constitution exists, a people no longer have the right to judge how that constitution ought to be administered. For suppose they had such a right and their judgment ran counter to that of the actual head of state: who is to decide which side is right? Neither one can act as a judge in his own case. To decide between the head and the people there would have to be a head above the head—which is self-contradictory.

Nor, by the way, can a sort of *right of necessity (ius in casu necessitatis)*—which supposed *right* to do *wrong* in extreme (physical) need is an absurdity anyway[5]—arise here to provide a way in which the barrier blocking the people's own power could be lifted. For the head of state is just as apt to justify his harsh treatment of the subjects by their recalcitrance as they are to justify their rebellion with complaints of their undue suffering at his hands. And who is to decide? The one who is in control of the supreme administration of public justice, and this is precisely the head of state—he alone can decide. And no one in the community can thus have a right to contest that control of his.

And yet there are estimable men who maintain that in certain circumstances the subject does have the right to oppose his superior with force. Among them I will here mention only Achenwall who, in presenting his doctrines of natural law,[6] exhibits great caution, precision, and modesty. He says: "If the danger from enduring further the injustice of its head poses a greater threat to the community than may be feared from taking up arms against him, then the people may resist him; on the strength of this right they may set aside their contract of submission and depose him as a tyrant." And he concludes: "In this fashion (respective to their former overlord) the people return to a state of nature."

I can well believe that in an actual case neither Achenwall nor any of the good men who have aired their minds in agreement with him on this point would ever have lent their counsel or consent to such dangerous undertakings. And as for the uprisings in which the Swiss, the Dutch, or even the British won their much vaunted constitutions, there can be hardly a doubt that if those revolts had miscarried, readers of their history would view the execution of their now so exalted initiators as nothing more than the well-earned punishment of high political criminals. For the outcome usually colors our judgment of the legal grounds, though it was uncertain while the latter are certain. As far as these legal grounds are concerned—granting even that such a rebellion might do no wrong to a prince (who may have violated, say, a *joyeuse entrée*, or an actual underlying contract with his people)—it is clear that the people by pursuing their rights in this manner have done the greatest wrong. For this manner, if adopted as a maxim, would render every legal constitution insecure and introduce a state of utter lawlessness *(status naturalis)* in which all rights would lose at least their effectiveness.

Since so many right-thinking authors have this tendency to argue the people's case (to the people's own ruin), I will note only that this is due, at times, to a common fallacy whereby, while talking of the principle of right, they shift the ground of their judgment to the principle of happiness. At other times, no document can be produced of a contract actually submitted to the community, accepted by its head, and sanctioned by both. Having assumed the idea of an original contract—an idea that always provides the rational basis—to be something that must have happened in *actual fact*, they believe the people to have always retained the right to depart from the contract whenever, in the people's own judgment, there is a gross violation of it.[7]

It is plain to see here what mischief the principle of happiness (and happiness is really incapable of any determinate principle) causes in constitutional law, just as it does in morality, despite the best intentions of those who teach it. The sovereign wants to make the people happy according to his own notions and becomes a despot; the people will not be deprived of the universal human claim to their own happiness and become rebels. If one had asked, to begin with, what is right—and the principles of this are a priori certain and cannot be bungled by any empiricist—the idea of the social contract would retain its unimpeachable prestige. It would not do so as a fact, as Danton would have it when he declares that without such a fact all property and all rights contained in the actually existing constitution are null and void. But the idea would retain its prestige solely as the rational principle for judging any public lawful constitution as such. And one would see that until a general will exists, the people possess no right at all to coerce their ruler, since it is only through him that they can legally coerce. Yet, once that general will exists, there can be no popular coercion of the rule, because then the people themselves would be the supreme ruler. Consequently, the people never have any right of coercion (any right to be refractory in word or deed) against the head of state.

This theory is also amply confirmed in practice. In Great Britain, whose people boast of their constitution as if it were the model for all the world, we nonetheless find the constitution completely silent on what the people have a right to do in case the monarch should transgress the contract of 1688. In other words: if he wanted to violate it, the constitution, in the absence of any specific law, secretly reserves the right to rebel. That the constitution should contain a law for such a case—a law to justify the overthrow of the existing constitution which is the source of all particular laws (even assuming a breach of contract)—is a clear contradiction, because then

it would have to contain a publicly constituted[8] opposing power, a second head of state to protect the people's right against the first. And there would have to be a third, then, to decide which of the two sides is right.

Worried, moreover, about such charges in the event their enterprise should fail, those popular guides (or guardians, if you will) who frightened the monarch away preferred to impute to him a voluntary surrender of the reins of government rather than to arrogate to themselves a right to depose him—a claim that would have brought the constitution into a flagrant contradiction with itself.

Surely I will not be accused of flattering the monarch too much with this kind of inviolability; and so I hope also to be spared the charge of favoring the people too much when I say that they, too, have inalienable rights against the head of state, even though these rights cannot be coercive.

Hobbes is of the opposite opinion. According to him (*de Cive*, Chapter 7, Section 14) the head of state is bound by no contractual obligation toward the people. He cannot wrong the citizens, he may dispose of them as he wishes. This thesis would be quite true if "wrong" were understood to give the injured a coercive right against the man who inflicted the wrong; but stated in such general terms the proposition is terrifying.

The nonrecalcitrant subject must be able to assume that his sovereign does not *want* to wrong him. On this assumption, since every man has inalienable rights which he cannot give up even if he would, and concerning which he is himself entitled to judge, the wrong that a citizen believes himself to have suffered can be due only to an error, or to the ignorance of certain consequences that follow from laws made by the supreme power. Accordingly the citizen must be free to inform the public of his views on whatever in the sovereign decrees appears to him as a wrong against the community, and he must have this freedom with the sovereign's own approval. For to assume that the head might never be in error, never in ignorance of anything, would be to imagine him graced with divine intuitions and exalted above all men. *Freedom of the pen*—within the bounds of respect and affection for the constitution one lives under, kept within those bounds by the subjects' liberal way of thinking which the constitution itself instills in them (and to which the pens automatically restrict one another, lest they lose their freedom)—this is the sole shield of popular rights. For to deny the people this freedom would not merely deprive them of every claim to justice in regard to the supreme commander (according to Hobbes); it would also deprive the supreme commander, whose will commands the subjects as citizens only by representing the general will of the people, of any knowledge of matters which he himself would change if only he knew them. Hence, to limit this freedom would bring him into contradiction with himself. But to make the head apprehensive that public unrest might be incited if men were to think for themselves and to think out loud amounts to arousing in him distrust of his own power or even hatred of his own people.

There is a universal principle by which a people must judge its rights *negatively*—i.e., must judge what the supreme legislature, in all good faith, might be deemed *not to have ordained*. This principle is contained in the proposition: *Whatever resolution the people cannot make about themselves, the lawmaker cannot make about the people.*

Suppose, for example, a law were to command the permanent establishment of a previously decreed state religion. Could this be viewed as expressing the lawmaker's real will and intent? One should first ask himself whether a people *may* enact a law to the effect that certain tenets of faith and outward religious forms, once adopted, should remain forever; that is, may a people prevent itself (in its future generations) from progressing in religious insight or from correcting what may be old errors? It will be clear then that an original contract in which the people made such a law would be null and void in itself, because it runs counter to the destiny and to the ends of mankind. A law so made is thus not to be regarded as the monarch's true will, and remonstrances may be made to him.

But in each case in which something of the kind has nevertheless been decreed by supreme legislation, general and public judgments on it may be offered, but resistance in word or deed must never be mobilized.

What must prevail in every community is *obedience*, bowing to coercive laws that suffer no exception within the mechanism of the state constitution. But at the same time a *spirit of freedom* must prevail, since in matters of universal human duty everyone wants to be rationally convinced of the justice of this coercion, lest he come into contradiction with himself. Obedience without the spirit of freedom is the effective cause of all *secret societies*. For it is a natural calling of mankind to communicate with one another, especially about what concerns man in general; with the cultivation of this freedom those societies would disappear.

And how else could a government obtain the knowledge that promotes its own essential intent than by allowing the spirit of freedom, a spirit so worthy of respect both in its origin and its effects, to express itself?

Nowhere will a practice that avoids all pure rational principles disparage theory more arrogantly than in the question of what a good state constitution requires. This is because a long-standing legal constitution gradually causes the people to make it their rule to judge both their happiness and their rights by the state of affairs in which everything so far has functioned peacefully—but not, conversely, to evaluate the state of affairs by concepts of both their rights and happiness with which reason supplies them. The rule is, rather, always to prefer that passive state to the perilous position of seeking a better one, a position to which Hippocrates' advice to physicians applies: *indicium anceps, experimentum periculosum*—decision is difficult, experiment perilous. All constitutions of sufficiently long standing, whatever their flaws and for all their differences, yield the same result: one is content with the constitution one lives under. Hence, from the viewpoint of *the people's welfare*, no theory properly applies to all; instead, everything rests on a practice submissive to experience.

But if there is something in reason which the term "constitutional law" can express, and if men who face each other in the antagonism of their freedom find in this concept a unifying force—if it shows them an objective, practical reality (and here no reference must be made to whatever well-being or ill-being it may cause them, for that can be learned only by experience)—it is based on a priori principles, because experience cannot teach us what is right. And then, there is a *theory* of constitutional law with which all practice, to be valid, must agree.

The only argument to be advanced against this thesis is that while men have in their heads the idea of rights that are their due, their hard hearts make them incapable and unworthy of being treated accordingly, so that they may and must be kept in order by a supreme power acting solely on rules of prudence. Yet this desperate leap (*salto mortale*) is such that, once we are talking not of right but of power only, the people may try their own power and jeopardize every legal constitution. Unless there is something which rationally compels immediate respect, such as human rights, all influences upon human choice will be incapable of curbing human freedom. But when the right, joined by benevolence, makes its voice heard, human nature shows itself not too depraved to listen diferentially. *(Tum pietate gravem meritisque si forte virum quem/Conspexere silent arrectisque auribus adstant:* Once they behold a man weighty with merits and righteousness, they stand in silence, pricking up their ears. Virgil.)

III. ON THE RELATION OF THEORY TO PRACTICE IN INTERNATIONAL LAW—A GENERAL-PHILANTHROPIC, I.E., COSMOPOLITAN VIEW[9]

(*contra* Mendelssohn)

Are we to love the human race as a whole, or is it an object to be viewed with displeasure, an object that has our best wishes (lest we become misanthropic) but never our best expectations, and from which, therefore, we would rather avert our eyes?

The answer to this question depends on our answer to another question. Are there tendencies in human nature which allow us to infer that the species will always progress toward the better, and that the evil of present and past times will be lost in the good of the future? If so, we could love the species at least for its constant approach to the good; if not, we would have to loathe or despise it, no matter what the affectations of a universal love of mankind—which would then be, at most, a well-meaning love, not a love well pleased—may say to the contrary. What is and remains evil, notably the evil and deliberate mutual violation of the most sacred human rights, this we cannot avoid loathing, even when we try our hardest to love it. We hate it—not that we would harm people, but that we would have as little to do with them as possible.

Moses Mendelssohn was of the latter opinion (*Jerusalem*, Section Two, pp. 44–47), opposing it to his friend Lessing's hypothesis of mankind undergoing a divine education. To him it is chimera "that the whole of mankind down here should be moving ever forward, perfecting itself in the sequence of times."

We see, he says, the human race as a whole "performing slight oscillations, and it has never taken a few forward steps without relapsing soon after, twice as fast, into its former condition." (This is exactly the boulder of Sisyphus; in this way one assumes, with the Hindus, that the earth is a place of penance for old sins now beyond recall.) "Men progress but mankind constantly wavers within the same fixed limits; viewed as a whole it maintains at all periods of time about the same level of morality, the same measure of religion and irreligion, virtue and vice, happiness(?) and misery."

He introduces this assertion (p. 46) by saying, "You want to guess what Providence intends for mankind? Forge no hypotheses" (earlier he had called them "theory"); "just look around at what is really happening, and if you can, survey the history of all ages and look at what has happened from the beginning. This is the fact; this must have been part of the intention; this must have been approved or at least included in the plans of wisdom."

I take a different view.

If it is a sight fit for a god to see a virtuous man wrestle with tribulations and temptations and yet stand firm, it is a sight most unfit, I will not say for a god, but for the commonest man of good will to see the human race from period to period take upward steps toward virtue, only to see it soon after relapsing just as deeply into vice and misery. To watch this tragedy for a while may perhaps be touching and instructive, but eventually the curtain has to fall. For in the long run the tragedy becomes a farce, and though the actors, fools that they are, do not tire of it, the spectator will. After one or two acts he has had enough of it; he can correctly assume that the neverending play is forever the same. If it is only a play, the punishment at the end may make up for his unpleasant sensations. But in real life to pile vice upon countless vice (though interrupted by virtues), just so that some day there will be plenty to punish, would be repugnant, at least by our conception, even to the morality of a wise creator and governor of the world.

I may be allowed to assume, therefore, that our species, progressing steadily in civilization as is its natural end, is also making strides for the better in regard to the moral end of its existence, and that this progress will be *interrupted* now and then, but never *broken off*. I do not have to prove this assumption; the burden of proof is on its opponent. I rest my case on this: I have the innate duty (though in respect of moral character required I am not so good as I should and hence could be) so to affect posterity through each member in the sequence of generations in which I live, simply as a human being, that future generations will become continually better (which also must be assumed to be possible), and that this duty may thus rightfully be passed on from one generation to the next. Let any number of doubts be drawn from history to dispute my hopes, doubts which, if conclusive, might move me to abandon a seemingly futile labor; but as long as the futility cannot be made

wholly certain, I cannot exchange my duty (as the *liquidum,*) for the rule of prudence not to attempt the unfeasible (as the *illiquidum,* because it is a mere hypothesis). I may always be and remain unsure whether an improvement in the human race can be hoped for; but this can invalidate neither the maxim nor its necessary presupposition that in a practical respect it be feasible.

Without this hope for better times the human heart would never have been warmed by a serious desire to do something useful for the common good; this hope has always influenced the labors of right-thinking men. Even the excellent Mendelssohn must have reckoned with it when he so zealously strove for the enlightenment and welfare of the nation to which he belonged. For he could not reasonably hope to accomplish them by himself, all alone, unless others after him continued advancing on the same path. Despite the depressing sight, not so much of ills that oppress mankind from natural causes as of those men inflict upon each other, the mind is cheered by the prospect that things may be better in future—a quite unselfish benevolence, since we shall long be in our graves and shall not reap the fruits which we have helped to sow. Empirical arguments against the success of these resolves, which rest on hope, are insufficient here. The argument that what has not succeeded so far will therefore never succeed, does not even justify the abandonment of a pragmatic or technological intention (as that of air travel by aerostatic balloons, for instance), much less than abandonment of a moral intention that becomes a duty unless its accomplishment is demonstrably impossible. Besides, there is a good deal of evidence to show that in our age, compared with all earlier ones, mankind has by and large really made considerable moral progress for the better. (Short-time arrests can prove nothing to the contrary.) And it can also be shown that the screaming about an irresistibly growing depravation of mankind comes from the very fact that, upon reaching a higher level of morality, we can see farther ahead, and that the severity of our judgments about what we are compared with what we ought to be—in other words, our self-criticism—increases the higher we have climbed on the moral ladder in all of what we have come to know of the world's course.

If we ask, then, by what means we might maintain and possibly accelerate this perpetual progress for the better, we soon see that this immeasurable success will depend not so much on what *we* do (on what education we give to the young, for instance), or on the method *we* ought to use to accomplish it. Instead, it will depend upon what human *nature* will do in and with us to *force* us into a track to which we would not easily accommodate ourselves on our own. For we can look only to nature, or rather, because the attainment of this end requires supreme wisdom, the *Providence* for a success that will affect the whole and thence the parts, while on the contrary, the *designs* of men start with the parts, if indeed they do not stop there. The whole as such is too large for men; they can extend their ideas to it, but not their influence, chiefly since the design of one man will repel another, so that they would hardly reach agreement on a design of their own free intention.

Just as universal violence and the resulting distress were finally bound to make a people decide that they should submit to the coercion of public laws, which reason itself prescribes for them as remedy, and found a state under a *civil constitution*, even so the distress of ceaseless warfare, in which states in turn seek to reduce or subjugate each other, must eventually bring the states under a *cosmopolitan* constitution even against their will. Such general peace may pose an even greater threat to freedom from another quarter by leading to the most terrible despotism, as has repeatedly happened in the case of oversized states. Yet the distress of ceaseless warfare must compel them to adopt a condition which, although not a cosmopolitan community under one head, is still lawful—a *federation* under jointly agreed *international law*.

For the advancing civilization of the states, accompanied by a growing inclination to expand by cunning or by force at the other's expense, means the multiplication of wars. To maintain standing armies, to add to them constantly more men at the same pay, to keep them in training and equip them with ever more numerous tools of war, all this is bound to produce higher and higher costs. The price of all necessities keeps rising, without any hope of a corresponding increase in the supply of the metals of which they are made. And no peace lasts long enough for the peacetime savings to match the cost of the next war, a complaint for which the invention of national debts is an ingenious but ultimately self-destructive nostrum. As a result, impotence must finally accomplish what good will ought to have done but did not: the organization of every state's internal affairs so that the decisive voice on whether or not to wage war is not that of the head of state—for whom the war costs actually nothing—but that of the people, who pay for it. (This necessarily presupposes, of course, the realization of that idea of the original contract.) For the people are hardly likely to plunge themselves into penury—which never touches the head of state—out of sheer lust of expansion or because of supposed purely verbal insults. And so their descendants will not be burdened with debts they have not brought on themselves; they too—due not to any love for them, but only to the self-love of each era—will be able to progress toward an ever better condition, even in a moral sense; because any community unable to harm others by force must rely on justice alone, and may have grounds to hope for help from other communities of the same constitution.

This, however, is just an opinion and mere hypothesis, as uncertain as all judgments claiming to state the sole adequate natural cause for an intended effect that is not wholly in our power. And, as has been shown above, even as such an hypothesis it contains no principle for its enforcement by the subjects of an existing state; rather, it contains an enforcement for uncoercible heads of state. In the usual order of things it is not in human nature to relinquish power voluntarily; yet, in pressing circumstances, it is not impossible. So we may consider it a not inadequate expression of the moral hopes and wishes of men (conscious of their weakness) to look to *Providence* for the circumstances required. They may hope that since it is the *purpose* of *mankind*, of the entire species, to achieve its final destiny by the free use of its powers as far as they go, Providence will bring about an outcome to which the purposes of *men*, considered separately, run directly counter. For this very counteraction of inclinations, the fonts of evil, gives reason free play to subjugate them all and to inaugurate a reign of the good that is self-sustaining, once it exists, in place of the reign of self-destructive evil.

Nowhere does human nature appear less lovable than in the relations of whole nations to each other. No state's independence or possessions are even for a moment safe from the others. The will to subjugate another, or encroach upon what belongs to him, is always present; and warlike preparations for defense, which often make peace more burdensome and more destructive of domestic welfare than war itself, may never be relaxed. For this the only possible remedy is international law based on public statutes backed by power, statutes to which every state would have to submit in analogy to civil or constitutional law for individuals. For an enduring universal peace by means of the so-called *balance of power in Europe* is a mere chimera, rather like Swift's house whose architect had built it in such perfect accordance with all the laws of equilibrium that a sparrow lighting on the roof made it promptly collapse.

"But states," it will be said, "will never submit to such coercive laws; and the proposal of a universal international state, whose authority all individual states should voluntarily accept and whose laws they should obey, may sound ever so nice in the theory of an Abbé de Saint-Pierre or a Rousseau, but it will not work in practice. Has it not always been ridiculed by great statesmen, and more yet by heads of state, as a pedantically childish academic idea?"

I for my part put my trust in the theory that proceeds from the principle of justice, concerning how relations between individuals and states

ought to be. The theory commends to the earthly demigods the maxim to proceed so that each of their quarrels become the introduction to such a universal international state and, thus, to assume as a practical possibility that it *can be.*

At the same time, however, I trust *(in subsidium)* in the nature of things, which compels one to go where he would rather not *(fata volentem ducunt, nolentem trahunt*—fate guides the willing and drags the unwilling). In this I also take human nature into account. Since respect for right and duty is still alive in human nature, I cannot, or will not, consider it so steeped in evil that in the end, after many unsuccessful attempts, moral-practical reason should not Triumph and show human nature also to be lovable. So, even from a cosmopolitan viewpoint my assertion stands: what is valid in theory, on rational grounds, is valid also in practice.

Notes

1. If we want to link the word "gracious" with a determinate concept differentiating it from "kind," "benevolent," "protective," and the like, we can use it only for a person who is not subject to legal coercion. In other words, since it is the head of the *state government* who effects and grants every benefit possible under public law (for the *sovereign* who gives those laws is invisible, as it were; he is the law personified, not its agent), that head alone, as the only one not subject to legal coercion, can rightly be titled "gracious lord." Even in an aristocracy, as in Venice for example, the *Senate* is the only "gracious lord." All the nobles who constitute it are subjects (not even the *Doge* excepted, for the Grand Council alone is the sovereign) and, as far as the execution of the laws is concerned, the equals of everyone else. Every subject has the right to coerce any one of them.

Princes—i.e., those who have a hereditary right to the rule—are styled "gracious lords" by courtesy, court fashion, on account of their prospects and claims; but in their proprietary status they are fellow subjects nonetheless, and their humblest servant must have the right to coerce them legally through the head of state.

As for the gracious (more properly, noble) ladies, it might be considered that it is their *status* together with their *sex* which gives them a claim to this title (a claim, consequently, only upon the male sex), and this owing to the refinement of manners (called gallantry), whereby the male believes to do himself greater honor in proportion as he concedes greater prerogatives to the fair sex.

2. The producer of an *opus* can convey it to another by transfer, just as if it were his property; but *praestatio operae* is not such a transfer. The domestic servant, the shop clerk, the laborer, even the hairdresser—these are mere *operarii*, not *artifices* in the broader sense, and they are not members of the state, hence not entitled to be citizens. Although my relations to the man I give my firewood to cut, and to the tailor to whom I give my cloth with which to make me a garment, seem altogether similar, yet the first differs from the second as the hairdresser differs from the wigmaker (even if I have given him the hair for my wig) or the day-laborer from the artist or craftsman who fashions a work that belongs to him until he has been paid. The latter, acting as a tradesman, will exchange his property *(opus)* with others; the former will permit others to use his services *(operam)*.

It is, I confess, somewhat difficult to determine just what it takes to be able to claim the status of being one's own master.

3. If, for example, a proportional war tax were levied on all subjects, the fact that it is onerous would not permit them to call it unjust on the grounds that the war, in their view, was unnecessary. This they have no right to judge, because there is always *the possibility* that the war is unavoidable and the tax indispensable, and hence must be considered lawful in the judgment of the subjects. But if in such a war the property of certain owners is onerously commandeered while others, equally situated, are spared this burden, it is easy to see chat all the people cannot consent to such a law, and because they cannot consider such an unequal distribution of burdens as just, they are entitled at least to remonstrate against it.

4. This includes certain import restrictions in order to promote the use of purchasing power for the subjects' own good rather than to benefit foreigners and to stimulate foreign industry; because the state, without a prosperous people, would not be strong enough to resist foreign enemies or to maintain itself as a community.

5. There is only one *casus necessitatis*—the case in which an *absolute duty* conflicts with one that, though perhaps major, is still only a *conditional duty*. For example, to save the state from calamity it may be necessary to betray one's relative, perhaps a father or son. To save the state from calamity is an unconditional duty, but it is only a conditional duty to avert the relative's unhappiness (as long as he has not become guilty of a crime against the state). Reporting a relative's plans to the authorities may be performed with extreme reluctance, but is compelled by necessity, to wit, moral necessity.

But when a shipwrecked man pushes another off his raft to save his own life, then to say that he had a right to do so because of his (physical) need is totally false. For I have a duty to save my life only on condition that I can do so without committing a crime. But I have an unconditional duty not to take the life of someone else who is not injuring me nor even causing the danger threatening mine. Even so, the professors of law are quite consistent in making legal allowance for such emergency acts. For the authorities cannot attach any *punishment* to this injunction, because that punishment would have to be death. And it would be an absurd law that threatened death to one who refuses to die voluntarily in a dangerous situation.

6. *Ius Naturae. Editio 5ta. Paris posterior*, Sections 203 to 206.

7. No matter how the people's real contract with their sovereign may be violated, they cannot immediately react *as a community*, but only as a mob. For the former constitution has been torn up by the people, while their organization as a new *community* is still to occur. This is when the state of anarchy arises with all its at least potential horrors. And the wrong in that situation is whatever each of the people's parties inflicts on the other. This also emerges from an example cited, where the rebellious subjects of that state finally sought to force on each other a constitution that would have become far more oppressive than the one discarded—namely, the prospect of being devoured by clerics and aristocrats instead of being able to look to an all-governing head for a more equitable distribution of the state's burdens.

8. No right in the state can be insidiously concealed, as it were, by way of a secret reservation, least of all the right which the people presume to be a part of the constitution. For all constitutional laws must be conceived as deriving from a public will. If the constitution were to permit rebellion, it would have to state publicly the right to rebel and the way to exercise it.

9. It is not immediately apparent how a general *philanthropic* presupposition relates to a *cosmopolitan* constitution, and how the latter relates to the foundation of international law as the only condition in which those human tendencies that make our species lovable can be property developed. The conclusion of this part will make that connection plain.

Perpetual Peace

We need not try to decide whether this satirical inscription, (once found on a Dutch innkeeper's signboard above the picture of a churchyard) is aimed at mankind in general, or at the rulers of states in particular, unwearying in their love of war, or perhaps only at the philosophers who cherish the sweet dream of perpetual peace. The author of the present sketch would make one stipulation, however. The practical politician stands upon a definite footing with the theorist: with great self-complacency he looks down upon him as a mere pedant whose empty ideas can threaten no danger to the state (starting as it does from principles derived from experience), and who may always be permitted to knock down his eleven skittles at once without a worldly-wise statesman needing to disturb himself. Hence, in the event of a quarrel arising between the two, the practical statesman must always act consistently, and not scent danger to the state behind opinions ventured by the theoretical politician at random and publicly expressed. With which saving clause *(clausula salvatoria)* the author will herewith consider himself duly and expressly protected against all malicious misinterpretation.

FIRST SECTION

Containing the Preliminary Articles of Perpetual Peace Between States

1. "No treaty of peace shall be regarded as valid, if made with the secret reservation of material for a future war."

For then it would be a mere truce, a mere suspension of hostilities, not peace. A peace signifies the end of all hostilities and to attach to it the epithet "eternal" is not only a verbal pleonasm, but matter of suspicion. The causes of a future war existing, although perhaps not yet known to the high contracting parties themselves, are entirely annihilated by the conclusion of peace, however acutely they may be ferreted out of documents in the public archives. There may be a mental reservation of old claims to be thought out at a future time, which are, none of them, mentioned at this stage, because both parties are too much exhausted to continue the war, while the evil intention remains of using the first favourable opportunity for further hostilities. Diplomacy of this kind only Jesuitical casuistry can justify: it is beneath the dignity of a ruler, just as acquiescence in such processes of reasoning is beneath the dignity of his minister, if one judges the facts as they really are.

If, however, according to present enlightened ideas of political wisdom, the true glory of a state lies in the uninterrupted development of its power by every possible means, this judgment must certainly strike one as scholastic and pedantic.

2. "No state having an independent existence—whether it be great or small—shall be acquired by another through inheritance, exchange, purchase or donation."

For a state is not a property *(patrimonium)*, as may be the ground on which its people are settled. It is a society of human beings over whom no one but itself has the right to rule and to dispose. Like the trunk of a tree, it has its own roots, and to

From "Perpetual Peace; A Photographical Essay," translated by M. Campbell Smith, Swan Sonnenschein & Co., Lim., 1903. Footnotes omitted.

graft it on to another state is to do away with its existence as a moral person, and to make of it a thing. Hence it is in contradiction to the idea of the original contract without which no right over a people is thinkable. Everyone knows to what danger the bias in favour of these modes of acquisition has brought Europe (in other parts of the world it has never been known). The custom of marriage between states, as if they were individuals, has survived even up to the most recent times and is regarded partly as a new kind of industry by which ascendency may be acquired through family alliances, without any expenditure of strength; partly as a device for territorial expansion. Moreover, the hiring out of the troops of one state to another to fight against an enemy not at war with their native country is to be reckoned in this connection; for the subjects are in this way used and abused at will as personal property.

3. "Standing armies *(miles perpetuus)* shall be abolished in course of time."

For they are always threatening other states with war by appearing to be in constant readiness to fight. They incite the various states to outrival one another in the number of their soldiers, and to this number no limit can be set. Now, since owing to the sums devoted to this purpose, peace at last becomes even more oppressive than a short war, these standing armies are themselves the cause of wars of aggression, undertaken in order to get rid of this burden. To which we must add that the practice of hiring men to kill or to be killed seems to imply a use of them as mere machines and instruments in the hand of another (namely, the state) which cannot easily be reconciled with the right of humanity in our own person. The matter stands quite differently in the case of voluntary periodical military exercise on the part of citizens of the state, who thereby seek to secure themselves and their country against attack from without.

The accumulation of treasure in a state would in the same way be regarded by other states as a menace of war, and might compel them to anticipate this by striking the first blow. For of the three forces, the power of arms, the power of

alliance and the power of money, the last might well become the most reliable instrument of war, did not the difficulty of ascertaining the amount stand in the way.

4. "No national debts shall be contracted in connection with the external affairs of the state."

This source of help is above suspicion, where assistance is sought outside or within the state, on behalf of the economic administration of the country (for instance, the improvement of the roads, the settlement and support of new colonies, the establishment of granaries to provide against seasons of scarcity, and so on). But, as a common weapon used by the Powers against one another, a credit system under which debts go on indefinitely increasing and are yet always assured against immediate claims (because all the creditors do not put in their claim at once) is a dangerous money power. This ingenious invention of a commercial people in the present century is, in other words, a treasure for the carrying on of war which may exceed the treasures of all the other states taken together, and can only be exhausted by a threatening deficiency in the taxes—an event, however, which will long be kept off by the very briskness of commerce resulting from the reaction of this system on industry and trade. The ease, then, with which war may be waged, coupled with the inclination of rulers towards it—an inclination which seems to be implanted in human nature—is a great obstacle in the way of perpetual peace. The prohibition of this system must be laid down as a preliminary article of perpetual peace, all the more necessarily because the final inevitable bankruptcy of the state in question must involve in the loss many who are innocent; and this would be a public injury to these states. Therefore other nations are at least justified in uniting themselves against such an one and its pretensions.

5. "No state shall violently interfere with the constitution and administration of another."

For what can justify it in so doing? The scandal which is here presented to the subjects of another state? The erring state can much more serve as a warning by exemplifying the great evils which a nation draws down on itself through its own law-lessness. Moreover, the bad example which one free person gives another, (as *scandalum accep-tum*) does no injury to the latter. In this connec-tion, it is true, we cannot count the case of a state which has become split up through internal cor-ruption into two parts, each of them representing by itself an individual state which lays claim to the whole. Here the yielding of assistance to one faction could not be reckoned as interference on the part of a foreign state with the consitution of another, for here anarchy prevails. So long, how-ever, as the inner strife has not yet reached this state the interference of other powers would be a violation of the rights of an independent nation which is only struggling with internal disease. It would therefore itself cause a scandal, and make the autonomy of all states insecure.

6. "No state at war with another shall coun-tenance such modes of hostility as would make mutual confidence impossible in a subsequent state of peace: such are the employment of assassins *(percussores)* or of poisoners *(venefici)*, breaches of capitulation, the instigating and making use of treachery *(perduellio)* in the hostile state."

These are dishonourable strategems. For some kind of confidance in the disposition of the enemy must exist even in the midst of war, as otherwise peace could not be concluded, and the hostilities would pass into a war of extermination *(bellum internecinum)*. War, however, is only our wretched expedient of asserting a right by force, an expedi-ent adopted in the state of nature, where no court of justice exists which could settle the matter in dispute. In circumstances like these, neither of the two parties can be called an unjust enemy, because this form of speech presupposes a legal decision: the issue of the conflict—just as in the case of the so-called judgments of God—decides on which side right is. Between states, however, no puni-tive war *(bellum punitivum)* is thinkable, because between them a relation of superior and inferior does not exist. Whence it follows that a war of extermination, where the process of annihilation would strike both parties at once and all right as

well, would bring about perpetual peace only in the great graveyard of the human race. Such a war then, and therefore also the use of all means which lead to it, must be absolutely forbidden. That the methods just mentioned do inevitably lead to this result is obvious from the fact that these infernal arts, already vile in themselves, on coming into use, are not long confined to the sphere of war. Take, for example, the use of spies *(uti explorato-ribus)*. Here only the dishonesty of others is made use of; but vices such as these, when once encour-aged, cannot in the nature of things be stamped out and would be carried over into the state of peace, where their presence would be utterly de-structive to the purpose of that state.

Although the laws stated are, objectively re-garded, (i.e. in so far as they affect the action of rulers) purely prohibitive laws *(leges prohibitivæ)*, some of them *(leges strictæ)* are strictly valid without regard to circumstances and urgently re-quire to be enforced. Such are Nos. 1, 5, 6. Others, again, (like Nos. 2, 3, 4) although not indeed ex-ceptions to the maxims of law, yet in respect of the practical application of these maxims allow subjectively of a certain latitude to suit particu-lar circumstances. The enforcement of these *leges latæ* may be legitimately put off, so long as we do not lose sight of the ends at which they aim. This purpose of reform does not permit of the defer-ment of an act of restitution (as, for example, the restoration to certain states of freedom of which they have been deprived in the manner described in article 2) to an infinitely distant date—as Au-gustus used to say, to the "Greek Kalends," a day that will never come. This would be to sanction non-restitution. Delay is permitted only with the intention that restitution should not be made too precipitately and so defeat the purpose we have in view. For the prohibition refers here only to the *mode of acquisition* which is to be no longer valid, and not to the *fact of possession* which, although indeed it has not the necessary title of right, yet at the time of so-called acquisition was held legal by all states, in accordance with the public opinion of the time.

SECOND SECTION

Containing the Definitive Articles of a Perpetual Peace Between States

A state of peace among men who live side by side is not the natural state *(status naturalis)*, which is rather to be described as a state of war: that is to say, although there is not perhaps always actual open hostility, yet there is a constant threatening that an outbreak may occur. Thus the state of peace must be *established*. For the mere cessation of hostilities is no guarantee of continued peaceful relations, and unless this guarantee is given by every individual to his neighbour—which can only be done in a state of society regulated by law—one man is at liberty to challenge another and treat him as an enemy.

First Definitive Article of Perpetual Peace

I. "The civil constitution of each state shall be republican."

The only constitution which has its origin in the idea of the original contract, upon which the lawful legislation of every nation must be based, is the republican. It is a constitution, in the first place, founded in accordance with the principle of the freedom of the members of society, as human beings: secondly, in accordance with the principle of the dependence of all, as subjects, on a common legislation: and, thirdly, in accordance with the law of the equality of the members as citizens. It is then, looking at the question of right, the only constitution whose fundamental principles lie at the basis of every form of civil constitution. And the only question for us now is, whether it is also the one constitution which can lead to perpetual peace.

Now the republican constitution apart from the soundness of its origin, since it arose from the pure source of the concept of right, has also the prospect of attaining the desired result, namely, perpetual peace. And the reason is this. If, as must be so under this constitution, the consent of the subjects is required to determine whether there shall be war or not, nothing is more natural than that they should weigh the matter well, before undertaking such a bad business. For in decreeing war, they would of necessity be resolving to bring down the miseries of war upon their country. This implies: they must fight themselves; they must hand over the costs of the war out of their own property; they must do their poor best to make good the devastation which it leaves behind; and finally, as a crowning ill, they have to accept a burden of debt which will embitter even peace itself, and which they can never pay off on account of the new wars which are always impending. On the other hand, in a government where the subject is not a citizen holding a vote, *i.e.* in a constitution which is not republican, the plunging into war is the least serious thing in the world. For the ruler is not a citizen, but the owner of the state, and does not lose a whit by the war, while he goes on enjoying the delights of his table or sport, or of his pleasure palaces and gala days. He can therefore decide on war for the most trifling reasons, as if it were a kind of pleasure party. Any justification of it that is necessary for the sake of decency he can leave without concern to the diplomatic corps who are always only too ready with their services.

The following remarks must be made in order that we may not fall into the common error of confusing the republican with the democratic constitution. The forms of the state *(civitas)* may be classified according to either of two principles of division:—the difference of the persons who hold the supreme authority in the state, and the manner in which the people are governed by their ruler whoever he may be. The first is properly called the form of sovereignty *(forma imperii)*, and there can be only three constitutions differing in this respect: where, namely, the supreme authority belongs to only one, to several individuals working together, or to the whole people constituting the civil society. Thus we have autocracy or the sovereignty of a monarch, aristocracy or the sovereignty of the nobility, and democracy or the sovereignty of the people. The second principle of division is the form of government (*forma regiminis*), and refers to the way in which the state makes use of its supreme power: for the manner of government is based on the constitution, itself the act of that universal will which transforms a multitude into a nation. In this respect the form of government is either republican or despotic. Republicanism is the political principle of severing the executive power of the government from the legislature. Despotism is that principle in pursuance of which the state arbitrarily puts into effect laws which it has itself made: consequently it is the administration of the public will, but this is identical with the private will of the ruler. Of these three forms of a state, democracy, in the proper sense of the word, is of necessity despotism, because it establishes an executive power, since all decree regarding—and, if need be, against—any individual who dissents from them. Therefore the "whole people," so-called, who carry their measure are really not all, but only a majority: so that here the universal will is in contradiction with itself and with the principle of freedom.

Every form of government in fact which is not representative is really no true constitution at all, because a law-giver may no more be, in one and the same person, the administrator of his own will, than the universal major premise of a syllogism may be, at the same time, the subsumption under itself of the particulars contained in the minor premise. And, although the other two constitutions, autocracy and aristocracy, are always defective in so far as they leave the way open for such a form of government, yet there is at least always a possibility in these cases, that they may take the form of a government in accordance with the spirit of a representative system. Thus Frederick the Great used at least to say that he was "merely the highest servant of the state." The democratic constitution, on the other hand, makes this impossible, because under such a government every one wishes to be master. We may therefore say that the smaller the staff of the executive—that is to say, the number of rulers—and the more

real, on the other hand, their representation of the people, so much the more is the government of the state in accordance with a possible republicanism; and it may hope by gradual reforms to raise itself to that standard. For this reason, it is more difficult under an aristocracy than under a monarchy—while under a democracy it is impossible except by a violent revolution—to attain to this, the one perfectly, lawful constitution. The kind of government, however, is of infinitely more importance to the people than the kind of constitution, although the greater or less aptitude of a people for this ideal greatly depends upon such external form. The form of government, however, if it is to be in accordance with the idea of right, must embody the representative system in which alone a republican form of administration is possible and without which it is despotic and violent, be the constitution what it may. None of the ancient so-called republics were aware of this, and they necessarily slipped into absolute despotism which, of all despotisms, is most endurable under the sovereignty of one individual.

Second Definitive Article of Perpetual Peace

II. "The law of nations shall be founded on a federation of free states."

Nations, as states, may be judged like individuals who, living in the natural state of society—that is to say, uncontrolled by external law—injure one another through their very proximity. Every state, for the sake of its own security, may—and ought to—demand that its neighbour should submit itself to conditions, similar to those of the civil society where the right of every individual is guaranteed. This would give rise to a federation of nations which, however, would not have to be a State of nations. That would involve a contradiction. For the term "state" implies the relation of one who rules to those who obey—that is to say, of lawgiver to the subject people: and many nations in one state would constitute only one nation, which contradicts our hypothesis, since here we have to consider the right of one nation against another, in so far as they are so many separate states and are not to be fused into one.

The attachment of savages to their lawless liberty, the fact that they would rather be at hopeless variance with one another than submit themselves to a legal authority constituted by themselves, that they therefore prefer their senseless freedom to a reason—governed liberty, is regarded by us with profound contempt as barbarism and uncivilisation and the brutal degradation of humanity. So one would think that civilised races, each formed into a state by itself, must come out of such an abandoned condition as soon as they possibly can. On the contrary, however, every state thinks rather that its majesty (the "majesty" of a people is an absurd expression) lies just in the very fact that it is subject to no external legal authority; and the glory of the ruler consists in this, that, without his requiring to expose himself to danger, thousands stand at his command ready to let themselves be sacrificed for a matter of no concern to them. The difference between the savages of Europe and those of America lies chiefly in this, that, while many tribes of the latter have been entirely devoured by their enemies, Europeans know a better way of using the vanquished than by eating them; and they prefer to increase through them the number of their subjects, and so the number of instruments at their command for still more widely spread war.

The depravity of human nature shows itself without disguise in the unrestrained relations of nations to each other, while in the law-governed civil state much of this is hidden by the check of government. This being so, it is astonishing that the word "right" has not yet been entirely banished from the policies of war as pedantic, and that no state has yet ventured to publicly advocate this point of view. For Hugo Grotius, Puffendorf, Vattel and others—Job's comforters, all of them—are always quoted in good faith to justify an attack, although their codes, whether couched in philosophical or diplomatic terms, have not—nor can have—the slightest legal force, because states, as such, are under no common external

authority; and there is no instance of a state having ever been moved by argument to desist from its purpose, even when this was backed up by the testimony of such great men. This homage which every state renders—in words at least—to the idea of right, proves that, although it may be slumbering, there is, notwithstanding, to be found in man a still higher natural moral capacity by the aid of which he will in time gain the mastery over the evil principle in his nature, the existence of which he is unable to deny. And he hopes the same of others; for otherwise the word "right" would never be uttered by states who wish to wage war, unless to deride it like the Gallic Prince who declared:—"The privilege which nature gives the strong is that the weak must obey them."

The method by which states prosecute their rights can never be by process of law—as it is where there is an external tribunal—but only by war. Through this means, however, and its favourable issue, victory, the question of right is never decided. A treaty of peace makes, it may be, an end to the war of the moment, but not to the conditions of war which at any time may afford a new pretext for opening hostilities; and this we cannot exactly condemn as unjust, because under these conditions everyone is his own judge. Notwithstanding, not quite the same rule applies to states according to the law of nations as holds good of individuals in a lawless condition according to the law of nature, namely, "that they ought to advance out of this condition." This is so, because, as states, they have already within themselves a legal constitution, and have therefore advanced beyond the stage at which others, in accordance with their ideas of right, can force them to come under a wider legal constitution. Meanwhile, however, reason, from her throne of the supreme law-giving moral power, absolutely condemns war as a morally lawful proceeding, and makes a state of peace, on the other hand, an immediate duty. Without a compact between the nations, however, this state of peace cannot be established or assured. Hence there must be an alliance of a particular kind which we may call a covenant of peace (*foedus pacificum*), which would differ from a treaty of peace (*pactum pacis*) in this respect, that the latter merely puts an end to one war, while the former would seek to put an end to war for ever. This alliance does not aim at the gain of any power whatsoever of the state, but merely at the preservation and security of the freedom of the state for itself and of other allied states at the same time. The latter do not, however, require, for this reason, to submit themselves like individuals in the state of nature to public laws and coercion. The practicability or objective reality of this idea of federation which is to extend gradually over all states and so lead to perpetual peace can be shrewn. For, if Fortune ordains that a powerful and enlightened people should form a republic,—which by its very nature is inclined to perpetual peace—this would serve as a centre of federal union for other states wishing to join, and thus secure conditions of freedom among the states in accordance with the idea of the law of nations. Gradually, through different unions of this kind, the federation would extend further and further.

It is quite comprehensible that a people should say:—"There shall be no war among us, for we shall form ourselves into a state, that is to say, constitute for ourselves a supreme legislative, administrative, and judicial power which will settle our disputes peaceably." But if this state says:—"There shall be no war between me and other states, although I recognise no supreme law-giving power which will secure me my rights and whose rights I will guarantee;" then it is not at all clear upon what grounds I could base my confidence in my right, unless it were the substitute for that compact on which civil society is based—namely, free federation which reason must necessarily connect with the idea of the law of nations, if indeed any meaning is to be left in that concept at all.

There is no intelligible meaning in the idea of the law of nations as giving a right to make war; for that must be a right to decide what is just, not in accordance with universal, external laws limiting the freedom of each individual, but by means

of one-sided maxims applied by force. We must then understand by this that men of such ways of thinking are quite justly served, when they destroy one another, and thus find perpetual peace in the wide grave which covers all the abominations of acts of violence as well as the authors of such deeds. For states, in their relation to one another, there can be, according to reason, no other way of advancing from that lawless condition which unceasing war implies, than by giving up their savage lawless freedom, just as individual men have done, and yielding to the coercion of public laws. Thus they can form a State of nations (*civitas gentium*), one, too, which will be ever increasing and would finally embrace all the peoples of the earth. States, however, in accordance with their understanding of the law of nations, by no means desire this, and therefore reject *in hypothesi* what is correct *in thesi*. Hence, instead of the positive idea of a world-republic, if all is not to be lost, only the negative substitute for it, a federation averting war, maintaining its ground and ever extending over the world may stop the current of this tendency to war and shrinking from the control of law. But even then there will be a constant danger that this propensity may break out.

"Furor impius intus—fremit horridus ore cruento." (Virgil.)

Third Definitive Article of Perpetual Peace

III. "The rights of men, as citizens of the world, shall be limited to the conditions of universal hospitality."

We are speaking here, as in the previous articles, not of philanthropy, but of right; and in this sphere hospitality signifies the claim of a stranger entering foreign territory to be treated by its owner without hostility. The latter may send him away again, if this can be done without causing his death; but, so long as he conducts himself peaceably, he must not be treated as an enemy. It is not a right to be treated as a guest to which the stranger can lay claim—a special friendly compact on his behalf would be required to make him for a given time an actual inmate—but he has a right of visitation. This right to present themselves to society belongs to all mankind in virtue of our common right of possession on the surface of the earth on which, as it is a globe, we cannot be infinitely scattered, and must in the end reconcile ourselves to existence side by side: at the same time, originally no one individual had more right than another to live in any one particular spot. Uninhabitable portions of the surface, ocean and desert, split up the human community, but in such a way that ships and camels—"the ship of the desert"—make it possible for men to come into touch with one another across these unappropriated regions and to take advantage of our common claim to the face of the earth with a view to a possible intercommunication. The inhospitality of the inhabitants of certain sea coasts—as, for example, the coast of Barbary—in plundering ships in neighbouring seas or making slaves of ship-wrecked mariners; or the behaviour of the Arab Bedouins in the deserts, who think that proximity to nomadic tribes constitutes a right to rob, is thus contrary to the law of nature. This right to hospitality, however—that is to say, the privilege of strangers arriving on foreign soil—does not amount to more than what is implied in a permission to make an attempt at intercourse with the original inhabitants. In this way far distant territories may enter into peaceful relations with one another. These relations may at last come under the public control of law, and thus the human race may be brought nearer the realisation of a cosmopolitan constitution.

Let us look now, for the sake of comparison, at the inhospitable behaviour of the civilised nations, especially the commercial states of our continent. The injustice which they exhibit on visiting foreign lands and races—this being equivalent in their eyes to conquest—is such as to fill us with horror. America, the negro countries, the Spice Islands, the Cape etc. were, on being discovered, looked upon as countries which belonged to nobody; for the native inhabitants were reckoned as nothing.

In Hindustan, under the pretext of intending to establish merely commercial depots, the Europeans introduced foreign troops; and, as a result, the different states of Hindustan were stirred up to far-spreading wars. Oppression of the natives followed, famine, insurrection, perfidy and all the rest of the litany of evils which can afflict mankind.

China and Japan (Nipon) which had made an attempt at receiving guests of this kind, have now taken a prudent step. Only to a single European people, the Dutch, has China given the right of access to her shores (but not of entrance into the country), while Japan has granted both these concessions; but at the same time they exclude the Dutch who enter, as if they were prisoners, from social intercourse with the inhabitants. The worst, or from the standpoint of ethical judgment the best, of all this is that no satisfaction is derived from all this violence, that all these trading companies stand on the verge of ruin, that the Sugar Islands, that seat of the most horrible and deliberate slavery, yield no real profit, but only have their use indirectly and for no very praiseworthy object—namely, that of furnishing men to be trained as sailors for the men-of-war and thereby contributing to the carrying on of war in Europe. And this has been done by nations who make a great ado about their piety, and who, while they are quite ready to commit injustice, would like, in their orthodoxy, to be considered among the elect.

The intercourse, more or less close, which has been everywhere steadily increasing between the nations of the earth, has now extended so enormously that a violation of right in one part of the world is felt all over it. Hence the idea of a cosmopolitan right is no fantastical, high-flown notion of right, but a complement of the unwritten code of law—constitutional as well as international law—necessary for the public rights of mankind in general and thus for the realisation of perpetual peace. For only by endeavouring to fulfil the conditions laid down by this cosmopolitan law can we flatter ourselves that we are gradually approaching that ideal.

FIRST SUPPLEMENT

Concerning the Guarantee of Perpetual Peace

This guarantee is given by no less a power than the great artist nature (*natura dædala rerum*) in whose mechanical course is clearly exhibited a predetermined design to make harmony spring from human discord, even against the will of man. Now this design, although called Fate when looked upon as the compelling force of a cause, the laws of whose operation are unknown to us, is, when considered as the purpose manifested in the course of nature, called Providence, the deep lying wisdom of a Higher Cause, directing itself towards the ultimate practical end of the human race and predetermining the course of things with a view to its realisation. This Providence we do not, it is true, perceive in the cunning contrivances [*Kunstanstalten*] of nature; nor can we even conclude from the fact of their existence that it is there; but, as in every relation between the form of things and their final cause, we can, and must, supply the thought of a Higher Wisdom, in order that we may be able to form an idea of the possible existence of these products after the analogy of human works of art [*Kunsthandlungen*]. The representation to ourselves of the relation and agreement of these formations of nature to the moral purpose for which they were made and which reason directly prescribes to us, is an Idea, it is true, which is in theory superfluous; but in practice it is dogmatic, and its objective reality is well established. Thus we see, for example, with regard to the ideal of perpetual peace, that it is our duty to make use of the mechanism of nature for the realisation of that end. Moreover, in a case like this where we are interested merely in the theory and not in the religious question, the use of the word "nature" is more appropriate than that of "providence," in view of the limitations of human reason, which, in considering the relation of effects to their causes, must keep within the limits of possible experience. And the term "nature" is also less presumptuous than the other. To speak of a Providence knowable by us would be boldly to put on the wings of Icarus in order to draw near to the mystery of its unfathomable purpose.

Before we determine the surety given by nature more exactly, we must first look at what ultimately makes this guarantee of peace necessary—the circumstances in which nature has carefully placed the actors in her great theatre. In the next place, we shall proceed to consider the manner in which she gives this surety.

The provisions she has made are as follows: (1) she has taken care that men *can* live in all parts of the world; (2) she has scattered them by means of war in all directions, even into the most inhospitable regions, so that these too might be populated; (3) by this very means she has forced them to enter into relations more or less controlled by law. It is surely wonderful that, on the cold wastes round the Arctic Ocean, there is always to be found moss for the reindeer to scrape out from under the snow, the reindeer itself either serving as food or to draw the sledge of the Ostiak or Samoyedes. And salt deserts which would otherwise be left unutilised have the camel, which seems as if created for travelling in such lands. This evidence of design in things, however, is still more clear when we come to know that, besides the fur-clad animals of the shores of the Arctic Ocean, there are seals, walruses and whales whose flesh furnishes food and whose oil fire for the dwellers in these regions. But the providential care of nature excites our wonder above all, when we hear of the driftwood which is carried—whence no one knows—to these treeless shores: for without the aid of this material the natives could neither construct their craft, nor weapons, nor huts for shelter. Here too they have so much to do, making war against wild animals, that they live at peace with one another. But what drove them originally into these regions was probably nothing but war.

Of animals, used by us as instruments of war, the horse was the first which man learned to tame and domesticate during the period of the peopling of the earth; the elephant belongs to the late period of the luxury of states already established.

In the same way, the art of cultivating certain grasses called cereals—no longer known to us in their original form—and also the multiplication and improvement, by transplanting and grafting, of the original kinds of fruit—in Europe, probably only two species, the crab-apple and wild pear—could only originate under the conditions accompanying established states where the rights of property are assured. That is to say it would be after man, hitherto existing in lawless liberty, had advanced beyond the occupations of a hunter, a fisherman or a shepherd to the life of a tiller of the soil, when salt and iron were discovered,—to become, perhaps, the first articles of commerce between different peoples,—and were sought far and near. In this way the peoples would be at first brought into peaceful relation with one another, and so come to an understanding and the enjoyment of friendly intercourse, even with their most distant neighbours.

Now while nature provided that men could live on all parts of the earth, she also at the same time despotically willed that they *should* live everywhere on it, although against their own inclination and even although this imperative did not presuppose an idea of duty which would compel obedience to nature with the force of a moral law. But, to attain this end, she has chosen war. So we see certain peoples, widely separated, whose common descent is made evident by affinity in their languages. Thus, for instance, we find the Samoyedes on the Arctic Ocean, and again a people speaking a similar language on the Altai Mts., 200 miles [*Meilen*] off, between whom has pressed in a mounted tribe, warlike in character and of Mongolian origin, which has driven one branch of the race far from the other, into the most inhospitable regions where their own inclination would certainly not have carried them. In the same way, through the intrusion of the Gothic and Sarmatian tribes, the Finns in the most northerly regions of Europe, whom we call Laplanders, have been separated by as great a distance from the Hungarians, with whose language their own is allied. And what but war

can have brought the Esquimos to the north of America, a race quite distinct from those of that country and probably European adventurers of prehistoric times? And war too, nature's method of populating the earth, must have driven the Pescherais, in South America as far as Patagonia. War itself, however, is in need of no special stimulating cause, but seems engrafted in human nature, and is even regarded, as something noble in itself to which man is inspired by the love of glory apart from motives of self-interest. Hence, among the savages of America as well as those of Europe in the age of chivalry, martial courage is looked upon as of great value in itself, not merely when a war is going on, as is reasonable enough, but in order that there should be war: and thus war is often entered upon merely to exhibit this quality. So that an intrinsic dignity is held to attach to war in itself, and even philosophers eulogise it as an ennobling, refining influence on humanity, unmindful of the Greek proverb, "War is evil, in so far as it makes more bad people than it takes away."

So much, then, of what nature does for her own ends with regard to the human race as members of the animal world. Now comes the question which touches the essential points in this design of a perpetual peace:—"What does nature do in this respect with reference to the end which man's own reason sets before him as a duty? and consequently what does she do to further the realisation of his moral purpose? How does she guarantee that what man, by the laws of freedom, ought to do and yet fails to do, he will do, without any infringement of his freedom by the compulsion of nature and that, moreover, this shall be done in accordance with the three forms of public right—constitutional or political law, international law and cosmopolitan law?" When I say of nature that she *wills* that this or that should take place, I do not mean that she imposes upon us the duty to do it—for only the free, unrestrained, practical reason can do that—but that she does it herself, whether we will or not. *"Fata volentem ducunt, nolentem trahunt."*

1. Even if a people were not compelled through internal discord to submit to the restraint of public laws, war would bring this about, working from without. For, according to the contrivance of nature which we have mentioned, every people finds another tribe in its neighbourhood, pressing upon it in such a manner that it is compelled to form itself internally into a state to be able to defend itself as a power should. Now the republican constitution is the only one which is perfectly adapted to the rights of man, but it is also the most difficult to establish and still more to maintain. So generally is this recognised that people often say the members of a republican state would require to be angels, because men, with their self-seeking propensities, are not fit for a constitution of so sublime a form. But now nature comes to the aid of the universal, reason-derived will which, much as we honour it, is in practice powerless. And this she does, by means of these very self-seeking propensities, so that it only depends—and so much lies within the power of man—on a good organisation of the state for their forces to be so pitted against one another, that the one may check the destructive activity of the other or neutralise its effect. And hence, from the standpoint of reason, the result will be the same as if both forces did not exist, and each individual is compelled to be, if not a morally good man, yet at least a good citizen. The problem of the formation of the state, hard as it may sound, is not insoluble, even for a race of devils, granted that they have intelligence. It may be put thus:—"Given a multitude of rational beings who, in a body, require general laws for their own preservation, but each of whom, as an individual, is secretly inclined to exempt himself from this restraint: how are we to order their affairs and how establish for them a constitution such that, although their private dispositions may be really antagonistic, they may yet so act as a check upon one another, that, in their public relations, the effect is the same as if they had no such evil sentiments." Such a problem must be capable of solution. For it deals, not with the moral reformation of mankind, but only with the mechanism of nature; and the problem is to learn how this mechanism of nature can be applied to men, in order so to regulate the antagonism of conflicting interests in a people that they may even compel one another to submit to compulsory laws and thus necessarily bring about the state of peace in which laws have force. We can see, in states actually existing, although very imperfectly organised, that, in externals, they already approximate very nearly to what the Idea of right prescribes, although the principle of morality is certainly not the cause. A good political constitution, however, is not to be expected as a result of progress in morality; but rather, conversely, the good moral condition of a nation is to be looked for, as one of the first fruits of such a constitution. Hence the mechanism of nature, working through the self-seeking propensities of man (which of course counteract one another in their external effects), may be used by reason as a means of making way for the realisation of her own purpose, the empire of right, and, as far as is in the power of the state, to promote and secure in this way internal as well as external peace. We may say, then, that it is the irresistible will of nature that right shall at last get the supremacy. What one here fails to do will be accomplished in the long run, although perhaps with much inconvenience to us. As Bouterwek says, "If you bend the reed too much it breaks: he who would do too much does nothing."

2. The idea of international law presupposes the separate existence of a number of neighbouring and independent states; and, although such a condition of things is in itself already a state of war, (if a federative union of these nations does not prevent the outbreak of hostilities) yet, according to the Idea of reason, this is better than that all the states should be merged into one under a power which has gained the ascendancy over its neighbours and gradually become a universal monarchy. For the wider the sphere of their jurisdiction, the more laws lose in force; and soulless despotism, when it has choked the seeds of good, at last sinks into anarchy. Nevertheless it is the desire of every state, or of its ruler, to attain to

a permanent condition of peace in this very way; that is to say, by subjecting the whole world as far as possible to its sway. But nature wills it otherwise. She employs two means to separate nations, and prevent them from intermixing: namely, the differences of language and of religion. These differences bring with them a tendency to mutual hatred, and furnish pretexts for waging war. But, none the less, with the growth of culture and the gradual advance of men to greater unanimity of principle, they lead to concord in a state of peace which, unlike the despotism we have spoken of, (the churchyard of freedom) does not arise from the weakening of all forces, but is brought into being and secured through the equilibrium of these forces in their most active rivalry.

3. As nature wisely separates nations which the will of each state, sanctioned even by the principles of international law, would gladly unite under its own sway by stratagem or force; in the same way, on the other hand, she united nations whom the principle of a cosmopolitan right would not have secured against violence and war. And this union she brings about through an appeal to their mutual interests. The commercial spirit cannot co-exist with war, and sooner or later it takes possession of every nation. For, of all the forces which lie at the command of a state, the power of money is probably the most reliable. Hence states find themselves compelled—not, it is true, exactly from motives of morality—to further the noble end of peace and to avert war, by means of mediation, wherever it threatens to break out, just as if they had made a permanent league for this purpose. For great alliances with a view to war can, from the nature of things, only very rarely occur, and still more seldom succeed.

In this way nature guarantees the coming of perpetual peace, through the natural course of human propensities: not indeed with sufficient certainty to enable us to prophesy the future of this ideal theoretically, but yet clearly enough for practical purposes. And thus this guarantee of nature makes it a duty that we should labour for this end, an end which is no mere chimera.

SECOND SUPPLEMENT

A Secret Article for Perpetual Peace

A secret article in negotiations concerning public rights is, when looked at objectively or with regard to the meaning of the term, a contradiction. When we view it, however, from the subjective standpoint, with regard to the character and condition of the person who dictates it, we see that it might quite well involve some private consideration, so that he would regard it as hazardous to his dignity to acknowledge such an article as originating from him.

The only article of this kind is contained in the following proposition:—"The opinions of philosophers, with regard to the conditions of the possibility of a public peace, shall be taken into consideration by states armed for war."

It seems, however, to be derogatory to the dignity of the legislative authority of a state—to which we must of course attribute all wisdom—to ask advise from subjects (among whom stand philosophers) about the rules of its behaviour to other states. At the same time, it is very advisable that this should be done. Hence the state will silently invite suggestion for this purpose, while at the same time keeping the fact secret. This amounts to saying that the state will allow philosophers to discuss freely and publicly the universal principles governing the conduct of war and establishment of peace; for they will do this of their own accord, if no prohibition is laid upon them. The arrangement between states, on this point, does not require that a special agreement should be made, merely for this purpose; for it is already involved in the obligation imposed by the universal reason of man which gives the moral law. We would not be understood to say that the state must give a preference to the principles of the philosopher, rather than to the opinions of the jurist, the representative of state authority; but only that he should be heard. The latter, who has chosen for a symbol the scales of right and the sword of justice, generally uses that sword not merely to keep off all outside influences from the scales; for, when one pan of the balance will not go down, he throws his sword into it; and then *Væ victis!* The jurist, not being a moral philosopher, is under the greatest temptation to do this, because it is his business only to apply existing laws and not to investigate whether these are not themselves in need of improvement; and this actually lower function of his profession he looks upon as the nobler, because it is linked to power (as is the case also in both the other faculties, theology and medicine). Philosophy occupies a very low position compared with this combined power. So that it is said, for example, that she is the handmaid of theology; and the same has been said of her position with regard to law and medicine. It is not quite clear, however, "whether she bears the torch before these gracious ladies, or carries the train."

That kings should philosophise, or philosophers become kings, is not to be expected. But neither is it to be desired; for the possession of power is inevitably fatal to the free exercise of reason. But it is absolutely indispensable, for their enlightenment as to the full significance of their vocations, that both kings and sovereign nations, which rule themselves in accordance with laws of equality, should not allow the class of philosophers to disappear, nor forbid the expression of their opinions, but should allow them to speak openly. And since this class of men, by their very nature, are incapable of instigating rebellion or forming unions for purposes of political agitation, they should not be suspected of propagandism.

EDMUND BURKE

~

INTRODUCTION

BURLEIGH T. WILKINS

Edmund Burke (1729–1797), was born in Dublin, Ireland, the son of a solicitor. He attended Trinity College in Dublin, and graduated in 1748. He began the study of law at the Middle Temple in London in 1750, but he did not complete his studies. He embarked instead on a literary career and formed friendships with a number of prominent literary figures, including Dr. Samuel Johnson. In 1757 he became secretary to Lord Rockingham, which was the beginning of a long, distinguished, and controversial political career. Burke represented the city of Bristol in Parliament, but following a defeat for reelection, he was given a seat from a safe "pocket borough" by Lord Rockingham. Burke was a leader of the Rockingham element of the Whig Party, and he was active on behalf of his native Ireland, in the prolonged impeachment proceedings against Warren Hastings, and as a critic of the French Revolution and its English admirers.

Burke's most famous works are a satire of Lord Bolingbrooke, *A Vindication of Natural Society* (1756), and *A Philosophical Inquiry into the Origins of Our Ideas of the Sublime and Beautiful* (1757), which influenced Kant's aesthetics, and the classic *Reflections on the Revolution in France* (1790).

Critics of conservatism often complain of being unable to isolate a distinctive body of conservative doctrine, but perhaps it is possible to discover a cohesive set of attitudes or beliefs shared by most if not all conservatives. Here it may be useful to regard Edmund Burke as the quintessential conservative. One conservative attitude Burke exemplifies is the tendency not so much to ignore principle as to place as narrow a construction on principle as possible. With his training in law and his parliamentary experience, Burke preferred to speak in terms of constitutional principles. Burke was a champion of the American colonists in their dispute with the British government, but unlike Jefferson who linked the dispute to the inalienable rights of man, Burke was content to insist that the Americans were simply defending their rights as Englishmen. Also, although Burke was an heir to the English Revolution of 1688 to 1689, he chose to interpret it as involving "a small and temporary deviation" from the strict order of regular hereditary succession.

Another conservative attitude Burke illustrates lies in his belief that "metaphysical" speculation, or the dogmatic assertion of "abstract" rights, is often pernicious, whether in the British government's insistence on its rights of taxation over the American colonies or in the French Third Estate's insistence on its rights against the monarchy and the aristocracy, Nowhere was the harmful effect more evident to Burke than in the French Declaration of the Rights of Man. Burke's condemnation of the Rights of Man was so harsh and sweeping that some scholars have concluded Burke believed only in historical rights resulting from orderly, constitutional change, but this is not the case. Like Locke, Burke believed that men have natural rights to life, liberty, and property, but he affirmed that the "real" rights of man lie in the advantages that civil society makes possible. He cautioned that the effective exercise of these rights depends very much on a proper understanding of the historical context and on a sense of prudence. Burke strongly opposed contemporary English proposals for universal manhood suffrage and for greater freedom for the dissenters on the ground that political and religious liberties were adequately provided for under existing laws.

In situations where no one could reasonably view governmental misconduct as simply an interruption or denial of historical constitutional rights, Burke appealed to the principles of natural law, as he did eloquently and repeatedly in the (unsuccessful) impeachment proceedings against Warren Hastings of the East India Company. Here Burke defended India against what he regarded as despotism and misrule by Englishmen, and, since no one could plausibly maintain that the people of India were being denied their rights as Englishmen, Burke rested his case squarely on the principles of natural law. Since Burke's commitment to the natural law has been questioned, it is important to note that Burke had read every defender of the natural law, with the possible exception of Aquinas, and as a devout Anglican Burke would have found it difficult to ignore the natural law tradition of the Anglican Church.

Religious faith is another attitude that Burke shares with most but not all conservatives. Burke saw the natural moral law as that portion of the divine law that is accessible to human reason and is applicable to all men. However, he believed that the ways in which it is applicable depend greatly on the historical circumstances of a people. Arrangements that promote the peace, prosperity, and liberty of a people depend on many variables, including, he thought, the participation of Divine Providence.

Another conservative attitude we find in Burke lies in his belief that a country consists of complementary and not opposed social classes or groups. Burke saw the legislator not as a spokesman for the particular interests of a given constituency but as a representative of the long-term interests of the nation as a whole. He saw no opposition between land and commerce, which helps explain the difficulty Marxists have experienced over whether to classify Burke as a champion of a dying feudal order or of an emerging commercial class. What Burke did believe in was the free market ideas of Adam Smith, but he also stressed the importance of charity.

Although he sometimes condemned factions, Burke, unlike James Madison, did not regard society as being typically subject to the pressures of opposed factions, and we find in Burke nothing like the American idea of a system of checks and balances in a federal system as a means of offsetting the divisiveness of faction.

Burke's belief in the essential harmony of classes and groups in society was subject to one important caveat. He distrusted intellectuals as a group, especially when they were no longer moored (as he had been) to an aristocratic patron or to the Church. In all matters of practical reason, Burke believed it important to remember (as one of our contemporary political philosophers has put it) that the view we adopt is always a view from somewhere, a fact that he believed his enemies, such as the French *philosophes*, failed to comprehend. Burke himself can be regarded as attempting to explain and justify the practices of what he believed to be on the whole a just constitutional regime. Although he was reluctant to appeal to first principles, this was due in large part to his belief that these principles had found satisfactory expression in the English constitutional monarchy. This may, of course, strike us as premature self-congratulation, but what is enduring perhaps is Burke's insight that, given the frailties of human nature and the vagaries of circumstance, we may never enjoy a point of view from which we can correctly say that a given society is entirely just. Although Burke believed the natural rights of man are "sacred," he rejected the view that the individuals who possess these rights are isolated and atomic. For Burke, an individual person is far more than the "rights bearer" that has been the focus of modern liberal thought. He is a member of a society with a common culture and set of traditions, and he has duties arising from his position in society.

A recent conservative critic has complained that when a tradition becomes Burkian it is already dead or dying, but this is because of the exaggerated importance he has attached to Burke's contrasts between tradition and reason and between the stability of tradition and conflict. For Burke, tradition, in a viable constitutional regime, is the product of successful conflict resolutions over many generations, and neither death nor stagnation need occur so long as we have change and piecemeal reform in which practical reason does not neglect the historical circumstances of a people. Burke's cherished ideas of prejudice, prescription, and presumption have the function of ensuring that conflict does not override the stability that tradition provides. Prejudice on Burke's view is the latent wisdom found in many but not all the opinions of a people; prescription is the recognition that rights may be established by the long exercise of their corresponding powers; and presumption is a lawyerly way of saying that rights based on prescription should prevail unless there is overwhelming evidence that they should be altered. This is Burke's (and Hume's) way of ensuring that change will not be at the expense of ordered liberty.

The definitive political biography of Burke is Carl B. Cone's two-volume *Burke and the Nature of Politics* (Lexington: University of Kentucky Press, 1957 and 1964). Two natural law interpretations of Burke that differ on important points are Peter J. Stanlis, *Edmund Burke and the Natural Law* (Ann Arbor: University of Michigan Press, 1958), and Burleigh Taylor Wilkins, *The Problem of Burke's Political Philosophy* (Oxford: Oxford University Press, 1967). For a Marxist critique of Burke, see C. B. MacPherson, *Edmund Burke* (Oxford: Oxford University Press, 1980). See also J. G. A. Pocock's *Introduction to Edmund Burke: Reflections on the Revolution in France* (Indianapolis: Hackett Publishing Company, 1987), and Alasdair MacIntyre, *After Virtue* (Notre Dame, Ind.: Notre Dame University Press, 1984).

Reflections on the Revolution in France

It looks to me as if I were in a great crisis, not of the affairs of France alone, but of all Europe, perhaps of more than Europe. All circumstances taken together, the French Revolution is the most astonishing that has hitherto happened in the world. The most wonderful things are brought about in many instances by means the most absurd and ridiculous; in the most ridiculous modes; and, apparently, by the most contemptible instruments. Everything seems out of nature in this strange chaos of levity and ferocity, and of all sorts of crimes jumbled together with all sorts of follies. In viewing this monstrous tragiccomic scene, the most opposite passions necessarily succeed, and sometimes mix with each other in the mind; alternate contempt and indignation; alternate laughter and tears; alternate scorn and horror.

It cannot, however, be denied, that to some this strange scene appeared in quite another point of view. Into them it inspired no other sentiments than those of exultation and rapture. They saw nothing in what has been done in France, but a firm and temperate exertion of freedom: so consistent, on the whole, with morals and with piety as to make it deserving not only of the secular applause of dashing Machiavellian politicians, but to render it a fit theme for all the devout effusions of sacred eloquence.

On the forenoon of the 4th of November last, Doctor Richard Price, a nonconforming minister of eminence, preached at the dissenting meeting-house of the Old Jewry, to his club or society, a very extraordinary miscellaneous sermon, in which there are some good moral and religious sentiments, and not ill expressed, mixed up in a sort of porridge of various political opinions and reflections; but the Revolution in France is the grand ingredient in the cauldron. . . .

His doctrines affect our constitution in its vital parts. He tells the Revolution Society in this political sermon, that his Majesty "is almost the *only* lawful king in the world, because the *only* one who owes his crown to the *choice of his people.*" . . .

This doctrine, as applied to the prince now on the British throne, either is nonsense, and therefore neither true or false, or it affirms a most unfounded, dangerous, illegal, and unconstitutional position. According to this spiritual doctor of politics, if his Majesty does not owe his crown to the choice of his people, he is no *lawful king*. Now nothing can be more untrue than that the crown of this kingdom is so held by his Majesty. Therefore if you follow their rule, the king of Great Britain, who most certainly does not owe his high office to any form of popular election, is in no respect better than the rest of the gang of usurpers, who reign, or rather rob, all over the face of this miserable world, without any sort of right or title to the allegiance of their people. . . .

If you admit this interpretation, how does their idea of election differ from our idea of inheritance? And how does the settlement of the crown in the Brunswick line derived from James the First come to legalize our monarchy, rather than that of any of the neighboring countries? At some time or other, to be sure, all the beginners of dynasties were chosen by those who called them to govern. There is ground enough for the opinion that all the kingdoms of Europe were, at a remote period, elective, with more or fewer limitations in the objects of choice. But whatever kings might have been here, or elsewhere, a thousand years ago, or in whatever manner the ruling dynasties of England or France may have begun, the king of Great Britain is at this day king by a fixed rule of succession, according to the laws of his country; and whilst the legal conditions of the compact of sovereignty are performed by him (as they are performed), he holds his crown in contempt of the choice of the Revolution Society, who have not a single vote for a king amongst them, either individually or collectively; though I make no doubt they would soon erect themselves into an electoral college, if things were ripe to give effect to their claim. His Majesty's heirs and successors, each in his time and order, will come to the crown with the same contempt of their choice with which his Majesty has succeeded to that he wears.

Whatever may be the success of evasion in explaining away the gross error of *fact*, which supposes that his Majesty (though he holds it in concurrence with the wishes) owes his crown to the choice of his people; yet nothing can evade their full explicit declaration, concerning the principle of a right in the people to choose; which right is directly maintained, and tenaciously adhered to. All the oblique insinuations concerning election bottom in this proposition, and are referable to it. Lest the foundation of the king's exclusive legal title should pass for a mere rant of adulatory freedom, the political divine proceeds dogmatically to assert, that, by the principles of the Revolution, the people of England have acquired three fundamental rights, all which, with him, compose one system, and lie together in one short sentence; namely, that we have acquired a right,

1. "To choose our own governors."
2. "To cashier them for misconduct."
3. "To frame a government for ourselves."

This new, and hitherto unheard-of, bill of rights, though made in the name of the whole people, belongs to those gentlemen and their faction only. The body of the people of England have no share in it. They utterly disclaim it. They will resist the practical assertion of it with their lives and fortunes. They are bound to do so by the laws of their country, made at the time of that very Revolution which is appealed to in favor of the fictitious rights claimed by the society which abuses its name.

These gentlemen of the Old Jewry, in all their reasonings on the Revolution of 1688, have a Revolution which happened in England about forty years before, and the late French Revolution, so much before their eyes, and in their hearts, that they are constantly confounding all the three together. It is necessary that we should separate what they confound. We must recall their erring fancies to the acts of the Revolution which we revere, for the discovery of its true *principles*. If the *principles* of the Revolution of 1688 are anywhere to be found, it is in the statute called the *Declaration of Right*. In that most wise, sober, and considerate declaration, drawn up by great lawyers and great statesmen, and not by warm and inexperienced enthusiasts, not one word is said, nor one suggestion made, of a general right "to choose our own *governers;* to cashier them for misconduct; and to *form* a government for *ourselves*." . . .

You will observe, that from Magna Charta to the Declaration of Right, it has been the uniform policy of our constitution to claim and assert our liberties, as an *entailed inheritance* derived to us from our forefathers, and to be transmitted to our posterity; as an estate specially belonging to the people of this kingdom without any reference whatever to any other more general or prior right. By this means our constitution preserves a unity in so great a diversity of its parts. We have an inheritable crown; an inheritable peerage; and a House of Commons and a people inheriting privileges, franchises, and liberties, from a long line of ancestors.

This policy appears to me to be the result of profound reflection; or rather the happy effect of following nature, which is wisdom without reflection, and above it. A spirit of innovation is generally the result of a selfish temper and confined views. People will not look forward to posterity, who never look backward to their ancestors. Besides, the people of England well know, that the idea of inheritance furnishes a sure principle of conservation, and a sure principle of transmission; without at all excluding a principle of improvement. It leaves acquisition free; but it secures what it acquires. Whatever advantages are obtained by a state proceeding on these maxims, are locked fast as in a sort of family settlement; grasped as in a kind of mortmain for ever. By a constitutional policy, working after the pattern of nature, we receive, we hold, we transmit our government and our privileges, in the same manner in which we enjoy and transmit our property and our lives. The institutions of policy, the goods of fortune, the gifts of providence, are handed down to us, and from us, in the same course and order. Our political system is placed in a just correspondence and symmetry with the order of the world, and with the mode of extensive decreed to a permanent body composed of transitory parts; wherein, by the disposition of a stupendous wisdom, moulding together the great mysterious incorporation of the human race, the whole, at one time, is never old, or middle-aged, or young, but, in a condition of unchangeable constancy, moves on through the varied tenor of perpetual decay, fall, renovation, and progression. Thus, by preserving the method of nature in the conduct of the state, in what we improve, we are never wholly new; in what we retain, we are never wholly obsolete. By adhering in this manner and on those principles to our forefathers, we are guided not by the superstition of antiquarians, but by the spirit of philosophic analogy. In this choice of inheritance we have given to our frame of polity the image of a relation in blood; binding up the constitution of our country with our dearest domestic ties; adopting our fundamental laws into the bosom of our family affections; keeping inseparable, and cherishing with the warmth of all their combined and mutually reflected charities, our state, our hearths, our sepulchres, and our altars.

Through the same plan of a conformity to nature in our artificial institutions, and by calling in the aid of her unerring and powerful instincts, to fortify the fallible and feeble contrivances of our reason, we have derived several other, and

those no small benefits, from considering our liberties in the light of an inheritance. Always acting as if in the presence of canonized forefathers, the spirit of freedom, leading in itself to misrule and excess, is tempered with an awful gravity. This idea of a liberal descent inspires us with a sense of habitual native dignity, which prevents that upstart insolence almost inevitably adhering to and disgracing those who are the first acquirers of any distinction. By this means our liberty becomes a noble freedom. It carries an imposing and majestic aspect. It has a pedigree and illustrious ancestors. It has its bearings, and its ensigns armorial. It has its gallery of portraits; its monumental inscriptions; its records, evidences, and titles. We procure reverence to our civil institutions on the principle upon which nature teaches us to revere individual men; on account of their age, and on account of those from whom they are descended. All you sophisters cannot produce anything better adapted to preserve a rational and manly freedom than the course that we have pursued, who have chosen our nature rather than our speculations, our breasts rather than our inventions, for the great conservatories and magazines of our rights and privileges.

You might, if you pleased, have profited of our example, and have given to your recovered freedom a correspondent dignity. Your privileges, though discontinued, were not lost to memory. Your constitution, it is true, whilst you were out of possession, suffered waste and dilapidation; but you possessed in some parts the walls, and, in all, the foundations, of a noble and venerable castle. You might have repaired those walls; you might have built on those old foundations. Your constitution was suspended before it was perfected; but you had the elements of a constitution very nearly as good as could be wished. In your old states you possessed that variety of parts corresponding with the various descriptions of which your community was happily composed; you had all the combination, and all that opposition of interests, you had that action and counteraction, which, in the natural and in the political world, from the reciprocal struggle of discordant powers, draws out the harmony of the universe. These opposed and conflicting interests, which you considered as so great a blemish in your old and in our present constitution, interpose a salutary check to all precipitate resolutions. They render deliberation a matter not of choice, but of necessity; they make all change a subject of *compromise*, which naturally begets moderation; they produce *temperaments* preventing the sore evil of harsh, crude, unqualified reformations; and rendering all the headlong exertions of arbitrary power, in the few or in the many, for ever impracticable. Through the diversity of members and interests, general liberty had as many securities as there were separate views in the several orders; whilst by pressing down the whole by the weight of a real monarchy, the separate parts would have been prevented from warping and starting from their allotted places.

You had all these advantages in your ancient states; but you chose to act as if you had never been moulded into civil society, and had everything to begin anew. You began ill, because you began by despising everything that belonged to you. You set up your trade without a capital. If the last generations of your country appeared without much lustre in your eyes, you might have passed them by, and derived your claims from a more early race of ancestors. Under a pious predilection for those ancestors, your imaginations would have realized in them a standard of virtue and wisdom, beyond the vulgar practice of the hour: and you would have risen with the example to whose imitation you aspired. Respecting your forefathers, you would have been taught to respect yourselves. You would not have chosen to consider the French as a people of yesterday, as a nation of lowborn servile wretches until the emancipating year of 1789. . . .

Compute your gains: see what is got by those extravagant and presumptuous speculations which have taught your leaders to despise all their predecessors, and all their contemporaries, and even to despise themselves, until the moment in which they became truly despicable. By following those false lights, France has bought undisguised calamities at a higher price than any nation has purchased the most unequivocal blessings! France has bought poverty by crime! France has not sacrificed her virtue to her interest, but she has abandoned her interest, that she might prostitute her virtue. All other nations have begun the fabric of a new government, or the reformation of an old, by establishing originally, or by enforcing with greater exactness, some rites or other of religion. All other people have laid the foundations of civil freedom in severer manners, and a system of a more austere and masculine morality. France, when she let loose the reins of regal authority, doubled the license of a ferocious dissoluteness in manners, and of an insolent irreligion in opinions and practices; and has extended through all ranks of life, as if she were communicating some privilege, or laying open some secluded benefit, all the unhappy corruptions that usually were the disease of wealth and power. This is one of the new principles of equality in France. . . .

Believe me, Sir, those who attempt to level, never equalise. In all societies, consisting of various descriptions of citizens, some description must be uppermost. The levellers therefore only change and pervert the natural order of things; they load the edifice of society, by setting up in the air what the solidity of the structure requires to be on the ground. The associations of tailors and carpenters, of which the republic (of Paris, for instance) is composed, cannot be equal to the situation, into which, by the worst of usurpations, an usurpation on the prerogatives of nature, you attempt to force them.

The Chancellor of France at the opening of the States, said, in a tone of oratorical flourish, that all occupations were honourable. If he meant only, that no honest employment was disgraceful, he would not have gone beyond the truth. But in asserting that anything is honourable, we imply some distinction in its favor. The occupation of a hair-dresser, or of a working tallow-chandler, cannot be a matter of honor to any person—to say nothing of a number of other more servile employments. Such descriptions of men ought not to suffer oppression from the state; but the state suffers oppression, if such as they, either individually or collectively, are permitted to rule. In this you think you are combating prejudice, but you are at war with nature.

I do not, my dear Sir, conceive you to be of that sophistical, captious spirit, or of that uncandid dulness, as to require, for every general observation or sentiment, an explicit detail of the correctives and exceptions, which reason will presume to be included in all the general propositions which come from reasonable men. You do not imagine, that I wish to confine power, authority, and distinction to blood, and names, and titles. No, Sir. There is no qualification for government but virtue and wisdom, actual or presumptive. Wherever they are actually found, they have, in whatever state, condition, profession or trade, the passport of Heaven to human place and honor. Woe to the country which would madly and impiously reject the service of the talents and virtues, civil, military, or religious, that are given to grace and serve it; and would condemn to obscurity everything formed to diffuse lustre and glory around a state. Woe to that country too, that, passing into the opposite extreme, considers a low education, a mean contracted view of things, a sordid, mercenary occupation, as a preferable title to command. Everything ought to be open; but not indifferently to every man. No rotation; no appointment by lot; no mode of election operating in the spirit of sortition, or rotation, can be generally good in a government conversant in extensive objects. Because they have no tendency, direct or indirect, to select the man with a view to the duty, or to accommodate the one to the other. I do not hesitate to say, that the road to eminence and power, from obscure condition, ought not to be made too easy, nor a thing too much of course. If rare merit be the rarest of all rare things, it ought to pass through some sort of probation. The temple of honor ought to be seated on an eminence. If it be opened through virtue, let it be remembered too, that virtue is never tried but by some difficulty and some struggle.

Nothing is a due and adequate representation of a state, that does not represent its ability, as well as its property. But as ability is a vigorous and active principle, and as property is sluggish, inert, and timid, it never can be safe from the invasions of ability, unless it be, out of all proportion, predominant in the representation. It must be represented too in great masses of accumulation, or it is not rightly protected. The characteristic essence of property, formed out of the combined principles of its acquisition and conservation, is to be *unequal*. The great masses therefore which excite envy, and tempt rapacity, must be put out of the possibility of danger. Then they form a natural rampart about the lesser properties in all their gradations. The same quantity of property, which is by the natural course of things divided among many, has not the same operation. Its defensive power is weakened as it is diffused. In this diffusion each man's portion is less than what, in the eagerness of his desires, he may flatter himself to obtain by dissipating the accumulations of others. The plunder of the few would indeed give but a share inconceivably small in the distribution to the many. But the many are not capable of making this calculation; and those who lead them to rapine never intend this distribution. . . .

It is said, that twenty-four millions ought to prevail over two hundred thousand. True; if the constitution of a kingdom be a problem of arithmetic. This sort of discourse does well enough with the lamp-post for its second: to men who *may* reason calmly, it is ridiculous. The will of the many and their interest must very often differ; and great will be the difference when they make an evil choice. A government of five hundred country attorneys and obscure curates is not good for twenty-four millions of men, though it were chosen by eight-and-forty millions; nor is it the better for being guided by a dozen of persons of quality, who have betrayed their trust in order to obtain that power. At present, you seem in everything to have strayed out of the high road of nature. The property of France does not govern it. Of course property is destroyed, and rational liberty has no existence. All you have got for the present is a paper circulation and a stock-jobbing constitution: and as to the future, do you seriously think that the territory of France, upon the republican system of eighty-three independent municipalities (to say nothing of the parts that compose them), can ever be governed as one body, or can ever be set in motion by the impulse of one mind? When the National Assembly has completed its work, it will have accomplished its ruin. These commonwealths will not long bear a state of subjection to the republic of Paris. They will not bear that this one body should monopolize the captivity of the king, and the dominion over the Assembly calling itself national. Each will keep its own portion of the spoil of the church to itself; and it will not suffer either that spoil, or the more just fruits of their industry, or the natural produce of their soil, to be sent to swell the insolence, or pamper the luxury, of the mechanics of Paris. In this they will see none of the equality, under the pretence of which they have been tempted to throw off their allegiance to their sovereign, as well as the ancient constitution of their country. There can be no capital city in such a constitution as they have lately made. They have forgot, that when they framed democratic governments, they had virtually dismembered their country. The person, whom they persevere in calling king, has not power left to him by the hundredth part sufficient to hold together this collection of republics. The republic of Paris will endeavor indeed to complete the debauchery of the army, and illegally to perpetuate the Assembly, without resort to its constituents, as the means of continuing its

despotism. It will make efforts, by becoming the heart of a boundless paper circulation, to draw everything to itself; but in vain. All this policy in the end will appear as feeble as it is now violent.

. . .

Far am I from denying in theory, full as far is my heart from withholding in practice (if I were of power to give or to withhold), the *real* rights of men. In denying their false claims of right, I do not mean to injure those which are real, and are such as their pretended rights would totally destroy. If civil society be made for the advantage of man, all the advantages for which it is made become his right. It is an institution of beneficence; and law itself is only beneficence acting by a rule. Men have a right to live by that rule; they have a right to do justice, as between their fellows, whether their fellows are in politic function or in ordinary occupation. They have a right to the fruits of their industry; and to the means of making their industry fruitful. They have a right to the acquisitions of their parents; to the nourishment and improvement of their offspring; to instruction in life, and to consolation in death. Whatever each man can separately do, without trespassing upon others, he has a right to do for himself; and he has a right to a fair portion of all which society, with all its combinations of skill and force, can do in his favor. In this partnership all men have equal rights; but not to equal things. He that has but five shillings in the partnership, has as good a right to it, as he that has five hundred pounds has to his larger proportion. But he has not a right to an equal dividend in the product of the joint stock; and as to the share of power, authority, and direction which each individual ought to have in the management of the state, that I must deny to be amongst the direct original rights of man in civil society; for I have in my contemplation the civil social man, and no other. It is a thing to be settled by convention.

If civil society be the offspring of convention, that convention must be its law. That convention must limit and modify all the descriptions of constitution which are formed under it. Every sort of legislative, judicial, or executory power are its creatures. They can have no being in any other state of things; and how can any man claim, under the conventions of civil society, rights which do not so much as suppose its existence? Rights which are absolutely repugnant to it? One of the first motives to civil society, and which becomes one of its fundamental rules, is, *that no man should be judge in his own case.* By this each person has at once divested himself of the first fundamental right of uncovenanted man, that is, to judge for himself, and to assert his own cause. He abdicates all right to be his own governor. He inclusively, in a great measure, abandons the right of self-defence, the first law of nature. Men can not enjoy the rights of an uncivil and of a civil state together. That he may obtain justice, he gives up his right of determining what it is in points the most essential to him. That he may secure some liberty, he makes a surrender in trust of the whole of it.

Government is not made in virtue of natural rights, which may and do exist in total independence of it; and exist in much greater clearness, and in a much greater degree of abstract perfection: but their abstract perfection is their practical defect. By having a right to everything they want everything. Government is a contrivance of human wisdom to provide for human *wants.* Men have a right that these wants should be provided for by this wisdom. Among these wants is to be reckoned the want, out of civil society, of a sufficient restraint upon their passions. Society requires not only that the passions of individuals should be subjected, but that even in the mass and body, as well as in the individuals, the inclinations of men should frequently be thwarted, their will controlled, and their passions brought into subjection. This can only be done *by a power out of themselves;* and not, in the exercise of its function, subject to that will and to those passions which it is its office to bridle and subdue. In this sense the restraints on men, as well as their liberties, are to be reckoned among their rights. But

as the liberties and the restrictions vary with times and circumstances, and admit of infinite modifications, they cannot be settled upon any abstract rule; and nothing is so foolish as to discuss them upon that principle.

The moment you abate anything from the full rights of men, each to govern himself, and suffer any artificial, positive limitation upon those rights, from that moment the whole organization of government becomes a consideration of convenience. This it is which makes the constitution of a state, and the due distribution of its powers, a matter of the most delicate and complicated skill. It requires a deep knowledge of human nature and human necessities, and of the things which facilitate or obstruct the various ends, which are to be pursued by the mechanism of civil institutions. The state is to have recruits to its strength, and remedies to its distempers. What is the use of discussing a man's abstract right to food or medicine? The question is upon the method of procuring and administering them. In that deliberation I shall always advise to call in the aid of the farmer and the physician, rather than the professor of metaphysics.

The science of constructing a commonwealth, or renovating it, or reforming it, is, like every other experimental science, not to be taught *à priori.* Nor is it a short experience that can instruct us in that practical science; because the real effects of moral causes are not always immediate; but that which in the first instance is prejudicial may be excellent in its remoter operation; and its excellence may arise even from the ill effects it produces in the beginning. The reverse also happens: and very plausible schemes, with very pleasing commencements, have often shameful and lamentable conclusions. In states there are often some obscure and almost latent causes, things which appear at first view of little moment, on which a very great part of its prosperity or adversity may most essentially depend. The science of government being therefore so practical in itself, and intended for such practical purposes, a matter which requires experience, and even more experience than any person can gain in his whole life, however sagacious and observing he may be, it is with infinite caution that any man ought to venture upon pulling down an edifice, which has answered in any tolerable degree for ages the common purposes of society, or on building it up again, without having models and patterns of approved utility before his eyes.

These metaphysic rights entering into common life, like rays of light which pierce into a dense medium, are, by the laws of nature, refracted from their straight line. Indeed in the gross and complicated mass of human passions and concerns, the primitive rights of men undergo such a variety of refractions and reflections, that it becomes absurd to talk of them as if they continued in the simplicity of their original direction. The nature of man is intricate; the objects of society are of the greatest possible complexity: and therefore no simple disposition or direction or power can be suitable either to man's nature, or to the quality of his affairs. When I hear the simplicity of contrivance aimed at and boasted of in any new political constitutions, I am at no loss to decide that the artificers are grossly ignorant of their trade, or totally negligent of their duty. The simple governments are fundamentally defective, to say no worse of them. If you were to contemplate society in but one point of view, all these simple modes of polity are infinitely captivating. In effect each would answer its single end much more perfectly than the more complex is able to attain in its complex purposes. But it is better that the whole should be imperfectly and anomalously answered, than that, while some parts are provided for with great exactness, others might be totally neglected, or perhaps materially injured, by the overcare of a favorite member.

The pretended rights of these theorists are all extremes: and in proportion as they are metaphysically true, they are morally and politically false. The rights of men are in a sort of *middle*, incapable of definition, but not impossible to be discerned. The rights of men in governments are their advantages; and these are often in balances between differences of good; in compromises sometimes between good and evil, and sometimes between evil and evil. Political reason is a computing principle; adding, subtracting, multiplying, and dividing, morally and not metaphysically, or mathematically, true moral denominations.

By these theorists the right of the people is almost always sophistically confounded with their power. The body of the community, whenever it can come to act, can meet with no effectual resistance; but till power and right are the same, the whole body of them has no right inconsistent with virtue, and the first of all virtues, prudence. Men have no right to what is not reasonable, and to what is not for their benefit. . . .

History will record, that on the morning of the 6th of October, 1789, the king and queen of France, after a day of confusion, alarm, dismay, and slaughter, lay down, under the pledged security of public faith, to indulge nature in a few hours of respite, and troubled, melancholy repose. From this sleep the queen was first startled by the voice of the sentinel at her door, who cried out to her to save herself by flight—that this was the last proof of fidelity he could give—that they were upon him, and he was dead. Instantly he was cut down. A band of cruel ruffians and assassins, reeking with his blood, rushed into the chamber of the queen, and pierced with a hundred strokes of bayonets and poniards the bed, from whence this persecuted woman had but just time to fly almost naked, and, through ways unknown to the murderers, had escaped to seek refuge at the feet of a king and husband, not secure of his own life for a moment.

This king, to say no more of him, and this queen, and their infant children (who once would have been the pride and hope of a great and generous people), were then forced to abandon the sanctuary of the most splendid palace in the world, which they left swimming in blood, polluted by massacre, and strewed with scattered limbs and mutilated carcasses. Thence they were conducted into the capital of their kingdom. Two had been selected from the unprovoked, unresisted, promiscuous slaughter, which was made of the gentlemen of birth and family who composed the king's body guard. These two gentlemen, with all the parade of an execution of justice, were cruelly and publicly dragged to the block, and beheaded in the great court of the palace. Their heads were stuck upon spears, and led the procession; whilst the royal captives who followed in train were slowly moved along, amidst the horrid yells, and shrilling screams, and frantic dances, and infamous contumelies, and all the unutterable abominations of the furies of hell, in the abused shape of the vilest of women. After they had been made to taste, drop by drop, more than the bitterness of death, in the slow torture of a journey of twelve miles, protracted to six hours, they were, under a guard, composed of those very soldiers who had thus conducted them through this famous triumph, lodged in one of the old palaces of Paris, now converted into a bastille for kings. . . .

It is now sixteen or seventeen years since I saw the queen of France, then the dauphiness, at Versailles; and surely never lighted on this orb, which she hardly seemed to touch, a more delightful vision. I saw her just above the horizon, decorating and cheering the elevated sphere she just began to move in,—glittering like the morning-star, full of life, and splendor, and joy. Oh! What a revolution! and what a heart must I have to contemplate without emotion that elevation and that fall! Little did I dream when she added titles of veneration to those of enthusiastic, distant, respectful love, that she should ever be obliged to carry the sharp antidote against disgrace concealed in that bosom; little did I dream that I should have lived to see such disasters fallen upon her in a nation of gallant men, in a nation of men of honor, and of cavaliers. I thought ten thousand swords must have leaped from their scabbards to avenge even a look that threatened her with insult. But the age of chivalry is gone. That of sophisters, economists,

and calculators, has succeeded; and the glory of Europe is extinguished for ever. Never, never more shall we behold that generous loyalty to rank and sex, that proud submission, that dignified obedience, that subordination of the heart, which kept alive, even in servitude itself, the spirit of an exalted freedom. The unbought grace of life, the cheap defence of nations, the nurse of manly sentiment and heroic enterprise, is gone! It is gone, that sensibility of principle, that chastity of honor, which felt a stain like a wound, which inspired courage whilst it mitigated ferocity, which ennobled whatever it touched, and under which vice itself lost half its evil, by losing all its grossness.

This mixed system of opinion and sentiment had its origin in the ancient chivalry; and the principle, though varied in its appearance by the varying state of human affairs, subsisted and influenced through a long succession of generations, even to the time we live in. If it should ever be totally extinguished, the loss I fear will be great. It is this which has given its character to modern Europe. It is this which has distinguished it under all its forms of government, and distinguished it to its advantage, from the states of Asia, and possibly from those states which flourished in the most brilliant periods of the antique world. It was this, which, without confounding ranks, had produced a noble equality, and handed it down through all the gradations of social life. It was this opinion which mitigated kings into companions, and raised private men to be fellows with kings. Without force or opposition, it subdued the fierceness of pride and power; it obliged sovereigns to submit to the soft collar of social esteem, compelled stern authority to submit to elegance, and gave a dominating vanquisher of laws, to be subdued by manners.

But now all is to be changed. All the pleasing illusions, which made power gentle and obedience liberal, which harmonized the different shades of life, and which, by a bland assimilation, incorporated into politics the sentiments which beautify and soften private society, are to be dissolved by this new conquering empire of light and reason. All the decent drapery of life is to be rudely torn off. All the super-added ideas, furnished from the wardrobe of a moral imagination, which the heart owns, and the understanding ratifies, as necessary to cover the defects of our naked, shivering nature, and to raise it to dignity in our own estimation, are to be exploded as a ridiculous, absurd, and antiquated fashion.

On this scheme of things, a king is but a man, a queen is but a woman; a woman is but an animal, and an animal not of the highest order. All homage paid to the sex in general as such, and without distinct views, is to be regarded as romance and folly. Regicide, and parricide, and sacrilege, are but fictions of superstition, corrupting jurisprudence by destroying its simplicity. The murder of a king, or a queen, or a bishop, or a father, are only common homicide; and if the people are by any chance, or in any way, gainers by it, a sort of homicide much the most pardonable, and into which we ought not to make too severe a scrutiny.

On the scheme of this barbarous philosophy, which is the offspring of cold hearts and muddy understandings, and which is as void of solid wisdom as it is destitute of all taste and elegance, laws are to be supported only by their own terrors, and by the concern which each individual may find in them from his own private speculations, or can spare to them from his own private interests. In the groves of *their* academy, at the end of every vista, you see nothing but the gallows. Nothing is left which engages the affections on the part of the commonwealth. On the principles of this mechanic philosophy, our institutions can never be embodied, if I may use the expression, in persons; so as to create in us love, veneration, admiration, or attachment. But that sort of reason which banishes the affections is incapable of filling their place. These public affections, combined with manners, are required sometimes as supplements, sometimes as correctives, always as aids to law. . . .

When the old feudal and chivalrous spirit of *fealty*, which, by freeing kings from fear, freed both kings and subjects from the precautions of tyranny, shall be extinct in the minds of men, plots and assassinations will be anticipated by preventive murder and preventive confiscation, and that long roll of grim and bloody maxims, which form the political code of all power, not standing on its own honor, and the honor of those who are to obey it. Kings will be tyrants from policy, when subjects are rebels from principle.

When ancient opinions and rules of life are taken away, the loss cannot possibly be estimated. From that moment we have no compass to govern us; nor can we know distinctly to what port we steer. Europe, undoubtedly, taken in a mass, was in a flourishing condition the day on which your revolution was completed. How much of that prosperous state was owing to the spirit of our old manners and opinions is not easy to say; but as such causes cannot be indifferent in their operation, we must presume, that, on the whole, their operation was beneficial.

We are but too apt to consider things in the state in which we find them, without sufficiently adverting to the causes by which they have been produced, and possibly may be upheld. Nothing is more certain than that our manners, our civilization, and all the good things which are connected with manners and with civilization, have, in this European world of ours, depended for ages upon two principles; and were indeed the result of both combined; I mean the spirit of a gentleman, and the spirit of religion. The nobility and the clergy, the one by profession, the other by patronage, kept learning in existence, even in the midst of arms and confusions, and whilst governments were rather in their causes, than formed. Learning paid back what it received to nobility and to priesthood; and paid it usury, by enlarging their ideas, and by furnishing their minds. Happy if they had all continued to know their indissoluble union, and their proper place! Happy if learning, not debauched by ambition, had been satisfied to continue the instructor, and not aspired to be the master! Along with its natural protectors and guardians, learning will be cast into the mire, and trodden down under the hoofs of a swinish multitude. . . .

I hear it is sometimes given out in France, that what is doing among you is after the example of England. I beg leave to affirm, that scarcely anything done with you has originated from the practice or the prevalent opinions of this people, either in the act or in the spirit of the proceeding. Let me add, that we are as unwilling to learn these lessons from France, as we are sure that we never taught them to that nation. The cabals here, who take a sort of share in your transactions, as yet consist of but a handful of people. . . .

As such cabals have not existed in England, so neither has the spirit of them had any influence in establishing the original frame of our constitution, or in any one of the several reparations and improvements it has undergone. The whole has been done under the auspices, and is confirmed by the sanctions of religion and piety. The whole has emanated from the simplicity of our national character, and from a sort of native plainness and directness of understanding, which for a long time characterized those men who have successively obtained authority amongst us. This disposition still remains, at least in the great body of the people.

We know, and what is better, we feel inwardly, that religion is the basis of civil society, and the source of all good and of all comfort. In England we are so convinced of this, that there is no rust of superstition, with which the accumulated absurdity of the human mind might have crusted it over in the course of ages, that ninety-nine in a hundred of the people of England would not prefer to impiety. We shall never be such fools as to call in an enemy to the substance of any system to remove its corruptions, to supply its defects, or to perfect its construction. If our religious tenets should ever want a further elucidation, we shall not call on atheism to explain them. We shall not light up our temple from that unhallowed fire. It will be illuminated with other lights. It will be perfumed with other incense, than the infectious stuff which is imported by the smugglers of adulterated

metaphysics. If our ecclesiastical establishment should want a revision, it is not avarice or rapacity, public or private, that we shall employ for the audit, or receipt, or application of its consecrated revenue. Violently condemning neither the Greek nor the Armenian, nor, since heats are subsided, the Roman system of religion, we prefer the Protestant; not because we think it has less of the Christian religion in it, but because, in our judgment, it has more. We are Protestants, not from indifference, but from zeal.

We know, and it is our pride to know, that man is by his constitution a religious animal; that atheism is against, not only our reason, but our instincts; and that it cannot prevail long. But if, in the moment of riot, and in a drunken delirium from the hot spirit drawn out of the alembic of hell, which in France is now so furiously boiling, we should uncover our nakedness by throwing off that Christian religion which has hitherto been our boast and comfort, and one great source of civilization amongst us, and amongst many other nations, we are apprehensive (being well aware that the mind will not endure a void) that some uncouth, pernicious, and degrading superstition might take place of it.

For that reason, before we take from our establishment the natural human means of estimation, and give it up to contempt, as you have done, and in doing it have incurred the penalties you well deserve to suffer, we desire that some other may be presented to us in the place of it. We shall then form our judgment.

On these ideas, instead of quarrelling with establishments, as some do, who have made a philosophy and a religion of their hostility to such institutions, we cleave closely to them. We are resolved to keep an established church, an established monarchy, an established aristocracy, and an established democracy, each in the degree it exists, and in no greater. . . .

Society is indeed a contract. Subordinate contracts for objects of mere occasional interest may be dissolved at pleasure—but the state ought not to be considered as nothing better than a partnership agreement in a trade of pepper and coffee, calico or tobacco, or some other such low concern, to be taken up for a little temporary interest, and to be dissolved by the fancy of the parties. It is to be looked on with other reverence; because it is not a partnership in things subservient only to the gross animal existence of a temporary and perishable nature, It is a partnership in all science; a partnership in all art; a partnership in every virtue, and in all perfection. As the ends of such a partnership cannot be obtained in many generations, it becomes a partnership not only between those who are living, but between those who are living, those who are dead, and those who are to be born. Each contract of each particular state is but a clause in the great primaeval contract of eternal society, linking the lower with the higher natures, connecting the visible and invisible world, according to a fixed compact sanctioned by the inviolable oath which holds all physical and all moral natures, each in their appointed place. This law is not subject to the will of those, who by an obligation above them, and infinitely superior, are bound to submit their will to that law. The municipal corporations of that universal kingdom are not morally at liberty at their pleasure, and on their speculations of a contingent improvement, wholly to separate and tear asunder the bands of their subordinate community, and to dissolve it into an unsocial, uncivil, unconnected chaos of elementary principles. It is the first and supreme necessity only, a necessity that is not chosen, but chooses, a necessity paramount to deliberation, that admits no discussion, and demands no evidence, which alone can justify a resort to anarchy. This necessity is no exception to the rule; because this necessity itself is a part too of that moral and physical disposition of things, to which man must be obedient by consent or force; but if that which is only submission to necessity should be made the object of choice, the law is broken, nature is disobeyed, and the rebellious are outlawed, cast forth, and exiled, from this world of reason, and order, and peace, and virtue, and fruitful penitence, into the antagonist world of madness, discord, vice, confusion, and unavailing sorrow. . . .

When all the frauds, impostures, violences, rapines, burnings, murders, confiscations, compulsory paper currencies, and every description of tyranny and cruelty employed to bring about and to uphold this Revolution, have their natural effect, that is, to shock the moral sentiments of all virtuous and sober minds, the abettors of this philosophic system immediately strain their throats in a declaration against the old monarchial government of France. . . . Have these gentlemen never heard, in the whole circle of the worlds of theory and practice, of anything between the despotism of the monarch and the despotism of the multitude? Have they never heard of a monarchy directed by laws, controlled and balanced by the great hereditary wealth and hereditary dignity of a nation; and both again controlled by a judicious check from the reason and feeling of the people at large, acting by a suitable and permanent organ? Is it then impossible that a man may be found, who, without criminal ill intention, or pitiable absurdity, shall prefer such a mixed and tempered government to either of the extremes; and who may repute that nation to be destitute of all wisdom and of all virtue, which, having in its choice to obtain such a government with ease, *or rather to confirm it when actually possessed*, thought proper to commit a thousand crimes, and to subject their country to a thousand evils, in order to avoid it? Is it then a truth so universally acknowledged, that a pure democracy is the only tolerable form into which human society can be thrown, that a man is not permitted to hesitate about its merits, without the suspicion of being a friend to tyranny, that is, of being a foe to mankind?

I do not know under what description to class the present ruling authority in France. It affects to be a pure democracy, though I think it in a direct train of becoming shortly a mischievous and ignoble oligarchy. But for the present

I admit it to be a contrivance of the nature and effect of what it pretends to. I reprobate no form of government merely upon abstract principles. There may be situations in which the purely democratic form will become necessary. There may be some (very few, and very particularly circumstanced) where it would be clearly desirable. This I do not take to be the case of France, or of any other great country. Until now, we have seen no examples of considerable democracies. The ancients were better acquainted with them. Not being wholly unread in the authors, who had seen the most of those constitutions, and who best understood them, I cannot help concurring with their opinion, that an absolute democracy, no more than absolute monarchy, is to be reckoned among the legitimate forms of government. They think it rather the corruption and degeneracy, than the sound constitution of a republic. If I recollect rightly, Aristotle observes, that democracy has many striking points of resemblance with a tyranny. Of this I am certain, that in a democracy, the majority of the citizens is capable of exercising the most cruel oppressions upon the minority, whenever strong divisions prevail in that kind of polity, as they often must; and that oppression of the minority will extend to far greater numbers, and will be carried on with much greater fury, than can almost ever be apprehended from the dominion of a single sceptre. In such a popular persecution, individual sufferers are in a much more deplorable condition than in any other. Under a cruel prince they have the balmy compassion of mankind to assuage the smart of their wounds; they have the plaudits of the people to animate their generous constancy under their sufferings: but those who are subjected to wrong under multitudes, are deprived of all external consolation. They seem deserted by mankind, overpowered by a conspiracy of their whole species. . . .

Corporate bodies are immortal for the good of the members, but not for their punishment. Nations themselves are such corporations. As well

might we in England think of waging inexpiable war upon all Frenchmen for the evils which they have brought upon us in the several periods of our mutual hostilities. You might, on your part, think yourselves justified in falling upon all Englishmen on account of the unparalleled calamities brought on the people of France by the unjust invasions of our Henrys and our Edwards. Indeed we should be mutually justified in this exterminatory war upon each other, full as much as you are in the unprovoked persecution of your present countrymen, on account of the conduct of men of the same name in other times.

We do not draw the moral lessons we might from history. On the contrary, without care it may be used to vitiate our minds and to destroy our happiness. In history a great volume is unrolled for our instruction, drawing the materials of future wisdom from the past errors and infirmities of mankind. It may, in the perversion, serve for a magazine, furnishing offensive and defensive weapons for parties in church and state, and supplying the means of keeping alive, or reviving, dissensions and animosities, and adding fuel to civil fury. History consists, for the greater part, of the miseries brought upon the world by pride, ambition, avarice, revenge, lust, sedition, hypocrisy, ungoverned zeal, and all the train of disorderly appetites, which shake the public with the same

> troublous storms that toss
> The private state, and render life unsweet. . . .

Your citizens of Paris formerly had lent themselves as the ready instruments to slaughter the followers of Calvin, at the infamous massacre of St. Bartholomew. What should we say to those who could think of retaliating on the Parisians of this day the abominations and horrors of that time? They are indeed brought to abhor *that* massacre. Ferocious as they are, it is not difficult to make them dislike it; because the politicians and fashionable teachers have no interest in giving their passions exactly the same direction. Still, however, they find it their interest to keep the same savage dispositions alive. It was but the other day that they caused this very massacre to be acted on the stage for the diversion of the descendants of those who committed it. In this tragic farce they produced the cardinal of Lorraine in his robes of function, ordering general slaughter. Was this spectacle intended to make the Parisians abhor persecution, and loathe the effusion of blood?—No; it was to teach them to persecute their own pastors; it was to excite them, by raising a disgust and horror of their clergy, to an alacrity in hunting down to destruction an order, which, if it ought to exist at all, ought to exist not only in safety, but in reverence. It was to stimulate their cannibal appetites (which one would think had been gorged sufficiently) by variety and seasoning; and to quicken them to an alertness in new murders and massacres, if it should suit the purpose of the Guises of the day. An Assembly, in which sat a multitude of priests and prelates, was obliged to suffer this indignity at its door. The author was not sent to the galleys, nor the players to the house of correction. Not long after this exhibition, those players came forward to the Assembly to claim the rites of that very religion which they had dared to expose, and to show their prostituted faces in the senate, whilst the archbishop of Paris, whose function was known to his people only by his prayers and benedictions, and his wealth only by his alms, is forced to abandon his house, and to fly from his flock (as from ravenous wolves), because, truly, in the sixteenth century, the cardinal of Lorraine was a rebel and a murderer.

Such is the effect of the perversion of history, by those, who, for the same nefarious purposes, have perverted every other part of learning. But those who will stand upon that elevation of reason, which places centuries under our eye, and brings things to the true point of comparison, which obscures little names, and effaces the colors of little parties, and to which nothing can ascend but the spirit and moral quality of human actions, will say to the teachers of the Palais Royal,—The cardinal of Lorraine was the murderer of the sixteenth century, you have the glory of being the murderers in the eighteenth; and this is the only difference between you. But history in the nineteenth century, better understood, and better employed, will, I trust, teach a civilized posterity to abhor the misdeeds of both these barbarous ages. It will teach future priests and magistrates not to retaliate upon the speculative and inactive atheists of future times, the enormities committed by the present practical zealots and furious fanatics of that wretched error, which, in its quiescent state, is more than punished, whenever it is embraced. It will teach posterity not to make war upon either religion or philosophy, for the abuse which the hypocrites of both have made of the two most valuable blessings conferred upon us by the bounty of the universal Patron, who in all things eminently favors and protects the race of man.

G. W. F. HEGEL

~

INTRODUCTION

STEVEN B. SMITH

G. W. F. Hegel (1770–1831) was born into a middle-class family in Stuttgart. He attended university at Tübingen where he was a classmate of the philosopher Schelling and the poet Holderlin. As legend has it, they celebrated together news of the outbreak of the French Revolution. Hegel held the post of lecturer at the University of Jena where he finished his first major book, *The Phenomenology of Spirit*, in 1807. It was here that he saw Napoleon ("this world soul on horse back") ride through the town. Due to the closing of the university, Hegel found employment first as a newspaper editor at Bamberg and later as the head master of a *Gymnasium* at Nuremberg. During these years he began work on his *Science of Logic* and was subsequently called to a professorship first at Heidelberg and then at Berlin, where he succeeded Fichte to a chair of philosophy. His major work of political philosophy, *Philosophy of Right*, was published in 1821. He died in 1831 in the midst of a typhus epidemic.

Philosophy of Right excited controversy almost immediately upon publication. In part because of his prefatory statement that "what is rational is actual and what is actual is rational," critics took the book to be a wholesale justification of the political status quo. Later in the century, it came to be regarded as a rearguard defense of the Prussian state, and during World War I it was thought to provide a defense for German militarism and imperialism. During the Cold War Hegelianism was associated with both the rise of German national socialism and Soviet communism, although Marxist defenders of Hegel regarded his dialectic as inherently progressive and liberating. Recently, *Philosophy of Right* has been reassessed as a classic work of reformist or gradualist liberalism in keeping with other great nineteenth-century works by liberals like Benjamin Constant, Alexis de Tocqueville, and John Stuart Mill.

Difficulties with *Philosophy of Right* often begin with the very title of the book. The subject matter of the work is stated in the introduction as "the idea of right." The German term for right (*Recht*) is ambiguous. It can mean either "law" in the relatively narrow sense of jurisprudence or "right" in the broader sense of the proper ordering of political relationships. The subtitle of the work, *Natural Right and Political Science in Outline*, indicates Hegel's preference for this wider meaning of the term. The idea of right refers to more than the structure of civil rights and liberties, but to the entire normative dimension of a people's way of life, their ethical norms and values, including their system of public morality and religion.

The opening paragraphs of *Philosophy of Right* provide an account of the source or ground of right in a theory of the human will (pars. 5–7). Like the entire modern tradition of moral and political philosophy as developed by philosophers from Hobbes to Kant, Hegel believes that the will is the ultimate source of political legitimacy. Hegel treats the will as consisting of three aspects or "moments." The first is defined by the will's ability to abstract freely from all content, from everything empirical or merely given in experience. This kind of freedom is associated with the element of pure "indeterminacy," the will's ability to choose anything and everything. This moment of sheer negativity is deeply resistant to any form of limitation. As such it is entirely empty.

The first moment of the will's activity leads dialectically to the second. Freedom of the will does not mean arbitrary choice. To will means to choose something determinate, the decision to be this rather than that. To will is not merely to declare one's independence from all content, it is to become something specific. The need for the will to be something concrete or specific is not a constraint on freedom, but is essential to it. Furthermore, willing is not an arbitrary choice, but an act of rational deliberation. So long as we understand the will to mean arbitrary choice, it is not truly free. The freedom identified with arbitrary choice (*Wilkur*) is associated by Hegel with slavery to natural appetites and passions. The self-determination of the rational will, by contrast, is characterized not just by a capacity for choice, but for reflection and deliberation over the ends we choose. Rational liberty consists in the ability to reflect evaluatively upon the kinds of things we ought to desire, including the kinds of persons we ought to become.

The final aspect of the will's activity consists in determining what kind of content is appropriate to freedom. To what ought the free will to give its consent? Despite his often fierce rejection of social contract theory, there is built into Hegel's theory of the will an idea of rational consent as the only plausible justification for modern political institutions. The person largely credited for recognizing this principle is Rousseau, who is congratulated for "adducing the will as the principle of the state" (par. 258). The aim of making the rational will the ultimate arbiter of the state is to make citizens feel "at home" in their world, to overcome the various forms of division (*Zerrissenheit*) that have previously alienated citizens from their public institutions. The major headings of the *Philosophy of Right* are thus given over to an account of the kinds of public institutions that the free will can ratify or affirm as its own. The whole domain of these institutions and practices constitutes the sphere of right.

Before indicating briefly how these institutions satisfy the conditions of rational freedom, Hegel's views must be distinguished from two positions with which he is frequently identified. The first maintains that Hegel has no independent theory of moral justification because he ultimately subordinates the rights of individual judgment and conscience to the will of the state. To be sure, there are more than enough passages in the work affirming such sentiments as "the state in and by itself is the ethical whole" (par. 260a). He frequently criticizes the standpoint of Kantian *Moralitat* as an "empty formalism" for its attempt to generate a universal principle of right action (par. 135). As he sometimes writes, there is no principle of right over and above the state. He enjoys recalling the ancient story of a man who asked a philosopher the best way of educating his son. The philosopher replied, "Make him a citizen of a state with good laws" (par. 153).

A second criticism turns on Hegel's frequently noted historicism. On this account Hegel subordinates the moral will to the forward or progressive march of history.

"Every individual," he notes in the preface to *Philosophy of Right*, "is a child of his time." Morality is thus made relative to time, place, and circumstance. History is advanced precisely by great leaders like Caesar and Napoleon who serve the cause of moral progress but at the expense of much misery and human suffering. In *Introduction to the Philosophy of History* Hegel presents these "World-Historical Individuals" as moral heroes whose greatness consists in embodying the dominant ethos or spirit of their times. "World-historical men," Hegel writes, "the heroes of an epoch, must therefore be recognized as its clear sighted ones: their deeds, their words are the best of that time." However, even the most farsighted of heroes play a limited role as the agents or instruments of a historical process they cannot in principle comprehend. Once they achieve their ends, they are fated to fade from the scene. "When their object is attained," Hegel hints darkly, "they fall off like empty hulls from the kernel."

Hegel's answer to these objections can be found in his concept of *Sittlichkeit* or ethical life that comprises the entire third part of *Philosophy of Right*. The German word for ethics, *Sitte*, emphasizes the role of practice, custom, and habituation in forming moral judgment and character (pars. 144, 151). In contrast to Kant's view of morality, Hegel stresses that moral reasoning is not something that applies to individuals in the abstract, but takes place within a context or tradition, a community of moral reasoners. Hegel's use of the term is intended to evoke the place of habituation and practice in the moral life. He enjoys tweaking the modern moral standpoint by evoking the largely unreflective and habitual character of ethical life. His conception of fully developed moral virtue takes the form of "rectitude," which involves little more than obeying the laws and fulfilling the duties of one's station (par. 150).

Many interpreters have seen in Hegel's conception of social ethics an incipient relativism according to which standards of right and wrong can come only from within existing conventions and institutions. His identification of *Sittlichkeit* with "absolutely valid laws and institutions" appears to give it a conservative dimension reminiscent of Burkean traditionalism. But this is to misidentify Hegel's conception of *Sittlichkeit*. Ethical life is not just a descriptive sociological term, but a term of moral classification and evaluation. It is not just a description of what institutions happen to exist; it is a rational account of what institutions must exist if rational freedom is to be possible. Institutions and practices are not called upon to be judges in their own case. Rather they are judged by their capacity to further and sustain the human desire for freedom.

Philosophy of Right is nothing less than an articulation of those institutions of modern ethical life that most completely correspond to the moral imperative of freedom. These institutions—the famous Hegelian triad of family, civil society, and state—are judged by how well they promote mutual recognition or respect between citizens. Hegel's conception of *Sittlichkeit* does not celebrate existing standards whatever they happen to be, but is tied to a distinctive conception of human agency and moral personality. "Be a person and respect others as persons" is his watchword (par. 36). Being a person means having a sense of one-self as an autonomous agent with a will and consciousness of one's own. Hegel reminds us that the attainment of personality is not just an individual but a social and even a historical accomplishment. The institutions of modern *Sittlichkeit*, chiefly a robust market economy and a developed constitutional state, provide the conditions for complete moral satisfaction.

Hegel's defense of the moral legitimacy of social institutions obviously makes sense only against the background of his general conception of philosophy. The aim of philosophy, he remarks in the preface to *Philosophy of Right*, is not to construct a Platonic utopia, but to discover the rationality in what exists. Philosophy, he avers, cannot give advice about what ought to be the case, but should seek to "reconcile" citizens to the world they actually inhabit. This is not a counsel of despair. For Hegel, the world we now inhabit is so arranged that we see ourselves perfectly expressed within the institutions of modern *Sittlichkeit*. Freedom need no longer be sought in an ideal world that perpetually eludes our grasp, but in the forms of social and political life now before us. For some, this strategy will seem far too accommodationist to prove satisfactory. However, to reverse Marx's famous dictum, the purpose of philosophy is not to change the world but to interpret it.

There are a number of excellent commentaries and interpretations of *Philosophy of Right*. Among works that interpret Hegel in a more liberal vein along roughly the lines developed here, see Charles Taylor, *Hegel and Modern Society* (Cambridge: Cambridge University Press, 1979); Manfred Riedel, *Between Tradition and Revolution: The Hegelian Transformation of Political Philosophy* (Cambridge: Cambridge University Press, 1984); Steven B. Smith, *Hegel's Critique of Liberalism: Rights in Context* (Chicago: University of Chicago Press, 1989); Allen Wood, *Hegel's Ethical Thought* (Cambridge: Cambridge University Press, 1990); Michael O. Hardimon, *Hegel's Social Philosophy: The Project of Reconciliation* (Cambridge: Cambridge University Press, 1994); Robert Pippin, "Hegel's Ethical Rationalism," in *Idealism as Modernism: Hegelian Variations* (Cambridge: Cambridge University Press, 1997), pp. 417–450; Paul Franco, *Hegel's Philosophy of Freedom* (New Haven, Conn.: Yale University Press, 1999); and John Rawls, "Hegel," in *Lectures on the History of Moral Philosophy*, edited by Barbara Herman (Cambridge, Mass.: Harvard University Press, 2000), pp. 329–371. For a comprehensive recent biography, see Terry Pinkard, *Hegel* (Cambridge: Cambridge University Press, 2000).

Philosophy of Right

PREFACE

. . . *What is rational is actual and what is actual is rational.* On this conviction the plain man like the philosopher takes his stand, and from it philosophy starts in its study of the universe of mind as well as the universe of nature. If reflection, feeling, or whatever form subjective consciousness may take, looks upon the present as something vacuous and looks beyond it with the eyes of superior wisdom, it finds itself in a vacuum, and because it is actual only in the present, it is itself mere vacuity. If on the other hand the Idea passes for "only an Idea," for something represented in an opinion, philosophy rejects such a view and shows that nothing is actual except the Idea. Once that is granted, the great thing is to apprehend in the show of the temporal and transient the substance which is immanent and the eternal which is present. For since rationality (which is synonymous with the Idea) enters upon external existence simultaneously with its actualization, it emerges with an infinite

From *The Philosophy of History*, translated by J. Sibree. Copyright © 1956 by Dover Publications, Inc. Reprinted by permission of the publisher.

wealth of forms, shapes, and appearances. Around its heart it throws a motley covering with which consciousness is at home to begin with, a covering which the concept has first to penetrate before it can find the inward pulse and feel it still beating in the outward appearances. But the infinite variety of circumstance which is developed in this externality by the light of the essence glinting in it—this endless material and its organization—this is not the subject matter of philosophy. To touch this at all would be to meddle with things to which philosophy is unsuited; on such topics it may save itself the trouble of giving good advice. Plato might have omitted his recommendation to nurses to keep on the move with infants and to rock them continually in their arms. And Fichte too need not have carried what has been called the "construction" of his passport regulations to such a pitch of perfection as to require suspects not merely to sign their passports but to have their likenesses painted on them. Along such tracks all trace of philosophy is lost, and such super-erudition it can the more readily disclaim since its attitude to this infinite multitude of topics should of course be most liberal. In adopting this attitude, philosophic science shows itself to be poles apart from the hatred with which the folly of superior wisdom regards a vast number of affairs and institutions, a hatred in which pettiness takes the greatest delight because only by venting it does it attain a feeling of its self-hood.

This book, then, containing as it does the science of the state, is to be nothing other than the endeavour to apprehend and portray the state as something inherently rational. As a work of philosophy, it must be poles apart from an attempt to construct a state as it ought to be. The instruction which it may contain cannot consist in teaching the state what it ought to be; it can only show how the state, the ethical universe, is to be understood. . . .

Hic Rhodus, *hic* saltus.

To comprehend what is, this is the task of philosophy, because what is, is reason. Whatever happens, every individual is a child of his time; so philosophy too is its own time apprehended in thoughts. It is just as absurd to fancy that a philosophy can transcend its contemporary world as it is to fancy that an individual can overleap his own age, jump over Rhodes. If his theory really goes beyond the world as it is and builds an ideal one as it ought to be, that world exists indeed, but only in his opinions, an unsubstantial element where anything you please may, in fancy, be built.

With hardly an alteration, the proverb just quoted would run:

Here is the rose, dance thou here.

What lies between reason as self-conscious mind and reason as an actual world before our eyes, what separates the former from the latter and prevents it from finding satisfaction in the latter, is the fetter of some abstraction or other which has not been liberated [and so transformed] into the concept. To recognize reason as the rose in the cross of the present and thereby to enjoy the present, this is the rational insight which reconciles us to the actual, the reconciliation which philosophy affords to those in whom there has once arisen an inner voice bidding them to comprehend, not only to dwell in what is substantive while still retaining subjective freedom, but also to possess subjective freedom while standing not in anything particular and accidental but in what exists absolutely.

It is this too which constitutes the more concrete meaning of what was described above rather abstractly as the unity of form and content; for form in its most concrete signification is reason as speculative knowing, and content is reason as the substantial essence of actuality, whether ethical or natural. The known identity of these two is the philosophical Idea. It is a sheer obstinacy, the obstinacy which does honour to mankind, to refuse to recognize in conviction anything not ratified by thought. This obstinacy is the characteristic of our epoch, besides being the principle peculiar to Protestantism. What Luther initiated as faith in feeling and in the witness of the spirit, is precisely what spirit, since become more mature, has striven to apprehend in the concept in order to free and so to find itself in the world as it exists to-day. The saying has become famous that "a half-philosophy leads away from God" and it is the same half-philosophy that locates knowledge in an "approximation" to truth—"while true philosophy leads to God"; and the same is true of philosophy and the state. Just as reason is not content with an approximation which, as something "neither cold nor hot," it will "spue out of its mouth," so it is just as little content with the cold despair which submits to the view that in this earthly life things are truly bad or at best only tolerable, though here they cannot be improved and that this is the only reflection which can keep us at peace with the world. There is less chill in the peace with the world which knowledge supplies.

One word more about giving instruction as to what the world ought to be. Philosophy in any case always comes on the scene too late to give it. As the thought of the world, it appears only when actuality is already there cut and dried after its process of formation has been completed. The teaching of the concept, which is also history's inescapable lesson, is that it is only when actuality is mature that the ideal first appears over against the real and that the ideal apprehends this same real world in its substance and builds it up for itself into the shape of an intellectual realm. When philosophy paints its grey in grey, then has a shape of life grown old. By philosophy's grey in grey it cannot be rejuvenated but only understood. The owl of Minerva spreads its wings only with the falling of the dusk.

But it is time to close this preface. After all, as a preface, its only business has been to make some external and subjective remarks about the standpoint of the book it introduces. If a topic is to be discussed philosophically, it spurns any but a scientific and objective treatment, and so too if criticisms of the author take any form other than a scientific discussion of the thing itself, they can count only as a personal epilogue and as capricious assertion, and he must treat them with indifference.

SECOND PART

Morality

105. The standpoint of morality is the standpoint of the will which is infinite not merely in itself but for itself. . . . In contrast with the will's implicit being, with its immediacy and the determinate characteristics developed within it at that level, this reflection of the will into itself and its explicit awareness of its identity makes the person into the subject.

106. It is as subjectivity that the concept has now been determined, and since subjectivity is distinct from the concept as such, i.e. from the implicit principle of the will, and since furthermore it is at the same time the will of the subject as a single individual aware of himself (i.e. still has immediacy in him), it constitutes the determinate *existence* of the concept. In this way a higher ground has been assigned to freedom; the Idea's existential aspect, or its moment of reality, is now the subjectivity of the will. Only in the will as subjective can freedom or the implicit principle of the will be actual.

> The second sphere, Morality, therefore throughout portrays the real aspect of the concept of freedom, and the movement of this sphere is as follows: the will, which at the start is aware only of its independence and which before it is mediated is only implicitly identical with the universal will or the principle of the will, is raised beyond its [explicit] difference from the universal will, beyond this situation in which it sinks deeper and deeper into itself, and is established as explicitly identical with the principle of the will. This process is accordingly the cultivation of the ground in which freedom is now set, i.e. subjectivity. What happens is that subjectivity, which is abstract at the start, i.e. distinct from the concept, becomes likened to it, and thereby the Idea acquires its genuine realization. The result is that the subjective will determines itself as objective too and so as truly concrete.

107. The self-determination of the will is at the same time a moment in the concept of the

will, and subjectivity is not merely its existential aspect but its own determinate character. . . . The will aware of its freedom and determined as subjective is at the start concept alone, but itself has determinate existence in order to exist as Idea. The moral standpoint therefore takes shape as the right of the subjective will. In accordance with this right, the will recognizes something and is something, only in so far as the thing is its own and as the will is present to itself there as something subjective.

> The same process through which the moral attitude develops (see the Remark to the preceding Paragraph) has from this point of view the form of being the development of the right of the subjective will, or of the mode of its existence. In this process the subjective will further determines what it recognizes as its own in its object (*Gegenstand*), so that this object becomes the will's own true concept, becomes objective (*objektiv*) as the expression of the will's own universality.

108. The subjective will, directly aware of itself, and distinguished from the principle of the will (see Remark to Paragraph 106), is therefore abstract, restricted, and formal. But not merely is subjectivity itself formal; in addition, as the infinite self-determination of the will, it constitutes the form of all willing. In this, its first appearance in the single will, this form has not yet been established as identical with the concept of the will, and therefore the moral point of view is that of relation, of ought-to-be, or demand. And since the self-difference of subjectivity involves at the same time the character of being opposed to objectivity as external fact, it follows that the point of view of consciousness comes on the scene here too. . . . The general point of view here is that of the will's self-difference, finitude, and appearance.

> The moral is not characterized primarily by its having already been opposed to the immoral, nor is right directly characterized by its opposition to

wrong. The point is rather that the general characteristics of morality and immorality alike rest on the subjectivity of the will.

109. This form of all willing primarily involves in accordance with its general character (*a*) the opposition of subjectivity and objectivity, and (*b*) the activity . . . related to this opposition. Now existence and specific determinacy are identical in the concept of the will . . . , and the will as subjective is itself this concept. Hence the moments of this activity consist more precisely in (*a*) distinguishing between objectivity and subjectivity and even ascribing independence to them both, and (*b*) establishing them as identical. In the will which is self-determining, (α) its specific determinacy is in the first place established in the will itself by itself as its inner particularization, as a content which it gives to itself. This is the first negation, and the formal limitation (*Grenze*) of this negation is that of being only something posited, something subjective. (β) As infinitely reflected into itself, this limitation exists for the will, and the will is the struggle to transcend this barrier (*Schranke*), i.e. it is the activity of translating this content in some way or other from subjectivity into objectivity, into an immediate existence. (γ) The simple identity of the will with itself in this opposition is the content which remains self-identical in both these opposites and indifferent to this formal distinction of opposition. In short, it is my aim [the purpose willed].

110. But, at the standpoint of morality, where the will is aware of its freedom, of this identity of the will with itself (see Paragraph 105), this identity of content acquires the more particularized character appropriate to itself.

(*a*) The content as "mine" has for me this character: by virtue of its identity in subject and object it enshrines for me my subjectivity, not merely as my inner purpose, but also inasmuch as it has acquired outward existence.

111. (*b*) Though the content does have in it something particular, whencesoever it may be derived, still it is the content of the will reflected

into itself in its determinacy and thus of the self-identical and universal will; and therefore:

(α) the content is inwardly characterized as adequate to the principle of the will or as possessing the objectivity of the concept;

(β) since the subjective will, as aware of itself, is at the same time still formal (see Paragraph 108), the content's adequacy to the concept is still only something demanded, and hence this entails the possibility that the content may *not* be adequate to the concept.

112. (*c*) Since in carrying out my aims I retain my subjectivity (see Paragraph 110), during this process of objectifying them I simultaneously supersede the immediacy of this subjectivity as well as its character as this my individual subjectivity. But the external subjectivity which is thus identical with me is the will of others. . . . The will's ground of existence is now subjectivity (see Paragraph 106) and the will of others is that existence which I give to my aim and which is at the same time to me an other. The achievement of my aim, therefore, implies this identity of my will with the will of others, it has a positive bearing on the will of others.

The objectivity of the aim achieved thus involves three meanings, or rather it has three moments present within it at once; it is:

(α) something existing externally and immediately (see Paragraph 109);

(β) adequate to the concept (see Paragraph 111);

(γ) *universal* subjectivity.

The subjectivity which maintains itself in this objectivity consists:

(α) in the fact that the objective aim is mine, so that in it I maintain myself as *this* individual (see Paragraph 110);

(β) and (γ), in moments which coincide with the moments (β) and (γ) above.

At the standpoint of morality, subjectivity and objectivity are distinct from one another, or

united only by their mutual contradiction; it is this fact more particularly which constitutes the finitude of this sphere or its character as mere appearance (see Paragraph 108), and the development of this standpoint is the development of these contradictions and their resolutions, resolutions, however, which within this field can be no more than relative.

113. The externalization of the subjective or moral will is action. Action implies the determinate characteristics here indicated:

(α) in its externality it must be known to me as *my* action;

(β) it must bear essentially on the concept as an "ought" [see Paragraph 131];

(γ) it must have an essential bearing on the will of others.

It is not until we come to the externalization of the moral will that we come to action. The existence which the will gives to itself in the sphere of formal rights is existence in an immediate thing and is itself immediate; to start with, it neither has in itself any express bearing on the concept, which is at that point not yet contrasted with the subjective will and so is not distinguished from it, nor has it a positive bearing on the will of others; in the sphere of right, command in its fundamental character is only prohibition. . . . In contract and wrong, there is the beginning of a bearing on the will of others; but the correspondence established in contract between one will and another is grounded in arbitrariness, and the essential bearing which the will has there on the will of the other is, as a matter of rights, something negative, i.e. one party retains his property (the value of it) and allows the other to retain his. On the other hand, crime in its aspect as issuing from the subjective will, and the question of the mode of its existence in that will, come before us now for consideration for the first time.

The content of an action at law (*actio*), as something determined by legal enactment, is not imputable to me. Consequently, such an action contains only some of the moments of a moral action proper, and contains them only incidentally. The aspect of an action in virtue of which it is properly moral is therefore distinct from its aspect as legal.

114. The right of the moral will involves three aspects:

(*a*) The abstract or formal right of action, the right that the content of the action as carried out in immediate existence, shall be in principle mine, that thus the action shall be the *Purpose* of the subjective will.

(*b*) The particular aspect of the action is its inner content (α) as I am aware of it in its general character; my awareness of this general character constitutes the worth of the action and the reason I think good to do it—in short my *Intention*. (β) Its content is my special aim, the aim of my particular, merely individual, existence, i.e. *Welfare*.

(*c*) This content (as something which is inward and which yet at the same time is raised to its universality as to absolute objectivity) is the absolute end of the will, the *Good*—with the opposition in the sphere of reflection, of *subjective* universality, which is now wickedness and now conscience.

SUBSECTION 1

Purpose and Responsibility

115. The finitude of the subjective will in the immediacy of acting consists directly in this, that its action *presupposes* an external object with a complex environment. The deed sets up an alteration in this state of affairs confronting the will, and my will has responsibility in general for its deed in so far as the abstract predicate "mine" belongs to the state of affairs so altered.

An event, a situation which has been produced, is a concrete external actuality which because of its concreteness has in it an indeterminable multiplicity of factors. Any and every single element which appears as the condition, ground, or cause of one such factor, and so has contributed its share to the event in question, may be looked upon as responsible for the event, or at least as sharing the responsibility for it. Hence, in the case of a complex event (e.g. the French Revolution) it is open to the abstract Understanding to choose which of an endless number of factors it will maintain to be responsible for it.

116. It is, of course, not my own doing if damage is caused to others by things whose owner I am and which as external objects stand and are effective in manifold connexions with other things (as may also be the case with my self as a bodily mechanism or as a living thing). This damage, however, is to some extent chargeable to me because the things that cause it are in principle mine, although it is true that they are subject to my control, vigilance, &c., only to an extent varying with their special character.

117. The freely acting will, in directing its aim on the state of affairs confronting it, has an idea of the attendant circumstances. But because the will is finite, since this state of affairs is presupposed, the objective phenomenon is contingent so far as the will is concerned, and may contain something other than what the will's idea of it contains. The will's right, however, is to recognize as its action, and to accept responsibility for, only those presuppositions of the deed of which it was conscious in its aim and those aspects of the deed which were contained in its purpose. The deed can be imputed to me only if my will is responsible for it—this is the right to know.

118. Further, action is translated into external fact, and external fact has connexions in the field of external necessity through which it develops itself in all directions. Hence action has a multitude of consequences. These consequences are the outward form whose inner soul is the aim of the action, and thus they are the consequences *of the action*, they belong to the action. At the same time, however, the action, as the aim posited in the external world, has become the prey of external forces which attach to it something totally different from what it is explicitly and drive it on into alien and distant consequences. Thus the will has the right to repudiate the imputation of all consequences except the first, since it alone was purposed.

To determine which results are accidental and which necessary is impossible, because the necessity implicit in the finite comes into determinate existence as an external necessity, as a relation of single things to one another, things which as self-subsistent are conjoined in indifference to one another and externally. The maxim: "Ignore the consequences of actions" and the other: "Judge actions by their consequences and make these the criterion of right and good" are both alike maxims of the abstract Understanding. The consequences, as the shape proper to the action and immanent within it, exhibit nothing but its nature and are simply the action itself; therefore the action can neither disavow nor ignore them. On the other hand, however, among the consequences there is also comprised something interposed from without and introduced by chance, and this is quite unrelated to the nature of the action itself.

The development in the external world of the contradiction involved in the *necessity* of the *finite* is just the conversion of necessity into contingency and vice versa. From this point of view, therefore, acting means surrendering oneself to this law. It is because of this that it is to the advantage of the criminal if his action has comparatively few bad consequences (while a good action must be content to have had no consequences or very few), and that the fully developed consequences of a crime are counted as part of the crime.

The self-consciousness of heroes (like that of Oedipus and others in Greek tragedy) had not advanced out of its primitive simplicity either to reflection on the distinction between act and action, between the external event and the purpose and knowledge of the circumstances, or to the subdivision of consequences. On the contrary, they accepted responsibility for the whole compass of the deed.

SUBSECTION 2

Intention and Welfare

119. An action as an external event is a complex of connected parts which may be regarded as divided into units *ad infinitum*, and the action may be treated as having touched in the first instance only one of these units. The truth of the single, however, is the universal; and what explicitly gives action its specific character is not an isolated content limited to an external unit, but a universal content, comprising in itself the complex of connected parts. Purpose, as issuing from a thinker, comprises more than the mere unit; essentially it comprises that universal side of the action, i.e. the intention.

Etymologically, *Absicht* (intention) implies abstraction, either the form of universality or the extraction of a particular aspect of the concrete thing. The endeavour to justify an action by the intention behind it involves the isolation of one or other of its single aspects which is alleged to be the essence of the action on its subjective side.

To judge an action as an external deed without yet determining its rightness or wrongness is simply to bestow on it a universal predicate, i.e. to describe it as burning, killing, &c.

The discrete character of the external world shows what the nature of that world is, namely a chain of external relations. Actuality is touched in the first instance only at a single point (arson, for instance, *directly* concerns only a tiny section of the firewood, i.e. is describable in a proposition, not a judgement), but the universal nature of this point entails its expansion. In a living thing, the single part is there in its immediacy not as a mere part, but as an organ in which the universal is really present as the universal; hence in murder, it is not a piece of flesh, as something isolated, which is injured, but life itself which is injured in that piece of flesh. It is subjective reflection, ignorant of the logical nature of the single and the universal, which indulges *ad libitum* in the subdivision of single parts and consequences; and yet it is the nature of the finite deed itself to contain such separable contingencies.—The device of *dolus indirectus* has its basis in these considerations.

120. The right of intention is that the universal quality of the action shall not merely be implicit but shall be known by the agent, and so shall have lain from the start in his subjective will. Vice versa, what may be called the right of the objectivity of

action is the right of the action to evince itself as known and willed by the subject as a *thinker*.

> This right to insight of this kind entails the complete, or almost complete, irresponsibility of children, imbeciles, lunatics, &c., for their actions.—But just as actions on their external side as events include accidental consequences, so there is involved in the subjective agent an indeterminacy whose degree depends on the strength and force of his self-consciousness and circumspection. This indeterminacy, however, may not be taken into account except in connexion with childhood or imbecility, lunacy, &c., since it is only such well marked states of mind that nullify the trait of thought and freedom of will, and permit us to treat the agent as devoid of the dignity of being a thinker and a will.

121. The universal quality of the action is the manifold content of the action as such, reduced to the simple form of universality. But the subject, an entity reflected into himself and so particular in correlation with the particularity of his object, has in his end his own particular content, and this content is the soul of the action and determines its character. The fact that this moment of the particularity of the agent is contained and realized in the action constitutes subjective freedom in its more concrete sense, the right of the subject to find his satisfaction in the action.

122. It is on the strength of this particular aspect that the action has subjective worth or interest for me. In contrast with this *end*—the content of the intention—the direct character of the action in its further content is reduced to a *means*. In so far as such an end is something finite, it may in its turn be reduced to a means to some further intention and so on *ad infinitum*.

123. For the content of these ends nothing is available at this point except (α) pure activity itself, i.e. the activity present owing to the fact that the subject puts himself into whatever he is to look upon and promote as his end. Men are willing to be *active* in pursuit of what interests them, or should interest them, as something which is

their own. (β) A more determinate content, however, the still abstract and formal freedom of subjectivity possesses only in its natural subjective embodiment, i.e. in needs, inclinations, passions, opinions, fancies, &c. The satisfaction of these is welfare or happiness, both in general and in its particular species—the ends of the whole sphere of finitude.

> Here—the standpoint of relation (see Paragraph 108), when the subject is characterized by his self-difference and so counts as a particular—is the place where the content of the natural will (see Paragraph 11) comes on the scene. But the will here is not as it is in its immediacy; on the contrary, this content now belongs to a will reflected into itself and so is elevated to become a universal end, the end of welfare or happiness; this happens at the level of the thinking which does not yet apprehend the will in its freedom but reflects on its content as on one natural and given—the level, for example, of the time of Croesus and Solon.

124. Since the subjective satisfaction of the individual himself (including the recognition which he receives by way of honour and fame) is also part and parcel of the achievement of ends of absolute worth, it follows that the demand that such an end alone shall appear as willed and attained, like the view that, in willing, objective and subjective ends are mutually exclusive, is an empty dogmatism of the abstract Understanding. And this dogmatism is more than empty, it is pernicious if it passes into the assertion that because subjective satisfaction is present, as it always is when any task is brought to completion, it is what the agent intended in essence to secure and that the objective end was in his eyes only a means to that.—What the subject is, is the series of his actions. If these are a series of worthless productions, then the subjectivity of his willing is just as worthless. But if the series of his deeds is of a substantive nature, then the same is true also of the individual's inner will.

> The right of the subject's particularity, his right to be satisfied, or in other words the right of

subjective freedom, is the pivot and centre of the difference between antiquity and modern times. This right in its infinity is given expression in Christianity and it has become the universal effective principle of a new form of civilization. Amongst the primary shapes which this right assumes are love, romanticism, the quest for the eternal salvation of the individual, &c.; next come moral convictions and conscience; and, finally, the other forms, some of which come into prominence in what follows as the principle of civil society and as moments in the constitution of the state, while others appear in the course of history, particularly the history of art, science, and philosophy.

Now this principle of particularity is, to be sure, one moment of the antithesis, and in the first place at least it is just as much identical with the universal as distinct from it. Abstract reflection, however, fixes this moment in its distinction from and opposition to the universal and so produces a view of morality as nothing but a bitter, unending, struggle against self-satisfaction, as the command: "Do with abhorrence what duty enjoins."

It is just this type of ratiocination which adduces that familiar psychological view of history which understands how to belittle and disparage all great deeds and great men by transforming into the main intention and operative motive of actions the inclinations and passions which likewise found their satisfaction from the achievement of something substantive, the fame and honour, &c., consequential on such actions, in a word their particular aspect, the aspect which it has decreed in advance to be something in itself pernicious. Such ratiocination assures us that, while great actions and the efficiency which has subsisted through a series of them have produced greatness in the world and have had as their consequences for the individual agent power, honour, and fame, still what belongs to the individual is not the greatness itself but what has accrued to him from it, this purely particular and external result; because this result is a consequence, it is therefore supposed to have been the agent's end and even his sole end. Reflection of this sort stops short at the subjective side of great men, since it itself stands on purely subjective ground, and consequently it overlooks what is substantive in

this emptiness of its own making. This is the view of those valet psychologists "for whom there are no heroes, not because there are no heroes, but because these psychologists are only valets."

125. The subjective element of the will, with its particular content—welfare, is reflected into itself and infinite and so stands related to the universal element, to the principle of the will. This moment of universality, posited first of all within this particular content itself, is the welfare of others also, or, specified completely, though quite emptily, the welfare of all. The welfare of many other unspecified particulars is thus also an essential end and right of subjectivity. But since the absolutely universal, in distinction from such a particular content, has not so far been further determined than as "the right," it follows that these ends of particularity, differing as they do from the universal, may be in conformity with it, but they also may not.

126. My particularity, however, like that of others, is only a right at all in so far as I am a free entity. Therefore it may not make claims for itself in contradiction to this its substantive basis, and an intention to secure my welfare or that of others (and it is particularly in this latter case that such an intention is called "moral") cannot justify an action which is wrong.

It is one of the most prominent of the corrupt maxims of our time to enter a plea for the so-called "moral" intention behind wrong actions and to imagine bad men with well-meaning hearts, i.e. hearts willing their own welfare and perhaps that of others also. This doctrine is rooted in the "benevolence" (*guten Herzens*) of the pre-Kantian philosophers and constitutes, e.g., the quintessence of well-known touching dramatic productions; but to-day it has been resuscitated in a more extravagant form, and inner enthusiasm and the heart, i.e. the form of particularity as such, have been made the criterion of right, rationality, and excellence. The result is that crime and the thoughts that lead to it, be they fancies however trite and empty, or opinions however wild, are to be regarded as right, rational, and excellent, simply because they issue from men's hearts and enthusiasms. . . .

Incidentally, however, attention must be paid to the point of view from which right and welfare are being treated here. We are considering right as abstract right and welfare as the particular welfare of the single agent. The so-called "general good," the welfare of the state, i.e. the right of mind actual and concrete, is quite a different sphere, a sphere in which abstract right is a subordinate moment like particular welfare and the happiness of the individual. As was remarked above, it is one of the commonest blunders of abstract thinking to make private rights and private welfare count as *absolute* in opposition to the universality of the state.

127. The particularity of the interests of the natural will, taken in their entirety as a single whole, is personal existence or life. In extreme danger and in conflict with the rightful property of someone else, this life may claim (as a right, not a mercy) a right of distress, because in such a situation there is on the one hand an infinite injury to a man's existence and the consequent loss of rights altogether, and on the other hand only an injury to a single restricted embodiment of freedom, and this implies a recognition both of right as such and also of the injured man's capacity for rights, because the injury affects only *this* property of his.

> The right of distress is the basis of *beneficium competentiae* whereby a debtor is allowed to retain of his tools, farming implements, clothes, or, in short, of his resources, i.e. of his creditor's property, so much as is regarded as indispensable if he is to continue to support life—to support it, of course, on his own social level.

128. This distress reveals the finitude and therefore the contingency of both right and welfare, of right as the abstract embodiment of freedom without embodying the particular person, and of welfare as the sphere of the particular will without the universality of right. In this way they are *established* as onesided and ideal, the character which in *conception* they already possessed. Right

has already (see Paragraph 106) determined its embodiment as the particular will; and subjectivity, in its particularity as a comprehensive whole, is itself the *embodiment* of freedom (see Paragraph 127), while as the infinite relation of the will to itself, it is implicitly the *universal* element in freedom. The two moments present in right and subjectivity, thus integrated and attaining their truth, their identity, though in the first instance still remaining *relative* to one another, are (*a*) the good (as the concrete, absolutely determinate, universal), and (*b*) conscience (as infinite subjectivity inwardly conscious and inwardly determining its content).

SUBSECTION 3

Good and Conscience

129. The good is the Idea as the unity of the concept of the will with the particular will. In this unity, abstract right, welfare, the subjectivity of knowing and the contingency of external fact, have their independent self-subsistence superseded, though at the same time they are still contained and retained within it in their essence. The good is thus freedom realized, the absolute end and aim of the world.

130. In this Idea, welfare has no independent validity as the embodiment of a single particular will but only as universal welfare and essentially as universal in principle, i.e. as according with freedom. Welfare without right is not a good. Similarly, right without welfare is not the good; *fiat justitia* should not be followed by *pereat mundus*. Consequently, since the good must of necessity be actualized through the particular will and is at the same time its substance, it has absolute right in contrast with the abstract right of property and the particular aims of welfare. If either of these moments becomes distinguished from the good, it has validity only in so far as it accords with the good and is subordinated to it.

131. For the subjective will, the good and the good alone is the essential, and the subjective will has value and dignity only in so far as its insight

and intention accord with the good. Inasmuch as the good is at this point still only this *abstract* Idea of good, the subjective will has not yet been caught up into it and established as according with it. Consequently, it stands in a *relation* to the good, and the relation is that the good *ought* to be substantive for it, i.e. it ought to make the good its aim and realize it completely, while the good on its side has in the subjective will its only means of stepping into actuality.

132. The right of the subjective will is that whatever it is to recognize as valid shall be seen by it as good, and that an action, as its aim entering upon external objectivity, shall be imputed to it as right or wrong, good or evil, legal or illegal, in accordance with its *knowledge* of the worth which the action has in this objectivity.

The good is in principle the essence of the will in its substantiality and universality, i.e. of the will in its truth, and therefore it exists simply and solely in thinking and by means of thinking. Hence assertions such as "man cannot know the truth but has to do only with phenomena," or "thinking injures the good will" are dogmas depriving mind not only of intellectual but also of all ethical worth and dignity.

The right of giving recognition only to what my insight sees as rational is the highest right of the subject, although owing to its subjective character it remains a formal right; against it the right which reason *qua* the objective possesses over the subject remains firmly established.

On account of its formal character, insight is capable equally of being true and of being mere opinion and error. The individual's acquisition of this right of insight is, on the principles of the sphere which is still moral only, part and parcel of his particular subjective education. I may demand from myself, and regard it as one of my subjective rights, that my insight into an obligation shall be based on good reasons, that I shall be convinced of the obligation and even that I shall apprehend it from its concept and fundamental nature. But whatever I may claim for the satisfaction of my conviction about the character of an action as good, permitted, or forbidden, and so about its

imputability in respect of this character, this in no way detracts from the right of objectivity.

This right of insight into the good is distinct from the right of insight in respect of action as such (see Paragraph 117); the form of the right of objectivity which corresponds to the latter is this, that since action is an alteration which is to take place in an actual world and so will have recognition in it, it must in general accord with what has validity there. Whoever wills to act in this world of actuality has *eo ipso* submitted himself to its laws and recognized the right of objectivity.

Similarly, in the state as the objectivity of the concept of reason, legal responsibility cannot be tied down to what an individual may hold to be or not to be in accordance with his reason, or to his subjective insight into what is right or wrong, good or evil, or to the demands which he makes for the satisfaction of his conviction. In this objective field, the right of insight is valid as insight into the legal or illegal, *qua* into what is recognized as right, and it is restricted to its elementary meaning, i.e. to knowledge in the sense of acquaintance with what is legal and to that extent obligatory. By means of the publicity of the laws and the universality of manners, the state removes from the right of insight its formal aspect and the contingency which it still retains for the subject at the level of morality. The subject's right to know action in its specific character as good or evil, legal or illegal, has the result of diminishing or cancelling in this respect too the responsibility of children, imbeciles, and lunatics, although it is impossible to delimit precisely either childhood, imbecility, &c., or their degree of irresponsibility. But to turn momentary blindness, the goad of passion, intoxication, or, in a word, what is called the strength of sensual impulse (excluding impulses which are the basis of the right of distress—see Paragraph 127) into *reasons* when the imputation, specific character, and culpability of a crime are in question, and to look upon such circumstances as if they took away the criminal's guilt, again means (compare Paragraph 100 and the Remark to Paragraph 120) failing to treat the criminal in accordance with the right and honour due to him as a man; for the nature of man consists precisely in the fact that he is essentially something universal, not a being whose knowledge is an abstractly momentary and piecemeal affair.

Just as what the incendiary really sets on fire is not the isolated square inch of wooden surface to which he applies his torch, but the universal in that square inch, e.g. the house as a whole, so, as subject, he is neither the single existent of this moment of time nor this isolated hot feeling of revenge. If he were, he would be an animal which would have to be knocked on the head as dangerous and unsafe because of its liability to fits of madness.

The claim is made that the criminal in the moment of his action must have had a "clear idea" of the wrong and its culpability before it can be imputed to him as a crime. At first sight, this claim seems to preserve the right of his subjectivity, but the truth is that it deprives him of his indwelling nature as intelligent, a nature whose effective presence is not confined to the "clear ideas" of Wolff's psychology, and only in cases of lunacy is it so deranged as to be divorced from the knowing and doing of isolated things.

The sphere in which these extenuating circumstances come into consideration as grounds for the mitigation of punishment is a sphere other than that of rights, the sphere of pardon.

133. The particular subject is related to the good as to the essence of his will, and hence his will's obligation arises directly in this relation. Since particularity is distinct from the good and falls within the subjective will, the good is characterized to begin with only as the universal abstract essentiality of the will, i.e. as duty. Since duty is thus abstract and universal in character, it should be done for duty's sake.

134. Because every action explicitly calls for a particular content and a specific end, while duty as an abstraction entails nothing of the kind, the question arises: what is my duty? As an answer nothing is so far available except: (*a*) to do the right, and (*b*) to strive after welfare, one's own welfare, and welfare in universal terms, the welfare of others (see Paragraph 119).

135. These specific duties, however, are not contained in the definition of duty itself; but since

both of them are conditioned and restricted, they *eo ipso* bring about the transition to the higher sphere of the unconditioned, the sphere of duty. Duty itself in the moral self-consciousness is the essence or the universality of that consciousness, the way in which it is inwardly related to itself alone; all that is left to it, therefore, is abstract universality, and for its determinate character it has identity without content, or the abstractly positive, the indeterminate.

However essential it is to give prominence to the pure unconditioned self-determination of the will as the root of duty, and to the way in which knowledge of the will, thanks to Kant's philosophy, has won its firm foundation and starting-point for the first time owing to the thought of its infinite autonomy, still to adhere to the exclusively moral position, without making the transition to the conception of ethics, is to reduce this gain to an empty formalism, and the science of morals to the preaching of duty for duty's sake. From this point of view, no immanent doctrine of duties is possible; of course, material may be brought in from outside and particular duties may be arrived at accordingly, but if the definition of duty is taken to be the absence of contradiction, formal correspondence with itself—which is nothing but abstract indeterminacy stabilized—then no transition is possible to the specification of particular duties nor, if some such particular content for acting comes under consideration, is there any criterion in that principle for deciding whether it is or is not a duty. On the contrary, by this means any wrong or immoral line of conduct may be justified.

Kant's further formulation, the possibility of visualizing an action as a *universal* maxim, does lead to the more concrete visualization of a situation, but in itself it contains no principle beyond abstract identity and the "absence of contradiction" already mentioned.

The absence of property contains in itself just as little contradiction as the non-existence of this or that nation, family, &c., or the death of the whole human race. But if it is already established on other grounds and presupposed that property and human life are to exist and be respected, then indeed it is a contradiction to commit theft or murder; a contradiction must be a contradiction of something, i.e. of some content presupposed from the start as a fixed principle. It is to a principle of that kind alone, therefore, that an action can be related either by correspondence or contradiction. But if duty is to be willed simply for duty's sake and not for the sake of some content, it is only a formal identity whose nature it is to exclude all content and specification.

The further antinomies and configurations of this never-ending ought-to-be, in which the exclusively moral way of thinking—thinking in terms of *relation*—just wanders to and fro without being able to resolve them and get beyond the ought-to-be, I have developed in my *Phenomenology of Mind*.

136. Because of the abstract characterization of the good, the other moment of the Idea—particularity in general—falls within subjectivity. Subjectivity in its universality reflected into itself is the subject's absolute inward certainty (*Gewissheit*) of himself, that which establishes the particular and is the determining and decisive element in him, his conscience (*Gewissen*).

137. True conscience is the disposition to will what is absolutely good. It therefore has fixed principles and it is aware of these as its explicitly objective determinants and duties. In distinction from this its content (i.e. truth), conscience is only the formal side of the activity of the will, which as *this* will has no special content of its own. But the objective system of these principles and duties, and the union of subjective knowing with this system, is not present until we come to the standpoint of ethical life. Here at the abstract standpoint of morality, conscience lacks this objective content and so its explicit character is that of infinite abstract self-certainty, which at the same time is for this very reason the self-certainty of *this* subject.

Conscience is the expression of the absolute title of subjective self-consciousness to know in itself and from within itself what is right and obligatory, to give recognition only to what it thus knows as good, and at the same time to maintain that whatever in this way it knows and wills is in truth right and obligatory. Conscience as this unity of subjective knowing with what is absolute is a sanctuary which it would be sacrilege to violate. But whether the conscience of a specific individual corresponds with this Idea of conscience, or whether what it takes or declares to be good is actually so, is ascertainable only from the content of the good it seeks to realize. What is right and obligatory is the absolutely rational element in the will's volitions and therefore it is not in essence the *particular* property of an individual, and its form is not that of feeling or any other private (i.e. sensuous) type of knowing, but essentially that of universals determined by thought, i.e. the form of laws and principles. Conscience is therefore subject to the judgement of its truth or falsity, and when it appeals only to itself for a decision, it is directly at variance with what it wishes to be, namely the rule for a mode of conduct which is rational, absolutely valid, and universal. For this reason, the state cannot give recognition to conscience in its private form as subjective knowing, any more than science can grant validity to subjective opinion, dogmatism, and the appeal to a subjective opinion. In true conscience, its elements are not different, but they may become so, and it is the determining element, the subjectivity of willing and knowing, which can sever itself from the true content of conscience, establish its own independence, and reduce that content to a form and a show. The ambiguity in connexion with conscience lies therefore in this: it is presupposed to mean the *identity* of subjective knowing and willing with the true good, and so is claimed and recognized to be something sacrosanct; and yet at the same time, as the mere subjective reflection of self-consciousness into itself, it still claims for itself the title due, solely on the strength of its absolutely valid rational *content*, to that identity alone.

At the level of morality, distinguished as it is in this book from the level of ethics, it is only formal conscience that is to be found. True conscience has been mentioned only to indicate its distinction from the other and to obviate the possible misunderstanding that here, where it is only formal conscience that is under consideration, the argument is about true conscience. The latter is part of the ethical disposition which comes before us for the first time in the following section.—The religious conscience, however, does not belong to this sphere at all.

THIRD PART

Ethical Life

142. Ethical life is the Idea of freedom in that on the one hand it is the good become alive—the good endowed in self-consciousness with knowing and willing and actualized by self-conscious action—while on the other hand self-consciousness has in the ethical realm its absolute foundation and the end which actuates its effort. Thus ethical life is the concept of freedom developed into the existing world and the nature of self-consciousness.

143. Since this unity of the concept of the will with its embodiment—i.e. the particular will—is knowing, consciousness of the distinction between these two moments of the Idea is present, but present in such a way that now each of these moments is in its own eyes the totality of the Idea and has that totality as its foundation and content.

144. (a) The objective ethical order, which comes on the scene in place of good in the abstract, is substance made concrete by subjectivity as infinite form. Hence it posits within itself distinctions whose specific character is thereby determined by the concept, and which endow the ethical order with a stable content independently necessary and subsistent in exaltation above subjective opinion and caprice. These distinctions are absolutely valid laws and institutions.

145. It is the fact that the ethical order is the system of these specific determinations of the Idea which constitutes its rationality. Hence the ethical order is freedom or the absolute will as what is objective, a circle of necessity whose moments are the ethical powers which regulate the life of individuals. To these powers individuals are related as accidents to substance, and it is in individuals that

these powers are represented, have the shape of appearance, and become actualized.

146. (b) The substantial order, in the self-consciousness which it has thus actually attained in individuals, knows itself and so is an object of knowledge. This ethical substance and its laws and powers are on the one hand an object over against the subject, and from his point of view they *are*— "are" in the highest sense of self-subsistent being. This is an absolute authority and power infinitely more firmly established than the being of nature.

> The sun, the moon, mountains, rivers, and the natural objects of all kinds by which we are surrounded, *are*. For consciousness they have the authority not only of mere being but also of possessing a particular nature which it accepts and to which it adjusts itself in dealing with them, using them, or in being otherwise concerned with them. The authority of ethical laws is infinitely higher, because natural objects conceal rationality under the cloak of contingency and exhibit it only in their utterly external and disconnected way.

147. On the other hand, they are not something alien to the subject. On the contrary, his spirit bears witness to them as to its own essence, the essence in which he has a feeling of his selfhood, and in which he lives as in his own element which is not distinguished from himself. The subject is thus directly linked to the ethical order by a relation which is more like an identity than even the relation of faith or trust.

> Faith and trust emerge along with reflection; they presuppose the power of forming ideas and making distinctions. For example, it is one thing to be a pagan, a different thing to believe in a pagan religion. This relation or rather this absence of relation, this identity in which the ethical order is the actual living soul of self-consciousness, can no doubt pass over into a relation of faith and conviction and into a relation produced by means of further reflection, i.e. into an *insight* due to reasoning starting perhaps from some particular purposes interests, and considerations, from

fear or hope, or from historical conditions. But adequate *knowledge* of this identity depends on thinking in terms of the concept.

148. As substantive in character, these laws and institutions are duties binding on the will of the individual, because as subjective, as inherently undetermined, or determined as particular, he distinguishes himself from them and hence stands related to them as to the substance of his own being.

The "doctrine of duties" in moral philosophy (I mean the objective doctrine, not that which is supposed to be contained in the empty principle of moral subjectivity, because that principle determines nothing—see Paragraph 134) is therefore comprised in the systematic development of the circle of ethical necessity which follows in this Third Part. The difference between the exposition in this book and the form of a "doctrine of duties" lies solely in the fact that, in what follows, the specific types of ethical life turn up as necessary relationships; there the exposition ends, without being supplemented in each case by the addition that "therefore men have a duty to conform to this institution."

A "doctrine of duties" which is other than a philosophical science takes its material from existing relationships and shows its connexion with the moralist's personal notions or with principles and thoughts, purposes, impulses, feelings, &c., that are forthcoming everywhere; and as reasons for accepting each duty in turn, it may tack on its further consequences in their bearing on the other ethical relationships or on welfare and opinion. But an immanent and logical "doctrine of duties" can be nothing except the serial exposition of the relationships which are necessitated by the Idea of freedom and are therefore actual in their entirety, to wit in the state.

149. The bond of duty can appear as a restriction only on indeterminate subjectivity or abstract freedom, and on the impulses either of the natural will or of the moral will which determines its indeterminate good arbitrarily. The truth is, however, that in duty the individual finds his liberation; first, liberation from dependence on mere natural impulse and from the depression which as a particular subject he cannot escape in his moral reflections on what ought to be and what might be; secondly, liberation from the indeterminate subjectivity which, never reaching reality or the objective determinacy of action, remains self-enclosed and devoid of actuality. In duty the individual acquires his substantive freedom.

150. Virtue is the ethical order reflected in the individual character so far as that character is determined by its natural endowment. When virtue displays itself solely as the individual's simple conformity with the duties of the station to which he belongs, it is rectitude.

In an *ethical* community, it is easy to say what man must do, what are the duties he has to fulfil in order to be virtuous: he has simply to follow the well-known and explicit rules of his own situation. Rectitude is the general character which may be demanded of him by law or custom. But from the standpoint of *morality*, rectitude often seems to be something comparatively inferior, something beyond which still higher demands must be made on oneself and others, because the craving to be something special is not satisfied with what is absolute and universal; it finds consciousness of peculiarity only in what is exceptional.

The various facets of rectitude may equally well be called virtues, since they are also properties of the individual, although not specially of him in contrast with others. Talk about virtue, however, readily borders on empty rhetoric, because it is only about something abstract and indeterminate; and furthermore, argumentative and expository talk of the sort is addressed to the individual as to a being of caprice and subjective inclination. In an existing ethical order in which a complete system of ethical relations has been developed and actualized, virtue in the strict sense of the word is in place and actually appears only in exceptional circumstances or when one obligation clashes with another. The clash, however, must be a genuine one, because moral reflection can manufacture clashes of all sorts to suit its purpose and give itself a consciousness of being something special and having made sacrifices. It is for this reason that the phenomenon of virtue proper is commoner when societies and communities are uncivilized, since in those circumstances ethical conditions and their actualization are more a matter of private choice or the natural genius of an exceptional individual. For instance, it was especially to Hercules that the ancients ascribed virtue. In the states of antiquity, ethical life had not grown into this free system of an objective order self-subsistently developed, and consequently it was by the personal genius of individuals that this defect had to be made good. It follows that if a "doctrine of virtues" is not a mere "doctrine of duties," and if therefore it embraces the particular facet of character, the facet grounded in natural endowment, it will be a natural history of mind.

Since virtues are ethical principles applied to the particular, and since in this their subjective aspect they are something indeterminate, there turns up here for determining them the quantitative principle of more or less. The result is that consideration of them introduces their corresponding defects or vices, as in Aristotle, who defined each particular virtue as strictly a mean between an excess and a deficiency.

The content which assumes the form of duties and then virtues is the same as that which also has the form of Impulses. . . . Impulses have the same basic content as duties and virtues, but in impulses this content still belongs to the immediate will and to instinctive feeling; it has not been developed to the point of becoming ethical. Consequently, impulses have in common with the content of duties and virtues only the abstract object on which they are directed, an object indeterminate in itself, and so devoid of anything to discriminate them as good or evil. Or in other words, impulses, considered abstractly in their positive aspect alone, are good, while, considered abstractly in their negative aspect alone, they are evil. . . .

151. But when individuals are simply identified with the actual order, ethical life (*das Sittliche*) appears as their general mode of conduct, i.e. as custom (*Sitte*), while the habitual practice of ethical living appears as a second nature which, put in the place of the initial, purely natural will, is the soul of custom permeating it through and through, the significance and the actuality of its existence. It is mind living and present as a world, and the substance of mind thus exists now for the first time as mind.

152. In this way the ethical substantial order has attained its right, and its right its validity. That is to say, the self-will of the individual has vanished together with his private conscience which had claimed independence and opposed itself to the ethical substance. For, when his character is ethical, he recognizes as the end which moves him to act the universal which is itself unmoved but is disclosed in its specific determinations as rationality actualized. He knows that his own dignity and the whole stability of his particular ends are grounded in this same universal, and it is therein that he actually attains these. Subjectivity is itself the absolute form and existent actuality of the substantial order, and the distinction between subject on the one hand and substance on the other, as the object, end, and controlling power of the subject, is the same as, and has vanished directly along with, the distinction between them in form.

> Subjectivity is the ground wherein the concept of freedom is realized (see Paragraph 106). At the level of morality, subjectivity is still distinct from freedom, the concept of subjectivity; but at the level of ethical life it is the realization of the concept in a way adequate to the concept itself.

153. The right of individuals to be subjectively destined to freedom is fulfilled when they belong to an actual ethical order, because their conviction of their freedom finds its truth in such an objective order, and it is in an ethical order that they are actually in possession of their own essence or their own inner universality (see Paragraph 147).

> When a father inquired about the best method of educating his son in ethical conduct, a Pythagorean replied: "Make him a citizen of a state with good laws." (The phrase has also been attributed to others.)

154. The right of individuals to their *particular* satisfaction is also contained in the ethical substantial order, since particularity is the outward appearance of the ethical order—a mode in which that order is existent.

155. Hence in this identity of the universal will with the particular will, right and duty coalesce, and by being in the ethical order a man has rights in so far as he has duties, and duties in so far as he has rights. In the sphere of abstract right, I have the right and another has the corresponding duty. In the moral sphere, the right of my private judgement and will, as well as of my happiness, has not, but only ought to have, coalesced with duties and become objective.

156. The ethical substance, as containing independent self-consciousness united with its concept, is the actual mind of a family and a nation.

157. The concept of this Idea has being only as mind, as something knowing itself and actual, because it is the objectification of itself, the movement running through the form of its moments. It is therefore

(A) ethical mind in its natural or immediate phase—the *Family*. This substantiality loses its unity, passes over into division, and into the phase of relation, i.e. into

(B) *Civil Society*—an association of members as self-subsistent individuals in a universality which, because of their self-subsistence, is only abstract. Their association is brought about by their needs, by the legal system—the means to security of person and property—and by an external organization for attaining their particular and common interests. This external state

(C) is brought back to and welded into unity in the *Constitution of the State* which is the end and actuality of both the substantial universal order and the public life devoted thereto.

Introduction to the Philosophy of History

. . . The inquiry into the *essential destiny* of Reason—as far as it is considered in reference to the World—is identical with the question, *what is the ultimate design of the World?* And the expression implies that that design is destined to be realized. Two points of consideration suggest themselves; first, the *import* of this design—its abstract definition; and secondly, its *realization*.

It must be observed at the outset, that the phenomenon we investigate—Universal History—belongs to the realm of *Spirit*. The term "*World*," includes both physical and psychical Nature. Physical Nature also plays its part in the World's History, and attention will have to be paid to the fundamental natural relations thus involved. But Spirit, and the course of its development, is our substantial object. Our task does not require us to contemplate Nature as a Rational System in itself—though in its own proper domain it proves itself such—but simply in its relation to *Spirit*. On the stage on which we are observing it—Universal History—Spirit displays itself in its most concrete reality. Notwithstanding this (or rather for the very purpose of comprehending the *general* principles which this, its form of *concrete reality*, embodies) we must premise some abstract characteristics of the *nature of Spirit*. Such an explanation, however, cannot be given here under any other form than that of bare assertion. The present is not the occasion for unfolding the idea of Spirit speculatively; for whatever has a place in an Introduction, must, as already observed, be taken

From *The Philosophy of History*, translated by J. Sibree. Copyright © 1956 by Dover Publications, Inc. Reprinted by permission of the publisher.

as simply historical; something assumed as having been explained and proved elsewhere; or whose demonstration awaits the sequel of the Science of History itself.

We have therefore to mention here:

1. The abstract characteristics of the nature of Spirit.
2. What means Spirit uses in order to realize its Idea.
3. Lastly, we must consider the shape which the perfect embodiment of Spirit assumes—the State.

(1) The nature of Spirit may be understood by a glance at its direct opposite—*Matter*. As the essence of Matter is Gravity, so, on the other hand, we may affirm that the substance, the essence of Spirit is Freedom. All will readily assent to the doctrine that Spirit, among other properties, is also endowed with Freedom; but philosophy teaches that all the qualities of Spirit exist only through Freedom; that all are but means for attaining Freedom; that all seek and produce this and this alone. It is a result of speculative Philosophy, that Freedom is the sole truth of Spirit. Matter possesses gravity in virtue of its tendency toward a central point. It is essentially composite; consisting of parts that *exclude* each other. It seeks its Unity; and therefore exhibits itself as self-destructive, as verging toward its opposite [an indivisible point]. If it could attain this, it would be Matter no longer, it would have perished. It strives after the realization of its Idea; for in Unity it exists *ideally*. Spirit, on the contrary, may be defined as that which has its centre in itself. It has not a unity outside itself, but has already found it; it exists *in* and *with itself*. Matter has its essence out of itself; Spirit is *self-contained existence* (Bei-sich-selbst-seyn). Now this is Freedom, exactly. For if I am dependent, my being is referred to something else which I am not; I cannot exist independently of something external. I am free, on the contrary, when my existence depends upon myself. This self-contained existence of Spirit is none other than

self-consciousness—consciousness of one's own being. Two things must be distinguished in consciousness; first, the fact *that I know;* secondly, *what I know*. In *self* consciousness these are merged in one; for Spirit *knows itself*. It involves an appreciation of its own nature, as also an energy enabling it to realize itself; to make itself *actually* that which it is *potentially*. According to this abstract definition it may be said of Universal History, that it is the exhibition of Spirit in the process of working out the knowledge of that which it is potentially. And as the germ bears in itself the whole nature of the tree, and the taste and form of its fruits, so do the first traces of Spirit virtually contain the whole of that History. The Orientals have not attained the knowledge that Spirit—Man *as such*— is free; and because they do not know this, they are not free. They only know that *one is free*. But on this very account, the freedom of that one is only caprice; ferocity—brutal recklessness of passion, or a mildness and tameness of the desires, which is itself only an accident of Nature—mere caprice like the former.—That *one* is therefore only a Despot; not a *free man*. The consciousness of Freedom first arose among the Greeks, and therefore they were free; but they, and the Romans likewise, knew only that *some* are free—not man as such. Even Plato and Aristotle did not know this. The Greeks, therefore, had slaves; and their whole life and the maintenance of their splendid liberty, was implicated with the institution of slavery: a fact moreover, which made that liberty on the one hand only an accidental, transient and limited growth; on the other hand, it constituted a rigorous thraldom of our common nature— of the Human. The German nations, under the influence of Christianity, were the first to attain the consciousness, that man, as man, is free: that it is the *freedom* of Spirit which constitutes its essence. This consciousness arose first in religion, the in-most region of Spirit; but to introduce the principle into the various relations of the actual world, involves a more extensive problem than its simple implantation; a problem whose solution and application require a severe and lengthened process of culture. In proof of this, we may note that slavery did not cease immediately on the reception of Cristianity. Still less did liberty predominate in States; or Governments and Constitutions adopt a rational organization, or recognize freedom as their basis. That application of the principle to political relations; the thorough moulding and interpenetration of the constitution of society by it, is a process identical with history itself. I have already directed attention to the distinction here involved, between a principle as such, and its *application; i.e.*, its introduction and carrying out in the actual phenomena of Spirit and Life. This is a point of fundamental importance in our science, and one which must be constantly respected as essential. And in the same way as this distinction has attracted attention in view of the *Christian* principle of self-consciousness—Freedom; it also shows itself as an essential one, in view of the principle of Freedom *generally*. The History of the world is none other than the progress of the consciousness of Freedom; a progress whose development according to the necessity of its nature, it is our business to investigate.

The general statement given above, of the various grades in the consciousness of Freedom—and which we applied in the first instance to the fact that the Eastern nations knew only that *one* is free; the Greek and Roman world only that *some* are free; while *we* know that all men absolutely (man *as man*) are free—supplies us with the natural division of Universal History, and suggests the mode of its discussion. This is remarked, however, only incidentally and anticipatively; some other ideas must be first explained.

The destiny of the spiritual World, and—since this is the *substantial World*, while the physical remains subordinate to it, or, in the language of speculation, has no truth *as against* the spiritual— *the final cause of the World at large*, we allege to be the *consciousness* of its own freedom on the part of Spirit, and *ipso facto*, the *reality* of that freedom. But that this term "Freedom," without further qualification, is an indefinite, and incalculable ambiguous term; and that while that which

it represents is the *ne plus ultra* of attainment, it is liable to an infinity of misunderstandings, confusions and errors, and to become the occasion for all imaginable excesses—has never been more clearly known and felt than in modern times. Yet, for the present, we must content ourselves with the term itself without farther definition. Attention was also directed to the importance of the infinite difference between a principle in the abstract, and its realization in the concrete. In the process before us, the essential nature of freedom—which involves in it absolute necessity—is to be displayed as coming to a consciousness of itself (for it is in its very nature, self-consciousness) and thereby realizing its existence. Itself is its own object of attainment, and the sole aim of Spirit. This result it is, at which the process of the World's History has been continually aiming; and to which the sacrifices that have ever and anon been laid on the vast altar of the earth, through the long lapse of ages, have been offered. This is the only aim that sees itself realized and fulfilled; the only pole of repose amid the ceaseless change of events and conditions, and the sole efficient principle that pervades them. This final aim is God's purpose with the world; but God is the absolutely perfect Being, and can, therefore, will nothing other than himself—his own Will. The Nature of His Will— that is, His Nature itself—is what we here call the Idea of Freedom; translating the language of Religion into that of Thought. The question, then, which we may next put, is: What means does this principle of Freedom use for its realization? This is the second point we have to consider.

(2) The question of the *means* by which Freedom develops itself to a World, conducts us to the phenomenon of History itself. Although Freedom is, primarily, an undeveloped idea, the means it uses are external and phenomenal; presenting themselves in History to our sensuous vision. The first glance at History convinces us that the actions of men proceed from their needs, their passions, their characters and talents; and impresses us with the belief that such needs, passions and interests are the sole springs of action—the efficient

agents in this scene of activity. Among these may, perhaps, be found aims of a liberal or universal kind—benevolence it may be, or noble patriotism; but such virtues and general views are but insignificant as compared with the World and its doings. We may perhaps see the Ideal of Reason actualized in those who adopt such aims, and within the sphere of their influence; but they bear only a trifling proportion to the mass of the human race; and the extent of that influence is limited accordingly. Passions, private aims, and the satisfaction of selfish desires, are on the other hand, most effective springs of action. Their power lies in the fact that they respect none of the limitations which justice and morality would impose on them; and that these natural impulses have a more direct influence over man than the artificial and tedious discipline that tends to order and self-restraint, law and morality. When we look at this display of passions, and the consequences of their violence; the Unreason which is associated not only with them, but even (rather we might say *especially*) with *good* designs and righteous aims; when we see the evil, the vice, the ruin that has befallen the most flourishing kingdoms which the mind of man ever created; we can scarce avoid being filled with sorrow at this universal taint of corruption: and, since this decay is not the work of mere Nature, but of the Human Will—a moral embitterment—a revolt of the Good Spirit (if it have a place within us) may well be the result of our reflections. Without rhetorical exaggeration, a simply truthful combination of the miseries that have overwhelmed the noblest of nations and polities, and the finest exemplars of private virtue—forms a picture of most fearful aspect, and excites emotions of the profoundest and most hopeless sadness, counterbalanced by no consolatory result. We endure in beholding it a mental torture, allowing no defence or escape but the consideration that what has happened could not be otherwise; that it is a fatality which no intervention could alter. And at last we draw back from the intolerable disgust with which these sorrowful reflections threaten us, into the more agreeable environment of our individual life—the Present formed by our private aims and interests. In short we retreat into the selfishness that stands on the quiet shore, and thence enjoys in safety the distant spectacle of "wrecks confusedly hurled." But even regarding History as the slaughter-bench at which the happiness of peoples, the wisdom of States, and the virtue of individuals have been victimized—the question involuntarily arises—to what principle, to what final aim these enormous sacrifices have been offered. From this point the investigation usually proceeds to that which we have made the general commencement of our inquiry. Starting from this we pointed out those phenomena which made up a picture so suggestive of gloomy emotions and thoughtful reflections—as *the very field* which we, for our part, regard as exhibiting only the means for realizing what we assert to be the essential destiny—the absolute aim, or—which comes to the same thing—the true *result* of the World's History. We have all along purposely eschewed "moral reflections" as a method of rising from the scene of historical specialties to the general principles which they embody. Besides, it is not the interest of such sentimentalities, really to rise above those depressing emotions; and to solve the enigmas of Providence which the considerations that occasioned them, present. It is essential to their character to find a gloomy satisfaction in the empty and fruitless sublimities of that negative result. We return them to the point of view which we have adopted; observing that the successive steps (Momente) of the analysis to which it will lead us, will also evolve the conditions requisite for answering the inquiries suggested by the panorama of sin and suffering that history unfolds.

The *first* remark we have to make, and which—though already presented more than once—cannot be too often repeated when the occasion seems to call for it—is that what we call *principle*, *aim*, *destiny*, or the nature and idea of Spirit, is something merely general and abstract. Principle—Plan of Existence—Law—is a hidden, undeveloped essence, which *as such*—however true in itself—is not completely real. Aims, principles, etc., have a place in our thoughts, in our subjective design only; but not yet in the sphere of reality. That which exists for itself only, is a possibility, a potentiality; but has not yet emerged into Existence. A *second* element must be introduced in order to produce actuality—viz., actuation, realization; and whose motive power is the Will—the activity of man in the widest sense. It is only by this activity that that Idea as well as abstract characteristics generally, are realized, actualized; for of themselves they are powerless. The motive power that puts them in operation, and gives them determinate existence, is the need, instinct, inclination, and passion of man. That some conception of mine should be developed into act and existence, is my earnest desire: I wish to assert my personality in connection with it: I wish to be satisfied by its execution. If I am to exert myself for any object, it must in some way or other be *my* object. In the accomplishment of such or such designs I must at the same time find *my* satisfaction; although the purpose for which I exert myself includes a complication of results, many of which have no interest for me. This is the absolute right of personal existence—to find *itself* satisfied in its activity and labor. If men are to interest themselves for anything, they must (so to speak) have part of their existence involved in it; find their individuality gratified by its attainment. Here a mistake must be avoided. We intend blame, and justly impute it as a fault, when we say of an individual, that he is "interested" (in taking part in such or such transactions), that is, seeks only his private advantage. In reprehending this we find fault with him for furthering his personal aims without any regard to a more comprehensive design; of which he takes advantage to promote his own interest, or which he even sacrifices with this view. But he who is active in *promoting an object*, is not simply "interested," but interested in that object itself. Language faithfully expresses this distinction.—Nothing therefore happens, nothing is accomplished, unless the individuals concerned, seek their own satisfaction in the issue. They are particular units of society; *i.e.*, they have special needs, instincts, and interests generally, peculiar to themselves. Among these needs are not only such as we usually call necessities—the stimuli of individual desire and volition—but also those connected with individual views and convictions; or—to use a term expressing less decision—leanings of opinion; supposing the impulses of reflection, understanding, and reason, to have been awakened. In these cases people demand, if they are to exert themselves in any direction, that the object should commend itself to them; that in point of opinion—whether as to its goodness, justice, advantage, profit—they should be able to "enter into it" (dabei seyn). This is a consideration of especial importance in our age, when people are less than formerly influenced by reliance on others, and by authority; when, on the contrary, they devote their activities to a cause on the ground of their own understanding, their independent conviction and opinion.

We assert then that nothing has been accomplished without interest on the part of the actors; and—if interest be called passion, inasmuch as the whole individuality, to the neglect of all other actual or possible interests and claims, is devoted to an object with every fibre of volition, concentrating all its desires and powers upon it—we may affirm absolutely that *nothing great in the World* has been accomplished without *passion*. Two elements, therefore, enter into the object of our investigation; the first the Idea, the second the complex of human passions; the one the warp, the other the woof of the vast arrasweb of Universal History. The concrete mean and union of the two is Liberty, under the conditions of morality in a State. We have spoken of the Idea of Freedom as the nature of Spirit, and the absolute goal of History. Passion is regarded as a thing of sinister aspect, as more or less immoral. Man is required to have no passions. Passion, it is true, is not quite the suitable word for what I wish to express. I mean here nothing more than the human activity as resulting from private interests—special, or if you will, self-seeking designs—with this qualification, that the whole energy of will and character is devoted to their attainment; that other interests (which would in themselves constitute attractive aims) or rather all things else, are sacrificed to them. The object in question is so bound up with the man's will, that it entirely and alone determines the "hue of resolution," and is inseparable from it. It has become the very essence of his volition. For a person is a specific existence; not man in general (a term to which no real existence corresponds) but a particular human being. The term "character" likewise expresses this idiosyncrasy of Will and Intelligence. But *Character* comprehends all peculiarities whatever; the way in which a person conducts himself in private relations, etc., and is not limited to his idiosyncrasy in its practical and active phase. I shall, therefore, use the term "passions"; understanding thereby the particular bent of character, as far as the peculiarities of volition are not limited to private interest, but supply the impelling and actuating force for accomplishing deeds shared in by the community at large. Passion is in the first instance the *subjective*, and therefore the *formal* side of energy, will, and activity—leaving the object or aim still undetermined. And there is a similar relation of formality to reality in merely individual conviction, individual views, individual conscience. It is always a question of essential importance, what is the purport of my conviction, what the object of my passion, in deciding whether the one or the other is of a true and substantial nature. Conversely, if it is so, it will inevitably attain actual existence—be realized.

From this comment on the second essential element in the historical embodiment of an aim, we infer—glancing at the institution of the State in passing—that a State is then well constituted and internally powerful, when the private interest of its citizens is one with the common interest of the State; when the one finds its gratification and realization in the other—a proposition in itself very important. But in a State many institutions must be adopted, much political machinery invented, accompanied by appropriate political arrangements—necessitating long struggles of the understanding before what is really appropriate can be discovered—involving, moreover, contentions with private interest and passions, and a

tedious discipline of these latter, in order to bring about the desired harmony. The epoch when a State attains this harmonious condition, marks the period of its bloom, its virtue, its vigor, and its prosperity. But the history of mankind does not begin with a *conscious* aim of any kind, as it is the case with the particular circles into which men form themselves of set purpose. The mere social instinct implies a conscious purpose of security for life and property; and when society has been constituted, this purpose becomes more comprehensive. The History of the World begins with *its general* aim—the *realization of the Idea* of Spirit—only in an *implicit* form (*an sich*) that is, as Nature; a hidden, most profoundly hidden, unconscious instinct; and the whole process of History (as already observed), is directed to rendering this unconscious impulse a conscious one. Thus appearing in the form of merely natural existence, natural will—that which has been called the subjective side—physical craving, instinct, passion, private interest, as also opinion and subjective conception—spontaneously present themselves at the very commencement. This vast congeries of volitions, interests and activities, constitute the instruments and means of the World-Spirit for attaining its object; bringing it to consciousness, and realizing it. And this aim is none other than finding itself—coming to itself—and contemplating itself in concrete actuality. But that those manifestations of vitality on the part of individuals and peoples, in which they seek and satisfy their own purposes, are, at the same time, the means and instruments of a higher and broader purpose of which they know nothing—which they realize unconsciously— might be made a matter of question; rather has been questioned, and in every variety of form negatived, decried and contemned as mere dreaming and "Philosophy." But on this point I announced my view at the very outset, and asserted our hypothesis—which, however, will appear in the sequel, in the form of a legitimate inference—and our belief, that Reason governs the world, and has consequently governed its history. In relation to this independently universal and substantial existence—all else is subordinate, subservient to it, and the means for its development.—The Union of Universal Abstract Existence generally with the Individual—the Subjective—that this alone is Truth, belongs to the department of speculation, and is treated in this general form in Logic.—But in the process of the World's History itself—as still incomplete—the abstract final aim of history is not yet made the distinct object of desire and interest. While these limited sentiments are still unconscious of the purpose they are fulfilling, the universal principle is implicit in them, and is realizing itself through them. The question also assumes the form of the union of *Freedom* and *Necessity*; the latent abstract process of Spirit being regarded as *Necessity*, while that which exhibits itself in the conscious will of men, as their interest, belongs to the domain of *Freedom*. As the metaphysical connection (*i.e.*, the connection in the Idea) of these forms of thought, belongs to Logic, it would be out of place to analyze it here. The chief and cardinal points only shall be mentioned.

Philosophy shows that the Idea advances to an infinite antithesis; that, viz., between the Idea in its free, universal form—in which it exists for itself—and the contrasted form of abstract introversion, reflection on itself, which is formal existence-for-self, personality, formal freedom, such as belongs to Spirit only. The universal Idea exists thus as the substantial totality of things on the one side, and as the abstract essence of free volition on the other side. This reflection of the mind on itself is individual self-consciousness—the polar opposite of the Idea in its general form, and therefore existing in absolute Limitation. This polar opposite is consequently limitation, particularization, for the universal absolute being; it is the side of its *definite existence*; the sphere of its formal reality, the sphere of the reverence paid to God.—To comprehend the absolute connection of this antithesis, is the profound task of metaphysics. This Limitation originates all forms of particularity of whatever kind. The formal volition [of which we have spoken] wills itself; desires to make its own personality valid in

all that it purposes and does: even the pious individual wishes to be saved and happy. This pole of the antithesis, existing for itself, is—in contrast with the Absolute Universal Being—a special separate existence, taking cognizance of specialty only, and willing that alone. In short it plays its part in the region of mere phenomena. This is the sphere of particular purposes, in effecting which individuals exert themselves on behalf of their individuality—give it full play and objective realization. This is also the sphere of happiness and its opposite. He is happy who finds his condition suited to his special character, will, and fancy, and so enjoys himself in that condition. The History of the World is not the theatre of happiness. Periods of happiness are blank pages in it, for they are periods of harmony—periods when the antithesis is in abeyance. Reflection on self—the Freedom above described—is abstractly defined as the formal element of the activity of the absolute Idea. The realizing *activity* of which we have spoken is the middle term of the Syllogism, one of whose extremes is the Universal essence, the *Idea*, which reposes in the penetralia of Spirit; and the other, the complex of external things—objective matter. That activity is the medium by which the universal latent principle is translated into the domain of objectivity.

I will endeavor to make what has been said more vivid and clear by examples.

The building of a house is, in the first instance, a subjective aim and design. On the other hand we have, as means, the several substances required for the work—Iron, Wood, Stones. The elements are made use of in working up this material: fire to melt the iron, wind to blow the fire, water to set wheels in motion, in order to cut the wood, etc. The result is, that the wind, which has helped to build the house, is shut out by the house; so also are the violence of rains and floods, and the destructive powers of fire, so far as the house is made fireproof. The stones and beams obey the law of gravity—press downward—and so high walls are carried up. Thus the elements are made use of in accordance with their nature, and yet to co-operate for a product, by which their operation is limited. Thus the passions of men are gratified; they develop themselves and their aims in accordance with their natural tendencies, and build up the edifice of human society; thus fortifying a position for Right and Order *against themselves*.

The connection of events above indicated, involves also the fact, that in history an additional result is commonly produced by human actions beyond that which they aim at and obtain—that which they immediately recognize and desire. They gratify their own interest; but something further is thereby accomplished, latent in the actions in question, though not present to their consciousness, and not included in their design. An analogous example is offered in the case of a man who, from a feeling of revenge—perhaps not an unjust one, but produced by injury on the other's part—burns that other man's house. A connection is immediately established between the deed itself and a train of circumstances not directly included in it, taken abstractedly. In itself it consisted in merely presenting a small flame to a small portion of a beam. Events not involved in that simple act follow of themselves. The part of the beam which was set fire to is connected with its remote portions; the beam itself is united with the woodwork of the house generally, and this with other houses; so that a wide conflagration ensues, which destroys the goods and chattels of many other persons besides his against whom the act of revenge was first directed; perhaps even costs not a few men their lives. This lay neither in the deed abstractedly, nor in the design of the man who committed it. But the action has a further general bearing. In the design of the doer it was only revenge executed against an individual in the destruction of his property, but it is moreover a crime, and that involves punishment also. This may not have been present to the mind of the perpetrator, still less in his intention; but his deed itself, the general principles it calls into play, its substantial content entails it. By this example I wish only to impress on you the consideration, that in a simple act, something further may be implicated than lies in the intention and

consciousness of the agent. The example before us involves, however, this additional consideration, that the substance of the act, consequently we may say the act itself, recoils upon the perpetrator—reacts upon him with destructive tendency. This union of the two extremes—the embodiment of a general idea in the form of direct reality, and the elevation of a speciality into connection with universal truth—is brought to pass, at first sight, under the conditions of an utter diversity of nature between the two, and an indifference of the one extreme towards the other. The aims which the agents set before them are limited and special; but it must be remarked that the agents themselves are intelligent thinking beings. The purport of their desires is interwoven with *general, essential* considerations of justice, good, duty, etc.; for mere desire—volition in its rough and savage forms—falls not within the scene and sphere of Universal History. Those general considerations, which form at the same time a norm for directing aims and actions, have a determinate purport; for such an abstraction as "good for its own sake," has no place in living reality. If men are to act, they must not only intend the Good, but must have decided for themselves whether this or that particular thing is a Good. What special course of action, however, is good or not, is determined, as regards the ordinary contingencies of private life, by the laws and customs of a State; and here no great difficulty is presented. Each individual has his position; he knows on the whole what a just, honorable course of conduct is. As to ordinary, private relations, the assertion that it is difficult to choose the right and good—the regarding it as the mark of an exalted morality to find difficulties and raise scruples on that score—may be set down to an evil or perverse will, which seeks to evade duties not in themselves of a perplexing nature; or, at any rate, to an idly reflective habit of mind—where a feeble will affords no sufficient exercise to the facultie—leaving them therefore to find occupation within themselves, and to expend themselves on moral self-adulation.

It is quite otherwise with the comprehensive relations that History has to do with. In this sphere are presented those momentous collisions between existing, acknowledged duties, laws, and rights, and those contingencies which are adverse to this fixed system; which assail and even destroy its foundations and existence; whose tenor may nevertheless seem good—on the large scale advantageous—yes, even indispensable and necessary. These contingencies realize themselves in History: they involve a general principle of a different order from that on which depends the *permanence* of a people or a State. This principle is an essential phase in the development of the *creating* Idea, of Truth striving and urging towards [consciousness of] itself. Historical men—*World-Historical Individuals*—are those in whose aims such a general principle lies.

Cæsar, in danger of losing a position, not perhaps at that time of superiority, yet at least of equality with the others who were at the head of the State, and of succumbing to those who were just on the point of becoming his enemies—belongs essentially to this category. These enemies—who were at the same time pursuing *their* personal aims—had the form of the constitution, and the power conferred by an appearance of justice, on their side. Cæsar was contending for the maintenance of his position, honor, and safety; and, since the power of his opponents included the sovereignty over the provinces of the Roman Empire, his victory secured for him the conquest of that entire Empire; and he thus became—though leaving the form of the constitution—the Autocrat of the State. That which secured for him the execution of a design, which in the first instance was of negative import—the Autocracy of Rome—was, however, at the same time an independently necessary feature in the history of Rome and of the world. It was not, then, his private gain merely, but an unconscious impulse that occasioned the accomplishment of that for which the time was ripe. Such are all great historical men—whose own particular aims involve those large issues which are the will of the World-Spirit. They may be called Heroes, inasmuch as they have derived their purposes and their vocation, not from the calm, regular course of things, sanctioned by the existing order; but from a concealed fount—one which has not attained to phenomenal, present existence—from that inner Spirit, still hidden beneath the surface, which, impinging on the outer world as on a shell, bursts it in pieces, because it is another kernel than that which belonged to the shell in question. They are men, therefore, who appear to draw the impulse of their life from themselves; and whose deeds have produced a condition of things and a complex of historical relations which appear to be only *their* interest, and *their* work.

Such individuals had no consciousness of the general Idea they were unfolding, while prosecuting those aims of theirs; on the contrary, they were practical, political men. But at the same time they were thinking men, who had an insight into the requirements of the time—*what was ripe for development*. This was the very Truth for their age, for their world; the species next in order, so to speak, and which was already formed in the womb of time. It was theirs to know this nascent principle; the necessary, directly sequent step in progress, which their world was to take; to make this their aim, and to expend their energy in promoting it. World-historical men—the Heroes of an epoch—must, therefore, be recognized as its clear-sighted ones; *their* deeds, *their* words are the best of that time. Great men have formed purposes to satisfy themselves, not others. Whatever prudent designs and counsels they might have learned from others, would be the more limited and inconsistent features in their career; for it was they who best understood affairs; from whom *others* learned, and approved, or at least acquiesced in—their policy. For that Spirit which had taken this fresh step in history is the inmost soul of all individuals; but in a state of unconsciousness which the great men in question aroused. Their fellows, therefore, follow these soul-leaders; for they feel the irresistible power of their own inner Spirit thus embodied. If we go on to cast a look at the fate of these World-Historical persons, whose vocation it was to be the agents of the World-Spirit— we shall find it to have been no happy one. They attained no calm enjoyment; their whole life was labor and trouble; their whole nature was nought else but their master-passion. When their object is attained they fall off like empty hulls from the kernel. They die early, like Alexander; they are murdered, like Cæsar; transported to St. Helena, like Napoleon. This fearful consolation—that historical men have not enjoyed what is called happiness, and of which only private life (and this may be passed under very various external circumstances) is capable—this consolation those may draw from history, who stand in need of it; and it is craved by Envy—vexed at what is great and transcendant—striving, therefore, to depreciate it, and to find some flaw in it. Thus in modern times it has been demonstrated *ad nauseam* that princes are generally unhappy on their thrones; in consideration of which the possession of a throne is tolerated, and men acquiesce in the fact that not themselves but the personages in question are its occupants. The Free Man, we may observe, is not envious, but gladly recognizes what is great and exalted, and rejoices that it exists.

It is in the light of those common elements which constitute the interest and therefore the passions of individuals, that these historical men are to be regarded. They are *great* men, because they willed and accomplished something great; not a mere fancy, a mere intention, but that which met the case and fell in with the needs of the age. This mode of considering them also excludes the so-called "psychological" view, which—serving the purpose of envy most effectually—contrives so to refer all actions to the heart—to bring them under such a subjective aspect—as that their authors appear to have done everything under the impulse of some passion, mean or grand—some *morbid craving*—and on account of these passions and cravings to have been not moral men. Alexander of Macedon partly subdued Greece, and then Asia; therefore he was possessed by a *morbid craving* for conquest. He is alleged to have acted from a craving for fame, for conquest; and the proof that these were the impelling motives is that he did that which resulted in fame. What

pedagogue has not demonstrated of Alexander the Great—of Julius Cæsar—that they were instigated by such passions, and were consequently immoral men?—whence the conclusion immediately follows that he, the pedagogue, is a better man than they, because he has not such passions; a proof of which lies in the fact that he does not conquer Asia—vanquish Darius and Porus—but while he enjoys life himself, lets others enjoy it too. These psychologists are particularly fond of contemplating those peculiarities of great historical figures which appertain to them as private persons. Man must eat and drink; he sustains relations to friends and acquaintances; he has passing impulses and ebullitions of temper. "No man is a hero to his *valet-de-chambre*," is a well-known proverb; I have added—and Goethe repeated it ten years later—"but not because the former is no hero, but because the latter is a valet." He takes off the hero's boots, assists him to bed, knows that he prefers champagne, etc. Historical personages waited upon in historical literature by such psychological valets, come poorly off; they are brought down by these their attendants to a level with—or rather a few degrees below the level of—the morality of such exquisite discerners of spirits. The Thersites of Homer who abuses the kings is a standing figure for all times. Blows—that is beating with a solid cudgel—he does not get in every age, as in the Homeric one; but his envy, his egotism, is the thorn which he has to carry in his flesh; and the undying worm that gnaws him is the tormenting consideration that his excellent views and vituperations remain absolutely without result in the world. But our satisfaction at the fate of Thersitism also, may have its sinister side.

A World-historical individual is not so unwise as to indulge a variety of wishes to divide his regards. He is devoted to the One Aim, regardless of all else. It is even possible that such men may treat other great, even sacred interests, inconsiderately; conduct which is indeed obnoxious to moral reprehension. But so mighty a form must trample down many an innocent flower—crush to pieces many an object in its path.

JEREMY BENTHAM

⌒

INTRODUCTION

JEREMY WALDRON

Jeremy Bentham is the best known of the English utilitarians, a group of philosophical radicals working at the end of the eighteenth and beginning of the nineteenth century to formulate and apply utilitarian principles as criteria for the detailed criticism and reform of law, politics, and social institutions.

Bentham was born in 1748; he was educated at Westminster School and Queen's College, Oxford. He was admitted to the English bar in 1769, but soon forswore the practice of law as it is for the more solitary, less remunerative, but temperamentally more congenial study of the law as it ought to be. In his earliest writings—*A Fragment on Government*, published in 1776, and *A Comment upon the Commentaries* (unpublished until 1928)—Bentham attacked the characterization of the common law and the English Constitution in William Blackstone's *Commentaries on the Laws of England* (1767), an attack that continues in the later chapters of the extract presented here.

Throughout his life, Bentham insisted that law could be understood only in terms of the determinate commands of an identifiable sovereign backed up by sanctions of some sort. He was a legal positivist, not in the sense that he thought law was or should be morally neutral or value-free, but in the sense that he rejected the idea of natural law, regarding laws instead as social facts, though of course *mutable* social facts that the community was entitled to take charge of and change and improve for the sake of the general welfare. Since law sprang from the human will, lawmaking was to be evaluated in the same way as all other conduct concerning other people—by its tendency to promote the happiness of those affected. On this account, the student of law and politics had a twofold function: first to find out what the existing state of the law was and the effects of its operation on society, and second, to work out what the greatest-happiness principle demanded in the particular circumstances of a given society, to propose rules and institutions for putting those demands into effect, and to persuade powerful sovereigns to include those proposals in the content of their sanctioned commands.

This utilitarian approach to law, politics, and ethics was a product of the intellectual optimism that dominated continental philosophy in the eighteenth century. Under the influence of Enlightenment figures like Cesare Beccaria and Claude Helvetius, Bentham developed a precisely formulated version of utilitarianism, which he set out in perhaps his best-known work, *An Introduction to the Principles of Morals and Legislation* (1789). (The extract that follows is from an adaptation of the *Introduction* published originally in French by Bentham's disciple Etienne Dumont.)

Bentham's utilitarianism is at once a psychological theory and a normative principle: "Nature has placed mankind under the governance of two sovereign masters, *pain* and *pleasure*. It is for them alone to determine what we ought to do, as well as to determine what we shall do." The "ought" side of this equation is pretty clear. The utilitarian principle approves or disapproves of actions, including legislative actions, by their effects on the happiness of the members of the community ("the greatest happiness of the greatest number"), and Bentham provided an elaborate account of the various dimensions on which pleasure and pain would have to be measured in the "moral arithmetic" that legislative calculations ought ideally to involve.

What is less clear is how this comports with the "is" side of his theory, the view about psychological motivation. If sovereigns are motivated in fact by pleasure and pain, they are likely to pass laws that promote their own interests rather than those of their subjects. Bentham never really came to terms with this difficulty in his earlier work, but by the beginning of the nineteenth century he had become convinced that the promotion of the greatest happiness of the greatest number could be secured only by giving the greatest number some degree of influence over the careers (and thus the happiness) of their legislators, making the latter effectively accountable to them. In this way the tension between the normative and the psychological sides of Benthamism generated a pretty powerful argument for democracy.

The paradigm of utilitarian moral calculation—adding costs and benefits to members of the community, multiplying each one by its intensity and discounting it by its uncertainty—dominated Bentham's thought throughout his life. He did not believe it could be applied meticulously "to every moral judgment or to every legislative operation." And he did believe it should be supplemented by what he called "axioms of mental pathology," that is, empirical generalizations "expressive of the connexion between such occurrences as are continually taking place, or liable to take place, and the pleasures and pains representing the result of them." (The law of the diminishing marginal utility of money is a good example.) But the calculus of utility was "always to be kept in view," if only as a way of discrediting other less consequentialist—and on Bentham's account less rational—approaches to politics, such as appeals to tradition, religion, or natural law.

In particular, it is Bentham's consequentialism that explains his antipathy to that other great reforming creed of his day, the doctrine of natural rights expounded by the American and French revolutionaries. Though Bentham supported both revolutions, he regarded the invocation of rights as a dangerous argument stopper in politics: "When I hear of natural rights . . . I always see in the background a cluster of daggers and pikes introduced into the National Assembly." The problem with rights was conceptual as well as political. Bentham's polemic *Anarchical Fallacies* (written in the 1790s as a response to the French Declaration of the Rights of Man and the Citizen) is famous for the quip "Natural rights is simple nonsense: natural and imprescriptible rights, rhetorical nonsense—nonsense upon stilts," and the word "nonsense" here is not just a term of abuse but the mark of another of Bentham's convictions: the need for analytical clarity and linguistic precision. This concern is apt to seem pedantic to us, or even cranky in the context of Bentham's obsession with elaborate taxonomies and coining of new terms such as "demosio-tameutic" to settle problems of definition. We forget, though, how riddled with confusion political and legal discourse was in Bentham's day and how often verbal equivocation was put to the service of reaction. Macaulay was not exaggerating when he described Bentham as "the man who found jurisprudence a gibberish and left it a science."

Much the same can be said about Bentham's more practical schemes for legal and social reform. In his later years, Bentham sent out a steady stream of legislative and constitutional proposals touching almost every aspect of public affairs, from the codification of civil law to the detailed design of prisons. The recipients included not only the government of his own country but also those of Russia, France, Spain, and particularly the new republics of North and South America. During this period, the previously solitary Bentham accumulated a number of acolytes who took on the task of making his often illegible and chaotic manuscripts available in orderly form to the general public. (This process continues, with no end in sight, to this day.) He died in 1832, surrounded by these acolytes and by well over seventy thousand pages of manuscript material.

That few of Bentham's proposals were ever taken up directly by those who received them might lead us to regard this body of work as the cranky production of a utilitarian Mad Hatter, closeted in his study and beguiled by the intricacies of his own crabbed system. In fact, his lasting legacy was the spirit of rational reform that came to dominate English politics through the work of those whose intelligence and political instincts were molded by Bentham's example. We tend to underestimate this legacy now, because we take for granted many of the reforms that were animated by the rational, radical, and calculating spirit of Benthamism. It is easy to forget how savage and chaotic the English criminal law was until the utilitarians set about campaigning for its reform and rationalization in the nineteenth century. It was not just the criminal law. One commentator offered this list in the London *Times*, a century after Bentham's death:

> The reform of the representative system in Parliament; the removal of defects in the jury system, the abolition of imprisonment for debt, the sweeping away of usury laws, reform of the law of evidence, reform of the Poor Law, the establishment of a national system of education, an extension of the idea of savings banks, cheap postage, a complete and uniform Register of Births, Deaths and Marriages, a Code for Merchant Shipping, protection of inventors, uniform and scientific methods of drafting Acts of Parliament, the passing of public health legislation. . . .

To us, the commentator remarked, the list makes quite dull reading. But in 1800 it was an heroic adventure, "for when Bentham set forth his polity all these things were impossible, absurd, ridiculous. Great intellects waved them away. . . ."

Thus we should read the extract that follows not just as a practical manifesto, but as an earnest, if rather labored, attempt to found a new political culture, not forgetting how hard it was at the beginning of the nineteenth century to sustain thinking in these or any similar terms in public life, against the baying of prejudice, terror, superstition, equivocation, and humbug that for time immemorial had greeted any attempt to rehabilitate the fabric of English society and its law.

There are excellent discussions of Bentham's political philosophy in Ross Harrison, *Bentham* (London: Routledge, 1983); in "The Arguments of the Philosophers" series, in Douglas Long, *Bentham on Liberty* (Toronto: University of Toronto Press, 1977); and in Nancy Rosenblum, *Bentham's Theory of the State* (Cambridge, Mass.: Harvard University Press, 1978). For his legal theory, see Gerald Postema, *Bentham and the Common Law Tradition* (Oxford: Clarendon Press, 1986), and *Essays on Bentham* (Oxford: Clarendon Press, 1983) by one of the twentieth century's most distinguished Bentham editors, H. L. A. Hart.

Principles of Legislation

CHAPTER I

The Principle of Utility

The Public Good ought to be the object of the legislator; General Utility ought to be the foundation of his reasonings. To know the true good of the community is what constitutes the science of legislation; the art consists in finding the means to realize that good.

The principle of *utility*, vaguely announced, is seldom contradicted; it is even looked upon as a sort of commonplace in politics and morals. But this almost universal assent is only apparent. The same ideas are not attached to this principle; the same value is not given to it; no uniform and logical manner of reasoning results from it.

To give it all the efficacy which it ought to have, that is, to make it the foundation of a system of reasonings, three conditions are necessary.

First,—To attach clear and precise ideas to the word *utility*, exactly the same with all who employ it.

Second,—To establish the unity and the sovereignty of this principle, by rigorously excluding every other. It is nothing to subscribe to it in general; it must be admitted without any exception.

Third,—To find the processes of a moral arithmetic by which uniform results may be arrived at.

The causes of dissent from the doctrine of utility may all be referred to two false principles, which exercise an influence, sometimes open and sometimes secret, upon the judgments of men. If these can be pointed out and excluded, the true principle will remain in purity and strength.

These three principles are like three roads which often cross each other, but of which only one leads to the wished-for destination. The traveller turns often from one into another, and loses in these wanderings more than half his time and strength. The true route is however the easiest; it has mile-stones which cannot be shifted, it has inscriptions, in a universal language, which cannot be effaced; while the two false routes have only contradictory direction in enigmatical characters. But without abusing the language of allegory, let us seek to give a clear idea of the true principle, and of its two adversaries.

Nature has placed man under the empire of *pleasure* and of *pain*. We owe to them all our ideas; we refer to them all our judgments and all the determinations of our life. He who pretends to withdraw himself from this subjection knows not what he says. His only object is to seek pleasure and to shun pain, even at the very instant that he rejects the greatest pleasures or embraces pains the most acute. These eternal and irresistible sentiments ought to be the great study of the moralist and the legislator. The *principle of utility* subjects everything to these two motives.

Utility is an abstract term. It expresses the property or tendency of a thing to prevent some evil or to procure some good. *Evil* is pain, or the

The Theory of Legislation (New York: Harcourt Brace 1931). Translated by Richard Hildreth.

cause of pain. *Good* is pleasure, or the cause of pleasure. That which is comfortable to the utility, or the interest of an individual, is what tends to augment the total sum of his happiness. That which is conformable to the utility, or the interest of a community, is what tends to augment the total sum of happiness of the individuals that compose it.

A *principle* is a first idea, which is made the beginning or basis of a system of reasonings. To illustrate it by a sensible image, it is a fixed point to which the first link of a chain is attached. Such a principle must be clearly evident—to illustrate and to explain it must secure its acknowledgment. Such are the axioms of mathematics; they are not proved directly; it is enough to show that they cannot be rejected without falling into absurdity.

The *logic of utility* consists in setting out, in all the operations of the judgment, from the calculation or comparison of pains and pleasures, and in not allowing the interference of any other idea.

I am a partisan of the *principle of utility* when I measure my approbation or disapprobation of a public or private act by its tendency to produce pleasure or pain; when I employ the words *just, unjust, moral, immoral, good, bad,* simply as collective terms including the ideas of certain pains or pleasures; it always being understood that I use the words *pain* and *pleasure* in their ordinary signification, without inventing any arbitrary definition for the sake of excluding certain pleasures or denying the existence of certain pains. In this matter we want no refinement, no metaphysics. It is not necessary to consult Plato, nor Aristotle. *Pain* and *pleasure* are what everybody feels to be such—the peasant and the prince, the unlearned as well as the philosopher.

He who adopts the *principle of utility*, esteems virtue to be a good only on account of the pleasures which result from it; he regards vice as an evil only because of the pains which it produces. Moral good is *good* only by its tendency to produce physical good. Moral evil is *evil* only by its tendency to produce physical evil; but when I say *physical*, I mean the pains and pleasures of the

soul as well as the pains and pleasures of sense. I have in view man, such as he is, in his actual constitution.

Programs for Reform

If the partisan of the *principle of utility* finds in the common list of virtues an action from which there results more pain than pleasure, he does not hesitate to regard that pretended virtue as a vice; he will not suffer himself to be imposed upon by the general error; he will not lightly believe in the policy of employing false virtues to maintain the true.

If he finds in the common list of offenses some indifferent action, some innocent pleasure, he will not hesitate to transport this pretended offence into the class of lawful actions; he will pity the pretended criminals, and will reserve his indignation for their persecutors.

CHAPTER II

The Ascetic Principle[1]

This principle is exactly the rival, the antagonist of that which we have just been examining. Those who follow it have a horror of pleasures. Everything which gratifies the senses, in their view, is odious and criminal. They found morality upon privations, and virtue upon the renouncement of one's self. In one word, the reverse of the partisans of utility, they approve everything which tends to diminish enjoyment, they blame everything, which tends to augment it.

This principle has been more or less followed by two classes of men, who in other respects have scarce any resemblance, and who even affect a mutual contempt. The one class are philosophers, the other, devotees. The ascetic philosophers, animated by the hope of applause, have flattered themselves with the idea of seeming to rise above humanity, by despising vulgar pleasures. They expect to be paid in reputation and in glory, for all the sacrifices which they seem to make to the severity of their maxims. The ascetic devotees are foolish people, tormented by vain terrors. Man, in their eyes, is but a degenerate being, who ought to punish himself without ceasing for the crime of being born, and never to turn off his thoughts from that gulf of eternal misery which is ready to open beneath his feet. Still, the martyrs to these absurd opinions have, like all others, a fund of hope. Independent of the worldly pleasures attached to the reputation of sanctity, these atrabilious pietists flatter themselves that every instant of voluntary pain here below will procure them an age of happiness in another life. Thus, even the ascetic principle reposes upon some false idea of utility. It acquired its ascendancy only through mistake.[2]

The devotees have carried the ascetic principle much further than the philosophers. The philosophical party has confined itself to censuring pleasures; the religious sects have turned the infliction of pain into a duty. The stoics said that pain was not an evil; the Jansenists maintained that it was actually a good. The philosophical party never reproved pleasures in the mass, but only those which it called gross and sensual, while it exalted the pleasures of sentiment and understanding. It was rather a preference for the one class, than a total exclusion of the other. Always despised, or disparaged under its true name, pleasure was received and applauded when it took the titles of *honour, glory, reputation, decorum,* or *self-esteem.*

Not to be accused of exaggerating the absurdity of the ascetics, I shall mention the least unreasonable origin which can be assigned to their system.

It was early perceived that the attraction of pleasure might seduce into pernicious acts; that is, acts of which the good was not equivalent to the evil. To forbid these pleasures, in consideration of their bad effects, is the object of sound morals and good laws. But the ascetics have made a mistake, for they have attacked pleasure itself; they have condemned it in general; they have made it the object of a universal prohibition, the sign of a reprobate nature; and it is only out of regard for human weakness that they have had the indulgence to grant some particular exemptions.

CHAPTER III

The Arbitrary Principle; or the Principle of Sympathy and Antipathy

This principle consists in approving or blaming by sentiment, without giving any other reason for the decision except the decision itself. *I love; I hate;* such is the pivot on which this principle turns. An action is judged to be good or bad, not because it is conformable, or on the contrary, to the interest of those whom it affects, but because it pleases or displeases him who judges. He pronounces sovereignly; he admits no appeal; he does not think himself obliged to justify his opinion by any consideration relative to the good of society. "It is my interior persuasion; it is my intimate conviction; I feel it; sentiment consults nobody; the worse for him who does not agree with me—he is not a man, he is a monster in human shape." Such is the despotic tone of these decisions.

But, it may be asked, are there men so unreasonable as to dictate their particular sentiments as laws, and to arrogate to themselves the privilege of infallibility? What you call the *principle of sympathy and antipathy* is not a principle of reasoning; it is rather the negation, the annihilation of all principle. A true anarchy of ideas results from it; since every man having an equal right to give *his* sentiments as a universal rule, there will no longer be any common measure, no ultimate tribunal to which we can appeal.

Without doubt the absurdity of this principle is sufficiently manifest. No man, therefore, is bold enough to say openly, "I wish you to think as I do, without giving me the trouble to reason with you." Every one would revolt against a pretension so absurd. Therefore, recourse is had to diverse inventions of disguise. Despotism is veiled under some ingenious phrase. Of this the greater part of philosophical systems are a proof.

One man tells you that he has in himself something which has been given him to teach what is good and what is evil; and this he calls either his *conscience* or his *moral sense*. Then, working at his case, he decides such a thing to be good, such another to be bad. Why? Because my moral sense tells me so; because my conscience approves or disapproves it.

Another comes and the phrase changes. It is no longer the moral sense,—it is *common sense* which tells him what is good and what is bad. This common sense is a sense, he says, which belongs to everybody; but then he takes good care in speaking of everybody to make no account of those who do not think as he does.

Another tells you that this moral sense and this common sense are but dreams; that the *understanding* determines what is good and what is bad. His understanding tells him so and so; all good and wise men have just such an understanding as he has. As to those who do not think in the same way, it is a clear proof that their understandings are defective or corrupt.

Another tells you that he has an *eternal and immutable rule of right*, which rule commands this and forbids that; then he details to you his own particular sentiments, which you are obliged to receive as so many branches of the eternal rule of right.

You hear a multitude of professors, of jurists, of magistrates, of philosophers, who make the *law of nature* echo in your ears. They all dispute, it is true, upon every point of their system; but no matter—each one proceeds with the same confident intrepidity, and utters his opinions as so many chapters of the *law of nature*. The phrase is sometimes modified, and we find in its place, *natural right, natural equity, the rights of man*, etc.

One philosopher undertakes to build a moral system upon what he calls *truth;* according to him, the only evil in the world is lying. If you kill your father, you commit a crime, because it is a particular fashion of saying that he is not your father. Everything which this philosopher does not like, he disapproves under the pretext that it is a sort of falsehood—since it amounts to asserting that we ought to do what ought not to be done. . . .

To sum up—the *ascetic principle* attacks utility in front. The *principle of sympathy* neither rejects it nor admits it; it pays no attention to it; it floats at hazard between good and evil. The ascetic principle is so unreasonable, that its most senseless followers have never attempted to carry it out. The principle of sympathy and antipathy does not prevent its partisans from having recourse to the principle of utility. This last alone neither asks nor admits any exceptions. *Qui non sub me contra me;* that which is not under me is against me; such is its motto. According to this principle, to legislate is an affair of observation and calculation; according to the ascetics, it is an affair of fanaticism; according to the principle of sympathy and antipathy, it is a matter of humour, of imagination, of taste. The first method is adapted to philosophers; the second to monks; the third is the favourite of wits, of ordinary moralists, of men of the world, of the multitude.

CHAPTER IV

Operation of These Principles Upon Legislation

. . . The principle which has exercised the greatest influence upon governments, is that of sympathy and antipathy. In fact, we must refer to that principle all those specious objects which governments pursue, without having the general good for a single and independent aim; such as good morals, equality, liberty, justice, power, commerce, religion; objects respectable in themselves, and which ought to enter into the views of the legislator; but which too often lead him astray, because he regards them as ends, not as means. He substitutes them for public happiness, instead of making them subordinate to it.

Thus, a government, entirely occupied with wealth and commerce, looks upon society as a workshop, regards men only as productive machines, and cares little how much it torments them, provided it makes them rich. The customs, the exchanges, the stocks, absorb all its thoughts. It looks with indifference upon a multitude of evils which it might easily cure. It wishes only for a great production of the means of enjoyment, while it is constantly putting new obstacles in the way of enjoying.

Other governments esteem power and glory as the sole means of public good. Full of disdain for those states which are able to be happy in a peaceful security, they must have intrigues, negotiations, wars and conquests. They do not consider of what misfortunes this glory is composed, and how many victims these bloody triumphs require. The *éclat* of victory, the acquisition of a province, conceal from them the desolation of their country, and make them mistake the true end of government.

Many persons do not inquire if a state be well administered; if the laws protect property and persons; if the people are happy. What they require, without giving attention to anything else, is political liberty—that is, the most equal distribution which can be imagined of political power. Wherever they do not see the form of government to which they are attached, they see nothing but slaves; and if these pretended slaves are well satisfied with their condition, if they do not desire to change it, they despise and insult them. In their fanaticism they are always ready to stake all the happiness of a nation upon a civil war, for the sake of transporting power into the hands of those whom an invincible ignorance will not permit to use it, except for their own destruction. . . .

CHAPTER VII

Pains and Pleasures Considered as Sanctions

The will cannot be influenced except by motives; but when we speak of *motives* we speak of *pleasures* or *pain*. A being whom we could not effect either by painful or pleasurable emotions would be completely independent of us.

The pain or pleasure which is attached to a law form what is called its sanction. The laws of one state are not laws in another because they have no sanction there, no obligatory force.

Pleasures and pains may be distinguished into four classes:

1st. Physical.
2nd. Moral.

3rd. Political.
4th. Religious.

Consequently, when we come to consider pains and pleasures under the character of punishments and rewards, attached to certain rules of conduct, we may distinguish four sanctions.

1st. Those pleasures and pains which may be expected from the ordinary course of nature, acting by itself, without human intervention, compose the *natural* or *physical sanction.*

2nd. The pleasures or pains which may be expected from the action of our fellow-men, in virtue of their friendship or hatred, of their esteem or their contempt—in one word, of their spontaneous disposition towards us, compose the *moral sanction;* or it may be called the *popular sanction, sanction of public opinion, sanction of honour, sanction of the pains and pleasures of sympathy.*

3rd. The pleasures or pains which may be expected from the action of the magistrate, in virtue of the laws, compose the *political sanction;* it may also be called the *legal sanction.*

4th. The pleasures or pains which may be expected in virtue of the threats or promises of religion, compose the *religious sanction.*

A man's house is destroyed by fire. Is it in consequence of his imprudence?—It is a pain of the natural sanction. Is it by the sentence of a judge? It is a pain of the political sanction. Is it by the malice of his neighbours? It is a pain of the popular sanction. Is it supposed to be the immediate act of an offended Divinity? In such a case it would be a pain of the religious sanction, or vulgarly speaking, a judgment of God.

It is evident from this example that the same sort of pains belong to all the sanctions. The only difference is in the circumstances which produce them.

This classification will be very useful in the course of this work. It is an easy and uniform nomenclature, absolutely necessary to distinguish and describe the different kinds of moral powers, those intellectual levers which constitute the machinery of the human heart.

These four sanctions do not act upon all men in the same manner, nor with the same degree of force. They are sometimes rivals, sometimes allies, and sometimes enemies. When they agree, they operate with an irresistible power; when they are in opposition, they mutually enfeeble each other; when they are rivals, they produce uncertainties and contradictions in the conduct of men.

Four bodies of laws may be imagined, corresponding to these four sanctions. The highest point of perfection would be reached if these four codes constituted but one. This perfection, however, is as yet far distant, though it may not be impossible to attain it. But the legislator ought always to recollect that he can operate directly only by means of the political sanction. The three others must necessarily be its rivals or its allies, its antagonists or its ministers. If he neglects them in his calculations, he will be deceived in his results; but if he makes them subservient to his views, he will gain an immense power. There is no chance of uniting them, except under the standard of utility.

The natural sanction is the only one which always acts; the only one which works of itself; the only one which is unchangeable in its principal characteristics. It insensibly draws all the others to it, corrects their deviations, and produces whatever uniformity there is in the sentiments and the judgments of men.

The popular sanction and the religious sanction are more variable, more dependant upon human caprices. Of the two, the popular sanction is more equal, more steady, and more constantly in accordance with the principle of utility. The force of the religious sanction is more unequal, more apt to change with times and individuals, more subject to dangerous deviations. It grows weak by repose, but revives by opposition.

In some respects the political sanction has the advantage of both. It acts upon all men with a more equal force; it is clearer and more precise in its precepts; it is surer and more exemplary in its operations; finally, it is more susceptible of being carried to perfection. Its progress has an immediate influence upon the progress of the other two; but it embraces only actions of a certain kind; it has not a sufficient hold upon the private conduct of individuals; it cannot proceed except upon proofs which it is often impossible to obtain; and secrecy, force, or stratagem are able to escape it. It thus appears, from considering what each of these sanctions can effect, and what they cannot, that neither ought to be rejected, but that all should be employed and directed towards the same end. They are like magnets, of which the virtue is destroyed when they are presented to each other by their contrary poles, while their power is doubled when they are united by the poles which correspond.

It may be observed, in passing, that the systems which have most divided men have been founded upon an exclusive preference given to one or the other of these sanctions. Each has had its partisans, who have wished to exalt it above the others. Each has had its enemies, who have sought to degrade it by showing its weak side, exposing its errors, and developing all the evils which have resulted from it, without making any mention of its good effects. Such is the true theory of all those paradoxes which elevate nature against society, politics against religion, religion against nature and government, and so on.

Each of these sanctions is susceptible of error, that is to say, of some applications contrary to the principle of utility. But by applying the nomenclature above explained, it is easy to indicate by a single word the seat of the evil. Thus, for example, the reproach which after the punishment of a criminal falls upon an innocent family is an error of the popular sanction. The offence of usury, that is, of receiving interest above the legal interest, is an error of the political sanction. Heresy and magic are errors of the religious sanction. Certain sympathies and antipathies are errors of the natural sanction. The first germ of mistake exists in some single sanction, whence it commonly spreads into the others. It is necessary, in all these cases, to discover the origin of the evil before we can select or apply the remedy.

CHAPTER VIII

The Measure of Pleasures and Pains

The sole object of the legislator is to increase pleasures and to prevent pains; and for this purpose
he ought to be well acquainted with their respective values. As pleasures and pains are the only
instruments which he employs, he ought carefully
to study their power.

If we examine the *value* of a pleasure, considered in itself, and in relation to a single individual, we shall find that it depends upon four
circumstances,—

> 1st. *Its intensity.*
> 2nd. *Its duration.*
> 3rd. *Its certainty.*
> 4th. *Its proximity.*

The value of a pain depends upon the same
circumstances.

But it is not enough to examine the value of
pleasures and pains as if they were isolated and
independent. Pains and pleasures may have other
pains and pleasures as their consequences. Therefore, if we wish to calculate the *tendency* of an
act from which there results an immediate pain
or pleasure, we must take two additional circumstances into the account, viz.—

> 5th. *Its productiveness.*
> 6th. *Its purity.*
> A *productive pleasure* is one which is likely to be
>   followed by other pleasures of the same kind.
> A *productive pain* is one which is likely to be
>   followed by other pains of the same kind.
> A *pure pleasure* is one which is not likely to
>   produce pains.
> A *pure pain* is one which is not likely to pro-
>   duce pleasures.
> When the calculation is to be made in relation
>   to a collection of individuals, yet another
>   element is necessary,—
> 7th. *Its extent.*

That is, the number of persons who are
likely to find themselves affected by this pain or
pleasure.

When we wish to value an action, we must
follow in detail all the operations above indicated. These are the elements of moral calculation; and legislation thus becomes a matter of
arithmetic. The *evil* produced is the outgo, the
good which results is the income. The rules of
this calculation are like those of any other. This
is a slow method, but a sure one; while what
is called sentiment is a prompt estimate, but
apt to be deceptive. It is not necessary to re-
commence this calculation upon every occasion. When one has become familiar with the
process; when he has acquired the justness of
estimate which results from it; he can compare
the sum of good and evil with so much promp-
titude as scarcely to be conscious of the steps
of the calculation. It is thus that we perform
many arithmetical calculations, almost without
knowing it. The analytical method, in all its details, becomes essential, only when some new or
complicated matter arises; when it is necessary
to clear up some disputed point, or to demonstrate a truth to those who are yet unacquainted
with it.

This theory of moral calculation, though never
clearly explained, has always been followed in
practice; at least, in every case where men have
had clear ideas of their interest. What is it, for example, that makes up the value of a landed estate?
Is it not the amount of pleasure to be derived
from it? and does not this value vary according
to the length of time for which the estate is to be
enjoyed; according to the nearness or the distance
of the moment when the possession is to begin;
according to the certainty or uncertainty of its
being retained?

Errors, whether in legislation or the moral
conduct of men, may be always accounted for by
a mistake, a forgetfulness, or a false estimate of
some one of these elements, in the calculation of
good and evil.

CHAPTER IX

Circumstances Which Affect Sensibility

All causes of pleasure do not give the same pleasure to all; all causes of pain do not always produce the same pain. It is in this that *difference of sensibility* consists. This difference is in degree, or in kind: in degree, when the impression of a given cause upon many individuals is uniform, but unequal; in kind, when the same cause produces opposite sensations in different individuals.

This difference of sensibility depends upon certain circumstances which influence the physical or moral condition of individuals, and which, being changed, produce a corresponding change in their feelings. This is an experimental fact. Things do not affect us in the same manner in sickness and ill health, in plenty and in poverty, in infancy and old age. But a view so general is not sufficient; it is necessary to go deeper into the human heart. Lyonet wrote a quarto volume upon the anatomy of the caterpillar; morals are in need of an investigator as patient and philosophical. I have not courage to imitate Lyonet. I shall think it sufficient if I open a new point of view—if I suggest a surer method to those who wish to pursue this subject.

The foundation of the whole is *temperament*, or the original constitution. By this word I understand that radical and primitive disposition which attends us from our birth, and which depends upon physical organization, and the nature of the soul.

But although this radical constitution is the basis of all the rest, this basis lies so concealed that it is very difficult to get at it, so as to distinguish those varieties of sensibility which it produces from those which belong to other causes.

It is the business of the physiologist to distinguish these temperaments; to follow out their mixtures; and to trace their effects. But these grounds are as yet too little known to justify the moralist or legislator in founding anything upon them. . . .

CHAPTER X

Analysis of Political Good and Evil—How They Are Diffused Through Society

It is with government as with medicine; its only business is the choice of evils. Every law is an evil, for every law is an infraction of liberty. Government, I repeat it, has but the choice of evils. In making that choice, what ought to be the object of the legislator? He ought to be certain of two things: 1st, that in every case, the acts which he undertakes to prevent are really evils; and, 2nd, that these evils are greater than those which he employs to prevent them.

He has then two things to note—the evil of the offence, and the evil of the law; the evil of the malady, and the evil of the remedy.

An evil seldom comes alone. A portion of evil can hardly fall upon an individual, without spreading on every side, as from a centre. As it spreads, it takes different forms. We see an evil of one kind coming out of an evil of another kind; We even see evil coming out of good, and good out of evil. . . .

The propagation of good is less rapid and less sensible than that of evil. The seed of good is not so productive in hopes as the seed of evil is fruitful in alarms. But this difference is abundantly made up, for good is a necessary result of natural causes which operate always; while evil is produced only by accident, and at intervals.

Society is so constituted that, in labouring for our particular good, we labour also for the good of the whole. We cannot augment our own means of enjoyment without augmenting also the means of others. Two nations, like two individuals, grow rich by a mutual commerce; and all exchange is founded upon reciprocal advantages.

It is fortunate also that the effects of evil are not always evil. They often assume the contrary quality. Thus, juridical punishments applied to offenses, although they produce an evil of the first order, are not generally regarded as evils, because they produce a good of the second order. They produce alarm and danger,—but for whom? Only for a class of evildoers, who are voluntary sufferers. Let them obey the laws, and they will be exposed neither to danger nor alarm.

We should never be able to subjugate, however imperfectly, the vast empire of evil, had we not learned the method of combatting one evil by another. It has been necessary to enlist auxiliaries among pains, to oppose other pains which attack us on every side. So, in the art of curing pains of another sort, poisons well applied have proved to be remedies.

CHAPTER XII

The Limits Which Separate Morals from Legislation

Morality in general is the art of directing the actions of men in such a way as to produce the greatest possible sum of good.

Legislation ought to have precisely the same object.

But although these two arts, or rather sciences, have the same end they differ greatly in extent. All actions, whether public or private, fall under the jurisdiction of morals. It is a guide which leads the individual, as it were, by the hand through all the details of his life, all his relations with his fellows. Legislation cannot do this; and, if it could, it ought not to exercise a continual interference and dictation over the conduct of men.

Morality commands each individual to do all that is advantageous to the community, his own personal advantages included. But there are many acts useful to the community which legislation ought not to command. There are also many injurious actions which it ought not to forbid, although morality does so. In a word, legislation has the same centre with morals, but it has not the same circumference.

There are two reasons for this difference: 1st. Legislation can have no direct influence upon the conduct of men, except by punishments. Now these punishments are so many evils, which are not justifiable, except so far as there results from them a greater sum of good. But, in many cases in which we might desire to strengthen a moral precept by a punishment, the evil of the punishment would be greater than the evil of the offence. The means necessary to carry the law into execution would be of a nature to spread through society a degree of alarm more injurious than the evil intended to be prevented.

2nd. Legislation is often arrested by the danger of overwhelming the innocent in seeking to punish the guilty. Whence comes this danger? From the difficulty of defining an offence, and giving a clear and precise idea of it. For example, hardheartedness, ingratitude, perfidy, and other vices which the popular sanction punishes, cannot come under the power of the laws, unless they are defined as exactly as theft, homicide, or perjury.

But, the better to distinguish the true limits of morals and legislation, it will be well to refer to the common classification of moral duties.

Private morality regulates the actions of men, either in that part of their conduct in which they alone are interested, or in that which may affect the interests of others. The actions which affect a man's individual interest compose a class called, perhaps improperly, *duties to ourselves;* and the quality or disposition manifested in the accomplishment of those duties receives the name of *prudence.* That part of conduct which relates to others composes a class of actions called *duties to others.* Now there are two ways of consulting the happiness of others: the one negative, abstaining from diminishing it; the other positive, labouring to augment it. The first constitutes *probity;* the second is *beneficence.*

Morality upon these three points needs the aid of the law; but not in the same degree, nor in the same manner.

I. The rules of prudence are almost always sufficient of themselves. If a man fails in what regards his particular private interest, it is not his will which is in fault, it is his understanding. If he does wrong, it can only be through mistake. The fear of hurting himself is a motive of repression sufficiently strong; it would be useless to add to it the fear of an artificial pain.

Does any one object, that facts show the contrary? That excesses of play, those of intemperance, the illicit intercourse between the sexes, attended so often by the greatest dangers, are enough to prove that individuals have not always sufficient prudence to abstain from what hurts them?

Confining myself to a general reply, I answer, in the first place, that, in the greater part of these cases, punishment would be so easily eluded, that it would be inefficacious; secondly, that the evil produced by the penal law would be much beyond the evil of the offence.

Suppose, for example, that a legislator should feel himself authorized to undertake the extirpation of drunkenness and fornication by direct laws. He would have to begin by a multitude of regulations. The first inconvenience would therefore be a complexity of laws. The easier it is to conceal these vices, the more necessary it would be to resort to severity of punishment, in order to destroy by the terror of examples the constantly recurring hope of impunity. This excessive rigour of laws forms a second inconvenience not less grave than the first. The difficulty of procuring proofs would be such that it would be necessary to encourage informers, and to entertain an army of spies. This necessity forms a third inconvenience, greater than either of the others. Let us compare the results of good and evil. Offenses of this nature, if that name can be properly given to imprudences, produce no alarm; but the pretended remedy would spread a universal terror; innocent or guilty, every one would fear for himself or his connexions; suspicions and accusations would render society dangerous; we should fly from it; we should involve ourselves in mystery and concealment; we should shun all the disclosures of confidence. Instead of suppressing one vice, the laws would produce other vices, new and more dangerous.

It is true that example may render certain excesses contagious; and that an evil which would be almost imperceptible, if it acted only upon a small number of individuals, may become important by its extent. All that the legislator can do in reference to offenses of this kind is, to submit them to some slight punishment in cases of scandalous notoriety. This will be sufficient to give them a taint of illegality, which will excite the popular sanction against them.

It is in cases of this kind that legislators have governed too much. Instead of trusting to the prudence of individuals, they have treated them like children, or slaves. They have suffered themselves to be carried away by the same passion which has influenced the founders of religious orders, who, to signalize their authority, and through a littleness of spirit, have held their subjects in the most abject dependence, and have traced for them, day by day, and moment by moment, their occupations, their food, their rising up, their lying down, and all the petty details of their life. There are celebrated codes, in which are found a multitude of clogs of this sort; there are useless restraints upon marriage; punishments decreed against celibacy; sumptuary laws regulating the fashion of dress, the expense of festivals, the furniture of houses, and the ornaments of women; there are numberless details about ailments, permitted or forbidden; about ablutions of such or such a kind; about the purifications which health or cleanliness require; and a thousand similar puerilities, which add, to all the inconveniences of useless restraint, that of besotting the people, by covering these absurdities with a veil of mystery, to disguise their folly.

Yet more unhappy are the States in which it is attempted to maintain by penal laws a uniformity of religious opinions. The choice of their religion ought to be referred entirely to the prudence of individuals. If they are persuaded that their eternal happiness depends upon a certain form of worship or a certain belief, what can a legislator oppose to an interest so great? It is not necessary to insist upon this truth—it is generally acknowledged; but, in tracing the boundaries of legislation, I cannot forget those which it is the most important not to overstep.

As a general rule, the greatest possible latitude should be left to individuals, in all cases in which they can injure none but themselves, for they are the best judges of their own interests. If they deceive themselves, it is to be supposed that the moment they discover their error they will alter their conduct. The power of the law need interfere only to prevent them from injuring each other. It is there that restraint is necessary; it is there that the application of punishments is truly useful, because the rigour exercised upon an individual becomes in such a case the security of all.

II. It is true that there is a natural connection between prudence and probity; for our own interest, well understood, will never leave us without motives to abstain from injuring our fellows. . . .

A man enlightened as to his own interest will not indulge himself in a secret offence through fear of contracting a shameful habit, which sooner or later will betray him; and because the having secrets to conceal from the prying curiosity of mankind leaves in the heart a sediment of disquiet, which corrupts every pleasure. All he can acquire at the expense of security cannot make up for the loss of that; and, if he desires a good reputation, the best guarantee he can have for it is his own esteem.

But, in order that an individual should perceive this connection between the interests of others and his own, he needs an enlightened spirit and a heart free from seductive passions. The greater part of men have neither sufficient light, sufficient strength of mind, nor sufficient moral sensibility to place their honesty above the aid of the laws. The legislator must supply the feebleness of this natural interest by adding to it an artificial interest, more steady and more easily perceived.

More yet. In many cases morality derives its existence from the law; that is, to decide whether the action is morally good or bad, it is necessary to know whether the laws permit or forbid it. It is so of what concerns property. A manner of selling or acquiring, esteemed dishonest in one country, would be irreproachable in another. It is the same with offenses against the state. The state exists only by law, and it is impossible to say what conduct in this behalf morality requires of us before

knowing what the legislator has decreed. There are countries where it is an offence to enlist into the service of a foreign power, and others in which such a service is lawful and honourable.[3]

III. As to beneficence some distinctions are necessary. The law may be extended to general objects, such as the care of the poor; but, for details, it is necessary to depend upon private morality. Beneficence has its mysteries, and loves best to employ itself upon evils so unforeseen or so secret that the law cannot reach them. Besides, it is to individual free will that benevolence owes its energy. If the same acts were commanded, they would no longer be benefits, they would lose their attractions and their essence. It is morality and especially religion, which here form the necessary complement to legislation, and the sweetest tie of humanity.

However, instead of having done too much in this respect, legislators have not done enough. They ought to erect into an offence the refusal or the omission of a service to humanity when it would be easy to render it, and when some distinct ill clearly results from the refusal; such, for example, as abandoning a wounded man in a solitary road without seeking any assistance for him; not giving information to a man who is ignorantly meddling with poisons; not reaching out the hand to one who has fallen into a ditch from which he cannot extricate himself; in these, and other similar cases, could any fault be found with a punishment, exposing the delinquent to a certain degree of shame, or subjecting him to a pecuniary responsibility for the evil which he might have prevented?

I will add, that legislation might be extended further than it is in relation to the interests of the inferior animals. I do not approve the laws of the Hindus on this subject. There are good reasons why animals should serve for the nourishment of man, and for destroying those which incommode us. We are the better for it, and they are not the worse; for they have not, as we have, long and cruel anticipations of the future; and the death which they receive at our hands may always be rendered less painful than that which awaits them in the inevitable course of nature. But what can be said to justify the useless torments they are made to suffer; the cruel caprices which are exercised upon them? Among the many reasons which might be given for making criminal such gratuitous cruelties, I confine myself to that which relates to my subject. It is a means of cultivating a general sentiment of benevolence, and of rendering men more mild; or at least of preventing that brutal depravity, which, after fleshing itself upon animals, presently demands human suffering to satiate its appetite.[4]

CHAPTER XIII

False Methods of Reasoning on the Subject of Legislation

It has been the object of this introduction to give a clear idea of the principle of utility, and of the method of reasoning conformable to that principle. There results from it a legislative logic, which can be summed up in a few words. What is it to offer a *good reason* with respect to a law? It is to allege the good or evil which the law tends to produce: so much good, so many arguments in its favour; so much evil, so many arguments against it; remembering all the time that good and evil are nothing else than pleasure and pain.

What is it to offer a *false reason?* It is the alleging for or against a law something else than its good or evil effects.

Nothing can be more simple, yet nothing is more new. It is not the principle of utility which is new; on the contrary, that principle is necessarily as old as the human race. All the truth there is in morality, all the good there is in the laws, emanate from it; but utility has often been followed by instinct, while it has been combatted by argument. If in books of legislation it throws out some sparks here and there, they are quickly extinguished in the surrounding smoke. BECCARIA is the only writer who deserves to be noted as an exception; yet even in his work there is some reasoning drawn from false sources.

It is upwards of two thousand years since Aristotle undertook to form, under the title of *Sophisms*, a complete catalogue of the different kinds of false reasoning. This catalogue, improved by the information which so long an interval might furnish, would here have its place and its uses. But such an undertaking would carry me too far. I shall be content with presenting some heads of error on the subject of legislation. By means of such a contrast, the principle of utility will be put into a clearer light.

1. *Antiquity Is Not a Reason.* The antiquity of a law may create a prejudice in its favour; but in itself, it is not a reason. If the law in question has contributed to the public good, the older it is, the easier it will be to enumerate its good effects, and to prove its utility by a direct process.

2. *The Authority of Religion Is Not a Reason.* Of late, this method of reasoning has gone much out of fashion, but till recently its use was very extensive. The work of Algernon Sidney is full of citation from the Old Testament, and he finds there the foundation of a system of Democracy, as Bossuet had found the principle of absolute power. Sidney wished to combat the partisans of divine right and passive obedience with their own weapons.

If we suppose that a law emanates from the Deity, we suppose that it emanates from supreme wisdom, and supreme bounty. Such a law, then, can only have for its object the most eminent utility; and this utility, put into a clear light, will always be an ample justification of the law.

3. *Reproach of Innovation Is Not a Reason.* To reject innovation is to reject progress; in what condition should we be, if that principle had been always followed? All which exists had had a beginning; all which is established has been innovation. Those very persons who approve a law today because

it is ancient, would have opposed it as new when it was first introduced.

4. *An Arbitrary Definition Is Not a Reason.* Nothing is more common, among jurists and political writers, than to base their reasonings, and even to write long works, upon a foundation of purely arbitrary definitions. This artifice consists in taking a work in a particular sense, foreign from its common usage; in employing that word as no one ever employed it before; and in puzzling the reader by an appearance of profoundness and of mystery.

Montesquieu himself has fallen into this fault in the very beginning of his work. Wishing to give a definition of law, he proceeds from metaphor to metaphor; he brings together the most discordant objects—the Divinity, the material world, superior intelligence, beasts and men. We learn, at last, that *laws are relations; and eternal relations.* Thus the definition is more obscure than the thing to be defined. The word *law*, in its proper sense, excites in every mind a tolerably clear idea, the word *relation* excites no idea at all. The word *law*, in its figurative sense, produces nothing, but equivocations; and Montesquieu, who ought to have dissipated the darkness has only increased it.

It is the character of a false definition, that it can only be employed in a particular way. That author, a little further on (ch. iii.), gives another definition. *Law in general*, he says, *is human reason, in so far as it governs all the people of the earth.* These terms are more familiar; but no clear idea results from them. Is it the fact, that so many laws, contradictory, ferocious, or absurd, and in a perpetual state of change, are always *human reason*? It would seem that reason, so far from being the law, is often in opposition to it.

This first chapter of Montesquieu has given occasion to an abundance of nonsense. The brain has been racked in search of metaphysical mysteries, where none in fact exist. Even Beccaria has suffered himself to be carried away by this obscure notion of *relations*. To interrogate a man in

order to know whether he is innocent or guilty, is to force him, he tells us, to accuse himself. To this procedure he objects; and why? because, as he says, it is to *confound all relations.*[5] But what does that mean? To enjoy, to suffer, to cause enjoyment, to cause suffering: those are expressions which I understand; but to follow relations and to confound relations, is what I do not understand at all. These abstract terms do not excite any idea in my mind; they do not awaken any sentiment. I am absolutely indifferent about *relations:—pleasures* and *pains* are what interest me.

Rousseau has not been satisfied with the definition of Montesquieu. He has given his own, which he announces as a great discovery. *Law*, he says, *is the expression of the general will.* There are, then, no laws except where the people have spoken in a body. There is no law except in an absolute democracy. Rousseau has suppressed, by this supreme decree, all existing laws; and at the same time he has deprived of the possibility of existence all those which are likely to be made hereafter,—the legislation of the republic of San Marino alone excepted.

5. *Metaphors Are Not Reasons.* I mean either metaphor properly so called, or allegory, used at first for illustration or ornament, but afterwards made the basis of an argument.

Blackstone, so great an enemy of all reform, that he has gone so far as to find fault with the introduction of the English language into the reports of cases decided by the courts, has rejected no means of inspiring his readers with the same prejudice. He represents the law as a castle, as a fortress, which cannot be altered without being weakened. I allow that he does not advance this metaphor as an argument; but why does he employ it? To gain possession of the imagination; to prejudice his readers against every idea of reform; to excite in them an artificial fear of all innovation in the laws. There remains in the mind a false image, which produces the same effect with false reasoning. He ought to have recollected that this allegory might be employed against himself. When they see the law turned into a castle, is it not natural for ruined suitors to represent it as a castle inhabited by robbers?

A man's house, say the English, is his castle. This poetical expression is certainly no reason; for if a man's house be his castle by night, why not by day? If it is an inviolable asylum for the owner, why is it not so for every person whom he chooses to receive there? The course of justice is sometimes interrupted in England by this puerile notion of liberty. Criminals seem to be looked upon like foxes; they are suffered to have their burrows, in order to increase the sports of the chase.

A church in Catholic countries is the *House of God*. This metaphor has served to establish asylums for criminals. It would be a mark of disrespect for the Divinity to seize by force those who had taken refuge in his house.

The *balance of trade* has produced a multitude of reasonings founded upon metaphor. It has been imagined that in the course of mutual commerce nations rose and sank like the scales of a balance loaded with unequal weights; people have been terribly alarmed at what appeared to them a want of equilibrium; for it has been supposed that what one nation gained the other must lose, as if a weight had been transferred from one scale to another.

The word *mother-country* has produced a great number of prejudices and false reasonings in all questions concerning colonies and the parent state. Duties have been imposed upon colonies, and they have been accused of offenses, founded solely upon the metaphor of their filial dependence.

6. *A Fiction Is Not a Reason*. I understand by fiction an assumed fact notoriously false, upon which one reasons as if it were true. . . .

Blackstone, in the seventh chapter of his first book, in speaking of the royal authority, has given himself up to all the puerility of fiction. The king, he tells us, is everywhere present; he can do no wrong; he is immortal.

These ridiculous paradoxes, the fruits of servility, so far from furnishing just ideas of the prerogatives of royalty, only serve to dazzle, to mislead, and to give to reality itself an air of fable and of prodigy. But these fictions are not mere sparkles of imagination. He makes them the foundation of many reasonings. He employs them to explain certain royal prerogatives, which might be justified by very good arguments, without perceiving how much the best cause is injured by attempting to prop it up by falsehoods. *The judges*, he tells us, *are mirrors, in which the image of the king is reflected*. What puerility! Is it not exposing to ridicule the very objects which he designs to render the most respectable?

But there are fictions more bold and more important, which have played a great part in politics, and which have produced celebrated works; these are *contracts*.

The *Leviathan* of Hobbes, a work now-a-days but little known, and detested through prejudice and at second-hand as a defence of despotism, is an attempt to base all political society upon a pretended contract between the people and the sovereign. The people by this contract have renounced their natural liberty, which produced nothing but evil; and have deposited all power in the hands of the prince. All opposing wills have been united in his, or rather annihilated by it. That which he wills is taken to be the will of all his subjects. When David brought about the destruction of Uriah, he acted in that matter with Uriah's consent, for Uriah had consented to all that David might command. The prince, according to this system, might sin against God, but he could not sin against man, because all his actions proceeded from the general consent. It was impossible to entertain the idea of resisting him, because such an idea implied the contradiction of resisting one's self.

Locke, whose name is as dear to the friends of liberty as that of Hobbes is odious, has also fixed the basis of government upon a contract. He agrees that there is a contract between the prince and the people; but according to him the prince takes an engagement to govern according to the laws, and for the public good; while the people, on their side, take an engagement of obedience so long, as the prince remains faithful to the conditions in virtue of which he receives the crown.

Rousseau rejects with indignation the idea of this bilateral contract between the prince and the people. He has imagined a *social contract*, by which all are bound to all, and which is the only legitimate basis of government. Society exists only by virtue of this free convention of associates.

These three systems—so directly opposed—agree, however, in beginning the theory of politics with a fiction, for these three contracts are equally fictitious. They exist only in the imagination of their authors. Not only we find no trace of them in history, but everywhere we discover proofs to the contrary. . . .

It is not necessary to make the happiness of the human race dependent on a fiction. It is not necessary to erect the social pyramid upon a foundation of sand, or upon a clay which slips from beneath it. Let us leave such trifling to children; men ought to speak the language of truth and reason.

The true political tie is the immense interest which men have in maintaining a government. Without a government there can be no security, no domestic enjoyments, no property, no industry. It is in this fact that we ought to seek the basis and the reason of all governments, whatever may be their origin and their form; it is by comparing them with their object that we can reason with solidity upon their rights and their obligations, without having recourse to pretended contracts which can only serve to produce interminable disputes.

    7. *Fancy Is Not a Reason.* Nothing is more common than to say, reason decides, eternal reason orders, etc. But what is this reason? If it is not a distinct view of good or evil, it is mere fancy; it is a despotism, which announces nothing but the interior persuasion of him who speaks. Let us see upon what foundation a distinguished jurist has sought to establish the paternal authority. A man of ordinary good sense

would not see much difficulty in that question; but your learned men find a mystery everywhere.

"The right of a father over his children," says Cocceiji, "is founded in reason;—for, 1st, Children are born in a house, of which the father is the master; 2nd, They are born in a family of which he is the chief; 3rd, They are of his seed, and a part of his body." These are the reasons from which he concludes, among other things, that a man of forty ought not to marry without the consent of a father, who in the course of nature must by that time be in his dotage. What there is common to these three reasons is, that none of them has any relation to the interests of the parties. The author consults neither the welfare of the father nor that of the children.

The right of a father is an improper phrase. The question is not of an unlimited, nor of an indivisible right. There are many kinds of rights which may be granted or refused to a father, each for particular reasons. . . .

And here we may remark an essential difference between false principles and the true one. The principle of utility, applying itself only to the interests of the parties, bends to circumstances, and accommodates itself to every case. False principles, being founded upon things which have nothing to do with individual interests, would be inflexible if they were consistent. Such is the character of this pretended right founded upon birth. The son naturally belongs to the father, because the matter of which the son is formed once circulated in the father's veins. No matter how unhappy he renders his son;—it is impossible to annihilate his right, because we cannot make his son cease to be his son. The corn of which your body is made formerly grew in my field; how is it that you are not my slave?

    8. *Antipathy and Sympathy Are Not Reasons.* Reasoning by antipathy is most common upon subjects connected with penal law; for we have antipathies against actions

reputed to be crimes; antipathies against individuals reputed to be criminals; antipathies against the ministers of justice; antipathies against such and such punishments. This false principle has reigned like a tyrant throughout this vast province of law. Beccaria first dared openly to attack it. His arms were of celestial temper; but if he did much towards destroying the usurper, he did very little towards the establishment of a new and more equitable rule.

It is the principle of antipathy which leads us to speak of offenses as *deserving* punishment. It is the corresponding principle of sympathy which leads us to speak of certain action as *meriting* reward. This word *merit* can only lead to passion and to error. It is *effects*, good or bad, which we ought alone to consider.

But when I say that *antipathies and sympathies are no reason*, I mean those of legislator; for the antipathies and sympathies of the people may be reasons, and very powerful ones. However odd or pernicious a religion, a law, a custom may be, it is of no consequence, so long as the people are attached to it. To take away an enjoyment or a hope, chimerical though it may be, is to do the same injury as if we took away a real hope, a real enjoyment. In such a case the pain of a single individual becomes, by sympathy, the pain of all. Thence results a crowd of evils; antipathy against a law which wounds the general prejudice; antipathy against the whole code of that law is a part; antipathy against the government which carries the laws into execution; a disposition not to aid in their execution; a disposition secretly to oppose it; a disposition to oppose it openly and by force; a disposition to destroy a government which sets itself in opposition to the popular will—all the evils produced by those offences, which, in a collective shape, form that sad compound called *rebellion* or *civil war*—all the evils produced by the punishments which are resorted to as a means of putting a stop to those offences. Such is the succession of fatal consequences which are always

ready to arise from fancies and prejudices violently opposed. The legislator ought to yield to the violence of a current which carries away everything that obstructs it. But let us observe, that in such a case, the fancies themselves are not the reason that determines the legislator; his reason is the evils which threaten to grow out of an opposition to those fancies.

But ought the legislator to be a slave to the fancies of those whom he governs? No. Between an imprudent opposition and a servile compliance there is a middle path, honourable and safe. It is to combat these fancies with the only arms that can conquer them—example and instruction. He must enlighten the people, he must address himself to the public reason; he must give time for error to be unmasked. Sound reasons, clearly set forth, are of necessity stronger than false ones. But the legislator ought not to show himself too openly in these instructions, for fear of compromising himself with the public ignorance. Indirect means will better answer his end.

It is to be observed, however, that too much deference for prejudices is a more common fault than the contrary excess. The best projects of laws are for ever stumbling against this common objection—"Prejudice is opposed to it; the people will be offended!" But how is that known? How has public opinion been consulted? What is its organ? Have the whole people but one uniform notion on this subject? Have all the individuals of the community the same sentiment, including perhaps nine out of ten, who never heard the subject spoken of? Besides, if the people are in error, are they compelled always to remain so? Will not an influx of light dissipate the darkness which produces error? Can we expect the people to possess sound knowledge, while it is yet unattained by their legislators, by those who are regarded as the wise men of the land? Have there not been examples of other nations who have come out of similar ignorance, and where triumphs have been achieved over the same obstacles?

After all, popular prejudice serves oftener as a pretext than as a motive. It is a convenient cover for the weakness of statesmen. The ignorance of the people is the favourite argument of pusillanimity and of indolence; while the real motives are prejudices from which the legislators themselves have not been able to get free. The name of the people is falsely used to justify their leaders.

9. *Begging the Question Is Not a Reason.* The petito principii, or begging the question, is one of the sophisms which is noted by Aristotle; but it is a Proteus which conceals itself artfully, and is reproduced under a thousand forms.

Begging the question, or rather assuming the question, consists in making use of the very proposition in dispute, as though it were already proved.

This false procedure insinuates itself into morals and legislation, under the disguise of *sentimental* or *impassioned* terms; that is, terms which, beside their principle sense, carry with them an accessory idea of praise or blame. Neuter terms are those which simply express the thing in question, without any attending presumption of good or evil; without introducing any foreign idea of blame or approbation.

Now it is to be observed that an impassioned term envelops a proposition not expressed, but understood, which always accompanies its employment, though in general unperceived by those who employ it. This concealed proposition implies either blame or praise; but the implication is always vague and undetermined.

Do I desire to connect an idea of utility with a term which commonly conveys an accessory idea of blame? I shall seem to advance a paradox, and to contradict myself. For example, should I say that such a piece of luxury is a good thing? The proposition astonishes those who are accustomed to attach to this word luxury a sentiment of disapprobation.

How shall I be able to examine this particular point without awakening a dangerous association? I must have recourse to a neuter word; I must say, for example, *such a manner of spending one's revenue* is good. This turn of expression runs counter to no prejudice, and permits an impartial examination of the object in question. When Helvetius advanced the idea that all actions have interest for their motive, the public cried out against his doctrine without stopping to understand it. Why? Because the word *interest* has an odious sense; a common acceptation, in which it seems to exclude every motive of pure attachment and of benevolence.

How many reasonings upon political subjects are founded upon nothing but impassioned terms! People suppose they are giving a reason for a law, when they say that it is conformable to the principles of monarchy or of democracy. But that meant nothing. If there are persons in whose minds these words are associated with an idea of approbation, there are others who attach contrary ideas to them. Let these two parties begin to quarrel, the dispute will never come to an end, except through the weariness of the combatants. For, before beginning a true examination, we must renounce these impassioned terms, and calculate the effects of the proposed law in good and evil.

Blackstone admires in the British constitution the combination of the three forms of government; and he hence concludes that it must possess the collected good qualities of monarchy, aristocracy, and democracy. How happened it that he did not perceive, that without changing his premises, a conclusion might be drawn from them, diametrically opposite, yet equally just; to wit, that the British constitution must unite all the particular *faults* of democracy, aristocracy, and monarchy?

To the word *independence*, there are attached certain accessory ideas of dignity and virtue; to the word *dependence*, accessory ideas of inferiority and corruption. Hence it is that the panegyrists of the British constitution admire the *independence* of the three powers of which the legislature is composed. This, in their eyes, is the masterpiece of politics; the happiest trait in that whole scheme of government. On the other side, those who would detract from the merits of that constitution, are always insisting upon the actual *dependence* of one or the other of its branches. Neither the praise nor the censure contain any reasons.

As to the fact, the pretended independence does not exist. The king and the greater part of the lords have a direct influence upon the election of the House of Commons. The king has the power of dissolving that House at any moment; a power of no little efficacy. The king exercises a direct influence by honourable and lucrative employments, which he gives or takes away at pleasure. On the other side, the king is dependent upon the two Houses, and particularly upon the Commons, since he cannot maintain himself without money and troops,—two principal and essential matters which are wholly under the control of the representatives of the people. What pretence has the House of Lords to be called independent, while the king can augment its number at pleasure, and change the vote in his favour by the creation of new lords; exercising too, as he does, an additional influence on the temporal peers, by the prospect of advancement in the ranks of the peerage; and on the bishops, by the bait of ecclesiastical promotion?

Instead of reasoning upon a deceptive word, let us consider effects. It is the reciprocal dependence of these three powers which produces their agreement; which subjects them to fixed rules, which gives them a steady and systematic operation. Hence the necessity of mutual respect, attention, concession, and moderation. If they were absolutely independent, there would be continual shocks between them. It would often be necessary to appeal to force; and the result would be a state of anarchy.

I cannot refrain from giving two other examples of this error of reasoning, founded upon the misuse of terms.

If we attempt a theory upon the subject of *national presentation*, in following out all that appears to be a natural consequence of that abstract idea, we come at last to the conclusion that *universal suffrage* ought to be established; and to the additional conclusion that the representatives ought to be re-chosen as frequently as possible, in order that the national representation may deserve to be esteemed such.

In deciding these same questions according to the principle of utility, it will not do to reason upon words; we must look only at effects. In the election of a legislative assembly, the right of suffrage should not be allowed except to those who are esteemed by the nation fit to exercise it; for a choice made by men who do not possess the national confidence will weaken the confidence of the nation in the assembly so chosen.

Men who would be thought fit to be electors, are those who cannot be presumed to possess political integrity, and a sufficient degree of knowledge. Now we cannot presume upon the political integrity of those whom want exposes to the temptation of selling themselves; nor of those who have no fixed abode; nor of those who have been found guilty in the courts of justice of certain offenses forbidden by the law. We cannot presume a sufficient degree of knowledge in women, whom their domestic condition withdraws from the conduct of public affairs; in children and adults beneath a certain age; in those who are deprived by their poverty of the first elements of education, etc. etc.

It is according to these principles, and others like them, that we ought to fix the conditions necessary for becoming an elector; and it is in like manner, upon the advantages and disadvantages of frequent elections, without paying any attention to arguments drawn from abstract terms, that we ought to reason in establishing the duration of a legislative assembly.

The last example I shall give will be taken from *contracts:* I mean those political fictions to which this name has been applied by their authors.

When Locke and Rousseau reason upon these pretended contracts; when they affirm that the social or political contract includes such and such a clause, can they prove it otherwise than by the general utility which is supposed to result from it? Grant that this contract which has never been reduced to writing is, however, in full existence.

On what depends all its force? It is not upon its utility? Why ought we to fulfil our engagements? Because the faith of promises is the basis of society. It is for the advantage of all that the promises of every individiual should be faithfully observed. There would no longer be any security among men, no commerce, no confidence;—it would be necessary to go back to the woods, if engagements did not possess an obligatory force. It is the same with these political contracts. It is their utility which makes them binding. When they become injurious, they lose their force. If a king had taken an oath to render his subjects unhappy, would such an engagement be valid? If the people were sworn to obey him at all events, would they be bound to suffer themselves to be exterminated by a Nero or a Caligula, rather than violate their promise? If there resulted from the contract effects universally injurious, could there be any sufficient reason for maintaining it? It cannot be denied, then, that the validity of a contract is at bottom only a question of utility—a little wrapped up, a little disguised, and, in consequence, more susceptible of false interpretations.

10. *An Imaginary Law Is Not a Reason.* Natural law, natural rights are two kinds of fictions or metaphors, which play so great a part in books of legislation that they deserve to be examined by themselves.

The primitive sense of the word *law*, and the ordinary meaning of the word, is—the will or command of a legislator. The *law of nature* is a figurative expression, in which nature is represented as a being; and such and such a disposition is attributed to her, which is figuratively called a law. In this sense, all the general inclinations of men, all those which appear to exist independently of human societies, and from which must proceed the establishment of political and civil law, are called *laws of nature*. This is the true sense of the phrase.

But this is not the way in which it is understood. Authors have taken it in a direct sense; as if there had been a real code of natural laws. They appeal to these laws; they cite them, and they oppose them, clause by clause, to the enactments of legislators. They do not see that these natural laws are laws of their own invention; that they are all at odds among themselves as to the contents of this pretended code; that they affirm without proof; that systems are as numerous as authors; and that, in reasoning in this manner, it is necessary to be always beginning anew, because every one can advance what he pleases touching laws which are only imaginary, and so keep on disputing for ever.

What is natural to man is sentiments of pleasure or pain, what are called inclinations. But to call these sentiments and these inclinations laws, is to introduce a false and dangerous idea. It is to set language in opposition to itself; for it is necessary to make *laws* precisely for the purpose of restraining these inclinations. Instead of regarding them as laws, they must be submitted to laws. It is against the strongest natural inclinations that it is necessary to have laws the most repressive. If there were a law of nature which directed all men towards their common good, laws would be useless; it would be employing a creeper to uphold an oak; it would be kindling a torch to add light to the sun.

Blackstone, in speaking of the obligation of parents to provide for the support of their children, says, "that it is a principle of natural law, a duty imposed by nature itself, and by the proper act of the parents in bringing the children into the world." Montesquieu, he adds, "observes with reason, that the natural obligation of the father to support his children, is what has caused the establishment of marriage, which points out the person who ought to fulfill this obligation" (Book i. Ch. 16).

Parents *are inclined* to support their children; parents *ought* to support their children; these are two distinct propositions. The first does not suppose the second; the second does not suppose the first. There are, without doubt, the strongest reasons for imposing upon parents the obligation to bring up their children. Why have not Blackstone and Montesquieu mentioned those reasons? Why do they refer us to what they call the law of nature? What is this law of nature, which needs to be propped up by a secondary law from another legislator? If this natural obligation exists, as Montesquieu says it does, far from serving as the foundation of marriage, it proves its inutility,—at least for the end which he assigns. One of the objects of marriage is, precisely to supply the insufficiency of natural affection. It is designed to convert into obligation that inclination of parents, which would not always be sufficiently strong to surmount the pains and embarrassments of education.

Men are very well disposed to provide for their own support. It has not been necessary to make laws to oblige them to that. If the disposition of parents to provide for the support of their children had been constantly and universally as strong, legislators never would have thought of turning it into an obligation.

The exposure of infants, so common in ancient Greece, is still practised in China, and to a greater extent. To abolish this practice, would it not be necessary to allege other reasons besides this pretended law of nature, which here is evidently at fault?

The word *rights*, the same as the word *law*, has two senses; the one a proper sense, the other a metaphorical sense. *Rights*, properly so called, are the creatures of *law* properly so called, real laws give birth to real rights. *Natural rights* are the creatures of natural law; they are a metaphor which derives its origin from another metaphor.

What there is natural in men is means,—faculties. But to call these means, these faculties, *natural rights*, is again to put language in opposition to itself. For *rights* are established to insure the exercise of means and faculties. The right is the *guarantee;* the faculty is the thing guaranteed. How can we understand each other with a language which confounds under the same term things so different? Where would be the nomenclature of the arts, if we gave to the *mechanic* who makes an article the same name as to the article itself?

Real rights are always spoken of in a legal sense; natural rights are often spoken of in a sense that may be called anti-legal. When it is said, for example, that *law cannot avail against natural rights*, the word *rights* is employed in a sense above the law; for, in this use of it, we acknowledge rights which attack the law; which overturn it, which annul it. In this anti-legal sense, the word *right* is the greatest enemy of reason, and the most terrible destroyer of governments.

There is no reasoning with fanatics, armed with *natural rights*, which each one understands as he pleases, and applies as he sees fit; of which nothing can be yielded, nor retrenched; which are inflexible, at the same time that they are unintelligible; which are consecrated as dogmas, from which it is a crime to vary. Instead of examining laws by their effects, instead of judging them as good or bad, they consider them in relation to these pretended natural rights; that is to say, they substitute for the reasoning of experience the chimeras of their own imaginations.

This is not a harmless error; it passes from speculation into practice. "Those laws must be obeyed, which are accordant with nature; the others are null in fact; and instead of obeying them, they ought to be resisted. The moment natural rights are attacked, every good citizen ought to rouse up in their defence. These rights, evidence in themselves, do not need to be proved; it is sufficient to declare them. How prove what is evident already? To doubt implies a want of sense, or a fault of intellect," &c.

But not to be accused of gratuitously ascribing such seditious maxims to these inspired politicians of nature, I shall cite a passage from Blackstone, directly to the point; and I choose Blackstone, because he is, of all writers, the one who has shown the most profound respect for the authority of governments. In speaking of these pretended laws of nature, and of the laws of revelation, he says: "Human laws must not be permitted to contradict these; if a human law commands a thing forbidden by the natural or divine law, we are bound to transgress that human law," &c. (1 Comm. p. 43).

Is not this arming every fanatic against all governments? In the immense variety of ideas respecting natural and Divine law, cannot some reason be found for resisting all human laws? Is there a single state which can maintain itself a day, if each individual holds himself bound in conscience to resist the laws, whenever they are not conformed to his particular ideas of natural or Divine law? What a cut-throat scene of it we should have between all the interpreters of the code of nature, and all the interpreters of the law of God!

"The pursuit of happiness is a natural right." The pursuit of happiness is certainly a natural inclination; but can it be declared to be a right? That depends on the way in which it is pursued. The assassin pursues his happiness, or what he esteems such, by committing an assassination. Has he a right to do so? If not, why declare that he has? What tendency is there in such a declaration to render men more happy or more wise?

Turgot was a great man; but he had adopted the general opinion without examining it. Inalienable and natural rights were the despotism or the dogmatism which he wished to exercise, without himself perceiving it. If he saw no reason to doubt a proposition; if he judged it evidently true; he referred it, without going further, to natural right, to eternal justice. Henceforward he made use of it as an article of faith, which he was no longer permitted to examine.

Utility having been often badly applied, understood in a narrow sense, and having lent its name to crimes, has appeared contrary to eternal justice. It thus became degraded, and acquired a mercenary reputation. It needs courage to restore it to honour, and to re-establish reasoning upon its true basis.

I propose a treaty of conciliation with the partisans of natural rights. If *nature* has made such or such a law, those who cite it with so much confidence, those who have modestly taken upon themselves to be its interpreters, must suppose that nature had some reasons for her law. Would it not be surer, shorter and more persuasive, to give us those reasons directly, instead of urging upon us the will of this unknown legislator, as itself an authority?

All these false methods of reasoning can always be reduced to one or the other of the two false principles. This fundamental distinction is very useful in getting rid of words, and rendering ideas more clear. To refer such or such an argument to one or another of the false principles, is like tying weeds into bundles, to be thrown into the fire.

I conclude with a general observation. The language of error is always obscure and indefinite. An abundance of words serves to cover a paucity and a falsity of ideas. The oftener terms are changed, the easier it is to delude the reader. The language of truth is uniform and simple. The same ideas are always expressed by the same terms. Everything is referred to pleasures or to pains. Every expression is avoided which tends to disguise or intercept the familiar idea, that from such and such actions result such and such pleasures and pains. Trust not to me, but to experience, and especially your own. Of two opposite methods of action, do you desire to know which should have the preference? Calculate their effects in good and evil, and prefer that which promises the greater sum of good.

Notes

1. *Ascetic*, by its etymology, signifies *one who exercises*. It was applied to the monks, to indicate their favorite practices of devotion and penitence.

2. This mistake consists in representing the Deity in words, as a being of infinite benevolence, yet ascribing to him prohibitions and threats which are the attributes of an implacable being, who uses his power only to satisfy his malevolence.

We might ask these ascetic theologians what life is good for, if not for the pleasures it procures us?—and what pledge we have for the goodness of God in another life, if he has forbidden the enjoyment of this?

3. Here we touch upon one of the most difficult of questions. If the law is not what it ought to be; if it openly combats the principle of utility; ought we to obey it? Ought we to violate it? Ought we to remain neutral between the law which commands an evil, and morality which forbids it? The solution of this question involves considerations both of prudence and benevolence. We ought to examine if it is more dangerous to violate the law than to obey it; we ought to consider whether the probable evils of disobedience are less or greater than the probable evils of obedience.

4. See *Barrow's Voyage to the Cape of Good Hope*, for the cruelties of the Dutch settlers toward their cattle and their slaves.

5. Beccaria. Chap. xii.

ALEXIS DE TOCQUEVILLE

~

INTRODUCTION

STEVEN B. SMITH

Alexis de Tocqueville (1805–1859) was born to a Norman family with an ancient lineage. His parents had been arrested during the French Revolution and were held in prison for almost a year. Only the fall of Robespierre in 1794 saved them from execution. Tocqueville was born under the reign of Napoleon. He studied law in Paris, and sometime during the late 1820s he made the acquaintance of another young aristocrat by the name of Gustave de Beaumont. In 1830 the two men received a commission from the new government of King Louis Philippe to go to the United States in order to study the prison system. Tocqueville's journey to America, which has been extensively documented, lasted a little over nine months, from May 1831 to February 1832. During that time he traveled as far north as New England, south to New Orleans, and west to the outer banks of Lake Michigan. The result of this visit was two large volumes that he called *Democracy in America*. The first volume appeared in 1835 when its author was only thirty years of age and the second volume five years later in 1840.

Democracy in America remains the most important book on democracy ever written. Ironically, the most famous book on American democracy was written by a French aristocrat. From the time of its first publication, the book was hailed as a "masterpiece," by no less an authority than John Stuart Mill. It is often assumed that Tocqueville was a kind of political journalist who visited America, like so many Europeans before and since, to chronicle the peculiar manners and habits of the New World. But that is inaccurate. As he would later say, America "was only the frame, my picture was democracy." What Tocqueville saw in America was what he believed would be the future of Europe; he saw the age of equality not as a local American phenomenon, but a phenomenon of potentially global significance. Tocqueville approached America as a philosopher hoping to educate European statesmen about how to navigate the new age of equality and to steer the ship of state between the shoals of reaction and revolution.

Democracy in America set out to answer two questions. The first concerns the gradual replacement of the *ancien regime*, the old aristocratic order based on the principles of hierarchy, deference, and inequality with a new democratic society based on equality. How did this happen, and what brought it about? The second, not explicitly asked but present on virtually every page of the book, concerns the difference between the form of democracy taken in America and the form taken in France during the revolutionary period. Why was American democracy relatively gentle or mild—what we might call a liberal democracy—and why did democracy in France veer dangerously toward terror and despotism? Tocqueville believed it to be virtually a providential fact of history that society was becoming increasingly democratic.

The opening sentence of *Democracy in America* is among the most famous in the work: "Among the new objects that attracted my attention during my stay in the United States, none struck my eye more vividly than the equality of conditions." Note that Tocqueville speaks of equality as a social state ("equality of conditions") rather than a feature of human nature. This is in part an expression of his sociological imagination. He does not ascribe equality to an original state of nature as did Hobbes, Locke, and Rousseau. Equality of conditions meant the absence of a traditional aristocracy that could hand down privileges and titles by fact of birth. Social equality was produced by the gradual weakening of the claims of aristocracy and is the cause from which democratic government arose. Modern democratic governments are only as old as the American and French Revolutions, but equality of conditions had been prepared by deep-rooted historical processes long before the modern age came into being.

Tocqueville writes about equality as an historical fact that has come to acquire almost providential force. His use of the term "providence" does not so much describe God as an historical process that is working, so to speak, even against the intentions of individual actors. The gradual spread of conditions of equality has two characteristics of providence: it is universal, and it always escapes the powers of human control. It is the very power of equality that makes it seem an irresistible force. Rather than the product of the modern age alone, Tocqueville shows how the steady emergence of the equality has been at the heart of European history for centuries.

It is in order to understand the scope of equality that Tocqueville turns to America of the 1830s. Indeed, there was much in American democracy that he found to admire, especially its traditions of local government, the practice of civil association, and its religious life. Unlike France with its long tradition of administrative centralization, Tocqueville admired the bottom up character of American democracy. It is through uniting and joining together in common endeavors that people develop a taste for liberty. Only through free associations—voluntary groups of all sorts—do we learn the habits of initiative, cooperation, and responsibility. Only such institutions can resist the power of centralized authority. It is through the whole sphere of civil society that we learn how to become democratic citizens.

But it was not just the institutional arrangements of America that Tocqueville found worthy of report: it was the manners, habits, and sentiments—"the habits of the heart"—that made these institutions possible in the first place. Not only a political theorist and sociologist, Tocqueville was a moral psychologist seeking to understand the inner workings of the democratic soul. Among the sentiments he singled out was the spirit of religion. Like other European observers, then as well as now, Tocqueville was perplexed by the fact that in America the spirit of democracy and the spirit of religion have worked hand in hand. From its beginnings, America was a uniquely Puritan democracy created by a people with strong religious habits who brought with them a suspicion of government and a strong desire for independence.

Tocqueville drew two theoretical conclusions from the fact of religious life in America. The first is that contrary to the European experience with its tradition of national churches, it is the separation of church and state that has done most not only to establish political liberty but to encourage the spread of religion. Religion fares best when it is made to fend for itself rather than be a monopoly of the government. The second is that it would be a terrible mistake to attempt to secularize society altogether. It was Tocqueville's belief that free societies rest on public morality and that morality cannot be effective without religion. Individuals may be able to derive moral guidance from reason alone, but societies cannot. The danger in attempting to eliminate religion from public life is that people will increasingly become wards of the state and look to government as surrogate object of worship.

Another habit that Tocqueville admired was the democratic virtue of "self-interest well understood." By this Tocqueville did not mean egoism or avarice. Tocqueville would not have been an admirer of contemporary forms of libertarianism or Gordon Gekko's slogan "Greed is good." While the term "interest" later came to be associated with economic advantage, Tocqueville took it to comprise anything that contributed to human well-being. It also indicated an element of reflection and calculation as to how our aspirations were fulfilled. Self-interest well understood was intended to provide a brake to excessive self-absorption and withdrawal from the life of the community that is ever present in democratic societies. It is a form of enlightened morality that promotes virtues such as honesty, thrift, industry, and personal responsibility. These habits may not reach the sublime heights of heroism and self-sacrifice lauded in aristocratic times, but signify a set of "bourgeois" virtues—virtues of the middle class—appropriate to men and women situated in a modern commercial order. Self-interest well understood is a form of practical utilitarianism that eschews brilliance, less grand and less ambitious than in the past, but, if conscientiously applied, allows people to achieve a modest and continual profit all the days of their lives.

Competing with Tocqueville's understanding of equality as the absence of legal barriers to self-advancement, however, was a second and more ominous understanding of equality as the absolute sovereignty of the people. He sometimes referred to the "omnipotence" of the majority to give the term an almost theological authority. Here is where Tocqueville launched a subtle but powerful criticism of James Madison and the American founders. The American Constitution had enshrined the sovereignty of the majority ("We the People") even as it sought to limit its power through a complex system of representation and checks and balances. Although Tocqueville devoted a lengthy chapter of *Democracy in America* to the federal structure of the Constitution, he was less impressed than Madison that the problem of majority faction has been solved. Rather than regarding the people in Madisonian terms as a shifting coalition of interest groups, he tended to regard the power of the majority as unlimited and unstoppable. Legal guarantees of minority rights were not likely to be effective in the face of mobilized opinion.

In *Democracy in America* Tocqueville treated the problem of "tyranny of the majority" largely in terms inherited from Aristotle and the *Federalist Papers*. In *Politics* Aristotle had associated democracy with rule of the many, generally the poor, for their own interests. The danger of democracy was precisely that it represented the self-interested rule of the largest class of the community over the minority. Democracy was thus always potentially a form of class struggle exercised by the poor over the rich often egged on by populist demagogues. The same theme was considered by the Federalist authors. Their ingenious solution to the problem of majority faction was to "enlarge the orbit" of government in order to prevent the creation of a permanent majority faction. The greater the number of factions, the less likely would any one of them be able to exercise despotic power over national politics.

Tocqueville identified a source of democratic tyranny that escaped the attention of Madison: the power of public opinion. The danger of a mobilized public opinion is something that the classical theorists of tyranny had not even considered, but that was specifically a product of the modern democratic age. This new power posed a special challenge to the freedom of thought and opinion. Public opinion draws a charmed circle around itself that allows little room for dissent or satire. It could perhaps be compared to the power of what today is called "political correctness." In a single arresting sentence Tocqueville wrote, "I do not know any country where, in general, less independence of mind and genuine freedom of discussion reign than in America."

Another source of this new form of democratic tyranny was the rise of the modern administrative state. Tocqueville drew a distinction, not always clear, between political and administrative centralization. Political or governmental centralization Tocqueville regarded as a good thing. The idea of a uniform center of legislation was greatly to be preferred to any system of competing or overlapping sovereignties. Governmental centralization is necessary to ensure that equal justice is afforded to every citizen, but administrative centralization is another matter. The science of administration concerns not the establishment of common rules, but the oversight of the details of conduct and the direction of the everyday affairs of citizens. It represents the slow penetration of the bureaucracy into every aspect of daily affairs. While governmental centralization is necessary for the purposes of law making and national defense, centralized administration is mainly preventative and produces nothing but languid and apathetic citizens. It was this kind of administrative centralization that he would later call "democratic despotism" to define "an immense tutelary power" that keeps its subjects in a perpetual state of political adolescence.

Tocqueville's democratic despotism was, to be sure, an imaginary condition. He was not predicting the future course of history either in the manner of a social scientist or a prophet. Such a future was not inevitable even though it was possible. His book was written as a warning to his contemporaries about what might be the case unless they acted to resist it. Tocqueville opposed all schemes of historical determinism that would submit the power of human agency to impersonal causes, tendencies, or destinies. He wrote not to imprison, but to empower his readers to direct their future.

Democracy in America is, above all, a work of political education written to guide future generations of citizens and statesmen. Will democracy be relatively open and tolerant or will it be centralized and despotic? Will liberty or equality be the dominant trend? Tocqueville preferred to leave this an open question offering his readers not a prediction but a challenge:

> There is in fact a manly and legitimate passion for equality that incites men to want all to be strong and esteemed. This passion tends to elevate the small to the rank of the great; but one also encounters a depraved taste for equality in the human heart that brings the weak to want to draw the strong to their level and that reduces men to preferring equality in servitude to inequality in freedom.

How we answer this challenge will determine what form the democracy of the future will take.

Raymond Aron, *Main Currents in Sociological Thought*, vol. 1 (New Brunswick, N. J.: Transaction Publishers, 1998), is a leading interpretation of Tocqueville as a social theorist. Jean-Claude Lamberti, *Tocqueville and His Two Democracies*, trans. Arthur Goldhammer (Cambridges: Mass. Harvard University Press, 1989), is the best biography of Tocqueville in any language. Bernard-Henri Lévy, *American Vertigo: Travelling America in the Footsteps of Tocqueville* (New York: Random House, 2006), is an attempt to update Tocqueville's journey through America by a leading French intellectual. Pierre Manent, *Tocqueville and the Nature of Democracy*, trans. John Waggoner (Lanham, Md.: Rowman & Littlefield, 1996), is a brilliant study that treats Tocqueville as a philosopher examining democracy and aristocracy as the two fundamental regime types. John Stuart Mill, "M. de Tocqueville on Democracy in America" in *The Philosophy of John Stuart Mill*, ed. Marshall Cohen (New York: Modern Library, 1961), is a major review by Tocqueville's leading English contemporary.

Democracy in America

PART TWO

Chapter 6

What Are the Real Advantages That American Society Derives from the Government of Democracy

Before beginning the present chapter I feel the need to recall to the reader what I have already indicated several times in the course of this book.

The political constitution of the United States appears to me to be one of the forms that democracy can give to its government; but I do not consider American institutions the only ones or the best that a democratic people should adopt.

In making known what goods the Americans derive from the government of democracy I am therefore far from claiming or thinking that such advantages can be obtained only with the aid of the same laws.

ON THE GENERAL TENDENCY OF THE LAWS UNDER THE EMPIRE OF AMERICAN DEMOCRACY, AND ON THE INSTINCT OF THOSE WHO APPLY THEM

The vices of democracy are seen all at once.— Its advantages are perceived only at length.— American democracy is often unskillful, but the general tendency of its laws is profitable.—Public officials under American democracy do not have permanent interests that differ from those of the greatest number. What results from this.

The vices and weaknesses of the government of democracy are seen without trouble; they are demonstrated by patent facts, whereas its salutary influence is exerted in an insensible and, so to speak, occult manner. Its faults strike one at first approach, but its [good] qualities are discovered only at length.

From *Democracy in America*, translated by Harvey C. Mansfield and Delba Winthrop (Chicago: University of Chicago Press, 2000). Reprinted by permission of the publisher. All notes omitted.

The laws of American democracy are often defective or incomplete; they may happen to violate acquired rights or to sanction dangerous ones: were they good, their frequency would still be a great evil. All this is perceived at first glance.

How is it therefore that the American republics maintain themselves and prosper?

In laws, one ought to distinguish carefully the goal they pursue from the manner in which they advance toward this goal; their absolute goodness, from that which is only relative.

Let me suppose that the object of the legislator is to favor the interests of the few at the expense of the many; his provisions are combined in such a fashion as to obtain the result that is proposed in the least time and with the least possible effort. The law will be well made, its goal bad; it will be dangerous in proportion to its very efficacy.

The laws of democracy generally tend to the good of the greatest number, for they emanate from the majority of all citizens, which can be mistaken, but cannot have an interest contrary to itself.

Those of aristocracy tend, on the contrary, to monopolize wealth and power in the hands of the few because aristocracy by its nature always forms a minority.

One can therefore say in a general manner that the object of democracy in its legislation is more useful to humanity than is the object of aristocracy in its.

But there its advantages end.

Aristocracy is infinitely more skillful in the science of the legislator than democracy can be. Master of itself, it is not subject to getting carried away in passing distractions; it has long designs that it knows how to ripen until a favorable occasion presents itself. Aristocracy proceeds wisely; it knows the art of making the collective force of all its laws converge at the same time toward the same point.

It is not so in democracy: its laws are almost always defective or unseasonable.

The means of democracy are therefore more imperfect than those of aristocracy: often it works against itself, without wanting to; but its goal is more useful.

Imagine a society that nature or its constitution has organized in such a manner as to bear the transient operation of bad laws, and that can await the result of the *general tendency* of the laws without perishing, and you will conceive that the government of democracy, despite its faults, is still the most appropriate of all to make this society prosper.

That is precisely what happens in the United States; I repeat here what I have already expressed elsewhere: the great privilege of the Americans is to be able to have repairable mistakes.

I shall say something analogous about public officials.

It is easy to see that American democracy is often mistaken in the choice of the men in whom it entrusts power; but it is not so easy to say why the state prospers in their hands.

Remark first that if those who govern in a democratic state are less honest or less capable, the governed are more enlightened and more attentive.

The people in democracies, constantly occupied as they are with their affairs, and jealous of their rights, prevent their representatives from deviating from a certain general line that their interest traces for them.

Remark again that if the democratic magistrate uses power worse than someone else, he generally possesses it for less time.

But there is a more general reason than that one, and more satisfying.

It is doubtless important to the good of nations that those who govern have virtues or talents; but what is perhaps still more important to them is that those who govern do not have interests contrary to the mass of the governed; for in that case the virtues could become almost useless and the talents fatal.

I said that it is important that those who govern not have interests contrary to or different from the mass of the governed; I did not say that it is important that they have interests like those of *all* the governed, because I do not know that the thing has ever been encountered.

A political form that equally favors the development and prosperity of all the classes of which society is composed has not been discovered up to now. These classes have continued to form almost so many distinct nations in the same nation, and experience has proven that it is nearly as dangerous to rely completely on any of them for the fate of the others, as to make one people the arbiter of the destinies of another people. When the rich govern alone, the interest of the poor is always in peril; and when the poor make the law, that of the rich runs great risks. What therefore is the advantage of democracy? The real advantage of democracy is not, as has been said, to favor the prosperity of all, but only to serve the well-being of the greatest number.

Those charged with directing the affairs of the public in the United States are often inferior in capacity and morality to the men that aristocracy would bring to power; but their interest intermingles and is identified with that of the majority of their fellow citizens. They can therefore commit frequent infidelities and grave errors, but they will never systematically follow a tendency hostile to that majority; and they cannot succeed in impressing an exclusive and dangerous style on the government.

Moreover, the bad administration of one magistrate under democracy is an isolated fact that has influence only for the short duration of that administration. Corruption and incapacity are not common interests that can bind men among themselves in a permanent manner.

A corrupt or incapable magistrate will not combine his efforts with another magistrate for the sole reason that the latter is incapable and corrupt like him, and these two men will never work in concert to make corruption and incapacity flourish in their posterity. On the contrary, the ambition and maneuvers of the one will serve to unmask the other. In democracies, the vices of the magistrate are in general wholly personal to him.

But public men under the government of aristocracy have a class interest which, if it is sometimes intermingled with that of the majority,

often remains distinct from it. That interest forms a common and lasting bond among them; it invites them to unite and to combine their efforts toward a goal that is not always the happiness of the greatest number: it not only binds those who govern with one another; it also unites them to a considerable portion of the governed; for many citizens, without being vested with any post, make up a part of the aristocracy.

The aristocratic magistrate therefore encounters constant support in society at the same time that he finds it in the government.

The common object that unites the magistrates in aristocracies to the interest of a part of their contemporaries also identifies them and subjects them, so to speak, to that of future races. They work for the future as well as for the present. The aristocratic magistrate is therefore pushed toward the same point all at once by the passions of the governed, by his own, and I could almost say by the passions of his posterity.

How be surprised if he does not resist? One often also sees the spirit of class in aristocracies carry along even those it does not corrupt and, little by little without their knowing it, make them accommodate the society to their use and prepare it for their descendants.

I do not know if an aristocracy as liberal as that of England has ever existed, which without interruption has furnished men as worthy and enlightened to the government of the country.

It is, however, easy to recognize that in English legislation the good of the poor has in the end often been sacrificed to that of the rich, and the rights of the greatest number to the privileges of some: thus England in our day unites within itself all the most extreme fortunes, and one meets with miseries there that almost equal its power and glory.

In the United States, where public officials have no class interest to make prevail, the general and continuous course of government is beneficent although those who govern are often unskillful and sometimes contemptible.

There is, therefore, at the base of democratic institutions, a hidden tendency that often makes men cooperate for the general prosperity despite their vices or errors, whereas in aristocratic institutions a secret inclination is sometimes discovered that, despite talents and virtues, brings them to contribute to the miseries of those like them. Thus it can happen that in aristocratic governments public men do evil without wanting to, and in democracies they produce good without having any thought of doing so.

ON PUBLIC SPIRIT IN THE UNITED STATES

Instinctive love of native country.—Reflective patriotism.—Their different characteristics.—That people ought to strive with all their strength toward the second when the first disappears.—Efforts the Americans have made to achieve this.—The interest of the individual intimately hound to that of the country.

There exists a love of native country that has its source principally in the unreflective, disinterested, and indefinable sentiment that binds the heart of the man to the place where the man was born. This instinctive love intermingles with the taste for old customs, with respect for ancestors and memory of the past; those who feel it cherish their country as one loves a paternal home. They love the tranquillity they enjoy; they hold to the peaceful habits they have contracted there; they are attached to the memories it presents to them, and even find some sweetness in living there obediently. Often that love of native country is further exalted by religious zeal, and then one sees prodigies done. It is a sort of religion itself; it does not reason, it believes, it feels, it acts. Peoples have been encountered who have, in some fashion, personified the native country and have caught a glimpse of it in the prince. They have therefore carried over to him a part of the sentiment of which patriotism is composed; they have become haughty with his triumphs and have taken pride in his power. There was a time, under the former monarchy, when the French experienced a sort of joy in feeling themselves delivered without

recourse to the arbitrariness of the monarch, and they used to say haughtily: "We live under the most powerful king in the world."

Like all unreflective passions, this love of country pushes one to great, fleeting efforts rather than to continuity of efforts. After having saved the state in a time of crisis, it often allows it to decline in the midst of peace.

When peoples are still simple in their mores and firm in their beliefs; when society rests gently on an old order of things whose legitimacy is not contested, one sees this instinctive love of native country reign.

There is another more rational than that one; less generous, less ardent perhaps, but more fruitful and more lasting; this one is born of enlightenment; it develops with the aid of laws, it grows with the exercise of rights, and in the end it intermingles in a way with personal interest. A man understands the influence that the well-being of the country has on his own; he knows that the law permits him to contribute to producing this well-being, and he interests himself in the prosperity of his country at first as a thing that is useful to him, and afterwards as his own work.

But sometimes a moment arrives in the lives of peoples when old customs are changed, mores destroyed, beliefs shaken, the prestige of memories faded away, and when, however, enlightenment remains incomplete and political rights are badly secured or restricted. Then men no longer perceive the native country except in a weak and doubtful light; they no longer place it in the soil, which has become a lifeless land in their eyes, nor in the usages of their ancestors, which they have been taught to regard as a yoke; nor in the religion which they doubt; nor in the laws they do not make, nor in the legislator whom they fear and scorn. They therefore see it nowhere, no more with its own features than with any other, and they withdraw into a narrow and unenlightened selfishness. These men escape prejudices without recognizing the empire of reason; they have neither the instinctive patriotism of the monarchy nor the reflective patriotism of the republic; but they have come to a stop between the two, in the midst of confusion and miseries.

What is one to do in such a state? Retreat. But peoples no more come back to the sentiments of their youth than do men to the innocent tastes of their first years; they can regret them, but not make them revive. One must therefore go further ahead and hasten to unite in the eyes of the people individual interest to the interest of the country, for disinterested love of one's native country is fleeing away without return.

I am surely far from claiming that, to arrive at this result, one ought to accord the exercise of political rights to all men all at once; but I say that the most powerful means, and perhaps the only one that remains to us, of interesting men in the fate of their native country is to make them participate in its government. In our day, the spirit of the city seems to me inseparable from the exercise of political rights; and I think that from now on one will see the number of citizens in Europe increase or diminish in proportion to the extension of these rights.

How is it that in the United States, where the inhabitants arrived yesterday on the soil they occupy, where they have brought neither usages nor memories; where they meet for the first time without knowing each other; where, to say it in a word, the instinct of the native country can scarcely exist; how is it that each is interested in the affairs of his township, of his district, and of the state as a whole as in his own? It is that each, in his sphere, takes an active part in the government of society.

In the United States, the man of the people understands the influence that general prosperity exerts on his happiness—an idea so simple and yet so little known by the people. Furthermore, he is accustomed to regarding this prosperity as his own work. He therefore sees in the public fortune his own, and he works for the good of the state not only out of duty or out of pride, but I would almost dare say out of cupidity.

One does not need to study the institutions and history of Americans to know the truth of what

precedes; mores advertise it enough to you. The American, taking part in all that is done in this country, believes himself interested in defending all that is criticized there; for not only is his country then attacked, he himself is: thus one sees his national pride have recourse to all the artifices and descend to all the puerilities of individual vanity.

There is nothing more annoying in the habits of life than this irritable patriotism of the Americans. A foreigner would indeed consent to praise much in their country; but he would want to be permitted to blame something, and this he is absolutely refused.

America is therefore a country of freedom where, in order not to wound anyone, the foreigner must not speak freely either of particular persons, or of the state, or of the governed, or of those who govern, or of public undertakings, or of private undertakings; or, finally, of anything one encounters except perhaps the climate and the soil; and still, one finds Americans ready to defend both as if they had helped to form them.

In our day one must know how to resign oneself and dare to choose between the patriotism of all and the government of the few, for one cannot at once unite the social force and activity given by the first with the guarantees of tranquillity sometimes furnished by the second.

ON THE IDEA OF RIGHTS IN THE UNITED STATES

There are no great peoples without an idea of rights.—What is the means of giving the idea of rights to the people.—Respect for rights in the United States.—How it arises.

After the general idea of virtue I know of none more beautiful than that of rights, or rather these two ideas are intermingled. The idea of rights is nothing other than the idea of virtue introduced into the political world.

It is with the idea of rights that men have defined what license and tyranny are. Enlightened by it, each could show himself independent without arrogance and submissive without baseness. The man who obeys violence bows and demeans himself; but when he submits to the right to command that he recognizes in someone like him, he raises himself in a way above the very one who commands him. There are no great men without virtue; without respect for rights, there is no great people: one can almost say that there is no society; for, what is a union of rational and intelligent beings among whom force is the sole bond?

I wonder what, in our day, is the means of inculcating in men the idea of rights and of making it, so to speak, fall upon their senses; and I see only one, which is to give the peaceful exercise of certain rights to all of them: one sees that well among children, who are men except for force and experience. When the child begins to move in the midst of external objects, instinct brings him to put to his use all that he encounters in his hands; he has no idea of the property of others, not even of its existence; but as he is made aware of the price of things and he discovers that he can be stripped of his in his turn, he becomes more circumspect and ends by respecting in those like him what he wants to be respected in himself.

What happens to the infant with his playthings happens later to the man with all the objects that belong to him. Why in America, country of democracy par excellence, does no one make heard those complaints against property in general that often ring out in Europe? Is there need to say it?—it is that in America there are no proletarians. Each one, having a particular good to defend, recognizes the right of property in principle.

In the political world it is the same. In America, the man of the people has conceived a lofty idea of political rights because he has political rights; so that his own are not violated, he does not attack those of others. And whereas in Europe this same man does not recognize sovereign authority, the American submits without murmur to the power of the least of its magistrates.

This truth appears even in the smallest details of the existence of peoples. In France there are few pleasures reserved exclusively for the upper classes of society; the poor man is admitted almost everywhere the wealthy man can enter: so he is seen to conduct himself with decency, and to respect everything that serves enjoyments he shares. In England, where wealth has the privilege of pleasure like the monopoly of power, they complain that when the poor man comes to introduce himself furtively into the place destined for the pleasures of the rich he likes to cause useless damage: how can one be surprised at this?—they have taken care that he has nothing to lose.

The government of democracy makes the idea of political rights descend to the least of citizens, as the division of goods puts the idea of the right of property in general within reach of all men. There is one of its greatest merits in my eyes.

I do not say that it is an easy thing to teach all men to make use of political rights; I say only that when that can be done, the resulting effects are great.

And I add that if there is a century in which such an undertaking ought to be attempted, that century is ours.

Do you not see that religions are weakening and that the divine notion of rights is disappearing? Do you not find that mores are being altered, and that with them the moral notion of rights is being effaced?

Do you not perceive on all sides beliefs that give way to reasoning, and sentiments that give way to calculations? If in the midst of that universal disturbance you do not come to bind the idea of rights to the personal interest that offers itself as the only immobile point in the human heart, what will then remain to you to govern the world, except fear?

Therefore when I am told that the laws are weak and the governed turbulent; that passions are lively and virtue without power, and that in this situation one must not think of augmenting the rights of democracy, I respond that it is because of these very things that I believe one must think of it; and in truth I think that governments have still more interest in it than society, for governments perish, and society cannot die.

Furthermore, I do not want to abuse the example of America.

In America, the people were vested with political rights at a period when it was difficult for them to make bad use of them, because the citizens were few and simple in mores. In becoming larger, Americans did not so to speak increase the powers of democracy; rather, they extended its domain.

One cannot doubt that the moment when one accords political rights to a people who have been deprived of them until then is a moment of crisis, a crisis often necessary, but always dangerous.

The child puts to death when he is ignorant of the price of life; he takes away the property of others before knowing that one can rob him of his. The man of the people, at the instant when he is accorded political rights, finds himself, in relation to his rights, in the same position as the child vis-à-vis all nature, and that is the case in which to apply to him these celebrated words: *Homo puer robustus.* [A man is a robust boy.—S.M.C.]

This truth is exposed in America itself. The states where citizens have enjoyed their rights longest are those where they know best how to make use of them.

One cannot say it too often: There is nothing more prolific in marvels than the art of being free; but there is nothing harder than the apprenticeship of freedom. It is not the same with despotism. Despotism often presents itself as the mender of all ills suffered; it is the support of good law, the sustainer of the oppressed, and the founder of order. Peoples fall asleep in the bosom of the temporary prosperity to which it gives birth; and when they awaken, they are miserable. Freedom, in contrast, is ordinarily born in the midst of storms, it is established painfully among civil discords, and only when it is old can one know its benefits.

ON RESPECT FOR THE LAW IN THE UNITED STATES

Respect of Americans for the law.—Paternal love that they feel for it.—Personal interest that each finds in increasing the power of the law.

It is not always permissible to call the entire people, either directly or indirectly, to the making of the law; but one cannot deny that when that is practicable, the law acquires great authority from it. That popular origin, which often harms the goodness and wisdom of legislation, contributes singularly to its power.

There is a prodigious force in the expression of the will of a whole people. When it is uncovered in broad daylight, the very imagination of those who would wish to struggle against it is overwhelmed.

The truth of this is well known to parties.

And so one sees them contest for a majority everywhere they can. When they lack it among those who have voted, they place it among those who have abstained from voting, and when it still happens to escape them there, they find it among those who did not have the right to vote.

In the United States, excepting slaves, domestics, and indigents nourished by the townships, there is no one who is not an elector, and whoever has this title concurs indirectly in the law. Those who want to attack the laws are therefore reduced to doing openly one of these two things: they must either change the opinion of the nation or ride roughshod over its will.

Add to this first reason, another more direct and more powerful, that in the United States each finds a sort of personal interest in everyone's obeying the laws; for whoever does not make up a part of the majority today will perhaps be in its ranks tomorrow; and the respect that he professes now for the will of the legislator he will soon have occasion to require for his. However distressing the law may be, the inhabitant of the United States submits to it without trouble, therefore, not only as the work of the greatest number, but also as his own; he considers it from the point of view of a contract to which he would have been a party.

One therefore does not see in the United States a numerous and always turbulent crowd, which, regarding the law as a natural enemy, casts only glances of fear and suspicion on it. On the contrary, it is impossible not to perceive that all classes show great confidence in the legislation that rules the country and feel a sort of paternal love for it.

I am mistaken in saying all classes. In America, the European ladder of powers being reversed, the rich are found in a position analogous to that of the poor in Europe; it is they who often mistrust the law. I have said it elsewhere: the real advantage of democratic government is not to guarantee the interests of all, as it has sometimes been claimed, but only to protect those of the greatest number. In the United States, where the poor man governs, the rich always have to fear lest he abuse his power against them.

This disposition of the mind of the rich can produce a muted discontent; but society is not violently troubled by it; because the same reason that prevents the rich man from granting his confidence to the legislator prevents him from defying his commandments. He does not make the law because he is rich, and he does not dare to violate it because of his wealth. In civilized nations it is generally only those who have nothing to lose who revolt. So, therefore, if the laws of democracy are not always respectable, they are almost always respected; for those who generally violate the laws cannot fail to obey those that they have made and from which they profit, and citizens who could have an interest in breaking them are brought by character and by position to submit to the will of the legislator, whatever it may be. Furthermore, the people in America obey the law not only because it is their work, but also because they can change it when by chance it hurts them; they submit to it in the first place as an evil that is imposed by themselves and after that as a passing evil.

ACTIVITY REIGNING IN ALL PARTS OF THE BODY POLITIC OF THE UNITED STATES; INFLUENCE THAT IT EXERTS ON SOCIETY

It is more difficult to conceive of the political activity reigning in the United States than of the freedom or equality encountered there.—The great movement that constantly agitates legislatures is only an episode, a prolongation of this universal movement.—Difficulty that the American finds in occupying himself only with his own affairs.—Political agitation spreads into civil society.—Industrial activity of the Americans coming in part from this cause.—Indirect advantages that society derives from the government of democracy.

When one passes from a free country into another that is not, one is struck by a very extraordinary spectacle: there, all is activity and movement; here, all seems calm and immobile. In the one, it is only a question of betterment and progress; one would say that society in the other, after having acquired all goods, aspires only to rest in order to enjoy them. Nevertheless, the country that gives itself so much agitation so as to be happy is generally richer and more prosperous than the one that appears so satisfied with its lot. And in considering them both, one has trouble conceiving how so many new needs make themselves felt daily in the first, whereas one seems to feel so few in the second.

If this remark is applicable to free countries that have preserved the monarchical form and to those where aristocracy dominates, it is still more so in democratic republics. There, it is no longer one portion of the people that undertakes to better the state of society; the entire people takes charge of this care. It is not only a question of providing for the needs and the conveniences of one class, but of all classes at the same time.

It is not impossible to conceive the immense freedom that Americans enjoy; one can get an idea of their extreme equality as well; but what one cannot comprehend without having already been witness to it is the political activity that reigns in the United States.

Scarcely have you descended on the soil of America when you find yourself in the midst of a sort of tumult; a confused clamor is raised on all sides; a thousand voices come to your ear at the same time, each of them expressing some social needs. Around you everything moves: here, the people of one neighborhood have gathered to learn if a church ought to be built; there, they are working on the choice of a representative; farther on, the deputies of a district are going to town in all haste in order to decide about some local improvements; in another place, the farmers of a village abandon their furrows to go discuss the plan of a road or a school. Citizens assemble with the sole goal of declaring that they disapprove of the course of government, whereas others gather to proclaim that the men in place are the fathers of their country. Here are others still who, regarding drunkenness as the principal source of the evils of the state, come solemnly to pledge themselves to give an example of temperance.

The great political movement that constantly agitates American legislatures, the only one that is perceived from the outside, is only one episode and a sort of prolongation of the universal movement that begins in the lowest ranks of the people and afterwards spreads gradually to all classes of citizens. One cannot work more laboriously at being happy.

It is difficult to say what place the cares of politics occupy in the life of a man in the United States. To meddle in the government of society and to speak about it is the greatest business and, so to speak, the only pleasure that an American knows. This is perceived even in the least habits of life: women themselves often go to political assemblies and, by listening to political discourses, take a rest from household tedium. For them, clubs replace theatergoing to a certain point. An American does not know how to converse, but he discusses; he does not discourse, but he holds forth. He always speaks to you as to an assembly; and if he happens by chance to become heated, he will say "sirs" in addressing his interlocutor.

In certain countries, the inhabitant only accepts with a sort of repugnance the political rights that the law accords him; it seems that to occupy him with common interests is to steal his time, and he likes to enclose himself in a narow selfishness of which four ditches topped by a hedge form the exact limits.

On the contrary, from the moment when an American were reduced to occupying himself only with his own affairs, he would have been robbed of half of his existence; he would feel an immense void in his days, and he would become incredibly unhappy.

I am persuaded that if despotism ever comes to be established in America, it will find more difficulties in defeating the habits to which freedom has given birth than in surmounting the love of freedom itself.

This agitation, constantly reborn, that the government of democracy has introduced into the political world, passes afterwards into civil society. I do not know if, all in all, that is not the greatest advantage of democratic government, and I praise it much more because of what it causes to be done than for what it does.

It is incontestable that the people often direct public affairs very badly; but the people cannot meddle in public affairs without having the scope of their ideas extended and without having their minds be seen to go outside their ordinary routine. The man of the people who is called to the government of society conceives a certain self-esteem. As he is then a power, very enlightened intellects put themselves at the service of his. People constantly address themselves to him to get his support, and in seeking to deceive him in a thousand different manners, they enlighten him. In politics, he participates in undertakings that he has not conceived, but that give him a general taste for undertakings. Every day people indicate to him new improvements to make to the common property; and he feels the desire being born to improve what is personal to him. He is perhaps neither more virtuous nor happier, but he is more enlightened and more active than his precursors. I do not doubt that democratic institutions, joined to the physical nature of the country, are not the direct cause, as so many people say, but the indirect cause of the prodigious motion of industry to be remarked in the United States. Laws do not give birth to it, but the people learn to produce it by making the law.

When the enemies of democracy claim that one alone does better what he takes charge of than the government of all, it seems to me that they are right. The government of one alone, supposing equality of enlightenment on both sides, puts more coherence into its undertakings than the multitude; it shows more perseverance, more of an idea of an ensemble, more perfection of detail, a more just discernment in the choice of men. Those who deny these things have never seen a democratic republic or have judged by only a few examples. Democracy, even if local circumstances and the dispositions of the people permit it to be maintained, does not present to the eye administrative regularity and methodical order in government; that is true. Democratic freedom does not execute each of its undertakings with the same perfection as intelligent despotism; often it abandons them before having received their fruit, or it risks dangerous ones: but in the long term democracy produces more than despotism; it does each thing less well, but it does more things. Under its empire, what is great is above all not what public administration executes but what is executed without it and outside it. Democracy does not give the most skillful government to the people, but it does what the most skillful government is often powerless to create; it spreads a restive activity through the whole social body, a superabundant force, an energy that never exists without it, and which, however little circumstances may be favorable, can bring forth marvels. Those are its true advantages.

In this century, when the destinies of the Christian world appear to be unresolved, some hasten to attack democracy as an enemy power while it is still getting larger; others already adore it as a new god that issues from nothingness; but both know the object of their hatred or their desire only imperfectly; they do combat in the shadows and strike only haphazardly.

What do you ask of society and its government? We must understand each other.

Do you want to give a certain loftiness to the human spirit, a generous way of viewing the things of this world? Do you want to inspire in men a sort of contempt for material goods? Do you desire to give birth to or to maintain profound convictions and to prepare for great devotions?

Is it a question for you of polishing mores, of elevating manners, of making the arts shine? Do you want poetry, renown, glory?

Do you intend to organize a people in such a manner as to act strongly on all others? Do you destine it to attempt great undertakings and, whatever may be the result of its efforts, to leave an immense mark on history?

If this is, according to you, the principal object that men ought to propose for themselves in society, do not take the government of democracy; it would surely not lead you to the goal.

But if it seems to you useful to turn the intellectual and moral activity of man to the necessities of material life and to employ it in producing well-being; if reason appears to you to be more profitable to men than genius; if your object is not to create heroic virtues but peaceful habits; if you would rather see vices than crimes, and if you prefer to find fewer great actions on condition that you will encounter fewer enormities; if instead of acting within a brilliant society it is enough for you to live in the midst of a prosperous society; if, finally, the principal object of a government, according to you, is not to give the most force or the most glory possible to the entire body of the nation, but to procure the most well-being for each of the individuals who compose it and to have each avoid the most misery, then equalize conditions and constitute the government of a democracy.

If there is no longer time to make a choice and if a force superior to man already carries you along toward one of the two governments without consulting your desires, seek at least to derive from it all the good that it can do; and knowing its good instincts as well as its evil penchants, strive to restrict the effects of the latter and develop the former.

Chapter 7

ON THE OMNIPOTENCE OF THE
MAJORITY IN THE UNITED STATES
AND ITS EFFECTS

*Natural force of the majority in democracies.—
Most of the American constitutions have artificially increased this natural force.—How.—
Imperative mandates.—Moral empire of the*

majority.—Opinion of its infallibility.—Respect for its rights. What augments it in the United States.

It is of the very essence of democratic governments that the empire of the majority is absolute; for in democracies, outside the majority there is nothing that resists it.

Most of the American constitutions have also sought to augment this natural force of the majority artificially.

Of all political powers, the legislature is the one that obeys the majority most willingly. Americans wanted the members of the legislature to be named *directly* by the people, and for a *very short* term, in order to oblige them to submit not only to the general views, but even to the daily passions of their constituents.

They have taken the members of the two houses from the same classes and named them in the same manner, so that the motions of the legislative body are almost as rapid and no less irresistible than those of a single assembly.

The legislature thus constituted, they have united almost all the government in it.

At the same time that the law increased the force of powers that were naturally strong, it enervated more and more those that were naturally weak. It accorded neither stability nor independence to the representatives of the executive power; and, in submitting them completely to the caprices of the legislature, it took away from them the little influence that the nature of democratic government would have permitted them to exert.

In several states it left the judicial power to the election of the majority, and in all, it made its existence depend in a way on the legislative power by leaving to the representatives the right to fix the salary of the judges each year.

Usages have gone still further than the laws.

A custom that in the end will make the guarantees of representative government vain is spreading more and more in the United States: it very frequently happens that electors, in naming a deputy, lay out a plan of conduct for him and impose a certain number of positive obligations on him from which he can in no way deviate. It is

as if, except for the tumult, the majority itself were deliberating in the public square.

Several particular circumstances also tend to render the power of the majority in America not only predominant, but irresistible.

The moral empire of the majority is founded in part on the idea that there is more enlightenment and wisdom in many men united than in one alone, in the number of legislators than in their choice. It is the theory of equality applied to intellects. This doctrine attacks the pride of man in its last asylum: so the minority accepts it only with difficulty; it habituates itself to it only in the long term. Like all powers, and perhaps more than any of them, therefore, the power of the majority needs to be lasting in order to appear legitimate. When it begins to establish itself, it makes itself obeyed by constraint; it is only after having lived for a long time under its laws that one begins to respect it.

The idea of the right to govern society that the majority possesses by its enlightenment was brought to the soil of the United States by its first inhabitants. This idea, which alone would suffice to create a free people, has passed into mores today, and one finds it in even the least habits of life.

The French under the former monarchy held as a constant that the king could never fail; and when he happened to do evil, they thought that the fault was in his counselors. That marvelously facilitated obedience. One could murmur against the law without ceasing to love and respect the legislator. The Americans have the same opinion of the majority.

The moral empire of the majority is also founded on the principle that the interests of the greatest number ought to be preferred to those of the few. Now, one understands without difficulty that the respect that is professed for the right of the greatest number naturally increases or diminishes according to the state of the parties. When a nation is partitioned among several great irreconcilable interests, the privilege of the majority is often unrecognized because it becomes too painful to submit to it.

If there existed in America a class of citizens whom the legislator was trying to strip of certain exclusive advantages possessed for centuries, and wanted to make them descend from an elevated situation so as to reduce them to the ranks of the multitude, it is probable that the minority would not easily submit to his laws.

But the United States having been peopled by men equal among themselves, there is not as yet a natural and permanent dissidence among the interests of its different inhabitants.

There is a certain social state in which the members of the minority cannot hope to attract the majority to them, because for that it would be necessary to abandon the very object of the struggle that they sustain against it. An aristocracy, for example, cannot become a majority while preserving its exclusive privileges, and it cannot let its privileges escape without ceasing to be an aristocracy.

In the United States, political questions cannot be posed in a manner so general and so absolute, and all the parties are ready to recognize the rights of the majority because they all hope to be able to exercise them to their profit one day.

The majority in the United States therefore has an immense power in fact, and a power in opinion almost as great; and once it has formed on a question, there are so to speak no obstacles that can, I shall not say stop, but even delay its advance, and allow it the time to hear the complaints of those it crushes as it passes.

The consequences of this state of things are dire and dangerous for the future.

HOW THE OMNIPOTENCE OF THE MAJORITY IN AMERICA INCREASES THE LEGISLATIVE AND ADMINISTRATIVE INSTABILITY THAT IS NATURAL TO DEMOCRACIES

How Americans increase the legislative instability that is natural to democracy by changing the legislator each year and arming him with a power almost without limits.—The same effect produced on administration.—In America the force brought to social improvements is infinitely greater, but less continuous than in Europe.

I have spoken previously of the vices that are natural to the government of democracy; there is not one of them that does not grow at the same time as the power of the majority.

And, to begin with, the most apparent of all:

Legislative instability is an evil inherent in democratic government because it is of the nature of democracies to bring new men to power. But this evil is more or less great according to the power and the means of action granted to the legislator.

In America they hand over sovereign power to the authority that makes the laws. It can indulge each of its desires rapidly and irresistibly, and every year it is given other representatives. That is to say, they have adopted precisely the combination that most favors democratic instability and that permits democracy to apply its changing will to the most important objects.

Thus in our day, of the world's countries, America is the one in which the laws have the least duration. Almost all the American constitutions have been amended within thirty years. There is therefore no American state that has not modified the principle of its laws during this period.

As for the laws themselves, it is enough to cast a glance at the archives of the different states of the Union to be convinced that in America the action of the legislator never slows. It is not that American democracy is more unstable than any other by its nature, but it has been given the means to follow the natural instability of its penchants in the forming of laws.

The omnipotence of the majority and the rapid and absolute manner in which its will is executed in the United States not only renders the law unstable, it also exerts the same influence on the execution of the law and on the action of public administration.

The majority being the sole power that is important to please, the works that it undertakes are eagerly agreed to; but from the moment that its attention goes elsewhere, all efforts cease; whereas in the free states of Europe, where the administrative power has an independent existence and a secure position, the will of the legislator continues to be executed even when it is occupied with other objects.

In America, much more zeal and activity is brought to certain improvements than is done elsewhere.

In Europe, a social force infinitely less great, but more continuous, is employed in these same things.

Several years ago, some religious men undertook to improve the state of the prisons. The public was moved by their voices, and the rehabilitation of criminals became a popular work.

New prisons were then built. For the first time, the idea of reforming the guilty penetrated the dungeon at the same time as the idea of punishment. But the happy revolution with which the public had associated itself so eagerly, and which the simultaneous efforts of citizens rendered irresistible, could not work in a moment.

Alongside the new penitentiaries, whose development was hastened by the wish of the majority, the old prisons still remained and continued to confine a great number of the guilty. The latter seemed to become more unhealthful and more corrupting as the new ones turned more to reform and became more healthful. This double effect is easily understood: the majority, preoccupied with the idea of founding the new establishment, had forgotten the one that already existed. Everyone then having turned his eyes from the object that no longer held the regard of the master, oversight had ceased. One first saw the salutary bonds of discipline slacken, and then, soon after, break. And alongside the prison, lasting monument to the mildness and the enlightenment of our time, was a dungeon that recalled the barbarism of the Middle Ages.

TYRANNY OF THE MAJORITY

How one must understand the principle of the sovereignty of the people.—Impossibility of conceiving a mixed government.—The sovereign power must be somewhere.—Precautions that ought to be taken to moderate its action.—These precautions have not been taken in the United States.—What results from this.

I regard as impious and detestable the maxim that in matters of government the majority of a people has the right to do everything, and nonetheless I place the origin of all powers in the will of the majority. Am I in contradiction with myself?

A general law exists that has been made or at least adopted not only by the majority of this or that people, but by the majority of all men, This law is justice.

Justice therefore forms the boundary of each people's right.

A nation is like a jury charged with representing the universal society and with applying the justice that is its law. Ought the jury that represents society have more power than the society itself for which it applies the laws?

Therefore, when I refuse to obey an unjust law, I do not deny to the majority the right to command; I only appeal from the sovereignty of the people to the sovereignty of the human race.

There are people who have not feared to say that a people, in the objects that interested only itself, could not go entirely outside the limits of justice and reason, and thus one must not fear giving all power to the majority that represents it. But that is the language of a slave.

What therefore is a majority taken collectively, if not an individual who has opinions and most often interests contrary to another individual that one names the minority? Now, if you accept that one man vested with omnipotence can abuse it against his adversaries, why not accept the same thing for a majority? Have men changed in character by being united? Have they become more patient before obstacles by becoming stronger? As for me, I cannot believe it; and I shall never grant to several the power of doing everything that I refuse to a single one of those like me.

It is not that I believe that in order to preserve freedom one can mix several principles in the same government in a manner that really opposes them to one another.

The government called mixed has always seemed to me to be a chimera. There is, to tell the truth, no mixed government (in the sense that one gives to this word), because in each society one discovers in the end one principle of action that dominates all the others.

England in the last century, which has been cited particularly as an example of these sorts of governments, was an essentially aristocratic state, although large elements of democracy were found within it; for laws and mores there had been established so that aristocracy always had to predominate in the long term and direct public affairs at its will.

The error has come from the fact that, seeing constantly the interests of the great doing battle with those of the people, one thought only of the struggle instead of paying attention to the result of that struggle, which was the important point. When a society really comes to have a mixed government, that is to say equally divided between contrary principles, it enters into revolution or it is dissolved.

I think, therefore, that one must always place somewhere one social power superior to all the others, but I believe freedom to be in peril when that power finds no obstacle before it that can restrain its advance and give it time to moderate itself.

Omnipotence seems to me to be an evil and dangerous thing in itself. Its exercise appears to me above the strength of man, whoever he may be, and I see only God who can be omnipotent without danger, because his wisdom and justice are always equal to his power. There is therefore no authority on earth so respectable in itself or vested with a right so sacred that I should wish to allow to act without control and to dominate without obstacles. Therefore, when I see the right and the ability to do everything granted to any power whatsoever, whether it is called people or king, democracy or aristocracy, whether it is exercised in a monarchy or in a republic, I say: there is the seed of tyranny, and I seek to go live under other laws.

What I most reproach in democratic government, as it has been organized in the United States, is not, as many people in Europe claim, its weakness, but on the contrary, its irresistible force. And what is most repugnant to me in America is not the extreme freedom that reigns there, it is the lack of a guarantee against tyranny.

When a man or a party suffers from an injustice in the United States, whom do you want him to address? Public opinion? that is what forms the majority; the legislative body? it represents the majority and obeys it blindly; the executive power? it is named by the majority and serves as its passive instrument; the public forces? the public forces are nothing other than the majority in arms; the jury? the jury is the majority vested with the right to pronounce decrees: in certain states, the judges themselves are elected by the majority. Therefore, however iniquitous or unreasonable is the measure that strikes you, you must submit to it.

Suppose on the contrary a legislative body composed in such a manner that it represents the majority without necessarily being the slave of its passions; an executive power with a force that is its own and a judicial power independent of the other two powers; you will still have democratic government, but there will be almost no more chance of tyranny.

I do not say that at the present time frequent use is made of tyranny in America, I say that no guarantee against it may be discovered, and that one must seek the causes of the mildness of government in circumstances and mores rather than in the laws.

EFFECTS OF THE OMNIPOTENCE OF
THE MAJORITY ON THE ARBITRARINESS
OF AMERICAN OFFICIALS

Freedom that American law leaves to officials within the circle that it has drawn.—Their power.

One must distinguish well arbitrariness from tyranny. Tyranny can be exercised by means of law itself, and then it is not arbitrariness; arbitrariness can be exercised in the interest of the governed, and then it is not tyrannical.

Tyranny ordinarily makes use of arbitrariness, but in case of need it knows how to do without it.

In the United States, at the same time that the omnipotence of the majority favors the legal despotism of the legislator, it favors the arbitrariness of the magistrate as well. The majority, being an absolute master in making the law and in overseeing its execution, having equal control over those who govern and over those who are governed, regards public officials as its passive agents and willingly deposits in them the care of serving its designs. It therefore does not enter in advance into the details of their duties and hardly takes the trouble to define their rights. It treats them as a master could do to his servants if, always seeing them act under his eye, he could direct or correct their conduct at each instant.

In general, the law leaves American officials much freer than ours within the circle that it draws around them. It sometimes even happens that the majority permits them to leave it. Guaranteed by the opinion of the greatest number and made strong by its concurrence, they then dare things that a European, habituated to the sight of arbitrariness, is still astonished at. Thus are formed, in the bosom of freedom, habits that can one day become fatal to it.

ON THE POWER THAT THE MAJORITY IN AMERICA EXERCISES OVER THOUGHT

In the United States, when the majority has irrevocably settled on a question, there is no more discussion.—Why.—Moral power that the majority exercises over thought.—Democratic republics make despotism immaterial.

When one comes to examine what the exercise of thought is in the United States, then one perceives very clearly to what point the power of the majority surpasses all the powers that we know in Europe.

Thought is an invisible and almost intangible power that makes sport of all tyrannies. In our day the most absolute sovereigns of Europe cannot prevent certain thoughts hostile to their authority from mutely circulating in their states and even in the heart of their courts. It is not the same in America: as long as the majority is doubtful, one speaks; but when it has irrevocably pronounced, everyone becomes silent and friends and enemies alike then seem to hitch themselves together to its wagon. The reason for this is simple: there is no monarch so absolute that he can gather in his hands all the strength of society and defeat resistance, as can a majority vested with the right to make the laws and execute them.

A king, moreover, has only a material power that acts on actions and cannot reach wills; but the majority is vested with a force, at once material and moral, that acts on the will as much as on actions, and which at the same time prevents the deed and the desire to do it.

I do not know any country where, in general, less independence of mind and genuine freedom of discussion reign than in America.

There is no religious or political theory that cannot be preached freely in the constitutional states of Europe and that does not penetrate the others; for there is no country in Europe so subject to one single power that he who wants to speak the truth does not find support capable of assuring him against the consequences of his independence. If he has the misfortune to live under an absolute government, he often has the people for him; if he inhabits a free country, he can take shelter behind royal authority if need be. The aristocratic fraction of the society sustains him in democratic regions, and the democracy in the others. But in the heart of a democracy organized as that of the United States, one encounters only a single power, a single element of force and success, and nothing outside it.

In America the majority draws a formidable circle around thought. Inside those limits, the writer is free; but unhappiness awaits him if he dares to leave them. It is not that he has to fear an auto-da-fé, but he is the butt of mortifications of all kinds and of persecutions every day. A political career is closed to him: he has offended the only power that has the capacity to open it up. Everything is refused him, even glory. Before publishing his opinions, he believed he had partisans; it seems to him that he no longer has any now that he has uncovered himself to all; for those who blame him express themselves openly, and those who think like him, without having his courage, keep silent and move away. He yields, he finally bends under the effort of each day and returns to silence as if he felt remorse for having spoken the truth.

Chains and executioners are the coarse instruments that tyranny formerly employed; but in our day civilization has perfected even despotism itself, which seemed, indeed, to have nothing more to learn.

Princes had so to speak made violence material; democratic republics in our day have rendered it just as intellectual as the human will that it wants to constrain. Under the absolute government of one alone, despotism struck the body crudely, so as to reach the soul; and the soul, escaping from those blows, rose gloriously above it; but in democratic republics, tyranny does not proceed in this way; it leaves the body and goes straight for the soul. The master no longer says to it: You shall think as I do or you shall die; he says: You are free not to think as I do; your life, your goods, everything remains to you; but from this day on, you are a stranger among us. You shall keep your privileges in the city, but they will become useless to you; for if you crave the vote of your fellow citizens, they will not grant it to you, and if you demand only their esteem, they will still pretend to refuse it to you. You shall remain among men, but you shall lose your rights of humanity. When you approach those like you, they shall flee you as being impure; and those who believe in your innocence, even they shall abandon you, for one would flee them in their turn. Go in peace, I leave you your life, but I leave it to you worse than death.

Absolute monarchies had dishonored despotism; let us be on guard that democratic republics do not rehabilitate it, and that in rendering it heavier for some, they do not remove its odious aspect and its demeaning character in the eyes of the greatest number.

In the proudest nations of the Old World, works destined to paint faithfully the vices and ridiculousness of contemporaries were published; La Bruyère lived at the palace of Louis XIV when he composed his chapter on the great, and Molière criticized the Court in plays that he had performed before courtiers. But the power that dominates in the United States does not intend to be made sport of like this. The slightest reproach wounds it, the least prickly truth alarms it; and one must praise it from the forms of its language to its most solid virtues. No writer, whatever his renown may be, can escape the obligation of singing the praises of his fellow citizens. The majority, therefore, lives in perpetual adoration of itself; only foreigners or experience can make certain truths reach the ears of the Americans.

If America has not yet had great writers, we ought not to seek the reasons for this elsewhere: no literary genius exists without freedom of mind, and there is no freedom of mind in America.

The Inquisition could never prevent books contrary to the religion of the greatest number from circulating in Spain. The empire of the majority does better in the United States: it has taken away even the thought of publishing them. One encounters nonbelievers in America, but disbelief finds so to speak no organ.

One sees governments that strive to protect mores by condemning the authors of licentious books. In the United States no one is condemned for these sorts of works; but no one is tempted to write them. It is not, however, that all the citizens have pure mores, but the majority is regular in its.

Here the use of power is doubtless good: so I speak only of the power in itself. This irresistible power is a continuous fact, and its good use is only an accident.

EFFECTS OF THE TYRANNY OF THE MAJORITY ON THE NATIONAL CHARACTER OF THE AMERICANS; ON THE SPIRIT OF A COURT IN THE UNITED STATES

Up to the present, the effects of the tyranny of the majority have made themselves felt more on mores than on the conduct of society.—They arrest the development of great characters.—Democratic republics organized like those of the United States put the spirit of a court within reach of the many.— Proofs of this spirit in the United States.—Why there is more patriotism in the people than in those who govern in its name.

The influence of the preceding still makes itself felt only feebly in political society; but one already remarks its distressing effects on the national character of the Americans. I think that the small number of remarkable men who show themselves on the political scene today must above all be attributed to the always growing activity of the despotism of the majority in the United States.

When the American Revolution broke out, a crowd of them appeared; public opinion then directed wills and did not tyrannize over them. The celebrated men of this period, associating freely in the movement of minds, had a greatness that was proper to them; they spread their brilliance over the nation and did not borrow [their brilliance] from it.

In absolute governments, the great who are near the throne flatter the passions of the master and voluntarily bend to his caprices. But the mass of the nation does not lend itself to servitude; it often submits to it out of weakness, out of habit, or out of ignorance; sometimes out of love of royalty or of the king. One has seen peoples take a kind of pleasure and pride in sacrificing their will to that of the prince, and so place a sort of independence of soul even in the midst of obedience. In these peoples one encounters much less degradation than misery. Besides, there is a great difference between doing what one does not approve of and feigning approval of what one does: the one is the part of a weak man, but the other belongs only to the habits of a valet.

In free countries, where each is more or less called to give his opinion about affairs of state; in democratic republics, where public life is incessantly mixed with private life, where the sovereign is approachable from all sides and where it is only a question of raising one's voice to reach its ear, one encounters many more people who seek to speculate about its weakness and to live at the expense of its passions than in absolute monarchies. It is not that men are naturally worse there than elsewhere, but the temptation there is very strong and is offered to more people at the same time. A much more general abasement of souls results from it.

Democratic republics put the spirit of a court within reach of the many and let it penetrate all classes at once. That is one of the principal reproaches that can be made against them.

That is above all true in democratic states organized like the American republics, where the majority possesses an empire so absolute and so irresistible that one must in a way renounce one's rights as a citizen and so to speak one's quality as a man when one wants to deviate from the path it has traced.

Among the immense crowd that flocks to a political career in the United States, I have seen few men indeed who show that virile candor, that manly independence of thought, that often distinguished Americans in previous times and that, everywhere it is found, forms the salient feature of great characters. One would say at first approach that in America, spirits have all been formed on the same model, so much do they follow exactly the same ways. The foreigner, it is true, sometimes encounters Americans who deviate from the rigor of formulas; they come to deplore the defectiveness of the laws, the volatility of democracy, and its lack of enlightenment; they often even go so far as to note the faults that alter the national character, and they point out the means that could be taken to correct them; but no one except you listens to them; and you, to whom they confide these secret thoughts, you are only a foreigner, and you pass on. They willingly deliver to you truths that are useless to you, and when they descend to the public square, they hold to another language.

If these lines ever come to America, I am sure of two things: first, that readers will all raise their voices to condemn me; second, that many among them will absolve me at the bottom of their consciences.

I have heard the native country spoken of in the United States. I have encountered genuine patriotism in the people; I have often sought it in vain in those who direct it. This is easily understood by analogy: despotism depraves the one who submits to it much more than the one who imposes it. In absolute monarchies, the king often has great virtues, but the courtiers are always base.

It is true that courtiers in America do not say "Sire" and "Your Majesty"—a great and capital difference; but they speak constantly of the natural enlightenment of their master; they do not hold a competition on the question of knowing which one of the virtues of the prince most merits being admired; for they are sure that he possesses all the virtues, without having acquired them and so to speak without wanting to do so; they do not give him their wives and their daughters so that he may deign to elevate them to the rank of his mistresses; but in sacrificing their opinions to him, they prostitute themselves.

Moralists and philosophers in America are not obliged to wrap their opinions in veils of allegory; but before hazarding a distressing truth they say: We know that we are speaking to a people too much above human weaknesses not to remain always master of itself. We would not use language like this if we did not address men whose virtues and enlightenment rendered them alone among all others worthy of remaining free.

How could the flatterers of Louis XIV do better?

As for me, I believe that in all governments, whatever they may be, baseness will attach itself to force and flattery to power. And I know only one

means of preventing men from being degraded: it is to grant to no one, along with omnipotence, the sovereign power to demean them.

THAT THE GREATEST DANGER OF THE AMERICAN REPUBLICS COMES FROM THE OMNIPOTENCE OF THE MAJORITY

It is by the bad use of their power, and not by powerlessness, that democratic republics are liable to perish.—The government of the American republics more centralized and more energetic than that of the monarchies of Europe.—Danger that results from this.—Opinions of Madison and Jefferson on this subject.

Governments ordinarily perish by powerlessness or by tyranny. In the first case power escapes them; in the other, it is torn from them.

Many people, on seeing democratic states fall into anarchy, have thought that government in these states was naturally weak and powerless. The truth is that when war among their parties has once been set aflame, government loses its action on society. But I do not think that the nature of democratic power is to lack force and resources; I believe, on the contrary, that almost always the abuse of its strength and the bad use of its resources bring it to perish. Anarchy is almost always born of its tyranny or its lack of skillfulness, but not of its powerlessness.

One must not confuse stability with force, the greatness of the thing and its duration. In democratic republics, the power that directs society is not stable, for it often changes hands and purpose. But everywhere it is brought, its force is almost irresistible.

The government of the American republics appears to me to be as centralized and more energetic than that of absolute monarchies of Europe. I therefore do not think that it will perish from weakness.

If ever freedom is lost in America, one will have to blame the omnipotence of the majority that will have brought minorities to despair and have forced them to make an appeal to material force. One will then see anarchy, but it will have come as a consequence of despotism.

President James Madison expressed the same thoughts. (See *Federalist* 51.)

"It is of great importance in a republic," he says, "not only to guard the society against the oppression of its rulers, but to guard one part of the society against the injustice of the other part. . . . Justice is the end of government. It is the end of civil society. It ever has been and ever will be pursued until it be obtained or until liberty be lost in the pursuit. In a society under the forms of which the stronger faction can readily unite and oppress the weaker, anarchy may as truly be said to reign as in the state of nature, where the weaker individual is not secured against the violence of the stronger; and as, in the latter state, even the stronger individuals are prompted, by the uncertainty of their condition, to submit to a government which may protect the weak as well as themselves; so, in the former state, will the more powerful factions or parties be gradually induced, by a like motive, to wish for a government which will protect all parties, the weaker as well as the more powerful. It can be little doubted that if the State of Rhode Island was separated from the confederacy and left to itself, the insecurity of rights under the popular form of government within such narrow limits would be displayed by such reiterated oppressions of factious majorities that some power altogether independent of the people would soon be called for by the voice of the very factions whose misrule had proved the necessity of it."

Jefferson as well said: "The executive in our governments is not the sole, it is scarcely the principal object of my jealousy. The tyranny of the legislatures is the most formidable dread at present, and will be for long years. That of the executive will come in its turn, but it will be at a remote period."

I like to cite Jefferson in preference to everyone else on this matter because I consider him to be the most powerful apostle that democracy has ever had.

KARL MARX AND FRIEDRICH ENGELS

~

INTRODUCTION

RICHARD MILLER

Karl Marx (1818–1883) was born in Trier, in a Prussian province along the Rhine. His family was upper middle class, nominally Protestant, and ethnically Jewish. From 1835 to 1841, Marx pursued his university studies, first at Bonn, then at Berlin, Hegel's old university, where his tenuous interest in the law shifted to a commitment to philosophy. Marx became one of the "Young Hegelians" who followed Hegel in viewing history as the rational development of the idea of freedom through the generation and resolution of contradictions, and, much more than Hegel, criticized received traditions and institutions as obstacles to this progress.

Although Marx earned a doctorate in philosophy in 1841, he turned to journalism as his most effective means of social criticism. But Prussian repression intervened. His newspaper was shut down in 1843, largely in response to Marx's investigations of poverty among the Rhenish peasantry.

Marx moved to Paris, where he combined more journalism with intensive study of English economists, French political historians, and "Communists," that is, advocates of communal ownership and the leveling of economic differences who had begun to attract a working-class following in France and Germany. The source of our first selection, a series of rough drafts now known as the *Economic and Philosophical Manuscripts of 1844*, was the most important product of this diverse ferment. First published in 1927, the *Manuscripts* mark a large step away from the rationalist reformism of the Young Hegelians and have served, since their publication, as an epitome of Marx's abiding spiritual concerns.

Often, Marx's project in these manuscripts is to use his experience and reading concerning economic life to transform certain diagnoses of psychological impoverishment that he had encountered in Hegel and in the atheist, materialist philosopher Ludwig Feuerbach (1804–1872). Both philosophers were concerned with processes of "alienation," in which aspects of human life through which people could potentially express themselves or their common humanity are instead confronted as external phenomena, opposed to self-expression. Marx's predecessors locate the roots of this self-estrangement in confused thinking: the self's overly rigid conceptualization of its relation to objective reality (Hegel), or humans' conversion of "species-being," our appreciation of our common humanity, into awe at an imagined God embodying our common strivings (Feuerbach). Marx accepts the devastating effect of estrangement from oneself and others but traces it to a specific feature of economic life under capitalism: the necessity that wage earners face of selling their life activity as a commodity in order to survive.

Unrestrained economic competition leads more and more people to lose control of means of production, forcing them to submit to the labor market. So the cure for alienation is not mere removal of political restrictions but the creation of a new kind of economy, based on common control of production in the interest of reciprocity, expressive work, and the satisfaction of the needs characteristic of cooperating human beings.

In 1845, the French government, under pressure from the Prussian monarchy, expelled Marx, who moved to Brussels. There, Marx began his lifelong collaboration with Friedrich Engels, with whom he had become friends in Paris. Engels (1820–1895) was born to a wealthy, devoutly Pietist family in Barmen, about 100 miles north of Marx's Trier, also in Prussian territory near the Rhine. The family business was an international textile-manufacturing firm, with a branch in Manchester, England. As he became part of the family business, Engels was increasingly appalled by the conditions he encountered among factory workers. This experience, together with his readings in philosophy and political economy, led him through the same phases as the young Marx had gone through, culminating in his widely read indictment of the most advanced capitalism of the time, *The Condition of the Working Class in England* (1845).

One of their first coauthored works, *The German Ideology* (finished in 1846, but unpublished until 1932), is the source of our second reading. As in the 1844 *Manuscripts*, the project is sometimes the economic explanation of spiritual ills, both alienation and the one-sided personal development that Marx and Engels trace to the division of labor. A new theme is the explanation of how social systems develop. In a vague outline that would be filled in and revised in much future work, Marx and Engels propose that the pursuit of enhanced powers of material production has the unintended consequence of creating new social relations of production, which, in turn, mold the political and cultural features of an era.

Along with this theoretical work, Marx and Engels were getting to know working-class radicals, especially members of the League of the Just, a conspiratorial Communist group with branches throughout western Europe. As they moved the League closer to their own views, they joined it. In a congress in London, the League renamed itself "The Communist League" and adopted guiding principles that Marx and Engels were asked to elaborate in a manifesto. The result, *Manifesto of the Communist Party*, our next selection, came off the presses in February 1848, just as a continental wave of revolutions began with the overthrow of the French monarchy.

The *Manifesto's* astounding mixture of advocacy, theorizing, and historical narration centers on a conception of capitalist society as based on an antagonistic relation that will, inevitably, destroy it, the relation between the proletariat and the bourgeoisie. Broadly speaking, the proletariat are those who control no significant means of production and must make a living by selling the use of their labor power to others who do. The bourgeoisie are these others, people exercising significant control over means of production and mainly deriving their income from the sale of what proletarians working these means produce. The two classes are "two great hostile camps," since the competitive bourgeois drive for profits creates relentless pressure to reduce wages and to eliminate individualized ways of working that conflict with industrial routines. Marx and Engels view political and cultural institutions (including "the modern representative state") as advancing the long-term interests of the bourgeoisie in this conflict. Yet, in the face of this "ruling class" dominance, the bourgeoisie "produces . . . , above all, its own grave-diggers." Economic interdependence, the reduced importance of master-craftsmen's expertise, mass literacy, and ease of communication are features of modern proletarian life due to the bourgeois drive to expand production. Yet their utterly unintended result is increased unity in resistance to the burdens of capitalist production, ultimately progressing to full-scale revolution and the creation of a proletarian ruling class. Marx and Engels see this as the basis for yet further transformations, ultimately including a stateless society in which work is motivated by a desire for mutual benefit.

Responding to the revolutionary fervor that coincided with the appearance of the *Manifesto*, Marx and Engels returned to Germany—Marx as organizer and main writer of a revolutionary newspaper, Engels both as journalist and officer in a revolutionary army. The failure of the revolutions brought Marx's final exile. He was expelled from Prussia in 1850 on account of the "dangerous tendencies" of his newspaper, soon settling in London, where he spent the rest of his life. The Marx family was desperately poor at the start, and, for the next two decades (after which Engels provided a stipend), Marx's struggle to make ends meet as a freelance journalist never kept them far from poverty.

Most of Marx's theoretical work in this second half of his life was devoted to the description of the economic "laws of motion" of capitalism, which eventually took the form of his multivolume treatise, *Capital*. Only the first volume appeared in Marx's lifetime, in 1867. Marx's most important political activity in London was his leading role in the International Workingmen's Association (1864–1876), an international group of predominantly working-class activists, which led demonstrations of English workers in favor of Irish independence, organized international strike support, and outraged the respectable classes of Europe by supporting the Paris Commune, a revolutionary government, including members of the International, which controlled Paris for two months at the end of the Franco-Prussian War.

Our next selection is the celebrated preface to an otherwise little-read work that prefigured parts of *Capital* I—*A Contribution to the Critique of Political Economy* (1859). Its fame rests on part of a paragraph in a brief autobiographical sketch, a few lines that contain Marx's most detailed statement of his general conception of social stability and social change. With the help of other writings by Marx and the many thousands of pages of commentary inspired by these few lines, some features of Marx's meaning here have become fairly well established. As in his analysis of capitalist society in the *Manifesto*, Marx takes relations of control that dominate material production to be the foundation on which political and cultural institutions rest: in other words, the most important features of these "super-structural" institutions are as they are because this helps to maintain the "economic structure" consisting of those "relations of production." Despite these stabilizing institutions, Marx thinks that there are processes internal to some social systems that make change inevitable. The ultimate origin of such internal change lies in the mode of production: the ensemble of relations of control, work relations, and technological capacities through which material goods are produced. In particular, people's locations in an initially stable economic structure may lead them to increase the productive capacity of resources they control until further productive improvement is inhibited by the old relations of production. Marx's paradigm is the inhibition of productive capitalist investment by guild rules, traditional overlord-tenant ties, and economically arbitrary grants of royal monopolies in late-feudal England. Eventually, the enhanced productive forces, together with their fettering, provide resources and motivations for an effective social revolution, so that the chains are broken and a new structure established, facilitating the growth of productive power.

The development of Marx's theory of capitalism in his London years, which led to our last selection, was sustained by countless hours of reading in the British Museum library. At the same time, the evolution of Marx's thinking reflected his personal contact with British trades unionism. While the *Manifesto* had emphasized spontaneous tendencies of capitalism to dissolve divisions among workers based on ethnicity, religion, or nation, Marx came to see the antagonism between ethnically English and ethnically Irish workers as "the secret of the impotence of the English working class," a division maintained by the mass media of the time, requiring organized opposition by groups such as the International. While the *Manifesto* had described a downward trend of wages and working conditions to the thresh-old of bare physical survival, Marx became acutely aware of the sustained upward trend in real wages in Britain and the benefits of the shortened working day.

Value, Price and Profit, the basis for talks Marx gave in the General Council of the International in 1865, reflects this combination of theoretical work and concrete experience. The first six chapters, omitted here, argue against a position advanced in Council discussions that trades union activity could do nothing to improve the economic situation of workers under capitalism. In our selection, Marx, in effect, gives a preview of aspects of Volume I of *Capital* in order to shed light on the actual limits of the capitalist labor market.

For purposes of economic theorizing, Marx measures the value of a commodity by the total time needed to produce it (both at the final stage and in the provision of equipment and raw materials) when work is done with current techniques at typical intensity. Under average conditions, then, the value that a worker adds to what a firm owns in the course of a working day will be the length of this working day. But the value of the use of a worker's labor power for that time will be the labor time needed to provide for the worker's existence for the day—a smaller magnitude in any firm with a hope of surviving. Marx calls the difference between these magnitudes *surplus value*. He takes it to be the most important source of all the various forms of profit on capital (interest included), while the values of commodities are the basic determinants of prices, including the wage paid for labor.

Marx's identification of the value of labor power with what is necessary to maintain and reproduce it suggests his earlier view that capitalism forces wages down to the minimum needed for physical subsistence. But in fact, Marx adds a further "historical or social element." It, too, comprises "necessities" for workers, but this is because people's needs are themselves determined, in part, by their social conditions. Marx does think that reduction to the physical minimum is "the tendency of *things* under capitalism." If workers only advance their interests as competing individuals in the labor market, they are bound to succumb to the superior bargaining power of capitalist employers—a superiority based, for example, on the desperation of a reserve army of the unemployed replenished by capitalists' recourse to laborsaving, capital-intensive innovations. But, Marx insists, workers can combine to resist the tendency of things, through militant trades union struggles and the forcing of favorable legislation such as the Ten Hours'

Act. Indeed, his judgment of the balance of forces, in *Capital*, is that workers will succeed in cashing in a constant proportionate share of gains from technological improvement when fluctuations in the business cycle are discounted. This gain in material possessions entails no increase in the value of labor power, because value is a matter of labor time expended with current techniques, regardless of their productivity.

Among the many questions about Marx's and Engels's meanings, some have proved especially apt to shed light on large issues in political and social theory. The Preface to *A Contribution to the Critique of Political Economy* seems to many readers to make technological innovation the ultimate source of social change, but Marx's specific historical explanations, including the economic histories in *Capital*, rarely give technology the leading role. Is there an underlying theory that fits both general statements and concrete practice? In the *Manifesto* and elsewhere, Marx and Engels seem to reject appeals to justice and even to morality as part of their "radical rupture with traditional ideas." Is there any sense in which the rejections are genuine, and, if so, what replaces justice and morality? Marx and Engels treat politics and culture as "superstructural," yet political goals and religious beliefs have obviously motivated conduct of socially important kinds. Can they admit that social processes are based on individual conduct that often has these motives, without watering down their intriguing claims into banalities about the need to eat and the presence of economic and technological processes as some of the many important sources of change? Recent works exploring these questions include Gerald Cohen, *Karl Marx's Theory of History* (Princeton, N.J.: Princeton University Press, 1978), a defense of a technological determinist interpretation; Jon Elster, *Making Sense of Marx* (Cambridge: Cambridge University Press, 1985), which defends a "methodological individualist" view of Marx; Alan Gilbert, *Marx's Politics* (New Brunswick, N.J.: Rutgers University Press, 1981), which questions economic deterministic understandings of Marx; Richard W. Miller, *Analyzing Marx* (Princeton, N.J.: Princeton University Press, 1984), with discussions of morality, the nature of the state, and (from an antitechnological-determinist perspective) history; and Allen Wood, *Karl Marx* (London: Routledge & Kegan Paul, 1981), which includes discussions of morality and alienation.

Economic and Philosophic Manuscripts of 1844

ESTRANGED LABOR

We have proceeded from the premises of political economy. We have accepted its language and its laws. We presupposed private property, the separation of labor, capital and land, and of wages, profit of capital and rent of land— likewise division of labor, competition, the concept of exchange-value, etc. On the basis of political economy itself, in its own words, we have shown that the worker sinks to the level of a commodity and becomes indeed the most wretched of commodities; that the wretchedness of the worker is in inverse proportion to the power and

---

Translated by Martin Milligan. Reprinted by permission of International Publishers.

magnitude of his production; that the necessary result of competition is the accumulation of capital in a few hands, and thus the restoration of monopoly in a more terrible form; and that finally the distinction between capitalist and land rentier, like that between the tiller of the soil and the factory worker, disappears and that the whole of society must fall apart into the two classes—the property *owners* and the propertyless *workers*.

Political economy starts with the fact of private property, but it does not explain it to us. It expresses in general, abstract formulas the *material* process through which private property actually passes, and these formulas it then takes for *laws*. It does not *comprehend* these laws, i.e., it does not demonstrate how they arise from the very nature of private property. Political economy does not disclose the source of the division between labor and capital, and between capital and land. When, for example, it defines the relationship of wages to profit, it takes the interest of the capitalists to be the ultimate cause, i.e., it takes for granted what it is supposed to explain. Similarly, competition comes in everywhere. It is explained from external circumstances. As to how far these external and apparently accidental circumstances are but the expression of a necessary course of development, political economy teaches us nothing. We have seen how exchange itself appears to it as an accidental fact. The only wheels which political economy sets in motion are *greed* and the war *amongst the greedy—competition*.

Precisely because political economy does not grasp the way the movement is connected, it was possible to oppose, for instance, the doctrine of competition to the doctrine of monopoly, the doctrine of the freedom of the crafts to the doctrine of the guild, the doctrine of the division of landed property to the doctrine of the big estate—for competition, freedom of the crafts and the division of landed property were explained and comprehended only as accidental, premeditated and violent consequences of monopoly, of the guild system, and of feudal property, not as their necessary, inevitable and natural consequences.

Now, therefore, we have to grasp the essential connection between private property; greed, and the separation of labor, capital and landed property; between exchange and competition, value and the devaluation of men, monopoly and competition, etc.—the connection between this whole estrangement and the *money* system.

Do not let us go back to a fictitious primordial condition as the political economist does, when he tries to explain. Such a primordial condition explains nothing; it merely pushes the question away into a gray nebulous distance. It assumes in the form of a fact, of an event, what the economist is supposed to deduce—namely, the necessary relationship between two things—between, for example, division of labor and exchange. Theology in the same way explains the origin of evil by the fall of man; that is, it assumes as a fact, in historical form, what has to be explained.

We proceed from an economic fact *of the present.*

The worker becomes all the poorer the more wealth he produces, the more his production increases in power and size. The worker becomes an ever cheaper commodity the more commodities he creates. With the *increasing value* of the world of things proceeds in direct proportion the *devaluation* of the world of men. Labor produces not only commodities: it produces itself and the worker as a *commodity*—and this in the same general proportion in which it produces commodities.

This fact expresses merely that the object which labor produces—labor's product—confronts it as *something* alien, as a *power independent* of the producer. The product of labor is labor which has been embodied in an object, which has become material: it is the objectification of labor. Labor's realization is its objectification. In the sphere of political economy this realization of labor appears as loss of *realization* for the workers; objectification as loss of the *object* and *bondage* to it; appropriation as *estrangement*, as *alienation*.

So much does labor's realization appear as loss of realization that the worker loses realization to the point of starving to death. So much does objectification appear as loss of the object that the worker is robbed of the objects most necessary not only for his life but for his work. Indeed, labor itself becomes an object which he can obtain only with the greatest effort and with the most irregular interruptions. So much does the appropriation of the object appear as estrangement that the more objects the worker produces the less he can possess and the more he falls under the sway of his product, capital.

All these consequences result from the fact that the worker is related to the *product of his labor* as to an *alien* object. For on this premise it is clear that the more the worker spends himself, the more powerful becomes the alien world of objects which he creates over and against himself, the poorer he himself—his inner world—becomes, the less belongs to him as his own. It is the same in religion. The more man puts into God, the less he retains in himself. The worker puts his life into the object; but now his life no longer belongs to him but to the object. Hence, the greater this activity, the greater is the worker's lack of objects. Whatever the product of his labor is, he is not. Therefore the greater this product, the less is he himself. The *alienation* of the worker in his product means not only that his labor becomes an object, an *external* existence, but that it exists *outside* him, independently, as something alien to him, and that it becomes a power on its own confronting him. It means that the life which he has conferred on the object confronts him as something hostile and alien.

Let us now look more closely at the *objectification*, at the production of the worker; and in it as the *estrangement*, the *loss* of the object, of his product.

The worker can create nothing without *nature*, without the *sensuous external world*. It is the material on which his labor is realized, in which it is active, from which and by means of which it produces.

But just as nature provides labor with the *means of life* in the sense that labor cannot live without objects on which to operate, on the other hand, it also provides the *means of life* in the more restricted sense, i.e., the means for the physical subsistence of the *worker* himself.

Thus the more the worker by his labor *appropriates* the external world, hence sensuous nature, the more he deprives himself of *means of life* in double manner: first, in that the sensuous external world more and more ceases to be an object belonging to his labor—to be his labor's *means of life*; and secondly, in that it more and more ceases to be *means of life* in the immediate sense, means for the physical subsistence of the worker.

In both respects, therefore, the worker becomes a slave of his object, first, in that he receives an *object of labor*, i.e., in that he receives *work*; and secondly, in that he receives *means of subsistence*. Therefore, it enables him to exist, first, as a *worker*; and, second as a *physical subject*. The height of this bondage is that it is only as a *worker* that he continues to maintain himself as a *physical subject*, and that is only as a *physical subject* that he is a *worker*.

(The laws of political economy express the estrangement of the worker in his object thus: the more the worker produces, the less he has to consume; the more values he creates, the more valueless, the more unworthy he becomes; the better formed his product, the more deformed becomes the worker; the more civilized his object, the more barbarous becomes the worker; the more powerful labor becomes, the more powerless becomes the worker; the more ingenious labor becomes, the less ingenious becomes the worker and the more he becomes nature's bondsman.)

Political economy conceals the estrangement inherent in the nature of labor by not considering the direct relationship between the worker (labor) *and production.* It is true that labor produces for the rich wonderful things—but for the worker it produces privation. It produces palaces—but for the worker, hovels. It produces beauty—but for the worker, deformity. It replaces labor by machines, but it throws a section of the workers back to a barbarous type of labor, and turns the other workers into machines. It produces intelligence—but for the worker stupidity, cretinism.

The direct relationship of labor to its products is the relationship of the worker to the objects of his production. The relationship of the man of means to the objects of production and to production itself is only a *consequence* of this first relationship—and confirms it. We shall consider this other aspect later.

When we ask, then, what is the essential relationship of labor we are asking about the relationship of the *worker* to production.

Till now we have been considering the estrangement, the alienation of the worker only in one of its aspects, i.e., the worker's *relationship to the products of his labor*. But the estrangement is manifested not only in the result but in the *act of production*, within the *producing activity*, itself. How would the worker come to face the product of his activity as a stranger, were it not that in the very act of production he was estranging himself from himself? The product is after all but the summary of the activity, of production. If then the product of labor is alienation, production itself must be active alienation, the alienation of activity, the activity of alienation. In the estrangement of the object of labor is merely summarized the estrangement, the alienation, in the activity of labor itself.

What, then, constitutes the alienation of labor?

First, the fact that labor is *external* to the worker, i.e., it does not belong to his essential being; that in his work, therefore, he does not affirm himself but denies himself, does not feel content but unhappy, does not develop freely his physical and mental energy but mortifies his body and ruins his mind. The worker therefore only feels himself outside his work, and in his work feels outside himself. He is at home when he is not working, and when he is working he is not at home. His labor is therefore not voluntary, but coerced; it is *forced labor*. It is therefore not the satisfaction of a need; it is merely a *means* to satisfy needs external to it. Its alien character emerges clearly in the fact that as soon as no physical or other compulsion exists, labor is shunned like the plague. External labor, labor in which man alienates himself, is a labor of self-sacrifice, of mortification. Lastly, the external

character of labor for the worker appears in the fact that it is not his own, but someone else's, that it does not belong to him, that in it he belongs, not to himself, but to another. Just as in religion the spontaneous activity of the human imagination, of the human brain and the human heart, operates independently of the individual—that is, operates on him as an alien, divine or diabolical activity—so is the worker's activity not his spontaneous activity. It belongs to another; it is the loss of his self.

As a result, therefore, man (the worker) only feels himself freely active in his animal functions—eating, drinking, procreating, or at most in his dwelling and in dressing-up, etc.; and in his human functions he no longer feels himself to be anything but an animal. What is animal becomes human and what is human becomes animal.

Certainly eating, drinking, procreating, etc., are also genuinely human functions. But abstractly taken, separated from the sphere of all other human activity and turned into sole and ultimate ends, they are animal functions.

We have considered the act of estranging practical human activity, labor, in two of its aspects. (1) The relation of the worker to the *product of labor* as an alien object exercising power over him. This relation is at the same time the relation to the sensuous external world, to the objects of nature, as an alien world inimically opposed to him. (2) The relation of labor to the *act of production* within the *labor* process. This relation is the relation of the worker to his own activity as an alien activity not belonging to him; it is activity as suffering, strength as weakness, begetting as emasculating, the worker's own physical and mental energy, his personal life indeed, what is life but activity?—as an activity which is turned against him, independent of him and not belonging to him. Here we have *self-estrangement*, as previously we had the estrangement of the *thing*.

We have still a third aspect of *estranged labor* to deduce from the two already considered.

Man is a species being, not only because in practice and in theory he adopts the species as his object (his own as well as those of other things), but—and this is only another way of expressing it—also because he treats himself as the actual, living species; because he treats himself as a *universal* and therefore a free being.

The life of the species, both in man and in animals, consists physically in the fact that man (like the animal) lives on inorganic nature; and the more universal man is compared with an animal, the more universal is the sphere of inorganic nature on which he lives. Just as plants, animals, stones, air, light, etc., constitute theoretically a part of human consciousness, partly as objects of natural science, partly as objects of art—his spiritual inorganic nature, spiritual nourishment which he must first prepare to make palatable and digestible—so also in the realm of practice they constitute a part of human life and human activity. Physically man lives only on these products of nature, whether they appear in the form of food, heating, clothes, a dwelling, etc. The universality of man appears in practice precisely in the universality which makes all nature his *inorganic body*—both inasmuch as nature is (1) his direct means of life, and (2) the material, the object, and the instrument of his life activity. Nature is man's *inorganic body*—nature, that is, in so far as it is not itself the human body. Man *lives* on nature—means that nature is his body, with which he must remain in continuous interchange if he is not to die. That man's physical and spiritual life is linked to nature means simply that nature is linked to itself, for man is a part of nature.

In estranging from man (1) nature, and (2) himself, his own active functions, his life activity, estranged labor estranges the *species* from man. It changes for him the *life of the species* into a means of individual life, and secondly it makes individual life in its abstract form the purpose of the life of the species, likewise in its abstract and estranged form.

Indeed, labor, *life-activity, productive life* itself, appears in the first place merely as a means of satisfying a need—the need to maintain physical existence. Yet the productive life is the life of the species. It is life-engendering life. The whole character of a species—its species character—is contained in the character of its life activity; and free, conscious activity is man's species character. Life itself appears only as a *means to life*.

The animal is immediately one with its life activity. It does not distinguish itself from it. It is *its life activity*. Man makes his life activity itself the object of his will and of his consciousness. He has conscious life activity. It is not a determination with which he directly merges. Conscious life activity distinguishes man immediately from animal life activity. It is just because of this that he is a species being. Or rather, it is only because he is a species being that he is a conscious being, i.e., that his own life is an object for him. Only because of that is his activity free activity. Estranged labor reverses this relationship, so that it is just because man is a conscious being that he makes his life activity, his *essential* being, a mere means to his *existence*.

In creating a *world of objects* by his practical activity, in *his work upon* inorganic nature, man proves himself a conscious species being, i.e., as a being that treats the species as its own essential being, or that treats itself as a species being. Admittedly animals also produce. They build themselves nests, dwellings, like the bees, beavers, ants, etc. But an animal only produces what it immediately needs for itself or its young. It produces one-sidedly, whilst man produces universally. It produces only under the dominion of immediate physical need, whilst man produces even when he is free from physical need and only truly produces in freedom therefrom. An animal produces only itself, whilst man reproduces the whole of nature. An animal's product belongs immediately to its physical body, whilst man freely confronts his product. An animal forms things in accordance with the standard and the need of the species to which it belongs, whilst man knows how to produce in accordance with the standard of every species, and knows how to apply everywhere the inherent standard to the object. Man therefore also forms things in accordance with the laws of beauty.

It is just in his work upon the objective world, therefore, that man first really proves himself to be a *species being*. This production is his active species life. Through and because of this production, nature appears as his work and his reality. The object of labor is, therefore, the *objectification of man's species life*: for he duplicates himself not only, as in consciousness, intellectually, but also actively, in reality, and therefore he contemplates himself in a world that he has created. In tearing away from man the object of his production, therefore, estranged labor tears from him his *species life*, his real objectivity as a member of the species and transforms his advantage over animals into the disadvantage that his inorganic body, nature, is taken away from him.

Similarly, in degrading spontaneous, free, activity, to a means, estranged labor makes man's species life a means to his physical existence.

The consciousness which man has of his species is thus transformed by estrangement in such a way that species life becomes for him a means.

Estranged labor turns thus: (3) *Man's species being*, both nature and his spiritual species property, into a being *alien* to him, into a *means* to his *individual existence*. It estranges from man his own body, as well as external nature and his spiritual essence, his *human* being. (4) An immediate consequence of the fact that man is estranged from the product of his labor, from his life activity, from his species being is the *estrangement of man* from *man*. When man confronts himself, he confronts the *other* man. What applies to a man's relation to his work, to the product of his labor and to himself, also holds of a man's relation to the other man, and to the other man's labor and object of labor.

In fact, the proposition that man's species nature is estranged from him means that one man is estranged from the other, as each of them is from man's essential nature.

The estrangement of man, and in fact every relationship in which man stands to himself, is first realized and expressed in the relationship in which a man stands to other men.

Hence within the relationship of estranged labor each man views the other in accordance with the standard and the relationship in which he finds himself as a worker.

We took our departure from a fact of political economy—the estrangement of the worker and his production. We have formulated this fact in conceptual terms as *estranged, alienated* labor. We have analyzed this concept—hence analyzing merely a fact of political economy.

Let us now see, further, how the concept of estranged, alienated labor must express and present itself in real life.

If the product of labor is alien to me, if it confronts me as an alien power, to whom, then, does it belong?

If my own activity does not belong to me, if it is an alien, a coerced activity, to whom, then, does it belong?

To a being *other* than myself.

Who is this being?

The *gods*? To be sure, in the earliest times the principal production (for example, the building of temples, etc., in Egypt, India and Mexico) appears to be in the service of the gods, and the product belongs to the gods. However, the gods on their own were never the lords of labor. No more was *nature*. And what a contradiction it would be if, the more man subjugated nature by his labor and the more the miracles of the gods were rendered superfluous by the miracles of industry, the more man were to renounce the joy of production and the enjoyment of the product in favor of these powers.

The *alien* being, to whom labor and the product of labor belongs, in whose service labor is done and for whose benefit the product of labor is provided, can only be *man* himself.

If the product of labor does not belong to the worker, if it confronts him as an alien power, then this can only be because it belongs to some *other man than the worker*. If the worker's activity is a torment to him, to another it must be *delight* and his life's joy. Not the gods, not nature, but only man himself can be this alien power over man.

We must bear in mind the previous proposition that man's relation to himself only becomes for him *objective* and *actual* through his relation to the other man. Thus, if the product of his labor, his labor *objectified*, is for him an *alien*, hostile, powerful object independent of him, then his position towards it is such that someone else is master of this object, someone who is alien, hostile, powerful, and independent of him. If his own activity is to him related as an unfree activity, then he is related to it as an activity performed in the service, under the dominion, the coercion, and the yoke of another man.

Every self-estrangement of man, from himself and from nature, appears in the relation in which he places himself and nature to men other than and differentiated from himself. For this reason religious self-estrangement necessarily appears in the relationship of the layman to the priest, or again to a mediator, etc., since we are here dealing with the intellectual world. In the real practical world self-estrangement can only become manifest through the real practical relationship to other men. The medium through which estrangement takes place is itself *practical*. Thus through estranged labor man not only creates his relationship to the object and to the act of production as to men that are alien and hostile to him; he also creates the relationship in which other men stand to his production and to his product, and the relationship in which he stands to these other men. Just as he creates his own production as the loss of his reality, as his punishment; his own product as a loss, as a product not belonging to him; so he creates the domination of the person who does not produce over production and over the product. Just as he estranges his own activity from himself, so he confers to the stranger an activity which is not his own.

We have until now only considered this relationship from the standpoint of the worker and later we shall be considering it also from the standpoint of the non-worker.

Through *estranged*, *alienated* labor, then, the worker produces the relationship to this labor of a man alien to labor and standing outside it. The relationship of the worker to labor creates the relation to it of the capitalist (or whatever one chooses to call the master of labor). *Private property* is thus the product, the result, the necessary consequence, of *alienated labor*, of the external relation of the worker to nature and to himself.

Private property thus results by analysis from the concept of alienated labor, of *alienated man*, of *estranged labor*, of estranged life, of estranged man.

True, it as a result of the *movement of private property* that we have obtained the concept of *alienated labor (of alienated life)* from political economy. But on analysis of this concept it becomes clear that though private property appears to be the source, the cause of alienated labor, it is rather its consequence, just as the gods are *originally* not the cause but the effect of man's intellectual confusion. Later this relationship becomes reciprocal.

Only at the last culmination of the development of private property does this, its secret, appear again, namely, that on the one hand it is the *product* of alienated labor, and that on the other it is the *means* by which labor alienates itself, the *realization of this alienation*.

This exposition immediately sheds light on various hitherto unsolved conflicts.

(1) Political economy starts from labor as the real soul of production; yet to labor it gives nothing, and to private property everything. Confronting this contradiction, Proudhon has decided in favor of labor it gives nothing, and to private property everything. Confronting this contradiction, Proudhon has decided in favor of labor against private property. We understand, however, that this apparent contradiction is the contradiction of *estranged labor* with itself, and that political economy has merely formulated the laws of estranged labor.

We also understand, therefore, that *wages* and *private property* are identical: since the product, as the object of labor pays for labor itself, therefore the wage is but a necessary consequence of labor's estrangement. After all, in the wage of labor, labor does not appear as an end in itself but as the servant of the wage. We shall develop this point later, and meanwhile will only derive some conclusions.

An enforced increase of wages (disregarding all other difficulties, including the fact that it would only be by force, too, that higher wages, being an anomaly, could be maintained) would therefore be nothing but *better payment for the slave*, and would not win either for the worker or for labor their human status and dignity.

Indeed, even the *equality of wages* demanded by Proudhon only transforms the relationship of the present-day worker to his labor into the relationship of all men to labor. Society is then conceived as an abstract capitalist.

Wages are a direct consequence of estranged labor, and estranged labor is the direct cause of private property. The downfall of the one must involve the downfall of the other.

(2) From the relationship of estranged labor to private property it follows further that the emancipation of society from private property, etc., from servitude, is expressed in the *political* form of the *emancipation of the workers*; not that *their* emancipation alone is at stake, but because the emancipation of the workers contains universal human emancipation—and it contains this, because the whole of human servitude is involved in the relation of the worker to production, and every relation of servitude is but a modification and consequence of this relation.

Just as we have derived the concept of *private property* from the concept of *estranged, alienated labor* by *analysis*, so we can develop every *category* of political economy with the help of these two factors; and we shall find again in each category, e.g., trade, competition, capital, money, only a *definite* and *developed expression* of these first elements.

Before considering this aspect, however, let us try to solve two problems.

(1) To define the general *nature of private property*, as it has arisen as a result of estranged labor, in its relation to *truly human* and *social property*.

(2) We have accepted the estrangement of labor, its alienation, as a fact, and we have analyzed this fact. How, we now ask, does man come to alienate, to estrange, his labor? How is this estrangement rooted in the nature of human development? We have already gone a long way to the solution of this problem by transforming the question of the origin of private property into the question of the relation of alienated labor to the course of humanity's development. For when one speaks of private property, one thinks of dealing with something external to man. When one speaks of labor, one is directly dealing with man himself. This new formulation of the question already contains its solution.

As to (1): The general nature of private property and its relation to truly human property.

Alienated labor has resolved itself for us into two elements which mutually condition one another, or which are but different expressions of one and the same relationship. *Appropriation* appears as *estrangement*, as *alienation*; and *alienation* appears as *appropriation*, *estrangement* as true introduction into society.

We have considered the one side—*alienated* labor in relation to the *worker* himself, i.e., *the relation of alienated labor to itself.* The *property relation of the non-worker to the worker and to labor* we have found as the product, the necessary outcome of this relationship. Private property, as the material, summary expression of alienated labor, embraces both relations—*the relation of the worker to work and to the product of his labor and to the non-worker*, and the relation of the *non-worker to the worker and to the product of his labor.*

Having seen that in relation to the worker who *appropriates* nature by means of his labor, this appropriation appears as estrangement, his own spontaneous activity as activity for another and as activity of another, vitality as a sacrifice of life, production of the object as loss of the object to an alien power, to an *alien* person—we shall now consider the relation to the worker, to labor and its object of this person who is *alien* to labor and the worker.

First it has to be noted that everything which appears in the worker as an *activity of alienation, of estrangement*, appears in the non-worker as a *state of alienation, of estrangement.*

Secondly, that the worker's *real, practical attitude* in production and to the product (as a state of mind) appears in the non-worker confronting him as a *theoretical* attitude.

Thirdly, the non-worker does everything against the worker which the worker does against himself; but he does not do against himself what he does against the worker.

Let us look more closely at these three relations. *[At this point the manuscript breaks off unfinished.]*

The German Ideology

Men can be distinguished from animals by consciousness, by religion or anything else you like. They themselves begin to distinguish themselves from animals as soon as they begin to *produce* their means of subsistence, a step which is conditioned by their physical organisation. By producing their means of subsistence men are indirectly producing their actual material life.

The way in which men produce their means of subsistence depends first of all on the nature of the actual means of subsistence they find in existence and have to reproduce. This mode of production must not be considered simply as being the production of the physical existence of the individuals. Rather it is a definite form of activity of these individuals, a definite form of expressing their life, a definite *mode of life* on their part. As individuals express their life, so they are. What they are, therefore, coincides with their production, both with *what* they produce and with *how* they produce. The nature of individuals thus depends on the material conditions determining their production.

This production only makes its appearance with the *increase of population*. In its turn this presupposes the *intercourse* [*Verkehr*] of individuals with one another. The form of this intercourse is again determined by production.

The relations of different nations among themselves depend upon the extent to which each has developed its productive forces, the division of labour and internal intercourse. This statement is generally recognised. But not only the relation of one nation to others, but also the whole internal structure of the nation itself depends on the stage of development reached by its production and its internal and external intercourse. How far the productive forces of a nation are developed is shown most manifestly by the degree to which the division of labour has been carried. Each new productive force, insofar as it is not merely a quantitative extension of productive forces already known (for instance the bringing into cultivation of fresh land), causes a further development of the division of labour.

The division of labour inside a nation leads at first to the separation of industrial and commercial from agricultural labour, and hence to the separation of *town* and *country* and to the conflict of their interests. Its further development leads to the separation of commercial from industrial labour. At the same time through the division of labour inside these various branches there develop various divisions among the individuals cooperating in definite kinds of labour. The relative position of these individual groups is determined by the methods employed in agriculture, industry and commerce (patriarchalism, slavery, estates, classes). These same conditions are to be seen (given a more developed intercourse) in the relations of different nations to one another.

Edited by C. J. Arthur. Reprinted by permission of International Publishers.

The various stages of development in the division of labour are just so many different forms of ownership, i.e. the existing stage in the division of labour determines also the relations of individuals to one another with reference to the material, instrument, and product of labour.

The first form of ownership is tribal [*Stammeigentum*] ownership. It corresponds to the undeveloped stage of production, at which a people lives by hunting and fishing, by the rearing of beasts or, the highest stage, agriculture. In the latter case it presupposes a great mass of uncultivated stretches of land. The division of labour is at this stage still very elementary and is confined to a further extension of the natural division of labour existing in the family. The social structure is, therefore, limited to an extension of the family; patriarchal family chieftains, below them the members of the tribe, finally slaves. The slavery latent in the family only develops gradually with the increase of population, the growth of wants, and with the extension of external relations, both of war and of barter.

The second form is the ancient communal and State ownership which proceeds especially from the union of several tribes into a *city* by agreement or by conquest, and which is still accompanied by slavery. Beside communal ownership we already find movable, and later also immovable, private property developing, but as an abnormal form subordinate to communal ownership. The citizens hold power over their labouring slaves only in their community, and on this account alone, therefore, they are bound to the form of communal ownership. It is the communal private property which compels the active citizens to remain in this spontaneously derived form of association over against their slaves. For this reason the whole structure of society based on this communal ownership, and with it the power of the people, decays in the same measure as, in particular, immovable private property evolves. The division of labour is already more developed. We already find the antagonism of town and country; later the antagonism between those states which represent town interests and those which represent country interests, and inside the towns themselves the antagonism between industry and maritime commerce. The class relation between citizens and slaves is now completely developed.

With the development of private property, we find here for the first time the same conditions which we shall find again, only on a more extensive scale, with modern private property. On the one hand, the concentration of private property, which began very early in Rome (as the Licinian agrarian law proves[1]) and proceeded very rapidly from the time of the civil wars and especially under the Emperors; on the other hand, coupled with this, the transformation of the plebeian small peasantry into a proletariat, which, however, owing to its intermediate position between propertied citizens and slaves, never achieved an independent development.

The third form of ownership is feudal or estate property. If antiquity started out from the *town* and its little territory, the Middle Ages started out from the *country*. This different starting-point was determined by the sparseness of the population at that time, which was scattered over a large area and which received no large increase from the conquerors. In contrast to Greece and Rome, feudal development at the outset, therefore, extends over a much wider territory, prepared by the Roman conquests and the spread of agriculture at first associated with it. The last centuries of the declining Roman Empire and its conquest by the barbarians destroyed a number of productive forces; agriculture had declined, industry had decayed for want of a market, trade had died out or been violently suspended, the rural and urban population had decreased. From these conditions and the mode of organisation of the conquest determined by them, feudal property developed under the influence of the Germanic military constitution. Like tribal and communal ownership, it is based again on a community; but the directly producing class standing over against it is not, as in the case of the ancient community, the slaves, but the enserfed small peasantry. As soon as feudalism is fully developed, there also arises antagonism to the towns. The hierarchical structure of land-ownership, and the armed bodies of retainers associated with it, gave the nobility power over the serfs. This feudal organisation was, just as much as the ancient communal ownership, an association against a subjected producing class; but the form of association and the relation to the direct producers were different because of the different conditions of production.

This feudal system of landownership had its counterpart in the *towns* in the shape of corporative property, the feudal organisation of trades. Here property consisted chiefly in the labour of each individual person. The necessity for association against the organised robber-nobility, the need for communal covered markets in an age when the industrialist was at the same time a merchant, the growing competition of the escaped serfs swarming into the rising towns, the feudal structure of the whole country: these combined to bring about the *guilds*. The gradually accumulated small capital of individual craftsmen and their stable numbers, as against the growing population, evolved the relation of journeyman and apprentice, which brought into being in the towns a hierarchy similar to that in the country.

Thus the chief form of property during the feudal epoch consisted on the one hand of landed property with serf labour chained to it, and on the other of the labour of the individual with small capital commanding the labour of journeymen. The organisation of both was determined by the restricted conditions of production—the small-scale and primitive cultivation of the land, and the craft type of industry. There was little division of labour in the heyday of feudalism. Each country bore in itself the antithesis of town and country; the division into estates was certainly strongly marked; but apart from the differentiation of princes, nobility, clergy and peasants in the country, and masters, journeymen, apprentices and soon also the rabble of casual labourers in the towns, no division of importance took place. In agriculture it was rendered difficult by

the strip-system, beside which the cottage industry of the peasants themselves emerged. In industry there was no division of labour at all in the individual trades themselves, and very little between them. The separation of industry and commerce was found already in existence in older towns; in the newer it only developed later, when the towns entered into mutual relations.

The grouping of larger territories into feudal kingdoms was a necessity for the landed nobility as for the towns. The organisation of the ruling class, the nobility, had, therefore, everywhere a monarch at its head.

The fact is, therefore, that definite individuals who are productively active in a definite way enter into these definite social and political relations. Empirical observation must in each separate instance bring out empirically, and without any mystification and speculation, the connection of the social and political structure with production. The social structure and the State are continually evolving out of the life-process of definite individuals, but of individuals, not as they may appear in their own or other people's imagination, but as they *really* are; i.e. as they operate, produce materially, and hence as they work under definite material limits, presuppositions and conditions independent of their will.

The production of ideas, of conceptions, of consciousness, is at first directly interwoven with the material activity and the material intercourse of men, the language of real life. Conceiving, thinking, the mental intercourse of men, appear at this stage as the direct efflux of their material behavior. The same applies to mental production as expressed in the language of politics, laws, morality, religion, metaphysics, etc. of a people. Men are the producers of their conceptions, ideas, etc.—real, active men, as they are conditioned by a definite development of their productive forces and of the intercourse corresponding to these, up to its furthest forms. Consciousness can never be anything else than conscious existence, and the existence of men is their actual life-process. If in all ideology men and their circumstances appear upside-down as in a *camera obscura*, this phenomenon arises just as much from their historical life-process as the inversion of objects on the retina does from their physical life-process.

In direct contrast to German philosophy which descends from heaven to earth, here we ascend from earth to heaven. That is to say, we do not set out from what men say, imagine, conceive, nor from men as narrated, thought of, imagined, conceived, in order to arrive at men in the flesh. We set out from real, active men, and on the basis of their real life-process we demonstrate the development of the ideological reflexes and echoes of this life-process. The phantoms formed in the human brain are also, necessarily, sublimates of their material life-process, which is empirically verifiable and bound to material premises. Morality, religion, metaphysics, all the rest of ideology and their corresponding forms of consciousness, thus no longer retain the semblance of independence. They have no history, no development; but men, developing their material production and their material intercourse, alter, along with this their real existence, their thinking and the products of their thinking. Life is not determined by consciousness, but consciousness by life. In the first method of approach the starting-point is consciousness taken as the living individual; in the second method, which conforms to real life, it is the real living individuals them-selves, and consciousness is considered solely as *their* consciousness.

This method of approach is not devoid of premises. It starts out from the real premises and does not abandon them for a moment. Its premises are men, not in any fantastic isolation and rigidity, but in their actual, empirically perceptible process of development under definite conditions. As soon as this active life-process is described, history ceases to be a collection of dead facts as it is with the empiricists (themselves still abstract), or an imagined activity of imagined subjects, as with the idealists.

Where speculation ends—in real life—there real, positive science begins: the representation of the practical activity, of the practical process of development of men. Empty talk about consciousness ceases, and real knowledge has to take its place. When reality is depicted, philosophy as an independent branch of knowledge loses its medium of existence. At the best its place can only be taken by a summing-up of the most general results, abstractions which arise from the observation of the historical development of men. Viewed apart from real history, these abstractions have in themselves no value whatsoever. They can only serve to facilitate the arrangements of historical materials, to indicate the sequence of its separate strata. But they by no means afford a recipe or schema, as does philosophy, for neatly trimming the epochs of history. On the contrary, our difficulties begin only when we set about the observation and the arrangement—the real depiction—of our historical material, whether of a past epoch or of the present. The removal of these difficulties is governed by premises which it is quite impossible to state here, but which only the study of the actual life-process and the activity of the individuals of each epoch will make evident. We shall select here some of these abstractions, which we use in contradistinction to the ideologists, and shall illustrate them by historical examples.

HISTORY: FUNDAMENTAL CONDITIONS

Since we are dealing with the Germans, who are devoid of premises, we must begin by stating the first premise of all human existence and, therefore, of all history, the premise, namely, that men must be in a position to live in order to be able to "make history." But life involves before everything else eating and drinking, a habitation, clothing and many other things. The first historical act is thus the production of the means to satisfy these needs, the production of material life itself. And indeed this is an historical act, a fundamental condition of all history, which today, as thousands of years ago, must daily and hourly be fulfilled merely in order to sustain human life.

Even when the sensuous world is reduced to a minimum, to a stick as with Saint Bruno [Bauer], it presupposes the action of producing the stick. Therefore in any interpretation of history one has first of all to observe this fundamental fact in all its significance and all its implications and to accord it its due importance. It is well known that the Germans have never done this, and they have never, therefore, had an *earthly* basis for history and consequently never an historian. The French and the English, even if they have conceived the relation of this fact with so-called history only in an extremely one-sided fashion, particularly as long as they remained in the toils of political ideology, have nevertheless made the first attempts to give the writing of history a materialistic basis by being the first to write histories of civil society, of commerce and industry.

The second point is that the satisfaction of the first need (the action of satisfying, and the instrument of satisfaction which has been acquired) leads to new needs; and this production of new needs is the first historical act. Here we recognise immediately the spiritual ancestry of the great historical wisdom of the Germans who, when they run out of positive material and when they can serve up neither theological nor political nor literary rubbish, assert that this is not history at all, but the "prehistoric era." They do not, however, enlighten us as to how we proceed from this nonsensical "prehistory" to history proper; although, on the other hand, in their historical speculation they seize upon this "prehistory" with especial eagerness because they imagine themselves safe there from interference on the part of "crude facts," and, at the same time, because there they can give full rein to their speculative impulse and set up and knock down hypotheses by the thousand.

The third circumstance which, from the very outset, enters into historical development, is that men, who daily remake their own life, begin to make other men, to propagate their kind: the relation between man and woman, parents and children, the *family*. The family, which to begin with is the only social relationship, becomes later,

when increased needs create new social relations and the increased population new needs, a subordinate one (except in Germany), and must then be treated and analysed according to the existing empirical data, not according to "the concept of the family," as is the custom in Germany. These three aspects of social activity are not of course to be taken as three different stages, but just as three aspects or, to make it clear to the Germans, three "moments," which have existed simultaneously since the dawn of history and the first men, and which still assert themselves in history today.

The production of life, both of one's own labour and of fresh life in procreation, now appears as a double relationship; on the one hand as a natural, on the other as a social relationship. By social we understand the co-operation of several individuals, no matter under what conditions, in what manner and to what end. It follows from this that a certain mode of production, or industrial stage, is always combined with a certain mode of co-operation, or social stage, and this mode of co-operation is itself a "productive force." Further, that the multitude of productive forces accessible to men determines the nature of society, hence, that the "history of humanity" must always be studied and treated in relation to the history of humanity and exchange. But it is also clear how in Germany it is impossible to write this sort of history, because the Germans lack not only the necessary power of comprehension and the material but also the "evidence of their senses," for across the Rhine you cannot have any experience of these things since history has stopped happening. Thus it is quite obvious from the start that there exists a materialistic connection of men with one another, which is determined by their needs and their mode of production, and which is as old as men themselves. This connection is ever taking on new forms, and thus presents a "history" independently of the existence of any political or religious nonsense which in addition may hold men together.

Only now, after having considered four moments, four aspects of the primary historical relationships, do we find that man also possesses "consciousness," but, even so, not inherent, not "pure" consciousness. From the start the "spirit" is afflicted with the curse of being "burdened" with matter, which here makes its appearance in the form of agitated layers of air, sounds, in short, of language. Language is as old as consciousness, language is practical consciousness that exists also for other men, and for that reason alone it really exists for me personally as well; language, like consciousness, only arises from the need, the necessity, of intercourse with other men. Where there exists a relationship, it exists for me: the animal does not enter into *"relations"* with anything, it does not enter into any relation at all. For the animal, its relation to others does not exist as a relation. Consciousness is, therefore, from the very beginning a social product, and remains so as long as men exist at all. Consciousness is at first, of course, merely consciousness concerning the *immediate* sensuous environment and consciousness of the limited connection with other persons and things outside the individual who is growing self-conscious. At the same time it is consciousness of nature, which first appears to men as a completely alien, all-powerful and unassailable force, with which men's relations are purely animal and by which they are overawed like beasts; it is thus a purely animal consciousness of nature (natural religion) just because nature is as yet hardly modified historically. (We see here immediately: this natural religion or this particular relation of men to nature is determined by the form of society and vice versa. Here, as everywhere, the identity of nature and man appears in such a way that the restricted relation of men to nature determines their restricted relation to one another, and their restricted relation to one another determines men's restricted relation to nature.) On the other hand, man's consciousness of the necessity of associating with the individuals around him is the beginning of the consciousness that he is living in society at all. This beginning is as animal as social life itself at this stage. It is mere herd-consciousness, and at this point man is only distinguished

from sheep by the fact that with him consciousness takes the place of instinct or that his instinct is a conscious one. This sheep-like or tribal consciousness receives its further development and extension through increased productivity, the increase of needs, and, what is fundamental to both of these, the increase of population. With these there develops the division of labour, which was originally nothing but the division of labour in the sexual act, then that division of labour which develops spontaneously or "naturally" by virtue of natural predisposition (e.g. physical strength), needs, accidents, etc. etc. Division of labour only becomes truly such from the moment when a division of material and mental labour appears. (The first form of ideologists, *priests*, is concurrent.) From this moment onwards consciousness *can* really flatter itself that it is something other than consciousness of existing practice, that it *really* represents something without representing something real; from now on consciousness is in a position to emancipate itself from the world and to proceed to the formation of "pure" theory, theology, philosophy, ethics, etc. But even if this theory, theology, philosophy, ethics, etc. comes into contradiction with the existing relations, this can only occur because existing social relations have come into contradiction with existing forces of production; this, moreover, can also occur in a particular national sphere of relations through the appearance of the contradiction, not within the national orbit, but between this national consciousness and the practice of other nations, i.e. between the national and the general consciousness of a nation (as we see it now in Germany).

Moreover, it is quite immaterial what consciousness starts to do on its own: out of all such muck we get only the one inference that these three moments, the forces of production, the state of society, and consciousness, can and must come into contradiction with one another, because the *division of labour* implies the possibility, nay the fact that intellectual and material activity—enjoyment and labour, production and consumption—devolve on different individuals, and that the only possibility of their not coming into contradiction lies in the negation in its turn of the division of labour. It is self-evident, moreover, that "spectres," "bonds," "the higher being," "concept," "scruple," are merely the idealistic, spiritual expression, the conception apparently of the isolated individual, the image of very empirical fetters and limitations, within which the mode of production of life and the form of intercourse coupled with it move.

Note

1. The building of houses. With savages each family has as a matter of course its own cave or hut like the separate family tent of the nomads. This separate domestic economy is made only the more necessary by the further development of private property. With the agricultural peoples a communal domestic economy is just as impossible as a communal cultivation of the soil. A great advance was the building of towns. In all previous periods, however, the abolition of individual economy, which is inseparable from the abolition of private property, was impossible for the simple reason that the material conditions governing it were not present. The setting-up of a communal domestic economy presupposes the development of machinery, of the use of natural forces and of many other productive forces—e.g. of water-supplies, of gas-lighting, steam-heating, etc., the removal [of the antagonism] of town and country. Without these conditions a communal economy would not in itself form a new productive force; lacking any material basis and resting on a purely theoretical foundation, it would be a mere freak and would end in nothing more than a monastic economy—What was possible can be seen in the towns brought about by condensation and the erection of communal buildings for various definite purposes (prisons, barracks, etc.). That the abolition of individual economy is inseparable from the abolition of the family is self-evident.

Manifesto of the Communist Party

A specter is haunting Europe—the specter of communism. All the powers of old Europe have entered into a holy alliance to exorcise this specter: Pope and Czar, Metternich and Guizot, French radicals and German police spies.

Where is the party in opposition that has not been decried as communistic by its opponents in power? Where the opposition that has not hurled back the branding reproach of communism against the more advanced opposition parties, as well as against its reactionary adversaries?

Two things result from this fact:

I. Communism is already acknowledged by all European powers to be itself a power.
II. It is high time that communists should openly, in the face of the whole world, publish their views, their aims, their tendencies, and meet this nursery tale of the specter of communism with a Manifesto of the party itself.

To this end, communists of various nationalities have assembled in London and sketched the following Manifesto, to be published in the English, French, German, Italian, Flemish, and Danish languages.

I. BOURGEOIS AND PROLETARIANS[1]

The history of all hitherto existing society[2] is the history of class struggles.

Free man and slave, patrician and plebeian, lord and serf, guild master[3] and journeyman, in a word, oppressor and oppressed, stood in constant opposition to one another, carried on an uninterrupted, now hidden, now open fight, a fight that each time ended either in a revolutionary reconstitution of society at large or in the common ruin of the contending classes.

In the earlier epochs of history we find almost everywhere a complicated arrangement of society into various orders, a manifold gradation of social rank. In ancient Rome we have patricians, knights, plebeians, slaves; in the Middle Ages, feudal lords, vassals, guild masters, journeymen, apprentices, serfs; in almost all of these classes, again, subordinate gradations.

The modern bourgeois society that has sprouted from the ruins of feudal society has not done away with class antagonisms. It has but established new classes, new conditions of oppression, new forms of struggle in place of the old ones.

Our epoch, the epoch of the bourgeoisie, possesses, however, this distinctive feature: it has simplified the class antagonisms. Society as a whole is more and more splitting up into two great hostile camps, into two great classes directly facing each other: bourgeoisie and proletariat.

From the serfs of the Middle Ages sprang the chartered burghers of the earliest towns. From these burgesses the first elements of the bourgeoisie were developed.

The discovery of America, the rounding of the Cape, opened up fresh ground for the rising bourgeoisie. The East Indian and Chinese markets, the colonization of America, trade with the colonies, the increase in the means of exchange and in commodities generally, gave to commerce, to navigation, to industry an impulse never before known, and thereby, to the revolutionary element in the tottering feudal society, a rapid development.

The feudal system of industry, under which industrial production was monopolized by closed guilds, now no longer sufficed for the growing wants of the new markets. The manufacturing system took its place. The guild masters were pushed on one side by the manufacturing middle class; division of labor between the different corporate guilds vanished in the face of division of labor in each single workshop.

Meantime the markets kept ever growing, the demand ever rising. Even manufacture no longer sufficed. Thereupon steam and machinery revolutionized industrial production. The place of manufacture was taken by the giant, modern industry, the place of the industrial middle class by industrial millionaires, the leaders of whole industrial armies, the modern bourgeois.

Modern industry has established the world market, for which the discovery of America paved the way. This market has given an immense development to commerce, to navigation, to communication by land. This development has, in its turn, reacted on the extension of industry; and in proportion as industry, commerce, navigation, railways extended, in the same proportion the bourgeoisie developed, increased its capital, and pushed into the background every class handed down from the Middle Ages.

We see, therefore, how the modern bourgeoisie is itself the product of a long course of development, of a series of revolutions in the modes of production and of exchange.

Each step in the development of the bourgeoisie was accompanied by a corresponding political advance of that class. An oppressed class under the sway of the feudal nobility, an armed and self-governing association in the medieval commune,[4] here independent urban republic (as in Italy and Germany), there taxable "third estate" of the monarchy (as in France), afterwards, in the period of manufacture proper, serving either the semi-feudal or the absolute monarchy as a counterpoise against the nobility, and, in fact, cornerstone of the great monarchies in general, the bourgeoisie has at last, since the establishment of modern industry and of the world market, conquered for itself, in the modern representative state, exclusive political sway. The executive of the modern state is but a committee for managing the common affairs of the whole bourgeoisie.

The bourgeoisie, historically, has played a most revolutionary part.

The bourgeoisie, wherever it has got the upper hand, has put an end to all feudal, patriarchal, idyllic relations. It has pitilessly torn asunder the motley feudal ties that bound man to his "natural superiors," and has left remaining no other nexus between man and man than naked self-interest, than callous "cash payment." It has drowned the most heavenly ecstasies of religious fervor, of chivalrous enthusiasm, of Philistine sentimentalism in the icy water of egotistical calculation. It has resolved personal worth into exchange value and, in place of the numberless indefeasible chartered freedoms, has set up that single, unconscionable freedom—free trade. In one word, for exploitation, veiled by religious and political illusions, it has substituted naked, shameless, direct, brutal exploitation.

The bourgeoisie has stripped of its halo every occupation hitherto honored and looked up to with reverent awe. It has converted the physician, the lawyer, the priest, the poet, the man of science into its paid wage laborers.

The bourgeoisie has torn away from the family its sentimental veil, and has reduced the family relation to a mere money relation.

The bourgeoisie has disclosed how it came to pass that the brutal display of vigor in the Middle Ages, which reactionists so much admire, found its fitting complement in the most slothful indolence. It has been the first to show what man's activity can bring about. It has accomplished wonders far surpassing Egyptian pyramids, Roman aqueducts, and Gothic cathedrals; it has conducted expeditions that put in the shade all former exoduses of nations and crusades.

The bourgeoisie cannot exist without constantly revolutionizing the instruments of production, and thereby the relations of production, and with them the whole relations of society. Conservation of the old modes of production in unaltered form was, on the contrary, the first condition of existence for all earlier industrial classes. Constant revolutionizing of production, uninterrupted disturbance of all social conditions, everlasting uncertainty and agitation distinguish the bourgeois epoch from all earlier ones. All fixed, fast-frozen relations, with their train of ancient and venerable prejudices and opinions, are swept away, all newformed ones become antiquated before they can ossify. All that is solid melts into air, all that is holy is profaned, and man is at last compelled to face with sober senses his real conditions of life and his relations with his kind.

The need of a constantly expanding market for its products chases the bourgeoisie over the whole surface of the globe. It must nestle everywhere, settle everywhere, establish connections everywhere.

The bourgeoisie has through its exploitation of the world market given a cosmopolitan character to production and consumption in every country. To the great chagrin of reactionists, it has drawn from under the feet of industry the national ground on which it stood. All old-established national industries have been destroyed or are daily being destroyed. They are dislodged by new industries, whose introduction becomes a life and death question for all civilized nations, by industries that no longer work up indigenous raw material, but raw material drawn from the remotest zones; industries whose products are consumed not only at home, but in every quarter of the globe. In place of the old wants, satisfied by the productions of the country, we find new wants, requiring for their satisfaction the products of distant lands and climes. In place of the old local and national seclusion and self-sufficiency we have intercourse in every direction, universal interdependence of nations. And as in material, so also in intellectual production. The intellectual creations of individual nations become common property. National onesidedness and narrow-mindedness become more and more impossible, and from the numerous national and local literatures there arises a world literature.

The bourgeoisie, by the rapid improvement of all instruments of production, by the immensely facilitated means of communication, draws all, even the most barbarian, nations into civilization. The cheap prices of its commodities are the heavy artillery with which it batters down all Chinese walls, with which it forces the barbarians' intensely obstinate hatred of foreigners to capitulate. It compels all nations, on pain of extinction, to adopt the bourgeois mode of production; it compels them to introduce what it calls civilization into their midst, i.e., to become bourgeois themselves. In one word, it creates a world after its own image.

The bourgeoisie has subjected the country to the rule of the towns. It has created enormous cities, has greatly increased the urban population as compared with the rural, and has thus rescued a considerable part of the population from the idiocy of rural life. Just as it has made the country dependent on the towns, so it has made barbarian and semi-barbarian countries dependent on the civilized ones, nations of peasants on nations of bourgeois, the East on the West.

The bourgeoisie keeps more and more doing away with the scattered state of the population, of the means of production, and of property. It has agglomerated population, centralized means of production, and has concentrated property in a few hands. The necessary consequence of this was political centralization. Independent, or but loosely connected provinces, with separate interests, laws, governments and systems of taxation, became lumped together into one nation, with one government, one code of laws, one national class interest, one frontier, and one customs tariff.

The bourgeoisie, during its rule of scarce one hundred years, has created more massive and more colossal productive forces than have all preceding generations together. Subjection of nature's forces to man, machinery, application of chemistry to industry and agriculture, steam navigation, railways, electric telegraphs, clearing of whole continents for cultivation, canalization of rivers, whole populations conjured out of the ground—what earlier century had even a presentiment that such productive forces slumbered in the lap of social labor?

We see then: the means of production and of exchange, on whose foundation the bourgeoisie built itself up, were generated in feudal society. At a certain stage in the development of these means of production and of exchange, the conditions under which feudal society produced and exchanged, the feudal organization of agriculture and manufacturing industry, in one word, the feudal relations of property, became no longer compatible with the already developed productive forces; they became so many fetters. They had to be burst asunder; they were burst asunder.

Into their place stepped free competition, accompanied by a social and political constitution adapted to it, and by the economic and political sway of the bourgeois class.

A similar movement is going on before our own eyes. Modern bourgeois society with its relations of production, of exchange, and of property, a society that has conjured up such gigantic means of production and of exchange, is like the sorcerer who is no longer able to control the powers of the nether world whom he has called up by his spells. For many a decade past, the history of industry and commerce is but the history of the revolt of modern productive forces against modern conditions of production, against the property relations that are the conditions for the existence of the bourgeoisie and of its rule. It is enough to mention the commercial crises that by their periodic return put on its trial, each time more threatening, the existence of the entire bourgeois society. In these crises a great part not only of the existing products but also of the previously created productive forces are periodically destroyed. In these crises there breaks out an epidemic that in all earlier epochs would have seemed an absurdity—the epidemic of overproduction. Society suddenly finds itself put back into a state of momentary barbarism; it appears as if a famine, a universal war of devastation had cut off the supply of every means of subsistence; industry and commerce seem to be destroyed; and why? Because there is too much civilization, too much means of subsistence, too much industry, too much commerce. The productive forces at the disposal of society no longer tend to further the development of the conditions of bourgeois property; on the contrary, they have become too powerful for these conditions, by which they are fettered, and as soon as they overcome these fetters they bring disorder into the whole of bourgeois society, endanger the existence of bourgeois property. The conditions of bourgeois society are too narrow to comprise the wealth created by them. And how does the bourgeoisie get over these crises? On the one hand, by enforced destruction of a mass of productive forces; on the other, by the conquest of new markets, and by the more thorough exploitation of the old ones. That is to say, by paving the way of more extensive and more destructive crises, and by diminishing the means whereby crises are prevented.

The weapons with which the bourgeoisie felled feudalism to the ground are now turned against the bourgeoisie itself.

But not only has the bourgeoisie forged the weapons that bring death to itself; it has also called into existence the men who are to wield those weapons—the modern working class—the proletarians.

In proportion as the bourgeoisie, i.e., capital, is developed, in the same proportion is the proletariat, the modern working class, developed—a class of laborers, who live only so long as they find work, and who find work only so long as their labor increases capital. These laborers, who must sell themselves piecemeal, are a commodity, like every other article of commerce, and are consequently exposed to all the vicissitudes of competition, to all the fluctuations of the market.

Owing to the extensive use of machinery and to division of labor, the work of the proletarians has lost all individual character and, consequently, all charm for the workman. He becomes an appendage of the machine, and it is only the simplest, most monotonous, and most easily acquired knack that is required of him. Hence the cost of production of a workman is restricted, almost entirely, to the means of subsistence that he requires for his maintenance and for the propagation of his race. But the price of a commodity, and therefore also of labor, is equal to its cost of production. In proportion, therefore, as the repulsiveness of the work increases, the wage decreases. Nay, more, in proportion as the use of machinery and division of labor increases, in the same proportion the burden of toil also increases, whether by prolongation of the working hours, by increase of the work exacted in a given time, or by increased speed of the machinery, etc.

Modern industry has converted the little workshop of the patriarchal master into the great factory of the industrial capitalist. Masses of laborers, crowded into the factory, are organized like soldiers. As privates of the industrial army they are placed under the command of a perfect hierarchy of officers and sergeants. Not only are they slaves of the bourgeois class, and of the bourgeois state; they are daily and hourly enslaved by the machine, by the overlooker, and, above all, by the individual bourgeois manufacturer himself. The more openly this despotism proclaims gain to be its end and aim, the more petty, the more hateful, and the more embittering it is.

The less the skill and exertion of strength implied in manual labor, in other words, the more modern industry becomes developed, the more is the labor of men superseded by that of women. Differences of age and sex have no longer any distinctive social validity for the working class. All are instruments of labor, more or less expensive to use, according to their age and sex.

No sooner is the exploitation of the laborer by the manufacturer over, to the extent that he receives his wages in cash, than he is set upon by the other portions of the bourgeoisie, the landlord, the shopkeeper, the pawnbroker, etc.

The lower strata of the middle class—the small tradespeople, shopkeepers, and retired tradesman generally, the handicraftsmen and peasants—all these sink gradually into the proletariat, partly because their diminutive capital does not suffice for the scale on which modern industry is carried on, and is swamped in the competition with the large capitalists, partly because their specialized skill is rendered worthless by new methods of production. Thus the proletariat is recruited from all classes of the population.

The proletariat goes through various stages of development. With its birth begins its struggle with the bourgeoisie. At first the contest is carried on by individual laborers, then by the workpeople of a factory, then by the operatives of one trade, in one locality, against the individual bourgeois who directly exploits them. They direct their attacks not against the bourgeois conditions of production, but against the instruments of production themselves; they destroy imported wares that compete with their labor, they smash to pieces machinery, they set factories ablaze, they seek to restore by force the vanished status of the workman of the Middle Ages.

At this stage the laborers still form an incoherent mass scattered over the whole country, and broken up by their mutual competition. If anywhere they unite to form more compact bodies, this is not yet the consequence of their own active union, but of the union of the bourgeoise, which class, in order to attain its own political ends, is compelled to set the whole proletariat in motion, and is moreover yet, for a time, able to do so. At this stage, therefore, the proletarians do not fight their enemies, but the enemies of their enemies, the remnants of absolute monarchy, the landowners, the non-industrial bourgeois, the petty bourgeoisie. Thus the whole historical movement is concentrated in the hands of the bourgeoisie; every victory so obtained is a victory for the bourgeoisie.

But with the development of industry the proletariat not only increases in number; it becomes concentrated in greater masses, its strength grows, and it feels that strength more. The various interests and conditions of life within the ranks of the proletariat are more and more equalized, in proportion as machinery obliterates all distinctions of labor and nearly everywhere reduces wages to the same low level. The growing competition among the bourgeois and the resulting commercial crises make the wages of the workers ever more fluctuating. The unceasing improvement of machinery, ever more rapidly developing, makes their livelihood more and more precarious; the collisions between individual workmen and individual bourgeois take more and more the character of collisions between two classes. Thereupon the workers begin to form combinations (trade unions) against the bourgeois; they club together in order to keep up the rate of wages; they found permanent associations in order to make provision beforehand for these occasional revolts. Here and there the contest breaks out into riots.

Now and then the workers are victorious, but only for a time. The real fruit of their battles lies not in the immediate result, but in the ever expanding union of the workers. This union is helped on by the improved means of communication that are created by modern industry and that place the workers of different localities in contact with one another. It was just this contact that was needed to centralize the numerous local struggles, all of the same character, into one national struggle between classes. But every class struggle is a political struggle. And that union, to attain which the burghers of the Middle Ages, with their miserable highways, required centuries, the modern proletarians, thanks to railways, achieve in a few years.

This organization of the proletarians into a class, and consequently into a political party, is continually being upset again by the competition between the workers themselves. But it ever rises up again, stronger, firmer, mightier. It compels legislative recognition of particular interests of the workers by taking advantage of the divisions among the bourgeoisie itself. Thus the ten-hour bill in England was carried.

Altogether collisions between the classes of the old society further, in many ways, the course of development of the proletariat. The bourgeoisie finds itself involved in a constant battle. At first with the aristocracy, later on with those portions of the bourgeoisie itself whose interests have become antagonistic to the progress of industry; at all times, with the bourgeoisie of foreign countries. In all these battles it sees itself compelled to appeal to the proletariat, to ask for help, and thus to drag it into the political arena. The bourgeoisie itself, therefore, supplies the proletariat with its own elements of political and general education: in other words, it furnishes the proletariat with weapons for fighting the bourgeoisie.

Further, as we have already seen, entire sections of the ruling classes are, by the advance of industry, precipitated into the proletariat, or are at least threatened in their conditions of existence. These also supply the proletariat with fresh elements of enlightenment and progress.

Finally, in times when the class struggle nears the decisive hour, the process of dissolution going on within the ruling class, in fact within the whole range of old society, assumes such a violent, glaring character that a small section of the ruling class cuts itself adrift and joins the revolutionary class, the class that holds the future in its hands. Just as, therefore, at an earlier period, a section of the nobility went over to the bourgeoisie, so now a portion of the bourgeoisie goes over to the proletariat, and in particular a portion of the bourgeois ideologists, who have raised themselves to the level of comprehending theoretically the historical movement as a whole.

Of all the classes that stand face to face with the bourgeoisie today, the proletariat alone is a really revolutionary class. The other classes decay and finally disappear in the face of modern industry; the proletariat is its special and essential product.

The lower-middle class, the small manufacturer, the shopkeeper, the artisan, the peasant, all these fight against the bourgeoisie, to save from extinction their existence as fractions of the middle class. They are therefore not revolutionary, but conservative. Nay, more, they are reactionary, for they try to roll back the wheel of history. If by chance they are revolutionary they are so only in view of their impending transfer into the proletariat; they thus defend not their present but their future interests, they desert their own standpoint to place themselves at that of the proletariat.

The "dangerous class," the social scum, that passively rotting mass thrown off by the lowest layers of old society, may, here and there, be swept into the movement by a proletarian revolution; its conditions of life, however, prepare it far more for the part of a bribed tool of reactionary intrigue.

In the conditions of the proletariat those of old society at large are already virtually swamped. The proletarian is without property; his relation to his wife and children has no longer anything in common with the bourgeois family relations; modern industrial labor, modern subjection to capital, the same in England as in France, in America as in Germany, has stripped him of every trace of national character. Law, morality, religion are to him so many bourgeois prejudices, behind which lurk in ambush just as many bourgeois interests.

All the preceding classes that got the upper hand sought to *fortify* their already acquired status by subjecting society at large to their conditions of appropriation. The proletarians cannot become masters of the productive forces of society, except by abolishing their own previous mode of appropriation, and thereby also every other previous mode of appropriation. They have nothing of their own to secure and to fortify; their mission is to destroy all previous securities for, and insurances of, individual property.

All previous historical movements were movements of minorities, or in the interest of minorities. The proletarian movement is the self-conscious, independent movement of the immense majority, in the interests of the immense majority. The proletariat, the lowest stratum of our present society, cannot stir, cannot raise itself up, without the whole superincumbent strata of official society being sprung into the air.

Though not in substance, yet in form, the struggle of the proletariat with the bourgeoisie is at first a national struggle. The proletariat of each country must, of course, first of all settle matters with its own bourgeoisie.

In depicting the most general phases of the development of the proletariat, we traced the more or less veiled civil war, raging within existing society, up to the point where that war breaks out into open revolution, and where the violent overthrow of the bourgeoisie lays the foundation for the sway of the proletariat.

Hitherto every form of society has been based, as we have already seen, on the antagonism of oppressing and oppressed classes. But in order to oppress a class certain conditions must be assured to it under which it can, at least, continue its slavish existence. The serf, in the period of serfdom, raised himself to membership in the commune just as the petty bourgeois, under the yoke of feudal absolutism, managed to develop into a bourgeois. The modern laborer, on the contrary, instead of rising with the progress of industry, sinks deeper and deeper below the conditions of existence of his own class. He becomes a pauper, and pauperism develops more rapidly than population and wealth. And here it becomes evident that the bourgeoisie is unfit any longer to be the ruling class in society, and to impose its conditions of existence upon society as an overriding law. It is unfit to rule because it is incompetent to assure an existence to its slave within his slavery, because it cannot help letting him sink into such a state that it has to feed him instead of being fed by him. Society can no longer live under this bourgeoisie: in other words, its existence is no longer compatible with society.

The essential condition for the existence, and for the sway of the bourgeois class, is the formation and augmentation of capital; the condition for capital is wage labor. Wage labor rests exclusively on competition between the laborers. The advance of industry, whose involuntary promoter is the bourgeoisie, replaces the isolation of the laborers, due to competition, by their revolutionary combination, due to association. The development of modern industry, therefore, cuts from under its feet the very foundation on which the bourgeoisie produces and appropriates products. What the bourgeoisie, therefore, produces, above all, is its own gravediggers. Its fall and the victory of the proletariat are equally inevitable.

II. PROLETARIANS AND COMMUNISTS

In what relation do the communists stand to the proletarians as a whole?

The communists do not form a separate party opposed to other working-class parties.

They have no interests separate and apart from those of the proletariat as a whole.

They do not set up any sectarian principles of their own, by which to shape and mold the proletarian movement.

The communists are distinguished from the other working-class parties by this only: 1. In the national struggles of the proletarians of the different countries they point out and bring to the front the common interests of the entire proletariat, independent of all nationality. 2. In the various stages of development which the struggle of the working class against the bourgeoisie has to pass through, they always and everywhere represent the interests of the movement as a whole.

The communists, therefore, are on the one hand, practically, the most advanced and resolute section of the working-class parties of every country, that section which pushes forward all others; on the other hand, theoretically, they have over the great mass of the proletariat the advantage of clearly understanding the line of march, the conditions, and the ultimate general results of the proletarian movement.

The immediate aim of the communists is the same as that of all the other proletarian parties: formation of the proletariat into a class, overthrow of the bourgeois supremacy, conquest of political power by the proletariat.

The theoretical conclusions of the communists are in no way based on ideas or principles that have been invented, or discovered, by this or that would-be universal reformer.

They merely express, in general terms, actual relations springing from an existing class struggle, from a historical movement going on under our very eyes. The abolition of existing property relations is not at all a distinctive feature of communism.

All property relations in the past have continually been subject to historical change consequent upon the change in historical conditions.

The French Revolution, for example, abolished feudal property in favor of bourgeois property.

The distinguishing feature of communism is not the abolition of property generally, but the abolition of bourgeois property. But modern bourgeois private property is the final and most complete expression of the system of producing and appropriating products that is based on antagonisms, on the exploitation of the many by the few.

In this sense the theory of the communists may be summed up in the single sentence: Abolition of private property.

We communists have been reproached with the desire of abolishing the right of personally acquiring property as the fruit of a man's own labor, which property is alleged to be the groundwork of all personal freedom, activity, and dependence.

Hard-won, self-acquired, self-earned property! Do you mean the property of the petty artisan and of the small peasant, a form of property that preceded the bourgeois form? There is no need to abolish that; the development of industry has to a great extent already destroyed it and is still destroying it daily.

Or do you mean modern bourgeois private property?

But does wage labor create any property for the laborer? Not a bit. It creates capital, i.e., that kind of property which exploits wage labor, and which cannot increase except upon condition of begetting a new supply of wage labor for fresh exploitation. Property, in its present form, is based on the antagonism of capital and wage labor. Let us examine both sides of this antagonism.

To be a capitalist is to have not only a purely personal but a social *status* in production. Capital is a collective product, and only by the united action of many members, nay, in the last resort only by the united action of all members of society, can it be set in motion.

Capital is, therefore, not a personal, it is a social power.

When, therefore, capital is converted into common property, into the property of all members of society, personal property is not thereby transformed into social property. It is only the social character of the property that is changed. It loses its class character.

Let us now take wage labor.

The average price of wage labor is the minimum wage, i.e., that quantum of the means of subsistence which is absolutely requisite to keep the laborer in bare existence as a laborer. What, therefore, the wage laborer appropriates by means of his labor merely suffices to prolong and reproduce a bare existence. We by no means intend to abolish this personal appropriation of the products of labor, an appropriation that is made for the maintenance and reproduction of human life, and that leaves no surplus wherewith to command the labor of others. All that we want to do away with is the miserable character of this appropriation, under which the laborer lives merely to increase capital, and is allowed to live only in so far as the interest of the ruling class requires it.

In bourgeois society living labor is but a means to increase accumulated labor. In communist society accumulated labor is but a means to widen, to enrich, to promote the existence of the laborer.

In bourgeois society, therefore, the past dominates the present; in communist society the present dominates the past. In bourgeois society capital is independent and has individuality, while the living person is dependent and has no individuality.

And the abolition of this state of things is called by the bourgeois abolition of individuality and freedom! And rightly so. The abolition of bourgeois individuality, bourgeois independence, and bourgeois freedom is undoubtedly aimed at.

By freedom is meant, under the present bourgeois conditions of production, free trade, free selling and buying.

But if selling and buying disappear, free selling and buying disappear also. This talk about free selling and buying, and all the other "brave words" of our bourgeoisie about freedom in general, have a meaning, if any, only in contrast with restricted selling and buying, with the fettered traders of the Middle Ages, but have no meaning when opposed to the communistic abolition of buying and selling, of the bourgeois conditions of production, and of the bourgeoisie itself.

You are horrified at our intending to do away with private property. But in your existing society private property is already done away with for nine tenths of the population; its existence for the few is solely due to its nonexistence in the hands of those nine tenths. You reproach us, therefore, with intending to do away with a form of property the necessary condition for whose existence is the non-existence of any property for the immense majority of society.

In one word, you reproach us with intending to do away with your property. Precisely so; that is just what we intend.

From the moment when labor can no longer be converted into capital, money, or rent, into a social power capable of being monopolized, i.e., from the moment when individual property can no longer be transformed into bourgeois property, into capital, from that moment, you say, individuality vanishes.

You must, therefore, confess that by "individual" you mean no other person than the bourgeois, than the middle-class owner of property. This person must, indeed, be swept out of the way and made impossible.

Communism deprives no man of the power to appropriate the products of society; all that it does is to deprive him of the power to subjugate the labor of others by means of such appropriation.

It has been objected that upon the abolition of private property all work will cease and universal laziness will overtake us.

According to this, bourgeois society ought long ago have gone to the dogs through sheer idleness, for those of its members who work acquire nothing and those who acquire anything do not work. The whole of this objection is but another expression of the tautology that there can no longer be any wage labor when there is no longer any capital.

All objections urged against the communistic mode of producing and appropriating material products have, in the same way, been urged against the communistic modes of producing and appropriating intellectual products. Just as, to the bourgeois, the disappearance of class property is the disappearance of production itself, so the disappearance of class culture is to him identical with the disappearance of all culture.

That culture, the loss of which he laments, is, for the enormous majority, a mere training to act as a machine.

But don't wrangle with us so long as you apply, to our intended abolition of bourgeois property, the standard of your bourgeois notions of freedom, culture, law, etc. Your very ideas are but the outgrowth of the conditions of your bourgeois production and bourgeois property, just as your jurisprudence is but the will of your class made into a law for all, a well whose essential character and direction are determined by the economic conditions of existence of your class.

The selfish misconception that induces you to transform into eternal laws of nature and of reason the social forms springing from your present mode of production and form of property—historical relations that rise and disappear in the progress of production—this misconception you share with every ruling class that has preceded you. What you see clearly in the case of ancient property, what you admit in the case of feudal property you are of course forbidden to admit in the case of your own bourgeois form of property.

Abolition of the family! Even the most radical flare up at this infamous proposal of the communists.

On what foundation is the present family, the bourgeois family, based? On capital, on private gain. In its completely developed form this family exists only among the bourgeoisie. But this state of things finds its complement in the practical absence of the family among the proletarians, and in public prostitution.

The bourgeois family will vanish as a matter of course when its complement vanishes, and both will vanish with the vanishing of capital.

Do you charge us with wanting to stop the exploitation of children by their parents? To this crime we plead guilty.

But, you will say, we destroy the most hallowed of relations when we replace home education by social.

And your education! Is not that also social, and determined by the social conditions under which you educate, by the intervention, direct or indirect, of society, by means of schools, etc.? The communists have not invented the intervention of society in education; they do but seek to alter the character of that intervention, and to rescue education from the influence of the ruling class.

The bourgeois claptrap about the family and education, about the hallowed co-relation of parent and child, becomes all the more disgusting, the more, by the action of modern industry, all family ties among the proletarians are torn asunder and their children transformed into simple articles of commerce and instruments of labor.

"But you communists would introduce community of women," screams the whole bourgeoisie in chorus.

The bourgeois sees in his wife a mere instrument of production. He hears that the instruments of production are to be exploited in common and, naturally, can come to no other conclusion than that the lot of being common to all will likewise fall to the women.

He has not even a suspicion that the real point aimed at is to do away with the status of women as mere instruments of production.

For the rest, nothing is more ridiculous than the virtuous indignation of our bourgeois at the community of women which, they pretend, is to be openly and officially established by the communists. The communists have no need to introduce community of women; it has existed almost from time immemorial.

Our bourgeois, not content with having the wives and daughters of their proletarians at their disposal, not to speak of common prostitutes, take the greatest pleasure in seducing each other's wives.

Bourgeois marriage is in reality a system of wives in common and thus, at the most, what the communists might possibly be reproached with is that they desire to introduce, in substitution for a hypocritically concealed, an openly legalized community of women. For the rest, it is self-evident that the abolition of the present system of production must bring with it the abolition of the community of women springing from that system, i.e., of prostitution, both public and private.

The communists are further reproached with desiring to abolish countries and nationality.

The workingmen have no country. We cannot take from them what they have not got. Since the proletariat must first of all acquire political supremacy, must rise to be the leading class of the nation, must constitute itself *the* nation, it is, so far, itself national, though not in the bourgeois sense of the word.

National differences and antagonisms between peoples are daily more and more vanishing, owing to the development of the bourgeoisie, to freedom of commerce, to the world market, to uniformity in the mode of production and in the conditions of life corresponding thereto.

The supremacy of the proletariat will cause them to vanish still faster. United action, of the leading civilized countries at least, is one of the first conditions for the emancipation of the proletariat.

In proportion as the exploitation of one individual by another is put to an end, the exploitation of one nation by another will also be put to an end. In proportion as the antagonism between classes within the nation vanishes, the hostility of one nation to another will come to an end.

The charges against communism made from a religious, a philosophical, and, generally, from an ideological standpoint are not deserving of serious examination.

Does it require deep intuition to comprehend that man's ideas, views, and conceptions, in one word, man's consciousness, change with every change in the conditions of his material existence, in his social relations, and in his social life?

What else does the history of ideas prove than that intellectual production changes its character in proportion as material production is changed? The ruling ideas of each age have ever been the ideas of its ruling class.

When people speak of ideas that revolutionize society they do but express the fact that within the old society the elements of a new one have been created, and that the dissolution of the old ideas keeps even pace with the dissolution of the old conditions of existence.

When the ancient world was in its last throes, the ancient religions were overcome by Christianity. When Christian ideas succumbed in the eighteenth century to rationalist ideas, feudal society fought its death battle with the then revolutionary bourgeoisie. The ideas of religious liberty and freedom of conscience merely gave expression to the sway of free competition within the domain of knowledge.

"Undoubtedly," it will be said, "religious, moral, philosophical, and juridical ideas have been modified in the course of historical development. But religion, morality, philosophy, political science, and law constantly survived this change.

There are, besides, eternal truths, such as freedom, justice, etc., that are common to all states of society. But communism abolishes eternal truths, it abolishes all religion, and all morality, instead of constituting them on a new basis; it therefore acts in contradiction to all past historical experience."

What does this accusation reduce itself to? The history of all past society has consisted in the development of class antagonisms, antagonisms that assumed different forms at different epochs.

But whatever form they may have taken, one fact is common to all past ages, viz., the exploitation of one part of society by the other. No wonder then that the social consciousness of past ages, despite all the multiplicity and variety it displays, moves within certain common forms, or general ideas, which cannot completely vanish except with the total disappearance of class antagonisms.

The communist revolution is the most radical rupture with traditional property relations; no wonder that its development involves the most radical rupture with traditional ideas.

But let us have done with the bourgeois objections to communism.

We have seen above that the first step in the revolution by the working class to raise the proletariat to the position of ruling class, to win the battle of democracy.

The proletariat will use its political supremacy to wrest, by degrees, all capital from the bourgeoisie, to centralize all instruments of production in the hands of the state, i.e., of the proletariat organized as the ruling class, and to increase the total of productive forces as rapidly as possible.

Of course, in the beginning this cannot be effected except by means of despotic inroads on the rights of property and on the conditions of bourgeois production; by means of measures, therefore, which appear economically insufficient and untenable, but which, in the course of the movement, outstrip themselves, necessitate further inroads upon the old social order, and are unavoidable as a means of entirely revolutionizing the mode of production.

These measures will of course be different in different countries.

Nevertheless, in the most advanced countries the following will be pretty generally applicable:

1. Abolition of property in land and application of all rents of land to public purposes.
2. A heavy progressive or graduated income tax.
3. Abolition of all right of inheritance.
4. Confiscation of the property of all emigrants and rebels.
5. Centralization of credit in the hands of the state, by means of a national bank with state capital and an exclusive monopoly.
6. Centralization of the means of communication and transport in the hands of the state.
7. Extension of factories and instruments of production owned by the state; the bringing into cultivation of wastelands, and the improvement of the soil generally in accordance with a common plan.
8. Equal liability of all to labor. Establishment of industrial armies, especially for agriculture.
9. Combination of agriculture with manufacturing industries; gradual abolition of the distinction between town and country, by a more equable distribution of the population over the country.
10. Free education for all children in public schools. Abolition of children's factory labor in its present form. Combination of education with industrial production, etc.

When, in the course of development, class distinctions have disappeared and all production has been concentrated in the hands of a vast association of the whole nation, the public power will lose its political character. Political power, properly so called, is merely the organized power of one class for oppressing another. If the proletariat during its contest with the bourgeoisie is compelled, by the force of circumstances, to organize itself as a class, if by means of a revolution, it makes itself the ruling class and, as such, sweeps away by force the old conditions of production, then it will, along with these conditions, have swept away the conditions for the existence of class antagonisms and of classes generally, and will thereby have abolished its own supremacy as a class.

In place of the old bourgeois society, with its classes and class antagonisms, we shall have an association in which the free development of each is the condition for the free development of all.

IV. POSITION OF THE COMMUNISTS IN RELATION TO THE VARIOUS EXISTING OPPOSITION PARTIES

Section II has made clear the relations of the communists to the existing working-class parties, such as the Chartists in England and the agrarian reformers in America.

The communists fight for the attainment of the immediate aims, for the enforcement of the momentary interests of the working class, but in the movement of the present they also represent and take care of the future of that movement. In France the communists ally themselves with the social democrats,[5] against the conservative and radical bourgeoisie, reserving, however, the right to take up a critical position in regard to phrases and illusions traditionally handed down from the Great Revolution.

In Switzerland they support the radicals, without losing sight of the fact that this party consists of antagonistic elements, partly of democratic socialists, in the French sense, partly of radical bourgeois.

In Poland they support the party that insists on an agrarian revolution as the prime condition for national emancipation, that party which fomented the insurrection of Cracow in 1846.

In Germany they fight with the bourgeoisie whenever it acts in a revolutionary way, against the absolute monarchy, the feudal squirearchy, and the petty bourgeoisie.

But they never cease, for a single instant, to instill into the working class the clearest possible recognition of the hostile antagonism between bourgeoisie and proletariat, in order that the German workers may straightway use, as so many weapons against the bourgeoisie, the social and political conditions that the bourgeoisie must necessarily introduce along with its supremacy, and in order that, after the fall of the reactionary classes in Germany, the fight against the bourgeoisie itself may immediately begin.

The communists turn their attention chiefly to Germany, because that country is on the eve of a bourgeois revolution that is bound to be carried out under more advanced conditions of European civilization, and with a much more developed proletariat, than that of England was in the seventeenth and of France in the eighteenth century, and because the bourgeois revolution in Germany will be but the prelude to an immediately following proletarian revolution.

In short, the communists everywhere support every revolutionary movement against the existing social and political order of things.

In all these movements they bring to the front, as the leading question in each, the property question, no matter what its degree of development at the time.

Finally, they labor everywhere for the union and agreement of the democratic parties of all countries.

The communists disdain to conceal their views and aims. They openly declare that their ends can be attained only by the forcible overthrow of all existing social conditions. Let the ruling classes tremble at a communistic revolution. The proletarians have nothing to lose but their chains. They have a world to win.

WORKING MEN OF ALL COUNTRIES, UNITE!

Notes

1. By "bourgeoisie" is meant the class of modern capitalists, owners of the means of social production and employers of wage labor. By proletariat, the class of modern wage laborers who, having no means of production of their own, are reduced to selling their labor power in order to live.

2. That is, all *written* history. In 1847 the pre-history of society, the social organization existing previous to recorded history, was all but unknown. Since then Haxthausen discovered common ownership of land in Russia, Maurer proved it to be the social foundation from which all Teutonic races started in history, and by and by village communities were found to be, or to have been the primitive form of society everywhere from India to Ireland. The inner organization of this primitive communistic society was laid bare, in its typical form, by Morgan's crowning discovery of the true nature of the *gens* and its relation to the *tribe*. With the dissolution of these primeval communities society begins to be differentiated into separate and finally antagonistic classes. I have attempted to retrace this process of dissolution in *Der Ursprung der Familie des Privateigenthums und des Staats* [*The Origin of the Family, Private Property and the State*], second edition, Stuttgart, 1886.

3. Guild master, that is, a full member of a guild, a master within, not a head of a guild.

4. "Commune" was the name taken, in France, by the nascent towns even before they had conquered from their feudal lords and masters local self-government and political rights as the "third estate." Generally speaking, for the economic development of the bourgeoisie, England is here taken as the typical country; for its political development, France.

5. The party then represented in Parliment by Ledru-Rollin, in literature by Louis Blanc, in the daily press by the *Réforme*. The name of social democracy signified, with these its inventors, a section of the democratic or republican party more or less tinged with socialism.

A Contribution to the Critique of Political Economy

PREFACE

... The general conclusion at which I arrived and which, once reached, became the guiding principle of my studies can be summarised as follows. In the social production of their existence, men inevitably enter into definite relations, which are independent of their will, namely relations of production appropriate to a given stage in the development of their material forces of production. The totality of these relations of production constitutes the economic structure of society, the real foundation, on which arises a legal and political superstructure and to which correspond definite forms of social consciousness. The mode of production of material life conditions the general process of social, political and intellectual life. It is not the consciousness of men that determines their existence, but their social existence that determines their consciousness. At a certain stage of development, the material productive forces of society come into conflict with the existing relations of production or—this merely expresses the same thing in legal terms—with the property relations within the framework of which they have operated hitherto. From forms of development of the productive forces these relations turn into their fetters. Then begins an era of social revolution. The changes in the economic foundation lead sooner or later to the transformation of the whole immense superstructure. In studying such transformations it is always necessary to distinguish between the material transformation of the economic conditions of production, which can be determined with the precision of natural science, and the legal, political, religious, artistic or

Translated by S. W. Ryazanskaya. Reprinted with permission of International Publishers.

philosophic—in short, ideological forms in which men become conscious of this conflict and fight it out. Just as one does not judge an individual by what he thinks about himself, so one cannot judge such a period of transformation by its consciousness, but, on the contrary, this consciousness must be explained from the contradictions of material life, from the conflict existing between the social forces of production and the relations of production. No social order is ever destroyed before all the productive forces for which it is sufficient have been developed, and new superior relations of production never replace older ones before the material conditions for their existence have matured within the framework of the old society. Mankind thus inevitably sets itself only such tasks as it is able to solve, since closer examination will always show that the problem itself arises only when the material conditions for its solution are already present or at least in the course of formation. In broad outline, the Asiatic, ancient, feudal and modern bourgeois modes of production may be designated as epochs marking progress in the economic development of society. The bourgeois mode of production is the last antagonistic form of the social process of production—antagonistic not in the sense of individual antagonism but of an antagonism that emanates from the individuals' social conditions of existence—but the productive forces developing within bourgeois society create also the material conditions for a solution of this antagonism. The prehistory of human society accordingly closes with this social formation.

Value, Price and Profit

VI

Value and Labour

Citizens, I have now arrived at a point where I must enter upon the real development of the question. I cannot promise to do this in a very satisfactory way because to do so I should be obliged to go over the whole field of political economy. I can, as the French would say, but *effleurer la question*, touch upon the main points.

The first question we have to put is: What is the *value* of a commodity? How is it determined?

At first sight it would seem that the value of a commodity is a thing quite *relative*, and not to be settled without considering one commodity in its relations to all other commodities. In fact, in speaking of the value, the value in exchange of a commodity, we mean the proportional quantities in which it exchanges with all other commodities. But then arises the question: How are the proportions in which commodities exchange with each other regulated?

We know from experience that these proportions vary infinitely. Taking one single commodity, wheat, for instance, we shall find that a quarter of wheat exchanges in almost countless variations of proportion with different commodities. Yet, *its value remaining always the same*, whether expressed in silk, gold, or any other commodity, it must be something distinct from, and independent of, these *different rates of exchange* with different articles. It must be possible to express, in a very different form, these various equations with various commodities.

Besides, if I say a quarter of wheat exchanges with iron in a certain proportion, or the value of a quarter of wheat is expressed in a certain amount of iron, I say that the value of wheat and its equivalent in iron are equal to *some third thing*, which is neither wheat nor iron, because I suppose them to express the same magnitude in two different

Reprinted by permission of International Publishers.

shapes. Either of them, the wheat or the iron, must, therefore, independently of the other, be reducible to this third thing which is their common measure.

To elucidate this point I shall recur to a very simple geometrical illustration. In comparing the areas of triangles of all possible forms and magnitudes, or comparing triangles with rectangles, or any other rectilinear figure, how do we proceed? We reduce the area of any triangle whatever to an expression quite different from its visible form. Having found from the nature of the triangle that its area is equal to half the product of its base by its height, we can then compare the different values of all sorts of triangles, and of all rectilinear figures whatever, because all of them may be resolved into a certain number of triangles.

The same mode of procedure must obtain with the values of commodities. We must be able to reduce all of them to an expression common to all, and distinguishing them only by the proportions in which they contain that same and identical measure.

As the *exchangeable values* of commodities are only *social functions* of those things, and have nothing at all to do with the *natural* qualities, we must first ask: What is the common *social substance* of all commodities? It is *labour*. To produce a commodity a certain amount of labour must be bestowed upon it, or worked up in it. And I say not only *labour*, but *social labour*. A man who produces an article for his own immediate use, to consume it himself, creates a *product*, but not a *commodity*. As a self-sustaining producer he has nothing to do with society. But to produce a *commodity*, a man must not only produce an article satisfying some *social* want, but his labour itself must form part and parcel of the total sum of labour expended by society. It must be subordinate to the *division of labour within society*. It is nothing without the other division of labour, and on its part is required to *integrate* them.

If we consider *commodities as values*, we consider them exclusively under the single aspect of *realised, fixed*, or, if you like, *crystallised social labour*. In this respect they can *differ* only by representing greater or smaller quantities of labour, as, for example, a greater amount of labour may be worked up in a silken handkerchief than in a brick. But how does one measure *quantities of labour*? By the *time the labour lasts*, in measuring the labour by the hour, the day, etc. Of course, to apply this measure, all sorts of labour are reduced to average or simple labour as their unit.

We arrive, therefore, at this conclusion. A commodity has a *value*, because it is a *crystallisation of social labour*. The greatness of its value, or its *relative* value, depends upon the greater or less amount of that social substance contained in it; that is to say, on the relative mass of labour necessary for its production. The *relative values of commodities* are, therefore, determined by the *respective quantities or amounts of labour, worked up, realised, fixed in them*. The *correlative* quantities of commodities which can be produced in the *same time of labour* are *equal*. Or the value of one commodity is to the value of another commodity as the quantity of labour fixed in the one is to the quantity of labour fixed in the other.

I suspect that many of you will ask: Does then, indeed, there exist such a vast, or any difference whatever, between determining of values of commodities by *wages*, and determining them by the *relative quantities of labour* necessary for their production? You must, however, be aware that the *reward* for labour, and *quantity* of labour, are quite disparate things. Suppose, for example, *equal quantities of labour* to be fixed in one quarter of wheat and one ounce of gold. I resort to the example because it was used by Benjamin Franklin in his first essay published in 1721, and entitled: *A Modest Enquiry into the Nature and Necessity of a Paper Currency*, where he, one of the first, hit upon the true nature of value. Well. We suppose, then, that one quarter of wheat and one ounce of gold are *equal values* or *equivalents*, because they are *crystallisations of equal amounts of average labour*, of so many days' or so many weeks' labour respectively fixed in them. In thus determining the relative values of gold and corn, do we refer in any way whatever to the *wages* of the agricultural labourer and the miner? Not a bit. We leave it quite *indeterminate how* their day's or week's labour was paid, or even whether wages labour was employed at all. If it was, wages may have been very unequal. The labourer whose labour is realised in the quarter of wheat may receive two bushels only, and the labourer employed in mining may receive one half of the ounce of gold. Or, supposing their wages to be equal, they may deviate in all possible proportions from the values of the commodities produced by them. They may amount to one half, one third, one fourth, one fifth, or any other proportional part of the one quarter of corn or the one ounce of gold. Their *wages* can, of course, not *exceed*, not be more than the values of the commodities they produced, but they can be *less* in every possible degree. Their *wages* will be *limited* by the *values* of the products, but the *values of their products* will not be limited by the wages. And above all, the values, the relative values of corn and gold, for example, will have been settled without any regard whatever to the value of the labour employed, that is to say, to *wages*. To determine the values of commodities by the *relative quantities of labour fixed in them*, is, therefore, a thing quite different from the tautological method of determining the values of commodities by the value of labour, or by wages. This point, however, will be further elucidated in the progress of our inquiry.

In calculating the exchangeable value of a commodity we must add to the quantity of labour *last* employed the quantity of labour *previously* worked up in the raw material of the commodity, and the labour bestowed on the implements, tools, machinery, and buildings, with which such labour is assisted. For example, the value of a certain amount of cotton yarn is the crystallisation of the quantity of labour added to the cotton during the spinning process, the quantity of labour previously realised in the cotton, itself, the quantity of labour realised in the coal, oil, and other auxiliary matter used, the quantity of labour fixed in the steam-engine, the spindles,

the factory building, and so forth. Instruments of production properly so-called such as tools, machinery, buildings, serve again and again for a longer or shorter period during repeated processes of production. If they were used up at once, like the raw material, their whole value would at once be transferred to the commodities they assist in producing. But as a spindle, for example, is but gradually used up, an average calculation is made, based upon the average time it lasts, and its average waste or wear and tear during a certain period, say a day. In this way we calculate how much of the value of the spindle is transferred to the yarn daily spun, and how much, therefore, of the total amount of labour realised in a pound of yarn, for example, is due to the quantity of labour previously realised in the spindle. For our present purpose it is not necessary to dwell any longer upon this point.

It might seem that if the value of a commodity is determined by the *quantity of labour bestowed upon its production*, the lazier a man, or the clumsier a man, the more valuable his commodity, because the greater the time of labour required for finishing the commodity. This, however, would be a sad mistake. You will recollect that I used the word *"social* labour," and many points are involved in this qualification of *"social."* In saying that the value of a commodity is determined by the *quantity of labour* worked up or crystallised in it, we mean *the quantity of labour necessary* for its production in a given state of society, under certain social average conditions of production, with a given social average intensity, and average skill of the labour employed. When, in England, the power-loom came to compete with the handloom, only one-half the former time of labour was wanted to convert a given amount of yarn into a yard of cotton or cloth. The poor handloom weaver now worked seventeen and eighteen hours daily, instead of the nine or ten hours he had worked before. Still the product of twenty hours of his labour represented now only ten social hours of labour, or ten hours of labour socially necessary for the conversion of a certain amount of yarn into textile stuffs. His product of twenty hours had, therefore, no more value than his former product of ten hours.

If then the quantity of socially necessary labour realised in commodities regulates their exchangeable values, every increase in the quantity of labour wanted for the production of a commodity must augment its value, as every diminution must lower it.

If the respective quantities of labour necessary for the production of the respective commodities remained constant, their relative values also would be constant. But such is not the case. The quantity of labour necessary for the production of a commodity changes continuously with the changes in the productive powers of the labour employed. The greater the productive powers of labour, the more produce is finished in a given time of labour; and the smaller the productive powers of labour, the less produce is finished in the same time. If, for example, in the progress of population it should become necessary to cultivate less fertile soils, the same amount of produce would be only attainable by a greater amount of labour spent, and the value of agricultural produce would consequently rise. On the other hand, if with the modern means of production, a single spinner converts into yarn, during one working day, many thousand times the amount of cotton which he could have spun during the same time with the spinning wheel, it is evident that every single pound of cotton will absorb many thousand times less of spinning labour than it did before, and, consequently, the value added by spinning to every single pound of cotton will be a thousand times less than before. The value of yarn will sink accordingly.

Apart from the different natural energies and acquired working abilities of different peoples, the productive powers of labour must principally depend:

Firstly. Upon the *natural* conditions of labour, such as fertility of soil, mines, and so forth.

Secondly. Upon the progressive improvement of the *social powers of labour*, such as are derived from production on a grand scale, concentration of capital and combination of labour, subdivision of labour, machinery, improved methods, appliance of chemical and other natural agencies, shortening of time and space by means of communication and transport, and every other contrivance by which science presses natural agencies into the service of labour, and by which the social or co-operative character of labour is developed. The greater the productive powers of labour, the less labour is bestowed upon a given amount of produce; hence the smaller the value of this produce The smaller the productive powers of labour, the more labour is bestowed upon the same amount of produce; hence the greater its value. As a general law we may, therefore, set it down that:

The values of commodities are directly as the times of labour employed in their production, and are inversely as the productive powers of the labour employed.

Having till now only spoken of *value*, I shall add a few words about *price*, which is a peculiar form assumed by value.

Price, taken by itself, is nothing but the *monetary expression of value*. The values of all commodities of this country, for example, are expressed in gold prices, while on the Continent they are mainly expressed in silver prices. The value of gold or silver, like that of all other commodities, is regulated by the quantity of labour necessary for getting them. You exchange a certain amount of your national products, in which a certain amount of your national labour is crystallised, for the produce of the gold and silver producing countries, in which a certain quantity of *their* labour is crystallised. It is in this way, in fact by barter, that you learn to express in gold and silver the values of all commodities, that is the respective quantities of labour bestowed upon them. Looking somewhat closer into *the monetary expression of value*, or what comes to the same, the *conversion of value into price*, you will find that it is a process by which you give to the *values* of all commodities an *independent* and *homogeneous form*, or by which you express them as quantities of *equal* social labour. So far as it is but the monetary expression of value, price has been called *natural price* by Adam Smith, *prix nécessaire* by the French physiocrats.

What then is the relation between *value* and *market prices*, or between *natural prices* and *market prices?* You all know that the *market price* is the *same* for all commodities of the same kind, however the conditions of production may differ for the individual producers. The market price expresses only the *average amount of social labour* necessary, under the average conditions of production, to supply the market with a certain mass of a certain article. It is calculated upon the whole lot of a commodity of a certain description.

So far the *market price* of a commodity coincides with its *value.* On the other hand, the oscillations of market prices, rising now over, sinking now under the value or natural price, depend upon the fluctuations of supply and demand. The deviations of market prices from values are continual, but as Adam Smith says: "The natural price is the central price to which the prices of commodities are continually gravitating. Different accidents may sometimes keep them suspended a good deal above it, and sometimes force them down even somewhat below it. But whatever may be the obstacles which hinder them from settling in this centre of repose and continuance, they are constantly tending towards it."

I cannot now sift this matter. It suffices to say that if supply and demand equilibrate each other, the market prices of commodities will correspond with their natural prices, that is to say with their values, as determined by the respective quantities of labour required for their production. But supply and demand *must* constantly tend to equilibrate each other, although they do so only by compensating one fluctuation by another, a rise by a fall, and *vice versa.* If instead of considering only the daily fluctuations you analyse the movement of market prices for longer periods, as Mr. Tooke, for example, has done in his *History of Prices*, you will find that the fluctuations of market prices, their deviations from values, their ups and downs, paralyse and compensate each other; so that apart from the effect of monopolies and some other modifications I must now pass by, all descriptions of commodities are, on the average, sold at their respective *values* or natural prices. The average periods during which the fluctuations of market prices compensate each other are different for different kinds of commodities, because with one kind it is easier to adapt supply to demand than with the other.

If then, speaking broadly, and embracing somewhat longer periods, all descriptions of commodities sell at their respective values, it is nonsense to suppose that profit, not in individual cases, but that the constant and usual profits of different trades spring from surcharging the prices of commodities or selling them at a price over and above their *value.* The absurdity of this notion becomes evident if it is generalised. What a man would constantly win as a seller he would as constantly lose as a purchaser. It would not do to say that there are men who are buyers without being sellers, or consumers without being producers. What these people pay to the producers, they must first get from them for nothing. If a man first takes your money and afterwards returns that money in buying your commodities, you will never enrich yourselves by selling your commodities too dear to that same man. This sort of transaction might diminish a loss, but would never help in realising a profit.

To explain, therefore, the *general nature of profits*, you must start from the theorem that, on an average, commodities are *sold at their real values*, and that *profits are derived from selling them at their values*, that is, in proportion to the quantity of labour realised in them. If you cannot explain profit upon this supposition, you cannot explain it at all. This seems paradox and contrary to everyday observation. It is also paradox that the earth moves round the sun, and that water consists of two highly inflammable gases. Scientific truth is always paradox, if judged by everyday experience, which catches only the delusive appearance of things.

VII

Labouring Power

Having now, as far as it could be done in such a cursory manner, analysed the nature of *Value*, of the *Value of any commodity whatever*, we must turn our attention to the specific *Value of Labour*. And here, again, I must startle you by a seeming paradox. All of you feel sure that what they daily sell is their Labour; that, therefore, Labour has a Price, and that, the price of a commodity being only the monetary expression of its value, there must certainly exist such a thing as the *Value of Labour*. However, there exists no such thing as the *Value of Labour* in the common acceptance of the word. We have seen that the amount of necessary labour crystallised in a commodity constitutes its value. Now, applying this notion of value, how could we define, say, the value of a ten hours' working day? How much labour is contained in that day? Ten hours' labour. To say that the value of a ten hours' working day is equal to ten hours' labour, or the quantity of labour contained in it, would be a tautological and, moreover, a nonsensical expression. Of course, having once found out the true but hidden sense of the expression "*Value of Labour*," we shall be able to interpret this irrational, and seemingly impossible application of value, in the same way that, having once made sure of the real movement of the celestial bodies, we shall be able to explain their apparent or merely phenomenal movements.

What the working man sells is not directly his *Labour*, but his *Labouring Power*, the temporary disposal of which he makes over to the capitalist. This is so much the case that I do not know whether by the English laws, but certainly by some Continental laws, the *maximum time* is fixed for which a man is allowed to sell his labouring power. If allowed to do so for any indefinite period whatever, slavery would be immediately restored. Such a sale, if it comprised his lifetime, for example, would make him at once the lifelong slave of his employer.

One of the oldest economists and most original philosophers of England—Thomas Hobbes—has already, in his *Leviathan*, instinctively hit upon this point overlooked by all his successors. He says: "*The value or worth of a man* is, as in all other things, his price: that is so much as would be given for the *Use of his Power*."

Proceeding from this basis, we shall be able to determine the *Value of Labour* as that of all other commodities.

But before doing so, we might ask, how does this strange phenomenon arise, that we find on the market a set of buyers, possessed of land, machinery, raw material, and the means of life, all of them, save land in its crude state, the *products of labour*, and on the other hand, a set of sellers who have nothing to sell except their labouring power, their working arms and brains? That the one set buys continually in order to make a profit and enrich themselves, while the other set continually sells in order to earn their livelihood? The inquiry into this question would be an inquiry into what the economists call "*Previous, or Original Accumulation*," but which ought to be called *Original Expropriation*. We should find that this so-called *Original Accumulation* means nothing but a series of historical processes, resulting in a *Decomposition of the Original Union* existing between the Labouring Man and his Means of Labour. Such an inquiry, however, lies beyond the pale of my present subject. The *Separation* between the Man of Labour and the Means of Labour once established, such a state of things will maintain itself and reproduce itself upon a constantly increasing scale, until a new and fundamental revolution in the mode of production should again overturn it, and restore the original union in a new historical form.

What, then, is the *Value of Labouring Power?*

Like that of every other commodity, its value is determined by the quantity of labour necessary to produce it. The labouring power of a man exists only in his living individuality. A certain mass of necessaries must be consumed by a man to grow up and maintain his life. But the man, like the machine, will wear out, and must be replaced by another man. Beside the mass of necessaries required for *his own* maintenance, he wants another amount of necessaries to bring up a certain quota of children that are to replace him on the labour marker and to perpetuate the race of labourers. Moreover, to develop his labouring power, and acquire a given skill, another amount of values must be spent. For our purpose it suffices to consider only average labour, the costs of whose education and development are vanishing magnitudes. Still I must seize upon this occasion to state that, as the costs of producing labouring powers of different quality do differ, so must differ the values of the labouring powers employed in different trades. The cry for an *equality of wages* rests, therefore, upon a mistake, is an inane wish never to be fulfilled. It is an offspring of that false and superficial radicalism that accepts premises and tries to evade conclusions. Upon the basis of the wages system the value of labouring power is settled like that of every other commodity; and as different kinds of labouring power have different values, or require different quantities of labour for their production, they *must* fetch different prices in the labour market. To clamour for *equal or even equitable retribution* on the basis of the wages system is the same as to clamour for *freedom* on the basis of the slavery system. What you think just or equitable is out of the question. The question is: What is necessary and unavoidable with a given system of production?

After what has been said, the *value of labouring power* is determined by the *value of the necessaries* required to produce, develop, maintain, and perpetuate the labouring power.

VIII

Production of Surplus Value

Now suppose that the average amount of the daily necessaries of a labouring man require *six hours of average labour* for their production. Suppose,

moreover, six hours of average labour to be also realised in a quantity of gold equal to 3*s*. Then 3*s*. would be the *Price*, or the monetary expression of the *Daily Value* of that man's *Labouring Power*. If he worked daily six hours he would daily produce a value sufficient to buy the average amount of his daily necessaries, or to maintain himself as a labouring man.

But our man is a wages labourer. He must, therefore, sell his labouring power to a capitalist. If he sells it at 3*s*. daily, or 18*s*. weekly, he sells it at its value. Suppose him to be a spinner. If he works six hours daily he will add to the cotton a value of 3*s*. daily. This value, daily added by him, would be an exact equivalent for the wages, or the price of his labouring power, received daily. But in that case no *surplus value* or *surplus produce* whatever would go to the capitalist. Here, then, we come to the rub.

In buying the labouring power of the workman, and paying its value, the capitalist, like every other purchaser, has acquired the right to consume or use the commodity bought. You consume or use the labouring power of a man by making him work, as you consume or use a machine by making it run. By paying the daily or weekly value of the labouring power of the workman, the capitalist has, therefore, acquired the right to use or make that labouring power work during the *whole day or week*. The working day or the working week has, of course, certain limits, but those we shall afterwards look more closely at.

For the present I want to turn your attention to one decisive point.

The *value* of the labouring power is determined by the quantity of labour necessary to maintain or reproduce it, but the *use* of that labouring power is only limited by the active energies and physical strength of the labourer. The daily or weekly value of the labouring power is quite distinct from the daily or weekly exercise of that power, the same as the food a horse wants and the time it can carry the horseman are quite distinct. The quantity of labour by which the *value* of the workman's labouring power is limited forms by no means a limit to the quantity of labour which his labouring power is apt to perform. Take the example of our spinner. We have seen that, to daily reproduce his labouring power, he must daily reproduce a value of three shillings, which he will do by working six hours daily. But this does not disable him from working ten or twelve or more hours a day. But by paying the daily or weekly *value* of the spinner's labouring power the capitalist has acquired the right of using that labouring power during *the whole day or week*. He will, therefore, make him work daily, say, twelve hours. *Over and above* the six hours required to replace his wages, or the value of his labouring power, he will, therefore, have to work *six other hours*, which I shall call hours of *surplus labour*, which surplus labour will realise itself in a *surplus value* and a *surplus produce*. If our spinner, for example, by his daily labour of six hours, added three shillings' value to the cotton, a value forming an exact equivalent to his wages, he will, in twelve hours, add six shillings' worth to the cotton, and produce a *proportional surplus of yarn*. As he has sold his labouring power to the capitalist, the whole value or produce created by him belongs to the capitalist, the owner *pro tem.* of his labouring power. By advancing three shillings, the capitalist will, therefore, realise a value of six shillings, because, advancing a value in which six hours of labour are crystallised, he will receive in return a value in which twelve hours of labour are crystallised. By repeating this same process daily, the capitalist will daily advance three shillings and daily pocket six shillings, one half of which will go to pay wages anew, and the other half of which will form the *surplus value*, for which the capitalist pays no equivalent. It is this *sort of exchange between capital and labour* upon which capitalistic production, or the wages system, is founded, and which must constantly result in reproducing the working man as a working man, and the capitalist as a capitalist.

The rate of surplus value, all other circumstances remaining the same, will depend on the proportion between that part of the working day necessary to reproduce the value of the labouring power and the *surplus time or surplus labour* performed for the capitalist. It will, therefore, depend on the *ratio in which the working day is prolonged over and above* that extent, by working which the working man would only reproduce the value of his labouring power, or replace his wages.

IX

Value of Labour

We must now return to the expression, *"Value, or Price of Labour."*

We have seen that, in fact, it is only the value of the labouring power, measured by the values of commodities necessary for its maintenance. But since the workman receives his wages *after* his labour is performed, and knows, moreover, that what he actually gives to the capitalist is his labour, the value or price of his labouring power necessarily appears to him as the *price* or *value of his labour itself*. If the price of his labouring power is three shillings, in which six hours of labour are realised, and if he works twelve hours, he necessarily considers these three shillings as the value or price of twelve hours of labour, although these twelve hours of labour realise themselves in a value of six shillings. A double consequence flows from this.

Firstly. *The value or price of the labouring power* takes the semblance of the *price or value of labour itself*, although, strictly speaking, value and price of labour are senseless terms.

Secondly. Although one part only of the workman's daily labour is *paid*, while the other part is *unpaid*, and while that unpaid or surplus labour constitutes exactly the fund out of which *surplus value* or *profit* is formed, it seems as if the aggregate labour was paid labour.

This false appearance distinguishes *wages labour* from other *historical* forms of labour. On the basis of the wages system even the *unpaid* labour seems to be *paid* labour. With the *slave*, on the contrary, even that part of his labour which is paid appears to be unpaid. Of course, in order to work the slave must live, and one part of his working day goes to replace the value of his own maintenance. But since no bargain is struck between him and his master, and no acts of selling and buying are going on between the two parties, all his labour seems to be given away for nothing.

Take, on the other hand, the peasant serf, such as he, I might say, until yesterday existed in the whole east of Europe. This peasant worked, for example, three days for himself on his own field or the field allotted to him, and the three subsequent days he performed compulsory and gratuitous labour on the estate of his lord. Here, then, the paid and unpaid parts of labour were visibly separated, separated in time and space; and our Liberals overflowed with moral indignation at the preposterous notion of making a man work for nothing.

In point of fact, however, whether a man works three days of the week for himself on his own field and three days for nothing on the estate of his lord, or whether he works in the factory or the workshop six hours daily for himself and six for his employer, comes to the same, although in the latter case the paid and unpaid portions of labour are inseparably mixed up with each other, and the nature of the whole transaction is completely masked by the *intervention of a contract* and the *pay* received at the end of the week. The gratuitous labour appears to be voluntarily given in the one instance, and to be compulsory in the other. That makes all the difference.

In using the word *"value of labour,"* I shall only use it as a popular slang term for *"value of labouring power."*

X

Profit Is Made by Selling a Commodity at Its Value

Suppose an average hour of labour to be realised in a value equal to sixpence, or twelve average hours of labour to be realised in six shillings. Suppose,

further, the value of labour to be three shillings or the produce of six hours' labour. If, then, in the raw material, machinery, and so forth, used up in a commodity, twenty-four average hours of labour were realised, its value would amount to twelve shillings. If, moreover, the workman employed by the capitalist added twelve hours of labour to those means of production, these twelve hours would be realised in an additional value of six shillings. The *total value of the product* would, therefore, amount to thirty-six hours of realised labour, and be equal to eighteen shillings. But as the value of labour, or the wages paid to the workman, would be three shillings only, no equivalent would have been paid by the capitalist for the six hours of surplus labour worked by the workman, and realised in the value of the commodity. By selling this commodity at its value for eighteen shillings, the capitalist would, therefore, realise a value of three shillings, for which he had paid no equivalent. These three shillings would constitute the surplus value or profit pocketed by him. The capitalist would consequently realise the profit of three shillings, not by selling his commodity at a price *over and above* its value, but by selling it *at its real value*.

The value of a commodity is determined by the *total quantity of labour* contained in it. But part of that quantity of labour is realised in a value, for which an equivalent has been paid in the form of wages; part of it is realised in a value for which *no* equivalent has been paid. Part of the labour contained in the commodity is *paid* labour; part is *unpaid* labour. By selling, therefore, the commodity *at its value*, that is, as the crystallisation of the *total quantity of labour* bestowed upon it, the capitalist must necessarily sell it at a profit. He sells not only what has cost him an equivalent, but he sells also what has cost him nothing, although it has cost the labour of his workman. The cost of the commodity to the capitalist and its real cost are different things. I repeat, therefore, that normal and average profits are made by selling commodities not *above*, but *at their real values*.

XI

The Different Parts into Which Surplus Value Is Decomposed

The *surplus value*, or that part of the total value of the commodity in which the *surplus labour* or *unpaid labour* of the working man is realised, I call *Profit*. The whole of that profit is not pocketed by the employing capitalist. The monopoly of land enables the landlord to take one part of that *surplus value*, under the name of *rent*, whether the land is used for agriculture or buildings or railways, or for any other productive purpose. On the other hand, the very fact that the possession of the *means of labour* enables the employing capitalist to produce a *surplus value*, or, what comes to the same, to *appropriate to himself a certain amount of unpaid labour*, enables the owner of the means of labour, which he lends wholly or partly to the employing capitalist—enables, in one word, the *money-lending capitalist* to claim for himself under the name of interest another part of that surplus value, so that there remains to the employing capitalist *as such* only what is called *industrial* or *commercial profit*.

By what laws this division of the total amount of surplus value amongst the three categories of people is regulated is a question quite foreign to our subject. This much, however, results from what has been stated.

Rent, Interest, and Industrial Profit are only *different names for different parts of the surplus value* of the commodity or the *unpaid labour realised in it*, and they are *equally derived from this source, and from this source alone*. They are not derived from *land* as such nor from *capital* as such, but land and capital enable their owners to get their respective shares out of the surplus value extracted by the employing capitalist from the labourer. For the labourer himself it is a matter of subordinate importance whether that surplus value, the result of his surplus labour, or unpaid labour, is altogether pocketed by the employing capitalist, or whether the latter is obliged to pay portions of it, under the names of rent and interest, away to third parties. Suppose the employing capitalist to use only his own capital and to be his own landlord, then the whole surplus value would go into his pocket.

It is the employing capitalist who immediately extracts from the labourer this surplus value, whatever part of it he may ultimately, be able to keep for himself. Upon this relation, therefore, between the employing capitalist and the wages labourer the whole wages system and the whole present system of production hinge. Some of the citizens who took part in our debate were, therefore, wrong in trying to mince matters, and to treat this fundamental relation between the employing capitalist and the working man as a secondary question, although they were right in stating that, under given circumstances, a rise of prices might affect in very unequal degrees the employing capitalist, the landlord, the moneyed capitalist, and, if you please, the tax-gatherer.

Another consequence follows from what has been stated.

That part of the value of the commodity which represents only the value of the raw materials, the machinery, in one word, the value of the means of production used up, forms *no revenue* at all, but replaces *only capital*. But, apart from this, it is false that the other part of the value of the commodity *which forms revenue*, or may be spent in the form of wages, profits, rent, interest, is *constituted* by the value of wages, the value of rent, the value of profit, and so forth. We shall, in the first instance, discard wages, and only treat industrial profits, interest, and rent. We have just seen that the *surplus value* contained in the commodity, or that part of its value in which *unpaid labour* is realised, resolves itself into different fractions, bearing three different names. But it would be quite the reverse of the truth to say that its value is *composed* of, or *formed* by, the *addition of the independent values of the three constituents*.

If one hour of labour realises itself in a value of sixpence, if the working day of the labourer comprises twelve hours, if half of this time is unpaid labour, that surplus labour will add to the commodity a *surplus value* of three shillings, that is of value for which no equivalent has been paid. This surplus value of three shillings constitutes the *whole fund* which the employing capitalist may divide, in whatever proportions, with the landlord and the money-lender. The value of these three shillings constitutes the limit of the value they have to divide amongst them. But it is not the employing capitalist who adds to the value of the commodity an arbitrary value for his profit, to which another value is added for the landlord, and so forth, so that the addition of these arbitrarily fixed values would constitute the total value. You see, therefore, the fallacy of the popular notion, which confounds the *decomposition* of a *given value* into three parts, with the *formation* of that value by the addition of three *independent values*, thus converting the aggregate value, from which rent, profit, and interest are derived, into an arbitrary magnitude.

If the total profit realised by a capitalist be equal to £100, we call this sum, considered as absolute magnitude, the *amount of profit*. But if we calculate the ratio which those £100 bear to the capital advanced, we call this *relative* magnitude, the *rate of profit*. It is evident that this rate of profit may be expressed in a double way.

Suppose £100 to be the capital *advanced in wages*. If the surplus value created is also £100— and this would show us that half the working day

of the labourer consists of unpaid labour—and if we measured this profit by the value of the capital advanced in wages, we should say that the *rate of profit* amounted to one hundred per cent, because the value advanced would be one hundred and the value realised would be two hundred.

If, on the other hand, we should not only consider the *capital advanced in wages*, but the *total capital* advanced, say, for example, £500, of which £400 represented the value of raw materials, machinery, and so forth, we should say that the *rate of profit* amounted only to twenty per cent, because the profit of one hundred would be but the fifth part of the total capital advanced.

The first mode of expressing the rate of profit is the only one which shows you the real ratio between paid and unpaid labour, the real degree of the *exploitation* (you must allow me this French word) *of labour*. The other mode of expression is that in common use, and is, indeed, appropriate for certain purposes. At all events, it is very useful for concealing the degree in which the capitalist extracts gratuitous labour from the workman.

In the remarks I have still to make I shall use the word *Profit* for the whole amount of the surplus value extracted by the capitalist without any regard to the division of that surplus value between different parties, and in using the words *Rate of Profit*, I shall always measure profits by the value of the capital advanced in wages.

JOHN STUART MILL

~

INTRODUCTION

JEREMY WALDRON

John Stuart Mill (1806–1873) was born in London and educated privately by his father, James Mill, a utilitarian, a friend and follower of Jeremy Bentham, and a considerable political thinker in his own right.

The story of Mill's peculiar education is notorious, largely through his own account of it in the *Autobiography* published shortly after his death. Under Bentham's guidance and (as the boy grew older) in the company of such distinguished thinkers as the economist David Ricardo and the jurist John Austin, Mill Senior set out to cultivate in his son the perfect utilitarian mind—an intellect equipped with the material and analytical skills that would enable it to focus without distraction on the Benthamite political agenda.

"Without distraction" turned out to mean without the benefit of any religion, art, poetry, or philosophy (besides the basic empiricism that Bentham's system required or presupposed), or more generally without any sense of the proper place the emotions should occupy in a healthy view of the world. These deficiencies surfaced in a mental crisis that beset the young man in 1826–1827, and Mill's realization that they *were* deficiencies meant that his own outlook and (because of the eventual importance of his work) utilitarian philosophy were never the same again. The young man who had worked so assiduously for social improvement—who among other things had been arrested in 1823 for distributing leaflets about birth control in London—became convinced that a Benthamite calculus of cost and benefit, pain and pleasure, was too crude to be deployed as a tool of social change. In its place, Mill sought to reconstruct utilitarianism, so that it incorporated elements of Romantic thought and embodied a sense that while happiness in general was good, certain experiences and enjoyments were qualitatively, not just quantitatively, better than others.

The distinction between the "higher" and "lower" pleasures elaborated in Mill's book *Utilitarianism* (1861)—"Better to be a human being dissatisfied than a pig satisfied"—can easily be made to sound elitist, or indulgently aestheticist. Three points are worth bearing in mind in assessing its influence in Mill's political theory. First, the higher pleasures were not understood as languid or effete enjoyments. What counted most for Mill was the cultivation and employment of our *active* faculties: our curiosity, our questioning, and our ability to make something of our lives and of the world we experience. Second, Mill was convinced—rightly or wrongly—that true happiness, even on his elevated definition, was not just the birthright of the few. Mill was an optimist: he believed that a life "of few and transitory pains, many and various pleasures, with a decided predominance of the active over the passive," was already the lot of many and that "the present wretched education, and wretched social arrangements, are the only real hindrance to its being available to all."

And so—thirdly—though he repudiated Bentham's psychology and theory of value, Mill never abandoned his commitment to forward-looking social reform in a broadly utilitarian spirit. On the contrary, the works included here represent a sustained effort to alter the "wretched social arrangements"—such as the subordination of women, the tyranny of mass culture, and the exclusion of the great majority of working people from participation in politics—which stood in the way of human happiness.

In each of these instances, a case was made by supporters of the status quo that people were often better off submitting to others' ideas of how to live their lives or letting others look after their interests. In each case, Mill responded, "What sort of human beings can be formed under such a regimen? What development can either their thinking or their active faculties attain under it?" And in each case he did his best, through his writings, to swing the spirit of reform in England away from paternalism and toward the cultivation of freedom and individuality of which he thought all men and women were capable. As he said at the beginning of *On Liberty*, he continued to "regard utility as the ultimate appeal on all ethical questions"—he remained Benthamite enough not to be interested in abstract theories of natural right—but it must, he said, be "utility in the largest sense, grounded on the permanent interests of man as a progressive being."

Thus, after his mental crisis, Mill did not retreat, under the influence of Schiller or Coleridge, into the indulgent life of a Victorian romantic, concerned only to protect beauty and feeling from the ravages of routinized utilitarianism. His whole career was one of public service, whether in the pages of the *London and Westminster Review*, which he founded in 1836 along with other young Benthamite radicals, or in the offices of the East India Company, where he worked from 1823 to 1858, or in Parliament where he served one term as M.P. for Westminster in the mid-1860s.

His political career in and out of Parliament was notable for his principled stands in favor of the rights of workers, the rights of political prisoners, and the rights of colonial peoples to a just and decent administration, stands that made him, in Isaiah Berlin's words, "the most passionate and best-known champion of the insulted and the oppressed" of his day. In 1862, he published an article entitled "The Contest in America" in which he attempted to influence public opinion in Britain against the Southern states and to impress on them that the issue was slavery, not just the right to secession—by no means an easy task even in the liberal circles in which he moved. In the House of Commons, Mill spoke against capital punishment and against the suspension of habeas corpus in Ireland and in favor of proportional representation, municipal reform, and women's suffrage.

In particular, his position on women's rights is a striking exception to the casual indifference of most liberal philosophers to the issue. It is explained in part by his association from 1830 with Harriet Taylor, a woman he described in the dedication to *On Liberty* as "the inspirer, and in part the author of all that is best in my writings." But though *The Subjection of Women* was written and published after her death in 1858, there is no reason to doubt the assertion in the opening lines of that tract that opposition to "the legal subordination of one sex to the other" was an opinion he had held from the earliest period of his moral and political thinking.

Harriet Taylor's influence is discernible in other areas of Mill's writing. There is no doubt that he was more favorably inclined to socialism than he would have been without her presence (though he believed that in an ideal world, capitalist arrangements were better, provided something could be done to mitigate the sources of inherited inequality). There is no doubt, either, that Mill's experience of an open and committed friendship with a married woman—for the two were wed only after the death of Harriet Taylor's husband in 1849—laid an important experiential foundation for the loathing of the repressive, moralistic, and, as Isaiah Berlin put it, "uniformitarian despotism" of contemporary public opinion expressed in *On Liberty*.

The works represented here—*Utilitarianism*, *On Liberty*, and *The Subjection of Women*—were all composed during a period of Mill's life (1854–1861) in which, as John Gray has pointed out, he thought that his life might be short, following a grave illness, and that he should say what he had to say on the issues he judged central in his time. But Mill's earlier writings are important too. *A System of Logic* (1843) and *Principles of Political Economy* (1848) quickly became standard texts in their respective subjects, and the essays collected in Mill's *Dissertations and Discussions*, including a long review of Alexis de Tocqueville's *Democracy in America*, add a dimension of sociological and cultural insight that often eludes those who confine themselves to his better-known works. In particular, the affinity with de Tocqueville helps us understand that Mill's primary concerns in *On Liberty* are to do with social and not just legal repression, and with the threat to individuality from mass society even more than majoritarian legislation.

There is an immense and growing literature on Mill's moral and political theory. Isaiah Berlin's essay, "John Stuart Mill and the Ends of Life," in his collection *Four Essays on Liberty* (Oxford: Oxford University Press, 1969), is an excellent starting point, while Alan Ryan, *The Philosophy of John Stuart Mill* (London: Macmillan, 1970), provides an authoritative overview of Mill's arguments. Much of the modern literature focuses on the essay *On Liberty*. Two good book-length studies are C. L. Ten, *Mill on Liberty* (Oxford: Clarendon Press, 1980), and John Gray, *Mill on Liberty—A Defence* (London: Routledge, 1983)—the latter arguing for the consistency of *On Liberty* and *Utilitarianism*. P. Radcliff has put together a useful collection of articles in *Limits of Liberty: Studies of Mill's On Liberty* (Belmont, Calif.: Wadsworth, 1966). D. F. Thompson, *John Stuart Mill and Representative Government* (Princeton, N.J.: Princeton University Press, 1976), is a useful study of Mill's democratic theory, and there is a fine discussion of Mill's feminism in Susan Moller Okin, *Women in Western Political Thought* (Princeton, N.J.: Princeton University Press, 1979).

Utilitarianism

CHAPTER II

What Utilitarianism Is

. . . The creed which accepts as the foundation of morals "utility" or the "greatest happiness principle" holds that actions are right in proportion as they tend to promote happiness; wrong as they tend to produce the reverse of happiness. By happiness is intended pleasure and the absence of pain; by unhappiness, pain and the privation of pleasure. To give a clear view of the moral

From John Stuart Mill, *Utilitarianism* (1863).

standard set up by the theory, much more requires to be said; in particular, what things it includes in the ideas of pain and pleasure, and to what extent this is left an open question. But these supplementary explanations do not affect the theory of life on which this theory of morality is grounded—namely, that pleasure and freedom from pain are the only things desirable as ends; and that all desirable things (which are as numerous in the utilitarian as in any other scheme) are desirable either for pleasure inherent in themselves or as means to the promotion of pleasure and the prevention of pain.

Now such a theory of life excites in many minds, and among them in some of the most estimable in feeling and purpose, inveterate dislike. To suppose that life has (as they express it) no higher end than pleasure—no better and nobler object of desire and pursuit—they designate as utterly mean and groveling, as a doctrine worthy only of swine. . . .

But there is no known . . . theory of life which does not assign to the pleasures of the intellect, of the feelings and imagination, and of the moral sentiments a much higher value as pleasures than to those of mere sensation. It must be admitted, however, that utilitarian writers in general have placed the superiority of mental over bodily pleasures chiefly in the greater permanency, safety, uncostliness, etc., of the former—that is, in their circumstantial advantages rather than in their intrinsic nature. And on all these points utilitarians have fully proved their case; but they might have taken the other and, as it may be called, higher ground with entire consistency. It is quite compatible with the principle of utility to recognize the fact that some kinds of pleasure are more desirable and more valuable than others. It would be absurd that, while in estimating all other things quality is considered as well as quantity, the estimation of pleasure should be supposed to depend on quantity alone.

If I am asked what I mean by difference in quality in pleasures, or what makes one pleasure more valuable than another, merely as a pleasure, except its being greater in amount, there is but

one possible answer. Of two pleasures, if there be one to which all or almost all who have experience of both give a decided preference, irrespective of any feeling of moral obligation to prefer it, that is the more desirable pleasure. If one of the two is, by those who are competently acquainted with both, placed so far above the other that they prefer it, even though knowing it to be attended with a greater amount of discontent, and would not resign it for any quantity of the other pleasure which their nature is capable of, we are justified in ascribing to the preferred enjoyment a superiority in quality so far outweighing quantity as to render it, in comparison, of small account.

Now it is an unquestionable fact that those who are equally acquainted with and equally capable of appreciating and enjoying both do give a most marked preference to the manner of existence which employs their higher faculties. Few human creatures would consent to be changed into any of the lower animals for a promise of the fullest allowance of a beast's pleasures; no intelligent human being would consent to be a fool, no instructed person would be an ignoramus, no person of feeling and conscience would be selfish and base, even though they should be persuaded that the fool, the dunce, or the rascal is better satisfied with his lot than they are with theirs. They would not resign what they possess more than he for the most complete satisfaction of all the desires which they have in common with him. If they ever fancy they would, it is only in cases of unhappiness so extreme that to escape from it they would exchange their lot for almost any other, however undesirable in their own eyes. A being of higher faculties requires more to make him happy, is capable probably of more acute suffering, and certainly accessible to it at more points, than one of an inferior type; but in spite of these liabilities, he can never really wish to sink into what he feels to be a lower grade of existence. . . .

It is better to be a human being dissatisfied than a pig satisfied; better to be Socrates dissatisfied than a fool satisfied. And if the fool, or the pig, are of a different opinion, it is because they only know their own side of the question. The other party to the comparison knows both sides.

It may be objected that many who are capable of the higher pleasures occasionally, under the influence of temptation, postpone them to the lower. But this is quite compatible with a full appreciation of the intrinsic superiority of the higher. Men often, from infirmity of character, make their election for the nearer good, though they know it to be the less valuable; and this no less when the choice is between two bodily pleasures than when it is between bodily and mental. They pursue sensual indulgences to the injury of health, though perfectly aware that health is the greater good. It may be further objected that many who begin with youthful enthusiasm for everything noble, as they advance in years, sink into indolence and selfishness. But I do not believe that those who undergo this very common change voluntarily choose the lower description of pleasures in preference to the higher. I believe that, before they devote themselves exclusively to the one, they have already become incapable of the other. Capacity for the nobler feelings is in most natures a very tender plant, easily killed, not only by hostile influences, but by mere want of sustenance; and in the majority of young persons it speedily dies away if the occupations to which their position in life has devoted them, and the society into which it has thrown them, are not favorable to keeping that higher capacity in exercise. Men lose their high aspirations as they lose their intellectual tastes, because they have not time or opportunity for indulging them; and they addict themselves to inferior pleasures, not because they deliberately prefer them, but because they are either the only ones to which they have access or the only ones which they are any longer capable of enjoying. It may be questioned whether anyone who has remained equally susceptible to both classes of pleasures ever knowingly and calmly preferred the lower, though many, in all ages, have broken down in an ineffectual attempt to combine both.

From this verdict of the only competent judges, I apprehend there can be no appeal. On a question which is the best worth having of two pleasures, or which of the two modes of existence is the most grateful to the feelings, apart from its moral attrwibutes and from its consequences, the judgment of these who are qualified by knowledge of both, or, if they differ, that of the majority among them, must be admitted as final. And there needs to be the less hesitation to accept this judgment respecting the quality of pleasures, since there is no other tribunal to be referred to even on the question of quantity. What means are there of determining which is the acutest of two pains, or the intensest of two pleasurable sensations, except the general suffrage of those who are familiar with both? . . .

I must again repeat what the assailants of utilitarianism seldom have the justice to acknowledge, that the happiness which forms the utilitarian standard of what is right in conduct is not the agent's own happiness but that of all concerned. As between his own happiness and that of others, utilitarianism requires him to be as strictly impartial as a disinterested and benevolent spectator. In the golden rule of Jesus of Nazareth, we read the complete spirit of the ethics of utility. "To do as you would be done by," and "to love your neighbor as your self," constitute the ideal perfection of utilitarian morality. As the means of making the nearest approach to this ideal, utility would enjoin, first, that laws and social arrangements should place the happiness or (as, speaking practically, it may be called) the interest of every individual as nearly as possible in harmony with the interest of the whole; and, secondly, that education and opinion, which have so vast a power over human character, should so use that power as to establish in the mind of every individual an indissoluble association between his own happiness and the good of the whole, especially between his own happiness and the practice of such modes of conduct, negative and positive, as regard for the universal happiness prescribes; so that not only he may be unable to conceive the possibility of happiness to himself, consistently with conduct opposed to the general good, but also that a direct impulse to promote the general good may be in every individual one of the habitual motives of action, and the sentiments connected therewith may fill a large and prominent place in every human being's sentient existence. If the impugners of the utilitarian morality represented it to their own minds in this its true character, I know not what recommendation possessed by any other morality they could possibly affirm to be wanting to it; what more beautiful or more exalted developments of human nature any other ethical system can be supposed to foster; or what springs of action, not accessible to the utilitarian, such systems rely on for giving effect to their mandates.

The objectors to utilitarianism cannot always be charged with representing it in a discreditable light. On the contrary, those among them who entertain anything like a just idea of its disinterested character sometimes find fault with its standard as being too high for humanity. They say it is exacting too much to require that people shall always act from the inducement of promoting the general interest of society. But this is to mistake the very meaning of a standard of morals and confound the rule of action with the motive of it. It is the business of ethics to tell us what are our duties, or by what test we may know them; but no system of ethics requires that the sole motive of all we do shall be a feeling of duty; on the contrary, ninety-nine hundredths of all our actions are done from other motives, and rightly so done if the rule of duty does not condemn them. It is the more unjust to utilitarianism that this particular misapprehension should be made a ground of objection to it, inasmuch as utilitarian moralists have gone beyond almost all others in affirming that the motive has nothing to do with the morality of the action, though much with the worth of the agent. He who saves a fellow creature from drowning does what is morally right, whether his motive be duty or the hope of being paid for his trouble; he who betrays the friend that trusts him is guilty of a crime, even if his object be to serve another friend to whom he is under greater obligations. But to speak only of actions done from the motive of duty, and in direct obedience to principle: it is a misapprehension of the utilitarian mode of thought to conceive it as implying that people should fix their minds upon so wide a generality as the world, or society at large. The greatest majority of good actions are intended not for the benefit of the world, but for that of individuals, of which the good of the world is made up; and the thoughts of the most virtuous man need not on these occasions travel beyond the particular persons concerned, except so far as is necessary to assure himself that in benefiting them he is not violating the rights, that is, the legitimate and authorized expectations, of anyone else. The multiplication of happiness is, according to the utilitarian ethics, the object of virtue: the occasions on which any person (except one in a thousand) has it in his power to do this on an extended scale—in other words, to be a public benefactor—are but exceptional; and on these occasions alone is he called on to consider public utility; in every other case, private utility, the interest or happiness of some few persons, is all he has to attend to. Those alone the influence of whose actions extends to society in general need concern themselves habitually about so large an object. In the case of abstinences indeed—of things which people forbear to do from moral considerations, though the consequences in the particular case might be beneficial—it would be unworthy of an intelligent agent not to be consciously aware that the action is of a class which, if practiced generally, would be generally injurious, and that this is the ground of the obligation to abstain from it. The amount of regard for the public interest implied in this recognition is no greater than is demanded by every system of morals, for they all enjoin to abstain from whatever is manifestly pernicious to society. . . .

Again, utility is often summarily stigmatized as an immoral doctrine by giving it the name of "expediency," and taking advantage of the popular use of that term to contrast it with principle. But the expedient, in the sense in which it is opposed to the right, generally means that which is expedient for the particular interest of the agent himself, as when a minister sacrifices the interests of his country to keep himself in place. When it means anything better than this, it means that which is expedient for some immediate object, some temporary purpose, but which violates a rule whose observance is expedient in a much higher degree. The expedient, in this sense, instead of being the same thing with the useful, is a branch of the hurtful. Thus it would often be expedient, for the purpose of getting over some momentary embarrassment, or attaining some object immediately useful to ourselves or others, to tell a lie. But inasmuch as the cultivation in ourselves of a sensitive feeling on the subject of veracity is one of the most useful, and the enfeeblement of that feeling one of the most hurtful, things to which our conduct can be instrumental; and inasmuch as any, even unintentional, deviation from truth does that much toward weakening the trustworthiness of human assertion, which is not only the principal support of all present social well-being, but the insufficiency of which does more than any one thing that can be named to keep back civilization, virtue, everything on which human happiness on the largest scale depends—we feel that the violation, for a present advantage, of a rule of such transcendent expediency is not expedient, and that he who, for the sake of convenience to himself or to some other individual, does what depends on him to deprive mankind of the good, and inflict upon them the evil, involved in the greater or less reliance which they can place in each other's words, acts the part of one of their worst enemies. Yet that even this rule, sacred as it is, admits of possible exceptions is acknowledged by all moralists, the chief of which is when the withholding of some fact (as of information from a malefactor, or of bad news from a person dangerously ill) would save an individual (especially an individual other than oneself) from great and unmerited evil, and when the withholding can only be effected by denial. But in order that the exception may not extend itself beyond the need, and may have the least possible effect in weakening

reliance on veracity, it ought to be recognized and, if possible, its limits defined; and, if the principle of utility is good for anything, it must be good for weighing these conflicting utilities against one another and marking out the region within which one or the other preponderates.

Again, defenders of utility often find themselves called upon to reply to such objections as this—that there is not time, previous to action, for calculating and weighing the effects of any line of conduct on the general happiness. This is exactly as if anyone were to say that it is impossible to guide our conduct by Christianity because there is not time, on every occasion on which anything has to be done, to read through the Old and New Testaments. The answer to the objection is that there has been ample time, namely, the whole past duration of the human species. During all that time mankind have been learning by experience the tendencies of actions, on which experience all the prudence as well as all the morality of life are dependent. People talk as if the commencement of this course of experience had hitherto been put off, and as if, at the moment when some man feels tempted to meddle with the property or life of another, he had to begin considering for the first time whether murder and theft are injurious to human happiness. Even then I do not think that he would find the question very puzzling; but, at all events, the matter is now done to his hand. It is truly a whimsical supposition that, if mankind were agreed in considering utility to be the test of morality, they would remain without any agreement as to what *is* useful, and would take no measures for having their notions on the subject taught to the young and enforced by law and opinion. There is no difficulty in proving any ethical standard whatever to work ill if we suppose universal idiocy to be conjoined with it; but on any hypothesis short of that, mankind must by this time have acquired positive beliefs as to the effects of some actions on their happiness; and the beliefs which have thus come down are the rules of morality for the multitude, and for the philosopher until he has succeeded in finding better. That philosophers might easily do this, even now, on many subjects; that the received code of ethics is by no means of divine right; and that mankind have still much to learn as to the effects of actions on the general happiness, I admit or rather earnestly maintain. The corollaries from the principle of utility, like the precepts of every practical art, admit of indefinite improvement, and, in a progressive state of the human mind, their improvement is perpetually going on. But to consider the rules of morality as improvable is one thing; to pass over the intermediate generalization entirely and endeavor to test each individual action directly by the first principle is another. It is a strange notion that the acknowledgment of a first principle is inconsistent with the admission of secondary ones. To inform a traveler respecting the place of his ultimate destination is not to forbid the use of landmarks and direction-posts on the way. The proposition that happiness is the end and aim of morality does not mean that no road ought to be laid down to that goal, or that persons going thither should not be advised to take one direction rather than another. Men really ought to leave off talking a kind of nonsense on this subject, which they would neither talk nor listen to on other matters of practical concernment. Nobody argues that the art of navigation is not founded on astronomy because sailors cannot wait to calculate the Nautical Almanac. Being rational creatures, they go to sea with it ready calculated; and all rational creatures go out upon the sea of life with their minds made up on the common questions of right and wrong, as well as on many of the far more difficult questions of wise and foolish. And this, as long as foresight is a human quality, it is to be presumed they will continue to do. Whatever we adopt as the fundamental principle of morality, we require subordinate principles to apply it by; the impossibility of doing without them, being common to all systems, can afford no argument against any one in particular; but gravely to argue as if no such secondary principles could be had, and as if mankind had remained till now, and always must remain, without drawing any general conclusions

from the experience of human life is as high a pitch, I think, as absurdity has ever reached in philosophical controversy. . . .

CHAPTER IV

Of What Sort of Proof the Principle of Utility Is Susceptible

. . . Questions about ends are, in other words, questions about what things are desirable. The utilitarian doctrine is that happiness is desirable and the only thing desirable as an end, all other things being only desirable as means to that end. What ought to be required of the doctrine, what conditions is it requisite that the doctrine should fulfill—to make good its claim to be believed?

The only proof capable of being given that an object is visible is that people actually see it. The only proof that a sound is audible is that people hear it; and so of the other sources of our experience. In like manner, I apprehend, the sole evidence it is possible to produce that anything is desirable is that people do actually desire it. If the end which the utilitarian doctrine proposes to itself were not, in theory and in practice, acknowledged to be an end, nothing could ever convince any person that it was so. No reason can be given why the general happiness is desirable, except that each person, so far as he believes it to be attainable, desires his own happiness. This, however, being a fact, we have not only all the proof which the case admits of, but all which it is possible to require, that happiness is a good, that each person's happiness is a good to that person, and the general happiness, therefore, a good to the aggregate of all persons. Happiness has made out its title as *one* of the ends of conduct and, consequently, one of the criteria of morality.

But it has not, by this alone, proved itself to be the sole criterion. To do that it would seem, by the same rule, necessary to show not only that people desire happiness but that they never desire anything else. Now it is palpable that they do desire things which, in common language, are decidedly distinguished from happiness. They desire, for example, virtue and the absence of vice no less really than pleasure and the absence of pain. The desire of virtue is not as universal, but it is as authentic a fact as the desire of happiness. And hence the opponents of the utilitarian standard deem that they have a right to infer that there are other ends of human action besides happiness, and that happiness is not the standard of approbation and disapprobation.

But does the utilitarian doctrine deny that people desire virtue, or maintain that virtue is not a thing to be desired? The very reverse. It maintains not only that virtue is to be desired, but that it is to be desired disinterestedly, for itself. Whatever may be the opinion of utilitarian moralists as to the original conditions by which virtue is made virtue, however they may believe (as they do) that actions and dispositions are only virtuous because they promote another end than virtue, yet this being granted, and it having been decided, from considerations of this description, what *is* virtuous, they not only place virtue at the very head of the things which are good as means to the ultimate end, but they also recognize as a psychological fact the possibility of its being, to the individual, a good in itself, without looking to any end beyond it; and hold that the mind is not in a right state, not in a state conformable to utility, not in the state most conducive to the general happiness, unless it does love virtue in this manner— as a thing desirable in itself, even although, in the individual instance, it should not produce those other desirable consequences which it ends to produce, and on account of which it is held to be virtue. This opinion is not, in the smallest degree, a departure from the happiness principle. The ingredients of happiness are very various, and each of them is desirable in itself, and not merely when considered as swelling an aggregate. The principle of utility does not mean that any given pleasure, as music, for instance, or any given exemption from pain, as for example health, is to be looked upon as means to a collective something termed happiness, and to be desired on that account. They are desired and desirable in and for themselves; besides being means, they are a part of the end. Virtue, according to the utilitarian doctrine, is not naturally and originally part of the end, but

it is capable of becoming so; and in those who live it disinterestedly it has become so, and is desired and cherished, not as a means to happiness, but to a part of their happiness.

To illustrate this further, we may remember that virtue is not the only thing originally a means, and which if it were not a means to anything else would be and remain indifferent, but which by association with what it is a means to comes to be desired for itself, and that too with the utmost intensity. What, for example, shall we say of the love of money? There is nothing originally more desirable about money than about any heap of glittering pebbles. Its worth is solely that of the things which it will buy; the desires for other things than itself, which it is a means of gratifying. Yet the love of money is not one of the strongest moving forces of human life, but money is, in many cases, desired in and for itself; the desire to possess it is often stronger than the desire to use it, and goes on increasing when all the desires which point to ends beyond it, to be compassed by it, are falling off. It may, then, be said truly that money is desired not for the sake of an end, but as part of the end. From being a means to happiness, it has come to be itself a principal ingredient of the individual's conception of happiness. The same may be said of the majority of the great objects of human life: power, for example, or fame, except that to each of these there is a certain amount of immediate pleasure annexed, which has at least the semblance of being naturally inherent in them—a thing which cannot be said of money. Still, however, the strongest natural attraction, both of power and of fame, is the immense aid they give to the attainment of our other wishes; and it is the strong association thus generated between them and all our objects of desire which gives to the direct desire of them the intensity it often assumes, so as in some characters to surpass in strength all other desires. In these cases the means have become a part of the end, and a more important part of it than any of the things which they are means to. What was once desired as an instrument for the attainment of happiness has come to be desired for its own sake. In being desired for its own sake it is, however, desired as *part* of happiness. The person is made, or thinks he would be made, happy by its mere possession and is made unhappy by failure to obtain it. The desire of it is not a different thing from the desire of happiness any more than the love of music or the desire of health. They are included in happiness. They are some of the elements of which the desire of happiness is made up. Happiness is not an abstract idea but a concrete whole; and these are some of its parts. And the utilitarian standard sanctions and approves their being so. Life would be a poor thing, very ill provided with sources of happiness, if there were not this provision of nature by which things originally indifferent, but conducive to, or otherwise associated with, the satisfaction of our primitive desires, become in themselves sources of pleasure more valuable than the primitive pleasures, both in permanency, in the space of human existence that they are capable of covering, and even in intensity.

Virtue, according to the utilitarian conception, is a good of this description. There was no original desire of it, or motive to it, save its conduciveness to pleasure, and especially to protection from pain. But through the association thus formed it may be felt a good in itself, and desired as such with as great intensity as any other good; and with this difference between it and the love of money, of power, or of fame—that all of these may, and often do, render the individual noxious to the other members of the society to which he belongs, whereas there is nothing which makes him so much a blessing to them as the cultivation of the disinterested love of virtue. And consequently, the utilitarian standard, while it tolerates and approves those other acquired desires, up to the point beyond which they would be more injurious to the general happiness than promotive of it, enjoins and requires the cultivation of the love of virtue up to the greatest strength possible, as being above all things important to the general happiness.

It results from the preceding considerations that there is in reality nothing desired except happiness. Whatever is desired otherwise than as a means to some end beyond itself, and ultimately to happiness, is desired as itself a part of happiness, and is not desired for itself until it has become so. Those who desire virtue for its own sake desire it either because the consciousness of it is a pleasure, or because the consciousness of being without it is a pain, or for both reasons united, as in truth the pleasure and pain seldom exist separately, but almost always together—the same person feeling pleasure in the degree of virtue attained, and pain in not having attained more. If one of these gave him no pleasure, and the other no pain, he would not love or desire virtue, or would desire it only for the other benefits which it might produce to himself or to persons whom he cared for.

We have now, then, an answer to the question, of what sort of proof the principle of utility is susceptible.

On Liberty

The grand, leading principle, towards which every argument unfolded in these pages directly converges, is the absolute and essential importance of human development in its richest diversity.

—*Wilhelm von Humboldt:* Sphere and Duties of Government

To the beloved and deplored memory of her who was the inspirer, and in part the author, of all that is best in my writings—the friend and wife whose exalted sense of truth and right was my strongest incitement, and whose approbation was my chief reward—I dedicate this volume. Like all that I have written for many years, it belongs as much to her as to me; but the work as it stands has had, in a very insufficient degree, the inestimable advantage of her revision; some of the most important portions having been reserved for a more careful re-examination, which they are now never destined to receive. Were I but capable of interpreting to the world one half the great thoughts and noble feelings which are buried in her grave, I should be the medium of a greater benefit to it, than is ever likely to arise from anything that I can write, unprompted and unassisted by her all but unrivaled wisdom.

CHAPTER I

Introductory

. . . The object of this essay is to assert one very simple principle, as entitled to govern absolutely the dealings of society with the individual in the way of compulsion and control, whether the means used be physical force in the form of legal penalties or the moral coercion of public opinion. That principle is that the sole end for which mankind are warranted, individually or collectively, in interfering with the liberty of action of any of their number is self-protection. That the only purpose for which power can be rightfully exercised over any member of a civilized community, against his will, is to prevent harm to others. His own good, either physical or moral, is not a sufficient warrant. He cannot rightfully be compelled to do or forbear because it will be better for him to do so, because it will make him happier, because, in the opinions of others, to do so would be wise or even right. These are good reasons for remonstrating with him, or reasoning with him, or persuading him, or entreating him, but not for compelling him or visiting him with any evil in case he do otherwise. To justify that, the conduct from which it is desired to deter him must be calculated to produce evil to someone else. The only part of the conduct of anyone for which he is amenable to society is that which concerns others. In the part which merely concerns himself, his independence is, of right, absolute. Over himself, over his own body and mind, the individual is sovereign. . . .

This, then, is the appropriate region of human liberty. It comprises, first, the inward domain of consciousness, demanding liberty of conscience in the most comprehensive sense, liberty of thought and feeling, absolute freedom of opinion and sentiment on all subjects, practical or speculative, scientific, moral, or theological. The liberty of expressing and publishing opinions may seem to fall under a different principle, since it belongs to that part of the conduct of an individual which concerns other people, but, being almost of as much importance as the liberty of thought itself and resting in great part on the same reasons, is practically inseparable from it. Secondly, the principle requires liberty of tastes and pursuits, of framing the plan of our life to suit our own character, of doing as we like, subject to such consequences as may follow, without impediment from our fellow creatures, so long as what we do does not harm them, even though they should think our conduct foolish, perverse, or wrong. Thirdly, from this liberty of each individual follows the liberty, within the same limits, of combination among individuals; freedom to unite for any purpose not involving harm to others: the persons combining being supposed to be of full age and not forced or deceived.

No society in which these liberties are not, on the whole, respected is free, whatever may be its form of government; and none is completely free in which they do not exist absolute and unqualified. The only freedom which deserves the name is that of pursuing our own good in our own way, so long as we do not attempt to deprive others of theirs or impede their efforts to obtain it. Each is the proper guardian of his own health, whether bodily *or* mental and spiritual. Mankind are greater gainers by suffering each other to live as seems good to themselves than by compelling each to live as seems good to the rest. . . .

It will be convenient for the argument if, instead of at once entering upon the general thesis, we confine ourselves in the first instance to a single branch of it on which the principle here stated is, if not fully, yet to a certain point, recognized by the current opinions. This one branch is the Liberty of Thought, from which it is impossible to separate the cognate liberty of speaking and of writing. Although these liberties, to some considerable amount, form part of the political morality of all countries which profess religious toleration and free institutions, the grounds, both philosophical and practical, on which they rest are perhaps not so familiar to the general mind, nor so thoroughly appreciated by many, even of the leaders of opinion, as might have been expected. Those grounds, when rightly understood, are of much wider application than to only one division of the subject, and a thorough consideration of this part of the question will be found the best introduction to the remainder. Those to whom nothing which I am about to say will be new may therefore, I hope, excuse me if on a subject which for now three centuries has been so often discussed I venture on one discussion more.

CHAPTER II

Of the Liberty of Thought and Discussion

The time, it is hoped, is gone by when any defense would be necessary of the "liberty of the press" as one of the securities against corrupt or tyrannical government. No argument, we may suppose, can now be needed against permitting a legislature or an executive, not identified in interest with the people, to prescribe opinions to them and determine what doctrines or what arguments they shall be allowed to hear. This aspect of the question, besides, has been so often and so triumphantly enforced by preceding writers that it needs not be specially insisted on in this place. Though the law of England, on the subject of the press, is as servile to this day as it was in the time of the Tudors, there is little danger of its being actually put in force against political discussion except during some temporary panic when fear of insurrection drives ministers and judges from their propriety; band, speaking generally, it is not, in constitutional countries, to be apprehended that the government, whether completely responsible to the

people or not, will often attempt to control the expression of opinion, except when in doing so it makes itself the organ of the general intolerance of the public. Let us suppose, therefore, that the government is entirely at one with the people, and never thinks of exerting any power of coercion unless in agreement with what it conceives to be their voice. But I deny the right of the people to exercise such coercion, either by themselves or by their government. The power itself is illegitimate. The best government has no more title to it than the worst. It is as noxious, or more noxious, when exerted in accordance with public opinion than when in opposition to it. If all mankind minus one were of one opinion, and only one person were of the contrary opinion, mankind would be no more justified in silencing that one person than he, if he had the power, would be justified in silencing mankind. Were an opinion a personal possession of no value except to the owner, if to be obstructed in the enjoyment of it were simply a private injury, it would make some difference whether the injury was inflicted only on a few persons or on many. But the peculiar evil of silencing the expression of an opinion is that it is robbing the human race, posterity as well as the existing generation—those who dissent from the opinion, still more than those who hold it. If the opinion is right, they are deprived of the opportunity of exchanging error for truth; if wrong, they lose, what is almost as great a benefit, the clearer perception and livelier impression of truth produced by its collision with error.

It is necessary to consider separately these two hypotheses, each of which has a distinct branch of the argument corresponding to it. We can never be sure that the opinion we are endeavoring to stifle is a false opinion; and if we were sure, stifling it would be an evil still.

First, the opinion which it is attempted to suppress by authority may possibly be true. Those who desire to suppress it, of course, deny its truth; but they are not infallible. They have no authority to decide the question for all mankind and exclude every other person from the means of judging. To refuse a hearing to an opinion because they are sure that it is false is to assume that *their* certainty is the same thing as *absolute* certainty. All silencing of discussion is an assumption of infallibility. Its condemnation may be allowed to rest on this common argument, not the worse for being common.

Unfortunately for the good sense of mankind, the fact of their fallibility is far from carrying the weight in their practical judgment which is always allowed to it in theory; for while everyone well knows himself to be fallible, few think it necessary to take any precautions against their own fallibility, or admit the supposition that any opinion of which they feel very certain may be one of the examples of the error to which they acknowledge themselves to be liable. Absolute princes, or others who are accustomed to unlimited deference, usually feel this complete confidence in their own opinions on nearly all subjects. People more happily situated, who sometimes hear their opinions disputed and are not wholly unused to be set right when they are wrong, place the same unbounded reliance only on such of their opinions as are shared by all who surround them, or to whom they habitually defer; for in proportion to a man's want of confidence in his own solitary judgment does he usually repose, with implicit trust, on the infallibility of "the world" in general. And the world, to each individual, means the part of it with which he comes in contact: his party, his sect, his church, his class of society; the man may be called, by comparison, almost liberal and large-minded to whom it means anything so comprehensive as his own country or his own age. Nor is his faith in this collective authority at all shaken by his being aware that other ages, countries, sects, churches, classes, and parties have thought, and even now think, the exact reverse. He devolves upon his own world the responsibility of being in the right against the dissentient worlds of other people; and it never troubles him that mere accident has decided which of these numerous worlds is the object of his reliance, and that the same causes which make him a churchman in London would have made him a Buddhist or a Confucian in Peking. Yet it is as evident in itself, as any amount of argument can make it, that ages are no more infallible than individuals—every age having held many opinions which subsequent ages have deemed not only false but absurd; and it is as certain that many opinions, now general, will be rejected by future ages, as it is that many, once general, are rejected by the present.

The objection likely to be made to this argument would probably take some such form as the following. There is no greater assumption of infallibility in forbidding the propagation of error than in any other thing which is done by public authority on its own judgment and responsibility. Judgment is given to men that they may use it. Because it may be used erroneously, are men to be told that they ought not to use it at all? To prohibit what they think pernicious is not claiming exemption from error, but fulfilling the duty incumbent on them, although fallible, of acting on their conscientious conviction. If we were never to act on our opinions, because those opinions may be wrong, we should leave all our interests uncared for, and all our duties unperformed. An objection which applies to all conduct can be no valid objection to any conduct in particular. It is the duty of governments, and of individuals, to form the truest opinions they can; to form them carefully, and never impose them upon others unless they are quite sure of being right. But when they are sure (such reasoners may say), it is not conscientiousness but cowardice to shrink from acting on their opinions and allow doctrines which they honestly think dangerous to the welfare of mankind, either in this life or in another, to be scattered abroad without restraint, because other people, in less enlightened times, have persecuted opinions now believed to be true. Let us take care, it may be said, not to make the same mistake; but governments and nations have made mistakes in other things which are not denied to be fit subjects for the exercise of authority: they have laid on bad taxes, made unjust wars. Ought we therefore to lay on no taxes and, under whatever provocation, make no wars? Men and governments must act to the best of their ability. There is no such thing as absolute certainty, but there is assurance sufficient for the purposes of human life. We may, and must, assume our opinion to be true for the guidance of our own conduct; and it is assuming no more when we forbid bad men to pervert society by the propagation of opinions which we regard as false and pernicious.

I answer, that it is assuming very much more. There is the greatest difference between presuming an opinion to be true because, with every opportunity for contesting it, it has not been refuted, and assuming its truth for the purpose of not permitting its refutation. Complete liberty of contradicting and disproving our opinion is the very condition which justifies us in assuming its truth for purposes of action; and on no other terms can a being with human faculties have any rational assurance of being right.

When we consider either the history of opinion or the ordinary conduct of human life, to what is it to be ascribed that the one and the other are no worse than they are? Not certainly to the inherent force of the human understanding, for on any matter not self-evident there are ninety-nine persons totally incapable of judging of it for one who is capable; and the capacity of the hundredth person is only comparative, for the majority of the eminent men of every past generation held many opinions now known to be erroneous, and did or approved numerous things which no one will now justify. Why is it, then, that there is on the whole a preponderance among mankind of rational opinions and rational conduct? If there really is this preponderance—which there must be unless human affairs are, and have always been, in an almost desperate state—it is owing to a quality of the human mind, the source of everything respectable in man either as an intellectual or as a moral being, namely, that his errors are corrigible. He is capable of rectifying his mistakes by discussion and experience. Not by experience alone. There must be discussion to show how experience is to be interpreted. Wrong opinions and practices gradually yield to fact and argument; but facts and arguments, to produce any effect on the mind, must be brought before it. Very few facts are able to tell their own story, without comments to bring out their meaning. The whole strength and value, then, of human judgment depending on the one property, that it can be set right when it is wrong, reliance can be placed on it only when the means of setting it right are kept constantly at hand. In the case of any person whose judgment is really deserving of confidence, how has it become so? Because he has kept his mind open to criticism of his opinions and conduct. Because it has been his practice to listen to all that could be said against him; to profit by as much of it as was just, and to expound to himself, and upon occasion to others, the fallacy of what was fallacious. Because he has felt that the only way in which a human being can make some approach to knowing the whole of a subject is by hearing what can be said about it by persons of every variety of opinion, and studying all modes in which it can be looked at by every character of mind. No wise man ever acquired his wisdom in any mode but this; nor is it in the nature of human intellect to become wise in any other manner. The steady habit of correcting and completing his own opinion by collating it with those of others, so far from causing doubt and hesitation in carrying it into practice, is the only stable foundation for a just reliance on it; for, being cognizant of all that can, at least obviously, be said against him, and having taken up his position against gainsayers—knowing that he has sought for objections and difficulties instead of avoiding them, and has shut out no light which can be thrown upon the subject from any quarter—he has a right to think his judgment better than that of any person, or any multitude, who have not gone through a similar process.

It is not too much to require that what the wisest of mankind, those who are best entitled to trust their own judgment, find necessary to warrant their relying on it, should be submitted to by that miscellaneous collection of a few wise and many foolish individuals called the public. The most intolerant of churches, the Roman Catholic

Church, even at the canonization of a saint admits, and listens patiently to, a "devil's advocate." The holiest of men, it appears, cannot be admitted to posthumous honors until all that the devil could say against him is known and weighed. If even the Newtonian philosophy were not permitted to be questioned, mankind could not feel as complete assurance of its truth as they now do. The beliefs which we have most warrant for have no safeguard to rest on but a standing invitation to the whole world to prove them unfounded. If the challenge is not accepted, or is accepted and the attempt fails, we are far enough from certainty still, but we have done the best that the existing state of human reason admits of: we have neglected nothing that could give the truth a chance of reaching us; if the lists are kept open, we may hope that, if there be a better truth, it will be found when the human mind is capable of receiving it; and in the meantime we may rely on having attained such approach to truth as is possible in our own day. This is the amount of certainty attainable by a fallible being, and this the sole way of attaining it.

Strange it is that men should admit the validity of the arguments for free discussion, but object to their being "pushed to an extreme," not seeing that unless the reasons are good for an extreme case, they are not good for any case. Strange that they should imagine that they are not assuming infallibility when they acknowledge that there should be free discussion on all subjects which can possibly be *doubtful*, but think that some particular principle or doctrine should be forbidden to be questioned because it is so *certain*, that is, because *they are certain* that it is certain. To call any proposition certain, while there is anyone who would deny its certainty if permitted, but who is not permitted, is to assume that we ourselves, and those who agree with us, are the judges of certainty, and judges without hearing the other side.

In the present age—which has been described as "destitute of faith, but terrified at skepticism"—in which people feel sure, not so much that their opinions are true as that they should not know what to do with them—the claims of an opinion

to be protected from public attack are rested not so much on its truth as on its importance to society. There are, it is alleged, certain beliefs so useful, not to say indispensable, to well-being that it is as much the duty of governments to uphold those beliefs as to protect any other of the interests of society. In a case of such necessity, and so directly in the line of their duty, something less than infallibility may, it is maintained, warrant, and even bind, governments to act on their own opinion confirmed by the general opinion of mankind. It is also often argued, and still oftener thought, that none but bad men would desire to weaken these salutary beliefs; and there can be nothing wrong, it is thought, in restraining bad men and prohibiting what only such men would wish to practice. This mode of thinking makes the justification of restraints on discussion not a question of the truth of doctrines but of their usefulness, and flatters itself by that means to escape the responsibility of claiming to be an infallible judge of opinions. But those who thus satisfy themselves do not perceive that the assumption of infallibility is merely shifted from one point to another. The usefulness of an opinion is itself matter of opinion—as disputable, as open to discussion, and requiring discussion as much as the opinion itself. There is the same need of an infallible judge of opinions to decide an opinion to be noxious as to decide it to be false, unless the opinion condemned has full opportunity of defending itself. And it will not do to say that the heretic may be allowed to maintain the utility or harmlessness of his opinion, though forbidden to maintain its truth. The truth of an opinion is part of its utility. If we would know whether or not it is desirable that a proposition should be believed, is it possible to exclude the consideration of whether or not it is true? In the opinion, not of bad men, but of the best men, no belief which is contrary to truth can be really useful; and can you prevent such men from urging that plea when they are charged with culpability for denying some doctrine which they are told is useful, but which they believe to be false? Those who are on the side of received opinions never fail to take all possible advantage of this plea; you do not find *them* handling the question of ability as if it could be completely abstracted from that of truth; on the contrary, it is, above all, because their doctrine is "the truth" that the knowledge or the belief of it is held to be so indispensable. There can be no fair discussion of the question of usefulness when an argument so vital may be employed on one side, but not on the other. And in point of fact, when law or public feeling do not permit the truth of an opinion to be disputed, they are just as little tolerant of a denial of its usefulness. The utmost they allow is an extenuation of its absolute necessity, or of the positive guilt of rejecting it.

In order more fully to illustrate the mischief of denying a hearing to opinions because we, in our own judgment, have condemned them, it will be desirable to fix down the discussion to a concrete case; and I choose, by preference, the cases which are least favorable to me—in which the argument against freedom of opinion, both on the score of truth and on that of utility, is considered the strongest. Let the opinions impugned be the belief in a God and in a future state, or any of the commonly received doctrines of morality. To fight the battle on such ground gives a great advantage to an unfair antagonist, since he will be sure to say (and many who have no desire to be unfair will say it internally), Are these the doctrines which you do not deem sufficiently certain to be taken under the protection of law? Is the belief in a God one of the opinions to feel sure of which you hold to be assuming infallibility? But I must be permitted to observe that it is not the feeling sure of a doctrine (be it what it may) which I call an assumption of infallibility. It is the undertaking to decide that question *for others*, without allowing them to hear what can be said on the contrary side. And I denounce and reprobate this pretension not the less if put forth on the side of my most solemn convictions. However positive anyone's persuasion may be, not only of the falsity but of the pernicious consequences—not only of the pernicious consequences, but (to adopt expressions which I

altogether condemn) the immorality and impiety of an opinion—yet if, in pursuance of that private judgment, though backed by the public judgment of his country or his contemporaries, he prevents the opinion from being heard in its defense, he assumes infallibility. And so far from the assumption being less objectionable or less dangerous because the opinion is called immoral or impious, this is the case of all others in which it is most fatal. These are exactly the occasions on which the men of one generation commit those dreadful mistakes which excite the astonishment and horror of posterity. It is among such that we find the instances memorable in history, when the arm of the law has been employed to root out the best men and the noblest doctrines; with deplorable success as to the men, though some of the doctrines have survived to be (as if in mockery) invoked in defense of similar conduct toward those who dissent from *them*, or from their received interpretation.

Mankind can hardly be too often reminded that there was once a man called Socrates, between whom and the legal authorities and public opinion of his time there took place a memorable collision. Born in an age and country abounding in individual greatness, this man has been handed down to us by those who best knew both him and the age as the most virtuous man in it; while *we* know him as the head and prototype of all subsequent teachers of virtue, the source equally of the lofty inspiration of Plato and the judicious utilitarianism of Aristotle, *"i maestri di color che sanno,"* the two headsprings of ethical as of all other philosophy. This acknowledged master of all the eminent thinkers who have since lived—whose fame, still growing after more than two thousand years, all but outweighs the whole remainder of the names which make his native city illustrious—was put to death by his countrymen, after a judicial conviction, for impiety and immorality. Impiety, in denying the gods recognized by the State; indeed, his accuser asserted (see the *Apologia*) that he believed in no gods at all. Immorality, in being, by his doctrines and instructions, a "corruptor of youth." Of these charges the tribunal, there is every ground for believing, honestly found him guilty, and condemned the man who probably of all then born had deserved best of mankind, to be put to death as a criminal.

To pass from this to the only other instance of judicial iniquity, the mention of which, after the condemnation of Socrates, would not be an anticlimax: the event which took place on Calvary rather more than eighteen hundred years ago. The man who left on the memory of those who witnessed his life and conversation such an impression of his moral grandeur that eighteen subsequent centuries have done homage to him as the Almighty in person, was ignominiously put to death, as what? As a blasphemer. Men did not merely mistake their benefactor, they mistook him for the exact contrary of what he was and treated him as that prodigy of impiety which they themselves are now held to be for their treatment of him. The feelings with which mankind now regard these lamentable transactions, especially the later of the two, render them extremely unjust in their judgment of the unhappy actors. These were, to all appearance, not bad men—not worse than men commonly are, but rather the contrary; men who possessed in a full, or somewhat more than a full measure, the religious, moral, and patriotic feelings of their time and people: the very kind of men who, in all times, our own included, have every chance of passing through life blameless and respected. The high priest who rent his garments when the words were pronounced, which, according to all the ideas of his country, constituted the blackest guilt, was in all probability quite as sincere in his horror and indignation as the generality of respectable and pious men now are in the religious and moral sentiments they profess; and most of those who now shudder at his conduct, if they had lived in his time, and been born Jews, would have acted precisely as he did. Orthodox Christians who are tempted to think that those who stoned to death the first martyrs must have been worse men than they themselves are, ought to remember that one of those persecutors was Saint Paul . . .

Let us now pass to the second division of the argument, and dismissing the supposition that any of the received opinions may be false, let us assume them to be true and examine into the worth of the manner in which they are likely to be held when their truth is not freely and openly canvassed. However unwillingly a person who has a strong opinion may admit the possibility that his opinion may be false, he ought to be moved by the consideration that, however true it may be, if it is not fully, frequently, and fearlessly discussed, it will be held as a dead dogma, not a living truth.

There is a class of persons (happily not quite so numerous as formerly) who think it enough if a person assents undoubtingly to what they think true, though he has no knowledge whatever of the grounds of the opinion and could not make a tenable defense of it against the most superficial objections. Such persons, if they can once get their creed taught from authority, naturally think that no good, and some harm, comes of its being allowed to be questioned. Where their influence prevails, they make it nearly impossible for the received opinion to be rejected wisely and considerately, though it may still be rejected rashly and ignorantly; for to shut out discussion entirely is seldom possible, and when it once gets in, beliefs not grounded on conviction are apt to give way before the slightest semblance of an argument. Waiving, however, this possibility—assuming that the true opinion abides in the mind, but abides as a prejudice, a belief independent of, and proof against, argument—this is not the way in which truth ought to be held by a rational being. This is not knowing the truth. Truth, thus held, is but one superstition the more, accidentally clinging to the words which enunciate a truth.

If the intellect and judgment of mankind ought to be cultivated, a thing which Protestants at least do not deny, on what can these faculties be more appropriately exercised by anyone than on the things which concern him so much that is it considered necessary for him to hold opinions on them? If the cultivation of the understanding consists in one thing more than in another, it is surely in learning the grounds of one's own opinions. Whatever people believe, on subjects on which it is of the first importance to believe rightly, they ought to be able to defend against at least the common objections. But, someone may say, "Let them be *taught* the grounds of their opinions. It does not follow that opinions must be merely parroted because they are never heard controverted. Persons who learn geometry do not simply commit the theorems to memory, but understand and learn likewise the demonstrations; and it would be absurd to say that they remain ignorant of the grounds of geometrical truths because they never hear anyone deny and attempt to disprove them." Undoubtedly: and such teaching suffices on a subject like mathematics, where there is nothing at all to be said on the wrong side of the question. The peculiarity of the evidence of mathematical truths is that all the argument is on one side. There are no objections, and no answers to objections. But on every subject on which difference of opinion is possible, the truth depends on a balance to be struck between two sets of conflicting reasons. Even in natural philosophy, there is always some other explanation possible of the same facts; some geocentric theory instead of heliocentric, some phlogiston instead of oxygen; and it has to be shown why that other theory cannot be the true one; and until this is shown, and until we know how it is shown, we do not understand the grounds of our opinion. But when we turn to subjects infinitely more complicated, to morals, religion, politics, social relations, and the business of life, three-fourths of the arguments for every disputed opinion consist in dispelling the appearances which favor some opinion different from it. The greatest orator, save one, of antiquity, has left it on record that he always studied his adversary's case with as great, if not still greater, intensity than even his own. What Cicero practiced as the means of forensic success requires to be imitated by all who study any subject in order to arrive at the truth. He who knows only his own side of the case knows little of that. His reasons may be good, and no one may have been able to

refute them. But if he is equally unable to refute the reasons on the opposite side, if he does not so much as know what they are, he has no ground for preferring either opinion. The rational position for him would be suspension of judgment, and unless he contents himself with that, he is either led by authority or adopts, like the generality of the world, the side to which he feels most inclination. Nor is it enough that he should hear the arguments of adversaries from his own teachers, presented as they state them, and accompanied by what they offer as refutations. That is not the way to do justice to the arguments or bring them into real contact with his own mind. He must be able to hear them from persons who actually believe them, who defend them in earnest and do their very utmost for them. He must know them in their most plausible and persuasive form; he must feel the whole force of the difficulty which the true view of the subject has to encounter and dispose of, else he will never really possess himself of the portion of truth which meets and removes that difficulty. Ninety-nine in a hundred of what are called educated men are in this condition, even of those who can argue fluently for their opinions. Their conclusion may be true, but it might be false for anything they know; they have never thrown themselves into the mental position of those who think differently from them, and considered what such persons may have to say; and, consequently, they do not, in any proper sense of the word, know the doctrine which they themselves profess. They do not know those parts of it which explain and justify the remainder—the considerations which show that a fact which seemingly conflicts with another is reconcilable with it, or that, of two apparently strong reasons, one and not the other ought to be preferred. All that part of the truth which turns the scale and decides the judgment of a completely informed mind, they are strangers to; nor is it ever really known but to those who have attended equally and impartially to both sides and endeavored to see the reasons of both in the strongest light. So essential is this discipline to a real understanding of moral and human subjects that, if opponents of all-important truths do not exist, it is indispensable to imagine them and supply them with the strongest arguments which the most skillful devil's advocate can conjure up. . . .

It still remains to speak of one of the principal causes which make diversity of opinion advantageous, and will continue to do so until mankind shall have entered a stage of intellectual advancement which at present seems at an incalculable distance. We have hitherto considered only two possibilities: that the received opinion may be false, and some other opinion, consequently, true; or that, the received opinion being true, a conflict with the opposite error is essential to a clear apprehension and deep feeling of its truth. But there is a commoner case than either of these: when the conflicting doctrines, instead of being one true and the other false, share the truth between them, and the nonconforming opinion is needed to supply the remainder of the truth of which the received doctrine embodies only a part. Popular opinions, on subjects not palpable to sense, are often true, but seldom or never the whole truth. They are a part of the truth, sometimes a greater, sometimes a smaller part, but exaggerated, distorted, and disjointed from the truths by which they ought to be accompanied and limited. Heretical opinions, on the other hand, are generally some of these suppressed and neglected truths, bursting the bonds which kept them down, and either seeking reconciliation with the truth contained in the common opinion, or fronting it as enemies, and setting themselves up, with similar exclusiveness, as the whole truth. The latter case is hitherto the most frequent, as, in the human mind, one-sidedness has always been the rule, and many-sidedness the exception. Hence, even in revolutions of opinion, one part of the truth usually sets while another rises. Even progress, which ought to superadd, for the most part only substitutes one partial and incomplete truth for another; improvement consisting chiefly in this, that the new fragment of truth is more wanted, more adapted to the needs of the time than that which it displaces. Such being the partial character of prevailing opinions, even

when resting on a true foundation, every opinion which embodies somewhat of the portion of truth which the common opinion omits ought to be considered precious, with whatever amount of error and confusion that truth may be blended. No sober judge of human affairs will feel bound to be indignant because those who force on our notice truths which we should otherwise have overlooked, overlook some of those which we see. Rather, he will think that so long as popular truth is one-sided, it is more desirable than otherwise that unpopular truth should have one-sided assertors, too, such being usually the most energetic and the most likely to compel reluctant attention to the fragment of wisdom which they proclaim as if it were the whole.

Thus, in the eighteenth century, when nearly all the instructed, and all those of the uninstructed who were led by them, were lost in admiration of what is called civilization, and of the marvels of modern science, literature, and philosophy, and while greatly overrating the amount of unlikeness between the men of modern and those of ancient times, indulged the belief that the whole of the difference was in their own favor; with what a salutary shock did the paradoxes of Rousseau explode like bombshells in the midst, dislocating the compact mass of one-sided opinion and forcing its elements to recombine in a better form and with additional ingredients. Not that the current opinions were on the whole farther from the truth than Rousseau's were; on the contrary, they were nearer to it; they contained more of positive truth, and very much less of error. Nevertheless there lay in Rousseau's doctrine, and has floated down the stream of opinion along with it, a considerable amount of exactly those truths which the popular opinion wanted; and these are the deposit which was left behind them when the flood subsided. The superior worth of simplicity of life, the enervating and demoralizing effect of the trammels and hypocrisies of artificial society are ideas which have never been entirely absent from cultivated minds since Rousseau wrote; and they will in time produce their due effect, though at present needing to be asserted as much as ever, and to be asserted by deeds; for words, on this subject, have nearly exhausted their power.

In politics, again, it is almost a commonplace that a party of order or stability and a party of progress or reform are both necessary elements of a healthy state of political life, until the one or the other shall have so enlarged its mental grasp as to be a party equally of order and of progress, knowing and distinguishing what is fit to be preserved from what ought to be swept away. Each of these modes of thinking derives its utility from the deficiencies of the other; but it is in a great measure the opposition of the other that keeps each within the limits of reason and sanity. Unless opinions favorable to democracy and to aristocracy, to property and to equality, to co-operation and to competition, to luxury and to abstinence, to sociality and individuality, to liberty and discipline, and all the other standing antagonisms of practical life, are expressed with equal freedom and enforced and defended with equal talent and energy, there is no chance of both elements obtaining their due; one scale is sure to go up, and the other down. Truth, in the great practical concerns of life, is so much a question of the reconciling and combining of opposites that very few have minds sufficiently capacious and impartial to make the adjustment with an approach to correctness, and it has to be made by the rough process of a struggle between combatants fighting under hostile banners. On any of the great open questions just enumerated, if either of the two opinions has a better claim than the other, not merely to be tolerated, but to be encouraged and countenanced, it is the one which happens at the particular time and place to be in a minority. That is the opinion which, for the time being, represents the neglected interests, the side of human well-being which is in danger of obtaining less than its share. I am aware that there is not, in this country, any intolerance of differences of opinion on most of these topics. They are adduced to show, by admitted and multiplied examples, the universality of the fact that only through diversity of opinion is there, in the existing state of human intellect, a chance of fair play to all sides of the truth. When there are persons to be found who form an exception to the apparent unanimity of the world on any subject, even if the world is in the right, it is always probable that dissentients have something worth hearing to say for themselves, and that truth would lose something by their silence.

It may be objected, "But *some* received principles, especially on the highest and most vital subjects, are more than half-truths. The Christian morality, for instance, is the whole truth on that subject, and if anyone teaches a morality which varies from it, he is wholly in error." As this is of all cases the most important in practice, none can be fitter to test the general maxim. But before pronouncing what Christian morality is or is not, it would be desirable to decide what is meant by Christian morality. If it means the morality of the New Testament, I wonder that any one who derives his knowledge of this from the book itself can suppose that it was announced, or intended, as a complete doctrine of morals. The Gospel always refers to a preexisting morality and confines its precepts to the particulars in which that morality was to be corrected or superseded by a wider and higher, expressing itself, moreover, in terms most general, often impossible to be interpreted literally, and possessing rather the impressiveness of poetry or eloquence than the precision of legislation. To extract from it a body of ethical doctrine has never been possible without eking it out from the Old Testament, that is, from a system elaborate indeed, but in many respects barbarous, and intended only for a barbarous people. St. Paul, a declared enemy to this Judaical mode of interpreting the doctrine and filling up the scheme of his Master, equally assumes a pre-existing morality, namely that of the Greeks and Romans; and his advice to Christians is in a great measure a system of accommodation to that, even to the extent of giving an apparent sanction to slavery. What is called Christian, but should rather be termed theological, morality was not the work of Christ or the Apostles, but is of much later origin, having been gradually built up by the Catholic Church of the first five centuries, and though not implicitly adopted by moderns and Protestants, has been much less modified by them than might have been expected. For the most part, indeed, they have contented themselves with cutting off the additions which had been made to it in the Middle Ages, each sect supplying the place by fresh additions, adapted to its own character and tendencies. That mankind owe a great debt to this morality, and to its early teachers, I should be the last person to deny, but I do not scruple to say of it that it is, in many important points, incomplete and one-sided, and that, unless ideas and feelings not sanctioned by it had contributed to the formation of European life and character, human affairs would have been in a worse condition than they now are. Christian morality (so called) has all the characters of a reaction; it is, in great part, a protest against paganism. Its ideal is negative rather than positive; passive rather than active; innocence rather than nobleness; abstinence from evil rather than energetic pursuit of good; in its precepts (as has been well said) "thou shalt not" predominates unduly over "though shalt." In its horror of sensuality, it made an idol of asceticism which has been gradually compromised away into one of legality. It holds out the hope of heaven and the threat of hell as the appointed and appropriate motives to a virtuous life: in this falling far below the best of the ancients, and doing what lies in it to give to human morality an essentially selfish character, by disconnecting each man's feelings of duty from the interests of his fellow creatures, except so far as a self-interested inducement is offered to him for consulting them. It is essentially a doctrine of passive obedience; it inculcates submission to all authorities found established; who indeed are not to be actively obeyed when they command what religion forbids, but who are not to be resisted, far less rebelled against, for any amount of wrong to ourselves. And while, in the morality of the best pagan nations, duty to the State holds even a disproportionate place, infringing on the just liberty of the individua in purely Christian ethics that

grand department of duty is scarcely noticed or acknowledged. It is in the Koran, not the New Testament, that we read the maxim: "A ruler who appoints any man to an office, when there is in his dominions another man better qualified for it, sins against God and against the State." What little recognition the idea of obligation to the public obtains in modern morality is derived from Greek and Roman sources, not from Christian; as, even in the morality of private life, whatever exists of magnanimity, high-mindedness, personal dignity, even the sense of honor, is derived from the purely human, not the religious part of our education, and never could have grown out of a standard of ethics in which the only worth, professedly recognized, is that of obedience.

I am as far as anyone from pretending that these defects are necessarily inherent in the Christian ethics in every manner in which it can be conceived, or that the many requisites of a complete moral doctrine which it does not contain do not admit of being reconciled with it. Far less would I insinuate this out of the doctrines and precepts of Christ himself. I believe that the sayings of Christ are all that I can see any evidence of their having been intended to be; that they are irreconcilable with nothing which a comprehensive morality requires; that everything which is excellent in ethics may be brought within them, with no greater violence to their language than has been done to it by all who have attempted to deduce from them any practical system of conduct whatever. But it is quite consistent with this to believe that they contain, and were meant to contain, only a part of the truth; that many essential elements of the highest morality are among the things which are not provided for, nor intended to be provided for, in the recorded deliverances of the Founder of Christianity, and which have been entirely thrown aside in the system of ethics erected on the basis of those deliverances by the Christian Church. And this being so, I think it a great error to persist in attempting to find in the Christian doctrine that complete rule for our guidance which its Author intended it to sanction and enforce, but only partially to provide. I believe, too, that this narrow theory is becoming a grave practical evil, detracting greatly from the moral training and instruction which so many well-meaning persons are now at length exerting themselves to promote. I much fear that by attempting to form the mind and feelings on an exclusively religious type, and discarding those secular standards (as for want of a better name they may be called) which heretofore coexisted with and supplemented the Christian ethics, receiving some of its spirits, and infusing into it some of theirs, there will result, and is even now resulting, a low, abject, servile type of character which, submit itself as it may to what it deems the Supreme Will, is incapable of rising to or sympathizing in the conception of Supreme Goodness. I believe that other ethics than any which can be evolved from exclusively Christian sources must exist side by side with Christian ethics to produce the moral regeneration of mankind; and that the Christian system is no exception to the rule that in an imperfect state of the human mind the interests of truth require a diversity of opinions. It is not necessary that in ceasing to ignore the moral truths not contained in Christianity men should ignore any of those which it does contain. Such prejudice or oversight, when it occurs, is altogether an evil, but it is one from which we cannot hope to be always exempt, and must be regarded as the price paid for an inestimable good. The exclusive pretension made by a part of the truth to be the whole must and ought to be protested against; and if a reactionary impulse should make the protestors unjust in their turn, this one-sidedness, like the other, may be lamented but must be tolerated. If Christians would teach infidels to be just to Christianity, they should themselves be just to infidelity. It can do truth no service to blink the fact, known to all who have the most ordinary acquaintance with literary history, that a large portion of the noblest and most valuable moral teaching has been the work, not only of men who did not know, but of men who knew and rejected, the Christian faith.

I do not pretend that the most unlimited use of the freedom of enunciating all possible opinions would put an end to the evils of religious or philosophical sectarianism. Every truth which men of narrow capacity are in earnest about is sure to be asserted, inculcated, and in many ways even acted on, as if no other truth existed in the world, or at all events none that could limit or qualify the first. I acknowledge that the tendency of all opinions to become sectarian is not cured by the freest discussion, but is often heightened and exacerbated thereby; the truth which ought to have been, but was not, seen, being rejected all the more violently because proclaimed by persons regarded as opponents. But it is not on the impassioned partisan, it is on the calmer and more disinterested bystander, that this collision of opinions works its salutary effect. Not the violent conflict between parts of the truth, but the quiet suppression of half of it, is the formidable evil; there is always hope when people are forced to listen to both sides; it is when they attend only to one that errors harden into prejudices, and truth itself ceases to have the effect of truth by being exaggerated into falsehood. And since there are few mental attributes more rare than that judicial faculty which can sit in intelligent judgment between two sides of a question, of which only one is represented by an advocate before it, truth has no chance but in proportion as every side of it, every opinion which embodies any fraction of the truth, not only finds advocates, but is so advocated as to be listened to.

We have now recognized the necessity to the mental well-being of mankind (on which all their other well-being depends) of freedom of opinion, and freedom of the expression of opinion, on four distinct grounds, which we will now briefly recapitulate:

First, if any opinion is compelled to silence, that opinion may, for aught we can certainly know, be true. To deny this is to assume our own infallibility.

Secondly, though the silenced opinion be an error, it may, and very commonly does, contain a portion of truth; and since the general or prevailing opinion on any subject is rarely or never the whole truth, it is only by the collision of adverse opinions that the remainder of the truth has any chance of being supplied.

Thirdly, even if the received opinion be not only true, but the whole truth; unless it is suffered to be, and actually is, vigorously and earnestly contested, it will, by most of those who receive it, be held in the manner of a prejudice, with little comprehension or feeling of its rational grounds. And not only this, but, fourthly, the meaning of the doctrine itself will be in danger of being lost or enfeebled, and deprived of its vital effect on the character and conduct: the dogma becoming a mere formal profession, inefficacious for good, but cumbering the ground and preventing the growth of any real and heartfelt conviction from reason or personal experience.

Before quitting the subject of freedom of opinion, it is fit to take some notice of those who say that the free expression of all opinions should be permitted on condition that the manner be temperate, and do not pass the bounds of fair discussion. Much might be said on the impossibility of fixing where these supposed bounds are to be placed; for if the test be offense to those whose opinions are attacked, I think experience testifies that this offense is given whenever the attack is telling and powerful, and that every opponent who pushes them hard, and whom they find it difficult to answer, appears to them, if he shows any strong feeling on the subject, an intemperate opponent. But this, though an important consideration in a practical point of view, merges in a more fundamental objection. Undoubtedly, the manner of asserting an opinion, even though it be a true one, may be very objectionable and may justly incur severe censure. But the principal offenses of the kind are such as it is mostly impossible, unless by accidental self-betrayal, to bring home to conviction. The gravest of them is, to argue sophistically, to suppress facts or arguments, to misstate the elements of the case, or misrepresent the opposite opinion. But all this, even to the most aggravated degree, is so continually done in perfect good faith by persons who are not considered, and in many other respects may not deserve to be considered, ignorant or incompetent, that it is rarely possible, on adequate grounds, conscientiously to stamp the misrepresentation as morally culpable, and still less could law presume to interfere with this kind of controversial misconduct. With regard to what is commonly meant by intemperate discussion, namely invective, sarcasm, personality, and the like, the denunciation of these weapons would deserve more sympathy if it were ever proposed to interdict them equally to both sides; but it is only desired to restrain the employment of them against the prevailing opinion; against the unprevailing they may not only be used without general disapproval, but will be likely to obtain for him who uses them the praise of honest zeal and righteous indignation. Yet whatever mischief arises from their use is greatest when they are employed against the comparatively defenseless; and whatever unfair advantage can be derived by any opinion from this mode of asserting it accrues almost exclusively to received opinions. The worst offense of this kind which can be committed by a polemic is to stigmatize those who hold the contrary opinion as bad and immoral men. To calumny of this sort, those who hold any unpopular opinion are peculiarly exposed, because they are in general few and uninfluential, and nobody but themselves feels much interested in seeing justice done them; but this weapon is, from the nature of the case, denied to those who attack a prevailing opinion: they can neither use it with safety to themselves, nor, if they could, would it do anything but recoil on their own cause. In general, opinions contrary to those commonly received can only obtain a hearing by studied moderation of language and the most cautious avoidance of unnecessary offense, from which they hardly ever deviate even in a slight degree without losing ground, while unmeasured vituperation employed on the side of the prevailing opinion really does deter people from professing contrary opinions and from listening to those who profess them. For the interest, therefore, of truth and justice it is far more important to restrain this employment of vituperative language than the other; and, for example, if it were necessary to choose, there would be much more need to discourage offensive attacks on infidelity than on religion. It is, however, obvious that law and authority have no business with restraining either, while opinion ought, in every instance, to determine its verdict by the circumstances of the individual case—condemning everyone, on whichever side of the argument he places himself, in whose mode of advocacy either want of candor, or malignity, bigotry, or intolerance of feeling manifest themselves; but not inferring these vices from the side which a person takes, though it be the contrary side of the question to our own; and giving merited honor to everyone, whatever opinion he may hold, who has calmness to see and honesty to state what his opponents and their opinions really are, exaggerating nothing to their discredit, keeping nothing back which tells, or can be supposed to tell, in their favor. This is the real morality of public discussion; and if often violated, I am happy to think that there are many controversialists who to a great extent observe it, and a still greater number who conscientiously strive toward it.

CHAPTER III

Of Individuality, as One of the Elements of Well-Being

Such being the reasons which make it imperative that human beings should be free to form opinions and to express their opinions without reserve; and such the baneful consequences to the intellectual, and through that to the moral nature of man, unless this liberty is either conceded or asserted in spite of prohibition; let us next examine whether the same reasons do not require that men should be free to act upon their opinions—to carry these out in their lives without hindrance, either physical or moral, from their fellow men, so long as it is at their own risk and peril. This last proviso is of course indispensable. No one pretends that actions should be as free as opinions. On the contrary, even opinions lose their immunity when the circumstances in which they are expressed are such

as to constitute their expression a positive instigation to some mischievous act. An opinion that corn dealers are starvers of the poor, or that private property is robbery, ought to be unmolested when simply circulated through the press, but may justly incur punishment when delivered orally to an excited mob assembled before the house of a corn dealer, or when handed about among the same mob in the form of a placard. Acts, of whatever kind, which without justifiable cause do harm to others may be, and in the more important cases absolutely require to be, controlled by the unfavorable sentiments, and, when needful, by the active interference of mankind. The liberty of the individual must be thus far limited; he must not make himself a nuisance to other people. But if he refrains from molesting others in what concerns them, and merely acts according to his own inclination and judgment in things which concern himself, the same reasons which show that opinion should be free prove also that he should be allowed, without molestation, to carry his opinions into practice at his own cost. That mankind are not infallible; that their truths, for the most part, are only half-truths; that unity of opinion, unless resulting from the fullest and freest comparison of opposite opinions, is not desirable, and diversity not an evil, but a good, until mankind are much more capable than at present of recognizing all sides of the truth, are principles applicable to men's modes of action not less than to their opinions. As it is useful that while mankind are imperfect there should be different opinions, so it is that there should be different experiments of living; that free scope should be given to varieties of character, short of injury to others; and that the worth of different modes of life should be proved practically, when anyone thinks fit to try them. It is desirable, in short, that in things which do not primarily concern others individuality should assert itself. Where not the person's own character but the traditions or customs of other people are the rule of conduct, there is wanting one of the principal ingredients of human happiness, and quite the chief ingredient of individual and social progress. . . .

The Subjection of Women

CHAPTER I

The object of this Essay is to explain, as clearly as I am able, the grounds of an opinion which I have held from the very earliest period when I had formed any opinions at all on social or political matters, and which, instead of being weakened or modified, has been constantly growing stronger by the progress of reflection and the experience of life: That the principle which regulates the existing social relations between the two sexes—the legal subordination of one sex to the other—is wrong in itself, and now one of the chief hindrances to human improvement; and that it ought to be replaced by a principle of perfect equality, admitting no power or privilege on the one side, nor disability on the other. . . .

The generality of a practice is in some cases a strong presumption that it is, or at all events once was, conducive to laudable ends. This is the case, when the practice was first adopted, or afterwards kept up, as a means to such ends, and was grounded on experience of the mode in which they could be most effectually attained. If the authority of men over women, when first established, had been the result of a conscientious comparison between different modes of constituting the government of society; if, after trying various other modes of social organization—the government of women over men, equality between the two, and such mixed and divided modes of government as might be invented—it had been decided, on the testimony of experience, that the mode in which women are wholly under the rule of men, having no share at all in public concerns, and each in private being under the legal obligation of obedience to the man with whom she has associated her destiny, was the arrangement most conducive to

the happiness and well-being of both; its general adoption might then be fairly thought to be some evidence that, at the time when it was adopted, it was the best: though even then the considerations which recommended it may, like so many other primeval social facts of the greatest importance, have subsequently, in the course of ages, ceased to exist. But the state of the case is in every respect the reverse of this. In the first place, the opinion in favour of the present system, which entirely subordinates the weaker sex to the stronger, rests upon theory only; for there never has been trial made of any other: so that experience, in the sense in which it is vulgarly opposed to theory, cannot be pretended to have pronounced any verdict. And in the second place, the adoption of this system of inequality never was the result of deliberation, or forethought, or any social ideas, or any notion whatever of what conduced to the benefit of humanity or the good order of society. It arose simply from the fact that from the very earliest twilight of human society, every woman (owing to the value attached to her by men, combined with her inferiority in muscular strength) was found in a state of bondage to some man. Laws and systems of polity always begin by recognizing the relations they find already existing between individuals. They convert what was a mere physical fact into a legal right, give it the sanction of society, and principally aim at the substitution of public and organized means of asserting and protecting these rights, instead of the irregular and lawless conflict of physical strength. Those who had already been compelled to obedience became in this manner legally bound to it. Slavery, from being a mere affair of force between the master and the slave, became regularized and a matter of compact among the masters, who, binding themselves to one another for common protection, guaranteed by their collective strength the private possessions of each, including his slaves. In early times, the great majority of the male sex were slaves, as well as the whole of the female. And many ages elapsed, some of them ages of high cultivation, before any thinker was bold enough to question the rightfulness, and the absolute social necessity, either of the one slavery or of the other. By degrees such thinkers did arise: and (the general progress of society assisting) the slavery of the male sex has, in all the countries of Christian Europe at least (though, in one of them, only within the last few years) been at length abolished, and that of the female sex has been gradually changed into a milder form of dependence. But this dependence, as it exists at present, is not an original institution, taking a fresh start from considerations of justice and social expediency— it is the primitive state of slavery lasting on, through successive mitigations and modifications occasioned by the same causes which have softened the general manners, and brought all human relations more under the control of justice and the influence of humanity. It has not lost the taint of its brutal origin. No presumption in its favour, therefore, can be drawn from the fact of its existence. The only such presumption which it could be supposed to have, must be grounded on its having lasted till now, when so many other things which came down from the same odious source have been done away with. And this, indeed, is what makes it strange to ordinary ears, to hear it asserted that the inequality of rights between men and women has no other source than the law of the strongest. . . .

But, it will be said, the rule of men over women differs from all these others in not being a rule of force: it is accepted voluntarily; women make no complaint, and are consenting parties to it. In the first place, a great number of women do not accept it. Ever since there have been women able to make their sentiments known by their writings (the only mode of publicity which society permits to them), an increasing number of them have recorded protests against their present social condition: and recently many thousands of them,

headed by the most eminent women known to the public, have petitioned Parliament for their admission to the Parliamentary Suffrage. The claim of women to be educated as solidly, and in the same branches of knowledge, as men, is urged with growing intensity, and with a great prospect of success; while the demand for their admission into professions and occupations hitherto closed against them, becomes every year more urgent. Though there are not in this country, as there are in the United States, periodical Conventions and an organized party to agitate for the Rights of Women, there is a numerous and active Society organized and managed by women, for the more limited object of obtaining the political franchise. Nor is it only in our own country and in America that women are beginning to protest, more or less collectively, against the disabilities under which they labour. France, and Italy, and Switzerland, and Russia now afford examples of the same thing. How many more women there are who silently cherish similar aspirations, no one can possibly know; but there are abundant tokens how many *would* cherish them, were they not so strenuously taught to repress them as contrary to the proprieties of their sex. It must be remembered, also, that no enslaved class ever asked for complete liberty at once. When Simon de Montfort called the deputies of the commons to sit for the first time in Parliament, did any of them dream of demanding that an assembly, elected by their constituents, should make and destroy ministries, and dictate to the king in affairs of State? No such thought entered into the imagination of the most ambitious of them. The nobility had already these pretensions; the commons pretended to nothing but to be exempt from arbitrary taxation, and from the gross individual oppression of the king's officers. It is a political law of nature that those who are under any power of ancient origin never begin by complaining of the power itself, but only of its oppressive exercise. There is never any want of women who complain of ill usage by their husbands. There would be infinitely more, if complaint were not the greatest of all provocatives to a repetition and increase of the ill usage. It is this which frustrates all attempts to maintain the power but protect the woman against its abuses. In no other case (except that of a child) is the person who has been proved judicially to have suffered an injury, replaced under the physical power of the culprit who inflicted it. Accordingly wives, even in the most extreme and protracted cases of bodily ill usage, hardly ever dare avail themselves of the laws made for their protection: and if, in a moment of irrepressible indignation, or by the interference of neighbours, they are induced to do so, their whole effort afterwards is to disclose as little as they can, and to beg off their tyrant from his merited chastisement.

All causes, social and natural, combine to make it unlikely that women should be collectively rebellious to the power of men. They are so far in a position different from all other subject classes, that their masters require something more from them than actual service. Men do not want solely the obedience of women, they want their sentiments. All men, except the most brutish, desire to have, in the woman most nearly connected with them, not a forced slave but a willing one; not a slave merely, but a favourite. They have therefore put everything in practice to enslave their minds. The masters of all other slaves rely, for maintaining obedience, on fear; either fear of themselves, or religious fears. The masters of women wanted more than simple obedience, and they turned the whole force of education to effect their purpose. All women are brought up from the very earliest years in the belief that their ideal of character is the very opposite to that of men; not self-will, and government by self-control, but submission, and yielding to the control of others. All the moralities tell them that it is the duty of women, and all the current sentimentalities that it is their nature, to live for others; to make complete abnegation of themselves, and to have no life but in their affections. And by their affections are meant the only ones they are allowed to have—those to the men with whom they are connected, or to the children who constitute an additional and indefeasible tie between them and a man. When we put together three things—first, the natural attraction between opposite sexes; secondly, the wife's entire dependence on the husband, every privilege or pleasure she has being either his gift, or depending entirely on his will; and lastly, that the principal object of human pursuit, consideration, and all objects of social ambition, can in general be sought or obtained by her only through him—it would be a miracle if the object of being attractive to men had not become the polar star of feminine education and formation of character. And, this great means of influence over the minds of women having been acquired, an instinct of selfishness made man avail themselves of it to the utmost as a means of holding women in subjection, by representing to them meekness, submissiveness, and resignation of all individual will into the hands of a man, as an essential part of sexual attractiveness. Can it be doubted that any of the other yokes which mankind have succeeded in breaking, would have subsisted till now if the same means had existed, and had been as sedulously used, to bow down their minds to it? . . .

Neither does it avail anything to say that the *nature* of the two sexes adapts them to their present functions and position, and renders these appropriate to them. Standing on the ground of common sense and the constitution of the human mind, I deny that any one knows, or can know, the nature of the two sexes, as long as they have only been seen in their present relation to one another. If men had ever been found in society without women, or women without men, or if there had been a society of men and women in which the women were not under the control of the men, something might have been positively known about the mental and moral differences which may be inherent in the nature of each. What is now called the nature of women is an eminently artificial thing—the result of forced repression in some directions, unnatural stimulation in others. It may be asserted without scruple, that no other class of dependents have had their character so entirely distorted from its natural proportions by their relation with their masters; for, if conquered and slave races have been, in some respects, more forcibly repressed, whatever in them has not been crushed down by an iron heel has generally been let alone, and if left with any liberty of development, it has developed itself according to its own laws; but in the case of women, a hothouse and stove cultivation has always been carried on of some of the capabilities of their nature, for the benefit and pleasure of their masters. Then, because certain products of the general vital force sprout luxuriantly and reach a great development in this heated atmosphere and under this active nurture and watering, while other shoots from the same root, which are left outside in the wintry air, with ice purposely heaped all round them, have a stunted growth, and some are burnt off with fire and disappear; men, with that inability to recognize their own work which distinguishes the unanalytic mind, indolently believe that the tree grows of itself in the way they have made it grow, and that it would die if one half of it were not kept in a vapour bath and the other half in the snow . . .

The general opinion of men is supposed to be, that the natural vocation of a woman is that of a wife and mother. I say, is supposed to be, because, judging from acts—from the whole of the present constitution of society—one might infer that their opinion was the direct contrary. They might be supposed to think that the alleged natural vocation of women was of all things the most repugnant to their nature; insomuch that if they are free to do anything else—if any other means of living, or occupation of their time and faculties, is open, which has any chance of appearing desirable to them—there will not be enough of them who will be willing to accept the condition said to be natural to them. If this is the real opinion of men in general, it would be well that it should be spoken out. I should like to hear somebody openly enunciating the doctrine (it is already implied in much that is written on the subject)—"It is necessary to society that women should marry and produce children. They will not do so unless they are compelled. Therefore it is necessary to compel them." The merits of the case would then be clearly defined. It would be exactly that of the slaveholders of South Carolina and Louisiana. "It is necessary that cotton and

sugar should be grown. White men cannot produce them. Negroes will not, for any wages which we choose to give. *Ergo* they must be compelled." . . .

CHAPTER II

It will be well to commence the detailed discussion of the subject by the particular branch of it to which the course of our observations has led us: the conditions which the laws of this and all other countries annex to the marriage contract. Marriage being the destination appointed by society for women, the prospect they are brought up to, and the object which it is intended should be sought by all of them, except those who are too little attractive to be chosen by any man as his companion; one might have supposed that everything would have been done to make this condition as eligible to them as possible, that they might have no cause to regret being denied the option of any other. Society, however, both in this, and, at first, in all other cases, has preferred to attain its object by foul rather than fair means: but this is the only case in which it has substantially persisted in them even to the present day. Originally women were taken by force, or regularly sold by their father to the husband. Until a late period in European history, the father had the power to dispose of his daughter in marriage at his own will and pleasure, without any regard to hers. The Church, indeed, was so far faithful to a better morality as to require a formal "yes" from the woman at the marriage ceremony; but there was nothing to show that the consent was other than compulsory; and it was practically impossible for the girl to refuse compliance if the father persevered, except perhaps when she might obtain the protection of religion by a determined resolution to take monastic vows. After marriage, the man had anciently (but this was anterior to Christianity) the power of life and death over his wife. She could invoke no law against him; he was her sole tribunal and law. For a long time he could repudiate her, but she had no corresponding power in regard to him. By the old laws of England, the husband was called the *lord* of the wife; he was literally regarded as her sovereign, inasmuch that the murder of a man by his wife was called treason *(petty* as distinguished from *high* treason), and was more cruelly avenged than was usually the case with high treason, for the penalty was burning to death. Because these various enormities have fallen into disuse (for most of them were never formally abolished, or not until they had long ceased to be practised) men suppose that all is now as it should be in regard to the marriage contract; and we are continually told that civilization and Christianity have restored to the woman her just rights. Meanwhile the wife is the actual bond-servant of her husband: no less so, as far as legal obligation goes, than slaves commonly so called. She vows a lifelong obedience to him at the altar, and is held to it all through her life by law. Casuists may say that the obligation of obedience stops short of participation in crime, but it certainly extends to everything else. She can do no act whatever but by his permission, at least tacit. She can acquire no property but for him; the instant it becomes hers, even if by inheritance, it becomes *ipso facto* his. In this respect the wife's position under the common law of England is worse than that of slaves in the laws of many countries: by the Roman law, for example, a slave might have his peculium, which to a certain extent the law guaranteed to him for his exclusive use. The higher classes in this country have given an analogous advantage to their women, through special contracts setting aside the law, by conditions of pin-money, &c.: since parental feeling being stronger with fathers than the class feeling of their own sex, a father generally prefers his own daughter to a son-in-law who is a stranger to him. By means of settlements, the rich usually contrive to withdraw the whole or part of the inherited property of the wife from the absolute control of the husband: but they do not succeed in keeping it under her own control; the utmost they can do only prevents the husband from squandering it, at the same time debarring the rightful owner from its use. The property itself is out of the reach of both; and as to the income derived from it, the form of settlement most favourable to the wife (that called "to her separate use") only precludes the husband from receiving it instead of her: it must pass through her hands, but if he takes it from her by personal violence as soon as she receives it, he can neither be punished, nor compelled to restitution. This is the amount of the protection which, under the laws of this country, the most powerful nobleman can give his own daughter as respects her husband. In the immense majority of cases there is no settlement: and the absorption of all rights, all property, as well as all freedom of action, is complete. The two are called "one person in law," for the purpose of inferring that whatever is hers is his, but the parallel inference is never drawn that whatever is his is hers; the maxim is not applied against the man, except to make him responsible to third parties for her acts, as a master is for the acts of his slaves or of his cattle. I am far from pretending that wives are in general no better treated than slaves; but no slave is a slave to the same lengths, and in so full a sense of the word, as a wife is. Hardly any slave, except one immediately attached to the master's person, is a slave at all hours and all minutes; in general he has, like a soldier, his fixed task, and when it is done, or when he is off duty, he disposes, within certain limits, of his own time, and has a family life into which the master rarely intrudes. "Uncle Tom" under his first master had his own life in his "cabin," almost as much as any man whose work takes him away from home, is able to have in his own family. But it cannot be so with the wife. Above all, a female slave has (in Christian countries) an admitted right, and is considered under a moral obligation, to refuse to her master the last familiarity. Not so the wife: however brutal a tyrant she may unfortunately be chained to—though she may know that he hates her, though it may be his daily pleasure to torture her, and though she may feel it impossible not to loathe him—he can claim from her and enforce the lowest degradation of a human being, that of being made the instrument of an animal function contrary to her inclinations. While she is held in this worst description of slavery as to her own person, what is her position in regard to the children in whom she and her master have a joint interest? They are by law his children. He alone has any legal rights over them. Not one act can she do towards or in relation to them, except by delegation from him. Even after he is dead she is not their legal guardian, unless he by will has made her so. He could even send them away from her, and deprive her of the means of seeing or corresponding with them, until this power was in some degree restricted by Serjeant Talfourd's Act. This is her legal state. And from this state she has no means of withdrawing herself. If she leaves her husband, she can take nothing with her, neither her children nor anything which is rightfully her own. If he chooses, he can compel her to return, by law, or by physical force; or he may content himself with seizing for his own use anything which she may earn, or which may be given to her by her relations. It is only legal separation by a decree of a court of justice, which entitles her to live apart, without being forced back into the custody of an exasperated jailer—or which empowers her to apply any earnings to her own use, without fear that a man whom perhaps she has not seen for twenty years will pounce upon her some day and carry all off. This legal separation, until lately, the courts of justice would only give at an expense which made it inaccessible to any one out of the higher ranks. Even now it is only given in cases of desertion, or of the extreme of cruelty; and yet complaints are made every day that it is granted too easily. Surely, if a woman is denied any lot in life but that of being the personal body-servant of a despot, and is dependent for everything upon the chance of finding one who may be disposed to make a favourite of her instead of merely a drudge, it is a very cruel aggravation of her fate that she should be allowed to try this chance only once. The natural sequel and corollary from this state of things would be, that since her all in life depends upon obtaining a good master, she should be allowed to change again

and again until she finds one. I am not saying that she ought to be allowed this privilege. That is a totally different consideration. The question of divorce, in the sense involving liberty of remarriage, is one into which it is foreign to my purpose to enter. All I now say is, that to those to whom nothing but servitude is allowed, the free choice of servitude is the only, though a most insufficient, alleviation. Its refusal completes the assimilation of the wife to the slave—and the slave under not the mildest form of slavery: for in some slave codes the slave could, under certain circumstances of ill usage, legally compel the master to sell him. But no amount of ill usage, without adultery superadded, will in England free a wife from her tormentor. . . .

Institutions, books, education, society, all go on training human beings for the old, long after the new has come; much more when it is only coming. But the true virtue of human beings is fitness to live together as equals; claiming nothing for themselves but what they as freely concede to every one else; regarding command of any kind as an exceptional necessity, and in all cases a temporary one; and preferring, whenever possible, the society of those with whom leading and following can be alternate and reciprocal. To these virtues, nothing in life as at present constituted gives cultivation by exercise. The family is a school of despotism, in which the virtues of despotism, but also its vices, are largely nourished. Citizenship, in free countries, is partly a school of society in equality; but citizenship fills only a small place in modern life, and does not come near the daily habits or inmost sentiments. The family, justly constituted, would be the real school of the virtues of freedom. It is sure to be a sufficient one of everything else. It will always be a school of obedience for the children, of command for the parents. What is needed is, that it should be a school of sympathy in equality, of living together in love, without power on one side or obedience on the other. This it ought to be between the parents. It would then be an exercise of those virtues which each requires to fit them for all other association, and a model to the children of the feelings and conduct which their temporary training by means of obedience is designed to render habitual, and therefore natural, to them. The moral training of mankind will never be adapted to the conditions of the life for which all other human progress is a preparation, until they practise in the family the same moral rule which is adapted to the normal constitution of human society. . . .

When the support of the family depends not on property, but on earnings, the common arrangement, by which the man earns the income and the wife superintends the domestic expenditure, seems to me in general the most suitable division of labour between the two persons. If, in addition to the physical suffering of bearing children, and the whole responsibility of their care and education in early years, the wife undertakes the careful and economical application of the husbands earnings to the general comfort of the family; she takes not only her fair share, but usually the larger share, of the bodily and mental exertion required by their joint existence. If she undertakes any additional portion, it seldom relieves her from this, but only prevents her from performing it properly. The care which she is herself disabled from taking of the children and the household, nobody else takes; those of the children who do not die, grow up as they best can, and the management of the household is likely to be so bad, as even in point of economy to be a great drawback from the value of the wife's earnings. In an otherwise just state of things, it is not, therefore, I think, a desirable custom, that the wife should contribute by her labour to the income of the family. In an unjust state of things, her doing so may be useful to her, by making her of more value in the eyes of the man who is legally her master; but, on the other hand, it enables him still farther to abuse his power, by forcing her to work, and leaving the support of the family to her exertions, while he spends most of his time in drinking and idleness. The *power* of earning is

essential to the dignity of a woman, if she has not independent property. But if marriage were an equal contract, not implying the obligation of obedience; if the connexion were no longer enforced to the oppression of those to whom it is purely a mischief, but a separation, on just terms (I do not now speak of a divorce), could be obtained by any woman who was morally entitled to it; and if she would then find all honourable employments as freely open to her as to men; it would not be necessary for her protection, that during marriage she should make this particular use of her faculties. Like a man when he chooses a profession, so, when a woman marries, it may in general be understood that she makes choice of the management of a household, and the bringing up of a family, as the first call upon her exertions, during as many years of her life as may be required for the purpose; and that she renounces, not all other objects and occupations, but all which are not consistent with the requirements of this. The actual exercise, in a habitual or systematic manner, of outdoor occupations, or such as cannot be carried on at home, would by this principle be practically interdicted to the greater number of married women. But the utmost latitude ought to exist for the adaptation of general rules to individual suitabilities; and there ought to be nothing to prevent faculties exceptionally adapted to any other pursuit, from obeying their vocation notwithstanding marriage: due provision being made for supplying otherwise any falling-short which might become inevitable, in her full performance of the ordinary functions of mistress of a family. These things, if once opinion were rightly directed on the subject, might with perfect safety be left to be regulated by opinion, without any interference of law. . . .

CHAPTER IV

When we consider the positive evil caused to the disqualified half of the human race by their disqualification—first in the loss of the most inspiriting and elevating kind of personal enjoyment, and next in the weariness, disappointment, and profound dissatisfaction with life, which are so often the substitute for it; one feels that among all the lessons which men require for carrying on the struggle against the inevitable imperfections of their lot on earth, there is no lesson which they more need, than not to add to the evils which nature inflicts, by their jealous and prejudiced restrictions on one another.

Their vain fears only substitute other and worse evils for those which they are idly apprehensive of: while every restraint on the freedom of conduct of any of their human fellow creatures (otherwise than by making them responsible for any evil actually caused by it), dries up *pro tanto* the principal fountain of human happiness, and leaves the species less rich, to an inappreciable degree, in all that makes life valuable to the individual human being.

FRIEDRICH NIETZSCHE

INTRODUCTION

RICHARD SCHACHT

Friedrich Nietzsche was born on October 15, 1844, in the small town of Röcken in what is now the eastern part of Germany. He was only four when his father, the pastor of the local Lutheran church, died; he and his sister were raised by their widowed mother under very modest circumstances in the nearby town of Naumburg. His early loves were literature and music (at which he showed some ability, both as a pianist and as a composer). The brilliance Nietzsche displayed in his university education in the classics led to an astonishingly early appointment (when he was but twenty-four) at the Swiss University of Basel, as professor of classical philology.

After just ten years (in 1879), poor health obliged him to resign. During the decade that followed he lived in boarding houses in Switzerland, Italy, and southern France, seeking a congenial environment and relief from the health problems that plagued him. Most of the writings for which he is best known today derive from that period. In early 1889, at the age of forty-four, he suffered a complete physical and mental collapse, from which he never recovered. He lived on for another eleven years, under first his mother's and then his sister's care, finally expiring in Weimar (to which his sister had moved him, to link him with Goethe and Schiller) on August 25, 1900; but his productive life had long since come to an end.

Nietzsche migrated intellectually from philology to philosophy on his own during his Basel years. He in effect invented himself as a philosopher, and found his way to the kind of philosophy he believed to be needed to address the issues with which he believed contemporary humanity to be confronted. He was an astute and severe critic of social, cultural, and political developments in the Europe of his time, as well as of the pretensions of religion, morality, science, and his philosophical predecessors alike. But he also sought new and more adequate ways of comprehending ourselves as human beings and of assessing the kinds of lives human beings have led and might lead.

Proclaiming "the death of God" (by which he meant the collapse of traditional religious and metaphysical ways of thinking, and the untenability of any absolutes beyond this life and this world by reference to which they might be assessed), Nietzsche was deeply concerned about the crisis that might well follow in its wake. He gave the name "nihilism" to this crisis, which he conceived as a paralyzing disillusionment with the very ideas of any sort of truth, value, and meaning by reference to which life might be conceived, assessed, and found endurable and worth living. While commonly considered a nihilist himself, he actually sought to go "beyond" nihilism as well as the addiction to absolutes he believed set the stage for it, to develop a new way of thinking about this life in this world making the affirmation of these absolutes possible.

Nietzsche's new interpretation, which he cast in terms of "will to power," was linked to a project he called the "revaluation of all values." It revolved around the ideas of an "enhancement of life" and an attainable "higher humanity" (symbolized by the image of the *Übermensch*, or "overman"), with creativity being the key to value and meaningfulness. He called for a "philosophy of the future" that would be "beyond good and evil" in its reinterpretive and revaluative endeavors.

Morals and politics, for Nietzsche, are among the means by which humanity has bootstrapped its way to forms of existence that are no longer merely animal. Morals and politics thus have helped to set the stage for further such developments, through the operation of similar or other educational devices, even if these morals and politics themselves have long tended and commonly continue to be and to employ crude techniques of human engineering, engendered in the service of all-too-human or even pathological social and psychological imperatives, with effects upon those whose lives they touch that are often mixed at best.

Nietzsche's political philosophy, like his moral philosophy, is both interpretive and evaluative. Its basic premise is that politics and morals alike are human phenomena best regarded as *forms of life*, interpreted accordingly, and assessed in terms of whatever sorts of positive, negative, or mixed significance they turn out to have "in the service of life"—which itself can mean quite different things. And much of what he says about various forms of both of them is put forward as a variety of observations of how things tend to go under such differing sorts of arrangements with their associated values, and of what their consequences tend to be for the fostering or hindering of the realization and development of sundry human possibilities.

As a first approximation, politics for Nietzsche might be said to have to do with the mobilization and direction of human resources and associated structurings of human life within and among groups and communities of varying sorts and sizes; with the ways in which such structures are engendered, established, maintained, and modified; and with their impact upon the character and quality of human life. As in the case of his moral philosophy, the analytical and interpretive part of his political philosophy involves an attempt to develop the perspectives and conceptual tools with which to be able to understand its genealogies, motivations, social and psychological functions, and consequences in the lives of those who adopt them, as well as to set the stage for their assessment.

The new "great politics" of which Nietzsche sometimes speaks—in contrast to the "power politics" he derides (e.g., *Twilight of the Idols*, VIII, 3)—is fundamentally a *politics of culture*, revolving around the shaping and reshaping of institutions and practices affecting the way cultural life develops and proceeds. If Nietzsche approaches politics with an eye to culture (and vice versa), that is because he thinks it a fact of life that political life and cultural life are intimately entangled as well as divergent. Their entanglement is only to be expected, for they both reflect and also redirect the needs, interests, desires, fears, and all else that expresses what he calls the "will to power" of various groups and types of human beings. As a dimension of human social life, politics is an arena of *cultural contest*. Different sets of cultural values and their institutional expressions confront each other in this arena; and that confrontation is commonly conflictual rather than harmonious. That fact of life is not necessarily to be lamented, and indeed may even turn out to result in forms of competition that invigorate both the forms of life involved and their participants.

Indeed, the whole issue of what to make of difference, competition, and conflict in this arena—as elsewhere in human life—is one of Nietzsche's central political-analytical interests. His speculations along these lines are often jarring; but the specific observations he hazards are secondary to his insistence upon the importance of thinking about this whole matter in a manner unblinkered by the moralism that views everything through the lenses of its highly problematic notions of "good and evil." Eschewing political and moral "correctness" by itself may contribute little of a positive nature to its proper comprehension, but it is a necessary condition of getting anywhere in that direction.

Political life, for Nietzsche, may ultimately be an expression of colliding and competing "wills to power" and of the resulting social dynamics; but it is more concretely (if also very broadly) a matter of the *contested mobilization* of human resources, in the service of various human purposes, interests, or goods. And it commonly involves the devising of ways to get people to do things serving purposes they understand poorly if at all. That, for Nietzsche, is just the way it is. It is only to be expected, therefore, that mobilization in support of almost any sort of human endeavor—and quite certainly any that involve the intensive cultivation of human abilities of one sort or another, and the pursuit of ever more creative, refined, and demanding forms of excellence—will typically require manipulation and exploitation. And one must reckon with the idea that strong bonds of some sort or other will be necessary to render most such arrangements durable enough to amount to anything. This is not a happy thought; but if it is right, neither is the alternative.

Politics becomes most interesting, for Nietzsche, when one gets down to cases and begins to consider what sorts of outcomes are worth going for and against; what the conditions of their possibility would seem to be; how they might be furthered in the former case and countered in the latter; and whether the prices to be paid in both instances would appear to be worth it. But at this point political theory gives way to agenda setting; and the issue becomes not how political life is to be understood, but rather what values are to prevail.

The paramount political as well as human questions, for Nietzsche, concern the sorts of humanly possible cultural life that will wind up being fostered and furthered, considered in terms of their significance for the human future and human worth—their "value for life" and its "enhancement." This is what Nietzschean "great politics" is really all about, beyond all Nietzschean political philosophizing. And it is the radical openness of these questions, together with the impossibility of specifying the outcomes that would be most desirable, that accounts for both the trepidation and the fascination that it does and should inspire. But this is neither to its discredit nor to its particular credit; for if Nietzsche is right, what warrants both reactions is not his kind of politics itself, but rather that to which his conception of political life is meant to be true: the open-endedness and uncanniness of human life itself.

Nietzsche discusses things political in many of his writings, from his early unpublished essay "Homer's Contest" and *Human, All Too Human* to *Beyond Good and Evil, On the Genealogy of Morals*, and *Twilight of the Idols*, but nowhere sets forth his political thinking systematically or definitively. Walter Kaufmann, *Nietzsche: Philosopher, Psychologist, Antichrist* (Princeton, N.J.: Princeton University Press, 1974) remains a useful introduction to Nietzsche. Richard Schacht, *Nietzsche* (London: Routledge,

1983) explores his philosophical thinking more comprehensively and systematically. Mark Warren, *Nietzsche and Political Thought* (Cambridge, Mass.: MIT Press, 1988), the first substantial book on this subject in English, has been followed by many other studies from differing perspectives, including Bruce Detweiler, *Nietzsche and the Politics of Aristocratic Radicalism* (Chicago: University of Chicago Press, 1990); Lawrence Hatab, *A Nietzschean Defense of Democracy* (Chicago: Open Court, 1995); David Owen, *Nietzsche, Politics and Modernity* (London: Sage, 1995); Daniel Conway, *Nietzsche and the Political* (London and New York: Routledge, 1997); and Fredrick Appel, *Nietzsche Contra Democracy* (Ithaca, N.Y.: Cornell University Press, 1999).

Beyond Good and Evil

SECTION FIVE

Towards a Natural History of Morals

199

In every age, for as long as there have been humans, there have also been human herds (family groups, congregations, tribes, peoples, nations, churches) and always a great many followers in proportion to the small number of commanders. Considering, then, that obedience has until now been bred and practised best and longest among humans, we can surely assume that everyone on average is born with a need to obey, as a kind of *formal conscience* that decrees: "Thou shalt do certain things without question, refrain from certain things without question," in short "thou shalt." This need seeks to satisfy its hunger and fill its form with some content; it helps itself according to how strong, impatient, or eager it is, indiscriminately, as a gross appetite, and accepts whatever may be shouted in its ear by whichever commander (parents, teachers, laws, class prejudices, public opinions). Human development has been so strangely restricted—so laggardly, protracted, often regressing and turning round and round—because the herd instinct of obedience is inherited best, and at the cost of the skill in commanding. If we imagine this instinct taken to its ultimate excesses, we find a complete absence of commanders or independent people; or else they suffer inwardly from a bad conscience and feel the need to dupe themselves first in order to be able to give commands, by acting as if they too were only following orders. This really is the case in Europe today: I call it the moral hypocrisy of commanders. The only way they know to protect themselves from their own bad conscience is to behave as if they were carrying out orders from before or from above (from ancestors, the constitution, the judicial system, the laws, or even from God) or else to adopt the herd phrases that are part of the herd mentality, such as "first servant of his people," or "instrument for the common good." The European herd man, on the other hand, puts on airs nowadays as if he were the only acceptable type of man, glorifying the characteristics that make him tame, docile, and useful to the herd as if they were the true human virtues: such as public spirit, benevolence, consideration, industriousness, moderation, modesty, concern, sympathy. In those cases, however, when a leader and bell-wether is thought to be indispensable, people nowadays keep trying to replace commanders with an aggregation of the cleverest

From Friedrich Nietzsche, *Beyond Good and Evil,* translated by Marion Faber, Oxford University Press, 1998. Notes are the translator's.

herd people: this is the origin of all representative constitutions, for example. But what a blessing despite everything, what salvation from an increasingly unbearable pressure the appearance of an absolute commander is for these European herd animals—this has been demonstrated most recently by the powerful impact Napoleon had when he came on the scene. The history of Napoleon's impact is virtually the history of the higher happiness which our entire century was able to achieve in its most valuable people and moments.

200

A person who lives in an age of disintegration that mixes all the races together, will carry in his body the heritage of his multifarious origins, that is to say, contradictory and often more than merely contradictory standards and instincts that struggle with one another and seldom come to rest. Such a person, in the dimming light of a late culture, will generally be a weak person: his most heartfelt desire is that the war that he *embodies* come to an end. In agreement with a medicine and a mentality that tranquillizes (Epicureanism or Christianity, for example), he takes happiness to be essentially the happiness of rest, of tranquillity, of satiety, of ultimate oneness, to be the "Sabbath of Sabbaths,"[1] in the words of the sainted rhetorician Augustine, who was that kind of a man himself.

But if someone with this kind of a nature experiences the warlike oppositions within him as one stimulant and incitement to life *the more*, and if on the other hand, along with his powerful and irreconcilable instincts, he has also inherited the true, inbred expertise and cunning in waging war with himself, that is to say, self-control, self-deception: then he may develop into one of those enchantingly elusive and unfathomable men, those mysterious people who are destined for victory and for seduction, expressed most beautifully in Alcibiades[2] and Caesar (in whose company I would like to include the *first* European to my taste, the Hohenstaufen Frederick II),[3] and among artists, perhaps, Leonardo da Vinci. They appear during just those epochs

when that other weak type, with its desire for rest, comes into the foreground: both types belong to one another and arise from the same causes.

201

As long as the utility that dominates moral judgements is still only the utility of the herd, as long as we confine our gaze solely to the preservation of the community, seeking out immorality exactly and exclusively in whatever seems dangerous to communal stability, there can be no "morality of neighbourly love." Assuming that here, too, there are already small ongoing acts of consideration, sympathy, fairness, gentleness, reciprocal help; and that at this stage of society, too, all the instincts are already at work that will later be designated by honourable names as "virtues" and finally fit the concept "morality"; during this period they are still in no way part of the realm of moral value judgements—they are still *extra-moral*. In the heyday of Rome for example, an act of pity was neither good nor evil, neither moral nor immoral; and even such praise as it may have received could well be accompanied by a kind of irritated disdain as soon as it was compared to an action that served to further the whole, the *res publica*.[4] Ultimately, "neighbourly love" is always something secondary, in part convention and a deliberate fiction in relation to *fear of one's neighbour*. Once the social structure appears to be more or less established and secured against external dangers, it is this fear of one's neighbour that once again creates new perspectives for moral value judgements. Certain strong and dangerous instincts, such as adventurousness, recklessness, vengefulness, slyness, rapacity, lust for power, were previously not only honoured (by names other than the ones above, of course) as beneficial to the community, but they also had to be cultivated and bred, because people continually had need of them in their common danger against common enemies. But now (when there are no drainage channels for them) these same instincts are felt to be doubly dangerous and are gradually stigmatized and slandered as immoral. Now the opposite drives and tendencies gain moral respect; step by step, the herd instinct draws its consequences. The moral perspective now considers how harmful or harmless an opinion, an emotional state, a will, a talent is to the community, to equality: here again, fear is the mother of morality. When an individual's highest and strongest instincts break forth with a passion, driving him far above and beyond the average, beyond the lowlands of the herd conscience, the community's self-regard is destroyed as a result; its belief in itself, its backbone, so to speak, is shattered: and that is why people do well to stigmatize and slander just these instincts above all. Exalted, self-directed spirituality, a will to solitude, even great powers of reason are felt as a danger; everything that raises an individual above the herd and causes his neighbour to fear him is henceforth called *evil*; a proper, modest, conforming, equalizing mentality, what is *average* on the scale of desires gains a moral name and respect. Finally, when conditions are very peaceable, there is less and less opportunity or necessity for educating one's feelings to be stern and harsh; and then every kind of sternness, even in matters of justice, begins to trouble the conscience; a harsh, exalted nobility or individual responsibility is almost considered offensive and awakens distrust, whereas "a lamb," or better yet, "a sheep" gains in esteem. There can come a point of such sickly morbidity and pampered indulgence in the history of a society that in all due seriousness it even takes the side of the one who does it harm, the *criminal*. Punishing: society thinks there is something unfair about it—it certainly finds the idea of "punishment" and the "need to punish" painful and frightening. "Isn't it enough just to render him *innocuous*? Why do we have to punish him too? Real punishment is awful!"—with this question the herd morality, the morality of timidity, draws its final conclusion. Assuming that we could entirely abolish the danger, the grounds for fear, then we would have abolished this morality as well: it would no longer be necessary, it *would deem itself* no longer necessary!

Anyone who examines the conscience of a present-day European will have to extract from his thousand moral crannies and hiding places the same imperative, the imperative of herdlike timidity: "At some point, we want there to be *nothing more to be afraid of*!" At some point—the will and the way *to that point* is what everyone in Europe today calls "progress."

202

Let us immediately say once again what we have already said a hundred times, for nowadays ears are reluctant to hear such truths—*our* truths. We know perfectly well how offensive it sounds when someone counts man among the animals plain and simple, without metaphorical intent; but we will almost be accounted a *criminal* for always using expressions such as "herd," "herd instincts," and the like when speaking about people of "modern ideas." What's the use! We can't do otherwise, for this is just what our new insight is about. We discovered that Europe, and those countries dominated by a European influence, are now of one mind in all their key moral judgements: it is obvious that Europeans nowadays *know* that which Socrates thought he did not know, and what that famous old serpent once promised to teach—people "know" what is good and evil. It must sound harsh and trouble the ears, then, if we insist over and over that it is the instinct of man the herd animal that thinks it knows, that glorifies itself and calls itself good whenever it allots praise or blame. This instinct has had a breakthrough, has come to predominance, has prevailed over the other instincts and continues to do so as a symptom of the increasing process of physiological approximations and resemblances. *Morality in Europe today is herd animal morality*—and thus, as we understand things, it is only one kind of human morality next to which, before which, after which many others, and especially *higher* moralities, are or should be possible. But this morality defends itself with all its strength against such "possibilities," against such "should be's." Stubbornly and relentlessly it says, "I am Morality itself, and nothing else is!" Indeed, with the help of a religion that played along with and flattered the most sublime desires of the herd animal, we have reached the point of finding an ever more visible expression of this morality even in political and social structures: the *democratic* movement is Christianity's heir. But its tempo is still far too slow and sleepy for the overeager, for patients or addicts of this above-mentioned instinct, as we can tell from the increasingly frantic howl, the ever more widely bared teeth of the anarchist dogs who now roam the alleys of European culture. They appear to be in conflict with the peaceably industrious democrats or ideologues of revolution, and even more with the foolish philosophasts and brotherhood enthusiasts who call themselves socialists and want a "free society"; but in reality they are united with those others in their fundamental and instinctive enmity towards every form of society other than *autonomous* herds (right up to the point of even rejecting the concepts "master" and "servant"— *ni dieu ni maître*[5] is a socialist motto); united in their tough resistance to every exceptional claim, every exceptional right and privilege (and thus ultimately to *all* rights, for no one needs "rights" any longer when everyone is equal); united in their distrust of any justice that punishes (as if it were a rape of the weaker party, unjust towards the *necessary* consequence of all earlier society); but also just as united in their religion of pity, in their empathy, wherever there are feelings, lives, or suffering (reaching down to the animal or up to "God"—the eccentric notion of "pity for God" suits a democratic age); united one and all in their impatient cry for pity, in their mortal hatred of any suffering, in their almost feminine incapacity to remain a spectator to it, to *allow* suffering; united in the involuntary depression and decadence which seems to hold Europe captive to a threatening new Buddhism; united in their belief in a morality of *communal* pity, as if it were Morality itself, the summit, the *conquered* summit of humankind, the only hope for the future, comfort in the present, the great redemption from all past guilt—united together in their belief in community as a *redeemer*, and thus a belief in the herd, a belief in "themselves." . . .

203

We who hold a different belief—we who consider the democratic movement not merely a decadent form of political organization, but a decadent (that is to say, diminished) form of the human being, one that mediocritizes him and debases his value: what can *we* set our hopes on?

On *new philosophers*, we have no other choice; on spirits that are strong and original enough to give impetus to opposing value judgements and to revalue, to reverse "eternal values"; on forerunners, on men of the future, who in the present will forge the necessary link to force a thousand-year-old will onto *new* tracks. They will teach humans that their future is their *will*, that the future depends on their human will, and they will prepare the way for great risk-taking and joint experiments in discipline and breeding in order to put an end to that terrible reign of nonsense and coincidence that until now has been known as "history" (the nonsense about the "greatest number" is only its most recent form). To accomplish this, new kinds of philosophers and commanders will eventually be necessary, whose image will make all the secretive, frightful, benevolent spirits that have existed in the world look pale and dwarfish. The image of such leaders is what hovers before *our* eyes—may I say it aloud, you free spirits? The circumstances that would have to be in part created, in part exploited to give rise to these leaders; the probable paths and tests by which a soul would grow so great and powerful that it would feel *compelled* to accomplish these projects; a revaluation of values, under whose new hammer and pressure the conscience would be transformed into steel, the heart into bronze, so that they could bear the weight of such responsibility; the indispensability of such leaders; on the other hand, the terrible danger that they might not arrive or might go astray and degenerate—those are really the things that concern and worry *us*—do you know that, you free spirits?—those are the distant oppressive thoughts and thunderstorms that pass across the sky of *our* life. There are few pains so raw as to have once observed, understood, sympathized while an extraordinary man strayed from his path or degenerated: but a person with the rare vision to see the general danger that "man" himself *is degenerating*, who has recognized as we have the tremendous randomness that thus far has been at play in determining the future of mankind (a play that has been guided by no one's hand, not even by "God's finger!"), who has guessed the fate that lies hidden in all the stupid innocence and blissful confidence of "modern ideas," and even more in the entire Christian-European morality: this person suffers from an anxiety that cannot be compared to any other. With one single glance he grasps everything that *mankind could be bred to be* if all its energies and endeavours were gathered together and heightened; with all the knowledge of his conscience, he knows how mankind's greatest possibilities have as yet been untapped, and how many mysterious decisions and new paths the human type has already encountered—he knows better yet, from his most painful memory, what kind of wretched things have usually caused the finest example of an evolving being to shatter, break apart, sink down, become wretched. The *overall degeneration of man*, right down to what socialist fools and flatheads call their "man of the future" (their ideal!); this degeneration and diminution of man into a perfect herd animal (or, as they call it, man in a "free society"); this bestialization of man into a dwarf animal with equal rights and claims is *possible*, no doubt about that! Anyone who has thought this possibility through to its end knows no disgust but other people—and also, perhaps, a new *project*! . . .

SECTION NINE

What Is Noble?

257

In the past, every elevation of the type "human being" was achieved by an aristocratic society—and this will always be the case: by a society that believes in a great ladder of hierarchy and value differentiation between people and that requires

slavery in one sense or another. Without the *grand feeling of distance* that grows from inveterate class differences, from the ruling caste's constant view downwards onto its underlings and tools, and from its equally constant practice in obeying and commanding, in holding down and holding at arm's length—without this grand attitude, that other, more mysterious attitude could never exist, that longing for ever greater distances within the soul itself, the development of ever higher, rarer, more far-flung, extensive, spacious inner states, in short, the elevation of the type "human being," the continual "self-overcoming of the human," to use a moral formula in a supra-moral sense. To be sure, we must not give in to any humanitarian delusions about these aristocratic societies' historical origins (that is, about the preconditions for that elevation of the type "human"): the truth is harsh. Let us not mince words in describing to ourselves the *beginnings* of every previous higher culture on earth! People who still had a nature that was natural, barbarians in every terrible sense of the word, predatory humans, whose strength of will and desire for power were still unbroken, threw themselves upon the weaker, more well-behaved, peaceable, perhaps trading or stockbreeding races, or upon old, crumbling cultures whose remaining life-force was flickering out in a brilliant fireworks display of wit and depravity. At the beginning, the noble caste was always the barbarian caste: its dominance was not due to its physical strength primarily, but rather to its spiritual—these were the *more complete* human beings (which at every level also means the "more complete beasts").

258

Corruption, as the expression of impending anarchy among the instincts and of the collapse of the emotional foundations called "life": this corruption will vary fundamentally according to the form of life in which it manifests itself. When for example an aristocracy like pre-Revolutionary France tosses away its privileges with sublime revulsion and sacrifices itself to its excess of moral feeling, this is corruption: it was really only the final act of that centuries-long corruption that caused the aristocracy to abandon its tyrannical authority bit by bit and reduce itself to a *function* of the monarchy (and ultimately in fact to its ornament and showpiece). The crucial thing about a good and healthy aristocracy, however, is that it does *not* feel that it is a function (whether of monarchy or community) but rather its *essence* and highest justification—and that therefore it has no misgivings in condoning the sacrifice of a vast number of people who must *for its sake* be oppressed and diminished into incomplete people, slaves, tools. Its fundamental belief must simply be that society can *not* exist for its own sake, but rather only as a foundation and scaffolding to enable a select kind of creature to ascend to its higher task and in general to its higher *existence*—much like those sun-loving climbing plants on Java (called *sipo matador*) whose tendrils encircle an oak tree so long and so repeatedly that finally, high above it but still supported by it, they are able to unfold their coronas in the free air and make a show of their happiness.—

259

To refrain from injuring, abusing, or exploiting one another; to equate another person's will with our own: in a certain crude sense this can develop into good manners between individuals, if the preconditions are in place (that is, if the individuals have truly similar strength and standards and if they are united within one single social body). But if we were to try to take this principle further and possibly even make it the *basic principle of society*, it would immediately be revealed for what it is: a will to *deny* life, a principle for dissolution and decline. We must think through the reasons for this and resist all sentimental frailty: life itself *in its essence* means appropriating, injuring, overpowering those who are foreign and weaker; oppression, harshness, forcing one's own forms on others, incorporation, and at the very least, at the very mildest, exploitation—but why should we

keep using this kind of language, that has from time immemorial been infused with a slanderous intent? Even that social body whose individuals, as we have just assumed above, treat one another as equals (this happens in every healthy aristocracy) must itself, if the body is vital and not moribund, do to other bodies everything that the individuals within it refrain from doing to one another: it will have to be the will to power incarnate, it will want to grow, to reach out around itself, pull towards itself, gain the upper hand—not out of some morality or immorality, but because it is *alive*, and because life simply *is* the will to power. This, however, more than anything else, is what the common European consciousness resists learning; people everywhere are rhapsodizing, even under the guise of science, about future social conditions that will have lost their "exploitative character"—to my ear that sounds as if they were promising to invent a life form that would refrain from all organic functions. "Exploitation" is not part of a decadent or imperfect, primitive society: it is part of the *fundamental nature* of living things, as its fundamental organic function; it is a consequence of the true will to power, which is simply the will to life.

Assuming that this is innovative as theory—as reality it is the *original fact* of all history: let us at least be this honest with ourselves!

260

While perusing the many subtler and cruder moral codes that have prevailed or still prevail on earth thus far, I found that certain traits regularly recurred in combination, linked to one another—until finally two basic types were revealed and a fundamental difference leapt out at me. There are *master moralities* and *slave moralities*. I would add at once that in all higher and more complex cultures, there are also apparent attempts to mediate between the two moralities, and even more often a confusion of the two and a mutual misunderstanding, indeed sometimes even their violent juxtaposition—even in the same person, within one single breast. Moral value distinctions have emerged either from among a masterful kind, pleasantly aware of how it differed from those whom it mastered, or else from among the mastered, those who were to varying degrees slaves or dependants. In the first case, when it is the masters who define the concept "good," it is the proud, exalted states of soul that are thought to distinguish and define the hierarchy. The noble person keeps away from those beings who express the opposite of these elevated, proud inner states: he despises them. Let us note immediately that in this first kind of morality the opposition "good" and "bad" means about the same thing as "noble" and "despicable"—the opposition "good" and "*evil*" has a different origin. The person who is cowardly or anxious or petty or concerned with narrow utility is despised; likewise the distrustful person with his constrained gaze, the self-disparager, the craven kind of person who endures maltreatment, the importunate flatterer, and above all the liar: all aristocrats hold the fundamental conviction that the common people are liars. "We truthful ones"—that is what the ancient Greek nobility called themselves. It is obvious that moral value distinctions everywhere are first attributed to *people* and only later and in a derivative fashion applied to *actions*: for that reason moral historians commit a crass error by starting with questions such as: "Why do we praise an empathetic action?" The noble type of person feels *himself* as determining value—he does not need approval, he judges that "what is harmful to me is harmful per se," he knows that he is the one who causes things to be revered in the first place, he *creates values*. Everything that he knows of himself he reveres: this kind of moral code is self-glorifying. In the foreground is a feeling of fullness, of overflowing power, of happiness in great tension, an awareness of a wealth that would like to bestow and share—the noble person will also help the unfortunate, but not, or not entirely, out of pity, but rather from the urgency created by an excess of power. The noble person reveres the power in himself, and also his power over himself, his ability to speak and to be silent, to enjoy the practice of severity and harshness towards himself and to respect everything that is severe and harsh. "Wotan placed a harsh heart within my breast," goes a line in an old Scandinavian saga: that is how it is written from the heart of a proud Viking—and rightly so. For this kind of a person is proud *not* to be made for pity; and so the hero of the saga adds a warning: "If your heart is not harsh when you are young, it will never become harsh." The noble and brave people who think like this are the most removed from that other moral code which sees the sign of morality in pity or altruistic behaviour or *désintéressement*,[6] belief in ourselves, pride in ourselves, a fundamental hostility and irony towards "selflessness"—these are as surely a part of a noble morality as caution and a slight disdain towards empathetic feelings and "warm hearts."

It is the powerful who *understand* how to revere, it is their art form, their realm of invention. Great reverence for old age and for origins (all law is based upon this twofold reverence), belief in ancestors and prejudice in their favour and to the disadvantage of the next generation—these are typical in the morality of the powerful; and if, conversely, people of "modern ideas" believe in progress and "the future" almost by instinct and show an increasing lack of respect for old age, that alone suffices to reveal the ignoble origin of these "ideas." Most of all, however, the master morality is foreign and embarrassing to current taste because of the severity of its fundamental principle: that we have duties only towards our peers, and that we may treat those of lower rank, anything foreign, as we think best or "as our heart dictates" or in any event "beyond good and evil"—pity and the like should be thought of in this context. The ability and duty to feel enduring gratitude or vengefulness (both only within a circle of equals), subtlety in the forms of retribution, a refined concept of friendship, a certain need for enemies (as drainage channels for the emotions of envy, combativeness, arrogance—in essence, in order to be a good *friend*): these are the typical signs of a noble morality, which, as we have suggested, is not the morality of "modern ideas" and is therefore difficult to sympathize with these days, also difficult to dig out and uncover.

It is different with the second type of morality, *slave morality*. Assuming that the raped, the oppressed, the suffering, the shackled, the weary, the insecure engage in moralizing, what will their moral value judgements have in common? They will probably express a pessimistic suspicion about the whole human condition, and they might condemn the human being along with his condition. The slave's eye does not readily apprehend the virtues of the powerful: he is sceptical and distrustful, he is *keenly* distrustful of everything that the powerful revere as "good"—he would like to convince himself that even their happiness is not genuine. Conversely, those qualities that serve to relieve the sufferers' existence are brought into relief and bathed in light: this is where pity, a kind, helpful hand, a warm heart, patience, diligence, humility, friendliness are revered—for in this context, these qualities are most useful and practically the only means of enduring an oppressive existence. Slave morality is essentially a morality of utility. It is upon this hearth that the famous opposition "good" and "*evil*" originates—power and dangerousness, a certain fear-inducing, subtle strength that keeps contempt from surfacing, are translated by experience into evil. According to slave morality, then, the "evil" person evokes fear; according to master morality, it is exactly the "good" person who evokes fear and wants to evoke it, while the "bad" person is felt to be despicable. The opposition comes to a head when, in terms of slave morality, a hint of condescension (it may be slight and well intentioned) clings even to those whom this morality designates as "good," since within a slave mentality a good person must in any event be *harmless*: he is good-natured, easily deceived, perhaps a bit stupid, a *bonhomme*.[7] Wherever slave morality gains the upper hand, language shows a tendency to make a closer association of the words "good" and "stupid."

A last fundamental difference: the longing for *freedom*, an instinct for the happiness and nuances of feeling free, is as necessarily a part of slave morals and morality as artistic, rapturous reverence and devotion invariably signal an aristocratic mentality and judgement.

From this we can immediately understand why *passionate* love (our European speciality) absolutely must have a noble origin: the Provençal poet-knights are acknowledged to have invented it, those splendid, inventive people of the "*gai saber*"[8] to whom Europe owes so much—virtually its very self.

261

Among the things that a noble person finds most difficult to understand is vanity. he will be tempted to deny its existence, even when a different kind of person thinks that he grasps it with both hands. He has trouble imagining beings who would try to elicit a good opinion about themselves that they themselves do not hold (and thus do not "deserve," either) and who then themselves nevertheless *believe* this good opinion. To him, that seems in part so tasteless and irreverent towards one's self, and in part so grotesquely irrational that he would prefer to consider vanity an anomaly and in most of the cases when it is mentioned, doubt that it exists. He will say, for example: "I may be wrong about my worth, but on the other hand require that others recognize the worth that I assign—but that is not vanity (rather it is arrogance, or more often what is called "humility," and also "modesty")." Or he will say: "There are many reasons to be glad about other people's good opinion of me, perhaps because I revere and love them and am happy about every one of their joys, or else perhaps because their good opinion underscores and strengthens my belief in my own private good opinion, or perhaps because the good opinion of others, even in the cases where I do not share it, is nevertheless useful or promises to be useful to me—but none of that is vanity." It takes compulsion, particularly with the help of history, for the noble person to realize that in every sort of dependent social class, from time immemorial, a common person *was* only what he was *thought to be*—completely unused to determining values himself, he also attributed to himself no other value than what his masters attributed to him (creating values is truly the *master's privilege*). We may understand it as the result of a tremendous atavism that even now, the ordinary person first *waits* for someone else to have an opinion about him, and then instinctively submits to it—and by no means merely to "good" opinions, but also to bad or improper ones (just think, for example, how most pious women esteem or under-esteem themselves in accordance with what they have learned from their father confessors, or what pious Christians in general learn from their Church). Now, in fact, in conformity with the slow emergence of a democratic order of things (this in turn caused by mixing the blood of masters and slaves), the originally noble and rare impulse to ascribe one's own value to oneself and to "think well" of oneself, is more and more encouraged and widespread: but always working against it is an older, broader, and more thoroughly entrenched tendency—and when it comes to "vanity," this older tendency becomes master of the newer. The vain person takes pleasure in *every* good opinion that he hears about himself (quite irrespective of any prospect of its utility, and likewise irrespective of truth or falsehood), just as he suffers at any bad opinion: for he submits himself to both, he *feels* submissive to both, from that old submissive instinct that breaks out in him.

It is the "slave" in the blood of the vain person, a remnant of the slave's craftiness (and how much of the "slave" is still left, for example, in women today!) that tries to *seduce* him to good opinions of himself; and it is likewise the slave who straightway kneels down before these opinions, as if he himself were not the one who had called them forth.

So I repeat: vanity is an atavism.

262

A *species* comes into being, a type grows strong and fixed, by struggling for a long time with essentially similar *unfavourable* conditions. Conversely, as we know from the experiences of stockbreeders, a species that is given over-abundant nourishment and extra protection and care generally shows an immediate and very pronounced tendency to variations in type, and is rich in marvels and monstrosities (and in monstrous vices, too). Now let us consider an aristocratic community, such as the ancient Greek *polis*, say, or Venice, as an organization whose voluntary or involuntary purpose is to *breed*: there are people coexisting in it, relying on one another, who want to further their species, chiefly because they *must* further it or run some sort of terrible risk of extermination. In such a case, good will, excess, and protection, those conditions that favour variation, are missing; the species needs to remain a species, something that by virtue of its very harshness, symmetry, and simplicity of form, can be furthered and in general endure throughout all its continual struggles with its neighbours or with oppressed peoples who threaten rebellion or revolt. From its most diverse experience the species learns which qualities have particularly contributed to its survival, to its continuing victory in defiance of all gods and peoples: these qualities it calls virtues, and these are the only virtues that it cultivates. It is done harshly, indeed it demands harshness; every aristocratic moral code is intolerant, be it in educating its children, in disposing of its women, in its marital customs, in the relations of its old and young, or in its punitive laws (which apply only to the deviant); even intolerance itself is counted as a virtue, going by the name of "justice." A type like this, with few but very strong characteristics, a species of severe, warlike, prudently taciturn, closed and uncommunicative people (and as such most subtly attuned to the charms and nuances of society) thus becomes established beyond generational change; as mentioned above, its continual struggle with the same *unfavourable* conditions causes the type to become fixed and harsh. Eventually, however, it arrives at a period of good fortune, the tremendous tension relaxes; perhaps there are no longer any enemies among its neighbours and its means for living, even for enjoying life, are plentiful. At one single stroke the coercing bond of the old discipline is torn apart: it is no longer felt to be essential, critical for existence—if such discipline wished to endure, it could do so only as a kind of *luxury*, as an archaic *taste*. Variation, whether as deviance (into something higher, finer, more rare) or as degeneration and monstrosity is suddenly on the scene in all its greatest fullness and splendour; the individual dares to be an individual and stand out. During these historical turning points, we see splendid, manifold, jungle-like upgrowths and upsurges coexisting and often inextricably tangled up with one another; competition for growth assumes a kind of *tropical* tempo and there is a tremendous perishing and causing-to-perish, owing to the wild egoisms that challenge one another with seeming explosiveness, struggling "for sun and light," and no longer knowing how to derive any set of limits, any restraint, any forbearance from their earlier moral code. It was this very moral code, in fact, that stored up the energy to such a monstrous extent, that tensed the bow so ominously—and now that code is, or is becoming "obsolete." The dangerous and sinister point is reached where the greater, more differentiated, richer life *survives beyond* the old morality; the "individual" is left standing, forced to be his own lawgiver, to create his own arts and wiles of self-preservation, self-advancement, self-redemption. Nothing left but new "What for?"s and new "How to?"s; no more common formulae; misunderstanding and mistrust in league with one another; decline, decay, and the greatest aspirations terribly entangled; the genius of the race spilling good and bad out of all the horns of plenty; an ominous simultaneity of spring and autumn, full of new delights and veils that are intrinsic to the new, still unplumbed, still unwearied decay. Danger is present once again, the mother of morality, the great danger, this time displaced into the individual, into the neighbour or friend, into the street, into our own children, into our own hearts, into everything that is most secretly our own of wishing and wanting: what will the moral philosophers who emerge during this period find to preach about? They will discover, these keen observers and idlers, that things are quickly going downhill, that everything around them is turning to decay and causing decay, that nothing lasts past tomorrow, with the exception of one single species of human being, the incurably *mediocre*. The mediocre alone have the prospect of continuing, of having descendants—they are the people of the future, the only survivors. "Be like them! Become mediocre!" will henceforth be the only moral code that still makes sense, that can still find an ear.

But it is hard to preach, this morality of the mediocre!—it can never admit to itself what it is and what it wants! It has to talk of proportion and dignity and duty and brotherly love—it will not find it easy to *hide its irony*!

263

There is an *instinct for rank* that more than anything else is itself the sign of *high* rank; there is a *joy* in the nuances of reverence that hints at a noble origin and habits. The subtlety, kindness, and greatness of a soul are dangerously tested when it encounters something that is of the first rank, but as yet unprotected by awe of authority against crude, intrusive poking; something unmarked, undiscovered, tentative, perhaps capriciously cloaked or disguised, going its way like a living touchstone. A person who has taken upon himself the task and habit of sounding out souls and who wishes to establish the ultimate value of a soul, its irrevocable, inherent hierarchical position, will make manifold use of one particular art above all others: he will test the soul for its *instinct for reverence*. *Différence engendre haine*:[9] when a holy vessel, a jewel from a locked shrine, or a book with the sign of a great destiny is borne past, the commonness of certain natures suddenly splatters forth like dirty water; and on the other hand, there can be an involuntary loss of words, a hesitation in the eye, a quieting of all gestures which conveys the fact that a soul *feels* the proximity of something most worthy of reverence. The way that Europeans have so far more or less continued to revere the *Bible* may be the best part of the discipline and refinement in manners that Europe owes to Christianity: books with this kind of depth and ultimate significance must be protected by a tyrannical external authority in order to win those thousands of years of *duration* that are required for their full exploration and comprehension. Much has been achieved when the great crowd (the shallow and diarrhoeal of every kind) has finally been trained to feel that it may not touch everything; that there are holy experiences in the presence of which it must remove its shoes and keep its dirty hands off—this is virtually its highest ascent to humanity. Conversely, the so-called educated people, believers in "modern ideas," stir our revulsion most of all perhaps by their lack of shame, their easy impertinent eyes and hands that go touching everything, licking, groping; and it is possible that among the common people, the low people, among today's peasants especially, there is *relatively* more nobility in taste and sense of reverence than in the newspaper-reading intellectual *demi-monde*, the educated.

264

There is no way to efface from a person's soul what his ancestors best and most regularly liked to do: whether they were avid economizers, say, appendages of their desks and money-boxes, modest and bourgeois in their desires, modest too in their virtues; or whether they lived in the habit of commanding from dawn to dusk, enjoying rough pleasures and along with them perhaps even rougher duties and responsibilities; or whether at a certain point they ultimately sacrificed their old privileges of birth and property in order to live for their beliefs (their "god"), as people of an unshakeable and sensitive conscience that blushes at every compromise. It is simply impossible that a person would *not* have his parents' and forefathers' qualities and preferences in his body—whatever appearances may say to the contrary. This is a problem of race. If we know something about the parents, then we are allowed a stab at the child: a certain repellent intemperance,

a certain narrow envy, a clumsy self-righteousness (these three together have ever made up the true rabble type)—these things will be passed on to the child as surely as corrupted blood; and all that the best upbringing or education can achieve is to *deceive* others about such an inheritance.

And what other intention do today's upbringing and education have! In our very popular, which is to say, rabble-like age, "upbringing" and "education" *must* be essentially the art of deception—deceiving away the origins, the inherited rabble in body and soul. Nowadays an educator who would preach truthfulness above all else and constantly call out to his charges, "Be genuine! Be natural! Be yourselves!"—before too long, even such a virtuous and naive idiot would learn to reach for that *furca* of Horace's, in order to *naturam expellere*: with what success? "Rabble" *usque recurret*.[10]

265

Running the risk of displeasing innocent ears, I would assert that egoism is part of the nature of noble souls—I mean that steadfast belief that other beings must naturally submit to "our" kind of being and sacrifice themselves to it. The noble soul accepts its egoistic condition without any sort of question mark, also without any feeling of harshness, coercion, or wilfulness, but rather as something that may be based in the primeval law of things: if a noble soul were to seek a name for this, it would say, "This is Justice itself." In certain circumstances that at first cause it to hesitate, the soul admits to itself that there are others with entitlements equal to its own; as soon as this question of rank has been clarified, it moves among these equally entitled equals as assured in its modesty or tender reverence as when dealing with itself—according to an inborn, heavenly mechanism that all the stars understand. This is one *more* aspect of the soul's egoism, this subtle self-limitation in the society of its equals (every star is this kind of egoist): in these equals and in the rights that it yields to them, it reveres *itself*; it has no doubt that mutual reverence and rights are the *essence* of all society and also part of the natural state of things. The noble soul gives as it takes, from out of the passionate and excitable instinct of requital that is at its core. The concept of "mercy" has no meaning *inter pares*,[11] no aroma: there may be a sublime way of letting ourselves be showered, as it were, with gifts from above, drinking them in thirstily like dewdrops—but the noble soul is not adept in arts or gestures of this kind. Its egoism stops it here: it never really likes to look "up"—preferring to look either *ahead*, horizontal and slow, or downwards: *it knows that it is above.*

266

"The only person we can really respect is one who is not *seeking* himself."—Goethe to Councillor Schlosser.

267

The Chinese have a saying which mothers even teach their children: *siao-sin,* "make your heart *small*!" This really is the fundamental tendency in late civilizations: I have no doubt that the first thing an ancient Greek would notice about us contemporary Europeans is that we make ourselves small—for that reason alone he would find us "offensive."

268

What does commonness really mean?

Words are acoustic signs for concepts; concepts, however, are more or less precise figurative signs for frequently recurring and simultaneous sensations, for groups of sensations. Using the same words is not enough to ensure mutual understanding: we must also use the same words for the same category of inner experiences; ultimately, we must have the same experiences in *common.* That is why the individuals of one single people understand one another better than the members of different peoples do, even when they are using the same language; or to put it better, when people have lived for a long time under similar conditions (of climate, soil, danger, necessities, work), then something *comes into being* as a result, something that "goes without saying," a people. In all their souls a similar number of often-recurring experiences has prevailed over others less frequent: because of these experiences, they understand one another quickly, and ever more quickly (the history of language is the history of a process of abbreviation); because of this quick understanding, they are connected, closely and ever more closely. The greater the danger, the greater the need to agree quickly and easily about what is necessary; not to be misunderstood in times of danger—people in society find this absolutely crucial. We carry out this test even in friendships or love affairs: both are doomed as soon as one person discovers that the same words have caused different feelings, thoughts, hunches, wishes, fears in the other person. (The fear of "eternal misunderstanding": that is the benevolent genius that so often keeps people of different sexes from an overhasty attachment when their senses and heart are urging it—and *not* some Schopenhauerian "genius of the species"—!) Which of the groups of sensations within a soul come alive most quickly, to speak or command—that decides the overall hierarchy of the soul's values and ultimately determines its table of goods. A person's value judgements reveal something about how his soul is *structured,* and what, in its view, constitutes the conditions essential to its life, its real necessity. If we now assume that necessity has always brought together only those people who could indicate by similar signs their similar needs, similar experiences: then this is as much as to say that the easy *communicability* of necessity (which ultimately means having experienced only average and *common* experiences) must, of all the forces that have heretofore controlled humans, have been the most forceful. The more similar, the more common people: these have always been and continue to be at an advantage, while those who are more select, subtle, rare, harder to understand are readily left alone, come to harm in their isolation, and rarely procreate. We have to call upon enormous counterforces in order to thwart this natural, all-too-natural *progressus in simile,*[12] the further development of humans who are similar, ordinary, average, herd-like—*common!*

Notes

1. *Sabbath of Sabbaths*: cf. Augustine's *City of God*, book XXII, section 30.

2. *Alcibiades*: Athenian general (450–404 BC), statesman, and pupil of Socrates, exiled to Sparta for sacrilege, but later elected Athenian commander-in-chief.

3. *Frederick II*: brilliant Hohenstaufen ruler (1194–1250), Emperor of the Holy Roman Empire from 1215 to 1250.

4. *res publica*: Latin: commonwealth.

5. *ni dieu ni maître*: French: neither God nor master.

6. *désintéressement*: French: disinterestedness.

7. *bonhomme*: French: Simple man.

8. *gai saber*: Provençal: gay science. This concept was first introduced by Nietzsche in the eponymous work of 1882.

9. *Différence engendre haine*: French: difference engenders hatred.

10. *furca . . . recurret*: a reference to Horace's *Epistles* 1. x. 24: Try to drive nature out (*naturam expellere*) with a pitchfork (*furca*), it always returns (*usque recurret*).

11. *inter pares*: Latin: among equals.

12. *progressus in simile*: Latin: continuation of the same thing.

W. E. B. DU BOIS

INTRODUCTION

DERRICK DARBY

William Edward Burghardt Du Bois was buried beyond the walls of Osu Castle in Accra, Ghana, on August 29, 1963. His tomb overlooks the Atlantic Ocean where European slave ships loaded their African cargo. The state funeral, hosted by President Kwame Nkrumah, was the day after Martin Luther King Jr. delivered his "I Have a Dream" speech during the March on Washington. Du Bois, cofounder of the National Association for the Advancement of Colored People (NAACP), pioneer of the U.S. civil rights movement, and champion of Pan-Africanism, worked tirelessly as a teacher, writer, and activist to tackle the color line problem—a legacy of modern slavery, colonialism, and imperialism. He paved the way for the historic event and resounding call for American democracy to fulfill its promises.

W. E. B. Du Bois was born on February 23, 1868, in Great Barrington, Massachusetts. He died in Ghana on August 23, 1963. His mother, Mary, descended from a West African slave owned by Dutchman Conrad Burghardt, one of the colonizers of western Massachusetts. His father, Alfred, descended from Dr. James Du Bois, a wealthy New York doctor of French Huguenot background, and his slave woman. After graduating as high school class valedictorian at sixteen and getting his undergraduate degree at Fisk University, Du Bois became the first African American to receive a Harvard doctorate. He worked at Wilberforce University and the University of Pennsylvania before landing a job teaching sociology at Atlanta University. There, in the Deep South, far from his New England upbringing, and after he traveled the world, Du Bois resolved to devote his life to Black uplift using social science, history, and journalism. He was a prolific and wide-ranging writer with books, novels, correspondence, and countless articles to his credit. As editor of *The Crisis*, the NAACP monthly magazine, he commanded an influential platform to address issues of race, racism, injustice, inequality, and imperialism in America and globally.

The Souls of Black Folk (1903) is Du Bois's most well-known work and is widely discussed within philosophy. He wanted whites to understand the truths about Blacks, their contributions to civilization, and race relations, with the hope that whites would be moved to redress racial wrongs. *Darkwater: Voices From Within the Veil* (1920) is Du Bois's most political work. He had faith that the races could take united action against the race problem. He presumed that whites would rally around democracy once they understood that race prejudice was harmful to all and that it jeopardized democracy worldwide. Du Bois's singular contribution to political philosophy is an argument for inclusive democracy. He believed that affording Blacks, women, and workers a seat at democracy's table empowered them to fight for freedom, equality, and jobs. His argument appears in chapter 6, "Of the Ruling of Men."

The nineteenth amendment to the U.S. Constitution, which passed when Du Bois was writing *Darkwater*, proscribed vote denial based on sex. Congress ratified it on August 18, 1920, the same year the book was published. With this new law the nation became a more inclusive democracy. More citizens gained the right to participate in democratic rule. While some African Americans worried that giving white women the vote would set back the struggle for Black freedom (giving more white people political power to oppose it), Du Bois argued for supporting the right to vote unconditionally. He defends democratic inclusion by rebutting what had been a familiar rationale for excluding women, African Americans, and others from democratic rule in the United States—namely, that they were too ignorant to participate in the ruling of men.

Democratic theorists spend considerable time defining democracy and identifying normative reasons to value it. Du Bois was not preoccupied with these philosophical exercises but did have thoughts about democracy's value and how to secure it. One reason we have to value democracy, normatively, is because of its potential to secure the broadest measure of justice for all. The more people we afford a hand in political rule, the greater chance for realizing this value. Voting is not the only way that citizens participate in democracy. They can serve as political representatives, lobbyists, campaign workers, and more. Du Bois focuses on the importance of voting in this essential text. His overarching thesis is that universal suffrage, affording as many citizens as possible the right to vote, is the surest way for democracy to realize its normative potential. Du Bois is primarily interested in America's failure to grant universal suffrage. He considers the historical reasons for this, paying special attention to claims that some groups, including Blacks and women, are too ignorant to participate in democratic rule. Inclusive democracy is a less compelling ideal if this epistemic rationale stands. We get a methodical and incisive rebuttal in "Of the Ruling of Men."

Du Bois's refutation of the epistemic justification for excluding so-called ignorant citizens from democratic rule unfolds in three steps. The first one takes the problem of ignorance seriously as a constraint on realizing the broadest measure of justice for all. If we assume that democratic rule requires knowledge and that some lack it, then democratic rule should be limited to those with knowledge. Du Bois situates this argument within history. Not only had it been used to exclude women and Blacks from democratic rule, it was deployed to exclude white men too—those considered not well born. Securing justice for all with inclusive democracy is an ideal he contrasts with stages in history, where political rule first sought the good of a monarch, then a selected few and a greater number of rich, privileged, and powerful persons. It is also the aim of democratic movements.

Du Bois marks the industrial age as a time when the titans of industry and the millionaire class used this argument to justify excluding labor from political and industrial democratic rule. The industrial age, when mass production of goods became the object of work, introduced complexities requiring knowledge about matters such as trade, business, and commerce that the masses lacked. And industrialists seized upon this to claim that rule should be in their hands. This led to hard times for all laborers, especially the lowest of them—African Americans who worked the hardest and got the least. It also invited a twist on the argument from ignorance that pitted white and Black laborers against one another. Blacks were deemed ignorant not merely in virtue of lacking knowledge of new industry, which they shared with white laborers, but by virtue of being members of a so-called inferior race. The industrial ruling class invited white workers to use this race prejudice-laced argument to claim higher rank in return for continued exploitation by the titans in the new regime.

The first step of Du Bois's argument shows that allowing the appeal to ignorance to stand, as a justification for limiting democratic rule, was used against white labor in precisely this way. And he observes the dire consequences: "This program, however, although it undoubtedly helped raise the scale of white labor, in much greater proportion put wealth and power in the hands of the great European Captains of Industry and made modern industrial imperialism possible."

Du Bois uses this result to interrogate "the roots of democracy." He asks, "Who may be excluded from a share in the ruling of men?" Here he takes up, and rebuts, several reasons for limiting the ballot—namely, that some are too ignorant, inexperienced, guarded, and unwilling to rule. If we suppose that civilized states must exclude the ignorant from political rule, rather than accept this, Du Bois contends that such states have a duty to educate citizens so that none are too ignorant to participate in democratic rule. As he puts it, "education is not a prerequisite to political control—political control is the cause of popular education." He dismisses the experience restriction, noting that this would not only stop the spread of democracy but would limit power to those born into the ruling class, caste, race, or sex. And he adds that democracy is a great experiment in living where we seek solutions to problems by trial and error.

To be sure, Du Bois's defense of democracy is not based on blind, uncritical devotion to it. Rather it is rooted in a pragmatic realism—democracy's not perfect, but it's the best game in town—and an abiding faith in the masses to better their own conditions when given a real opportunity. In a conference paper published by the *American Historical Review* in 1910, Du Bois states: "The theory of democratic government is not that the will of the people is always right, but rather that normal human beings of average intelligence will, if given a chance, learn the right and best course by bitter experience." He admitted that democracy can make the wrong calls. But the answer is not to go for less democracy. It is to have more voices at the table.

With his reply to the claim that only persons not under benevolent guardianship—presumably rich, privileged, and powerful white men—should rule, and that excluded groups do not really want to vote, Du Bois advances to the second step of his rebuttal of the epistemic rationale for limited rule. And here he does not let the assumption of ignorance stand. The critics of extending the ballot say that women don't need the vote because the more intelligent sex, men, can take care of their interests; they assert that this is the same with Blacks, where the more intelligent race, whites, can take care of their interests. And these critics add that women and Blacks don't really want to vote, preferring to leave political matters to those that know best. Du Bois replies that voting is not a mere privilege, and not just a method of meeting needs and satisfying preferences, but a way to secure the broadest measure of justice. And he says that this requires all possible knowledge. He pushes back by identifying important knowledge that the excluded masses—women and Blacks—possess and argues that this knowledge is needed for democratic rule to realize its normative potential of securing justice for all.

Du Bois contends that all individuals know their own "souls," and that this knowledge is vital for securing democracy's normative aim. It is also necessary for improving culture and achieving a greater world. When political rule is left to aristocracies or the select few, relying solely on the knowledge they possess, it is doomed to fail from lack of knowledge. The excluded groups or excluded person may not know some things such as the business side of industrial manufacturing, but Du Bois says, "he knows when something hurts and he alone knows how that hurt feels." Even if the masses don't know the remedy for their pains, this intimate knowledge of their condition is essential to building a just society. Because of this, all citizens must have a hand in choosing and evaluating political rulers. The excluded wisdom of the masses is essential for just government.

Du Bois's third and final step in rebutting the epistemic rationale for exclusion is a response to a sound objection. If we suppose that the masses do indeed have knowledge needed for securing justice in society, one may object that they need not be given the ballot to secure it. Perhaps we only need to consult with them, say by conducting surveys of what they think, and then others can use this knowledge to secure justice. Du Bois answers this objection by arguing that the ballot is also necessary for self-defense. Women need to vote because they can be counted on, more than men, to secure the neglected rights of women and children. Similarly, Blacks can be counted on, more than whites, to secure protection from lynching, discrimination, and other basic rights. The same holds for federations of nations that exclude nations of darker races (Black, brown, or yellow): excluded nations must have an equal vote to defend themselves against exploitation and imperialism.

Du Bois admits that making political rule more inclusive will have costs and raise real challenges. Men will resent sharing democratic rule with women. Whites will resent sharing it with Blacks. And whiter nations will resent sharing it with darker ones. The transition to more inclusive democracy may need to proceed gradually, with temporary exclusions, until the "ignorant and their children are taught, or to avoid too sudden an influx of inexperienced voters." However, Du Bois insists, "such exclusions can be but temporary if justice is to prevail." He concludes the argument with this: "Democracy alone is the method of showing the whole experience of the race for the benefit of the future and if democracy tries to exclude women or Negroes or the poor or any class because of innate characteristics which do not interfere with intelligence, then that democracy cripples itself and belies its name."

All persons, even the so-called ignorant masses, are what might be thought of as *sage souls*. Du Bois's multifaceted defense of democracy—highlighting this and the necessity of including them in political rule to achieve democracy's normative potential—is an epistemic argument. The reason why *all* must rule, and not only those thought to have certain experience, ability, or knowledge the masses lack, is because democracy is a way for society to secure the broadest measure of justice and this can only be done if all souls have a hand in democratic rule. While the historically excluded souls are not omniscient because no mortals are, each person knows things that others do not and this excluded wisdom is indispensable for our collective striving toward perfect democracy.

"The real argument for democracy," says Du Bois, "is, then, that in the people we have the source of that endless life and unbounded wisdom which the rulers of men must have." A society steadfastly and sincerely pursuing the democratic ideal has a dual imperative: (a) to make the class of ignorant persons as small as possible, and (b) to make the class of mature voting age persons as large as possible. Because when sage souls can speak for themselves politically, which they can do with the ballot, they can take steps to secure the full schedule of rights needed to undo the circumstances of democratic failure. This is how the excluded masses contribute to democracy's survival.

For the definitive two volume biography of Du Bois's life, see David Levering Lewis, *W. E. B. Du Bois: Biography of a Race, 1868–1919* (New York: Henry Holt, 1993), and David Levering Lewis, *W. E. B. Du Bois: The Fight for Equality and the American Century, 1919–1963* (New York: Henry Holt, 2000). Important critical studies of Du Bois's political thought include Manning Marable, *W. E. B. Du Bois: Black Radical Democrat* (Boston: Twayne, 1986); Adolph Reed Jr., *W. E. B. Du Bois and American Political Thought: Fabianism and the Color Line* (Oxford: Oxford University Press, 1997); and Robert Gooding Williams, *In the Shadow of Du Bois: Afro Modern Political Thought in America* (Cambridge, Mass.: Harvard University Press, 2009). For articles on Du Bois's thoughts about race, gender, culture, and pan-Africanism, see *W. E. B. Du Bois on Race and Culture: Philosophy, Politics, and Poetics*, edited by Bernard W. Bell, Emily Grosholz, and James B. Stewart (New York: Routledge, 1996). Also see *A Political Companion to W. E. B. Du Bois*, edited by Nick Bromell (Lexington: University of Kentucky Press, 2018). For an essay reconstructing the argument in "Of the Ruling of Men," see Derrick Darby, "Du Bois's Defense of Democracy," in *Democratic Failure*: NOMOS LXIII, edited by Melissa Schwartzberg and Daniel Viehoff (New York: New York University Press, 2020).

Of the Ruling of Men

THE RULING of men is the effort to direct the individual actions of many persons toward some end. This end theoretically should be the greatest good of all, but no human group has ever reached this ideal because of ignorance and selfishness. The simplest object would be rule for the Pleasure of One, namely the Ruler; or of the Few—his favorites; or of many—the Rich, the Privileged, the Powerful. Democratic movements inside groups and nations are always taking place and they are the efforts to increase the number of beneficiaries of the ruling. In 18th century Europe, the effort became so broad and sweeping that an attempt was made at universal expression and the philosophy of the movement said that if All ruled they would rule for All and thus Universal Good was sought through Universal Suffrage.

The unrealized difficulty of this program lay in the widespread ignorance. The mass of men, even of the more intelligent men, not only knew little about each other but less about the action of men in groups and the technique of industry in general. They could only apply universal suffrage, therefore, to the things they knew or knew partially: they knew personal and menial service, individual craftsmanship, agriculture and barter, taxes or the taking of private property for public ends and the rent of land. With these matters then they attempted to deal. Under the cry of "Freedom" they greatly relaxed the grip of selfish interests by restricting menial service, securing the right of property in handiwork and regulating public taxes; distributing land ownership and freeing trade and barter.

From W. E. B. Du Bois, *Dark Water: Voices From Within the Veil*, Harcourt, Brace and Company, 1920.

While they were doing this against stubborn resistance, a whole new organization of work suddenly appeared. The suddenness of this "Industrial Revolution" of the 19th century was partly fortuitous—in the case of Watt's teakettle—partly a natural development, as in the matter of spinning, but largely the determination of powerful and intelligent individuals to secure the benefits of privileged persons, as in the case of foreign slave trade.

The result was on the one hand a vast and unexampled development of industry. Life and civilization in the late 19th and early 20th century were Industry in its whole conception, language, and accomplishment: the object of life was to make goods. Now before this giant aspect of things, the new democracy stood aghast and impotent. It could not rule because it did not understand: an invincible kingdom of trade, business, and commerce ruled the world, and before its threshold stood the Freedom of 18th century philosophy warding the way. Some of the very ones who were freed from the tyranny of the Middle Age became the tyrants of the industrial age.

There came a reaction. Men sneered at "democracy" and politics, and brought forth Fate and Philanthropy to rule the world—Fate which gave divine right to rule to the Captains of Industry and their created Millionaires; Philanthropy which organized vast schemes of relief to stop at least the flow of blood in the vaster wounds which industry was making.

It was at this time that the lowest laborers, who worked hardest, got least and suffered most, began to mutter and rebel, and among these were the American Negroes. Lions have no historians, and therefore lion hunts are thrilling and satisfactory human reading. Negroes had no bards, and therefore it has been widely told how American philanthropy freed the slave. In truth the Negro revolted by armed rebellion, by sullen refusal to work, by poison and murder, by running away to the North and Canada, by giving point and powerful example to the agitation of the abolitionists and by furnishing 200,000 soldiers and many

times as many civilian helpers in the Civil War. This war was not a war for Negro freedom, but a duel between two industrial systems, one of which was bound to fail because it was an anachronism, and the other bound to succeed because of the Industrial Revolution.

When now the Negro was freed the Philanthropists sought to apply to his situation the Philosophy of Democracy handed down from the 18th century.

There was a chance here to try democratic rule in a new way, that is, against the new industrial oppression with a mass of workers who were not yet in its control. With plenty of land widely distributed, staple products like cotton, rice, and sugar cane, and a thorough system of education, there was a unique chance to realize a new modern democracy in industry in the southern United States which would point the way to the world. This, too, if done by black folk, would have tended to a new unity of human beings and an obliteration of human hatreds festering along the color line.

Efforts were begun. The 14th and 15th amendments gave the right to vote to white and black laborers, and they immediately established a public school system and began to attack the land question. The United States government was seriously considering the distribution of land and capital—"40 acres and a mule"—and the price of cotton opened an easy way to economic independence. Co-operative movements began on a large scale.

But alas! Not only were the former slaveowners solidly arrayed against this experiment, but the owners of the industrial North saw disaster in any such beginnings of industrial democracy. The opposition based its objections on the color line, and Reconstruction became in history a great movement for the self-assertion of the white race against the impudent ambition of degraded blacks, instead of, in truth, the rise of a mass of black and white laborers.

The result was the disfranchisement of the blacks of the South and a world-wide attempt to restrict democratic development to white races and to distract them with race hatred against the darker races. This program, however, although it undoubtedly helped raise the scale of white labor, in much greater proportion put wealth and power in the hands of the great European Captains of Industry and made modern industrial imperialism possible.

This led to renewed efforts on the part of white European workers to understand and apply their political power to its reform through democratic control.

Whether known as Communism or Socialism or what not, these efforts are neither new nor strange nor terrible, but world-old and seeking an absolutely justifiable human ideal—the only ideal that can be sought: the direction of individual action in industry so as to secure the greatest good of all. Marxism was one method of accomplishing this, and its panacea was the doing away with private property in machines and materials. Two mighty attacks were made on this proposal. One was an attack on the fundamental democratic foundation: modern European white industry does not even theoretically seek the good of all, but simply of all Europeans. This attack was virtually unanswered—indeed some Socialists openly excluded Negroes and Asiatics from their scheme. From this it was easy to drift into that form of syndicalism which asks socialism for the skilled laborer only and leaves the common laborer in his bonds.

This throws us back on fundamentals. It compels us again to examine the roots of democracy.

Who may be excluded from a share in the ruling of men? Time and time again the world has answered:

The Ignorant
The Inexperienced
The Guarded
The Unwilling

That is, we have assumed that only the intelligent should vote, or those who know how to rule men, or those who are not under benevolent guardianship, or those who ardently desire the right.

These restrictions are not arguments for the wide distribution of the ballot—they are rather reasons for restriction addressed to the self-interest of the present real rulers. We say easily, for instance, "The ignorant ought not to vote." We would say, "No civilized state should have citizens too ignorant to participate in government," and this statement is but a step to the fact: that no state is civilized which has citizens too ignorant to help rule it. Or, in other words, education is not a prerequisite to political control—political control is the cause of popular education.

Again, to make experience a qualification for the franchise is absurd: it would stop the spread of democracy and make political power hereditary, a prerequisite of a class, caste, race, or sex. It has of course been soberly argued that only white folk or Englishmen, or men, are really capable of exercising sovereign power in a modern state. The statement proves too much: only yesterday it was Englishmen of high descent, or men of "blood," or sovereigns "by divine right" who could rule. Today the civilized world is being ruled by the descendants of persons who a century ago were pronounced incapable of ever developing a self-ruling people. In every modern state there must come to the polls every generation, and indeed every year, men who are inexperienced in the solutions of the political problems that confront them and who must experiment in methods of ruling men. Thus and thus only will civilization grow.

Again, what is this theory of benevolent guardianship for women, for the masses, for Negroes—for "lesser breeds without the law"? It is simply the old cry of privilege, the old assumption that there are those in the world who know better what is best for others than those others know themselves, and who can be trusted to do this best.

In fact no one knows himself but that self's own soul. The vast and wonderful knowledge of this marvelous universe is locked in the bosoms of its individual souls. To tap this mighty reservoir of experience, knowledge, beauty, love, and deed we must appeal not to the few, not to some souls, but to all. The narrower the appeal, the poorer the culture; the wider the appeal the more magnificent are the possibilities. Infinite is human nature. We make it finite by choking back the mass of men, by attempting to speak for others, to interpret and act for them, and we end by acting for ourselves and using the world as our private property. If this were all, it were crime enough—but it is not all: by our ignorance we make the creation of the greater world impossible; we beat back a world built of the playing of dogs and laughter of children, the song of Black Folk and worship of Yellow, the love of women and strength of men, and try to express by a group of doddering ancients the Will of the World.

There are people who insist upon regarding the franchise, not as a necessity for the many, but as a privilege for the few. They say of persons and classes: "They do not need the ballot." This is often said of women. It is argued that everything which women with the ballot might do for themselves can be done for them; that they have influence and friends "at court," and that their enfranchisement would simply double the number of ballots. So, too, we are told that American Negroes can have done for them by other voters all that they could possibly do for themselves with the ballot and much more because the white voters are more intelligent.

Further than this, it is argued that many of the disfranchised people recognize these facts. "Women do not want the ballot" has been a very effective counter war-cry, so much so that many men have taken refuge in the declaration: "When they want to vote, why, then——" So, too, we are continually told that the "best" Negroes stay out of politics.

Such arguments show so curious a misapprehension of the foundation of the argument for democracy that the argument must be continually restated and emphasized. We must remember that if the theory of democracy is correct, the right to vote is not merely a privilege, not simply a method of meeting the needs of a particular group, and least of all a matter of recognized want or desire. Democracy is a method of realizing the broadest measure of justice to all human beings. The world has, in the past, attempted various methods of

attaining this end, most of which can be summed up in three categories:

The method of the benevolent tyrant.
The method of the select few.
The method of the excluded groups.

The method of intrusting the government of a people to a strong ruler has great advantages when the ruler combines strength with ability, unselfish devotion to the public good, and knowledge of what that good calls for. Such a combination is, however, rare and the selection of the right ruler is very difficult. To leave the selection to force is to put a premium on physical strength, chance, and intrigue; to make the selection a matter of birth simply transfers the real power from sovereign to minister. Inevitably the choice of rulers must fall on electors.

Then comes the problem, who shall elect. The earlier answer was: a select few, such as the wise, the best born, the able. Many people assume that it was corruption that made such aristocracies fail. By no means. The best and most effective aristocracy, like the best monarchy, suffered from lack of knowledge. The rulers did not know or understand the needs of the people and they could not find out, for in the last analysis only the man himself, however humble, knows his own condition. He may not know how to remedy it, he may not realize just what is the matter; but he knows when something hurts and he alone knows how that hurt feels. Or if sunk below feeling or comprehension or complaint, he does not even know that he is hurt, God help his country, for it not only lacks knowledge, but has destroyed the sources of knowledge.

So soon as a nation discovers that it holds in the heads and hearts of its individual citizens the vast mine of knowledge, out of which it may build a just government, then more and more it calls those citizens to select their rulers and to judge the justice of their acts.

Even here, however, the temptation is to ask only for the wisdom of citizens of a certain grade or those of recognized worth. Continually some classes are tacitly or expressly excluded. Thus women have been excluded from modern democracy because of the persistent theory of female subjection and because it was argued that their husbands or other male folks would look to their interests. Now, manifestly, most husbands, fathers, and brothers will, so far as they know how or as they realize women's needs, look after them. But remember the foundation of the argument,— that in the last analysis only the sufferer knows his sufferings and that no state can be strong which excludes from Its expressed wisdom the knowledge possessed by mothers, wives, and daughters. We have but to view the unsatisfactory relations of the sexes the world over and the problem of children to realize how desperately we need this excluded wisdom.

The same arguments apply to other excluded groups: if a race, like the Negro race, is excluded, then so far as that race is a part of the economic and social organization of the land, the feeling and the experience of that race are absolutely necessary to the realization of the broadest justice for all citizens. Or if the "submerged tenth" be excluded, then again, there is lost from the world an experience of untold value, and they must be raised rapidly to a place where they can speak for themselves. In the same way and for the same reason children must be educated, insanity prevented, and only those put under the guardianship of others who can in no way be trained to speak for themselves.

The real argument for democracy is, then, that in the people we have the source of that endless life and unbounded wisdom which the rulers of men must have. A given people today may not be intelligent, but through a democratic government that recognizes, not only the worth of the individual to himself, but the worth of his feelings and experiences to all, they can educate, not only the individual unit, but generation after generation, until they accumulate vast stores of wisdom. Democracy alone is the method of showing the whole experience of the race for the benefit of the

future and if democracy tries to exclude women or Negroes or the poor or any class because of innate characteristics which do not interfere with intelligence, then that democracy cripples itself and belies its name.

From this point of view we can easily see the weakness and strength of current criticism of extension of the ballot. It is the business of a modern government to see to it, first, that the number of ignorant within its bounds is reduced to the very smallest number. Again, it is the duty of every such government to extend as quickly as possible the number of persons of mature age who can vote. Such possible voters must be regarded, not as sharers of a limited treasure, but as sources of new national wisdom and strength.

The addition of the new wisdom, the new points of view, and the new interests must, of course, be from time to time bewildering and confusing. Today those who have a voice in the body politic have expressed their wishes and sufferings. The result has been a smaller or greater balancing of their conflicting interests. The appearance of new interests and complaints means disarrangement and confusion to the older equilibrium. It is, of course, the inevitable preliminary step to that larger equilibrium in which the interests of no human soul will be neglected. These interests will not, surely, be all fully realized, but they will be recognized and given as full weight as the conflicting interests will allow. The problem of government thereafter would be to reduce the necessary conflict of human interests to the minimum.

From such a point of view one easily sees the strength of the demand for the ballot on the part of certain disfranchised classes. When women ask for the ballot, they are asking, not for a privilege, but for a necessity. You may not see the necessity, you may easily argue that women do not need to vote. Indeed, the women themselves in considerable numbers may agree with you. Nevertheless, women do need the ballot. They need it to right the balance of a world sadly awry because of its brutal neglect of the rights of women and children. With the best will and knowledge, no man can know women's wants as well as women themselves. To disfranchise women is deliberately to turn from knowledge and grope in ignorance.

So, too, with American Negroes: the South continually insists that a benevolent guardianship of whites over blacks is the ideal thing. They assume that white people not only know better what Negroes need than Negroes themselves, but that they are anxious to supply these needs. As a result they grope in ignorance and helplessness. They cannot "understand" the Negro; they cannot protect him from cheating and lynching; and, in general, instead of loving guardianship we see anarchy and exploitation. If the Negro could speak for himself in the South instead of being spoken for, if he could defend himself instead of having to depend on the chance sympathy of white citizens, how much healthier a growth of democracy the South would have.

So, too, with the darker races of the world. No federation of the world, no true inter-nation—can exclude the black and brown and yellow races from its counsels. They must equally and according to number act and be heard at the world's council.

It is not, for a moment, to be assumed that enfranchising women will not cost something. It will for many years confuse our politics. It may even change the present status of family life. It will admit to the ballot thousands of inexperienced persons, unable to vote intelligently. Above all, it will interfere with some of the present prerogatives of men and probably for some time to come annoy them considerably.

So, too, Negro enfranchisement meant reconstruction, with its theft and bribery and incompetency as well as its public schools and enlightened, social legislation. It would mean today that black men in the South would have to be treated with consideration, have their wishes respected and their manhood rights recognized. Every white Southerner, who wants peons beneath him, who believes in hereditary menials and a privileged aristocracy, or who hates certain races because of their characteristics, would resent this.

Notwithstanding this, if America is ever to become a government built on the broadest justice to every citizen, then every citizen must be enfranchised. There may be temporary exclusions, until the ignorant and their children are taught, or to avoid too sudden an influx of inexperienced voters. But such exclusions can be but temporary if justice is to prevail.

The principle of basing all government on the consent of the governed is undenied and undeniable. Moreover, the method of modern democracy has placed within reach of the modern state larger reserves of efficiency, ability, and even genius than the ancient or mediaeval state dreamed of. That this great work of the past can be carried further among all races and nations no one can reasonably doubt.

Great as are our human differences and capabilities there is not the slightest scientific reason for assuming that a given human being of any race or sex cannot reach normal, human development if he is granted a reasonable chance. This is, of course, denied. It is denied so volubly and so frequently and with such positive conviction that the majority of unthinking people seem to assume that most human beings are not human and have no right to human treatment or human opportunity. All this goes to prove that human beings are, and must be, woefully ignorant of each other. It always startles us to find folks thinking like ourselves. We do not really associate with each other, we associate with our ideas of each other, and few people have either the ability or courage to question their own ideas. None have more persistently and dogmatically insisted upon the inherent inferiority of women than the men with whom they come in closest contact. It is the husbands, brothers, and sons of women whom it has been most difficult to induce to consider women seriously or to acknowledge that women have rights which men are bound to respect. So, too, it is those people who live in closest contact with black folk who have most unhesitatingly asserted the utter impossibility of living beside Negroes who are not industrial or political slaves or social pariahs. All this proves that none are so blind as those nearest the thing seen, while, on the other hand, the history of the world is the history of the discovery of the common humanity of human beings among steadily-increasing circles of men.

If the foundations of democracy are thus seen to be sound, how are we going to make democracy effective where it now fails to function—particularly in industry? The Marxists assert that industrial democracy will automatically follow public ownership of machines and materials. Their opponents object that nationalization of machines and materials would not suffice because the mass of people do not understand the industrial process. They do not know:

What to do
How to do it
Who could do it best
      or
How to apportion the resulting goods.

There can be no doubt but that monopoly of machines and materials is a chief source of the power of industrial tyrants over the common worker and that monopoly today is due as much to chance and cheating as to thrift and intelligence. So far as it is due to chance and cheating, the argument for public ownership of capital is incontrovertible even though it involves some interference with long vested rights and inheritance. This is being widely recognized in the whole civilized world. But how about the accumulation of goods due to thrift and intelligence—would democracy in industry interfere here to such an extent as to discourage enterprise and make impossible the intelligent direction of the mighty and intricate industrial process of modern times?

The knowledge of what to do in industry and how to do it in order to attain the resulting goods rests in the hands and brains of the workers and managers, and the judges of the result are the public. Consequently it is not so much a question as to whether the world will admit democratic control here as how can such control be long

avoided when the people once understand the fundamentals of industry. How can civilization persist in letting one person or a group of persons, by secret inherent power, determine what goods shall be made—whether bread or champagne, overcoats or silk socks? Can so vast a power be kept from the people?

But it may be opportunely asked: has our experience in electing public officials led us to think that we could run railways, cotton mills, and department stores by popular vote? The answer is clear: no, it has not, and the reason has been lack of interest in politics and the tyranny of the Majority. Politics have not touched the matters of daily life which are nearest the interests of the people—namely, work and wages; or if they have, they have touched it obscurely and indirectly. When voting touches the vital, everyday interests of all, nominations and elections will call for more intelligent activity. Consider too the vast unused and misused power of public rewards to obtain ability and genius for the service of the state. If millionaires can buy science and art, cannot the Democratic state outbid them not only with money but with the vast ideal of the common weal?

There still remains, however, the problem of the Majority.

What is the cause of the undoubted reaction and alarm that the citizens of democracy continually feel? It is, I am sure, the failure to feel the full significance of the change of rule from a privileged minority to that of an omnipotent majority, and the assumption that mere majority rule is the last word of government; that majorities have no responsibilities, that they rule by the grace of God. Granted that government should be based on the consent of the governed, does the consent of a majority at any particular time adequately express the consent of all? Has the minority, even though a small and unpopular and unfashionable minority, no right to respectful consideration?

I remember that excellent little high school text book, "Nordhoff's Politics," where I first read of government, saying this sentence at the beginning of its most important chapter: "The first duty of a minority is to become a majority." This is a statement which has its underlying truth, but it also has its dangerous falsehood; viz., any minority which cannot become a majority is not worthy of any consideration. But suppose that the outvoted minority is necessarily always a minority? Women, for instance, can seldom expect to be a majority; artists must always be the few; ability is always rare, and black folk in this land are but a tenth. Yet to tyrannize over such minorities, to browbeat and insult them, to call that government a democracy which makes majority votes an excuse for crushing ideas and individuality and self-development, is manifestly a peculiarly dangerous perversion of the real democratic ideal. It is right here, in its method and not in its object, that democracy in America and elsewhere has so often failed. We have attempted to enthrone any chance majority and make it rule by divine right. We have kicked and cursed minorities as upstarts and usurpers when their sole offense lay in not having ideas or hair like ours. Efficiency, ability, and genius found often no abiding place in such a soil as this. Small wonder that revolt has come and high-handed methods are rife, of pretending that policies which we favor or persons that we like have the anointment of a purely imaginary majority vote.

Are the methods of such a revolt wise, howsoever great the provocation and evil may be? If the absolute monarchy of majorities is galling and inefficient, is it any more inefficient than the absolute monarchy of individuals or privileged classes have been found to be in the past? Is the appeal from a numerous-minded despot to a smaller, privileged group or to one man likely to remedy matters permanently? Shall we step backward a thousand years because our present problem is baffling?

Surely not and surely, too, the remedy for absolutism lies in calling these same minorities to council. As the king-in-council succeeded the king by the grace of God, so in future democracies the toleration and encouragement of minorities and the willingness to consider as "men" the crankiest, humblest and poorest and blackest peoples, must

be the real key to the consent of the governed. Peoples and governments will not in the future assume that because they have the brute power to enforce momentarily dominant ideas, it is best to do so without thoughtful conference with the ideas of smaller groups and individuals. Proportionate representation in physical and spiritual form must come.

That this method is virtually coming in vogue we can see by the minority groups of modern legislatures. Instead of the artificial attempts to divide all possible ideas and plans between two great parties, modern legislatures in advanced nations tend to develop smaller and smaller minority groups, while government is carried on by temporary coalitions. For a time we inveighed against this and sought to consider it a perversion of the only possible method of practical democracy. Today we are gradually coming to realize that government by temporary coalition of small and diverse groups may easily become the most efficient method of expressing the will of man and of setting the human soul free. The only hindrance to the faster development of this government by allied minorities is the fear of external war which is used again and again to melt these living, human, thinking groups into inhuman, thoughtless, and murdering machines.

The persons, then, who come forward in the dawn of the 20th century to help in the ruling of men must come with the firm conviction that no nation, race, or sex, has a monopoly of ability or ideas; that no human group is so small as to deserve to be ignored as a part, and as an integral and respected part, of the mass of men; that, above all, no group of twelve million black folk, even though they are at the physical mercy of a hundred million white majority, can be deprived of a voice in their government and of the right to self-development without a blow at the very foundations of all democracy and all human uplift; that the very criticism aimed today at universal suffrage is in reality a demand for power on the part of consciously efficient minorities,—but these minorities face a fatal blunder when they assume that less democracy will give them and their kind greater efficiency. However desperate the temptation, no modern nation can shut the gates of opportunity in the face of its women, its peasants, its laborers, or its socially damned. How astounded the future world-citizen will be to know that as late as 1918 great and civilized nations were making desperate endeavor to confine the development of ability and individuality to one sex,—that is, to one-half of the nation; and he will probably learn that similar effort to confine humanity to one race lasted a hundred years longer.

The doctrine of the divine right of majorities leads to almost humorous insistence on a dead level of mediocrity. It demands that all people be alike or that they be ostracized. At the same time its greatest accusation against rebels is this same desire to be alike: the suffragette is accused of wanting to be a man, the socialist is accused of envy of the rich, and the black man is accused of wanting to be white. That any one of these should simply want to be himself is to the average worshiper of the majority inconceivable, and yet of all worlds, may the good Lord deliver us from a world where everybody looks like his neighbor and thinks like his neighbor and is like his neighbor.

The world has long since awakened to a realization of the evil which a privileged few may exercise over the majority of a nation. So vividly has this truth been brought home to us that we have lightly assumed that a privileged and enfranchised majority cannot equally harm a nation. Insane, wicked, and wasteful as the tyranny of the few over the many may be, it is not more dangerous than the tyranny of the many over the few. Brutal physical revolution can, and usually does, end the tyranny of the few. But the spiritual losses from suppressed minorities may be vast and fatal and yet all unknown and unrealized because idea and dream and ability are paralyzed by brute force.

If, now, we have a democracy with no excluded groups, with all men and women enfranchised, what is such a democracy to do? How will it function? What will be its field of work?

The paradox which faces the civilized world today is that democratic control is everywhere limited in its control of human interests. Mankind is engaged in planting, forestry, and mining, preparing food and shelter, making clothes and machines, transporting goods and folk, disseminating news, distributing products, doing public and private personal service, teaching, advancing science, and creating art.

In this intricate whirl of activities, the theory of government has been hitherto to lay down only very general rules of conduct, marking the limits of extreme anti-social acts, like fraud, theft, and murder.

The theory was that within these bounds was Freedom—the Liberty to think and do and move as one wished. The real realm of freedom was found in experience to be much narrower than this in one direction and much broader in another. In matters of Truth and Faith and Beauty, the Ancient Law was inexcusably strait and modern law unforgivably stupid. It is here that tire future and mighty fight for Freedom must and will be made. Here in the heavens and on the mountaintops, the air of Freedom is wide, almost limitless, for here, in the highest stretches, individual freedom harms no man, and, therefore, no man has tire right to limit it.

On the other hand, in the valleys of the hard, unyielding laws of matter and the social necessities of time production, and human intercourse, the limits on our freedom are stern and unbending if we would exist and thrive. This does not say that everything here is governed by incontrovertible "natural" law which needs no human decision as to raw materials, machinery, prices, wages, news-dissemination, education of children, etc.; but it does mean that decisions here must be limited by brute facts and based on science and human wants.

Today the scientific and ethical boundaries of our industrial activities are not in the hands of scientists, teachers, and thinkers; nor is the intervening opportunity for decision left in the control of the public whose welfare such decisions guide. On the contrary, the control of industry is largely in the hands of a powerful few, who decide for their own good and regardless of the good of others. The making of the rules of Industry, then, is not in the hands of All, but in the hands of the Few. The Few who govern industry envisage, not the wants of mankind, but their own wants. They work quietly, often secretly, opposing Law, on the one hand, as interfering with the "freedom of industry"; opposing, on the other hand, free discussion and open determination of the rules of work and wealth and wages, on the ground that harsh natural law brooks no interference by Democracy.

These things today, then, are not matters of free discussion and determination. They are strictly controlled. Who controls them? Who makes these inner, but powerful, rules? Few people know. Others assert and believe these rules are "natural"—a part of our inescapable physical environment. Some of them doubtless are; but most of them are just as clearly the dictates of self-interest laid down by the powerful private persons who today control industry. Just here it is that modern men demand that Democracy supplant skilfully concealed, but all too evident, Monarchy.

In industry, monarchy and the aristocracy rule, and there are those who, calling themselves democratic, believe that democracy can never enter here. Industry, they maintain, is a matter of technical knowledge and ability, and, therefore, is the eternal heritage of the few. They point to the failure of attempts at democratic control in industry, just as we used to point to Spanish-American governments, and they expose, not simply the failures of Russian Soviets,—they fly to arms to prevent that greatest experiment in industrial democracy which the world has yet seen. These are the ones who say: We must control labor or civilization will fail; we must control white labor in Europe and America; above all, we must control yellow labor in Asia and black labor in Africa and the South, else we shall have no tea, or rubber, or cotton. And yet,—and yet is it so easy to give up the dream of

democracy? Must industry rule men or may men rule even industry? And unless men rule industry, can they ever hope really to make laws or educate children or create beauty?

That the problem of the democratization of industry is tremendous, let no man deny. We must spread that sympathy and intelligence which tolerates the widest individual freedom despite the necessary public control; we must learn to select for public office ability rather than mere affability. We must stand ready to defer to knowledge and science and judge by result rather than by method; and finally we must face the fact that the final distribution of goods—the question of wages and income is an ethical and not a mere mechanical problem and calls for grave public human judgment and not secrecy and closed doors. All this means time and development. It comes hot complete by instant revolution of a day, nor yet by the deferred evolution of a thousand years—it comes daily, bit by bit and step by step, as men and women learn and grow and as children are trained in Truth.

These steps are in many cases clear: the careful, steady increase of public democratic ownership of industry, beginning with the simplest type of public utilities and monopolies, and extending gradually as we learn the way; the use of taxation to limit inheritance and to take the unearned increment for public use beginning (but not ending) with a "single tax" on monopolized land values; the training of the public in business technique by co-operation in buying and selling, and in industrial technique by the shop committee and manufacturing guild.

But beyond all this must come the Spirit— the Will to Human Brotherhood of all Colors, Races, and Creeds; the Wanting of the Wants of All. Perhaps the finest contribution of current Socialism to the world is neither its light nor its dogma, but the idea back of its one mighty word—Comrade!

HANNAH ARENDT

~

INTRODUCTION

MICHAEL MCCARTHY

Hannah Arendt (1906–1975) was one of the most important political thinkers of the twentieth century. A European by birth, culture, and education, she was raised in Königsberg, Prussia, and spent her youth and adolescence amidst the political instability of Weimar Germany. During her extended university career she studied with three of Germany's most important thinkers, Edmund Husserl (Freiburg), Martin Heidegger (Marburg), and Karl Jaspers (Heidelberg). Her earliest theoretical interests were theological rather than political, and are reflected in her doctoral dissertation completed under Jaspers on St. Augustine's understanding of love. She emigrated from Nazi Germany to Paris in 1933. After the fall of France, she fled from Europe with her mother and husband to seek exile in the United States, where she became a citizen in 1951. She traveled widely in her new political home, teaching at Princeton, Berkeley, Chicago, Wesleyan, and the New School for Social Research (1967–1975).

Hannah Arendt's political thinking developed over several decades. It began with her exploration and appraisal of *The Origins of Totalitarianism* (1951). It expanded with her critical retrieval of the active life (*via activa*) in *The Human Condition* (1958). These early works provided the intellectual horizon for her genealogical critique of "our tradition of political thought." In developing that critique, she amplified her civic republican vision by contrasting it with the dominant political visions of the West: *Between Past and Future* (1961); *On Revolution* (1963); *Eichmann in Jerusalem* (1963); and *Lectures on Kant's Political Philosophy* (1982). In the last decade of her life, she applied her distinctive political insights to *The Crises of the Republic* (1972) and augmented her earlier study of the active life with a complementary account of *The Life of the Mind* (1978).

To understand Arendt's turn to political questions it is critical to remember that she reached maturity during what Eric Hobsbawm has called the age of catastrophe. Between 1914 and 1945 the stabilizing structures of modern Europe collapsed. While the parliamentary democracies of England and France remained impotent, fascist regimes consolidated their power in Italy and Spain, and popularly supported totalitarian governments emerged in Hitler's Germany and Stalin's Soviet Union. Totalitarianism was an unprecedented form of human domination, based on ideology and terror, that slaughtered millions of innocent people in the name of global utopian prophecies. Although Nazi Germany was defeated eventually, the two world wars had transformed Europe from the center of world civilization to a demoralized continent in ruins. From Arendt's critical perspective, the political and economic collapse of Europe extended to its intellectual, moral, and cultural traditions as well. The vital human connection between the past and the present had been severed; conscientious citizens were now forced "to think without bannisters" (*denken ohne Geländer*).

At the end of the Second World War when the horrors of the Holocaust became known, Arendt committed herself to a work of remembrance and reflection. Intellectual integrity demanded that we comprehend and articulate the genesis of totalitarian terror. What earlier spiritual and moral collapse had made totalitarianism possible? What was the basis of its evident mass appeal? To what cultural resources and political institutions could we turn to prevent its recurrence? After long years of study, Arendt concluded that the deepest crisis of the modern world was political, and that the continuing appeal of totalitarian mass movements demonstrated how profound that crisis had become.

The crisis she identified could be discerned on four distinct but interconnected levels: cultural, theoretical, institutional, and normative. The world alienation of modernity had promoted a mass culture antithetical to republican self-government and particularly prone to ideological manipulation. Our theoretical capacity to critique this culture and the ideologies it spawns is compromised because our inherited traditions have systematically misrepresented political experience. By substituting making (*poiesis*) for action (*praxis*), command and coercion for persuasion and argument, and technical mastery for political excellence and judgment our traditional theorists, ancient and modern, have darkened the common perception of politics and reduced it to a servant of economic needs and concerns. The striking rise of economics to its present cultural supremacy has transformed the public realm into a sphere of necessity rather than freedom, while the enduring attractions of freedom have been largely confined to the individual pursuit of private happiness. As a result, the demoralized individuals who live within mass societies lack the informed commitment to public liberty that is needed to sustain the republican spirit. And without that spirit, the lost spirit of the great democratic revolutions, modern citizens no longer know what to require of themselves and their political leaders, nor how to judge responsibly their public conduct and speech.

For Arendt, the modern political crisis is also a crisis of humanism. The radical totalitarian experiment was rooted in two fundamentally distorted images of the human being. The agents of terror believed in the limitless power generated by collective organization, a power wielded and justified by appeal to historical necessity. The victims of terror, by contrast, were systematically dehumanized by the ruling ideology, and then brutally deprived of their political and legal rights and their moral and existential dignity. Hannah Arendt's political humanism explicitly challenges both these distorting images, the first because it dangerously inflates human power, the second because it subverts human freedom and agency. Human beings living together on the earth, in a humanly constructed world and within a web of fragile human connections, are neither sovereign masters nor superfluous animals. Rather, they are singular and unique persons capable of distinguishing themselves through action and speech, and requiring both a public realm of freedom and justice and a private realm of security and intimacy to protect and enhance their dignity.

In the tradition of civic republican thinkers that stretches from Aristotle and Cicero to Charles Taylor and Michael Sandel, Arendt made the concepts of public liberty, civic virtue, and public happiness essential to her understanding of genuine citizenship.

Equipped with these normative resources, she openly criticized the reductive modern anthropologies that had reduced human beings to calculating economic animals. The ideological reduction of the human person had not only been used to justify totalitarian terror; it had also contributed to the political alienation of democratic citizens in contemporary liberal societies. If we are to recover a more authentic understanding of the human, we will need a much richer and deeper account of citizenship than conservatism, liberalism, or Marxism provides.

Hannah Arendt's spirited defense of republican citizenship was not a case of disinterested scholarship. For her, the most dangerous threats to human dignity were caused by extreme political alienation. It was the alienation of the European masses from parliamentary democracy that led to the rise of totalitarian governments. Even in liberal democracies, like England and the United States, where civic alienation is less advanced, there has been a striking decline in political legitimacy. Evidence of this decline can be found in the loss of governmental authority, a diminished sense of civic obligation, low levels of electoral participation and a growing contempt for traditional political parties and their leaders. On Arendt's historical analysis, these are not transient phenomena easily corrected with the passage of time. They are instead structural features of the modern world directly connected to the modern understanding of human existence and freedom.

If these critical suspicions are justified, the contemporary political thinker is faced with a formidable challenge. The deep political alienation of modernity threatens human dignity and freedom, but "our tradition of political thought" lacks the resources to address that threat effectively. When our inherited traditions can no longer be trusted, the need for free and independent thinking (*selbst denken*) becomes urgent. Hannah Arendt aspired to be such a thinker and modeled her reflection on the philosophers she most admired: Socrates, Augustine, Scotus, Lessing, Kant, and Heidegger. Independent thinking of the sort Arendt attempted is not systematic and progressive, but foundational and critical. Faced with a crisis in politics, we need to rethink the basic principles of human association. Faced with a systemic assault on human dignity, we need to rethink its foundation in the constitution of the human person. Faced with an erosion of public liberty, we need to reestablish the inter-dependence of plurality and freedom. These foundational tasks are obligatory for the critical thinker who challenges the answers of the tradition but does not dismiss them, who seeks to recover the retrievable past and not to forget it (*Between Past and Future*).

Perhaps Arendt's greatest strength as a thinker was her ability to resist the modern propensity for half-truths. She is difficult to classify in conventional political categories because she combined and connected what modern ideologies have fiercely opposed. She deeply distrusted the sterile oppositions between left and right, progressive and conservative, communitarian and individualist. "Nothing compromises the understanding of political issues and their meaningful debate more seriously than the automatic thought reactions conditioned by the beaten path of ideologies born in the wake and aftermath of the French Revolution" (*On Revolution*). Since the early nineteenth century, our dominant political traditions have tended to treat complementary principles as mutually exclusive polarities. But it is only against the background of a common world of meaning that individual differences can truly reveal themselves. And it is only in the midst of a community of peers that personal distinction and excellence can be appreciated. A credible political philosophy needs to connect what the ideologists of left and right have consistently separated: an old world with young citizens; the spirit of conservation with a commitment to civic initiative; worldly permanence with the eruption of miraculous novelty; and the security and equality of law with institutions of republican freedom.

Hannah Arendt never forgot the example of the European death camps. For her, they served as a warning against many things: the threatening potential of political mass movements, the inherent dangers in an atomized and fragmented society, and the profound instability of the European moral inheritance in our secular age. But they also provided an inverted model of what political action should really be striving for. If the death camps were holes of oblivion and anonymity, then an authentic political community should be a site of remembrance and personal distinction. If the camps had eliminated spontaneity and driven human beings into brute-like silence, then the public realm should be a space of freedom where human beings reveal their uniqueness in word and deed. If the camps systematically destroyed human dignity through ideology and terror, then a true republic must render dignity secure by guaranteeing each citizen's legal and political rights and by ensuring that all persons will be publicly judged based on opinions they freely express and actions they really perform. If the camps turned human beings into naked and submissive animals, then genuine politics should create an enduring world where they can think, speak, and act like free men and women.

Though Arendt's appraisal of our political situation is harsh, it is not fatalistic. Historical inevitability does not govern the conduct of human affairs. Each of the elements in our political crisis is subject to challenge and redress, and as her own life reveals, the individual person is not condemned to impotence and despair. The critical thinker can challenge the oversights and distortions of traditional political theory, the dedicated teacher can oppose the culture of *humanitas* to the complacent egoism of our consumer society, the gifted storyteller can remind us of both the greatness and misery of our common past, and the individual citizen can speak and act cooperating with peers in the unending work of protecting human dignity and renewing human liberty.

For an excellent account of Arendt's personal and intellectual development, see Elisabeth Young-Bruehl, *Hannah Arendt: For Love of the World* (New Haven Conn.: Yale University Press, 1982). Important critical studies of Arendt include: Margaret Canovan, *A Reinterpretation of Her Political Thought* (Cambridge: Cambridge University Press, 1992); Seyla Benhabib; *The Reluctant Modernism of Hannah Arendt* (Thousand Oaks, Calif.: Sage Books, 1996); Julia Kristeva, *Hannah Arendt* (New York: Columbia University Press, 2001); Hannah Pitkin, *The Attack of the Blob* (Chicago: University of Chicago Press, 1998); Dana Villa, *Arendt and Heidegger: The Fate of the Political* (Princeton, N.J.: Princeton University Press, 1995); and Michael Mc Carthy, *The Political Humanism of Hannah Arendt* (Lanham, Md.: Lexington Books, 2012). *Hannah Arendt*, a recent film directed by Margarethe Von Trotta, explores the intense controversy generated by Arendt's analysis and appraisal of the Israeli government's trial and conviction of Adolph Eichmann.

The Origins of Totalitarianism

X

A Classless Society

. . . Totalitarian movements are possible wherever there are masses who for one reason or another have acquired the appetite for political organization. Masses are not held together by a consciousness of common interest and they lack that specific class articulateness which is expressed in determined, limited, and obtainable goals. The term masses applies only where we deal with people who either because of sheer numbers, or indifference, or a combination of both, cannot be integrated into any organization based on common interest, into political parties or municipal governments or professional organizations or trade unions. Potentially, they exist in every country and form the majority of those large numbers of neutral, politically indifferent people who never join a party and hardly ever go to the polls.

It was characteristic of the rise of the Nazi movement in Germany and of the Communist movements in Europe after 1930 that they recruited their members from this mass of apparently indifferent people whom all other parties had given up as too apathetic or too stupid for their attention. The result was that the majority of their membership consisted of people who never before had appeared on the political scene. This permitted the introduction of entirely new methods into political propaganda, and indifference to the arguments of political opponents; these movements not only placed themselves outside and against the party system as a whole, they found a membership that

had never been reached, never been "spoiled" by the party system. Therefore they did not need to refute opposing arguments and consistently preferred methods which ended in death rather than persuasion, which spelled terror rather than conviction. They presented disagreements as invariably originating in deep natural, social, or psychological sources beyond the control of the individual and therefore beyond the power of reason. This would have been, a shortcoming only if they had sincerely entered into competition with other parties; it was not if they were sure of dealing with people who had reason to be equally hostile to all parties.

The success of totalitarian movements among the masses meant the end of two illusions of democratically ruled countries in general and of European nation-states and their party system in particular. The first was that the people in its majority had taken an active part in government and that each individual was in sympathy with one's own or somebody else's party. On the contrary, the movements showed that the politically neutral and indifferent masses could easily be the majority in a democratically ruled country, that therefore a democracy could function according to rules which are actively recognized by only a minority. The second democratic illusion exploded by the totalitarian movements was that these politically indifferent masses did not matter, that they were truly neutral and constituted no more than the inarticulate backward setting for the political life of the nation. Now they made apparent what no other organ of public opinion had ever been able to show, namely, that democratic government had rested as much on the silent approbation and tolerance of the indifferent

From Hannah Arendt, *The Origins of Totalitarianism*, new edition with added prefaces, Harcourt, Inc., 1985. Reprinted by permission of the publisher. Footnotes omitted.

and inarticulate sections of the people as on the articulate and visible institutions and organizations of the country. Thus when the totalitarian movements invaded Parliament with their contempt for parliamentary government, they merely appeared inconsistent: actually, they succeeded in convincing the people at large that parliamentary majorities were spurious and did not necessarily correspond to the realities of the country, thereby undermining the self-respect and the confidence of governments which also believed in majority rule rather than in their constitutions. . . .

Totalitarian movements are mass organizations of atomized, isolated individuals. Compared with all other parties and movements, their most conspicuous external characteristic is their demand for total, unrestricted, unconditional, and unalterable loyalty of the individual member. This demand is made by the leaders of totalitarian movements even before they seize power. It usually precedes the total organization of the country under their actual rule and it follows from the claim of their ideologies that their organization will encompass, in due course, the entire human race. Where, however, totalitarian rule has not been prepared by a totalitarian movement (and this, in contradistinction to Nazi Germany, was the case in Russia), the movement has to be organized afterward and the conditions for its growth have artificially to be created in order to make total loyalty—the psychological basis for total domination—at all possible. Such loyalty can be expected only from the completely isolated human being who, without any other social ties to family, friends, comrades, or even mere acquaintances, derives his sense of having a place in the world only from his belonging to a movement, his membership in the party.

Total loyalty is possible only when fidelity is emptied of all concrete content, from which changes of mind might naturally arise. The totalitarian movements, each in its own way, have done their utmost to get rid of the party programs which specified concrete content and which they inherited from earlier, nontotalitarian stages of development. No matter how radically they might have been phrased, every definite political goal which does not simply assert or circumscribe the claim to world rule, every political program which deals with issues more specific than "ideological questions of importance for centuries" is an obstruction to totalitarianism. Hitler's greatest achievement in the organization of the Nazi movement, which he gradually built up from the obscure crackpot membership of a typically nationalistic little party, was that he unburdened the movement of the party's earlier program, not by changing or officially abolishing it, but simply by refusing to talk about it or discuss its points, whose relative moderateness of content and phraseology were very soon outdated. Stalin's task in this as in other respects was much more formidable; the socialist program of the Bolshevik party was a much more troublesome burden. . . . But Stalin achieved eventually, after having abolished the factions of the Russian party, the same result through the constant zigzag of the Communist Party lines, and the constant reinterpretation and application of Marxism which voided the doctrine of all its content because it was no longer possible to predict what course or action it would inspire. The fact that the most perfect education in Marxism and Leninism was no guide whatsoever for political behavior—that, on the contrary, one could follow the party line only if one repeated each morning what Stalin had announced the night before—naturally resulted in the same state of mind, the same concentrated obedience, undivided by any attempt to understand what one was doing, that Himmler's ingenious watchword for his SS-men expressed: "My honor is my loyalty." . . .

What is more disturbing to our peace of mind than the unconditional loyalty of members of totalitarian movements, and the popular support of totalitarian regimes, is the unquestionable attraction these movements exert on the elite, and not only on the mob elements in society. It would be rash indeed to discount, because of artistic vagaries or scholarly naïveté, the terrifying roster of distinguished men whom totalitarianism can count among its sympathizers, fellow-travelers, and inscribed party members. . . .

. . . There is no doubt that the elite was pleased whenever the underworld frightened respectable society into accepting it on an equal footing. The members of the elite did not object at all to paying a price, the destruction of civilization, for the fun of seeing how those who had been excluded unjustly in the past forced their way into it. They were not particularly outraged at the monstrous forgeries in historiography of which all totalitarian regimes are guilty and which announce themselves clearly enough in totalitarian propaganda. They had convinced themselves that traditional historiography was a forgery in any case, since it had excluded the underprivileged and oppressed from the memory of mankind. Those who were rejected by their own time were usually forgotten by history, and insult added to injury had troubled all sensitive consciences ever since faith in a hereafter where the last would be the first had disappeared. Injustices in the past as well as the present became intolerable when there was no longer any hope that the scales of justice eventually would be set right. Marx's great attempt to rewrite world history in terms of class struggles fascinated even those who did not believe in the correctness of his thesis, because of his original intention to find a device by which to force the destinies of those excluded from official history into the memory of posterity.

The temporary alliance between the elite and the mob rested largely on this genuine delight with which the former watched the latter destroy respectability. This could be achieved when the German steel barons were forced to deal with and to receive socially Hitler the housepainter and self-admitted former derelict, as it could be with the crude and vulgar forgeries perpetrated by the totalitarian movements in all fields of intellectual life, insofar as they gathered all the subterranean, nonrespectable elements of European history into one consistent picture. . . .

To this aversion of the intellectual elite for official historiography, to its conviction that history, which was a forgery anyway, might as well be the playground of crackpots, must be added the terrible, demoralizing fascination in the possibility that gigantic lies and monstrous falsehoods can eventually be established as unquestioned facts, that man may be free to change his own past at will, and that the difference between truth and falsehood may cease to be objective and become a mere matter of

power and cleverness, of pressure and infinite repetition. Not Stalin's and Hitler's skill in the art of lying but the fact that they were able to organize the masses into a collective unit to back up their lies with impressive magnificence, exerted the fascination. Simple forgeries from the viewpoint of scholarship appeared to receive the sanction of history itself when the whole marching reality of the movements stood behind them and pretended to draw from them the necessary inspiration for action. . . .

In all fairness to those among the elite, on the other hand, who at one time or another have let themselves be seduced by totalitarian movements, and who sometimes, because of their intellectual abilities, are even accused of having inspired totalitarianism, it must be stated that what these desperate men of the twentieth century did or did not do had no influence on totalitarianism whatsoever, although it did play some part in earlier, successful, attempts of the movements to force the outside world to take their doctrines seriously. Wherever totalitarian movements seized power, this whole group of sympathizers was shaken off even before the regimes proceeded toward their greatest crimes. Intellectual, spiritual, and artistic initiative is as dangerous to totalitarianism as the gangster initiative of the mob, and both are more dangerous than mere political opposition. The consistent persecution of every higher form of intellectual activity by the new mass leaders springs from more than their natural resentment against everything they cannot understand. Total domination does not allow for free initiative in any field of life, for any activity that is not entirely predictable. Totalitarianism in power invariably replaces all first-rate talents, regardless of their sympathies, with those crackpots and fools whose lack of intelligence and creativity is still the best guarantee of their loyalty.

XI

The Totalitarian Movement

. . . A mixture of gullibility and cynicism had been an outstanding characteristic of mob mentality before it became an everyday phenomenon of masses. In an ever-changing, incomprehensible world the masses had reached the point where they would, at the same time, believe everything and nothing, think that everything was possible and that nothing was true. The mixture in itself was remarkable enough, because it spelled the end of the illusion that gullibility was a weakness of unsuspecting primitive souls and cynicism the vice of superior and refined minds. Mass propaganda discovered that its audience was ready at all times to believe the worst, no matter how absurd, and did not particularly object to being deceived because it held every statement to be a lie anyhow. The totalitarian mass leaders based their propaganda on the correct psychological assumption that, under such conditions, one could make people believe the most fantastic statements one day, and trust that if the next day they were given irrefutable proof of their falsehood, they would take refuge in cynicism; instead of deserting the leaders who had lied to them, they would protest that they had known all along that the statement was a lie and would admire the leaders for their superior tactical cleverness.

What had been a demonstrable reaction of mass audiences became an important hierarchical principle for mass organizations. A mixture of gullibility and cynicism is prevalent in all ranks of totalitarian movements, and the higher the rank the more cynicism weighs down gullibility. The essential conviction shared by all ranks, from fellow-traveler to leader, is that politics is a game of cheating and that the "first commandment" of the movement: "The Fuehrer is always right," is as necessary for the purposes of world politics, i.e., world-wide cheating, as the rules of military discipline are for the purposes of war.

The machine that generates, organizes, and spreads the monstrous falsehoods of totalitarian movements depends again upon the position of the Leader. To the propaganda assertion that all happenings are scientifically predictable according to the laws of nature or economics, totalitarian organization adds the position of one man who has monopolized this knowledge and whose principal quality is that he "was always right and will always be right." To a member of a totalitarian movement this knowledge has nothing to do with truth and this being right nothing to do with the objective truthfulness of the Leader's statements which cannot be disproved by facts, but only by future success or failure. The Leader is always right in his actions and since these are planned for centuries to come, the ultimate test of what he does has been removed beyond the experience of his contemporaries.

The only group supposed to believe loyally and textually in the Leader's words are the sympathizers whose confidence surrounds the movement with an atmosphere of honesty and simple-mindedness, and helps the Leader to fulfill half his task, that is, to inspire confidence in the movement. The party members never believe public statements and are not supposed to, but are complimented by totalitarian propaganda on that superior intelligence which supposedly distinguishes them from the nontotalitarian outside world, which, in turn, they know only from the abnormal gullibility of sympathizers. Only Nazi sympathizers believed Hitler when he swore his famous legality oath before the supreme court of the Weimar Republic; members of the movement knew very well that he lied, and trusted him more than ever because he apparently was able to fool public opinion and the authorities. When in later years Hitler repeated the performance for the whole world, when he swore to his good intentions and at the same time most openly prepared his crimes, the admiration of the Nazi membership naturally was boundless. Similarly, only Bolshevik fellow-travelers believed in the dissolution of the Comintern, and only the nonorganized masses of the Russian people and the fellow-travelers abroad were meant to take at face value Stalin's prodemocratic statements during the war. Bolshevik party members were explicitly warned not to be fooled by tactical maneuvers and were asked to admire their Leader's shrewdness in betraying his allies. . . .

The topmost layer in the organization of totalitarian movements is the intimate circle around the Leader, which can be a formal institution, like the Bolshevik Politburo, or a changing clique of men who do not necessarily hold office, like the entourage of Hitler. To them ideological clichés are mere devices to organize the masses, and they feel no compunction about changing them according to the needs of circumstances if only the organizing principle is kept intact. . . .

It is this freedom from the content of their own ideologies which characterizes the highest rank of the totalitarian hierarchy. These men consider everything and everybody in terms of organization, and this includes the Leader who to them is neither an inspired talisman nor the one who is infallibly right, but the simple consequence of this type of organization; he is needed, not as a person, but as a function, and as such he is indispensable to the movement. In contrast, however, to other despotic forms of government, where frequently a clique rules and the despot plays only the representative role of a puppet ruler, totalitarian leaders are actually free to do whatever they please and can count on the loyalty of their entourage even if they choose to murder them.

The more technical reason for this suicidal loyalty is that succession to the supreme office is not regulated by any inheritance or other laws. A successful palace revolt would have as disastrous results for the movement as a whole as a military defeat. It is in the nature of the movement that once the Leader has assumed his office, the whole organization is so absolutely identified with him that any admission of a mistake or removal from office would break the spell of infallibility which surrounds the office of the Leader and spell doom to all those connected with the movement. It is not the truthfulness of the Leader's words but the infallibility of his actions which is the basis for the structure. Without it and in the heat of a discussion which presumes fallibility, the whole fictitious world of totalitarianism goes to pieces, overwhelmed at once by the factuality of the real world which only the movement steered in an infallibly right direction by the Leader was able to ward off.

XII

Totalitarianism in Power

History teaches that rise to power and responsibility affects deeply the nature of revolutionary parties. Experience and common sense were perfectly justified in expecting that totalitarianism in power would gradually lose its revolutionary momentum and utopian character, that the everyday business of government and the possession of real power would moderate the pre-power claims of the movements and gradually destroy the fictitious world of their organizations. It seems, after all, to be in the very nature of things, personal or public, that extreme demands and goals are checked by objective conditions; and reality, taken as a whole, is only to a very small extent determined by the inclination toward fiction of a mass society of atomized individuals.

Many of the errors of the nontotalitarian world in its diplomatic dealings with totalitarian governments (the most conspicuous ones being confidence in the Munich pact with Hitler and the Yalta agreements with Stalin) can clearly be traced to an experience and a common sense which suddenly proved to have lost its grasp on reality. Contrary to all expectations, important concessions and greatly heightened international prestige did not help to reintegrate the totalitarian countries into the comity of nations or induce them to abandon their lying complaint that the whole world had solidly lined up against them. And far from preventing this, diplomatic victories clearly precipitated their recourse to the instruments of violence and resulted in all instances in increased hostility against the powers that had shown themselves willing to compromise. . . .

The trouble with totalitarian regimes is not that they play power politics in an especially ruthless way, but that behind their politics is hidden an entirely new and unprecedented concept of power, just as behind their *Realpolitik* lies an entirely new and unprecedented concept of reality. Supreme disregard for immediate consequences rather than ruthlessness; rootlessness and neglect of national interests rather than nationalism; contempt for utilitarian motives rather than unconsidered pursuit of self-interest; "idealism," i.e., their unwavering faith in an ideological fictitious world, rather than lust for power—these have all introduced into international politics a new and more disturbing factor than mere aggressiveness would have been able to do.

Power, as conceived by totalitarianism, lies exclusively in the force produced through organization. Just as Stalin saw every institution, independent of its actual function, only as a "transmission belt connecting the party with the people" and honestly believed that the most precious treasures of the Soviet Union were not the riches of its soil or the productive capacity of its huge manpower, but the "cadres" of the party (i.e., the police), so Hitler, as early as 1929, saw the "great thing" of the movement in the fact that sixty thousand men "have outwardly become almost a unit, that actually these members are uniform not only in ideas, but that even the facial expression is almost the same. Look at these laughing eyes, this fanatical enthusiasm and you will discover . . . how a hundred thousand men in a movement become a single type." Whatever connection power had in the minds of Western man with earthly possessions, with wealth, treasures, and riches, has been dissolved into a kind of dematerialized mechanism whose every move generates power as friction or galvanic currents generate electricity. The totalitarian division of states into Have and Have-not countries is more than a demagogic device; those who make it are actually convinced that the power of material possessions is negligible and only stands in the way of the development of organizational power. To Stalin constant growth and development of police cadres were incomparably more important than the oil in Baku, the coal and ore in the Urals, the granaries in the Ukraine, or the potential treasures of Siberia—in

short the development of Russia's full power arsenal. The same mentality led Hitler to sacrifice all Germany to the cadres of the SS; he did not consider the war lost when German cities lay in rubble and industrial capacity was destroyed, but only when he learned that the SS troops were no longer reliable. To a man who believed in organizational omnipotence against all mere material factors, military or economic, and who, moreover, calculated the eventual victory of his enterprise in centuries, defeat was not military catastrophe or threatened starvation of the population, but only the destruction of the elite formations which were supposed to carry the conspiracy for world rule through a line of generations to its eventual end.

The structurelessness of the totalitarian state, its neglect of material interests, its emancipation from the profit motive, and its nonutilitarian attitudes in general have more than anything else contributed to making contemporary politics well-nigh unpredictable. The inability of the nontotalitarian world to grasp a mentality which functions independently of all calculable action in terms of men and material, and is completely indifferent to national interest and the well-being of its people, shows itself in a curious dilemma of judgment: those who rightly understand the terrible efficiency of totalitarian organization and police are likely to overestimate the material force of totalitarian countries, while those who understand the wasteful incompetence of totalitarian economics are likely to underestimate the power potential which can be created in disregard of all material factors. . . .

The concentration and extermination camps of totalitarian regimes serve as the laboratories in which the fundamental belief of totalitarianism that everything is possible is being verified. Compared with this, all other experiments are secondary in importance—including those in the field of medicine whose horrors are recorded in detail in the trials against the physicians of the Third Reich—although it is characteristic that these laboratories were used for experiments of every kind.

Total domination, which strives to organize the infinite plurality and differentiation of human beings as if all of humanity were just one individual, is possible only if each and every person can be reduced to a never-changing identity of reactions, so that each of these bundles of reactions can be exchanged at random for any other. The problem is to fabricate something that does not exist, namely, a kind of human species resembling other animal species whose only "freedom" would consist in "preserving the species." Totalitarian domination attempts to achieve this goal both through ideological indoctrination of the elite formations and through absolute terror in the camps; and the atrocities for which the elite formations are ruthlessly used become, as it were, the practical application of the ideological indoctrination—the testing ground in which the latter must prove itself—while the appalling spectacle of the camps themselves is supposed to furnish the "theoretical" verification of the ideology.

The camps are meant not only to exterminate people and degrade human beings, but also serve the ghastly experiment of eliminating, under scientifically controlled conditions, spontaneity itself as an expression of human behavior and of transforming the human personality into a mere thing, into something that even animals are not; for Pavlov's dog, which, as we know, was trained to eat not when it was hungry but when a bell rang, was a perverted animal. . . .

The uselessness of the camps, their cynically admitted anti-utility, is only apparent. In reality they are more essential to the preservation of the regime's power than any of its other institutions. Without concentration camps, without the undefined fear they inspire and the very well-defined training they offer in totalitarian domination, which can nowhere else be fully tested with all of its most radical possibilities, a totalitarian state can neither inspire its nuclear troops with fanaticism nor maintain a whole people in complete apathy. The dominating and the dominated would only too quickly sink back into the "old bourgeois routine"; after early "excesses," they would succumb to everyday life with its human laws; in short, they would develop in the direction which all observers counseled by common sense were so prone to predict. The tragic fallacy of all these prophecies; originating in a world that was still safe, was to suppose that there was such a thing as one human nature established for all time, to identify this human nature with history, and thus to declare that the idea of total domination was not only inhuman but also unrealistic. Meanwhile we have learned that the power of man is so great that he really can be what he wishes to be.

It is in the very nature of totalitarian regimes to demand unlimited power. Such power can only be secured if literally all men, without a single exception, are reliably dominated in every aspect of their life. In the realm of foreign affairs new neutral territories must constantly be subjugated, while at home ever-new human groups must be mastered in expanding concentration camps, or, when circumstances require liquidated to make room for others. The question of opposition is unimportant both in foreign and domestic affairs. Any neutrality, indeed any spontaneously given friendship, is from the standpoint of totalitarian domination just as dangerous as open hostility, precisely because spontaneity as such, with its incalculability, is the greatest of all obstacles to total domination over man. . . .

What makes conviction and opinion of any sort so ridiculous and dangerous under totalitarian conditions is that totalitarian regimes take the greatest pride in having no need of them, or of any human help of any kind. Men insofar as they are more than animal reaction and fulfillment of functions are entirely superfluous to totalitarian regimes. Totalitarianism strives not toward despotic rule over men, but toward a system in which men are superfluous. Total power can be achieved and safeguarded only in a world of conditioned reflexes, of marionettes without the slightest trace of spontaneity. Precisely because man's resources are so great, he can be fully dominated only when he becomes a specimen of the animal-species man.

Therefore character is a threat and even the most unjust legal rules are an obstacle; but individuality, anything indeed that distinguishes one man from another, is intolerable. As long as all men have not been made equally superfluous—and this has been accomplished only in concentration camps—the ideal of totalitarian domination has not been achieved. Totalitarian states strive constantly, though never with complete success, to establish the superfluity of man—by the arbitrary selection of various groups for concentration camps, by constant purges of the ruling apparatus, by mass liquidations. Common sense protests desperately that the masses are submissive and that all this gigantic apparatus of terror is therefore superfluous; if they were capable of telling the truth, the totalitarian rulers would reply: The apparatus seems superfluous to you only because it serves to make men superfluous. . . .

XIII

Ideology and Terror: A Novel Form of Government

In the preceding chapters we emphasized repeatedly that the means of total domination are not only more drastic but that totalitarianism differs essentially from other forms of political oppression known to us such as despotism, tyranny and dictatorship. Wherever it rose to power, it developed entirely new political institutions and destroyed all social, legal and political traditions of the country. No matter what the specifically national tradition or the particular spiritual source of its ideology, totalitarian government always transformed classes into masses, supplanted the party system, not by one-party dictatorships, but by a mass movement, shifted the center of power from the army to the police, and established a foreign policy openly directed toward world domination. Present totalitarian governments have developed from one-party systems; whenever these became truly totalitarian, they started to operate

according to a system of values so radically different from all others, that none of our traditional legal, moral, or common sense utilitarian categories could any longer help us to come to terms with, or judge, or predict their course of action.

If it is true that the elements of totalitarianism can be found by retracing the history and analyzing the political implications of what we usually call the crisis of our century, then the conclusion is unavoidable that this crisis is no mere threat from the outside, no mere result of some aggressive foreign policy of either Germany or Russia, and that it will no more disappear with the death of Stalin than it disappeared with the fall of Nazi Germany. It may even be that the true predicaments of our time will assume their authentic form—though not necessarily the cruelest—only when totalitarianism has become a thing of the past.

It is in the line of such reflections to raise the question whether totalitarian government, born of this crisis and at the same time its clearest and only unequivocal symptom, is merely a makeshift arrangement, which borrows its methods of intimidation, its means of organization and its instruments of violence from the well-known political arsenal of tyranny, despotism and dictatorships, and owes its existence only to the deplorable, but perhaps accidental failure of the traditional political forces—liberal or conservative, national or socialist, republican or monarchist, authoritarian or democratic. Or whether, on the contrary, there is such a thing as the *nature* of totalitarian government, whether it has its own essence and can be compared with and defined like other forms of government such as Western thought has known and recognized since the times of ancient philosophy. If this is true, then the entirely new and unprecedented forms of totalitarian organization and course of action must rest on one of the few basic experiences which men can have whenever they live together, and are concerned with public affairs. If there is a basic experience which finds its political expression in totalitarian domination, then, in view of the novelty of the totalitarian form of government, this must be an experience which, for whatever reason, has never before served as the foundation of a body politic and whose general mood—although it may be familiar in every other respect—never before has pervaded, and directed the handling of, public affairs.

If we consider this in terms of the history of ideas, it seems extremely unlikely. For the forms of government under which men live have been very few; they were discovered early, classified by the Greeks and have proved extraordinarily long-lived. If we apply these findings, whose fundamental idea, despite many variations, did not change in the two and a half thousand years that separate Plato from Kant, we are tempted at once to interpret totalitarianism as some modern form of tyranny, that is a lawless government where power is wielded by one man. Arbitrary power, unrestricted by law, wielded in the interest of the ruler and hostile to the interests of the governed, on one hand, fear as the principle of action, namely fear of the people by the ruler and fear of the ruler by the people, on the other—these have been the hallmarks of tyranny throughout our tradition.

Instead of saying that totalitarian government is unprecedented, we could also say that it has exploded the very alternative on which all definitions of the essence of governments have been based in political philosophy, that is the alternative between lawful and lawless government, between arbitrary and legitimate power. That lawful government and legitimate power, on one side, lawlessness and arbitrary power on the other, belonged together and were inseparable has never been questioned. Yet, totalitarian rule confronts us with a totally different kind of government. It defies, it is true, all positive laws, even to the extreme of defying those which it has itself established (as in the case of the Soviet Constitution of 1936, to quote only the most outstanding example) or which it did not care to abolish (as in the case of the Weimar Constitution which the Nazi government never revoked). But it operates neither without guidance of law nor is it arbitrary, for it claims to obey strictly and unequivocally those laws of Nature or of History from which all positive laws always have been supposed to spring.

It is the monstrous, yet seemingly unanswerable claim of totalitarian rule that, far from being "lawless," it goes to the sources of authority from which positive laws received their ultimate legitimation, that far from being arbitrary it is more obedient to these suprahuman forces than any government ever was before, and that far from wielding its power in the interest of one man, it is quite prepared to sacrifice everybody's vital immediate interests to the execution of what it assumes to be the law of History or the law of Nature. Its defiance of positive laws claims to be a higher form of legitimacy which, since it is inspired by the sources themselves, can do away with petty legality. Totalitarian lawfulness pretends to have found a way to establish the rule of justice on earth—something which the legality of positive law admittedly could never attain. The discrepancy between legality and justice could never be bridged because the standards of right and wrong into which positive law translates its own source of authority—"natural law" governing the whole universe, or divine law revealed in human history, or customs and traditions expressing the law common to the sentiments of all men—are necessarily general and must be valid for a countless and unpredictable number of cases, so that each concrete individual case with its unrepeatable set of circumstances somehow escapes it.

Totalitarian lawfulness, defying legality and pretending to establish the direct reign of justice on earth, executes the law of History or of Nature without translating it into standards of right and wrong for individual behavior. It applies the law directly to mankind without bothering with the behavior of men. The law of Nature or the law of History, if properly executed, is expected to produce mankind as its end product; and this expectation lies behind the claim to global rule of all totalitarian governments. Totalitarian policy claims to transform the human species into an active unfailing carrier of a law to which human beings otherwise would only passively and reluctantly be subjected. If it is true that the link between totalitarian countries and the civilized world was broken through the monstrous crimes of totalitarian regimes, it is also true that this criminality was not due to simple aggressiveness, ruthlessness, warfare and treachery, but to a conscious break of that *consensus iuris* which, according to Cicero, constitutes a "people," and which, as international law, in modern times has constituted the civilized world insofar as it remains the foundation-stone of international relations even under the conditions of war. Both moral judgment and legal punishment presuppose this basic consent; the criminal can be judged justly only because he takes part in the *consensus iuris*, and even the revealed law of God can function among men only when they listen and consent to it.

At this point the fundamental difference between the totalitarian and all other concepts of law comes to light. Totalitarian policy does not replace one set of laws with another, does not establish its own *consensus iuris*, does not create, by one revolution, a new form of legality. Its defiance of all, even its own positive laws implies that it believes it can do without any *consensus iuris* whatever, and still not resign itself to the tyrannical state of lawlessness, arbitrariness and fear. It can do without the *consensus iuris* because it promises to release the fulfillment of law from all action and will of man; and it promises justice on earth because it claims to make mankind itself the embodiment of the law.

This identification of man and law, which seems to cancel the discrepancy between legality and justice that has plagued legal thought since ancient times, has nothing in common with the *lumen naturale* or the voice of conscience, by which Nature or Divinity as the sources of authority for the *ius naturale* or the historically revealed commands of God, are supposed to announce their authority in man himself. This never made man a walking embodiment of the law, but on the contrary remained distinct from him as the authority which demanded consent and obedience. Nature or Divinity as the source of authority for positive laws were thought of as permanent and eternal; positive laws were changing and changeable according to circumstances, but they possessed a relative permanence as compared with the much more rapidly changing actions of men; and they derived this permanence from the eternal presence of their source of authority. Positive laws, therefore, are primarily designed to function as stabilizing factors for the ever changing movements of men.

In the interpretation of totalitarianism, all laws have become laws of movement. When the Nazis talked about the law of nature or when the Bolsheviks talk about the law of history, neither nature nor history is any longer the stabilizing source of authority for the actions of mortal men; they are movements in themselves. . . .

Terror is the realization of the law of movement; its chief aim is to make it possible for the force of nature or of history to race freely through mankind, unhindered by any spontaneous human action. As such, terror seeks to "stabilize" men in order to liberate the forces of nature or history. It is this movement which singles out the foes of mankind against whom terror is let loose, and no free action of either opposition or sympathy can be permitted to interfere with the elimination of the "objective enemy" of History or Nature, of the class or the race. Guilt and innocence become senseless notions; "guilty" is he who stands in the way of the natural or historical process which has passed judgment over "inferior races," over individuals "unfit to live," over "dying classes and decadent peoples." Terror executes these judgments, and before its court, all concerned are subjectively innocent: the murdered because they did nothing against the system, and the murderers because they do not really murder but execute a death sentence pronounced by some higher tribunal. The rulers themselves do not claim to be just or wise, but only to execute historical or natural laws; they do not apply laws, but execute a movement in accordance with its inherent law. Terror is lawfulness, if law is the law of the movement of some suprahuman force, Nature or History.

Terror as the execution of a law of movement whose ultimate goal is not the welfare of men or the interest of one man but the fabrication of mankind, eliminates individuals for the sake of the species, sacrifices the "parts" for the sake of the "whole." The suprahuman force of Nature or History has its own beginning and its own end, so that it can be hindered only by the new beginning and the individual end which the life of each man actually is.

Positive laws in constitutional government are designed to erect boundaries and establish channels of communication between men whose community is continually endangered by the new men born into it. With each new birth, a new beginning is born into the world, a new world has potentially come into being. The stability of the laws corresponds to the constant motion of all human affairs, a motion which can never end as long as men are born and die. The laws hedge in each new beginning and at the same time assure its freedom of movement, the potentiality of something entirely new and unpredictable; the boundaries of positive laws are for the political existence of man what memory is for his historical existence: they guarantee the pre-existence of a common world, the reality of some continuity which transcends the individual life span of each generation, absorbs all new origins and is nourished by them.

Total terror is so easily mistaken for a symptom of tyrannical government because totalitarian government in its initial stages must behave like a tyranny and raze the boundaries of man-made law. But total terror leaves no arbitrary lawlessness behind it and does not rage for the sake of some arbitrary will or for the sake of despotic power of one man against all, least of all for the sake of a war of all against all. It substitutes for the boundaries and channels of communication between individual men a band of iron which holds them so tightly together that it is as though their plurality had disappeared into One Man of gigantic dimensions. To abolish the fences of laws between men—as tyranny does—means to take away man's liberties and destroy freedom as a living political reality; for the space between men as it is hedged in by laws, is the living space of freedom. Total terror uses this old instrument of tyranny but destroys at the same time also the lawless, fenceless wilderness of fear and suspicion which tyranny leaves behind. This desert, to be sure, is no longer a living space of freedom, but it still provides some room for the fear-guided movements and suspicion-ridden actions of its inhabitants.

By pressing men against each other, total terror destroys the space between them; compared to the condition within its iron band, even the desert of tyranny, insofar as it is still some kind of space, appears like a guarantee of freedom. Totalitarian government does not just curtail liberties or abolish essential freedoms; nor does it, at least to our limited knowledge, succeed in eradicating the love for freedom from the hearts of man. It destroys the one essential prerequisite of all freedom which is simply the capacity of motion which cannot exist without space.

Total terror, the essence of totalitarian government, exists neither for nor against men. It is supposed to provide the forces of nature or history with an incomparable instrument to accelerate their movement. This movement, proceeding according to its own law, cannot in the long run be hindered; eventually its force will always prove more powerful than the most powerful forces engendered by the actions and the will of men. But it can be slowed down and is slowed down almost inevitably by the freedom of man, which even totalitarian rulers cannot deny, for this freedom—irrelevant and arbitrary as they may deem it—is identical with the fact that men are being born and that therefore each of them *is* a new beginning, begins, in a sense, the world anew. From the totalitarian point of view, the fact that men are born and die can be only regarded as an annoying interference with higher forces. Terror, therefore, as the obedient servant of natural or historical movement has to eliminate from the process not only freedom in any specific sense, but the very source of freedom which is given with the fact of the birth of man and resides in his capacity to make a new beginning. In the iron band of terror, which destroys the plurality of men and makes out of many the One who unfailingly will act as though he himself were part of the course of history or nature, a device has been found not only to liberate the historical and natural forces, but to accelerate them to a speed they never would reach if left to themselves. Practically speaking, this means that terror executes on the spot the death sentences which Nature is supposed to have pronounced on races or individuals who are "unfit to live," or History on "dying classes," without waiting for the slower and less efficient processes of nature or history themselves. . . .

In a perfect totalitarian government, where all men have become One Man, where all action aims at the acceleration of the movement of nature or history, where every single act is the execution of a death sentence which Nature or History has already pronounced, that is, under conditions where terror can be completely relied upon to keep the movement in constant motion, no principle of action separate from its essence would be needed at all. Yet as long as totalitarian rule has not conquered the earth and with the iron band of terror made each single man a part of one mankind, terror in its double function as essence of government and principle, not of action, but of motion, cannot be fully realized. Just as lawfulness in constitutional government is insufficient to inspire and guide men's actions, so terror in totalitarian government is not sufficient to inspire and guide human behavior.

While under present conditions totalitarian domination still shares with other forms of government the need for a guide for the behavior of its citizens in public affairs, it does not need and could not even use a principle of action strictly speaking, since it will eliminate precisely the capacity of man to act. Under conditions of total terror not even fear can any longer serve as an advisor of how to behave, because terror chooses its victims without reference to individual actions or thoughts, exclusively in accordance with the objective necessity of the natural or historical process. Under totalitarian conditions, fear probably is more widespread

than ever before; but fear has lost its practical usefulness when actions guided by it can no longer help to avoid the dangers man fears. The same is true for sympathy or support of the regime; for total terror not only selects its victims according to objective standards; it chooses its executioners with as complete a disregard as possible for the candidate's conviction and sympathies. The consistent elimination of conviction as a motive for action has become a matter of record since the great purges in Soviet Russia and the satellite countries. The aim of totalitarian education has never been to instill convictions but to destroy the capacity to form any. The introduction of purely objective criteria into the selective system of the SS troops was Himmler's great organizational invention; he selected the candidates from photographs according to purely racial criteria. Nature itself decided, not only who was to be eliminated, but also who was to be trained as an executioner.

No guiding principle of behavior, taken itself from the realm of human action, such as virtue, honor, fear, is necessary or can be useful to set into motion a body politic which no longer uses terror as a means of intimidation, but whose essence *is* terror. In its stead, it has introduced an entirely new principle into public affairs that dispenses with human will to action altogether and appeals to the craving need for some insight into the law of movement according to which the terror functions and upon which, therefore, all private destinies depend.

The inhabitants of a totalitarian country are thrown into and caught in the process of nature or history for the sake of accelerating its movement; as such, they can only be executioners or victims of its inherent law. The process may decide that those who today eliminate races and individuals or the members of dying classes and decadent peoples are tomorrow those who must be sacrificed. What totalitarian rule needs to guide the behavior of its subjects is a preparation to fit each of them equally well for the role of executioner and the role of victim. This two-sided preparation, the substitute for a principle of action, is the ideology.

ISAIAH BERLIN

~

INTRODUCTION

ROBERT B. TALISSE

Isaiah Berlin was born in Riga, Latvia, in 1909. While he was still a boy, his family relocated to St. Petersburg (then Petrograd), where Berlin witnessed the Russian Revolutions of 1917 and the emergence of the Bolshevik regime. After a troubled return to Riga for a brief period, Berlin's family moved to London in 1921. Berlin studied classics at Corpus Christi College, Oxford, and was eventually appointed to a fellowship at All Souls College, Oxford. During World War II, he worked as a reporter and correspondent for the British Ministry of Information, a post that brought him to live in New York, Moscow, and Washington, D.C. After the war, Berlin returned to Oxford, where he spent the rest of his life as a distinguished and influential academic and public intellectual. In 1957 Berlin was appointed the Chichele Professor of Social and Political Theory at All Souls; in 1966 he was appointed the founding president of Wolfson College, Oxford. He was elected to the British Academy in 1957. Berlin died in 1997, at the age of eighty-eight.

Although Berlin's earliest work is engaged with technical questions in the philosophy of language, Berlin quickly turned his attention almost exclusively toward social and political thought. His work in this area reveals a persistent focus on human freedom, a concern that Berlin claimed to derive from his earlier encounters with Soviet communism and fascism. These formative experiences help to explain Berlin's turn toward a methodology that he associated with a "history of ideas" rather than philosophy. That is, in contrast with much of twentieth-century philosophy, which tends to proceed by way of the analysis of abstract concepts, Berlin tends to fix on individual thinkers and the historical traditions of thought associated with the Enlightenment, romanticism, Marxism, and liberalism. This is not to say that Berlin's writings are purely descriptive; he aims not simply to interpret the great thinkers of the past, but rather to examine the role of philosophical ideas in history, ultimately for the purpose of criticizing philosophies from the perspective of how they have worked in practice. Accordingly, apart from his first book, *Karl Marx: His Life and Environment* (1939), Berlin's works consist mainly of collections of essay-length studies of thinkers and trends, including his *Russian Thinkers* (1978), *Against the Current* (1979), and *The Crooked Timber of Humanity* (1990). His most influential essays are "John Stuart Mill and the Ends of Life" and the lecture reprinted here, "Two Concepts of Liberty," both of which were published in a collection titled *Four Essays on Liberty* (1969), which is currently published under the title *Liberty* (2002).

Although Berlin writes about a broad range of thinkers and events, much of his work is given to the critical evaluation of the philosophical origins of the forms of tyranny that marred the twentieth century—communism and fascism—and the defense of the Enlightenment values of liberal individualism and tolerance. These themes take center stage in "Two Concepts of Liberty," which was originally delivered in 1958 as Berlin's inaugural lecture upon his appointment as the Chichele Professor.

"Two Concepts of Liberty" contrasts two prominent visions of human freedom. Although Berlin is not the first to distinguish between *negative* and *positive* liberty, his formulation of this distinction remains the most influential. Berlin's central argument is that although both conceptions capture important aspects of freedom, only the ideal presented by the negative conception is compatible with a free and tolerant society. Accordingly, Berlin maintains that it is the negative vision that a society ought to embrace.

The negative conception of liberty, associated with Enlightenment philosophers such as John Locke, Immanuel Kant, and John Stuart Mill, takes freedom to consist in the absence of external impediments to human action. This is to say that one is free insofar as one is able to choose what to do without interference. Of course, Berlin quickly notes that there is of course no loss of liberty in the fact that one cannot jump tall buildings in a single bound; there are indeed constraints on what one can do that are not infringements upon one's liberty. Liberty is lessened only when constraints upon action are *imposed by others*, either through force or the threat thereof. One's liberty, then, concerns only the things that it is possible for one to do; one is free to the degree that one can in fact act without others' obstruction.

Berlin contrasts this view of liberty with the positive conception, a vision associated with pre-Enlightenment and romantic philosophers, including Plato, Aristotle, Jean-Jacques Rousseau, G. W. F. Hegel, and Karl Marx. According to the positive conception, freedom is *self-mastery*. One's freedom does not consist in the absence of external impediments to action, but is rather a matter of the presence of internal capacities for self-determination. One is free insofar as one's actions are within one's control and not caused by alien forces.

The distinction can be made clear by considering what each view takes to be a paradigmatic example of the loss of freedom. According to the negative liberty theorist, prison cells are the fundamental tools of unfreedom. A prisoner is greatly constrained in his options for action; there is a vast number of actions he could perform but for his cell, and his lack of freedom consists in that fact. For the positive liberty theorist, the fundamental sources of unfreedom are internal to the agent. They are psychological forces such as ignorance, irrationality, delusion, and obsession. The unfree man lacks self-control due to features of his inner life that are, despite being internal, nonetheless alien. On the positive conception, then, the addict paradigmatically lacks liberty, for the addict's actions are driven by forces within him that are not really his own. When feeding his addiction, the addict may *in some sense* act as he chooses, yet he is not really in control of himself. Moreover, he does not get what he truly wants; he desires his drug, but more fundamentally he wants to not want it. He is a slave to his addiction.

The addict is of course only an especially extreme case of someone lacking positive freedom. Less extreme cases include those in which an individual is *paralyzed* by fear, or *blinded* by ignorance, or *in the grip* of anxiety. Here the question of the individual's freedom turns not on external obstacles preventing him from doing what he could otherwise do, but rather on the internal mechanisms affecting his will in ways that he cannot fully endorse. The addict may enjoy broad negative freedom; there may be few obstacles in the way of his action. Yet he may lack freedom because he is ultimately not his own master.

Berlin's argument is not that the negative conception is correct and the positive erroneous. Berlin's question is decidedly political: which is the more fitting political vision of human freedom? His answer is clear. Berlin insists that whatever one may think of the positive conception of liberty, it is a *dangerous* view when adopted as an ideal by society. This danger emerges from the fact that the positive conception draws a distinction between an individual's true and merely apparent self. Once this distinction is drawn, the positive conception then associates freedom with the realization of the true self, and the corresponding suppression of the merely apparent self. Berlin contends that this feature of the positive conception threatens to transform liberty into its opposite—that is, into a kind of submission. The positive view, when adopted as a political ideal, is a betrayal of freedom.

To see how this argument works, consider again the addict. It is natural to say that although he *seems* to want his drug, he *really* does not want it at all. After all, as he is an addict, the drives within him are not *truly* his. So we may say that in *denying* him his drug, we *unshackle* him; we may even say that when we forcibly block his drug-procuring actions, we *enhance* his freedom, perhaps we even begin to *liberate* him. As Rousseau put it in formulating his theory of positive liberty, we force him to be free.

The very thought that one can be forced to be free seems odd. But, according to Berlin, the positive conception must go even further than this. The positive liberty theorist must ultimately say that when we apply force to the addict's merely apparent self for the sake of liberating his true (unaddicted) self, we do not really coerce anyone. Recall that the positive view's core claim is that the addicted individual is not *truly* an addict, but rather a free man caught in the grip of addiction. Consequently, by suppressing the alien drives to which he is subject, we dismantle the addict, thereby liberating the true man. Ultimately, then, we do not force the addict to be free; instead, we destroy the addict, and free the man.

Berlin contends that this feature of the positive conception renders it a dangerous political ideal. Once freedom is seen as realization of the true self, and the overcoming of the merely apparent self, the door is open for governments to allege that the individual's true self is the citizen, or the member of a specific economic class, or a member of some political party. The diversity among individuals, the variety of choices they may make and lifestyles they pursue, can then be suppressed in the name of freedom itself. This, Berlin argues, is a perversion of freedom, a transformation of liberty into submission. He concludes that, when taken as a social ideal, the positive conception is ultimately an enemy of liberty.

Berlin closes his essay by locating the flaw of positive liberty within a broader theoretical failure. He alleges that the positive conception rests upon a false theory of value, which he calls *monism*. Monism holds that all goods fit together into a single unified system of value; monists hence claim that all conflicts among values at least *in principle* admit of a single, uniquely rational resolution. Contrast this view with Berlin's own theory of value, *pluralism*. The pluralist holds that there are objective goods that nonetheless conflict with each other. Berlin's favorite example is the conflict between liberty and equality; these two objective goods cannot be reconciled, as any increase in one involves a loss of the other. When faced with the conflict between the two, we must make a choice, thereby suffering an inevitable moral loss of the good we do not choose.

The pluralist idea, then, is that not all of the worthy goals and important goods can be fit together neatly into a single life or society; moral variety is irreducible and therefore moral loss is inescapable. Berlin thinks that this pluralist vision of inevitable moral conflict favors the negative conception of liberty because this conception understands freedom as the ability to make choices without obstruction. Monism, by contrast, sees all value as unified, and so could allow individual choice and idiosyncrasy to be violated in pursuit of an allegedly encompassing moral ideal. Berlin holds that historically the various forms of tyranny have adopted the monist vision.

Berlin's ideas remain influential. Those looking for more information about Berlin and a bibliography of his writings should consult Wolfson College's *The Isaiah Berlin Virtual Library* (http://berlin.wolf.ox.ac.uk/index.html). Michael Ignatieff has written an excellent intellectual biography, *Isaiah Berlin: A Life* (New York: Metropolitan Books, 1998). Critical yet sympathetic overviews of Berlin's philosophy can be found in John Gray, *Isaiah Berlin: An Interpretation of His Thought* (Princeton, N.J.: Princeton University Press, 2013) and George Crowder, *Isaiah Berlin: Liberty, Pluralism, and Liberalism* (London: Polity, 2004). Berlin's thought is canvassed in two recent collections of essays, *The Legacy of Isaiah Berlin,* edited by Mark Lilla (New York: New York Review of Books, 2001), and *The One and the Many*, edited by George Crowder and Henry Hardy (Amherst, N.Y.: Prometheus Books, 2007). A recent work that critiques Berlin's views is Ronald Dworkin, *Justice for Hedgehogs* (Cambridge, Mass.: Harvard University Press, 2011).

Two Concepts of Liberty

I

To coerce a man is to deprive him of freedom—freedom from what? Almost every moralist in human history has praised freedom. Like happiness and goodness, like nature and reality, the meaning of this term is so porous that there is little interpretation that it seems able to resist. I do not propose to discuss either the history or the more than two hundred senses of this protean word recorded by historians of ideas. I propose to examine no more than two of these senses—but those central ones, with a great deal of human history behind them, and, I dare say, still to come. The first of these political senses of freedom or liberty (I shall use both words to mean the same), which (following much precedent) I shall call the "negative" sense, is involved in the answer to the question "What is the area within which the subject—a person or group of persons—is or should be left to do or be what he is able to do or be, without interference by other persons?" The second, which I shall call the positive sense, is involved in the answer to the question "What, or who, is the source of control or interference that can determine someone to do, or be, this rather than that?" The two questions are clearly different, even though the answers to them may overlap.

The Notion of "Negative" Freedom

I am normally said to be free to the degree to which no man or body of men interferes with my activity. Political liberty in this sense is simply the

From *Four Essays on Liberty*, Oxford University Press, 1969. Reprinted by permission of the publisher.

area within which a man can act unobstructed by others. If I am prevented by others from doing what I could otherwise do, I am to that degree unfree; and if this area is contracted by other men beyond a certain minimum, I can be described as being coerced, or, it may be, enslaved. Coercion is not, however, a term that covers every form of inability. If I say that I am unable to jump more than ten feet in the air, or cannot read because I am blind, or cannot understand the darker pages of Hegel, it would be eccentric to say that I am to that degree enslaved or coerced. Coercion implies the deliberate interference of other human beings within the area in which I could otherwise act. You lack political liberty or freedom only if you are prevented from attaining a goal by human beings.[1] Mere incapacity to attain a goal is not lack of political freedom.[2] This is brought out by the use of such modern expressions as "economic freedom" and its counterpart, "economic slavery." It is argued, very plausibly, that if a man is too poor to afford something on which there is no legal ban—a loaf of bread, a journey round the world, recourse to the law courts—he is as little free to have it as he would be if it were forbidden him by law. If my poverty were a kind of disease, which prevented me from buying bread, or paying for the journey round the world or getting my case heard, as lameness prevents me from running, this inability would not naturally be described as a lack of freedom, least of all political freedom. It is only because I believe that my inability to get a given thing is due to the fact that other human beings have made arrangements whereby I am, whereas others are not, prevented from having enough money with which to pay for it, that I think myself a victim of coercion or slavery. In other words, this use of the term depends on a particular social and economic theory about the causes of my poverty or weakness. If my lack of material means is due to my lack of mental or physical capacity, then I begin to speak of being deprived of freedom (and not simply about poverty) only if I accept the theory.[3] If, in addition, I believe that I am being kept in want

by a specific arrangement which I consider unjust or unfair, I speak of economic slavery or oppression. "The nature of things does not madden us, only ill will does," said Rousseau. The criterion of oppression is the part that I believe to be played by other human beings, directly or indirectly, with or without the intention of doing so, in frustrating my wishes. By being free in this sense I mean not being interfered with by others. The wider the area of non-interference the wider my freedom.

This is what the classical English political philosophers meant when they used this word.[4] They disagreed about how wide the area could or should be. They supposed that it could not, as things were, be unlimited, because if it were, it would entail a state in which all men could boundlessly interfere with all other men; and this kind of "natural" freedom would lead to social chaos in which men's minimum needs would not be satisfied; or else the liberties of the weak would be suppressed by the strong. Because they perceived that human purposes and activities do not automatically harmonize with one another, and because (whatever their official doctrines) they put high value on other goals, such as justice, or happiness, or culture, or security, or varying degrees of equality, they were prepared to curtail freedom in the interests of other values and, indeed, of freedom itself. For, without this, it was impossible to create the kind of association that they thought desirable. Consequently, it is assumed by these thinkers that the area of men's free action must be limited by law. But equally it is assumed, especially by such libertarians as Locke and Mill in England, and Constant and Tocqueville in France, that there ought to exist a certain minimum area of personal freedom which must on no account be violated; for if it is overstepped, the individual will find himself in an area too narrow for even that minimum development of his natural faculties which alone makes it possible to pursue, and even to conceive, the various ends which men hold good or right or sacred. It follows that a frontier must be drawn between the area of private life and that of public authority. Where it is to be drawn is a matter of argument, indeed of haggling. Men are largely interdependent, and no man's activity is so completely private as never to obstruct the lives of others in any way. "Freedom for the pike is death for the minnows"; the liberty of some must depend on the restraint of others. "Freedom for an Oxford don," others have been known to add, "is a very different thing from freedom for an Egyptian peasant."

This proposition derives its force from something that is both true and important, but the phrase itself remains a piece of political claptrap. It is true that to offer political rights, or safeguards against intervention by the state, to men who are half-naked, illiterate, underfed, and diseased is to mock their condition; they need medical help or education before they can understand, or make use of, an increase in their freedom. What is freedom to those who cannot make use of it? Without adequate conditions for the use of freedom, what is the value of freedom? First things come first: there are situations, as a nineteenth-century Russian radical writer declared, in which boots are superior to the works of Shakespeare; individual freedom is not everyone's primary need. For freedom is not the mere absence of frustration of whatever kind; this would inflate the meaning of the word until it meant too much or too little. The Egyptian peasant needs clothes or medicine before, and more than, personal liberty, but the minimum freedom that he needs today, and the greater degree of freedom that he may need tomorrow, is not some species of freedom peculiar to him, but identical with that of professors, artists, and millionaires.

What troubles the consciences of Western liberals is not, I think, the belief that the freedom that men seek differs according to their social or economic conditions, but that the minority who possess it have gained it by exploiting, or, at least, averting their gaze from, the vast majority who do not. They believe, with good reason, that if individual liberty is an ultimate end for human beings, none should be deprived of it by others; least of all that some should enjoy it at the expense of

others. Equality of liberty; not to treat others as I should not wish them to treat me; repayment of my debt to those who alone have made possible my liberty or prosperity or enlightenment; justice, in its simplest and most universal sense—these are the foundations of liberal morality. Liberty is not the only goal of men. I can, like the Russian critic Belinsky, say that if others are to be deprived of it—if my brothers are to remain in poverty, squalor, and chains—then I do not want it for myself, I reject it with both hands and infinitely prefer to share their fate. But nothing is gained by a confusion of terms. To avoid glaring inequality or widespread misery I am ready to sacrifice some, or all, of my freedom: I may do so willingly and freely: but it is freedom that I am giving up for the sake of justice or equality or the love of my fellow men. I should be guilt-stricken, and rightly so, if I were not, in some circumstances, ready to make this sacrifice. But a sacrifice is not an increase in what is being sacrificed, namely freedom, however great the moral need or the compensation for it. Everything is what it is: liberty is liberty, not equality or fairness or justice or culture, or human happiness or a quiet conscience. If the liberty of myself or my class or nation depends on the misery of a number of other human beings, the system which promotes this is unjust and immoral. But if I curtail or lose my freedom, in order to lessen the shame of such inequality, and do not thereby materially increase the individual liberty of others, an absolute loss of liberty occurs. This may be compensated for by a gain in justice or in happiness or in peace, but the loss remains, and it is a confusion of values to say that although my "liberal," individual freedom may go by the board, some other kind of freedom—"social" or "economic" is increased. Yet it remains true that the freedom of some must at times be curtailed to secure the freedom of others. Upon what principle should this be done? If freedom is a sacred, untouchable value, there can be no such principle. One or other of these conflicting rules or principles must, at any rate in practice, yield: not always for reasons which can be clearly stated, let alone generalized into rules or universal maxims. Still, a practical compromise has to be found.

Philosophers with an optimistic view of human nature and a belief in the possibility of harmonizing human interests, such as Locke or Adam Smith and, in some moods, Mill, believed that social harmony and progress were compatible with reserving a large area for private life over which neither the state nor any other authority must be allowed to trespass. Hobbes, and those who agreed with him, especially conservative or reactionary thinkers, argued that if men were to be prevented from destroying one another and making social life a jungle or a wilderness, greater safeguards must be instituted to keep them in their places; he wished correspondingly to increase the area of centralized control and decrease that of the individual. But both sides agreed that some portion of human existence must remain independent of the sphere of social control. To invade that preserve, however small, would be despotism. The most eloquent of all defenders of freedom and privacy, Benjamin Constant, who had not forgotten the Jacobin dictatorship, declared that at the very least the liberty of religion, opinion, expression, property, must be guaranteed against arbitrary invasion. Jefferson, Burke, Paine, Mill, compiled different catalogues of individual liberties, but the argument for keeping authority at bay is always substantially the same. We must preserve a minimum area of personal freedom if we are not to "degrade or deny our nature." We cannot remain absolutely free, and must give up some of our liberty to preserve the rest. But total self-surrender is self-defeating. What then must the minimum be? That which a man cannot give up without offending against the essence of his human nature. What is this essence? What are the standards which it entails? This has been, and perhaps always will be, a matter of infinite debate. But whatever the principle in terms of which the area of non-interference is to be drawn, whether it is that of natural law or natural rights, or of utility or the pronouncements of a categorical imperative, or the sanctity of the social contract, or any other concept with which men have sought to clarify and justify their convictions, liberty in this sense means liberty *from*; absence of interference beyond the shifting, but always recognizable, frontier. "The only freedom which deserves the name is that of pursuing our own good in our own way," said the most celebrated of its champions. If this is so, is compulsion ever justified? Mill had no doubt that it was. Since justice demands that all individuals be entitled to a minimum of freedom, all other individuals were of necessity to be restrained, if need be by force, from depriving anyone of it. Indeed, the whole function of law was the prevention of just such collisions: the state was reduced to what Lassalle contemptuously described as the functions of a night-watchman or traffic policeman.

What made the protection of individual liberty so sacred to Mill? In his famous essay he declares that, unless men are left to live as they wish "in the path which merely concerns themselves," civilization cannot advance; the truth will not, for lack of a free market in ideas, come to light; there will be no scope for spontaneity, originality, genius, for mental energy, for moral courage. Society will be crushed by the weight of "collective mediocrity." Whatever is rich and diversified will be crushed by the weight of custom, by men's constant tendency to conformity, which breeds only "withered capacities," "pinched and hidebound," "cramped and warped" human beings. "Pagan self-assertion is as worthy as Christian self-denial." "All the errors which a man is likely to commit against advice and warning are far outweighed by the evil of allowing others to constrain him to what they deem is good." The defence of liberty consists in the "negative" goal of warding off interference. To threaten a man with persecution unless he submits to a life in which he exercises no choices of his goals; to block before him every door but one, no matter how noble the prospect upon which it opens, or how benevolent the motives of those who arrange this, is to sin against the truth that he is a man, a being with a life of his own to live. This is liberty as it has been conceived by liberals in the modern world from the days of Erasmus (some would say of Occam) to our own. Every plea for civil liberties and individual rights, every protest against exploitation and humiliation, against the encroachment of public authority, or the mass hypnosis of custom or organized propaganda, springs from this individualistic, and much disputed, conception of man.

Three facts about this position may be noted. In the first place Mill confuses two distinct notions. One is that all coercion is, in so far as it frustrates human desires, bad as such, although it may have to be applied to prevent other, greater evils; while non-interference, which is the opposite of coercion, is good as such, although it is not the only good. This is the "negative" conception of liberty in its classical form. The other is that men should seek to discover the truth, or to develop a certain type of character of which Mill approved—critical, original, imaginative, independent, non-conforming to the point of eccentricity, and so on—and that truth can be found, and such character can be bred, only in conditions of freedom. Both these are liberal views, but they are not identical, and the connexion between them is, at best, empirical. No one would argue that truth or freedom of self-expression could flourish where dogma crushes all thought. But the evidence of history tends to show (as, indeed, was argued by James Stephen in his formidable attack on Mill in his *Liberty, Equality, Fraternity*) that integrity, love of truth, and fiery individualism grow at least as often in severely disciplined communities among, for example, the puritan Calvinists of Scotland or New England, or under military discipline, as in more tolerant or indifferent societies; and if this is so, Mill's argument for liberty as a necessary condition for the growth of human genius falls to the ground. If his two goals proved incompatible, Mill would be faced with a cruel dilemma, quite apart from the further difficulties created by the inconsistency of his doctrines with strict utilitarianism, even in his own humane version of it.[5]

In the second place, the doctrine is comparatively modern. There seems to be scarcely any discussion of individual liberty as a conscious political ideal (as opposed to its actual existence) in the ancient world. Condorcet had already remarked that the notion of individual rights was absent from the legal conceptions of the Romans and Greeks; this seems to hold equally of the Jewish, Chinese, and all other ancient civilizations that have since come to light.[6] The domination of this ideal has been the exception rather than the rule, even in the recent history of the West. Nor has liberty in this sense often formed a rallying cry for the great masses of mankind. The desire not to be impinged upon, to be left to oneself, has been a mark of high civilization both on the part of individuals and communities. The sense of privacy itself, of the area of personal relationships as something sacred in its own right, derives from a conception of freedom which, for all its religious roots, is scarcely older, in its developed state, than the Renaissance or the Reformation.[7] Yet its decline would mark the death of a civilization, of an entire moral outlook.

The third characteristic of this notion of liberty is of greater importance. It is that liberty in this sense is not incompatible with some kinds of autocracy, or at any rate with the absence of self-government. Liberty in this sense is principally concerned with the area of control, not with its source. Just as a democracy may, in fact, deprive the individual citizen of a great many liberties which he might have in some other form of society, so it is perfectly conceivable that a liberal-minded despot would allow his subjects a large measure of personal freedom. The despot who leaves his subjects a wide area of liberty may be unjust, or encourage the wildest inequalities, care little for order, or virtue, or knowledge; but provided he does not curb their liberty, or at least curbs it less than many other régimes, he meets with Mill's specification.[8] Freedom in this sense is not, at any rate logically, connected with democracy or self-government. Self-government may, on the whole, provide a better guarantee of the preservation of civil liberties than other régimes, and has been defended as such by libertarians. But there is no necessary connexion between individual liberty and democratic rule. The answer to the question "Who governs me?" is logically distinct from the question "How far does government interfere with me?" It is in this difference that the great contrast between the two concepts of negative and positive liberty, in the end, consists.[9] For the "positive" sense of liberty comes to light if we try to answer the question, not "What am I free to do or be?," but "By whom am I ruled?" or "Who is to say what I am, and what I am not, to be or do?" The connexion between democracy and individual liberty is a good deal more tenuous than it seemed to many advocates of both. The desire to be governed by myself, or at any rate to participate in the process by which my life is to be controlled, may be as deep a wish as that of a free area for action, and perhaps historically older. But it is not a desire for the same thing. So different is it, indeed, as to have led in the end to the great clash of ideologies that dominates our world. For it is this—the "positive" conception of liberty: not freedom from, but freedom to—to lead one prescribed form of life—which the adherents of the "negative" notion represent as being, at times, no better than a specious disguise for brutal tyranny.

II

The Notion of Positive Freedom

The "positive" sense of the word "liberty" derives from the wish on the part of the individual to be his own master. I wish my life and decisions to depend on myself, not on external forces of whatever kind. I wish to be the instrument of my own, not of other men's, acts of will. I wish to be a subject, not an object; to be moved by reasons, by conscious purposes, which are my own, not by causes which affect me, as it were, from outside. I wish to be somebody, not nobody; a doer—deciding, not being decided for, self-directed and not acted upon by external nature or by other men as if I were a thing, or an animal, or a slave incapable of playing a human role, that is, of conceiving goals and policies of my own and realizing them. This is at least part of what I mean when I say that I am rational, and that it is my reason that distinguishes me as a human being from the rest of the world. I wish, above all, to be conscious of myself as a thinking, willing, active being, bearing responsibility for my choices and able to explain them by references to my own ideas and purposes. I feel free to the degree that I believe this to be true, and enslaved to the degree that I am made to realize that it is not.

The freedom which consists in being one's own master, and the freedom which consists in not being prevented from choosing as I do by other men, may, on the face of it, seem concepts at no great logical distance from each other—no more than negative and positive ways of saying much the same thing. Yet the "positive" and "negative" notions of freedom historically developed in divergent directions not always by logically reputable steps, until, in the end, they came into direct conflict with each other.

One way of making this clear is in terms of the independent momentum which the, initially perhaps quite harmless, metaphor of self-mastery acquired. "I am my own master"; "I am slave to no man"; but may I not (as Platonists or Hegelians tend to say) be a slave to nature? Or to my own "unbridled" passions? Are these not so many species of the identical genus "slave" some political or legal, others moral or spiritual? Have not men had the experience of liberating themselves from spiritual slavery, or slavery to nature, and do they not in the course of it become aware, on the one hand, of a self which dominates, and, on the other, of something in them which is brought to heel? This dominant self is then variously identified with reason, with my "higher nature," with the self which calculates and aims at what will satisfy it in the long run, with my "real," or "ideal," or "autonomous" self, or with my self "at its best"; which is then contrasted with irrational impulse, uncontrolled desires, my "lower" nature, the pursuit of immediate pleasures, my "empirical" or "heteronomous" self, swept by every gust of desire and passion, needing to be rigidly disciplined if it is ever to rise to the full height of its "real" nature. Presently the two selves may be represented as divided by an even larger gap: the real self may be conceived as something wider than the individual (as the term is normally understood), as a social "whole" of which the individual is an element or aspect: a tribe, a race, a church, a state, the great society of the living and the dead and the yet unborn. This entity is then identified as being the "true" self which, by imposing its collective, or "organic," single will upon its recalcitrant "members," achieves its own, and therefore their, "higher" freedom. The perils of using organic metaphors to justify the coercion of some men by others in order to raise them to a "higher" level of freedom have often been pointed out. But what gives such plausibility as it has to this kind of language is that we recognize that it is possible, and at times justifiable, to coerce men in the name of some goal (let us say, justice or public health) which they would, if they were more enlightened, themselves pursue, but do not, because they are blind or ignorant or corrupt. This renders it easy for me to conceive of myself as coercing others for their own sake, in their, not my, interest. I am then claiming that I know what they truly need better than they know it themselves. What, at most, this entails is that they would not resist me if they were rational and as wise as I and understood their interests as I do. But I may go on to claim a good deal more than this. I may declare that they are actually aiming at what in their benighted state they consciously resist, because there exists within them an occult entity—their latent rational will, or their "true" purpose—and that this entity, although it is belied by all that they overtly feel and do and say, is their "real" self, of which the poor empirical self in space and time may know nothing or little; and that this inner spirit is the

only self that deserves to have its wishes taken into account.[10] Once I take this view, I am in a position to ignore the actual wishes of men or societies, to bully, oppress, torture them in the name, and on behalf, of their "real" selves, in the secure knowledge that whatever is the true goal of man (happiness, performance of duty, wisdom, a just society, self-fulfilment) must be identical with his freedom—the free choice of his "true," albeit often submerged and inarticulate, self.

This paradox has been often exposed. It is one thing to say that I know what is good for X, while he himself does not; and even to ignore his wishes for its—and his—sake; and a very different one to say that he has *eo ipso* chosen it, not indeed consciously, not as he seems in everyday life, but in his role as a rational self which his empirical self may not know—the "real" self which discerns the good, and cannot help choosing it once it is revealed. This monstrous impersonation, which consists in equating what X would choose if he were something he is not, or at least not yet, with what X actually seeks and chooses, is at the heart of all political theories of self-realization. It is one thing to say that I may be coerced for my own good which I am too blind to see: this may, on occasion, be for my benefit; indeed it may enlarge the scope of my liberty. It is another to say that if it is my good, then I am not being coerced, for I have willed it, whether I know this or not, and am free (or "truly" free) even while my poor earthly body and foolish mind bitterly reject it, and struggle against those who seek however benevolently to impose it, with the greatest desperation.

This magical transformation, or sleight of hand (for which William James so justly mocked the Hegelians), can no doubt be perpetrated just as easily with the "negative" concept of freedom, where the self that should not be interfered with is no longer the individual with his actual wishes and needs as they are normally conceived, but the "real" man within, identified with the pursuit of some ideal purpose not dreamed of by his empirical self. And, as in the case of the "positively" free self, this entity may be inflated into some super-personal entity—a state, a class, a nation, or the march of history itself, regarded as a more "real" subject of attributes than the empirical self. But the "positive" conception of freedom as self-mastery, with its suggestion of a man divided against himself, has, in fact, and as a matter of history, of doctrine and of practice, lent itself more easily to this splitting of personality into two: the transcendent, dominant controller, and the empirical bundle of desires and passions to be disciplined and brought to heel. It is this historical fact that has been influential. This demonstrates (if demonstration of so obvious a truth is needed) that conceptions of freedom directly derive from views of what constitutes a self, a person, a man. Enough manipulation with the definition of man, and freedom can be made to mean whatever the manipulator wishes. Recent history has made it only too clear that the issue is not merely academic.

The consequences of distinguishing between two selves will become even clearer if one considers the two major forms which the desire to be self-directed—directed by one's "true" self—has historically taken: the first, that of self-abnegation in order to attain, independence; the second, that of self-realization, or total self-identification with a specific principle or ideal in order to attain the selfsame end.

III

The Retreat to the Inner Citadel

I am the possessor of reason and will; I conceive ends and I desire to pursue them; but if I am prevented from attaining them I no longer feel master of the situation. I may be prevented by the laws of nature, or by accidents, or the activities of men, or the effect, often undesigned, of human institutions. These forces may be too much for me. What am I to do to avoid being crushed by them? I must liberate myself from desires that I know I cannot realize. I wish to be master of my kingdom, but my frontiers are long and insecure,

therefore I contract them in order to reduce or eliminate the vulnerable area. I begin by desiring happiness, or power, or knowledge, or the attainment of some specific object. But I cannot command them. I choose to avoid defeat and waste, and therefore decide to strive for nothing that I cannot be sure to obtain. I determine myself not to desire what is unattainable. The tyrant threatens me with the destruction of my property, with imprisonment, with the exile or death of those I love. But if I no longer feel attached to property, no longer care whether or not I am in prison, if I have killed within myself my natural affections, then he cannot bend me to his will, for all that is left of myself is no longer subject to empirical fears or desires. It is as if I had performed a strategic retreat into an inner citadel—my reason, my soul, my "noumenal" self—which, do what they may, neither external blind force, nor human malice, can touch. I have withdrawn into myself; there, and there alone, I am secure. It is as if I were to say: "I have a wound in my leg. There are two methods of freeing myself from pain. One is to heal the wound. But if the cure is too difficult or uncertain, there is another method. I can get rid of the wound by cutting off my leg. If I train myself to want nothing to which the possession of my leg is indispensable, I shall not feel the lack of it." This is the traditional self-emancipation of ascetics and quietists, of stoics or Buddhist sages, men of various religions or of none, who have fled the world, and escaped the yoke of society or public opinion, by some process of deliberate self-transformation that enables them to care no longer for any of its values, to remain, isolated and independent, on its edges, no longer vulnerable to its weapons.[11] All political isolationism, all economic autarky, every form of autonomy, has in it some element of this attitude. I eliminate the obstacles in my path by abandoning the path; I retreat into my own sect, my own planned economy, my own deliberately insulated territory, where no voices from outside need be listened to, and no external forces can have effect. This is a form of the search for security; but it has also been called the search for personal or national freedom or independence. . . .

It is perhaps worth remarking that in its individualistic form the concept of the rational sage who has escaped into the inner fortress of his true self seems to arise when the external world has proved exceptionally arid, cruel, or unjust. "He is truly free," said Rousseau, "who desires what he can perform, and does what he desires." In a world where a man seeking happiness or justice or freedom (in whatever sense) can do little, because he finds too many avenues of action blocked to him, the temptation to withdraw into himself may become irresistible. It may have been so in Greece, where the Stoic ideal cannot be wholly unconnected with the fall of the independent democracies before centralized Macedonian autocracy. It was so in Rome, for analogous reasons, after the end of the Republic.[12] It arose in Germany in the seventeenth century, during the period of the deepest national degradation of the German states that followed the Thirty Years War, when the character of public life, particularly in the small principalities, forced those who prized the dignity of human life, not for the first or last time, into a kind of inner emigration. The doctrine that maintains that what I cannot have I must teach myself not to desire; that a desire eliminated, or successfully resisted, is as good as a desire satisfied, is a sublime, but, it seems to me, unmistakable, form of the doctrine of sour grapes: what I cannot be sure of, I cannot truly want.

This makes it clear why the definition of negative liberty as the ability to do what one wishes—which is, in effect, the definition adopted by Mill—will not do. If I find that I am able to do little or nothing of what I wish, I need only contract or extinguish my wishes, and I am made free. If the tyrant (or "hidden persuader") manages to condition his subjects (or customers) into losing their original wishes and embrace ("internalize") the form of life he has invented for them, he will, on this definition, have succeeded in liberating them. He will, no doubt, have made them *feel* free—as Epictetus feels freer than his master (and

the proverbial good man is said to feel happy on the rack). But what he has created is the very antithesis of political freedom.

Ascetic self-denial may be a source of integrity or serenity and spiritual strength, but it is difficult to see how it can be called an enlargement of liberty. If I save myself from an adversary by retreating indoors and locking every entrance and exit, I may remain freer than if I had been captured by him, but am I freer than if I had defeated or captured him? If I go too far, contract myself into too small a space, I shall suffocate and die. The logical culmination of the process of destroying everything through which I can possibly be wounded is suicide. While I exist in the natural world, I can never be wholly secure. Total liberation in this sense (as Schopenhauer correctly perceived) is conferred only by death. . . .[13]

IV

Self-Realization

. . . Marx and his disciples maintained that the path of human beings was obstructed not only by natural forces, or the imperfections of their own character, but, even more, by the workings of their own social institutions, which they had originally created (not always consciously) for certain purposes, but whose functioning they systematically came to misconceive,[14] and which thereupon became obstacles in their creators' progress. He offered social and economic hypotheses to account for the inevitability of such misunderstanding, in particular of the illusion that such man-made arrangements were independent forces, as inescapable as the laws of nature. As instances of such pseudo-objective forces, he pointed to the laws of supply and demand, or of the institution of property, or of the eternal division of society into rich and poor, or owners and workers, as so many unaltering human categories. Not until we had reached a stage at which the spells of these illusions could be broken, that is, until enough men reached a social stage that alone enabled them to understand that these laws and institutions were themselves the work of human minds and hands, historically needed in their day, and later mistaken for inexorable, objective powers, could the old world be destroyed, and more adequate and liberating social machinery substituted.

We are enslaved by despots—institutions or beliefs or neuroses—which can be removed only by being analysed and understood. We are imprisoned by evil spirits which we have ourselves—albeit not consciously—created, and can exorcize them only by becoming conscious and acting appropriately: indeed, for Marx understanding *is* appropriate action. I am free if, and only if, I plan my life in accordance with my own will; plans entail rules; a rule does not oppress me or enslave me if I impose it on myself consciously, or accept it freely, having understood it, whether it was invented by me or by others, provided that it is rational, that is to say, conforms to the necessities of things. To understand why things must be as they must be is to will them to be so. Knowledge liberates not by offering us more open possibilities amongst which we can make our choice, but by preserving us from the frustration of attempting the impossible. To want necessary laws to be other than they are is to be prey to an irrational desire—a desire that what must be X should also be not X. To go further, and believe these laws to be other than what they necessarily are, is to be insane. That is the metaphysical heart of rationalism. The notion of liberty contained in it is not the "negative" conception of a field (ideally) without obstacles, a vacuum in which nothing obstructs me, but the notion of self-direction or self-control. I can do what I will with my own. I am a rational being; whatever I can demonstrate to myself as being necessary, as incapable of being otherwise in a rational society—that is, in a society directed by rational minds, towards goals such as a rational being would have—I cannot, being rational, wish to sweep out of my way. I assimilate it into my substance as I do the laws of logic, of mathematics, of physics, the rules of art, the principles that govern everything of which I understand,

and therefore will, the rational purpose, by which I can never be thwarted, since I cannot want it to be other than it is.

This is the positive doctrine of liberation by reason. Socialized forms of it, widely disparate and opposed to each other as they are, are at the heart of many of the nationalist, communist, authoritarian, and totalitarian creeds of our day. It may, in the course of its evolution, have wandered far from its rationalist moorings. Nevertheless, it is this freedom that, in democracies and in dictatorships, is argued about, and fought for, in many parts of the earth today. Without attempting to trace the historical evolution of this idea, I should like to comment on some of its vicissitudes.

V

The Temple of Sarastro

Those who believed in freedom as rational self-direction were bound, sooner or later, to consider how this was to be applied not merely to a man's inner life, but to his relations with other members of his society. Even the most individualistic among them—and Rousseau, Kant, and Fichte certainly began as individualists—came at some point to ask themselves whether a rational life not only for the individual, but also for society, was possible, and if so, how it was to be achieved. I wish to be free to live as my rational will (my "real self") commands, but so must others be. How am I to avoid collisions with their wills? Where is the frontier that lies between my (rationally determined) rights and the identical rights of others? For if I am rational, I cannot deny that what is right for me must, for the same reasons, be right for others who are rational like me. A rational (or free) state would be a state governed by such laws as all rational men would freely accept; that is to say, such laws as they would themselves have enacted had they been asked what, as rational beings, they demanded; hence the frontiers would be such as all rational men would consider to be the right frontiers for rational beings. But who, in fact, was to determine what these frontiers were? Thinkers of this type argued that if moral and political problems were genuine—as surely they were—they must in principle be soluble; that is to say, there must exist one and only one true solution to any problem. All truths could in principle be discovered by any rational thinker, and demonstrated so clearly that all other rational men could not but accept them; indeed, this was already to a large extent the case in the new natural sciences. On this assumption, the problem of political liberty was soluble by establishing a just order that would give to each man all the freedom to which a rational being was entitled. My claim to unfettered freedom can prima facie at times not be reconciled with your equally unqualified claim; but the rational solution of one problem cannot collide with the equally true solution of another, for two truths cannot logically be incompatible; therefore a just order must in principle be discoverable—an order of which the rules make possible correct solutions to all possible problems that could arise in it. This ideal, harmonious state of affairs was sometimes imagined as a Garden of Eden before the Fall of Man, from which we were expelled, but for which we were still filled with longing; or as a golden age still before us, in which men, having become rational, will no longer be "other-directed," nor "alienate" or frustrate one another. In existing societies justice and equality are ideals which still call for some measure of coercion, because the premature lifting of social controls might lead to the oppression of the weaker and the stupider by the stronger or abler or more energetic and unscrupulous. But it is only irrationality on the part of men (according to this doctrine) that leads them to wish to oppress or exploit or humiliate one another. Rational men will respect the principle of reason in each other, and lack all desire to fight or dominate one another. The desire to dominate is itself a symptom of irrationality, and can be explained and cured by rational methods. Spinoza offers one kind of explanation and remedy, Hegel another, Marx a third. Some of these theories may perhaps, to some degree, supplement each other, others are not combinable. But they all assume that in a society of perfectly rational beings the lust for domination over men will be absent or ineffective. The existence of, or craving for, oppression will be the first symptom that the true solution to the problems of social life has not been reached.

This can be put in another way. Freedom is self-mastery, the elimination of obstacles to my will, whatever these obstacles may be—the resistance of nature, of my ungoverned passions, of irrational institutions, of the opposing wills or behaviour of others. Nature I can, at least in principle, always mould by technical means, and shape to my will. But how am I to treat recalcitrant human beings? I must, if I can, impose my will on them too, "mould" them to my pattern, cast parts for them in my play. But will this not mean that I alone am free, while they are slaves? They will be so if my plan has nothing to do with their wishes or values, only with my own. But if my plan is fully rational, it will allow for the full development of their "true" natures, the realization of their capacities for rational decisions "for making the best of themselves" as a part of the realization of my own "true" self. All true solutions to all genuine problems must be compatible: more than this, they must fit into a single whole: for this is what is meant by calling them all rational and the universe harmonious. Each man has his specific character, abilities, aspirations, ends. If I grasp both what these ends and natures are, and how they all relate to one another, I can, at least in principle, if I have the knowledge and the strength, satisfy them all, so long as the nature and the purposes in question are rational. Rationality is knowing things and people for what they are: I must not use stones to make violins, nor try to make born violin players play flutes. If the universe is governed by reason, then there will be no need for coercion; a correctly planned life for all will coincide with full freedom—the freedom of rational self-direction—for all. This will be so if, and only if, the plan is the true plan—the one unique pattern which alone fulfils the claims of reason. Its laws will be the rules which reason prescribes: they will only seem irksome to those whose reason is dormant, who do not understand the true "needs" of their own "real" selves. So long as each player recognizes and plays the part set him by reason—the faculty that understands his true nature and discerns his true ends—there can be no conflict. Each man will be a liberated, self-directed actor in the cosmic drama. Thus Spinoza tells us that "children, although they are coerced, are not slaves," because "they obey orders given in their own interests," and that "The subject of a true commonwealth is no slave, because the common interests must include his own." Similarly, Locke says "Where there is no law there is no freedom," because rational laws are directions to a man's "proper interests" or "general good"; and adds that since such laws are what "hedges us from bogs and precipices" they "ill deserve the name of confinement," and speaks of desires to escape from such laws as being irrational, forms of "licence," as "brutish," and so on. Montesquieu, forgetting his liberal moments, speaks of political liberty as being not permission to do what we want, or even what the law allows, but only "the power of doing what we ought to will," which Kant virtually repeats. Burke proclaims the individual's "right" to be restrained in his own interest, because "the presumed consent of every rational creature is in unison with the predisposed order of things." The common assumption of these thinkers (and of many a schoolman before them and Jacobin and Communist after them) is that the rational ends of our "true" natures must coincide, or be made to coincide, however violently our poor, ignorant, desire-ridden, passionate, empirical selves may cry out against this process. Freedom is not freedom to do what is irrational, or stupid, or wrong. To force empirical selves into the right pattern is no tyranny, but liberation.[15] Rousseau tells me that if I freely surrender all the parts of my life to society, I create an entity which, because it has been built by an equality of sacrifice of all its members, cannot wish to hurt any one of them; in such a society, we are informed, it can be nobody's interest to damage anyone else. "In giving myself to all, I give myself to none," and get back as much as I lose, with enough new force to preserve my new gains. Kant tells us that when "the individual has entirely abandoned his wild, lawless freedom, to find it again, unimpaired, in a state of dependence according to law," that alone is true freedom, "for this dependence is the work of my own will acting as a lawgiver." Liberty, so far from being incompatible with authority, becomes virtually identical with it. This is the thought and language of all the declarations of the rights of man in the eighteenth century, and of all those who look upon society as a design constructed according to the rational laws of the wise lawgiver, or of nature, or of history, or of the Supreme Being. Bentham, almost alone, doggedly went on repeating that the business of laws was not to liberate but to restrain: "Every law is an infraction of liberty" even if such "infraction" leads to an increase of the sum of liberty.

If the underlying assumptions had been correct—if the method of solving social problems resembled the way in which solutions to the problems of the natural sciences are found, and if reason were what rationalists said that it was, all this would perhaps follow. In the ideal case, liberty coincides with law: autonomy with authority. A law which forbids me to do what I could not, as a sane being, conceivably wish to do is not a restraint of my freedom. In the ideal society, composed of wholly responsible beings, rules, because I should scarcely be conscious of them, would gradually wither away. Only one social movement was bold enough to render this assumption quite explicit and accept its consequences—that of the Anarchists. But all forms of liberalism founded on a rationalist metaphysics are less or more watered-down versions of this creed.

In due course, the thinkers who bent their energies to the solution of the problem on these lines came to be faced with the question of how in practice men were to be made rational in this way. Clearly they must be educated. For the uneducated are irrational, heteronomous, and need to be coerced, if only to make life tolerable for the rational if they are to live in the same society and not be compelled to withdraw to a desert or some Olympian height. But the uneducated cannot be expected to understand or co-operate with the purposes of their educators. Education, says Fichte, must inevitably work in such a way that "you will later recognize the reasons for what I am doing now." Children cannot be expected to understand why they are compelled to go to school, nor the ignorant—that is, for the moment, the majority of mankind—why they are made to obey the laws that will presently make them rational. "Compulsion is also a kind of education." You learn the great virtue of obedience to superior persons. If you cannot understand your own interests as a rational being, I cannot be expected to consult you, or abide by your wishes, in the course of making you rational. I must, in the end, force you to be protected against smallpox, even though you may not wish it. Even Mill is prepared to say that I may forcibly prevent a man from crossing a bridge if there is not time to warn him that it is about to collapse, for I know, or am justified in assuming, that he cannot wish to fall into the water. Fichte knows what the uneducated German of his time wishes to be or do better than he can possibly know them for himself. The sage knows you better than you know yourself, for you are the victim of your passions, a slave living a heteronomous life, purblind, unable to understand your true goals. You want to be a human being. It is the aim of the state to satisfy your wish. "Compulsion is justified by education for future insight." The reason within me, if it is to triumph, must eliminate and suppress my "lower" instincts, my passions and desires, which render me a slave; similarly (the fatal transition from individual to social concepts is almost imperceptible) the higher elements in society—the better educated, the more rational, those who "possess the highest insight of their time and people" may exercise compulsion to rationalize the irrational section of society. For—so Hegel, Bradley,

Bosanquet have often assured us—by obeying the rational man we obey ourselves: not indeed as we are, sunk in our ignorance and our passions, weak creatures afflicted by diseases that need a healer, wards who require a guardian, but as we could be if we were rational; as we could be even now, if only we would listen to the rational element which is, *ex hypothesi*, within every human being who deserves the name. . . .

The same attitude was pointedly expressed by Auguste Comte, who asked "If we do not allow free thinking in chemistry or biology, why should we allow it in morals or politics?" Why indeed? If it makes sense to speak of political truths—assertions of social ends which all men, because they are men, must, once they are discovered, agree to be such; and if, as Comte believed, scientific method will in due course reveal them; then what case is there for freedom of opinion or action—at least as an end in itself, and not merely as a stimulating intellectual climate, either for individuals or for groups? Why should any conduct be tolerated that is not authorized by appropriate experts? Comte put bluntly what had been implicit in the rationalist theory of politics from its ancient Greek beginnings. There can, in principle, be only one correct way of life; the wise lead it spontaneously, that is why they are called wise. The unwise must be dragged towards it by all the social means in the power of the wise; for why should demonstrable error be suffered to survive and breed? The immature and untutored must be made to say to themselves: "Only the truth liberates, and the only way in which I can learn the truth is by doing blindly today, what you, who know it, order me, or coerce me, to do, in the certain knowledge that only thus will I arrive at your clear vision, and be free like you."

We have wandered indeed from our liberal beginnings. This argument, employed by Fichte in his latest phase, and after him by other defenders of authority, from Victorian schoolmasters and colonial administrators to the latest nationalist or communist dictator, is precisely what the Stoic and Kantian morality protests against most bitterly in the name of the reason of the free individual following his own inner light. In this way the rationalist argument, with its assumption of the single true solution, has led by steps which, if not logically valid, are historically and psychologically intelligible, from an ethical doctrine of individual responsibility and individual self-perfection to an authoritarian state obedient to the directives of an *élite* of Platonic guardians.

VI

The Search for Status

... No doubt every interpretation of the word liberty, however unusual, must include a minimum of what I have called "negative" liberty. There must be an area within which I am not frustrated. No society literally suppresses all the liberties of its members; a being who is prevented by others from doing anything at all on his own is not a moral agent at all, and could not either legally or morally be regarded as a human being, even if a physiologist or a biologist, or even a psychologist, felt inclined to classify him as a man. But the fathers of liberalism—Mill and Constant—want more than this minimum: they demand a maximum degree of non-interference compatible with the minimum demands of social life. It seems unlikely that this extreme demand for liberty has ever been made by any but a small minority of highly civilized and self-conscious human beings. The bulk of humanity has certainly at most times been prepared to sacrifice this to other goals: security, status, prosperity, power, virtue, rewards in the next world; or justice, equality, fraternity, and many other values which appear wholly, or in part, incompatible with the attainment of the greatest degree of individual liberty, and certainly do not need it as a pre-condition for their own realization. It is not a demand for *Lebensraum* for each individual that has stimulated the rebellions and wars of liberation for which men were ready to die in the past, or, indeed, in the present. Men who have fought for freedom have commonly

fought for the right to be governed by themselves or their representatives—sternly governed, if need be, like the Spartans, with little individual liberty, but in a manner which allowed them to participate, or at any rate to believe that they were participating, in the legislation and administration of their collective lives. And men who have made revolutions have, as often as not, meant by liberty no more than the conquest of power and authority by a given sect of believers in a doctrine, or by a class, or by some other social group, old or new. Their victories certainly frustrated those whom they ousted, and sometimes repressed, enslaved, or exterminated vast numbers of human beings. Yet such revolutionaries have usually felt it necessary to argue that, despite this, they represented the party of liberty, or "true" liberty, by claiming universality for their ideal, which the "real selves" of even those who resisted them were also alleged to be seeking, although they were held to have lost the way to the goal, or to have mistaken the goal itself owing to some moral or spiritual blindness. All this has little to do with Mill's notion of liberty as limited only by the danger of doing harm to others. It is the non-recognition of this psychological and political fact (which lurks behind the apparent ambiguity of the term "liberty") that has, perhaps, blinded some contemporary liberals to the world in which they live. Their plea is clear, their cause is just. But they do not allow for the variety of basic human needs. Nor yet for the ingenuity with which men can prove to their own satisfaction that the road to one ideal also leads to its contrary.

VII

Liberty and Sovereignty

The French Revolution, like all great revolutions, was, at least in its Jacobin form, just such an eruption of the desire for "positive" freedom of collective self-direction on the part of a large body of Frenchmen who felt liberated as a nation, even though the result was, for a good many of them, a severe restriction of individual freedoms. Rousseau had spoken exultantly of the fact that the laws of liberty might prove to be more austere than the yoke of tyranny. Tyranny is service to human masters. The law cannot be a tyrant. Rousseau does not mean by liberty the "negative" freedom of the individual not to be interfered with within a defined area, but the possession by all, and not merely by some, of the fully qualified members of a society of a share in the public power which is entitled to interfere with every aspect of every citizen's life. The liberals of the first half of the nineteenth century correctly foresaw that liberty in this "positive" sense could easily destroy too many of the "negative" liberties that they held sacred. They pointed out that the sovereignty of the people could easily destroy that of individuals. Mill explained, patiently and unanswerably, that government by the people was not, in his sense, necessarily freedom at all. For those who govern are not necessarily the same "people" as those who are governed, and democratic self-government is not the government "of each by himself" but, at best, of "each by the rest." Mill and his disciples spoke of the tyranny of the majority and of the tyranny of "the prevailing feeling and opinion," and saw no great difference between that and any other kind of tyranny which encroaches upon men's activities beyond the sacred frontiers of private life.

No one saw the conflict between the two types of liberty better, or expressed it more clearly, than Benjamin Constant. He pointed out that the transference by a successful rising of the unlimited authority, commonly called sovereignty, from one set of hands to another does not increase liberty, but merely shifts the burden of slavery. He reasonably asked why a man should deeply care whether he is crushed by a popular government or by a monarch, or even by a set of oppressive laws. He saw that the main problem for those who desire "negative," individual freedom is not who wields this authority, but how much authority should be placed in any set of hands. For unlimited authority in anybody's grasp was bound, he

believed, sooner or later, to destroy somebody. He maintained that usually men protested against this or that set of governors as oppressive, when the real cause of oppression lay in the mere fact of the accumulation of power itself, wherever it might happen to be, since liberty was endangered by the mere existence of absolute authority as such. "It is not the arm that is unjust," he wrote, "but the weapon that is too heavy—some weights are too heavy for the human hand." Democracy may disarm a given oligarchy, a given privileged individual or set of individuals, but it can still crush individuals as mercilessly as any previous ruler. In an essay comparing the liberty of the moderns with that of the ancients he said that an equal right to oppress—or interfere—is not equivalent to liberty. Nor does universal consent to loss of liberty somehow miraculously preserve it merely by being universal, or by being consent. If I consent to be oppressed, or acquiesce in my condition with detachment or irony, am I the less oppressed? If I sell myself into slavery, am I the less a slave? If I commit suicide, am I the less dead because I have taken my own life freely? "Popular government is a spasmodic tyranny, monarchy a more efficiently centralized despotism." Constant saw in Rousseau the most dangerous enemy of individual liberty, because he had declared that "by giving myself to all I give myself to none." Constant could not see why, even though the sovereign is "everybody," it should not oppress one of the "members" of its indivisible self, if it so decided. I may, of course, prefer to be deprived of my liberties by an assembly, or a family, or a class, in which I am a minority. It may give me an opportunity one day of persuading the others to do for me that to which I feel I am entitled. But to be deprived of my liberty at the hands of my family or friends or fellow citizens is to be deprived of it just as effectively. Hobbes was at any rate more candid: he did not pretend that a sovereign does not enslave: he justified this slavery, but at least did not have the effrontery to call it freedom.

Throughout the nineteenth century liberal thinkers maintained that if liberty involved a limit upon the powers of any man to force me to do what I did not, or might not, wish to do, then, whatever the ideal in the name of which I was coerced, I was not free; that the doctrine of absolute sovereignty was a tyrannical doctrine in itself. If I wish to preserve my liberty, it is not enough to say that it must not be violated unless someone or other—the absolute ruler, or the popular assembly, or the King in Parliament, or the judges, or some combination of authorities, or the laws themselves—for the laws may be oppressive—authorizes its violation. I must establish a society in which there must be some frontiers of freedom which nobody should be permitted to cross. Different names or natures may be given to the rules that determine these frontiers: they may be called natural rights, or the word of God, or Natural Law, or the demands of utility or of the "permanent interests of man"; I may believe them to be valid a priori, or assert them to be my own ultimate ends, or the ends of my society or culture. What these rules or commandments will have in common is that they are accepted so widely, and are grounded so deeply in the actual nature of men as they have developed through history, as to be, by now, an essential part of what we mean by being a normal human being. Genuine belief in the inviolability of a minimum extent of individual liberty entails some such absolute stand. For it is clear that it has little to hope for from the rule of majorities; democracy as such is logically uncommitted to it, and historically has at times failed to protect it, while remaining faithful to its own principles. Few governments, it has been observed, have found much difficulty in causing their subjects to generate any will that the government wanted. "The triumph of despotism is to force the slaves to declare themselves free." It may need no force; the slaves may proclaim their freedom quite sincerely: but they are none the less slaves. Perhaps the chief value for liberals of political—"positive" rights, of participating in the government, is as a means for protecting what they hold to be an ultimate value, namely individual—"negative" liberty.

But if democracies can, without ceasing to be democratic, suppress freedom, at least as liberals have used the word, what would make a society truly free? For Constant, Mill, Tocqueville, and the liberal tradition to which they belong, no society is free unless it is governed by at any rate two interrelated principles: first, that no power, but only rights, can be regarded as absolute, so that all men, whatever power governs them, have an absolute right to refuse to behave inhumanly; and, second, that there are frontiers, not artificially drawn, within which men should be inviolable, these frontiers being defined in terms of rules so long and widely accepted that their observance has entered into the very conception of what it is to be a normal human being, and, therefore, also of what it is to act inhumanly or insanely; rules of which it would be absurd to say, for example, that they could be abrogated by some formal procedure on the part of some court or sovereign body. When I speak of a man as being normal, a part of what I mean is that he could not break these rules easily, without a qualm of revulsion. It is such rules as these that are broken when a man is declared guilty without trial, or punished under a retroactive law; when children are ordered to denounce their parents, friends to betray one another, soldiers to use methods of barbarism; when men are tortured or murdered, or minorities are massacred because they irritate a majority or a tyrant. Such acts, even if they are made legal by the sovereign, cause horror even in these days, and this springs from the recognition of the moral validity—irrespective of the laws—of some absolute barriers to the imposition of one man's will on another. The freedom of a society, or a class or a group, in this sense of freedom, is measured by the strength of these barriers, and the number and importance of the paths which they keep open for their members—if not for all, for at any rate a great number of them.[16]

This is almost at the opposite pole from the purposes of those who believe in liberty in the "positive" self-directive—sense. The former want to curb authority as such. The latter want it placed in their own hands. That is a cardinal issue. These are not two different interpretations of a single concept, but two profoundly divergent and irreconcilable attitudes to the ends of life. It is as well to recognize this, even if in practice it is often necessary to strike a compromise between them. For each of them makes absolute claims. These claims cannot both be fully satisfied. But it is a profound lack of social and moral understanding not to recognize that the satisfaction that each of them seeks is an ultimate value which, both historically and morally, has an equal right to be classed among the deepest interests of mankind.

VIII

The One and the Many

One belief, more than any other, is responsible for the slaughter of individuals on the altars of the great historical ideals—justice or progress or the happiness of future generations, or the sacred mission or emancipation of a nation or race or class, or even liberty itself, which demands the sacrifice of individuals for the freedom of society. This is the belief that somewhere, in the past or in the future, in divine revelation or in the mind of an individual thinker, in the pronouncements of history or science, or in the simple heart of an uncorrupted good man, there is a final solution. This ancient faith rests on the conviction that all the positive values in which men have believed must, in the end, be compatible, and perhaps even entail one another. "Nature binds truth, happiness, and virtue together as by an indissoluble chain," said one of the best men who ever lived, and spoke in similar terms of liberty, equality, and justice.[17] But is this true? It is a commonplace that neither political equality nor efficient organization nor social justice is compatible with more than a modicum of individual liberty, and certainly not with unrestricted laissez-faire; that justice and generosity, public and private loyalties, the demands of genius and the claims of society, can conflict violently with each other. And it is no great way from

that to the generalization that not all good things are compatible, still less all the ideals of mankind. But somewhere, we shall be told, and in some way, it must be possible for all these values to live together, for unless this is so, the universe is not a cosmos, not a harmony; unless this is so, conflicts of values may be an intrinsic, irremovable element in human life. To admit that the fulfilment of some of our ideals may in principle make the fulfilment of others impossible is to say that the notion of total human fulfilment is a formal contradiction, a metaphysical chimaera. For every rationalist metaphysician, from Plato to the last disciples of Hegel or Marx, this abandonment of the notion of a final harmony in which all riddles are solved, all contradictions reconciled, is a piece of crude empiricism, abdication before brute facts, intolerable bankruptcy of reason before things as they are, failure to explain and to justify, to reduce everything to a system, which "reason" indignantly rejects. But if we are not armed with an *a priori* guarantee of the proposition that a total harmony of true values is somewhere to be found—perhaps in some ideal realm the characteristics of which we can, in our finite state, not so much as conceive— we must fall back on the ordinary resources of empirical observation and ordinary human knowledge. And these certainly give us no warrant for supposing (or even understanding what would be meant by saying) that all good things, or all bad things for that matter, are reconcilable with each other. The world that we encounter in ordinary experience is one in which we are faced with choices between ends equally ultimate, and claims equally absolute, the realization of some of which must inevitably involve the sacrifice of others. Indeed, it is because this is their situation that men place such immense value upon the freedom to choose; for if they had assurance that in some perfect state, realizable by men on earth, no ends pursued by them would ever be in conflict, the necessity and agony of choice would disappear, and with it the central importance of the freedom to choose. Any method of bringing this final state nearer would then seem fully justified, no matter how much freedom were sacrificed to forward its advance. It is, I have no doubt, some such dogmatic certainty that has been responsible for the deep, serene, unshakeable conviction in the minds of some of the most merciless tyrants and persecutors in history that what they did was fully justified by its purpose. I do not say that the ideal of self-perfection—whether for individuals or nations or churches or classes—is to be condemned in itself, or that the language which was used in its defence was in all cases the result of a confused or fraudulent use of words, or of moral or intellectual perversity. Indeed, I have tried to show that it is the notion of freedom in its "positive" sense that is at the heart of the demands for national or social self-direction which animate the most powerful and morally just public movements of our time, and that not to recognize this is to misunderstand the most vital facts and ideas of our age. But equally it seems to me that the belief that some single formula can in principle be found whereby all the diverse ends of men can be harmoniously realized is demonstrably false. If, as I believe, the ends of men are many, and not all of them are in principle compatible with each other, then the possibility of conflict—and of tragedy—can never wholly be eliminated from human life, either personal or social. The necessity of choosing between absolute claims is then an inescapable characteristic of the human condition. This gives its value to freedom as Acton had conceived of it—as an end in itself, and not as a temporary need, arising out of our confused notions and irrational and disordered lives, a predicament which a panacea could one day put right.

I do not wish to say that individual freedom is, even in the most liberal societies, the sole, or even the dominant, criterion of social action. We compel children to be educated, and we forbid public executions. These are certainly curbs to freedom. We justify them on the ground that ignorance, or a barbarian upbringing, or cruel pleasures and excitements are worse for us than the amount of restraint needed to repress them. This judgment in turn depends on how we determine good and evil, that is to say, on our moral, religious, intellectual, economic, and aesthetic values; which are, in their turn, bound up with our conception of man, and of the basic demands of his nature. In other words, our solution of such problems is based on our vision, by which we are consciously or unconsciously guided, of what constitutes a fulfilled human life, as contrasted with Mill's "cramped and warped," "pinched and hidebound" natures. To protest against the laws governing censorship or personal morals as intolerable infringements of personal liberty presupposes a belief that the activities which such laws forbid are fundamental needs of men as men, in a good (or, indeed, any) society. To defend such laws is to hold that these needs are not essential, or that they cannot be satisfied without sacrificing other values which come higher—satisfy deeper needs—than individual freedom, determined by some standard that is not merely subjective, a standard for which some objective status—empirical or *a priori*—is claimed.

The extent of a man's, or a people's, liberty to choose to live as they desire must be weighed against the claims of many other values, of which equality, or justice, or happiness, or security, or public order are perhaps the most obvious examples. For this reason, it cannot be unlimited. We are rightly reminded by R. H. Tawney that the liberty of the strong, whether their strength is physical or economic, must be restrained. This maxim claims respect, not as a consequence of some *a priori* rule, whereby the respect for the liberty of one man logically entails respect for the liberty of others like him; but simply because respect for the principles of justice, or shame at gross inequality of treatment, is as basic in men as the desire for liberty. That we cannot have everything is a necessary, not a contingent, truth. Burke's plea for the constant need to compensate, to reconcile, to balance; Mill's plea for novel "experiments in living" with their permanent possibility of error, the knowledge that it is not merely in practice but in principle impossible to reach clear-cut and certain answers, even in an ideal world of wholly good and rational men and wholly clear ideas—may madden those who seek for final solutions and single, all-embracing systems, guaranteed to be eternal. Nevertheless, it is a conclusion that cannot be escaped by those who, with Kant, have learnt the truth that out of the crooked timber of humanity no straight thing was ever made.

There is little need to stress the fact that monism, and faith in a single criterion, has always proved a deep source of satisfaction both to the intellect and to the emotions. Whether the standard of judgment derives from the vision of some future perfection, as in the minds of the *philosophes* in the eighteenth century and their technocratic successors in our own day, or is rooted in the past—*la terre et les morts*—as maintained by German historicists or French theocrats, or neo-Conservatives in English-speaking countries, it is bound, provided it is inflexible enough, to encounter some unforeseen and unforeseeable human development, which it will not fit; and will then be used to justify the *a priori* barbarities of Procrustes—the vivisection of actual human societies into some fixed pattern dictated by our fallible understanding of a largely imaginary past or a wholly imaginary future. To preserve our absolute categories or ideals at the expense of human lives offends equally against the principles of science and of history; it is an attitude found in equal measure on the right and left wings in our days, and is not reconcilable with the principles accepted by those who respect the facts.

Pluralism, with the measure of "negative" liberty that it entails, seems to me a truer and more humane ideal than the goals of those who seek in the great, disciplined, authoritarian structures the ideal of "positive" self-mastery by classes, or peoples, or the whole of mankind. It is truer, because it does, at least, recognize the fact that human goals are many, not all of them commensurable, and in perpetual rivalry with one another. To assume that all values can be graded on one scale, so that it is a mere matter of inspection to determine the highest, seems to me to falsify our knowledge that men are free agents, to represent moral decision as an operation which a slide-rule could, in principle, perform. To say that in some

ultimate, all-reconciling, yet realizable synthesis, duty *is* interest, or individual freedom *is* pure democracy or an authoritarian state, is to throw a metaphysical blanket over either self-deceit or deliberate hypocrisy. It is more humane because it does not (as the system builders do) deprive men, in the name of some remote, or incoherent, ideal, of much that they have found to be indispensable to their life as unpredictably self-transforming human beings.[18] In the end, men choose between ultimate values; they choose as they do, because their life and thought are determined by fundamental moral categories and concepts that are, at any rate over large stretches of time and space, a part of their being and thought and sense of their own identity; part of what makes them human.

It may be that the ideal of freedom to choose ends without claiming eternal validity for them, and the pluralism of values connected with this, is only the late fruit of our declining capitalist civilization: an ideal which remote ages and primitive societies have not recognized, and one which posterity will regard with curiosity, even sympathy, but little comprehension. This may be so; but no sceptical conclusions seem to me to follow. Principles are not less sacred because their duration cannot be guaranteed. Indeed, the very desire for guarantees that our values are eternal and secure in some objective heaven is perhaps only a craving for the certainties of childhood or the absolute values of our primitive past. "To realise the relative validity of one's convictions," said an admirable writer of our time, "and yet stand for them unflinchingly, is what distinguishes a civilised man from a barbarian." To demand more than this is perhaps a deep and incurable metaphysical need; but to allow it to determine one's practice is a symptom of an equally deep, and more dangerous, moral and political immaturity.

Notes

1. I do not, of course, mean to imply the truth of the converse.

2. Helvétius made this point very clearly: "The free man is the man who is not in irons, nor imprisoned in a

gaol, nor terrorized like a slave by the fear of punishment . . . it is not lack of freedom not to fly like an eagle or swim like a whale."

3. The Marxist conception of social laws is, of course, the best-known version of this theory, but it forms a large element in some Christian and utilitarian, and all socialist, doctrines.

4. "A free man," said Hobbes, "is he that . . . is not hindered to do what he hath the will to do." Law is always a "fetter," even if it protects you from being bound in chains that are heavier than those of the law, say, some more repressive law or custom, or arbitrary despotism or chaos. Bentham says much the same.

5. This is but another illustration of the natural tendency of all but a very few thinkers to believe that all the things they hold good must be intimately connected, or at least compatible, with one another. The history of thought, like the history of nations, is strewn with examples of inconsistent, or at least disparate, elements artificially yoked together in a despotic system, or held together by the danger of some common enemy. In due course the danger passes, and conflicts between the allies arise, which often disrupt the system, sometimes to the great benefit of mankind.

6. See the valuable discussion of this in Michel Villey, *Leçons d'histoire de la philosophie du droit*, who traces the embryo of the notion of subjective rights to Occam.

7. Christian (and Jewish or Moslem) belief in the absolute authority of divine or natural laws, or in the equality of all men in the sight of God, is different from belief in freedom to live as one prefers.

8. Indeed, it is arguable that in the Prussia of Frederick the Great or in the Austria of Josef II men of imagination, originality, and creative genius, and, indeed, minorities of all kinds, were less persecuted and felt the pressure, both of institutions and custom, less heavy upon them than in many an earlier or later democracy.

9. "Negative liberty" is something the extent of which, in a given case, it is difficult to estimate. It might, prima facie, seem to depend simply on the power to choose between at any rate two alternatives. Nevertheless, not all choices are equally free, or free at all. If in a totalitarian state I betray my friend under threat of torture, perhaps even if I act from fear of losing my job, I can reasonably say that I did not act freely. Nevertheless, I did, of course, make a choice, and could, at any rate in theory, have chosen to be killed or tortured or imprisoned. The mere existence of alternatives is not, therefore, enough to make my action free (although it may be voluntary) in the normal sense of the word. The extent of my freedom seems to depend on

(*a*) how many possibilities are open to me (although the method of counting these can never be more than impressionistic. Possibilities of action are not discrete entities like apples, which can be exhaustively enumerated); (*b*) how easy or difficult each of these possibilities is to actualize; (*c*) how important in my plan of life, given my character and circumstances, these possibilities are when compared with each other; (*d*) how far they are closed and opened by deliberate human acts; (*e*) what value not merely the agent, but the general sentiment of the society in which he lives, puts on the various possibilities. All these magnitudes must be "integrated," and a conclusion, necessarily never precise, or indisputable, drawn from this process. It may well be that there are many incommensurable kinds and degrees of freedom, and that they cannot be drawn up on any single scale of magnitude. Moreover, in the case of societies, we are faced by such (logically absurd) questions as "Would arrangement X increase the liberty of Mr. A more than it would that of Messrs. B, C, and D between them, added together?" The same difficulties arise in applying utilitarian criteria. Nevertheless, provided we do not demand precise measurement, we can give valid reasons for saying that the average subject of the King of Sweden is, on the whole, a good deal freer today than the average citizen of Spain or Albania. Total patterns of life must be compared directly as wholes, although the method by which we make the comparison, and the truth of the conclusions, are difficult or impossible to demonstrate. But the vagueness of the concepts, and the multiplicity of the criteria involved, is an attribute of the subject-matter itself, not of our imperfect methods of measurement, or incapacity for precise thought.

10. "The ideal of true freedom is the maximum of power for all the members of human society alike to make the best of themselves," said T. H. Green in 1881. Apart from the confusion of freedom with equality, this entails that if a man chose some immediate pleasure—which (in whose view?) would not enable him to make the best of himself (what self?)—what he was exercising was not "true" freedom: and if deprived of it, would not lose anything that mattered. Green was a genuine liberal: but many a tyrant could use this formula to justify his worse acts of oppression.

11. "A wise man, though he be a slave, is at liberty, and from this it follows that though a fool rule, he is in slavery," said St. Ambrose. It might equally well have been said by Epictetus or Kant.

12. It is not perhaps far-fetched to assume that the quietism of the Eastern sages was, similarly, a response to the

despotism of the great autocracies, and flourished at periods when individuals were apt to be humiliated, or at any
rate ignored or ruthlessly managed, by those possessed of
the instruments of physical coercion.

13. It is worth remarking that those who demanded—
and fought for—liberty for the individual or for the nation
in France during this period of German quietism did not
fall into this attitude. Might this not be precisely because,
despite the despotism of the French monarchy and the arrogance and arbitrary behaviour of privileged groups in
the French state, France was a proud and powerful nation,
where the reality of political power was not beyond the
grasp of men of talent, so that withdrawal from battle
into some untroubled heaven above it, whence it could be
surveyed dispassionately by the self-sufficient philosopher,
was not the only way out? The same holds for England in
the nineteenth century and well after it, and for the United
States today.

14. In practice even more than in theory.

15. On this Bentham seems to me to have said the last
word: "Is not liberty to do evil, liberty? If not, what is it?
Do we not say that it is necessary to take liberty from idiots
and bad men, because they abuse it?" Compare with this
a typical statement made by a Jacobin club of the same
period: "No man is free in doing evil. To prevent him is to
set him free." This is echoed in almost identical terms by
British Idealists at the end of the following century.

16. In Great Britain such legal power is, of course, constitutionally vested in the absolute sovereign—the King in
Parliament. What makes this country comparatively free,
therefore, is the fact that this theoretically omnipotent entity is restrained by custom or opinion from behaving as
such. It is clear that what matters is not the form of these
restraints on power—whether they are legal, or moral, or
constitutional—but their effectiveness.

17. Condorcet, from whose *Esquisse* these words are
quoted, declares that the task of social science is to show
"by what bonds Nature has united the progress of enlightenment with that of liberty, virtue, and respect for
the natural rights of man; how these ideals, which alone
are truly good, yet so often separated from each other
that they are even believed to be incompatible, should, on
the contrary, become inseparable, as soon as enlightenment has reached a certain level simultaneously among a
large number of nations." He goes on to say that: "Men
still preserve the errors of their childhood, of their country, and of their age long after having recognized all the
truths needed for destroying them." Ironically enough,
his belief in the need and possibility of uniting all good
things may well be precisely the kind of error he himself
so well described.

18. On this also Bentham seems to me to have spoken
well: "Individual interests are the only real interests . . . can
it be conceived that there are men so absurd as to . . . prefer
the man who is not to him who is; to torment the living,
under pretence of promoting the happiness of them who
are not born, and who may never be born?" This is one
of the infrequent occasions when Burke agrees with Bentham; for this passage is at the heart of the empirical, as
against the metaphysical, view of politics.

CHARLES TAYLOR

INTRODUCTION

ROBERT B. TALISSE

Charles Taylor, born in Montreal in 1931, earned his undergraduate degree in history from McGill University. He later studied at Oxford University as a Rhodes Scholar and continued at Oxford to complete his D.Phil. under the supervision of the distinguished philosopher and intellectual historian Isaiah Berlin. Taylor has held the Chichele Professorship at Oxford and been a fellow of All Souls College. He spent most of his career at McGill University, where he is currently professor emeritus. Taylor also holds an appointment as Board of Trustees Professor of Law and Philosophy at Northwestern University. He is a fellow of Royal Society of Canada, the British Academy, and the American Academy of Arts and Sciences. In 2007 he was awarded the prestigious Templeton Prize for Progress Toward Research or Discoveries About Spiritual Realities; in 2008 he won the Kyoto Prize in Arts and Philosophy.

Although Taylor is best known for his academic achievements, he is also highly active in Canadian politics. On three occasions he was a New Democratic Party candidate for election to the Canadian House of Commons. In 2007, Taylor was appointed to cochair a commission of inquiry charged with examining possibilities for accommodating the claims of minority cultures in Quebec.

Contemporary philosophers commonly focus their research on a single specialized area or problem in philosophy; however, Taylor's philosophical work spans the entire discipline. He has written on topics in philosophy of history, philosophy of language, action theory, ethics, epistemology, phenomenology, philosophy of social science, the philosophy of Hegel, philosophy of religion, and political philosophy. Despite its broad scope, Taylor's work is unified by an overarching concern to develop a philosophical account of *the self*. This theme is evident in the titles of his major works: *The Explanation of Behaviour* (1963); *Sources of the Self* (1989); *The Ethics of Authenticity* (1992); and *A Secular Age* (2007). The essays collected in two volumes of his philosophical papers—*Human Agency and Language* (1985) and *Philosophy and the Human Sciences* (1985)—similarly demonstrate both the breadth and unity of Taylor's thought.

The way issues concerning the nature of the self shape Taylor's views in political philosophy is apparent in the influential essay reprinted here. Taylor is well known for criticizing dominant understandings of individual liberty and corresponding conceptions of liberalism.

Though the term "liberalism" is in popular settings used to denote a particular collection of public policy initiatives, such as progressive taxation and governmental assistance to the poor, it is used in political philosophy to refer to a tradition of thought that emphasizes individual rights and liberty, and sees political institutions—including states—as instruments aimed solely at protecting individuals and their rights.

Thus liberalism in this sense is not to be contrasted with "conservatism," but rather with views, like those of Aristotle and others, that consider humans *essentially* members of a state. Liberalism takes individuals and their rights, independent from social associations, as the starting point of political theory. All political associations—from states and cities to smaller social communities, such as neighborhoods—exist not by nature (as Aristotle held) but by convention. In other words, liberals see political association as *voluntary*, the product of individual choices that serve individual interests.

No wonder the contract theory of society is popular among liberal political philosophers. Such views, as that of John Locke, begin with pre-social individuals concerned to further their interests and try to show why they would choose to live within a state. Thus liberals seem committed to the idea that individuals exist prior to their social associations. How else could consent be required for the legitimation of those associations?

Another contrast with Aristotle will help to complete our picture of liberalism. Aristotle held that since human beings were essentially "social animals," the good of human beings could be achieved only within a political community; hence Aristotle held that the purpose of political association was the moral development of human beings. States exist, then, for the sake of making their citizens good; consequently, Aristotle thought that states had the authority to morally educate citizens to be virtuous (and to punish and discourage vice).

Liberals, however, reject the view that states exist for the sake of making people good. Rather, they hold that states exist for the sake of protecting individuals from interference by others. The aim of the state is to secure individual liberty, not moral development. Accordingly, liberty is understood as the ability to decide for oneself what is of value, how to act, and what makes a life good, subject to the condition that one must not interfere with the right of others to decide those matters in their own ways. Accordingly, individual liberty is taken to consist strictly in the absence of external constraints; one is free to the extent that there are no obstacles preventing one from doing what one wants. This view is called the *negative* conception of liberty.

In "What's Wrong with Negative Liberty," Taylor criticizes this conception. He argues that, in its most common formulations, the negative conception of liberty is internally unstable.

Taylor begins by noting that the chief virtue of the negative conception of liberty is its apparent simplicity. If liberty consists in the absence of external obstacles, then the question of how free a person is seems simple to answer: one is free insofar as one is able to act without hindrance. As Taylor emphasizes, the negative conception sees liberty as an *opportunity* concept rather than an *exercise* concept. One need not examine what individuals actually choose in order to assess their degree of liberty; liberty simply increases with the number of options available to individuals, and decreases as options are reduced. On such a view, the paradigmatically unfree person is the prisoner, as being in handcuffs drastically restricts the number of actions one can perform.

Contrast this with a competing conception of liberty, known as the *positive* conception, which holds that liberty is not the absence of external obstacles, but the presence of a specified internal capacity, such as rationality or self-control. Here an individual's liberty is not a matter of the number of actions he is able to perform, but rather of what actions he is inclined to perform. Liberty on this view is hence associated with the *presence* of the right behavioral tendencies or dispositions. Accordingly, the positive view treats liberty as an *exercise* concept. To judge whether an individual is free, one must evaluate what he in fact does; liberty increases with the increase of an individual's powers of rational self-control, and decreases to the extent that his actions are irrational or impulsive. The positive view sees the addict or the person in the grip of a psychosis, whose actions are driven by internal forces that are irrational and out of the agent's control, as paradigmatically unfree.

Thus the simplicity of the negative conception comes into view. The positive conception can assess an individual's degree of freedom only by examining his internal workings and evaluating his actions; the positive theorist can assess an individual's freedom only by referring to some conception of the individual's *proper aims* or *rational ends*. The negative conception has no need for such scrutinizing: a free person can yet be an irrational or fundamentally flawed agent; one can be free whole devoting one's life to vicious or meaningless ends. And this simplicity also helps to explain the appeal of the negative conception of liberty among liberals. On the negative conception, the state can secure liberty without taking a stand on how individuals should exercise their liberty; it serves liberty simply by protecting as broad a range of choices as possible, and need not assess what or how individuals make their choices.

But, as Taylor argues, the simplicity of the negative conception is ultimately illusory. Consider his compelling example: Albania has a tyrannical government that has outlawed public expressions of religion, but also has very lax traffic laws and so uses very few traffic lights. Britain, by contrast, is democratically governed and religious expression is largely unconstrained, but there is a large number of traffic lights. Arguably, the presence of high numbers of traffic lights occasions far more instances of interference with a person's actions than a ban on religious expression. Yet, as Taylor rightly notes, it would be absurd to call Albania a free nation. Can the negative liberty theorist accommodate this highly intuitive view that people in Britain are free and those in Albania are not?

Taylor thinks that the judgment that Britain is free and Albania not rests on an assessment of the relative *importance* of activities of religious exercise as compared with unrestricted driving through city streets. The latter, Taylor claims, is *trivial*, whereas the former is highly significant. And this significance derives from the fact that humans are, as Taylor says, "purposive beings." We adopt aims, projects, plans, and commitments; what is more, we experience our different purposes as ranked in a rough order of significance. That is, some of our projects are experienced as *more central* to our identities, and thus more significant to our lives, than others. According to Taylor, this feature of human nature is what underlies the strong intuition that the high number of traffic lights in Britain poses a negligible reduction of the liberty of its citizens, whereas the laws forbidding public religious expression in Albania suffice to render that society unfree. The thought, roughly, is that religious commitments are so central to the lives of those who have them that a restriction on religious expression must be experienced by them as a significant assault on their identities, a thwarting of their most exalted purposes. The obstructions produced by even a vast system of traffic lights never have this kind of impact on individuals' lives.

Taylor reasons that if negative liberty theorists are to escape the absurd implication that Albania is free in virtue of its lax traffic laws, they must admit that the question of whether an individual is free is in part a question about the aims, goals, and purposes that the individual experiences as significant. At the very least, then, freedom would not be the simple absence of obstacles, but the absence of obstacles to our significant purposes.

Taylor argues that once negative liberty theorists incorporate the idea of significant purposes into their conception, they have embraced the idea of positive liberty. He reasons that an individual's significant purposes can be thwarted not only by external constraints, but by internal obstacles such as ignorance, phobia, and irrationality. Consequently, liberty, when understood as the absence of obstacles to our significant purposes, requires a degree of self-knowledge and self-control on the part of the individual. Taylor claims this renders freedom an *exercise* concept; in order to be free, one's internal workings—one's rational and affective capacities, for example—must be functioning properly. And that is the core idea of the positive conception of liberty.

Taylor's views are widely discussed in the professional literature. A comprehensive bibliography of Taylor's writings and of work written about him is maintained online by Ruth Abbey; it can be found at http://www.nd.edu/~rabbey1/index.htm. Professor Abbey's *Charles Taylor* (Princeton, N.J.: Princeton University Press, 2001) provides an accessible brief overview of Taylor's philosophy. Nicholas H. Smith's *Charles Taylor: Meaning, Morals, and Modernity* (London: Polity, 2002) offers a more detailed survey. Taylor's philosophy is the subject of three collections of essays, *Philosophy in an Age of Pluralism: The Philosophy of Charles Taylor* (Cambridge: Cambridge University Press, 1995), edited by James Tully and Daniel Weinstock; *Charles Taylor* (Cambridge: Cambridge University Press, 2004), edited by Ruth Abbey; and *Varieties of Secularism in a Secular Age* (Cambridge, Mass.: Harvard University Press, 2013), edited by Michael Warner, Jonathan VanAntwerpen, and Craig Calhoun.

What's Wrong with Negative Liberty?

This is an attempt to resolve one of the issues that separate "positive" and "negative" theories of freedom, as these have been distinguished in Isaiah Berlin's seminal essay, "Two Concepts of Liberty." Although one can discuss almost endlessly the detailed formulation of the distinction, I believe it is undeniable that there are two such families of conceptions of political freedom abroad in our civilisation.

Thus there clearly are theories, widely canvassed in liberal society, which want to define freedom exclusively in terms of the independence of the individual from interference by others, be these governments, corporations or private persons; and equally clearly these theories are challenged by those who believe that freedom resides at least in part in collective control over the common life. We unproblematically recognize theories descended from Rousseau and Marx as fitting in this category.

There is quite a gamut of views in each category. And this is worth bearing in mind, because it is

From *The* Idea *of Freedom*, ed. Alan Ryan, Oxford University Press, 1979. Reprinted by permission of the publisher.

too easy in the course of polemic to fix on the extreme, almost caricatural variants of each family. When people attack positive theories of freedom, they generally have some Left totalitarian theory in mind, according to which freedom resides exclusively in exercising collective control over one's destiny in a classless society, the kind of theory which underlies, for instance, official Communism. This view, in its caricaturally extreme form, refuses to recognise the freedoms guaranteed in other societies as genuine. The destruction of "bourgeois freedoms" is no real loss of freedom, and coercion can be justified in the name of freedom if it is needed to bring into existence the classless society in which alone men are properly free. Men can, in short, be forced to be free.

Even as applied to official Communism, this portrait is a little extreme, although it undoubtedly expresses the inner logic of this kind of theory. But it is an absurd caricature if applied to the whole family of positive conceptions. This includes all those views of modern political life which owe something to the ancient republican tradition, according to which men's ruling themselves is seen as an activity valuable in itself, and not only for instrumental reasons. It includes in its scope thinkers like Tocqueville, and even arguably the J. S. Mill of *On Representative Government*. It has no necessary connection with the view that freedom consists *purely and simply* in the collective control over the common life, or that there is no freedom worth the name outside a context of collective control. And it does not therefore generate necessarily a doctrine that men can be forced to be free.

On the other side, there is a corresponding caricatural version of negative freedom which tends to come to the fore. This is the tough-minded version, going back to Hobbes, or in another way to Bentham, which sees freedom simply as the absence of external physical or legal obstacles. This view will have no truck with other less immediately obvious obstacles to freedom, for instance, lack of awareness, or false consciousness, or repression, or other inner factors of this kind. It holds firmly

to the view that to speak of such inner factors as relevant to the issue about freedom, to speak for instance of someone's being less free because of false consciousness, is to abuse words. The only clear meaning which can be given to freedom is that of the absence of external obstacles.

I call this view caricatural as a representative portrait of the negative view, because it rules out of court one of the most powerful motives behind the modern defence of freedom as individual independence, viz., the post-Romantic idea that each person's form of self-realisation is original to him/her, and can therefore only be worked out independently. This is one of the reasons for the defence of individual liberty by among others J. S. Mill (this time in his *On Liberty*). But if we think of freedom as including something like the freedom of self-fulfilment, or self-realisation according to our own pattern, then we plainly have something which can fail for inner reasons as well as because of external obstacles. We can fail to achieve our own self-realisation through inner fears, or false consciousness, as well as because of external coercion. Thus the modern notion of negative freedom which gives weight to the securing of each person's right to realise him/herself in his/her own way cannot make do with the Hobbes/ Bentham notion of freedom. The moral psychology of these authors is too simple, or perhaps we should say too crude, for its purposes.

Now there is a strange asymmetry here. The extreme caricatural views tend to come to the fore in the polemic, as I mentioned above. But whereas the extreme "forced-to-be-free" view is one which the opponents of positive liberty try to pin on them, as one would expect in the heat of argument, the proponents of negative liberty themselves often seem anxious to espouse their extreme, Hobbesian view. Thus even Isaiah Berlin, in his eloquent exposition of the two concepts of liberty, seems to quote Bentham approvingly and Hobbes as well. Why is this?

To see this we have to examine more closely what is at stake between the two views. The negative theories, as we saw, want to define freedom in terms of individual independence from others; the positive also want to identify freedom with collective self-government. But behind this lie some deeper differences of doctrines.

Isaiah Berlin points out that negative theories are concerned with the area in which the subject should be left without interference, whereas the positive doctrines are concerned with who or what controls. I should like to put the point behind this in a slightly different way. Doctrines of positive freedom are concerned with a view of freedom which involves essentially the exercising of control over one's life. On this view, one is free only to the extent that one has effectively determined oneself and the shape of one's life. The concept of freedom here is an exercise-concept.

By contrast, negative theories can rely simply on an opportunity-concept, where being free is a matter of what we can do, of what it is open to us to do, whether or not we do anything to exercise these options. This certainly is the case of the crude, original Hobbesian concept. Freedom consists just in there being no obstacle. It is a sufficient condition of one's being free that nothing stand in the way.

But we have to say that negative theories *can* rely on an opportunity-concept, rather than that they necessarily do so rely, for we have to allow for that part of the gamut of negative theories mentioned above which incorporates some notion of self-realisation. Plainly this kind of view can't rely simply on an opportunity-concept. We can't say that someone is free, on a self-realisation view, if he is totally unrealised, if for instance he is totally unaware of his potential, if fulfilling it has never even arisen as a question for him, or if he is paralysed by the fear of breaking with some norm which he has internalised but which does not authentically reflect him. Within this conceptual scheme, some degree of exercise is necessary for a man to be thought free. Or if we want to think of the internal bars to freedom as obstacles on all fours with the external ones, then being in a position to exercise freedom, having the opportunity, involves removing the internal barriers;

and this is not possible without having to some extent realised myself. So that with the freedom of self-realisation, having the opportunity to be free requires that I already be exercising freedom. A pure opportunity-concept is impossible here.

But if negative theories can be grounded on either an opportunity- or an exercise-concept, the same is not true of positive theories. The view that freedom involves at least partially collective self-rule is essentially grounded on an exercise-concept. For this view (at least partly) identifies freedom with self-direction, i.e., the actual exercise of directing control over one's life.

But this already gives us a hint towards illuminating the above paradox, that while the extreme variant of positive freedom is usually pinned on its protagonists by their opponents, negative theorists seem prone to embrace the crudest versions of their theory themselves. For if an opportunity-concept is incombinable with a positive theory, but either it or its alternative can suit a negative theory, then one way of ruling out positive theories in principle is by firmly espousing an opportunity-concept. One cuts off the positive theories by the root, as it were, even though one may also pay a price in the atrophy of a wide range of negative theories as well. At least by taking one's stand firmly on the crude side of the negative range, where only opportunity concepts are recognised, one leaves no place for a positive theory to grow.

Taking one's stand here has the advantage that one is holding the line around a very simple and basic issue of principle, and one where the negative view seems to have some backing in common sense. The basic intuition here is that freedom is a matter of being able to do something or other, of not having obstacles in one's way, rather than being a capacity that we have to realise. It naturally seems more prudent to fight the Totalitarian Menace at this last-ditch position, digging in behind the natural frontier of this simple issue, rather than engaging the enemy on the open terrain of exercise-concepts, where one will have to fight to discriminate the good from the bad among such concepts; fight, for instance, for a view of individual self-realisation against various notions of collective self-realisation, of a nation, or a class. It seems easier and safer to cut all the nonsense off at the start by declaring all self-realisation views to be metaphysical hog-wash. Freedom should just be tough-mindedly defined as the absence of external obstacles.

Of course, there are independent reasons for wanting to define freedom tough-mindedly. In particular there is the immense influence of the anti-metaphysical, materialist, natural-science-oriented temper of thought in our civilisation. Something of this spirit at its inception induced Hobbes to take the line that he did, and the same spirit goes marching on today. Indeed, it is because of the prevalence of this spirit that the line is so easy to defend, forensically speaking, in our society.

Nevertheless, I think that one of the strongest motives for defending the crude Hobbes-Bentham concept, that freedom is the absence of external obstacles, physical or legal, is the strategic one above. For most of those who take this line thereby abandon many of their own intuitions, sharing as they do with the rest of us in a post-Romantic civilisation which puts great value on self-realisation, and values freedom largely because of this. It is fear of the Totalitarian Menace, I would argue, which has led them to abandon this terrain to the enemy.

I want to argue that this not only robs their eventual forensic victory of much of its value, since they become incapable of defending liberalism in the form we in fact value it, but I want to make the stronger claim that this Maginot Line mentality actually ensures defeat, as is often the case with Maginot Line mentalities. The Hobbes-Bentham view, I want to argue, is indefensible as a view of freedom.

To see this, let's examine the line more closely, and the temptation to stand on it. The advantage of the view that freedom is the absence of external obstacles is its simplicity. It allows us to say that freedom is being able to do what you want, where what you want is unproblematically understood as what the agent can identify as his desires. By

contrast an exercise-concept of freedom requires that we discriminate among motivations. If we are free in the exercise of certain capacities, then we are not free, or less free, when these capacities are in some way unfulfilled or blocked. But the obstacles can be internal as well as external. And this must be so, for the capacities relevant to freedom must involve some self-awareness, self-understanding, moral discrimination and self-control, otherwise their exercise couldn't amount to freedom in the sense of self-direction; and this being so, we can fail to be free because these internal conditions are not realised. But where this happens, where, for example, we are quite self-deceived, or utterly fail to discriminate properly the ends we seek, or have lost self-control, we can quite easily be doing what we want in the sense of what we can identify as our wants, without being free; indeed, we can be further entrenching our unfreedom.

Once one adopts a self-realisation view, or indeed, any exercise-concept of freedom, then being able to do what one wants can no longer be accepted as a sufficient condition of being free. For this view puts certain conditions on one's motivation. You are not free if you are motivated, through fear, inauthentically internalised standards, or false consciousness, to thwart your self-realisation. This is sometimes put by saying that for a self-realisation view, you have to be able to do what you really want, or to follow your real will, or to fulfil the desires of your own true self. But these formulas, particularly the last, may mislead, by making us think that exercise concepts of freedom are tied to some particular metaphysic, in particular that of a higher and lower self. We shall see below that this is far from being the case, and that there is a much wider range of bases for discriminating authentic and inauthentic desires.

In any case, the point for our discussion here is that for an exercise-concept of freedom, being free can't just be a question of doing what you want in the unproblematic sense. It must also be that what you want doesn't run against the grain of your basic purposes, or your self-realisation. Or to put the issue in another way, which converges on the same point, the subject himself can't be the final authority on the question whether he is free; for he cannot be the final authority on the question whether his desires are authentic, whether they do or do not frustrate his purposes.

To put the issue in this second way is to make more palpable the temptation for defenders of the negative view to hold their Maginot Line. For once we admit that the agent himself is not the final authority on his own freedom, do we not open the way to totalitarian manipulation? Do we not legitimate others, supposedly wiser about his purposes than himself, redirecting his feet on the right path, perhaps even by force, and all this in the name of freedom?

The answer is that of course we don't. Not by this concession alone. For there may also be good reasons for holding that others are not likely to be in a better position to understand his real purposes. This indeed plausibly follows from the post-Romantic view above that each person has his/her own original form of realisation. Some others, who know us intimately, and who surpass us in wisdom, are undoubtedly in a position to advise us, but no official body can possess a doctrine or a technique whereby they could know how to put us on the rails, because such a doctrine or technique cannot in principle exist if human beings really differ in their self-realisation.

Or again, we may hold a self-realisation view of freedom, and hence believe that there are certain conditions on my motivation necessary to my being free, but also believe that there are other necessary conditions which rule out my being forcibly led towards some definition of my self-realisation by external authority. Indeed, in these last two paragraphs I have given a portrait of what I think is a very widely held view in liberal society, a view which values self-realisation, and accepts that it can fail for internal reasons, but which believes that no valid guidance can be provided in principle by social authority, because of human diversity and originality, and holds that the attempt to impose such guidance will destroy other necessary conditions of freedom.

It is however true that totalitarian theories of positive freedom do build on a conception which involves discriminating between motivations. Indeed, one can represent the path from the negative to the positive conceptions of freedom as consisting of two steps: the first moves us from a notion of freedom as doing what one wants to a notion which discriminates motivations and equates freedom with doing what we really want, or obeying our real will, or truly directing our lives. The second step introduces some doctrine purporting to show that we cannot do what we really want, or follow our real will, outside of a society of a certain canonical form, incorporating true self-government. It follows that we can only be free in such a society, and that being free *is* governing ourselves collectively according to this canonical form.

We might see an example of this second step in Rousseau's view that only a social contract society in which all give themselves totally to the whole preserves us from other-dependence and ensures that we obey only ourselves; or in Marx's doctrine of man as a species-being who realises his potential in a mode of social production, and who must thus take control of this mode collectively.

Faced with this two-step process, it seems safer and easier to stop it at the first step, to insist firmly that freedom is just a matter of the absence of external obstacles, that it therefore involves no discrimination of motivation and permits in principle no second-guessing of the subject by any one else. This is the essence of the Maginot Line strategy. It is very tempting. But I want to claim that it is wrong. I want to argue that we cannot defend a view of freedom which doesn't involve at least some qualitative discrimination as to motive, i.e., which doesn't put some restrictions on motivation among the necessary conditions of freedom, and hence which could rule out second-guessing in principle.

There are some considerations one can put forward straight off to show that the pure Hobbesian concept won't work, that there are some discriminations among motivations which are essential to the concept of freedom as we use it. Even where we think of freedom as the absence of external obstacles, it is not the absence of such obstacles *simpliciter*. For we make discriminations between obstacles as representing more or less serious infringements of freedom. And we do this, because we deploy the concept against a background understanding that certain goals and activities are more significant than others.

Thus we could say that my freedom is restricted if the local authority puts up a new traffic light at an intersection close to my home; so that where previously I could cross as I liked, consistently with avoiding collision with other cars, now I have to wait until the light is green. In a philosophical argument, we might call this a restriction of freedom, but not in a serious political debate. The reason is that it is too trivial, the activity and purposes inhibited here are not really significant. It is not just a matter of our having made a trade-off, and considered that a small loss of liberty was worth fewer traffic accidents, or less danger for the children, we are reluctant to speak here of a loss of liberty at all; what we feel we are trading off is convenience against safety.

By contrast a law which forbids me from worshipping according to the form I believe in is a serious below to liberty; even a law which tried to restrict this to certain times (as the traffic light restricts my crossing of the intersection to certain times) would be seen as a serious restriction. Why this difference between the two cases? Because we have a background understanding, too obvious to spell out, of some activities and goals as highly significant for human beings and others as less so. One's religious belief is recognised, even by atheists, as supremely important, because it is that by which the believer defines himself as a moral being. By contrast my rhythm of movement through the city traffic is trivial. We don't want to speak of these two in the same breath. We don't even readily admit that liberty is at stake in the traffic light case. . . .

But this recourse to significance takes us beyond a Hobbesian scheme. Freedom is no longer just the absence of external obstacle *tout court*, but the absence of external obstacle to significant action, to what is important to man. There are discriminations to be made; some restrictions are more serious than others, some are utterly trivial. About many, there is of course controversy. But what the judgement turns on is some sense of what is significant for human life. Restricting the expression of people's religious and ethical convictions is more significant than restricting their movement around uninhabited parts of the country; and both are more significant than the trivia of traffic control.

But the Hobbesian scheme has no place for the notion of significance. It will allow only for purely quantitative judgements. On the toughest-minded version of his conception, where Hobbes seems to be about to define liberty in terms of the absence of physical obstacles, one is presented with the vertiginous prospect of human freedom being measurable in the same way as the degrees of freedom of some physical object, say a lever. Later we see that this won't do, because we have to take account of legal obstacles to my action. But in any case, such a quantitative conception of freedom is a non-starter.

Consider the following diabolical defence of Albania as a free country. We recognise that religion has been abolished in Albania, whereas it hasn't been in Britain. But on the other hand there are probably far fewer traffic lights per head in Tirana than in London. (I haven't checked for myself, but this is a very plausible assumption.) Suppose an apologist for Albanian Socialism were nevertheless to claim that this country was freer than Britain, because the number of acts restricted was far smaller. After all, only a minority of Londoners practise some religion in public places, but all have to negotiate their way through traffic. Those who do practise a religion generally do so on one day of the week, while they are held up at traffic lights every day. In sheer quantitative terms, the number of acts restricted by traffic lights must be greater than that restricted by a ban on public religious practice. So if Britain is considered a free society, why not Albania?

So the application even of our negative notion of freedom requires a background conception of what is significant, according to which some restrictions are seen to be without relevance for freedom altogether, and others are judged as being of greater and lesser importance. So some discrimination among motivations seems essential to our concept of freedom. A minute's reflection shows why this must be so. Freedom is important to us because we are purposive beings. But then there must be distinctions in the significance of different kinds of freedom based on the distinction in the significance of different purposes.

But of course, this still doesn't involve the kind of discrimination mentioned above, the kind which would allow us to say that someone who was doing what he wanted (in the unproblematic sense) wasn't really free, the kind of discrimination which allows us to put conditions on people's motivations necessary to their being free, and hence to second-guess them. All we have shown is that we make discriminations between more or less significant freedoms, based on discriminations among the purposes people have.

This creates some embarrassment for the crude negative theory, but it can cope with it by simply adding a recognition that we make judgements of significance. Its central claim that freedom just is the absence of external obstacles seems untouched, as also its view of freedom as an opportunity-concept. It is just that we now have to admit that not all opportunities are equal.

But there is more trouble in store for the crude view when we examine further what these qualitative discriminations are based on. What lies behind our judging certain purposes/feelings as more significant than others? One might think that there was room here again for another quantitative theory; that the more significant purposes are those we want more. But this account is either vacuous or false.

It is true but vacuous if we take wanting more just to mean being more significant. It is false as soon as we try to give wanting more an independent criterion, such as, for instance, the urgency

or force of a desire, or the prevalence of one desire over another, because it is a matter of the most banal experience that the purposes we know to be more significant are not always those which we desire with the greatest urgency to encompass, nor the ones that actually always win out in cases of conflict of desires.

When we reflect on this kind of significance, we come up against what I have called elsewhere the fact of strong evaluation, the fact that we human subjects are not only subjects of first-order desires, but of second-order desires, desires about desires. We experience our desires and purposes as qualitatively discriminated, as higher or lower, noble or base, integrated or fragmented, significant or trivial, good and bad. This means that we experience some of our desires and goals as intrinsically more significant than others: some passing comfort is less important than the fulfilment of our lifetime vocation, our *amour propre* less important than a love relationship; while we experience some others as bad, not just comparatively, but absolutely: we desire not to be moved by spite, or some childish desire to impress at all costs. And these judgements of significance are quite independent of the strength of the respective desires: the craving for comfort may be overwhelming at this moment, we may be obsessed with our *amour propre*, but the judgement of significance stands.

But then the question arises whether this fact of strong evaluation doesn't have other consequences for our notion of freedom, than just that it permits us to rank freedoms in importance. Is freedom not at stake when we find ourselves carried away by a less significant goal to override a highly significant one? Or when we are led to act out of a motive we consider bad or despicable?

The answer is that we sometimes do speak in this way. Suppose I have some irrational fear, which is preventing me from doing something I very much want to do. Say the fear of public speaking is preventing me from taking up a career that I should find very fulfilling, and that I should be quite good at, if I could just get over this "hang-up." It is clear that we experience this fear as an obstacle, and that we feel we are less than we would be if we could overcome it.

Or again, consider the case where I am very attached to comfort. To go on short rations, and to miss my creature comforts for a time, makes me very depressed. I find myself making a big thing of this. Because of this reaction I can't do certain things that I should like very much to do, such as going on an expedition over the Andes, or a canoe trip in the Yukon. Once again, it is quite understandable if I experience this attachment as an obstacle, and feel that I should be freer without it.

Or I could find that my spiteful feelings and reactions which I almost can't inhibit are undermining a relationship which is terribly important to me. At times, I feel as though I am almost assisting as a helpless witness at my own destructive behaviour, as I lash out again with my unbridled tongue at her. I long to be able not to feel this spite. As long as I feel it, even control is not an option, because it just builds up inside until it either bursts out, or else the feeling somehow communicates itself, and queers things between us. I long to be free of this feeling.

These are quite understandable cases, where we can speak of freedom or its absence without strain. What I have called strong evaluation is essentially involved here. For these are not just cases of conflict, even cases of painful conflict. If the conflict is between two desires with which I have no trouble identifying, there can be no talk of lesser freedom, no matter how painful or fateful. Thus if what is breaking up my relationship is my finding fulfilment in a job which, say, takes me away from home a lot, I have indeed a terrible conflict, but I would have no temptation to speak of myself as less free.

Even seeing a great difference in the significance of the two terms doesn't seem to be a sufficient condition of my wanting to speak of freedom and its absence. Thus my marriage may be breaking up because I like going to the pub and playing cards on Saturday nights with the boys. I may feel quite unequivocally that my marriage is much more important than the release and comradeship of the Saturday night bash. But nevertheless I wouldn't want to talk of my being freer if I could slough off this desire.

The difference seems to be that in this case, unlike the ones above, I still identify with the less important desire, I still see it as expressive of myself, so that I couldn't lose it without altering who I am, losing something of my personality. Whereas my irrational fear, my being quite distressed by discomfort, my spite—these are all things which I can easily see myself losing without any loss whatsoever to what I am. This is why I can see them as obstacles to my purposes, and hence to my freedom, even though they are in a sense unquestionably desires and feelings of mine.

Before exploring further what's involved in this, let's go back and keep score. It would seem that these cases make a bigger breach in the crude negative theory. For they seem to be cases in which the obstacles to freedom are internal; and if this is so, then freedom can't simply be interpreted as the absence of *external* obstacles; and the fact that I'm doing what I want, in the sense of following my strongest desire, isn't sufficient to establish that I'm free. On the contrary, we have to make discriminations among motivations, and accept that acting out of some motivations, for example irrational fear or spite, or this too great need for comfort, is not freedom, is even a negation of freedom.

But although the crude negative theory can't be sustained in the face of these examples, perhaps something which springs from the same concerns can be reconstructed. For although we have to admit that there are internal, motivational, necessary conditions for freedom, we can perhaps still avoid any legitimation of what I called above the second-guessing of the subject. If our negative theory allows for strong evaluation, allows that some goals are really important to us, and that other desires are seen as not fully ours, then can it not retain the thesis that freedom is being able to do what I want, that is, what I can identify myself as wanting, where this means not just what I identify as my strongest desire, but what I identify as my true, authentic desire or purpose? The subject would still be the final arbiter of his being free/unfree, as indeed he is clearly capable of discerning this in the examples above, where I relied precisely on the subject's own experience of constraint, of motives with which he can't identify. We should have sloughed off the untenable Hobbesian reductive-materialist metaphysics, according to which only external obstacles count, as though action were just movement, and there could be no internal, motivational obstacles to our deeper purposes. But we would be retaining the basic concern of the negative theory, that the subject is still the final authority as to what his freedom consists in, and cannot be second-guessed by external authority. Freedom would be modified to read: the absence of internal or external obstacle to what I truly or authentically want. But we would still be holding the Maginot Line. Or would we?

I think not, in fact. I think that this hybrid or middle position is untenable, where we are willing to admit that we can speak of what we truly want, as against what we most strongly desire, and of some desires as obstacles to our freedom, while we still will not allow for second-guessing. For to rule this out in principle is to rule out in principle that the subject can ever be wrong about what he truly wants. And how can he never, in principle, be wrong, unless there is nothing to be right or wrong about in this matter?

That in fact is the thesis our negative theorist will have to defend. And it is a plausible one for the same intellectual (reductive-empiricist) tradition from which the crude negative theory springs. On this view, our feelings are brute facts about us; that is, it is a fact about us that we are affected in such and such a way, but our feelings can't themselves be understood as involving some perception or sense of what they relate to, and hence as potentially veridical or illusory, authentic or inauthentic. On this scheme, the fact that a certain desire represented one of our fundamental purposes, and another a mere force with which we cannot identify, would concern merely the brute

quality of the affect in both cases. It would be a matter of the raw feel of these two desires that this was their respective status.

In such circumstances, the subject's own classification would be incorrigible. There is no such thing as an imperceptible raw feel. If the subject failed to experience a certain desire as fundamental, and if what we meant by "fundamental" applied to desire was that the felt experience of it has a certain quality, then the desire couldn't be fundamental. We can see this if we look at those feelings which we can agree are brute in this sense: for instance, the stab of pain I feel when the dentist jabs into my tooth, or the crawling unease when someone runs his fingernail along the blackboard. There can be no question of misperception here. If I fail to "perceive" the pain, I am not in pain. Might it not be so with our fundamental desires, and those which we repudiate?

The answer is clearly no. For first of all, many of our feelings and desires, including the relevant ones for these kinds of conflicts, are not brute. By contrast with pain and the fingernail-on-blackboard sensation, shame and fear, for instance, are emotions which involve our experiencing the situation as bearing a certain import for us, as being dangerous or shameful. This is why shame and fear can be inappropriate, or even irrational, where pain and a frisson cannot. Thus we can be in error in feeling shame or fear. We can even be consciously aware of the unfounded nature of our feelings, and this is when we castigate them as irrational.

Thus the notion that we can understand all our feelings and desires as brute, in the above sense, is not on. But more, the idea that we could discriminate our fundamental desires, or those which we want to repudiate, by the quality of brute affect is grotesque. When I am convinced that some career, or an expedition in the Andes, or a love relationship, is of fundamental importance to me (to recur to the above examples), it cannot be just because of the throbs, *élans* or tremors I feel; I must also have some sense that these are of great significance for me, meet important, long-lasting needs, represent a fulfilment of something central to me, will bring me closer to what I really am, or something of the sort. The whole notion of our identity, whereby we recognise that some goals, desires, allegiances are central to what we are, while others are not or are less so, can make sense only against a background of desires and feelings which are not brute, but what I shall call import-attributing, to invent a term of art for the occasion.

Thus we have to see our emotional life as made up largely of import-attributing desires and feelings, that is, desires and feelings which we can experience mistakenly. And not only can we be mistaken in this, we clearly must accept, in cases like the above where we want to repudiate certain desires, that we are mistaken.

For let us consider the distinction mentioned above between conflicts where we feel fettered by one desire, and those where we do not, where, for instance, in the example mentioned above, a man is torn between his career and his marriage. What made the difference was that in the case of genuine conflict both desires are the agent's, whereas in the cases where he feels fettered by one, this desire is one he wants to repudiate.

But what is it to feel that a desire is not truly mine? Presumably, I feel that I should be better off without it, that I don't lose anything in getting rid of it, I remain quite complete without it. What could lie behind this sense?

Well, one could imagine feeling this about a brute desire. I may feel this about my addiction to smoking, for instance—wish I could get rid of it, experience it as a fetter, and believe that I should be well rid of it. But addictions are a special case; we understand them to be unnatural, externally-induced desires. We couldn't say in general that we are ready to envisage losing our brute desires without a sense of diminution. On the contrary, to lose my desire for, and hence delectation in, oysters, mushroom pizza, or Peking duck would be a terrible deprivation. I should fight against such a change with all the strength at my disposal.

So being brute is not what makes desires repudiable. And besides, in the above examples the repudiated desires aren't brute. In the first case, I am chained by unreasoning fear, an import-attributing emotion, in which the fact of being mistaken is already recognised when I identify the fear as irrational or unreasoning. Spite, too, which moves me in the third case, is an import-attributing emotion. To feel spite is to see oneself and the target of one's resentment in a certain light; it is to feel in some way wounded, or damaged, by his success or good fortune, and the more hurt the more he is fortunate. To overcome feelings of spite, as against just holding them in, is to come to see self and other in a different light, in particular, to set aside self-pity, and the sense of being personally wounded by what the other does and is.

(I should also like to claim that the obstacle in the second example, the too great attachment to comfort, while not itself import-attributing, is also bound up with the way we see things. The problem is here not just that we dislike discomfort, but that we are too easily depressed by it; and this is something which we overcome only by sensing a different order of priorities, whereby small discomforts matter less. But if this is thought too dubious, we can concentrate on the other two examples.)

Now how can we feel that an import-attributing desire is not truly ours? We can do this only if we see it as mistaken, that is, the import or the good it supposedly gives us a sense of is not a genuine import or good. The irrational fear is a fetter, because it is irrational; spite is a fetter because it is rooted in a self-absorption which distorts our perspective on everything, and the pleasures of venting it preclude any genuine satisfaction. Losing these desires we lose nothing, because their loss deprives us of no genuine good or pleasure or satisfaction. In this they are quite different from my love of oysters, mushroom pizza and Peking duck.

It would appear from this that to see our desires as brute gives us no clue as to why some of them are repudiable. On the contrary it is precisely their not being brute which can explain this. It is because they are import-attributing desires which are mistaken that we can feel that we would lose nothing in sloughing them off. Everything which is truly important to us would be safeguarded. If they were just brute desires, we couldn't feel this unequivocally, as we certainly do not when it comes to the pleasures of the palate. True, we also feel that our desire to smoke is repudiable, but there is a special explanation here, which is not available in the case of spite.

Thus we can experience some desires as fetters, because we can experience them as not ours. And we can experience them as not ours because we see them as incorporating a quite erroneous appreciation of our situation and of what matters to us. We can see this again if we contrast the case of spite with that of another emotion which partly overlaps, and which is highly considered in some societies, the desire for revenge. In certain traditional societies this is far from being considered a despicable emotion. On the contrary, it is a duty of honour on a male relative to avenge a man's death. We might imagine that this too might give rise to conflict. It might conflict with the attempts of a new regime to bring some order to the land. The government would have to stop people taking vengeance, in the name of peace.

But short of a conversion to a new ethical outlook, this would be seen as a trade-off, the sacrifice of one legitimate goal for the sake of another. And it would seem monstrous were one to propose reconditioning people so that they no longer felt the desire to avenge their kin. This would be to unman them.[1]

Why do we feel so different about spite (and for that matter also revenge)? Because the desire for revenge for an ancient Icelander was his sense of a real obligation incumbent on him, something it would be dishonourable to repudiate; while for us, spite is the child of a distorted perspective on things.

We cannot therefore understand our desires and emotions as all brute, and in particular we cannot make sense of our discrimination of some desires as more important and fundamental, or of our repudiation of others, unless we understand our feelings to be import-attributing. This is essential to there being what we have called strong

evaluation. Consequently the half-way position which admits strong evaluation, admits that our desires may frustrate our deeper purposes, admits therefore that there may be inner obstacles to freedom, and yet will not admit that the subject may be wrong or mistaken about these purposes—this position doesn't seem tenable. For the only way to make the subject's assessment incorrigible in principle would be to claim that there was nothing to be right or wrong about here; and that could only be so if experiencing a given feeling were a matter of the qualities of brute feeling. But this it cannot be if we are to make sense of the whole background of strong evaluation, more significant goals, and aims that we repudiate. This whole scheme requires that we understand the emotions concerned as import-attributing, as, indeed, it is clear that we must do on other grounds as well.

But once we admit that our feelings are import-attributing, then we admit the possibility of error, or false appreciation. And indeed, we have to admit a kind of false appreciation which the agent himself detects in order to make sense of the cases where we experience our own desires as fetters. How can we exclude in principle that there may be other false appreciations which the agent does not detect? That he may be profoundly in error, that is, have a very distorted sense of his fundamental purposes? Who can say that such people can't exist? All cases are, of course, controversial; but I should nominate Charles Manson and Andreas Baader for this category, among others. I pick them out as people with a strong sense of some purposes and goals as incomparably more fundamental than others, or at least with a propensity to act as having such a sense so as to take in even themselves a good part of the time, but whose sense of fundamental purpose was shot through with confusion and error. And once we recognise such extreme cases, how do we avoid admitting that many of the rest of mankind can suffer to a lesser degree from the same disabilities?

What has this got to do with freedom? Well, to resume what we have seen: our attributions of freedom make sense against a background sense of more and less significant purposes, for the question of freedom/unfreedom is bound up with the frustration/fulfilment of our purposes. Further, our significant purposes can be frustrated by our own desires, and where these are sufficiently based on misappreciation, we consider them as not really ours, and experience them as fetters. A man's freedom can therefore be hemmed in by internal, motivational obstacles, as well as external ones. A man who is driven by spite to jeopardise his most important relationships, in spite of himself, as it were, or who is prevented by unreasoning fear from taking up the career he truly wants, is not really made more free if one lifts the external obstacles to his venting his spite or acting on his fear. Or at best he is liberated into a very impoverished freedom.

If through linguistic/ideological purism one wants to stick to the crude definition, and insist that men are equally freed from whom the same external obstacles are lifted, regardless of their motivational state, then one will just have to introduce some other term to mark the distinction, and say that one man is capable of taking proper advantage of his freedom, and the other (the one in the grip of spite, or fear) is not. This is because in the meaningful sense of "free," that for which we value it, in the sense of being able to act on one's important purposes, the internally fettered man is not free. If we choose to give "free" a special (Hobbesian) sense which avoids this issue, we'll just have to introduce another term to deal with it.

Moreover since we have already seen that we are always making judgements of degrees of freedom, based on the significance of the activities or purposes which are left unfettered, how can we deny that the man, externally free but still stymied by his repudiated desires, is less free than one who has no such inner obstacles?

But if this is so, then can we not say of the man with a highly distorted view of his fundamental purpose, the Manson or Baader of my discussion above, that he may not be significantly freer when we lift even the internal barriers to his doing what is in line with this purpose, or at best may

be liberated into a very impoverished freedom? Should a Manson overcome his last remaining compunction against sending his minions to kill on caprice, so that he could act unchecked, would we consider him freer, as we should undoubtedly consider the man who had done away with spite or unreasoning fear? Hardly, and certainly not to the same degree. For what he sees as his purpose here partakes so much of the nature of spite and unreasoning fear in the other cases, that is, it is an aspiration largely shaped by confusion, illusion and distorted perspective.

Once we see that we make distinctions of degree and significance in freedoms depending on the significance of the purpose fettered/enabled, how can we deny that it makes a difference to the degree of freedom not only whether one of my basic purposes is frustrated by my own desires but also whether I have grievously misidentified this purpose? The only way to avoid this would be to hold that there is no such thing as getting it wrong, that your basic purpose is just what you feel it to be. But there is such a thing as getting it wrong, as we have seen, and the very distinctions of significance depend on this fact.

But if this is so, then the crude negative view of freedom, the Hobbesian definition, is untenable. Freedom can't just be the absence of external obstacles, for there may also be internal ones. And nor may the internal obstacles be just confined to those that the subject identifies as such, so that he is the final arbiter; for he may be profoundly mistaken about his purposes and about what he wants to repudiate. And if so, he is less capable of freedom in the meaningful sense of the word. Hence we cannot maintain the incorrigibility of the subject's judgements about his freedom, or rule out second-guessing, as we put it above. And at the same time, we are forced to abandon the pure opportunity-concept of freedom.

For freedom now involves my being able to recognise adequately my more important purposes, and my being able to overcome or at least neutralise my motivational fetters, as well as my way being free of external obstacles. But clearly the first condition (and, I would argue, also the second) require me to have become something, to have achieved a certain condition of self-clairvoyance and self-understanding. I must be actually exercising self-understanding in order to be truly or fully free. I can no longer understand freedom just as an opportunity-concept.

In all these three formulations of the issue—opportunity- versus exercise-concept; whether freedom requires that we discriminate among motivations; whether it allows of second-guessing the subject—the extreme negative view shows up as wrong. The idea of holding the Maginot Line before this Hobbesian concept is misguided not only because it involves abandoning some of the most inspiring terrain of liberalism, which is concerned with individual self-realisation, but also because the line turns out to be untenable. The first step from the Hobbesian definition to a positive notion, to a view of freedom as the ability to fulfil my purposes, and as being greater the more significant the purposes, is one we cannot help taking. Whether we must also take the second step, to a view of freedom which sees it as realisable or fully realisable only within a certain form of society; and whether in taking a step of this kind one is necessarily committed to justifying the excesses of totalitarian oppression in the name of liberty; these are questions which must now be addressed. What is certain is that they cannot simply be evaded by a philistine definition of freedom which relegates them by fiat to the limbo of metaphysical pseudo-questions. This is altogether too quick a way with them.

Note

1. Compare the unease we feel at the reconditioning of the hero of Anthony Burgess's *A Clockwork Orange*.

JOHN RAWLS

~

INTRODUCTION

JOSHUA COHEN

John Rawls (1921–2003) was born in Baltimore, Maryland. He graduated from Princeton University, and then, after serving in the U.S. Army in the Pacific during World War II, returned to Princeton, where he received a Ph.D. in philosophy in 1950. An influential teacher of several generations of moral and political philosophers, Rawls taught at Cornell in the 1950s, moved to the Massachusetts Institute of Technology in 1960, and then to Harvard's philosophy department in 1962, where he remained until his retirement in 1991. From the time he received his Ph.D. until 1971, Rawls's principal intellectual project was a book about justice. That book appeared in 1971 under the title *A Theory of Justice* and provided a comprehensive statement of a theory that Rawls called "justice as fairness." After the book's publication, Rawls spent nearly twenty years rethinking the foundations of justice as fairness, with the aim of making the presentation of his outlook more consistent with the religious and philosophical pluralism characteristic of modern democracies. The fruits of those labors appeared in 1993 in his *Political Liberalism* (New York: Columbia University Press). In 1999, Rawls published *The Law of Peoples* (Cambridge, Mass.: Harvard University Press), which extended his ideas about justice to the international system.

For much of the past century, the idea of an egalitarian-liberal political philosophy seemed to many a contradiction in terms. Egalitarians troubled by vast differences between the lives of rich and poor commonly condemned liberalism for paying excessive attention to legal rights and liberties while exhibiting indifference to the real fate of ordinary people. Equality, they argued, could be found only in the rarified atmosphere of liberal legal and political discourse—with its claims about equality of persons before the law and of citizens in the state—in disturbing isolation from life on earth. Liberals concerned to ensure individual rights would condemn egalitarianism for being paternalistic and willing to sacrifice human freedom in the name of a bland sameness of circumstance or future utopia. Practically speaking, democratic welfare states tried, with more or less success, to respect liberal and egalitarian values: to ensure basic individual rights to personal and political liberties while protecting individuals from the contingencies of the market. But the philosophical options seemed starkly opposed. In between Friedrich Hayek's classical liberalism and Karl Marx's egalitarianism, everything was an unstable political compromise, or an ad hoc balancing of competing values.

Rawls's *Theory of Justice* reshaped this philosophical terrain. Rawls proposed a conception of justice committed to the individual rights associated with traditional liberalism, to an egalitarian ideal of fair distribution conventionally associated with socialist and radical democratic traditions, and to a reasonable faith in the practical possibility of a form of constitutional democracy ensuring both liberty and equality. In summarizing his view, he said that justice as fairness aims to effect a "reconciliation of liberty and equality."

To appreciate the force of this reconciliation, consider the two principles of justice that Rawls explains and defends in *A Theory of Justice*. Rawls's first principle—a principle of *equal basic liberties*—says that each citizen has an equal right to the most extensive system of equal basic personal and political liberties compatible with a similar system of liberties for others. This principle does not assert a right to "liberty as such," that is, a right that would condemn restrictions on all manner of choices. Instead, the first principle requires stringent protections for certain *specific* liberties: liberty of thought and conscience; political liberty; freedom of association; liberty and integrity of the person; and the rights and liberties associated with the rule of law, and its requirements of generality and predictability. Rawls's first principle also includes a demanding norm of political equality, which holds that political liberty is to be assured a fair value—that the chance to hold office and to exercise influence on the political system ought to be independent of socioeconomic position. So citizens who have the motivation and ability to play an active political role should not be disadvantaged in their efforts by a lack of sufficient private wealth, or advantaged by their greater wealth.

Rawls's second principle of justice expresses egalitarian ideals of distributive justice. The second principle has two components, both of which set limits on acceptable socioeconomic inequalities. The first component states that when inequalities are attached to offices and positions—say, when different jobs are differently rewarded—those offices and positions must be open to everyone under conditions of *fair equality of opportunity*. In particular, people who are equally talented and motivated must have equal chances to attain desirable positions, regardless of their class background. Access to responsible and well-compensated work should not depend on the social circumstances in which people happen to have been born and raised.

But even a society that protects each person's basic personal and political liberties, and ensures fair equality of opportunity, might still have troubling inequalities. Thus, suppose some people, partly because of their native endowments, possess scarce talents that command high returns in the market, while others lack such skills. Assume people in both groups work hard and contribute according to their abilities. Still, they will reap substantially different rewards, and those differences will have a large impact on their lives. But these inequalities of reward are founded on natural contingencies, bare undeserved luck in life's lottery, and "there is no more reason to permit the distribution of income and wealth to be settled by the distribution of natural assets than by historical and social fortune." So a second part of Rawls's second principle—the difference principle—requires an economic structure that mitigates inequalities in income and wealth owing to differences in natural talent. Instead of permitting differences of reward simply to reflect differences of native endowment, the difference principle requires that we maximize the lifetime expectations of those who are in the least advantaged social position. Thus someone might legitimately be paid more than someone else because the higher income compensates for expensive training and education that enable the person to take on socially desirable tasks; or inequalities might make sense as incentives that encourage people to take on tasks they would otherwise be unable or simply unwilling to take on. According to the difference principle, such inequalities are fully just only if they are to the greatest benefit of those who are least well-off.

While the requirement of fair equality of opportunity, then, condemns a society in which class background is a source of social or economic privilege, the difference principle condemns a society in which, as the sociologist Emile Durkheim put it, "social inequalities exactly express natural inequalities." In effect, then, Rawls urges us to reject the idea that our economic system is a race or talent contest, designed to reward the swift and gifted. Instead, it is one part of a fair scheme of cooperation, designed to ensure a reasonable life for all. "In justice as fairness," Rawls says, "men agree to share one another's fate. In designing institutions they undertake to avail themselves of the accidents of nature and social circumstance *only when* doing so is for the common benefit."

To see how justice as fairness reconciles liberty and equality, then, consider the joint operation of the two principles of justice. Assume that what matters to people is not only to have basic liberties that are legally protected from interferences by others, but that the legally protected liberties provide a meaningful or valuable liberty, that the liberties are worth something to us. Assume, too, that the worth of our liberty to us reflects the resources we have available for using the liberty. In particular, assume that the value of my liberties to me is an increasing function of the resources over which I exercise control: as my command of resources increases, I can do more with my liberties.

Now put the two principles together: the first principle ensures equal basic liberties, and the difference principle guarantees that the minimum level of resources is maximized. If, as I just suggested, the worth of a person's liberty—its value to the person—is an increasing function of the level of that person's resources, then by maximizing the minimum level of resources, we also maximize the minimum worth of liberty. Thus the two principles together require that society "maximize the worth to the least advantaged of the complete scheme of equal liberty shared by all." Maximizing the minimum worth of liberty "defines," Rawls says, "the end of social justice"—what justice aims ultimately to achieve.

The central idea of justice as fairness, then, is that an egalitarian-liberal conception comprising the two principles of justice is the most reasonable conception of justice "for a democratic society." Abraham Lincoln said that the United States was conceived in liberty and dedicated to the proposition that all men are created equal. Justice as fairness argues that the two principles of justice are the most reasonable theory of justice for a society with that conception and dedication—more reasonable than, for example, utilitarianism, or libertarianism, or a less liberal egalitarianism, or a less egalitarian liberalism.

To argue for the two principles of justice over alternatives, Rawls revives the social contract idea associated with Hobbes, Locke, Rousseau, and Kant. The social contract idea is that the most reasonable ordering of a society is the ordering that the members themselves would unanimously agree to as the basis for their own association. So Rawls asks us to imagine ourselves in a hypothetical situation—he calls it "the Original Position"—in which we are to choose the principles of justice that will be used in our own society. Whereas the Hobbesian social contract was based on certain fundamental truths about human nature, the construction of the Original Position is designed to reflect the moral idea that we are free and equal moral persons—with a capacity to cooperate with others on fair terms, to choose our ends and devotions, and to pursue the ends we set for ourselves—and that the principles of justice for our society should treat us as such. So certain of our characteristics—those that distinguish among free and equal persons—are irrelevant in deciding what we are entitled to as a matter of justice. Specifically, our social class position, natural talents, sex or race, and conception of the good are irrelevant from the standpoint of justice. When we imagine ourselves making a choice of principles of justice, then, we are to imagine choosing from behind a "veil of ignorance" in which we are assumed to lack knowledge of the irrelevant features. We know that we are free and equal moral persons, but we do not know our class background, native endowments, sex or race, and conception of the good. We do not know, in short, whether the natural and social contingencies have worked in our favor.

When we reason from behind the veil of ignorance, then, we focus only on interests we share as free and equal moral persons, and put aside what distinguishes us from one another. Thus the parties in the original position know only that they represent a person who has some conception of the good (though they do not know what that conception is); an interest in being able to choose and revise their ends; and an interest in forming and acting on a sense of justice. Moreover, advancing those shared interests requires certain goods, called "social primary goods," and so the parties to the social contract know that they need these goods—in particular, the basic liberties; freedom of movement and occupational choice; powers and prerogatives of office and positions of responsibility; income and wealth; and the social bases of self-respect.

Why would parties in the original position choose Rawls's principles? The argument is complicated, but the intuitive idea is reasonably straightforward. You are asked to choose principles for your society under conditions of ignorance about your talents, ideals, and social position, ignorance that models the irrelevance of these properties from the point of view of justice. You do not know which person you will be, but have to live with the principles you choose, so you want to be sure—if this is possible—that your situation is acceptable whatever it turns out to be: you want to be sure that the society is acceptable from the point of view of each person, because you do not know which person you are. In particular, you want to be sure that it will be acceptable even if you land in the lowest social position, where acceptability is least likely. And, according to Rawls, this is precisely the "downside protection," the insurance that the two principles provide. They ensure that social arrangements are acceptable to all members of a society of equals, in particular because they guarantee basic liberties to all, and ensure an acceptable worth of liberty, even at the minimum position.

Starting from the fundamental ideal of fair cooperation among free and equal moral persons, then, we are led to the social contract idea of finding principles that would be the object of an initial agreement. And that initial agreement, made under conditions of ignorance, would endorse an egalitarian-liberal political conception that promises to maximize the minimum worth of liberty and thus to provide terms that are acceptable to all members of a democratic society. It is an inspiring political vision, and in a better world than our own, it would guide the political judgment of democratic citizens.

In *Political Liberalism*, Rawls preserves the key elements of justice as fairness: the two principles of justice, the central role of the idea of fair cooperation among free and equal moral persons, and the original position as a point of view for evaluating conceptions of justice. But he addresses a fundamental problem that was inadequately treated in *Theory of Justice*.

In modern democratic societies, Rawls says, citizens face deep and unresolvable disagreements on religious, moral, and philosophical doctrines. These doctrines are not confined to politics, but provide guidance on a very broad range of practical and metaphysical questions. Because of that breadth, Rawls calls them "comprehensive doctrines." Thus, modern democratic societies are characterized by a "reasonable pluralism" of comprehensive doctrines. *A Theory of Justice*, however, presents justice as fairness as founded on one particular, comprehensive doctrine—as an extension to politics the Kantian idea that persons are autonomous agents and that morality is the self-legislation of such agents. If that is right, however, then we are left with the suggestion, deeply troubling to Rawls, that only moral liberals—with comprehensive moralities based on notions of individuality and autonomy—have good reason to embrace liberal political ideas. Those ideas would be at odds with, for example, the convictions of religious citizens who think that morality is based on natural laws given by God, not moral laws we impose on ourselves.

Political Liberalism responds to this challenge. Rawls argues that we have reason to hope that the diverse comprehensive doctrines—both religious and secular—embraced by the members of a well-ordered democratic society would provide reasons for endorsing justice as fairness, or at least for endorsing some liberal conception of justice. Rawls calls the result—conflicting comprehensive doctrines but shared political ideas—an "overlapping consensus." In a modern democratic society, an overlapping consensus provides the most reasonable basis for social unity. And the political ideas that provide the focus of that consensus can in turn provide the basis for public discussion—for a "public reason" that citizens can use in conducting political debate in the public forum.

Fundamental disagreement does not demand, then, that we rethink our ideas about what justice requires. But it does demand that we formulate those ideas in ways that can be embraced by equal citizens with profoundly different convictions. With that formulation, Rawls proposed, we will see that liberal political ideas can provide common ground in the face of our unresolvable disagreements on the answers to basic moral, religious, and philosophical questions.

In addition to Rawls's three main books, his articles are available in John Rawls, *Collected Papers*, edited by Samuel Freeman (Cambridge, Mass.: Harvard University Press, 1999). Some of his lectures, particularly on Kant, have been published in *Lectures on the History of Moral Philosophy*, edited by Barbara Herman (Cambridge, Mass.: Harvard University Press, 2000). His lectures on political philosophy have been published in *Lectures on the History of Political Philosophy*, edited by Samuel Freeman (Cambridge, Mass.: Harvard University Press, 2008). And a reformulation of justice as fairness in light of the ideas in *Political Liberalism* is now available in *Justice as Fairness: A Restatement*, edited by Erin Kelly (Cambridge, Mass.: Harvard University Press, 2001). Rawls's work is also the topic of a vast secondary literature. The discussion of Rawls in Brian Barry, *Theories of Justice* (Berkeley: University of California Press, 1989) is especially illuminating. *Reading Rawls*, edited by Norman Daniels (Stanford, Calif.: Stanford University Press, 1989), contains some of the classic early papers on *Theory of Justice*, including important articles by Thomas Nagel, Ronald Dworkin, and H. L. A. Hart. In chapter 7 of *Anarchy, State, and Utopia* (New York: Basic Books, 1974), Robert Nozick advances a forceful libertarian critique of justice as fairness. Susan Okin, *Justice, Gender, and the Family* (New York: Basic Books, 1989) presents a feminist critique of justice as fairness. In *Liberalism and the Limits of Justice*, 2d ed. (Cambridge: Cambridge University Press, 1998), Michael Sandel argues that there is a fundamental tension between the liberal and egalitarian commitments of justice as fairness—that Rawls's liberalism is founded on an individualistic outlook, whereas his egalitarianism suggests a communitarian philosophy. In *Rescuing Justice and Equality* (Cambridge, Mass.: Harvard University Press, 2008), G. A. Cohen argues that Rawls's willingness to countenance "incentive inequalities" represents an accommodation to injustice as the heart of his principles of justice. The articles in *The Cambridge Companion to Rawls*, edited by Samuel Freeman (Cambridge: Cambridge University Press, 2002), provide illuminating explorations of the central ideas in Rawls's political philosophy.

A Theory of Justice

3. THE MAIN IDEA OF THE THEORY OF JUSTICE

My aim is to present a conception of justice which generalizes and carries to a higher level of abstraction the familiar theory of the social contract as found, say, in Locke, Rousseau, and Kant.[1] In order to do this we are not to think of the original contract as one to enter a particular society or to set up a particular form of government. Rather, the guiding idea is that the principles of justice for the basic structure of society are the object of the original agreement. They are the principles that free and rational persons concerned to further their own interests would accept in an initial position of equality as defining the fundamental terms of their association. These principles are to regulate all further agreements; they specify the kinds of social cooperation that can be entered into and the forms of government that can be established. This way of regarding the principles of justice I shall call justice as fairness.

Thus we are to imagine that those who engage in social cooperation choose together, in one joint act, the principles which are to assign basic rights and duties and to determine the division of social benefits. Men are to decide in advance how they are to regulate their claims against one another and what is to be the foundation charter of their society. Just as each person must decide by rational reflection what constitutes his good, that is, the system

of ends which it is rational for him to pursue, so a group of persons must decide once and for all what is to count among them as just and unjust. The choice which rational men would make in this hypothetical situation of equal liberty, assuming for the present that this choice problem has a solution, determines the principles of justice.

In justice as fairness the original position of equality corresponds to the state of nature in the traditional theory of the social contract. This original position is not, of course, thought of as an actual historical state of affairs, much less as a primitive condition of culture. It is understood as a purely hypothetical situation characterized so as to lead to a certain conception of justice.[2] Among the essential features of this situation is that no one knows his place in society, his class position or social status, nor does any one know his fortune in the distribution of natural assets and abilities, his intelligence, strength, and the like. I shall even assume that the parties do not know their conceptions of the good or their special psychological propensities. The principles of justice are chosen behind a veil of ignorance. This ensures that no one is advantaged or disadvantaged in the choice of principles by the outcome of natural chance or the contingency of social circumstances. Since all are similarly situated and no one is able to design principles to favor his particular condition, the principles of justice are the result of a fair agreement or bargain. For given the circumstances of the original position, the symmetry

From *A Theory of Justice: Revised Edition*, by John Rawls, Cambridge, Mass.: Harvard University Press, © 1999 by The President and Fellows of Harvard College.

of everyone's relations to each other, this initial situation is fair between individuals as moral persons, that is, as rational beings with their own ends and capable, I shall assume, of a sense of justice. The original position is, one might say, the appropriate initial status quo, and thus the fundamental agreements reached in it are fair. This explains the propriety of the name "justice as fairness": it conveys the idea that the principles of justice are agreed to in an initial situation that is fair. The name does not mean that the concepts of justice and fairness are the same, any more than the phrase "poetry as metaphor" means that the concepts of poetry and metaphor are the same.

Justice as fairness begins, as I have said, with one of the most general of all choices which persons might make together, namely, with the choice of the first principles of a conception of justice which is to regulate all subsequent criticism and reform of institutions. Then, having chosen a conception of justice, we can suppose that they are to choose a constitution and a legislature to enact laws, and so on, all in accordance with the principles of justice initially agreed upon. Our social situation is just if it is such that by this sequence of hypothetical agreements we would have contracted into the general system of rules which defines it. Moreover, assuming that the original position does determine a set of principles (that is, that a particular conception of justice would be chosen), it will then be true that whenever social institutions satisfy these principles those engaged in them can say to one another that they are cooperating on terms to which they would agree if they were free and equal persons whose relations with respect to one another were fair. They could all view their arrangements as meeting the stipulations which they would acknowledge in an initial situation that embodies widely accepted and reasonable constraints on the choice of principles. The general recognition of this fact would provide the basis for a public acceptance of the corresponding principles of justice. No society can, of course, be a scheme of cooperation which men enter voluntarily in a literal sense; each person finds himself placed at birth in some particular position in some particular society, and the nature of this position materially affects his life prospects. Yet a society satisfying the principles of justice as fairness comes as close as a society can to being a voluntary scheme, for it meets the principles which free and equal persons would assent to under circumstances that are fair. In this sense its members are autonomous and the obligations they recognize self-imposed.

One feature of justice as fairness is to think of the parties in the initial situation as rational and mutually disinterested. This does not mean that the parties are egoists, that is, individuals with only certain kinds of interests, say in wealth, prestige, and domination. But they are conceived as not taking an interest in one another's interests. They are to presume that even their spiritual aims may be opposed, in the way that the aims of those of different religions may be opposed. Moreover, the concept of rationality must be interpreted as far as possible in the narrow sense, standard in economic theory, of taking the most effective means to given ends. I shall modify this concept to some extent, as explained later, but one must try to avoid introducing into it any controversial ethical elements. The initial situation must be characterized by stipulations that are widely accepted.

In working out the conception of justice as fairness one main task clearly is to determine which principles of justice would be chosen in the original position. To do this we must describe this situation in some detail and formulate with care the problem of choice which it presents. These matters I shall take up in the immediately succeeding chapters. It may be observed, however, that once the principles of justice are thought of as arising from an original agreement in a situation of equality, it is an open question whether the principle of utility would be acknowledged. Off-hand it hardly seems likely that persons who view themselves as equals, entitled to press their claims upon one another, would agree to a principle which may require lesser life prospects for some simply for the sake of a greater sum of advantages enjoyed by others. Since each desires to protect his interests, his capacity to advance his conception of the good, no one has a reason to acquiesce in an enduring loss for himself in order to bring about a greater net balance of satisfaction. In the absence of strong and lasting benevolent impulses, a rational man would not accept a basic structure merely because it maximized the algebraic sum of advantages irrespective of its permanent effects on his own basic rights and interests. Thus it seems that the principle of utility is incompatible with the conception of social cooperation among equals for mutual advantage. It appears to be inconsistent with the idea of reciprocity implicit in the notion of a well-ordered society. Or, at any rate, so I shall argue.

I shall maintain instead that the persons in the initial situation would choose two rather different principles: the first requires equality in the assignment of basic rights and duties, while the second holds that social and economic inequalities, for example inequalities of wealth and authority, are just only if they result in compensating benefits for everyone, and in particular for the least advantaged members of society. These principles rule out justifying institutions on the grounds that the hardships of some are offset by a greater good in the aggregate. It may be expedient but it is not just that some should have less in order that others may prosper. But there is no injustice in the greater benefits earned by a few provided that the situation of persons not so fortunate is thereby improved. The intuitive idea is that since everyone's well-being depends upon a scheme of cooperation without which no one could have a satisfactory life, the division of advantages should be such as to draw forth the willing cooperation of everyone taking part in it, including those less well situated. The two principles mentioned seem to be a fair basis on which those better endowed, or more fortunate in their social position, neither of which we can be said to deserve, could expect the willing cooperation of others when some workable scheme is a necessary condition of the welfare of all.[3] Once we decide to look for a conception of justice that prevents the use of the accidents of natural endowment and the contingencies of social circumstance as counters in a quest for political and economic advantage, we are led to these principles. They express the result of leaving aside those aspects of the social world that seem arbitrary from a moral point of view.

The problem of the choice of principles, however, is extremely difficult. I do not expect the answer I shall suggest to be convincing to everyone. It is, therefore, worth noting from the outset that justice as fairness, like other contract views, consists of two parts: (1) an interpretation of the initial situation and of the problem of choice posed there, and (2) a set of principles which, it is argued, would be agreed to. One may accept the first part of the theory (or some variant thereof), but not the other, and conversely. The concept of the initial contractual situation may seem reasonable although the particular principles proposed are rejected. To be sure, I want to maintain that the most appropriate conception of this situation does lead to principles of justice contrary to utilitarianism and perfectionism, and therefore that the contract doctrine provides an alternative to these views. Still, one may dispute this contention even though one grants that the contractarian method is a useful way of studying ethical theories and of setting forth their underlying assumptions.

Justice as fairness is an example of what I have called a contract theory. Now there may be an objection to the term "contract" and related expressions, but I think it will serve reasonably well. Many words have misleading connotations which at first are likely to confuse. The terms "utility" and "utilitarianism" are surely no exception. They too have unfortunate suggestions which hostile critics have been willing to exploit; yet they are clear enough for those prepared to study utilitarian doctrine. The same should be true of the term "contract" applied to moral theories. As I have mentioned, to understand it one has to keep in mind that it implies a certain level of abstraction. In particular, the content of the relevant agreement is not to enter a given society or to adopt a given form of government, but to accept certain moral principles. Moreover, the undertakings referred to are purely hypothetical: a contract view holds that certain principles would be accepted in a well-defined initial situation.

The merit of the contract terminology is that it conveys the idea that principles of justice may be conceived as principles that would be chosen by rational persons, and that in this way conceptions of justice may be explained and justified. The theory of justice is a part, perhaps the most significant part, of the theory of rational choice. Furthermore, principles of justice deal with conflicting claims upon the advantages won by social cooperation; they apply to the relations among several persons or groups. The word "contract" suggests this plurality as well as the condition that the appropriate division of advantages must be in accordance with principles acceptable to all parties. The condition of publicity for principles of justice is also connoted by the contract phraseology. Thus, if these principles are the outcome of an agreement, citizens have a knowledge of the principles that others follow. It is characteristic of contract theories to stress the public nature of political principles. Finally there is the long tradition of the contract doctrine. Expressing the tie with this line of thought helps to define ideas and accords with natural piety. There are then several advantages in the use of the term "contract." With due precautions taken, it should not be misleading. . . .

4. THE ORIGINAL POSITION AND JUSTIFICATION

I have said that the original position is the appropriate initial status quo which insures that the fundamental agreements reached in it are fair. This fact yields the name "justice as fairness." It is clear, then, that I want to say that one conception of justice is more reasonable than another, or justifiable with respect to it, if rational persons in the initial situation would choose its principles over those of the other for the role of justice. Conceptions of justice are to be ranked by their acceptability to persons so circumstanced. Understood in this way the question of justification is settled by working out a problem of deliberation: we have to ascertain which principles it would be

rational to adopt given the contractual situation. This connects the theory of justice with the theory of rational choice.

If this view of the problem of justification is to succeed, we must, of course, describe in some detail the nature of this choice problem. A problem of rational decision has a definite answer only if we know the beliefs and interests of the parties, their relations with respect to one another, the alternatives between which they are to choose, the procedure whereby they make up their minds, and so on. As the circumstances are presented in different ways, correspondingly different principles are accepted. The concept of the original position, as I shall refer to it, is that of the most philosophically favored interpretation of this initial choice situation for the purposes of a theory of justice.

But how are we to decide what is the most favored interpretation? I assume, for one thing, that there is a broad measure of agreement that principles of justice should be chosen under certain conditions. To justify a particular description of the initial situation one shows that it incorporates these commonly shared presumptions. One argues from widely accepted but weak premises to more specific conclusions. Each of the presumptions should be itself be natural and plausible; some of them may seem innocuous or even trivial. The aim of the contract approach is to establish that taken together they impose significant bounds on acceptable principles of justice. The ideal outcome would be that these conditions determine a unique set of principles; but I shall be satisfied if they suffice to rank the main traditional conceptions of social justice.

One should not be misled, then, by the somewhat unusual conditions which characterize the original position. The idea here is simply to make vivid to ourselves the restrictions that it seems reasonable to impose on arguments for principles of justice, and therefore on these principles themselves. Thus it seems reasonable and generally acceptable that no one should be advantaged or disadvantaged by natural fortune or social circumstances in the choice of principles. It also seems widely agreed that it should be impossible to tailor principles to the circumstances of one's own case. We should insure further that particular inclinations and aspirations, and persons' conceptions of their good do not affect the principles adopted. The aim is to rule out those principles that it would be rational to propose for acceptance, however little the chance of success, only if one knew certain things that are irrelevant from the standpoint of justice. For example, if a man knew that he was wealthy, he might find it rational to advance the principle that various taxes for welfare measures be counted unjust; if he knew that he was poor, he would most likely propose the contrary principle. To represent the desired restrictions one imagines a situation in which everyone is deprived of this sort of information. One excludes the knowledge of those contingencies which sets men at odds and allows them to be guided by their prejudices. In this manner the veil of ignorance is arrived at in a natural way. This concept should cause no difficulty if we keep in mind the constraints on arguments that it is meant to express. At any time we can enter the original position, so to speak, simply by following a certain procedure, namely, by arguing for principles of justice in accordance with these restrictions.

It seems reasonable to suppose that the parties in the original position are equal. That is, all have the same rights in the procedure for choosing principles; each can make proposals, submit reasons for their acceptance, and so on. Obviously the purpose of these conditions is to represent equality between human beings as moral persons, as creatures having a conception of their good and capable of a sense of justice. The basis of equality is taken to be similarity in these two respects. Systems of ends are not ranked in value; and each man is presumed to have the requisite ability to understand and to act upon whatever principles are adopted. Together with the veil of ignorance, these conditions define the principles of justice as those which rational persons concerned to advance their interests would consent to as equals when none are known to be advantaged or disadvantaged by social and natural contingencies.

There is, however, another side to justifying a particular description of the original position. This is to see if the principles which would be chosen match our considered convictions of justice or extend them in an acceptable way. We can note whether applying these principles would lead us to make the same judgments about the basic structure of society which we now make intuitively and in which we have the greatest confidence; or whether, in cases where our present judgments are in doubt and given with hesitation, these principles offer a resolution which we can affirm on reflection. There are questions which we feel sure must be answered in a certain way. For example, we are confident that religious intolerance and racial discrimination are unjust. We think that we have examined these things with care and have reached what we believe is an impartial judgment not likely to be distorted by an excessive attention to our own interests. These convictions are provisional fixed points which we presume any conception of justice must fit. But we have much less assurance as to what is the correct distribution of wealth and authority. Here we may be looking for a way to remove our doubts. We can check an interpretation of the initial situation, then, by the capacity of its principles to accommodate our firmest convictions and to provide guidance where guidance is needed.

In searching for the most favored description of this situation we work from both ends. We begin by describing it so that it represents generally shared and preferably weak conditions. We then see if these conditions are strong enough to yield a significant set of principles. If not, we look for further premises equally reasonable. But if so, and these principles match our considered convictions of justice, then so far well and good. But presumably there will be discrepancies. In this case we have a choice. We can either modify the account of the initial situation or we can revise our existing judgments, for even the judgments we take provisionally as fixed points are liable to revision.

By going back and forth, sometimes altering the conditions of the contractual circumstances, at others withdrawing our judgments and conforming them to principle, I assume that eventually we shall find a description of the initial situation that both expresses reasonable conditions and yields principles which match our considered judgments duly pruned and adjusted. This state of affairs I refer to as reflective equilibrium.[4] It is an equilibrium because at last our principles and judgments coincide; and it is reflective since we know to what principles our judgments conform and the premises of their derivation. At the moment everything is in order. But this equilibrium is not necessarily stable. It is liable to be upset by further examination of the conditions which should be imposed on the contractual situation and by particular cases which may lead us to revise our judgments. Yet for the time being we have done what we can to render coherent and to justify our convictions of social justice. We have reached a conception of the original position.

I shall not, of course, actually work through this process. Still, we may think of the interpretation of the original position that I shall present as the result of such a hypothetical course of reflection. It represents the attempt to accommodate within one scheme both reasonable philosophical conditions on principles as well as our considered judgments of justice. In arriving at the favored interpretation of the initial situation there is no point at which an appeal is made to self-evidence in the traditional sense either of general conceptions or particular convictions. I do not claim for the principles of justice proposed that they are necessary truths or derivable from such truths. A conception of justice cannot be deduced from self-evident premises or conditions on principles; instead, its justification is a matter of the mutual support of many considerations, of everything fitting together into one coherent view.

A final comment. We shall want to say that certain principles of justice are justified because they would be agreed to in an initial situation of equality. I have emphasized that this original position is purely hypothetical. It is natural to ask why, if this agreement is never actually entered into, we should take any interest in these principles, moral or otherwise. The answer is that the conditions embodied in the description of the original position are ones that we do in fact accept. Or if we do not, then perhaps we can be persuaded to do so by philosophical reflection. Each aspect of the contractual situation can be given supporting grounds. Thus what we shall do is to collect together into one conception a number of conditions on principles that we are ready upon due consideration to recognize as reasonable. These constraints express what we are prepared to regard as limits on fair terms of social cooperation. One way to look at the idea of the original position, therefore, is to see it as an expository device which sums up the meaning of these conditions and helps us to extract their consequences. On the other hand, this conception is also an intuitive notion that suggests its own elaboration, so that led on by it we are drawn to define more clearly the standpoint from which we can best interpret moral relationships. We need a conception that enables us to envision our objective from afar: the intuitive notion of the original position is to do this for us.[5]

11. TWO PRINCIPLES OF JUSTICE

I shall now state in a provisional form the two principles of justice that I believe would be agreed to in the original position. The first formulation of these principles is tentative. As we go on I shall consider several formulations and approximate step by step the final statement to be given much later. I believe that doing this allows the exposition to proceed in a natural way.

The first statement of the two principles reads as follows.

First: each person is to have an equal right to the most extensive scheme of equal basic liberties compatible with a similar scheme of liberties for others.

Second: social and economic inequalities are to be arranged so that they are both (a) reasonably expected to be to everyone's advantage, and (b) attached to positions and offices open to all. . . .

These principles primarily apply, as I have said, to the basic structure of society and govern the assignment of rights and duties and regulate the distribution of social and economic advantages. Their formulation presupposes that, for the purposes of a theory of justice, the social structure may be viewed as having two more or less distinct parts, the first principle applying to the one, the second principle to the other. Thus we distinguish between the aspects of the social system that define and secure the equal basic liberties and the aspects that specify and establish social and economic inequalities. Now it is essential to observe that the basic liberties are given by a list of such liberties. Important among these are political liberty (the right to vote and to hold public office) and freedom of speech and assembly; liberty of conscience and freedom of thought; freedom of the person, which includes freedom from psychological oppression and physical assault and dismemberment (integrity of the person); the right to hold personal property and freedom from arbitrary arrest and seizure as defined by the concept of the rule of law. These liberties are to be equal by the first principle.

The second principle applies, in the first approximation, to the distribution of income and wealth and to the design of organizations that make use of differences in authority and responsibility. While the distribution of wealth and income need not be equal, it must be to everyone's advantage, and at the same time, positions of authority and responsibility must be accessible to all. One applies the second principle by holding positions open, and then, subject to this constraint, arranges social and economic inequalities so that everyone benefits.

These principles are to be arranged in a serial order with the first principle prior to the second. This ordering means that infringements of the basic equal liberties protected by the first principle cannot be justified, or compensated for, by greater social and economic advantages. These

liberties have a central range of application within which they can be limited and compromised only when they conflict with other basic liberties. Since they may be limited when they clash with one another, none of these liberties is absolute; but however they are adjusted to form one system, this system is to be the same for all. It is difficult, and perhaps impossible, to give a complete specification of these liberties independently from the particular circumstances—social, economic, and technological—of a given society. The hypothesis is that the general form of such a list could be devised with sufficient exactness to sustain this conception of justice. Of course, liberties not on the list, for example, the right to own certain kinds of property (e.g., means of production) and freedom of contract as understood by the doctrine of laissez-faire are not basic; and so they are not protected by the priority of the first principle. Finally, in regard to the second principle, the distribution of wealth and income, and positions of authority and responsibility, are to be consistent with both the basic liberties and equality of opportunity.

The two principles are rather specific in their content, and their acceptance rests on certain assumptions that I must eventually try to explain and justify. For the present, it should be observed that these principles are a special case of a more general conception of justice that can be expressed as follows.

> All social values—liberty and opportunity, income and wealth, and the social bases of self-respect—are to be distributed equally unless an unequal distribution of any, or all, of these values is to everyone's advantage.

Injustice, then, is simply inequalities that are not to the benefit of all. Of course, this conception is extremely vague and requires interpretation.

As a first step, suppose that the basic structure of society distributes certain primary goods, that is, things that every rational man is presumed to want. These goods normally have a use whatever a person's rational plan of life. For simplicity, assume that the chief primary goods at the disposition of society are rights, liberties, and opportunities, and income and wealth. (Later on in Part Three the primary good of self-respect has a central place.) These are the social primary goods. Other primary goods such as health and vigor, intelligence and imagination, are natural goods; although their possession is influenced by the basic structure, they are not so directly under its control. Imagine, then, a hypothetical initial arrangement in which all the social primary goods are equally distributed: everyone has similar rights and duties, and income and wealth are evenly shared. This state of affairs provides a benchmark for judging improvements. If certain inequalities of wealth and differences in authority would make everyone better off than in this hypothetical starting situation, then they accord with the general conception.

Now it is possible, at least theoretically, that by giving up some of their fundamental liberties men are sufficiently compensated by the resulting social and economic gains. The general conception of justice imposes no restrictions on what sort of inequalities are permissible; it only requires that everyone's position be improved. We need not suppose anything so drastic as consenting to a condition of slavery. Imagine instead that people seem willing to forego certain political rights when the economic returns are significant. It is this kind of exchange which the two principles rule out; being arranged in serial order they do not permit exchanges between basic liberties and economic and social gains except under extenuating circumstances. . . .

The fact that the two principles apply to institutions has certain consequences. First of all, the rights and basic liberties referred to by these principles are those which are defined by the public rules of the basic structure. Whether men are free is determined by the rights and duties established by the major institutions of society. Liberty is a certain pattern of social forms. The first principle simply requires that certain sorts of rules, those defining basic liberties, apply to everyone equally and that they allow the most extensive liberty compatible with a like liberty for all. The only reason for circumscribing basic liberties and making them less extensive is that otherwise they would interfere with one another.

Further, when principles mention persons, or require that everyone gain from an inequality, the reference is to representative persons holding the various social positions, or offices established by the basic structure. Thus in applying the second principle I assume that it is possible to assign an expectation of well-being to representative individuals holding these positions. This expectation indicates their life prospects as viewed from their social station. In general, the expectations of representative persons depend upon the distribution of rights and duties throughout the basic structure. Expectations are connected: by raising the prospects of the representative man in one position we presumably increase or decrease the prospects of representative men in other positions. Since it applies to institutional forms, the second principle (or rather the first part of it) refers to the expectations of representative individuals. As I shall discuss below, neither principle applies to distributions of particular goods to particular individuals who may be identified by their proper names. The situation where someone is considering how to allocate certain commodities to needy persons who are known to him is not within the scope of the principles. They are meant to regulate basic institutional arrangements. We must not assume that there is much similarity from the standpoint of justice between an administrative allotment of goods to specific persons and the appropriate design of society. Our common sense intuitions for the former may be a poor guide to the latter.

Now the second principle insists that each person benefit from permissible inequalities in the basic structure. This means that it must be reasonable for each relevant representative man defined by this structure, when he views it as a going concern, to prefer his prospects with the inequality to his prospects without it. One is not allowed to justify differences in income or in positions of authority and responsibility on the ground that the disadvantages of those in one position are outweighed by the greater advantages of those in another. Much less can infringements of liberty be counterbalanced in this way. It is obvious, however, that there are indefinitely many ways in which all may be advantaged when the initial arrangement of equality is taken as a benchmark. How then are we to choose among these possibilities? The principles must be specified so that they yield a determinate conclusion. . . .

13. DEMOCRATIC EQUALITY AND THE DIFFERENCE PRINCIPLE

The democratic interpretation . . . is arrived at by combining the principle of fair equality of opportunity with the difference principle. . . . Assuming the framework of institutions required by equal liberty and fair equality of opportunity, the higher expectations of those better situated are just if and only if they work as part of a scheme which improves the expectations of the least advantaged members of society. The intuitive idea is that the social order is not to establish and secure the more attractive prospects of those better off unless doing so is to the advantage of those less fortunate. . . .

To illustrate the difference principle, consider the distribution of income among social classes. Let us suppose that the various income groups correlate with representative individuals by reference to whose expectations we can judge the distribution. Now those starting out as members of the entrepreneurial class in property-owning democracy, say, have a better prospect than those who begin in the class of unskilled laborers. It seems likely that this will be true even when the social injustices which now exist are removed. What, then, can possibly justify this kind of initial inequality in life prospects? According to the difference principle, it is justifiable only if the difference in expectation is to the advantage of the representative man who is worse off, in this case the representative unskilled worker. The inequality in expectation is permissible only if lowering it would make the working class even more worse off. Supposedly, given the rider in the second principle concerning open positions, and the principle of liberty generally, the greater expectations allowed to entrepreneurs encourages them to do things which raise the prospects of the laboring class. Their better prospects act as incentives so that the economic process is more efficient, innovation proceeds at a faster pace, and so on. I shall not consider how far these things are true. The point is that something of this kind must be argued if these inequalities are to satisfy by the difference principle. . . .

17. THE TENDENCY TO EQUALITY

I wish to conclude this discussion of the two principles by explaining the sense in which they express an egalitarian conception of justice. Also I should like to forestall the objection to the principle of fair opportunity that it leads to a meritocratic society. In order to prepare the way for doing this, I note several aspects of the conception of justice that I have set out.

First we may observe that the difference principle gives some weight to the considerations singled out by the principle of redress. This is the principle that undeserved inequalities call for redress; and since inequalities of birth and natural endowment are undeserved, these inequalities are to be somehow compensated for.[6] Thus the principle holds that in order to treat all persons equally, to provide genuine equality of opportunity, society must give more attention to those with fewer native assets and to those born into the less favorable social positions. The idea is to redress the bias of contingencies in the direction of equality. In pursuit of this principle greater resources might be spent on the education of the less rather than the more intelligent, at least over a certain time of life, say the earlier years of school.

Now the principle of redress has not to my knowledge been proposed as the sole criterion of justice, as the single aim of the social order. It is plausible as most such principles are only as a prima facie principle, one that is to be weighed in the balance with others. For example, we are to weigh it against the principle to improve the average standard of life, or to advance the common good.[7] But whatever other principles we hold, the claims of redress are to be taken into account. It is thought to represent one of the elements in our conception of justice. Now the difference principle is not of course the principle of redress. It does not require society to try to even out handicaps as if all were expected to compete on a fair basis in the same race. But the difference principle would allocate resources in education, say, so as to improve the long-term expectation of the least favored. If this end is attained by giving more attention to the better endowed, it is permissible; otherwise not. And in making this decision, the value of education should not be assessed solely in terms of economic efficiency and social welfare. Equally if not more important is the role of education in enabling a person to enjoy the culture of his society and to take part in its affairs, and in this way to provide for each individual a secure sense of his own worth.

Thus although the difference principle is not the same as that of redress, it does achieve some of the intent of the latter principle. It transforms the aims of the basic structure so that the total scheme of institutions no longer emphasizes social efficiency and technocratic values. The difference principle represents, in effect, an agreement to regard the distribution of natural talents as in some respects a common asset and to share in the greater social and economic benefits made possible by the complementarities of this distribution. Those who have been favored by nature, whoever they are, may gain from their good fortune only on terms that improve the situation of those who have lost out. The naturally advantaged are not to gain merely because they are more gifted, but only to cover the costs of training and education and for using their endowments in ways that help the less fortunate as well. No one deserves his greater natural capacity nor merits a more favorable starting place in society. But, of course, this is no reason to ignore, much less to eliminate these distinctions. Instead, the basic structure can be arranged so that these contingencies work for the good of the least fortunate. Thus we are led to the difference principle if we wish to set up the social system so that no one gains or loses from his arbitrary place in the distribution of natural assets or his initial position in society without giving or receiving compensating advantages in return.

In view of these remarks we may reject the contention that the ordering of institutions is always defective because the distribution of natural talents and the contingencies of social circumstance are unjust, and this injustice must inevitably carry over to human arrangements. Occasionally this reflection is offered as an excuse for ignoring injustice, as if the refusal to acquiesce in injustice is on a par with being unable to accept death. The natural distribution is neither just nor unjust; nor is it unjust that persons are born into society at some particular position. These are simply natural facts. What is just and unjust is the way that institutions deal with these facts. Aristocratic and caste societies are unjust because they make these contingencies the ascriptive basis for belonging to more or less enclosed and privileged social classes. The basic structure of these societies incorporates the arbitrariness found in nature. But there is no necessity for men to resign themselves to these contingencies. The social system is not an unchangeable order beyond human control but a pattern of human action. In justice as fairness men agree to avail themselves of the accidents of nature and social circumstance only when doing so is for the common benefit. The two principles are a fair way of meeting the arbitrariness of fortune; and while no doubt imperfect in other ways, the institutions which satisfy these principles are just.

A further point is that the difference principle expresses a conception of reciprocity. It is a principle of mutual benefit. At first sight, however, it may appear unfairly biased towards the least favored. To consider this question in an intuitive way, suppose for simplicity that there are only two groups in society, one noticeably more fortunate than the other. Subject to the usual constraints (defined by the priority of the first principle and fair equality of opportunity), society could maximize the expectations of either group but not both, since we can maximize with respect to only one aim at a time. It seems clear that society should not do the best it can for those initially more advantaged; so if we reject the difference principle, we must prefer maximizing some weighted mean of the two expectations. But if we give any weight to the more fortunate, we are valuing for their own sake the gains to those already more favored by natural and social contingencies. No one had an antecedent claim to be benefited in this way, and so to maximize a weighted mean is, so to speak, to favor the more fortunate twice over. Thus the more advantaged, when they view the matter from a general perspective, recognize that the well-being of each depends on a scheme of social cooperation without which no one could have a satisfactory life; they recognize also that they can expect the willing cooperation of all only if the terms of the scheme are reasonable. So they regard themselves as already compensated, as it were, by the advantages to which no one (including themselves) had a prior claim. They forego the idea of maximizing a weighted mean and regard the difference principle as a fair basis for regulating the basic structure.

One may object that those better situated deserve the greater advantages they could acquire for themselves under other schemes of cooperation whether or not these advantages are gained in ways that benefit others. Now it is true that given a just system of cooperation as a framework of public rules, and the expectations set up by it, those who, with the prospect of improving their condition, have done what the system announces it will reward are entitled to have their expectations met. In this sense the more fortunate have title to their better situation; their claims are legitimate expectations established by social institutions and the community is obligated to fulfill them. But this sense of desert is that of entitlement. It presupposes the existence of an ongoing cooperative scheme and is irrelevant to the question whether this scheme itself is to be designed in accordance with the difference principle or some other criterion.

Thus it is incorrect that individuals with greater natural endowments and the superior character that has made their development possible have a right to a cooperative scheme that enables them to obtain even further benefits in ways that do not contribute to the advantages of others. We do not deserve our place in the distribution of native endowments, any more than we deserve our initial starting place in society. That we deserve the superior character that enables us to make the effort to cultivate our abilities is also problematic; for such character depends in good part upon fortunate family and social circumstances in early life for which we can claim no credit. The notion of desert does not apply here. To be sure, the more advantaged have a right to their natural assets, as does everyone else; this right is covered by the first principle under the basic liberty protecting the integrity of the person. And so the more advantaged are entitled to whatever they can acquire in accordance with the rules of a fair system of social cooperation. Our problem is how this scheme, the basic structure of society, is to be designed. From a suitably general standpoint, the difference principle appears acceptable to both the more advantaged and the less advantaged individual. Of course, none of this is strictly speaking an argument for the principle, since in a contract theory arguments are made from the point of view of the original position. But these intuitive considerations help to clarify the principle and the sense in which it is egalitarian. . . .

24. THE VEIL OF IGNORANCE

The idea of the original position is to set up a fair procedure so that any principles agreed to will be just. The aim is to use the notion of pure procedural justice as a basis of theory. Somehow we must nullify the effects of specific contingencies which put men at odds and tempt them to exploit social and natural circumstances to their own advantage. Now in order to do this I assume that the parties are situated behind a veil of ignorance. They do not know how the various alternatives will affect their own particular case and they are obliged to evaluate principles solely on the basis of general considerations.[8]

It is assumed, then, that the parties do not know certain kinds of particular facts. First of all, no one knows his place in society, his class position or social status; nor does he know his fortune in the distribution of natural assets and abilities, his intelligence and strength, and the like. Nor, again, does anyone know his conception of the good, the particulars of his rational plan of life, or even the special features of his psychology such as his aversion to risk or liability to optimism or pessimism. More than this, I assume that the parties do not know the particular circumstances of their own society. That is, they do not know its economic or political situation, or the level of civilization and culture it has been able to achieve. The persons in the original position have no information as to which generation they belong. These broader restrictions on knowledge are appropriate in part because questions of social justice arise between generations as well as within them, for example, the question of the appropriate rate of capital saving and of the conservation of natural resources and the environment of nature. There is also, theoretically anyway, the question of a reasonable genetic policy. In these cases too, in order to carry through the idea of the original position, the parties must not know the contingencies that set them in opposition. They must choose principles the consequences of which they are prepared to live with whatever generation they turn out to belong to.

As far as possible, then, the only particular facts which the parties know is that their society is subject to the circumstances of justice and whatever this implies. It is taken for granted, however, that they know the general facts about human society. They understand political affairs and the principles of economic theory; they know the basis of social organization and the laws of human psychology. Indeed, the parties are presumed to know whatever general facts affect the choice of the principles of justice. There are no limitations on general information, that is, on general laws and theories, since conceptions of justice must be adjusted to the characteristics of the systems of social cooperation which they are to regulate, and there is no reason to rule out these facts. It is, for example, a consideration against a conception of justice that, in view of the laws of moral psychology, men would not acquire a desire to act upon it even when the institutions of their society satisfied it. For in this case there would be difficulty in securing the stability of social cooperation. An important feature of a conception of justice is that it should generate its own support. Its principles should be such that when they are embodied in the basic structure of society men tend to acquire the corresponding sense of justice and develop a desire to act in accordance with its principles. In this case a conception of justice is stable. This kind of general information is admissible in the original position.

The notion of the veil of ignorance raises several difficulties. Some may object that the exclusion of nearly all particular information makes it difficult to grasp what is meant by the original position. Thus it may be helpful to observe that one or more persons can at any time enter this position, or perhaps better, simulate the deliberations of this hypothetical situation, simply by reasoning in accordance with the appropriate restrictions. In arguing for a conception of justice we must be sure that it is among the permitted alternatives and satisfies the stipulated formal constraints. No considerations can be advanced in its favor unless they would be rational ones for us to urge were we to lack the kind of knowledge that is excluded. The evaluation of principles must proceed in terms of the general consequences of their public recognition and universal application, it being assumed that they will be complied with by everyone. To say that a certain conception of justice would be chosen in the original position is equivalent to saying that rational deliberation satisfying certain conditions and restrictions would reach a certain conclusion. If necessary, the argument to this result could be set out more formally. I shall, however, speak throughout in terms of the notion of the original position. It is more economical and suggestive, and brings out certain essential features that otherwise one might easily overlook.

These remarks show that the original position is not to be thought of as a general assembly which includes at one moment everyone who will live at some time or, much less, as an assembly of everyone who could live at some time. It is not a gathering of all actual or possible persons. If we conceived of the original position in either of these ways, the conception would cease to be a natural guide to intuition and would lack a clear sense. In any case, the original position must be interpreted so that one can at any time adopt its perspective. It must make no difference when one takes up this viewpoint, or who does so: the restrictions must be such that the same principles are always chosen. The veil of ignorance is a key condition in meeting this requirement. It insures not only that the information available is relevant, but that it is at all times the same.

It may be protested that the condition of the veil of ignorance is irrational. Surely, some may object, principles should be chosen in the light of all the knowledge available. There are various replies to this contention. Here I shall sketch those which emphasize the simplifications that need to be made if one is to have any theory at all. . . . To begin with, it is clear that since the differences among the parties are unknown to them, and everyone is equally rational and similarly situated, each is convinced by the same arguments.

Therefore, we can view the agreement in the original position from the standpoint of one person selected at random. If anyone after due reflection prefers a conception of justice to another, then they all do, and a unanimous agreement can be reached. We can, to make the circumstances more vivid, imagine that the parties are required to communicate with each other through a referee as intermediary, and that he is to announce which alternatives have been suggested and the reasons offered in their support. He forbids the attempt to form coalitions, and he informs the parties when they have come to an understanding. But such a referee is actually superfluous, assuming that the deliberations of the parties must be similar.

Thus there follows the very important consequence that the parties have no basis for bargaining in the usual sense. No one knows his situation in society nor his natural assets, and therefore no one is in a position to tailor principles to his advantage. We might imagine that one of the contractees threatens to hold out unless the others agree to principles favorable to him. But how does he know which principles are especially in his interests? The same holds for the formation of coalitions: if a group were to decide to band together to the disadvantage of the others, they would not know how to favor themselves in the choice of principles. Even if they could get everyone to agree to their proposal, they would have no assurance that it was to their advantage, since they cannot identify themselves either by name or description. The one case where this conclusion fails is that of saving. Since the persons in the original position know that they are contemporaries (taking the present time of entry interpretation), they can favor their generation by refusing to make any sacrifices at all for their successors; they simply acknowledge the principle that no one has a duty to save for posterity. Previous generations have saved or they have not; there is nothing the parties can now do to affect that. So in this instance the veil of ignorance fails to secure the desired result. Therefore, to handle the question of justice between generations, I modify the motivation assumption and add a further constraint. . . . With these adjustments, no generation is able to formulate principles especially designed to advance its own cause and some significant limits on savings principles can be derived. . . . Whatever a person's temporal position, each is forced to choose for all.[9]

The restrictions on particular information in the original position are, then, of fundamental importance. Without them we would not be able to work out any definite theory of justice at all. We would have to be content with a vague formula stating that justice is what would be agreed to without being able to say much, if anything, about the substance of the agreement itself. The formal constraints of the concept of right, those applying to principles directly; are not sufficient for our purpose. The veil of ignorance makes possible a unanimous choice of a particular conception of justice. Without these limitations on knowledge the bargaining problem of the original position would be hopelessly complicated. Even if theoretically a solution were to exist, we would not, at present anyway, be able to determine it. . . .

26. THE REASONING LEADING TO THE TWO PRINCIPLES OF JUSTICE

. . . It seems from these remarks that the two principles are at least a plausible conception of justice. The question, though, is how one is to argue for them more systematically. Now there are several things to do. One can work out their consequences for institutions and note their implications for fundamental social policy. In this way they are tested by a comparison with our considered judgments of justice. . . .

But one can also try to find arguments in their favor that are decisive from the standpoint of the original position. In order to see how this might be done, it is useful as a heuristic device to think of the two principles as the maximin solution to the problem of social justice. There is a relation between the two principles and the maximin rule

for choice under uncertainty.[10] This is evident from the fact that the two principles are those a person would choose for the design of a society in which his enemy is to assign him his place. The maximin rule tells us to rank alternatives by their worst possible outcomes: we are to adopt the alternative the worst outcome of which is superior to the worst outcomes of the others.[11] The persons in the original position do not, of course, assume that their initial place in society is decided by a malevolent opponent. As I note below, they should not reason from false premises. The veil of ignorance does not violate this idea, since an absence of information is not misinformation. But that the two principles of justice would be chosen if the parties were forced to protect themselves against such a contingency explains the sense in which this conception is the maximin solution. And this analogy suggests that if the original position has been described so that it is rational for the parties to adopt the conservative attitude expressed by this rule, a conclusive argument can indeed be constructed for these principles. Clearly the maximin rule is not, in general, a suitable guide for choices under uncertainty. But it holds only in situations marked by certain special features. My aim, then, is to show that a good case can be made for the two principles based on the fact that the original position has these features to a very high degree.

Now there appear to be three chief features of situations that give plausibility to this unusual rule.[12] First, since the rule takes no account of the likelihoods of the possible circumstances, there must be some reason for sharply discounting estimates of these probabilities. Offhand, the most natural rule of choice would seem to be to compute the expectation of monetary gain for each decision and then to adopt the course of action with the highest prospect. . . . Thus it must be, for example, that the situation is one in which a knowledge of likelihoods is impossible, or at best extremely insecure. In this case it is unreasonable not to be skeptical of probabilistic calculations unless there is no other way out, particularly if the decision is a fundamental one that needs to be justified to others.

The second feature that suggests the maximin rule is the following: the person choosing has a conception of the good such that he cares very little, if anything, for what he might gain above the minimum stipend that he can, in fact, be sure of by following the maximin rule. It is not worthwhile for him to take a chance for the sake of a further advantage, especially when it may turn out that he loses much that is important to him. This last provision brings in the third feature, namely, that the rejected alternatives have outcomes that one can hardly accept. The situation involves grave risks. Of course these features work most effectively in combination. The paradigm situation for following the maximin rule is when all three features are realized to the highest degree.

Let us review briefly the nature of the original position with these three special features in mind. To begin with, the veil of ignorance excludes all knowledge of likelihoods. The parties have no basis for determining the probable nature of their society, or their place in it. Thus they have no basis for probability calculations. They must also take into account the fact that their choice of principles should seem reasonable to others, in particular their descendants, whose rights will be deeply affected by it. These considerations are strengthened by the fact that the parties know very little about the possible states of society. Not only are they unable to conjecture the likelihoods of the various possible circumstances, they cannot say much about what the possible circumstances are, much less enumerate them and foresee the outcome of each alternative available. Those deciding are much more in the dark than illustrations by numerical tables suggest. It is for this reason that I have spoken only of a relation to the maximin rule.

Several kinds of arguments for the two principles of justice illustrate the second feature. Thus, if we can maintain that these principles provide a workable theory of social justice, and that they are compatible with reasonable demands of efficiency, then this conception guarantees a satisfactory minimum. There may be, on reflection, little reason for trying to do better. Thus much of the argument . . . is to show, by their application to some main questions of social justice, that the two principles are a satisfactory conception. These details have a philosophical purpose. Moreover, this line of thought is practically decisive if we can establish the priority of liberty. For this priority implies that the persons in the original position have no desire to try for greater gains at the expense of the basic equal liberties. The minimum assured by the two principles in lexical order is not one that the parties wish to jeopardize for the sake of greater economic and social advantages.

Finally, the third feature holds if we can assume that other conceptions of justice may lead to institutions that the parties would find intolerable. For example, it has sometimes been held that under some conditions the utility principle (in either form) justifies, if not slavery or serfdom, at any rate serious infractions of liberty for the sake of greater social benefits. We need not consider here the truth of this claim. For the moment, this contention is only to illustrate the way in which conceptions of justice may allow for outcomes which the parties may not be able to accept. And having the ready alternative of the two principles of justice which secure a satisfactory minimum, it seems unwise, if not irrational, for them to take a chance that these conditions are not realized. . . .

Notes

1. As the text suggests, I shall regard Locke's *Second Treatise of Government*, Rousseau's *The Social Contract*, and Kant's ethical works beginning with *The Foundations of the Metaphysics of Morals* as definitive of the contract tradition. For all of its greatness, Hobbes's *Leviathan* raises special problems. A general historical survey is provided by J. W. Gough, *The Social Contract*, 2nd ed. (Oxford, The Clarendon Press, 1957), and Otto Gierke, *Natural Law and the Theory of Society*, trans. with an introduction by Ernest Barker (Cambridge, The University Press, 1934). A presentation of

the contract view as primarily an ethical theory is to be found in G. R. Grice, *The Grounds of Moral Judgment* (Cambridge, The University Press, 1967). . . .

2. Kant is clear that the original agreement is hypothetical. See *The Metaphysics of Morals*, pt. I (*Recht-slehre*), especially §§47, 52; and pt. II of the essay "Concerning the Common Saying: This May Be True in Theory but It Does Not Apply in Practice," in *Kant's Political Writings*, ed. Hans Reiss and trans. by H. B. Nisbet (Cambridge, The University Press, 1970), pp. 73–87. See Georges Vlachos, *La Pensée politique de Kant* (Paris, Presses Universitaires de France, 1962), pp. 326–335; and J. G. Murphy, *Kant: The Philosophy of Right* (London, Macmillan, 1970), pp. 109–112, 133–136, for a further discussion.

3. For the formulation of this intuitive idea I am indebted to Allan Gibbard.

4. The process of mutual adjustment of principles and considered judgments is not peculiar to moral philosophy. See Nelson Goodman, *Fact, Fiction, and Forecast* (Cambridge, Mass., Harvard University Press, 1955), pp. 65–68, for parallel remarks concerning the justification of the principles of deductive and inductive inference.

5. Henri Poincaré remarks: "Il nous faut une faculté qui nous fasse voir le but de loin, et, cette faculté, c'est l'intuition." *La Valeur de la science* (Paris, Flammarion, 1909), p. 27.

6. See Herbert Spiegelberg, "A Defense of Human Equality," *Philosophical Review*, vol. 53 (1944), pp. 101, 113–123; and D. D. Raphael, "Justice and Liberty," *Proceedings of the Aristotelian Society*, vol. 51 (1950–1951), pp. 187f.

7. See, for example, Spiegelberg, pp. 120f.

8. The veil of ignorance is so natural a condition that something like it must have occurred to many. The formulation in the text is implicit, I believe, in Kant's doctrine of the categorical imperative, both in the way this procedural criterion is defined and the use Kant makes of it. Thus when Kant tells us to test our maxim by considering what would be the case were it a universal law of nature, he must suppose that we do not know our place within this imagined system of nature. See, for example, his discussion of the topic of practical judgment in *The Critique of Practical Reason*, Academy Edition, vol. 5, pp. 68–72. A similar restriction on information is found in J. C. Harsanyi, "Cardinal Utility in Welfare Economics and in the Theory of Risk-taking," *Journal of Political Economy*, vol. 61 (1953).

However, other aspects of Harsanyi's view are quite different, and he uses the restriction to develop a utilitarian theory. . . .

9. Rousseau, *The Social Contract*, bk. II, ch. IV, par. 5.

10. An accessible discussion of this and other rules of choice under uncertainty can be found in W. J. Baumol, *Economic Theory and Operations Analysis*. 2nd ed. (Englewood Cliffs, N.J., Prentice-Hall Inc., 1965), ch. 24. Baumol gives a geometric interpretation of these rules . . . to illustrate the difference principle. See pp. 558–562. See also R. D. Luce and Howard Raiffa, *Games and Decisions* (New York, John Wiley and Sons, Inc., 1957), ch. XIII, for a fuller account.

11. Consider the gain-and-loss table below. It represents the gains and losses for a situation which is not a game of strategy. There is no one playing against the person making the decision; instead he is faced with several possible circumstances which may or may not obtain. Which circumstances happen to exist does not depend upon what the person choosing decides or whether he announces his moves in advance. The numbers in the table are monetary values (in hundreds of dollars) in comparison with some initial situation. The gain (g) depends upon the individual's decision (d) and the circumstances (c). Thus $g = f(d, c)$. Assuming that there are three possible decisions and three possible circumstances, we might have this gain-and-loss table.

Decisions	Circumstances		
	$c1$	$c2$	$c3$
d_1	−7	8	12
d_2	−8	7	14
d_3	5	6	8

The maximin rule requires that we make the third decision. For in this case the worst that can happen is that one gains five hundred dollars, which is better than the worst for the other actions. If we adopt one of these we may lose either eight or seven hundred dollars. Thus, the choice of d_3 maximizes $f(d, c)$ for that value of c, which for a given d, minimizes f. The term "maximin" means the *maximum minimorum*; and the rule directs our attention to the worst that can happen under any proposed course of action, and to decide in the light of that.

12. Here I borrow from William Fellner, *Probability and Profit* (Homewood, Ill., R. D. Irwin, Inc., 1965), pp. 140–142, where these features are noted.

Political Liberalism

INTRODUCTION

The aims of *Theory* . . . were to generalize and carry to a higher order of abstraction the traditional doctrine of the social contract. I wanted to show that this doctrine was not open to the more obvious objections often thought fatal to it. I hoped to work out more clearly the chief structural features of this conception—which I called "justice as fairness"—and to develop it as an alternative systematic account of justice that is superior to utilitarianism. I thought this alternative conception was, of the traditional moral conceptions, the best approximation to our considered convictions of justice and constituted the most appropriate basis for the institutions of a democratic society.

The aims of these lectures are quite different. Note that in my summary of the aims of *Theory*, the social contract tradition is seen as part of moral philosophy and no distinction is drawn between moral and political philosophy. In *Theory* a moral doctrine of justice general in scope is not distinguished from a strictly political conception of justice. Nothing is made of the contrast between comprehensive philosophical and moral doctrines and conceptions limited to the domain of the political. In the lectures in this volume, however, these distinctions and related ideas are fundamental.

Indeed, it may seem that the aim and content of these lectures mark a major change from those of *Theory*. Certainly, as I have indicated, there are important differences. But to understand the nature and extent of the differences, one must see

them as arising from trying to resolve a serious problem internal to justice as fairness. . . .

To explain: the serious problem I have in mind concerns the unrealistic idea of a well-ordered society as it appears in *Theory*. An essential feature of a well-ordered society associated with justice as fairness is that all its citizens endorse this conception on the basis of what I now call a comprehensive philosophical doctrine. They accept, as rooted in this doctrine, its two principles of justice. Similarly, in the well-ordered society associated with utilitarianism citizens generally endorse that view as a comprehensive philosophical doctrine and they accept the principle of utility on that basis. Although the distinction between a political conception of justice and a comprehensive philosophical doctrine is not discussed in *Theory*, once the question is raised, it is clear, I think, that the text regards justice as fairness and utilitarianism as comprehensive, or partially comprehensive, doctrines.

Now the serious problem is this. A modern democratic society is characterized not simply by a pluralism of comprehensive religious, philosophical, and moral doctrines but by a pluralism of incompatible yet reasonable comprehensive doctrines. No one of these doctrines is affirmed by citizens generally. Nor should one expect that in the foreseeable future one of them, or some other reasonable doctrine, will ever be affirmed by all, or nearly all, citizens. Political liberalism assumes that, for political purposes, a plurality of reasonable yet incompatible comprehensive doctrines is the normal result of the exercise of human reason within the framework of the free institutions of a

From John Rawls, *Political Liberalism*, Columbia University Press, 1993. Reprinted by permission of the publisher. Footnotes omitted.

constitutional democratic regime. . . . The problem of political liberalism is: How is it possible that there may exist over time a stable and just society of free and equal citizens profoundly divided by reasonable though incompatible religious, philosophical, and moral doctrines? Put another way: How is it possible that deeply opposed though reasonable comprehensive doctrines may live together and all affirm the political conception of a constitutional regime? What is the structure and content of a political conception that can gain the support of such an overlapping consensus? . . .

LECTURE I

Fundamental Ideas

§ 1. Addressing Two Fundamental Questions

3. I return . . . to our first question and ask: How might political philosophy find a shared basis for settling such a fundamental question as that of the most appropriate family of institutions to secure democratic liberty and equality? Perhaps the most that can be done is to narrow the range of disagreement. Yet even firmly held convictions gradually change: religious toleration is now accepted, and arguments for persecution are no longer openly professed; similarly, slavery, which caused our Civil War, is rejected as inherently unjust, and however much the aftermath of slavery may persist in social policies and unavowed attitudes, no one is willing to defend it. We collect such settled convictions as the belief in religious toleration and the rejection of slavery and try to organize the basic ideas and principles implicit in these convictions into a coherent political conception of justice. These convictions are provisional fixed points that it seems any reasonable conception must account for. We start, then, by looking to the public culture itself as the shared fund of implicitly recognized basic ideas and principles. We hope to formulate these ideas and principles clearly enough to be combined into a political conception of justice congenial to our

most firmly held convictions. We express this by saying that a political conception of justice, to be acceptable, must accord with our considered convictions, at all levels of generality, on due reflection, or in what I have called elsewhere "reflective equilibrium."

The public political culture may be of two minds at a very deep level. Indeed, this must be so with such an enduring controversy as that concerning the most appropriate understanding of liberty and equality. This suggests that if we are to succeed in finding a basis for public agreement, we must find a way of organizing familiar ideas and principles into a conception of political justice that expresses those ideas and principles in a somewhat different way than before. Justice as fairness tries to do this by using a fundamental organizing idea within which all ideas and principles can be systematically connected and related. This organizing idea is that of society as a fair system of social cooperation between free and equal persons viewed as fully cooperating members of society over a complete life. It lays a basis for answering the first fundamental question. . . .

4. Now suppose justice as fairness were to achieve its aims and a publicly acceptable political conception were found. Then this conception provides a publicly recognized point of view from which all citizens can examine before one another whether their political and social institutions are just. It enables them to do this by citing what are publicly recognized among them as valid and sufficient reasons singled out by that conception itself. Society's main institutions and how they fit together into one system of social cooperation can be assessed in the same way by each citizen, whatever that citizen's social position or more particular interests.

The aim of justice as fairness, then, is practical: it presents itself as a conception of justice that may be shared by citizens as a basis of a reasoned, informed, and willing political agreement. It expresses their shared and public political reason. But to attain such a shared reason, the conception of justice should be, as far as possible, independent of the opposing and conflicting philosophical and religious doctrines that citizens affirm. In formulating such a conception, political liberalism applies the principle of toleration to philosophy itself. The religious doctrines that in previous centuries were the professed basis of society have gradually given way to principles of constitutional government that all citizens, whatever their religious view, can endorse. Comprehensive philosophical and moral doctrines likewise cannot be endorsed by citizens generally, and they also no longer can, if they ever could, serve as the professed basis of society.

Thus, political liberalism looks for a political conception of justice that we hope can gain the support of an overlapping consensus of reasonable religious, philosophical, and moral doctrines in a society regulated by it. Gaining this support of reasonable doctrines lays the basis for answering our second fundamental question as to how citizens, who remain deeply divided on religious, philosophical, and moral doctrines, can still maintain a just and stable democratic society. To this end, it is normally desirable that the comprehensive philosophical and moral views we are wont to use in debating fundamental political issues should give way in public life. Public reason—citizens' reasoning in the public forum about constitutional essentials and basic questions of justice—is now best guided by a political conception the principles and values of which all citizens can endorse (VI). That political conception is to be, so to speak, political and not metaphysical.

Political liberalism, then, aims for a political conception of justice as a freestanding view. It offers no specific metaphysical or epistemological doctrine beyond what is implied by the political conception itself. As an account of political values, a free-standing political conception does not deny there being other values that apply, say, to the personal, the familial, and the associational; nor does it say that political values are separate from, or discontinuous with, other values. One aim, as I have said, is to specify the political domain and its conception of justice in such a way that its

institutions can gain the support of an overlapping consensus. In this case, citizens themselves, within the exercise of their liberty of thought and conscience, and looking to their comprehensive doctrines, view the political conception as derived from, or congruent with, or at least not in conflict with, their other values.

§ 6. The Idea of a Well-Ordered Society

1. I have said that in justice as fairness the fundamental idea of society as a fair system of cooperation over generations is developed in conjunction with two companion ideas: the idea of citizens as free and equal persons, and the idea of a well-ordered society as a society effectively regulated by a public political conception of justice. . . .

To say that a society is well-ordered conveys three things: first (and implied by the idea of a publicly recognized conception of justice), it is a society in which everyone accepts, and knows that everyone else accepts, the very same principles of justice; and second (implied by the idea of the effective regulation of such a conception), its basic structure—that is, its main political and social institutions and how they fit together as one system of cooperation—is publicly known, or with good reason believed, to satisfy these principles. And third, its citizens have a normally effective sense of justice and so they generally comply with society's basic institutions, which they regard as just. In such a society the publicly recognized conception of justice establishes a shared point of view from which citizens' claims on society can be adjudicated.

This is a highly idealized concept. Yet any conception of justice that cannot well order a constitutional democracy is inadequate as a democratic conception. This might happen because of the familiar reason that its content renders it self-defeating when it is publicly recognized. It might also happen because. . . . a democratic society is marked by the fact of reasonable pluralism. Thus, a conception of justice may fail because it cannot gain the support of reasonable citizens who affirm reasonable comprehensive doctrines; or as I shall often say, it cannot gain the support of a reasonable overlapping consensus. Being able to do this is necessary for an adequate political conception of justice.

2. The reason for this is that the political culture of a democratic society is characterized (I assume) by three general facts understood as follows.

The first is that the diversity of reasonable comprehensive religious, philosophical, and moral doctrines found in modern democratic societies is not a mere historical condition that may soon pass away; it is a permanent feature of the public culture of democracy. Under the political and social conditions secured by the basic rights and liberties of free institutions, a diversity of conflicting and irreconcilable—and what's more, reasonable—comprehensive doctrines will come about and persist if such diversity does not already obtain.

This fact of reasonable pluralism must be distinguished from the fact of pluralism as such. It is the fact that free institutions tend to generate not simply as a variety of doctrines and views, as one might expect from peoples' various interests and their tendency to focus on narrow points of view. Rather, it is the fact that among the views that develop are a diversity of reasonable comprehensive doctrines. These are the doctrines that reasonable citizens affirm and that political liberalism must address. They are not simply the upshot of self- and class interests, or of people's understandable tendency to view the political world from a limited standpoint. Instead, they are in part the work of free practical reason within the framework of free institutions. Thus, although historical doctrines are not, of course, the work of free reason alone, the fact of reasonable pluralism is not an unfortunate condition of human life. In framing the political conception so that it can, at the second stage, gain the support of reasonable comprehensive doctrines, we are not so much adjusting that conception to brute forces of the world but to the inevitable outcome of free human reason.

A second and related general fact is that a continuing shared understanding on one comprehensive religious, philosophical, or moral doctrine can be maintained only by the oppressive use of state power. If we think of political society as a community united in affirming one and the same comprehensive doctrine, then the oppressive use of state power is necessary for political community. In the society of the Middle Ages, more or less united in affirming the Catholic faith, the Inquisition was not an accident; its suppression of heresy was needed to preserve that shared religious belief. The same holds, I believe, for any reasonable comprehensive philosophical and moral doctrine, whether religious or nonreligious. A society united on a reasonable form of utilitarianism, or on the reasonable liberalisms of Kant or Mill, would likewise require the sanctions of state power to remain so. Call this "the fact of oppression."

Finally, a third general fact is that an enduring and secure democratic regime, one not divided into contending doctrinal confessions and hostile social classes, must be willingly and freely supported by at least a substantial majority of its politically active citizens. Together with the first general fact, this means that to serve as a public basis of justification for a constitutional regime a political conception of justice must be one that can be endorsed by widely different and opposing though reasonable comprehensive doctrines.

3. Since there is no reasonable religious, philosophical, or moral doctrine affirmed by all citizens, the conception of justice affirmed in a well-ordered democratic society must be a conception limited to what I shall call "the domain of the political" and its values. The idea of a well-ordered democratic society must be framed accordingly. I assume, then, that citizens' overall views have two parts: one part can be seen to be, or to coincide with, the publicly recognized political conception of justice; the other part is a (fully or partially) comprehensive doctrine to which the political conception is in some manner related. How it may be related I note later in IV. The point

to stress here is that, as I have said, citizens individually decide for themselves in what way the public political conception all affirm is related to their own more comprehensive views.

With this understood, I note briefly how a well-ordered democratic society meets a necessary (but certainly not sufficient) condition of realism and stability. Such a society can be well-ordered by a political conception of justice so long as, first, citizens who affirm reasonable but opposing comprehensive doctrines belong to an overlapping consensus: that is, they generally endorse that conception of justice as giving the content of their political judgments on basic institutions; and second, unreasonable comprehensive doctrines (these, we assume, always exist) do not gain enough currency to undermine society's essential justice. These conditions do not impose the unrealistic—indeed, the utopian—requirement that all citizens affirm the same comprehensive doctrine, but only, as in political liberalism, the same public conception of justice.

4. The idea of an overlapping consensus is easily misunderstood given the idea of consensus used in everyday politics. Its meaning for us arises thus: we suppose a constitutional democratic regime to be reasonably just and workable, and worth defending. Yet given the fact of reasonable pluralism, how can we frame our defense of it so that it can win sufficiently wide support to achieve stability?

To this end, we do not look to the comprehensive doctrines that in fact exist and then draw up a political conception that strikes some kind of balance of forces between them. To illustrate: in specifying a list of primary goods, say, we can proceed in two ways. One is to look at the various comprehensive doctrines actually found in society and specify an index of such goods so as to be near to those doctrines' center of gravity, so to speak; that is, so as to find a kind of average of what those who affirmed those views would need by way of institutional claims and protections and all-purpose means. Doing this might seem the best way to insure that the index provides the

basic elements necessary to advance the conceptions of the good associated with existing doctrines and thus improve the likelihood of securing an overlapping consensus.

This is not how justice as fairness proceeds; to do so would make it political in the wrong way. Rather, it elaborates a political conception as a freestanding view working from the fundamental idea of society as a fair system of cooperation and its companion ideas. The hope is that this idea, with its index of primary goods arrived at from within, can be the focus of a reasonable overlapping consensus. We leave aside comprehensive doctrines that now exist, or that have existed, or that might exist. The thought is not that primary goods are fair to comprehensive conceptions of the good associated with such doctrines, by striking a fair balance among them, but rather fair to free and equal citizens as those persons who have those conceptions.

The problem, then, is how to frame a conception of justice for a constitutional regime such that those who support, or who might be brought to support, that kind of regime might also endorse the political conception provided it did not conflict too sharply with their comprehensive views. This leads to the idea of a political conception of justice as a freestanding view starting from the fundamental ideas of a democratic society and presupposing no particular wider doctrine. We put no doctrinal obstacles to its winning allegiance to itself, so that it can be supported by a reasonable and enduring overlapping consensus.

LECTURE IV

The Idea of an Overlapping Consensus

§ 3. Three Features of an Overlapping Consensus

2. There are at least four objections likely to be raised against the idea of social unity founded on an overlapping consensus on a political conception of justice. I begin with perhaps the most

obvious of these, namely, that an overlapping consensus is a mere modus vivendi.

To fix ideas I shall use a model case of an overlapping consensus to indicate what is meant; and I shall return to this example from time to time. It contains three views: one affirms the political conception because its religious doctrine and account of free faith lead to a principle of toleration and underwrite the fundamental liberties of a constitutional regime; while the second view affirms the political conception on the basis of a comprehensive liberal moral doctrine such as those of Kant or Mill. The third, however, is not systematically unified: besides the political values formulated by a freestanding political conception of justice, it includes a large family of nonpolitical values. It is a pluralist view, let us say, since each subpart of this family has its own account based on ideas drawn from within it, leaving all values to be balanced against one another, either in groups or singly, in particular kinds of cases.

In this model case the religious doctrine and the liberalisms of Kant and Mill are taken to be general and comprehensive. The third view is only partially comprehensive but holds, with political liberalism, that under reasonably favorable conditions that make democracy possible, political values normally outweigh whatever nonpolitical values conflict with them. The previous views agree with the last in this respect and so all views lead to roughly the same political judgments and thus overlap on the political conception.

3. To begin with the objection: some will think that even if an overlapping consensus were sufficiently stable, the idea of political unity founded on an overlapping consensus must still be rejected, since it abandons the hope of political community and settles instead for a public understanding that is at bottom a mere modus vivendi. To this objection, we say that the hope of political community must indeed be abandoned, if by such a community we mean a political society united in affirming the same comprehensive doctrine. This possibility is excluded by the fact of reasonable pluralism together with the rejection of the oppressive use of the state power to overcome it. The substantive question concerns the significant features of such a consensus and how these features affect social concord and the moral quality of public life. I turn to why an overlapping consensus is not a mere modus vivendi.

A typical use of the phrase "modus vivendi" is to characterize a treaty between two states whose national aims and interests put them at odds. In negotiating a treaty each state would be wise and prudent to make sure that the agreement proposed represents an equilibrium point: that is, that the terms and conditions of the treaty are drawn up in such a way that it is public knowledge that it is not advantageous for either state to violate it. The treaty will then be adhered to because doing so is regarded by each as in its national interest, including its interest in its reputation as a state that honors treaties. But in general both states are ready to pursue their goals at the expense of the other, and should conditions change they may do so. This background highlights the way in which such a treaty is a mere modus vivendi. A similar background is present when we think of social consensus founded on self-or group interests, or on the outcome of political bargaining: social unity is only apparent, as its stability is contingent on circumstances remaining such as not to upset the fortunate convergence of interests.

4. That an overlapping consensus is quite different from a modus vivendi is clear from our model case. In that example, note two aspects: first, the object of consensus, the political conception of justice, is itself a moral conception. And second, it is affirmed on moral grounds, that is, it includes conceptions of society and of citizens as persons, as well as principles of justice, and an account of the political virtues through which those principles are embodied in human character and expressed in public life. An overlapping consensus, therefore, is not merely a consensus on accepting certain authorities, or on complying with certain institutional arrangements, founded on a convergence of self- or group interests. All those who affirm the political conception start

from within their own comprehensive view and draw on the religious, philosophical, and moral grounds it provides. The fact that people affirm the same political conception on those grounds does not make their affirming it any less religious, philosophical, or moral, as the case may be, since the grounds sincerely held determine the nature of their affirmation.

The preceding two aspects of an overlapping consensus—moral object and moral grounds—connect with a third aspect, that of stability. This means that those who affirm the various views supporting the political conception will not withdraw their support of it should the relative strength of their view in society increase and eventually become dominant. So long as the three views are affirmed and not revised, the political conception will still be supported regardless of shifts in the distribution of political power. Each view supports the political conception for its own sake, or on its own merits. The test for this is whether the consensus is stable with respect to changes in the distribution of power among views. This feature of stability highlights a basic contrast between an overlapping consensus and a modus vivendi, the stability of which does depend on happenstance and a balance of relative forces.

This becomes clear once we change our example and include the views of Catholics and Protestants in the sixteenth century. At that time there was not an overlapping consensus on the principle of toleration. Both faiths held that it was the duty of the ruler to uphold the true religion and to repress the spread of heresy and false doctrine. In such a case the acceptance of the principle of toleration would indeed be a mere modus vivendi, because if either faith becomes dominant, the principle of toleration would no longer be followed. Stability with respect to the distribution of power is lacking. So long as such views as those of Catholic and Protestant in the sixteenth century are very much in the minority, and are likely to remain so, they do not significantly affect the moral quality of public life and the basis of social concord. For the vast majority in society

are confident that the distribution of power will range over and be widely shared by views in the consensus that affirm the political conception of justice for its own sake. But should this situation change, the moral quality of political life will also change in ways that are obvious and require no comment.

LECTURE VI

The Idea of Public Reason

§ 4. The Content of Public Reason

2. Now it is essential that a liberal political conception include, besides its principles of justice, guidelines of inquiry that specify ways of reasoning and criteria for the kinds of information relevant for political questions. Without such guidelines substantive principles cannot be applied and this leaves the political conception incomplete and fragmentary. That conception has, then, two parts:

  a. first, substantive principles of justice for the basic structure; and
  b. second, guidelines of inquiry: principles of reasoning and rules of evidence in the light of which citizens are to decide whether substantive principles properly apply and to identify laws and policies that best satisfy them.

Hence liberal political values are likewise of two kinds:

  a. The first kind—the values of political justice—fall under the principles of justice for the basic structure: the values of equal political and civil liberty; equality of opportunity; the values of social equality and economic reciprocity; and let us add also values of the common good as well as the various necessary conditions for all these values.
  b. The second kind of political values—the values of public reason—fall under the

guidelines for public inquiry, which make that inquiry free and public. Also included here are such political virtues as reasonableness and a readiness to honor the (moral) duty of civility, which as virtues of citizens help to make possible reasoned public discussion of political questions.

3. As we have said, on matters of constitutional essentials and basic justice, the basic structure and its public policies are to be justifiable to all citizens, as the principle of political legitimacy requires. We add to this that in making these justifications we are to appeal only to presently accepted general beliefs and forms of reasoning found in common sense, and the methods and conclusions of science when these are not controversial. The liberal principle of legitimacy makes this the most appropriate, if not the only, way to specify the guidelines of public inquiry. What other guidelines and criteria have we for this case?

This means that in discussing constitutional essentials and matters of basic justice we are not to appeal to comprehensive religious and philosophical doctrines—to what we as individuals or members of associations see as the whole truth—nor to elaborate economic theories of general equilibrium, say, if these are in dispute. As far as possible, the knowledge and ways of reasoning that ground our affirming the principles of justice and their application to constitutional essentials and basic justice are to rest on the plain truths now widely accepted, or available, to citizens generally. Otherwise, the political conception would not provide a public basis of justification. . . .

5. Keep in mind that political liberalism is a kind of view. It has many forms, depending on the substantive principles used and how the guidelines of inquiry are set out. These forms have in common substantive principles of justice that are liberal and an idea of public reason. Content and idea may vary within these limits.

Accepting the idea of public reason and its principle of legitimacy emphatically does not mean, then, accepting a particular liberal conception of justice down to the last details of the principles defining its content. We may differ about these principles and still agree in accepting a conception's more general features. We agree that citizens share in political power as free and equal, and that as reasonable and rational they have a duty of civility to appeal to public reason, yet we differ as to which principles are the most reasonable basis of public justification. The view I have called "justice as fairness" is but one example of a liberal political conception; its specific content is not definitive of such a view.

The point of the ideal of public reason is that citizens are to conduct their fundamental discussions within the framework of what each regards as a political conception of justice based on values that the others can reasonably be expected to endorse and each is, in good faith, prepared to defend that conception so understood. This means that each of us must have, and be ready to explain, a criterion of what principles and guidelines we think other citizens (who are also free and equal) may reasonably be expected to endorse along with us. We must have some test we are ready to state as to when this condition is met. I have elsewhere suggested as a criterion the values expressed by the principles and guidelines that would be agreed to in the original position. Many will prefer another criterion.

Of course, we may find that actually others fail to endorse the principles and guidelines our criterion selects. That is to be expected. The idea is that we must have such a criterion and this alone already imposes very considerable discipline on public discussion. Not any value is reasonably said to meet this test, or to be a political value; and not any balance of political values is reasonable. It is inevitable and often desirable that citizens have different views as to the most appropriate political conception; for the public political culture is bound to contain different fundamental ideas that can be developed in different ways. An orderly contest between them over time is a reliable way to find which one, if any, is most reasonable.

ROBERT NOZICK

~

INTRODUCTION

THOMAS CHRISTIANO

Robert Nozick (1938–2003) was born in Brooklyn, New York, graduated from Columbia College and received his Ph.D. from Princeton University. He was Pellegrino University Professor at Harvard University, a past president of the American Philosophical Association (Eastern Division), a Fellow of the American Academy of Arts and Sciences, a Corresponding Fellow of the British Academy, and a Senior Fellow in the Society of Fellows at Harvard University.

While Nozick wrote pathbreaking works in an unusually wide variety of areas in philosophy, his most famous book, winner of the 1975 National Book Award, was *Anarchy, State, and Utopia*. It revived classical liberalism as a serious option in political philosophy, offered the first full-length challenge to John Rawls's *A Theory of Justice*, and defended a version of libertarianism. Nozick's book *Philosophical Explanations* (1981) made lasting contributions to epistemology and our understanding of personal identity, free will, and the foundations of ethics. *The Examined Life* (1989) explored the nature of the good life and the meaning of life. *The Nature of Rationality* (1993) culminated a lifelong study of theories of rational decision and rational belief. Nozick also published *Socratic Puzzles* (1997), a collection of essays, and *Invariances* (2001), a book on the notion of an objective world and the role that invariance plays in it, including topics in philosophy of science, philosophy of mind, metaphysics, and ethics.

In *Anarchy, State, and Utopia*, Nozick's arguments proceed in the Lockean tradition of natural rights to liberty and property. For Nozick, justice entails absolute constraints on the behavior of people toward others. No one may abridge the liberty of another, harm the other in life or limb, or take property from another, without the other's consent. Persons have the right to act in self-defense, and rectification is appropriate if the rights to property and liberty have been violated. In short, whatever comes about by the voluntary consent of people who do not violate the rights of others is just. Any attempt to interfere with this process is an illegitimate interference with liberty. These theses imply a radical criticism of contemporary welfare states, inasmuch as modern states impose taxes on their citizens and to that extent regulate their behavior in the pursuit of economic and political aims. These views also entail a radical rejection of much contemporary and classical theorizing in political philosophy. Aristotelian, utilitarian, egalitarian, and various forms of contractarian theory, and many contemporary accounts of liberalism, such as that of John Rawls, run afoul of Nozick's stringent restrictions on what persons may do to one another. Much as these theories may celebrate human freedom or dignity, all are committed to ideals of politics that require individuals to relate in ways to which they may not consent.

Nozick's entitlement theory of justice asserts three basic principles. The principle of entitlement in acquisition regulates how each person may acquire holdings in previously unowned things. The principle of entitlement in transfer states that each may legitimately acquire holdings from another if and only if one has the other's voluntary consent and the other has legitimately acquired the holdings. The principle of rectification calls for appropriate rectification for any violation of the two first principles.

A key support for the three principles is the Kantian idea that one must never treat persons as mere means but always as ends in themselves. According to Nozick, treating persons as ends requires the persons' consent to their treatment. This interpretation of the Kantian principle, however, leaves unanswered questions. Why doesn't it also require that everyone help persons to pursue their reasonable ends even at the expense of those who have more than enough? If I value a person's rational nature, aren't I sometimes under a duty to enhance a person's capacity to exercise that nature? Doesn't treating persons as ends require that one ensure that one's relations and exchanges with them take place under fair conditions, such as an adequate supply of goods that enable those persons to avoid mistreatment?

Nozick argues that persons may act as they wish so long as they do not interfere with others. Hence, individuals may commit suicide or sell themselves into slavery. For Kant, by contrast, a person is not permitted to do these things, because both of these actions amount to treating oneself as a mere means and not as an end.

Another of Nozick's foundational notions is that each person is an owner of himself or herself. This principle is widely accepted but has been interpreted variously. Locke thought that self-ownership did not imply ownership of one's body, which is the property of God; one owns one's self and the activities of the self. For Nozick, a person owns his or her body, and Nozick infers that if I violate another's entitlement to be unmolested, I am acting as if I were part owner of that person. Nozick employs this idea in a defense of property rights; in a striking illustration he argues that if a group taxes a person without the person's consent from the product of that person's labor, then the group is acting as if it were part owner of the person by appropriating a proportion of his or her labor for its own aims. But doing so forces the person to work for the group, which can be permitted only if the group owns the person, at least in part. So, according to Nozick, taxation is a form of forced labor or slavery, which is forbidden without the person's consent.

To the extent that Nozick can found the entitlement theory on the idea that no one may own another without that other's consent, his view has a strong intuitive foundation. The crucial question concerns the relation between self-ownership and the ownership of external things.

But someone's taking something from me does not appear to involve taking any part of me, molesting me, or even exercising control over me. It does involve exercising control over something I own. For instance, if I am taxed, I am still free to do whatever job I please or not do any job at all. Perhaps taxation is theft, but not obviously because taxation is forced labor.

In addition, one can assert some control over another for a just cause, such as self-defense. Or if someone has violated my rights, I may attempt to rectify the situation by taking something back in return. Whether these are cases of asserting part-ownership over another is unclear. If they are not, then the notion of ownership appears to pre-suppose some principles of justice. If they are, then the notion of self-ownership appears not to be absolute in the face of competing ideas of justice.

Nozick also bases his entitlement theory on a conception of liberty, which plays an intuitive role in his use of the Wilt Chamberlain example: Wilt offers to play basketball for his adoring fans on condition that they pay an extra twenty-five cents, which goes directly to him and not to the team. If a million fans go to see him, he ends up a quarter-million dollars wealthier than anyone else. Nozick asks us to imagine this scenario against the backdrop of some particular conception of distributive justice. For instance, if we suppose that justice requires that each person begins with an equal share of the wealth of the society, then while Wilt and the fans and the players all start out with equal wealth, Wilt ends up a quarter-million dollars wealthier than the others. The egalitarian must now decide whether to redistribute the money Wilt received or allow the inequality that has arisen from the transactions. Nozick believes the egalitarian faces a dilemma. To ban the transactions would be to say that the fans were not legitimately in possession of their holdings. To say that the subsequent unequal distribution accords with equality would surely be puzzling. So, the egalitarian seems committed to say that equality conflicts with liberty, for to maintain any pattern of distribution requires interventions in social life to restore the damage to that pattern done by consenting adults. In other words, patterns of distribution are always under threat, when people are free to do what they want with their goods. By contrast, the entitlement theory, which does not require that any pattern of distribution be maintained, does not conflict with liberty. According to Nozick, the theory is a historical conception of justice, which says that whatever results from persons' just uses of justly held goods is itself just. Since the fans justly hold their money and pay to see Wilt play, the outcome of the exchanges is just.

The Wilt Chamberlain example points to the disturbing prospect of a state, concerned with maintaining patterned distributions, constantly but unpredictably intruding in the lives of its citizens. Nozick challenges pattern theorists to show how one can maintain a pattern while at the same time establishing the conditions for autonomous, long-term planning under predictable and secure circumstances.

One may transfer holdings to others only if one has legitimately received the holdings from others or legitimately acquired them from what is unowned. Every exchange is legitimate on condition that the holdings in question were previously legitimately held. With the exception of the parts of one's body, no one is born with legitimate holdings. Thus, a major question for Nozick is how things can be legitimately acquired from unowned things. When one legitimately acquires something previously unowned, one in effect restricts others from using it. Hence, through legitimate acquisition one can limit the liberty of others without their consent. But, isn't this conclusion at odds with one of the founding ideas of the entitlement theory?

Locke argues that one may acquire property from previously unowned things in order to satisfy needs. So the origin of property is linked to the importance of the preservation of oneself and others. And Locke ascribes the same foundation to liberty. He claims that one legitimately acquires property from what is unowned by mixing one's labor with it. Philosophers have interpreted this suggestive idea in a number of ways. Some have said that one makes oneself part of the thing, thus extending the right of self-ownership to it. Others have said that one deserves to own the thing because of one's work put into it. Locke also imposes limits on what can be acquired, arguing that, based on the equal importance of everyone's need, one ought not waste the things one acquires and, secondly, one must leave enough and as good for others.

Nozick accepts Locke's second proviso but rejects his labor-mixing idea on the grounds that it is not clear whether by working one has gained a possession or lost one's labor. Nozick does not offer a complete account of the basis of acquisition or of its justification but tells us that acquisition of unowned things is legitimate as long as the second proviso is satisfied. In other words, what I can acquire is constrained by the needs of others.

However, questions remain. What about future generations that no longer have access to acquisition of unowned external goods? Is the proviso violated in their cases? Or is it sufficient that they have opportunities to live decent lives by virtue of the acquisition and productive efforts of others? What does "as good and enough for others" imply in this circumstance? Nozick responds that the capitalist society justified by his entitlement theory would be so productive that it would obviate any worries about later generations.

For an excellent edition of critical essays on Nozick's book, see Jeffrey Paul (ed.), *Reading Nozick: Essays on Anarchy, State and Utopia* (Lanham, Md.: Rowman & Littlefield, 1981). A recent critical study devoted largely to a discussion of Nozick's political theory is G. A. Cohen, *Self-Ownership, Freedom and Equality* (Cambridge: Cambridge University Press, 1995). For a collection of essays by leading contemporary philosophers on different aspects of Nozick's work but devoted in major part to his political philosophy, see David Schmidtz (ed.), *Robert Nozick: Contemporary Philosophers in Focus* (New York: Cambridge University Press, 2001).

Anarchy, State, and Utopia

CHAPTER 7

Distributive Justice

The minimal state is the most extensive state that can be justified. Any state more extensive violates people's rights. Yet many persons have put forth reasons purporting to justify a more extensive state. It is impossible within the compass of this book to examine all the reasons that have been put forth. Therefore, I shall focus upon those generally acknowledged to be most weighty and influential, to see precisely wherein they fail. In this chapter we consider the claim that a more extensive state is justified, because necessary (or the best instrument) to achieve distributive justice. . . .

From *Anarchy, State, and Utopia* by Robert Nozick. Copyright © 1974 by Basic Books, Inc. Reprinted by permission of Basic Books, Inc., Publishers.

The term "distributive justice" is not a neutral one. Hearing the term "distribution," most people presume that some thing or mechanism uses some principle or criterion to give out a supply of things. Into this process of distributing shares some error may have crept. So it is an open question, at least, whether *re*distribution should take place; whether we should do again what has already been done once, though poorly. However, we are not in the position of children who have been given portions of pie by someone who now makes last minute adjustments to rectify careless cutting. There is no *central* distribution, no person or group entitled to control all the resources, jointly deciding how they are to be doled out. What each person gets, he gets from others who give to him in exchange for something, or as a gift. In a free society, diverse persons control different resources, and new holdings arise out of the voluntary exchanges and actions of persons. There is no more a distributing or distribution of shares than there is a distributing of mates in a society in which persons choose whom they shall marry. The total result is the product of many individual decisions which the different individuals involved are entitled to make. Some uses of the term "distribution," it is true, do not imply a previous distributing appropriately judged by some criterion (for example, "probability distribution"); nevertheless, despite the title of this chapter, it would be best to use a terminology that clearly is neutral. We shall speak of people's holdings; a principle of justice in holdings describes (part of) what justice tells us (requires) about holdings. I shall state first what I take to be the correct view about justice in holdings, and then turn to the discussion of alternate views.

Section I

THE ENTITLEMENT THEORY

The subject of justice in holdings consists of three major topics. The first is the *original acquisition of holdings*, the appropriation of unheld things. This includes the issues of how unheld things may come to be held, the process, or processes, by which unheld things may come to be held, the things that may come to be held by these processes, the extent of what comes to be held by a particular process, and so on. We shall refer to the complicated truth about this topic, which we shall not formulate here, as the principle of justice in acquisition. The second topic concerns the *transfer of holdings* from one person to another. By what processes may a person transfer holdings to another? How may a person acquire a holding from another who holds it? Under this topic come general descriptions of voluntary exchange, and gift and (on the other hand) fraud, as well as reference to particular conventional details fixed upon in a given society. The complicated truth about this subject (with placeholders for conventional details) we shall call the principle of justice in transfer. (And we shall suppose it also includes principles governing how a person may divest himself of a holding, passing it into an unheld state.)

If the world were wholly just, the following inductive definition would exhaustively cover the subject of justice in holdings.

1. A person who acquires a holding in accordance with the principle of justice in acquisition is entitled to that holding.
2. A person who acquires a holding in accordance with the principle of justice in transfer, from someone else entitled to the holding, is entitled to the holding.
3. No one is entitled to a holding except by (repeated) applications of 1 and 2.

The complete principle of distributive justice would say simply that a distribution is just if everyone is entitled to the holdings they possess under the distribution.

A distribution is just if it arises from another just distribution by legitimate means. The legitimate means of moving from one distribution to another are specified by the principle of justice in transfer. The legitimate first "moves" are specified by the principle of justice in acquisition.[1] Whatever arises from a just situation by just steps is itself just. The means of change specified by the principle of justice in transfer preserve justice. As correct rules of inference are truth-preserving, and any conclusion deduced via repeated application of such rules from only true premises is itself true, so the means of transition from one situation to another specified by the principle of justice in transfer are justice-preserving, and any situation actually arising from repeated transitions in accordance with the principle from a just situation is itself just. The parallel between justice-preserving transformations and truth-preserving transformations illuminates where it fails as well as where it holds. That a conclusion could have been deduced by truth-preserving means from premises that are true suffices to show its truth. That from a just situation a situation *could* have arisen via justice-preserving means does *not* suffice to show its justice. The fact that a thief's victims voluntarily *could* have presented him with gifts does not entitle the thief to his ill-gotten gains. Justice in holdings is historical; it depends upon what actually has happened. We shall return to this point later.

Not all actual situations are generated in accordance with the two principles of justice in holdings: the principle of justice in acquisition and the principle of justice in transfer. Some people steal from others, or defraud them, or enslave them, seizing their product and preventing them from living as they choose, or forcibly exclude others from competing in exchanges. None of these are permissible modes of transition from one situation to another. And some persons acquire holdings by means not sanctioned by the principle of justice in acquisition. The existence of past injustice (previous violations of the first two principles of justice in holdings) raises the third major topic under justice in holdings: the rectification of injustice in holdings. If past injustice has shaped present holdings in various ways, some identifiable and some not, what now, if anything, ought to be done to rectify these injustices? What obligations do the performers of injustice have toward those whose position is worse than it would have been had the injustice not been done? Or, than it would have been had compensation been paid promptly? How, if at all, do things change if the beneficiaries and those made worse off are not the direct parties in the act of injustice, but, for example, their descendants? Is an injustice done to someone whose holding was itself based upon an unrectified injustice? How far back must one go in wiping clean the historical slate of injustices? What may victims of injustice permissibly do in order to rectify the injustices being done to them, including the many injustices done by persons acting through their government? I do not know of a thorough or theoretically sophisticated treatment of such issues.[2] Idealizing greatly, let us suppose theoretical investigation will produce a principle of rectification. This principle uses historical information about previous situations and injustices done in them (as defined by the first two principles of justice and rights against interference), and information about the actual course of events that flowed from these injustices, until the present, and it yields a description (or descriptions) of holdings in the society. The principle of rectification presumably will make use of its best estimate of subjunctive information about what would have occurred (or a probability distribution over what might have occurred, using the expected value) if the injustice had not taken place. If the actual description of holdings turns out not to be one of the descriptions yielded by the principle, then one of the descriptions yielded must be realized.[3]

The general outlines of the theory of justice in holdings are that the holdings of a person are just if he is entitled to them by the principles of justice in acquisition and transfer, or by the principle of rectification of injustice (as specified by the first two principles). If each person's holdings are just, then the total set (distribution) of holdings is just. To turn these general outlines into a specific theory we would have to specify the details of each of the three principles of justice in holdings: the principle of acquisition of holdings, the principle of transfer of holdings, and the principle of rectification of violations of the first two principles. I shall not attempt that task here.

HISTORICAL PRINCIPLES AND END-RESULT PRINCIPLES

The general outlines of the entitlement theory illuminate the nature and defects of other conceptions of distributive justice. The entitlement theory of justice in distribution is *historical*; whether a distribution is just depends upon how it came about. In contrast, *current time-slice principles* of justice hold that the justice of a distribution is determined by how things are distributed (who has what) as judged by some *structural* principle(s) of just distribution. A utilitarian who judges between any two distributions by seeing which has the greater sum of utility and, if the sums tie, applies some fixed equality criterion to choose the more equal distribution, would hold a current time-slice principle of justice. As would someone who had a fixed schedule of trade-offs between the sum of happiness and equality. According to a current time-slice principle, all that needs to be looked at, in judging the justice of a distribution, is who ends up with what; in comparing any two distributions one need look only at the matrix presenting the distributions. No further information need be fed into a principle of justice. It is a consequence of such principles of justice that any two structurally identical distributions are equally just. (Two distributions are structurally identical if they present the same profile, but perhaps have different persons occupying the particular slots. My having ten and your having five, and my having five and your having ten are structurally identical distributions.) Welfare economics is the theory of current time-slice principles of justice. The subject is conceived as operating on matrices representing only current information about distribution. This, as well as some of the usual conditions (for example, the choice of distribution is invariant under relabeling of columns), guarantees that welfare

economics will be a current time-slice theory, with all of its inadequacies.

Most persons do not accept current time-slice principles as constituting the whole story about distributive shares. They think it relevant in assessing the justice of a situation to consider not only the distribution it embodies, but also how that distribution came about. If some persons are in prison for murder or war crimes, we do not say that to assess the justice of the distribution in the society we must look only at what this person has, and that person has, and that person has, . . . at the current time. We think it relevant to ask whether someone did something so that he *deserved* to be punished, deserved to have a lower share. Most will agree to the relevance of further information with regard to punishments and penalties. Consider also desired things. One traditional socialist view is that workers are entitled to the product and full fruits of their labor; they have earned it; a distribution is unjust if it does not give the workers what they are entitled to. Such entitlements are based upon some past history. No socialist holding this view would find it comforting to be told that because the actual distribution A happens to coincide structurally with the one he desires D, A therefore is no less just than D; it differs only in that the "parasitic" owners of capital receive under A what the workers are entitled to under D, and the workers receive under A what the owners are entitled to under D, namely very little. This socialist rightly, in my view, holds onto the notions of earning, producing, entitlement, desert, and so forth, and he rejects current time-slice principles that look only to the structure of the resulting set of holdings. (The set of holdings resulting from what? Isn't it implausible that how holdings are produced and come to exist has no effect at all on who should hold what?) His mistake lies in his view of what entitlements arise out of what sorts of productive processes.

We construe the position we discuss too narrowly by speaking of *current* time-slice principles. Nothing is changed if structural principles operate upon a time sequence of current time-slice profiles and, for example, give someone more now to counterbalance the less he has had earlier. A utilitarian or an egalitarian or any mixture of the two over time will inherit the difficulties of his more myopic comrades. He is not helped by the fact that *some* of the information others consider relevant in assessing a distribution is reflected, unrecoverably, in past matrices. Henceforth, we shall refer to such unhistorical principles of distributive justice, including the current time-slice principles, as *end-result principles* or *end-state principles*.

In contrast to end-result principles of justice, *historical principles* of justice hold that past circumstances or actions of people can create differential entitlements or differential deserts to things. An injustice can be worked by moving from one distribution to another structurally identical one, for the second, in profile the same, may violate people's entitlements or deserts; it may not fit the actual history.

The entitlement principles of justice in holdings that we have sketched are historical principles of justice. To better understand their precise character, we shall distinguish them from another subclass of the historical principles. Consider, as an example, the principle of distribution according to moral merit. This principle requires that total distributive shares vary directly with moral merit; no person should have a greater share than anyone whose moral merit is greater. (If moral merit could be not merely ordered but measured on an interval or ratio scale, stronger principles could be formulated.) Or consider the principle that results by substituting "usefulness to society" for "moral merit" in the previous principle. Or instead of "distribute according to moral merit," or "distribute according to usefulness to society," we might consider "distribute according to the weighted sum of moral merit, usefulness to society, and need," with the weights of the different dimensions equal. Let us call a principle of distribution *patterned* if it specifies that a distribution is to vary along with some natural dimension, weighted sum of natural dimensions, or lexicographic ordering of natural dimensions. And let us say a distribution is patterned if it accords with some patterned principle. (I speak of natural dimensions, admittedly without a general criterion for them, because for any set of holdings some artificial dimensions can be gimmicked up to vary along with the distribution of the set.) The principle of distribution in accordance with moral merit is a patterned historical principle, which specifies a patterned distribution. "Distribute according to I.Q." is a patterned principle that looks to information not contained in distributional matrices. It is not historical, however, in that it does not look to any past actions creating differential entitlements to evaluate a distribution; it requires only distributional matrices whose columns are labeled by I.Q. scores. The distribution in a society, however, may be composed of such simple patterned distributions, without itself being simply patterned. Different sectors may operate different patterns, or some combination of patterns may operate in different proportions across a society. A distribution composed in this manner, from a small number of patterned distributions, we also shall term "patterned." And we extend the use of "pattern" to include the overall designs put forth by combinations of end-state principles.

Almost every suggested principle of distributive justice is patterned: to each according to his moral merit, or needs, or marginal product, or how hard he tries, or the weighted sum of the foregoing, and so on. The principle of entitlement we have sketched is *not* patterned.[4] There is no one natural dimension or weighted sum or combination of a small number of natural dimensions that yields the distributions generated in accordance with the principle of entitlement. The set of holdings that results when some persons receive their marginal products, others win at gambling, others receive a share of their mate's income, others receive gifts from foundations, others receive interest on loans, others receive gifts from admirers, others receive returns on investment, others make for themselves much of what they have, others find things, and so on, will not be patterned. Heavy strands of patterns will run through it; significant portions of the variance in holdings will be accounted for by pattern-variables. If most people most of the time choose to transfer some of their entitlements to others only in exchange for something from them, then a large part of what many people hold will vary with what they held that others wanted. More details are provided by the theory of marginal productivity. But gifts to relatives, charitable donations, bequests to children, and the like, are not best conceived, in the first instance, in this manner. Ignoring the strands of pattern, let us suppose for the moment that a distribution actually arrived at by the operation of the principle of entitlement is random with respect to any pattern. Though the resulting set of holdings will be unpatterned, it will not be incomprehensible, for it can be seen as arising from the operation of a small number of principles. These principles specify how an initial distribution may arise (the principle of acquisition of holdings) and how distributions may be transformed into others (the principle of transfer of holdings). The process whereby the set of holdings is generated will be intelligible, though the set of holdings itself that results from this process will be unpatterned.

The writings of F. A. Hayek focus less than is usually done upon what patterning distributive justice requires. Hayek argues that we cannot know enough about each person's situation to distribute to each according to his moral merit (but would justice demand we do so if we did have this knowledge?); and he goes on to say, "our objection is against all attempts to impress upon society a deliberately chosen pattern of distribution, whether it be an order of equality or of inequality."[5] However, Hayek concludes that in a free society there will be distribution in accordance with value rather than moral merit; that is, in accordance with the perceived value of a person's actions and services to others. Despite his rejection of a patterned conception of distributive justice, Hayek himself suggests a pattern he thinks justifiable: distribution in accordance with

the perceived benefits given to others, leaving room for the complaint that a free society does not realize exactly this pattern. Stating this patterned strand of a free capitalist society more precisely, we get "To each according to how much he benefits others who have the resources for benefiting those who benefit them." This will seem arbitrary unless some acceptable initial set of holdings is specified, or unless it is held that the operation of the system over time washes out any significant effects from the initial set of holdings. As an example of the latter, if almost anyone would have bought a car from Henry Ford, the supposition that it was an arbitrary matter who held the money then (and so bought) would not place Henry Ford's earnings under a cloud. In any event, *his* coming to hold it is not arbitrary. Distribution according to benefits to others *is* a major patterned strand in a free capitalist society, as Hayek correctly points out, but it is only a strand and does not constitute the whole pattern of a system of entitlements (namely, inheritance, gifts for arbitrary reasons, charity, and so on) or a standard that one should insist a society fit. Will people tolerate for long a system yielding distributions that they believe are unpatterned?[6] No doubt people will not long accept a distribution they believe is *unjust*. People want their society to be and to look just. But must the look of justice reside in a resulting pattern rather than in the underlying generating principles? We are in no position to conclude that the inhabitants of a society embodying an entitlement conception of justice in holdings will find it unacceptable. Still, it must be granted that were people's reasons for transferring some of their holdings to others always irrational or arbitrary, we would find this disturbing. (Suppose people always determined what holdings they would transfer, and to whom, by using a random device.) We feel more comfortable upholding the justice of an entitlement system if most of the transfers under it are done for reasons. This does not mean necessarily that all deserve what holdings they receive. It means only that there is a purpose or point to someone's transferring a holding to one person rather than to another; that usually we can see what the transferrer thinks he's gaining, what cause he thinks he's serving, what goals he thinks he's helping to achieve, and so forth. Since in a capitalist society people often transfer holdings to others in accordance with how much they perceive these others benefiting them, the fabric constituted by the individual transactions and transfers is largely reasonable and intelligible.[7] (Gifts to loved ones, bequests to children, charity to the needy also are nonarbitrary components of the fabric.) In stressing the large strand of distribution in accordance with benefit to others, Hayek shows the point of many transfers, and so shows that the system of transfer of entitlements is not just spinning its gears aimlessly. The system of entitlements is defensible when constituted by the individual aims of individual transactions. No overarching aim is needed, no distributional pattern is required.

To think that the task of a theory of distributive justice is to fill in the blank in "to each according to his _____" is to be predisposed to search for a pattern; and the separate treatment of "from each according to his _____" treats production and distribution as two separate and independent issues. On an entitlement view these are *not* two separate questions. Whoever makes something, having bought or contracted for all other held resources used in the process (transferring some of his holdings for these cooperating factors), is entitled to it. The situation is *not* one of something's getting made, and there being an open question of who is to get it. Things come into the world already attached to people having entitlements over them. From the point of view of the historical entitlement conception of justice in holdings, those who start afresh to complete "to each according to his _____" treat objects as if they appeared from nowhere, out of nothing. A complete theory of justice might cover this limit case as well; perhaps here is a use for the usual conceptions of distributive justice.[8]

So entrenched are maxims of the usual form that perhaps we should present the entitlement conception as a competitor. Ignoring acquisition and rectification, we might say:

> From each according to what he chooses to do, to each according to what he makes for himself (perhaps with the contracted aid of others) and what others choose to do for him and choose to give him of what they've been given previously (under this maxim) and haven't yet expended or transferred.

This, the discerning reader will have noticed, has its defects as a slogan. So as a summary and great simplification (and not as a maxim with any independent meaning) we have:

> *From each as they choose, to each as they are chosen.*

HOW LIBERTY UPSETS PATTERNS

It is not clear how those holding alternative conceptions of distributive justice can reject the entitlement conception of justice in holdings. For suppose a distribution favored by one of these nonentitlement conceptions is realized. Let us suppose it is your favorite one and let us call this distribution D_1; perhaps everyone has an equal share, perhaps shares vary in accordance with some dimension you treasure. Now suppose that Wilt Chamberlain is greatly in demand by basketball teams, being a great gate attraction. (Also suppose contracts run only for a year, with players being free agents.) He signs the following sort of contract with a team: In each home game, twenty-five cents from the price of each ticket of admission goes to him. (We ignore the question of whether he is "gouging" the owners, letting them look out for themselves.) The season starts, and people cheerfully attend his team's games; they buy their tickets, each time dropping a separate twenty-five cents of their admission price into a special box with Chamberlain's name on it. They are excited about seeing him play; it is worth the total admission price to them. Let us suppose that in one season one million persons attend his home games, and Wilt Chamberlain winds up with $250,000, a much larger sum than the average income and larger even than anyone else has. Is he entitled to this income? Is this new distribution D_2, unjust? If so, why? There is *no* question about whether each of the people was entitled to the control over the resources they held in D_1; because that was the distribution (your favorite) that (for the purposes of argument) we assumed was acceptable. Each of these persons *chose* to give twenty-five cents of their money to Chamberlain. They could have spent it on going to the movies, or on candy bars, or on copies of *Dissent* magazine, or of *Monthly Review*. But they all, at least one million of them, converged on giving it to Wilt Chamberlain in exchange for watching him play basketball. If D_1 was a just distribution, and people voluntarily moved from it to D_2, transferring parts of their shares they were given under D_1 (what was it for if not to do something with?), isn't D_2 also just? If the people were entitled to dispose of the resources to which they were entitled (under D_1), didn't this include their being entitled to give it to, or exchange it with, Wilt Chamberlain? Can anyone else complain on grounds of justice? Each other person already has his legitimate share under D_1. Under D_1, there is nothing that anyone has that anyone else has a claim of justice against. After someone transfers something to Wilt Chamberlain, third parties *still* have their legitimate shares; *their* shares are not changed. By what process could such a transfer among two persons give rise to a legitimate claim of distributive justice on a portion of what was transferred, by a third party who had no claim of justice on any holding of the others *before* the transfer?[9] To cut off objections irrelevant here, we might imagine the exchanges occurring in a socialist society, after hours. After playing whatever basketball he does in his daily work, or doing whatever other daily work he does, Wilt Chamberlain decides to put in *overtime* to earn additional money. (First his work quota is set; he works time over that.) Or imagine it is a skilled juggler people like to see, who puts on shows after hours.

Why might someone work overtime in a society in which it is assumed their needs are satisfied? Perhaps because they care about things other than needs. I like to write in books that I read, and to have easy access to books for browsing at odd hours. It would be very pleasant and convenient to have the resources of Widener Library in my back yard. No society, I assume, will provide such resources close to each person who would like them as part of his regular allotment (under D_1). Thus, persons either must do without some extra things that they want, or be allowed to do something extra to get some of these things. On what basis could the inequalities that would eventuate be forbidden? Notice also that small factories would spring up in a socialist society, unless forbidden. I melt down some of my personal possessions (under D_1) and build a machine out of the material. I offer you, and others, a philosophy lecture once a week in exchange for your cranking the handle on my machine, whose products I exchange for yet other things, and so on. (The raw materials used by the machine are given to me by others who possess them under D_1, in exchange for hearing lectures.) Each person might participate to gain things over and above their allotment under D_1. Some persons even might want to leave their job in socialist industry and work full time in this private sector. I shall say something more about these issues in the next chapter. Here I wish merely to note how private property even in means of production would occur in a socialist society that did not forbid people to use as they wished some of the resources they are given under the socialist distribution D_1.[10] The socialist society would have to forbid capitalist acts between consenting adults.

The general point illustrated by the Wilt Chamberlain example and the example of the entrepreneur in a socialist society is that no end-state principle or distributional patterned principle of justice can be continuously realized without continuous interference with people's lives. Any favored pattern would be transformed into one unfavored by the principle, by people choosing to act in various ways; for example, by people exchanging goods and services with other people, or giving things to other people, things the transferrers are entitled to under the favored distributional pattern. To maintain a pattern one must either continually interfere to stop people from transferring resources as they wish to, or continually (or periodically) interfere to take from some persons resources that others for some reason chose to transfer to them. (But if some time limit is to be set on how long people may keep resources others voluntarily transfer to them, why let them keep these resources for *any* period of time? Why not have immediate confiscation?) It might be objected that all persons voluntarily will choose to refrain from actions which would upset the pattern. This presupposes unrealistically (1) that all will most want to maintain the pattern (are those who don't, to be "reeducated" or forced to undergo "self-criticism"?), (2) that each can gather enough information about his own actions and the ongoing activities of others to discover which of his actions will upset the pattern, and (3) that diverse and far-flung persons can coordinate their actions to dovetail into the pattern. Compare the manner in which the market is neutral among persons' desires, as it reflects and transmits widely scattered information via prices, and coordinates persons' activities.

It puts things perhaps a bit too strongly to say that every patterned (or end-state) principle is liable to be thwarted by the voluntary actions of the individual parties transferring some of their shares they receive under the principle. For perhaps some *very* weak patterns are not so thwarted.[11] Any distributional pattern with any egalitarian component is overturnable by the voluntary actions of individual persons over time; as is every patterned condition with sufficient content so as actually to have been proposed as presenting the central core of distributive justice. Still, given the possibility that some weak conditions or patterns may not be unstable in this way, it would be better to formulate an explicit description of the kind of interesting and contentful patterns under discussion, and to prove a theorem about their instability. Since the weaker the patterning, the more likely it is that the entitlement system itself satisfies it, a plausible conjecture is that any patterning either is unstable or is satisfied by the entitlement system.

LOCKE'S THEORY OF ACQUISITION

. . . We must introduce an additional bit of complexity into the structure of the entitlement theory. This is best approached by considering Locke's attempt to specify a principle of justice in acquisition. Locke views property rights in an unowned object as originating through someone's mixing his labor with it. This gives rise to many questions. What are the boundaries of what labor is mixed with? If a private astronaut clears a place on Mars, has he mixed his labor with (so that he comes to own) the whole planet, the whole uninhabited universe, or just a particular plot? Which plot does an act bring under ownership? The minimal (possibly disconnected) area such that an act decreases entropy in that area, and not elsewhere? Can virgin land (for the purposes of ecological investigation by high-flying airplane) come under ownership by a Lockean process? Building a fence around a territory presumably would make one the owner of only the fence (and the land immediately underneath it).

Why does mixing one's labor with something make one the owner of it? Perhaps because one owns one's labor, and so one comes to own a previously unowned thing that becomes permeated with what one owns. Ownership seeps over into the rest. But why isn't mixing what I own with what I don't own a way of losing what I own rather than a way of gaining what I don't? If I own a can of tomato juice and spill it in the sea so that its molecules (made radioactive, so I can check this) mingle evenly throughout the sea, do I thereby come to own the sea, or have I foolishly dissipated my tomato juice? Perhaps the idea, instead, is that laboring on something improves it and makes it more valuable; and anyone is entitled to own a thing whose value he has created. (Reinforcing this, perhaps, is the view that laboring is unpleasant. If some people made things effortlessly, as the cartoon characters in *The Yellow Submarine* trail flowers in their wake, would they have lesser claim to their own products whose making didn't *cost* them anything?) Ignore the fact that laboring on something may make it less valuable (spraying pink enamel paint on a piece of drift-wood that you have found). Why should one's entitlement extend to the whole object rather than just to the *added value* one's labor has produced? (Such reference to value might also serve to delimit the extent of ownership; for example, substitute "increases the value of" for "decreases entropy in" in the above entropy criterion.) No workable or coherent value-added property scheme has yet been devised, and any such scheme presumably would fall to objections (similar to those) that fell the theory of Henry George.

It will be implausible to view improving an object as giving full ownership to it, if the stock of unowned objects that might be improved is limited. For an object's coming under one person's ownership changes the situation of all others. Whereas previously they were at liberty (in Hohfeld's sense) to use the object, they now no longer are. This change in the situation of others (by removing their liberty to act on a previously unowned object) need not worsen their situation. If I appropriate a grain of sand from Coney Island, no one else may now do as they will with *that* grain of sand. But there are plenty of other grains of sand left for them to do the same with. Or if not grains of sand, then other things. Alternatively, the things I do with the grain of sand I appropriate might improve the position of others, counterbalancing their loss of the liberty to use that grain. The crucial point is whether appropriation of an unowned object worsens the situation of others.

Locke's proviso that there be "enough and as good left in common for others" (sect. 27) is meant to ensure that the situation of others is not worsened. . . .

Is the situation of persons who are unable to appropriate (there being no more accessible and useful unowned objects) worsened by a system allowing appropriation and permanent property? Here enter the various familiar social considerations favoring private property: it increases the social product by putting means of production in the hands of those who can use them most efficiently (profitably); experimentation is encouraged, because with separate persons controlling resources, there is no one person or small group whom someone with a new idea must convince to try it out; private property enables people to decide on the pattern and types of risks they wish to bear, leading to specialized types of risk bearing; private property protects future persons by leading some to hold back resources from current consumption for future markets; it provides alternate sources of employment for unpopular persons who don't have to convince any one person or small group to hire them, and so on. These considerations enter a Lockean theory to support the claim that appropriation of private property satisfies the intent behind the "enough and as good left over" proviso, *not* as a utilitarian justification of property. They enter to rebut the claim that because the proviso is violated no natural right to private property can arise by a Lockean process. The difficulty in working such an argument to show that the proviso is satisfied is in fixing the appropriate base line for comparison. Lockean appropriation makes people no worse off than they would be *how*?[12] This question of fixing the baseline needs more detailed investigation than we are able to give it here. It would be desirable to have an estimate of the general economic importance of original appropriation in order to see how much leeway there is for differing theories of appropriation and of the location of the baseline. Perhaps this importance can be measured by the percentage of all income that is based upon untransformed raw materials and given resources (rather than upon human actions), mainly rental income representing the unimproved value of land, and the price of raw material *in situ*, and by the percentage of current wealth which represents such income in the past.[13]

We should note that it is not only persons favoring *private* property who need a theory of how property rights legitimately originate. Those believing in collective property, for example those believing that a group of persons living in an area jointly own the territory, or its mineral resources, also must provide a theory of how such property rights arise; they must show why the persons living there have rights to determine what is done with the land and resources there that persons living elsewhere don't have (with regard to the same land and resources).

THE PROVISO

... A theory which includes this proviso in its principle of justice in acquisition must also contain a more complex principle of justice in transfer. Some reflection of the proviso about appropriation constrains later actions. If my appropriating all of a certain substance violates the Lockean proviso, then so does my appropriating some and purchasing all the rest from others who obtained it without otherwise violating the Lockean proviso. If the proviso excludes someone's appropriating all the drinkable water in the world, it also excludes his purchasing it all. (More weakly, and messily, it may exclude his charging certain prices for some of his supply.) This proviso (almost?) never will come into effect; the more someone acquires of a scarce substance which others want, the higher the price of the rest will go, and the more difficult it will become for him to acquire it all. But still, we can imagine, at least, that something like this occurs: someone makes simultaneous secret bids to the separate owners of a substance, each of whom sells assuming he can easily purchase more from the other owners; or some natural catastrophe destroys all of the supply of something except that in one person's possession. The total supply could not be permissibly appropriated by one person at the beginning. His later acquisition of it all does not show that the original appropriation violated the proviso. ... Rather, it is the combination of the original appropriation *plus* all the later transfers and actions that violates the Lockean proviso.

Each owner's title to his holding includes the historical shadow of the Lockean proviso on appropriation. This excludes his transferring it into an agglomeration that does violate the Lockean proviso and excludes his using it in a way, in co-ordination with others or independently of them, so as to violate the proviso by making the situation of others worse than their baseline situation. Once it is known that someone's ownership runs afoul of the Lockean proviso, there are stringent limits on what he may do with (what it is difficult any longer unreservedly to call) "his property." Thus a person may not appropriate the only water hole in a desert and charge what he will. Nor may he charge what he will if he possesses one, and unfortunately it happens that all the water holes in the desert dry up, except for his. This unfortunate circumstance, admittedly no fault of his, brings into operation the Lockean proviso and limits his property rights.[14] Similarly, an owner's property right in the only island in an area does not allow him to order a castaway from a shipwreck off his island as a trespasser, for this would violate the Lockean proviso. ...

The fact that someone owns the total supply of something necessary for others to stay alive does *not* entail that his (or anyone's) appropriation of anything left some people (immediately or later) in a situation worse than the baseline one. A medical researcher who synthesizes a new substance that effectively treats a certain disease and who refuses to sell except on his terms does not worsen the situation of others by depriving them of whatever he has appropriated. The others easily can possess the same materials he appropriated; the researcher's appropriation or purchase of chemicals didn't make those chemicals scarce in a way so as to violate the Lockean proviso. Nor would someone else's purchasing the total supply of the synthesized substance from the medical researcher. The fact that the medical researcher uses easily available chemicals to synthesize the drug no more violates the Lockean proviso than does the fact that the only surgeon able to perform a particular operation eats easily obtainable food in order to stay alive and to have the energy to work. This shows that the Lockean proviso is not an "end-state principle"; it focuses on a particular way that appropriative actions affect others, and not on the structure of the situation that results.

Intermediate between someone who takes all of the public supply and someone who makes the total supply out of easily obtainable substances is someone who appropriates the total supply of something in a way that does not deprive the others of it. For example, someone finds a new substance in an out-of-the-way place. He discovers that it effectively treats a certain disease and appropriates the total supply. He does not worsen the situation of others; if he did not stumble upon the substance no one else would have, and the others would remain without it. However, as time passes, the likelihood increases that others would have come across the substance; upon this fact might be based a limit to his property right in the substance so that others are not below their baseline position; for example, its bequest might be limited. The theme of someone worsening another's situation by depriving him of something he otherwise would possess may also illuminate the example of patents. An inventor's patent does not deprive others of an object which would not exist if not for the inventor. Yet patents would have this effect on others who independently invent the object. Therefore, these independent inventors, upon whom the burden of proving independent discovery may rest, should not be excluded from utilizing their own invention as they wish (including selling it to others). Furthermore, a known inventor drastically lessens the chances of actual independent invention. For persons who know of an invention usually will not try to reinvent it, and the notion of independent discovery here would be murky at best. Yet we may assume that in the absence of the original invention, sometime later someone else would have come up with it. This suggests placing a time limit on patents, as a rough rule of thumb to approximate how long it would have taken, in the absence of knowledge of the invention, for independent discovery.

I believe that the free operation of a market system will not actually run afoul of the Lockean proviso. . . . If this is correct, the proviso will not play a very important role in the activities of protective agencies and will not provide a significant opportunity for future state action. Indeed, were it not for the effects of previous *illegitimate* state action, people would not think the possibility of the proviso's being violated as of more interest than any other logical possibility. (Here I make an empirical historical claim; as does someone who disagrees with this.) This completes our indication of the complication in the entitlement theory introduced by the Lockean proviso.

Notes

1. Applications of the principle of justice in acquisition may also occur as part of the move from one distribution to another. You may find an unheld thing now and appropriate it. Acquisitions also are to be understood as included when, to simplify, I speak only of transitions by transfers.

2. See, however, the useful book by Boris Bittker, *The Case for Black Reparations* (New York: Random House, 1973).

3. If the principle of rectification of violations of the first two principles yields more than one description of holdings, then some choice must be made as to which of these is to be realized. Perhaps the sort of considerations about distributive justice and equality that I argue against play a legitimate role in *this* subsidiary choice. Similarly, there may be room for such considerations in deciding which otherwise arbitrary features a statute will embody, when such features are unavoidable because other considerations do not specify a precise line; yet a line must be drawn.

4. One might try to squeeze a patterned conception of distributive justice into the framework of the entitlement conception, by formulating a gimmicky obligatory "principle of transfer" that would lead to the pattern. For example, the principle that if one has more than the mean income one must transfer everything one holds above the mean to persons below the mean so as to bring them up to (but not over) the mean. We can formulate a criterion for a "principle of transfer" to rule out such obligatory transfers, or we can say that

no correct principle of transfer, no principle of transfer in a free society will be like this. The former is probably the better course, though the latter also is true.

Alternatively, one might think to make the entitlement conception instantiate a pattern, by using matrix entries that express the relative strength of a person's entitlements as measured by some real-valued function. But even if the limitation to natural dimensions failed to exclude this function, the resulting edifice would *not* capture our system of entitlements to *particular* things.

5. F. A. Hayek, *The Constitution of Liberty* (Chicago: University of Chicago Press, 1960), p. 87.

6. This question does not imply that they will tolerate any and every patterned distribution. In discussing Hayek's views, Irving Kristol has recently speculated that people will not long tolerate a system that yields distributions patterned in accordance with value rather than merit. ("'When Virtue Loses All Her Loveliness'—Some Reflections on Capitalism and 'The Free Society,'" *The Public Interest*, Fall 1970, pp. 3–15.) Kristol, following some remarks of Hayek's, equates the merit system with justice. Since some case can be made for the external standard of distribution in accordance with benefit to others, we ask about a weaker (and therefore more plausible) hypothesis.

7. We certainly benefit because great economic incentives operate to get others to spend much time and energy to figure out how to serve us by providing things we will want to pay for. It is not mere paradox mongering to wonder whether capitalism should be criticized for most rewarding and hence encouraging, not individualists like Thoreau who go about their own lives, but people who are occupied with serving others and winning them as customers. But to defend capitalism one need not think businessmen are the finest human types. (I do not mean to join here the general maligning of businessmen, either.) Those who think the finest should acquire the most can try to convince their fellows to transfer resources in accordance with *that* principle.

8. Varying situations continuously from that limit situation to our own would force us to make explicit the underlying rationale of entitlements and to consider whether entitlement considerations lexicographically precede the considerations of the usual theories of distributive justice, so that the *slightest* strand of entitlement outweighs the considerations of the usual theories of distributive justice.

9. Might not a transfer have instrumental effects on a third party, changing his feasible options? (But what if the two parties to the transfer independently had used their holdings in this fashion?) I discuss this question below, but note here that this question concedes the point for distributions of ultimate intrinsic noninstrumental goods (pure utility experiences, so to speak) that are transferrable. It also might be objected that the transfer might make a third party more envious because it worsens his position relative to someone else. I find it incomprehensible how this can be thought to involve a claim of justice. . . .

Here and elsewhere in this chapter, a theory which incorporates elements of pure procedural justice might find what I say acceptable, *if* kept in its proper place; that is, if background institutions exist to ensure the satisfaction of certain conditions on distributive shares. But if these institutions are not themselves the sum or invisible-hand result of people's voluntary (nonaggressive) actions, the constraints they impose require justification. At no point does *our* argument assume any background institutions more extensive than those of the minimal night-watchman state, a state limited to protecting persons against murder, assault, theft, fraud, and so forth.

10. See the selection from John Henry MacKay's novel. *The Anarchists*, reprinted in Leonard Krimmerman and Lewis Perry, eds., *Patterns of Anarchy* (New York: Doubleday Anchor Books, 1966), in which an individualist anarchist presses upon a communist anarchist the following question: "Would you, in the system of society which you call 'free Communism' prevent individuals from exchanging their labor among themselves by means of their own medium of exchange? And further: Would you prevent them from occupying land for the purpose of personal use?" The novel continues: "[the] question was not to be escaped. If he answered 'Yes!' he admitted that society had the right of control over the individual and threw overboard the autonomy of the individual which he had always zealously defended; if on the other hand, he answered 'No!' he admitted the right of private property which he had just denied so emphatically. . . . Then he answered 'In Anarchy any number of men must have the right of forming a voluntary association, and so realizing their ideas in practice. Nor can I understand how any one could justly be driven from the land and house which he uses and occupies . . . every serious man must declare himself: for Socialism, and thereby for force and against liberty, or for Anarchism, and thereby for liberty and against force.'" In contrast, we find Noam Chomsky

writing, "Any consistent anarchist must oppose private ownership of the means of production," "the consistent anarchist then . . . will be a socialist . . . of a particular sort." Introduction to Daniel Guerin, *Anarchism: From Theory to Practice* (New York: Monthly Review Press, 1970), pp. XIII, XV.

11. Is the patterned principle stable that requires merely that a distribution be Pareto-optimal? One person might give another a gift or bequest that the second could exchange with a third to their mutual benefit. Before the second makes this exchange, there is not Pareto-optimality. Is a stable pattern presented by a principle choosing that among the Pareto-optimal positions that satisfies some further condition C? It may seem that there cannot be a counterexample, for won't any voluntary exchange made away from a situation show that the first situation wasn't Pareto-optimal? (Ignore the implausibility of this last claim for the case of bequests.) But principles are to be satisfied over time, during which new possibilities arise. A distribution that at one time satisfies the criterion of Pareto-optimality might not do so when some new possibilities arise (Wilt Chamberlain grows up and starts playing basketball); and though people's activities will tend to move then to a new Pareto-optimal position, *this* new one need not satisfy the contentful condition C. Continual interference will be needed to insure the continual satisfaction of C. (The theoretical possibility of a pattern's being maintained by some invisible-hand process that brings it back to an equilibrium that fits the pattern when deviations occur should be investigated.)

12. Compare this with Robert Paul Wolff's "A Refutation of Rawls' Theorem on Justice," *Journal of Philosophy*, March 31, 1966, sect. 2. Wolff's criticism does not apply to Rawls' conception under which the baseline is fixed by the difference principle.

13. I have not seen a precise estimate. David Friedman. *The Machinery of Freedom* (N.Y.: Harper & Row, 1973), pp. XIV, XV, discusses this issue and suggests 5 percent of U.S. national income as an upper limit for the first two factors mentioned. However he does not attempt to estimate the percentage of current wealth which is based upon such income in the past. (The vague notion of "based upon" merely indicates a topic needing investigation.)

14. I discuss overriding and its moral traces in "Moral Complications and Moral Structures," *Natural Law Forum*, 1968, pp. 1–50.

JÜRGEN HABERMAS

~

INTRODUCTION

THOMAS A. MCCARTHY

Jürgen Habermas is the leading contemporary representative of the Frankfurt School of Critical Theory, the first generation of which included thinkers like Max Horkheimer, Theodor Adorno, Herbert Marcuse, and Walter Benjamin. Born in 1929 in Düsseldorf, Germany, he studied at the universities of Göttingen, Zurich, and Bonn after World War II, receiving the doctorate in 1954. From 1956 to 1959 he was Adorno's assistant at the Institute for Social Research in Frankfurt. After habilitating at Marburg University in 1961, he taught philosophy and sociology at the universities of Heidelberg and Frankfurt before becoming codirector-director of the Max Planck Institute in Starnberg in 1971. In 1983 he returned to the University of Frankfurt where he was a professor of philosophy until his retirement in 1994.

Habermas's life and work have been deeply influenced by the traumatic events of his youth under national socialism. From the time of his involvement with the German student movement in the 1960s, he has been one of Germany's most prominent public intellectuals, speaking out on a wide array of issues, from violations of civil liberties and attempts to "historicize" the Holocaust, to German reunification and European integration. These public interventions in the form of essays and lectures have been collected in the twelve volumes of his *Kleine Politische Schriften*.

Habermas's scholarly work, which aspires to a comprehensive critical theory of modern society, ranges across many of the humanities and social sciences. His earliest and latest theoretical writings focused on the normative foundations and empirical preconditions of democratic self-governance. Thus *The Structural Transformation of the Public Sphere* (1962) was a historical, sociological, and philosophical account of the rise of the classical liberal "public sphere" as an arena for critical public discussion of matters of general concern. While the historical features of the bourgeois public sphere reflected the particular constellation of interests that gave rise to it, Habermas argued, the idea it claimed to embody, of legitimating political authority through rational discussion and reasoned agreement, remained central to democratic theory. Thirty years later Habermas returned to these themes in his major political-theoretical work, *Between Facts and Norms* (1992), where he elaborated a "discourse theory" of deliberative democracy around the idea of legitimation by appeal to reasons that are tested in public discourse among free and equal citizens of a constitutional democracy.

One could read Habermas's extensive writings in the intervening years as a protracted examination of the cultural, psychological, and social preconditions for and barriers to the effective realization of this form of deliberative democracy. In the 1960s, in such works as *Theory and Practice* (1963), *On the Logic of the Social Sciences* (1967), and *Knowledge and Human Interests* (1968), he launched a methodological and episte-mological critique of positivism to clear the way for critical social theory as a means of enlightening political consciousness and guiding political practice. Over the next two decades, in such works as *Legitimation Crisis* (1973), *Communication and the Evolution of Society* (1976), *Moral Consciousness and Communicative Action* (1983), and *The Philosophical Discourse of Modernity* (1985), he developed the detailed accounts of communication, socialization, sociocultural development, rationality, morality, and legitimacy that were to serve as the underpinnings of his critical theory of modern society. That theory was given its most systematic statement in the two volumes of his monumental *Theory of Communicative Action* (1981), which highlighted the tendencies in contemporary society toward a "colonization of the lifeworld" by forces arising from the economy and the state, such that markets and bureaucracies have come increasingly to dominate in more and more spheres of modern life. Their relentless attack upon the "communicative infrastructures" of society can be contained, Habermas argued, only by a countervailing expansion of the power of public communication, in particular by effectively subordinating the operations of the economy and the government to in-formed, critical, public discourse.

In the years since the publication of *Between Facts and Norms*. Habermas has further elaborated his conception of deliberative democracy and demonstrated its relevance to current debates on multiculturalism, nationalism, globalization, and cosmopolitan-ism in a series of essays collected in such works as *The Inclusion of the Other* (1996), *The Post-national Constellation* (1998), *Between Naturalism and Religion* (2005) and *The Crisis of the European Union* (2011). The two essays included in this volume are taken from the first collection and are concerned more with conceptual and norma-tive issues in the theory of democracy than with empirical and critical questions of its actual practice. A central theme of both essays is what Habermas takes to be the "internal relation" in democratic theory between, on the one hand, the liberal stress on constitutionally guaranteed "negative liberties" that secure individual freedom of choice and, on the other hand, the republican emphasis on the "positive liberties" of political participation that underwrite popular sovereignty. The function of the system of basic citizenship rights, he argues, is simultaneously to secure *both* personal *and* po-litical autonomy; and the medium in which this is accomplished is modern positive law. Individual rights and liberties are an "enabling condition" of such law, and agreements arrived at through public discourse and negotiation are its only source of legitimation.

Universal morality alone cannot legitimate positive, enacted law. Rather, moral justi-fication is only one element of democratic decision-making processes that also include negotiation and compromise, pragmatic considerations, and "ethical" questions having to do with collective goods, values, and identities central to the self-understandings of particular democratic polities. As a result, constitutional "projects" to articulate and actualize the basic principles of democratic government and the basic rights of citizens ineluctably also express the particular cultural contexts and historical circumstances in which they are founded and developed. They are situated and continuing efforts, in ever changing circumstances, to interpret and embody in practices and institutions the ideal of democratic self-determination by free and equal citizens.

An important implication of Habermas's view of the internal relation between the basic values of liberal individualism and civic republicanism is that equal individual rights can be secured only through democratic public life; for substantive—in contrast to merely formal—equality requires coming to some common understanding about the specific respects in which citizens will be treated equally. As his remarks on the politics of women's equality illustrate, this in turn requires sensitivity to the systematic causes of de facto inequalities in citizens' capacities to exercise de jure equal rights. And that can be fostered and sustained, he argues, only through citizens' participation in public political discourse, for there is no other nonpaternalistic way to determine the concrete meaning and preconditions of equal rights, equal respect, equal consideration, equal treatment, and the like.

In this view, a central feature of democratic society is the political public sphere, about which Habermas wrote at the very beginning of his intellectual career. It is only through the informed, critical, public discussion of the governed that the administrative powers of government can be effectively monitored and channeled by the "communicative power" of citizens. Independent public forums, voluntary associations, social movements, and other networks and processes of unofficial communication in civil society, including the mass media, are the organs of democratic self-governance. And the culturally and politically mobilized publics who make use of them to identify, interpret, and debate social problems are its lifeblood. Not even constitutional principles are exempt from this public use of reason. Because public discourse is inherently open and reflexive, our understanding of the principles of justice must remain so as well. Normative political theory can do no more than spell out the basic conditions and presuppositions of democratic deliberation and leave all substantive matters to the public use of reason by participants themselves. Anything beyond this should be understood as a contribution to public debate and thus susceptible to all its vicissitudes.

There is a vast and growing secondary literature on Habermas in English. One might begin with his own account of his life and work in the collection of interviews edited by P. Dews, *Autonomy and Solidarity* (London: Verso, 1992), and with a general overview by D. Ingram, *Habermas: Introduction and Analysis* (Ithaca, N.Y.: Cornell University Press, 2010), B. Fultner (ed.), *Habermas: Key Concepts* (Durham, U.K.: Acumen, 2011), or K. Baynes, *Habermas* (New York: Routledge, 2013). General discussions of his work in the 1960s and 1970s can be found in T. McCarthy, *The Critical Theory of Jürgen Habermas* (Cambridge, Mass.: MIT Press, 1978), and of his work into the 1980s in S. Benhabib, *Critique, Norm, and Utopia* (New York: Columbia University Press, 1986). Raymond Geuss offers a critical study of Habermas's earlier work in *The Idea of a Critical Theory* (Cambridge: Cambridge University Press, 1982), and J. M. Bernstein of his later work in *Recovering Ethical Life* (London: Routledge, 1995). W. Rehg's *Insight and Solidarity* (Berkeley: University of California Press, 1994) provides a systematic treatment of Habermas's moral theory; various aspects of his political theory are examined in J. Bohman, *Public Deliberation: Pluralism, Complexity, and Democracy* (Cambridge, Mass.: MIT Press, 1996), C. Zurn, *Deliberative Democracy and Judicial Review* (Cambridge: Cambridge University Press, 2007), and T. Hedrick, *Rawls and Habermas* (Stanford, Calif.: Stanford University Press, 2007). Among the collections of critical essays on Habermas's work that contain useful discussions of his political thought are C. Calhoun (ed.), *Habermas and the Public Sphere* (Cambridge, Mass.: MIT Press, 1992), S. White (ed.), *The Cambridge Companion to Habermas* (Cambridge: Cambridge University Press, 1995), J. Meehan (ed.), *Feminists Read Habermas* (New York: Routledge, 1995), M. Rosenfeld and A. Arato (eds.), *Habermas on Law and Democracy* (Berkeley: University of California Press, 1998), and R. vom Schomberg and K. Baynes (eds.), *Discourse and Democracy* (Berkeley: University of California Press, 2002). Extensive bibliographies of other works by and on Habermas can be found at the *Habermas Forum* www.habermasforum.dk.

Three Normative Models of Democracy

In what follows I refer to the idealized distinction between the "liberal" and the "republican" understanding of politics—terms which mark the fronts in the current debate in the United States initiated by the so-called communitarians. Drawing on the work of Frank Michelman, I will begin by describing the two polemically contrasted models of democracy with specific reference to the concept of the citizen, the concept of law, and the nature of processes of political will-formation. In the second part, beginning with a critique of the "ethical overload" of the republican model, I introduce a third, procedural model of democracy for which I propose to reserve the term "deliberative politics."

I

The crucial difference between liberalism and republicanism consists in how the role of the democratic process is understood. According to the "liberal" view, this process accomplishes the task of programming the state in the interest of society, where the state is conceived as an apparatus of public administration, and society is conceived as a system of market-structured interactions of private persons and their labor. Here politics (in the sense of the citizens' political will-formation) has the function of bundling together and bringing to bear private social interests against a state apparatus that specializes in the administrative employment of political power for collective goals.

On the republican view, politics is not exhausted by this mediating function but is constitutive for the socialization process as a whole. Politics is conceived as the reflexive form of substantial ethical life. It constitutes the medium in which the members of quasi-natural solidary communities become aware of their dependence on one another and, acting with full deliberation as citizens, further shape and develop existing relations of reciprocal recognition into an association of free and equal consociates under law. With this, the liberal architectonic of government and society undergoes an important change. In addition to the hierarchical regulatory apparatus of sovereign state authority and the decentralized regulatory mechanism of the market—that is, besides administrative power and self-interest—*solidarity* appears as a third source of social integration.

This horizontal political will-formation aimed at mutual understanding or communicatively achieved consensus is even supposed to enjoy priority, both in a genetic and a normative sense. An autonomous basis in civil society independent of public administration and market-mediated private commerce is assumed as a precondition for the practice of civic self-determination. This

From *The Inclusion of the Other: Studies in Political Theory*, Cambridge, Mass.: The MIT Press, 1998. Reprinted by permission of The MIT Press.

basis prevents political communication from being swallowed up by the government apparatus or assimilated to market structures. Thus, on the republican conception, the political public sphere and its base, civil society, acquire a strategic significance. Together they are supposed to secure the integrative power and autonomy of the communicative practice of the citizens.[1] The uncoupling of political communication from the economy has as its counterpart a coupling of administrative power with the communicative power generated by political opinion- and will-formation.

These two competing conceptions of politics have different consequences.

(a) In the first place, their concepts of the citizen differ. According to the liberal view, the citizen's status is determined primarily by the individual rights he or she has vis-à-vis the state and other citizens. As bearers of individual rights citizens enjoy the protection of the government as long as they pursue their private interests within the boundaries drawn by legal statutes—and this includes protection against state interventions that violate the legal prohibition on government interference. Individual rights are negative rights that guarantee a domain of freedom of choice within which legal persons are freed from external compulsion. Political rights have the same structure: they afford citizens the opportunity to assert their private interests in such a way that, by means of elections, the composition of parliamentary bodies, and the formation of a government, these interests are finally aggregated into a political will that can affect the administration. In this way the citizens in their political role can determine whether governmental authority is exercised in the interest of the citizens as members of society.[2]

According to the republican view, the status of citizens is not determined by the model of negative liberties to which these citizens can lay claim as private persons. Rather, political rights—preeminently rights of political participation and communication—are positive liberties. They do not guarantee freedom from external compulsion, but guarantee instead the possibility of participating in a common practice, through which the citizens can first make themselves into what they want to be—politically responsible subjects of a community of free and equal citizens.[3] To this extent, the political process does not serve just to keep government activity under the surveillance of citizens who have already acquired a prior social autonomy through the exercise of their private rights and prepolitical liberties. Nor does it act only as a hinge between state and society, for democratic governmental authority is by no means an original authority. Rather, this authority proceeds from the communicative power generated by the citizens' practice of self-legislation, and it is legitimated by the fact that it protects this practice by institutionalizing public freedom.[4] The state's *raison d'être* does not lie primarily in the protection of equal individual rights but in the guarantee of an inclusive process of opinion- and will-formation in which free and equal citizens reach an understanding on which goals and norms lie in the equal interest of all. In this way the republican citizen is credited with more than an exclusive concern with his or her private interests.

(b) The polemic against the classical concept of the legal person as bearer of individual rights reveals a controversy about the concept of law itself. Whereas on the liberal conception the point of a legal order is to make it possible to determine which individuals in each case are entitled to which rights, on the republican conception these "subjective" rights owe their existence to an "objective" legal order that both enables and guarantees the integrity of an autonomous life in common based on equality and mutual respect. On the one view, the legal order is conceived in terms of individual rights; on the other, their objective legal content is given priority.

To be sure, this conceptual dichotomy does not touch on the *intersubjective* content of rights that demand reciprocal respect for rights and duties in symmetrical relations of recognition. But the republican concept at least points in the direction of a concept of law that accords equal weight to both the integrity of the individual and the integrity of the community in which persons as both individuals and members can first accord one another reciprocal recognition. It ties the legitimacy of the laws to the democratic procedure by which they are generated and thereby preserves an internal connection between the citizens' practice of self-legislation and the impersonal sway of the law:

> For republicans, rights ultimately are nothing but determinations of prevailing political will, while for liberals, some rights are always grounded in a "higher law" of transpolitical reason or revelation. . . . In a republican view, a community's objective, common good substantially consists in the success of its political endeavor to define, establish, effectuate, and sustain the set of rights (less tendentiously, laws) best suited to the conditions and *mores* of that community. Whereas in a contrasting liberal view, the higher-law rights provide the transactional structures and the curbs on power required so that pluralistic pursuit of diverse and conflicting interests may proceed as satisfactorily as possible.[5]

The right to vote, interpreted as a positive right, becomes the paradigm of rights as such, not only because it is constitutive for political self-determination, but because it shows how inclusion in a community of equals is connected with the individual right to make autonomous contributions and take personal positions on issues:

> The claim is that we all take an interest in each others' enfranchisement because (i) our choice lies between hanging together and hanging separately; (ii) hanging together depends on reciprocal assurances to all of having one's vital interests heeded by others; and (iii) in the deeply pluralized conditions of contemporary American society, such assurances are not attainable through virtual representation, but only by maintaining at least the semblance of a politics in which everyone is conceded a voice.[6]

This structure, read off from the political rights of participation and communication, is extended to *all* rights via the legislative process constituted by political rights. Even the authorization guaranteed by private law to pursue private, freely chosen goals simultaneously imposes an obligation to respect the limits of strategic action which are agreed to be in the equal interest of all.

(c) The different ways of conceptualizing the role of citizen and the law express a deeper disagreement about the nature of the political process. On the liberal view, politics is essentially a struggle for positions that grant access to administrative power. The political process of opinion- and will-formation in the public sphere and in parliament is shaped by the competition of strategically acting collectives trying to maintain or acquire positions of power. Success is measured by the citizens' approval of persons and programs, as quantified by votes. In their choices at the polls, voters express their preferences. Their votes have the same structure as the choices of participants in a market, in that their decisions license access to positions of power that political parties fight over with a success-oriented attitude similar to that of players in the market. The input of votes and the output of power conform to the same pattern of strategic action.

According to the republican view, the political opinion- and will-formation in the public sphere and in parliament does not obey the structures of market processes but rather the obstinate structures of a public communication oriented to mutual understanding. For politics as the citizens' practice of self-determination, the paradigm is not the market but dialogue. From this perspective there is a structural difference between communicative power, which proceeds from political communication in the form of discursively generated majority decisions, and the administrative power possessed by the governmental apparatus. Even the parties that struggle over access to positions of governmental power must bend themselves to the deliberative style and the stubborn character of political discourse:

> Deliberation . . . refers to a certain attitude toward social cooperation, namely, that of openness to persuasion by reasons referring to

the claims of others as well as one's own. The deliberative medium is a good faith exchange of views—including participants' reports of their own understanding of their respective vital interests—. . . in which a vote, if any vote is taken, represents a pooling of judgments.[7]

Hence the conflict of opinions conducted in the political arena has legitimating force not just in the sense of an authorization to occupy positions of power; on the contrary, the ongoing political discourse also has binding force for the way in which political authority is exercised. Administrative power can only be exercised on the basis of policies and within the limits laid down by laws generated by the democratic process.

II

So much for the comparison between the two models of democracy that currently dominate the discussion between the so-called communitarians and liberals, above all in the US. The republican model has advantages and disadvantages. In my view it has the advantage that it preserves the radical democratic meaning of a society that organizes itself through the communicatively united citizens and does not trace collective goals back to "deals" made between competing private interests. Its disadvantage, as I see it, is that it is too idealistic in that it makes the democratic process dependent on the virtues of citizens devoted to the public weal. For politics is not concerned in the first place with questions of ethical self-understanding. The mistake of the republican view consists in an ethical foreshortening of political discourse.

To be sure, ethical discourses aimed at achieving a collective self-understanding—discourses in which participants attempt to clarify how they understand themselves as members of a particular nation, as members of a community or a state, as inhabitants of a region, etc., which traditions they wish to cultivate, how they should treat each other, minorities, and marginal groups, in what sort of society they want to live—constitute an

important part of politics. But under conditions of cultural and social pluralism, behind politically relevant goals there often lie interests and value-orientations that are by no means constitutive of the identity of the political community as a whole, that is, for the totality of an intersubjectively shared form of life. These interests and value-orientations, which conflict with one another within the same polity without any prospect of consensual resolution, need to be counterbalanced in a way that cannot be effected by ethical discourse, even though the results of this nondiscursive counterbalancing are subject to the proviso that they must not violate the basic values of a culture. The balancing of interests takes the form of reaching a compromise between parties who rely on their power and ability to sanction. Negotiations of this sort certainly presuppose a readiness to cooperate, that is, a willingness to abide by the rules and to arrive at results that are acceptable to all parties, though for different reasons. But compromise-formation is not conducted in the form of a rational discourse that neutralizes power and excludes strategic action. However, the fairness of compromises is measured by presuppositions and procedures which for their part are in need of rational, indeed normative, justification from the standpoint of justice. In contrast with ethical questions, questions of justice are not by their very nature tied to a particular collectivity. Politically enacted law, if it is to be legitimate, must be at least in harmony with moral principles that claim a general validity that extends beyond the limits of any concrete legal community.

The concept of deliberative politics acquires empirical relevance only when we take into account the multiplicity of forms of communication in which a common will is produced, that is, not just ethical self-clarification but also the balancing of interests and compromise, the purposive choice of means, moral justification, and legal consistency-testing. In this process the two types of politics which Michelman distinguishes in an ideal-typical fashion can interweave and complement one another in a rational manner.

"Dialogical" and "instrumental" politics can *interpenetrate* in the medium of deliberation if the corresponding forms of communication are sufficiently institutionalized. Everything depends on the conditions of communication and the procedures that lend the institutionalized opinion- and will-formation their legitimating force. The third model of democracy, which I would like to propose, relies precisely on those conditions of communication under which the political process can be presumed to produce rational results because it operates deliberatively at all levels.

Making the proceduralist conception of deliberative politics the cornerstone of the theory of democracy results in differences both from the republican conception of the state as an ethical community and from the liberal conception of the state as the guardian of a market society. In comparing the three models, I take my orientation from that dimension of politics which has been our primary concern, namely, the democratic opinion- and will-formation that issue in popular elections and parliamentary decrees.

According to the liberal view, the democratic process takes place exclusively in the form of compromises between competing interests. Fairness is supposed to be guaranteed by rules of compromise-formation that regulate the general and equal right to vote, the representative composition of parliamentary bodies, their order of business, and so on. Such rules are ultimately justified in terms of liberal basic rights. According to the republican view, by contrast, democratic will-formation is supposed to take the form of an ethical discourse of self-understanding; here deliberation can rely for its content on a culturally established background consensus of the citizens, which is rejuvenated through the ritualistic reenactment of a republican founding act. Discourse theory takes elements from both sides and integrates them into the concept of an ideal procedure for deliberation and decision making. Weaving together negotiations and discourses of self-understanding and of justice, this democratic procedure grounds the presumption that under

such conditions reasonable or fair results are obtained. According to this proceduralist view, practical reason withdraws from universal human rights or from the concrete ethical life of a specific community into the rules of discourse and forms of argumentation that derive their normative content from the validity-basis of action oriented to reaching understanding, and ultimately from the structure of linguistic communication.[8]

These descriptions of the structures of democratic process set the stage for different normative conceptualizations of state and society. The sole presupposition is a public administration of the kind that emerged in the early modern period together with the European state system and in functional interconnection with a capitalist economic system. According to the republican view, the citizens' political opinion- and will-formation forms the medium through which society constitutes itself as a political whole. Society is centered in the state; for in the citizens' practice of political self-determination the polity becomes conscious of itself as a totality and acts on itself via the collective will of the citizens. Democracy is synonymous with the political self-organization of society. This leads to a polemical understanding of politics as directed against the state apparatus. In Hannah Arendt's political writings one can see the thrust of republican arguments: in opposition to the civic privatism of a depoliticized population and in opposition to the acquisition of legitimation through entrenched parties, the political public sphere should be revitalized to the point where a regenerated citizenry can, in the forms of a decentralized self-governance, (once again) appropriate the governmental authority that has been usurped by a self-regulating bureaucracy.

According to the liberal view, this separation of the state apparatus from society cannot be eliminated but only bridged by the democratic process. However, the weak normative connotations of a regulated balancing of power and interests stands in need of constitutional channeling. The democratic will-formation of self-interested citizens, construed in minimalist terms, constitutes just one element within a constitution that disciplines governmental authority through normative constraints (such as basic rights, separation of powers, and legal regulation of the administration) and forces it, through competition between political parties, on the one hand, and between government and opposition, on the other, to take adequate account of competing interests and value orientations. This state-centered understanding of politics does not have to rely on the unrealistic assumption of a citizenry capable of acting collectively. Its focus is not so much the input of a rational political will-formation but the output of successful administrative accomplishments. The thrust of liberal arguments is directed against the disruptive potential of an administrative power that interferes with the independent social interactions of private persons. The liberal model hinges not on the democratic self-determination of deliberating citizens but on the legal institutionalization of an economic society that is supposed to guarantee an essentially nonpolitical common good through the satisfaction of the private aspirations of productive citizens.

Discourse theory invests the democratic process with normative connotations stronger than those of the liberal model but weaker than those of the republican model. Once again, it takes elements from both sides and fits them together in a new way. In agreement with republicanism, it gives center stage to the process of political opinion- and will-formation, but without understanding the constitution as something secondary; on the contrary, it conceives the basic principles of the constitutional state as a consistent answer to the question of how the demanding communicative presuppositions of a democratic opinion- and will-formation can be institutionalized. Discourse theory does not make the success of deliberative politics depend on a collectively acting citizenry but on the institutionalization of corresponding procedures. It no longer operates with the concept of a social whole centered in the state and conceived as a goal-oriented subject writ large. But neither does it localize the whole in a system of constitutional norms mechanically regulating the interplay of powers and interests in accordance with the market model. Discourse theory altogether jettisons the assumptions of the philosophy of consciousness, which invite us either to ascribe the citizens' practice of self-determination to one encompassing macro-subject or to apply the anonymous rule of law to competing individuals. The former approach represents the citizenry as a collective actor which reflects the whole and acts for its sake; on the latter, individual actors function as dependent variables in systemic processes that unfold blindly because no consciously executed collective decisions are possible over and above individual acts of choice (except in a purely metaphorical sense).

Discourse theory works instead with the *higher-level intersubjectivity* of communication processes that unfold in the institutionalized deliberations in parliamentary bodies, on the one hand, and in the informal networks of the public sphere, on the other. Both within and outside parliamentary bodies geared to decision making, these subjectless modes of communication form arenas in which a more or less rational opinion- and will-formation concerning issues and problems affecting society as a whole can take place. Informal opinion-formation result in institutionalized election decisions and legislative decrees through which communicatively generated power is transformed into administratively utilizable power. As on the liberal model, the boundary between state and society is respected; but here civil society, which provides the social underpinning of autonomous publics, is as distinct from the economic system as it is from the public administration. This understanding of democracy leads to the normative demand for a new balance between the three resources of money, administrative power, and solidarity from which modern societies meet their need for integration and regulation. The normative implications are obvious: the integrative force of solidarity, which can no longer be drawn solely from sources of communicative action, should develop through widely expanded autonomous public spheres as well as through legally institutionalized procedures of democratic deliberation and decision making and gain sufficient strength to hold its own against the other two social forces—money and administrative power.

III

This view has implications for how one should understand legitimation and popular sovereignty. On the liberal view, democratic will-formation has the exclusive function of *legitimating* the exercise of political power. The outcomes of elections license the assumption of governmental power, though the government must justify the use of power to the public and parliament. On the republican view, democratic will-formation has the significantly stronger function of *constituting* society as a political community and keeping the memory of this founding act alive with each new election. The government is not only empowered by the electorate's choice between teams of leaders to exercise a largely open mandate, but is also bound in a programmatic fashion to carry out certain policies. More a committee than an organ of the state, it is part of a self-governing political community rather than the head of a separate governmental apparatus. Discourse theory, by contrast, brings a third idea into play: the procedures and communicative presuppositions of democratic opinion- and will-formation function as the most important sluices for the discursive rationalization of the decisions of a government and an administration bound by law and statute. On this view, *rationalization* signifies more than mere legitimation but less than the constitution of political power. The power available to the administration changes its general character once it is bound to a process of democratic opinion- and will-formation that does not merely retrospectively monitor the exercise of political power but also programs it in a certain way. Notwithstanding this discursive rationalization, only the political system itself can "act." It is a subsystem specialized for collectively binding decisions, whereas the communicative structures of the public sphere comprise a far-flung network of sensors that respond to the pressure of society-wide problems and stimulate influential opinions. The public opinion which is worked up via democratic procedures into communicative power cannot itself "rule" but can only channel the use of administrative power in specific directions.

The concept of *popular sovereignty* stems from the republican appropriation and revaluation of the early modern notion of sovereignty originally associated with absolutist regimes. The state, which monopolizes the means of legitimate violence, is viewed as a concentration of power which can overwhelm all other temporal powers. Rousseau transposed this idea, which goes back to Bodin, to the will of the united people, fused it with the classical idea of the self-rule of free and equal citizens, and sublimated it into the modern concept of autonomy. Despite this normative sublimation, the concept of sovereignty remained bound to the notion of an embodiment in the (at first actually physically assembled) people. According to the republican view, the at least potentially assembled people are the bearers of a sovereignty that cannot in principle be delegated: in their capacity as sovereign, the people cannot let themselves be represented by others. Constitutional power is founded on the citizens' practice of self-determination, not on that of their representatives. Against this, liberalism offers the more realistic view that, in the constitutional state, the authority emanating from the people is exercised only "by means of elections and voting and by specific legislative, executive, and judicial organs."[9]

These two views exhaust the alternatives only on the dubious assumption that state and society must be conceived in terms of a whole and its parts, where the whole is constituted either by a sovereign citizenry or by a constitution. By contrast to the discourse theory of democracy corresponds the image of a *decentered* society, though with the political public sphere it sets apart an arena for the detection, identification, and interpretation of problems affecting society as a whole.

If we abandon the conceptual framework of the philosophy of the subject, sovereignty need neither be concentrated in the people in a concretistic manner nor banished into the anonymous agencies established by the constitution. The "self" of the self-organizing legal community disappears in the subjectless forms of communication that regulate the flow of discursive opinion- and will-formation whose fallible results enjoy the presumption of rationality. This is not to repudiate the intuition associated with the idea of popular sovereignty but rather to interpret it in intersubjective terms. Popular sovereignty, even though it has become anonymous, retreats into democratic procedures and the legal implementation of their demanding communicative presuppositions only to be able to make itself felt as communicatively generated power. Strictly speaking, this communicative power springs from the interactions between legally institutionalized will-formation and culturally mobilized publics. The latter for their part find a basis in the associations of a civil society distinct from the state and the economy alike.

The normative self-understanding of deliberative politics does indeed call for a discursive mode of socialization for the *legal community;* but this mode does not extend to the whole of the society in which the constitutionally established political system is *embedded.* Even on its own proceduralist self-understanding, deliberative politics remains a component of a complex society, which as a whole resists the normative approach of legal theory. In this regard, the discourse-theoretic reading of democracy connects with an objectifying sociological approach that regards the political system neither as the peak nor the center, nor even as the structuring model of society, but as just *one* action system among others. Because it provides a kind of surety for the solution of the social problems that threaten integration, politics must indeed be able to communicate, via the medium of law, with all of the other legitimately ordered spheres of action, however these may be structured and steered. But the political system remains dependent on other functional mechanisms, such as the revenue-production of the economic system, in

more than just a trivial sense; on the contrary, deliberative politics, whether realized in the formal procedures of institutionalized opinion- and will-formation or only in the informal networks of the political public sphere, stands in an internal relation to the contexts of a rationalized lifeworld that meets it halfway. Deliberatively filtered political communications are especially dependent on the resources of the lifeworld—on a free and open political culture and an enlightened political socialization, and above all on the initiatives of opinion-shaping associations. These resources emerge and regenerate themselves spontaneously for the most part—at any rate, they can only with difficulty be subjected to political control.

Notes

1. Cf. H. Arendt, *On Revolution* (New York, 1965); *On Violence* (New York, 1970).

2. Cf. F. I. Michelman, "Political Truth and the Rule of Law," *Tel Aviv University Studies in Law* 8 (1988): 283: "The political society envisioned by bumper-sticker republicans is the society of private rights bearers, an association whose first principle is the protection of the lives, liberties, and estates of its individual members. In that society, the state is justified by the protection it gives to those prepolitical interests; the purpose of the constitution is to ensure that the state apparatus, the government, provides such protection for the people at large rather than serves the special interests of the governors or their patrons; the function of citizenship is to operate the constitution and thereby to motivate the governors to act according to that protective purpose; and the value to you of your political franchise—your right to vote and speak, to have your views heard and counted—is the handle it gives you on influencing the system so that it will adequately heed and protect *your* particular, prepolitical rights and other interests."

3. On the distinction between positive and negative freedom see Ch. Taylor, "What is Human Agency?" in *Human Agency and Language: Philosophical Papers 1* (Cambridge, 1985), pp. 15–44.

4. Michelman, "Political Truth and the Rule of Law," p. 284: "In [the] civic constitutional vision, political society is primarily the society not of rights bearers, but of citizens, an association whose first principle is the creation and provision of a public realm within

which a people, together, argue and reason about the right terms of social coexistence, terms that they will set together and which they understand as comprising their common good. . . . Hence, the state is justified by its purpose of establishing and ordering the public sphere within which persons can achieve freedom in the sense of self-government by the exercise of reason in public dialogue."

5. Michelman, "Conceptions of Democracy in American Constitutional Argument: Voting Rights," *Florida Law Review* 41 (1989): 446f. (hereafter "Voting Rights").

6. Michelman, "Voting Rights," p. 484.

7. Michelman, "Conceptions of Democracy in American Constitutional Argument: The Case of Pornography Regulation," *Tennessee Law Review* 291 (1989): 293.

8. Cf. J. Habermas, "Popular Sovereignty as Procedure," in *Between Facts and Norms*, trans. W. Rehg (1996), pp. 463–490.

9. Cf. *The Basic Law of the Federal Republic of Germany*, article 20, sec. 2.

On the Internal Relation Between the Rule of Law and Democracy

In academia we often mention law and politics in the same breath, yet at the same time we are accustomed to consider law, the rule of law, and democracy as subjects of different disciplines: jurisprudence deals with law, political science with democracy, and each deals with the constitutional state in its own way—jurisprudence in normative terms, political science from an empirical standpoint. The scholarly division of labor continues to operate even when legal scholars attend to law and the rule of law, on the one hand, and will-formation in the constitutional state, on the other; or when social scientists, in the role of sociologists of law, examine law and the constitutional state and, in the role of political scientists, examine the democratic process. The constitutional state and democracy appear to us as entirely separate objects. There are good reasons for this. Because political rule is always exercised in the form of law, legal systems exist where political force has not yet been domesticated by the constitutional state. And constitutional states exist where the power to govern has not yet been democratized. In short, there are legally ordered governments without constitutional institutions and there are constitutional states without democratic constitutions. Of course, these empirical grounds for a division of labor in the academic treatment of the two subjects by no means imply that from a normative

standpoint, the constitutional state could exist without democracy.

In this paper I want to treat several aspects of this internal relation between the rule of law and democracy. This relation results from the concept of modern law itself (section 1) as well as from the fact that positive law can no longer draw its legitimacy from a higher law (section 2). Modern law is legitimated by the autonomy guaranteed equally to each citizen, and in such a way that private and public autonomy reciprocally presuppose each other (section 3). This conceptual interrelation also makes itself felt in the dialectic of legal and factual equality. It was this dialectic that first elicited the social-welfare paradigm of law as a response to the liberal understanding of law, and today this same dialectic necessitates a proceduralist self-understanding of constitutional democracy (section 4). In closing I will elucidate this proceduralist legal paradigm with the example of the feminist politics of equality (section 5).

1 FORMAL PROPERTIES OF MODERN LAW

Since Locke, Rousseau, and Kant, a certain concept of law has gradually prevailed not only in philosophical thought but in the constitutional reality of Western societies. This concept is supposed to account simultaneously for both the positivity and the freedom-guaranteeing character of coercible law. The positivity of law—the fact that norms backed by the threat of state sanction stem from the changeable decisions of a political lawgiver—is bound up with the demand for legitimation. According to this demand, positively enacted law should guarantee the autonomy of all legal persons equally; and the democratic procedure of legislation should in turn satisfy this demand. In this way, an internal relation is established between the coercibility and changeability of positive law on the one hand, and a mode of lawmaking that engenders legitimacy on the other. Hence from a normative perspective there is a conceptual or internal relation—and not simply a historically, accidental relation—between law and democracy, between legal theory and democratic theory.

At first glance, the establishment of this internal relation has the look of a philosophical trick. Yet, as a matter of fact, the relation is deeply rooted in the presuppositions of our everyday practice of law. For in the mode of validity that attaches to law, the facticity of the state's legal enforcement is intermeshed with the legitimating force of a legislative procedure that claims to be rational in that it guarantees freedom. This is shown in the peculiar ambivalence with which the law presents itself to its addressees and expects their obedience: that is, it leaves its addressees free to approach the law in either of two ways. They can either consider norms merely as factual constraints on their freedom and take a strategic approach to the calculable consequences of possible rule-violations, or they can comply with legal statutes in a performative attitude, indeed comply out of respect for results of a common will-formation that claim legitimacy. Kant already expressed this point with his concept of "legality," which highlighted the connection between these two moments without which legal obedience cannot be reasonably expected: legal norms must be fashioned so that they can be viewed simultaneously in two ways, as coercive and as laws of freedom. These two aspects belong to our understanding of modern law: we consider the validity of a legal norm as equivalent to the explanation that the state can simultaneously guarantee factual enforcement and legitimate enactment—thus it can guarantee, on the one hand, the legality of behavior in the sense of average compliance, which can if necessary be compelled by sanctions; and, on the other hand, the legitimacy of the rule itself, which must always make it possible to comply with the norm out of respect for the law.

Of course, this immediately raises the question of how the legitimacy of rules should be grounded when the rules in question can be changed at any time by the political legislator. Constitutional norms too are changeable; and even the basic norms that the constitution itself has declared nonamendable share with all positive law the fate that they can be abrogated, say, after a change of regime. As long as one was able to fall back on a religiously or metaphysically grounded natural law, the whirlpool of temporality enveloping positive law could be held in check by morality. Situated in a hierarchy of law, temporalized positive law was supposed to remain *subordinate* to an eternally valid moral law, from which it was to receive its lasting orientations. But even aside from the fact that in pluralistic societies such integrating worldviews and collectively binding comprehensive doctrines have in any case disintegrated, modern law, simply by virtue of its formal properties, resists the direct control of a posttraditional morality of conscience, which is, so to speak, all we have left.

2 THE COMPLEMENTARY RELATION BETWEEN POSITIVE LAW AND AUTONOMOUS MORALITY

Modern legal systems are constructed on the basis of individual rights. Such rights have the character of releasing legal persons from moral obligations in a carefully circumscribed manner. By introducing rights that concede to agents the latitude to act according to personal preferences, modern law as a whole implements the principle that whatever is not explicitly prohibited is permitted. Whereas in morality an inherent symmetry exists between rights and duties, legal duties are a consequence of entitlements, that is, they result only from statutory constraints on individual liberties. This basic conceptual privileging of rights over duties is explained by the modern concepts of the "legal person" and of the "legal community." The moral universe, which is *unlimited* in social space and historical time, includes *all natural persons* with their complex life histories; morality itself extends to the protection of the integrity of fully individuated persons (*Einzelner*). By contrast, the legal community, which is always localized in space and time, protects the integrity of its members precisely insofar as they acquire the artificial status of *rights bearers*. For this reason, the relation between law and morality is more one of complementarity than of subordination.

The same is true if one compares their relative scope. The matters that require legal regulation are at once both narrower and broader in scope than morally relevant concerns: narrower inasmuch as legal regulation has access only to external, that is, coercible, behavior, and broader inasmuch as law, as an organizational form of politics, pertains not only to the regulations of interpersonal conflicts but also to the pursuit of political goals and the implementation of policies. Hence legal regulations touch not only on moral questions in the narrow sense, but also on pragmatic and ethical questions, and on forming compromises among conflicting interests. Moreover, unlike the clearly delimited normative validity claimed by moral norms, the *legitimacy* claimed by legal norms is based on various sorts of reasons. The legislative practice of justification depends on a complex network of discourses and bargaining, and not just on moral discourse.

The idea from natural law of a hierarchy of laws at different levels of dignity is misleading. Law is better understood as a functional complement to morality. As positively valid, legitimately enacted, and actionable, law can relieve the morally judging and acting person of the considerable cognitive, motivational, and organizational demands of a morality based entirely on individual conscience. Law can compensate for the weaknesses of a highly demanding morality that—if we judge from its empirical results—provides only cognitively indeterminate and motivationally unreliable results. Naturally, this does not absolve legislators and judges from the concern that the law be in harmony with morality. But legal regulations are too concrete to be legitimated solely through their compatibility with moral principles. From what, then, can positive law borrow its legitimacy, if not from a superior moral law?

Like morality, law too is supposed to protect the autonomy of all persons equally. Law too must prove its legitimacy under this aspect of securing freedom. Interestingly enough, though, the positive character of law forces autonomy to split up in a peculiar way, which has no parallel in morality. Moral self-determination in Kant's sense is a unified concept insofar as it demands of each person, *in propria persona*, that she obey just those norms that she herself posits according to her own impartial judgment, or according to a judgment reached in common with all other persons. However, the binding quality of legal norms does not stem solely from processes of opinion- and will-formation, but arises also from the collectively binding decisions of authorities who make and apply law. This circumstance makes it conceptually necessary to distinguish the role of authors who make (and adjudicate) law from that of addressees who are subject to established law. The autonomy that in the moral domain is all of a piece, so to speak, appears in the legal domain only in the dual form of private and public autonomy.

However, these two moments must then be mediated in such a way that the one form of autonomy does not detract from the other. Each form of autonomy, the individual liberties of the subject of private law and the public autonomy of the citizen, makes the other form possible. This reciprocal relation is expressed by the idea that legal persons can be autonomous only insofar as they can understand themselves, in the exercise of their civic rights, as authors of just those rights which they are supposed to obey as addressees.

3 THE MEDIATION OF POPULAR SOVEREIGNTY AND HUMAN RIGHTS

It is therefore not surprising that modern natural law theories have answered the legitimation question by referring, on the one hand, to the principle of *popular sovereignty* and, on the other, to the *rule of law* as guaranteed by human rights. The principle of popular sovereignty is expressed in rights of communication and participation that secure the public autonomy of citizens; the rule of law is expressed in those classical basic rights that guarantee the private autonomy of members of society. Thus the law is legitimated as an instrument for the equal protection of private and public autonomy. To be sure, political philosophy has never really been able to strike a balance between popular sovereignty and human rights, or between the "freedom of the ancients" and the "freedom of the moderns." The political autonomy of citizens is supposed to be embodied in the self-organization of a community that gives itself its laws through the sovereign will of the people. The private autonomy of citizens, on the other hand, is supposed to take the form of basic rights that guarantee the anonymous rule of law. Once the issue is set up in this way, either idea can be upheld only at the expense of the other. The intuitively plausible co-originality of both ideas falls by the wayside.

Republicanism, which goes back to Aristotle and the political humanism of the Renaissance, has always given the public autonomy of citizens priority over the prepolitical liberties of private persons. *Liberalism*, which goes back to John Locke, has invoked the danger of tyrannical majorities and postulated the priority of human rights. According to republicanism, human rights owed their legitimacy to the ethical self-understanding and sovereign self-determination achieved by a political community; in liberalism, such rights were supposed to provide, from the very start, legitimate barriers that prevented the sovereign will of the people from encroaching on inviolable spheres of individual freedom. In their concepts of the legal person's autonomy, Rousseau and Kant certainly aimed to conceive of sovereign will and practical reason as unified in such a way that popular sovereignty and human rights would reciprocally interpret one another. But even they failed to do justice to the co-originality of the two ideas; Rousseau suggests more of a republican reading, Kant more of a liberal one. They missed the intuition they wanted to articulate: that the idea of human rights, which is expressed in the right to equal individual liberties, must neither be merely imposed on the sovereign legislator as an external barrier, nor be instrumentalized as a functional requisite for legislative goals.

To express this intuition properly it helps to view the democratic procedure—which alone provides legitimating force to the law-making process in the context of social and ideological pluralism—from a discourse-theoretical standpoint. Here I assume a principle that I cannot discuss in detail, namely, that a regulation may claim legitimacy only if all those possibly affected by it could consent to it after participating in rational discourses. Now, if discourses—and bargaining processes as well, whose fairness is based on discursively grounded procedures—represent the place where a reasonable political will can develop, then the presumption of reasonability, which the democratic procedure is supposed to ground, ultimately rests on an elaborate communicative arrangement: the presumption depends on the conditions under which one can legally institutionalize the forms of communication necessary for legitimate law-making. In that case, the desired internal relation between human rights and popular sovereignty consists in this: human rights themselves are what satisfy the requirement that a civic practice of the public use of communicative freedom be legally institutionalized. Human rights, which make the exercise of popular sovereignty legally possible, cannot be imposed on this practice as an external constraint. Enabling conditions must not be confused with such constraints.

Naturally, this analysis is at first plausible only for those political civil rights, specifically the rights of communication and participation, that safeguard the exercise of political autonomy. It is less plausible for the classical human rights that guarantee the citizens' private autonomy. Here we think in the first instance of the fundamental right to the greatest possible degree of equal individual liberties, though also of basic rights that constitute membership status in a state and provide the individual with comprehensive legal protection. These rights, which are meant to guarantee everyone an equal opportunity to pursue his or her private conception of the good, have an intrinsic value, or at least they are not reducible to their instrumental value for democratic will-formation. We will do justice to the intuition that the classical liberties are co-original with political rights only if we state more precisely the thesis that human rights legally enable the citizens' practice of self-determination. I turn now to this more precise statement.

4 THE RELATION BETWEEN PRIVATE AND PUBLIC AUTONOMY

However well-grounded human rights are, they may not be paternalistically foisted, as it were, on a sovereign. Indeed, the idea of citizens' legal autonomy demands that the addressees of law be able to understand themselves at the same time as its authors. It would contradict this idea if the democratic legislator were to discover human rights as though they were (preexisting) moral facts that one merely needs to enact as positive law. At the same time, one must also not forget that when citizens occupy the role of co-legislators they are no longer free to choose the medium in which alone they can realize their autonomy. They participate in legislation only as legal subjects; it is no longer in their power to decide which language they will make use of. The democratic idea of self-legislation *must* acquire its validity in the medium of law itself.

However, when citizens judge in the light of the discourse principle whether the law they make is legitimate, they do so under communicative presuppositions that must themselves be legally institutionalized in the form of political civil rights, and for such institutionalization to occur, the legal code as such must be available. But in order to establish this legal code it is necessary to create the status of legal persons who as bearers of individual rights belong to a voluntary association of citizens and when necessary effectively claim their rights. There is no law without the private autonomy of legal persons in general. Consequently, without basic rights that secure the private autonomy of citizens there is also no medium for legally institutionalizing the conditions under which these citizens, as citizens of a state, can make use of their public autonomy. Thus private and public autonomy mutually presuppose each other in such a way that neither human rights nor popular sovereignty can claim primacy over its counterpart.

This mutual presupposition expresses the intuition that, on the one hand, citizens can make adequate use of their public autonomy only if, on the basis of their equally protected private autonomy, they are sufficiently independent; but that, on the other hand, they can arrive at a consensual regulation of their private autonomy only if they make adequate use of their political autonomy as enfranchised citizens.

The internal relation between the rule of law and democracy has been concealed long enough by the competition between the legal paradigms that have been dominant up to the present. The liberal legal paradigm reckons with an economic society that is institutionalized through private law—above all through property rights and contractual freedom—and left to the spontaneous workings of the market. Such a "private law society" is tailored to the autonomy of legal subjects who as market participants more or less rationally pursue their personal life-plans. This model of society is associated with the normative expectation that social justice can be realized by guaranteeing such a negative legal status, and thus solely by delimiting spheres of individual freedom. The well-founded critique of this supposition gave rise to the social welfare model. The objection is obvious: if the free "capacity to have and acquire" is supposed to guarantee social justice, then an equality in "legal capacity" must exist. As a matter of fact, however, the growing inequalities in economic power, assets, and living conditions have increasingly destroyed the factual preconditions for an equal opportunity to make effective use of equally distributed legal powers. If the normative content of legal equality is not to be inverted, then two correctives are necessary. On the one hand, existing norms of private law must be substantively specified, and on the other, basic social rights must be introduced, rights that ground claims to a more just distribution of socially produced wealth and to more effective protection against socially produced dangers.

In the meantime, of course, this *materialization* of law has in turn created the unintended side effects of welfare paternalism. Clearly, efforts to compensate for actual living conditions and power positions must not lead to "normalizing" interventions of a sort that once again restrict the presumptive beneficiaries' pursuit of an autonomous life-project. The further development of the dialectic of legal and factual equality has shown that both legal paradigms are equally committed to the productivist image of an economic society based on industrial capitalism. This society is supposed to function in such a way that the expectation of social justice can be satisfied by securing each individual's private pursut of his or her conception of the good life. The only dispute between the two paradigms concerns whether private autonomy can be guaranteed directly by negative liberties (*Freiheitsrechte*), or whether on the contrary the conditions for private autonomy must be secured through the provision of welfare entitlements. In both cases, however, the internal relation between private and public autonomy drops out of the picture.

5   AN EXAMPLE: THE FEMINIST POLITICS OF EQUALITY

In closing, I want to examine the feminist politics of equality to show that policies and legal strategies oscillate helplessly between the conventional paradigms as long as they remain limited to securing private autonomy and disregard how the individual rights of private persons are related to the public autonomy of citizens engaged in lawmaking. For, in the final analysis, private legal subjects cannot enjoy even equal individual liberties if they themselves do not jointly exercise their civic autonomy in order to specify clearly which interests and standards are justified, and to agree on the relevant respects that determine when like cases should be treated alike and different cases differently.

Initially, the goal of liberal policies was to uncouple the acquisition of status from gender identity and to guarantee to women equal opportunities in the competition for jobs, social recognition, education, political power, etc., regardless of the outcome. However, the formal equality that was partially achieved merely made more obvious the ways in which women were *in fact* treated unequally. Social welfare politics responded, especially in the areas of social, labor, and family law, by passing special regulations relating, for example, to pregnancy and child care, or to social hardship in the case of divorce. In the meantime feminist critique has targeted not only the unredeemed demands, but also the ambivalent consequences of successfully implemented welfare programs—for example, the higher risk of women losing their jobs as a result of compensatory regulations, the over-representation of women in lower wage brackets, the problematic issue of "what is in the child's best interests," and in general the progressive feminization of poverty. From a legal standpoint, one reason for this reflexively generated discrimination is found in the overgeneralized classifications used to label disadvantaged situations and disadvantaged groups of persons, because these "false" classifications lead to "normalizing" interventions into how people conduct their lives, interventions that transform what was intended as compensation for damages into new forms of discrimination. Thus instead of guaranteeing liberty, such overprotection stifles it. In areas of law that are of concern to feminism, welfare paternalism takes on a literal meaning to the extent that legislation and adjudication are oriented by traditional patterns of interpretation and thus serve to buttress existing stereotypes of sexual identity.

The classification of gender-specific roles and differences touches on fundamental levels of a society's cultural self-understanding. Radical feminism has only now made us aware of the fallible character of this self-understanding, an understanding that is essentially contested and in need of revision. It rightly insists that the appropriate interpretation of needs and criteria be a matter of public debate in the political public sphere. It is here that citizens must clarify the aspects that determine which differences between the experiences and living situations of (specific groups of) men and women are relevant for an equal opportunity to exercise individual liberties. Thus, this struggle for the equal status of women is a particularly good example of the need for a change of the legal paradigm.

The dispute between the two received paradigms—whether the autonomy of legal persons is better secured through individual liberties for private competition or through publicly guaranteed entitlements for clients of welfare bureaucracies—is superseded by a *proceduralist conception of law*. According to this conception, the democratic process must secure private and public autonomy at the same time: the individual rights that are meant to guarantee to women the autonomy to pursue their lives in the private sphere cannot even be adequately formulated unless the affected persons themselves first articulate and justify in public debate those aspects that are relevant to equal or unequal treatment in typical cases. The private autonomy of equally entitled citizens can be secured only insofar as citizens actively exercise their civic autonomy.

MICHEL FOUCAULT

~

INTRODUCTION

THOMAS A. MCCARTHY

Michel Foucault (1926–1984) was born in Poitiers and studied at the École Normale Supérieure, where he earned degrees in both philosophy and psychology. After occupying various academic and cultural positions in France, Sweden, Poland, and Germany in the 1950s, he presented his major thesis for the doctorat ès lettres, *Madness and Civilization*, in 1961. Following professorships at the universities of Clermont-Ferrand and Vincennes, separated by a visiting professorship in Tunisia, he was elected in 1969 to the Collège de France, where he designated his chair as in the "History of the Systems of Thought." In 1971 he helped found an organization for monitoring and improving prison conditions in France, an interest that remained central to his various activities as a public intellectual until he died of an AIDS-related condition in 1984.

Foucault's work can be viewed as falling into several phases. Under the deep and lasting influence of Nietzsche, he adopted early on a critical, historical— "genealogical"—mode of conceptual inquiry that, following the lead of such philosophically oriented French historians of science as his mentor Georges Canguilhem, he applied to the development of the "sciences of man." Thus his 1961 study of the history of madness and of the circumstances under which the mentally ill began to be confined was at the same time a study of the origins of modern psychiatry in practices of delimiting rationality from irrationality. And the soon-to-follow *Birth of the Clinic* (1963) subjected the development of clinical medicine to the same sort of internal-external analysis. Later in the same decade, in *The Order of Things* (1966), a study of the transmutations in the classical sciences of language, wealth, and living beings from the seventeenth to the nineteenth century, and in *The Archeology of Knowledge* (1969), an extended reflection on method, Foucault elaborated the structuralist dimension of his approach. Archeology investigates "discursive formations," their rules and regularities, the relations that obtain between discourse and nondiscursive practices and institutions, and the transformations that such formations undergo.

In his publications of the 1970s, particularly in *Discipline and Punish* (1975) and *The History of Sexuality*, Volume I: *An Introduction* (1976), he amplified the genealogical dimension of his approach in critical social histories of the "will to truth." In these works, as well as in numerous essays, lectures, and interviews of the period, Foucault stressed the internal relationship between knowledge and power, in particular that the development of the human sciences was closely bound up with the development and deployment of practices, institutions, and techniques for monitoring, controlling, and "normalizing" human beings. Genealogy examines the "lowly origins" of the sciences' central ideas—humankind, reason, normality, criminality, sexuality, and the like—in contingent historical circumstances and traces their functional implications in relations of force. It directs our attention to the rules and prescriptions that are constitutive of epistemic practices in these domains, to the relations of hierarchy these rules and prescriptions encode, and to the ways in which they include and exclude, validate and invalidate, dismiss or invest with authority. It also examines the relations of such theoretical discourses to the practical ways in which they are applied by judges, administrators, social workers, therapists, physicians, and others, as well as to the institutional practices with which they are interwoven in courts, prisons, clinics, hospitals, schools, bureaucracies, and the like. In short, what genealogy seeks to demonstrate is that the "politics" of knowledge about the human world does not begin only with the production of ideology but already with the production of truth itself.

In the last phase of his work, roughly the early 1980s, Foucault's attention shifted to ethics. In volumes 2 and 3 of *The History of Sexuality* (1984), *The Use of Pleasure* and *The Care of the Self*, he concerned himself with the ways in which human beings become subjects. In the 1970s he had viewed subjectivity largely as the product of subjugation; that is, different kinds of subjects were analyzed as the effects of different kinds of power. Now, however, he investigated the ways in which individuals could act upon themselves and transform themselves, with reference to the sexual ethics of ancient Greece (vol. 2) and the care of the self in the Roman world of the first two centuries of the common era (vol. 3). This conception of ethics as a form of relation of the self to the self, which Foucault contrasted with the conception of morality as obedience to a code of rules that came to predominate in Christianity, opened up the prospect of attempting to elaborate one's life as a personal work of art.

The selection included here is taken from "Two Lectures" delivered in the mid-1970s, the most influential phase of Foucault's thought. In it we have one of his clearest statements of how the genealogical analysis of "power/knowledge regimes" relates to political theory as traditionally practiced. The classical liberal, or "juridical," conception of power—as something that is possessed by individuals and can be transferred through a social contract that constitutes a legitimate sovereign and relations of "right" or law—is contrasted with the Freudian-Marxist conceptualization of power in terms of conflict, struggle, domination, and repression. Prior to this (1976), Foucault's own treatment of power was clearly close to the latter conception. That is, he analyzed social and political power as "war continued by other means": relations of power legitimized by right rest upon and sanction relations of force that result from conflict and struggle and get inscribed in everything from social institutions and economic inequalities to standard languages and docile bodies. Now he suggests that this "domination-repression" schema itself requires modification if it is to be adequate to the realities of "disciplinary" power. His recent studies of penal reform had shown that truth does not so much limit power as function in its service: the relations of power that permeate modern societies cannot be established and maintained without the production and dissemination of supporting truths. Critical social and political theory has, accordingly, to detect and analyze the multiple forms of domination and subjugation that are transmitted and sanctioned in and through discourses of truth and right. This new mode of analyzing power focuses not on the central power of the sovereign but on "power at the extremities," on the techniques, instruments, practices, and institutions through which it is exercised; not on power at the level of conscious intention but on power as invested in practices, on the "how" of ongoing subjugation; not on the unified will of rational subjects, but on how subjects are formed by subjugation, on how individuals are simultaneously the effects and vehicles of power; not on class domination and ideology, but on the grids and networks of power relations through which power circulates, and on the apparatuses, techniques, and discourses through which it is deployed.

This is Foucault at his Nietzschean best. It is not surprising that the notions of "power/knowledge" regimes, "disciplinary" power, "normalizing" techniques, and the like that he sketches here have exerted a vast influence on critical-theoretical strategies in the humanities and the social sciences. Particularly when combined with his injunction in the first lecture to abjure global, unitary theories as the matrix for critical studies and attempt instead to promote the "insurrection of subjugated knowledges," they have lent themselves to fruitful adaptation in the theory and criticism of gender, race, ethnicity, sexuality, and postcolonialism, among other things.

In scattered essays and the posthumously published *Lectures at the College de France*, edited by A. Davidson (New York: Macmillan, 2003), especially in his course lectures from the late 1970s and early 1980s, Foucault provided a new perspective on the multiple forms and practices of power he had examined—from power-knowledge and normalization to selfcare and biopolitics—under the rubric of "governmentality." This approach has proved to be of particular interest to political theorists as it offers an analytics of government in the broadest sense, comprising all organized practices through which the conduct of subjects and populations is rendered governable, especially in relation to political economy and security apparatuses.

In addition to the works by Foucault mentioned above, there are a number of valuable collections of his interviews, lectures, essays, and other writings: D. Bouchard (ed.), *Language, Counter-Memory, Practice* (Ithaca, N.Y.: Cornell University Press, 1977); C. Gordon (ed.), *Power/Knowledge* (New York: Pantheon, 1980); P. Rabinow (ed.), *The Foucault Reader* (New York: Pantheon, 1984); L. D. Kritzman (ed.), *Michel Foucault: Politics, Philosophy, Culture* (London: Routledge, 1988); J. Bernauer and D. Rasmussen (eds.), *The Final Foucault* (Cambridge, Mass.: MIT Press, 1988), with a bibliography of Foucault's writings; S. Lotringer (ed.), *Foucault Live* (New York: Semiotext(e), 1989); and G. Burchell, C. Gordon, and P. Miller (eds.), *The Foucault Effect: Studies in Governmentality* (Chicago: University of Chicago Press, 1991). The secondary literature on Foucault is immense. D. Eribon's *Michel Foucault* (Cambridge, Mass.: Harvard University Press, 1991) and David Macey's *The Lives of Michel Foucault* (New York: Pantheon, 1993) are good biographies. L. McNay, *Foucault: A Critical Introduction* (New York: Continuum, 1994), provides an introductory overview of his thought. General interpretations and discussions can be found in G. Deleuze, *Foucault*, translated by S. Hand (Minneapolis: University of Minnesota Press, 1988), and G. Gutting, *Michel Foucault's Archeology of Scientific Reason* (Cambridge: Cambridge University Press, 1989). Studies that focus on aspects of Foucault's social and political thought are Mark Poster, *Foucault, Marxism, and History* (Cambridge: Polity Press, 1984); Jana Sawicki, *Disciplining Foucault: Feminism, Power, and the Body* (New York: Routledge, 1991); M. Dean, *Governmentality: Power and Rule in Modern Society* (London: Sage, 1998); and N. Rose, *Powers of Freedom: Reforming Political Thought* (Cambridge: Cambridge University Press 1999). Critical essays with that focus can be found in the following collections: D. Hoy (ed.), *Foucault: A Critical Reader* (Oxford: Blackwell, 1986); I. Diamond and L. Quinby (eds.), *Feminism and Foucault* (Boston: Northeastern University Press, 1988); M. Kelly (ed.), *Critique and Power: Rethinking the Foucault/Habermas Debate* (Cambridge, Mass.: MIT Press, 1994); G. Gutting (ed.), *The Cambridge Companion to Foucault* (Cambridge: Cambridge University Press, 1994); and S. Ashenden & D. Owen (eds.), *Foucault Contra Habermas* (London: Sage, 1999). For additional bibliography and other resources, see www.michel-foucault.com.

Power/Knowledge

LECTURE ONE

. . . What has emerged in the course of the last ten or fifteen years is a sense of the increasing vulnerability to criticism of things, institutions, practices, discourses. A certain fragility has been discovered in the very bedrock of existence—even, and perhaps above all, in those aspects of it that are most familiar, most solid and most intimately related to our bodies and to our everyday behaviour. But together with this sense of instability and this amazing efficacy of discontinuous, particular and local criticism, one in fact also discovers something that perhaps was not initially foreseen, something one might describe as precisely the inhibiting effect of global, *totalitarian theories*. It is not that these global theories have not provided nor continue to provide in a fairly consistent fashion useful tools for local research: Marxism and psychoanalysis are proofs of this. But I believe these tools have only been provided on the condition that the theoretical unity of these discourses was in some sense put in abeyance, or at least curtailed, divided, overthrown, caricatured, theatricalised, or what you will. In each case, the attempt to think in terms of a totality has in fact proved a hindrance to research.

So, the main point to be gleaned from these events of the last fifteen years, their predominant feature, is the *local* character of criticism. That should not, I believe, be taken to mean that its qualities are those of an obtuse, naive or primitive empiricism; nor is it a soggy eclecticism, an opportunism that laps up any and every kind of theoretical approach; nor does it mean a self-imposed ascetism which taken by itself would reduce to the worst kind of theoretical impoverishment. I believe that what this essentially local character of criticism indicates in reality is an autonomous, non-centralised kind of theoretical production, one that is to say whose validity is not dependent on the approval of the established régimes of thought.

Reprinted from *Power/Knowledge*, translated by Colin Gordon, Leo Marshall, John Mepham, and Kate Soper. New York: Pantheon Books, 1980. Reprinted by permission of Harvester Books, Inc.

It is here that we touch upon another feature of these events that has been manifest for some time now: it seems to me that this local criticism has proceeded by means of what one might term "a return of knowledge." What I mean by that phrase is this: it is a fact that we have repeatedly encountered, at least at a superficial level, in the course of most recent times, an entire thematic to the effect that it is not theory but life that matters, not knowledge but reality, not books but money etc.; but it also seems to me that over and above, and arising out of this thematic, there is something else to which we are witness, and which we might describe as an *insurrection of subjugated knowledges*.

By subjugated knowledges I mean two things: on the one hand, I am referring to the historical contents that have been buried and disguised in a functionalist coherence or formal systemisation. Concretely, it is not a semiology of the life of the asylum, it is not even a sociology of delinquency, that has made it possible to produce an effective criticism of the asylum and likewise of the prison, but rather the immediate emergence of historical contents. And this is simply because only the historical contents allow us to rediscover the ruptural effects of conflict and struggle that the order imposed by functionalist or systematising thought is designed to mask. Subjugated knowledges are thus those blocs of historical knowledge which were present but disguised within the body of functionalist and systematising theory and which criticism—which obviously draws upon scholarship—has been able to reveal.

On the other hand, I believe that by subjugated knowledges one should understand something else, something which in a sense is altogether different, namely, a whole set of knowledges that have been disqualified as inadequate to their task or insufficiently elaborated: naive knowledges, located low down on the hierarchy, beneath the required level of cognition or scientificity. I also believe that it is through the reemergence of these low-ranking knowledges, these unqualified, even directly disqualified knowledges (such as that of the psychiatric patient, of the ill person, of the nurse, of the

doctor—parallel and marginal as they are to the knowledge of medicine—that of the delinquent etc.), and which involve what I would call a popular knowledge (*le savoir des gens*) though it is far from being a general commonsense knowledge, but is on the contrary a particular, local, regional knowledge, a differential knowledge incapable of unanimity and which owes its force only to the harshness with which it is opposed by everything surrounding it—that it is through the re-appearance of this knowledge, of these local popular knowledges, these disqualified knowledges, that criticism performs its work.

However, there is a strange kind of paradox in the desire to assign to this same category of subjugated knowledges what are on the one hand the products of meticulous, erudite, exact historical knowledge, and on the other hand local and specific knowledges which have no common meaning and which are in some fashion allowed to fall into disuse whenever they are not effectively and explicitly maintained in themselves. Well, it seems to me that our critical discourses of the last fifteen years have in effect discovered their essential force in this association between the buried knowledges of erudition and those disqualified from the hierarchy of knowledges and sciences.

In the two cases—in the case of the erudite as in that of the disqualified knowledges—with what in fact were these buried, subjugated knowledges really concerned? They were concerned with a *historical knowledge of struggles*. In the specialised areas of erudition as in the disqualified, popular knowledge there lay the memory of hostile encounters which even up to this day have been confined to the margins of knowledge.

What emerges out of this is something one might call a genealogy, or rather a multiplicity of genealogical researches, a painstaking rediscovery of struggles together with the rude memory of their conflicts. And these genealogies, that are the combined product of an erudite knowledge and a popular knowledge, were not possible and could not even have been attempted except on one condition, namely that the tyranny of globalising discourses

with their hierarchy and all their privileges of a theoretical *avantgarde* was eliminated.

Let us give the term *genealogy* to the union of erudite knowledge and local memories which allows
us to establish a historical knowledge of struggles
and to make use of this knowledge tactically today.
This then will be a provisional definition of the genealogies which I have attempted to compile with
you over the last few years.

You are well aware that this research activity,
which one can thus call genealogical, has nothing
at all to do with an opposition between the abstract
unity of theory and the concrete multiplicity of
facts. It has nothing at all to do with a disqualification of the speculative dimension which opposes to
it, in the name of some kind of scientism, the rigour
of well established knowledges. It is not therefore
via an empiricism that the genealogical project unfolds, nor even via a positivism in the ordinary sense
of that term. What it really does is to entertain the
claims to attention of local, discontinuous, disqualified, illegitimate knowledges against the claims of
a unitary body of theory which would filter, hier-
archise and order them in the name of some true
knowledge and some arbitrary idea of what constitutes a science and its objects. Genealogies are
therefore not positivistic returns to a more careful
or exact form of science. They are precisely anti-
sciences. Not that they vindicate a lyrical right to
ignorance or non-knowledge: it is not that they are
concerned to deny knowledge or that they esteem
the virtues of direct cognition and base their practice upon an immediate experience that escapes en-
capsulation in knowledge. It is not that with which
we are concerned. We are concerned, rather, with
the insurrection of knowledges that are opposed
primarily not to the contents, methods or concepts
of a science, but to the effects of the centralising
powers which are linked to the institution and functioning of an organised scientific discourse within a
society such as ours. Nor does it basically matter all
that much that this institutionalisation of scientific
discourse is embodied in a university, or, more generally, in an educational apparatus, in a theoretical-
commercial institution such as psychoanalysis or

within the framework of reference that is provided
by a political system such as Marxism; for it is really
against the effects of the power of a discourse that
is considered to be scientific that the genealogy
must wage its struggle. . . .

By comparison, then, and in contrast to the
various projects which aim to inscribe knowledges
in the hierarchical order of power associated with
science, a genealogy should be seen as a kind of
attempt to emancipate historical knowledges from
that subjection, to render them, that is, capable of
opposition and of struggle against the coercion of a
theoretical, unitary, formal and scientific discourse.
It is based on a reactivation of local knowledges—
of minor knowledges, as Deleuze might call them—
in opposition to the scientific hierarchisation of
knowledges and the effects intrinsic to their power:
this, then, is the project of these disordered and
fragmentary genealogies. If we were to characterise
it in two terms, then "archaeology" would be the
appropriate methodology of this analysis of local
discursivities, and "genealogy" would be the tactics
whereby, on the basis of the descriptions of these
local discursivities, the subjected knowledges which
were thus released would be brought into play. . . .

It will be no part of our concern to provide a
solid and homogeneous theoretical terrain for all
these dispersed genealogies, nor to descend upon
them from on high with some kind of halo of
theory that would unite them. Our task, on the contrary, will be to expose and specify the issue at stake
in this opposition, this struggle, this insurrection of
knowledges against the institutions and against effects of the knowledge and power that invests scientific discourse.

What is at stake in all these genealogies is the
nature of this power which has surged into view
in all its violence, aggression and absurdity in the
course of the last forty years, contemporane-
ously, that is, with the collapse of Fascism and the
decline of Stalinism. What, we must ask, is this
power—or rather, since that is to give a formulation to the question that invites the kind of theoretical coronation of the whole which I am so keen
to avoid—what are these various contrivances of

power, whose operations extend to such differing levels and sectors of society and are possessed of such manifold ramifications? What are their mechanisms, their effects and their relations? The issue here can, I believe, be crystallised essentially in the following question: is the analysis of power or of powers to be deduced in one way or another from the economy? Let me make this question and my reasons for posing it somewhat clearer. It is not at all my intention to abstract from what are innumerable and enormous differences; yet despite, and even because of these differences, I consider there to be a certain point in common between the juridical, and let us call it, liberal, conception of political power (found in the *philosophes* of the eighteenth century) and the Marxist conception, or at any rate a certain conception currently held to be Marxist. I would call this common point an economism in the theory of power. By that I mean that in the case of the classic, juridical theory, power is taken to be a right, which one is able to possess like a commodity, and which one can in consequence transfer or alienate, either wholly or partially, through a legal act or through some act that establishes a right, such as takes place through cession or contract. Power is that concrete power which every individual holds, and whose partial or total cession enables political power or sovereignty to be established. This theoretical construction is essentially based on the idea that the constitution of political power obeys the model of a legal transaction involving a contractual type of exchange (hence the clear analogy that runs through all these theories between power and commodities, power and wealth). In the other case—I am thinking here of the general Marxist conception of power—one finds none of all that. Nonetheless, there is something else inherent in this latter conception, something which one might term an economic functionality of power. This economic functionality is present to the extent that power is conceived primarily in terms of the role it plays in the maintenance simultaneously of the relations of production and of a class domination which the development and specific forms of the forces of production have rendered possible. On this view, then,

the historical *raison d'être* of political power is to be found in the economy. Broadly speaking, in the first case we have a political power whose formal model is discoverable in the process of exchange, the economic circulation of commodities; in the second case, the historical *raison d'être* of political power and the principle of its concrete forms and actual functioning, is located in the economy. Well then, the problem involved in the researches to which I refer can, I believe, be broken down in the following manner: in the first place, is power always in a subordinate position relative to the economy? Is it always in the service of, and ultimately answerable to, the economy? Is its essential end and purpose to serve the economy? Is it destined to realise, consolidate, maintain and reproduce the relations appropriate to the economy and essential to its functioning? In the second place, is power modelled upon the commodity? Is it something that one possesses, acquires, cedes through force or contract, that one alienates or recovers, that circulates, that voids this or that region? Or, on the contrary, do we need to employ varying tools in its analysis—even, that is, when we allow that it effectively remains the case that the relations of power do indeed remain profoundly enmeshed in and with economic relations and participate with them in a common circuit? If that is the case, it is not the models of functional subordination or formal isomorphism that will characterise the interconnection between politics and the economy. Their indissolubility will be of a different order, one that it will be our task to determine.

What means are available to us today if we seek to conduct a non-economic analysis of power? Very few, I believe. We have in the first place the assertion that power is neither given, nor exchanged, nor recovered, but rather exercised, and that it only exists in action. Again, we have at our disposal another assertion to the effect that power is not primarily the maintenance and reproduction of economic relations, but is above all a relation of force. The questions to be posed would then be these: if power is exercised, what sort of exercise does it involve? In what does it consist? What is its mechanism? There is an immediate answer that many contemporary analyses would appear to offer: power is essentially that which represses. Power represses nature, the instincts, a class, individuals. Though one finds this definition of power as repression endlessly repeated in present day discourse, it is not that discourse which invented it—Hegel first spoke of it, then Freud and later Reich. In any case, it has become almost automatic in the parlance of the times to define power as an organ of repression. So should not the analysis of power be first and foremost an analysis of the mechanisms of repression?

Then again, there is a second reply we might make: if power is properly speaking the way in which relations of forces are deployed and given concrete expression, rather than analysing it in terms of cession, contract or alienation, or functionally in terms of its maintenance of the relations of production, should we not analyse it primarily in terms of *struggle, conflict* and *war*? One would then confront the original hypothesis, according to which power is essentially repression, with a second hypothesis to the effect that power is war, a war continued by other means. This reversal of Clausewitz's assertion that war is politics continued by other means has a triple significance: in the first place, it implies that the relations of power that function in a society such as ours essentially rest upon a definite relation of forces that is established at a determinate, historically specifiable moment, in war and by war. Furthermore, if it is true that political power puts an end to war, that it installs, or tries to install, the reign of peace in civil society, this by no means implies that it suspends the effects of war or neutralises the disequilibrium revealed in the final battle. The role of political power, on this hypothesis, is perpetually to re-inscribe this relation through a form of unspoken warfare; to reinscribe it in social institutions, in economic inequalities, in language, in the bodies themselves of each and everyone of us.

So this would be the first meaning to assign to the inversion of Clausewitz's aphorism that war is politics continued by other means. It consists in seeing politics as sanctioning and upholding the disequilibrium of forces that was displayed in war. But there is also something else that the inversion signifies, namely, that none of the political struggles, the conflicts waged over power, with power, for power, the alterations in the relations of forces, the favouring of certain tendencies, the reinforcements etc., etc., that come about within this "civil peace" that none of these phenomena in a political system should be interpreted except as the continuation of war. They should, that is to say, be understood as episodes, factions and displacements in that same war. Even when one writes the history of peace and its institutions, it is always the history of this war that one is writing. The third, and final, meaning to be assigned to the inversion of Clausewitz's aphorism, is that the end result can only be the outcome of war, that is, of a contest of strength, to be decided in the last analyses by recourse to arms. The political battle would cease with this final battle. Only a final battle of that kind would put an end, once and for all, to the exercise of power as continual war.

So, no sooner do we attempt to liberate ourselves from economistic analyses of power, than two solid hypotheses offer themselves: the one argues that the mechanisms of power are those of repression. For convenience sake, I shall term this Reich's hypothesis. The other argues that the basis of the relationship of power lies in the hostile engagement of forces. Again for convenience, I shall call this Nietzsche's hypothesis.

These two hypotheses are not irreconcilable; they even seem to be linked in a fairly convincing manner. After all, repression could be seen as the political consequence of war, somewhat as oppression, in the classic theory of political right, was seen as the abuse of sovereignty in the juridical order.

One might thus contrast two major systems of approach to the analysis of power: in the first place, there is the old system as found in the *philosophes* of the eighteenth century. The conception of power as an original right that is given up in the establishment of sovereignty, and the contract, as matrix of political power, provide its points of articulation. A power so constituted risks becoming oppression when ever it over-extends itself, whenever—that is—it goes beyond the terms of the contract. Thus we have contract-power, with oppression as its limit, or rather as the transgression of this limit. In contrast, the other system of approach no longer tries to analyse political power according to the schema of contract-oppression, but in accordance with that of war-repression, and, at this point, repression no longer occupies the place that oppression occupies in relation to the contract, that is, it is not abuse, but is, on the contrary, the mere effect and continuation of a relation of domination. On this view, repression is none other than the realisation, within the continual warfare of this pseudo-peace, of a perpetual relationship of force.

Thus we have two schemes for the analysis of power. The contract-oppression schema, which is the juridical one, and the domination-repression or war-repression schema for which the pertinent opposition is not between the legitimate and illegitimate, as in the first schema, but between struggle and submission.

It is obvious that all my work in recent years has been couched in the schema of struggle-repression, and it is this—which I have hitherto been attempting to apply—which I have now been forced to reconsider, both because it is still insufficiently elaborated at a whole number of points, and because I believe that these two notions of repression and war must themselves be considerably modified if not ultimately abandoned. In any case, I believe that they must be submitted to closer scrutiny.

I have always been especially diffident of this notion of repression: it is precisely with reference to those genealogies of which I was speaking just now—of the history of penal right, of psychiatric power, of the control of infantile sexuality etc.— that I have tried to demonstrate to you the extent to which the mechanisms that were brought into operation in these power formations were something quite other, or in any case something much more, than repression. The need to investigate this notion of repression more thoroughly springs therefore from the impression I have that it is wholly inadequate to the analysis of the mechanisms and effects

of power that it is so pervasively used to characterise today.

LECTURE TWO

The course of study that I have been following until now—roughly since 1970/71—has been concerned with the *how* of power. I have tried, that is, to relate its mechanisms to two points of reference, two limits: on the one hand, to the rules of right that provide a formal delimitation of power; on the other, to the effects of truth that this power produces and transmits, and which in their turn reproduce this power. Hence we have a triangle: power, right, truth.

Schematically, we can formulate the traditional question of political philosophy in the following terms: how is the discourse of truth, or quite simply, philosophy as that discourse which *par excellence* is concerned with truth, able to fix limits to the rights of power? That is the traditional question. The one I would prefer to pose is rather different. Compared to the traditional, noble and philosophic question it is much more down to earth and concrete. My problem is rather this: what rules of right are implemented by the relations of power in the production of discourses of truth? Or alternatively, what type of power is susceptible of producing discourses of truth that in a society such as ours are endowed with such potent effects? What I mean is this: in a society such as ours, but basically in any society, there are manifold relations of power which permeate, characterise and constitute the social body, and these relations of power cannot themselves be established, consolidated nor implemented without the production, accumulation, circulation and functioning of a discourse. There can be no possible exercise of power without a certain economy of discourses of truth which operates through and on the basis of this association. We are subjected to the production of truth through power and we cannot exercise power except through the production of truth. This is the case for every society, but I believe that in ours the relationship between power, right and truth is organised in a highly specific fashion.

If I were to characterise, not its mechanism itself, but its intensity and constancy, I would say that we are forced to produce the truth of power that our society demands, of which it has need, in order to function: we *must* speak the truth; we are constrained or condemned to confess or to discover the truth. Power never ceases its interrogation, its inquisition, its registration of truth: it institutionalises, professionalises and rewards its pursuit. In the last analysis, we must produce truth as we must produce wealth, indeed we must produce truth in order to produce wealth in the first place. In another way, we are also subjected to truth in the sense in which it is truth that makes the laws, that produces the true discourse which, at least partially, decides, transmits and itself extends upon the effects of power. In the end, we are judged, condemned, classified, determined in our undertakings, destined to a certain mode of living or dying, as a function of the true discourses which are the bearers of the specific effects of power.

So, it is the rules of right, the mechanisms of power, the effects of truth or if you like, the rules of power and the powers of true discourses, that can be said more or less to have formed the general terrain of my concern, even if, as I know full well, I have traversed it only partially and in a very zig-zag fashion. I should like to speak briefly about this course of research, about what I have considered as being its guiding principle and about the methodological imperatives and precautions which I have sought to adopt. As regards the general principle involved in a study of the relations between right and power, it seems to me that in Western societies since Medieval times it has been royal power that has provided the essential focus around which legal thought has been elaborated. It is in reponse to the demands of royal power, for its profit and to serve as its instrument or justification, that the juridical edifice of our own society has been developed. Right in the West is the King's right. Naturally everyone is familiar with the famous, celebrated, repeatedly emphasised role of the jurists in the organisation of royal power. We must not forget that the re-vitalisation of Roman Law in the twelfth century was the

major event around which, and on whose basis, the juridical edifice which had collapsed after the fall of the Roman Empire was reconstructed. This resurrection of Roman Law had in effect a technical and constitutive role to play in the establishment of the authoritarian, administrative, and, in the final analysis, absolute power of the monarchy. And when this legal edifice escapes in later centuries from the control of the monarch, when, more accurately, it is turned against that control, it is always the limits of this sovereign power that are put in question, its prerogatives that are challenged. In other words, I believe that the King remains the central personage in the whole legal edifice of the West. When it comes to the general organisation of the legal system in the West, it is essentially with the King, his rights, his power and its eventual limitations, that one is dealing. Whether the jurists were the King's henchmen or his adversaries, it is of royal power that we are speaking in every case when we speak of these grandiose edifices of legal thought and knowledge.

There are two ways in which we do so speak. Either we do so in order to show the nature of the juridical armoury that invested royal power, to reveal the monarch as the effective embodiment of sovereignty, to demonstrate that his power, for all that it was absolute, was exactly that which befitted his fundamental right. Or, by contrast, we do so in order to show the necessity of imposing limits upon this sovereign power, of submitting it to certain rules of right, within whose confines it had to be exercised in order for it to remain legitimate. The essential role of the theory of right, from medieval times onwards, was to fix the legitimacy of power; that is the major problem around which the whole theory of right and sovereignty is organised.

When we say that sovereignty is the central problem of right in Western societies, what we mean basically is that the essential function of the discourse and techniques of right has been to efface the domination intrinsic to power in order to present the latter at the level of appearance under two different aspects: on the one hand, as the legitimate rights of sovereignty, and on the other, as the legal obligation to obey it. The system of right is centred entirely upon the King, and it is therefore designed to eliminate the fact of domination and its consequences.

My general project over the past few years has been, in essence, to reverse the mode of analysis followed by the entire discourse of right from the time of the Middle Ages. My aim, therefore, was to invert it, to give due weight, that is, to the fact of domination, to expose both its latent nature and its brutality. I then wanted to show not only how right is, in a general way, the instrument of this domination—which scarcely needs saying—but also to show the extent to which, and the forms in which, right (not simply the laws but the whole complex of apparatuses, institutions and regulations responsible for their application) transmits and puts in motion relations that are not relations of sovereignty, but of domination. Moreover, in speaking of domination I do not have in mind that solid and global kind of domination that one person exercises over others, or one group over another, but the manifold forms of domination that can be exercised within society. Not the domination of the King in his central position, therefore, but that of his subjects in their mutual relations: not the uniform edifice of sovereignty, but the multiple forms of subjugation that have a place and function within the social organism.

The system of right, the domain of the law, are permanent agents of these relations of domination, these polymorphous techniques of subjugation. Right should be viewed, I believe, not in terms of a legitimacy to be established, but in terms of the methods of subjugation that it instigates.

The problem for me is how to avoid this question, central to the theme of right, regarding sovereignty and the obedience of individual subjects in order that I may substitute the problem of domination and subjugation for that of sovereignty and obedience. Given that this was to be the general line of my analysis, there were a certain number of methodological precautions that seemed requisite to its pursuit. In the very first place, it seemed important to accept that the analysis in question should not concern itself with the regulated and legitimate forms of power in their central locations, with the

general mechanisms through which they operate, and the continual effects of these. On the contrary, it should be concerned with power at its extremities, in its ultimate destinations, with those points where it becomes capillary, that is, in its more regional and local forms and institutions. Its paramount concern, in fact, should be with the point where power surmounts the rules of right which organise and delimit it and extends itself beyond them, invests itself in institutions, becomes embodied in techniques, and equips itself with instruments and eventually even violent means of material intervention. To give an example: rather than try to discover where and how the right of punishment is founded on sovereignty, how it is presented in the theory of monarchical right or in that of democratic right, I have tried to see in what ways punishment and the power of punishment are effectively embodied in a certain number of local, regional, material institutions, which are concerned with torture or imprisonment, and to place these in the climate—at once institutional and physical, regulated and violent—of the effective apparatuses of punishment. In other words, one should try to locate power at the extreme points of its exercise, where it is always less legal in character.

A second methodological precaution urged that the analysis should not concern itself with power at the level of conscious intention or decision; that it should not attempt to consider power from its internal point of view and that it should refrain from posing the labyrinthine and unanswerable question: "Who then has power and what has he in mind? What is the aim of someone who possesses power?" Instead, it is a case of studying power at the point where its intention, if it has one, is completely invested in its real and effective practices. What is needed is a study of power in its external visage, at the point where it is in direct and immediate relationship with that which we can provisionally call its object, its target, its field of application, there—that is to say—where it installs itself and produces its real effects.

Let us not, therefore, ask why certain people want to dominate, what they seek, what is their overall strategy. Let us ask, instead, how things work at the level of on-going subjugation, at the level of those continuous and uninterrupted processes which subject our bodies, govern our gestures, dictate our behaviours etc. In other words, rather than ask ourselves how the sovereign appears to us in his lofty isolation, we should try to discover how it is that subjects are gradually, progressively, really and materially constituted through a multiplicity of organisms, forces, energies, materials, desires, thoughts etc. We should try to grasp subjection in its material instance as a constitution of subjects. This would be the exact opposite of Hobbes' project in *Leviathan*, and of that, I believe, of all jurists for whom the problem is the distillation of a single will—or rather, the constitution of a unitary, singular body animated by the spirit of sovereignty—from the particular wills of a multiplicity of individuals. Think of the scheme of Leviathan: insofar as he is a fabricated man, Leviathan is no other than the amalgamation of a certain number of separate individualities, who find themselves reunited by the complex of elements that go to compose the State; but at the heart of the State, or rather, at its head, there exists something which constitutes it as such, and this is sovereignty, which Hobbes says is precisely the spirit of Leviathan. Well, rather than worry about the problem of the central spirit, I believe that we must attempt to study the myriad of bodies which are constituted as peripheral *subjects* as a result of the effects of power.

A third methodological precaution relates to the fact that power is not to be taken to be a phenomenon of one individual's consolidated and homogeneous domination over others, or that of one group or class over others. What, by contrast, should always be kept in mind is that power, if we do not take too distant a view of it, is not that which makes the difference between those who exclusively possess and retain it, and those who do not have it and submit to it. Power must by analysed as something which circulates, or rather as something which only functions in the form of a chain. It is never localised here or there, never in anybody's hands, never

appropriated as a commodity or piece of wealth. Power is employed and exercised through a net-like organisation. And not only do individuals circulate between its threads; they are always in the position of simultaneously undergoing and exercising this power. They are not only its inert or consenting target; they are always also the elements of its articulation. In other words, individuals are the vehicles of power, not its points of application.

The individual is not to be conceived as a sort of elementary nucleus, a primitive atom, a multiple and inert material on which power comes to fasten or against which it happens to strike, and in so doing subdues or crushes individuals. In fact, it is already one of the prime effects of power that certain bodies, certain gestures, certain discourses, certain desires, come to be identified and constituted as individuals. The individual, that is, is not the *vis-à-vis* of power; it is, I believe, one of its prime effects. The individual is an effect of power, and at the same time, or precisely to the extent to which it is that effect, it is the element of its articulation. The individual which power has constituted is at the same time its vehicle.

There is a fourth methodological precaution that follows from this: when I say that power establishes a network through which it freely circulates, this is true only up to a certain point. In much the same fashion we could say that therefore we all have a fascism in our heads, or, more profoundly, that we all have a power in our bodies. But I do not believe that one should conclude from that that power is the best distributed thing in the world, although in some sense that is indeed so. We are not dealing with a sort of democratic or anarchic distribution of power through bodies. That is to say, it seems to me—and this then would be the fourth methodological precaution—that the important thing is not to attempt some kind of deduction of power starting from its centre and aimed at the discovery of the extent to which it permeates into the base, of the degree to which it reproduces itself down to and including the most molecular elements of society. One must rather conduct an *ascending* analysis of power, starting, that is, from its infinitesimal mechanisms, which each have their own history, their own trajectory, their own techniques and tactics, and then see how these mechanisms of power have been—and continue to be—invested, colonised, utilised, involuted, transformed, displaced, extended etc., by ever more general mechanisms and by forms of global domination. It is not that this global domination extends itself right to the base in a plurality of repercussions: I believe that the manner in which the phenomena, the techniques and the procedures of power enter into play at the most basic levels must be analysed, that the way in which these procedures are displaced, extended and altered must certainly be demonstrated; but above all what must be shown is the manner in which they are invested and annexed by more global phenomena and the subtle fashion in which more general powers or economic interests are able to engage with these technologies that are at once both relatively autonomous of power and act as its infinitesimal elements. In order to make this clearer, one might cite the example of madness. The descending type of analysis, the one of which I believe one ought to be wary, will say that the bourgeoisie has, since the sixteenth or seventeenth century, been the dominant class; from this premise, it will then set out to deduce the internment of the insane. One can always make this deduction, it is always easily done and that is precisely what I would hold against it. It is in fact a simple matter to show that since lunatics are precisely those persons who are useless to industrial production, one is obliged to dispense with them. One could argue similarly in regard to infantile sexuality—and several thinkers, including Wilhelm Reich have indeed sought to do so up to a certain point. Given the domination of the bourgeois class, how can one understand the repression of infantile sexuality? Well, very simply—given that the human body had become essentially a force of production from the time of the seventeenth and eighteenth century, all the forms of its expenditure which did not lend themselves to the constitution of the productive forces—and were therefore exposed as redundant—were banned, excluded and repressed. These kinds of deduction are always possible. They are simultaneously correct and false. Above all they are too glib, because one can always do exactly the opposite and show, precisely by appeal to the principle of the dominance of the bourgeois class, that the forms of control of infantile sexuality could in no way have been predicted. On the contrary, it is equally plausible to suggest that what was needed was sexual training, the encouragement of a sexual precociousness, given that what was fundamentally at stake was the constitution of a labour force whose optimal state, as we well know, at least at the beginning of the nineteenth century, was to be infinite: the greater the labour force, the better able would the system of capitalist production have been to fulfil and improve its functions.

I believe that anything can be deduced from the general phenomenon of the domination of the bourgeois class. What needs to be done is something quite different. One needs to investigate historically, and beginning from the lowest level, how mechanisms of power have been able to function. In regard to the confinement of the insane, for example, or the repression and interdiction of sexuality, we need to see the manner in which, at the effective level of the family, of the immediate environment, of the cells and most basic units of society, these phenomena of repression or exclusion possessed their instruments and their logic, in response to a certain number of needs. We need to identify the agents responsible for them, their real agents (those which constituted the immediate social *entourage*, the family, parents, doctors etc.), and not be content to lump them under the formula of a generalised bourgeoisie. We need to see how these mechanisms of power, at a given moment, in a precise conjuncture and by means of a certain number of transformations, have begun to become economically advantageous and politically useful. I think that in this way one could easily manage to demonstrate that what the bourgeoisie needed, or that in which its system discovered its real interests, was not the exclusion of the mad or the surveillance and prohibition of infantile masturbation (for, to repeat, such a system can perfectly well tolerate quite opposite practices), but rather, the techniques and procedures themselves of such an exclusion. It is the mechanisms of that exclusion that are necessary, the apparatuses of surveillance, the medicalisation of sexuality, of madness, of delinquency, all the micro-mechanisms of power, that came, from a certain moment in time, to represent the interests of the bourgeoisie. Or even better, we could say that to the extent to which this view of the bourgeoisie and of its interests appears to lack content, at least in regard to the problems with which we are here concerned, it reflects the fact that it was not the bourgeoisie itself which thought that madness had to be excluded or infantile sexuality repressed. What in fact happened instead was that the mechanisms of the exclusion of madness, and of the surveillance of infantile sexuality, began from a particular point in time, and for reasons which need to be studied, to reveal their political usefulness and to lend themselves to economic profit, and that as a natural consequence, all of a sudden, they came to be colonised and maintained by global mechanisms and the entire State system. It is only if we grasp these techniques of power and demonstrate the economic advantages or political utility that derives from them in a given context for specific reasons, that we can understand how these mechanisms come to be effectively incorporated into the social whole.

To put this somewhat differently: the bourgeoisie has never had any use for the insane; but the procedures it has employed to exclude them have revealed and realised—from the nineteenth century onwards, and again on the basis of certain transformations—a political advantage, on occasion even a certain economic utility, which have consolidated the system and contributed to its overall functioning. The bourgeoisie is interested in power, not in madness, in the system of control of infantile sexuality, not in that phenomenon itself. The bourgeoisie could not care less about delinquents, about their punishment and rehabilitation, which economically have little importance, but it is concerned about the complex of mechanisms with which delinquency is controlled, pursued, punished and reformed etc.

As for our fifth methodological precaution: it is quite possible that the major mechanisms of power

have been accompanied by ideological productions. There has, for example, probably been an ideology of education, an ideology of the monarchy, an ideology of parliamentary democracy etc.; but basically I do not believe that what has taken place can be said to be ideological. It is both much more and much less than ideology. It is the production of effective instruments for the formation and accumulation of knowledge—methods of observation, techniques of registration, procedures for investigation and research, apparatuses of control. All this means that power, when it is exercised through these subtle mechanisms, cannot but evolve, organise and put into circulation a knowledge, or rather apparatuses of knowledge, which are not ideological constructs.

By way of summarising these five methodological precautions, I would say that we should direct our researches on the nature of power not towards the juridical edifice of sovereignty, the State apparatuses and the ideologies which accompany them, but towards domination and the material operators of power, towards forms of subjection and the inflections and utilisations of their localised systems, and towards strategic apparatuses. We must eschew the model of Leviathan in the study of power. We must escape from the limited field of juridical sovereignty and State institutions, and instead base our analysis of power on the study of the techniques and tactics of domination.

This, in its general outline, is the methodological course that I believe must be followed, and which I have tried to pursue in the various researches that we have conducted over recent years on psychiatric power, on infantile sexuality, on political systems, etc. Now as one explores these fields of investigation, observing the methodological precautions I have mentioned, I believe that what then comes into view is a solid body of historical fact, which will ultimately bring us into confrontation with the problems of which I want to speak this year.

This solid, historical body of fact is the juridical-political theory of sovereignty of which I spoke a moment ago, a theory which has had four roles to play. In the first place, it has been used to refer to a mechanism of power that was effective under the feudal monarchy. In the second place, it has served as instrument and even as justification for the construction of the large scale administrative monarchies. Again, from the time of the sixteenth century and more than ever from the seventeenth century onwards, but already at the time of the wars of religion, the theory of sovereignty has been a weapon which has circulated from one camp to another, which has been utilised in one sense or another, either to limit or else to re-inforce royal power: we find it among Catholic monarchists and Protestant anti-monarchists, among Protestant and more-or-less liberal monarchists, but also among Catholic partisans of regicide or dynastic transformation. It functions both in the hands of aristocrats and in the hands of parliamentarians. It is found among the representatives of royal power and among the last feudatories. In short, it was the major instrument of political and theoretical struggle around systems of power of the sixteenth and seventeenth centuries. Finally, in the eighteenth century, it is again this same theory of sovereignty, re-activated through the doctrine of Roman Law, that we find in its essentials in Rousseau and his contemporaries, but now with a fourth role to play: now it is concerned with the construction, in opposition to the administrative, authoritarian and absolutist monarchies, of an alternative model, that of parliamentary democracy. And it is still this role that it plays at the moment of the Revolution.

Well, it seems to me that if we investigate these four roles there is a definite conclusion to be drawn: as long as a feudal type of society survived, the problems to which the theory of sovereignty was addressed were in effect confined to the general mechanisms of power, to the way in which its forms of existence at the higher level of society influenced its exercise at the lowest levels. In other words, the relationship of sovereignty, whether interpreted in a wider or a narrower sense, encompasses the totality of the social body. In effect, the mode in which power was exercised could be defined in its essentials in terms of the relationship sovereign-subject. But in the seventeenth and eighteenth centuries,

we have the production of the an important phenomenon, the emergence, or rather the invention, of a new mechanism of power possessed of highly specific procedural techniques, completely novel instruments, quite different apparatuses, and which is also, I believe, absolutely incompatible with the relations of sovereignty.

This new mechanism of power is more dependent upon bodies and what they do than upon the Earth and its products. It is a mechanism of power which permits time and labour, rather than wealth and commodities, to be extracted from bodies. It is a type of power which is constantly exercised by means of surveillance rather than in a discontinuous manner by means of a system of levies or obligations distributed over time. It presupposes a tightly knit grid of material coercions rather than the physical existence of a sovereign. It is ultimately dependent upon the principle, which introduces a genuinely new economy of power, that one must be able simultaneously both to increase the subjected forces and to improve the force and efficacy of that which subjects them.

This type of power is in every aspect the antithesis of that mechanism of power which the theory of sovereignty described or sought to transcribe. The latter is linked to a form of power that is exercised over the Earth and its products, much more than over human bodies and their operations. The theory of sovereignty is something which refers to the displacement and appropriation on the part of power, not of time and labour, but of goods and wealth. It allows discontinuous obligations distributed over time to be given legal expression but it does not allow for the codification of a continuous surveillance. It enables power to be founded in the physical existence of the sovereign, but not in continuous and permanent systems of surveillance. The theory of sovereignty permits the foundation of an absolute power in the absolute expenditure of power. It does not allow for a calculation of power in terms of the minimum expenditure for the maximum return.

This new type of power, which can no longer be formulated in terms of sovereignty, is, I believe, one of the great inventions of bourgeois society. It has been a fundamental instrument in the constitution of industrial capitalism and of the type of society that is its accompaniment. This non-sovereign power, which lies outside the form of sovereignty, is disciplinary power. Impossible to describe in the terminology of the theory of sovereignty from which it differs so radically, this disciplinary power ought by rights to have led to the disappearance of the grand juridical edifice created by that theory. But in reality, the theory of sovereignty has continued not only to exist as an ideology of right, but also to provide the organising principle of the legal codes which Europe acquired in the nineteenth century, beginning with the Napoleonic Code.

Why has the theory of sovereignty persisted in this fashion as an ideology and an organising principle of these major legal codes? For two reasons, I believe. On the one hand, it has been, in the eighteenth and again in the nineteenth century, a permanent instrument of criticism of the monarchy and of all the obstacles that can thwart the development of disciplinary society. But at the same time, the theory of sovereignty, and the organisation of a legal code centred upon it, have allowed a system of right to be superimposed upon the mechanisms of discipline in such a way as to conceal its actual procedures, the element of domination inherent in its techniques, and to guarantee to everyone, by virtue of the sovereignty of the State, the exercise of his proper sovereign rights. The juridical systems—and this applies both to their codification and to their theorisation—have enabled sovereignty to be democratised through the constitution of a public right articulated upon collective sovereignty, while at the same time this democratisation of sovereignty was fundamentally determined by and grounded in mechanisms of disciplinary coercion.

To put this in more rigorous terms, one might say that once it became necessary for disciplinary constraints to be exercised through mechanisms of domination and yet at the same time for their effective exercise of power to be disguised, a theory of sovereignty was required to make an appearance at the level of the legal apparatus, and to re-emerge in its codes. Modern society, then, from the nineteenth century up to our own day, has been characterised on the one hand, by a legislation, a discourse, an organisation based on public right, whose principle of articulation is the social body and the delegative status of each citizen; and, on the other hand, by a closely linked grid of disciplinary coercions whose purpose is in fact to assure the cohesion of this same social body. Though a theory of right is a necessary companion to this grid, it cannot in any event provide the terms of its endorsement. Hence these two limits, a right of sovereignty and a mechanism of discipline, which define, I believe, the arena in which power is exercised. But these two limits are so heterogeneous that they cannot possibly be reduced to each other. The powers of modern society are exercised through, on the basis of, and by virtue of, this very heterogeneity between a public right of sovereignty and a polymorphous disciplinary mechanism. This is not to suggest that there is on the one hand an explicit and scholarly system of right which is that of sovereignty, and, on the other hand, obscure and unspoken disciplines which carry out their shadowy operations in the depths, and thus constitute the bedrock of the great mechanism of power. In reality, the disciplines have their own discourse. They engender, for the reasons of which we spoke earlier, apparatuses of knowledge (*savoir*) and a multiplicity of new domains of understanding. They are extraordinarily inventive participants in the order of these knowledge-producing apparatuses. Disciplines are the bearers of a discourse, but this cannot be the discourse of right. The discourse of discipline has nothing in common with that of law, rule, or sovereign will. The disciplines may well be the carriers of a discourse that speaks of a rule, but this is not the juridical rule deriving from sovereignty, but a natural rule, a norm. The code they come to define is not that of law but that of normalisation. Their reference is to a theoretical horizon which of necessity has nothing in common with the edifice of right. It is human science which constitutes their domain, and clinical knowledge their jurisprudence.

In short, what I have wanted to demonstrate in the course of the last few years is not the manner in which at the advance front of the exact sciences the uncertain, recalcitrant, confused dominion of human behaviour has little by little been annexed to science: it is not through some advancement in the rationality of the exact sciences that the human sciences are gradually constituted. I believe that the process which has really rendered the discourse of the human sciences possible is the juxtaposition, the encounter between two lines of approach, two mechanisms, two absolutely heterogeneous types of discourse: on the one hand there is the re-organisation of right that invests sovereignty, and on the other, the mechanics of the coercive forces whose exercise takes a disciplinary form. And I believe that in our own times power is exercised simultaneously through this right and these techniques and that these techniques and these discourses, to which the disciplines give rise invade the area of right so that the procedures of normalisation come to be ever more constantly engaged in the colonisation of those of law. I believe that all this can explain the global functioning of what I would call a *society of normalisation*. I mean, more precisely, that disciplinary normalisations come into ever greater conflict with the juridical systems of sovereignty: their incompatibility with each other is ever more acutely felt and apparent; some kind of arbitrating discourse is made ever more necessary, a type of power and of knowledge that the sanctity of science would render neutral. It is precisely in the extension of medicine that we see, in some sense, not so much the linking as the perpetual exchange or encounter of mechanisms of discipline with the principle of right. The developments of medicine, the general medicalisation of behaviours, conducts, discourses, desires etc., take place at the point of intersection between the two heterogeneous levels of discipline and sovereignty. For this reason, against these usurpations by the disciplinary mechanisms, against this ascent of a power that is tied to scientific knowledge, we find that there is no solid recourse available to us today, such being our situation, except that which lies precisely in the return to a theory of right organised around sovereignty and articulated upon its ancient principle. When today one wants to object in some way to the disciplines and all the effects of power and knowledge that are linked to them, what is it that one does, concretely, in real life, what do the Magistrates Union[1] or other similar institutions do, if not precisely appeal to this canon of right, this famous, formal right, that is said to be bourgeois, and which in reality is the right of sovereignty? But I believe that we find ourselves here in a kind of blind alley: it is not through recourse to sovereignty against discipline that the effects of disciplinary power can be limited, because sovereignty and disciplinary mechanisms are two absolutely integral constituents of the general mechanism of power in our society.

If one wants to look for a non-disciplinary form of power, or rather, to struggle against disciplines and disciplinary power, it is not towards the ancient right of sovereignty that one should turn, but towards the possibility of a new form of right, one which must indeed be anti-disciplinarian, but at the same time liberated from the principle of sovereignty. It is at this point that we once more come up against the notion of repression, whose use in this context I believe to be doubly unfortunate. On the one hand, it contains an obscure reference to a certain theory of sovereignty, the sovereignty of the sovereign rights of the individual, and on the other hand, its usage introduces a system of psychological reference points borrowed from the human sciences, that is to say, from discourses and practices that belong to the disciplinary realm. I believe that the notion of repression remains a juridical-disciplinary notion whatever the critical use one would make of it. To this extent the critical application of the notion of repression is found to be vitiated and nullified from the outset by the two-fold juridical and disciplinary reference it contains to sovereignty on the one hand and to normalisation on the other.

Note

1. This Union, established after 1968, has adopted a radical line on civil rights, the law and the prisons.

MICHAEL J. SANDEL

~

INTRODUCTION

ROBERT B. TALISSE

Michael Sandel was born in 1953 and grew up in Minneapolis and Los Angeles. He graduated from Brandeis University in 1975, and completed his graduate work in philosophy as a Rhodes Scholar at Balliol College, Oxford, in 1981. He currently is Anne T. and Robert M. Bass Professor of Government in the Department of Government at Harvard University. The recipient of many awards and distinctions, Sandel delivered both the Tanner Lectures on Human Values and the BBC Reith Lectures in 2009. He served on the President's Council on Bioethics from 2002 until 2005, and is a member of the American Academy of Arts and Sciences. For more than twenty years, Sandel has taught a course at Harvard titled "Justice," which is the most popular course in the history of the institution; over 15,000 Harvard students have taken the course, and it was recently filmed as a PBS television series titled *Justice: What's the Right Thing to Do?* Harvard has made Sandel's class available for free online at http://www.justiceharvard.org/.

Sandel's work engages a wide variety of issues in ethics, social philosophy, and political philosophy. He has written influentially about social justice, community, citizenship, genetic engineering, biotechnology, and the moral limits of markets. The broad scope of his thought reflects Sandel's commitment to the ideas that philosophy is a kind of public activity and that academic philosophy can be presented in a way that is accessible to a general audience. Accordingly his works include academic monographs, like his *Liberalism and the Limits of Justice* (Cambridge, Mass.: Cambridge University Press, 1982, revised edition 1998) and *Democracy's Discontent* (Cambridge, Mass.: Harvard University Press, 1996) as well as philosophical books aimed at a popular general readership, including *The Case Against Perfection* (Cambridge, Mass.: Harvard University Press, 2007), a collection of short essays titled *Public Philosophy* (Cambridge, Mass.: Harvard University Press, 2005), and *Justice: What's The Right Thing to Do?* (New York: Farrar, Straus, and Giroux, 2009).

Sandel's various philosophical endeavors are united by a central concern with liberalism as a framework for political theory. Although parlance in the United States associates liberalism with the political policy initiatives of the Democratic Party, in philosophy, liberalism is the name of a distinctive approach to political theory. Liberalism in the philosophical sense is an approach that is common among theorists otherwise as divided as John Locke, John Stuart Mill, and John Rawls. Liberalism is often contrasted with a family of views known as *communitarianism* or *civic republicanism*, which has its intellectual origins in the philosophy of Aristotle and can be found in the work of Jean-Jacques Rousseau, G. W. F. Hegel, and Charles Taylor. From his earliest writing to the present day, Sandel is a leading proponent of what is called the "communitarian critique of liberalism." The essay reprinted here captures the core of Sandel's criticism of liberalism and presents a sketch of his communitarian alternative.

The central thesis of Sandel's "The Procedural Republic and the Unencumbered Self" has two components. The first is that contemporary democratic politics in the United States (and elsewhere) is organized around a distinctively liberal conception of politics—that is, liberalism is our public philosophy. The second is that, although this conception offers an attractive individualist image of society, it is ultimately unable to sustain a healthy democracy. Accordingly, Sandel concludes that our liberal public philosophy must be replaced by a communitarian one.

Sandel devotes most of his essay to the characterization of liberalism. In the most general terms, liberalism is the view according to which states and political associations exist for the sake of protecting individuals and their rights. Liberalism thus holds that political associations exist because individuals *choose* to create them; this in turn suggests the idea that political bodies such as states derive their authority from the consent of those they govern. Sandel argues that this familiar view of the nature of political association rests upon a deeper, and ultimately suspicious, philosophical doctrine, namely, the thesis that the right is prior to the good.

The thesis that the right is prior to the good combines two commitments. First, liberals hold that the right is prior to the good in the sense that individual rights are understood as "trumps" against claims about the public good—that is, when an individual's right comes into conflict with the public good, the right takes precedence. This is why, for example, liberalism countenances a firm distinction between *allowing* someone to do something and *approving* of his doing it. This distinction is embedded in familiar attitudes toward, say, offensive speech; a common thought is that individuals have a right to say offensive things, even though everyone would be better off were they not to speak that way. Having a right to free speech simply means that one may speak even when doing so frustrates the common good. Liberals often claim that this is precisely what it means to have the right.

On Sandel's account, there is a second sense in which liberal holds that priority of the right to the good. They claim also that individual rights can be specified and defended without appealing to any controversial premises about what is good for humans, or what makes a human life a good one. One need not specify a vision of the good life in order to determine what rights an individual has; the right is prior in the sense that the theory of individual rights is *independent* of the theory of the good. The second sense of the priority of the right to the good fits together with the liberal commitment to the moral neutrality of the state. Liberals hold that as individuals disagree about what makes a life good, the liberal state must avoid legislating on the basis of any controversial view of the good life; the state must attend rather only to individuals' rights, not their good. This is why, for example, the state banned cigarette smoking in enclosed public spaces only after data were available demonstrating the dangers of secondhand smoke. That smoking is addictive and poses significant health risks to those who choose to smoke is no reason for the liberal state to constrain it. According to the liberal view, individuals have a right to decide whether to take risks with their health; consequently, smoking can be legally constrained only when the practice poses a threat to others. Hence the liberal state professes to serve the rights of individuals without implicating itself in judgments about what is good; this is what Sandel calls the "procedural republic."

These features of liberalism are evident in the theory of justice proposed by John Rawls, who Sandel takes as his main target. Rawls argues that the way to discover the correct principles of justice for a society is to imagine individuals in an "original position" where they must choose from among competing conceptions of justice; those principles that they would all agree to are, on Rawls's view, the correct principles. Thus far, Rawls's view is only a slight variant on traditional social contract view as found in Locke and Kant. But Rawls introduces the further element of the "veil of ignorance"; in the original position, individuals are to be understood to be ignorant of their talents, socioeconomic status, ethnicity, gender, religious conviction, and conception of the good life. Rawls reasons that the veil of ignorance ensures that the agreement reached the original position is fair. Since individuals in the original position are ignorant of their identities, they cannot bargain or haggle over principles of justice; individuals must instead weigh different conceptions as if they were going to assume the position of the worst off within each option. Rawls holds that his famous two principles of justice would be chosen under such conditions.

There is of course much more to say about Rawls's theory. But this simple sketch is enough to elucidate Sandel's criticism. Sandel argues that the thesis of the priority of the right to the good presupposes a particular theory of the human self that is in fact false.

To explain, Sandel contends that the priority of the right to the good depends upon a view according to which the self is prior to its ends. This is the thesis that the most important moral fact about individuals is that they are *choosers* of their conception of the good life. Rawls's view manifests this commitment when it stipulates that principles of justice must be selected from a condition in which individuals are ignorant of their personal conceptions of the good life. Sandel claims that liberalism is hence committed to a voluntarist conception of the self, a view according to which the self always stands at a distance from its moral convictions. The voluntarist conception thus denies that there could be moral commitments that *constitute* the self; it says that moral commitments are always things that individuals *have*, and never things that individuals *are*. The voluntarist view claims that selves are essentially "unencumbered," to use Sandel's memorable term.

Sandel argues that the voluntarist conception of the self is unsustainable because we are intrinsically encumbered selves. Consider the example of religious commitments. Individuals typically *identify* themselves with their religion; one does not "have" Christianity as much as one *is* Christian. A similar thought holds for national and familial loyalties. These are things we *are*, not things we *possess*; in some cases, we might say that such commitments *possess* us, they are *constitutive* of who we are, we are *encumbered* by them.

The most important feature of these constitutive commitments is that they are *unchosen*. Again, religious conviction provides a handy example. Individuals typically see their religious commitments as things they did not choose, but were *chosen for* them (sometimes by God himself). It is fitting, then, that when someone changes his religious conviction, we do not say that he merely changed his mind; we tend to employ stronger language to describe the phenomenon: we say that he converted, was transformed, was born again, and so on. This is because a shift in constitutive commitments marks a significant change in the person.

Sandel argues that once we see that our most central moral commitments are constitutive and not chosen, and that we are essentially encumbered selves, the very idea that the question of justice should be decided from behind a veil of ignorance will seem strikingly alien. Sandel reasons that the question of justice is ultimately the question of what we, as fellow citizens sharing a common civic enterprise, owe to each other. This question, he maintains, necessarily invokes our larger moral ideals and commitments; it cannot be adequately addressed from the point of view of asocial contractors in the Rawlsian original position or Lockean state of nature.

Sandel employs this critique of liberalism as a diagnostic tool for addressing what he sees as our "present predicament" as a democratic society. The liberal image of the unencumbered voluntarist self is ultimately too anemic to sustain a properly democratic politics of shared responsibility and common purposes. The idea that the state ought to see its citizens simply as rights holders rather than as participants in the common moral enterprise of democratic self-government has led to a social condition in which individuals are dislocated, disconnected, and ultimately disempowered. Sandel concludes that democracy needs to be reformulated on a communitarian rather than liberal public philosophy.

Sandel's critique of liberalism and his communitarian alternative is widely discussed in the contemporary professional literature. The collection *Debating Democracy's Discontent*, edited by Anita Allen and Milton Regan (New York: Oxford University Press, 1999), contains critical responses to Sandel's views and arguments. Those looking for a detailed overview of the debates between liberals and communitarians should consult *Liberals and Communitarians* by Stephen Mulhall and Adam Swift (Oxford: Blackwell, 1996) and *Contemporary Political Philosophy* by Will Kymlicka (New York: Oxford University Press, 2001).

The Procedural Republic and the Unencumbered Self

Political philosophy seems often to reside at a distance from the world. Principles are one thing, politics another, and even our best efforts to "live up" to our ideals typically founder on the gap between theory and practice.[1]

But if political philosophy is unrealizable in one sense, it is unavoidable in another. This is the sense in which philosophy inhabits the world from the start; our practices and institutions are embodiments of theory. To engage in a political practice is already to stand in relation to theory.[2] For all our uncertainties about ultimate questions of political philosophy—of justice and value and the nature of the good life—the one thing we know is that we live *some* answer all the time.

From *Political Theory* 12 (1984). Copyright © 1984 by Sage Publications, Inc. Reprinted by permission of the publisher.

In this essay I will try to explore the answer we live now, in contemporary America. What is the political philosophy implicit in our practices and institutions? How does it stand, as philosophy? And how do tensions in the philosophy find expression in our present political condition?

It may be objected that it is a mistake to look for a single philosophy, that we live no "answer," only answers. But a plurality of answers is itself a kind of answer. And the political theory that affirms this plurality is the theory I propose to explore.

THE RIGHT AND THE GOOD

We might begin by considering a certain moral and political vision. It is a liberal vision, and like most liberal visions gives pride of place to justice, fairness, and individual rights. Its core thesis is this: a just society seeks not to promote any particular ends, but enables its citizens to pursue their own ends, consistent with a similar liberty for all; it therefore must govern by principles that do not presuppose any particular conception of the good. What justifies these regulative principles above all is not that they maximize the general welfare, or cultivate virtue, or otherwise promote the good, but rather that they conform to the concept of *right*, a moral category given prior to the good, and independent of it.

This liberalism says, in other words, that what makes the just society just is not the *telos* or purpose or end at which it aims, but precisely its refusal to choose in advance among competing purposes and ends. In its constitution and its laws, the just society seeks to provide a framework within which its citizens can pursue their own values and ends, consistent with a similar liberty for others.

The ideal I've described might be summed up in the claim that the right is prior to the good, and in two senses: The priority of the right means first, that individual rights cannot be sacrificed for the sake of the general good (in this it opposes utilitarianism), and second, that the principles of

justice that specify these rights cannot be premised on any particular vision of the good life. (In this it opposes teleological conceptions in general.)

This is the liberalism of much contemporary moral and political philosophy, most fully elaborated by Rawls, and indebted to Kant for its philosophical foundations.[3] But I am concerned here less with the lineage of this vision than with what seem to me three striking facts about it.

First, it has a deep and powerful philosophical appeal. Second, despite its philosophical force, the claim for the priority of the right over the good ultimately fails. And third, despite its philosophical failure, this liberal vision is the one by which we live. For us in late twentieth century America, it is our vision, the theory most thoroughly embodied in the practices and institutions most central to our public life. And seeing how it goes wrong as philosophy may help us to diagnose our present political condition. So first, its philosophical power; second, its philosophical failure; and third, however briefly, its uneasy embodiment in the world.

But before taking up these three claims, it is worth pointing out a central theme that connects them. And that is a certain conception of the person, of what it is to be a moral agent. Like all political theories, the liberal theory I have described is something more than a set of regulative principles. It is also a view about the way the world is, and the way we move within it. At the heart of this ethic lies a vision of the person that both inspires and undoes it. As I will try to argue now, what make this ethic so compelling, but also, finally, vulnerable, are the promise and the failure of the unencumbered self.

KANTIAN FOUNDATIONS

The liberal ethic asserts the priority of right, and seeks principles of justice that do not presuppose any particular conception of the good.[4] This is what Kant means by the supremacy of the moral law, and what Rawls means when he writes that "justice is the first virtue of social institutions."[5]

Justice is more than just another value. It provides the framework that *regulates* the play of competing values and ends; it must therefore have a sanction independent of those ends. But it is not obvious where such a sanction could be found.

Theories of justice, and for that matter, ethics, have typically founded their claims on one or another conception of human purposes and ends. Thus Aristotle said the measure of a *polis* is the good at which it aims, and even J.S. Mill, who in the nineteenth century called "justice the chief part, and incomparably the most binding part of all morality," made justice an instrument of utilitarian ends.[6]

This is the solution Kant's ethic rejects. Different persons typically have different desires and ends, and so any principle derived from them can only be contingent. But the moral law needs a *categorical* foundation, not a contingent one. Even so universal a desire as happiness will not do. People still differ in what happiness consists of, and to install any particular conception as regulative would impose on some the conceptions of others, and so deny at least to some the freedom to choose their *own* conceptions. In any case, to govern ourselves in conformity with desires and inclinations, given as they are by nature or circumstance, is not really to be *self*-governing at all. It is rather a refusal of freedom, a capitulation to determinations given outside us.

According to Kant, the right is "derived entirely from the concept of freedom in the external relationships of human beings, and has nothing to do with the end which all men have by nature [i.e., the aim of achieving happiness] or with the recognized means of attaining this end."[7] As such, it must have a basis prior to all empirical ends. Only when I am governed by principles that do not presuppose any particular ends am I free to pursue my own ends consistent with a similar freedom for all.

But this still leaves the question of what the basis of the right could possibly be. If it must be a basis prior to all purposes and ends, unconditioned even by what Kant calls "the special circumstances of human nature,"[8] where could such a basis conceivably be found? Given the stringent demands of the Kantian ethic, the moral law would seem almost to require a foundation in nothing, for any empirical precondition would undermine its priority. "Duty!" asks Kant at his most lyrical, "What origin is there worthy of thee, and where is to be found the root of thy noble descent which proudly rejects all kinship with the inclinations?"[9]

His answer is that the basis of the moral law is to be found in the *subject*, not the object of practical reason, a subject capable of an autonomous will. No empirical end, but rather "a subject of ends, namely a rational being himself, must be made the ground for all maxims of action."[10] Nothing other than what Kant calls "the subject of all possible ends himself" can give rise to the right, for only this subject is also the subject of an autonomous will. Only this subject could be that "something which elevates man above himself as part of the world of sense" and enables him to participate in an ideal, unconditioned realm wholly independent of our social and psychological inclinations. And only this thoroughgoing independence can afford us the detachment we need if we are ever freely to choose for ourselves, unconditioned by the vagaries of circumstance.[11]

Who or what exactly *is* this subject? It is, in a certain sense, *us*. The moral law, after all, is a law we give *ourselves*; we don't *find* it, we *will* it. That is how it (and we) escape the reign of nature and circumstance and merely empirical ends. But what is important to see is that the "we" who do the willing are not "we" qua particular persons, you and me, each for ourselves—the moral law is not up to us as individuals—but "we" qua participants in what Kant calls "pure practical reason," "we" qua participants in a transcendental subject.

Now what is to guarantee that I *am* a subject of this kind, capable of exercising pure practical reason? Well, strictly speaking, there *is* no guarantee; the transcendental subject is only a possibility. But it is a possibility I must *presuppose* if I am to think of myself as a free moral agent. Were

I wholly an empirical being, I would not be capable of freedom, for every exercise of will would be conditioned by the desire for some object. All choice would be heteronomous choice, governed by the pursuit of some end. My will could never be a first cause, only the effect of some prior cause, the instrument of one or another impulse or inclination. "When we think of ourselves as free," writes Kant, "we transfer ourselves into the intelligible world as members and recognize the autonomy of the will."[12] And so the notion of a subject prior to and independent of experience, such as the Kantian ethic requires, appears not only possible but indispensable, a necessary presupposition of the possibility of freedom.

How does all of this come back to politics? As the subject is prior to its ends, so the right is prior to the good. Society is best arranged when it is governed by principles that do not presuppose any particular conception of the good, for any other arrangement would fail to respect persons as being capable of choice; it would treat them as objects rather than subjects, as means rather than ends in themselves.

We can see in this way how Kant's notion of the subject is bound up with the claim for the priority of right. But for those in the Anglo-American tradition, the transcendental subject will seem a strange foundation for a familiar ethic. Surely, one may think, we can take rights seriously and affirm the primacy of justice without embracing the *Critique of Pure Reason*. This, in any case, is the project of Rawls.

He wants to save the priority of right from the obscurity of the transcendental subject. Kant's idealist metaphysic, for all its moral and political advantage, cedes too much to the transcendent, and wins for justice its primacy only by denying it its human situation. "To develop a viable Kantian conception of justice," Rawls writes, "the force and content of Kant's doctrine must be detached from its background in transcendental idealism" and recast within the "canons of a reasonable empiricism."[13] And so Rawls' project is to preserve Kant's moral and political teaching by replacing Germanic obscurities with a domesticated metaphysic more congenial to the Anglo-American temper. This is the role of the original position.

FROM TRANSCENDENTAL SUBJECT TO UNENCUMBERED SELF

The original position tries to provide what Kant's transcendental argument cannot—a foundation for the right that is prior to the good, but still situated in the world. Sparing all but essentials, the original position works like this: It invites us to imagine the principles we would choose to govern our society if we were to choose them in advance, before we knew the particular persons we would be—whether rich or poor, strong or weak, lucky or unlucky before we knew even our interests or aims or conceptions of the good. These principles—the ones we would choose in that imaginary situation—are the principles of justice. What is more, if it works, they are principles that do not presuppose any particular ends.

What they *do* presuppose is a certain picture of the person, of the way we must be if we are beings for whom justice is the first virtue. This is the picture of the unencumbered self, a self understood as prior to and independent of purposes and ends.

Now the unencumbered self describes first of all the way we stand toward the things we have, or want, or seek. It means there is always a distinction between the values I *have* and the person I *am*. To identify any characteristics as *my* aims, ambitions, desires, and so on, is always to imply some subject "me" standing behind them, at a certain distance, and the shape of this "me" must be given prior to any of the aims or attributes I bear. One consequence of this distance is to put the self *itself* beyond the reach of its experience, to secure its identity once and for all. Or to put the point another way, it rules out the possibility of what we might call *constitutive* ends. No role or commitment could define me so completely that I could not understand myself without it. No project could be so essential that turning away from it would call into question the person I am.

For the unencumbered self, what matters above all, what is most essential to our personhood, are not the ends we choose but our capacity to choose them. The original position sums up this central claim about us. "It is not our aims that primarily reveal our nature," writes Rawls, "but rather the principles that we would acknowledge to govern the background conditions under which these aims are to be formed . . . We should therefore reverse the relation between the right and the good proposed by teleological doctrines and view the right as prior."[14]

Only if the self is prior to its ends can the right be prior to the good. Only if my identity is never tied to the aims and interests I may have at any moment can I think of myself as a free and independent agent, capable of choice.

This notion of independence carries consequences for the kind of community of which we are capable. Understood as unencumbered selves, we are of course free to join in voluntary association with others, and so are capable of community in the cooperative sense. What is denied to the unencumbered self is the possibility of membership in any community bound by moral ties antecedent to choice; he cannot belong to any community where the self *itself* could be at stake. Such a community—call it constitutive as against merely cooperative—would engage the identity as well as the interests of the participants, and so implicate its members in a citizenship more thoroughgoing than the unencumbered self can know.

For justice to be primary, then, we must be creatures of a certain kind, related to human circumstance in a certain way. We must stand to our circumstance always at a certain distance, whether as transcendental subject in the case of Kant, or as unencumbered selves in the case of Rawls. Only in this way can we view ourselves as subjects as well as objects of experience, as agents and not just instruments of the purposes we pursue.

The unencumbered self and the ethic it inspires, taken together, hold out a liberating vision. Freed from the dictates of nature and the sanction of social roles, the human subject is installed as sovereign, cast as the author of the only moral meanings there are. As participants in pure practical reason, or as parties to the original position, we are free to construct principles of justice unconstrained by an order of value antecedently given. And as actual, individual selves, we are free to choose our purposes and ends unbound by such an order, or by custom or tradition or inherited status. So long as they are not unjust, our conceptions of the good carry weight, whatever they are, simply in virtue of our having chosen them. We are, in Rawls' words, "self-originating sources of valid claims."[15]

This is an exhilarating promise, and the liberalism it animates is perhaps the fullest expression of the Enlightenment's quest for the self-defining subject. But is it true? Can we make sense of our moral and political life by the light of the self-image it requires? I do not think we can, and I will try to show why not by arguing first within the liberal project, then beyond it.

JUSTICE AND COMMUNITY

We have focused so far on the foundations of the liberal vision, on the way it derives the principles it defends. Let us turn briefly now to the substance of those principles, using Rawls as our example. Sparing all but essentials once again, Rawls' two principles of justice are these: first, equal basic liberties for all, and second, only those social and economic inequalities that benefit the least-advantaged members of society (the difference principle).

In arguing for these principles, Rawls argues against two familiar alternatives—utilitarianism and libertarianism. He argues against utilitarianism that it fails to take seriously the distinction between persons. In seeking to maximize the general welfare, the utilitarian treats society as a whole as if it were a single person; it conflates our many, diverse desires into a single system of desires, and tries to maximize. It is indifferent to the distribution of satisfactions among persons, except insofar as this may affect the overall sum. But this fails to respect our plurality and distinctness. It uses some as means to the happiness of all, and so fails to respect each as an end in himself. While utilitarians may sometimes defend individual rights, their defense must rest on the calculation that respecting those rights will serve utility in the long run. But this calculation is contingent and uncertain. So long as utility is what Mill said it is, "the ultimate appeal on all ethical questions,"[16] individual rights can never be secure. To avoid the danger that their life prospects might one day be sacrificed for the greater good of others, the parties to the original position therefore insist on certain basic liberties for all, and make those liberties prior.

If utilitarians fail to take seriously the distinctness of persons, libertarians go wrong by failing to acknowledge the arbitrariness of fortune. They define as just whatever distribution results from an efficient market economy, and oppose all redistribution on the grounds that people are entitled to whatever they get, so long as they do not cheat or steal or otherwise violate someone's rights in getting it. Rawls opposes this principle on the ground that the distribution of talents and assets and even efforts by which some get more and others get less is arbitrary from a moral point of view, a matter of good luck. To distribute the good things in life on the basis of these differences is not to do justice, but simply to carry over into human arrangements the arbitrariness of social and natural contingency. We deserve, as individuals, neither the talents our good fortune may have brought, nor the benefits that flow from them. We should therefore regard these talents as common assets, and regard one another as common beneficiaries of the rewards they bring. "Those who have been favored by nature, whoever they are, may gain from their good fortune only on terms that improve the situation of those who have lost out . . . In justice as fairness, men agree to share one another's fate."[17]

This is the reasoning that leads to the difference principle. Notice how it reveals, in yet another guise, the logic of the unencumbered self.

I cannot be said to deserve the benefits that flow from, say, my fine physique and good looks, because they are only accidental, not essential facts about me. They describe attributes I *have*, not the person I *am*, and so cannot give rise to a claim of desert. Being an unencumbered self, this is true of *everything* about me. And so I cannot, as an individual, deserve anything at all.

However jarring to our ordinary understandings this argument may be, the picture so far remains intact; the priority of right, the denial of desert, and the unencumbered self all hang impressively together.

But the difference principle requires more, and it is here that the argument comes undone. The difference principle begins with the thought, congenial to the unencumbered self, that the assets I have are only accidentally mine. But it ends by assuming that these assets are therefore *common* assets and that society has a prior claim on the fruits of their exercise. But this assumption is without warrant. Simply because I, as an individual, do not have a privileged claim on the assets accidentally residing "here," it does not follow that everyone in the world collectively does. For there is no reason to think that their location in society's province or, for that matter, within the province of humankind, is any *less* arbitrary from a moral point of view. And if their arbitrariness within *me* makes them ineligible to serve *my* ends, there seems no obvious reason why their arbitrariness within any particular society should not make them ineligible to serve that society's ends as well.

To put the point another way, the difference principle, like utilitarianism, is a principle of sharing. As such, it must presuppose some prior moral tie among those whose assets it would deploy and whose efforts it would enlist in a common endeavor. Otherwise, it is simply a formula for using some as means to others' ends, a formula this liberalism is committed to reject.

But on the cooperative vision of community alone, it is unclear what the moral basis for this sharing could be. Short of the constitutive conception, deploying an individual's assets for the sake of the common good would seem an offense against the "plurality and distinctness" of individuals this liberalism seeks above all to secure.

If those whose fate I am required to share really are, morally speaking, *others*, rather than fellow participants in a way of life with which my identity is bound, the difference principle falls prey to the same objections as utilitarianism. Its claim on me is not the claim of a constitutive community whose attachments I acknowledge, but rather the claim of a concatenated collectivity whose entanglements I confront.

What the difference principle requires, but cannot provide, is some way of identifying those *among* whom the assets I bear are properly regarded as common, some way of seeing ourselves as mutually indebted and morally engaged to begin with. But as we have seen, the constitutive aims and attachments that would save and situate the difference principle are precisely the ones denied to the liberal self; the moral encumbrances and antecedent obligations they imply would undercut the priority of right.

What, then, of those encumbrances? The point so far is that we cannot be persons for whom justice is primary, and also be persons for whom the difference principle is a principle of justice. But which must give way? Can we view ourselves as independent selves, independent in the sense that our identity is never tied to our aims and attachments?

I do not think we can, at least not without cost to those loyalties and convictions whose moral force consists partly in the fact that living by them is inseparable from understanding ourselves as the particular persons we are-as members of this family or community or nation or people, as bearers of that history, as citizens of this republic. Allegiances such as these are more than values I happen to have, and to hold, at a certain distance. They go beyond the obligations I voluntarily incur and the "natural duties" I owe to human beings as such. They allow that to some I owe more than justice requires or even permits, not by reason of agreements I have made but instead in virtue of those more or less enduring attachments and commitments that, taken together, partly define the person I am.

To imagine a person incapable of constitutive attachments such as these is not to conceive an ideally free and rational agent, but to imagine a person wholly without character, without moral depth. For to have character is to know that I move in a history I neither summon nor command, which carries consequences nonetheless for my choices and conduct. It draws me closer to some and more distant from others; it makes some aims more appropriate, others less so. As a self-interpreting being, I am able to reflect on my history and in this sense to distance myself from it, but the distance is always precarious and provisional, the point of reflection never finally secured outside the history itself. But the liberal ethic puts the self beyond the reach of its experience, beyond deliberation and reflection. Denied the expansive self-understandings that could shape a common life, the liberal self is left to lurch between detachment on the one hand, and entanglement on the other. Such is the fate of the unencumbered self, and its liberating promise.

THE PROCEDURAL REPUBLIC

But before my case can be complete, I need to consider one powerful reply. While it comes from a liberal direction, its spirit is more practical than philosophical. It says, in short, that I am asking too much. It is one thing to seek constitutive attachments in our private lives; among families and friends, and certain tightly knit groups, there may be found a common good that makes justice and rights less pressing. But with public life—at least today, and probably always—it is different. So long as the nation-state is the primary form of political association, talk of constitutive community too easily suggests a darker politics rather than a brighter one; amid echoes of the moral majority, the priority of right, for all its philosophical faults, still seems the safer hope.

This is a challenging rejoinder, and no account of political community in the twentieth century can fail to take it seriously. It is challenging not least because it calls into question the status of political philosophy and its relation to the world. For if my argument is correct, if the liberal vision we have considered is not morally self-sufficient but parasitic on a notion of community it officially rejects, then we should expect to find that the political practice that embodies this vision is not *practically* self-sufficient either—that it must draw on a sense of community it cannot supply and may even undermine. But is that so far from the circumstance we face today? Could it be that through the original position darkly, on the far side of the veil of ignorance, we may glimpse an intimation of our predicament, a refracted vision of ourselves?

How does the liberal vision—and its failure—help us make sense of our public life and its predicament? Consider, to begin, the following paradox in the citizen's relation to the modern welfare state. In many ways, we in the 1980s stand near the completion of a liberal project that has run its course from the New Deal through the Great Society and into the present. But notwithstanding the extension of the franchise and the expansion of individual rights and entitlements in recent decades, there is a widespread sense that, individually and collectively, our control over the forces that govern our lives is receding rather than increasing. This sense is deepened by what appear simultaneously as the power and the powerlessness of the nation-state. On the one hand, increasing numbers of citizens view the state as an overly intrusive presence, more likely to frustrate their purposes than advance them. And yet, despite its unprecedented role in the economy and society, the modern state seems itself disempowered, unable effectively to control the domestic economy, so respond to persisting social ills, or to work America's will in the world.

This is a paradox that has fed the appeals of recent politicians (including Carter and Reagan), even as it has frustrated their attempts to govern.

To sort it out, we need to identify the public philosophy implicit in our political practice, and to reconstruct its arrival. We need to trace the advent of the procedural republic, by which I mean a public life animated by the liberal vision and self-image we've considered.

The story of the procedural republic goes back in some ways to the founding of the republic, but its central drama begins to unfold around the turn of the century. As national markets and large-scale enterprise displaced a decentralized economy, the decentralized political forms of the early republic became outmoded as well. If democracy was to survive, the concentration of economic power would have to be met by a similar concentration of political power. But the Progressives understood, or some of them did, that the success of democracy required more than the centralization of government; it also required the nationalization of politics. The primary form of political community had to be a recast on a national scale. For Herbert Croly, writing in 1909, the "nationalizing of American political, economic, and social life" was "an essentially formative and enlightening political transformation." We would become more of a democracy only as we became "more of a nation . . . in ideas, in institutions, and in spirit."[18]

This nationalizing project would be consummated in the New Deal, but for the democratic tradition in America, the embrace of the nation was a decisive departure. From Jefferson to the populists, the party of democracy in American political debate had been, roughly speaking, the party of the provinces, of decentralized power, of small-town and small-scale America. And against them had stood the party of the nation—first Federalists, then Whigs, then the Republicans of Lincoln—a party that spoke for the consolidation of the union. It was thus the historic achievement of the New Deal to unite, in a single party and political program, what Samuel Beer has called "liberalism and the national idea."[19]

What matters for our purpose is that, in the twentieth century, liberalism made its peace with concentrated power. But it was understood at the start that the terms of this peace required a strong sense of national community, morally and politically to underwrite the extended involvements of a modern industrial order. If a virtuous republic of small-scale, democratic communities was no longer a possibility, a national republic seemed democracy's next best hope. This was still, in principle at least, a politics of the common good. It looked to the nation, not as a neutral framework for the play of competing interests, but rather as a formative community, concerned to shape a common life suited to the scale of modern social and economic forms.

But this project failed. By the mid- or late twentieth century, the national republic had run its course. Except for extraordinary moments, such as war, the nation proved too vast a scale across which to cultivate the shared self-understandings necessary to community in the formative, or constitutive sense. And so the gradual shift, in our practices and institutions, from a public philosophy of common purposes to one of fair procedures, from a politics of good to a politics of right, from the national republic to the procedural republic.

OUR PRESENT PREDICAMENT

A full account of this transition would take a detailed look at the changing shape of political institutions, constitutional interpretation, and the terms of political discourse in the broadest sense. But I suspect we would find in the *practice* of the procedural republic two broad tendencies foreshadowed by its philosophy: first, a tendency to crowd out democratic possibilities; second, a tendency to undercut the kind of community on which it nonetheless depends.

Where liberty in the early republic was understood as a function of democratic institutions and dispersed power,[20] liberty in the procedural republic is defined in opposition to democracy,

as an individual's guarantee against what the majority might will. I am free insofar as I am the bearer of rights, where rights are trumps.[21] Unlike the liberty of the early republic, the modern version permits—in fact even requires—concentrated power. This has to do with the universalizing logic of rights. Insofar as I have a right, whether to free speech or a minimum income, its provision cannot be left to the vagaries of local preferences but must be assured at the most comprehensive level of political association. It cannot be one thing in New York and another in Alabama. As rights and entitlements expand, politics is therefore displaced from smaller forms of association and relocated at the most universal form—in our case, the nation. And even as politics flows to the nation, power shifts away from democratic institutions (such as legislatures and political parties) and toward institutions designed to be insulated from democratic pressures, and hence better equipped to dispense and defend individual rights (notably the judiciary and bureaucracy).

These institutional developments may begin to account for the sense of powerlessness that the welfare state fails to address and in some ways doubtless deepens. But it seems to me a further clue to our condition that recalls even more directly the predicament of the unencumbered self—lurching, as we left it, between detachment on the one hand, the entanglement on the other. For it is a striking feature of the welfare state that it offers a powerful promise of individual rights, and also demands of its citizens a high measure of mutual engagement. But the self-image that attends the rights cannot sustain the engagement.

As bearers of rights, where rights are trumps, we think of ourselves as freely choosing, individual selves, unbound by obligations antecedent to rights, or to the agreements we make. And yet, as citizens of the procedural republic that secures these rights, we find ourselves implicated willy-nilly in a formidable array of dependencies and expectations we did not choose and increasingly reject.

In our public life, we are more entangled, but less attached, than ever before. It is as though the unencumbered self presupposed by the liberal ethic had begun to come true—less liberated than disempowered, entangled in a network of obligations and involvements unassociated with any act of will, and yet unmediated by those common identifications or expansive self-definitions that would make them tolerable. As the scale of social and political organization has become more comprehensive, the terms of our collective identity have become more fragmented, and the forms of political life have outrun the common purpose needed to sustain them.

Something like this, it seems to me, has been unfolding in America for the past half-century or so. I hope I have said at least enough to suggest the shape a fuller story might take. And I hope in any case to have conveyed a certain view about politics and philosophy and the relation between them—that our practices and institutions are themselves embodiments of theory, and to unravel their predicament is, at least in part, to seek after the self-image of the age.

Notes

1. An excellent example of this view can be found in Samuel Huntington, *American Politics: The Promise of Disharmony* (Cambridge: Harvard University Press, 1981). See especially his discussion of the "ideals versus institutions" gap, pp. 10–12, 39–41, 61–84, 221–62.

2. See, for example, the conceptions of a "practice" advanced by Alasdair MacIntyre and Charles Taylor. MacIntyre, *After Virtue* (Notre Dame: University of Notre Dame Press, 1981), pp. 175–209. Taylor, "Interpretation and the Sciences of Man," *Review of Metaphysics* 25, (1971): 3–51.

3. John Rawls, *A Theory of Justice* (Oxford: Oxford University Press, 1972). Immanuel Kant, *Groundwork of the Metaphysics of Morals*, trans. H. J. Paton. (1785;

New York: Harper & Row, 1956). Kant, *Critique of Pure Reason*, trans. Norman Kemp Smith (1781, 1787; London: Macmillan, 1929). Kant, *Critique of Practical Reason*, trans. L. W. Beck (1788; Indianapolis: Bobbs-Merrill, 1956). Kant, "On the Common Saying: 'This May Be True in Theory, But It Does Not Apply in Practice,'" in Hans Reiss, ed., *Kant's Political Writings* (1793; Cambridge: Cambridge University Press, 1970). Other recent versions of the claim for the priority of the right over good can be found in Robert Nozick, *Anarchy, State and Utopia* (New York: Basic Books, 1974); Ronald Dworkin, *Taking Rights Seriously* (London: Duckworth, 1977); Bruce Ackerman, *Social Justice in the Liberal State* (New Haven: Yale University Press, 1980).

4. This section, and the two that follow, summarize arguments developed more fully in Michael Sandel, *Liberalism and the Limits of Justice* (Cambridge: Cambridge University Press, 1982).

5. Rawls (1971), p. 3.

6. John Stuart Mill, *Utilitarianism*, in *The Utilitarians* (1893; Garden City: Doubleday, 1973), p. 465. Mill, *On Liberty*, in *The Utilitarians*, p. 485 (originally published 1849).

7. Kant (1793), p. 73.

8. Kant (1785), p. 92.

9. Kant (1788), p. 89.

10. Kant (1785), p. 105.

11. Kant (1788), p. 89.

12. Kant (1785), p. 121.

13. Rawls, "The Basic Structure as Subject," *American Philosophical Quarterly* (1977): 165.

14. Rawls (1971), p. 560.

15. Rawls, "Kantian Constructivism in Moral Theory," *Journal of Philosophy* 77 (1980): 543.

16. Mill (1849), p. 485.

17. Rawls (1971), pp. 101–2.

18. Croly, *The Promise of American Life* (Indianapolis: Bobbs-Merrill, 1965), pp. 270–3.

19. Beer, "Liberalism and the National Idea," *The Public Interest*, Fall (1966): 70–82.

20. See, for example, Laurence Tribe, *American Constitutional Law* (Mineola: The Foundation Press, 1978), pp. 2–3.

21. See Ronald Dworkin, "Liberalism," in Stuart Hampshire, ed., *Public and Private Morality* (Cambridge: Cambridge University Press, 1978), p. 136.

VIRGINIA HELD

INTRODUCTION

CHESHIRE CALHOUN

Virginia Held, born in Mendham, New Jersey, in 1929, graduated cum laude from Barnard College, earned graduate certificates in philosophy and psychology at the University of Strasbourg, and in 1968 received her Ph.D. in philosophy from Columbia University. She is currently Distinguished Professor of Philosophy at the City University of New York Graduate Center and Professor Emerita at CUNY's Hunter College. In 1981 she was chosen as President of the International Association of Philosophy of Law and Social Philosophy, American Section, and in 2001 she was elected President of the Eastern Division of the American Philosophical Association. In 1992 the Society for Women in Philosophy honored Held with its Distinguished Woman Philosopher award.

Beginning as a lecturer at Barnard and Columbia University in 1964, Held entered philosophy when women constituted approximately 7 percent of the profession, gender neutral language had not yet become the norm, and feminist philosophy had not yet emerged as a distinct sub-discipline. She was among the earliest critics of contractual theories of moral and political philosophy as well as market approaches to supplying human needs for education, health care, and cultural products. She was also among the pioneers in developing an ethics of care and continues to be its leading exponent, extending its scope beyond personal relations to include social welfare policy, global human concerns, and issues of war and terrorism. Her books on care ethics include *Feminist Morality: Transforming Culture, Society, Politics* (1993); an edited collection, *Justice and Care: Essential Readings in Feminist Ethics* (1995); and *The Ethics of Care: Personal, Political, and Global* (2005).

A major strand of feminist political philosophy, originating in critiques of gender bias in dominant modes of ethical and political thought, is devoted to reconceiving the central problems, paradigms, and forms of theorizing from what might loosely be described as a woman's perspective. Held's essay is a highly influential example of this approach.

It was impacted by the groundbreaking work of educational psychologist Carol Gilligan, who had argued in her book *In a Different Voice* (Cambridge, Mass.: Harvard University Press, 1982) that the theory of moral development offered by her mentor, Lawrence Kohlberg, was gender biased, representing the developmental trajectory of boys and men: Gilligan argued that women's moral development often follows a different path and went on to distinguish an ethics of justice, characterized by an appeal to abstract moral principles and the ranking of rights, from an ethics of care, characterized by responsiveness to the needs of particular others and concern with sustaining webs of relationships. The influence of that distinction between justice and care is evident in Held's essay.

In her political philosophy Held rejects the standard methodological assumption that the goal of social theorizing is to develop a single theory for addressing all the normative questions that arise in moral or political life. Instead, she advocates methodological pluralism, arguing that rights-based theories, utilitarianism, and care ethics are each especially well suited to address normative questions in particular domains. Rights-based theories of justice, for example, are particularly useful in the domain of law; utilitarian ethical theories in the domain of the market, where preference satisfaction is a central concern; and an ethics of care in the domain of family and personal relationships. However, we may need to invoke multiple theories in a single domain. For example, important issues of justice need to be addressed with respect to the family, while in the public spheres of market and government we should consider how citizens could be better cared for and their needs better responded to, taking into account the vulnerabilities and responsibilities created by national and global interdependency. Indeed, one of Held's aims throughout her work is to show how an ethics of care is better equipped than rights-based and utilitarian theories to address some of the moral and political problems that arise in civil society, the market, and the political arena. In the essay presented here, "Non-contractual Society: A Feminist View," she considers the implications of conceiving relations in the public sphere on the model of caring familial relations between child and mothering person rather than on the model of contractual relations between rationally self-interested, independent individuals.

The problem, as she sees it, is not that contractual approaches to moral and political questions are altogether wrong, but that they are inherently limited. They work from a single paradigm of humans as "economic man," that is, as independent, self-interested or mutually disinterested individuals, whose primary motive is to maximize the satisfaction of their own preferences and whose fundamental moral and political relationship to others is a contractual one. Thus she says, "to the extent that some of our relations should be seen as contractual, we should recognize how essentially limited rather than general such relations are."

Held's recommendation that we begin our moral and political thinking from a woman's perspective, or more specifically, from the perspective of the relation between child and mothering person, serves a dual purpose. On the one hand, it draws attention to the level of gender bias in moral and political philosophy. Not only have women been denied the same political rights as men (consider, for example, Kant's defense of the disenfranchisement of women on the grounds that they are economically dependent on fathers and husbands), but their subordination to men in the family has either been defended (as Held observes of Rousseau) or not been addressed (Rawls, for example, assumes in *A Theory of Justice* that the contractors in the original position are heads of household, so that non–heads of household, presumably women, are not even contractors). Had political theorizing begun from the perspective of women, these inequalities might have seemed less obviously defensible. Such failures of contractual approaches might, of course, be remedied by a more gender egalitarian defense of rights in the public sphere and an extension of principles of justice to the institution of the family. Held intends, however, to draw attention to a deeper form of gender bias, namely, the failure to take the kinds of interpersonal relations, motives, and activities of those in caretaking roles—roles which are more likely to be occupied by women—as paradigmatically human. She argues that mothering is misdescribed when considered a natural,

biological function rather than a distinctively human activity. Indeed, we should consider starting our moral and political thinking from a maternal paradigm, thus enabling
us to see "what is most seriously overlooked by a contractual view of society, and to see
how important what is overlooked is."

What do contractual views overlook? Held begins by observing that contractual
views are not descriptively accurate. In fact, social arrangements are often the product
of illegitimate exercises of power—exploitation, racism, economic might, and war and
conquest. Although she does not pursue this point, one might follow her lead here and
argue that one test of a fully adequate normative theory is whether it acknowledges the
discrepancy between normative ideal and actual social reality and takes social critique
to be part of its task rather than deferring application of abstract theoretical principles
into an indefinite future.

More important, Held argues that contractual models do not even provide us with
the best normative paradigm. Contract models are especially well designed to address
the question of what makes the use of political coercion legitimate and to determine the
constraints on the pursuit of self-interest that moral or political actors are obligated to
observe. Other equally important questions, however, need to be addressed. On what
kinds of social relations does the stability of a polity or moral practice depend? What
enables the flourishing of individuals within a society? And what are the fundamental
ties that ought to bind persons together?

Held observes that a purely contractual society, in which the primary motive is rational self-interest, is unstable unless adult contractors have earlier learned attitudes of
trust, cooperation, loyalty, and moral concern. "Perhaps," she says, "what are needed
for even adequate levels of social cohesion are persons tied together by relations of
concern and caring and empathy and trust rather than merely by contracts it may be in
their interests to disregard." Fundamentally, any political arrangement or moral practice depends on the mothering labor that produces from infants social persons equipped
with a language, a familiarity with their culture, and the skills that enable them to be
independent individuals and thus contractors.

As to what conditions enable the flourishing of individuals within society, the focus
of contractual and rights-based approaches tends to be on rights to noninterference.
However important such rights might be, human flourishing depends on much more.
Consider children, whose development into autonomous adults depends on mothering
persons responding to children's needs, fostering transformative growth, and supplying affection and the bases for trusting others. We do not, as Held observes, fulfill our
obligations to children merely through noninterference. That morality demands more
of us than respect for the rights of others is especially salient in the mothering context,
but the moral demand to be responsive to the needs of particular others also characterizes our relation to adults. In Held's view, "seeing how unsatisfactory rights merely to
be left alone are as an interpretation of the rights of children may help us to recognize
a similar truth about other persons."

What are the fundamental ties that ought to bind persons together? Held claims that
contractual approaches offer us "an impoverished view of human aspiration." Contract
theories do not provide us with an account of the kinds of morally worthwhile human
relations to which we should aspire. These might be qualitatively described as caring
relations, for example, those in which vulnerable others count on us to accept and live

up to our, often unchosen, responsibility to attend to their needs. Held's detailed description of the mother/child relation draws our attention to human relationships that are nonvoluntary, that impose noncontractual responsibilities where the primary motive is concern for another's welfare, and that sustain such goods as mutual affection, trust, and shared joy. In the mother/child relation, as in some other dependency relations, equality is not best construed in terms of equal rights but in terms of equal consideration. In both moral and political contexts we should aspire not only to live up to our contractual obligations but to maintain caring, need-responsive relations with others.

An important work along the lines of Held's critique of contract approaches is Annette Baier, *Moral Prejudice* (Cambridge, Mass.: Harvard University Press, 1982). Discussions of the distinction between acceptable and unacceptable idealization in ethical and political theorizing may be found in Onora O'Neill, "Abstraction, Idealization and Ideology in Ethics," *Philosophy* 22, Supp. (1987): 55–69; and in Charles Mills, "Ideal Theory as Ideology," *Hypatia* 20, no. 3 (2005): 165–184. Developed critiques of gender and racial bias in contract theory may be found in Carole Pateman and Charles Mills, *Contract and Domination* (Cambridge: Polity, 2007); Charles Mills, *The Racial Contract* (Ithaca, N.Y.: Cornell University Press, 1997); and Carole Pateman, *The Sexual Contract* (Stanford, Calif.: Stanford University Press, 1988).

Another strand of feminist political philosophy creates new conceptual tools for addressing the nature, causes, and remedies for oppression. Consider, for example, Susan Okin's extension of Rawlsian liberalism to justice within the family in her *Justice, Gender, and the Family* (New York: Basic Books, 1989) or Iris Marion Young, *Justice and the Politics of Difference* (Princeton, N.J.: Princeton University Press, 1990), in which she critiques distributive conceptions of justice and advocates understanding justice in terms of nondomination of decision-making processes and the absence of oppression. Another example is Martha Nussbaum, *Sex and Social Justice* (New York: Oxford University Press, 1999), which develops a capabilities approach to articulating a liberal political theory. Also see Seyla Benhabib, *Situating the Self: Gender, Community, and Postmodernism in Contemporary Ethics* (New York: Routledge, 1992) and Nancy J. Hirschmann (ed.), *Revisioning the Political: Feminist Reconstructions of Traditional Concepts in Western Political Theory* (Boulder, Colo.: Westview Press, 1996).

For further discussion of the importance of attending to vulnerability see Robert E. Goodin, *Protecting the Vulnerable: A Reanalysis of Our Social Responsibilities* (Chicago: University of Chicago Press, 1985); Eva Feder Kittay, *Love's Labor: Essays on Women, Equality and Dependency* (New York: Routledge, 1999); and Martha C. Nussbaum, "The Future of Feminist Liberalism," *Setting the Moral Compass*, edited by Cheshire Calhoun (New York: Oxford University Press, 2004). For extended developments of an ethics of care see Joan Tronto, *Moral Boundaries: A Political Argument for an Ethic of Care* (London: Routledge, 1993), and Michael Slote, *The Ethics of Care and Empathy* (New York: Routledge, 2007). For discussions of the nature and importance of trust, see Annette Baier, "Trust and Anti-Trust" (in *Moral Prejudices*), and Onora O'Neill, *A Question of Trust. The BBC Reith Lectures 2002* (Cambridge: Cambridge University Press, 2002). For influential early reflections on mothering and ethics see Sara Ruddick, *Maternal Thinking: Toward a Politics of Peace* (Boston: Beacon Press, 1989), and Joyce Trebilcot (ed.), *Mothering: Essays in Feminist Theory* (Lanham, Md.: Rowman & Littlefield, 1983).

Non-contractual Society: A Feminist View

Contemporary society is in the grip of contractual thinking. Realities are interpreted in contractual terms, and goals are formulated in terms of rational contracts. The leading current conceptions of rationality begin with assumptions that human beings are independent, self-interested or mutually disinterested, individuals; they then typically argue that it is often rational for human beings to enter into contractual relationships with each other.

On the side of description, assumptions characteristic of a contractual view of human relations underlie the dominant attempts to view social realities through the lenses of the social sciences.[1] They also underlie the principles upon which most persons in contemporary Western society claim their most powerful institutions to be founded. We are told that modern democratic states rest on a social contract,[2] that their economies should be thought of as a free market where producers and consumers, employers and employees make contractual agreements.[3] And we should even, it is suggested, interpret our culture as a free market of ideas.[4]

On the side of prescription, leading theories of justice and equality such as those of Rawls, Nozick, and Dworkin, suggest what social arrangements should be like to more fully reflect the requirements of contractual rationality.[5] And various philosophers claim that even morality itself is best understood in contractual terms.[6] The vast domain of rational choice theory, supposedly applicable to the whole range of human activity and experience, makes the same basic assumptions about individuals, contractual relations, and rationality, as are by now familiar in the social contract tradition.[7] And contractual solutions are increasingly suggested for problems which arise in areas not hitherto thought of in contractual terms, such as in dealing with unruly patients in treatment contexts, in controlling inmates in prisons, and even in bringing up children.

When subjected to examination, the assumptions and conceptions of contractual thinking seem highly questionable. As descriptions of reality they can be seriously misleading. Actual societies are the results of war, exploitation, racism, and patriarchy far more than of social contracts. Economic and political realities are the outcomes of economic strength triumphing over economic weakness more than of a free market. And rather than a free market of ideas, we have a culture in which the loudspeakers that are the mass media drown out the soft voices of free expression. As expressions of normative concern, moreover, contractual theories hold out an impoverished view of human aspiration.

To see contractual relations between self-interested or mutually disinterested individuals as constituting a paradigm of human relations is to take a certain historically specific conception of "economic man" as representative of humanity. And it is, many feminists are beginning to agree, to overlook or to discount in very fundamental ways the experience of women.

I will try in this paper to look at society from a thoroughly different point of view than that of economic man. I will take the point of view of women, and especially of mothers, as the basis for trying to rethink society and its possible goals. Certainly there is no single point of view of women; the perspectives of women are potentially as diverse as those of men. But since the perspectives of women have all been to a large extent discounted,

From *Science, Morality, and Feminist Theory*, ed. Marsha Hanen and Kai Nielsen, *Canadian Journal of Philosophy*, Supplementary Volume 13. Calgary: University of Calgary Press, 1987. Reprinted by permission of the publisher. Revised by the author for this book.

across the spectrum, I will not try to deal here with diversity among such views, but rather to give voice to one possible feminist outlook.

The social contract tradition and bourgeois conceptions of rationality have already been criticized for some time from Marxian and other continental perspectives. These perspectives, however, usually leave out the perspective of mothers as fully as do those they criticize, so I will not try to deal here with these alternatives either. I will try instead to imagine what society would look like, for both descriptive and prescriptive purposes, if we replaced the paradigm of "economic man" and substituted for it the paradigm of mother and child. I will try to explore how society and our goals for it might appear if, instead of thinking of human relations as contractual, we thought of them as *like* relations between mothers and children. What would social relations look like? What would society look like if we would take the relation between mother and child as not just one relation among many, but as the *primary* social relation? And what sorts of aspirations might we have for such a society?

On the face of it, it seems plausible to take the relation between child and mother as *the* primary social relation, since before there could have been any self-sufficient, independent men in a hypothetical state of nature, there would have had to have been mothers, and the children these men would have had to have been. And the argument could be developed in terms of a conceptual as well as a causal primacy. However, let me anticipate a likely reaction and say before I begin this exploration that I doubt that the view I am going to present is the one we should end up with. I doubt that we should take any one relation as paradigmatic for all the others. And I doubt that morality should be based on any one type of human relation. In my recent book *Rights and Goods* I argue for different moral approaches for different contexts, and try to map out which approaches are suitable for which contexts.[8] Perhaps this book will turn out to be a mere stage in my thinking, and I will eventually suppose that relations between children and mothers should be thought of as primary, and as the sort of human relation all other

human relations should resemble or reflect. But I am inclined at this point to think that we will continue to need conceptions of different types of relations for different domains, such as the domains of law, of economic activity, and of the family.

To think of relations between mothers and children as paradigmatic, however, may be an important stage to go through in reconstructing a view of human relationships that will be adequate from a feminist point of view. Since the image of rational economic man in contractual relations is pervasive in this society, and expanding constantly, it may be a useful endeavor to try to see everything in this different way, as if the primary social relation is that between child and mother and as if all the others could and should be made over in the image of this one, or be embedded in a framework of such relations. In any case, if we pay attention to this neglected relation between mother and child, perhaps we can put a stop to the imperialism of the model of economic man, and assert with conviction that at least there are some or perhaps many domains where this model is definitely not appropriate. And perhaps we can show that morality must be as relevant to, and moral theory as appropriately based on, the context of mothering as the context of contracting. To the extent that some of our relations should be seen as contractual, we should recognize how essentially limited rather than general such relations are. And to the extent that some of morality should be understood in terms of what rational contractors would agree to, we should recognize that such a morality can only be suitable for a particular domain of human relations, and should not be supposed to be a model for morality in general.

Rational choice theorists point out that their theories are formulated for just those situations where individuals do seek to maximize their own interests and are uninterested in each others' interests. Their theories, they suggest, are not intended to deal with people in love. But the questions I am trying to raise in this paper have to do with how we ought to treat, conceptually, a great variety of human relations. Of course we *can*, theoretically, treat them *as* contractual, but *should* we do so? Is it plausible to do so? And when we ask these questions we can see that of course it is not only in special cases that persons can be and perhaps should be and often are bound together in social ties of a non-contractual kind.

To see society in terms of family rather than marketplace relationships is not new. Feudal conceptions, for instance, drew analogies between monarchs and the heads of households. But these were views based on relations between patriarchal fathers and their wives and children, not views of society seen in terms of mothering. To explore the latter is not to suggest a return to pre-contractual society, but to consider what further progress is needed.

Since it is the practice of mothering with which I will be concerned in what follows, rather than with women in the biological sense, I will use the term "mothering person" rather than "mother." A "mothering person" can be male or female. So I will speak of "mothering persons" in the same gender-neutral way that various writers now try to speak of "rational contractors." If men feel uncomfortable being referred to as, or even more so in being, "mothering persons," this may possibly mirror the discomfort many mothers feel adapting to the norms and practices, and language, of "economic man."

It is important to emphasize that I will look at the practice of mothering not as it has in fact existed in any patriarchal society, but in terms of what the characteristic features of this practice would be without patriarchal domination. In method this may be comparable to what has been done in developing a concept of rational contracting. This concept of course developed while large segments of society were in fact still feudal, and of course actual human beings are not in fact fully rational. These realities have not prevented the contractual relation from being taken as paradigmatic.

Furthermore, it may well be that the concept of the mother/child relation that I will develop is somewhat historically specific. But perhaps no concept can avoid being that. My aim is only to have the conception I will try to develop capable of being considered an alternative to the conception of economic man in contractual relations, that is, of being no more historically limited, and contextually dependent, than that. To the extent that

the mother/child relation will be an idealization, I hope it will not be more severely idealized than the relation between rational contractors that it is to replace; for the purposes of my exploration, it does not need to be less of an idealization.

I. WOMEN AND FAMILY

A first point to note in trying to imagine society from the point of view of women is that the contractual model was hardly ever applied, as either description or ideal, to women or to relations within the family. The family was imagined to be "outside" the polis and "outside" the market in a "private" domain. This private domain was contrasted with the public domain, and with what, by the time of Hobbes and Locke, was thought of as the contractual domain of citizen and state and tradesman and market. Although women have always worked, and although both women and children were later pressed into work in factories, they were still thought of as outside the domain in which the contractual models of "equal men" were developed. Women were not expected to demand equal rights either in the public domain or at home. Women were not expected to be "economic men." And children were simply excluded from the realm of what was being interpreted in contractual terms as distinctively human.

The clearest example of the extraordinary bias to which such views can lead can be seen in the writings of Rousseau. Moral principles were to be applied to men and to women in ways thoroughly inconsistent with each other. Rousseau argued that in the polity no man should surrender his freedom. He thought that government could be based on a social contract in which citizens under law will be as free as in the state of nature because they will give the law to themselves.[9] The argued, within the household, the man must rule and the woman must submit to this rule.[10] Rousseau maintained that women must be trained from the beginning to serve and to submit to men. Since the essence of being fully human was for Rousseau being free from submission to the will of another, women were to be denied the essential condition for being fully human. And he thought that if women were accorded equality with men in the household (which was the only domain to be open to them) this would bring about the dissolution of society. Human society, Rousseau thought, was incompatible with extending the principles of contractual society to women and the family.

The contrast, in this view, is total: complete freedom and equality in the exclusively male polity; absolute male authority and female submission in the household. And Rousseau seems not to have considered the implications of such a view. If one really believes that two persons in a household, with ties of affection and time for discussion, can never reach decisions by consensus, or by taking turns at deciding, but must always have one person in full authority to have the final word, what hope could there possibly be for the larger democratic, participatory, consensual political life Rousseau so eloquently advocated? On the other hand, if decisions in the political realm *can* be arrived at in such a way that the will of no man needs to be overpowered, as Rousseau thought, why cannot such concern for avoiding coercion be extended to relations between men and women in the family?

One way in which the dominant patterns of thought have managed to overlook such inconsistencies has been to see women as primarily mothers, and mothering as a primarily biological function. Then it has been supposed that while contracting is a specifically human activity, women are engaged in an activity which is not specifically human. Women have accordingly been thought to be closer to nature than men, to be enmeshed in a biological function involving processes more like those in which other animals are involved than like the rational contracting of distinctively human "economic man." The total or relative exclusion of women from the domain of voluntary contracting has then been thought to be either inevitable or appropriate.

The view that women are more governed by biology than are men is still prevalent. It is as questionable as many other traditional misinterpretations of women's experience. Human mothering is an extremely different activity from the mothering engaged in by other animals. It is as different from the mothering of other animals as is the work and speech of men different from the "work" and "speech" of other animals. Since humans are also animals, one should not exaggerate the differences between humans and other animals. But to whatever extent it is appropriate to recognize a difference between "man" and other animals, so would it be appropriate to recognize a comparable difference between human mothering and the mothering of other animals.

Human mothering shapes language and culture, and forms human social personhood. Human mothering develops morality, it does not merely transmit techniques of survival; impressive as the latter can be, they do not have built into them the aims of morality. Human mothering teaches consideration for others based on moral concern; it does not merely follow and bring the child to follow instinctive tendency. Human mothering creates autonomous persons; it does not merely propagate a species. It can be fully as creative an activity as most other human activities; to create *new* persons, and new types of *persons*, is surely as creative as to make new objects, products, or institutions. Human mothering is no more "natural" than any other human activity. It may include many dull and repetitive tasks, as does farming, industrial production, banking, and work in a laboratory. But degree of dullness has nothing to do with degree of "naturalness." In sum, human mothering is as different from animal mothering as humans are from animals.

On a variety of grounds there are good reasons to have mothering become an activity performed by men as well as by women.[11] We may wish to continue to use the term "mothering" to designate the activity, in recognition of the fact that it has been overwhelmingly women who have engaged in this activity,[12] and because for the foreseeable future it is the point of view of women, including women engaged in mothering, which should be called on to provide a contrast with the point of view of men. A time may come when a term such as "the nurturing of children" would be preferable to "mothering."[13]

Clearly, the view that contractual relations are a model for human relations generally is especially unsuitable for considering the relations between mothering persons and children. It stretches credulity even further than most philosophers can tolerate to imagine babies as little rational calculators contracting with their mothers for care. Of course the fundamental contracts have always been thought of as hypothetical rather than real. But one cannot imagine hypothetical babies contracting either. And mothering persons, in their care of children, demonstrate hardly any of the "trucking" or trading instinct claimed by Adam Smith to be the *most* characteristic aspect of human nature.[14] If the epitome of what it is to be human is thought to be a disposition to be a rational contractor, human persons creating other human persons through the processes of human mothering are overlooked. And human children developing human personhood are not recognized as engaged in a most obviously human activity.

David Hume, whom some admire for having moral views more compatible with "women's moral sense" than most philosophers have had,[15] had the following to say about the passion of avarice: "Avarice, or the desire of gain, is a universal passion which operates at all times, in all places, and upon all persons."[16] Surely we can note that in the relation between mothering person and child, not only as it should be but often enough as it is, avarice is hard to find. One can uncover very many emotions in the relation, but the avarice that fuels the model of "economic man" with his rational interest is not prominent among them.

There is an exchange in Charlotte Perkins Gilman's *Herland* that illustrates the contrast between the motives ascribed to rational economic man building contractual society, and those central to the practice of mothering. Herland is an imaginary society composed entirely of women. They reproduce by parthenogenesis, and there are only mothers and daughters in the society. Everything is arranged to benefit the next generation and the society has existed peacefully for hundreds of years, with a high level of technological advancement but without any conception of a "survival of the fittest" ethic. Three young men from twentieth century America manage to get to Herland. They acknowledge that

in Herland there are no wars, no kings, no priests, no aristocracies, that the women are all like sisters to each other and work together not by competition but by united action. But they argue that things are much better at home. In one exchange they try to explain how important it is to have competition. One of them expounds on the advantages of competition, on how it develops fine qualities, saying that "without it there would be 'no stimulus to industry.'"[17] He says competition is necessary to provide an incentive to work; "competition," he explains, "is the motor power" of society.

The women of Herland are genuinely curious and good-naturedly skeptical, as they so often are in Gilman's novel. "Do you mean," they ask, "that no mother would work for her children without the stimulus of competition?" In Herland, the entire, industrious society works on the strong motivation of making the society better for the children. As one woman explains, "The children in this country are the one center and focus of all our thoughts. Every step of our advance is always considered in its effects on them . . . You see, we are *Mothers*."[18]

Of course, this is an idealized picture of mothering. But I am contrasting it with an idealized picture of rationally contracting. Quite probably we would not want a society devoted entirely to mothering. But then we might not want a society devoted entirely to better bargains either. In developing these suggestions, it is instructive to see what is most seriously overlooked by a contractual view of society, and to see how important what is overlooked is.

II. FAMILY AND SOCIETY

In recent years, many feminists have demanded that the principles of justice and freedom and equality on which it is claimed that democracy rests be extended to women and the family. They have demanded that women be treated as equals in the polity, in the workplace, and, finally, at home. They have demanded, in short, to be accorded full rights to enter freely the contractual relations of modem society. They have asked that these be extended to take in the family.

But some feminists are now considering whether the arguments should perhaps, instead, run the other way. Instead of importing into the household principles derived from the marketplace, perhaps we should export to the wider society the relations suitable for mothering persons and children. This approach suggests that just as relations between persons within the family should be based on concern and caring, rather than on egoistic or non-tuistic contracts, so various relations in the wider society should be characterized by more care and concern and openness and trust and human feeling than are the contractual bargains that have developed so far in political and economic life, or even than are aspired to in contractarian prescriptions. Then, the household instead of the marketplace might provide a model for society. Of course what we would mean by the household would not be the patriarchal household which was, before the rise of contractual thinking, also thought of as a model of society. We would now mean the relations between children and mothering persons *without* the patriarch. We would take our conception of the *post*-patriarchal family as a model.

The model of the social contract was certainly an improvement over that of political patriarchy. Locke's prescriptions for political order are so clearly better than Filmer's that almost no one still reads the arguments made by philosophers such as Filmer, whose views were completely dominant until replaced by those of contractualists like Locke. Filmer thought that political authority should be based on correct inheritance: God gave the world to Adam, and authority to govern was transferred from Adam through the ancient patriarchs to the legitimate monarchs of any historical period. Democracy, to Filmer, was dangerous nonsense. Of course no feminist would wish to go back to such views as Filmer's, nor to those of Aristotle if interpreted as holding that the polity should be a version on a grander scale of the patriarchal household. But to consider whether we should generalize the relation between mothering person and child to any regions beyond the home is to consider generalizing a quite different relation from that which has existed within the patriarchal household, even between mothers and children within patriarchal society. It is to explore what relations between children and mothering persons should be in non-patriarchal societies, and to consider how a transformed household might contribute to a transformed society.

These questions lead us to focus on the family as a social institution of the utmost importance. The family is a set of relations creating human persons. Societies are composed of families. And a family is a small society. The family is undergoing profound change at the present time, and the attendant upheavals in the personal lives of many persons hold out the promise of remarkable social change, quite possibly for the better.

The family is only beginning to receive the central attention from feminists that it deserves, partly because feminist theory is still in such exploratory stages, trying to understand all at once the multiplicity of forces—social, economic, political, legal, psychological, sexual, biological, and cultural—that affect women. Multiple causes shape the sex/gender structures within which human females and males develop feminine and masculine characteristics and come to occupy the roles that existing societies designate as female and male. We need to understand empirically how this happens. We also need normative theories of the family. Jane Flax, surveying recent feminist writing on the family, writes that to develop alternatives to the oppressive relations that now prevail, we need to think through

> what kinds of child care are best for parents and children; what family structures are best for persons at various stages of the life cycle . . . how the state and political processes should affect families; and how work and the organization of production should be transformed to support whatever family forms are preferred.[19]

It is an enormous task, but recent years have provided more new thought on these subjects than many previous decades.[20]

The major question remains: what are the possibilities of remaking society by remaking what have been thought of as "personal" relations? Societies are composed of persons in relation to one another. The "personal" relations among persons are the most affective and influential in many ways. But the extent to which they are central to wider social relations, or could possibly provide a model for social and political relations of a kind that has been thought of as "public," remains an open question.

Western liberal democratic thought has been built on the concept of the "individual" seen as a theoretically isolatable entity. This entity can assert interests, have rights, and enter into contractual relations with other entities. But this individual is not seen as related to other individuals in inextricable or intrinsic ways. This individual is assumed to be motivated primarily by a desire to pursue his own interests, though he can recognize the need to agree to contractual restraints on the ways everyone may pursue their interests. To the extent that groups have been dealt with at all, they have been treated *as* individuals.

The difficulties of developing trust and cooperation and society itself on the sands of self-interested individuals pursuing their own gain are extreme.[21] Contractual society is society perpetually in danger of breaking down. Perhaps what are needed for even adequate levels of social cohesion are persons tied together by relations of concern and caring and empathy and trust rather than merely by contracts it may be in their interests to disregard. Any enforcement mechanisms put in place to keep persons to their contracts will be as subject to disintegration as the contracts themselves; at some point contracts must be embedded in social relations that are non-contractual.

The relation between mothering person and child, hardly understandable in contractual terms, may be a more fundamental human relation, and a more promising one on which to build our recommendations for the future, than is any relation between rational contractors. Perhaps we should look to the relation between child and mothering person for suggestions of how better describe such society as we now have. And perhaps we should look to it especially for a view of a future more fit for our children than a global battle-ground for rational, egoistic entities trying, somehow, to restrain their antagonisms by fragile contracts.

The Marxian view of the relations between human beings is in various ways more satisfactory than the contractual one and more capable of accounting for social relations in general. However, the Marxian view of our history split into classes and driven by economic forces, is hardly more capable of encompassing, and does not lend itself to reflecting, the experience of the relation between mothering person and child either. So I will continue to develop here the contrast between the relation between child and mothering person on the one hand, and the contractual exchanges of "economic man" on the other.

III. THE MOTHER/CHILD RELATION

Let us examine in more detail the relation between mothering person and child. A first aspect of the relation that we can note is the extent to which it is not voluntary and, for this reason among others, not contractual. The ties that bind child and mothering persons are affectional and solicitous on the one hand, and emotional and dependent on the other. The degree to which bearing and caring for children has been voluntary for most mothers throughout most of history has been extremely limited; it is still quite limited for most mothering persons. The relation *should* be voluntary for the mothering person but it cannot possibly be voluntary for the young child, and it can only become, gradually, slightly more voluntary.

A woman can have decided voluntarily to have a child, but once that decision has been made, she will never again be unaffected by the fact that she has brought this particular child into existence. And even if the decision to have a child is voluntary, the decision to have this particular child, for either parent, cannot be. Technological developments can continue to reduce the uncertainties of childbirth, but unpredictable aspects are likely to remain great for most parents. Unlike that contract where buyer and seller can know what is being exchanged, and which is void if the participants cannot know what they are agreeing to, a parent cannot know what a particular child will be like. And children are totally unable to choose their parents and, for many years, any of their caretakers.

The recognition of how limited are the aspects of voluntariness in the relation between child and mothering person may help us to gain a closer approximation to reality in our understanding of most human relations, especially at a global level, than we can gain from imagining the purely voluntary trades entered into by rational economic contractors to be characteristic of human relations in other domains.

Society may impose certain reciprocal obligations: on parents to care for children when the children are young, and on children to care for parents when the parents are old. But if there is any element of a bargain in the relation between mothering person and child, it is very different from the bargain supposedly characteristic of the marketplace. If a parent thinks, "I'll take care of you now so you'll take care of me when I'm old," it must be based, unlike the contracts of political and economic bargains, on enormous trust and on a virtual absence of enforcement.[22] And few mothering persons have any such exchange in mind when they engage in the activities of mothering. At least the bargain would only be resorted to when the callousness or poverty of the society made the plight of the old person desperate. This is demonstrated in survey after survey; old persons certainly hope not to have to be a burden on their children.[23] And they prefer social arrangements that will allow them to refuse to cash in on any such bargain. So the intention and goal of mothering is to give of one's care without obtaining a return of a self-interested kind. The emotional satisfaction of a mothering person is a satisfaction in the well-being and happiness of another human being, and a satisfaction in the health of the relation between the two persons, not the gain that results from an egoistic bargain. The motive behind the activity of mothering is thus entirely different from that behind a market transaction. And so is, perhaps even more clearly, the motive behind the child's project of growth and development.

A second aspect of the contrast between market relations and relations between mothering person and child is found in the qualities of permanence and non-replaceability. The market makes of everything, even human labor and artistic expression and sexual desire, a commodity to be bought and sold, with one unit of economic value replaceable by any other of equivalent value. To the extent that political life reflects these aspects of the market, politicians are replaceable and political influence is bought and sold. Though rights may be thought of as outside the economic market, in contractual thinking they are seen as inside the wider market of the social contract, and can be traded against each other. But the ties between parents and children are permanent ties, however strained or slack they become at times. And no person within a family should be a commodity to any other. Although various persons may participate in mothering a given child, and a given person may mother many children, still no child and no mothering person is to the other a merely replaceable commodity. The extent to which more of our attitudes, for instance toward our society's cultural productions, should be thought of in these terms rather than in the terms of the marketplace, should be considered.

A third aspect of the relation between mothering person and child that may be of interest is the insight it provides for our notions of equality. It shows us unmistakably that equality is not equivalent to having equal legal rights. All feminists are committed to equality and to equal rights in contexts where rights are what are appropriately at issue. But in many contexts, concerns other than rights are more salient and appropriate. And the equality that is at issue in the relation between child and mothering person is the equal consideration of persons, not a legal or contractual notion of equal rights.

Parents and children should not have equal rights in the sense that what they are entitled to decide or to do or to have should be the same. A family of several small children, an adult or two, and an aged parent should not, for instance, make its decisions by majority vote in most cases.[24] But every member of a family is worthy of equal respect and consideration. Each person in a family is as important as a person as every other.

Sometimes the interests of children have been thought in some sense to count for more, justifying "sacrificing for the children." Certainly, the interests of mothers have often counted for less than those of either fathers or children. Increasingly, we may come to think that the interests of all should count equally, but we should recognize that this claim is appropriately invoked only if the issue should be thought of as one of interest. Often, it should not. Much of the time we can see that calculations of interest, and of equal interests, are as out of place as are determinations of equal rights. Both the rights and the interests of individuals seen as separate entities, and equality between them all, should not exhaust our moral concerns. The flourishing of shared joy, of mutual affection, of bonds of trust and hope between mothering persons and children can illustrate this as clearly as anything can. Harmony, love, and cooperation cannot be broken down into individual benefits or burdens. They are goals we ought to share and relations *between* persons. And although the degree of their intensity may be different, many and various relations *between* persons are important also at the level of communities or societies. We can consider, of a society, whether the relations between its members are trusting and mutually supportive, or suspicious and hostile. To focus only on contractual relations and the gains and losses of individuals obscures these often more important relational aspects of societies.

A fourth important feature of the relation between child and mothering person is that we obviously do not fulfil our obligations by merely leaving people alone. If one leaves an infant alone he will starve. If one leaves a two-year old alone she will rapidly harm herself. The whole tradition that sees respecting others as constituted by non-interference with them is most effectively shown up as inadequate. It assumes that people can fend for themselves and provide through their own initiatives and efforts what they need. This Robinson Crusoe image of "economic man" is false for almost everyone, but it is totally and obviously false in the case of infants and children, and recognizing this can be salutary. It can lead us to see very vividly

how unsatisfactory are those prevalent political views according to which we fulfil our obligations merely by refraining from interference. We ought to acknowledge that our fellow citizens, and fellow inhabitants of the globe, have moral rights to what they need to live—to the food, shelter, and medical care that are the necessary conditions of living and growing—and that when the resources exist for honoring such rights there are few excuses for not doing so. Such rights are not rights to be left to starve unimpeded. Seeing how unsatisfactory rights merely to be left alone are as an interpretation of the rights of children may help us to recognize a similar truth about other persons. And the arguments—though appropriately in a different form—can be repeated for interests as distinct from rights.[25]

A fifth interesting feature of the relation between mothering person and child is the very different view it provides of privacy. We come to see that to be in a position where others are *not* making demands on us is a rare luxury, not a normal state. To be a mothering person is to be subjected to the continual demands and needs of others. And to be a child is to be subjected to the continual demands and expectations of others. Both mothering persons and children need to extricate themselves from the thick and heavy social fabric in which they are entwined in order to enjoy any pockets of privacy at all.

Here the picture we form of our individuality and the concept we form of a "self" is entirely different from the one we get if we start with the self-sufficient individual of the "state of nature." If we begin with the picture of rational contractor entering into agreements with others, the "natural" condition is seen as one of individuality and privacy, and the problem is the building of society and government. From the point of view of the relation between mothering person and child, on the other hand, the problem is the reverse. The starting condition is an enveloping tie, and the problem is individuating oneself. The task is to carve out a gradually increasing measure of privacy in ways appropriate to a constantly shifting independency. For the child, the problem is to become gradually more interdependent. For the mothering person, the problem is to free oneself from an all-consuming involvement. For both, the progression is from society to greater individuality rather than from self-sufficient individuality to contractual ties.

Psychology and psychoanalysis have long been interested in the process by which children develop and individuate themselves. Especially relevant now are feminist explorations of the different development of a sense of self in boys and in girls, and of a possibly different moral sense. Philosophers are just beginning to consider the normative issues involved. And social philosophers are just beginning to consider what we should think about social relations if we take women as our starting point. That we need not start with the family in forming our concepts of society has been recognized for several centuries, ever since Locke won out over Filmer, but the family has been assumed to be patriarchal. That it might be instructive to begin with the point of view of women, and within that with the relation between mothering person and child, to try to reconceptualize society and our goals for better societies, is a new idea. A new concept of the "self" may be at the heart of such reconceptualizations. And we should expect that a new concept of "self" or "person" should have as much significance for our views of politics and society, and for our conceptualizations of the supposedly "impersonal" and "public" domain distinct from the supposedly "personal" and "private" sphere of the family, as has the concept of the self as rational calculator and the conceptualization of society as contractual. The same real "persons" can act in and inhabit both marketplace and household contexts. It is open to them to decide what sorts of institutions to encourage for the sake of what sorts of persons.

A sixth aspect of the relation between child and mothering person which is noteworthy is the very different view of power it provides. We are accustomed to thinking of power as something that can be wielded by one person over another, as a means by which one person can bend another to his will. An ideal has been to equalize power so that agreements can be forged and conflicts defused. But consider now the very different view of power in the relation between mothering person and child.

The superior power of the mothering person over the child is relatively useless for most of what the mothering person aims to achieve in bringing up the child. The mothering person seeks to *empower* the child to act responsibly, she neither wants to "wield" power nor to defend herself against the power "wielded" by the child. The relative powerlessness of the child is largely irrelevant to most of the project of growing up. When the child is physically weakest, as in infancy and illness, the child can "command" the greatest amount of attention and care from the mothering person because of the seriousness of the child's needs.

The mothering person's stance is characteristically one of caring, of being vulnerable to the needs and pains of the child, and of fearing the loss of the child before the child is ready for independence. It is not characteristically a stance of domination. The child's project is one of developing, of gaining ever greater control over his or her own life, of relying on the mothering person rather than of submitting to superior strength. Of course the relation may in a degenerate form be one of domination and submission, but this only indicates that the relation is not what it should be. In a form in which the relation between mothering person and child is even adequately exemplified, the conceptions of power with which we are familiar, from Hobbes and Locke to Hegel and Marx, are of little use for understanding the aspects of power involved in the relation.[26] The power of a mothering person to empower others, to foster transformative growth, is a different sort of power than that of a stronger sword or dominant will. And the power of a child to call forth tenderness and care is perhaps more different still.

IV. MOTHERING AND MORAL THEORY

A final aspect of the relation between mothering person and child about which I would like to speculate is what a focus on this relation might imply for our views of morality itself, and of ethical theory itself.

Hobbes thought we could build society on the equal vulnerability of every man to the sword of his fellows. Women have never fit into that picture. We are more vulnerable to the sword. And yet the sword is powerless to create new wielders of it. Only the power of mothers can in the long run triumph. But the power of mothers is continually being eclipsed by the power of children.

The vulnerability of men may bring them to seek peace and to covenant against violence. We can hope for whatever progress can be made in curbing the murderous conflicts, tempered by truces and treaties, to which this has led, though our expectations under current conditions must realistically be very modest.

But let us speculate about a different vulnerability and a different development. Mothering persons are vulnerable to the demands and needs of children. We do not know if this is instinctive or innate, or not. Some claim that women lack a mothering instinct. Others claim that the experiences of carrying a child, of laboring and suffering to give birth, of suckling, inevitably cause mothers to be especially sensitive to the cries and needs of a child. Others claim that fathers, placed in the position of being the only persons capable of responding to the needs of a child, develop similar responsiveness. Whatever the truth, one can admit that no one can become a mothering person without becoming sensitive to the needs of relatively helpless or less powerful others. And to become thus sensitive is to become vulnerable. If the vulnerability is chosen, so much the better. Mothering persons become in this way vulnerable to the claims of morality.

It is not, however, the morality of following abstract, universal rules so much as the morality of being responsive to the needs of actual, particular others in relations with us. The traditional view, reasserted in the psychological studies of Lawrence Kohlberg, that women are less likely than men to be guided by the highest forms of morality, would only be plausible if morality were no more than the abstract and rational rules of pure and perfect principle.[27] For traditional morality, increasingly recognizable as developed from a male point of view, there seems to be either the pure principle of

the rational law-giver, or the self-interest of the individual contractor. There is the unreal universality of *all*, or the real *self* of individual interest.

Both views, however, lose sight of acting *for* particular others in actual contexts. Mothering persons cannot lose sight of the particularity of the child being mothered nor of the actuality of the circumstances in which the activity is taking place. Mothering persons may tend to resist harming or sacrificing those particular others for the sake of abstract principles or total faith; on the other hand, it is for the sake of *others*, or for the sake of relationships between persons, rather than to further their own interests, that such resistance is presented by mothering persons. Morality, for mothering persons, must guide us in our relations with actual, particular children, enabling them to develop their own lives and commitments. For mothering persons, morality can never seem adequate if it offers no more than ideal rules for hypothetical situations: morality must connect with the actual context of real, particular others in need. At the same time, morality, for mothering persons, cannot possibly be a mere bargain between rational contractors. That morality in this context could not be based on self-interest or mutual disinterest directly is obvious; that a contractual escape is unavailable or inappropriate is clear enough.

The morality that could offer guidance for those engaged in mothering might be a superior morality to those available at present. It would be a morality based on caring and concern for actual human others, and it would have to recognize the limitations of both egoism and perfect justice.[28] When we would turn to the social and political theories that would be compatible with such a view of morality, we would see that they would have to be very different not only from the patriarchial models of pre-contractual conceptions, but also from the contractual models that so dominate current thinking. Contractual relations would not be ruled out, but they would cease to seem paradigmatic of human relations, and the regions within which they could be thought to be justified would be greatly reduced.

V. THE CHILD'S PERSPECTIVE

What about the point of view of the child? A most salient characteristic of the relation between mothering person and child is the child's relative powerlessness. The child cannot possibly rely on the Hobbesian safeguard of the equal vulnerability of the caretaker. Not even when the caretaker is asleep is she vulnerable to the sword of the small child, and it will be years, if ever, before the child can match the caretaker in even physical strength, let alone social and economic and psychological power. Whatever claims the child makes against a mothering person must be based on something else than superior strength, and the child should come to trust the restraint of one who could but does not wish to cause the child harm.

The child in relation to the mothering person is permanently in the best possible position from which to recognize that right is *not* equivalent to might, that power, including the power to teach and enforce a given morality, is not equivalent to morality itself. Becoming a person is not so much learning a morality that is being taught as it is developing the ability to decide for oneself what morality requires of one. Children characteristically go beyond the mothering persons in their lives, becoming autonomous beings. They do not characteristically then respond to the mothering persons they leave behind with proposals for better bargains for themselves now that they have the power to enforce their terms. The relation between mothering person and child is such that disparities of power are given. Though the positions may reverse themselves, unequal power is almost ever present. But it is often also irrelevant to the relation.

When young men are invited to enter the public realm of contractual relations they are encouraged to forget their past lack of power and to assume a position of equality or superiority. But we should probably none of us ever forget what it is like to lack power. Taking the relation between child and mothering person as the primary social relation might encourage us to remember the point of view of those who cannot rely on the power of arms to uphold their moral claims. It

might remind us of the distinction between the morality that, as developed autonomous persons, we come to construct for ourselves, and the moral injunctions which those with superior force can hold us to. Though I cannot develop these suggestions further in this particular paper, *much* more needs to be felt from the point of view of children.

VI. MODELS FOR SOCIETY

The relation between child and mothering person seems especially worth exploring to see what implications and insights it might suggest for a transformed society.

There are good reasons to believe that a society resting on no more than bargains between self-interested or mutually disinterested individuals will not be able to withstand the forces of egoism and dissolution pulling such societies apart. Although there may be some limited domains in which rational contracts are the appropriate form of social relations, as a foundation for the fundamental ties which ought to bind human beings together, they are clearly inadequate. Perhaps we can learn from a non-patriarchal household better than from further searching in the marketplace what the sources might be for justifiable trust, cooperation, and caring.

Many persons can imagine human society on the model of "economic man," society built on a contract between rationally self-interested persons, because these are the theories they have been brought up with. But they cannot imagine society[29] resembling a group of persons tied together by on-going relations of caring and trust between persons in positions such as those of mothers and children where, as adults, we would sometimes be one and sometimes the other. Suppose now we ask: in the relation between mothering person and child, who are the contractors? Where is the rational self-interest? The model of "economic man" makes no sense in this context. Anyone in the social contract tradition who has noticed the relation of child and mothering person at all has supposed it to belong to some domain outside the realm of the "free market" and outside the "public" realm of politics and the law. Such theorists have supposed the context of mothering to be of much less significance for human history and of much less relevance for moral theory than the realms of trade and government, or they have imagined mothers and children as somehow outside human society altogether in a region labelled "nature," and engaged wholly in "reproduction." But mothering is at the heart of human society.

If the dynamic relation between child and mothering person is taken as the primary social relation, then it is the model of "economic man" that can be seen to be deficient as a model for society and morality, and unsuitable for all but a special context. A domain such as law, if built on no more than contractual foundations, can then be recognized as one limited domain among others; law protects some moral rights when people are too immoral or weak to respect them without the force of law. But it is hardly a majestic edifice that can serve as a model for morality. Neither can the domain of politics, if built on no more than self-interest or mutual disinterest, provide us with a model with which to understand and improve society and morality. And neither, even more clearly, can the market itself.

When we explore the implications of these speculations we may come to realize that instead of seeing the family as an anomalous island in a sea of rational contracts composing economic and political and social life, perhaps it is instead "economic man" who belongs on a relatively small island surrounded by social ties of a less hostile, cold, and precarious kind.

Notes

1. As Carole Pateman writes, "One of the most striking features of the past two decades is the extent to which the assumptions of liberal individualism have permeated the whole of social life." Carole Pateman, *The Problem of Political Obligation: A Critique of Liberal Theory* (Berkeley: University of California Press 1985), 182–3. All those fields influenced by rational choice theory—and that includes most of the social sciences—thus "hark back to classical liberal contract doctrines," Pateman writes, "and claims that social order is founded on the interactions of self-interested,

utility-maximizing individuals, protecting and enlarging their property in the capitalist market" (183).

2. E.g. Thomas Hobbes, *Leviathan*, C. B. Macpherson, ed. (Baltimore: Penguin 1971); John Locke, *Two Treatises of Government*, Peter Laslett, ed. (New York: Mentor 1965); Jean-Jacques Rousseau, The *Social Contract*, Charles Frankel, ed. (New York: Hafner 1947); The U.S. Declaration of Independence; and of course a literature too vast to mention. As Carole Pateman writes of this tradition, "a corollary of the liberal view. . . . is that social contract theory is central to liberalism. Paradigmatically, contract is the act through which two free and equal individuals create social bonds, or a collection of such individuals creates the state" (180).

3. E.g. Adam Smith, *The Wealth of Nations*, M. Lerner, ed. (New York: Random House 1937) and virtually the whole of classical and neo-classical economics.

4. The phrase has been entrenched in judicial and social discussion since Oliver Wendell Holmes used it in *Abrams v. United States* (250 U.S. 616, 630 [1919]).

5. E.g. John Rawls, *A Theory of Justice* (Cambridge, MA: Harvard University Press 1971); Robert Nozick, *Anarchy, State, and Utopia* (New York: Basic Books 1974); and Ronald Dworkin, *Taking Rights Seriously* (Cambridge, MA: Harvard University Press 1977).

6. E.g. David A. J. Richards, *A Theory of Reasons for Action* (New York: Oxford University Press 1971); and David Gauthier, *Morals By Agreement* (New York: Oxford University Press 1986).

7. For a recent sample, see the symposium "Explanation and Justification in Social Theory," in Ethics 97, 1.

8. Virginia Held, *Rights and Goods: Justifying Social Action* (New York: Free Press/Macmillan 1984).

9. J.-J. Rousseau, *The Social Contract*.

10. J.-J. Rousseau, *Emile*, trans. B. Foxley (New York: Dutton 1911).

11. See especially Nancy Chodorow, *The Reproduction of Mothering: Psychoanalysis and the Sociology of Gender* (Berkeley, CA: University of California Press 1978); and Joyce Trebilcot, ed., *Mothering: Essays in Feminist Theory* (Totowa, NJ: Rowman and Allanheld 1984).

12. See e.g. Susan Peterson, "Against 'Parenting,'" in Trebilcot, *Mothering*.

13. By then "parenting" might also be acceptable to those who find it presently misleading.

14. Adam Smith, Book I, Chap. II.

15. See, e.g., Annette Baier, "Hume: The Women's Moral Theorist?" in *Women and Moral Theory*, Eva Kittay and Diana Meyers, eds. (Totowa, NJ: Rowman and Littlefield 1986).

16. David Hume, *Essays Moral, Political, and Literary*, Vol. 1, Green and T. H. Grose, eds, (London: Longmans 1898), 176.

17. Charlotte Perkins Gilman, *Herland* (New York: Pantheon 1979), 60; orginally publ. 1915.

18. Ibid., 66.

19. Jane Flax, "The Family in Contemporary Feminist Thought: A Critical Review," in *The Family in Political Thought*, Jean Belhke Elshtain, ed. (Amherst: The University of Massachusetts Press 1982), 252.

20. The collection of readings in Barrie Thorne, ed., *Rethinking the Family* (New York: Longmans 1982) is a useful source. Joyce Trebilcot's *Mothering* is another helpful collection. And among the best sources of suggestions are feminist utopian novels, e.g. Marge Piercy's *Woman on the Edge of Time* (New York: Fawcett 1976).

21. See especially Virginia Held, *Rights and Goods*, chapter 5.

22. In some societies social pressures to conform with the norms of reciprocal care—of children by parents and later of parents by children—can be very great. But these societies are usually of a kind which are thought to be at a stage of development antecedent to that of contractual society.

23. The gerontologist Elaine Brody says about old people that "what we hear over and over again—and I'm talking gross numbers of 80 to 90 percent in survey after survey—is 'I don't want to be a burden on my children.'" Interview by Lindsy Van Gelder, *Ms.* Magazine (January 1986), 48.

24. For a different view see Howard Cohen, *Equal Rights for Children* (Totowa, NJ: Littlefield, Adams 1980).

25. See Virginia Held, *Rights and Goods*.

26. For related discussions see Nancy Hartsock, *Money, Sex and Power: Toward a Feminist Historical Materialism* (New York: Longmans 1983); and Sara Ruddick, "Maternal Thinking," in Trebilcot, *Mothering*.

27. For examples of the view that women are more deficient than men in understanding morality and acting morally, see e.g. Mary Mahowald, ed., *Philosophy of Woman: Classical to Current Concepts* (Indianapolis: Hackett 1978). See also Lawrence Kohlberg, *The Philosophy of Moral Development* (San Francisco: Harper and Row 1981), and L. Kohlberg and R. Kramer, "Continuities and Discontinuities in Child and Adult Moral Development," *Human Development* 12 (1969) 93–120. For critique and a different view, see Carol Gilligan, *In a Different Voice: Psychological Theory and Women's Development* (Cambridge, MA: Harvard University Press, 1982).

28. For further discussion, see Virginia Held, "Feminism and Moral Theory," in *Women and Moral Theory*, Eva Kittay and Diana Meyers, eds. (Totowa, NJ: Rowman & Littlefield 1987).

29. Virginia Held, "Marx, Sex, and the Transformation of Society," *The Philosophical Forum* 5, 1–2 (Fall-Winter 1973–74).

IRIS MARION YOUNG

~

INTRODUCTION

ANN E. CUDD

Iris Marion Young was born in 1949 and grew up in Astoria, Queens, in New York City. She graduated from Queens College in 1970 and earned her Ph.D. from Pennsylvania State University in 1974. She began college with the ambition of becoming a poet, but amid the Vietnam War and other social upheaval of the late 1960s she was drawn to social philosophy and political activism. Her work includes important contributions to feminist philosophy, phenomenology, political philosophy, and social theory. Among her many books, perhaps most famous is *Justice and the Politics of Difference* (1990), which received the American Political Science Association's Victoria Schuck Award for the best book on Women in Politics, and which includes a reworking of "Five Faces of Oppression" as one of its chapters. At the time of her death in 2006 she was a professor of political science at the University of Chicago, having been appointed previously in philosophy departments at Miami University and Worcester Polytechnic Institute, and in the Graduate School of Public and International Affairs at the University of Pittsburgh.

Young both argued for the importance of, and personally engaged in, grass-roots political activism. She worked actively on causes such as women's human rights, debt relief for Africa, and workers' rights, and considered herself a "citizen-theorist." Young could be found marching in picket lines with striking workers, visiting with employers to improve working conditions, and using her considerable skill as a writer to persuade people at all levels of influence and power to do the right thing.

Young's philosophical work concerned themes of difference, oppression, democracy, and collective responsibility. Her earliest published work described the embodied experience of women and argued for full appreciation and respect for their differences from men, which she explicated in essays collected in *Throwing Like a Girl and Other Essays in Feminist Philosophy and Social Theory* (Indiana University Press, 1990), and then revised and extended in *On Female Body Experience: "Throwing Like a Girl" and Other Essays* (Oxford University Press, 2005). Young argued against the prevailing currents of liberal deliberative democractic theory and communitarianism (as represented by Michael Sandel and Charles Taylor), and for maintaining and respecting cultural difference and the inclusion of multiple voices and modes of expression in democratic decision making. She explores these ideas in the aforementioned *Justice and the Politics of Difference*, then in *Intersecting Voices: Dilemmas of Gender, Political Philosophy, and Policy* (1997), and *Inclusion and Democracy* (2000). Finally, Young recognized that motivating social change requires that we recognize our responsibility for unjust social conditions, and developed an original and influential theory of how we can be held collectively responsible for injustice despite our lack of knowledge or intention to oppress others in two posthumously published books: *Global Challenges: War, Self-Determination, and Responsibility for Justice* (2007) and *Responsibility for Justice* (2010).

Mainstream political philosophy of the 1970s and 1980s was dominated in the English-speaking world by liberalism and in particular the work of John Rawls. The New Left offered a distinct alternative to liberalism, expounded in the work of feminist and radical activists and grounded in the philosophy Karl Marx as interpreted by European philosophers, such as Jürgen Habermas and Jacques Derrida, and the phenomenology of Martin Heidegger. This alternative political theory considers oppression to be a primary form of injustice. As Young explains in "Five Faces of Oppression," liberalism is an individualist philosophy that assigns responsibility to individual agents only for their conscious, intentional actions. Many of the harms that the New Left considers oppressive, however, are not caused by intentional actions. Rawls discusses the injustice of discrimination in his *Theory of Justice*, but his theory did not comprehend the kinds of systematic but unconscious harms suffered by women, the aged, the working class, or sexual and ethnic minorities, which leftists held to be at least as significant. Thus Young sets out to characterize and analyze these harms as part of the meaning of "oppression."

Young's primary thesis is that "oppression" does not name a single phenomenon but rather a set of related but irreducible harms, which she calls the "five faces" of oppression. They are related in that they are group-based, systematic harms of the social system that benefits other groups. This contrasts with the old use of "oppression" as tyranny by a ruler or ruling group. On the old conception oppression happens strictly within the political system and consists in the intentional actions of one political class to dominate others. A liberal democratic society could not support oppression on this view. But to Young and other social critics from the Left, oppression seemed not to have disappeared with the advent of legal, democratic equality. The new meaning of oppression Young wishes to characterize in this essay "names vast and deep injustices some groups suffer as consequence of frequently unconscious assumption and reactions of well-meaning people in ordinary interactions . . . of everyday life." These are the social harms that blacks, women, homosexuals, non-Christians, the elderly, and the disabled suffer through their everyday experiences of disrespect, material deprivation, and hate-inspired violence.

Oppression in this new sense happens to persons as members of social groups. A social group is neither an intentionally formed association (such as a track team) nor an accidental collection of persons (such as the people who just happen to be on the same plane together), but rather a social identity that is given by the social relations one finds oneself in with others. "To be in a group," Young writes, "is to share with others a way of life that defines a person's identity and by which other people identify him or her." For example, a woman has certain characteristic relations with other women that are different from those she has with men, and others identify her as a woman and relate to her accordingly. No individual can create anew the meanings of these identities and relations, but each approaches them as "always already there," in the words of Heidegger. Modern society, Young argues, inevitably renews and produces social group difference among persons. Although in this essay Young emphasizes the role of group identification in individual experience, she later characterized social groups as even less voluntary than that; a person would be placed in a social group because others treated her as a member of that group even if she herself did not identify as such.

A key aspect of the new concept of oppression is that it is systematic, caused by the very structure of society. Society is structured by everyday practices, norms, assumptions, behaviors, and institutional rules. These structures harm oppressed groups and benefit others. For example, the double sexual standard that assigns women responsibility for any reproductive outcomes of sexual intercourse, while men remain free of this responsibility, favors men at women's expense. Such social norms are neither due to nor changeable by any particular individual's actions or intentions (though, of course, concerted collective action can change them). Thus another feature of oppression's systematicity is that there need not be an oppressor, though for every oppressed group there will be another group that is privileged.

Young offers five categories of oppressive harms—the "five faces" of oppression—and claims that with these categories "the oppression of any group can be described." These five faces are exploitation, marginalization, powerlessness, cultural imperialism, and violence. Each category is a sufficient condition for claiming that a group is oppressed, although most oppressed groups suffer from more than one of these harms, and some suffer from all of them. They are also jointly necessary conditions for oppression; if a group does not suffer from any of these categories of harm, then it cannot claim to be oppressed.

In keeping with the Marxist grounding of her theory, the first three of the categories are facets of the way capitalism structures modern society, and are matters of concrete power differences. Exploitation is the first and, judging by the care with which she discusses it, for her the most important category of oppression. A group is exploited when its labor is systematically used for the benefit of another group through a process that maintains the power of the benefited group to continue to benefit from the labor of the oppressed. While exploitation was conceived by Marx as a primarily economic matter, Young invokes the feminist argument that women's sexual and reproductive labor is exploited by men. She offers an original analysis of the menial labor of workers of color as exploitation in terms of status as well as wealth.

Marginalization, the second category of oppressive harm, occurs when a social group is rendered invisible by the economic structure of society. In a capitalist economy both capitalists and workers have status, even if it is unequal, but one who neither works nor owns capital lacks status entirely. Groups who fall into this category include the disabled, the elderly, and those who are unable to find work because of discrimination, segregation, or a lack of skills. Because marginalization entails invisibility, groups who suffer from this harm are in danger of being completely neglected or even exterminated, and thus Young holds this to be the most dangerous category of oppressive harm.

Young's third category, powerlessness, afflicts those who are not considered professionals in modern society. The harm they suffer is disrespect and an unappealing work activity. This harm is less significant than the others, and more subject to change in different social contexts. For example, would a well-trained plumber or electrician count as a professional? Yet the importance of being seen as "respectable" has often been noted by social philosophers and psychologists, and lack of professional status makes it necessary to prove oneself respectable.

The fourth category of oppressive harm, cultural imperialism, happens when a dominant group establishes its experiences, tastes, and beliefs as norms for all. Anyone for whom these norms do not obtain is seen as the Other. This is a form of disrespect, but it can be even more damaging if the dominant group forcefully represses other norms, as happened to Jews in Nazi Germany or to homosexuals in nearly every society.

The final category of oppressive harm, violence, is given very short notice in Young's essay, perhaps because it is the most obvious form of harm. Yet because oppressive violence can seem random and is unprovoked, it may be overlooked as an accidental feature of social life. Oppressive violence is systematic, however, because it targets only members of certain social groups, but otherwise randomly targets individuals within them. Young holds that such violence is irrationally motivated, yet useful for the dominant group, because it helps maintain dominance. This duality is puzzling, but Young does not explore it further.

Armed with the five categories of oppressive harm, Young is able to explain why sexism, racism, ageism, and heterosexism are all forms of oppressions, yet in quite different ways. Women suffer from a different set of the five categories of oppressive harms than blacks, or the elderly, or gays and lesbians. Furthermore, in different societies or different times, these groups may suffer from a different set of categories, or perhaps, as we may someday hope, from none.

Other important philosophical work on oppression includes Marilyn Frye's classic "Oppression," in *The Politics of Reality* (Berkeley, Calif.: The Crossing Press, 1983), from which Young takes the basic definition of oppression as immobilizing or reducing a group. Jean Harvey, in *Civilized Oppression* (Lanham, Md.: Rowman & Littlefield, 1999) continues Young's exploration of cultural forms of oppression and considers the question of resistance. Ann E. Cudd, *Analyzing Oppression* (New York: Oxford University Press, 2006) offers, contrary to Young's thesis here, a unifying definition of oppression that covers a wider set of harms, including those that Young recognized. A collection of essays that provide excellent overview of and critical engagement with Young's work can be found in Ann Ferguson and Mechthild Nagel, *Dancing with Iris: The Philosophy of Iris Marion Young* (New York: Oxford University Press, 2009).

Five Faces of Oppression

Politics is partly a struggle over the language people use to describe social and political experience. Most people in the United States would not use the term "oppression" to name injustice in this society. For a minority of Americans, on the other hand—such as socialists, radical feminists, American Indian activists, black activists, gay and lesbian activists, and others identifying with new left social movements of the 1960s and '70s—oppression is a central category of political discourse. Speaking the political language in which oppression is a central word involves adopting a whole mode of analyzing and evaluating social structures and practices that is quite incommensurate with the language of liberal individualism that dominates political discourse in the United States.

From Iris Marion Young, "Five Faces of Oppression," *The Philosophical Forum*, vol. XIX, no. 4 (1988). Reprinted by permission of the journal.

Consequently, those of us who identify with at least one of the movements I have named have a major political project: we must persuade people that the discourse of oppression makes sense of much of our social experience. We are ill prepared for this task, however, if we have no clear account of the meaning of the concept of oppression. While we commonly find the term used in the diverse philosophical and theoretical literature spawned by radical social movements in the United States, we find little direct discussion of the meaning of the concept of oppression as used by these movements.

In this chapter I offer some explication of the concept as I understand its use by new social movements in the United States since the 1960s. I offer you an explication of this concept, an unfolding of its meaning. I do not think the concept of oppression can be strictly defined, that is, corralled within one clear boundary. There is no attribute or set of attributes that all oppressed people have in common.

In the following account of oppression I reflect on the situation and experience of those groups said by new left social movements to be oppressed in U.S. society: at least women, blacks, Chicanos, Puerto Ricans, and most other Spanish-speaking Americans, Native Americans, Jews, lesbians, gay men, Arabs, Asians, old people, working-class people, poor people, and physically or mentally disabled people.

Obviously, these groups are not oppressed to the same degree or in the same ways. In the most general sense, all oppressed people share some inhibition of their ability to develop and exercise their capacities and express their needs, thoughts, and feelings. Nevertheless, reflection on the concrete uses of the term "oppression" in radical political discourse convinces me that the term refers to several distinct structures or situations. I label these with five disparate categories: exploitation, marginality, powerlessness, cultural imperialism, and violence. Before I unfold these categories, though, I need to discuss some issues of social ontology relevant to placing the concept of oppression.

NEW LEFT REVISION OF THE CONCEPT OF OPPRESSION

One of the reasons that many people would not use the term "oppression" to describe our society is that they do not understand the term in the same way as do radicals. In its traditional usage, which most people retain, "oppression" means the exercise of tyranny by a ruling group. Thus, many Americans would agree with radicals in applying the term to the situation of black South Africans under apartheid. Traditionally, "oppression" also carries a strong connotation of conquest and colonial domination, The Hebrews were oppressed in Egypt, and many uses of the term in the West invoke this paradigm.

Dominant political discourse may use the term to describe societies other than our own, usually communist or purportedly communist societies. Within this anticommunist rhetoric, both tyrannical and colonialist implications of the term appear. For the anticommunist, communism denotes precisely the exercise of brutal tyranny over a whole people by a few rulers, and the will to conquer the world, bringing now independent peoples under that tyranny. In dominant political discourse, it is not legitimate to use the term to describe our society because "oppression" is the evil perpetrated by the "others."

New left social movements of the 1960s and '70s, however, shifted the meaning of the concept. In its new usage, "oppression" designates the disadvantage and injustice some people suffer not because a tyrannical power intends to keep them down, but because of the everyday practices of a well-intentioned liberal society. In this new left usage, the tyranny of a ruling group over another, as in South Africa, must certainly be called oppressive. But "oppression" also refers to systemic and structural phenomena that are not necessarily the result of the intentions of a tyrant. Oppression in the structural sense is part of the basic fabric of a society, not a function of a few people's choice or policies. You won't eliminate this structural oppression by getting rid of the rulers or making some new laws, because oppressions are systematically reproduced in major economic, political, and cultural institutions. Thus, one reason that "oppression" is not commonly used to describe injustice in our society is that the prevailing political discourse does not have a place in its social ontology for structuration and social groups.

Mirroring majority political discourse, philosophical discussions of justice and injustice rarely use the term "oppression," using instead the term "discrimination" to refer to some of the injustices radicals call oppression. Even radical philosophers tend to avoid the term "oppression." Although his analysis is clearly influenced by Black Marxism and Black Power movements, Bernard Boxill, for example, consistently uses the term "discrimination" to designate the injustice that blacks have suffered and continue to suffer in U.S. society.[1] This is a symptom of the hold majority political discourse has over our thinking, perhaps especially over philosophers, who in turn help legitimate that discourse by using it and giving it technical precision. By "discrimination" I mean conscious actions and policies by which members of a group are excluded from institutions or confined to inferior positions. Discrimination is often an instrument of oppression, and discriminatory practices are certainly part of some oppressions, but the concept of oppression is neither coincident with nor reducible to discrimination.

Discrimination is a methodologically individualist concept.[2] In recent years most courts have found that there has been discrimination only if particular victims of discrimination can be individually identified, that a particular agent can be identified as responsible for discrimination, and it can be shown that the agent knew its actions or policies were discriminatory. To be sure, the concept of discrimination can make reference to groups insofar as a discriminatory policy excludes a whole class of persons from some position or activity. Even when concerning groups, however, discrimination is usually an individualist concept

insofar as it presupposes an identifiable agent who discriminates, and that the sum of discrimination is the sum of discriminatory acts.

The difference between the concept of discrimination and the concept of oppression emerges most clearly with the insight that oppression often exists in the absence of overt discrimination. Though actions and policies that explicitly discriminated against members of particular groups were common in the United States not long ago and have by no means disappeared, legislation and litigation in the past twenty years have greatly lessened overt policies of discrimination against most groups, with the outrageous exception of lesbians and gay men. Socialists, feminists, antiracism activists, insist, however, that this serious reduction in overt and conscious policies of exclusion and segregation has done little to reduce the oppression that many groups have suffered and continue to suffer. This concept cites the vast and deep injustices some groups suffer as a consequence of frequently unconscious assumptions and reactions of well-meaning people in ordinary interactions, media and cultural stereotypes, and structural features of bureaucratic hierarchy and market mechanisms, in short, the normal ongoing processes of everyday life. As Marilyn Frye puts it, oppression refers to "an enclosing structure of forces and barriers which tends to be the immobilization and reduction of a group or category of people."[3]

THE CONCEPT OF SOCIAL GROUP

Oppression refers to structural phenomena that immobilize or reduce a group. But what is a group? To be in a group is to share with others a way of life that defines a person's identity and by which other people identify him or her. Political philosophy typically has no place for a specific concept of social group. When philosophers and political theorists discuss groups, they tend to conceive them either on the model of aggregates or associations, both of which are methodologically individualist concepts. Along with Marilyn Friedman and Larry May, I think it is important to distinguish the concept of group from both aggregate and association.[4]

Liberal sentiments sometimes prompt us to assert that grouping by race, sex, religion, ethnicity, region, and so on, ought to carry no more significance than grouping by hair color, height, or the make of car we drive. Such an invocation calls for groups to be considered as mere aggregates, a classification of persons according to some attribute they share. The logic of aggregates presumes a substantial notion of the person to whom attributes are attached, and in that logical sense the person is prior to the collective. If we consider social groups as aggregates we imply that group membership does not define that person, but merely is a set of attributes, and that the collective is nothing other than the sum of the individuals with those attributes.

Political theorists tend to elide social groups more often with associations than aggregates.[5] By an association I mean a formally organized institution, such as a club, corporation, political party, church, college, union, etc. An individualist contract model of society applies to associations but not to groups. Individuals constitute associations; they come together as already formed persons and set them up, establishing rules, positions, and offices. Groups, on the other hand, constitute individuals. A subject's particular sense of history, sense of identity, affinity, and separateness, even the person's mode of reasoning, evaluating, and expressing feeling are constituted at least partly by his or her group affinities. This does not mean that persons have no individual styles or are unable to transcend or reject a group-related identity, and it does not preclude persons having many aspects that are independent of these group identities. Since the form of group differentiation in modern societies implies that a single person usually belongs to several groups, it follows that individual subjects are not unified, but multiple, heterogeneous, and sometimes perhaps incoherent.

A person joins an association, and even if membership in it fundamentally affects one's life, one does not take that association membership to define one's very identity, in the way, for example, being Navajo might. Group affinity, on the other hand, has the character of what Heidegger calls "thrownness": one *finds oneself* as a member of a group, whose existence and relations one experiences as always already having been. For a person's identity is defined in relation to how others identify him or her, and they do so in terms of groups that always already have specific attributes, stereotypes, and norms associated with them, in reference to which a person's identity will be formed. From the thrownness of group affinity, it does not follow that one cannot leave groups and enter new ones. Many women become lesbian after identifying as heterosexual, and anyone who lives long enough becomes old. These cases illustrate thrownness precisely because such changes in group affinity are experienced as a transformation in one's identity.

Despite the modern myth of a decline of parochial attachments and ascribed identities, group differentiation is endemic to modern society. As markets and administration increase the web of social interdependency on a world scale, and as more people encounter one another as strangers in cities and states, they retain and renew ethnic, locale, age, sex, and occupational group identifications, and form new ones in the processes of encounter.[6] No social group, moreover, is itself homogeneous, but mirrors in its own differentiations many of the groups in the wider society. Patterns of group differentiation are fluid, often undergoing rapid change. Before the nineteenth century, for example, homosexuality did not serve as a basis of group ascription and identification.[7]

Some writers, such as Milton Fisk, understand class as a primary example of a social group.[8] Others might be inclined to distinguish the concept of group from class on the grounds that class is a structural concept that does not include subjectivity or identity, and a group as I have defined it includes reference to identity and interaction.[9]

In a way I agree with both approaches. As used in technical Marxian economic theory, the concept of class is more abstract and structural than the concept of social group. It refers specifically to a relation to the major means of production, whether one owns it and/or has major decision-making power about the movement of capital, how it is invested, and so on. Class denotes a relation to capitalist profit: who gets it, who decides who gets it and how it will be gotten, who contributes to its getting without getting it, or does none of these. These structural positions in themselves are too narrow to define social groups.

In a more colloquial and empirical sense, however, the term "class" also refers to a basis for interaction and conflict, an identity by which people recognize one another, and to that degree class names social groups as well as structural positions. The ruling class in the United States, and in most other societies, is a social group whose members tend to bond with a shared culture and world view, to have common interests, and to move within specific institutions. There is, however, no single social group of the working class correlated to that ruling class.[10] Whatever the difficulties of locating it in technical Marxian analysis, middle-class professionals and managers must be understood as a social group distinct from working-class manufacturing, clerical, and service workers and their families. Poor people, or what some theorists call the "underclass," may also constitute a social group.

Insofar as economic location and occupation significantly determine a person's self-understanding, perception of social relations and others, and insofar as such economic location in our society tends to be reproduced across generations, classes are certainly social groups in the sense I have discussed. Just how class will be defined will depend on the uses of the definition, for example, to understand the structural imperatives of accumulation or to understand the motivation of particular persons to support certain policies.

Group differentiation does not necessarily imply oppression, however; groups can exist that are not oppressed. In the United States, Catholics are a group in the sense I have discussed, but they are no longer an oppressed group. In Northern Ireland, on the other hand, Catholics are an oppressed group. Whether a group is oppressed depends on whether it is subject to one or more of the five conditions I shall discuss below. Despite the modern myth of a decline of parochial attachments and ascribed identities, I think that group differentiation is both an inevitable and desirable aspect of modern social processes. Social justice, then, requires not the melting away of differences, but institutions that promote reproduction of and respect for group difference without oppression.

I have suggested that oppression is the inhibition of a group through a vast network of everyday practices, attitudes, assumptions, behaviors, and institutional rules; it is structural or systemic. The systemic character of oppression implies that an oppressed group need not have a correlate oppressing group. While structural oppression in our society involves relations among groups, these relations do not generally fit the paradigm of one group's consciously and intentionally keeping another down. Foucault suggests that to understand the meaning and operation of power in modern society we should look beyond the model of power as "sovereignty," a dyadic relation of ruler and subject, and instead analyze the exercise of power as the effect of liberal and humanized practices of education, bureaucratic administration, production and distribution of consumer goods, medical practice, and so on. The conscious actions of many individuals daily contribute to maintaining and reproducing oppression, but those people are usually simply doing their jobs or living their lives, not understanding themselves as agents of oppression. Defining oppression as structural is an innovation of the new left usage of the term to describe our society. Many people understand oppression to refer only to a conscious tyranny of one individual or group over another and for that reason will not use the term to describe injustices in our own society.

By denying that structural oppression is perpetrated by an identifiable agent of oppression I do not mean to suggest that within this system of oppression individual persons do not intentionally do things to harm others in oppressed groups. The raped woman, the beaten black youth, the locked-out worker, and the gay man harassed on the street are victims of intentional behavior by identifiable agents. Nor do I mean to suggest that specific groups are not beneficiaries of the oppression of other groups, and thus have an interest in their continued oppression. On the contrary, for every oppressed group there is a group that is *privileged* in relation to that group.

The concept of oppression has been used among radicals since the 1960s, partly in reaction to some Marxist attempts to reduce the injustices of racism and sexism, for example, to the effects of class domination or bourgeois ideology. Racism, sexism, ageism, and homophobia, some social movements asserted, are distinct forms of oppression with their own dynamics apart from the dynamics of class, even though they might interact with class oppression. From often heated discussions among socialists, feminists, and anti-racism activists in the last ten years, a consensus is emerging that many different groups must be said to be oppressed in our society, and that no group's or form of oppression can claim causal or moral primacy.[11] The same discussion has also come to understand that group differences cross individual lives in a multiplicity of ways that can entail privilege and oppression for the same person in different respects. Only a plural explication of the concept of oppression can appropriately capture these insights (cf. Maynard and Brittan, 2–8).

Accordingly, in the following sections I offer an explication of five faces of oppression as a useful set of categories and distinctions that I believe is comprehensive, in the sense that it covers all the groups said by new left social movements to be oppressed and covers all the ways they are oppressed. I derive the five faces of oppression from reflection on the condition of these groups. Because different factors, or combinations of factors, constitute the oppression of different groups, making their oppression irreducible, I believe it is not possible to have one essential definition of oppression. With the following five categories, however, the oppression of any group can be described, as well as its similarities with and differences from the oppression of other groups.

Exploitation

The central function of Marx's theory of exploitation is to explain how class structure can exist in the absence of legally and normatively sanctioned class distinctions. In precapitalist societies domination is overt and carried on through direct political means. In both slave society and feudal society the right to appropriate the product of the labor of others partly defines class privilege, and these societies legitimate class distinctions with ideologies of natural superiority and inferiority.

Capitalist society, on the other hand, removes traditional juridically enforced class distinctions and promotes a belief in the legal freedom of persons. Workers freely contract with employers, receive a wage, and no formal mechanisms of law or custom force them to work for that employer or any employer. Thus, the mystery of capitalism arises: when everyone is formally free, how can there be class domination? Why does there continue to be class distinction between the wealthy, who own the means of production, and the mass of people, who work for them? The theory of exploitation answers this question.

Profit, the basis of capitalist power and wealth, is a mystery if we assume that in the market goods exchange at their values. Marx's use of the labor theory of value, however, dispels this mystery. Every commodity's value is a function of the labor time necessary for the production of labor power. Labor power is the one commodity that in the process of being consumed produces new value. Profit then comes from the difference between the actual labor and the value of that capacity to labor that the capitalist purchases and puts to work. The owner of capital appropriates this surplus value, which accounts for the possibility of realizing a profit.

In recent years there has been considerable controversy among Marxist scholars about the viability of the labor theory of value on which this account of exploitation relies.[12] John Roemer, for example, develops a theory of exploitation that claims to preserve the theoretical and practical purposes of Marx's theory, but without assuming a distinction between values and prices and without being restricted to a concept of abstract, homogeneous labor.[13] My purpose here is not to engage in technical economic disputes, but to indicate the place of a concept of exploitation in a conception of oppression.

Marx's theory of exploitation lacks an explicitly normative meaning, even though the judgment that workers are exploited clearly has normative as well as descriptive power in Marxian theory.[14] C. B. MacPherson reconstructs the Marxian idea of exploitation in a more explicitly normative form.[15] The injustice of capitalist society consists in the fact that some people exercise their capacities under the control, according to the purposes, and for the benefit of other people. Through the institutions of private ownership of the means of production, and through markets that allocate labor and the ability to buy goods, capitalism systematically transfers the powers of some persons to others, thereby augmenting their powers. In this process of the transfer of powers, moreover, according to MacPherson, the capitalist class acquires and maintains extractive power, which gives it the continued ability to extract benefits from workers. Not only are powers transferred from workers to capitalists, but also the powers of workers diminish by more than the amount of transfer because workers suffer deprivation, a lack of control, and hence a lack of self-respect. Justice, then, requires eliminating the institutional forms that enable and enforce this process of transfer. Justice requires replacing them with institutional forms that enable all to develop and use their capacities in a way that do not inhibit, but rather enhance, others developing and using theirs.

The central insight expressed with the concept of exploitation, then, is that domination occurs through a steady process of the transfer of the results of the labor of some people to benefit others. The injustice of class division does not consist only in the fact that some people have great wealth while most people have little and some are severely deprived.[16] The theory of exploitation shows that this relation of power and inequality is produced and reproduced through a systematic process in which the energies of the have-nots are continuously expended to maintain and augment the power, status, and wealth of the haves.

Many writers have cogently argued that the Marxian concept of exploitation is too narrow to encompass all forms of domination and oppression.[17] In particular, by confining itself to examining class domination and oppression, the Marxist concept of exploitation does not contribute to an understanding of such group oppressions as sexism and racism. The question, then, is whether the concept of exploitation can be broadened to include other ways that the labor and energy expenditure of one group benefits another, thus reproducing a relation of domination between them.

Feminists have had little difficulty showing that women's oppression consists partly in a systematic and unreciprocated transfer of powers from women to men. Women's oppression consists not merely in an inequality of status, power, and wealth resulting from men's excluding women from privileged activities. The freedom, power, status, and self-realization of men is possible precisely because women work for them. Gender exploitation has two aspects, transfer of the fruits of material labor to men, and the transfer of nurturing and sexual energies to men.

Christine Delphy, for example, theorizes marriage as a class relation in which women's labor benefits men without comparable remuneration.[18] She makes it clear that the exploitation consists not in the sort of work that women do in the home, for it might be various kinds of tasks, but the fact that they perform tasks for someone else on whom they are dependent. Thus, for example, in most systems of agricultural production in the world, men take to market goods women have produced, and more often than not men receive the status and often the entire income from this labor.

With the concept of sex-affective production, Ann Ferguson identifies another form of the transfer of women's energies to men.[19] Women provide men and children with emotional care and provide men with sexual satisfaction, and as a class receive little of either from men.[20] The gender socialization of women makes us tend to be more attentive to interactive dynamics than men, and makes women good at providing empathy and support for people's feelings and at smoothing over interactive tensions. Both men and women look to women as nurturers of their personal lives, and women frequently complain that when they look to men for emotional support they do not receive it.[21] The norms of heterosexuality, moreover, are oriented around male pleasure, and consequently many women receive little satisfaction from their sexual interaction with men.[22]

Most feminist theories of gender exploitation have concentrated on the institutional structure of the patriarchal family. Recently, however, feminists have begun to theorize relations of gender exploitation enacted in the contemporary workplace and through the state. Carol Brown argues that as men have removed themselves from responsibility for children, many women have become dependent on the state for subsistence as they continue to bear nearly total responsibility for child rearing.[23] This creates a new system of the exploitation of women's domestic labor mediated by those state institutions, which she calls public patriarchy.

In twentieth-century capitalist economies, the workplaces that women have been entering in increasing numbers serve as another important site of gender exploitation. David Alexander argues that most typically feminine jobs have gender tasks involving sexual labor, nurturing, caring for a person's body, or smoothing over relations through personality.[24] In these ways, women's energies are expended in workplaces that enhance the status of, please, or comfort others, usually men; and these gender-based labors of waitresses, clerical workers, nurses, and other caretakers often go unnoticed and undercompensated.

To summarize, women are exploited in the Marxian sense to the degree that they are wage workers. Some have argued that women's domestic labor is also a form of capitalist class exploitation insofar as it is labor covered by the wages a family receives. As a class, however, women undergo specific forms of gender exploitation—ways the energies and power of women are expended, often unnoticed and unacknowledged, usually to benefit men by releasing them for more important and creative work, enhancing their status or the environment around them, or providing men with sexual or emotional service.

Race is a structure of oppression at least as basic as class or gender. Are there, then, racially specific forms of exploitation? This is different from the question of whether racial groups are subjected to intense capitalist exploitation. Racial groups in the United States, especially blacks and Latinos, are oppressed through capitalist superexploitation resulting from a segmented labor market that tends to reserve skilled, high-paying, unionized jobs for whites. There is wide disagreement about whether such superexploitation benefits whites as a group or only benefits the capitalist class, and I do not intend to resolve that dispute here.[25]

However one answers the question about capitalist superexploitation of racial groups, is it also possible to conceptualize a form of exploitation that is racially specific on analogy with the gender-specific forms I have discussed? The category of *menial* labor might provide an opening for such conceptualization. In its derivation "menial" means the labor of servants. Wherever there is racism, including the United States today, there is the assumption, more or less enforced, that members of the oppressed racial groups are or ought to be servants of those, or some of those, in the privileged group. In white racist societies this generally means that many white people have dark-or yellow-skinned domestic servants, and in the United States today there remains significant race structuring of private household service.

In the United States today much service labor has gone public: anybody can have servants if they go to a good hotel, a good restaurant, or hire a cleaning service. Servants often attend the daily—and nightly—activities of business executives, government officials, and other high-status professionals. In our society there remains strong cultural pressure to fill servant jobs—like bell hop, porter, chamber maid, bus boy, and so on—with black and Latin workers. These jobs entail a transfer of energies whereby the servers enhance the status of the served, to place them in an aristocracy—the rule of the best.

Menial labor today refers to more than service, however; it refers to any servile, unskilled, low-paying work lacking in autonomy, and in which a person is subject to orders from several people. Menial work tends to be auxiliary work, instrumental to another person's work, in which that other person receives primary recognition for doing the job. Laborers on a construction site, for example, are at the beck and call of welders, electricians, carpenters, and other skilled workers, who receive recognition for the job done. In the history of the United States, explicit racial discrimination reserved menial work for blacks, Chicanos, American Indians, and Chinese, and menial work still tends to be linked to black and Latino workers.[26] I offer this category of menial labor as a form of racially specific exploitation, only as a proposal, however, that needs discussion.

Marginalization

Increasingly in the United States, racial oppression occurs more in the form of marginalization than exploitation. Marginals are people the system of labor markets cannot or will not employ. Not only in Third World capitalist countries, but also in most Western capitalist societies, there is a growing underclass of people permanently confined to lives of social marginality, the majority of whom are racially marked—blacks or Indians in Latin America, blacks, East Indians, Eastern Europeans, or North Africans in Europe.

Marginalization is by no means the fate only of racially marked groups, however. In the United States a shamefully large proportion of the population is marginal: old people, and increasingly people who are not very old but get laid off from their jobs and cannot find new work; young people, especially black or Latino, who cannot find first or second jobs; many single mothers and their children; other people involuntarily unemployed; many mentally or physically disabled people; and American Indians, especially those on reservations.

Marginalization is perhaps the most dangerous form of oppression. A whole category of people is expelled from useful participation in social life, then potentially subject to severe material deprivation and even extermination. The material deprivation marginalization often causes certainly is unjust, especially in a society in which others have plenty. Contemporary advanced capitalist societies in principle have acknowledged the injustice of material deprivation caused by marginalization, and have taken some steps to address it by providing welfare payments and services. The continuance of this welfare state is by no means assured, and in most welfare-state societies, especially the United States, benefits are not sufficient to eliminate large-scale suffering and deprivation.

Material deprivation, which can be addressed by redistributive social policies, is not, however, the extent of the harm caused by marginalization. Two categories of injustice beyond distribution are associated with marginality in advanced capitalist societies. The provision of welfare itself produces new injustice when it deprives dependent persons of rights and freedoms that others have. If justice requires that every person have the opportunity to develop and exercise his or her capacities, finally, then marginalization is unjust primarily because it blocks such opportunity to exercise capacities in socially defined and recognized ways.

Liberalism traditionally asserts the right of all rational autonomous agents to equal citizenship.

Early bourgeois liberalism made explicit that citizenship excluded all those whose reason was questionable or not fully developed and all those not independent.[27] Thus, poor people, women, the mad and the feeble-minded, and children were explicitly excluded from citizenship, and many of these were housed in institutions modeled on the modern prison: poor houses, insane asylums, schools.

In our own society the exclusion of dependent persons from equal citizenship rights is only barely hidden beneath the surface. Because they are dependent on bureaucratic institutions for support or services, old people, poor people, and mentally or physically disabled people are subject to patronizing, punitive, demeaning, and arbitrary treatment by the policies and people associated with welfare bureaucracies. Being a dependent in this society implies being legitimately subject to often arbitrary and invasive authority of social service providers and other public and private bureaucrats, who enforce rules with which the marginal must comply, and otherwise exercise power over the conditions of his or her life. In meeting needs of the marginalized, with the aid of social scientific disciplines, the welfare agencies also construct the needs themselves. Medical and social service professionals know what is good for those they serve, and the marginals and dependents themselves do not have the right to claim to know what is good for them.[28] Dependency thus implies in this society, as it has in all liberal societies, a sufficient condition to suspend rights to privacy, respect, and individual choice.

Although dependency thus produces conditions of injustice in our society, dependency in itself should not and need not be oppressive. We cannot imagine a society in which some people would not need to be dependent on others at least some of the time: children, sick people, women recovering from childbirth, old people who have become frail, and depressed or otherwise emotionally needy persons have the moral right to be dependent on others for subsistence and support.

An important contribution of feminist moral theory has consisted in questioning the deeply held assumption that moral agency and full citizenship require that a person be autonomous and independent. Feminists have exposed such an assumption as inappropriately individualistic and derived from a specifically male experience of social relations, valuing competition and solitary achievement.[29] Female experience of social relations, arising both from women's typical domestic care responsibilities and from the kinds of paid work that many women do, tends to recognize dependence as a basic human condition. Whereas in the autonomy model a just society would as much as possible give people the opportunity to be independent, the feminist model instead envisions justice as according respect and decision-making participation to those who are dependent as well as those who are independent.[30] Dependence should not be a reason to be deprived of choice and respect, and much of the oppression many marginals experience would diminish if a less individualistic model of rights prevailed.

Marginalization does not cease to be oppressive when one has shelter and food. Many old people, for example, have sufficient means to live comfortably but remain oppressed in their marginal status. Even if marginals were provided a comfortable material life within institutions that respected their freedom and dignity, injustices of marginality would remain in the form of uselessness, boredom, and lack of self-respect. Most of this society's productive and recognized activities take place in contexts of organized social cooperation, and social structures and processes that close persons out of participation in such social cooperation are unjust.

The fact of marginalization raises basic structural issues of justice. In particular, we must consider what is just about a connection between participation in productive activities of social cooperation, on the one hand, and acquisition of the means of consumption, on the other. As marginalization is increasing, with no sign of abatement, some social policy analysts have introduced the idea of a "social wage" as a socially provided, guaranteed income not tied to the wage system.

Restructuring activities of production and service provision to ensure that everyone able and willing has socially recognized work to do, moreover, also implies organization of socially productive activity at least partly outside of a wage system.[31]

Powerlessness

As I have indicated, the Marxian idea of class is important because it helps reveal the structure of exploitation: that some people have their power and wealth because they profit from the labor of others. For this reason I reject the claim of some that a traditional class exploitation model fails to capture the structure of contemporary society. It is still the case that the labor of most people in the society augments the power of a few; whatever their differences from nonprofessional workers, most professional workers share with them not being members of the capitalist class.

An adequate conception of oppression, however, cannot ignore the experience of social division colloquially referred to as the difference between the "middle class" and the "working class," a division structured by the social division of labor between professionals and nonprofessionals. Rather than expanding or revising the Marxian concept of class to take account of this experience, as some writers do, I suggest that we follow Weber and describe this as a difference in *status* rather than class.[32] Being a professional entails occupying a status position that nonprofessionals lack, creating a condition of oppression that nonprofessionals suffer. I shall call this kind of oppression "powerlessness."

The absence of genuine democracy in the United States means that most people do not participate in making decisions that regularly affect the conditions of their lives and actions. In this sense most people lack significant power. Powerlessness, however, describes the lives of people who have little or no work autonomy, exercise little creativity or judgment in their work, have no technical expertise or authority, express themselves awkwardly, especially in public or bureaucratic

settings, and do not command respect. Powerlessness names the oppressive situations Sennet and Cobb describe in their famous study of working class men.[33]

The clearest way for me to think of this powerless status is negatively: the powerless lack the status and sense of self that professionals tend to have. There are three aspects of status privilege that professionals have, the lack of which produces oppression for nonprofessionals.

First, acquiring and practicing a profession has an expansive, progressive character. Being professional usually requires a college education and learning a specialized knowledge that entails working with symbols and concepts. In acquiring one's profession, a person experiences progress in learning the necessary expertise, and usually when one begins practicing one enters a career, that is, a working life of growth or progress in professional development. The life of the non-professional by comparison is powerless in the sense that it lacks this orientation toward the progressive development of one's capacities.

Second, while most professionals have supervisors and do not have power to affect many decisions or the action of very many people, most nevertheless have considerable day-to-day work autonomy. Professionals usually have some authority over others, moreover, either over workers they supervise or over auxiliaries or clients. Nonprofessionals, on the other hand, lack autonomy, and both in their working lives and in their consumer-client lives, they often stand under the authority of professionals.

Though having its material basis in a division of labor between mental and manual work, the group division between middle class and working class designates not a division only in working life, but also in nearly all aspects of social life. Professionals and nonprofessionals belong to different cultures in the United States. The two groups tend to live in segregated neighborhoods or even different towns, not least because of the actions and decisions of real estate people. They tend to have different tastes in food, decor, clothes, music, and vacations. Members of the two groups socialize for the most part with others in the same status group. While there is some intergroup mobility between generations, for the most part the children of professionals become professionals and the children of nonprofessionals do not.

Thus, third, the privileges of the professional extend beyond the workplace to elevate a whole way of life, which consists in being "respectable." To treat someone with respect is to be prepared to listen to what they have to say or to do what they request because they have some authority, expertise, or influence.

The norms of respectability in our society are associated specifically with professional culture. Professional dress, speech, tastes, and demeanor all connote respectability. Generally professionals expect and receive respect from others. In restaurants, banks, hotels, real estate offices, and many other such public places, professionals typically receive more respectful treatment than nonprofessionals. For this reason nonprofessionals seeking a loan or a job, or to buy a house or a car, will often try to look "professional" and "respectable" in these settings. The privilege of this professional respectability starkly appears in the dynamics of racism and sexism. In daily interchange women and men of color must prove their respectability. At first they are often not treated by strangers with respectful distance or deference. Once people discover that this woman or that Puerto Rican man is a college teacher or a business executive, however, people often behave more respectfully toward her or him. Working-class white men, on the other hand, are often treated with respect until their working class status is revealed.

Cultural Imperialism

Exploitation, marginality, and powerlessness all refer to relations of power and oppression that occur by virtue of the social division of labor: who works for whom, who does not work, and how the content of work in one position is defined in relation to others. These three categories refer to the structural and institutional relations that delimit people's material lives, including but not limited to the resources they have access to, the concrete opportunity they have or do not have to develop and exercise capacities in involving, socially recognized ways that enhance rather than diminish their lives. These kinds of oppression are a matter of concrete power in relation to others, who benefits from whom, and who is dispensable.

Recent theorists of movements of group liberation, especially feminists and black liberation theorists, have also given prominence to a rather different experience of oppression, which I shall call cultural imperialism.[34] This is the experience of existing in a society whose dominant meanings render the particular perspectives and point of view of one's own group invisible at the same time as they stereotype one's group and mark it out as "other."

Cultural imperialism consists in the universalization of one group's experience and culture and its establishment as the norm. Some groups have exclusive or primary access to what Nancy Fraser calls the means of interpretation and communication in a society.[35] As a result, the dominant cultural products of the society, that is, those most widely disseminated, express the experience, values, goals, and achievements of the groups that produce them. The cultural products also express their perspective on and interpretation of events and elements in the society, including the other groups in the society, insofar as they are noticed at all. Often without noticing they do so, the dominant groups project their own experience as representative of humanity as such.

An encounter with groups different from the dominant group, however, challenges its claim to universality. The dominant group saves its position by bringing the other group under the measure of its dominant norms. Consequently, the difference of women from men, Native Americans or Africans from Europeans, Jews from Christians, homosexuals from heterosexuals, or workers from professionals becomes reconstructed as deviance and inferiority. The dominant groups and their cultural expressions are the normal, the universal, and thereby unremarkable. Since the dominant group's cultural expressions are the only expressions that receive wide dissemination, the dominant groups construct the differences that some groups exhibit as lack and negation in relation to the norms, and those groups become marked out as "other."

Victims of cultural imperialism experience a paradoxical oppression in that they are both marked out by stereotypes and rendered invisible. As remarkable, deviant beings, the culturally dominated are stamped with an essence. In contrast, the privileged are indefinable because they are individual; each is whatever he or she wants to be, they are what they do, and by their doings they are judged. The stereotype marks and defines the culturally dominated, confines them to a nature that is usually attached in some way to their bodies, and thus that cannot easily be denied. These stereotypes so permeate the society that they are not noticed as contestable. Just as everyone knows that the earth goes around the sun, so everyone knows that gay people are promiscuous, that Indians are alcoholics, and that women are good with children.

Those living under cultural imperialism find themselves defined from the outside, positioned, and placed by a system of dominant meanings they experience as arising from elsewhere, from those with whom they do not identify and who do not identify with them. The dominant culture's stereotyped, marked, and inferiorized images of the group must be internalized by group members at least to the degree that they are forced to react to behaviors of others that express or are influenced by those images. This creates for the culturally oppressed the experience that W. E. B. DuBois called "double consciousness." "This sense of always looking at one's self through the eyes of others, of measuring one's soul by the tape of a world that looks on in amused contempt and pity."[36] This consciousness is double because the oppressed subject refuses to coincide with these devalued, objectified, stereotyped visions of herself or himself. The subject desires recognition as human, capable of activity, full of hope and possibility, but receives from the dominant culture only the judgment that he or she is different, marked, or inferior.

People in culturally oppressed groups often maintain a sense of positive subjectivity because they can affirm and recognize one another as sharing similar experiences and perspectives on social life. The group defined by the dominant culture as deviant, as a stereotyped other, *is* culturally different from the dominant group because the status of otherness creates specific experiences not shared by the dominant group and because culturally oppressed groups also are often socially segregated and occupy specific positions in the social division of labor. They express their specific group experiences and interpretations of the world to one another, developing and perpetuating their own culture. Double consciousness, then, occurs because one finds one's being defined by two cultures: a dominant and a subordinate culture.

Cultural imperialism involves the paradox of experiencing oneself as invisible at the same time that one is marked out and noticed as different. The perspectives of other groups dominate the culture without their noticing it as a perspective, and their cultural expressions are widely disseminated. These dominant cultural expressions often simply pay no attention to the existence and experience of those other groups, only to mention or refer to them in stereotyped or marginalized ways. This, then, is the injustice of cultural imperialism: that the oppressed group's experience and interpretation of social life finds no expression that touches the dominant culture, while that same culture imposes on the oppressed group its experience and interpretations of social life.

Violence

Finally, many groups suffer the oppression of systematic and legitimized violence. The members of some groups live with the fear of random, unprovoked attacks on their persons or property, which have no motive but to damage, humiliate, or destroy them. In U.S. society women, blacks, Asians, Arabs, gay men, and lesbians live under such threats of violence, and in at least some regions Jews, Puerto Ricans, Chicanos, and other Spanish-speaking Americans must fear such violence as well. Violation may also take the form of name-calling or petty harassment intended to degrade or humiliate, and always signals an underlying threat of physical attack.

Such violence is systematic because it is directed at any member of the group simply because he or she is a member of that group. Any woman, for example, has reason to fear rape. The violence to which these oppressed groups are subject, moreover, is usually legitimate in the sense that most people regard it as unsurprising, and so it usually goes unpunished. Police beatings or killings of black youths, for example, are rarely publicized, rarely provoke moral outrage on the part of most white people, and rarely receive punishment.

An important aspect of the kind of random but systematic violence I am referring to here is its utter irrationality. Xenophobic violence is different from the violence of state or ruling-class repression. Repressive violence has a rational, though evil, motive: rulers use it as a coercive tool to maintain their power. Many accounts of racist, sexist, or homophobic violence try to explain it as motivated by a desire to maintain group privilege or domination. I agree that fear of violence functions to help keep these oppressed groups subordinate. I think the causes of such violence must be traced to unconscious structures of identity formation that project onto some groups the fluid, bodily aspect of the subject that threatens the rigid unity of that identity.

CONCLUSION

The five faces of oppression that I have explicated here function as criteria of oppression, not as a full theoretical account of oppression. With them we can tell whether a group is oppressed, according to objective social structures and behaviors. Being subject to any one of these five conditions is sufficient for calling a group oppressed. Most

of the groups I listed earlier as oppressed in U.S. society experience more than one of these forms, and some experience all five.

Nearly all, if not all, groups said by contemporary social movements to be oppressed in our society suffer cultural imperialism. Which other oppressions are experienced by which groups, however, is quite variable. Working-class people are exploited and powerless, for example, but if employed and white do not experience marginalization and violence. Gay men, on the other hand, are not *qua* gay exploited or powerless, but they experience severe cultural imperialism and violence. Similarly, Jews and Arabs as groups are victims of cultural imperialism and violence, though many members of these groups also suffer exploitation or powerlessness. Old people are oppressed by marginalization and cultural imperialism, and this is also true of physically or mentally disabled people. As a group women are subject to gender-based exploitation, powerlessness, cultural imperialism, and violence. Racism in the United States associates blacks and Latinos with marginalization, even though many members of these groups escape that condition; members of these groups often suffer all five forms of oppression.

With these criteria I have specifically avoided defining structures and kinds of oppression according to the groups oppressed: racism, classism, sexism, heterosexism, ageism. The forms of group oppression these terms name are not homologous, and the five criteria can help describe how and why not. The five criteria also help show that while no group oppression is reducible to or explained by any other group oppression, the oppression of one group is not a closed system with its own attributes, but overlaps with the oppression of other groups. With these criteria, moreover, we can claim that one group is more oppressed than another, insofar as it is subject to more of these five conditions, without thereby theoretically privileging a particular form of oppression or one oppressed group.

Are there any connections among these five forms of oppression? Why are particular groups subject to various combinations of them? The answers to these questions are beyond the scope of this chapter. My project here is analytical and descriptive, not explanatory. Answering these questions is important to the theoretical project of understanding oppression. I believe they cannot be answered by an a priori account, however, but require a specific explanatory account of the connections among forms of oppression for each social context and for each group.

Notes

1. Bernard Boxill, *Blacks and Social Justice* (Totowa, N.J.: Rowman and Allenheld, 1984).

2. Marlene Fried, "The Invisibility of Oppression," *The Philosophical Forum* XI, no. 1 (1979):18–29.

3. Marilyn Frye, "Oppression" in *The Politics of Reality* (Trumansburg, N.Y.: The Crossing Press, 1983), 1–16.

4. Marilyn Friedman and Larry May, "Harming Women as a Group," *Social Theory and Practice*, 11, no. 2 (1985):207–34.

5. Peter French, "Types of Collectivities and Blame," *The Personalist* 56 (1975):160–69.

6. Cf. Jeffrey Ross, Introduction to *The Mobilization of Collective Identity*, eds. Ross and Cottrell (Lanham, Md.: University Press of America, 1980); also, Joseph Rothschild, *Ethnopolitics* (New York: Columbia University Press, 1981).

7. Dennis Altman, *The Homosexualization of America* (Boston: Beacon Press, 1982).

8. Milton Fisk, *Ethics and Society* (New York: New York University Press, 1980), Part I.

9. E.g., Nicos Poulantzas, *Classes in Contemporary Capitalism* (London: Verso Books, 1975).

10. Cf. Manuel Castells, *The Economic Crisis and American Society* (Princeton, N.J.: Princeton University Press, 1980), 138–61.

11. See Roger Gottlieb, *History and Subjectivity* (Philadelphia: Temple University Press, 1987).

12. See R. P. Wolff, *Understanding Marx* (Princeton, N.J.: Princeton University Press, 1984).

13. John Roemer, *A General Theory of Exploitation and Class* (Cambridge: Harvard University Press, 1982).

14. Alan Buchanan, *Marx and Justice* (Totowa, N.J.: Rowman and Allenheld, 1980).

15. C. B. MacPherson, *Democratic Theory: Essays in Retrieval* (Oxford: Clarendon Press, 1973), especially Chapter III.

16. Cf. Buchanan, *Marx and Justice*, 44–49; Nancy Holmstrom, "Exploitation," *Canadian Journal of Philosophy*, VII, no. 2 (1977):353–69.

17. Anthony Giddens, *A Contemporary Critique of Historical Materialism* (Berkeley: University of California Press, 1981), 242; Arthur Brittan and Mary Maynard, *Sexism, Racism and Oppression* (Oxford: Basil Blackwell, 1984), 93; Raymond Murphy, "Exploitation or Exclusion?" *Sociology* 19, no. 2 (May, 1985):225–43; Herbert Gintis and Samuel Bowles, *Capitalism and Democracy* (New York: Basic Books, 1986).

18. Christine Delphy, *Close to Home: A Materialist Analysis of Women's Oppression* (Amherst: University of Massachusetts Press, 1984).

19. See her "Women as a New Revolutionary Class" in *Between Labor and Capital*, ed. Pat Walker (Boston: South End Press, 1979) and "On Conceiving Motherhood and Sexuality: A Feminist Materialist Approach" in *Mothering: Essays in Feminist Theory*, ed. Joyce Trebilco (Totowa, N.J.: Rowman and Allenheld, 1984).

20. Cf. Brittan and Maynard, *Sexism*, 142–48.

21. Barbara Easton, "Feminism and the Contemporary Family," *Socialist Review* 39 (May/June 1978):11–36.

22. Rhonda Gottlieb, "The Political Economy of Sexuality," *Review of Radical Political Economy* 16, no. 1 (1984): 143–65.

23. Carol Brown, "Mothers, Fathers and Children: From Private to Public Patriarchy" in *Women and Revolution*, ed. Lydia Sargent (Boston: South End Press, 1981), 239–68; cf. Ellen Boris and Peter Bardaglio, "The Transformation of Patriarchy; The Historic Role of the State" in *Families, Politics and Public Policy*, ed. Irene Diamond (New York: Longman, 1983), 79–93; Kathy Ferguson, *The Feminist Case Against Bureaucracy* (Philadelphia: Temple University Press, 1984).

24. David Alexander, "Gendered Job Traits and Women's Occupations" (Ph.D. Dissertation, University of Massachusetts, 1987).

25. Michael Reich, *Racial Inequality* (Princeton, N.J.: Princeton University Press, 1981).

26. Al Symanski, "The Structure of Race," *Review of Radical Political Economy* 17, no. 4 (1985):106–20.

27. Gintis and Bowles, 1986.

28. Nancy Fraser, "Women, Welfare, and the Politics of Need Interpretation," *Hypatia: A Journal of Feminist Philosophy* 2, no. 1 (Winter, 1987):103–22; Ferguson, *The Feminist Case*, 1984, Chapter 4.

29. Carol Gilligan, *In a Different Voice* (Cambridge, Harvard University Press, 1982); Marilyn Friedman,

"Care and Context in Moral Reasoning" in *Moral Dilemmas: Philosophical and Psychological Issues in the Development of Moral Reasoning*, ed. Carol Harding (Chicago: Precedent, 1985).

30. Virginia Held, "A Non-Contractual Society" (paper given at Conference on Feminist Moral, Legal and Political Theory, University of Cincinnati, November, 1986).

31. Claus Offe, *Disorganized Capitalism: Contemporary Transformation of Work and Politics* (Cambridge: M.I.T. Press, 1986), Chapters 1–3.

32. Max Weber, "Classes, Status Groups and Parties" in *Weber: Selections in Translation*, ed. W. G. Runciman (Cambridge: Cambridge University Press, 1978), 43–64; David Beetham, *Max Weber and the Theory of Modern Politics* (Oxford: Polity Press, 1985), 79–82.

33. Richard Sennet and Jonathan Cobb, *The Hidden Injuries of Class* (New York: Vintage Books, 1972).

34. Maria C. Lugones and Elizabeth V. Spelman, "Have We Got a Theory for You! Feminist Theory, Cultural Imperialism and the Demand for 'The Woman's Voice,' " *Women's Studies International Forum* 6, no. 6 (1983):573–81.

35. Nancy Fraser, "Social Movements vs. Disciplinary Bureaucracies: The Discourses of Social Needs," CHS Occasional Paper #8 (Center for Humanistic Studies, University of Minnesota, 1987), 1–37.

36. W. E. B. DuBois, *The Souls of Black Folks* (New York: Signet, 1903, 1969).

SUSAN MOLLER OKIN

~

INTRODUCTION

DEBRA SATZ

Susan Moller Okin was a feminist political theorist whose work spanned concerns from the exclusion of women in Western political thought to problems of global justice and nuclear disarmament. Okin was born in Auckland, New Zealand, in 1946 and graduated from the University of Auckland in 1967. She earned a master's degree at Oxford University in 1970 and was awarded her doctorate in political science at Harvard University in 1975. A prolific writer and an inspiring teacher, Okin taught at Vassar College and Brandeis University before joining the faculty at Stanford University in 1990. She received numerous awards during her career, including in 1989 the American Political Science Association's Victoria Schuck Prize for the best book on women and politics: *Justice, Gender, and the Family,* and in 2002 the Allan V. Cox Medal for Faculty Excellence Fostering Undergraduate Research.

Okin died in 2004 at the age of fifty-seven. At the time of her death she was the Marta Sutton Weeks Professor of Ethics in Society at Stanford University and held the Matina S. Horner Distinguished Visiting Professorship at the Radcliffe Institute for Advanced Study, a one-year fellowship at Harvard University. Although her career was cut short, her writings have had a lasting influence.

Okin, riding on a wave of feminist activism in the 1970s, was a scholarly maverick who sought to bring concerns that had been traditionally on the margins of political philosophy into its core, particularly concerns that relate to the nature and persistence of gender inequality. Gender issues belong at the core, not at the margins, of our theories of justice, she argued, because as long as women bear most responsibility for the care of the family, social justice can never be fully achieved. In her groundbreaking first book, *Women in Western Political Thought* (1979), Okin asked "whether the existing traditions of political philosophy can sustain the inclusion of women in its subject matter." Her answer was that they could not, because classical liberal thinkers assumed the male-headed family as a given unit whose structure and culture fell outside of the bounds of justice. Even John Stuart Mill, an early philosophical advocate of women's equality, assigned primary parenting responsibilities to women. Once the interests of women were included, she maintained, many of the ideals advocated by these thinkers could not be sustained or were in need of serious reform.

Okin thought that contemporary political philosophy suffered from similar limitations. Although today's philosophers accept principles of sex and gender equality, Okin argued that this commitment does not extend to relations within the family. The result of this limitation is that the unequal division of labor within the family is given freedom to shape gender inequality in the public sphere. Once the interplay of inequality in the family and inequality in public life is recognized, all aspects of society, including the organization of work, stand in need of change. Indeed, her subsequent writings can be seen as perceptive, if distressing, sequels to *Women in Western Political Thought*.

Justice, Gender, and the Family (1989) examines four major political theorists and philosophers—Alasdair MacIntyre, Robert Nozick, John Rawls, and Michael Walzer—and argues that fully taking account of women as the moral equals to men would radically change the central points on which the arguments of each of these philosophers rests. To take one example, Okin criticizes Rawls's *A Theory of Justice* for assuming that, given natural sympathy, children will be properly cared for. But this presupposition implicitly assumes, Okin argues, that children will naturally be looked after by their mothers. A fundamental source of women's subordination is thus removed from the agenda of justice.

In her brave and controversial book *Is Multiculturalism Bad for Women?* (1999) Okin argued against acceptance of gender inequalities rooted in cultural and religious communities, provoking attacks from both the right and the left. Feminists, she claimed, should not tolerate gender injustice within nonliberal communities, even if those communities were themselves subjects of oppression. Okin was not only a feminist but a liberal, who believed that the values of individual freedom and equality put limits on both cultural relativism and "anti-essentialism." While women's experiences differ and are not homogeneous, Okin believed that most cultures "have as one of their principal aims the control of women by men," and she insisted that there are disadvantages women face simply as women.

Justice, Gender, and the Family is written from what Okin describes as a "humanist perspective" that values the freedom and equality of every individual. From that perspective, the traditional division of the family is seen as wanting. In fact, at times Okin argues that the family is the "linchpin" of gender inequality and oppression. But given how her view is elaborated, it is probably fairer to characterize the family as part of an interlocking structure. It supports and reinforces inequality outside the family, and the gendered division of labor is in turn supported and reinforced by inequalities in the labor market. Women who assume primary responsibilities for parenting and the household cannot generally pursue high-paid careers involving long hours. Such careers reward investment in human capital, not in raising children, and are structured on the assumption that the worker has a wife at home who devotes herself to the household. At the same time, discrimination and stereotyping lead to women's receiving lower pay for work than men receive for comparable jobs, and this factor reinforces the gendered allocation of work within the family. Under these conditions, withdrawing women's labor from the labor market for childcare needs is rational, because women earn less than men. After women leave the labor force, they become increasingly economically dependent on their husbands.

Even those women who manage to combine both work and family face serious obstacles, including the lack of good quality subsidized day care; jobs with little flexibility for those who need to care for a sick child; school schedules premised on having a parent at home; and the social expectation that working women will continue to work a "second shift," assuming the responsibility for the bulk of household labor. This self-reproducing "cycle of vulnerability" renders women dependent and unequal. Okin argues that this system is also not good for children, cramping the possibilities of boys as well as girls, and exposing them all at an early age to a model of injustice.

How can we dismantle this cycle of vulnerability? In looking at Okin's answers to this question, we confront some familiar tensions between liberalism and egalitarianism. Consider some ways that the gender system of inequality could be dismantled. Society could define unequal domestic labor as an illegal form of sex discrimination; it could install cameras in people's homes to clock the time that men and women spend on household tasks; or as a form affirmative action it could offer parental leave only to fathers and require that they take it. None of these policies figure in Okin's policy recommendations. The reason I think that they do not is that they run afoul of Okin's liberalism and her commitment to a sphere of life in which individuals are free to adopt their own conceptions of value. Some of those conceptions will involve different understandings of the relationship between men and women. Traditional choices about the family, so long as they do not violate equal liberty and self-respect of all, are worthy of consideration. Okin recommended "equal sharing" between men and women within the family, but she did not mandate it. And while she emphatically rejected the idea of the family as part of a separate sphere beyond justice's reach, her argument does rest on some distinction between a private sphere of life and a public sphere.

Drawing on the work of John Rawls, Okin argued that individuals in a Rawlsian original position—under a veil of ignorance in which these individuals do not know their social class, their race or gender, or their own particular view of life and value— would agree to policies which substantially lessen the role of gender. Such a conclusion would be acceptable to those with traditional beliefs about the family, because it would allow the gendered division of labor in the family as long as the vulnerable were protected.

The policy measures Okin endorses do not directly seek to regulate individual choices but rather help shape them by changing the background incentives and opportunities. For example, Okin suggests that employers be required to provide accommodations based on the recognition that for some part of their working lives, workers are also parents. These accommodations could include flexible work time, paid parental leave, and high-quality subsidized day care. She argues that public education should expose students to the complex issues around gender, so that children have opportunities to explore other understandings than those found in their own families, and perhaps most radically, she advocates giving both partners an equal legal entitlement to all labor market earnings.

A range of other policy options are available to liberals who accept a plurality of reasonable conceptions of life and value, but unfortunately Okin does not take up these alternatives, although they would provide additional incentives and help structure a wider range of choices for women. These possibilities include labor market regulations such as equal pay for equal work and greater security for part-time workers. But I do not think that anything in her view precludes these policy proposals.

Thus we can see that Okin's list of policy options is meant to be compatible with different understandings of gender. Accommodations that are offered need not be taken up: families can forgo publicly available childcare, and women can choose to continue to bear the unequal burdens of domestic labor. Hers is a *liberal* form of egalitarianism.

Suppose, however, that women and men continue to choose an unequal gendered world. This world would not only represent the choices of adults but also shape the choices of children. And such choices are an important piece of the cycle of vulnerability reproduced over generations. For that reason, some feminist egalitarians are not liberals.

I believe that the liberalism of Okin's proposals can be seen as a bet: if men and women had more equal choices open to them, they would choose ways of life that better promote their flourishing. Not only would women benefit from ending the gendered division of labor, but men, too, would benefit from spending more time with their children and having greater opportunities to engage in care. Mill had earlier made such a bet in *The Subjection of Women*, arguing that we have no idea what men and women would choose if they were unshackled by a system predicated on women's subordination. We cannot look at how people are today for evidence about the limits of what they might be. Perhaps, then, the gendered system of inequality might be overturned.

Reasons can be offered for skepticism about such rosy prognoses regarding what we together might achieve. At the same time, there is room for hope. Okin's work forces us to confront the injustices wrought by our gender system and challenges us to work toward rectifying those injustices. Since we ourselves are part of the causal production of what it possible, we will not know where the limits for gender justice are unless we try to achieve it.

Okin's work has generated a significant amount of critical and engaged discussion. *Toward a Humanist Justice: The Political Philosophy of Susan Moller Okin* (Oxford: Oxford University Press, 2009), edited by Debra Satz and Rob Reich, assembles critical responses to her work from leading political and moral philosophers. *Justice, Gender, and the Family* has been the subject of extended commentary by Will Kymlicka in "Rethinking the Family: Justice Gender and the Family," *Philosophy and Public Affairs* 20, no. 1 (Winter 1991); Joshua Cohen in "Justice, Gender and the Family," *Canadian Journal of Philosophy* 22, no. 2 (1992); and Martha Nussbaum, in "A Feminist Theory of Justice," *New York Review of Books* 39, no. 16 (1992). Okin's papers, including her illuminating correspondence with Rawls and Nozick, among others, are deposited in the Schlesinger Library of the Radcliffe Institute.

Toward a Humanist Justice

. . . [F]amily life as typically practiced in our society is not just, either to women or to children. Moreover, it is not conducive to the rearing of citizens with a strong sense of justice. In spite of all the rhetoric about equality between the sexes, the traditional or quasi-traditional division of family labor still prevails. Women are made vulnerable by constructing their lives around the expectation that they will be primary parents; they become more vulnerable within marriages in which they fulfill this expectation, whether or not they also work for wages; and they are most vulnerable in

From Susan Moller Okin, *Justice, Gender, and the Family*, New York: Basic Books, 1989. Reprinted by permission of the publisher.

the event of separation or divorce, when they usually take over responsibility for children without adequate support from their ex-husbands. Since approximately half of all marriages end in divorce, about half of our children are likely to experience its dislocations, often made far more traumatic by the socioeconomic consequences of both gender-structured marriage and divorce settlements that fail to take account of it. . . . How can we address this injustice?

This is a complex question. It is particularly so because we place great value on our freedom to live different kinds of lives, there is no current consensus on many aspects of gender, and we have good reason to suspect that many of our beliefs about sexual difference and appropriate sex roles are heavily influenced by the very fact that we grew up in a gender-structured society. All of us have been affected, in our very psychological structures, by the fact of gender in our personal pasts, just as our society has been deeply affected by its strong influence in our collective past. Because of the lack of shared meanings about gender, it constitutes a particularly hard case for those who care deeply about both personal freedom and social justice. The way we divide the labor and responsibilities in our personal lives seems to be one of those things that people should be free to work out for themselves, but because of its vast repercussions it belongs clearly within the scope of things that must be governed by principles of justice. . . .

I shall argue here that any just and fair solution to the urgent problem of women's and children's vulnerability must encourage and facilitate the equal sharing by men and women of paid and unpaid work, of productive and reproductive labor. We must work toward a future in which all will be likely to choose this mode of life. A just future would be one without gender. In its social structures and practices, one's sex would have no more relevance than one's eye color or the length of one's toes. No assumptions would be made about male and female roles; childbearing would be so conceptually separated from child rearing

and other family responsibilities that it would be a cause for surprise, and no little concern, if men and women were not equally responsible for domestic life or if children were to spend much more time with one parent than the other. It would be a future in which men and women participated in more or less equal numbers in every sphere of life, from infant care to different kinds of paid work to high-level politics. Thus it would no longer be the case that having no experience of raising children would be the practical prerequisite for attaining positions of the greatest social influence. Decisions about abortion and rape, about divorce settlements and sexual harassment, or about any other crucial social issues would not be made, as they often are now, by legislatures and benches of judges overwhelmingly populated by men whose power is in large part due to their advantaged position in the gender structure. If we are to be at all true to our democratic ideals, moving away from gender is essential. Obviously, the attainment of such a social world requires major changes in a multitude of institutions and social settings outside the home, as well as within it.

Such changes will not happen overnight. Moreover, any present solution to the vulnerability of women and children that is just and respects individual freedom must take into account that most people currently live in ways that are greatly affected by gender, and most still favor many aspects of current, gendered practices. Sociological studies confirm what most of us already infer from our own personal and professional acquaintances: there are no currently shared meanings in this country about the extent to which differences between the sexes are innate or environmental, about the appropriate roles of men and women, and about which family forms and divisions of labor are most beneficial for partners, parents, and children.[1] There are those, at one extreme, for whom the different roles of the two sexes, especially as parents, are deeply held tenets of religious belief. At the other end of the spectrum are those of us for whom the sooner all social differentiation between the sexes vanishes, the better it will be for all of us. And there are a thousand varieties of view in between. Public policies must respect people's views and choices. But they must do so only insofar as it can be ensured that these choices do not result, as they now do, in the vulnerability of women and children. Special protections must be built into our laws and public policies to ensure that, for those who choose it, the division of labor between the sexes does not result in injustice. In the face of these difficulties—balancing freedom and the effects of past choices against the needs of justice—I do not pretend to have arrived at any complete or fully satisfactory answers. But I shall attempt . . . to suggest some social reforms, including changes in public policies and reforms of family law, that may help us work toward a solution to the injustices of gender.

Marriage has become an increasingly peculiar contract, a complex and ambiguous combination of anachronism and present-day reality. There is no longer the kind of agreement that once prevailed about what is expected of the parties to a marriage. Clearly, at least in the United States, it is no longer reasonable to assume that marriage will last a lifetime, since only half of current marriages are expected to. And yet, in spite of the increasing legal equality of men and women and the highly publicized figures about married women's increased participation in the labor force, many couples continue to adhere to more or less traditional patterns of role differentiation. As a recent article put it, women are "out of the house but not out of the kitchen."[2] Consequently, often working part-time or taking time out from wage work to care for family members, especially children, most wives are in a very different position from their husbands in their ability to be economically self-supporting. This is reflected, as we have seen, in power differentials between the sexes within the family. It means also, in the increasingly common event of divorce, usually by mutual agreement, that it is the mother who in 90% of cases will have physical custody of the children. But whereas the greater need for money goes one way, the bulk of the earning power almost always goes the other.

This is one of the most important causes of the feminization of poverty, which is affecting the life chances of ever larger numbers of children as well as their mothers. The division of labor within families has always adversely affected women, by making them economically dependent on men. Because of the increasing instability of marriage, its effects on children have now reached crisis proportions.

Some who are critical of the present structure and practices of marriage have suggested that men and women simply be made free to make their own agreements about family life, contracting with each other, much as business contracts are made.[3] But this takes insufficient account of the history of gender in our culture and our own psychologies, of the present substantive inequalities between the sexes, and, most important, of the well-being of the children who result from the relationship. As has long been recognized in the realm of labor relations, justice is by no means always enhanced by the maximization of freedom of contract, if the individuals involved are in unequal positions to start with. Some have even suggested that it is consistent with justice to leave spouses to work out their own divorce settlement.[4] By this time, however, the two people ending a marriage are likely to be far more unequal. Such a practice would be even more catastrophic for most women and children than is the present system. Wives in any but the rare cases in which they as individuals have remained their husbands' socioeconomic equals could hardly be expected to reach a just solution if left "free" to "bargain" the terms of financial support or child custody. What would they have to bargain with? . . .

Let us first try to imagine ourselves, as far as possible, in the [Rawlsian] original position, knowing neither what our sex nor any other of our personal characteristics will be once the veil of ignorance is lifted. Neither do we know our place in society or our particular conception of the good life. Particularly relevant in this context, of course, is our lack of knowledge of our beliefs about the characteristics of men and women and our related convictions about the appropriate division of labor between the sexes. Thus the positions we represent must include a wide variety of beliefs on these matters. We may, once the veil of ignorance is lifted, find ourselves feminist men or feminist women whose conception of the good life includes the minimization of social differentiation between the sexes. Or we may find ourselves traditionalist men or women, whose conception of the good life, for religious or other reasons, is bound up in an adherence to the conventional division of labor between the sexes. The challenge is to arrive at and apply principles of justice having to do with the family and the division of labor between the sexes that can satisfy these vastly disparate points of view and the many that fall between.

There are some traditionalist positions so extreme that they ought not be admitted for consideration, since they violate such fundamentals as equal basic liberty and self-respect. We need not, and should not, that is to say, admit for consideration views based on the notion that women are inherently inferior beings whose function is to fulfill the needs of men. Such a view is no more admissible in the construction of just institutions for a modern pluralist society than is the view, however deeply held, that some are naturally slaves and others naturally and justifiably their masters. We need not, therefore, consider approaches to marriage that view it as an inherently and desirably hierarchical structure of dominance and subordination. Even if it were conceivable that a person who did not know whether he or she would turn out to be a man or a woman in the society being planned would subscribe to such views, they are not admissible. Even if there were no other reasons to refuse to admit such views, they must be excluded for the sake of children, for everyone in the original position has a high personal stake in the quality of childhood. Marriages of dominance and submission are bad for children as well as for their mothers, and the socioeconomic outcome of divorce after such a marriage is very likely to damage their lives and seriously restrict their opportunities.

With this proviso, what social structures and public policies regarding relations between the sexes, and the family in particular, could we agree on in the original position? I think we would arrive at a basic model that would absolutely minimize gender. I shall first give an account of some of what this would consist in. We would also, however, build in carefully protective institutions for those who wished to follow gender-structured modes of life. These too I shall try to spell out in some detail.

MOVING AWAY FROM GENDER

First, public policies and laws should generally assume no social differentiation of the sexes. Shared parental responsibility for child care would be both assumed and facilitated. Few people outside of feminist circles seem willing to acknowledge that society does not have to choose between a system of female parenting that renders women and children seriously vulnerable and a system of total reliance on day care provided outside the home. While high-quality day care, subsidized so as to be equally available to all children, certainly constitutes an important part of the response that society should make in order to provide justice for women and children, it is only one part.[5] If we start out with the reasonable assumption that women and men are equally parents of their children, and have equal responsibility for both the unpaid effort that goes into caring for them and their economic support, then we must rethink the demands of work life throughout the period in which a worker of either sex is a parent of a small child. We can no longer cling to the by now largely mythical assumption that every worker has "someone else" at home to raise "his" children.

The facilitation and encouragement of equally shared parenting would require substantial changes.[6] It would mean major changes in the workplace, all of which could be provided on an entirely (and not falsely) gender-neutral basis. Employers must be required by law not only completely to eradicate sex discrimination, including sexual harassment. They should also be required to make positive provision for the fact that most workers, for differing lengths of time in their working lives, are also parents, and are sometimes required to nurture other family members, such as their own aging parents. Because children are borne by women but can (and, I contend, should) be raised by both parents equally, policies relating to pregnancy and birth should be quite distinct from those relating to parenting, Pregnancy and childbirth, to whatever varying extent they require leave from work, should be regarded as temporarily disabling conditions like any others, and employers should be mandated to provide leave for all such conditions.[7] Of course, pregnancy and childbirth are far more than simply "disabling conditions," but they should be treated as such for leave purposes, in part because their disabling effects vary from one woman to another. It seems unfair to mandate, say, eight or more weeks of leave for a condition that disables many women for less time and some for much longer, while not mandating leave for illnesses or other disabling conditions. Surely a society as rich as ours can afford to do both.

Parental leave during the postbirth months must be available to mothers and fathers on the same terms, to facilitate shared parenting; they might take sequential leaves or each might take half-time leave. All workers should have the right, without prejudice to their jobs, seniority, benefits, and so on, to work less than full-time during the first year of a child's life, and to work flexible or somewhat reduced hours at least until the child reaches the age of seven. Correspondingly greater flexibility of hours must be provided for the parents of a child with any health problem or disabling condition, The professions whose greatest demands (such as tenure in academia or the partnership hurdle in law) coincide with the peak period of child rearing must restructure their demands or provide considerable flexibility for those of their workers who are also participating parents. Large-scale employers should also be required to provide high-quality on-site day care for children from infancy up to school age. And to ensure equal quality of day care for all young children, *direct government subsidies* (not tax credits, which benefit the better-off) should make up the difference between the cost of high-quality day care and what less well paid parents could reasonably be expected to pay.

There are a number of things that schools, too, must do to promote the minimization of gender. As Amy Gutmann has recently noted, in their present authority structures (84% of elementary school teachers are female, while 99% of school superintendents are male), "schools do not simply reflect, they perpetuate the social reality of gender preferences when they educate children in a system in which men rule women and women rule children." She argues that, since such sex stereotyping is "a formidable obstacle" to children's rational deliberation about the lives they wish to lead, sex should be regarded as a relevant qualification in the hiring of both teachers and administrators, until these proportions have become much more equal.[8]

An equally important role of our schools must be to ensure in the course of children's education that they become fully aware of the politics of gender. This does not only mean ensuring that women's experience and women's writing are included in the curriculum, although this in itself is undoubtedly important.[9] Its political significance has become obvious from the amount of protest that it has provoked. Children need also to be taught about the present inequalities, ambiguities, and uncertainties of marriage, the facts of workplace discrimination and segregation, and the likely consequences of making life choices based on assumptions about gender. They should be discouraged from thinking about their futures as *determined* by the sex to which they happen to belong. For many children, of course, personal experience has already "brought home" the devastating effects of the traditional division of labor between the sexes. But they do not necessarily come away from this experience with positive ideas about how to structure their own future family lives differently. As Anita Shreve has recently suggested, "the old home-economics courses that used to teach girls how to cook and sew might give way to the new home economics: teaching girls *and* boys how to combine working and parenting."[10] Finally, schools should be required to provide high-quality after-school programs, where children can play safely, do their homework, or participate in creative activities.

The implementation of all these policies would significantly help parents to share the earning and the domestic responsibilities of their families, and children to grow up prepared for a future in which the significance of sex difference is greatly diminished. Men could participate equally in the nurturance of their children, from infancy and throughout childhood, with predictably great effects on themselves, their wives or partners, and their children. And women need not become vulnerable through economic dependence. In addition, such arrangements would alleviate the qualms many people have about the long hours that some children spend in day care. If one parent of a preschooler worked, for example, from eight to four o'clock and the other from ten to six o'clock, a preschool child would be at day care for only six hours (including nap time), and with each one or both of her or his parents the rest of the day. If each parent were able to work a six-hour day, or a four-day week, still less day care would be needed. Moreover, on-site provision of day care would enable mothers to continue to nurse, if they chose, beyond the time of their parental leave.[11]

The situation of single parents and their children is more complicated, but it seems that it too, for a number of reasons, would be much improved in a society in which sex difference was accorded an absolute minimum of social significance. Let us begin by looking at the situation of never-married mothers and their children. First, the occurrence of pregnancy among single teenagers, which is almost entirely unintended, would presumably be reduced if girls grew up more assertive and self-protective, and with less tendency

to perceive their futures primarily in terms of motherhood. It could also be significantly reduced by the wide availability of sex education and contraception.[12] Second, the added weight of responsibility given to fatherhood in a gender-free society would surely give young men more incentive than they now have not to incur the results of careless sexual behavior until they were ready to take on the responsibilities of being parents. David Ellwood has outlined a policy for establishing the paternity of all children of single mothers at the time of birth, and for enforcing the requirement that their fathers contribute to their support throughout childhood, with provision for governmental backup support in cases where the father is unable to pay. These proposals seem eminently fair and sensible, although the minimum levels of support suggested ($1,500 to $2,000 per year) are inadequate, especially since the mother is presumed to be either taking care of the child herself or paying for day care (which often costs far more than this) while she works.[13]

Third, never-married mothers would benefit greatly from a work structure that took parenthood seriously into account, as well as from the subsidization of high-quality day care. Women who grew up with the expectation that their work lives would be as important a part of their futures as the work lives of men would be less likely to enter dead-ended, low-skilled occupations, and would be better able to cope economically with parenthood without marriage.

Most single parenthood results, however, not from single mothers giving birth, but from marital separation and divorce. And this too would be significantly altered in a society not structured along the lines of gender. Even if rates of divorce were to remain unchanged (which is impossible to predict), it seems inconceivable that separated and divorced fathers who had shared equally in the nurturance of their children from the outset would be as likely to neglect them, by not seeing them or not contributing to their support, as many do today. It seems reasonable to expect that children after divorce would still have two actively involved parents, and two working adults economically responsible for them. Because these parents had shared equally the paid work and the family work, their incomes would be much more equal than those of most divorcing parents today. Even if they were quite equal, however, the parent without physical custody should be required to contribute to the child's support, *to the point where the standards of living of the two households were the same.* This would be very different from the situation of many children of divorced parents today, dependent for both their nurturance and their economic support solely on mothers whose wage work has been interrupted by primary parenting.

It is impossible to predict all the effects of moving toward a society without gender. Major current injustices to women and children would end. Men would experience both the joys and the responsibilities of far closer and more sustained contact with their children than many have today. Many immensely influential spheres of life—notably politics and the professional occupations— would for the first time be populated more or less equally by men and women, most of whom were also actively participating parents. This would be in great contrast to today, when most of those who rise to influential positions are either men who, if fathers, have minimal contact with their children, or women who have either forgone motherhood altogether or hired others as full-time caretakers for their children because of the demands of their careers. These are the people who make policy at the highest levels—policies not only about families and their welfare and about the education of children, but about the foreign policies, the wars and the weapons that will determine the future or the lack of future for all these families and children. Yet they are almost all people who gain the influence they do in part by never having had the day-to-day experience of nurturing a child. This is probably the most significant aspect of our gendered division of labor, though the least possible to grasp. The effects of changing it could be momentous.

PROTECTING THE VULNERABLE

The pluralism of beliefs and modes of life is fundamental to our society, and the genderless society I have just outlined would certainly not be agreed upon by all as desirable. Thus when we think about constructing relations between the sexes that could be agreed upon in the original position, and are therefore just from all points of view, we must also design institutions and practices acceptable to those with more traditional beliefs about the characteristics of men and women, and the appropriate division of labor between them. It is essential, if men and women are to be allowed to so divide their labor, as they must be if we are to respect the current pluralism of beliefs, that society protect the vulnerable. Without such protection, the marriage contract seriously exacerbates the initial inequalities of those who entered into it, and too many women and children live perilously close to economic disaster and serious social dislocation; too many also live with violence or the continual threat of it. It should be noted here that the rights and obligations that the law would need to promote and mandate in order to protect the vulnerable need not—and should not—be designated in accordance with sex, but in terms of different functions or roles performed. There are only a minute percentage of "househusbands" in this country, and a very small number of men whose work lives take second priority after their wives'. But they can quite readily be protected by the same institutional structures that can protect traditional and quasi-traditional wives, so long as these are designed without reference to sex.

Gender-structured marriage, then, needs to be regarded as a currently necessary institution (because still chosen by some) but one that is socially problematic. It should be subjected to a number of legal requirements, at least when there are children.[14] (I see no reason why what I propose here should be restricted to couples who are legally married. It should apply equally to "common law" relationships that produce children, and in which a division of labor is practiced.) Most important, there is no need for the division of labor between the sexes to involve the economic dependence, either complete or partial, of one partner on the other. Such dependence can be avoided if both partners have *equal legal entitlement* to all earnings coming into the household, The clearest and simplest way of doing this would be to have employers make out wage checks equally divided between the earner and the partner who provides all or most of his or her unpaid domestic services. In many cases, of course, this would not change the way couples actually manage their finances; it would simply codify what they already agree on— that the household income is rightly shared, because in a real sense jointly earned. Such couples recognize the fact that the wage-earning spouse is no more supporting the homemaking and child-rearing spouse than the latter is supporting the former; the form of support each offers the family is simply different. Such couples might well take both checks, deposit them in a joint account, and really share the income, just as they now do with the earnings that come into the household.

In the case of some couples, however, altering the entitlement of spouses to the earned income of the household as I have suggested *would* make a significant difference. It would make a difference in cases where the earning or higher-earning partner now directly exploits this power, by refusing to make significant spending decisions jointly, by failing to share the income, or by psychologically or physically abusing the nonearning or low-earning partner, reinforced by the notion that she (almost always the wife) has little option but to put up with such abuse or to take herself and her children into a state of destitution. It would make a difference, too, in cases where the higher-earning partner indirectly exploits this earning power in order to perpetuate the existing division of labor in the family. In such instances considerable changes in the balance of power would be likely to result from the legal and societal recognition that the partner who does most of the domestic work of the family contributes to its well-being just as much, and therefore rightly *earns* just as

much, as the partner who does most of the workplace work.

What I am suggesting is *not* that the wage-working partner pay the homemaking partner for services rendered. I do not mean to introduce the cash nexus into a personal relationship where it is inappropriate. I have simply suggested that since both partners in a traditional or quasi-traditional marriage work, there is no reason why only one of them should get paid, or why one should be paid far more than the other. The equal splitting of wages would constitute public recognition of the fact that the currently unpaid labor of families is just as important as the paid labor. If we do not believe this, then we should insist on the complete and equal sharing of both paid and unpaid labor, as occurs in the genderless model of marriage and parenting described earlier. It is only if we *do* believe it that society can justly allow couples to distribute the two types of labor so unevenly. But in such cases, given the enormous significance our society attaches to money and earnings, we should insist that the earnings be recognized as equally earned by the two persons. . . .

It is also important to point out that this proposal does not constitute unwarranted invasion of privacy or any more state intervention into the life of families than currently exists. It would involve only the same kind of invasion of privacy as is now required by such things as registration of marriages and births, and the filing of tax returns declaring numbers and names of dependents. And it *seems* like intervention in families only because it would alter the existing relations of power within them. If a person's capacity to fulfill the terms of his or her work is dependent on having a spouse at home who raises the children and in other ways sustains that worker's day-to-day life, then it is no more interventionist to pay both equally for their contributions than only to pay one.

The same fundamental principle should apply to separation and divorce, to the extent that the division of labor has been practiced within a marriage. Under current divorce laws, as we have seen, the terms of exit from marriage are disadvantageous for almost all women in traditional or quasi-traditional marriages. Regardless of the consensus that existed about the division of the family labor, these women lose most of the income that has supported them and the social status that attached to them because of their husband's income and employment, often at the same time as suddenly becoming single parents, and prospective wage workers for the first time in many years. This combination of prospects would seem to be enough to put most traditional wives off the idea of divorcing even if they had good cause to do so. In addition, since divorce in the great majority of states no longer requires the consent of both spouses, it seems likely that wives for whom divorce would spell economic and social catastrophe would be inhibited in voicing their dissatisfactions or needs within marriage. The terms of exit are very likely to affect the use and the power of voice in the ongoing relationship. At worst, these women may be rendered virtually defenseless in the face of physical or psychological abuse. This is not a system of marriage and divorce that could possibly be agreed to by persons in an original position in which they did not know whether they were to be male or female, traditionalist or not. It is a fraudulent contract, presented as beneficial to all but in fact to the benefit only of the more powerful.

For all these reasons, it seems essential that the terms of divorce be redrawn so as to reflect the gendered or nongendered character of the marriage that is ending, to a far greater extent than they do now.[15] The legal system of a society that allows couples to divide the labor of families in a traditional or quasi-traditional manner *must* take responsibility for the vulnerable position in which marital breakdown places the partner who has completely or partially lost the capacity to be economically self-supporting. When such a marriage ends, it seems wholly reasonable to expect a person whose career has been largely unencumbered by domestic responsibilities to support financially the partner who undertook these responsibilities. This support, in the form of combined alimony

and child support, should be far more substantial than the token levels often ordered by the courts now. *Both postdivorce households should enjoy the same standard of living*. Alimony should not end after a few years, as the (patronizingly named) "rehabilitative alimony" of today does; it should continue for at least as long as the traditional division of labor in the marriage did and, in the case of short-term marriages that produced children, until the youngest child enters first grade and the custodial parent has a real chance of making his or her own living. After that point, child support should continue at a level that enables the children to enjoy a standard of living equal to that of the noncustodial parent. There can be no reason consistent with principles of justice that some should suffer economically vastly more than others from the breakup of a relationship whose asymmetric division of labor was mutually agreed on.

I have suggested two basic models of family rights and responsibilities, both of which are currently needed because this is a time of great transition for men and women and great disagreement about gender. Families in which roles and responsibilities are equally shared regardless of sex are far more in accord with principles of justice than are typical families today. So are families in which those who undertake more traditional domestic roles are protected from the risks they presently incur. In either case, justice as a whole will benefit from the changes. Of the two, however, I claim that the genderless family is more just; . . . it is more just to women; it is more conducive to equal opportunity both for women and for children of both sexes; and it creates a more favorable environment for the rearing of citizens of a just society. Thus, while protecting those whom gender now makes vulnerable, we must also put our best efforts into promoting the elimination of gender.

The increased justice to women that would result from moving away from gender is readily apparent. Standards for just social institutions could no longer take for granted and exclude from considerations of justice much of what women now do, since men would share in it equally. Such central components of justice as what counts as productive labor, and what count as needs and deserts, would be greatly affected by this change. Standards of justice would become *humanist*, as they have never been before. One of the most important effects of this would be to change radically the situation of women as citizens. With egalitarian families, and with institutions such as workplaces and schools designed to accommodate the needs of parents and children, rather than being based as they now are on the traditional assumption that "someone else" is at home, mothers would not be virtually excluded from positions of influence in politics and the workplace. They would be represented at every level in approximately equal numbers with men.

In a genderless society, children too would benefit. They would not suffer in the ways that they do now because of the injustices done to women. It is undeniable that the family in which each of us grows up has a deeply formative influence on us—on the kind of persons we want to be as well as the kind of persons we are.[16] This is one of the reasons why one *cannot* reasonably leave the family out of "the basic structure of society," to which the principles of justice are to apply. Equality of opportunity to become what we want to be would be enhanced in two important ways by the development of families without gender and by the public policies necessary to support their development. First, the growing gap between the economic well-being of children in single-parent and those in two-parent families would be reduced. Children in single-parent families would benefit significantly if fathers were held equally responsible for supporting their children, whether married to their mothers or not; if more mothers had sustained labor force attachment; if high-quality day care were subsidized; and if the workplace were designed to accommodate parenting. These children would be far less likely to spend their formative years in conditions of poverty, with one parent struggling to fulfill the functions of two. Their life chances would be significantly enhanced.

Second, children of both sexes in gender-free families would have (as some already have) much more opportunity for self-development free from sex-role expectations and sex-typed personalities than most do now. Girls and boys who grow up in highly traditional families, in which sex difference is regarded as a determinant of everything from roles, responsibilities, and privileges to acceptable dress, speech, and modes of behavior, clearly have far less freedom to develop into whatever kind of person they want to be than do those who are raised without such constraints. It is too early for us to know a lot about the developmental outcomes and life choices of children who are equally parented by mothers and fathers, since the practice is still so recent and so rare. Persuasive theories such as Chodorow's, however, would lead us to expect much less differentiation between the sexes to result from truly shared parenting.[17] Even now, in most cases without men's equal fathering, both the daughters and the sons of wage-working mothers have been found to have a more positive view of women and less rigid views of sex roles; the daughters (like their mothers) tend to have greater self-esteem and a more positive view of themselves as workers, and the sons, to expect equality and shared roles in their own future marriages.[18] We might well expect that with mothers in the labor force and with fathers as equal parents, children's attitudes and psychologies will become even less correlated with their sex. In a very crucial sense, their opportunities to become the persons they want to be will be enlarged.

Finally, it seems undeniable that the enhancement of justice that accompanies the disappearance of gender will make the family a much better place for children to develop a sense of justice. We can no longer deny the importance of the fact that families are where we first learn, by example and by how we are treated, not only how people do relate to each other but also how they *should*. How would families not built on gender be better schools of moral development? First, the example of co-equal parents with shared roles, combining love with justice, would provide a far better example of human relations for children than the domination and dependence that often occur in traditional marriage. The fairness of the distribution of labor, the equal respect, and the *inter*dependence of his or her parents would surely be a powerful first example to a child in a family with equally shared roles. Second, . . . having a sense of justice requires that we be able to empathize, to abstract from our own situation and to think about moral and political issues from the points of view of others. We cannot come to either just principles or just specific decisions by thinking, as it were, as if we were nobody, or thinking from nowhere; we must, therefore, learn to think from the point of view of others, including others who are different from ourselves.

To the extent that gender is de-emphasized in our nurturing practices, this capacity would seem to be enhanced, for two reasons. First, if female primary parenting leads, as it seems to, to less distinct ego boundaries and greater capacity for empathy in female children, and to a greater tendency to self-definition and abstraction in males, then might we not expect to find the two capacities better combined in children of both sexes who are reared by parents of both sexes? Second, the experience of *being* nurturers, throughout a significant portion of our lives, also seems likely to result in an increase in empathy, and in the combination of personal moral capacities, fusing feelings with reason, that just citizens need.[19]

For those whose response to what I have argued here is the practical objection that it is unrealistic and will cost too much, I have some answers and some questions. Some of what I have suggested would not cost anything, in terms of public spending, though it would redistribute the costs and other responsibilities of rearing children more evenly between men and women. Some policies I have endorsed, such as adequate public support for children whose fathers cannot contribute, may cost more than present policies, but may not, depending on how well they work.[20] Some, such as subsidized high-quality day care, would

be expensive in themselves, but also might soon be offset by other savings, since they would enable those who would otherwise be full-time child carers to be at least part-time workers.

All in all, it seems highly unlikely that the *long-term* costs of such programs—even if we count only monetary costs, not costs in human terms—would outweigh the long-term benefits. In many cases, the cycle of poverty could be broken—and children enabled to escape from, or to avoid falling into, it—through a much better early start in life.[21] But even if my suggests would cost, and cost a lot, we have to ask: How much do we care about the injustices of gender? How much do we care that women who have spent the better part of their lives nurturing others can be discarded like used goods? How ashamed are we that one-quarter of our children, in one of the richest countries in the world, live in poverty? How much do we care that those who raise children, *because* of this choice, have restricted opportunities to develop the rest of their potential, and very little influence on society's values and direction? How much do we care that the family, our most intimate social grouping, is often a school of day-to-day injustice? How much do we want the just families that will produce the kind of citizens we need if we are ever to achieve a just society?

Notes

1. See chap. 3, 67–68.
2. "Women: Out of the House But Not Out of the Kitchen," *New York Times*, February 24, 1988, pp. A1, C10.
3. See, for example, Marjorie Maguire Schultz, "Contractual Ordering of Marriage: A New Model for State Policy," *California Law Review* 70, no. 2 (1982); Lenore Weitzman, *The Marriage Contract: Spouses, Lover, and the Law* (New York: *The Free Press*, 1981), parts 3–4.
4. See, for example, David L. Kirp, Mark G. Yudof, and Marlene Strong Franks, *Gender Justice* (Chicago: University of Chicago Press, 1986), pp. 183–85. Robert H. Mnookin takes an only slightly less laissez-faire approach, in "Divorce Bargaining: The Limits on Private

Ordering," *University of Michigan Journal of Law Reform*, 18, no. 4 (1985).

5. It seems reasonable to conclude that the effects of day care on children are probably just as variable as the effects of parenting—that is to say, very widely variable depending on the quality of the day care and of the parenting. There is no doubt that good out-of-home day care is expensive—approximately $100 per full-time week in 1987, even though child-care workers are now paid only about two-thirds as much per hour as other comparably educated women workers (Victor Fuchs, *Women's Quest for Economic Equality* [Cambridge: Harvard University Press, 1988], pp. 137–38). However, it is undoubtedly easier to control its quality than that of informal "family day care." In my view, based in part on my experience of the excellent day-care center that our children attended for a total of seven years, good-quality day care must have small-scale "home rooms" and a high staff-to-child ratio, and should pay staff better than most centers now do. For balanced studies of the effects of day care on a poor population, see Sally Provence, Audrey Naylor, June Patterson, *The Challenge of Daycare* (New Haven: Yale University Press, 1977); and, most recently, Lisbeth B. Schorr (with Daniel Schorr), *Within Our Reach—Breaking the Cycle of Disadvantage* (New York: Anchor Press, Doubleday, 1988), chap. 8.

6. Much of what I suggest here is not new; it has formed part of the feminist agenda for several decades, and I first made some of the suggestions I develop here in the concluding chapter of *Women in Western Political Thought* (Princeton: Princeton University Press, 1979). Three recent books that address some of the policies discussed here are Fuchs, *Women's Quest*, chap. 7; Philip Green, *Retrieving Democracy: In Search of Civic Equality* (Totowa, N.J.: Rowman and Allanheld, 1985), pp. 96–108; and Anita Shreve, *Remaking Motherhood: How Working Mother Are Shaping Our Children's Future* (New York: Fawcett Columbine, 1987) pp. 173–78. In Fuch's chapter he carefully analyzes the potential economic and social effects of alternative polices to improve women's economic status, and concludes that "child-centered policies" such as parental leave and subsidized day care are likely to have more of a positive impact on women's economic position than "labor market policies" such as antidiscrimination, comparable pay for comparable worth, and affirmative action have had and are likely to have. Some potentially very effective polices, such as on-side day care and flexible

and/or reduced working hours for parents of young or "special needs" children, seem to fall within both of his categories.

7. The dilemma faced by feminists in the recent California case *Guerra v. California Federal Savings and Loan Association*, 107 S. Ct. 683 (1987) was due to the fact that state law mandated leave for pregnancy and birth that it did *not* mandate for other disabling conditions. Thus to defend the law seemed to open up the dangers of discrimination that the earlier protection of women in the workplace had resulted in. (For a discussion of this general issue of equality versus difference, see, for example, Wendy W. Williams, "The Equality Crisis: Some Reflections on Culture, Courts, and Feminism," *Women's Rights Law Reporter* 7, no. 3 [1982].) The Supreme Court upheld the California law on the grounds that it treaded workers equally in terms of their rights to become parents.

8. Amy Gutmann, *Democratic Education* (Princeton: Princeton University Press, 1987), pp. 112–15 quotation from pp. 113–14. See also Elisabeth Hansot and David Tyack, "Gender in American Public Schools: Thinking Institutionally," *Signs* 13, no. 4 (1988).

9. A classic text on this subject is Dale Spender, eds., *Men's Studies Modified: The Impact of Feminism on the Academic Disciplines* (Oxford: Pergamon Press, 1981).

10. Shreve, *Remaking Motherhood*, p. 237.

11. Although 51 percent of infants are breast-fed at birth, only 14 percent are entirely breast-fed at six weeks of age. Cited from P. Leach, *Babyhood* (New York: Alfred A. Knopf, 1983), by Sylvia Ann Hewlett, in *A Lesser Life: The Myth of Women's Liberation in America* (New York: Morrow, 1986), p. 409n34. Given this fact, it seems quite unjustified to argue that lactation dictates that mothers be the primary parents, even during infancy.

12. In Sweden, where the liberalization of abortion in the mid-1970s was accompanied by much expanded birth-control education and information and reduced-cost contraceptives, the rates of both teenage abortion and teenage birth decreased significantly. The Swedish teenage birth-rate was by 1982 less than half what it had been in the 1970s. Mary Ann Glendon, *Abortion and Divorce in Western Law* (Cambridge: Harvard University Press, 1987), p. 23 and n65. Chapter 3 of Schorr's *Within Our Reach* gives an excellent account of programs in the United States that have proven effective in reducing early and unplanned pregnancies. Noting the strong correlation between emotional and

economic deprivation and early pregnancy, she emphasizes the importance, if teenagers are to have the incentive not to become pregnant, of their believing that they have a real stake in their own futures, and developing the aspirations and self-assertiveness that go along with this. As Victor Fuchs points out, approximately two-thirds of unmarried women who give birth are twenty or older (Women's Quest, p. 68). However, these women are somewhat more likely to have work skills and experience, and it seems likely that many live in informal "common law marriage" heterosexual or lesbian partnerships, rather than being in fact single parents.

13. David Ellwood, *Poor Support: Poverty in the American Family* (New York: Basic Books, 1988), pp. 163–74. He estimates that full-time day care for each child can be bought for $3,000 per year, and half-time for $1,000. He acknowledges that these estimated costs are "modest." I think they are unrealistic, unless the care is being provided by a relative or close friend. Ellwood reports that, as of 1985, only 18 percent of never-married fathers were ordered to pay child support, and only 11 percent actually paid any (p. 158).

14. Mary Ann Glendon has set out a "children first" approach to divorce (Glendon, *Abortion and Divorce*, pp. 94ff.); here I extend the same idea to ongoing marriage, where the arrival of a child is most often the point at which the wife becomes economically dependent.

15. My suggestions for protecting traditional and quasi-traditional wives in the event of divorce are similar to those of Lenore Weitzman in *The Divorce Revolution: The Unexpected Social and Economic Consequences for Women and Children in America* (New York: The Free Press, 1985), chap. 11, and Mary Ann Glendon in *Abortion and Divorce*, chap. 2. Although they would usually in practice protect traditional wives, the laws should be gender-neutral so that they would equally protect divorcing men who had undertaken the primary functions of parenting and homemaking.

16. Here I paraphrase Rawls's wording in explaining why the basic structure of society is basic. "The Basic Structure as Subject," *American Philosophical Quarterly* 14, no. 2 (1977): 160.

17. See chap. 6 $n58$ in this volume.

18. Shreve, *Remaking Motherhood*, chaps. 3–7.

19. See, for example, Sara Ruddick, "Maternal Thinking," *Feminist Studies* 6, no. 2 (1980); Diane Ehrensaft, "When Women and Men Mother," in *Mothering: Essays in Feminist Theory*, ed. Joyce Trebilcot (Totowa, NJ: Rowman and Allanheld, 1984); Judith Kegan Gardiner, "Self Psychology as Feminist Theory," *Signs* 12, no, 4 (1987), esp. 778–80.

20. David Ellwood estimates that "if most absent fathers contributed the given percentages, the program would actually save money" (*Poor Support*, p. 169).

21. Schorr's *Within Our Reach* documents the ways in which the cycle of disadvantage can be effectively broken, even for those in the poorest circumstances.

ELIZABETH S. ANDERSON

~

INTRODUCTION

REKHA NATH

Elizabeth Anderson was born in 1959 and grew up in Manchester, Connecticut. She graduated from Swarthmore College and went on to complete her Ph.D. in philosophy at Harvard University in 1987. Since then she has taught at the University of Michigan, where she is Arthur F. Thurnau Professor and John Dewey Distinguished University Professor of Philosophy and Women's Studies. She has served as president of the American Philosophical Association's Central Division and has been the recipient of numerous honors and awards, including the MacArthur Foundation's prestigious "Genius Grant." In 2015, she delivered the Tanner Lectures on Human Values, which became the basis of her 2017 book, *Private Government: How Employers Rule Our Lives (and Why We Don't Talk about It)*. She has published prolifically in wide-ranging areas that include philosophy of economics and the social sciences, history of ethics, philosophy of science, and social and feminist epistemology. She is best known for her work in social and political philosophy, especially on equality, democracy, race, and the ethical limits of markets.

Anderson's philosophical contributions are guided by a Dewey-inspired pragmatism. Her pragmatist leanings distinguish her work from an approach to normative theorizing that is dominant in contemporary analytic philosophy: the "ideal theory" approach, which often relies on highly stylized thought experiments in an effort to formulate and refine moral principles. The ideal theory approach tends to yield principles ill-suited to the actual, far-from-ideal circumstances that obtain at present. Anderson embraces a nonideal approach to normative theorizing that takes real-world social problems as its starting point. She seeks out remedies to such problems that not only conform with worthy moral ideals but are actually attainable. A cornerstone of her methodology is an insistence that moral inquiries be pursued holistically, in tandem with analyses of the social realities that they concern. She writes, "Pragmatism urges us to view social scientific, humanistic, and ethical inquiry as interconnected aspects of a joint enterprise."

This pragmatist approach can be seen in her early work, such as in her first book, *Value in Ethics and Economics* (1993). There she asks: Is there a single way in which people value things? Many economists and moral philosophers think so. But Anderson argues that they are wrong. She criticizes prevailing consequentialist theories of rational choice and monistic theories of value (such as hedonism) for failing to pay sufficient attention to the considerable nuance and diversity in how people actually value things. She articulates and defends a pluralist theory of value and practical action, arguing that it offers a superior framework for addressing pressing social and economic issues. In other work too, she sets out to expose flaws of standard economic models, explaining the disconnect between the idealizing assumptions upon which they are predicated and relevant empirical realities.

Anderson's pragmatist methodology is even more evident in her two most recent books. In her 2010 book *The Imperative of Integration*, she engages extensively with findings in psychology, sociology, history, economics, and other disciplines, to build a case for bringing an end to racial segregation in American society. In her view, to know what form meaningful progress should take, we must be savvy about evidence from the social sciences. We must understand much about, for example, the historical and present-day causes and effects of segregation; the successes and failures of the civil rights movement; and the important role that various cognitive biases play in fueling persistent racial inequalities. She therefore gives sustained consideration to issues often left unaddressed by moral and political philosophers engaged in ideal theorizing. This is characteristic of her body of work. She asks: What obstacles stand in the way of our making progress? How can reflecting on the past help us achieve a deeper understanding of current social problems? She pursues this enterprise in myriad ways, which includes engaging with people other than professional philosophers, through radio and podcast interviews as well as through contributions to social science journals and various nonacademic venues. Fostering interpersonal dialogue is central to her pragmatism. In her view, morality is a matter of the mutual demands that we, as persons who find ourselves unavoidably bound up in relations of social, political, and economic interdependence, can reasonably place on one another. And determining what those moral demands are depends, in part, on how particular arrangements work in practice for those subject to them. Indeed, she thinks moral ideals and principles can be tested by engaging in social "experiments in living," to use John Stuart Mill's well-known phrase, which Anderson frequently invokes.

In *Private Government*, Anderson argues that a majority of American workers endure profound threats to their basic freedom in the workplace: for instance, bosses are legally permitted to search subordinates' bodies and personal belongings without probable cause, and they can sanction employees for off-duty behavior such as their sexual choices and political activities. If this is so, however, why does it so often go unnoticed? According to Anderson, this grave injustice is obscured by widely accepted free-market ideology, and clarity on this matter can be attained by understanding where that ideology came from. Free-market ideology is often traced to heralded thinkers from the seventeenth and eighteenth centuries such as Adam Smith. But as Anderson argues, although Smith (along with John Locke, Thomas Paine, and others) extolled the virtues of free markets they did so on the basis of progressive agendas. Those thinkers did not subscribe to the reigning free-market ideology of our time that has made the injustice *Private Government* exposes hard to see. On the contrary, they celebrated free markets for their potential to promote the values of freedom and equality—values that fail to be embodied in the labor markets of our own time, which differ radically from the context in which those authors envisioned free markets operating. An underlying issue here, concerning how people's beliefs can come to be so deeply at odds with reality, as well as how such misconceptions can be corrected, is one that occupies Anderson in much of her work.

Perhaps the best known of Anderson's academic writings is her 1999 essay, "What Is the Point of Equality?" When she wrote this piece, several important contributions to debates about equality in analytic political philosophy focused on the distinction between luck and choice. A key issue here was how to distinguish chance-based inequalities from those that can be traced to choices for which individuals should be held responsible. That focus can in part be seen as being inspired by an idea advanced by John Rawls in *A Theory of Justice* (1971): the idea that there is something morally objectionable about people's relative life prospects being determined by matters that lie outside of their control, such as being born to impoverished rather than to wealthy parents. For Rawls, however, this idea is but one of several that he draws on in devising a theory of the substantive demands of egalitarian justice. By contrast, in the 1980s and '90s, a number of authors, including Ronald Dworkin, G. A. Cohen, and Richard Arneson, set out to formulate egalitarian theories in which the luck/choice distinction is central. On such theories, *all* luck-based inequalities—those due to such factors as one's social starting point in life as well as to natural differences, such as in the talents, personality traits, or looks one is born with—must, as a matter of justice, be remedied. Further, inequalities resulting not from luck but from differences in individuals' genuine choices are permissible.

Anderson coins a name for variants of the egalitarian theory favored by Dworkin et al., which has since become widely adopted by its proponents and critics alike: *luck egalitarianism* (she sometimes also refers to them as *equality of fortune*). In her view, luck egalitarianism is deeply misguided. For one thing, she disagrees that luck egalitarianism follows from Rawls's egalitarian commitments, as some contend. But her primary interest is not in how to interpret Rawls (with whom she studied at Harvard). She is occupied with a more serious concern: that mainstream thinking about equality in the post-Rawls era has gone astray. In "What Is the Point of Equality?" she sets out to reorient egalitarian thinking in fundamental ways. Part of the essay is critical. She provides a detailed analysis of luck egalitarianism's central assumptions and advances influential criticisms of them (many details of these criticisms are omitted in the abridged version of the article that follows). The essay is also constructive. Anderson sketches an alternative egalitarian theory, which she there calls *democratic equality*, detailing its contours and highlighting its comparative merits.

In the two decades since the publication of Anderson's seminal essay, there have been numerous attempts to formulate, refine, and criticize views of the sort that she sketches. It is now common for such views to be referred to as versions of *relational egalitarianism* or *social egalitarianism*. Views of this sort depart from prevailing egalitarian views on the matter of how we should conceive of equality, both in terms of what it is and why its pursuit is valuable. Luck egalitarians embrace a distributive conception, on which equality is construed "as a pattern of distribution" and individuals are equal "so long as they enjoy equal amounts of some distributable good—income, resources, opportunities for welfare, and so forth." By contrast, on Anderson's *relational* conception, social relations are the fundamental object of egalitarian concern. Equality is fundamentally a matter of people living together as equals, rather than of how goods are distributed.

What, according to Anderson, does it mean for people to live together as equals? In explicating this notion, her primary focus is on investigating what relations of equality would look like between those who belong to the same state. But the theory could, in her view, be applied to relations between people belonging to different states. For individuals to enjoy relations of equality requires that they not interact in certain ways: in particular, relational egalitarianism is incompatible with oppressive social relations whereby "some people dominate, exploit, marginalize, demean, and inflict violence upon others." Such oppressive relationships must be abolished. Furthermore, belonging to an egalitarian community requires that all members be positioned to have and to do certain things. Specifically, for fellow citizens to stand as equals, they all must be enabled "to participate in and enjoy the goods of society, and to participate in democratic self-government." Ensuring equal standing in these domains is called for because we owe one another justification for the character of the social arrangements that we jointly uphold. Consider what the latter requirement would entail for deaf individuals. Egalitarian justice, on this view, demands that being deaf not compromise a person's ability to participate as an equal in educational settings or the workforce, to navigate public spaces, or to engage in democratic deliberation alongside one's fellow citizens. To the extent that one's ability to do such things is compromised—for example, by schools in which sign-language translations of auditory learning materials are not provided to deaf students—this requirement of egalitarian justice would be violated.

The deafness case is but one of many real-world cases Anderson uses to support and explain relational egalitarianism and to reveal shortcomings of luck egalitarianism (she also discusses gay and lesbian individuals facing hostility and being denied equal rights, women's subjection to oppressive gender norms, and other cases). As she observes, luck egalitarians see no morally relevant difference between disadvantages that have a social versus a natural cause. They treat all unchosen disadvantages as being on a par. But as Anderson argues, that result does not reflect what oppressed people themselves tend to care about. Deaf individuals do not ask for handouts to rectify the "supposed cosmic injustice" of missing out on various pleasures experienced by the nondeaf, such as listening to music. Indeed, many deaf people object to their lives being portrayed as deficient. Rather, their demands concern the ways that society places them at a disadvantage. They have long fought against social operations being skewed in favor of the hearing, thereby preventing or limiting their inclusion in the workforce and in civil society. Unlike luck egalitarianism, relational egalitarianism provides a reasoned basis for such demands—a basis that does not extend implausibly to demands the deaf do not make. Further, on luck egalitarianism, deafness is cast as an unfortunate, even a pitiable, deficiency, and that theory's rationale for what society owes the deaf is demeaning toward them. By contrast, on relational egalitarianism, a commitment to equality is reflected not just in the distributive shares that people have but also in the regard that they are shown by others and whether they are treated with respect. In light of the value of individuals being recognized as equals, relational egalitarianism calls for assessment of how social policies and practices might problematically convey to some that they are inferior.

The fact that Anderson's relational egalitarianism yields prescriptions that align with demands for justice advanced by real-world egalitarian social movements reflects her methodology. Theorizing about the demands of egalitarian justice must, she contends, be informed by the experiences and perspectives of victims of actual injustices. Otherwise, our reflections might be distorted by biases of dominant social groups—for instance, resulting in an account of egalitarian justice that erroneously assumes an ableist perspective that casts all disabilities as unfortunate—and be too detached from real-world circumstances to provide useful guidance in addressing status quo injustices.

"What Is the Point of Equality?" was not the only piece of its time that voiced relational egalitarian concerns. Others include essays by David Miller and by Richard Norman, which can be found in Andrew Mason (ed.), *Ideals of Equality* (Oxford: Blackwell, 1998). Relational egalitarian concerns are also discussed by T. M. Scanlon in an essay reprinted in Matthew Clayton and Andrew Williams (eds.), *The Ideal of Equality* (Basingstoke: Palgrave Macmillan, 2000) as well as in his *Why Does Inequality Matter?* (Oxford: Oxford University Press, 2018). For a defense of relational egalitarianism that, like Anderson's, is motivated by serious misgivings about luck egalitarianism, see Samuel Scheffler's essays that are reprinted as chapters 7 and 8 of his *Equality and Tradition* (New York: Oxford University Press, 2010). For a collection bringing together more recent work on relational egalitarianism, see Carina Fourie, Fabian Schuppert, and Ivo Wallimann-Helmer (eds.), *Social Equality: On What It Means to Be Equals* (New York: Oxford University Press, 2015). That volume includes an essay by Jonathan Wolff, another author who, like Anderson in the late 1990s, pointed to distinctively relational egalitarian values being sidelined by mainstream egalitarian theorizing. For an earlier work that raises related concerns, from a communitarian perspective, see Michael Walzer, *Spheres of Justice: A Defense of Pluralism and Equality* (New York: Basic Books, 1983).

Anderson's views are firmly rooted in feminist theory. Her embrace of a relational theory that places oppressive relationships at the heart of egalitarian concern is influenced by the writings of Iris Marion Young—most prominently, her *Justice and the Politics of Difference* (Princeton, N.J.: Princeton University Press, 1990). Anderson's call for egalitarians to pay attention to demands of recognition in addition to distributive matters draws on Nancy Fraser's work, such as *Justice Interruptus: Critical Reflections on the "Postsocialist" Condition* (New York: Routledge, 1997). And in pressing the need for egalitarian justice to apply broadly—to include in its purview such things as social norms, practices, habits, and attitudes rather than the narrower Rawlsian focus on institutions—Anderson echoes a line of thought long advanced by feminist theorists such as, for instance, Susan Moller Okin, in *Justice, Gender, and the Family* (New York: Basic Books, 1989).

Anderson invites her reader to reflect on not only the point of equality but the point of normative theorizing more generally. In her view, the point of such theorizing is to deepen our understanding of the serious injustices that confront us, so as to make us better equipped to address them. In recent years, this approach to normative theorizing has become more widely embraced by analytic philosophers. Anderson's work can therefore be seen as connected to a diverse body of contemporary writings on group-based hierarchy and oppression such as the following: Miranda Fricker, *Epistemic Injustice: Power and the Ethics of Knowing* (Oxford: Oxford University Press, 2007); Sally Haslanger, *Resisting Reality: Social Construction and Social Critique* (Oxford: Oxford University Press, 2012); Christopher J. Lebron, *The Color of Our Shame: Race and*

Justice in Our Time (New York: Oxford University Press, 2013); Elizabeth Barnes, *The Minority Body: A Theory of Disability* (Oxford: Oxford University Press, 2016); Kate Manne, *Down Girl: The Logic of Misogyny* (Oxford: Oxford University Press, 2018).

For some of Dewey's work that has influenced Anderson, see *The Public and Its Problems* (1927); *Ethics*, coauthored with James Tufts (revised edition, 1932); and "Creative Democracy: The Task Before Us" (1939). All of these pieces can be found in Jo Ann Boydston (ed.), *The Later Works of John Dewey, 1925–1953* (Carbondale: Southern Illinois University Press, 1981).

What Is the Point of Equality?

If much recent academic work defending equality had been secretly penned by conservatives, could the results be any more embarrassing for egalitarians? Consider how much of this work leaves itself open to classic and devastating conservative criticisms. Ronald Dworkin defines equality as an "envy-free" distribution of resources.[1] This feeds the suspicion that the motive behind egalitarian policies is mere envy. Philippe Van Parijs argues that equality in conjunction with liberal neutrality among conceptions of the good requires the state to support lazy, able-bodied surfers who are unwilling to work.[2] This invites the charge that egalitarians support irresponsibility and encourage the slothful to be parasitic on the productive. Richard Arneson claims that equality requires that, under certain conditions, the state subsidize extremely costly religious ceremonies that its citizens feel bound to perform.[3] G. A. Cohen tells us that equality requires that we compensate people for being temperamentally gloomy or for being so incurably bored by inexpensive hobbies that they can get fulfilling recreation only from expensive diversions.[4]

These proposals bolster the objection that egalitarians are oblivious to the proper limits of state power and permit coercion of others for merely private ends. Van Parijs suggests that to fairly implement the equal right to get married, when male partners are scarce, every woman should be given an equal tradable share in the pool of eligible bachelors and have to bid for whole partnership rights, thus implementing a transfer of wealth from successful brides to compensate the losers in love.[5] This supports the objection that egalitarianism, in its determination to correct perceived unfairness everywhere, invades our privacy and burdens the personal ties of love and affection that lie at the core of family life.

Those on the left have no less reason than conservatives and libertarians to be disturbed by recent trends in academic egalitarian thought. First, consider those whom recent academic egalitarians have singled out for special attention: beach bums, the lazy and irresponsible, people who can't manage to entertain themselves with simple pleasures, religious fanatics. Thomas Nagel and Gerald Cohen give us somewhat more sympathetic but also pitiable characters in taking stupid, talentless, and bitter people to be exemplary beneficiaries of egalitarian concern.[6] What has happened to the concerns of the politically oppressed? What about inequalities of race, gender, class, and caste? Where are the victims of nationalist genocide, slavery, and ethnic subordination?

Second, the agendas defined by much recent egalitarian theorizing are too narrowly focused

Adapted by Elizabeth S. Anderson from her article "What is the Point of Equality?" *Ethics* 109, vol. 2 (1999). Copyright c 1999 by University of Chicago Press and reprinted with permission of the Press.

on the distribution of divisible, privately appropriated goods, such as income and resources, or
privately enjoyed goods, such as welfare. This
neglects the much broader agendas of actual
egalitarian political movements. For example, gay
and lesbian people seek the freedom to appear in
public as who they are without shame or fear of
violence, the right to get married and enjoy benefits of marriage, to adopt and retain custody
of children. The disabled have drawn attention
to the ways the configuration of public spaces
has excluded and marginalized them, and cam-
paigned against demeaning stereotypes that cast
them as stupid, incompetent, and pathetic. Thus,
with respect to both the targets of egalitarian concern and their agendas, recent egalitarian writing
seems strangely detached from existing egalitarian political movements.

What has gone wrong here? I shall argue that
these problems stem from a flawed understanding
of the point of equality. Recent egalitarian writing has come to be dominated by the view that
the fundamental aim of equality is to compensate
people for undeserved bad luck—being born with
poor native endowments, bad parents, and disagreeable personalities, suffering from accidents
and illness, and so forth. I shall argue that in focusing on correcting a supposed cosmic injustice,
recent egalitarian writing has lost sight of the
distinctively political aims of egalitarianism. The
proper negative aim of egalitarian justice is not to
eliminate the impact of brute luck from human
affairs, but to end oppression, which by definition
is socially imposed. Its proper positive aim is not
to ensure that everyone gets what they morally deserve, but to create a community in which people
stand in relations of equality to others.

The theory I shall defend can be called "democratic equality." In seeking the construction
of a community of equals, democratic equality
integrates principles of distribution with the expressive demands of equal respect. Democratic
equality guarantees all law-abiding citizens effective access to the social conditions of their
freedom at all times. It justifies the distributions

required to secure this guarantee by appealing to
the obligations of citizens in a democratic state.
In such a state, citizens make claims on one another in virtue of their equality, not their inferiority, to others. Because the fundamental aim of
citizens in constructing a state is to secure everyone's freedom, democratic equality's principles of
distribution neither presume to tell people how to
use their opportunities nor attempt to judge how
responsible people are for choices that lead to unfortunate outcomes. Instead, it avoids bankruptcy
at the hands of the imprudent by limiting the
range of goods provided collectively and expecting individuals to take personal responsibility for
the other goods in their possession.

WHAT IS THE POINT OF EQUALITY?

It is helpful to recall how egalitarian political
movements have historically conceived of their
aims. What have been the inegalitarian systems
that they have opposed? Inegalitarianism asserted the justice or necessity of basing social
order on a hierarchy of human beings, ranked
according to intrinsic worth. Inequality referred
not so much to distributions of goods as to relations between superior and inferior persons.
Those of superior rank were thought entitled to
inflict violence on inferiors, to exclude or seg-
regate them from social life, to treat them with
contempt, to force them to obey, to work without reciprocation, and to abandon their own cultures. These are what Iris Young has identified as
the faces of oppression: marginalization, status
hierarchy, domination, exploitation, and cultural
imperialism.[7] Such unequal social relations generate, and were thought to justify, inequalities in
the distribution of freedoms, resources, and welfare. This is the core of inegalitarian ideologies
of racism, sexism, nationalism, caste, class, and
eugenics.

Egalitarian political movements oppose such
hierarchies. They assert the equal moral worth
of persons. This assertion does not mean that all
have equal virtue or talent. Negatively, the claim

repudiates distinctions of moral worth based on birth or social identity—on family membership, inherited social status, race, ethnicity, gender, or genes. There are no natural slaves, plebeians, or aristocrats. Positively, the claim asserts that all competent adults are equally moral agents: everyone equally has the power to develop and exercise moral responsibility, to cooperate with others according to principles of justice, to shape and fulfill a conception of their good.[8]

Egalitarians base claims to social and political equality on the fact of universal moral equality. These claims also have a negative and a positive aspect. Negatively, egalitarians seek to abolish oppression—that is, forms of social relationship by which some people dominate, exploit, marginalize, demean, and inflict violence upon others. Diversities in socially ascribed identities, distinct roles in the division of labor, or differences in personal traits, whether these be neutral biological and psychological differences, valuable talents and virtues, or unfortunate disabilities and infirmities, never justify the unequal social relations listed above. Nothing can justify treating people in these ways, except just punishment for crimes and defense against violence. Positively, egalitarians seek a social order in which persons stand in relations of equality. They seek to live together in a democratic community, as opposed to a hierarchical one. Democracy is here understood as collective self-determination by means of open discussion among equals in accordance with rules acceptable to all. To stand as an equal before others in discussion means that one is entitled to participate, that others recognize an obligation to listen respectfully and respond to one's arguments, that no one need bow and scrape before others or represent themselves as inferior to others as a condition of having their claim heard.[9]

Contrast this democratic conception of equality with equality of fortune. First, democratic equality aims to abolish socially created oppression. Equality of fortune aims to correct what it takes to be injustices generated by the natural order. Second, democratic equality is what I shall call a relational theory of equality: it views equality as a social relationship. Equality of fortune is a distributive theory of equality: it conceives of equality as a pattern of distribution. Thus, equality of fortune regards two people as equal so long as they enjoy equal amounts of some distributable good—income, resources, opportunities for welfare, and so forth. Social relationships are largely seen as instrumental to generating such patterns of distribution. By contrast, democratic equality regards two people as equal when each accepts the obligation to justify their actions by principles acceptable to the other, and in which they take mutual consultation, reciprocation, and recognition for granted. Certain patterns in the distribution of goods may be instrumental to securing such relationships, follow from them, or even be constitutive of them. But democratic egalitarians are fundamentally concerned with the relationships within which goods are distributed, not only with the distribution of goods themselves. This implies, third, that democratic equality is sensitive to the need to integrate the demands of equal recognition with those of equal distribution.[10] Goods must be distributed according to principles and processes that express respect for all. People must not be required to grovel or demean themselves before others as a condition of laying claim to their share of goods. The basis for people's claims to distributed goods is that they are equals, not inferiors, to others.

This gives us a rough conception of equality. How do we derive principles of justice from it? Our investigation of equality of fortune has not been completely fruitless: from its failures, we have gleaned some desiderata for egalitarian principles. First, such principles must identify certain goods to which all citizens must have effective access over the course of their whole lives. Some goods are more important from an egalitarian point of view than others, within whatever space of equality is identified as of particular concern for egalitarians. And starting-gate theories, or any other principles that allow law-abiding citizens to lose access to adequate levels of these goods, are unacceptable. Second, egalitarians should be able to justify such guarantees of lifetime accessibility without resorting to paternalism. Third, egalitarian principles should offer remedies that match the type of injustice being corrected. Private satisfactions cannot make up for public oppression. Fourth, egalitarian principles should uphold the responsibility of individuals for their own lives without passing demeaning and intrusive judgments on their capacities for exercising responsibility or on how well they have used their freedoms. Finally, such principles should be possible objects of collective willing. They should be capable of supplying sufficient reasons for citizens acting together to collectively guarantee the particular goods of concern to egalitarians.

Let us take up the last desideratum first. The determination of what can or must be collectively willed has been the traditional task of social contract theory. In liberal democratic versions of social contract theory, the fundamental aim of the state is to secure the liberty of its members. Since the democratic state is nothing more than citizens acting collectively, it follows that the fundamental obligation of citizens to one another is to secure the social conditions of everyone's freedom.[11] Because libertarians also embrace this formula, it might be thought to lead to inegalitarian implications. Instead of repudiating this formula, democratic equality interprets it. It claims that the social condition of living a free life is that one stand in relations of equality with others.

This claim might seem paradoxical, given the prevailing view that represents equality and freedom as conflicting ideals. We can see how it is true by considering the oppressive relationships that social equality negates. Equals are not subject to arbitrary violence or physical coercion by others. Choice unconstrained by arbitrary physical coercion is one of the fundamental conditions of freedom. Equals are not marginalized by others. They are therefore free to participate in politics and the major institutions of civil society. Equals are not

dominated by others; they do not live at the mercy of others' wills. This means that they govern their lives by their own wills, which is freedom. Equals are not exploited by others. This means they are free to secure the fair value of their labor. Equals are not subject to cultural imperialism; they are free to practice their own culture, subject to the constraint of respecting everyone else. To live in an egalitarian community, then, is to be free from oppression to participate in and enjoy the goods of society, and to participate in democratic self-government.

Egalitarians thus differ from libertarians in advocating a more expansive understanding of the social conditions of freedom. Importantly, they view private relations of domination, even those entered into by consent or contract, as violations of individual freedom. Libertarians tend to identify freedom with formal, negative freedom: enjoying the legal right to do what one wants without having to ask anyone else's permission and without interference from others. This definition of freedom neglects the importance of having the means to do what one wants. In addition, the definition implicitly assumes that, given the material means and internal capacity to do what one wants, the absence of interference from others is all one needs to do what one wants. This ignores the fact that most of the things people want to do require participation in social activities, and hence communication and interaction with others. One cannot do these things if others make one an outcast. A libertarian might argue that freedom of association entails the right of people to refuse to associate with others on any grounds. Yet a society embodying such an unconditional right hardly needs physical coercion to force others to obey the wishes of those with the power to exclude others from participation in social life. The same point applies to a society in which property is so unequally distributed that some adults live in abject dependence on others, and so live at the mercy of others. Societies that permit the creation of outcasts and subordinate classes can be as repressive as any despotic regime.

EQUALITY IN THE SPACE OF FREEDOM: A CAPABILITIES APPROACH

Amartya Sen has proposed a better way to understand freedom. Consider the states of being and doing that constitute a person's well-being: a person can be healthy, well nourished, physically fit, literate, an active participant in community life, mobile, happy, respected, confident, and so forth. A person may also care about other states of being and doing that reflect her autonomous ends: she may want to be outgoing, raise children, practice medicine, play soccer, make love, and so forth. Call such states functionings. A person's capabilities consist of the sets of functionings she can achieve, given the personal, material, and social resources available to her. Capabilities measure not actually achieved functionings, but a person's freedom to achieve valued functionings. A person enjoys more freedom the greater the range of effectively accessible, significantly different opportunities she has for functioning or leading her life in ways she values most.[12] We can understand the egalitarian aim to secure for everyone the social conditions of their freedom in terms of capabilities. Following Sen, I say that egalitarians should seek equality for all in the space of capabilities.

Sen's capability egalitarianism leaves open a large question, however: Which capabilities does society have an obligation to equalize? Some people care about playing cards well, others about enjoying luxury vacations in Tahiti. Must egalitarians, in the name of equal freedom, offer free card-playing lessons and state-subsidized vacations in exotic lands? Surely there are limits to which capabilities citizens are obligated to provide one another. We should heed our first desideratum: to identify particular goods within the space of equality that are of special egalitarian concern.

Reflection on the negative and positive aims of egalitarianism helps us meet this requirement. Negatively, people are entitled to whatever capabilities are necessary to enable them to avoid or escape entanglement in oppressive social relationships.

Positively, they are entitled to the capabilities necessary for functioning as an equal citizen in a democratic state. While the negative and positive aims of egalitarianism overlap to a large extent, they are not identical. If functioning as an equal citizen were all that egalitarians cared about, they could not object to forced clitoridectomy, by which men control women's sexuality in private relations. But egalitarians also aim at abolishing private relations of domination, and therefore support the functionings needed for individual sexual autonomy. If having the capabilities needed to avoid oppression were all that mattered, then egalitarians would not oppose discrimination among the relatively privileged—for example, the glass ceiling for female executives. But egalitarians also aim at enabling all citizens to stand as equals to one another in civil society, and this requires that careers be open to talents.

Democratic equality thus aims for equality across a wide range of capabilities. But it does not support comprehensive equality in the space of capabilities. Being a poor card player does not make one oppressed. More precisely, the social order can and should be arranged so that one's skill at cards does not determine one's status in civil society. Nor is being a good card player necessary for functioning as a citizen. Society therefore has no obligation to provide free card lessons to citizens. Democratic equality satisfies the first desideratum of egalitarian theory.

Consider further the capabilities that democratic equality does guarantee to citizens. Let us focus on the capabilities necessary for functioning as an equal citizen. Citizenship involves functioning not only as a political agent—voting, engaging in political speech, petitioning government, and so forth—but participating as an equal in civil society. Civil society is the sphere of social life that is open to the general public and is not part of the state bureaucracy in charge of the administration of laws. Its institutions include public streets and parks; public accommodations such as restaurants, shops, theaters, buses and airlines; communications systems such as broadcasting, telephones, and the Internet; public libraries; hospitals; schools; and so forth. Enterprises engaged in production for the market are also part of civil society, because they sell their products to any customer and draw their employees from the general public. One of the important achievements of the civil rights movement was to vindicate an understanding of citizenship that includes the right to participate as an equal in civil society as well as in government affairs. A group that is excluded from or segregated within the institutions of civil society, or subject to discrimination on the basis of ascribed social identities by institutions in civil society, has been relegated to second-class citizenship, even if its members enjoy all of their political rights.

So, to be capable of functioning as an equal citizen involves the ability not just to effectively exercise specifically political rights, but also to participate in the various activities of civil society more broadly, including participation in the economy. And functioning in these ways presupposes functioning as a human being. Consider, then, three aspects of individual functioning: as a human being, as a participant in a system of cooperative production, and as a citizen of a democratic state. To be capable of functioning as a human being requires effective access to the means of sustaining one's biological existence—food, shelter, clothing, medical care—and access to the basic conditions of human agency—knowledge of one's circumstances and options; the ability to deliberate about means and ends; the psychological conditions of autonomy, including the self-confidence to think and judge for oneself; freedom of thought and movement. To be capable of functioning as an equal participant in a system of cooperative production requires effective access to the means of production, access to the education needed to develop one's talents, freedom of occupational choice, the right to make contracts and enter into cooperative agreements with others, the right to receive fair value for one's labor, and recognition by others of one's productive contributions. To be capable of functioning as a citizen requires rights to political participation, such as freedom of speech and the franchise, and also effective access to the goods and relationships of civil society. This entails freedom of association, access to public spaces such as roads, parks, and public accommodations including public transportation, the postal service, and telecommunications. This also entails the social conditions of being accepted by others, such as the ability to appear in public without shame, and not being ascribed outcast status. The freedom to form relationships in civil society also requires effective access to private spaces, since many such relationships can only function when protected from the scrutiny and intrusions of others. Homelessness—that is, having only public dwelling—is a condition of profound unfreedom.

Three points should be made about the structure of egalitarian guarantees in the space of freedom or capabilities. First, democratic equality guarantees not actual levels of functioning, but effective access to those levels. Individuals are free to choose to function at a lower level than they are guaranteed. For example, they might choose to join a religious group that discourages political participation. Moreover, democratic equality can make access to certain functionings—those requiring an income—conditional upon working for them, provided that citizens have effective access to those conditions—they are physically capable of performing the work, doing so is consistent with their other duties, they can find a job, and so forth. Effective access to a level of functioning means that people can achieve that functioning by deploying means already at their disposal, not that the functioning is unconditionally guaranteed without any effort on their own part. Thus, democratic equality is consistent with constructing the incentive systems needed for a modern economy to support the production needed to support egalitarian guarantees in the first place.

Second, democratic equality guarantees not effective access to equal levels of functioning but effective access to levels of functioning sufficient to stand as an equal in society. For some functionings, equal citizenship requires equal levels. For example, each citizen is entitled to the same number of votes in an election as everyone else. But for other functionings, standing as an equal does not require equal levels of functioning. To be capable of standing as an equal in civil society requires literacy. But in the U.S. context, it does not require literacy in any language other than English, or the ability to interpret obscure works of literary theory. Democratic equality does not object if not everyone knows a foreign language, and only a few have a Ph.D.-level training in literature. In other countries, multilingual literacy might be required for equal standing.

Third, democratic equality guarantees effective access to a package of capabilities sufficient for standing as an equal over the course of an entire life. It is not a starting-gate theory in which people could lose their access to equal standing through bad option luck. Access to the egalitarian capabilities is also market-inalienable: contracts whereby individuals irrevocably transfer their fundamental freedoms to others are null and void.[13] The rationale for establishing such inalienable rights might seem difficult to grasp from the point of view of the rights holder. Why shouldn't she be free to trade some of her egalitarian-guaranteed freedoms for other goods that she prefers? Isn't it paternalistic to deny her the freedom to trade?

We can avoid this thought by considering the point of view of the obligation holder. The counterpart to an individual's inalienable right to the social conditions of her freedom is the unconditional obligation of others to respect her dignity or moral equality. Kant would put the point as follows: every individual has a worth or dignity that is not conditional upon anyone's desires or preferences, not even the individual's own desires. This implies that there are some things one may never do to other people, such as to enslave them, even if one has their permission or consent. Contracts into slavery or servitude are therefore invalid. In basing inalienable rights on what others are obligated to do rather than on the rights bearer's own subjective interests, democratic equality satisfies the second desideratum of egalitarian theory: to justify lifetime guarantees without resorting to paternalism.

One advantage of the capabilities approach to equality is that it allows us to analyze injustices in regard to other matters besides the distribution of resources and other divisible goods. One's capabilities are a function not just of one's fixed personal traits and divisible resources, but also of one's mutable traits, social relations and norms, and the structure of opportunities, public goods, and public spaces. Egalitarian political movements have never lost sight of the whole range of targets of egalitarian assessment. For example, feminists work to overcome the internal obstacles to choice—self-abnegation, lack of confidence, and low self-esteem—that women often face from internalizing norms of femininity. Gays and lesbians seek the ability to publicly reveal their identities without shame or fear, which requires significant changes in social relations of contempt and hostility, and changes in norms of gender and sexuality. The disabled aim to reconfigure public spaces to make them accessible and adapt work situations to their needs, so that they can participate in productive activity. No mere redistribution of divisible resources can secure the freedoms these groups seek.

Of course, democratic equality is also concerned with the distribution of divisible resources. It requires that everyone have effective access to enough resources to avoid being oppressed by others and to function as an equal in civil society. What counts as "enough" varies with cultural norms, the natural environment, and individual circumstance. For example, cultural norms and climate influence what kind of clothing one needs to be able to appear in public without shame and with adequate protection from the elements. Individual circumstances, such as disabilities, influence how much resources one needs to function as an equal. People without use of their legs may need more resources—wheelchairs, specially adapted vans—to achieve mobility comparable to that of ambulatory persons. Equality in the space of capabilities may therefore demand an unequal division of resources to accommodate the disabled.[14] What citizens ultimately owe one another are the social conditions of the freedoms people need to function as equal citizens. Because of differences in their internal capacities and social situations, people are not equally able to convert resources into capabilities for functioning. They are therefore entitled to different amounts of resources so that they can enjoy freedom as equals.

Suppose we abstract from the fact that people have different internal physical and mental capabilities. Would democratic equality demand that external resources be divided equally from the start, as equality of fortune holds? There is no reason to think so. The capabilities relevant to functioning as a human being, as a participant in the system of social cooperation, and as an equal citizen do not include all functionings or all levels of functioning. To function as a human being, one needs adequate nutrition. To eat without being relegated to a subhuman status, one needs access to sources of nutrition besides pet food or the dumpster. But to be able to function as a dignified human being, one does not need the quantity or quality of food intake of a gourmet. Democratic equality therefore requires that everyone have effective access to adequate nutrition, as well as sources of nutrition that one's society considers dignified—fit for consumption in social gatherings. It does not require that everyone have the resources needed for an equal opportunity to function as a gourmet. It therefore does not require criteria for equality of resources that depend on the morally dubious idea that the distribution of resources should be sensitive to considerations of envy.

PARTICIPATION AS AN EQUAL IN A SYSTEM OF COOPERATIVE PRODUCTION

So far we have considered what citizens are obligated to provide one another. But how are such things to be produced, and by what means and principles shall they be distributed? In stressing the concept of obligation, democratic equality heads off the thought that in an egalitarian society everyone somehow could have a right to receive goods without anyone having an obligation to produce them. Democratic equality seeks equality in the capability or effective freedom to achieve functionings that are part of citizenship, broadly construed. For

those capable of working and with access to jobs, the actual achievement of these functionings is, in the normal case, conditional on participating in the productive system. Contrary to Van Parijs's view, citizens do not owe one another the real freedom to function as beach bums. Most able-bodied citizens, then, will get access to the divisible resources they need to function by earning a wage or some equivalent compensation due to them on account of their filling some role in the division of labor.

In deciding principles for a just division of labor and a just division of the fruits of that labor, workers are to regard the economy as a system of cooperative, joint production.[15] I want to contrast this image of joint production with the more familiar image that invites us to regard the economy as if it were a system of self-sufficient Robinson Crusoes, producing everything all by themselves until the point of trade. By "joint production," I mean that people regard every product of the economy as jointly produced by everyone working together. From the point of view of justice, the attempt, independent of moral principles, to credit specific bits of output to specific bits of input by specific individuals represents an arbitrary cut in the causal web that in fact makes everyone's productive contribution dependent on what everyone else is doing. Each worker's capacity to labor depends on a vast array of inputs produced by other people—food, schooling, parenting, and the like. It even depends on workers in the recreation and entertainment industries, since enjoyment of leisure activities helps restore energy and enthusiasm for work. In addition, the productivity of a worker in a specific role depends not only on her own efforts, but also on other people performing their roles in the division of labor. Michael Jordan could not make so many baskets if no one kept the basketball court swept clean. Millions of people could not even get to work if public transportation workers went on strike. The comprehensiveness of the division of labor in a modern economy implies that no one produces everything, or indeed anything, they consume by their own efforts alone. In regarding the division of labor as a comprehensive system of joint production, workers and consumers regard themselves as collectively commissioning everyone else to perform their chosen role in the economy. In performing their role in an efficient division of labor, each worker is regarded as an agent for the people who consume their products and for the other workers who, in being thereby relieved from performing that role, become free to devote their talents to more productive activities.

In regarding the economy as a cooperative venture, workers accept the demand of what G. A. Cohen has defined as the principle of interpersonal justification:[16] any consideration offered as a reason for a policy must serve to justify that policy when uttered by anyone to anyone else who participates in the economy as a worker or a consumer. The principles that govern the division of labor and the assignment of particular benefits to the performance of roles in the division of labor must be acceptable to everyone in this sense. To see how interpersonal justification works within the context of the economy considered as a system of cooperative, joint production, consider three of the cases equality of fortune gets wrong: disability compensation for workers in dangerous occupations, federal disaster relief, and dependent caretakers with their children.

Eric Rakowski argues that workers who choose particularly dangerous occupations, such as farming, fishing, mining, forestry, firefighting, and policing, have no claims to medical care, rehabilitation, or compensation if they are injured on the job.[17] Since they engage in these occupations by choice, any bad fortune they suffer on the job is a form of option luck, the consequences of which must be born by the worker alone. Cohen's test invites us to consider how persuasive this argument is when uttered to the disabled workers by the consumers who eat the food, use the metal and wood, and enjoy the protection from fire and crime that these workers provide. These consumers are not free to disclaim all responsibility for the bad luck that befalls workers in dangerous occupations. For they commissioned these workers to perform those dangerous tasks on their own behalf. The workers were acting as agents

for the consumers of their labor. It cannot be just to designate a work role in the division of labor that entails such risks and then assign a package of benefits to performance in the role that fails, given the risks, to secure the social conditions of freedom to those who occupy the role. The principle "let us be served by occupations so inadequately compensated that those in them shall lack the means necessary to secure their freedom, given the risks and conditions of their work" cannot survive the test of interpersonal justification.

Similar reflections apply to those who choose to live and work in areas prone to particularly severe natural disasters, such as residents near the San Andreas Fault. Rakowski argues that such residents should be excluded from federal disaster relief because they live there by choice.[18] But they live there because other citizens have, through their demand for California products, commissioned them to exploit the natural resources in California. To deny them federal disaster relief is to invoke the rejected principle above. Economists may object that, on balance, it may not be efficient to continue production in a particular region, and that disaster relief, in subsidizing the costs of living in disaster-prone regions, perpetuates a costly error. However, if, on balance, citizens decide that a region should be designated uninhabitable, because the costs of relief are too high, the proper response is not to leave its residents in the lurch but to designate their relief toward helping them relocate. Citizens are not to be deprived of basic capabilities on account of where they live.[19]

The case of non-wage-earning dependent caretakers and children might seem to fall outside the purview of society as system of cooperation. But this is to confuse the economy with the market sector.[20] Non-wage-earning dependent caretakers contribute to production in at least three ways. First, most engage in household production—cleaning, cooking, and so forth—which services, if not performed, would have to be hired out. Second, they raise the future workers of the economy and help rehabilitate the sick and injured ones so that they can return to work. Third, in discharging the obligations everyone has to dependents, considered as human beings, and the obligations all family members have toward their dependent kin, they relieve others of such responsibility and thereby free them to participate in the market economy. Fathers would not be so productive in the market if the non-wage-earning or part-time working mothers of their children did not relieve them of so much of their responsibility to engage in direct caretaking.[21] The principle "let us assign others to discharge our caretaking obligations to dependents, and attach such meager benefits to performance in this role that these caretakers live at our mercy" cannot survive interpersonal justification either. Dependent caretakers are entitled to enough of a share of their partner's income that they are not vulnerable to domination and exploitation within the relationship. This principle supports Susan Moller Okin's proposal that paychecks be split between husband and wife.[22] If this is not sufficient to eliminate caretakers' vulnerability in domestic partnership, a case can be made for socializing some of the costs of dependent care through a child-care (or elder-care) subsidy, as is common in western Europe. Ultimately, full equality may not be achievable simply through the redistribution of material resources. Equality may require a change in social norms by which men as well as women would be expected to share in caretaking responsibilities.[23]

Against the proposal to socialize the costs of dependent care, Rakowski insists that children are entitled only to resources from their parents, not from others. Even if they will provide benefits to others when they grow up and participate in the economy, it is unjust to make people pay for benefits they never asked for, and in any event most of those benefits will accrue to other family members.[24] If the economy consisted of isolated, economically self-sufficient family groups, as in a primitive hunter-gatherer society, one could see Rakowski's point. But in a society with an extensive division of labor, his assumptions make no sense. As long as one doesn't plan to commit suicide once the next generation enters the workforce, one can't help but demand the labor services of future generations. Moreover,

most of what people produce in a market economy is consumed by non-family members. In regarding the whole society as a system of cooperation that jointly produces the economy's entire output, democratic equality acknowledges everyone's profound mutual dependency in modern society. It rejects the atomistic norm of individual self-sufficiency as based on a failure to recognize the dependency of wage earners on the work of those whose labor is not for sale. In adjusting entitlements to account for the fact that adults have moral responsibilities to take care of dependents, democratic equality also rejects equality of fortune's reduction of moral obligations to expensive tastes and its consequent guarantee of equality only to egoists. Democratic equality says that no one should be reduced to an inferior status because they fulfill obligations to care for others.

The conception of society as a system of cooperation provides a safety net through which even the imprudent are never forced to fall. It provides that no role in the productive system shall be assigned such inadequate benefits that, given the risks and requirements of the job, people could be deprived of the social conditions of their freedom because they have fulfilled its requirements. Society may not define work roles that amount to peonage or servitude, nor, if it can avoid it, pay them so little that an able-bodied person working full-time would still lack basic capabilities.[25] One mechanism for achieving a decent minimum would be a minimum wage. A minimum wage need not raise unemployment if low-wage workers are given sufficient training to make them more productive or if the higher wage induces employers to supply their workers with productivity-enhancing tools. Benefits could also be attached to work by other means, such as socially provided disability and old-age pension schemes, and tax credits for earned income. Democratic equality also favors a qualified entitlement to work on the part of willing, able-bodied adults. Unemployment insurance is a poor substitute for work, given the central importance of participation in productive activity to living life as an equal in civil society. So is "workfare" if, as is typically the case in the United States, it means forcing people to engage in make-work for aid while depriving them of the dignity of a real job with a real wage.

It is instructive to consider what democratic equality says to those with low talents. Equality of fortune would offer compensation to those with low talents, precisely because their innate inferiority makes their labor so relatively worthless to others, as judged by the market. Democratic equality calls into question the very idea that inferior native endowments have much to do with observed income inequalities in capitalist economies. The biggest fortunes are made not by those who work but by those who own the means of production. Even among wage workers, most of the differences are due to the fact that society has invested far more in developing some people's talents than others and that it puts very unequal amounts of capital at the disposal of each worker. Productivity attaches mainly to work roles, not to individuals. Democratic equality deals with these facts by stressing the importance of educating the less advantaged and by offering firms incentives to increase the productivity of low-wage jobs through capital investment.

Moreover, in regarding society as a system of cooperation, democratic equality has a less demeaning rationale than equality of fortune for state interventions designed to raise the wages of low-wage workers. Society need not try to make the impossible and insulting judgment of whether low-wage workers are there by choice or by the fact that their meager native endowments prevent them from getting better work. Instead, it focuses on appreciation for the roles that low-wage workers fill. In performing routine, low-skill tasks, these workers free other people to make more productive uses of their talents. Those occupying more productive roles owe much of their productivity to the fact that those occupying less productive roles have freed them from the need to spend their time on low-skill tasks. Fancy corporate executives could not cut so many lucrative deals if they had to answer their own telephone calls. Such reflections express appreciation for the ways that everyone benefits from the diversity of talents and roles in society. They also undermine the thought that workers at the top make a lopsided contribution to the social product and thereby help motivate a conception of reciprocity that would squeeze the gap between the highest- and lowest-paid workers.

Would democratic equality support a wage-squeezing policy as demanding as John Rawls's difference principle? This would forbid all income inequalities that do not improve the incomes of the worst off.[26] In giving absolute priority to the worst off, the difference principle might require considerable sacrifices in the lower middle ranks for trifling gains at the lowest levels. Democratic equality would urge a less demanding form of reciprocity. Once all citizens enjoy a decent set of freedoms, sufficient for functioning as an equal in society, income inequalities beyond that point do not seem so troubling in themselves. The degree of acceptable income inequality would depend in part on how easy it was to convert income into status inequality—differences in the social bases of self-respect, influence over elections, and the like. The stronger the barriers against commodifying social status, political influence, and the like, the more acceptable are significant income inequalities.[27] The moral status of free-market allocations is strengthened the more carefully defined is the domain in which these allocations have free rein.

DEMOCRATIC EQUALITY, PERSONAL RESPONSIBILITY, AND PATERNALISM

Democratic equality guarantees effective access to the social conditions of freedom to all citizens, regardless of how imprudently they conduct their lives. It does not deprive negligent or self-destructive citizens of necessary medical care. It does not discriminate among the disabled depending on how much they can be held responsible for their disability. Under democratic equality, citizens refrain from making intrusive, moralizing judgments about how people ought to have used the opportunities open to them or about how capable they were of exercising personal responsibility. It need not make such judgments, because it does not condition citizens' enjoyment of their capabilities on whether they use them responsibly. The sole exception to this principle concerns criminal conduct. Only the commission of a crime can justify taking away a person's basic liberties and status as an equal in civil society. Even convicted criminals, however, retain their status as equal human beings, and so are still entitled to basic human functionings such as adequate nutrition, shelter, and medical care.

One might object to democratic equality on the grounds that all these guarantees invite personal irresponsibility, just as critics of equality have long suspected. If people are going to be bailed out of the situations they get into because of their own imprudence, then why act prudently? Egalitarians must face up to the need to uphold personal responsibility, if only to avoid bankrupting the state. There are two general strategies for doing so. One is to insure only against certain causes of loss: to distinguish between the losses for which people are responsible and those for which they are not, and to indemnify individuals only against the latter. This is the approach of luck egalitarianism, which leads to Poor Law thinking, and intrusive and disrespectful judgments of individuals. The second strategy is to insure only against the losses of certain types of goods: to distinguish between guaranteed and unguaranteed types of goods within the space of egalitarian concern, and to insure individuals only against the loss of the former. This is the approach of democratic equality.

Democratic equality does not indemnify individuals against all losses due to their imprudent conduct. It only guarantees a set of capabilities necessary to functioning as a free and equal citizen and avoiding oppression. Individuals must bear many other losses on their own. For example, a person who smokes would be entitled to treatment for resulting lung cancer, regardless of their degree of responsibility for smoking. But she would not be entitled to compensation for the loss of enjoyment of life brought about by her confinement

in the hospital and reduced lung capacity, for the dread she feels upon contemplating her mortality, or for the reproach of her relatives who disapprove of her lifestyle. Individuals thus have plenty to lose from their irresponsible conduct, and therefore have an incentive to behave prudently. Luck egalitarianism can't take advantage of this incentive structure, because it indemnifies individuals against the loss of all kinds of goods (kinds of resources or sources of welfare) within its space of egalitarian concern. It therefore must resort to moral judgments about the cause of loss in order to promote individual responsibility.

Democratic equality has two further strategies for promoting individual responsibility. First, it offers equality in the space of capabilities, which is to say opportunities or freedoms. Individuals still have to exercise responsible agency to achieve most of the functionings effective access to which society guarantees. In the typical case of an able-bodied adult, for instance, access to a decent income would be conditioned on responsible performance of one's duties in one's job, assuming a job was available.

Second, most of the freedoms that democratic equality guarantees are prerequisites to exercising responsible agency. Responsible agency requires real options, awareness of these options, deliberative skills, and the self-respect needed to trust one's own judgment. Democratic equality guarantees the education needed to know and deliberate about one's options, and the social bases of self-respect. Moreover, people will do almost anything to secure what they need to survive. In ensuring effective access to the means of subsistence through legitimate routes, democratic equality prevents the criminal behavior that would be spurred by a society that let people fall below subsistence or that deprived people of dignified legitimate means of subsistence. It also avoids the powerful incentives to deny personal responsibility that are built into equality of fortune, because it ensures that people will always have legitimate means at their disposal to get access to their basic capabilities without having to resort to deception about their role in getting into their predicament.

It might be objected that democratic equality, in guaranteeing such goods as medical care to all, still requires an objectionable subsidy of irresponsible behavior. Why should prudent nonsmokers have to pay more for universal health insurance, because so many fools choose to smoke? If the costs of some particularly dangerous activity are high, and if the activity is not performed in one's capacity as a participant in the productive system, then justice permits a tax on that activity to cover the extra costs of medical care for those injured by engaging in it. A tax on each pack of cigarettes, adjusted to cover the medical costs of treating smokers, would force smokers to absorb the extra costs of their behavior.

If it is just to force smokers to absorb these costs ex ante, why isn't it equally just to force them to absorb these costs ex post, as some luck egalitarians hold? John Roemer's plan does this by discounting the medical subsidy people are entitled to according to their degree of personal responsibility.[28] Besides entangling the state in intrusive moralizing judgments of personal responsibility, Roemer's plan leaves people vulnerable to such a deprivation of their capabilities that they cannot function as an equal. This is unjust. By making smokers pay for the costs of their behavior ex ante, democratic equality preserves their freedom and equality over the course of their whole lives.

It might be objected that democratic equality, in guaranteeing a specific set of capabilities to citizens, paternalistically violates the freedom of citizens and violates the requirement of liberal neutrality among conceptions of the good. Suppose a smoker would prefer to have cheaper cigarettes than to be provided medical care? Shouldn't citizens be free to choose what goods they prefer to have? Thus, citizens should be entitled to the welfare equivalent of medical care and not be forced to consume medical care at the cost of other things they might prefer. This line of thought supports equality in the space of opportunities for welfare, rather than in capabilities for equal citizenship.

These objections fail to appreciate the distinction between what people want and what other people are obligated to give them. The basic duty of citizens, acting through the state, is not to make everyone happy but to secure the conditions of everyone's freedom. In securing for citizens only the capabilities they need to function as equal citizens, the state is not declaring that these capabilities are more important for individual happiness than some others that they might prefer. It leaves individuals free to decide for themselves how useful or important are the goods that the state guarantees to them. It guarantees certain capabilities to citizens not because these are the most important ones as judged from the standpoint of the best conception of the good, but because these are the ones citizens are obligated to provide one another in common.

But why can't any given citizen waive his right to guaranteed health care in return for its welfare equivalent? Citizens can, with justice, refuse to provide what any individual regards as the welfare equivalent of health care. As Thomas Scanlon has stressed, the fact that someone would rather have help in building a temple to his god than to be decently fed does not generate a greater claim on others to subsidize his temple than to ensure his access to adequate nutrition.[29] Furthermore, the obligation to provide health care is unconditional and can't be rescinded, even with the permission of the person to whom the obligation is owed. We are not permitted to abandon people dying by the side of the road just because they gave us permission to deny them emergency medical care.[30]

One might object that democratic equality fails to respect neutrality among competing conceptions of the good. Some citizens will find the capability sets guaranteed them far more useful than others. For example, those whose conception of the good involves widespread participation in civil society will find their good more fully secured by democratic equality than those who prefer to lead their lives in insular religious cults. Democratic equality is therefore biased in favor of certain conceptions of the good.

This objection misunderstands the point of neutrality. As Rawls has stressed, given the fact the people hold conflicting conceptions of the good, liberal states need some basis for judging claims of justice that does not rest on partisan views of the good. The point of view of citizens acting collectively—the political point of view—does not claim authority in virtue of promoting the objectively best or most important goods but in virtue of being a possible object of collective willing. Neutral goods are the goods we can reasonably agree to collectively provide, given the fact of pluralism.[31] Thus, the capabilities citizens need to function as equals in civil society count as neutral goods for purposes of justice not because everyone finds these capabilities equally valuable, but because reasonable people can recognize that these form a legitimate basis for making moral claims on one another.[32] By contrast, reasonable persons need not recognize the desire to build a temple to their god as a legitimate basis for a claim to public subsidy. A person who does not worship that god could reasonably object to the state taxing her to subsidize someone else's involuntarily expensive religious desires.

Consider now what equality of fortune and democratic equality have to say to the person who decides, prudently or imprudently, not to purchase health insurance for himself. According to equality of fortune, there are two options. One is to allow the person to decline health insurance and abandon him if he needs emergency care. The other is to tell him, "You are too stupid to run your own life. Therefore, we will force you to purchase health insurance, because we know better than you what is for your own good." Democratic equality passes no judgment on whether it would be prudent or imprudent for any given individual to purchase health insurance. It tells the person who would not purchase insurance for himself, "You have a moral worth that no one can disregard. We recognize this worth in your inalienable right to our aid in an emergency. You are free to refuse this aid once we offer it. But this freedom does not absolve you of the obligation to come

to the aid of others when their health needs are urgent. Since this is an obligation we all owe to our fellow citizens, everyone shall be taxed for this good, which we shall provide to everyone. This is part of your rightful claim as an equal citizen." Which rationale for providing health insurance better expresses respect for its recipients?

THE DISABLED, THE UGLY, AND OTHER VICTIMS OF BAD LUCK

According to democratic equality, the distribution of nature's good or bad fortune is neither just nor unjust. Considered in itself, nothing in this distribution calls for any correction by society. No claims to compensation can be generated by nature's effects alone. This may seem an unduly harsh doctrine. Does it not leave the congenitally disabled, ugly, and stupid out in the cold, even though they do not deserve their sorry fates?

Democratic equality says no. Although the distribution of natural assets is not a matter of justice, what people do in response to this distribution is.[33] People may not make the possession of a disability, repugnant appearance, or low intelligence the occasion for excluding people from civil society, dominating them, beating them up, or otherwise oppressing them. In a liberal democratic state, all citizens are entitled to the social conditions of their freedom and standing as equals in civil society, regardless of handicap, physical appearance, or intelligence.[34] Moreover, these conditions are sensitive to variations in people's circumstances, including their disabilities. People who can't walk are entitled to accommodation in civil society: to wheelchairs, ramps on public buildings, and so forth. However, these conditions are not sensitive to variations in people's tastes. Everyone has an entitlement to the same package of capabilities, whatever else they may have, and regardless of what they would prefer to have. Thus, if a person who needs a wheelchair to get around has an involuntarily expensive taste for engaging in particular religious rituals, and would prefer having this taste satisfied to having a wheelchair, democratic equality does not substitute a subsidy for her rituals for the wheelchair. For individuals need to be able to move around civil society to have equal standing as citizens, but they do not need to be able to worship in particularly expensive ways in order to function as equals.

Richard Arneson objects to this distinction between disabled people and people with involuntarily expensive tastes. For disabilities are just another kind of involuntarily expensive taste. It's not the disabled individual's fault that it costs more for her to get around in a wheelchair than it takes ambulatory people to make the same journey. Once we see that it is the involuntariness of the costs of her tastes that entitles her to special subsidy, one must allow people with other involuntarily expensive tastes to make equal claims on behalf of their preferences. Arneson claims that only an illegitimate perfectionist doctrine—the claim that mobility is intrinsically more important than worship—can support discrimination between the disabled and those with other involuntarily expensive tastes.[35]

Democratic equality takes no stand on what goods individuals should value more when they are thinking only of their own interests. It provides the social conditions for equal citizenship, and not the conditions for equal ability to fulfill the demands of one's gods, because citizens are obligated to provide the first and are not obligated to provide the second. Arneson argues that capabilities are diverse, and the resources available to provide them scarce. Some trade-offs among capabilities must therefore be accepted. Some index is therefore needed to rank the importance of different capabilities. If one rejects perfectionist doctrines , the only basis for constructing an index of capabilities is subjective, based on the importance to the individual of having that capability.[36]

Against Arneson, democratic equality follows Scanlon in insisting that the weight that a citizen's claim has on others depends solely on the content of her interest and not on the importance she places on it in her own conception of the good.[37] In some cases, the weight of an interest can be determined by considering its impact on a person's standing as an equal in society. Some deprivations of capabilities express greater disrespect than others in ways any reasonable person can recognize. From a public point of view, it is more disrespectful to deny a person in a wheelchair access to the public schools than it is to deny her access to an amusement park ride that only accommodates the walking. This is true even if she'd rather go through the Fun House than learn how to read. In other cases, where the concepts of equal standing and respect don't yield a determinate answer to how capabilities should be ranked, the ranking may legitimately be left up to democratic legislation. Even here, voters are not to ask themselves what priorities they give to different capabilities for citizenship in their private choices, but what priorities they want the state to assign to these different capabilities, given that these goods shall be provided in common. The answers to the questions are likely to diverge, if only because many capabilities are more valuable to others than to their possessors. Most people gain much more from other people's freedom of speech than from their own.[38]

It might be argued that democratic equality is still too harsh to those who are disabled through bad brute luck. It would not compensate them for all of the miseries they face. For example, democratic equality would ensure that the deaf have equal access to civil society, but not that they be compensated for the loss of the pleasures of hearing itself. Yet the lives of the deaf are less happy for lacking these pleasures, and should be compensated on that account.

It is useful to ask what the deaf demand on their own account, in the name of justice. Do they bemoan the misery of not being able to hear, and demand compensation for this lack? On the contrary, like the disabled more generally, they resent being cast as poster children for the abled to pity, because they do not want to have to cast their claims as appeals to the condescending benevolence of kindly patrons. Many deaf people identify as part of a separate Deaf community that repudiates the intrinsic choice-worthiness of hearing itself. They insist that sign language is just as valuable a form of communication as is speech and that the other goods obtainable through hearing, such as appreciation of music, are dispensable parts of any conception of good. One needn't pass judgment on the intrinsic choiceworthiness of hearing to appreciate the rhetorical uses of denying it: the Deaf want to cut the hearing down to size, to purge the arrogant assumption of the hearing that the lives of the Deaf are somehow less worth living. They want to make claims on the hearing in a manner that expresses the dignity they see in their lives and community, rather than in a manner that appeals to pity for their condition.[39] They do this by denying that their condition, considered in itself, is anything to be pitied.

Equality of fortune, despite the fact that it considers the treatment of the disabled as a core case, has difficulty with such ideas. This is due to the fact that it relies on subjective measures of welfare or of the worth of personal assets. Subjective measures invite all the wrong thoughts on the part of the abled. Van Parijs's criterion of undominated diversity allows the disabled to make claims of justice regarding their disability only if everyone regards their condition as so wretched that everyone would prefer being someone else. This test asks the abled to take the horror they feel upon imagining that they had a disability as their reason for compensating the disabled. To regard the condition of the disabled as intrinsically horrible is insulting to the disabled people who lead their lives with dignity. Arneson's criterion of equal opportunity for welfare implies that as long as the disabled have equal chances for happiness, they have no claims to special accommodation. Survey research shows that the disabled experience the same range of happiness as the abled.[40] Thus, by Arneson's criterion, it is all right to exclude the disabled from public life because they are happy enough without being included.

Subjective measures of people's condition generate either pity for the disabled or reluctance to consider their claims of justice. The way to escape this dilemma is to take seriously what the disabled are actually complaining about. They do not ask that they be compensated for the disability itself. Rather, they ask that the social disadvantages others impose on them for having the disability be removed. "The inequality of people mobilizing in wheelchairs . . . manifests itself not in the inability to walk but in exclusion from bathrooms, theaters, transportation, places of work, [and] life-saving medical treatment."[41] Democratic equality can handle this distinction. It demands, for instance, that the disabled have good enough access to public accommodations that they can function as equals in civil society. To be capable of functioning as an equal does not require that one's access be equally fast, comfortable, or convenient, or that one get equal subjective utility from using public accommodations. There may be no way to achieve this. But the fact that, with current technology, it takes an extra minute to get into city hall does not compromise one's standing as an equal citizen.

Democratic equality thus supports the use of objective tests of unjust disadvantage. Such tests fit the claims of justice that the disabled make on their own behalf. For example, what the Deaf find objectionable is not that they can't hear, but that everyone else has rigged the means of communication in ways that leave them out of the conversation. One can detect this injustice without investigating anyone's preferences or subjective states. The test for a satisfactory remedy is equally objective. The Americans with Disabilities Act, for example, embodies an objective standard of accommodation. "Rather than speculating on how the *subjective personal response* of unimpaired agents would be transfigured by the onset of physical or mental impairment, this standard calls for projecting how *objective social practice* would be transformed were unimpaired functioning so *atypical* as to be of merely marginal importance for social policy."[42] The act asks us to imagine how communications in civil society would be arranged if nearly everyone were deaf, and then try to offer to the deaf arrangements approximating this.

The objective standards of injustice and remedy proposed by democratic equality have several advantages over those proposed by equality of fortune. They match the remedy to the injustice: if the injustice is exclusion, the remedy is inclusion. Democratic equality does not attempt to use private satisfactions to justify public oppression. Objective standards do not insultingly represent the disabled as deserving aid because of their pitiful internal condition. They locate the unjust disadvantage of disability in the way others treat the disabled. Democratic equality also does not assimilate the disabled to the situation of those suffering from involuntarily expensive tastes. Having a disability is not like being so spoiled that one can't help wanting expensive toys.

Should other victims of bad brute luck be treated like the handicapped? Equality of fortune thinks so—it extends its concern to the ugly, the stupid, and the untalented as well. Democratic equality does not pass judgment on the worth of people's native endowments, and so has nothing special to say to the stupid and the untalented. Instead, it focuses on the productive roles that people occupy in recognition of the fact that society attaches economic benefits to performance in a role rather than to the possession of talent in itself. Democratic equality requires that sufficient benefits be attached to performance in every role so that all workers can function as equals in society. Talent brings noneconomic advantages as well, such as the admiration of others. Democratic equality finds no injustice in this advantage, because one doesn't need to be admired to be able to function as an equal citizen. As justice requires, most residents of modern democracies live in a state of civilization where the attainment of honor is not a condition of enjoying basic freedoms. In places where this is not so, such as certain tough inner-city neighborhoods, it is clear that the injustice lies not in the fact that some individuals are unfortunately born with lower native endowments of courage, but that the social order is arranged so that only those willing to display uncommonly high degrees of ruthlessness can enjoy personal security.

What about the ugly? Are they not entitled to compensation for their repugnant appearance, which makes them so unwelcome in social settings? Some luck egalitarians would view this bad luck as calling for a remedy, perhaps in the form of publicly subsidized plastic surgery. Democratic equality refuses to publicly endorse the demeaning private judgments of appearance that are the basis of such claims to compensation. Instead, it asks whether the norms based on such judgments are oppressive. Consider a birth defect, affecting only a person's appearance, that is considered so abhorrent by current social norms that people tend to shun those who have it. Since the capability to participate in civil society as an equal citizen is a fundamental freedom, egalitarians demand that some remedy be provided for this. But the remedy need not consist in plastic surgery that corrects the defect. An alternative would be to persuade everyone to adopt new norms of acceptable physical appearance, so that people with the birth "defect" were no longer treated as pariahs. This is not to call for the abolition of norms of beauty altogether. The norms need only be flexible enough to deem the person an acceptable presence in civil society. They need not entitle such a person to claim equal beauty to others, since successful functioning as a contestant in a beauty pageant, or as a hot prospect for a Saturday night date, is not among the capabilities one needs to function as an equal citizen.

By directing attention to oppressive social norms of beauty, democratic equality avoids the disparaging scrutiny of the ugly through the lens of the oppressive norms themselves. This lets us see that the injustice lies not in the natural misfortune of the ugly but in the social fact that people shun others on account of their appearance. To change the person rather than the norm insultingly suggests that the defect lies in the person rather than in society. Other things equal, then, democratic equality prefers altering social norms to redistributing material resources in response to the disadvantages faced by the unsightly. Of course, other things are often not equal. It may be very difficult and costly to change prevailing norms of beauty that cruelly dictate who cannot appear in public without provoking shock and rejection. The liberal state can't do too much in this regard without overstepping its proper bounds; thus, this task must be delegated mainly to egalitarian social movements, which vary in their abilities to transform social norms. Under these conditions the better option may well be to supply the plastic surgery. Democratic equality, in focusing on equality as a social relationship rather than simply as a pattern of distribution, at least enables us to see that we have a choice between redistributing material resources and changing other aspects of society to meet the demands of equality.

DEMOCRATIC EQUALITY AND THE OBLIGATIONS OF CITIZENS

Democratic equality refocuses egalitarian theorizing in several ways. It conceives of justice as a matter of obligations that are not defined by the satisfaction of subjective preferences. This ensures that people's rights do not depend on arbitrary variations in individual tastes and that people may not claim rights without accepting corresponding obligations to others. Democratic equality applies judgments of justice to human arrangements, not to the natural order. This helps us see that people, not nature, are responsible for turning the natural diversity of human beings into oppressive hierarchies. It locates unjust deficiencies in the social order rather than in people's innate endowments. Instead of lamenting the human diversity of talents and trying to make up for what is represented as innate deficiencies in talent, democratic equality offers a way of conceiving and harnessing human diversity so that it benefits everyone and is recognized as doing so. Democratic equality conceives of equality as a relationship among people

rather than merely as a pattern in the distribution of divisible goods. This helps us see how egalitarians can take other features of society besides the distribution of goods, such as social norms, as subject to critical scrutiny. It lets us see how injustices may be better remedied by changing social norms and the structure of public goods than by redistributing resources. And it allows us to integrate the demands of equal distribution and equal respect, ensuring that the principles by which we distribute goods, however equal resulting patterns may be, do not in fact express contemptuous pity for the beneficiaries of egalitarian concern. Democratic equality thus offers a superior way to understand the expressive demands of justice—the demand to act only on principles that express respect for everyone. Finally, in refocusing academic egalitarian theorizing, democratic equality holds out the promise of reestablishing connections with actually existing egalitarian movements. It is not a moral accident that beach bums and people who find themselves slaves to their expensive hobbies are not organizing to make claims of justice on behalf of their lifestyles. Nor is it irrelevant that the disabled are repudiating forms of charity that appeal to pity for their condition and are straggling for respect from others, not just handouts. Democratic equality helps articulate the demands of genuine egalitarian movements in a framework that offers some hope of broader appeal.

Notes

1. Ronald Dworkin, "What Is Equality? II. Equality of Resources," *Philosophy and Public Affairs* 10 (1981): 283–345, at 285.

2. Philippe Van Parijs, "Why Surfers Should Be Fed: The Liberal Case for an Unconditional Basic Income," *Philosophy and Public Affairs* 20 (1991): 101–31.

3. Richard Arneson, "Equality and Equal Opportunity for Welfare," in *Equality: Selected Readings*, edited by Louis Pojman and Robert Westmoreland (New York: Oxford University Press, 1997), 231.

4. G. A. Cohen, "On the Currency of Egalitarian Justice," *Ethics* 99 (1989): 906–44, at 922–23, 930–31.

5. Philippe Van Parijs, *Real Freedom for All* (Oxford: Clarendon Press, 1995), 127.

6. Thomas Nagel, "The Policy of Preference," in his *Mortal Questions* (Cambridge: Cambridge University Press, 1979), 91–105.

7. Iris Marion Young, *Justice and the Politics of Difference* (Princeton, NJ: Princeton University Press, 1990).

8. John Rawls, "Kantian Constructivism in Moral Theory," *Journal of Philosophy* 77 (1980): 515–72, at 525. The use of "equally" to modify "moral agents" might seem otiose. Why not just say that all competent adults are moral agents? Egalitarians deny a hierarchy of types of moral agency—e.g., any theory that says there is a lower type of human only able to follow moral commands issued by others and a higher type able to issue or discover moral commands for themselves.

9. Elizabeth Anderson, 'The Democratic University: The Role of Justice in the Production of Knowledge," *Social Philosophy and Policy* 12 (1995): 186–219. Does this requirement mean that we must always listen patiently to those who have proven themselves to be stupid, cranky, or dishonest? No. It means that (1) everyone must be granted the initial benefit of the doubt, (2) a person can be ignored or excluded from discussion only on demonstrated grounds of communicative incompetence or unwillingness to engage in fair discussion, and (3) reasonable opportunities must be available to the excluded to demonstrate their communicative competence and thereby win back a place in the conversation.

10. Nancy Fraser, "From Redistribution to Recognition? Dilemmas of Justice in a 'Post-socialist' Age," in her *Justice Interruptus* (New York: Routledge, 1997), 11–39; Axel Honneth, *The Struggle for Recognition*, translated by Joel Anderson (Cambridge: Polity Press, 1995).

11. Christine Korsgaard, "Commentary on G. A. Cohen and Amartya Sen," in *The Quality of Life*, edited by Martha Nussbaum and Amartya Sen (Oxford: Clarendon Press, 1993).

12. Amartya Sen, *Inequality Reexamined* (Cambridge, MA: Harvard University Press, 1992), 39–42, 49.

13. Margaret Radin, "Market Inalienability," *Harvard Law Review* 100 (1987): 1849–1937. A person might have to forfeit some of her market-inalienable freedoms, however, if she is convicted of a serious crime.

14. Sen, *Inequality Reexamined*, 79–84.

15. I shift from talk of "citizens" to talk of "workers" in part because the moral implications of regarding the economy as a system of cooperative production cross international boundaries. As the economy becomes global, we are all implicated in an international division of labor subject to assessment from an egalitarian point of view. We have obligations not only to the citizens of our country but to our fellow workers, who are now found in virtually every part of the globe. We also have global humanitarian obligations to everyone, considered simply as human beings—to relieve famine and disease, avoid fomenting or facilitating aggressive warfare, and the like. Alas, I do not have the space to consider the international implications of democratic equality.

16. G. A. Cohen, "Incentives, Inequality, and Community," in *Equal Freedom*, edited by Stephen Darwall (Ann Arbor: University of Michigan Press, 1995), 348.

17. Eric Rakowski, *Equal Justice* (New York: Oxford University Press, 1991), 79.

18. Ibid.

19. What about rich people who build their vacation homes in disaster-prone areas? They haven't been commissioned by others to live there, nor does it seem fair to force taxpayers to insure their luxurious estates. Democratic equality cannot allow even unproductive citizens to lose everything, but it does not indemnify them against all their losses either. It only guarantees sufficient relief to get them back on their feet, not to shod them in luxurious footwear. If even this relief seems too expensive, an egalitarian state can forbid people from inhabiting disaster-prone areas, or tax people who do to cover the excess costs of disaster relief. What it may not do is let them live there at their own risk and then abandon them in their hour of need. Such action treats even the imprudent with impermissible contempt.

20. Marilyn Waring, *If Women Counted* (San Francisco: HarperCollins, 1990).

21. Joan Williams, "Is Coverture Dead?" *Georgetown Law Journal* 82 (1994): 2227–90, at 2227.

22. Susan Moller Okin, *Justice, Gender, and the Family* (New York: Basic Books, 1989), 180–82,

23. Nancy Fraser, "After the Family Wage: A Postindustrial Thought Experiment," in *Justice Interruptus*, 41–66.

24. Rakowski, *Equal Justice*, 153.

25. It might be thought that poor societies cannot afford even basic capabilities for all workers. However,

Sen's studies of the standard of living in India and China show that even extremely poor societies can supply an impressive set of basic capabilities—decent nutrition, health, literacy, and the like—to all of their members if they apply themselves to the task. See, e.g., Amartya Sen, *Commodities and Capabilities* (Amsterdam, the Netherlands: North-Holland, 1985).

26. John Rawls, *A Theory of Justice*, rev. ed. (Cambridge, MA: Harvard University Press, 1999), 75–78.

27. Michael Walzer, *Spheres of Justice* (New York: Basic Books, 1983); Mickey Kaus, *The End of Equality* (New York: Basic Books, 1992).

28. John Roemer, "A Pragmatic Theory of Responsibility for the Egalitarian Planner," in his *Egalitarian Perspectives* (Cambridge: Cambridge University Press, 1994), 179–96.

29. Thomas Scanlon, "Preference and Urgency," *Journal of Philosophy* 72 (1975): 655–69, at 659–60.

30. This point is entirely distinct from the right to refuse medical care. It is one thing for an individual to exercise the right to refuse medical care when offered, quite another for others to refuse to offer medical care when needed.

31. John Rawls, *Political Liberalism* (New York: Columbia University Press, 1993).

32. Peter De Marneffe, "Liberalism, Liberty, and Neutrality," *Philosophy and Public Affairs* 19 (1990): 253–74, at 255–58.

33. Rawls, *A Theory of Justice*, 102.

34. Some exceptions would have to be made for those so severely mentally disabled or insane that they cannot function as agents. In addition, children are entitled not immediately to all of the freedoms of adults, but to the social conditions for the development of their capacities to function as free and equal citizens.

35. Richard Arneson, "'Liberalism, Distributive Subjectivism, and Equal Opportunity for Welfare," *Philosophy and Public Affairs* 19 (1990): 158, 187, 190–94.

36. Arneson, "Equality and Equality of Opportunity for Welfare," 236–37.

37. Scanlon, "Preference and Urgency," 659.

38. Joseph Raz, "Rights and Individual Well-Being," in his *Ethics in the Public Domain* (Oxford: Clarendon Press, 1994), 52–55.

39. Owen Wrigley, *The Politics of Deafness* (Washington, DC: Gallaudet University Press, 1996), discusses the potentials and problems of reconceiving disability (being deaf) as community (being Deaf) after the manner of identity politics.

40. Anita Silvers, "Reconciling Equality to Difference: Caring (f)or Justice for People with Disabilities," *Hypatia* 10 (1995): 30–55, at 54n9.

41. Ibid., 48.

42. Ibid., 49.

MARTHA C. NUSSBAUM

∼

INTRODUCTION

EVA FEDER KITTAY

Martha Craven Nussbaum was born in Bryn Mawr, Pennsylvania in 1949. She attended Wellesley College, and then New York University, from which she graduated with a degree in classics. She received her advanced degrees in classical philology from Harvard University, becoming the first woman to be accepted into Harvard's Society of Fellows. She subsequently taught at Harvard and at Brown University and is currently Ernst Freund Professor of Law and Ethics at the University of Chicago, where she holds appointments in the Law School, the School of Divinity, and the departments of philosophy and classics. She served as president of the Central Division of the American Philosophical Association, received in 2016 the Kyoto Prize, Japan's highest prize for achievement in the arts and sciences, and in 2018 the Berggruen Prize for Philosophy and Culture. She is not only a prolific author but has also had a significant presence as a public intellectual, serving as a research advisor at the U.N.-sponsored World Institute for Development Economics Research and a consultant to the United Nations Development Program.

Nussbaum's political philosophy relies on the work of Aristotle, the Stoics, Kant, Mill, and Rawls. From the Stoics and Kant she draws accounts of human dignity and liberty; from Mill the ideals of equality and individualism that support women's aspirations; from Rawls the ideal of political liberalism; and from Aristotle the universal human capabilities implicit in a flourishing life, applicable to all regardless of cultural differences, gender and sexual distinction, race, age, or ability.

She also acknowledges her admiration for feminist philosophy. She credits it with putting new questions on the moral and political agenda and infusing them with passion and urgency.

The essay reprinted here is a succinct version of capability theory that she has developed from Amartya Sen's theoretical approach to economic and political theory. She has applied this view to normative concerns such as disability, animal welfare, and development ethics, as well as questions of sexual orientation, pornography, and religious freedom.

Sen presented capability theory as a theory of equality. He argued that important inequalities in well-being would persist if we did not attend to the way in which resources are converted into functioning. He argued that the reason equality is important is that people want an equal chance to do and be what is valuable to them.

Sen proposed capability theory as a corrective to liberal theories of distributive justice, such as that of Rawls, that regarded justice as a fair distribution of resources within a system of social cooperation. On such theories, equality is meant to enable as equal a distribution of resources as was compatible with other societal important goals.

Sen's theory was also a corrective to utilitarian theories of justice which regarded the welfare of persons as the satisfaction of preferences. In these theories the aim of equality is to allow people an equal ability to satisfy their preferences. Sen argued that what mattered was less how many resources a person had and more what the person could do with them. A wheelchair user, for example, may have the money to purchase a meal in a restaurant of her choice, but if the restaurant had no ramp access then the financial means do not translate to enjoying a meal with a friend at the restaurant. Similarly, two people may have an equal amount of food available, but if one is small and inactive and needs little while the other is a large active person, they do not have the same capability to be well-nourished. The equality of resources (food in this instance) does not imply that they have an equal capability to get their nutritional needs met.

Furthermore, Sen argued that what mattered to a person's well-being was not mere preference satisfaction, since the preferences one had may have been shaped in conditions of unfreedom. Consider a woman living in poverty who declares herself satisfied with five hundred calories a day, while her husband and children receive most of the available food. Even if she claims satisfaction with her near starvation diet, she is still malnourished. When people feel incapable of altering an unjust or oppressive situation, they sometimes adapt their preferences to make their condition livable. Their unjust circumstances curtail not only their capabilities but the desire to acquire capabilities that humans generally regard as valuable beings and doings. Even as people form "adaptive preferences," they lose important freedoms to function that are due to them as people with an equal right to live flourishing lives.

In the essay reprinted here, Nussbaum motivates adopting the conception of capabilities through the contrast not only with resource and preference-based distributive theories but also with the closely allied notion of rights. Rights within liberal theory are often conceived of as negative rights, rights not to be interfered with, or political rights, rights to have a say in the government under which one lives. Capabilities are more closely aligned to positive rights (rights to food, shelter, and so forth) insofar as capabilities are meant to secure access to the things one needs and values. To state that one has a right to food or shelter, for instance, does not necessarily make the demand on the state to enable or empower its members to acquire the food to which they have a right. Capabilities, unlike rights, demand that states empower its members to have the important freedoms to function that are pronounced in declarations of rights. Nussbaum understands these demands as so fundamental that they ought to be included in a nation's constitution.

The capability approach was also introduced by Sen as an alternative to the gross national product (GNP) in measuring how successful developing countries are in lifting themselves out of poverty. For while the gross domestic product (GDP) can tell us how wealthy the country is as a whole, it will not tell us if members of that state have equal access to a good education, adequate housing, quality nutrition, and healthcare. Even in wealthy societies with an impressive GDP, unjust arrangements can nonetheless result in inequalities in the capabilities of its members. Sen prefers to leave the choice of capabilities that are to be the index of interpersonal well-being to the members of the societies themselves.

For two reasons, however, Nussbaum is critical of such an approach. First, she is sensitive to ways in which many, if not most, societies are male-dominated, and the freedoms sought by the dominant group may be predicated on women's lack of freedom. For example, if women are expected to stay home and do domestic work, men (and women) may claim that a basic education would be a waste of resources, so women not having the capability to have an adequate education is the price paid for men having more resources to turn into capabilities. Therefore Nussbaum believes it important not to leave the content of the capabilities up to societies whose unjust governing structures may be used to perpetuate injustice.

Second, Nussbaum is influenced by the Aristotlean conception of human flourishing, *eudemonia*, and by the Marxian notion of "the rich human being with rich human needs"—as Marx wrote in his *Economic and Philosophic Manuscript of 1844*. Over many years, Nussbaum has advanced a list of capabilities that, on the one hand, is derived from the Aristotlean and Marxian conceptions, and, on the other hand, is refined by speaking to women from different parts of the globe who face limitations imposed by their poverty and male-domination. The components of a flourishing life may look somewhat different in different cultures but are based on what is it to live, as Nussbaum puts it, a "truly human" life—a life that cultivates the good for human beings.

Capabilities as designating the flourishing life has become the hallmark of Nussbaum's political philosophy. The list of central human capabilities includes (1) life; (2) bodily health; (3) bodily integrity; (4) senses, imagination, thought; (5) emotions; (6) practical reason; (7) affiliation: (a) being able to live with and toward one another, and (b) having the social bases of self-respect; (8) other species; (9) play; and (10) control over one's environment: (a) political, and (b) material. The capabilities listed are proposed in a form that allows them to be differently realized by people in different cultures and with different religious convictions.

Although she does not make the argument in the essay in this volume, the capabilities approach allows Nussbaum to offer a critique of liberal contemporary "contract theory"—the view that society is an association of mutually self-interested persons who "contract" as equals to share the benefits and burdens of social cooperation. In *Frontiers of Justice*, Nussbaum argues that contract theory cannot adequately account for why people with disabilities, especially people with cognitive disabilities, should be granted justice. Similarly, she argues that contract theory cannot explain why human beings owe anything to or should be concerned with the welfare of animals—an increasingly urgent concern for moral and political theory. Finally, contract theory reigns only within state borders—contractors are those who form a government together to rule over themselves. That theory, however, has little to say about whether we, either as individuals or as states, owe anything to those who do not live within our borders.

Nussbaum argues that the strength of capabilities theory is demonstrated by how well it can provide answers to these important political questions, which remain unresolved in contract theory, yet which dominate discussions in political philosophy. She believes capabilities theory demonstrates that we owe people with disabilities the freedom to function simply because they, too, require these freedoms to live flourishing lives. Furthermore, her theory recognizes from the outset that we must provide for people in ways that fit the different needs presented by different abilities, bodies and minds, all the while recognizing the commonality of capabilities needed to flourish. She also interprets the capabilities in a way that are applicable to nonhuman animals who have their own species way of flourishing. To the extent we can prevent interfering with their flourishing, or we have the power to enable their functioning, we ought to do so. Thus capability theory shows how to treat nonhuman animals justly, and shows that treating animals justly requires recognizes the capabilities they need to flourish, capabilities that are largely similar to what humans require. Finally, capabilities are not confined to national boundaries—they are universal. As such, a just response to those outside our borders is to promote their capabilities, especially by seeing to it that our own states assist other states to ensure that people within their borders have the where-withal to realize their capabilities.

One worry about capabilities is that it seems to be a Procrustean bed that all must fit, if we are to take this list as prescriptive for how we live our lives. Doing so seems illiberal. In response, Nussbaum stresses in *Capabilities and Social Justice* that the list of capabilities is not a list of functionings, but instead it is a list of *freedoms* to function. A just state will ensure that people have the capability to play, for example, not that people *must* play. One may have good reasons not to play, for instance if one is engaged in life-saving work, and play would distract one from accomplishing something of urgent importance. Nonetheless, the ability to play is important to secure for all, even for those who may choose not to do so.

The distinction between what a society is obligated to provide for persons and what persons choose to avail themselves of can be tricky. When a woman is not well nourished, is it because she is sacrificing food so that her children will have more to eat? Is it because she is following a religious command to fast? Or is it because she fasts to protest the maltreatment of others?

In the first case, one can say that a society that does not make food sufficiently available to nourish all its members is failing to provide the capability for all to maintain life and bodily health. In the second case, we can say that the woman is living in a society that provides these capabilities, but her conception of her own good dictates that she fast as part of her religious commitment. In the third case, she may be living in a society in which the capability to maintain her bodily needs for food exists, but the society has traded off that capability for the capability of others to live free from bodily harm.

The last case illustrates an important aspect of Nussbaum's vision: no trade-offs among capabilities are permitted. Just societies must make *all* the capabilities available. They cannot, for example, trade off the capability of political engagement for capability for affinitive relations that would allow someone to choose a same-sex partner. It is useful to recognize that the emphasis on freedom for people to choose how to live life that they regard as flourishing is an indication that Nussbaum is very much a liberal, even with an Aristotelian strain of perfectionism, the position that the goal of life is pursuit of a perfect ideal of character and action.

Like rights, the capabilities on the list are to be understood as universal, and are equally applicable regardless of cultural differences, gender and sexual distinctions, race, age or ability. And even though they are schematic, they are to apply to societies in diverse historical periods, religions, and cultures. Although Nussbaum wishes to re-spect such differences, she insists upon the universalism of capabilities. A diminution in any of the capabilities is morally unacceptable whether it occurs in India or in Indiana; whether the person involved is male or female, homosexual or heterosexual, white or Black. Like Nussbaum's contention that a list of capabilities is necessary, her insistence on the universalism of the capabilities is inspired both by the social constraints imposed on women globally and by concerns for the internalized perverse preferences that leave women unable to flourish fully.

Yet despite her efforts to accommodate cultural and religious difference, her universalism and her unwillingness to capitulate to any form of relativism has left Nussbaum at odds with a number of postcolonial and transnational feminists, many of whom have grown suspicious of any form of universalism. In addition, some critics have questioned the ability of a commanding Western woman with authority to be able to elicit the genuine concerns of the poor women with whom she spoke. Others worry that even a list of general capabilities cannot reflect values held dear by women in different cultural, economic, and social conditions.

Still another concern is that the capabilities capture what is a "truly human life." Some lives simply cannot take advantage of each of these capabilities. For example, a person with significant cognitive disability will lack the ability to enjoy the capability for practical reason. Unlike the person who chooses not to eat but to fast for religious or political reasons, the cognitively disabled person is not choosing not to deliberate or engage in practical reason. Is it then the case that such a person cannot live a "truly human life"? That is, does the list present a normative view of a person such that some human beings are excluded from being "truly human?" If the list of capabilities serves as a heuristic instead of a norm, this matter would not be a concern, but it would weaken the theory considerably. Nussbaum has since asserted that being born of two human parents was sufficient to be fully human. It remains somewhat unclear how this squares with the normative picture of the human being as it is presented in the list of capabilities.

Nussbaum's unwavering liberalism has also drawn fire. At a time when many leftist intellectuals have virtually abandoned liberalism, Nussbaum has remained its ardent defender, producing some powerful tracts that attempt to reconcile feminists and liberalism, or more precisely, with the core or deepest commitments of liberalism. In combining a feminist liberalism with capabilities approach, Nussbaum at once highlights features of liberalism that are consistent with an international feminism and reinterprets liberalism so that it accommodates the insights of feminist advocates.

Feminist philosophers have questioned whether liberal theories, such as Rawls's theory of justice, were adequate to answering a set of concerns raised by the traditional gendered division of labor. Liberal theories strongly support women's right to enter the world of waged labor. But when women enter the labor force, they leave behind those who they have traditionally cared for and assisted and who will continue to need care: the young, the frail elderly and those who need assistance because of illness or disability. Who is to do this labor? Too often these responsibilities overburden and disadvantage women both because men have not been accustomed to take over such tasks, and because the workplace does not accommodate the flexibility needed for parents to both be employed and do carework. The social expectations that women do carework means that women are disadvantaged in the workplace as they attempt to take their place alongside men in the public sphere. Thus feminists have argued that for theories that do not take seriously the needs of dependents and those who care for them, gender equality will continue to be elusive, even in the absence of formal barriers to women's equality.

Furthermore, some feminist theorists have argued that there are virtues and moral emotions that are cultivated in carework. These, too, have been ignored by political theorists of all stripes. In short, the importance of the work and the values of care have not adequately been integrated into political theory. Nussbaum sees the capabilities approach as a way of including the urgent concerns of this central domain of human life—the values, needs, and virtues of care—into political theory. By showing how care infuses all the capabilities, as Nussbaum does toward the end of the essay, she hopes to demonstrate why the capabilities approach can answer a vexing problem that women have raised about extant political theory.

An encyclopedia entry that offers an excellent overview of the capabilities approach as developed by Sen and Nussbaum as well as subsequent debates is Ingrid Robeyns, "The Capability Approach," in the *Stanford Encyclopedia of Philosophy* (Winter 2016 Edition), edited by Edward N. Zalta, available at https://plato.stanford.edu/archives/ win2016/entries/capability-approach.

An early article by Nussbaum that presents Aristotle as a major influence on her formulation of the capabilities approach is "Nature, Functioning and Capability: Aristotle on Political Distribution," *Oxford Studies in Ancient Philosophy* 6 (Supplementary Volume, 1988): 145–84. For a fuller exposition of the views presented in this selection, an essential volume that applies the capabilities approach to the blight of women in developing countries is Martha C. Nussbaum, *Women and Human Development: The Capabilities Approach*, The John Robert Seeley Lectures (Cambridge: Cambridge University Press, 2000). In *Frontiers of Justice: Disability, Nationality, Species Membership*, the Tanner Lectures on Human Values (Cambridge, Mass.: Harvard University Press, 2006), Nussbaum expands her capabilities approach to questions of justice toward the disabled, to nonhuman animals, and to a global population. It is the most expansive and boundary-breaking use of the capabilities approach.

Nussbaum's debt to the work of Sen and her partnership with him in developing the capabilities approach is best understood by studying his work. He develops the capabilities approach as a way of addressing inequality in "Equality of What?" in *Tanner Lectures on Human Values*, edited by S. McMurrin (Cambridge: Cambridge University Press, 1980) and in *Inequality Re-examined* (Oxford: Clarendon Press, 1992). The capabilities approach as a way of promoting the freedom to be and to do what was of value to the individual has always been central to the capabilities approach. The subject is explored both on the individual and societal level as the key aim for developing nations in Amartya Sen, *Development as Freedom* (New York: Knopf, 1999). For Sen's most recent statement and defense of the capabilities approach, see "Capability: Reach and Limit," in *Debating Global Society: Reach and Limit of the Capability Approach*, edited by E. Chipper-Martinetti (Milan: Feltrinelli, 2009), 15–28.

Thomas Pogge provides a critique of the capabilities approach from a Rawlsian resource perspective of equality and justice in "Can the Capability Approach be Justified?," *Philosophical Topics* 30, no. 2 (2002): 167–228. A defense and critiques of the capabilities approach to justice, as well as important applications to new concerns, is found in Harry Brighouse and Ingrid Robeyns (eds.), *Measuring Justice: Primary Goods and Capabilities* (Cambridge: Cambridge University Press, 2010).

Eva Kittay argues for the central importance of care in theories of justice and equality in her *Love's Labor: Essays on Women, Equality and Dependency*, 2nd ed. (New York: Routledge, 2019). Joan Tronto was a pioneer in introducing care into the discourse of political philosophy and raises important questions that are implicit in Nussbaum's discussion of care as implicated in all the capabilities. See her *Moral Boundaries: A Political Argument for an Ethic of Care* (New York: Routledge, 1994).

Nussbaum has received criticism of her liberal feminism from other feminists, primarily those who reject much of the humanist tradition from which Nussbaum works. See Carol Quillen, "Feminist Theory, Justice, and the Lure of the Human,'" *Signs* 27, no. 1 (2001): 87–122. Nussbaum responds in the same issue of the journal: "Comment on Quillen's 'Feminist Theory, Justice, and the Lure of the Human,'" *Signs* 27, no. 1 (2001): 123–35. An article that offers a critique of Nussbaum's universalism from the perspective of postcolonial feminism is S. Charusheela, "Social Analysis and the Capabilities Approach: A Limit to Martha Nussbaum's Universalist Ethics," *Cambridge Journal of Economics* 33, no. 6 (November 2009): 1135–1152.

Capabilities and Social Justice

Women in much of the world lack support for fundamental functions of a human life. Unequal social and political circumstances give women unequal human capabilities. This essay critiques other approaches to these inequalities and offers a version of the capabilities approach. The central question asked by the capabilities approach is not "How satisfied is this woman?" or "How much in the way of resources is she able to command?" It is, instead, "What is she actually able to do and to be?" The core idea seems to be that of the human being as a dignified free being who shapes his or her own life, rather than being passively shaped or pushed around by the world in the manner of a flock or herd animal. The basic intuition from which the capabilities approach

begins, in the political arena, is that human abilities exert a moral claim that they should be developed. Capability, not functioning, is the appropriate political goal.

> It will be seen how in place of the wealth and poverty of political economy come the rich human being and rich human need. The rich human being is . . . the human being in need of a totality of human life-activities.
> —Marx, *Economic and Philosophical Manuscripts of 1844*

> *I found myself beautiful as a free human mind.*
> —Mrinal, heroine of Rabindranath Tagore's "Letter from a Wife" (1914)

From Martha Nussbaum, "Capabilities and Social Justice," *International Studies Review* 4, no. 2 (2002). Reprinted by permission of the journal.

I. DEVELOPMENT AND SEX EQUALITY

Women in much of the world lack support for fundamental functions of a human life. They are less well nourished than men, less healthy, more vulnerable to physical violence and sexual abuse. They are much less likely than men to be literate, and still less likely to have preprofessional or technical education. Should they attempt to enter the workplace, they face greater obstacles, including intimidation from family or spouse, sex discrimination in hiring, and sexual harassment in the workplace—all, frequently, without effective legal recourse. Similar obstacles often impede their effective participation in political life. In many nations women are not full equals under the law: they do not have the same property rights as men, the same rights to make a contract, the same rights of association, mobility, and religious liberty.[1] Burdened, often, with the "double day" of taxing employment and full responsibility for housework and child care, they lack opportunities for play and the cultivation of their imaginative and cognitive faculties. All these factors take their toll on emotional well-being: women have fewer opportunities than men to live free from fear and to enjoy rewarding types of love—especially when, as often, they are married without choice in childhood and have no recourse from a bad marriage. In all these ways, unequal social and political circumstances give women unequal human capabilities.

According to the *Human Development Report 1999* of the United Nations Development Programme (UNDP), there is no country that treats its women as well as its men, in areas ranging from basic health and nutrition to political participation and economic activity.

One area of life that contributes especially greatly to women's inequality is the area of care. Women are the world's primary, and usually only, caregivers for people in a condition of extreme dependency: young children, the elderly, those whose physical or mental handicaps make them incapable of the relative (and often temporary) independence that characterizes so-called normal human lives. Women perform this crucial work, often, without pay and without recognition that it is work. At the same time, the fact that they need to spend long hours caring for the physical needs of others makes it more difficult for them to do what they want to do in other areas of life, including employment, citizenship, play, and self-expression.[2]

My aim in this brief presentation will be first to indicate why I believe other approaches to these inequalities are not fully adequate and the capabilities approach is needed. Then I shall mention some very general features of the capabilities approach to show how it can handle the problems other approaches fail to handle.

II. DEFICIENCIES OF OTHER APPROACHES

Prior to the shift in thinking that is associated with the work of Amartya Sen,[3] and with the *Human Development Reports* of the UNDP,[4] the most prevalent approach to measuring quality of life in a nation used to be simply to ask about GNP per capita. This approach tries to weasel out of making any cross-cultural claims about what has value—although, notice, it does assume the universal value of opulence. What it omits, however, is much more significant. We are not even told about the distribution of wealth and income, and countries with similar aggregate figures can exhibit great distributional variations. (Thus South Africa always did very well among developing nations, despite its enormous inequalities and violations of basic justice.) Circus girl Sissy Jupe, in Dickens's novel *Hard Times*, already saw the problem with this absence of normative concern for distribution. She says that her economics lesson didn't tell her "who has got the money and whether any of it is mine."[5] So too with women around the world: the fact that one nation or region is in general more prosperous than another is only a part of the story; it doesn't tell us what government has done for women in various social classes, or how they are doing. To know that, we'd need to look at their lives. But then we need to specify, beyond distribution of wealth and income itself, what parts of lives we ought to look at—such as life expectancy, infant mortality, educational opportunities, health care, employment opportunities, land rights, political liberties. Seeing what is absent from the GNP account nudges us sharply in the direction of mapping out these and other basic goods in a universal way, so that we can use the list of basic goods to compare quality of life across societies.

A further problem with all resource-based approaches, even those that are sensitive to distribution, is that individuals vary in their ability to convert resources into functionings. (This is the problem that has been stressed for some time by Amartya Sen in his writings about the capabilities approach.) Some of these differences are straightforwardly physical. Nutritional needs vary with age, occupation, and sex. A pregnant or lactating woman needs more nutrients than a nonpregnant woman. A child needs more protein than an adult. A person whose limbs work well needs few resources to be mobile, whereas a person with paralyzed limbs needs many more resources to achieve the same level of mobility. Many such variations can escape our notice if we live in a prosperous nation that can afford to bring all individuals to a high level of physical attainment; in the developing world we must be highly alert to these variations in need. Again, some of the pertinent variations are social, connected with traditional hierarchies. If we wish to bring all citizens of a nation to the same level of educational attainment, we will need to devote more resources to those who encounter obstacles from traditional hierarchy or prejudice: thus women's literacy will prove more expensive than men's literacy in many parts of the world. If we operate only with an index of resources, we will frequently reinforce inequalities that are highly relevant to well-being. As my examples

suggest, women's lives are especially likely to raise these problems; therefore, any approach that is to deal adequately with women's issues must be able to deal well with these variations.

If we turn from resource-based approaches to preference-based approaches, we encounter another set of difficulties.[6] Such approaches have one salient advantage over the GNP approach: they look at people, and assess the role of resources as they figure in improving actual people's lives. But users of such approaches typically assume without argument that the way to assess the role of resources in people's lives is simply to ask them about their satisfaction with their current preferences. The problem with this idea is that preferences are not exogenous, given independently of economic and social conditions. They are at least in part constructed by those conditions. Women often have no preference for economic independence before they learn about avenues through which women like them might pursue this goal; nor do they think of themselves as citizens with rights that were being ignored before they learn of their rights and are encouraged to believe in their equal worth. All of these ideas, and the preferences based on them, frequently take shape for women in programs of education sponsored by women's organizations of various types. Men's preferences, too, are socially shaped and often misshaped. Men frequently have a strong preference that their wives should do all the child care and all the housework—often in addition to working an eight-hour day. Such preferences, too, are not fixed in the nature of things: they are constructed by social traditions of privilege and subordination. Thus a preference-based approach typically will reinforce inequalities: especially those inequalities that are entrenched enough to have crept into people's very desires.

Once again, although this is a fully general problem, it has special pertinence to women's lives. Women have especially often been deprived of education and information, which are necessary, if by no means sufficient, to make preferences a reliable indicator of what public policy

should pursue. They have also often been socialized to believe that a lower living standard is what
is right and fitting for them, and that some great
human goods (for example, education, political
participation) are not for them at all. They may be
under considerable social pressure to say they are
satisfied without such things, and yet we should
not hastily conclude that public policy should
not work to extend these functions to women. In
short, looking at women's fives helps us see the
inadequacy of traditional approaches; and the urgency of women's problems gives us a very strong
motivation to prefer a nontraditional approach.

Finally, let us consider the influential human
rights approach. This approach has a great deal
to say about these inequalities, and the language
of rights has proven enormously valuable for
women, both in articulating their demands for
justice and in finking those demands to the earlier
demands of other subordinated groups. And yet
the rights framework is shaky in several respects.
First, it is intellectually contested: there are many
different conceptions of what rights are, and what
it means to secure a right to someone. (Are rights
prepolitical, or artifacts of laws and institutions?
Do they belong to individual persons only, or
also to groups? Are they always correlated with
duties, and who has the duties correlated with
human rights? And what are human rights rights
to? Freedom from state interference primarily, or
also a certain positive level of well-being and opportunity?) Thus to use the language of rights all
by itself is not very helpful: it just invites a host
of further questions about what is being recommended. Second, the language of rights has been
associated historically with political and civil
liberties, and only more recently with economic
and social entitlements. But the two are not only
of comparable importance in human lives, they
are also thoroughly intertwined: the liberties of
speech and association, for example, have material prerequisites. A woman who has no opportunities to work outside the home does not have
the same freedom of association as one who does.
Women deprived of education are also deprived

of much meaningful participation in politics and
speech. Third, the human rights approach has
typically ignored urgent claims of women to protection from domestic violence and other abuses
of their bodily integrity. It has also typically ignored urgent issues of justice within the family:
its distribution of resources and opportunities
among its members, the recognition of women's
work as work. This neglect is not accidental, because the rights approach is linked with the tradition of liberal political philosophy that typically
recognizes a distinction between the public and
the private realms, and puts the family off-limits
for purposes of state action. Fourth and finally,
the rights approach is often linked with the idea
of negative liberty, and with the idea of protecting the individual from state action. Although
rights of course need not be understood in this
way, their history, at least in the Lockean tradition, does lend itself to that sort of interpretation, and the focus on such areas of negative
liberty has been a persistent obstacle to making
progress for women in areas ranging from compulsory education to the reform of marriage.

III. HUMAN DIGNITY AND HUMAN CAPABILITIES

I shall now argue that a reasonable answer to all
these concerns—capable of giving good guidance
to governments establishing basic constitutional
principles and to international agencies assessing
the quality of life—is given by a version of the
capabilities approach.

The central question asked by the capabilities
approach is not "How satisfied is this woman?"
or even "How much in the way of resources is
she able to command?" It is, instead, "What
is she actually able to do and to be?" Taking a
stand for political purposes on a working list of
functions that would appear to be of central importance in human life, users of this approach
ask, "Is the person capable of this, or not?" They
ask not only about the person's satisfaction with
what she does, but also about what she does, and

what she is in a position to do (what her opportunities and liberties are). They ask not just about the resources that are present, but also about how those do or do not go to work, enabling the woman to function.

To introduce the intuitive idea behind the approach, it is useful to start from this passage of Marx's 1844 *Economic and Philosophical Manuscripts*, written at a time when he was reading Aristotle and was profoundly influenced by Aristotelian ideas of human capability and functioning: "It is obvious that the *human* eye gratifies itself in a way different from the crude, non-human eye; the human *ear* different from the crude ear, etc. . . . The *sense* caught up in crude practical need has only a *restricted* sense. For the starving man, it is not the human form of food that exists, but only its abstract being as food; it could just as well be there in its crudest form, and it would be impossible to say wherein this feeding activity differs from that of *animals*."

Marx here singles out certain human functions—eating and the use of the senses, which seem to have a particular centrality in any life one might live. He then claims that there is something that it is to be able to perform these activities in a fully human way—by which he means a way infused by reasoning and sociability. But human beings don't automatically have the opportunity to perform their human functions in a fully human way. Some conditions in which people live—conditions of starvation, or of educational deprivation—bring it about that a being who is human has to live in an animal way. Of course what he is saying is that these conditions are unacceptable, and should be changed.

Similarly, the intuitive idea behind my version of the capabilities approach is twofold. First, that there are certain functions that are particularly central in human life, in the sense that their presence or absence is typically understood to be a mark of the presence or absence of human life. Second, and this is what Marx found in Aristotle, that there is something that it is to do these

functions in a truly human way, not a merely animal way. We judge, frequently enough, that a life has been so impoverished that it is not worthy of the dignity of the human being, that it is a life in which one goes on living, but more or less like an animal, not being able to develop and exercise one's human powers. In Marx's example, a starving person just grabs at the food in order to survive, and the many social and rational ingredients of human feeding can't make their appearance. Similarly, the senses of a human being can operate at a merely animal level—if they are not cultivated by appropriate education, by leisure for play and self-expression, by valuable associations with others; and we should add to the list some items that Marx probably would not endorse, such as expressive and associational liberty, and the freedom of worship. The core idea seems to be that of the human being as a dignified free being who shapes his or her own life, rather than being passively shaped or pushed around by the world in the manner of a flock or herd animal. . . .

Notice that the approach makes each person a bearer of value, and an end. Marx, like his bourgeois forebears, holds that it is profoundly wrong to subordinate the ends of some individuals to those of others. That is at the core of what exploitation is: to treat a person as a mere object for the use of others. What this approach is after is a society in which individuals are treated as each worthy of regard, and in which each has been put in a position to live really humanly.

I think we can produce an account of these necessary elements of truly human functioning that commands a broad cross-cultural consensus, a list that can be endorsed for political purposes by people who otherwise have very different views of what a complete good life for a human being would be. The list is supposed to provide a focus for quality-of-life assessment and for political planning, and it aims to select capabilities that are of central importance, whatever else the person pursues. They therefore have a special claim to be supported for political purposes in a pluralistic society.[7]

The list is, emphatically, a list of separate components. We cannot satisfy the need for one of them by giving people a larger amount of another one. All are of central importance, and all are distinct in quality. The irreducible plurality of the list limits the trade-offs that it will be reasonable to make, and thus limits the applicability of quantitative cost-benefit analysis.

The basic intuition from which the capability approach begins, in the political arena, is that human abilities exert a moral claim that they should be developed. Human beings are creatures such that, provided with the right educational and material support, they can become fully capable of these human functions. That is, they are creatures with certain lower-level capabilities (which I call "basic capabilities"[8]) to perform the functions in question. When these capabilities are deprived of the nourishment that would transform them into the high-level capabilities that figure on my list, they are fruitless, cut off, in some way but a shadow of themselves. If a turtle were given a life that afforded a merely animal level of functioning, we would have no indignation, no sense of waste and tragedy. When a human being is given a life that blights powers of human action and expression, that does give us a sense of waste and tragedy—the tragedy expressed, for example, in the statement made by Tagore's heroine to her husband, when she says, "I am not one to die easily." In her view, a life without dignity and choice, a life in which she can be no more than an appendage, was a type of death of her humanity.

IV. FUNCTIONING AND CAPABILITY

I have spoken both of functioning and of capability. How are they related? Getting clear about this is crucial in defining the relation of the "capabilities approach" to our concerns about paternalism and pluralism. For if we were to take functioning itself as the goal of public policy, a liberal pluralist would rightly judge that we were precluding many choices that citizens may make in accordance with

their own conceptions of the good. A deeply religious person may prefer not to be well nourished, but to engage in strenuous fasting. Whether for religious or for other reasons, a person may prefer a celibate life to one containing sexual expression. A person may prefer to work with an intense dedication that precludes recreation and play. Am I declaring, by my very use of the list, that these are not fully human or flourishing lives? And am I instructing government to nudge or push people into functioning of the requisite sort, no matter what they prefer?

It is important that the answer to this question is no. Capability, not functioning, is the appropriate political goal. This is so because of the very great importance the approach attaches to practical reason, as a good that both suffuses all the other functions, making them fully human, and also figures, itself, as a central function on the list. The person with plenty of food may always choose to fast, but there is a great difference between fasting and starving, and it is this difference that we wish to capture. Again, the person who has normal opportunities for sexual satisfaction can always choose a life of celibacy, and the approach says nothing against this. What it does speak against (for example) is the practice of female genital mutilation, which deprives individuals of the opportunity to choose sexual functioning (and indeed, the opportunity to choose celibacy as well).[9] A person who has opportunities for play can always choose a workaholic life; again, there is a great difference between that chosen life and a life constrained by insufficient maximum-hour protections and/or the "double day" that makes women unable to play in many parts of the world.

Once again, we must stress that the objective is to be understood in terms of *combined capabilities*. To secure a capability to a person, it is not sufficient to produce good internal states of readiness to act. It is necessary, as well, to prepare the material and institutional environment so that people are actually able to function. Women burdened by the "double day" may be *internally* incapable of play—if, for example, they have been kept indoors and zealously guarded since infancy, married at age six, and forbidden to engage in the kind of imaginative exploration of the environment that male children standardly enjoy. Young girls in poor areas of rural Rajasthan, India, for example, have great difficulty *learning* to play in an educational program run by local activists—because their capacity for play has not been nourished early in childhood. On the other hand, there are also many women in the world who are perfectly capable of play in the internal sense, but who are unable to play because of the crushing demands of the "double day." Such a woman does not have the *combined capability* for play in the sense intended by the list. Capability is thus a demanding notion. In its focus on the environment of choice, it is highly attentive to the goal of functioning, and instructs governments to keep it always in view. On the other hand, it does not push people into functioning: once the stage is fully set, the choice is theirs.

One might worry that any approach as committed as is the capabilities approach to identifying a number of substantive areas of state action, and urging the state to promote capability in all of these areas by affirmative and not just negative measures, would ride roughshod over citizens' liberties and preferences, and thus become ultimately an illiberal approach. There are several distinct ways in which my version of the capabilities approach tries to meet this concern. One way is by specifying the capabilities at a high level of generality and allowing a lot of latitude for different interpretations of a capability that suit the history and traditions of the nation in question. A free-speech right that works well for the U.S. may not be right for Germany, which has expressed a commitment to the prohibition of anti-Semitic literature and expression that seems entirely appropriate, given its history. A second way, as this example shows, is that the standard political and civil liberties figure prominently within the content of the capabilities list. But the most important way in which the approach protects diversity and pluralism, or so it seems to me, is that it aims at capability rather than actual functioning, at the empowering of citizens rather than at dragooning them into one total mode of life.

V. CAPABILITIES AND CARE

Let me now return to the other approaches and briefly indicate how the capabilities approach goes beyond them. It appears superior to the focus on opulence and GNP, because it (a) treats each and every human being as an end, and (b) explicitly attends to the provision of well-being in a wide range of distinct areas of human functioning. It appears superior to resource-based approaches because it looks at the variable needs human beings have for resources and the social obstacles that stand between certain groups of people and the equal opportunity to function. It provides a rationale for affirmative measures addressing those discrepancies. It appears superior to preference-based approaches because it recognizes that preferences are endogenous, the creation of laws and institutions and traditions, and refuses to hold human equality hostage to the status quo. Finally, the approach is a close ally of the human rights approach and is complementary with some versions of it. But it has, I believe, a superior clarity in the way in which it defines both the goal of political action and its rationale. And it makes fully clear the fact that the state has not done its job if it simply fails to intervene with human functioning: affirmative shaping of the material and social environment is required to bring all citizens up to the threshold level of capability.

Finally, there is one salient issue on which, or so it seems to me, the capabilities approach goes well beyond all other approaches stemming from the liberal tradition: this is the issue of care and our need both to receive care and to give it. All human beings begin their lives as helpless children; if they live long enough, they are likely to end their lives in helplessness, whether physical or also mental. During the prime of life, most human beings encounter periods of extreme dependency; and some human beings remain dependent on the daily bodily care of others throughout their lives. Of course putting it this way suggests, absurdly, that "normal" human beings do not depend on others for bodily care and survival; but political thought should recognize that some phases of life, and some lives, generate more profound dependency than others.

The capabilities approach, more Aristotelian than Kantian, sees human beings from the first as animal beings whose lives are characterized by profound neediness as well as by dignity. It addresses the issue of care in many ways: under "life" it is stressed that people should be enabled to complete a "normal" human life span; under "health" and "bodily integrity" the needs of different phases of life are implicitly recognized; "sense," "emotions" and "affiliation" also target needs that vary with the stage of life. "Affiliation" is of particular importance, since it mentions the need for both compassion and self-respect, and it also mentions nondiscrimination. What we see, then, is that care must be provided in such a way that the capability for self-respect of the receiver is not injured, and also in such a way that the caregiver is not exploited and discriminated against on account of performing that role. In other words, a good society must arrange to provide care for those in a condition of extreme dependency without exploiting women as they have traditionally been exploited, and thus depriving them of other important capabilities. This huge problem will rightly shape the way states think about all the other capabilities.[10]

The capabilities approach has a great advantage in this area over traditional liberal approaches that use the idea of a social contract. Such approaches typically generate basic political principles from a hypothetical contract situation in which all participants are independent adults. John Rawls, for example, uses the phrase "fully cooperating members of society over a complete life."[11] But of course no human being is that. And the fiction distorts the choice of principles in a central way, effacing the issue of extreme dependency and care from the agenda of the contracting parties, when they choose the principles that shape society's basic structure. And yet such a fundamental issue cannot well be postponed for later consideration, since it profoundly shapes the way social institutions will be designed.[12] The capabilities approach, using a different concept of the human being, one that builds in need and dependency into the first phases of political thinking, is better suited to good deliberation on this urgent set of issues.

The capabilities approach may seem to have one disadvantage in comparison to some other approaches: it seems difficult to measure human capabilities. If this difficulty arises already when we think about such obvious issues as health and mobility, it most surely arises in a perplexing form for my own list, which has added so many apparently intangible items, such as development of the imagination, and the conditions of emotional health. We know, however, that anything worth measuring, in human quality of life, is difficult to measure. Resource-based approaches simply substitute something easy to measure for what really ought to be measured, a heap of stuff for the richness of human functioning. Preference-based approaches do even worse, because they not only don't measure what ought to be measured; they also get into quagmires of their own concerning how to aggregate preferences—and whether there is any way of doing that task that does not run afoul of the difficulties shown in the social choice literature. The capabilities approach as so far developed in the *Human Development Reports* is admittedly not perfect: years of schooling, everyone would admit, are an imperfect proxy for education. We may expect that any proxies we find as we include more capabilities in the study will be highly imperfect also—especially if it is data supplied by the nations that we need to rely on. On the other hand, we are at least working in the right place and looking at the right thing; and over time, as data-gathering responds to our concerns, we may expect increasingly adequate information, and better ways of aggregating that information. As has already happened with human rights approaches, we need to rely on the ingenuity of those who suffer from deprivation: they will help us find ways to describe, and even to quantify, their predicament.

Notes

1. For examples of these inequalities, see Martha Nussbaum, *Women and Human Development: The Capabilities Approach* (Cambridge: Cambridge University Press, 2000), chap. 3, my "Religion and Women's Human Rights," in *Religion and Contemporary Liberalism*, edited by Paul Weithman (Notre Dame, IN: University of Notre Dame Press, 1997), 93–137, and my *Sex and Social Justice* (New York: Oxford University Press, 1999).

2. See Eva Kittay, *Love's Labor: Essays on Women, Equality, and Dependency* (New York: Routledge, 1999); Nancy Folbre, "Care and the Global Economy," background paper for United Nations Development Programme, *Human Development Report 1999* (New York: Oxford University Press, 1999); Mona Harrington, *Care and Equality: Inventing a New Family Politics* (New York: Knopf, 1999); and Joan Williams, *Unbending Gender: Why Family and Work Conflict and What to Do About It* (New York: Oxford University Press, 1999).

3. The initial statement is in Amartya Sen, "Equality of What?" in *Tanner Lectures on Human Values*, edited by S. McMurrin, vol. 1 (Cambridge: Cambridge University Press, 1980), reprinted in Amartya Sen, *Choice, Welfare, and Measurement* (Oxford: Basil Blackwell, 1982; and Cambridge, MA: MIT Press, 1982). See also various essays by Amartya Sen in *Resources, Values, and Development* (Oxford: Basil Blackwell, 1984; and Cambridge, MA: Basil Blackwell and MIT Press, 1984), and *Commodities and Capabilities* (Amsterdam, the Netherlands: North-Holland, 1985). See also Amartya Sen, "Well-Being, Agency, and Freedom," The Dewey Lectures 1984, *Journal of Philosophy* 82 (1985): 169–221, "Capability and Well-Being," in *The Quality of Life*, edited by

Martha Nussbaum and Amartya Sen (Oxford: Clarendon Press, 1993), 30–53, "Gender Inequality and Theories of Justice," in *Women, Culture, and Development*, edited by Martha Nussbaum and Jonathon Glover (Oxford: Clarendon Press, 1995), 153–98, and *Inequality Reexamined* (Oxford: Clarendon Press, 1995; and Cambridge, MA: Harvard University Press, 1992). See also Jean Drèze and Amartya Sen, *Hunger and Public Action* (Oxford: Clarendon Press, 1989), and *India: Economic Development and Social Opportunity* (Delhi, India: Oxford University Press, 1995).

4. United Nations Development Programme, *Human Development Reports: 1993, 1994, 1995, 1996* (New York: Oxford University Press, 1993, 1994, 1995, 1996). For related approaches in economics, see Partha Dasgupta, *An Inquiry into Well-Being and Destitution* (Oxford: Clarendon Press, 1993); Bina Agarwal, *A Field of One's Own: Gender and Land Rights in South Asia* (Cambridge: Cambridge University Press, 1994); Sabina Alkire, "Operationalizing Amartya Sen's Capability Approach to Human Development: A Framework for Identifying Valuable Capabilities," D.Phil. diss., Oxford University, 1999; S. Anand and C. Harris, "Choosing a Welfare Indicator," *American Economic Association Papers and Proceedings* 84 (1993): 226–49; Frances Stewart, "Basic Needs, Capabilities, and Human Development," in *In Pursuit of the Quality of Life*, edited by Avner Offer (Oxford: Oxford University Press, 1996); Prasanta Pattanaik, "Cultural Indicators of Well-Being: Some Conceptual Issues," in UNESCO, *World Culture Report: Culture, Creativity, and Markets* (Paris: UNESCO Publishing, 1998), 333–39; Meghnad Desai, "Poverty and Capability: Towards an Empirically Implementable Measure," *Suntory-Toyota International Centre Discussion Paper* No. 27 (London: London School of Economics Development Economics Research Program, 1990); and Achin Chakraborty, "The Concept and Measurement of the Standard of Living," Ph.D. diss., University of California at Riverside, 1996. For discussion of the approach, see K. Aman, ed., *Ethical Principles for Development: Needs, Capabilities, or Rights* (Montclair, NJ: Montclair State University Press, 1991); and K. Basu, P. Pattanaik, and K. Suzumura, eds., *Choice, Welfare, and Development: A Festschrift in Honour of Amartya K. Sen* (Oxford: Clarendon Press, 1995).

5. See the discussion of this example in Martha Nussbaum and Amartya Sen's "Introduction" to *The Quality of Life*.

6. Chapter 2 of my Women and Human Development gives an extensive account of economic preference-based approaches, arguing that they are defective without reliance on a substantive list of goals such as that provided by the capabilities approach. Again, this is a theme that has repeatedly been stressed by Sen in his writings on the topic (see note 3).

7. Obviously, I am thinking of the political more broadly than do many theorists in the Western liberal tradition, for whom the nation-state remains the basic unit. I am envisaging not only domestic deliberations but also cross-cultural quality-of-life assessments and other forms of international deliberation and planning.

8. See the fuller discussion in my *Women and Human Development*, chap. 1.

9. See my *Sex and Social Justice*, chaps. 3 and 4.

10. See my "The Future of Feminist Liberalism," a *Presidential Address to the Central Division of the American Philosophical Association*, April 22, 2000, *Proceedings and Addresses of the American Philosophical Association* 74, 2 (November 2000): 47–79.

11. A frequent phrase. See John Rawls, *Political Liberalism* (New York: Columbia University Press, 1993), 20, 21, 183, and elsewhere. For detailed discussion of Rawls's views on this question, see my "Rawls and Feminism," in *The Cambridge Companion to Rawls*, edited by Samuel Freeman (Cambridge: Cambridge University Press, 2002). See also my "The Future of Feminist Liberalism."

12. See the excellent argument in Kittay, *Love's Labor*.

KWAME ANTHONY APPIAH

~

INTRODUCTION

TOMMIE SHELBY

Kwame Anthony Akroma-Ampim Kusi Appiah was born in 1954 in London and raised in Kumasi, in the Ashanti region of Ghana. His Ghanaian father, Joseph Emmanuel Appiah, was a lawyer and politician, and his English mother Peggy Appiah was a writer and philanthropist. Appiah earned his Ph.D. in philosophy from Cambridge University in 1982. He has held faculty positions at Yale, Cornell, Duke, Harvard, Princeton, and, beginning fall 2014, New York University. A prolific and wide-ranging author, Appiah's writings encompass ethics, philosophy of language and mind, political theory, literary and cultural criticism, and African and African American intellectual history. The recipient of numerous honors, he has been president of the American Philosophical Association (Eastern Division) and was awarded the National Humanities Medal by President Barack Obama.

His earliest philosophical books were *Assertion and Conditionals* (1985) and *For Truth in Semantics* (1986), which defended a realist theory of meaning by offering a probabilistic semantics for assertions. He is best known, however, for his philosophical writings on race, culture, social identities, and cosmopolitanism. Appiah's most important books on these topics include *In My Father's House* (1992), *Color Conscious*, with Amy Gutmann (1996), *The Ethics of Identity* (2005), *Cosmopolitanism* (2006), and *The Honor Code* (2010). His politico-philosophical writing, always eloquent and graceful, is marked by his frequent invocations of autobiography (including family history) and literary references, his tremendous facility with a number of languages, and his remarkably broad knowledge of world history and cultures.

Appiah argues forcefully against the biological idea of *race*. The concept of race rests, he believes, on the doctrine of *racialism*: there are distinct groups, each associated with a geographic continent, who possess a cluster of heritable traits—physical, moral, and cognitive—which explain why group members look and behave the way they do. Relying on his knowledge of the biological sciences and philosophy of language, he contends that there are no such groups and thus racialism is false. He is similarly skeptical of the concept of *culture*. The Western idea of culture comes from counter-Enlightenment German romanticism, but has now acquired so many conflicting meanings that its usefulness for political theory and ethical life is in doubt. The culture concept also leads to confusions, such as the implicit assumption that cultures are vulnerable to external transgression, can "belong" to particular groups, should be distributed equitably, are irreducible social goods, and can perish if they change. Things are made worse by the unfortunate tendency to conflate race and culture, as people often do when they use the notion of *ethnicity*.

What truth there is in our talk of "racial" or "cultural" differences should be, Appiah claims, reconceptualized in terms of the idea of *collective identity*—for example, our identities as men and women, Muslims and Jews, blacks and whites, Americans and Africans, and so on. Collective identities acquire their structure through three processes—labeling, identification, and treatment-as. Labeling is the social process through which a term of categorization becomes publicly available for use in picking out the members of a group. The application of a label to a group or its members generally follows a set of well-known (though often contested) criteria and relies on generalizations about how group members should behave or what typical members of the group are like. Identification is the process through which group members internalize and shape their various projects by reference to the group's label. Treatment-as is the corresponding pattern of conduct (negative or positive) toward members of a group because they (are believed to) fit an identity label.

In theorizing the place of identity in human life, Appiah relies on a distinction between *morality* (our inescapable duties to one another as human beings) and *ethics* (our attempts to fulfill our ambitions and to create and experience things of significance). He claims that our ethical lives inevitably rely on identities. Identities are sources of value: they give meaning to our aims and expand the import of our achievements. Identities enable forms of solidarity and make joint projects possible. Collective identities also have *scripts*, that is, conventional narratives that individuals use in the stories they tell about themselves. Such narratives help us make sense of our lives. But identities can also be a threat to liberty. Identity scripts can sometimes be a burden when they are rigid or aggressively policed by those who embody them. Because treatment-as can be unjust treatment, identities can also be instruments of domination, exclusion, and exploitation. And some identity categories are created to serve the ends of oppression. Even when treatment-as is not, per se, maltreatment, an individual may be constrained if he or she refuses to identify with an identity category that others insist on applying to him or her.

Appiah insists on the importance of *individuality* to our ethical lives. Individuality is understood as self-creation or living the life one has chosen for oneself, which is closely related to liberal value of autonomy. There is value in my choosing my life plan even if that plan is less good, objectively speaking, than one someone else might choose for me. However, the pursuit of individuality is not to be understood as a solitary enterprise. Nor need the choices that flow from self-creation be arbitrary. For the self that one creates is fashioned out of collective identities. Through identification with identity categories, our identities partially define what it means to live a successful life; they represent challenges that we must meet to find our lives worthwhile. We can exhibit considerable creativity in wielding identities, but we can't make of them whatever we please. Identities have a history and a conceptual and normative structure. And, importantly, they are developed and change through dialogue and social interaction.

This ethical vision contrasts with two that Appiah rejects. The ethics of *authenticity* calls on us to discover and conform to what we "really" already are. This is the injunction to find one's essence and then steadfastly affirm and stay true to it. *Existentialist* ethics suggests that we must make our lives out of nothing, a kind of radical freedom in which we have no guidance about how to live, nor any constraints on our choices. This is life as pure invention. Neither vision is attractive: one undervalues autonomy; the other overvalues it.

Turning now to politics, what stance should a liberal state take toward its members' collective identities? Departing from multiculturalism, Appiah does not believe the state has a positive duty to ensure the preservation or survival of existing collective identities. Nor does he think the state has an obligation to recognize or respect our identities as such. But he does believe that the state should treat individuals of diverse identities with *equal respect*, which means it should not disadvantage a person because of his or her identity.

But he doesn't maintain that a liberal state, in order to respect our autonomy, must stop at *tolerance* of diverse identities. Unlike liberals who believe the state should remain neutral with respect to conceptions of the good, Appiah thinks it may sometimes be permissible for the state to intervene in the ethical lives of citizens to increase their prospects of attaining their chosen ambitions. Such state interventions can take place at the site of collective identities—for instance, in acts that create new identities and sustain or alter existing ones—so that these identities might be available or more useful to those who would embody them. For example, an identity might have inconsistent constitutive norms or be stigmatized by demeaning stereotypes, thus inhibiting the success of projects carried about through that identity. Some racial and ethnic identities, given their reliance on faulty ideas of "race" and "culture," might fit this characterization. A state's interventions to reform these identities, which he calls *soul making*, can be justified on grounds of individuality. States may therefore help in providing and sustaining identity options without illegitimately interfering with individual liberty.

Rejecting strong forms of nationalism, Appiah believes we should aspire to be "citizens of the world." We should see our bonds with others extending beyond our loyalty to those with whom we share a polity or national identity. This is not a call for the establishment of a world-state to govern the planet. Cosmopolitanism is a philosophy for living together on our shared planet, a specification of how we ought to relate to strangers. It denies that our co-citizens should exhaust the scope of our moral attention, because individuals, not peoples or nations, should be the fundamental units of moral concern. But because we do not share a world-state, we cannot settle our differences or coordinate our actions through the same overarching state authority. And mere tolerance for our differences with distant others may show insufficient concern for their interests and reveal arrogance and unfounded certitude.

One worry about this vision is that is doesn't seem to leave room for *ethical partiality*—special concern for and loyalty to family and friends, comrades and compatriots. If all should be of equal concern, how can I have special duties to some that permit, and maybe require, me to give priority to their interests over others? We can see that the question is confused, Appiah argues, once we recognize that moral concern is not like a resource to be distributed equally and that while states have a duty to treat all impartially, individuals do not. Giving each what he or she is due morally is perfectly compatible with treating some persons better than others. What is more, partiality toward particular others is a part of ethical life, not morality, and so it is properly sensitive to our chosen projects and thus to our collective identities.

The selection included here is taken from the closing chapter of *The Ethics of Identity*. Its discussion of cosmopolitan conversation and of how to secure wide agreement on human rights takes place against the background of Appiah's theory of the place of identity and difference in our ethical, moral, and political lives. He sees dialogue, within and across nations, as a joint search for truth and justice. But he does not think it is helpful to see these sometimes difficult conversations as hampered by "cultural differences." Nor does he think we should seek common ground by searching for universal and necessary principles grounded in a human essence. There is, he observes, a wide range of views on the metaphysical foundations of human rights, often rooted in religious disagreements. Yet he believes we can often find agreement in our local and contingent judgments about concrete cases. We may still find agreement difficult to achieve, but agreement is often no easier among those who supposedly share "a culture." Most geopolitical conflict is not over "cultural differences" either, but over scarce goods, such as land and natural resources, that everyone values.

Appiah favors a pragmatic and minimal conception of human rights. We can all agree, regardless of the traditions within which we are embedded, that there ought to be inviolable constraints on the pursuit of our social and personal aims. Regardless of their available resources or the condition of existing social institutions, both private individuals and states can and should refrain from such acts as murder, torture, rape, and genocide. And the institutionalization of these minimal rights has worked reasonably well in international contexts without agreement on their metaphysical grounding, and has commanded assent from peoples of diverse traditions. We can expand this minimal scheme of rights by using it as a basis for ongoing conversation, genuine conversation, which requires not just speaking (so as to convert) but listening and learning from others, including distant others, strangers. We can often understand and relate to others, even across time and place, because of our capacity to understand and be moved by narratives. And thus this conversation can proceed from a variety of starting points, diverse narratives, and different identities.

Appiah's views on the relationship between "race" and identity are contested in Lucius T. Outlaw, *On Race and Philosophy* (New York: Routledge, 1996), Paul C. Taylor, *Race* (Malden, Mass.: Polity, 2004), and Linda M. Alcoff, *Visible Identities* (New York: Oxford University Press, 2006). A classic debate about multiculturalism, which includes a contribution from Appiah, can be found in *Multiculturalism*, edited by Amy Gutmann (Princeton, N.J.: Princeton University Press, 1994). Two wide-ranging selections of readings on the political significance of cultural difference are *The Rights of Minority Cultures*, edited by Will Kymlicka (New York: Oxford University Press, 1995), and *Democracy and Difference*, edited by Seyla Benhabib (Princeton, N.J.: Princeton University Press, 1996). Martha Nussbaum, Michelle Moody-Adams, and Jorge Gracia each critically respond to the argument of *The Ethics of Identity* in the *Journal of Social Philosophy*, vol. 37 (2006). *The Political Philosophy of Cosmopolitanism*, edited by Gillian Brock and Harry Brighouse (Cambridge: Cambridge University Press, 2005), provides a range of competing conceptions of cosmopolitanism.

The Ethics of Identity

CHAPTER SIX

Rooted Cosmopolitanism

A Worldwide Web

When my father died, my sisters and I found a handwritten draft of the final message he had meant to leave us. It began by reminding us of the history of our two families, his in Ghana and our mother's in England, which he took to be a summary account of who we were. But then he wrote, "Remember that you are citizens of the world." He told us that wherever we chose to live—and, as citizens of the world, we could surely choose to live anywhere that would have us—we should endeavor to leave that place "better than you found it." "Deep inside of me," he went on, "is a great love for mankind and an abiding desire to see mankind, under God, fulfill its highest destiny."

That notion of leaving a place "better than you found it" was a large part of what my father understood by citizenship. It wasn't just a matter of belonging to a community; it was a matter of taking responsibility with that community for its destiny. As evidenced by his long-term practical commitment to the United Nations and a host of other international organizations, he felt this responsible solidarity with all humanity. But he was also intensely engaged with many narrower, overlapping communities. He titled the account he wrote of his life, *The Autobiography of an African Patriot*: and what he meant by this epithet was not just that he was an African and a patriot of Ghana, but that he was a patriot of Africa as well. He felt about the continent and its people what he felt about Ghana and Ghanaians: that they were fellows, that they had a shared destiny. And he felt the same thing, in a more intimate way, about Ashanti, the region of Ghana where he and I were raised, the residuum of the great Asante empire that had dominated our region before its conquest by the British.

Growing up with this father and an English mother, who was both deeply connected to our family in England and fully rooted in Ghana, where she has now lived for half a century, I never found it hard to live with many such loyalties. Our community was Asante, was Ghana, was Africa, but it was also (in no particular order) England, the Methodist Church, the Third World: and, in his final words of love and guidance, my father insisted that it was also all humanity.

Is there sense in the sentiment? Is being a citizen of the world—a "cosmopolitan," in the word's root sense—something one can, or should, aspire to? If we "dip into the future" do we really anticipate "the Parliament of man, the Federation of the world." People have offered reasons for skepticism, and from a range of perspectives. Some deny that the notion . . . can be reconciled with the constitutive role of our local and positional attachments. "Cosmopolitanism," in their view, gives to aery nothing a local habitation and a name: but aery nothing it remains. Others view it not as unattainable but as objectionable; for them it is a distinctively modern mode of deracination—something essentially parasitic upon the tribalisms it disdains, the posturing *de haut en bas* of privilege. Cosmopolitan values, it has been said, are really imperial ones—a

From Kwame Anthony Appiah, *The Ethics of Identity*, Princeton University Press, 2005. Reprinted by permission of the publisher. Ellipsis on p. 1079 is the author's.

parochialism, yet again, puffed up with universalist pretensions; liberalism on safari. And, as we'll see, even for sympathetic souls, cosmopolitanism poses a congeries of paradoxes. . . .

Traveling Tales

The cosmopolitanism I want to defend is not the name for a dialogue among static closed cultures, each of which is internally homogenous and different from all the others; not a celebration of the beauty of a collection of closed boxes. What I want to make plausible is, instead, a form of universalism that is sensitive to the ways in which historical context may shape the significance of a practice. At the same time, I want to elaborate on the notion that we often don't need robust theoretical agreement in order to secure shared practices. . . .

Far from relying on a common understanding of our common human nature or a common articulation (through principles) of a moral sphere, we often respond to the situations of others with shared judgments about particular cases. We in our settings are able to find many moments when we share with people from different settings a sense that something has gone right or gone wrong. It isn't principle that brings the missionary doctor and the distressed mother together at the hospital bedside of a child with cholera: it is a shared concern for this particular child. And you do not need to be a missionary or an ethnographer to discover such moments: it happens also when we read. What we find in the epic or novel, which is always a message in a bottle from some other position, even if it was written and published last week in your hometown, derives not from a theoretical understanding of us as having a commonly understood common nature—not, then, from an understanding that we (we readers and writers) all share—but from an invitation to respond in imagination to narratively constructed situations. In short, what makes the cosmopolitan experience possible for us, whether as readers or as travelers, is not that we share beliefs and values

because of our common capacity for reason: in the novel, at least, it is not "reason" but a different human capacity that grounds our sharing: namely, the grasp of a narrative logic that allows us to construct the world to which our imaginations respond. That capacity is to be found up the Amazon, the Mississippi, the Congo, the Indus, and the Yellow rivers, just as it is found on the banks of the Avon and the Dordogne. . . . And the basic human capacity to grasp stories, even strange stories, is also what links us, powerfully, to others, even strange others.

I am insisting on agreement about particulars rather than about universals and on the role of the narrative imagination—our response to a sequence of particulars—because they are neglected elements in our accounts of how we respond to people who are different from ourselves. I do not deny that agreement about universals occurs, too. And the gift, and grasp, of narrative is not the only thing we share. . . . We can learn from each other's stories only if we share both human capacities and a single world: relativism about either is a reason not to converse but to fall silent.

Cosmopolitanism imagines a world in which people and novels and music and films and philosophies travel between places where they are understood differently, because people are different and welcome to their difference. Cosmopolitanism can work because there can be common conversations about these shared ideas and objects. But what makes the conversations possible is not always shared "culture"; not even, as the older humanists imagined, universal principles or values (though, as I say, people from far away can discover that their principles meet); nor yet shared understanding (though people with very different experiences can end up agreeing about the darnedest things). What works in encounters with other human beings across gaps of space, time, and experience is enormously various. For stories—epic poems as well as modern forms like novels and films, for example—it is the capacity to follow a narrative and conjure a world: and, it turns out, there are people everywhere more than willing to do this. This is the moral epistemology that makes cosmopolitanism possible.

The agenda of liberal cosmopolitanism focuses on conversations among places: but the case for those conversations applies for conversations among cities, regions, classes, genders, races, sexualities, across all the dimensions of difference. For we do learn something about humanity in responding to the worlds people conjure with words in the narrative framework of the folktale, or with images in the frame of film: we learn about the extraordinary diversity of human responses to our world and the myriad points of intersection of those various responses. If there is a critique of the Enlightenment to be made, it is not that the *philosophes* believed in human nature, or the universality of reason: it is rather that they were so dismally unimaginative about the range of what we have in common. . . .

I have said that what two people or two societies have in common as a basis for dialogue will generally include an odd hodgepodge of particular and general: narrative imagination, the capacity for love and reason, some principles, judgments about the rightness and wrongness of particular cases, the appreciation of certain objects. But that dodges such key questions as whether there really are Asian values that differ from Western values, for example, in placing a lesser moral weight on individuality than on the collective. What's at issue isn't whether what we can share is various—it is—but whether or not it includes respect for certain fundamental moral values, among them, in particular, the fundamental human rights.

And, to insist on a point, I am not concerned only with whether we all have these rights—I believe we do . . . but then I *would*, since, to the extent that there is something called the West, I am pretty firmly intellectually ensconced in it. I *am* concerned with what I called the practical question of whether we can expect everybody in the world (or at any rate almost everybody, once they give us a reasonable degree of attention) to come around to *agreeing* that we have those rights.

This is, of course, too large a question to answer here: and it is, in a certain sense, a question whose answer is developing before our eyes. We are watching a world in which people are facing each other with different ideas about what matters in human life, and influences are traveling, through the media and popular culture and evangelism and, no doubt, in many other ways. But in order to think clearly about what is at stake here, we must be clear about what picture of rights we are endorsing.

Globalizing Human Rights

Human rights as they actually exist are, above all, creatures of something like law: they are the results of agreements promulgated by states, agreements that set rule-governed constraints on the actions of states and individuals, sometimes requiring action, sometimes forbidding it. They are used by officials to justify actions both within and across states, and they are called upon by citizens of many states claiming protection from abuse. The wide diversity of people who call upon them includes, to be sure, a substantial diversity of opinion on matters metaphysical—on religion in particular—and even if there is a single truth to be had about these matters, it is not one that we shall all come to soon.

The major advantage of instruments that are not framed as the working out of a metaphysical tradition is, obviously, that people from different metaphysical traditions can accept them. The major disadvantage is that without some grounding—metaphysical or not—it is hard to see why they should have any power or effect. The mere making of declarations that one should behave this way or that does not in general lead people to act in conformity with them, especially in the absence of mechanisms of enforcement. Granted the fact that they are so weakly philosophically grounded, there is a puzzle about what gives human rights instruments their power.

As Michael Ignatieff has observed in a thoughtful discussion of the matter, "human rights has gone global by going local." People around the world, working in different religious and juridical traditions, have nevertheless found reasons to support various human rights instruments because those instruments embody protections that they both want and need. "Human rights is the only universally available moral vernacular that validates the claims of women and children against the oppression they experience in patriarchal and tribal societies; it is the only vernacular that enables dependent persons to perceive themselves as moral agents and to act against practices— arranged marriages, purdah, civic disenfranchisement, genital mutilation, domestic slavery, and so on—that are ratified by the weight and authority of their cultures," Ignatieff writes. "These agents seek out human rights protection precisely because it legitimizes their protests against oppression."[1] The moral individualism of human-rights discourse, as he insists, is what enables it to play this role, and so we cannot say that the notion of human rights is metaphysically *naked*; but it is, or should be, scantily clad, conceptually speaking. Certainly, we do not need to agree that we are all created in the image of God, or that we have natural rights that flow from our human essence, to agree that we do not want to be tortured by government officials, that we do not want to be subjected to arbitrary arrest, or have our lives, families, and property forfeited.

Still, it must be acknowledged that talk of human rights has long had a tendency to overflow its banks. You could see this tendency even in the Universal Declaration of Human Rights (UDHR), which the United Nations proclaimed in 1948, and it has been much in evidence since. The concern here is not that human rights are a Western parochialism; much of the UDHR is devoted to repudiating "traditional" Western values, including various forms of discrimination. No doubt some human-rights claims will be rejected, especially outside the nations of the developed world, when they are controversial, presuming too "thick" a conception of the human good. But sometimes we go wrong, too, when we use the glory term "human rights" to refer to objectives that aren't remotely controversial. Everybody can agree that it's a bad thing to starve to death. But (as I shall suggest in a moment) there's good reason to use "human rights" to designate something like side-constraints or conditions on the achievement of social goods, rather than those goods in themselves.[2] By contrast, the UDHR noticeably helps itself to both. To say, with the UDHR, that everyone has a right to education (to be compulsory through elementary school), and that higher education shall be equally available to all, according to merit, and that everyone has the right to ample food, clothing, medical care, and social services is to say—what? That these are terribly important things. And so they are. To say these things shouldn't be called rights isn't to say they're less important than rights; often they're *more* important. But they aren't things that an impoverished state, however well meaning, can simply provide. Unlike, say, a prohibition on torture, their realization depends on resources, not just on political will; they cannot simply be decreed. To think of human rights as side-constraints, as Robert Nozick did, is to say that if you have a right to X, then no one may deprive you of it. "Individuals have rights," he says, on the first page of *Anarchy, State and Utopia*, "and there are things no person or group may do to them (without violating their rights)." Side-constraints, then, are boundaries that it is always morally wrong to cross. We may pursue all sorts of goals, both moral and personal, but, on this view, we may do so only in ways that avoid violating the rights of others. Criticism of this idea has focused on Nozick's view that the constraints in question are infinitely stringent; for him, they are boundaries we must respect no matter what. And it is, indeed, more plausible to suppose that human rights may sometimes be abridged not only because there are circumstances where rights conflict and we must chose between them, but also because sufficiently substantial considerations of cost may sometimes be enough to outweigh a right. Take something as seemingly fundamental as freedom of expression ("through any media and regardless of frontiers," in the rhetoric of the UDHR). Suppose that abridging your freedom of expression significantly reduced the chances of an outbreak of rioting that would cause much damage to life and property. Here rights conflict. Or suppose that the problem is only that, because many people would be gravely offended, protecting your speech in these circumstances would be extraordinarily expensive. Here a right conflicts with considerations of cost.[3] Still, once we conceive of human rights as constraints on the pursuit of social ends, we should not include among them demands that states cannot meet. That is why negative rights to do something—where other people have the obligation not to hinder me if I do choose to do it—are so prominent in the basic human rights instruments: abstaining from action is almost always possible.

Now human rights are rights you have not just against states but against all other people: my right to life is not a right only against the government. So in committing ourselves to human rights in international law, we are requiring states not just to respect them, but also to attempt to enforce respect for these rights on the part of those they govern. Even if the right in question is a negative right, protecting it will require more of a state than that it abstain from infringing it itself. And this can already take states beyond the realm of what they have the resources to do. In a society in which marriages are thought of as arrangements between families, where the choice or even the consent of the woman is not required, merely passing a law requiring that marriages require consent will not protect the rights of women. And many governments may rightly judge that they simply do not have the legitimacy to enforce such a law (they may not be able, for example, to get their police to take it seriously); and, even if they can, the financial costs of effective enforcement might leave them unable to carry out their other obligations.

You could extend the claims of human rights beyond the realm of negative rights. You could say, for example, that states ought affirmatively to guarantee certain basic needs—for nutrition and for nurture in infancy, say—either by requiring others to provide them (as when we require parents to sustain their children) or by providing them themselves (as when governments guarantee a minimum level of welfare, so long as they have the resources to do so). But such extensions increase the risk, already present, as we saw, in the case of negative rights, that we will be announcing that people have an entitlement that cannot in fact be met; which amounts, in effect, to declaring that a state has a duty to do what it cannot in fact do. Such pronouncements not only offend against the fundamental moral requirement that "ought implies can"; in doing so, they discredit the regime of human rights.

None of this is to deny the importance of international agreements establishing (or, if you like, recording) norms other than human rights: the World Health Organization and UNAIDS make declarations and policies for combating AIDS; UNESCO selects World Heritage Properties and nations pay money into the World Heritage Fund to provide resources for their protection; UNICEF promotes breastfeeding and clean water; and there are many international accounting conventions and Internet protocols that are sustained directly neither by governments nor by intergovernmental organizations. Who could be against any of this? All I am insisting is that not every good needs to be explained in the language of human rights, a language that makes most sense if it is kept within bounds.

Mission creep is not the only thing that bedevils talk of human rights. Consider the problem of indeterminacy. The predicate "arbitrary"—as when one seeks to prohibit arbitrary arrest, or arbitrary interference with privacy, family, home—typically gets a vigorous workout in the formal language of human rights, but what counts as "arbitrary" is irreducibly a matter of judgment. And so it is with what constitutes "degrading" treatment; in various patriarchal societies, measures that we might consider part of the subjugation of women are justified, sincerely, as measures to protect women's dignity. (Many members of these societies would hold that the woman whose genitals have not been properly "feminized" by surgery, or whose visage can be gazed upon without barrier by lascivious men, has been subjected to degrading treatment.) Such practices are frequently "thickly" embedded, fraught with social significances. . . . [Different] societies evince greater agreement about the bad than about the good; but . . . people think of their acts "under descriptions," and public actors seldom intend (or, at any rate, admit they intend) opprobrious deeds under opprobrious descriptions.

In raising these few perplexities, I have taken only a brief glimpse into a vast and crowded armory. On the subject of rights, you will find a great deal of conceptual ammunition for any position you wish to take. The basic dilemma is a familiar one. A conception of rights that's highly determinate in its application may not be thin enough to win widespread agreement; a conception of rights that's thin enough to win widespread agreement risks indeterminacy or impotence.

And yet the impressive thing about human rights, it seems to me, is how effectively they have functioned despite all their manifest limitations and obscurities. Yes, the promulgation of human rights, by international institutions, hardly guarantees assent—and even assent hardly guarantees anything in particular. The miracle is how well we've done without such guarantees. The substance of these rights will indeed always be contested and interpreted; but that doesn't mean they aren't useful instruments for drawing attention to the many ways in which people are brutal to one another. Like Ignatieff, I prefer to see human rights as a language for deliberation, or argument, or some other form of conversation.

And it is conversation, not mere conversion, that we should seek; we must be open to the prospect of gaining insight from our interlocutors. Let me take one example out of many. As Joseph Chan and others have remarked, the Confucian tradition holds it important that children take care of their elderly parents; from this perspective, the

elderly would seem to have a right to our care similar to the claim that young children have on our nurture.[4] Certainly, in the wake of what happened in Paris during a recent heat wave that coincided with *le grand depart*—when thousands of elderly residents died alone in their apartments (some of whose children, according to news reports, declined to cut short their holidays to collect the bodies)—one wonders whether our "Western" attitude toward the care of the elderly isn't in need of reform. Now I have already expressed skepticism about the extension of such positive rights— which the right to care from your children surely is—so I offer this not as an example of a proposal I endorse, but as an example of a place where the flow of insight seems to be not from Us to Them, but in Our direction.

Though we've often been served notice that other societies, or their self-appointed spokesmen, resist talk of human rights—mistrusting them as a distinctively Western imposition, as excessively "individualist"—we should also be alert to the ways in which human rights, especially in their thinner conceptions, have managed to root themselves in a wide variety of social contexts. In effect, the reason why we do not need to ground human rights in any particular metaphysics is that many of them are already grounded in many metaphysics and can already derive sustenance from those many sources. A simple example, which I've used before, comes from the traditions of Asante, where I grew up. Free Asante citizens—both men and women—in the period before the state was conquered by Britain as well as since, are preoccupied with notions of personal dignity, with respect and self-respect. Treating others with the respect that is their due is central to Asante social life, as is a reciprocal anxiety about loss of respect, shame, and disgrace. Just as European liberalism—and democratic sentiment—grew by extending to every man and (then) woman the dignity that feudal society offered only to the aristocracy, and thus presupposes, in some sense, aspects of that feudal understanding of dignity, so modern Ghanaian thinking about politics depends, in part, on the prior grasp of concepts such as *animuonyam* (respect). Well-known Akan proverbs make it clear that, in the past, respect was precisely not something that belonged to everybody: *Agya Kra ne Agya Kwakyerēmē, emu biara mu nni animuonyam*. (Father Soul and Father Slave Kyerēmē, neither is respected; that is, whatever you call him, a slave is still a slave.) But just as *dignitas*, which was once, by definition, the property of an elite, has grown into human dignity, which is the property of every man and woman, so *animuonyam* can be the basis of the respect for all others that lies at the heart of a commitment to human rights. . . .

When it comes to those cases where the different traditions part, a richer metaphysical grounding would not help us. For when someone argues—in the name of Confucian values or Maoism or Hinduism or Islam—that the human-rights tradition is overly individualist and so certain individual rights have a lesser weight than community interests, the return to first principles will simply take us from one terrain of disagreement to another where there seems no reason to expect greater hope of resolution.

Cass Sunstein has defended what he calls "incompletely theorized agreements" in the context of American constitutional law.[5] I would like to defend a similar freedom from the demand for high doctrine in the development of the internal practices of human-rights law. We should be able to defend our treaties by arguing that they offer people protections against governments that most of their citizens desire, and that are important enough that they also want other peoples, through their governments, to help sustain them. Once we seek to defend these rights in this pragmatic way, we can appeal to a highly diverse set of arguments: perhaps some rights—to freedom of expression, for example—are not only necessary for dignity and the maintenance of respect but also helpful in the development of economies and the stabilization of polities. And all of these are things that are wanted by most people everywhere. Sunstein's account of "incompletely theorized agreement" goes together with a proposal

for a certain kind of judicial modesty: and, as I say, we do not go wrong if we resist designating everything we should devoutly hope for a "fundamental human right."

To make this pragmatic point—to argue for basic rights in a way that is receptive to a metaphysical ecumenism, responsive to the moral vocabularies we find on the ground—is not to hold, as some have suggested, that the foundation of the legitimacy of human rights is the consent of a majority of our species. After all, our most fundamental rights restrain majorities, and their consent to the system that embodies those restraints does not entail their consent to the rights themselves—otherwise there would be no need of them. (As Louis Menand has memorably observed, "Coercion is natural; freedom is artificial.")[6] If consent is an empirical notion, then most Americans do not consent to many rights that they actually have: for example, their right to marry even if they are condemned for capital crimes. The remarkable currency that human-rights discourse has gained around the world demonstrates that it speaks to people in a diversity of positions and traditions; this chord of resonating agreement explains why we can find global support for the human rights system. One reason for articulating these ideas in international documents, which are widely circulated and advertised, is just to draw attention to that core of agreement, however narrow, and to help to give it practical force. We needn't be unduly troubled by the fact that metaphysical debate is unlikely to yield consensus, because human rights can, and therefore should, be sustained without metaphysical consensus.

Cosmopolitan Conversation

The roots of the cosmopolitanism I am defending are liberal: and they are responsive to liberalism's insistence on human dignity. It has never been easy to say what this entails, and, indeed, it seems to me that exploring what it might mean is liberalism's historic project. . . . I would insist . . . that the individual whose self-creation is being valued here is not, in the justly censorious sense of the term, individualist. Nothing I have said is inconsistent with the recognition of the many ways in which we human beings are naturally and inevitably social. First, because we are incapable of developing on our own, because we need human nurture, moral and intellectual education, practice with language, if we are to develop into full persons. This is a sociality of mutual dependence. Second, because we desire relationship with others: friends, lovers, parents, children, the wider family, colleagues, neighbors. This is sociality as an end. And third, because many other things we value—literature, and the arts, the whole world of culture; education; money; and, in the modern world, food and housing— depend essentially on society for their production. This is instrumental sociality. . . .

This picture acknowledges that identity is at the heart of human life: liberalism . . . takes this picture seriously, and tries to construct a state and society that take account of the ethics of identity without losing sight of the values of personal autonomy. But the cosmopolitan impulse is central to this view, too, because it sees a world of cultural and social variety as a precondition for the self-creation that is at the heart of a meaningful human life. Let me be clear. Cosmopolitanism values human variety for what it makes possible for human agency, and some kinds of cultural variety constrain more than they enable. The cosmopolitan's high appraisal of variety flows, . . . from the human choices it enables, but variety is not something we value no matter what. (This is one reason why I think it is not helpful to see cosmopolitanism as expressing an aesthetic ideal.) There are other values. You can have an enormous amount of diversity between societies, even if they are all, in some sense, democratic.[7] But the fundamental idea that every society should respect human dignity and personal autonomy is more basic than the cosmopolitan love of variety; indeed, as I say, it is the autonomy that variety enables that is its fundamental justification. Cosmopolitans do not ask other people to maintain the diversity of the species at the price of their individual autonomy. We can't require others to provide us with a cultural museum to tour through or to visit on satellite television's endless virtual safari; nor can we demand an assortment of Shangri-las to enlarge the range of our own options for identity. The options we need in order for our choices to be substantial must be freely sustained, as must the human variety whose existence is, for the cosmopolitan, an endless source of insight and pleasure. In theory, . . . a whole society could come to be centered on a single set of values without coercion. I might be skeptical about the virtues of such a homogenized society as a place for myself to live (even if the values it was centered on were in some sense mine). I would think it might risk many cultural and economic and moral perils, because it might require in the end a kind of closing oneself off from the rest of the world. But those in such a society would no doubt have things to say in response—or might refuse to discuss the matter with me at all—and, in the end, they might well find their considerations weightier than mine. Freely chosen homogeneity, then, raises no problems for me: in the end, I would say, Good luck to them. But, as I have said, there is no ground for thinking that people are rushing toward homogeneity; and, in fact, in a world more respectful of human dignity and personal autonomy such movement toward homogeneity as there is would probably slow down.

Skepticism about the genuinely cosmopolitan character of the view I have been defending may flow in part from the thought that it seems so much a creature of Europe and its liberal tradition.[8] So it may be well to insist, in closing, that my own attachment to these ideas comes, as much as anything, from my father, who grew up in Asante, at a time when the independence of its moral climate from that of European Enlightenment was extremely obvious. Now, it would be preposterous to claim that he came to his cosmopolitanism or his faith in human rights and the rule of law unaffected by European traditions. But it would be equally untenable to deny that the view he arrived at had roots in Asante (indeed, as one travels the world, reviewing the liberal nationalisms of South Asia and Africa in the mid-twentieth century, one is impressed not only by their similarities but also by their local inflections). Two things, in particular, strike me about the local character of the source of my father's increasing commitment to individual rights: first, that it grew out of experience of illiberal government; second, that it depended on a sense of his own dignity and the dignity of his fellow citizens that was the product of Asante conceptions.

The first point—about experience—is crucial to the case for liberalism. The historical experience of the dangers of intolerance—religious intolerance in Europe in the seventeenth century, for example, for Locke; racial intolerance in the colonial context, for Gandhi (or for African independence leaders like my father)—often underlies the common liberal skepticism about state intervention in the lives of individuals. My father saw the colonial state's abuses of his fellows (and himself) and, in particular, the refusal to pay them the respect that was their due. As a lawyer and a member of the opposition, he traveled Ghana in the years after independence defending people whose rights were being abused by the post-colonial state. The political tradition of liberalism flows from these experiences of illiberal government. That liberal restraint on government recommends itself to people rooted in so many different traditions shows its grasp of a truth about human beings and about modern politics. Just as the centrality of murderous religious warfare in the period leading up to Locke's *Treatises* placed religious toleration at the core of Locke's understanding of the liberalism he defended, so the persecution of political dissenters by postcolonial despots has made protection of political dissent central to the liberalism of those who resist postcolonial states in Africa. (My father worried little about the state's entanglement with religion; once, I remember, as we sat in front of the television in the late evening, my father sang along with the national hymn, which was played some evenings as an alternative to the more secular national anthem, to end the day. "This would be a much better national anthem," he said to me. And I replied, ever the good liberal, "But the anthem

has the advantage that you don't have to believe in God to sing it sincerely." "No one in Ghana is silly enough not to believe in God," my father replied.[9] I now think he was right not to be worried about the entanglement: there was no history of religious intolerance in Ghana of the sort that makes necessary the separation of church and state; a genial ecumenism had been the norm at least until the arrival of American TV evangelism.) But more important yet to my father's concern with individual human dignity was its roots in the preoccupation that I said free Asante citizens—both men and women—have with notions of respect and self-respect. *Dignitas*, as understood by Cicero, reflects much that was similar between republican Roman ideology and the views of the *animuonyam*-prizing nineteenth-century Asante elite; it was, I think, as an Asante that my father recognized and admired Cicero, not as a British subject.

Although I've argued for the importance of stories, you shouldn't let my own storytelling convince you that the prospects for a liberal cosmopolitanism are as rosy as I am making them out to be. Pessimists can cite a dismal litany to the contrary. Still, it's hard to ignore the conceptual currency that the fundamental human rights have enjoyed among millions of ordinary people around the world. Inasmuch as we are, already, fellow citizens of a world, we do not have to wait for institutional change to exercise our common citizenship: to engage in dialogue with others around the world about the questions great and small that we must solve together, about the many projects in which we can learn from each other, is already to live as fellow citizens. . . . I have been arguing that there is a great range among the starting points we have for these conversations, the shared points of entry from which we can proceed. This is as true of conversations between Confucians from Shanghai and Pentecostals from Peoria as it is for conversations between people who differ in class and gender, or profession, or along a whole range of dimensions of identity. From these conversations we can be led to common action—for our shared environment, for human rights, for the simple enjoyment of comity. And such comity is as likely to prevail among those who revere different totems as among those who revere the same ones.

If this book has a totem, it is, of course, John Stuart Mill, and we should not be surprised to find that he himself has pithily expressed the cosmopolitan ideal: "To human beings, who, as hitherto educated, can scarcely cultivate even a good quality without running it into a fault, it is indispensable to be perpetually comparing their own notions and customs with the experience and example of persons in different circumstances from themselves: and there is no nation which does not need to borrow from others, not merely particular arts or practices, but essential points of character in which its own type is inferior."[10] Mill would join us, then, in rejecting a form of humanism that requires us to put our differences aside; the cosmopolitan believes, with him, that sometimes it is the differences we bring to the table that make it rewarding to interact at all. But he would also concede, as we should, that what we share can be important, too, though the cosmopolitan will insist that what we share with others is not always ethnonational in character: sometimes it will just be that you and I both like to fish or . . . make excellent strudel. Perhaps we have read and admired Goethe in translation, or responded with the same sense of wonder to a postcard of Angkor Wat or the Parthenon, or believe, as lawyers with very different trainings, in the ideal of the rule of law. This is, perhaps, the anglophone voice of cosmopolitanism. But, in the cosmopolitan spirit, let me end with a similar thought from my father's tradition. *Kuro korō mu nni nyansa*, the proverb says: In a single πολις there is no wisdom.[11]

Notes

1. Michael Ignatieff, *Human Rights as Politics and Idolatry* (Princeton: Princeton University Press, 2001), 7, 68.

2. See L. W. Sumner's fine discussion in "The Analysis of Rights," in *The Moral Foundation of Rights* (Oxford: Clarendon Press, 1987), especially 15–31.

3. In most respects, the United States has a singularly expansive free-expression regime, and yet even here, freedom of expression is tightly corseted, and legitimately so. The First Amendment does not protect a contract killer's verbal contract; it does not protect a fraudulent or defamatory claim; it does not protect expression that is a means of pursuing a tortious or criminal action. Then there's a matter of venue—of *where* this right is to be enjoyed. A student cannot say whatever he wants whenever he wants in a classroom; an employee has no First Amendment rights to expression in a private-sector workplace; a shopper at Macy's cannot display a placard touting the prices at Bloomingdale's. Even in places that look more like a "public forum," you'll find that signage is limited by zoning restrictions and the like. So this freedom, while real and important, doesn't fully apply in the places where you spend much of your life.

4. See Joseph Chan, "A Confucian Perspective on Human Rights for Contemporary China," in *The East Asian Challenge for Human Rights*, ed. Joanne R. Bauer and Daniel A. Bell (Cambridge: Cambridge University Press, 1999), 212–37; and Joseph Chan, "The Asian Challenge to Universal Human Rights: A Philosophical Appraisal," in *Human Rights and International Relations in the Asia-Pacific Region*, ed. James T. H. Tang (New York: St. Martin's Press, 1995). . . .

5. Cass R. Sunstein, "Incompletely Theorized Agreements," *Harvard Law Review* 108 (1995): 1733–72.

6. He continues, "Freedoms are socially engineered spaces where parties engaged in specified pursuits enjoy protection from parties who would otherwise naturally seek to interfere in those pursuits. One person's freedom is therefore always another person's restriction: we would not have even the concept of freedom if the reality of coercion were not already present." Louis Menand, "The Limits of Academic Freedom," in *The Future of Academic Freedom* (Chicago: University of Chicago Press, 1996), 1.

7. There is no reason to think that every society needs to implement the idea of popular choice in the same way; so different democratic institutions in different societies are consistent with the basic respect for autonomy, too.

8. I should explicitly record my opposition to the view that this origin in any way discredits these ideas, either for non-Europeans or, for that matter, for Europeans. The issues I want to explore have to do with the ways in which these views can be rooted in different

traditions. I am not interested in the nativist project of arguing for these principles in the name of authentically Asante (or African) roots. The issues raised in the following paragraphs are thus historical, not justificatory.

9. My father's thought clearly wasn't that there weren't any atheists in Ghana but that their views didn't matter. Locke, of course, agreed: "Those are not at all to be tolerated who deny the being of a God. Promises, covenants, and oaths, which are the bonds of human society, can have no hold upon an atheist. The taking away of God, though but even in thought, dissolves all." "A Letter Concerning Toleration," in *Political Writings of John Locke*, ed. David Wootton (New York: Mentor, 1993), 426.

10. Mill, *Principles of Political Economy*, *CWM* 3:594.

11. *Kuro* is usually translated as "town" or "hometown": but towns were relatively self-governing in the Asante past, so πολις looks like a translation that gets the right sense.

GILLIAN BROCK

~

INTRODUCTION

NICOLE HASSOUN

Gillian Brock is Professor of Philosophy at the University of Auckland. She was born in South Africa and studied at the University of Cape Town, completing her Ph.D. in 1993 at Duke University, where she wrote on the moral importance of needs. In 2018, she became a Fellow of the Royal Society of New Zealand and the Royal Society of Arts in the United Kingdom. She is one of the leading scholars working today on global justice, human needs, immigration, and corruption.

Brock has written or edited thirteen books and hundreds of articles. In her first book, *Necessary Goods: Our Responsibility to Meet Others' Needs* (Lanham, Md.: Rowman & Littlefield, 1998), she joined with others in considering which needs matter, what obligations they generate, and who has responsibility for meeting them. Her other collections, including (with Darrel Moellendorf) *Current Debates in Global Justice* (Dordrecht: Springer, 2005), *The Political Philosophy of Cosmopolitanism* (Cambridge: Cambridge University Press, 2005), and (with Solomon Benatar) *Global Health and Global Health Ethics* (Cambridge: Cambridge University Press, 2011), explore just war theory, climate change, health justice, patriotism, nationalism, and cosmopolitanism (the idea that we are all members of a single human community, so that national borders have no fundamental moral significance). In addition to *Global Justice: A Cosmopolitan Account* (Oxford: Oxford University Press, 2009) from which our excerpt is drawn, Brock has coauthored with Michael Blake a groundbreaking book on migration justice, *Debating Brain Drain: May Governments Restrict Emigration?* (New York: Oxford University Press, 2015), in which they consider how to address the problems that occur when talented workers, taking their skills with them, immigrate from poor countries. Her book *Justice for People on the Move: Migration in Challenging Times* (Cambridge: Cambridge University Press, 2020) offers a comprehensive framework for considering issues of migration justice, especially challenges faced by current migrants.

As globalization, immigration, climate change, and most recently the coronavirus pandemic reshape our social world, philosophers have considered issues of global justice. How can we treat each other fairly in a world marked by conflict and inequality? Different theories offer different answers. While some advocate global equality, others suggest that our obligations beyond borders are quite limited, requiring only respect for all decent societies and minimal foreign aid. Philosophers also disagree about how we should deal with international conflict and address such issues as trade, poverty, health, and the environment.

An influential contemporary book on global justice is John Rawls's *The Law of Peoples* (Cambridge, Mass.: Harvard University Press, 2001). Rawls rejects cosmopolitanism on the grounds that it does not leave enough room for nationalist and other legitimate group affiliations. Rather, he argues that we should respect the right to self-determination for all decent societies that uphold human rights, but not intervene in their affairs. Rawls's international theory differs from his earlier work regarding what we owe people within our own society. Previously he argued that we should ask what rules we would choose for our society if we were in an "original position" where we did not know who we would be in that society, or such basic information as how many people would be rich and poor. Rawls thought that in that situation we would endorse the "difference principle," distributing primary goods, those all people need no matter what their life plans, by maximizing the position of the least well off, allowing only inequalities that serve that end.

The first wave of work on global justice responded to Rawls's *The Law of Peoples* by arguing instead for cosmopolitanism, such as Thomas Pogge, *World Poverty and Human Rights* (Cambridge: Polity Press, 2008) and Charles Beitz, *Political Theory*. In the book from which the following selection is drawn, Brock defends a version of global justice that acknowledges the equal moral worth of persons but also is compatible with nationalism. She addresses two different sorts of global justice skeptics. One type argues that cosmopolitanism may be fine in theory but does not work in practice. Another contends that cosmopolitanism ignores important forms of group affiliation and identification, such as nationalism. The first part of *Global Justice* presents Brock's cosmopolitan theory of global justice; the second offers concrete proposals for making public policy more just; the third explains how her account of good practice informs her theory.

Our selection focuses on Brock's innovative argument against the position defended by Rawls, Pogge, and Beitz. She defends the view that people in a global original position would care about meeting their basic needs, and she appeals to empirical evidence that seeks to replicate the original position. In the relevant experiments, researchers told people they would be paid for work they would complete but asked if they wanted to plan to redistribute any gains from their efforts. They could choose to split the profits equally, help the least well off as much as possible, or keep their own payments, for instance. After discussion, people chose to give everyone a basic minimum. Researchers said they observed people balancing concern for incentives, entitlements, and needs, and found that people were happy with the results after the work was completed and the money redistributed (and productivity increased). Brock suggests that Rawlsians, in light of their concern for stability, should support a minimum floor principle because it is in the greatest interest of the least well off.

In subsequent sections of *Global Justice* Brock supports democratic self-determination that helps everyone live decent lives. She considers how we might address global poverty by changing international tax and other laws. She also discusses when international intervention is justified, which immigration reforms are required, and how to adjust international trade law and economic activity to promote global justice. Her account leaves room for a legitimate form of nationalism so long as people interact fairly with others, meeting their basic needs and maintaining sufficient freedom. To address the feasibility skeptic, Brock explains that her goals are realizable, that people can be motivated to pursue them, and that we can make (and track) progress toward global justice. Ultimately, she supports a strategy that reconciles cosmopolitanism with other commitments such as nationalism.

Canonical books on cosmopolitanism and global justice are Henry Shue, *On Basic Rights* (Princeton, N.J.: Princeton University Press, 1980); Martha Nussbaum, *Women and Human Development: The Capabilities Approach* (Cambridge: Cambridge University Press, 2000); Amartya Sen, *Development as Freedom* (New York: Random House, 1999); David Miller, *National Responsibility and Global Justice* (Oxford: Oxford University Press, 2007); Michael Blake, *Justice and Foreign Policy* (Oxford: Oxford University Press, 2013); Darrel Moellendorf, *Global Inequality Matters* (London: Palgrave Macmillan, 2009); Mattias Risse, *On Global Justice* (Princeton, N.J.: Princeton University Press, 2012); Kok-Chor Tan, *Justice, Institutions, and Luck: The Site, Ground, and Scope of Equality* (Oxford: Oxford University Press, 2012); and Nicole Hassoun, *Globalization and Global Justice* (Cambridge: Cambridge University Press, 2012).

Other important works on global governance offering practical proposals for positive change include Carol Gould, *Globalizing Democracy and Human Rights* (Cambridge: Cambridge University Press, 2009); Jeff McMahan, *Killing in War* (Oxford: Oxford University Press, 2004); Christian Barry and Sanjay Reddy, *International Trade and Labor Standards* (New York: Columbia University Press, 2008); Leif Wenar, *Blood Oil: Tyrants, Violence, and the Rules* (Oxford: Oxford University Press, 2017); and Nicole Hassoun, *Global Health Impact: Extending. Access to Essential Medicines* (New York: Oxford University Press, 2020).

Global Justice: A Cosmopolitan Account

AN ALTERNATIVE RAWLSIAN-STYLE NORMATIVE THOUGHT EXPERIMENT

I begin by sketching a normative thought experiment that models ideal deliberating conditions. It offers a systematic way for thinking through issues concerning global justice as well. I take my inspiration for the thought experiment from Rawls, though crucial details of my view are quite different from Rawls's account. Rawlsian-style thought experiments are well suited to examining what an ideal world might require of us. When properly set up, they are a good way to flesh out

what we can reasonably expect of one another in a way that avoids inappropriate partiality: if people do not know what positions they might find themselves in during the lottery of life, they will pay more attention to what would constitute fair arrangements.[1]

So, on to the normative thought experiment. What should we assume about the ideal world we are asked to contemplate? To assist our deliberation, in this exercise I try to make the ideal world easy to imagine by making it reflect our actual situation as much as possible. The ideal world is divided into communities that are variously organized. Some communities may be

From *Global Justice: A Cosmopolitan Account*. (New York: Oxford University Press, 2009), reprinted by permission of the publisher.

overlapping, others may not be; some divisions may be sharp, others blurred. Some of the most obvious divisions are along political lines. Other divisions exist among national, religious, cultural, or linguistic groups. I do not assume that all people everywhere form one community, nor do I assume homogeneity within communities. I do not assume, further, that people are necessarily altruistic, or even mutually concerned, so as not to bias the outcome towards what one might expect will be the sorts of conclusions I wish to endorse. To avoid the charge of bias and so that my conclusions have maximum reach with opponents, I assume that persons are instructed to be self-interested (understood in a fairly narrow sense). It is not that I think people are only self-interested and never other-regarding. It is more that people tend to have limited sympathies or impaired moral imagination. If we can be helped to feel the force of having to occupy another's position—of how that might be not for them, but as a real option for us—our moral imagination can be extended. The idea is to harness people's limited sympathies in ways that result in fairer solutions for everyone.[2]

An easy way to enter the thought experiment is to imagine that a global conference has been organized. You have been *randomly selected* to be a decision-making delegate to this conference.[3] You are to participate in deciding what would be a fair framework for interactions and relations among the world's inhabitants. Though you have been invited to the decision-making forum, you do not know anything about what allegiances you have (or may have after the conference concludes), but you do know that decisions made at this conference will be binding. It may turn out that you find that you belong to a developing nation, occupy a territory with poor natural resources, belong to a generation that does not yet exist, and so forth. Given these sorts of possibilities, you are provided with reasons to care about what you would be prepared to tolerate in a range of different circumstances.

You can have access to any information you like about various subjects (such as history,

psychology, or economics), but so far as possible, very little (if any) information about subjects like the demographics of world population should be made available. The idea is that you should not have access to information that could lead you to deduce the odds of your being in some circumstances as against others. For instance, if you know that over one billion of the six billion people alive today are Indian, you might be tempted to gamble that you are going to turn out to be Indian, and so try to ensure Indians get better treatment than others. I want to eliminate scope for this sort of gambling. I contend that, if a rational individual does not know the odds, it is not rational to gamble (at least under the conditions described). She will have to think seriously about what "the strains of commitment"[4] will really involve and what she will honestly be prepared to tolerate. For these reasons, delegates do not know where they live, the territory's size, how numerous or powerful the people are, what level of economic development is dominant in that territory, how well endowed it is with natural resources, and so forth.

Some information will be made available to all delegates. This includes data about our urgent global collective problems and how we will have to cooperate to solve them. Delegates will be informed about various threats to peace and security, including threats we face as a result of the increasing number of people who have access to weapons (especially weapons of mass destruction) and the activities of terrorists and drug traffickers. Delegates will be made aware of various environmental challenges, such as, the destruction of the ozone layer and climate change. Information about risks to health, such as highly infectious diseases or global pandemics, will also be included. This will make clear that these problems have global reach and require global cooperation if they are to be resolved. Some of this material will also maintain that the people of the world are in a state of interdependence and mutual vulnerability; they have to rely on each other if they are to achieve an acceptable level of peace, security, or well-being, both now and in the future.[5]

The main issue delegates must entertain concerns what *basic* framework governing the world's inhabitants we can reasonably expect to agree on as fair. Delegates will be aware that any entitlements selected will generate financial obligations. First, we consider what is the *minimum* set of protections and entitlements we could reasonably be prepared to tolerate. What would be the minimum reasonable lot for people to agree to? As individual contractors have no particular knowledge of how they will be positioned, of who they will be once the conference adjourns, it would not be prudent for them to agree to any arrangements that would be unbearable, since they may find themselves occupying the position of such a person. So, delegates would agree only to those policies that did not have unbearable effects on people, because they might end up being on the receiving end of such policies. More positively, whatever else they choose, delegates would find it prudent and reasonable for each person to be able to enjoy the prospects for a decent life, and much discussion would be about the (minimum) content of such a life. I submit we would centre the terms of agreement around two primary guidelines of roughly equal importance—namely, that everyone should enjoy *some* equal basic liberties and that everyone should be protected from certain real (or highly probable) risks of serious harms.

Reasonable people will care, at least minimally, about enjoying a certain level of freedom. Freedom may not be the only thing they care about, of course, and often they may not care about it very much when other issues are at stake about which they care more deeply. Nevertheless, reasonable people will care at least a little about enjoying *some* freedoms. Many kinds of freedoms will be of interest, but, importantly, they would include freedom from assault or extreme coercion (such as slavery) and *some* basic freedoms governing movement, association, and speech. We need to be permitted to evaluate and revise the central ideas that govern our lives should we choose to do this. Delegates should recognize that it is possible that they could find themselves in a society whose major organizing values, principles, and commitments are ones they

disagree with. In such a situation, it would be prudent to have—indeed, some might reasonably insist on having—the scope to question and revise the values operative in the society, or at least to have a certain freedom to live their lives in accordance with values they find more congenial. Recognizing this, they would, therefore, endorse a degree of freedom of dissent, conscience, speech, and the freedom to exit a society. Delegates would want minimum guarantees about what counts as permissible treatment. Heading the list would be guarantees against assault, torture, imprisonment without trial or sufficient warrant, or extreme coercion of various kinds. As I have also suggested, it would be reasonable for them to add some freedoms governing dissent, conscience, speech, association, and movement. . . .

In addition to caring about protecting freedom, rational decision-makers will also want protection from real risks of serious harms to which they could be vulnerable (and potentially powerless to resist) in certain cases. Under some kinds of arrangements, there could be enormous risk of harms. For instance, multinational corporations operating in unregulated market economies can threaten abilities to subsist in various ways—for example, they can pollute the soil and water so that crops no longer grow properly (or, perhaps more controversially, they can control labour markets so that wages are set at bare or below subsistence levels). In such cases, capacities to subsist may be significantly undermined. Indeed, those considering what arrangements to adopt would be vigilant to ensure that meeting their needs are within their reach, since being unable to meet our basic needs must be one of the greatest harms that we can face. Reflecting on the gravity of such harm in particular, more positively, but in a similar vein, we would find it reasonable to have certain guaranteed minimal opportunities and those would be strongly influenced by a certain baseline minimum—namely, what is necessary for us to meet our basic needs for ourselves.

Furthermore, adopting the perspective of self-interested persons (as the instructions to delegates require), delegates should consider the possibility that they are permanently disabled, and they should also consider the actual periods of extreme dependence that naturally occur in the human life-cycle. Self-interested individuals then would want adequate protections to be guaranteed should the need arise. Self-interested individuals (or, at least, reasonable people adopting the guise of such persons) reflecting behind an appropriate veil of ignorance should be strongly motivated to ensure not only the availability of baseline opportunities to meet our needs for ourselves, but also that persons should have adequate provision for assistance with need-satisfaction, should they not be in a position to meet their needs themselves.

So far my claim is that, in the ideal choosing situation, the minimum package it would be reasonable to agree to specifies that we should all be adequately positioned to enjoy the prospects for a decent life, as understood to include what is necessary to be enabled to meet our basic needs and those of our dependants (but with provisions firmly in place for the permanently or temporarily disabled to be adequately cared for), and certain protections for basic freedom.[6] We would use this as a baseline and endorse social and political arrangements that can ensure and underwrite at least these important goods. The minimum package that is endorsed will have implications for most spheres of human activity, especially economic activity and political organization. For instance, economic activity must be sensitive to everyone's prospects for a decent life and regulations must be devised to ensure this. Extensive sets of rules would need to be outlined to make plain for all just what would constitute important threats to people's prospects for decent lives. Organizations that can monitor and enforce these rules must be established.

What governance structure would we adopt? There are many arrangements we could choose, but two key guiding principles would operate: we would want our vital interests (such as, our ability to subsist) protected, and it can be anticipated that we would want to retain as much control over affairs that directly affect us as is consistent with protection of those vital interests. Any governing authorities we endorse will have the protection of our vital interests as a high priority and their legitimacy will rest on their ability to do an adequate job of this. Given that my ideal world (strongly coloured by the actual world) is already divided into political communities, delegates might find it reasonable to use those divisions in some of their prescriptions. They might agree that governments of those territories have primary authority to underwrite people's abilities to meet their needs and protect their freedoms, but when those governments are unable to do so, the duties should be distributed more effectively. Mixed forms of governance might reasonably be chosen, such that in some matters local bodies have complete control, while in others—where protection of vital interests can be secured only if there is widespread cooperation across states—joint sovereignty might reasonably be chosen. At any rate, whatever governing structures we endorse would (at a minimum) have as the central part of their mandate to ensure that people are so positioned that meeting their basic needs is within their reach, and that their basic liberties are protected. They would also select arrangements that can secure fair terms of cooperation in joint undertakings and practices. This minimally involves a notion of fair reciprocity—for instance, that there should be a fair distribution of benefits and burdens in collective endeavours.[7]

There are other important reasons why delegates might find it worthwhile to choose to retain states rather than endorse a world government. An important one has to do with what it would be prudent to choose, given the uncertainties involved. The grounding for this concern lies in the conjunction of two considerations. First, given the gravity of what is at stake, it would be prudent to be risk-averse under the decision-making circumstances, and this ensures a cautious approach. Second, there is a legitimate concern about what might transpire if world government turns out to be very bad. Bernard Boxill notices the problem and gives a good statement of the reasoning: "If a world state is inclined to be just, it could be very just. But if it is inclined to be unjust, the consequences could be appalling. An unjust world state would have no comparable independent power capable of restraining it. Nor could there be any escape from it. Backs to the wall, people would be either despairing or desperate. This suggests it is wiser to take our chances with a world of states."[8] That world order at least has some safeguards: citizens can defect to other states and there are other states that can help restrain the worst offenders in cases of grave injustices.[9]

Delegates are aware that all entitlements chosen need to be financed. Resources will be needed to fund the arrangements that are chosen. We will need to address the issue of what counts as fair ownership of resources, but the account of fair ownership of resources we endorse cannot block the funding of those reasonable arrangements that are necessary to underwrite the basic framework, since obligations to set up and do our part in supporting the basic framework are more fundamental.

There is more to say about all of the arguments covered in this section and throughout the book we return to the normative thought experiment where this is useful or necessary to further discussion.

I have suggested that one guiding principle we would choose is to have social and political arrangements that allow reasonable opportunities enabling us to meet our basic needs. But would we want more? Would we find it reasonable to endorse a global difference principle, or more substantive equality? As I maintain in the next section, a threshold principle is the more compelling choice.

EMPIRICAL EVIDENCE
FOR THE VIEW

A sceptic might complain that such armchair theorizing is all well and good, but what evidence is there that anything like what I suggest would actually be chosen? Why, for instance, would delegates not choose the more demanding difference principle? I am happy to report that there is quite a bit of encouraging evidence to support my claims. The work of Norman Frohlich and Joe Oppenheimer is particularly instructive, and I discuss it next.[10]

Frohlich and Oppenheimer argue that the key to understanding issues of distributive justice is choosing under conditions of impartiality (that is, where one must set aside certain particular interests one actually has that might skew one's judgements about fairness). They designed experiments to set up conditions of impartiality so they could assess what principles would be chosen and how stable these choices are over time. Imperfect information can generate ideal conditions for impartiality to operate, so the experiments were structured so that subjects did not know what was in their immediate self-interest, yet must choose as a group the principle of distributive justice by which they would run their affairs. Frohlich and Oppenheimer (and others) repeated the experiments in different countries to ensure the results were generalizable. They were particularly interested to see whether John Harsanyi's principle of maximizing the average income[11] or Rawls's idea of maximizing the income for the worst off would be chosen. They offered participants four principles, but allowed them also to choose any other they could think of:

1. Maximizing the floor income: "The most just distribution of income is that which maximizes the floor (or lowest) income in the society."
2. Maximizing the average income: "The most just distribution of income is that which maximizes the average income in the society."
3. Maximizing the average with a floor constraint of $: "The most just distribution of income is that which maximizes the average income only after a certain specified minimum income is guaranteed to everyone."

4. Maximizing the average with a range constraint of $: "The most just distribution of income is that which attempts to maximize the average income only after guaranteeing that the difference between the poorest and the richest individuals (i.e., the range of income) in the society is not greater than a specified amount."

Individual subjects then ranked which of these principles they preferred and how confident they felt about their rankings. Those choosing principles in which there is a dollar sign followed by a blank space were asked to fill in the blank.

There were several stages to the experiments, such as checking that participants understood all the principles, appreciated that their selection would determine their income, and that they would be randomly assigned to an income class. The participants also had to deliberate and decide as a group which principle they supported. After the group selection was made, subjects drew chits from a bag to be assigned to an income category (low, middle, or high income). Later in the experiments, they were given the chance to perform income-earning tasks[12] and to have redistributive policies applied to see whether they were able to live with their choices.

Unanimous agreement was reached on a single principle in all cases in which the experiments were run properly. Interestingly, the principles chosen in the experiment do not support either Rawls's or Harsanyi's models. Indeed, there was almost no support for the difference principle (i.e., maximizing the floor income); it was certainly the least popular choice and chosen in only about 1 per cent of cases. By far the most popular choice in all countries was the principle with the guaranteed floor constraint. Around 78 per cent chose the floor constraint principle, 12 per cent chose to maximize the average income, 9 per cent chose the range constraint principle, and 1 per cent chose the difference principle. Overwhelmingly, groups "wanted an income floor to be guaranteed to the worst-off individual. This floor was to act as a

safety net for all individuals. But after this constraint was set, they wished to preserve incentives so as to maximize production and hence average income."

What arguments were used for the floor-constraint principle? In just about all groups, there was a concern that individuals not fall below some minimum level of income, guaranteeing that they have enough to meet their basic needs.[13] But concern was also raised about how to set the floor so that it did not undermine incentives to work. There was also tension expressed between "the desire to preserve entitlements and to ensure that people at the bottom were not too badly off." Overall, three factors dominated the discussion: balancing people's basic needs against entitlements and incentives.

Since there was such a high level of support for a floor-constraint principle, can we say the principle is a fair rule? Frohlich and Oppenheimer check extensively whether various factors may have undermined the execution and design of the experiments. They argue that the subjects are not so homogenous in values or background that the resulting choices simply reflect that homogeneity rather than universal preference. They are particularly concerned to confirm that they are not merely reporting people's antecedent preferences. If that were the case, the experiments would be of little value. They say: "If the groups' choices are to have ethical validity, the answer to the following central question must be positive: Does the structure of the experiments affect the subjects' preferences and choices? . . . Participating in the experiments must have a meaningful impact on the subjects if the experiments are to reveal anything about distributive justice." They go on to show how the experiments did make a difference to participants' views, since their rankings, preferences, and confidence levels all changed significantly during the experiments. In fact,

in 74 percent of the cases some individuals had a preferred principle that differed from the one chosen by the group. It is relevant to these results that

Rawls indicated that a unanimous group decision need not reflect complete agreement among individuals regarding a principle. Rather, it was to reflect a workable political consensus. Our results support that interpretation: the decision is usually the result of political compromise, at least by some of the individuals.

After extensive analysis of the shifts that occurred, they conclude that the changes in preferences and confidence levels constitute clear evidence showing that the learning and decision phases made the relevant difference.

As we see, then, needs matter in considering issues of justice, but even more important is the balance between needs, entitlements, and incentives. People seek to harmonize these three considerations. What we find when we examine the dialogue participants actually had under conditions modelling impartiality is that a balance was sought *and found* among the three central ideas: they could arrive at a reasoned view of the weight to give a commitment to meeting basic needs that does not thwart entitlement or dampen incentives. It is not the case that they cared only about the worst off, nor is it the case that consideration of entitlements and incentives drowned out their appropriate concern with needs. As the empirical evidence shows, concern for needs is strong and robust, all things considered. But, importantly, it is strikingly not the case that, under conditions of impartiality, people want to arrange things so that they concern themselves only with maximizing the position of the worst off. This tells rather dramatically against the difference principle.

To reiterate, the negotiation for a principle of justice is concerned with balancing needs, (just) entitlement, and incentives, rather than making things best for the worst off. Notice also that the principle chosen is a compromise principle—it is not most people's first choice—but the principle is overwhelmingly chosen as a good compromise or balancing principle between competing considerations.

How stable are the choices when people must live with their decisions? Do the high producers feel they are not getting their due when part of what they earn is redistributed to others? What

happens to productivity? Importantly, Frohlich and Oppenheimer found ongoing firm support for the floor constraint principle and, in fact, both confidence in the principle and productivity increased when people experienced the results of having their decisions implemented.

COULD A GLOBAL DIFFERENCE PRINCIPLE BE COEXTENSIVE WITH A NEEDS-BASED MINIMUM FLOOR?

I have argued that in an appropriate cosmopolitan original position, a needs-based minimum floor principle would be chosen, rather than a global difference principle. I offered two central grounds for my view here. First, I presented a theoretical argument as to why we should focus on being well-positioned to meet our needs, if we are in a cosmopolitan original position. Second, I presented relevant empirical evidence that bears out the conclusion of the theoretical argument. What we would and should choose has to take account of how people actually reason under conditions of impartiality and how they are able to live with the decisions they then make. As the experiment showed, the preference for the minimum floor principle shows stability over time; people become more rather than less confident when they have to live with the results of their choices.

Rather than forcing a choice between the two principles, though, there is a way we can see that the choice of a global difference principle and a principle focusing on needs may be coextensive. If we follow the global difference principle and inequalities are arranged such that they are to be maximally in the interests of the worst off over the long term, then the recommendations of the difference principle might converge with those of a needs-based minimum floor principle. Why? Because, presumably, it is strongly in the interests of the worst off to have people's (considered) preferences for the systems governing distribution be quite stable. A system that balances needs, entitlement, and incentives in an appropriate way, in a way people overwhelmingly judge to be fair in conditions modelling impartiality, and in a way they grow increasingly rather than less confident about, strikes me as one that is strongly in the interests of the worst off.

Notes

1. In arguing for what we are all owed as human beings, I argue for what our reasonable expectations of one another should be, especially in situations of ongoing cooperation. The set-up of a normative thought experiment simply aims to make this more vivid to us, but the basic idea can be argued for independently of that framework.

2. The motivation of the parties in the original position is thus a mix of self-interest (as they are instructed to be self-interested) and fairness (they must arrive at a decision about what would be fair). This motivation is different, then, from the typical Rawlsian story. Delegates must reach agreement on a fair basic framework, but I try to highlight how we can show what it is reasonable to expect, by leaning almost entirely on what is prudent (i.e., what rational, self-interested delegates would find of benefit). The original position helps shield them from knowledge of their identity and so helps to harness the power of self-interest. The beauty of appealing later to the experiments of psychologists Frohlich and Oppenheimer is that we do not have to make any assumptions about how the participants are motivated. We simply put them in a situation that suitably models impartiality and we see what they choose.

3. I prefer to have my delegates randomly selected rather than being representatives for a range of reasons having to do with the problematic nature of representation, especially in this context. The notion of representation does, and can do, no real work here.

4. This is Rawls's term, and here it means that whatever decisions are made at this conference will be binding ones. You will have to live with the results knowing this imposes "the strains of commitment." See, for instance, John Rawls, *Justice as Fairness: A Restatement* (Cambridge, Mass.: Belknap, 2001), 103–4.

5. They will also have information about those who dissent from these common views. Notice how this recognition, though seemingly obvious, is decidedly lacking in Rawls's account as discussed in *Law of Peoples*.

6. From now, when I use the phrase "enabled to meet our needs," this is to be understood as including the needs of our dependants and also that provisions

are in place for the permanently or temporarily disabled to be adequately cared for as well. These provisions for disability should be understood to attend all subsequent statements of what the normative thought experiment would yield.

7. Perhaps this also involves that there should be a fitting and proportionate response to certain kinds of benefits received, but nothing crucial in my argument here hangs on this. For an excellent account of reciprocity, see Lawrence Becker, *Reciprocity* (New York: Routledge, 1986).

8. Bernard Boxill, "Global Equality of Opportunity," *Social Philosophy and Policy*, 5 (1987), 143–68.

9. It may be thought that another reason can be found in the fact that many people enjoy being in a cultural community that is composed of like-minded others. This adds significant value to their lives, which cannot be discounted if we are to take people as they actually are. Though this argument goes some way, it does not necessarily get us all the way to a society of *states*, because by this argument we may need to carve up the world rather differently to ensure cultural communities and states correspond better, perhaps leading to some smaller and some larger political units. Perhaps such reorganization would be selected, however, in that reshaping process, we could as well argue for larger regional political units as smaller ones.

10. Norman Frohlich and Joe Oppenheimer, Choosing *Justice: An Experimental Approach to Ethical Theory* (Berkeley, Calif. and Los Angeles, Calif.: University of California Press, 1992).

11. John Harsanyi, "Cardinal Utility in Welfare Economics and the Theory of Risk-taking," *Journal of Political Economy*, 61 (1953), 434–5; and John Harsanyi, "Cardinal Welfare, Individualistic Ethics, and Interpersonal Comparisons of Utility," *Journal of Political Economy*, 63 (1955), 309–21.

12. The tasks consisted of correcting spelling mistakes.

13. Typical of such points were these two sets of comments: (1) "I would like to see that everyone at least has the basic things. After that I don't really care. [If the floor is too low] . . . a lot of people are going to be starving, and they will be without shelter and housing" (Transcripts, 99); (2) "If you have people that are really poor . . . they have a tendency to just stay there because you know there isn't enough nutrition, they can't get an education, and all these kinds of things. But if you put it on a certain minimum, then they have a chance to get out of that situation. They have a chance" (Transcripts, 72).

SARAH SONG

~

I N T R O D U C T I O N

S HELLEY W ILCOX

Born in South Korea, Sarah Song immigrated with her family to the United States at the age of six. Her father originally came to the U.S. as a student, but he soon received a religious-worker visa, which allowed him to sponsor his family. While her parents served various immigrant churches in the Midwest and Northeast, Song attended local public K–12 schools. She went on to earn a B.A. in social studies from Harvard University, an M.Phil in politics from Oxford, and a Ph.D. (with distinction) in political science from Yale. Song is currently Professor of Law and Political Science and Director of the Kadish Center for Morality, Law, and Public Affairs at U.C. Berkeley, where she is the first Korean American woman to receive tenure at the Berkeley Law School and in the Political Science Department. She has been awarded many prizes and distinctions, including fellowships from the Woodrow Wilson National Fellowship Foundation and the American Academy of Arts and Sciences.

Song's work engages democratic theory and feminist theory to explore issues surrounding citizenship, migration, and multiculturalism. Her book *Justice, Gender, and the Politics of Multiculturalism* (2007) examines the challenges of religious and cultural diversity, focusing on the tension between accommodating the cultural rights of minority groups and achieving gender justice within these groups. This book was awarded the 2008 Ralph Bunche Award, which honors the best scholarly work in political science on issues of ethnic and cultural pluralism. *Immigration and Democracy* (2018), from which this excerpt is drawn, addresses some of the most important ethical questions raised by contemporary migration: What moral and political values ought to guide our thinking about migration? Which immigration policies can democratic states legitimately adopt?

Song explores these questions in the context of the so-called open borders debate among philosophers and political theorists. This debate centers on the issue of whether liberal democratic states have a moral right to restrict migration. On one side of the debate, closed borders theorists argue that, with few exceptions, states are morally free to exclude prospective migrants. On the other, open borders advocates insist that a commitment to fundamental liberal democratic values, including freedom and equality, requires states to maintain open borders, welcoming nearly all prospective migrants.

Song stakes out a distinctive, middle-ground position in this polarized debate. In her view, democratic states have a general right to control migration, but this right is presumptive, not absolute. It must be balanced against the moral claims of prospective migrants. When migrants have particularly strong moral claims to admission, these outweigh the right to control migration. In practice, this principle means that states must admit certain categories of prospective migrants, including refugees and the family of current members. States, however, maintain broad discretion over migration; they need not open their borders to all prospective migrants. In Song's words, what justice requires "is neither closed nor open borders but controlled borders and open doors."

To defend her position successfully, Song must provide a credible justification of the state's presumptive right to control migration. According to her, the right is rooted in collective self-determination, the idea that a political community ought to able to determine the terms of its common life—that is, that a people (or nation) should be self-governing. In the current international context, peoples exercise self-determination through the states they have authorized to act on their behalf. Since collective self-determination is widely regarded as a fundamental right, Song's argument provides a compelling justification of the right to control migration, provided that the connection between collective self-determination and migration control can be established.

Song regards the right to control migration as essential to collective self-determination in two respects. The first pertains to the effects of immigration on receiving societies. Specifically, immigration can negatively impact various collective goods, as well as the social conditions that enable democratic participation. For instance, some economists claim that increased labor migration depresses the wages and working conditions of domestic workers. Other theorists worry that ethnically diverse migration erodes the social trust necessary for widespread support of social welfare programs. Because the state, on behalf of the people, is charged with protecting these collective goods, and discretionary control over migration is necessary to do so, the right to control migration is essential to self-determination.

This line of argument invites a number of empirical questions. For instance, one might ask whether migration impacts wages across the board or only in certain industries that domestic workers tend to avoid, such as meatpacking and agriculture. We might also wonder whether the cultural changes generated by immigration are rapid and substantial enough to diminish social trust. Such questions expose the limitations of Song's initial argument: it makes the right to control migration contingent upon empirical assumptions that may not hold in all cases.

Song's second argument avoids this problem by offering a deontic justification of the right to control migration. For our purposes, a deontic justification claims that a proposed right is an essential feature of another widely recognized concept or right. According to Song, regardless of the effects of immigration, the right to control migration is a constitutive element of the right to democratic self-determination. States generally need various territorial rights in order to exercise collective self-determination on behalf of their constituents, including the right to territorial jurisdiction and the right to control borders. Moreover, Song argues, the right to control migration is essential to democratic self-determination. Democratic self-governance requires that all members of the political community are able to participate as equals in collective decision-making processes. Given this commitment to equality, decisions about who the people *is* are among the most important decisions that a democratic political community can make. Because policies that specify who is admitted into the territory play an essential role in defining the people, the right to control migration is an essential component of democratic self-determination. Thus, because the democratic state is authorized to exercise self-determination on behalf of the people it represents, the state has a right to control immigration.

It is important to remember that the right to control migration is a presumptive right, not an absolute right. States must balance the interests of members against those of prospective migrants. As we have seen, this means that states must admit prospective migrants who have particularly urgent moral claims to entry, including refugees and family members. This principle also has implications for other aspects of migration policy. For instance, Song argues that temporary worker programs are permissible so long as they include robust rights protections for migrant workers, but exclusions based on race, religion, ethnicity, sexuality, and gender are ruled out. Also, although a state may in principle deport migrants who are present illegally, it must recognize that regardless of immigration status, long-term residents acquire legal rights over time, including the right to membership.

One of the primary strengths of Song's normative approach is that it "takes seriously both the claims of political community and the claims of migrants." In doing so, it accommodates the core moral intuitions underlying both opposing positions in the open borders debate: on the one side, that democratic states should have broad discretion to enact migration policies that serve the national interest, and on the other, and that states must respect the fundamental interests of prospective migrants. As a result, Song's middle-ground position will appeal to thinkers across a broad political spectrum.

A second virtue of Song's theory is its generous understanding of the categories of migrants that states are morally required to admit—namely, refugees and the family members. Whereas the 1951 UN Refugee Convention defines a refugee as a person who is forced to flee her country due to persecution, war, or violence, Song insists anyone whose basic needs can only be met by providing her with safe haven in a new country should qualify as a refugee. She also encourages states to adopt a pluralistic conception of the family, which emphasizes individual autonomy by allowing members to decide for themselves which intimate and personal relationships count as familial. Nonetheless, perhaps the most daunting objections to Song's position charge that it does not take the moral claims of migrants seriously enough. Specifically, open borders theorists claim that justice requires not just bigger open doors but fully open borders.

Song defends her view against these challenges in the selections included in this excerpt. If her arguments are successful, they lend considerable plausibility to her self-determination argument for the state's right to control migration. However, Song's criticisms will be interesting even to readers who ultimately reject her positive position, as they raise powerful objections to the main arguments for open borders, which tend to dominate the philosophical debate on the ethics of migration. Song addresses two lines of open borders argument. The first claims that open borders are necessary to achieve global distributive justice. Like other cosmopolitan arguments, this argument begins with the core principle that all people, regardless of nationality, are morally equal. Open borders advocates interpret this principle as requiring that equal opportunity be extended to all human beings. However, in the current global context, citizens of wealthy countries have vastly different opportunities than citizens of poor countries. Thus, proponents argue, justice requires states to maintain open borders so people are able to access opportunities wherever they are located.

Song contends that the global distributive justice argument for open borders is based on two faulty assumptions: (1) that global justice requires universal equal opportunity, and (2) that global distributive justice entails open borders. Justice does not demand that equal opportunity be applied universally because safeguarding equal opportunity is an associative obligation, not a universal obligation. It aims to prevent discrimination and marginalization *within* a political community, not *among* countries, and it applies only to people who are governed by shared institutions that are able to enforce it.

Song also denies that global distributive justice requires open borders. This is because a general policy of open borders is neither necessary nor sufficient to remedy the forms of global inequality that constitute injustice. Song recognizes several forms of inequality as unjust, including inequalities resulting from historical injustice, domination, and procedural unfairness, as well as those in which some people fall below a minimal standard of decent living while others enjoy an excess of wealth. Consider the latter, for example. For many theorists, global justice requires not eliminating inequality per se, but rather bringing all human beings over a threshold of decent life prospects—that is, alleviating global poverty. Song endorses this view, but she denies that a general policy of open borders is an appropriate strategy for accomplishing it. For one thing, open borders would not benefit the world's poorest people, who lack the knowledge, skills, and financial resources necessary to move to a new country. The emigration of highly skilled workers, such as doctors and engineers, can also harm those who are left behind, especially because the remittances they send home tend to benefit the privileged members of the societies to which they are sent. Given these considerations, Song concludes that other policies, such as development assistance and targeted admissions policies, are more effective remedies to global injustice than open borders.

The second open borders challenge to Song's view claims that justice requires open borders because freedom of international movement is a basic human right. There are several versions of this argument. Some proponents argue that free migration is a basic right in itself. Others claim that the right to freedom of international movement is a logical extension of existing basic rights, including the right to free domestic movement and the right to exit. Still others, most notably libertarians, maintain that the right to migrate is entailed by a commitment to individual freedom of association and contract.

Song contends that the freedom of movement argument is based on two implausible claims: (1) that people have a fundamental interest in free migration, and (2) that this interest is sufficiently weighty to ground a corresponding duty to maintain open borders. Consider, for instance, the first formulation of the argument, which maintains that the right to migrate is a basic human right in itself. To establish this claim, proponents must prove that people have a fundamental human interest in being able to migrate freely. It is widely acknowledged that people have a fundamental interest in securing the necessities of a decent human life, which includes access to the things that give our lives meaning—such as friends, civic associations, religions, occupations, cultural activities, and life partners. Advocates of open borders argue that in order to access the full range of these valuable options, people need the right to migrate to the countries of their choosing. Song, however, points out that free domestic movement is usually sufficient to guarantee access to an adequate range of options, and in such cases, the interest in free migration, though significant, does not warrant protection as a basic human right. Of course, the ability to migrate does constitute a fundamental interest for those people who lack access to basic necessities in their home country. However, this fact merely establishes that the freedom of international movement is a remedial moral right and not, as proponents claim, a basic human right.

Some theorists attempt to avoid this objection by arguing that free migration is itself a fundamental human interest, regardless of its usefulness for accessing other valuable options. In their view, people have a fundamental interest in being able to move wherever they want as long as they do not violate the rights of others. However, Song again has a ready rejoinder: even if free migration were a fundamental human interest, this fact alone does not entail a general duty to maintain open borders. To establish that a proposed right entails a duty, proponents must show that the interest that the right is designed to protect is strong enough to outweigh countervailing considerations. Thus, to establish that states have a duty to maintain open borders, advocates must show that prospective migrants' interest in free migration outweighs the receiving society's interest in controlling migration. However, this condition is not met in every case. Consider, for instance, the migration of so-called expats from wealthy countries to poorer, less powerful countries. Unrestricted migration of this type may undermine the collective self-determination of destination societies, thereby exacerbating global injustice. Thus, Song concludes, the freedom of movement argument fails to establish that a basic human right to free migration requires states to maintain open borders. In her words, "if there is a right to migrate, it is contextual and depends on its effects not only on migrants but also on sending and receiving countries."

Reviews of *Immigration and Democracy* appear in *Law & Politics Book Review*, *Perspectives in Politics*, *The Political Theory Review* podcast, and *Public Books*. Related articles by Song include "Political Theories of Migration," *Annual Review of Political Science* (2018), pp. 385–402; "The Boundary Problem in Democratic Theory: Why the Demos Should Be Bounded by the State," *International Theory* (2012) volume 4, issue 1, pp. 39–68; "Democracy and Noncitizen Voting Rights," *Citizenship Studies* (2009) volume 13, issue 6, pp. 607–620; and "Majority Norms, Multiculturalism, and Gender Equality," *American Political Science Review* (2005) volume 99, issue 4, pp. 473–489. Influential books on the ethics of immigration include Joseph Carens, *The Ethics of Immigration* (New York: Oxford University Press, 2013), David Miller, *Strangers in Our Midst: The Political Philosophy of Immigration* (Cambridge, Mass.: Harvard University Press, 2016), and Phillip Cole and Christopher Heath Wellman, *Debating the Ethics of Immigration: Is There a Right to Exclude?* (New York: Oxford University Press, 2011).

Immigration and Democracy

DOES JUSTICE REQUIRE OPEN BORDERS?

Until the 1980s political theorists and philosophers had been mostly silent on the issue of immigration. They took for granted that their theories applied in the context of the nation-state. To take one prominent example, Rawls says his theory of justice is "for the basic structure of society conceived for the time being as a closed system isolated from other societies."[1] Rawls was not alone in assuming that the legitimacy of state borders and the obligations of distributive justice were based on political membership. Political theorists and philosophers have increasingly turned their attention to immigration over the last several decades. It is not an exaggeration to say that the open borders position has emerged as the dominant normative position.

The case for open borders begins with the premise that all human beings are morally equal and pursues one of two main lines of argument: equality arguments about the demands of global distributive justice and freedom-based arguments about the right to free movement. This chapter focuses on the distributive justice argument. The next chapter examines freedom-based arguments. This chapter begins by laying out the global distributive justice argument for open borders. I argue that it rests on two faulty assumptions: (1) that global distributive justice requires global equality of opportunity, and (2) that global distributive justice requires open borders. I cast doubt on the coherence and desirability of a global equality of opportunity principle and argue that objections to global inequality are better captured by

concerns about historical injustice, domination, procedural unfairness, and global poverty. Yet an open borders policy is unlikely to provide an adequate remedy to these concerns.

In showing how the leading arguments for open borders fall short, my aim is not to argue for a policy of closed borders. What is required is neither closed nor open borders but controlled borders and open doors. Considerations of global inequality support some degree of openness toward immigration, but this does not establish a right to entirely uncontrolled immigration.

The Global Distributive Justice Argument for Open Borders

The distributive justice argument for open borders is part of a broader conception of global distributive justice that expands the scope of obligations of justice beyond citizens of one state to include all of humanity. . . .

Ensuring equality of opportunity for fellow compatriots is not enough; what is required is *global* equality of opportunity . . . because open borders allow individuals to access opportunities. . . .

One problem with the global equality of opportunity principle is that it presupposes a universal metric for measuring opportunities, ignoring cultural differences between societies in how different opportunities are valued. Perhaps it is more plausible to say that global equality of opportunity requires that people have *equivalent,* not the same, opportunity sets. So the child from rural Mozambique should have an equal chance to attain a senior executive post in a bank somewhere, not necessarily in Switzerland, with the

From Sarah Song, *Immigration and Democracy* (New York: Oxford University Press, 2019). Reprinted by permission of the publisher.

same salary and benefits as a similarly talented and motivated child of a Swiss banker. In order to decide whether the two opportunity sets are equivalent, however, we still need a universal metric or standard of equality that applies globally. We might be able to reach some agreement on certain items that should be included in the global list of equal opportunities, but given the culturally pluralistic understandings of what counts as opportunities, we may run into difficulties in reaching agreement on a globally shared meaning. How can we judge whether a child in Mozambique has better or worse educational opportunities than a child in Switzerland? We can certainly find metrics for making comparisons (literacy, numeracy, etc.), but we encounter another difficulty: how to decide whether it is appropriate to merge specific metrics into more general ones. For example, we might say that people in one country have better educational opportunities but that people in another country have better cultural or leisure opportunities. The valuation of all metrics into more general metrics will vary from society to society, based in part on the community's shared values. The fact of pluralism between societies about what constitutes the relevant metric for a global equality of opportunity principle poses serious, though perhaps not insurmountable, challenges.

A second, more serious problem with the global equality of opportunity principle is that it gives little weight to relationships and group memberships as a source of obligations. For proponents of global equal opportunity, what matters is whether one is a human being, not whether we stand in particular relationships or institutional contexts with others. By contrast, a relational approach to equality holds that distinctive obligations arise out of the particular relationships and group memberships that we have with others. . . .

For example, when we claim that equality of opportunity in education has been denied, we assume that there is a government or some set of institutions that can make and enforce policies that outlaw discrimination in school admissions and ensure that academic standards are applied uniformly across different schools. The problem with the global equal opportunity principle is that there is no global agent responsible for ensuring global equality of opportunity in education. Proponents of open borders might argue that the absence of global governance structures does not undermine the claim that children in Mozambique are entitled to equality of opportunity in education on a level playing field with children in the United States and that leveling the playing field requires allowing children to go to where the opportunities are. But this response misses the relational point that claims of equal opportunity only apply to a group of people governed by shared institutions that have the power and authority to ensure equal opportunity. We lack such institutions at the global level. We need to look to other principles to capture injustices at the global level.

What Is Objectionable about Inequality and Its Relationship to Injustice

Now, one might reject the relational view that we have special obligations by virtue of our particular relationships and memberships and instead endorse the claim made by proponents of global equality of opportunity: because the distribution of citizenship is morally arbitrary, and being born a citizen of a wealthy country is hugely unfair given the enormous inequalities of wealth and opportunity that exist between countries, people should be permitted to migrate to where the opportunities are. This section is intended to speak to nonrelational egalitarians and to relational egalitarians by considering different kinds of inequality and whether they constitute injustice. I consider a diversity of reasons for objecting to inequality and then examine the implications for the global distributive justice argument for open borders. My aim is to cast doubt on the claim that combatting unjust forms of global inequality requires open borders. What follows is by no means intended as an exhaustive list; I focus on what I take to be some leading reasons for objecting to inequality.

Historical Injustice

One circumstance in which we might think global inequalities are unjust is where one country's wealth or poverty is the direct result of conquest, theft, or exploitation by another country. Whether past injustices should be rectified or whether they might be "superseded" are hard questions. Some argue that past injustices per se do not make an existing order unjust; we need to show how past injustices have contributed to injustice that persists into the present day. It is difficult to determine causal responsibility for persisting injustices, and connecting causal responsibility with moral responsibility for remedying ongoing injustices is also difficult. If we can determine who bears remedial responsibility for the injustice, for our task at hand—considering whether global justice requires open borders—we need to ask, Is the appropriate response to historical injustice the provision of global equality of opportunity via open borders or some more narrowly tailored response that more directly addresses the historical injustice and its persisting effects?

Considerations of historical injustice do not offer a clear-cut case for open borders. In the context of immigration, rectification arguments have been made on behalf of particular groups of people who have suffered injustices, not on behalf of everyone who wants to migrate. . . . Such backward-looking remedial arguments offer more compelling responses to what is owed to those harmed by historical injustice than a general policy of open borders, which applies to everyone in the world.

Domination

Another reason why inequality might be objectionable is that it gives some people an unacceptable degree of power over the lives of others. Economic power is an obvious example. Those who have vastly greater resources not only have more materially comfortable lives; they also get to determine what gets produced, how resources get distributed, and so on. The economically powerful have greater control over government and the media, which reinforces their dominant position in the economy. When it comes to relations between countries, when rich countries or powerful corporations interact with much poorer countries, the former set the terms of interaction in their favor. For example, wealthy countries use their power to establish terms of trade, lending, and conventions about the permissible use of military force in ways that favor their interests at the expense of those of developing countries. . . . As with historical injustice, the underlying concern here is not with ensuring equality of opportunity for everyone across the globe but with the violation of the rights of the poor.

What does the domination objection to inequality imply for immigration? A policy of open borders is neither necessary nor sufficient to reduce inequalities of power between countries. Open borders may improve the economic position of those migrants who move from poor to rich countries, but such migration is unlikely to reduce intercountry inequalities of power in any serious way and may even contribute to worsening intercountry inequalities via brain drain, which I discuss later in the chapter. There is a mismatch in the unit of analysis here: if a country as a collective entity is dominated, how is that domination addressed by the migration of individual citizens of that country to other countries? A more radical argument about power would be to call into question the legitimacy of the entire system of states on the grounds that the global order premised on the state system harms much of the world's population in the sense of thwarting their interests, but we would have no need to debate open borders in a world without states.

Furthermore, open borders may exacerbate global economic inequalities, reinforcing domination of already vulnerable individuals. The implicit sociology underlying the open borders position is a benign liberal cosmopolitan scenario: in a world of open borders, it would be people from poor countries migrating to wealthier countries. But a neoliberal scenario seems more likely: wealthy individuals moving across borders in search of beautiful natural landscapes, attractive cultural opportunities, and even better economic opportunities than what they already enjoy. After all, the wealthy have resources that facilitate migration and settlement in other countries, including in poorer countries with attractive landscapes. They can buy up property and take control of economic and political life in those areas. If this were to happen—and proponents of open borders haven't given us reason to think it wouldn't—open borders would reinforce rather than ameliorate the economic vulnerability of people in poor countries.

Procedural Unfairness

Another reason we might be concerned about inequality is that it undermines the fairness of basic social and political institutions. To take a familiar example, great inequality in family income and wealth contributes to inequality in people's prospects of success in the marketplace. The basic idea is that procedural fairness requires equality of starting places. This is weakly egalitarian because even after equal starting positions are provided, large inequalities could result and they would not be objectionable so long as they did not impair a fair process. . . .

What are the implications of the procedural fairness objection to inequality for immigration? Opening borders is not likely to lead to greater procedural fairness in interactions between countries. In the domestic context, one way to try to prevent inequalities of income and wealth from creating unfairness is through regulatory measures, such as employment contracts, inheritance taxes, and campaign finance restrictions. In the international realm, we can insist on the duty of fair dealing among countries, including nonexploitation; the duty to curb the capacity of one country's citizens or corporations to harm or exploit citizens of other states; and doing one's fair share to address common global problems. Since such regulatory measures are unlikely to be enacted on a global scale anytime soon, another

strategy would be one in which richer countries compete with one another, thereby checking each other's power vis-à-vis third parties. Neither strategy depends on opening borders.

Insufficiency

Perhaps the strongest objection to inequality arises from the concern to alleviate human suffering and deprivation. Consider the following facts about global poverty:

- 1.1 billion people lack access to safe drinking water;
- 795 million people (about one in nine people in the world) suffer from chronic undernourishment;
- 2.4 billion people lack access to improved sanitation (flush toilets or latrines with a slab), and 950 million people practice open defecation for lack of other options;
- 1.6 billion people lack adequate shelter.

These facts describe extreme deprivation and provoke a sense of moral urgency, but our motivation to respond is not rooted in opposition to inequality per se. . . . [T]he central concern is to improve the situation of the world's worst off above some threshold. . . . Along these lines, Harry Frankfurt has argued for replacing the concern for equality with a principle of sufficiency: "What is important from the moral point of view is not that everyone should have *the same* but that each should have *enough*. If everyone had enough, it would be of no moral consequence whether some had more than others."[2] On this view, the existence of economic inequality is not in itself objectionable. . . .

My aim is not to argue for the sufficiency principle as the best account of our domestic or global distributive obligations. Instead, my point is that the concern for sufficiency captures the core concern of the global distributive justice argument for open borders: to raise all human beings above some basic level of well-being. . . .

If that is the true concern, then what global justice requires is not a general principle of global equality of opportunity or a general policy of open borders but the wealthiest countries opening their borders to the world's poorest people. I turn now to assessing this claim.

The Limits of Open Borders as a Response to Global Poverty

You might agree that not all global inequalities per se constitute injustice yet nonetheless argue that a policy of open borders is required to alleviate global poverty. Compared with the most advantaged human beings, the level of opportunity enjoyed by the world's least advantaged is far below what justice would allow. So, a global sufficientarian might argue:

1. Global distributive justice requires that the opportunity-level of the least advantaged be raised considerably so that it reaches an adequacy threshold.
2. There is no reasonable prospect for raising the level sufficiently unless a regime of open borders is established.

As I argued earlier, open borders are neither necessary nor sufficient for meeting a strict equality of opportunity principle applied globally. I believe the same is true of meeting the opportunity threshold applied globally. I offer both normative and empirical arguments to cast doubt on the notion that open borders will alleviate global poverty.

First, proponents of open borders assume that open borders will reduce global poverty in part by permitting the poor to migrate to wealthier countries, but empirical studies suggest that it is not the poorest but those who have some financial means and access to human and social capital who are more likely to migrate. . . . The poorest citizens lack the knowledge, skills, and resources necessary to undertake the risks of migrating. Migration is, of course, regulated by the immigration laws of receiving countries, so current flows should not be taken as definitive of who is likely to migrate if borders were opened. But we have good reasons to think that those most likely to migrate would not be the world's poorest people but those who are already more advantaged in terms of skills and resources. . . .

Second, we also need to consider the impact of migration on those who stay behind. The emigration of large groups of skilled individuals is not likely to improve, and may worsen, the position of those who are left behind. Emigrants do send remittances back home, but because the emigrants are typically not from the poorest class, the money they send goes to the more privileged in the poor countries that receive the remittances. Some of these funds may trickle down to assist the poorest members of the sending countries, but the remittances may also reinforce existing inequalities within the sending countries. Remittances aside, those who are left behind would suffer from the departure of their more educated compatriots who possess the skills necessary to demand and build better institutions in their home country. This is the concern that has come to be called the brain-drain problem. Although the negative effects vary by country and by sector, emigration, especially of more productive members of society, is likely to hurt the institutional development of developing countries.

Third, the simple fact of moving to a wealthy country does not ensure that one will get a job. As Rainer Bauböck has argued, the most likely effect is a reduction in wage differentials between sending and receiving countries, but this is an average effect and the side effects of deregulating labor markets may well lead to even greater inequality and no net reduction of poverty worldwide.[3]

Finally, we see how truly limited a policy of open borders targeted at the world's poorest would be when we consider the sheer number of people who are in desperate need. There are 795 million people, about one in nine people, in the world who suffer from chronic undernourishment. Even if hundreds of thousands of them were able to migrate to wealthy countries, mil-lions more would be left in need. The sheer scale of migration that would be necessary to alleviate global poverty through migration gives us reasons to doubt the feasibility of an open borders policy as a primary answer to global poverty. These em-pirical claims about feasibility do not block the normative claim that we *should* accept a policy of open borders as one tool for alleviating global poverty. But . . . such empirical considerations should be brought to bear in reflecting on how to pursue the goal of alleviating global poverty.

. . . I think we should re-channel the norma-tive force of the open borders *argument* by linking it directly to another tool in the broader debate about global distributive justice: development as-sistance. If alleviating global poverty really is the animating concern behind the open borders ar-gument, it is both more desirable and feasible to turn to development assistance aimed at address-ing global poverty rather than opening borders to everyone. Remedying certain forms of injustice will sometimes require targeted admissions poli-cies, as in the case of countries that have contrib-uted to the creation of refugee crises. Otherwise, the global redistribution of resources is a more ef-fective and desirable alternative to open borders. Development assistance can take many forms, including not only money transfers but also as-sistance in building institutions. Money transfers cannot happen without a reliable way of distrib-uting funds to individuals who may not have bank accounts they can access and an environment in which individuals can spend money. What is needed are institutional improvements in build-ing up infrastructure in banking, medicine, and education.

In sum, immigration policy is just one tool—and not the best tool—for discharging our global obligations. The central focus of a theory of global distributive justice should be not on moving people from poorer to richer countries but on improving conditions and opportunities in poorer countries. The global distributive justice argument for open borders points to an important

qualification of the right of states to restrict immi-gration: wealthy states cannot exclude the world's poorest people if they do not do their part to al-leviate global poverty by providing development assistance and through other measures aimed at ensuring a minimally adequate standard of living for all.

IS THERE A RIGHT TO FREE MOVEMENT ACROSS BORDERS?

Residents of Ohio enjoy the right to move to California if they wish. Residents of Ontario or Oaxaca may want to move to California for the same reason. Why shouldn't they be able to? In arguing for freedom of international movement as a basic right, some appeal to international human rights documents. Article 13.1 of the Universal Declaration of Human Rights states, "Everyone has the right to freedom of movement and residence within the borders of each state." Article 12 of the International Covenant on Civil and Political Rights also says: "Everyone lawfully within the territory of a State shall, within that territory, have the right to liberty of movement and freedom to choose his residence"; "Every-one shall be free to leave any country, includ-ing his own"; and "No one shall be arbitrarily deprived of the right to enter his own country." But these international human rights documents restrict the scope of free movement. They refer to the right of free movement of those lawfully *within* a country, the right to *leave* any country, and the right to *enter one's own* country. There is no general right of international freedom of movement under current international law. What about as a matter of morality?

This chapter examines several freedom-based arguments in support of a general moral right to freedom of international movement. The first claims freedom of movement is a fundamen-tal human right in itself. The second adopts a "cantilever" strategy, arguing that freedom of international movement is a logical extension of existing fundamental rights, including the right of domestic free movement and the right to exit one's country. The third argument, developed by libertarians, is that international free movement is necessary to respect individual freedom of association and contract. This chapter shows how these arguments fall short of justifying a general right to free movement across borders.

A Human Right to Migration

The most direct argument for a general right of migration rests on the premise that freedom of movement is a fundamental right in itself. . . . In arguing that we have a human right to immigrate, proponents are really making two claims: first, that people have an interest in immigration that is fundamental to their well-being, and second, that this interest is of sufficient weight to ground a duty on others to respect her right to immigrate.

To assess whether we have a human right to immigrate, we need a theory of human rights that tells us what the purpose and grounds of human rights are. Theories of human rights tend to be grounded on some account of basic human needs or fundamental human interests. The content of human rights is far from settled, but most accounts include a list of basic rights encompassing core human needs necessary for a decent human life. The basic rights included in the key human rights conventions in international law are

> the right to life, the right to security of the person, and the right against torture;
> the right against enslavement;
> the right to resources for subsistence;
> the rights of due process and equality before the law;
> the right to freedom from religious persecution and against at least the more systematic forms of religious discrimination;
> the right to freedom of expression;
> the right to association; and
> the right against persecution and against at least the more systematic forms of discrimination on grounds of ethnicity, race,

gender, and sexual orientation.

The direct argument for a human right to immigrate depends on showing that immigration is necessary for people to live decent lives. . . .

A conception of human rights should reflect general interests that people have, but when it comes to determining the specific form these interests should take, it should take account of what is feasible. Under conditions of moderate scarcity, saying everyone should have access to a full range of options seems radically utopian. . . . What constitutes an adequate range of options is famously difficult to specify, but a good place to start is an account of basic human interests of the sort reflected in the list above.

There are cases in which international migration is necessary for individuals to have their basic interests met, but in many cases, respecting people's freedom to move about *within* their country seems sufficient to protect their basic interests. If one has the right to security, subsistence, and freedom of religion and expression within one's country, international freedom of movement is not required to vindicate these basic interests. There are circumstances in which international migration *is* morally required to meet people's basic interests. The paradigmatic cases involve those fleeing persecution and violence. In such cases, international migration is necessary to secure basic interests, but the right to migrate in such cases derives not from a human right to immigrate. Rather, it is a *remedial right* that is justified by the fact that the person's basic interests cannot be met in the country where she resides because of state persecution or the state's failure to secure an individual's freedom from persecution by third parties.

While the adequacy account is attractive in certain respects, it runs into a serious problem: it restricts not only international migration but also domestic migration. Say a resident of Ohio wants to move to California; but if she has access to an adequate range of options in Ohio, she would not be permitted to migrate across the country. While our interest in having an adequate range of options provides some justification for the right to domestic migration, which many take to be a fundamental right, it does not show why that right should extend across the entire territory of the country. This suggests the need to look elsewhere for the grounds of domestic free movement.

Proponents of the human right to immigrate point to another problem with the adequacy view: it misses the fundamental interest at stake for migrants. As [Joseph] Carens puts it, people have a "vital interest in being able to go where you want to go and do what you want to do, so long as you do not violate anyone else's rights." The vital interest he refers to is "freedom itself."[4] But the appeal to freedom *as such* doesn't get us very far. One person's right to freedom as such comes into conflict with everyone else's freedom as such. A regime of property rights infringes on your freedom as such by preventing you from entering my house uninvited. Sexual harassment law infringes on your freedom as such by regulating your conduct toward your colleagues in the workplace. A plausible theory of rights must be more precise, developing a set of rights that are broadly consistent with one another such that we don't include rights whose exercise would interfere with other rights we regard as fundamental. Freedom of movement is instrumentally valuable: we must move to pursue relationships, engage in religious worship, and pursue educational and job opportunities. Most of the time, domestic freedom of movement is sufficient to exercise these basic freedoms.

This reply will not satisfy those who think freedom of movement is not merely instrumentally valuable but also intrinsically valuable as a constituent of what is good in itself. This intrinsic view is echoed in the 2009 UN Human Development Report's definition of freedom of movement: "people's ability to choose the place they call home is a dimension of human freedom that we refer to as *human mobility*." It is "a dimension of freedom that is part of development— with intrinsic as well as potential instrumental value."[5] Even if we grant the view that freedom of movement has intrinsic value, we would still have to show that the interest in free movement is of sufficient weight to hold others under a duty. To establish that others have a duty to respect my right of free movement, we must compare the strength of the interests protected under the proposed right against the strength of countervailing interests. Whether a right generates a duty depends not only on the basis of that right but also on the absence of conflicting considerations.

In the case of immigration, there are countervailing considerations that support principled constraints on my right of freedom of movement, including your right to bodily integrity and your property rights. Another countervailing consideration is a political community's right of self-determination. To return to the 2009 UN Human Development Report on migration, its authors do not advocate "wholesale liberalization of international mobility" because they "recognize that people at destination places have a right to shape their societies, and that borders are one way in which people delimit the sphere of their obligations to those whom they see as members of their community."[6] . . .

To return to an earlier example, imagine there were open borders between Cuba and the United States with the attendant openness to American economic might. If American billionaires decided that Cuba's natural beauty could be used for unrestricted tourism and started buying up land in Cuba, there is very little . . . that would allow them to be excluded. Given a world characterized by global inequalities of the kinds discussed in chapter 5, unrestricted migration would involve not only the world's less advantaged moving to rich countries but the world's most privileged moving to poor countries. There is the real possibility that unrestricted migration would undermine the ability of members of less-advantaged states from exercising collective self-determination, thereby exacerbating political injustice. If there is a right to migrate, it is contextual and depends on its effects not only on migrants but also on sending and receiving countries.

Let me now turn to the "cantilever" arguments for the moral right of freedom of international movement. These arguments begin with rights we regard as fundamental and argue that international free movement is a logical extension of these rights. There are two consistency claims. The first rests on an analogy between domestic and international free movement. The second rests on an analogy between exit and entry.

From Domestic to International Freedom of Movement?

Some proponents of open borders analogize domestic migration and international migration, arguing that the reasons that support domestic freedom of movement also support international freedom of movement. . . .

What are the grounds of the right to domestic free movement and can they be extended to international free movement? . . .

There are two distinct components of autonomy at stake. The first has to do with the necessity of domestic migration to access an adequate range of options. As discussed above, the force of the personal autonomy interest depends on the circumstances of the individual seeking to migrate. If someone living in Ohio has access to an adequate range of options, then his personal autonomy interest does not justify his claim to migrate to California. The same logic applies to the context of international migration. A citizen of Syria might have a strong personal autonomy interest in migrating, but a citizen of Canada might not. . . . This is because the argument about personal autonomy is strongest for people whose life choices are extremely limited to begin with. The adequate options component of personal autonomy is thus a limited basis for justifying the right to domestic migration, as well as to international migration.

Another component of personal autonomy is freedom from coercion. . . . Liberal democratic governments are justified in coercing their citizens in certain ways. For example, I am justifiably

subject to the traffic laws that forbid me to drive through a red light because, although the law infringes on my freedom, it provides significant benefits to others. But if California were to put armed guards at its borders to prevent Nevadans from entering, we should object unless California could demonstrate a compelling justification for doing so. When governments have imposed restrictions on domestic free movement, they have done so to target particular groups for exclusion and discrimination. Historical examples abound: the Soviet Union's forced resettlement policies of the 1930s and 1940s, Jewish ghettos created by the Third Reich during World War II, the apartheid regime in South Africa, and restrictions on the movement of poor people by state governments in the United States. The right to domestic free movement serves as an important check on state domination of vulnerable minorities within the political community. The right to domestic migration is grounded in a concern to protect citizens against abuses of government power. . . .

This takes us to another value underlying the right to domestic migration in US law, the value of social cohesion. . . . The claim about cohesion is that a country is stronger and more prosperous when its citizens feel they are part of a common cause and regard themselves as one people. The right to domestic migration is important, even for those who already have access to an adequate range of options, because the country is stronger and more cohesive when citizens enjoy freedom of movement within the country. . . .

Carens argues that cohesion is not threatened by international migration because the cohesion of more local communities has not been threatened by permitting domestic free movement.[7] For example, there is freedom of movement between Georgia and New York, and yet they have maintained distinctive communities of character, so why should we think social cohesion in the United States would be threatened by an influx of immigrants from around the world?

It is true that states and localities within the United States have maintained distinctive cultures in spite of widespread movement, but Carens's argument is too quick to assume that the differences between countries are essentially the same as differences between states and localities in the United States. The latter are bound together by a shared set of political and legal institutions that shape the cultural character of the country. If someone from Georgia moves to New York, she will already share with her new co-residents a common language and cultural idioms and practices, such as celebrating many of the same national holidays and watching the same TV shows and sporting events. By contrast, the cultural distance will be much greater for international migrants to the United States, whether they are from Norway or Ethiopia, because they do not have the experience of living under common political institutions and sharing cultural idioms and practices. The nature and degree of cultural differences are empirical questions that require further study, but even if Carens is right that international migrants do not pose greater challenges to social cohesion than domestic migrants do, he still has not succeeded in equating international migration with domestic migration with respect to social cohesion. . . . Thus, his cantilever argument, whether based on extending the value of social cohesion or personal autonomy, falls short of justifying a right to international freedom of movement.

Does the Right of Exit Entail the Right of Entry?

The second argument in the cantilever strategy begins with the premise that people have a moral right to *exit* their countries and extends the same logic to justify the right to *enter* another country. Article 13.2 of the Universal Declaration of Human Rights states, "Everyone has the right to leave any country, including his own, and to return to his country." Article 12 of the International Covenant on Civil and Political Rights upholds a similar right. Both international documents declare a right of *emigration* but are silent on the question of *immigration*. Theorists have argued

that if we accept that individuals have a right to *exit* their native country, we must also accept that they have an unrestricted right to *enter* another country. . . . To assess whether freedom of exit and freedom of entry stand or fall together, let us look more closely at the different normative positions on exit and entry. . . .

There is a structural difference between exit and entry. Exit restrictions involve not only interfering with voluntary acquisition of new forms of personal relationships as entry restrictions do. . . . If someone no longer wishes to be a member, then the state cannot force her to remain. Even if my basic interests are met in the state of which I'm a member, being forced to remain in a political relationship that I want to leave behind violates something morally important. Preventing an individual from exiting the country for the sake of the good of other members of the society fails to adequately respect, in Rawls's words, the separateness of persons. On this view, the right of exit is a strong right, stronger than a right of entry.

Although the right of exit is strong, it is not unconstrained. . . . It may . . . be justifiable to restrict emigration for a limited period of time in order to minimize brain drain from developing countries

What is the right thing to do in response? . . . Temporary restrictions on freedom of exit may . . . be justifiable. As Gillian Brock has argued, prospective migrants themselves should bear some responsibility for remedying the losses caused by their departure. For example, those who have received government funding of tertiary education should be subject to a short period of compulsory service or required to pay back the costs of their education as a condition of exiting their native countries. The principle at work here is reciprocity or fair play. If one's home country has collectively contributed scarce resources toward one's education and training, the beneficiary incurs some obligations to his country, and the country is entitled to claim some compensation from the beneficiary.[8] . . .

The right of exit does not entail an unrestricted right to enter any country of one's choice. There are many rights whose exercise depends on finding cooperative partners with whom to exercise the right. Consider the case of marriage. The right to marry is a right that allows people to marry partners of their choice, but it is not a right to have a partner provided for you. Similarly, the right of exit is a right held by an individual, which grounds a duty on the individual's state of residence not to prevent her from leaving, but the right of exit does not entail a duty on another particular state to let that person in. Of course, if no state is willing to admit the person, then the right of exit cannot be exercised. If states are willing to consider entry applications from people who want to migrate, and if those people get offers from at least one of those states, then the right of exit can meaningfully be exercised. Where a person's basic interests are not protected by the states where they reside, as in the case of refugees, then states with integrative capabilities have an obligation to take in their fair share of refugees. . . In the case of those whose human rights are being met in their home countries, their right of exit must be weighed against the right of states to restrict entry. . . .

An Instrumental Argument from Freedom of Association and Contract

I turn now to consider a third argument for the right of free movement, based on the value of individual freedom of association and contract. . . .

Drawing on Locke, contemporary libertarian philosophers take individuals as having natural rights to acquire and use property. Individual property holders are viewed as forming a social contract for the purpose of protecting their persons and their property. The libertarian state is a voluntary association among consenting property owners. Although neither Locke nor Nozick wrote directly about migration, one can see how a libertarian might interpret the right of freedom of association as including the freedom to invite foreigners onto one's property for some mutually agreed upon enterprise. On such a view, the state

would not be justified in restricting immigration. If the owners of large American farms want to employ workers from Mexico, the US government would have no right to prohibit such a contract. So long as migrant workers do not violate the security and property rights of others, a Nozickean minimal state could not prevent such migration. That would violate individual rights of freedom of association and contract. . . .

Despite . . . efforts at appropriating Locke for libertarian purposes, [t]he libertarian argument fails to justify open borders for several reasons. First, the political community is not merely an aggregation of . . . associations. . . . When American farm owners contract with foreign workers, their contracts presuppose the broader context of the political community, including both the system of laws within which their contracts are made and enforced and the provision of public roads by which the worker travels to his employer. When a foreign worker sets foot on his American employer's property, he not only enters a parcel of private property; he also enters the territorial space of the political community. In other words, the libertarian case for open borders fails to differentiate between the private property rights of individuals and the jurisdictional rights of states.

Second, the scope of freedom of movement need not be unlimited to respect the right of freedom of association. In many cases, ensuring domestic freedom of movement is sufficient for the vindication of basic human interests, including the interest in freedom of association. This is not to suggest that levels of immigration should not be much higher than they currently are in liberal democratic societies, but rather that government restriction of American employers' access to foreign labor does not necessarily constitute a violation of their interest in freedom of association and contract if there are domestic laborers who are able and willing to perform the job.

Finally, it is interesting to note that the value of freedom of association has cut both ways in the immigration debate. It has been marshaled in favor of open borders . . . and in favor of the state's right to exclude. . . . Appealing to the value of freedom of association by itself leaves undetermined whether the right of association of those who want to exclude trumps, or is trumped by, the right of association of those who want to admit new migrants. This suggests that appealing to freedom of association alone cannot help us resolve questions about the scope of freedom of movement.

Notes

1. John Rawls, *A Theory of Justice* (Cambridge, MA: Belknap Press of Harvard University Press, 1971), 8.

2. Harry Frankfurt, "Equality as a Moral Ideal," *Ethics* 98, no. 1 (1987): 21.

3. Rainer Baub6ck, "Citizenship and Free Movement," in *Citizenship, Borders, and Human Needs*, ed. Rogers Smith (PhiladelphiaL University of Pennsylvania Press, 2011), 355.

4. United Nations Development Programme, *Human Development Report 2009*,15.

5. United Nations Development Programme, *Human Development Report 2009*, 17.

6. Shapiro v. Thompson, 394 U.S. 618, 643 (1969) concurring opinion.

7. Joseph H. Carens, "Aliens and Citizens: The Case for Open Borders," *Review of Politics* 49, no. 2 (1987): 266–67.

8. Brock offers other grounds for the emigrant's responsibility to his home country: redress for the creation of disadvantage, thwarting governments' attempts to discharge their duties, thwarting citizens' abilities to support their governments, and duties of loyalty. She suggests these are jointly sufficient to build a case that emigrating citizens bear a duty to compensate for the resulting losses. Gillian Brock, "Part I," in *Debating Brain Drain: May Governments Restrict Emigration?*, ed. Gillian Brock and Michael Blake (Oxford: Oxford University Press, 2015), 65–68.

DOCUMENTS AND ADDRESSES

~

PERICLES

This address was delivered by the Athenian leader Pericles (c. 495–429 BCE) at a funeral ceremony in memory of those soldiers who had died in the Peloponnesian War against Sparta.

Funeral Oration

"Many of those who have spoken here in the past have praised the institution of this speech at the close of our ceremony. It seemed to them a mark of honour to our soldiers who have fallen in war that a speech should be made over them. I do not agree. These men have shown themselves valiant in action, and it would be enough, I think, for their glories to be proclaimed in action, as you have just seen it done at this funeral organized by the state. Our belief in the courage and manliness of so many should not be hazarded on the goodness or badness of one man's speech. Then it is not easy to speak with a proper sense of balance, when a man's listeners find it difficult to believe in the truth of what one is saying. The man who knows the facts and loves the dead may well think that an oration tells less than what he knows and what he would like to hear: others who do not know so much may feel envy for the dead, and think the orator over-praises them, when he speaks of exploits that are beyond their own capacities. Praise of other people is tolerable only up to a certain point, the point where one still believes that one could do oneself some of the things one is hearing about. Once you get beyond this point, you will find people becoming jealous and incredulous.

However, the fact is that this institution was set up and approved by our forefathers, and it is my duty to follow the tradition and do my best to meet the wishes and the expectations of every one of you.

"I shall begin by speaking about our ancestors, since it is only right and proper on such an occasion to pay them the honour of recalling what they did. In this land of ours there have always been the same people living from generation to generation up till now, and they, by their courage and their virtues, have handed it on to us, a free country. They certainly deserve our praise. Even more so do our fathers deserve it. For to the inheritance they had received they added all the empire we have now, and it was not without blood and toil that they handed it down to us of the present generation. And then we ourselves, assembled here today, who are mostly in the prime of life, have, in most directions, added to the power of our empire and have organized our State in such a way that it is perfectly well able to look after itself both in peace and in war.

"I have no wish to make a long speech on subjects familiar to you all: so I shall say nothing about the warlike deeds by which we acquired our power or the battles in which we or our fathers gallantly resisted

From Thucydides, *History of the Peloponnesian War*, translated by Rex Warner, Penguin Group. 1954. Reprinted by permission of the publisher.

our enemies, Greek or foreign. What I want to do is, in the first place, to discuss the spirit in which we faced our trials and also our constitution and the way of life which has made us great. After that I shall speak in praise of the dead, believing that this kind of speech is not inappropriate to the present occasion, and that this whole assembly, of citizens and foreigners, may listen to it with advantage.

"Let me say that our system of government does not copy the institutions of our neighbours. It is more the case of our being a model to others, than of our imitating anyone else. Our constitution is called a democracy because power is in the hands not of a minority but of the whole people. When it is a question of settling private disputes, everyone is equal before the law; when it is a question of putting one person before another in positions of public responsibility, what counts is not membership of a particular class, but the actual ability which the man possesses. No one, so long as he has it in him to be of service to the state, is kept in political obscurity because of poverty. And, just as our political life is free and open, so is our day-to-day life in our relations with each other. We do not get into a state with our next-door neighbour if he enjoys himself in his own way, no do we give him the kind of black looks which, though they do no real harm, still do hurt people's feelings. We are free and tolerant in our private lives; but in public affairs we keep to the law. This is because it commands our deep respect.

"We give our obedience to those whom we put in positions of authority, and we obey the laws themselves, especially those which are for the protection of the oppressed, and those unwritten laws which it is an acknowledged shame to break.

"And here is another point. When our work is over, we are in a position to enjoy all kinds of recreation for our spirits. There are various kinds of contests and sacrifices regularly throughout the year; in our own homes we find a beauty and a good taste which delight us every day and which drive away our cares. Then the greatness of our city brings it about that all the good things from all over the world flow in to us, so that to us it

seems just as natural to enjoy foreign goods as our own local products.

"Then there is a great difference between us and our opponents, in our attitude towards military security. Here are some examples: Our city is open to the world, and we have no periodical deportations in order to prevent people observing or finding out secrets which might be of military advantage to the enemy. This is because we rely, not on secret weapons, but on our own real courage and loyalty. There is a difference, too, in our educational systems. The Spartans, from their earliest boyhood, are submitted to the most laborious training in courage; we pass our lives without all these restrictions, and yet are just as ready to face the same dangers as they are. Here is a proof of this: When the Spartans invade our land, they do not come by themselves, but bring all their allies with them; whereas we, when we launch an attack abroad, do the job by ourselves, and, though fighting on foreign soil, do not often fail to defeat opponents who are fighting for their own hearths and homes. As a matter of fact none of our enemies has ever yet been confronted with our total strength, because we have to divide our attention between our navy and the many missions on which our troops are sent on land. Yet, if our enemies engage a detachment of our forces and defeat it, they give themselves credit for having thrown back our entire army; or, if they lose, they claim that they were beaten by us in full strength. There are certain advantages, I think, in our way of meeting danger voluntarily, with an easy mind, instead of with a laborious training, with natural rather than with state-induced courage. We do not have to spend our time practising to meet sufferings which are still in the future; and when they are actually upon us we show ourselves just as brave as these others who are always in strict training. This is one point in which, I think, our city deserves to be admired. There are also others:

"Our love of what is beautiful does not lead to extravagance; our love of the things of the mind does not make us soft. We regard wealth as something to be properly used, rather than as something to boast about. As for poverty, no one need be ashamed to admit it: the real shame is in not taking practical measures to escape from it. Here each individual is interested not only in his own affairs but in the affairs of the state as well: even those who are mostly occupied with their own business are extremely well-informed on general politics—this is a peculiarity of ours: we do not say that a man who takes no interest in politics is a man who minds his own business; we say that he has no business here at all. We Athenians, in our own persons, take our decisions on policy or submit them to proper discussions: for we do not think that there is an incompatibility between words and deeds; the worst thing is to rush into action before the consequences have been properly debated. And this is another point where we differ from other people. We are capable at the same time of taking risks and of estimating them beforehand. Others are brave out of ignorance; and, when they stop to think, they begin to fear. But the man who can most truly be accounted brave is he who best knows the meaning of what is sweet in life and of what is terrible, and then goes out undeterred to meet what is to come.

"Again, in questions of general good feeling there is a great contrast between us and most other people. We make friends by doing good to others, not by receiving good from them. This makes our friendship all the more reliable, since we want to keep alive the gratitude of those who are in our debt by showing continued goodwill to them: whereas the feelings of one who owes us something lack the same enthusiasm, since he knows that, when he repays our kindness, it will be more like paying back a debt than giving something spontaneously. We are unique in this. When we do kindnesses to others, we do not do them out of any calculations of profit or loss: we do them without afterthought, relying on our free liberality. Taking everything together then, I declare that our city is an education to Greece, and I declare that in my opinion each single one of our citizens, in all the manifold aspects of life, is able to show himself the rightful lord and owner of his own person, and do this,

moreover, with exceptional grace and exceptional versatility. And to show that this is no empty boasting for the present occasion, but real tangible fact, you have only to consider the power which our city possesses and which has been won by those very qualities which I have mentioned. Athens, alone of the states we know, comes to her testing time in a greatness that surpasses what was imagined of her. In her case, and in her case alone, no invading enemy is ashamed at being defeated, and no subject can complain of being governed by people unfit for their responsibilities. Mighty indeed are the marks and monuments of our empire which we have left. Future ages will wonder at us, as the present age wonders at us now. We do not need the praises of a Homer, or of anyone else whose words may delight us for the moment, but whose estimation of facts will fall short of what is really true. For our adventurous spirit has forced an entry into every sea and into every land; and everywhere we have left behind us everlasting memorials of good done to our friends or suffering inflicted on our enemies.

"This, then, is the kind of city for which these men, who could not bear the thought of losing her, nobly fought and nobly died. It is only natural that every one of us who survive them should be willing to undergo hardships in her service. And it was for this reason that I have spoken at such length about our city, because I wanted to make it clear that for us there is more at stake than there is for others who lack our advantages; also I wanted my words of praise for the dead to be set in the bright light of evidence. And now the most important of these words has been spoken. I have sung the praises of our city; but it was the courage and gallantry of these men, and of people like them, which made her splendid. Nor would you find it true in the case of many of the Greeks, as it is true of them, that no words can do more than justice to their deeds.

"To me it seems that the consummation which has overtaken these men shows us the meaning of manliness in its first revelation and in its final proof. Some of them, no doubt, had their faults; but what we ought to remember first is their gallant conduct against the enemy in defence of their native land. They have blotted out evil with good, and done more service to the commonwealth than they ever did harm in their private lives. No one of these men weakened because he wanted to go on enjoying his wealth: no one put off the awful day in the hope that he might live to escape his poverty and grow rich. More to be desired than such things, they chose to check the enemy's pride. This, to them, was a risk most glorious, and they accepted it, willing to strike down the enemy and relinquish everything else. As for success or failure, they left that in the doubtful hands of Hope, and when the reality of battle was before their faces, they put their trust in their own selves. In the fighting, they thought it more honourable to stand their ground and suffer death than to give in and save their lives. So they fled from the reproaches of men, abiding with life and limb the brunt of battle; and, in a small moment of time, the climax of their lives, a culmination of glory, not of fear, were swept away from us.

"So and such they were, these men—worthy of their city. We who remain behind may hope to be spared their fate, but must resolve to keep the same daring spirit against the foe. It is not simply a question of estimating the advantages in theory. I could tell you a long story (and you know it as well as I do) about what is to be gained by beating the enemy back. What I would prefer is that you should fix your eyes every day on the greatness of Athens as she really is, and should fall in love with her. When you realize her greatness, then reflect that what made her great was men with a spirit of adventure, men who knew their duty, men who were ashamed to fall below a certain standard. If they ever failed in an enterprise, they made up their minds that at any rate the city should not find their courage lacking to her, and they gave to her the best contribution that they could. They gave her their lives, to her and to all of us, and for their own selves they won praises that never grow old, the most splendid of sepulchres—not the sepulchre in which their bodies are laid, but where their glory remains eternal in men's minds,

always there on the right occasion to stir others to speech or to action. For famous men have the whole earth as their memorial: it is not only the inscriptions on their graves in their own country that mark them out; no, in foreign lands also, not in any visible form but in people's hearts, their memory abides and grows. It is for you to try to be like them. Make up your minds that happiness depends on being free, and freedom depends on being courageous. Let there be no relaxation in face of the perils of the war. The people who have most excuse for despising death are not the wretched and unfortunate, who have no hope of doing well for themselves, but those who run the risk of a complete reversal in their lives, and who would feel the difference most intensely, if things went wrong for them. Any intelligent man would find a humiliation caused by his own slackness more painful to bear than death, when death comes to him unperceived, in battle, and in the confidence of his patriotism.

"For these reasons I shall not commiserate with those parents of the dead, who are present here. Instead I shall try to comfort them. They are well aware that they have grown up in a world where there are many changes and chances. But this is good fortune—for men to end their lives with honour, as these have done, and for you honourably to lament them: their life was set to a measure where death and happiness went hand in hand. I know that it is difficult to convince you of this. When you see other people happy you will often be reminded of what used to make you happy too. One does not feel sad at not having some good thing which is outside one's experience: real grief is felt at the loss of something which one is used to. All the same, those of you who are of the right age must bear up and take comfort in the thought of having more children. In your own homes these new children will prevent you from brooding over those who are no more, and they will be a help to the city, too, both in filling the empty places, and in assuring her security. For it is impossible for a man to put forward fair and honest views about our affairs if he has not, like everyone else, children whose lives may be at stake. As for those of you who are now too old to have children, I would ask you to count as gain the greater part of your life, in which you have been happy, and remember that what remains is not long, and let your hearts be lifted up at the thought of the fair fame of the dead. One's sense of honour is the only thing that does not grow old, and the last pleasure, when one is worn out with age, is not, as the poet said, making money, but having the respect of one's fellow men.

"As for those of you here who are sons or brothers of the dead, I can see a hard struggle in front of you. Everyone always speaks well of the dead, and, even if you rise to the greatest heights of heroism, it will be a hard thing for you to get the reputation of having come near, let alone equalled, their standard. When one is alive, one is always liable to the jealousy of one's competitors, but when one is out of the way, the honour one receives is sincere and unchallenged.

"Perhaps I should say a word or two on the duties of women to those among you who are now widowed. I can say all I have to say in a short word of advice. Your great glory is not to be inferior to what God has made you, and the greatest glory of a woman is to be least talked about by men, whether they are praising you or criticizing you. I have now, as the law demanded, said what I had to say. For the time being our offerings to the dead have been made, and for the future their children will be supported at the public expense by the city, until they come of age. This is the crown and prize which she offers, both to the dead and to their children, for the ordeals which they have faced. Where the rewards of valour are the greatest, there you will find also the best and bravest spirits among the people. And now, when you have mourned for your dear ones, you must depart."

EDMUND BURKE

These remarks were delivered by Edmund Burke on November 3, 1774, in Bristol, England, where he had just been elected a Member of Parliament.

Speech to the Electors of Bristol

. . . I cannot conclude without saying a word on a topic touched upon by my worthy colleague. I wish that topic had been passed by at a time when I have so little leisure to discuss it. But since he has thought proper to throw it out, I owe you a clear explanation of my poor sentiments on that subject.

He tells you that "the topic of instructions has occasioned much altercation and uneasiness in this city"; and he expresses himself (if I understand him rightly) in favor of the coercive authority of such instructions.

Certainly, Gentlemen, it ought to be the happiness and glory of a representative to live in the strictest union, the closest correspondence, and the most unreserved communication with his constituents. Their wishes ought to have great weight with him; their opinions high respect; their business unremitted attention. It is his duty to sacrifice his repose, his pleasure, his satisfactions, to theirs,—and above all, ever, and in all cases, to prefer their interest to his own.

But his unbiased opinion, his mature judgment, his enlightened conscience, he ought not to sacrifice to you, to any man, or to any set of men living. These he does not derive from your pleasure,—no, nor from the law and the Constitution. They are a trust from Providence, for the abuse of which he is deeply answerable. Your representative owes you, not his industry only, but his judgment; and he betrays, instead of serving you, if he sacrifices it to your opinion.

My worthy colleague says, his will ought to be subservient to yours. If that be all, the thing is innocent. If government were a matter of will upon any side, yours, without question, ought to be superior. But government and legislation are matters of reason and judgment, and not of inclination; and what sort of reason is that in which the determination precedes the discussion, in which one set of men deliberate and another decide, and where those who form the conclusion are perhaps three hundred miles distant from those who hear the arguments?

To deliver an opinion is the right of all men; that of constituents is a weighty and respectable opinion, which a representative ought always to rejoice to hear, and which he ought always most seriously to consider. But *authoritative* instructions, *mandates* issued, which the member is bound blindly and implicitly to obey, to vote, and to argue for, though contrary to the clearest conviction of his judgment and conscience,—these are things utterly unknown to the laws of this land, and which arise from a fundamental mistake of the whole order and tenor of our Constitution.

Parliament is not a *congress* of ambassadors from different and hostile interests, which interests each must maintain, as an agent and advocate, against other agents and advocates; but Parliament is a *deliberate* assembly of *one* nation, with *one* interest, that of the whole—where not local purposes, not local prejudices, ought to guide, but the general good, resulting from the general reason of the whole. You choose a member, indeed; but when you have chosen him, he is not a member of Bristol, but he is a member of *Parliament*. If the local constituent should have an interest or should form an hasty opinion evidently opposite to the real good of the rest of the community, the member for that place ought to be as far as any other from any endeavor to give it effect. I beg pardon for saying so much on this subject; I have been unwillingly drawn into it; but I shall ever use a respectful frankness of communication with you. Your faithful friend, your devoted servant, I shall be to the end of my life: a flatterer you do not wish for. On this point of instructions, however, I think it scarcely possible we ever can have any sort of difference. Perhaps I may give you too much, rather than too little trouble.

From the first hour I was encouraged to court your favor, to this happy day of obtaining it, I have never promised you anything but humble and persevering endeavors to do my duty. The weight of that duty, I confess, makes me tremble; and whoever well considers what it is, of all things in the world, will fly from what has the least likeness to a positive and precipitate engagement. To be a good member of Parliament is, let me tell you, no easy task,—especially at this time, when there is so strong a disposition to run into the perilous extremes of servile compliance or wild popularity. To unite circumspection with vigor is absolutely necessary, but it is extremely difficult. We are now members for a rich commercial *city*; this city, however, is but a part of a rich commercial *nation*, the interests of which are various, multiform, and intricate. We are members for that great nation, which, however, is itself but part of a great *empire*, extended by our virtue and our fortune to the farthest limits of the East and of the West. All these widespread interests must be considered,—must be compared,—must be reconciled, if possible. We are members for a *free* country; and surely we all know that the machine of a free constitution is no simple thing, but as intricate and as delicate as it is valuable. We are members in a great and ancient *monarchy*; and we must preserve religiously the true, legal rights of the sovereign, which form the keystone that binds together the noble and well-constructed arch of our empire and our Constitution. A constitution made up of balanced powers must ever be a critical thing. As such I mean to touch that part of it which comes within my reach. I know my inability, and I wish for support from every quarter.

THE DECLARATION OF INDEPENDENCE

Thomas Jefferson (1743–1826) was the primary author of this foundational statement of American principles.

In Congress, July 4th, 1776
The Unanimous Declaration Of The Thirteen States of America

When in the Course of human events, it becomes necessary for one people to dissolve the political bands which have connected them with another, and to assume among the Powers of the earth, the separate and equal station to which the Laws of Nature and of Nature's God entitle them, a decent respect to the opinions of mankind requires that they should declare the causes which impel them to the separation.

We hold these truths to be self-evident, that all men are created equal, that they are endowed by their Creator with certain unalienable Rights, that among these are Life, Liberty and the pursuit of Happiness. That to secure these rights, Governments are instituted among Men, deriving their just powers from the consent of the governed, That whenever any Form of Government becomes destructive of these ends, it is the Right of the People to alter or to abolish it, and to institute new Government, laying its foundation on such principles and organizing its powers in such form, as to them shall seem most likely to effect their Safety and Happiness. Prudence, indeed, will dictate that Governments long established should not be changed for light and transient causes; and accordingly all experience hath shown, that mankind are more disposed to suffer, while evils are sufferable, than to right themselves by abolishing the forms to which they are accustomed. But when a long train of abuses and usurpations, pursuing invariably the same Object evinces a design to reduce them under absolute Despotism, it is their right, it is their duty, to throw off such Government, and to provide new Guards for their future security.—Such has been the patient sufferance of these Colonies; and such is now the necessity which constrains them to alter their former Systems of Government. The history of the present King of Great Britain is a history of repeated injuries and usurpations, all having in direct object the establishment of an absolute Tyranny over these States. To prove this, let Facts be submitted to a candid world.

He has refused his Assent to Laws, the most wholesome and necessary for the public good.

He has forbidden his Governors to pass Laws of immediate and pressing importance, unless suspended in their operation till his Assent should be obtained; and when so suspended, he has utterly neglected to attend to them.

He has refused to pass other Laws for the accommodation of large districts of people, unless those people would relinquish the right of Representation in the Legislature, a right inestimable to them and formidable to tyrants only.

He has called together legislative bodies at places unusual, uncomfortable, and distant from the depository of their Public Records, for the sole purpose of fatiguing them into compliance with his measures.

He has dissolved Representative Houses repeatedly, for opposing with manly firmness his invasions on the rights of the people.

He has refused for a long time, after such dissolutions, to cause others to be elected; whereby the Legislative Powers, incapable of Annihilation, have returned to the People at large for their exercise; the State remaining in the mean time exposed to all the dangers of invasion from without, and convulsions within.

He has endeavoured to prevent the population of these States; for that purpose obstructing the Laws of Naturalization of Foreigners; refusing to pass others to encourage their migration hither, and raising the conditions of new Appropriations of Lands.

He has obstructed the Administration of Justice, by refusing his Assent to Laws for establishing Judiciary Powers.

He has made Judges dependent on his Will alone, for the tenure of their offices, and the amount and payment of their salaries.

He has erected a multitude of New Offices, and sent hither swarms of Officers to harass our People, and eat out their substance.

He has kept among us, in times of peace, Standing Armies without the Consent of our legislature.

He has affected to render the Military independent of and superior to the Civil Power.

He has combined with others to subject us to a jurisdiction foreign to our constitution, and unacknowledged by our laws; giving his Assent to their acts of pretended legislation:

For quartering large bodies of armed troops among us:

For protecting them, by a mock Trial, from Punishment for any Murders which they should commit on the Inhabitants of these States:

For cutting off our Trade with all parts of the world:

For imposing taxes on us without our Consent:

For depriving us in many cases, of the benefits of Trial by Jury:

For transporting us beyond Seas to be tried for pretended offences:

For abolishing the free System of English Laws in a neighbouring Province, establishing therein an Arbitrary government, and enlarging its Boundaries so as to render it at once an example and fit instrument for introducing the same absolute rule into these Colonies:

For taking away our Charters, abolishing our most valuable Laws, and altering fundamentally the Forms of our Governments:

For suspending our own Legislature, and declaring themselves invested with Power to legislate for us in all cases whatsoever.

He has abdicated Government here, by declaring us out of his Protection and waging War against us.

He has plundered our seas, ravaged our Coasts, burnt our towns, and destroyed the lives of our people.

He is at this time transporting large armies of foreign mercenaries to compleat the works of death, desolation and tyranny, already begun with circumstances of Cruelty & perfidy scarcely paralleled in the most barbarous ages, and totally unworthy the Head of a civilized nation.

He has constrained our fellow Citizens taken Captive on the high Seas to bear Arms against their Country, to become the executioners of their friends and Brethren, or to fall themselves by their Hands.

He has excited domestic insurrections amongst us, and has endeavoured to bring on the inhabitants of our frontiers, the merciless Indian Savages, whose known rule of warfare, is an undistinguished destruction of all ages, sexes and conditions.

In every stage of these Oppressions We have Petitioned for Redress in the most humble terms: Our repeated Petitions have been answered only by repeated injury. A Prince, whose character is thus marked by every act which may define a Tyrant, is unfit to be the ruler of a free People.

Nor have We been wanting in attention to our British brethren. We have warned them from time to time of attempts by their legislature to extend an unwarrantable jurisdiction over us. We have reminded them of the circumstances of our emigration and settlement here. We have appealed to their native justice and magnanimity, and we have conjured them by the ties of our common kindred to disavow these usurpations, which, would inevitably interrupt our connections and correspondence. They too have been deaf to the voice of justice and of consanguinity. We must, therefore, acquiesce in the necessity, which denounces our Separation, and hold them, as we hold the rest of mankind, Enemies in War, in Peace Friends.

We, therefore, the Representatives of the united States of America, in General Congress, Assembled, appealing to the Supreme Judge of the world for the rectitude of our intentions, do, in the Name, and by Authority of the good People of these Colonies, solemnly publish and declare, That these United Colonies are, and of Right ought to be Free and Independent States; that they are Absolved from all Allegiance to the British Crown, and that all political connection between them and the State of Great Britain, is and ought to be totally dissolved; and that as Free and Independent States, they have full Power to levy War, conclude Peace, contract Alliances, establish Commerce, and to do all other Acts and Things which Independent States may of right do. And for the support of this Declaration, with a firm reliance on the Protection of Divine Providence, we mutually pledge to each other our Lives, our Fortunes and our sacred Honor.

John Hancock

New York
William Floyd
Philip Livingston
Francis Lewis
Lewis Morris

New Jersey
Richard Stockton
John Witherspoon
Francis Hopkinson
John Hart
Abraham Clark

Pennsylvania
Robert Morris
Benjamin Rush
Benjamin Franklin
John Morton
George Clymer
James Smith
George Taylor
James Wilson
George Ross

Delaware
Caesar Rodney
George Read
Thomas McKean

Maryland
Samuel Chase
William Paca
Thomas Stone
Charles Carroll of
    Carrollton

Virginia
George Wythe
Richard Henry Lee
Thomas Jefferson
Benjamin Harrison
Thomas Nelson, Jr.
Francis Lightfoot Lee
Carter Braxton

North Carolina
William Hooper
Joseph Hewes
John Penn

South Carolina
Edward Rutledge
Thomas Heyward, Jr.
Thomas Lynch, Jr.
Arthur Middleton

Georgia
Button Gwinnett
Lyman Hall
George Walton

THE CONSTITUTION
OF THE UNITED STATES

The Constitution of the United States was drawn up at the Constitutional Convention in
Philadelphia in 1787 and went into effect in 1789.

We the people of the United States, in Order to form a more perfect Union, establish justice, insure domestic Tranquillity, provide for the common defence, promote the general Welfare, and secure the Blessings of Liberty to ourselves and our Posterity, do ordain and establish this Constitution of the United States of America.

ARTICLE I

Sec. 1. All legislative Powers herein granted shall be vested in a Congress of the United States, which shall consist of a Senate and House of Representatives.

Sec. 2. The House of Representatives shall be composed of Members chosen every second Year by the People of the several States, and the Electors in each State shall have the Qualifications requisite for Electors of the most numerous Branch of the State Legislature.

No Person shall be a Representative who shall not have attained to the Age of twenty five Years, and been seven Years a Citizen of the United States, and who shall not, when elected, be an Inhabitant of that State in which he shall be chosen.

Representatives and direct Taxes shall be apportioned among the several States which may be included within this Union, according to their respective Numbers, which shall be determined by adding to the whole Number of free Persons, including those bound to Service for a Term of Years, and excluding Indians not taxed, three fifths of all other Persons. The

actual Enumeration shall be made within three Years after the first Meeting of the Congress of the United States, and within every subsequent Term of ten Years, in such Manner as they shall by Law direct. The Number of Representatives shall not exceed one for every thirty Thousand, but each State shall have at Least one Representative; and until such enumeration shall be made, the State of New Hampshire shall be entitled to chuse three, Massachusetts eight, Rhode-Island and Providence Plantations one, Connecticut five, New-York six, New Jersey four, Pennsylvania eight, Delaware one, Maryland six, Virginia ten, North Carolina five, South Carolina five, and Georgia three.

When vacancies happen in the Representation from any State, the Executive Authority thereof shall issue Writs of Election to fill such Vacancies.

The House of Representatives shall chuse their Speaker and other Officers; and shall have the sole Power of Impeachment.

Sec. 3. The Senate of the United States shall be composed of two Senators from each State, chosen by the Legislature thereof, for six Years; and each Senator shall have one Vote.

Immediately after they shall be assembled in Consequence of the first Election, they shall be divided as equally as may be into three Classes. The Seats of the Senators of the first Class shall be vacated at the Expiration of the second Year, of the second Class at the Expiration of the fourth Year, and of the third Class at the Expiration of the sixth Year, so that one third may be chosen every second

Year; and if Vacancies happen by Resignation, or otherwise, during the Recess of the Legislature of any State, the Executive thereof may make temporary Appointments until the next Meeting of the Legislature, which shall then fill such Vacancies.

No Person shall be a Senator who shall not have attained to the Age of thirty Years, and been nine Years a Citizen of the United States, and who shall not, when elected, be an Inhabitant of that State for which he shall be chosen.

The Vice President of the Untied States shall be President of the Senate, but shall have no Vote, unless they be equally divided.

The Senate shall chuse their other, Officers, and also a President pro tempore, in the Absence of the Vice President, or when he shall exercise the Office of President of the United States.

The Senate shall have the sole Power to try all Impeachments. When sitting for that Purpose, they shall be on Oath or Affirmation. When the President of the United States is tried, the Chief justice shall preside: And no Person shall be convicted without the Concurrence of two thirds of the Members present.

Judgment in Cases of Impeachment shall not extend further than to removal from Office, and disqualification to hold and enjoy any Office of honor, Trust or Profit under the United States: but the Party convicted shall nevertheless be liable and subject to Indictment, Trial, Judgment and Punishment, according to Law.

Sec. 4. The Times, Places and Manner of holding elections for Senators and Representatives, shall be prescribed in each State by the Legislature thereof; but the Congress may at any time by Law make or alter such Regulations, except as to the Places of Chusing Senators.

The Congress shall assemble at least once in every Year, and such Meeting shall be on the first Monday in December, unless they shall by Law appoint a different Day.

Sec. 5. Each House shall be the Judge of the Elections, Returns and Qualifications of its own Members, and a Majority of each shall constitute a Quorum to do business; but a smaller Number may adjourn from day to day, and may be authorized to compel the Attendance of absent Members, in such Manner, and under such Penalties as each House may provide.

Each House may determine the Rules of its Proceedings, punish its Members for disorderly Behaviour, and with the Concurrence of two thirds, expel a Member.

Each House shall keep a Journal of its Proceedings, and from time to time publish the same, excepting such Parts as may in their judgment require Secrecy; and the Yeas and Nays of the Members of either House on any question shall, at the Desire of one fifth of those Present, be entered on the Journal.

Neither House, during the Session of Congress, shall, without the Consent of the other, adjourn for more than three days, nor to any other Place than that in which the two Houses shall be sitting.

Sec. 6. The Senators and Representatives shall receive a Compensation for their Services, to be ascertained by Law, and paid out of the Treasury of the United States. They shall in all Cases, except Treason, Felony and Breach of the Peace, be privileged from Arrest during their Attendance at the Session of their respective Houses, and in going to and returning from the same; and for any Speech or Debate in either House, they shall not be questioned in any other Place.

No Senator or Representative shall, during the Time for which he was elected, be appointed to any civil Office under the Authority of the United States which shall have been created, or the Emoluments whereof shall have been encreased during such time; and no Person holding any Office under the United States, shall be a Member of either House during his Continuance in Office.

Sec. 7. All Bills for raising Revenue shall originate in the House of Representatives; but the Senate may propose or concur with Amendments as on other Bills.

Every Bill which shall have passed the House of Representatives and the Senate, shall, before it become a Law, be presented to the President of the United States; If he approve he shall sign it, but if not he shall return it, with his Objections to the House in which it shall have originated, who shall enter the Objections at large on their Journal, and proceed to reconsider it. If after such Reconsideration two thirds of that House shall agree to pass the Bill, it shall be sent, together with the Objections, to the other House, by which it shall likewise be reconsidered, and if approved by two thirds of that House, it shall become a Law. But in all such Cases the Votes of both Houses shall be determined by Yeas and Nays, and the Names of the Persons voting for and against the Bill shall be entered on the journal of each House respectively. If any Bill shall not be returned by the President within ten Days (Sundays excepted) after it shall have been presented to him, the Same shall be a Law, in like Manner as if he had signed it, unless the Congress by their Adjournment prevent its Return, in which Case it shall not be a Law.

Every Order, Resolution, or Vote to which the Concurrence of the Senate and House of Representatives may be necessary (except on a question of Adjournment) shall be presented to the President of the United States; and before the Same shall take Effect, shall be approved by him, or being disapproved by him, shall be repassed by two thirds of the Senate and House of Representatives, according to the Rules and Limitations prescribed in the Case of a Bill.

Sec. 8. The Congress shall have Power to lay and collect Taxes, Duties, Imposts and Excises, to pay the Debts and provide for the common Defence and general Welfare of the United States; but all Duties, Imposts and Excises shall be uniform throughout the United States;

To borrow Money on the credit of the United States;

To regulate Commerce with foreign Nations, and among the several States, and with the Indian Tribes;

To establish an uniform Rule of Naturalization, and uniform Laws on the Subject of Bankruptcies throughout the United States;

To coin Money, regulate the Value Thereof, and of foreign Coin, and fix the standard of Weights and Measures;

To provide for the Punishment of counterfeiting the Securities and current Coin of the United States;

To establish Post Offices and post Roads;

To promote the Progress of Science and useful Arts, by securing for limited Times to Authors and Inventors the exclusive Right to their respective Writings and Discoveries;

To constitute Tribunals inferior to the supreme Court;

To define and punish Piracies and Felonies committed on the high Seas, and Offences against the Law of Nations;

To declare War, grant Letters of Marque and Reprisal, and make Rules concerning Captures on Land and Water;

To raise and support Armies, but no Appropriation of Money to that Use shall be for a longer Term than two Years;

To provide and maintain a Navy;

To make Rules for the Government and Regulation of the land and naval Forces;

To provide for calling forth the Militia to execute the Laws of the Union, suppress Insurrections and repel Invasions;

To provide for organizing, arming, and disciplining the Militia, and for governing such Part of them as may be employed in the Service of the United States, reserving to the States respectively, the Appointment of the Officers, and the Authority of training the Militia according to the discipline prescribed by Congress;

To exercise exclusive Legislation in all Cases whatsoever, over such District (not exceeding ten Miles square) as may, by Cession of particular States, and the Acceptance of Congress, become the Seat of the Government of the United States, and to exercise like Authority over all Places purchased by the Consent of the Legislature of the State in which the Same shall be, for the Erection of Forts, Magazines, Arsenals, dock-Yards, and other needful Buildings;—And

To make all Laws which shall be necessary and proper for carrying into Execution the foregoing Powers, and all other Powers vested by this Constitution in the Government of the United States, or in any Department or Officer thereof.

Sec. 9. The Migration or Importation of such Persons as any of the States now existing shall think proper to admit, shall not be prohibited by the Congress prior to the Year one thousand eight hundred and eight, but a Tax or duty may be imposed on such Importation, not exceeding ten dollars for each Person.

The Privilege of the Writ of Habeas Corpus shall not be suspended, unless when in Cases of Rebellion or Invasion the public Safety may require it.

No Bill of Attainder or ex post facto Law shall be passed.

No Capitation, or other direct, Tax shall be laid, unless in Proportion to the Census or Enumeration herein before directed to be taken.

No Tax or Duty shall be laid on Articles exported from any State.

No Preference shall be given by any Regulation of Commerce or Revenue to the Ports of one State over those of another: nor shall Vessels bound to, or from, one State, be obliged to enter, clear, or pay Duties in another.

No Money shall be drawn from the Treasury, but in Consequence of Appropriations made by Law; and a regular Statement and Account of the Receipts and Expenditures of all public Money shall be published from time to time.

No Title of Nobility shall be granted by the United States: And no Person holding any Office of Profit or Trust under them, shall, without the Consent of the Congress, accept of any present, Emolument, Office, or Title, of any kind whatever, from any King, Prince or Foreign State.

Sec. 10. No State shall enter into any Treaty, Alliance, or Confederation; grant Letters of Marque and Reprisal; coin Money; emit Bills of Credit; make any Thing but gold and silver Coin a Tender in Payment of Debts; pass any Bill of Attainder, ex post facto Law, or Law impairing the Obligation of Contracts, or grant any Title of Nobility.

No State shall, without the Consent of the Congress, lay any Imposts or Duties on Imports or Exports, except what may be absolutely necessary for executing its inspection Laws: and the net Produce of all Duties and Imposts, laid by any State on Imports or Exports, shall be for the Use of the Treasury of the United States, and all such Laws shall be subject to the Revision and Controul of the Congress.

No State shall, without the Consent of Congress, lay any Duty of Tonnage, keep Troops, or Ships of War in time of Peace, enter in any Agreement or Compact with another State, or with a foreign Power, or engage in War, unless actually invaded, or in such imminent Danger as will not admit of delay.

ARTICLE II

Sec. 1. The executive Power shall be vested in a President of the United States of America. He shall hold his Office during the Term of four Years, and, together with the Vice President, chosen for the same Term, be elected, as follows.

Each State shall appoint, in such Manner as the Legislature thereof may direct, a Number of Electors, equal to the whole Number of Senators and Representatives to which the State may be entitled in the Congress: but no Senator or Representative, or Person holding an Office of Trust or Profit under the United States, shall be appointed an Elector.

The Electors shall meet in their respective States, and vote by Ballot for two Persons, of whom one at least shall not be an Inhabitant of the same State with themselves. And they shall make a List of all the Persons voted for, and of the Number of Votes for each; which List they shall sign and certify, and transmit sealed to the Seat of the Government of the United States, directed to the President of the Senate. The President of the Senate shall, in the Presence of the Senate and House of Representatives, open all the Certificates, and the Votes shall then be counted. The Person having the greatest Number of Votes shall be the President, if such Number be a Majority of the whole Number of Electors appointed; and if there be more than one who have such Majority, and have an equal Number of Votes, then the House of Representatives shall immediately chuse by Ballot one of them for President; and if no person have a Majority, then from the five highest on the List the said House shall in like Manner chuse the President. But in chusing the President, the Votes shall be taken by States, the Representation from each State having one Vote; A quorum for this Purpose shall consist of a Member or Members from two thirds of the States, and a majority of all the States shall be necessary to a Choice. In every Case, after the Choice of the President, the Person having the greatest Number of Votes of the Electors shall be the Vice President. But if there should remain two or more who have equal Votes, the Senate shall chuse from them by Ballot the Vice President.

The Congress may determine the Time of chusing the Electors, and the Day on which they shall give their Votes; which Day shall be the same throughout the United States.

No Person except a natural born Citizen, or a Citizen of the United States, at the time of the Adoption of this Constitution, shall be eligible to the Office of President; neither shall any Person be eligible to that Office who shall not have attained to the Age of thirty five Years, and been fourteen Years a Resident within the United States.

In Case of the Removal of the President from Office, or of his Death, Resignation, or Inability to discharge the Powers and Duties of the said Office, the Same shall devolve on the Vice President, and the Congress may by law provide for the Case of Removal, Death, Resignation or Inability, both of the President and Vice President, declaring what Officer shall then act as President, and such Office shall act accordingly, until the Disability be removed, or a President shall be elected.

The President shall, at stated Times, receive for his Services, a Compensation, which shall neither be encreased nor diminished during the Period for which he shall have been elected, and he shall not receive within that Period any other Emolument from the United States, or any of them.

Before he enter on the Execution of his Office, he shall take the following Oath or Affirmation:— "I do solemnly swear (or affirm) that I will faithfully execute the Office of President of the United States, and will to the best of my Ability, preserve, protect and defend the Constitution of the United States."

Sec. 2. The President shall be commander in Chief of the Army and Navy of the United States, and of the Militia of the several States, when called into the actual Service of the United States; he may require the Opinion, in writing, of the principal Officer in each of the executive Departments, upon any Subject relating to the Duties of their respective Officers, and he shall have Power to grant Reprieves and Pardons for Offenses against the United States, except in Cases of Impeachment.

He shall have Power, by and with the Advice and Consent of the Senate, to make Treaties, provided two thirds of the Senators present concur; and he shall nominate, and by and with the Advice and Consent of the Senate, shall appoint Ambassadors, other public Ministers and Consuls, Judges of the supreme Court, and all other Officers of the United States, whose Appointments are not herein otherwise provided for, and which shall be established by Law: but the Congress may by Law vest the Appointment of such inferior Officers, as they think proper, in the President alone, in the Courts of Law, or in the Heads of Departments.

The President shall have Power to fill up all Vacancies that may happen during the Recess of the Senate, by granting Commissions which shall expire at the End of their next Session.

Sec. 3. He shall from time to time give to the Congress Information of the State of the Union, and recommend to their consideration such Measures as he shall judge necessary and expedient; he may, on extraordinary Occasion, convene both Houses, or either of them, and in Case of Disagreement between them, with Respect to the Time of Adjournment, he may adjourn them to such Time as he shall think proper; he shall receive Ambassadors and other public Ministers; he shall take Care that the Laws be faithfully executed, and shall Commission all the Officers of the United States.

Sec. 4. The President, Vice President and all civil Officers of the United States, shall be removed from Office on Impeachment for, and Conviction of, Treason, Bribery, or other high Crimes and Misdemeanors.

ARTICLE III

Sec. 1. The judicial Power of the United States, shall be vested in one supreme Court, and in such inferior Courts as the Congress may from time to time ordain and establish. The judges, both of the supreme and inferior Courts, shall hold their Offices during good Behaviour, and shall, at stated Times, receive for their Services, a Compensation, which shall not be diminished during their Continuance in Office.

Sec. 2. The judicial Power shall extend to all Cases, in Law and Equity, arising under this Constitution, the Laws of the United States, and Treaties made, or which shall be made, under their Authority;—to all Cases Affecting Ambassadors, other public Ministers and Consuls;—to all Cases of admiralty and maritime jurisdiction;—to Controversies to which the United States shall be a Party;—to Controversies between two or more States;—between a State and Citizens of another State;—between Citizens of different States;—between

Citizens of the same State claiming Lands under Grants of different States, and between a State, or the citizens thereof, and foreign States, Citizens or Subjects.

In all Cases affecting Ambassadors, other public Ministers and Consuls, and those in which a State shall be Party, the supreme Court shall have original jurisdiction. In all the other cases before mentioned, the supreme Court shall have appellate jurisdiction, both as to Law and Fact, with such Exceptions, and under such Regulations as the Congress shall make.

The Trial of all Crimes, except in Cases of Impeachment, shall be by jury; and such Trial shall be held in the State where the said Crimes shall have been committed; but when not committed within any State, the Trial shall be at such Place or Places as the Congress may by Law have directed.

Sec. 3. Treason against the United States, shall consist only in levying War against them, or in adhering to their Enemies, giving them Aid and Comfort. No Person shall be convicted of Treason unless on the Testimony of two Witnesses to the same overt Act, or on Confession in open Court.

The Congress shall have Power to declare the Punishment of Treason, but no Attainder of Treason shall work Corruption of Blood, or Forfeiture except during the Life of the Person attainted.

ARTICLE IV

Sec. 1. Full Faith and Credit shall be given in each State to the Public Acts, Records, and judicial Proceedings of every other State. And the Congress may by general Laws prescribe the Manner in which such Acts, Records and Proceedings shall be proved, and the Effect thereof.

Sec. 2. The Citizens of each State shall be entitled to all Privileges and Immunities of Citizens in the Several States.

A Person charged in any State with Treason, Felony, or other Crime, who shall flee from justice, and be found in another State, shall on Demand of the executive Authority of the State from which he fled, be delivered up, to be removed to the State having jurisdiction of the Crime.

No Person held to Service or Labour in one State, under the Laws thereof, escaping into another, shall, in Consequence of any Law or Regulation therein, be discharged from such Service or Labour, but shall be delivered up on Claim of the Party to whom such Service or Labour may be due.

Sec. 3. New States may be admitted by the Congress into this Union; but no new States shall be formed or erected within the jurisdiction of any other State; nor any State be formed by the junction of two or more States, or Parts of States, without Consent of the Legislatures of the States concerned as well as of the Congress.

The Congress shall have Power to dispose of and make all needful Rules and Regulations respecting the Territory or other Property belonging to the United States; and nothing in this Constitution shall be so construed as to Prejudice any Claims of the United States, or of any particular State.

Sec. 4. The United States shall guarantee to every State in this Union a Republican Form of Government, and shall protect each of them against Invasion; and on Application of the Legislature, or of the Executive (when the Legislature cannot be convened) against domestic Violence.

ARTICLE V

The Congress, whenever two thirds of both Houses shall deem it necessary, shall propose Amendments to this Constitution, or, on the Application of the Legislatures of two thirds of the several States, shall call a Convention for proposing Amendments, which, in either Case, shall be valid to all Intents and Purposes, as Part of this Constitution, when ratified by the Legislatures of three fourths of the several States, or by Conventions in three fourths thereof, as the one or the other Mode of Ratification may be proposed by the Congress; Provided that no Amendment which may be made prior to the Year One thousand eight hundred and eight shall in any Manner affect the first and fourth Clauses in the Ninth Section of the first Article; and that no State, without its Consent, shall be deprived of its equal Suffrage in the Senate.

ARTICLE VI

All Debts contracted and Engagements entered into, before the Adoption of this Constitution, shall be as valid against the United States under this Constitution, as under the Confederation.

This Constitution, and the Laws of the United States which shall be made in Pursuance thereof; and all Treaties made, or which shall be made, under the Authority of the United States, shall be the supreme Law of the Land; and the judges in every State shall be bound thereby, any Thing in the Constitution or Laws of any State to the Contrary notwithstanding.

The Senators and Representatives before mentioned, and the Members of the several State Legislatures, and all executive and judicial Officers, both of the United States and of the several States, shall be bound by Oath or Affirmation, to support this Constitution; but no religious Test shall ever be required as a Qualification to any Office or public Trust under the United States.

ARTICLE VII

The Ratification of the Conventions of nine States, shall be sufficient for the Establishment of this Constitution between the States so ratifying the Same.

Done in Convention by the Unanimous Consent of the States present the Seventeenth Day of September in the Year of our Lord one thousand seven hundred and Eighty seven and of the Independence of the United States of America the Twelfth. In witness whereof We have hereunto subscribed our Names,

Attest William Jackson Secretary

Delaware
Geo: Read
Gunning Bedford junr
John Dickinson
Richard Bassett
Jaco: Broom

Maryland
James McHenry
Dan of St Thos. Jenifer
Danl Carroll

Virginia
John Blair—
James Madison Jr.

North Carolina
Wm. Blount
Richd. Dobbs Spaight.
Hu Williamson

South Carolina
J. Rutledge
Charles Cotesworth Pinckney
Charles Pinckney
Pierce Butler

Georgia
William Few
Abr Baldwin

Geo: Washington—Presidt.
and deputy from Virginia

New Hampshire
John Langdon
Nicholas Gilman

Massachusetts
Nathaniel Gorham
Rufus King

Connecticut
Wm: Saml. Johnson
Roger Sherman

New York
Alexander Hamilton

New Jersey
Wil: Livingston
David Brearley
Wm. Paterson.
Jona: Dayton

Pennsylvania
B Franklin
Thomas Mifflin
Robt Morris
Geo. Clymer
Thos. FitzSimons
Jared Ingersoll
James Wilson
Gouv. Morris

Articles in Addition to, and Amendment of, the Constitution of the United States of America, proposed by Congress, and ratified by the Legislatures of the several States, pursuant to the fifth Article of the original Constitution.

AMENDMENT I

Congress shall make no law respecting an establishment of religion, or prohibiting the free exercise thereof; or abridging the freedom of speech, or of the press; or the right of the people peaceably to assemble, and to petition the government for a redress of grievances.

AMENDMENT II

A well regulated Militia, being necessary to the Security of a free State, the right of the people to keep and bear Arms, shall not be infringed.

AMENDMENT III

No Soldier shall, in time of peace be quartered in any house, without the consent of the Owner, nor in time of war, but in a manner to be prescribed by law.

AMENDMENT IV

The right of the people to be secure in their persons, houses, papers, and effects, against unreasonable searches and seizures, shall not be violated, and no Warrants shall issue, but upon probable cause, supported by Oath or affirmation, and particularly describing the place to be searched, and the persons or things to be seized.

AMENDMENT V

No person shall be held to answer for a capital, or otherwise infamous crime, unless on a presentment or indictment of a Grand Jury, except in cases arising in the land or naval forces, or in the Militia, when in actual service in time of War or public danger; nor shall any person be subject for the same offence to be twice put in jeopardy of life or limb; nor shall be compelled in any criminal case to be a witness against himself, nor be deprived of life, liberty, or property, without due process of law; nor shall private property be taken for public use, without just compensation.

AMENDMENT VI

In all criminal prosecutions, the accused shall enjoy the right to a speedy and public trial, by an impartial jury of the State and district wherein the crime shall have been committed, which district shall have been previously ascertained by law, and to be informed of the nature and cause of the accusation; to be confronted with the witnesses against him; to have compulsory process for obtaining witnesses in his favor, and to have the Assistance of Counsel for his defence.

AMENDMENT VII

In Suits at common law, where the value in controversy shall exceed twenty dollars, the right of trial by jury shall be preserved, and no fact tried by a jury, shall be otherwise re-examined in any Court of the United States, than according to the rules of the common law.

AMENDMENT VIII

Excessive bail shall not be required, nor excessive fines imposed, nor cruel and unusual punishments inflicted.

AMENDMENT IX

The enumeration in the Constitution, of certain rights, shall not be construed to deny or disparage others retained by the people.

AMENDMENT X

The powers not delegated to the United States by the Constitution, nor prohibited by it to the States, are preserved to the States respectively, or to the people.

AMENDMENT XI

The Judicial power of the United States shall not be construed to extend to any suit in law or equity, commenced or prosecuted against one of the United States by Citizens of another State, or by Citizens or Subjects of any Foreign State.

AMENDMENT XII

The Electors shall meet in their respective states, and vote by ballot for President and Vice-President, one of whom, at least, shall not be an inhabitant of the same state with themselves;

they shall name in their ballots the person voted for as President, and in distinct ballots the person voted for as Vice-President, and they shall make distinct lists of all persons voted for as President, and of all persons voted for as Vice-President, and of the number of votes for each, which lists they shall sign and certify, and transmit sealed to the seat of the government of the United States, directed to the President of the Senate;—The President of the Senate shall, in the presence of the Senate and House of Representatives, open all the certificates and the votes shall then be counted;—The person having the greatest number of votes for President, shall be the President, if such number be a majority of the whole number of Electors appointed; and if no person have such majority, then from the persons having the highest numbers not exceeding three on the list of those voted for as President, the House of Representatives shall choose immediately, by ballot, the President. But in choosing the President the votes shall be taken by states, the representation from each state having one vote; a quorum for this purpose shall consist of a member or members from two-thirds of the states, and a majority of all the states shall be necessary to a choice. And if the House of Representatives shall not choose a President whenever the right of choice shall devolve upon them, before the fourth day of March next following, then the Vice-President shall act as President, as in the case of the death or other constitutional disability of the President.—The person having the greatest number of votes as Vice-President shall be the Vice-President, if such number be a majority of the whole number of Electors appointed, and if no person have a majority, then from the two highest numbers on the list the Senate shall choose the Vice-President; a quorum for the purpose shall consist of two-thirds of the whole number of Senators, and a majority of the whole number shall be necessary to a choice. But no person constitutionally ineligible to the office of President shall be eligible to that of Vice-President of the United States.

AMENDMENT XIII

Sec. 1. Neither slavery nor involuntary servitude, except as a punishment for crime whereof the party shall have been duly convicted, shall exist within the United States, or any place subject to their jurisdiction.

Sec. 2. Congress shall have power to enforce this article by appropriate legislation.

AMENDMENT XIV

Sec. 1. All persons born or naturalized in the United States, and subject to the jurisdiction thereof, are citizens of the United States and of the State wherein they reside. No State shall make or enforce any law which shall abridge the privileges or immunities of citizens of the United States; nor shall any State deprive any person of life, liberty, or property, without due process of law; nor deny to any person within its jurisdiction the equal protection of the laws.

Sec. 2. Representatives shall be apportioned among the several States according to their respective numbers, counting the whole number of persons in each State, excluding Indians not taxed. But when the right to vote at any election for the choice of electors for President and Vice President of the United States, Representatives in Congress, the Executive and Judicial officers of a State, or the members of the Legislature thereof, is denied to any of the male inhabitants of such State, being twenty-one years of age, and citizens of the United States, or in any way abridged, except for participation in rebellion, or other crime, the basis of representation therein shall be reduced in the proportion which the number of such male citizens shall bear to the whole number of male citizens twenty-one years of age in such State.

Sec. 3. No person shall be a Senator or Representative in Congress, or elector of President and Vice President, or hold any office, civil or military, under the United States, or under any State, who, having previously taken an oath, as a member of Congress, or as an officer of the United States, or as a member of any State legislature, or as an executive or judicial officer of any State, to support the Constitution of the United States, shall have engaged in insurrection or rebellion against the same, or given aid or comfort to the enemies thereof. But Congress may by a vote of two-thirds of each House, remove such disability.

Sec. 4. The validity of the public debt of the United States, authorized by law, including debts incurred for payment of pensions and bounties for services in suppressing insurrection or rebellion, shall not be questioned. But neither the United States nor any State shall assume or pay any debt or obligation incurred in aid of insurrection or rebellion against the United States, or any claim for the loss or emancipation of any slave; but all such debts, obligations and claims shall be held illegal and void.

Sec. 5. The Congress shall have power to enforce, by appropriate legislation, provisions of this article.

AMENDMENT XV

Sec. 1. The right of citizens of the United States to vote shall not be denied or abridged by the United States or by any State on account of race, color, or previous condition of servitude.

Sec. 2. The Congress shall have power to enforce this article by appropriate legislation.

AMENDMENT XVI

The Congress shall have power to lay and collect taxes on incomes, from whatever source derived, without apportionment among the several States, and without regard to any census or enumeration.

AMENDMENT XVII

The Senate of the United States shall be composed of two Senators from each State, elected by the people thereof, for six years; and each Senator shall have one vote. The electors in each State shall have the qualifications requisite for electors of the most numerous branch of the State legislatures.

When vacancies happen in the representation of any State in the Senate, the executive authority of such State shall issue writs of election to fill such vacancies: *Provided,* That the legislature of any State may empower the executive thereof to make temporary appointments until the people fill the vacancies by election as the legislature may direct.

This amendment shall not be so construed as to affect the election or term of any Senator chosen before it becomes valid as part of the Constitution.

AMENDMENT XVIII

Sec. 1. After one year from the ratification of this article the manufacture, sale, or transportation of intoxicating liquors within, the importation thereof into, or the exportation thereof from the United States and all territory subject to the jurisdiction thereof for beverage purposes is hereby prohibited.

Sec. 2. The Congress and the several States shall have concurrent power to enforce this article by appropriate legislation.

Sec. 3. This article shall be inoperative unless it shall have been ratified as an amendment to the Constitution by the legislatures of the several States, as provided in the Constitution, within seven years from the date of the submission hereof to the States by the Congress.

AMENDMENT XIX

The right of citizens of the United States to vote shall not be denied or abridged by the United States or by any State on account of sex.

Congress shall have power to enforce this article by appropriate legislation.

AMENDMENT XX

Sec. 1. The terms of the President and Vice President shall end at noon on the 20th day of January, and the terms of Senators and Representatives at noon on the 3d day of January, of the years in which such terms would have ended if this article had not been ratified; and the terms of their successors shall then begin.

Sec. 2. The Congress shall assemble at least once in every year, and such meeting shall begin at noon on the 3d day of January, unless they shall by law appoint a different day.

Sec. 3. If, at the time fixed for the beginning of the term of the President, the President elect shall have died, the Vice President elect shall become President. If a President shall not have been chosen before the time fixed for the beginning of his term, or if the President elect shall have failed to qualify, then the Vice President elect shall act as President until a President shall have qualified; and the Congress may by law provide for the case wherein neither a President elect nor a Vice President elect shall have qualified, declaring who shall then act as President, or the manner in which one who is to act shall be selected, and such person shall act accordingly until a President or Vice President shall have qualified.

Sec. 4. The Congress may by law provide for the case of the death of any of the persons from whom the House of Representatives may choose a President whenever the right of choice shall have devolved upon them, and for the case of the death of any of the persons from whom the Senate may choose a Vice President whenever the right of choice shall have devolved upon them.

Sec. 5. Sections 1 and 2 shall take effect on the 15th day of October following the ratification of this article.

Sec. 6. This article shall be inoperative unless it shall have been ratified as an amendment to the Constitution by the legislatures of three-fourths of the several States within seven years from the date of its submission.

AMENDMENT XXI

Sec. 1. The eighteenth article of amendment to the Constitution of the United States is hereby repealed.

Sec. 2. The transportation or importation into any State, Territory, or possession of the United States for delivery or use therein of intoxicating liquors, in violation of the laws thereof, is hereby prohibited.

Sec. 3. This article shall be inoperative unless it shall have been ratified as an amendment to the Constitution by conventions in the several States, as provided in the Constitution, within seven years from the date of the submission hereof to the States by the Congress.

AMENDMENT XXII

Sec. 1. No person shall be elected to the office of the President more than twice, and no person who has held the office of President, or acted as President, for more than two years of a term to which some other person was elected President shall be elected to the office of the President more than once. But this Article shall not apply to any person holding the office of President when this

Article was proposed by the Congress, and shall not prevent any person who may be holding the office of President, or acting as President during the term within which this Article becomes operative from holding the office of President or acting as President during the remainder of such term.

Sec. 2. This article shall be inoperative unless it shall have been ratified as an amendment to the Constitution by the legislatures of three-fourths of the several States within seven years from the date of its submission to the States by the Congress.

AMENDMENT XXIII

Sec. 1. The District constituting the seat of Government of the United States shall appoint in such manner as the Congress may direct:

A number of electors of President and Vice President equal to the whole number of Senators and Representatives in Congress to which the District would be entitled if it were a State, but in no event more than the least populous State; they shall be in addition to those appointed by the States, but they shall be considered, for the purposes of the election of President and Vice President, to be electors appointed by a State; and they shall meet in the District and perform such duties as provided by the twelfth article of amendment.

Sec. 2. The Congress shall have power to enforce this article by appropriate legislation.

AMENDMENT XXIV

The right of citizens of the United States to vote in any primary or other election for President or Vice President, for electors for President or Vice President, or for Senator or Representative in Congress, shall not be denied or abridged by the United States or any State by reason of failure to pay any poll tax or other tax.

Sec. 2. The Congress shall have power to enforce this article by appropriate legislation.

AMENDMENT XXV

Sec. 1. In case of the removal of the President from office or of his death or resignation, the Vice President shall become President.

Sec. 2. Whenever there is a vacancy in the office of the Vice President, the President shall nominate a Vice President who shall take office upon confirmation by a majority vote of both Houses of Congress.

Sec. 3. Whenever the President transmits to the President pro tempore of the Senate and the Speaker of the House of Representatives his written declaration that he is unable to discharge the powers and duties of his office, and until he transmits to them a written declaration to the contrary, such powers and duties shall be discharged by the Vice President as Acting President.

Sec. 4. Whenever the Vice President and a majority of either the principal officers of the executive departments or of such other body as Congress may by law provide, transmit to the President pro tempore of the Senate and the Speaker of the House of Representatives their written declaration that the President is unable to discharge the powers and duties of his office, the Vice President shall immediately assume the powers and duties of the office as Acting President.

Thereafter, when the President transmits to the President pro tempore of the Senate and the Speaker of the House of Representatives his written declaration that no inability exists, he shall resume the powers and duties of his office unless the Vice President and a majority of either the principal officers of the executive department or of such other body as Congress may by law provide, transmit within four days to the President pro tempore of the Senate and the Speaker of the House of Representatives their written declaration that the President is unable to discharge the powers and duties of his office. Thereupon Congress shall decide the issue, assembling within forty-eight hours for that purpose if not in session. If the Congress, within twenty-one days after receipt of the latter written declaration, or, if Congress is not in session, within twenty-one days after Congress is required to assemble, determines by two-thirds vote of both Houses that the President is unable to discharge the powers and duties of his office, the Vice President shall continue to discharge the same as Acting President; otherwise, the President shall resume the powers and duties of his office.

AMENDMENT XXVI

Sec. 1. The right of citizens of the United States, who are eighteen years of age or older, to vote shall not be denied or abridged by the United States or by any State on account of age.

Sec. 2. The Congress shall have power to enforce this article by appropriate legislation.

AMENDMENT XXVII

No law, varying the compensation for the services of the Senators and Representatives, shall take effect, until an election of Representatives shall have intervened.

THE FEDERALIST PAPERS

In 1787, at the time debate raged as to whether the Constitution should be adopted, Alexander Hamilton (1755–1804), later to become the first United States Secretary of the Treasury, James Madison (1751–1836), later to become the fourth President of the United States, and John Jay (1745–1829), later to become the first Chief Justice of the United States Supreme Court, wrote a series of eighty-five articles for New York newspapers urging adoption of the Constitution. These essays, which were published under the pseudonym "Publius," were eventually collected in book form as The Federalist Papers.

NUMBER 10

Among the numerous advantages promised by a well-constructed Union, none deserves to be more accurately developed than its tendency to break and control the violence of faction. The friend of popular governments never finds himself so much alarmed for their character and fate, as when he contemplates their propensity to this dangerous vice. He will not fail, therefore, to set a due value on any plan which, without violating the principles to which he is attached, provides a proper cure for it. The instability, injustice, and confusion introduced into the public councils, have, in truth, been the mortal diseases under which popular

governments have everywhere perished; as they continue to be the favorite and fruitful topics from which the adversaries to liberty derive their most specious declamations. The valuable improvements made by the American constitutions on the popular models, both ancient and modern, cannot certainly be too much admired; but it would be an unwarrantable partiality, to contend that they have as effectually obviated the danger on this side, as was wished and expected. Complaints are everywhere heard from our most considerate and virtuous citizens, equally the friends of public and private faith, and of public and personal liberty, that our governments are too unstable, that the public good is disregarded in the conflicts of rival parties, and that measures are too often decided, not according to the rules of justice and the rights of the minor party, but by the superior force of an interested and overbearing majority. However anxiously we may wish that these complaints had no foundation, the evidence of known facts will not permit us to deny that they are in some degree true. It will be found, indeed, on a candid review of our situation, that some of the distresses under which we labor have been erroneously charged on the operation of our governments; but it will be found, at the same time, that other causes will not alone account for many of our heaviest misfortunes; and, particularly, for that prevailing and increasing distrust of public engagements, and alarm for private rights, which are echoed from one end of the continent to the other. These must be chiefly, if not wholly, effects of the unsteadiness and injustice with which a factious spirit has tainted our public administrations.

By a faction, I understand a number of citizens, whether amounting to a majority or minority of the whole, who are united and actuated by some common impulse of passion, or of interest, adverse to the rights of other citizens, or to the permanent and aggregate interests of the community.

There are two methods of curing the mischiefs of faction: the one, by removing its causes; the other, by controlling its effects.

There are again two methods of removing the causes of faction: the one, by destroying the liberty which is essential to its existence; the other, by giving to every citizen the same opinions, the same passions, and the same interests.

It could never be more truly said than of the first remedy, that it was worse than the disease. Liberty is to faction what air is to fire, an aliment without which it instantly expires. But it could not be less folly to abolish liberty, which is essential to political life, because it nourishes faction, than it would be to wish the annihilation of air, which is essential to animal life, because it imparts to fire its destructive agency.

The second expedient is as impracticable as the first would be unwise. As long as the reason of man continues fallible, and he is at liberty to exercise it, different opinions will be formed. As long as the connection subsists between his reason and his selflove, his opinions and his passions will have a reciprocal influence on each other; and the former will be objects to which the latter will attach themselves. The diversity in the faculties of men, from which the rights of property originate, is not less an insuperable obstacle to a uniformity of interests. The protection of these faculties is the first object of government. From the protection of different and unequal faculties of acquiring property, the possession of different degrees and kinds of property immediately results; and from the influence of these on the sentiments and views of the respective proprietors, ensues a division of the society into different interests and parties.

The latent causes of faction are thus sown in the nature of man; and we see them everywhere brought into different degrees of activity, according to the different circumstances of civil society. A zeal for different opinions concerning religion, concerning government, and many other points, as well of speculation as of practice; an attachment to different leaders ambitiously contending for pre-eminence and power; or to persons of other descriptions whose fortunes have been interesting to the human passions, have, in turn, divided mankind into parties, inflamed them with mutual animosity, and rendered them much more disposed to vex and oppress each other than to co-operate for their common good. So strong is this propensity of mankind to fall into mutual animosities, that where no substantial occasion presents itself, the most frivolous and fanciful distinctions have been sufficient to kindle their unfriendly passions and excite their most violent conflicts. But the most common and durable source of factions has been the various and unequal distribution of property. Those who hold and those who are without property have ever formed distinct interests in society. Those who are creditors, and those who are debtors, fall under a like discrimination. A landed interest, a manufacturing interest, a mercantile interest, a moneyed interest, with many lesser interests, grow up of necessity in civilized nations, and divide them into different classes, actuated by different sentiments and views. The regulation of these various and interfering interests forms the principal task of modern legislation, and involves the spirit of party and faction in the necessary and ordinary operations of the government.

No man is allowed to be a judge in his own cause, because his interest would certainly bias his judgment, and, not improbably, corrupt his integrity. With equal, nay with greater reason, a body of men are unfit to be both judges and parties at the same time; yet what are many of the most important acts of legislation, but so many judicial determinations, not indeed concerning the rights of single persons, but concerning the rights of large bodies of citizens? And what are the different classes of legislators but advocates and parties to the causes which they determine? Is a law proposed concerning private debts? It is a question to which the creditors are parties on one side and the debtors on the other. Justice ought to hold the balance between them. Yet the parties are, and must be, themselves the judges; and the most numerous party, or, in other words, the most powerful faction must be expected to prevail. Shall domestic manufactures be encouraged, and in what degree, by restrictions on foreign manufactures? are questions which would be differently decided by the landed and the manufacturing classes, and probably by neither with a sole regard to justice and the public good. The apportionment of taxes on the various descriptions of property is an act which seems to require the most exact impartiality; yet there is, perhaps, no legislative act in which greater opportunity and temptation are given to a predominant party to trample on the rules of justice. Every shilling with which they overburden the inferior number, is a shilling saved to their own pockets.

It is in vain to say that enlightened statesmen will be able to adjust these clashing interests, and render them all subservient to the public good. Enlightened statesmen will not always be at the helm. Nor, in many cases, can such an adjustment be made at all without taking into view indirect and remote considerations, which will rarely prevail over the immediate interest which one party may find in disregarding the rights of another or the good of the whole.

The inference to which we are brought is, that the *causes* of faction cannot be removed, and that relief is only to be sought in the means of controlling its *effects*.

If a faction consists of less than a majority, relief is supplied by the republican principle, which enables the majority to defeat its sinister views by regular vote. It may clog the administration, it may convulse the society; but it will be unable to execute and mask its violence under the forms of the Constitution. When a majority is included in a faction, the form of popular government, on the other hand, enables it to sacrifice to its ruling passion or interest both the public good and the rights of other citizens. To secure the public good and private rights against the danger of such a faction, and at the same time to preserve the spirit and the form of popular government, is then the great object to which our inquiries are directed. Let me add that it is the great desideratum by which this form of government can be rescued from the opprobrium under which it has so long labored, and be recommended to the esteem and adoption of mankind.

By what means is this object attainable? Evidently by one of two only. Either the existence of the same passion or interest in a majority at the same time must be prevented, or the majority, having such coexistent passion or interest, must be rendered, by their number and local situation, unable to concert and carry into effect schemes of oppression. If the impulse and the opportunity be suffered to coincide, we well know that neither moral nor religious motives can be relied on as an adequate control. They are not found to be such on the injustice and violence of individuals, and lose their efficacy in proportion to the number combined together, that is, in proportion as their efficacy becomes needful.

From this view of the subject it may be concluded that a pure democracy, by which I mean a society consisting of a small number of citizens, who assemble and administer the government in person, can admit of no cure for the mischiefs of faction. A common passion or interest will, in almost every case, be felt by a majority of the whole: a communication and concert result from the form of government itself; and there is nothing to check the inducements to sacrifice the weaker party or an obnoxious individual. Hence it is that such democracies have ever been spectacles of turbulence and contention; have ever been found incompatible with personal security or the rights of property; and have in general been as short in their lives as they have been violent in their deaths. Theoretic politicians, who have patronized this species of government, have erroneously supposed that by reducing mankind to a perfect equality in their political rights, they would, at the same time, be perfectly equalized and assimilated in their possessions, their opinions, and their passions.

A republic, by which I mean a government in which the scheme of representation takes place, opens a different prospect, and promises the cure for which we are seeking. Let us examine the points in which it varies from pure democracy, and we shall comprehend both the nature of the cure and the efficacy which it must derive from the Union.

The two great points of difference between a democracy and a republic are: first, the delegation of the government, in the latter, to a small number of citizens elected by the rest; secondly, the greater number of citizens, and greater sphere of country, over which the latter may be extended.

The effect of the first difference is, on the one hand, to refine and enlarge the public views, by passing them through the medium of a chosen body of citizens, whose wisdom may best discern the true interest of their country, and whose patriotism and love of justice will be least likely to sacrifice it to temporary or partial considerations. Under such a regulation, it may well happen that the public voice, pronounced by the representatives of the people, will be more consonant to the public good than if pronounced by the people themselves, convened for the purpose. On the other hand, the effect may be inverted. Men of factious tempers, of local prejudices, or of sinister designs, may, by intrigue, by corruption, or by other means, first obtain the suffrages, and then betray the interests, of the people. The question resulting is, whether small or extensive republics are more favorable to the election of proper guardians of the public weal; and it is clearly decided in favor of the latter by two obvious considerations:

In the first place, it is to be remarked that, however small the republic may be, the representatives must be raised to a certain number, in order to guard against the cabals of a few; and that, however large it may be, they must be limited to a certain number, in order to guard against the confusion of a multitude. Hence, the number of representatives in the two cases not being in proportion to that of the two constituents, and being proportionally greater in the small republic, it follows that, if the proportion of fit characters be not less in the large than in the small republic, the former will present a greater option, and consequently a greater probability of a fit choice. In the next place, as each representative will be chosen by a greater number of citizens in the large than in the small republic, it will be more difficult for unworthy candidates to practice with success the vicious arts by which elections are too often carried; and the suffrages of the people being more free, will be more likely to centre in men who possess the most attractive merit and the most diffusive and established characters.

It must be confessed that in this, as in most other cases, there is a mean, on both sides of which inconveniences will be found to lie. By enlarging too much the number of electors, you render the representative too little acquainted with all their local circumstances and lesser interests; as by reducing it too much, you render him unduly attached to these, and too little fit to comprehend and pursue great and national objects. The federal Constitution forms a happy combination in this respect;

the great and aggregate interests being referred to the national, the local and particular to the State legislatures.

The other point of difference is, the greater number of citizens and extent of territory which may be brought within the compass of republican than of democratic government; and it is this circumstance principally which renders factious combinations less to be dreaded in the former than in the latter. The smaller the society, the fewer probably will be the distinct parties and interests composing it; the fewer the distinct parties and interests, the more frequently will a majority be found of the same party; and the smaller the number of individuals composing a majority, and the smaller the compass within which they are placed, the more easily will they concert and execute their plans of oppression. Extend the sphere and you take in a greater variety of parties and interests; you make it less probable that a majority of the whole will have a common motive to invade the rights of other citizens; or if such a common motive exists, it will be more difficult for all who feel it to discover their own strength, and to act in unison with each other. Besides other impediments, it may be remarked that, where there is a consciousness of unjust or dishonorable purposes, communication is always checked by distrust in proportion to the number whose concurrence is necessary.

Hence, it clearly appears, that the same advantage which a republic has over a democracy, in controlling the effects of faction, is enjoyed by a large over a small republic—is enjoyed by the Union over the States composing it. does the advantage consist in the substitution of representatives whose enlightened views and virtuous sentiments render them superior to local prejudices and to schemes of injustice? It will not be denied that the representation of the Union will be most likely to possess these requisite endowments. does it consist in the greater security afforded by a greater variety of parties, against the event of any one party being able to outnumber and oppress the rest? In an equal degree does the increased variety of parties comprised within the Union, increase this security. does it, in fine, consist in the greater obstacles opposed to the concert and accomplishment of the secret wishes of an unjust and interested majority? Here, again, the extent of the Union gives it the most palpable advantage.

The influence of factious leaders may kindle a flame within their particular States, but will be unable to spread a general conflagration through the other States. A religious sect may degenerate into a political faction in a part of the Confederacy; but the variety of sects dispersed over the entire face of it must secure the national councils against any danger from that source. A rage for paper money, for an abolition of debts, for an equal division of property, or for any other improper or wicked project, will be less apt to pervade the whole body of the Union than a particular member of it; in the same proportion as such a malady is more likely to taint a particular county or district, than an entire State.

In the extent and proper structure of the Union, therefore, we behold a republican remedy for the diseases most incident to republican government. And according to the degree of pleasure and pride we feel in being republicans, ought to be our zeal in cherishing the spirit and supporting the character of Federalists.

Publius [Madison]

NUMBER 51

To what expedient, then, shall we finally resort, for maintaining in practice the necessary partition of power among the several departments, as laid down in the Constitution? The only answer that can be given is, that as all these exterior provisions are found to be inadequate the defect must be supplied, by so contriving the interior structure of the government as that its several constituent parts may, by their mutual relations, be the means of keeping each other in their proper places. Without presuming to undertake a full development of this important idea, I will hazard a few general observations, which may perhaps place it in a clearer light, and enable us to form a more correct judgment of the principles and structure of the government planned by the convention.

In order to lay a due foundation for that separate and distinct exercise of the different powers of government, which to a certain extent is admitted on all hands to be essential to the preservation of liberty, it is evident that each department should have a will of its own; and consequently should be so constituted that the members of each should have as little agency as possible in the appointment of the members of the others. Were this principle rigorously adhered to, it would require that all the appointments for the supreme executive, legislative, and judiciary magistracies should be drawn from the same fountain of authority, the people, through channels having no communication whatever with one another. Perhaps such a plan of constructing the several departments would be less difficult in practice than it may in contemplation appear. Some difficulties, however, and some additional expense would attend the execution of it. Some deviations, therefore, from the principle must be admitted. In the constitution of the judiciary department in particular, it might be inexpedient to insist rigorously on the principle: first, because peculiar qualifications being essential in the members, the primary consideration ought to be to select that mode of choice which best secures these qualifications; secondly, because the permanent tenure by which the appointments are held in that department, must soon destroy all sense of dependence on the authority conferring them.

It is equally evident, that the members of each department should be as little dependent as possible on those of the others, for the emoluments annexed to their offices. Were the executive magistrate, or the judges, not independent of the legislature in this particular, their independence in every other would be merely nominal.

But the great security against a gradual concentration of the several powers in the same department,

consists in giving to those who administer each department the necessary constitutional means and personal motives to resist encroachments of the others. The provision for defence must in this, as in all other cases, be made commensurate to the danger of attack. Ambition must be made to counteract ambition. The interest of the man must be connected with the constitutional rights of the place. It may be a reflection on human nature, that such devices should be necessary to control the abuses of government. But what is government itself, but the greatest of all reflections on human nature? If men were angels, no government would be necessary. If angels were to govern men, neither external nor internal controls on government would be necessary. In framing a government which is to be administered by men over men, the great difficulty lies in this: you must first enable the government to control the governed; and in the next place oblige it to control itself. A dependence on the people is, no doubt, the primary control on the government; but experience has taught mankind the necessity of auxiliary precautions.

This policy of supplying, by opposite and rival interests, the defect of better motives, might be traced through the whole system of human affairs, private as well as public. We see it particularly displayed in all the subordinate distributions of power, where the constant aim is to divide and arrange the several offices in such a manner as that each may be a check on the other—that the private interest of every individual may be a sentinel over the public rights. These inventions of prudence cannot be less requisite in the distribution of the supreme powers of the State.

But it is not possible to give to each department an equal power of self-defence. In republican government, the legislative authority necessarily predominates. The remedy for this inconveniency is to divide the legislature into different branches; and to render them, by different modes of election and different principles of action, as little connected with each other as the nature of their common functions and their common dependence on the society will admit. It may even be necessary to guard against dangerous encroachments by still further precautions. As the weight of the legislative authority requires that it should be thus divided, the weakness of the executive may require, on the other hand, that it should be fortified. An absolute negative on the legislature appears, at first view, to be the natural defence with which the executive magistrate should be armed. But perhaps it would be neither altogether safe nor alone sufficient. On ordinary occasions it might not be exerted with the requisite firmness, and on extraordinary occasions it might be perfidiously abused. May not this defect of an absolute negative be supplied by some qualified connection between this weaker department and the weaker branch of the stronger department, by which the latter may be led to support the constitutional rights of the former, without being too much detached from the rights of its own department?

If the principles on which these observations are founded be just, as I persuade myself they are, and they be applied as a criterion to the several State constitutions, and to the federal Constitution, it will be found that if the latter does not perfectly correspond with them, the former are infinitely less able to bear such a test.

There are, moreover, two considerations particularly applicable to the federal system of America, which place that system in a very interesting point of view.

First. In a single republic, all the power surrendered by the people is submitted to the administration of a single government; and the usurpations are guarded against by a division of the government into distinct and separate departments. In the compound republic of America, the power surrendered by the people is first divided between two distinct governments, and then the portion allotted to each subdivided among distinct and separate departments. Hence a double security arises to the rights of the people. The different governments will control each other, at the same time that each will be controlled by itself.

Second. It is of great importance in a republic not only to guard the society against the oppression of its rulers, but to guard one part of the society against the injustice of the other part. different interests necessarily exist in different classes of citizens. If a majority be united by a common interest, the rights of the minority will be insecure. There are but two methods of providing against this evil: the one by creating a will in the community independent of the majority—that is, of the society itself; the other, by comprehending in the society so many separate descriptions of citizens as will render an unjust combination of a majority of the whole very improbable, if not impracticable. The first method prevails in all governments possessing an hereditary or self-appointed authority. This, at best, is but a precarious security; because a power independent of the society may as well espouse the unjust views of the major, as the rightful interests of the minor party, and may possibly be turned against both parties. The second method will be exemplified in the federal republic of the United States. Whilst all authority in it will be derived from and dependent on the society, the society itself will be broken into so many parts, interests and classes of citizens, that the rights of individuals, or of the minority, will be in little danger from interested combinations of the majority. In a free government the security for civil rights must be the same as that for religious rights. It consists in the one case in the multiplicity of interests, and in the other in the multiplicity of sects. The degree of security in both cases will depend on the number of interests and sects; and this may be presumed to depend on the extent of country and number of people comprehended under the same government. This view of the subject must particularly recommend a proper federal system to all the sincere and considerate friends of republican government, since it shows that in exact proportion as the territory of the Union may be formed into more circumscribed Confederacies, or States, oppressive combinations of a majority will be facilitated; the best security, under the republican forms, for the rights of every class of citizens, will be diminished; and consequently the stability and independence of some member of the government, the only other security, must be proportionally increased. Justice is the end of government. It is the end of civil society. It ever has been and ever will be pursued until it be obtained, or until liberty be lost in the pursuit. In a society under the forms of which the stronger faction can readily unite and oppress the weaker, anarchy may as truly be said to reign as in a state of nature, where the weaker individual is not secured against the violence of the stronger; and as, in the latter state, even the stronger individuals are prompted, by the uncertainty of their condition, to submit to a government which may protect the weak as well as themselves; so, in the former state, will the more powerful factions or parties be gradually induced, by a like motive, to wish for a government which will protect all parties, the weaker as well as the more powerful. It can be little doubted that if the State of rhode Island was separated from the Confederacy and left to itself, the insecurity of rights under the popular form of government within such narrow limits would be displayed by such reiterated oppressions of factious majorities that some power altogether independent of the people would soon be called for by the voice of the very factions whose misrule had proved the necessity of it. In the extended republic of the United States, and among the great variety of interests, parties, and sects which it embraces, a coalition of a majority of the whole society could seldom take place on any other principles than those of justice and the general good; whilst there being thus less danger to a minor from the will of a major party, there must be less pretext, also, to provide for the security of the former, by introducing into the government a will not dependent on the latter, or, in other words, a will independent of the society itself. It is no less certain than it is important, notwithstanding the contrary opinions which have been entertained, that the larger the society, provided it lie within a practical sphere, the more duly capable it will be of selfgovernment. And happily for the *republican cause*, the practicable sphere may be carried to a very great extent, by a judicious modification and mixture of the *federal principle*.

Publius [Madison]

THE DECLARATION OF THE RIGHTS OF MAN AND OF THE CITIZEN

The Declaration was adopted August 26, 1789, by the French Constituent Assembly and served as a preamble to the French constitution of 1791.

The representatives of the people of France, formed into a National Assembly, considering that ignorance, neglect, or contempt of human rights, are the sole causes of public misfortunes and corruptions of Government, have resolved to set forth in a solemn declaration, these natural, imprescriptible, and inalienable rights: that this declaration being constantly present to the minds of the members of the body social, they may be for ever kept attentive to their rights and their duties; that the acts of the legislative and executive powers of government, being capable of being every moment compared with the end of political institutions, may be respected; and also, that the future claims

Translated by Thomas Paine.

of the citizens, being directed by simple and incontestable principles, may tend to the maintenance of the Constitution, and the general happiness.

For these reasons, the National Assembly doth recognize and declare, in the presence of the Supreme Being, and with the hope of his blessing and favour, the following *sacred* rights of men and of citizens:

I. Men are born, and always continue, free and equal in respect of their rights. Civil distinctions, therefore, can be founded only on public utility.

II. The end of all political associations, is the preservation of the natural and imprescriptible rights of man; and these rights are liberty, property, security, and resistance of oppression.

III. The nation is essentially the source of all sovereignty; nor can any individual, or any body of men, be entitled to any authority which is not expressly derived from it.

IV. Political liberty consists in the power of doing whatever does not injure another. The exercise of the natural rights of every man, has no other limits than those which are necessary to secure to every *other* man the free exercise of the same rights; and these limits are determinable only by the law.

V. The law ought to prohibit only actions hurtful to society. What is not prohibited by the law, should not be hindered; nor should any one be compelled to that which the law does not require.

VI. The law is an expression of the will of the community. All citizens have a right to concur, either personally, or by their representatives, in its formation. It should be the same to all, whether it protects or punishes; and all being equal in its sight, are equally eligible to all honours, places, and employments, according to their different abilities, without any other distinction than that created by their virtues and talents.

VII. No man should be accused, arrested, or held in confinement, except in cases determined by the law, and according to the forms which it has prescribed. All who promote, solicit, execute, or cause to be executed, arbitrary orders, ought to be punished, and every citizen called upon, or apprehended by virtue of the law, ought immediately to obey, and renders himself culpable by resistance.

VIII. The law ought to impose no other penalties but such as are absolutely and evidently necessary; and no one ought to be punished, but in virtue of a law promulgated before the offence, and legally applied.

IX. Every man being presumed innocent till he has been convicted, whenever his detention becomes indispensable, all rigour to him, more than is necessary to secure his person, ought to be provided against by the law.

X. No man ought to be molested on account of his opinions, not even on account of his *religious* opinions, provided his avowal of them does not disturb the public order established by law.

XI. The unrestrained communication of thoughts and opinions being one of the most precious rights of man, every citizen may speak, write, and publish freely, provided he is responsible for the abuse of this liberty, in cases determined by law.

XII. A public force being necessary to give security to the rights of men and of citizens, that force is instituted for the benefit of the community and not for the particular benefit of the persons to whom it is intrusted.

XIII. A common contribution being necessary for the support of the public force, and for defraying the other expenses of government, it ought to be divided equally among the members of the community, according to their abilities.

XIV. Every citizen has a right, either by himself or his representative, to a free voice in determining the necessity of public contributions, the appropriation of them, and their account, mode of assessment, and duration.

XV. Every community has had a right to demand of all its agents an account of their conduct.

XVI. Every community in which a separation of powers and a security of rights is not provided for, wants a constitution.

XVII. The right to property being inviolable and sacred, no one ought to be deprived of it, except in cases of evident public necessity, legally ascertained, and on condition of a previous just indemnity.

FREDERICK DOUGLASS

Frederick Douglass (1818–1895) was born into slavery, escaped at age twenty, became an abolitionist, then entered a career in journalism, wrote several best-selling autobiographies, and held various government appointments, including consul-general to Haiti. He was also a renowned public speaker, who in 1852 delivered to the Ladies' Anti-Slavery Society of Rochester, New York, this Fourth of July oration.

What to the Slave is the Fourth of July?

Mr. President, Friends and Fellow Citizens:

He who could address this audience without a quailing sensation, has stronger nerves than I have. I do not remember ever to have appeared as a speaker before any assembly more shrinkingly, nor with greater distrust of my ability, than I do this day. A feeling has crept over me, quite unfavorable to the exercise of my limited powers of speech. The task before me is one which requires much previous thought and study for its proper performance. I know that apologies of this sort are generally considered flat and unmeaning. I trust, however, that mine will not be so considered. Should I seem at ease, my appearance would much misrepresent me. The little experience I have had in addressing public meetings, in country school houses, avails me nothing on the present occasion.

The papers and placards say, that I am to deliver a 4th [of] July oration. This certainly, sounds large, and out of the common way, for me. It is true that I have often had the privilege to speak in this beautiful Hall, and to address many who now honor me with their presence. But neither their familiar faces, nor the perfect gage I think I have of Corinthian Hall, seems to free me from embarrassment.

The fact is, ladies and gentlemen, the distance between this platform and the slave plantation, from which I escaped, is considerable—and the difficulties to be overcome in getting from the latter to the former, are by no means slight. That I am here to-day, is, to me, a matter of astonishment as well as of gratitude. You will not, therefore, be surprised, if in what I have to say, I evince no elaborate preparation, nor grace my speech with any high sounding exordium. With little experience and with less learning, I have been able to throw my thoughts hastily and imperfectly together; and trusting to your patient and generous indulgence, I will proceed to lay them before you.

This, for the purpose of this celebration, is the 4th of July. It is the birthday of your National Independence, and of your political freedom. This, to you, is what the Passover was to the emancipated people of God. It carries your minds back to the day, and to the act of your great deliverance; and to the signs, and to the wonders, associated with that act, and that day. This celebration also marks the beginning of another year of your national life; and reminds you that the Republic of America is now 76 years old. I am glad, fellow-citizens, that your nation is so young. Seventy-six years, though a good old age for a man, is but a mere speck in the life of a nation. Three score years and ten is the allotted time for individual men; but nations number their years by thousands. According to this fact, you are, even now only in the beginning of you national career, still lingering in the period of childhood. I repeat, I am glad this is so. There is hope in the thought, and hope is much needed, under the dark clouds which lower above the horizon. The eye of the reformer is met with angry flashes, portending disastrous times; but his heart may well beat lighter at the thought that America is young, and that she is still in the impressible stage of her existence. May he not hope that high lessons of wisdom, of justice and of truth, will yet give direction to her destiny? Were the nation older, the patriot's heart might be sadder, and the reformer's brow heavier. Its future might be shrouded in gloom, and the hope of its prophets go out in sorrow. There is consolation in the thought, that America is young.—Great streams are not easily turned from channels, worn deep in the course of ages. They may sometimes rise in quiet and stately majesty, and inundate the land, refreshing and fertilizing the earth with their mysterious properties. They may also rise in wrath and fury, and bear away, on their angry waves, the accumulated wealth of years of toil and hardship. They, however, gradually flow back to the same old channel, and flow on as serenely as ever. But, while the river may not be turned aside, it may dry up, and leave nothing behind but the withered branch, and the unsightly rock, to howl in the abyss-sweeping wind, the sad tale of departed glory. As with rivers so with nations.

Fellow-citizens, I shall not presume to dwell at length on the associations that cluster about this day. The simple story of it is, that, 76 years ago, the people of this country were British subjects. The style and title of your "sovereign people" (in which you now glory) was not then born. You were under the British Crown. Your fathers esteemed the English Government as the home government; and England as the fatherland. This home government, you know, although a considerable distance from your home, did, in the exercise of its parental prerogatives, impose upon its colonial children, such restraints, burdens and limitations, as, in its mature judgment, it deemed wise, right and proper.

But, your fathers, who had not adopted the fashionable idea of this day, of the infallibility of government, and the absolute character of its acts, presumed to differ from the home government in respect to the wisdom and the justice of some of those burdens and restraints. They went so far in their excitement as to pronounce the measures of government unjust, unreasonable, and oppressive, and altogether such as ought not to be quietly submitted to. I scarcely need say, fellow-citizens, that my opinion of those measures fully accords with that of your fathers. Such a declaration of agreement on my part, would not be worth much to anybody. It would, certainly, prove nothing, as to what part I might have taken, had I lived during the great controversy of 1776. To say *now* that America was right, and England wrong, is exceedingly easy. Everybody can say it; the dastard, not less than the noble brave, can flippantly discant on the tyranny of England towards the American Colonies. It is fashionable to do so; but there was a time when, to pronounce against England, and in favor of the cause of the colonies, tried men's souls. They who did so were accounted in their day, plotters of mischief, agitators and rebels, dangerous men. To side with the right, against the wrong, with the weak against the strong, and with the oppressed against the oppressor! *here* lies the merit, and the one which, of all others, seems unfashionable in our day. The cause of liberty may be stabbed by the men who glory in the deeds of your fathers. But, to proceed.

Feeling themselves harshly and unjustly treated, by the home government, your fathers, like men of honesty, and men of spirit, earnestly sought redress. They petitioned and remonstrated; they did so in a decorous, respectful, and loyal manner. Their conduct was wholly unexceptionable. This, however, did not answer the purpose. They saw themselves treated with sovereign indifference, coldness and scorn. Yet they persevered. They were not the men to look back.

As the sheet anchor takes a firmer hold, when the ship is tossed by the storm, so did the cause of your fathers grow stronger, as it breasted the chilling blasts of kingly displeasure. The greatest and best of British statesmen admitted its justice, and the loftiest eloquence of the British Senate came to its support. But, with that blindness which seems to be the unvarying characteristic of tyrants, since Pharaoh and his hosts were drowned in the Red sea, the British Government persisted in the exactions complained of.

The madness of this course, we believe, is admitted now, even by England; but we fear the lesson is wholly lost on our present rulers.

Oppression makes a wise man mad. Your fathers were wise men, and if they did not go mad, they became restive under this treatment. They felt themselves the victims of grievous wrongs, wholly incurable in their colonial capacity. With brave men there is always a remedy for oppression. Just here, the idea of a total separation of the colonies from the crown was born! It was a startling idea, much more so, than we, at this distance of time, regard it. The timid and the prudent (as has been intimated) of that day, were, of course, shocked and alarmed by it.

Such people lived then, had lived before, and will, probably, ever have a place on this planet; and their course, in respect to any great change, (no matter how great the good to be attained, or the wrong to be redressed by it,) may be calculated with as much precision as can be the course of the stars. They hate all changes, but silver, gold and copper change! Of this sort of change they are always strongly in favor.

These people were called tories in the days of your fathers; and the appellation, probably, conveyed the same idea that is meant by a more modern, though a somewhat less euphonious term, which we often find in our papers, applied to some of our old politicians.

Their opposition to the then dangerous thought was earnest and powerful; but, amid all their terror and affrighted vociferations against it, the alarming and revolutionary idea moved on, and the country with it.

On the 2d of July, 1776, the old Continental Congress, to the dismay of the lovers of ease, and the worshippers of property, clothed that dreadful idea with all the authority of national sanction. They did so in the form of a resolution; and as we seldom hit upon resolutions, drawn up in our day, whose transparency is at all equal to this, it may refresh your minds and help my story if I read it.

Resolved, That these united colonies *are*, and of right, ought to be free and Independent States; that they are absolved from all allegiance to the British Crown; and that all political connection between them and the State of Great Britain *is*, and ought to be, dissolved.

Citizens, your fathers made good that resolution. They succeeded; and to-day you reap the fruits of their success. The freedom gained is yours; and you, therefore, may properly celebrate this anniversary. The 4th of July is the first great fact in your nation's history—the very ring-bolt in the chain of your yet undeveloped destiny.

Pride and patriotism, not less than gratitude, prompt you to celebrate and to hold it in perpetual remembrance. I have said that the Declaration of Independence is the RINGBOLT to the chain of your nation's destiny; so, indeed, I regard it. The principles contained in that instrument are saving principles. Stand by those principles, be true to them on all occasions, in all places, against all foes, and at whatever cost.

From the round top of your ship of state, dark and threatening clouds may be seen. Heavy billows, like mountains in the distance, disclose to the leeward huge forms of flinty rocks! That *bolt* drawn, that *chain* broken, and all is lost. *Cling to this day—cling to it*, and to its principles, with the grasp of a storm-tossed mariner to a spar at midnight.

The coming into being of a nation, in any circumstances, is an interesting event. But, besides general considerations, there were peculiar circumstances which make the advent of this republic an event of special attractiveness.

The whole scene, as I look back to it, was simple, dignified and sublime.

The population of the country, at the time, stood at the insignificant number of three millions. The country was poor in the munitions of war. The population was weak and scattered, and the country a wilderness unsubdued. There were then no means of concert and combination, such as exist now. Neither steam nor lightning had then been reduced to order and discipline. From the Potomac to the Delaware was a journey of many days. Under these, and innumerable other disadvantages, your fathers declared for liberty and independence and triumphed.

Fellow Citizens, I am not wanting in respect for the fathers of this republic. The signers of the Declaration of Independence were brave men. They were great men too—great enough to give fame to a great age. It does not often happen to a nation to raise, at one time, such a number of truly great men. The point from which I am compelled to view them is not, certainly the most favorable; and yet I cannot contemplate their great deeds with less than admiration. They were statesmen, patriots and heroes, and for the good they did, and the principles they contended for, I will unite with you to honor their memory.

They loved their country better than their own private interests; and, though this is not the highest form of human excellence, all will concede that it is a rare virtue, and that when it is exhibited, it ought to command respect. He who will, intelligently, lay down his life for his country, is a man whom it is not in human nature to despise. Your fathers staked their lives, their fortunes, and their sacred honor, on the cause of their country. In their admiration of liberty, they lost sight of all other interests.

They were peace men; but they preferred revolution to peaceful submission to bondage. They were quiet men; but they did not shrink from agitating against oppression. They showed forbearance; but that they knew its limits. They believed in order; but not in the order of tyranny. With them, nothing

was "*settled*" that was not right. With them, justice, liberty and humanity were "*final*;" not slavery and oppression. You may well cherish the memory of such men. They were great in their day and generation. Their solid manhood stands out the more as we contrast it with these degenerate times.

How circumspect, exact and proportionate were all their movements! How unlike the politicians of an hour! Their statesmanship looked beyond the passing moment, and stretched away in strength into the distant future. They seized upon eternal principles, and set a glorious example in their defence. Mark them!

Fully appreciating the hardships to be encountered, firmly believing in the right of their cause, honorably inviting the scrutiny of an onlooking world, reverently appealing to heaven to attest their sincerity, soundly comprehending the solemn responsibility they were about to assume, wisely measuring the terrible odds against them, your fathers, the fathers of this republic, did, most deliberately, under the inspiration of a glorious patriotism, and with a sublime faith in the great principles of justice and freedom, lay deep, the corner-stone *of the* national superstructure, which has risen and still rises in grandeur around you.

Of this fundamental work, this day is the anniversary. Our eyes are met with demonstrations of joyous enthusiasm. Banners and penants wave exultingly on the breeze. The din of business, too, is hushed. Even mammon seems to have quitted his grasp on this day. The ear-piercing fife and the stirring drum unite their accents with the ascending peal of a thousand church bells. Prayers are made, hymns are sung, and sermons are preached in honor of this day; while the quick martial tramp of a great and multitudinous nation, echoed back by all the hills, valleys and mountains of a vast continent, bespeak the occasion one of thrilling and universal interest—a nation's jubilee.

Friends and citizens, I need not enter further into the causes which led to this anniversary. Many of you understand them better than I do. You could instruct me in regard to them. That is a branch of knowledge in which you feel, perhaps, a much deeper interest than your speaker. The causes which led to the separation of the colonies from the British crown have never lacked for a tongue. They have all been taught in your common schools, narrated at your firesides, unfolded from your pulpits, and thundered from your legislative halls, and are as familiar to you as household words. They form the staple of your national poetry and eloquence.

I remember, also, that, as a people, Americans are remarkably familiar with all facts which make in their own favor. This is esteemed by some as a national trait—perhaps a national weakness. It is a fact, that whatever makes for the wealth or for the reputation of Americans, and can be had *cheap!* will be found by Americans. I shall not be charged with slandering Americans, if I say I think the American side of any question may be safely left in American hands.

I leave, therefore, the great deeds of your fathers to other gentlemen whose claim to have been regularly descended will be less likely to be disputed than mine!

THE PRESENT

My business, if I have any here to-day, is with the present. The accepted time with God and his cause is the ever-living now.

> "Trust no future, however pleasant,
> Let the dead past bury its dead;
> Act, act in the living present,
> Heart within, and God overhead."

We have to do with the past only as we can make it useful to the present and to the future. To all inspiring motives, to noble deeds which can be gained from the past, we are welcome. But now is the time, the important time. Your fathers have lived, died, and have done their work, and have done much of it well. You live and must die, and you must do your work. You have no right

to enjoy a child's share in the labor of your fathers, unless your children are to be blest by your labors. You have no right to wear out and waste the hard-earned fame of your fathers to cover your indolence. Sydney Smith tells us that men seldom eulogize the wisdom and virtues of their fathers, but to excuse some folly or wickedness of their own. This truth is not a doubtful one. There are illustrations of it near and remote, ancient and modern. It was fashionable, hundreds of years ago, for the children of Jacob to boast, we have "Abraham to our father," when they had long lost Abraham's faith and spirit. That people contented themselves under the shadow of Abraham's great name, while they repudiated the deeds which made his name great. Need I remind you that a similar thing is being done all over this country to-day? Need I tell you that the Jews are not the only people who built the tombs of the prophets, and garnished the sepulchres of the righteous? Washington could not die till he had broken the chains of his slaves. Yet his monument is built up by the price of human blood, and the traders in the bodies and souls of men, shout— "We have Washington to *our father.*"—Alas! that it should be so; yet so it is.

> "The evil that men do, lives after them,
> The good is oft' interred with their bones."

Fellow-citizens, pardon me, allow me to ask, why am I called upon to speak here to-day? What have I, or those I represent, to do with your national independence? Are the great principles of political freedom and of natural justice, embodied in that Declaration of Independence, extended to us? and am I, therefore, called upon to bring our humble offering to the national altar, and to confess the benefits and express devout gratitude for the blessings resulting from your independence to us?

Would to God, both for your sakes and ours, that an affirmative answer could be truthfully returned to these questions! Then would my task be light, and my burden easy and delightful. For *who* is there so cold, that a nation's sympathy could not warm him? Who so obdurate and dead to the claims of gratitude, that would not thankfully acknowledge such priceless benefits? Who so stolid and selfish, that would not give his voice to swell the hallelujahs of a nation's jubilee, when the chains of servitude had been torn from his limbs? I am not that man. In a case like that, the dumb might eloquently speak, and the "lame man leap as an hart."

But, such is not the state of the case. I say it with a sad sense of the disparity between us. I am not included within the pale of this glorious anniversary! Your high independence only reveals the immeasurable distance between us. The blessings in which you, this day, rejoice, are not enjoyed in common. The rich inheritance of justice, liberty, prosperity and independence, bequeathed by your fathers, is shared by you, not by me. The sunlight that brought life and healing to you, has brought stripes and death to me. This Fourth [of] July is *yours*, not *mine*. *You* may rejoice, *I* must mourn. To drag a man in fetters into the grand illuminated temple of liberty, and call upon him to join you in joyous anthems, were inhuman mockery and sacrilegious irony. Do you mean, citizens, to mock me, by asking me to speak to-day? If so, there is a parallel to your conduct. And let me warn you that it is dangerous to copy the example of a nation whose crimes, towering up to heaven, were thrown down by the breath of the Almighty, burying that nation in irrecoverable ruin! I can to-day take up the plaintive lament of a peeled and woe-smitten people!

"By the rivers of Babylon, there we sat down. Yea! we wept when we remembered Zion. We hanged our harps upon the willows in the midst thereof. For there, they that carried us away captive, required of us a song; and they who wasted us required of us mirth, saying, Sing us one of the songs of Zion. Flow can we sing the Lord's song in a strange land? If I forget thee, O Jerusalem, let my right hand forget her cunning. If I do not remember thee, let my tongue cleave to the roof of my mouth."

Fellow-citizens; above your national, tumultous joy, I hear the mournful wail of millions! whose chains, heavy and grievous yesterday, are, to-day, rendered more intolerable by the jubilee shouts that reach them. If I do forget, if I do not faithfully remember those bleeding children of sorrow this day, "may my right hand forget her cunning, and may my tongue cleave to the roof of my mouth!" To forget them, to pass lightly over their wrongs, and to chime in with the popular theme, would be treason most scandalous and shocking, and would make me a reproach before God and the world. My subject, then, fellow-citizens, is AMERICAN SLAVERY. I shall see, this day, and its popular characteristics, from the slave's point of view. Standing, there, identified with the American bondman, making his wrongs mine, I do not hesitate to declare, with all my soul, that the character and conduct of this nation never looked blacker to me than on this 4th of July! Whether we turn to the declarations of the past, or to the professions of the present, the conduct of the nation seems equally hideous and revolting. America is false to the past, false to the present, and solemnly binds herself to be false to the future. Standing with God and the crushed and bleeding slave on this occasion, I will, in the name of humanity which is outraged, in the name of liberty which is fettered, in the name of the constitution and the Bible, which are disregarded and trampled upon, dare to call in question and to denounce, with all the emphasis I can command, everything that serves to perpetuate slavery—the great sin and shame of America! "I will not equivocate; I will not excuse;" I will use the severest language I can command; and yet not one word shall escape me that any man, whose judgment is not blinded by prejudice, or who is not at heart a slaveholder, shall not confess to be right and just.

But I fancy I hear some one of my audience say, it is just in this circumstance that you and your brother abolitionists fail to make a favorable impression on the public mind. Would you argue more, and denounce less, would you persuade more, and rebuke less, your cause would be much more likely to succeed. But, I submit, where all is plain there is nothing to be argued. What point in the anti-slavery creed would you have me argue? On what branch of the subject do the people of this country need light? Must I undertake to prove that the slave is a man? That point is conceded already. Nobody doubts it. The slave-holders themselves acknowledge it in the enactment of laws for their government. They acknowledge it when they punish disobedience on the part of the slave. There are seventy-two crimes in the State of Virginia, which, if committed by a black man, (no matter how ignorant he be,) subject him to the punishment of death; while only two of the same crimes will subject a white man to the like punishment.—What is this but the acknowledgement that the slave is a moral, intellectual and responsible being. The manhood of the slave is conceded. It is admitted in the fact that Southern statute books are covered with enactments forbidding, under severe fines and penalties, the teaching of the slave to read or to write.—When you can point to any such laws, in reference to the beasts of the field, then I may consent to argue the manhood of the slave. When the dogs in your streets, when the fowls of the air, when the cattle on your hills, when the fish of the sea, and the reptiles that crawl, shall be unable to distinguish the slave from a brute, *then* will I argue with you that the slave is a man!

For the present, it is enough to affirm the equal manhood of the negro race. Is it not astonishing that, while we are ploughing, planting and reaping, using all kinds of mechanical tools, erecting houses, constructing bridges, building ships, working in metals of brass, iron, copper, silver and gold; that, while we are reading, writing and cyphering, acting as clerks, merchants and secretaries, having among us lawyers, doctors, ministers, poets, authors, editors, orators and teachers; that, while we are engaged in all manner of enterprises common to other men, digging gold in California, capturing the whale in the Pacific, feeding sheep and cattle on the hillside, living, moving, acting, thinking, planning,

living in families as husbands, wives and children, and, above all, confessing and worshipping the Christian's God, and looking hopefully for life and immortality beyond the grave, we are called upon to prove that we are men!

Would you have me argue that man is entitled to liberty? that he is the rightful owner of his own body? You have already declared it. Must I argue the wrongfulness of slavery? Is that a question for Republicans? Is it to be settled by the rules of logic and argumentation, as a matter beset with great difficulty, involving a doubtful application of the principle of justice, hard to be understood? How should I look to-day, in the presence of Americans, dividing, and subdividing a discourse, to show that men have a natural right to freedom? speaking of it relatively, and positively, negatively, and affirmatively, lo do so, would be to make myself ridiculous, and to offer an insult to your understanding.—There is not a man beneath the canopy of heaven, that does not know that slavery is wrong *for him*.

What, am I to argue that it is wrong to make men brutes, to rob them of their liberty, to work them without wages, to keep them ignorant of their relations to their fellow men, to beat them with sticks, to flay their flesh with the lash, to load their limbs with irons, to hunt them with dogs, to sell them at auction, to sunder their families, to knock out their teeth, to burn their flesh, to starve them into obedience and submission to their masters? Must I argue that a system thus marked wit blood, and stained with pollution, is *wrong*? No I will not. I have better employment for my time and strength, than such arguments would imply.

What, then, remains to be argued? Is it that slavery is not divine; that God did not establish it; that our doctors of divinity are mistaken? There is blasphemy in the thought. That which is inhuman, cannot be divine! *Who* can reason on such a proposition? They that can, may; I cannot. The time for such argument is past.

At a time like this, scorching irony, not convincing argument, is needed. O! had I the ability, and could I reach the nation's ear, I would, to-day, pour out a fiery stream of biting ridicule, blasting reproach, withering sarcasm, and stern rebuke. For it is not light that is needed, but fire; it is not the gentle shower, but thunder. We need the storm, the whirlwind, and the earthquake. The feeling of the nation must be quickened; the conscience of the nation must be roused; the propriety of the nation must be startled; the hypocrisy of the nation must be exposed; and its crimes against God and man must be proclaimed and denounced.

What, to the American slave, is your 4th of July? I answer; a day that reveals to him, more than all other days in the year, the gross injustice and cruelty to which he is the constant victim. To him, your celebration is a sham; your boasted liberty, an unholy license; your national greatness, swelling vanity; your sounds of rejoicing are empty and heartless; your denunciations of tyrants, brass fronted impudence; your shouts of liberty and equality, hollow mockery; your prayers and hymns, your sermons and thanksgivings, with all your religious parade, and solemnity, are, to him, mere bombast, fraud, deception, impiety, and hypocrisy—a thin veil to cover up crimes which would disgrace a nation of savages. There is not a nation on the earth guilty of practices, more shocking and bloody, than are the people of these United States, at this very hour.

Go where you may, search where you will, roam through all the monarchies and despotisms of the old world, travel through South America, search out every abuse, and when you have found the last, lay your facts by the side of the every day practices of this nation, and you will say with me, that, for revolting barbarity and shameless hypocrisy, America reigns without a rival.

THE INTERNAL SLAVE TRADE

Take the American slave-trade, which we are told by the papers, is especially prosperous just now. Ex-Senator Benton tells us that the price of men was never higher than now. He mentions the fact to show that slavery is in no danger. This trade is one of the peculiarities of American institutions. It is carried on in all the large towns and cities in one half of this confederacy; and millions are pocketed every year, by dealers in this horrid traffic. In several states, this trade is a chief source of wealth. It is called (in contradistinction to the foreign slave-trade) "*the internal slave-trade.*" It is, probably, called so, too, in order to divert from it the horror with which the foreign slave-trade is contemplated. That trade has long since been denounced by this government, as piracy. It has been denounced with burning words, from the high places of the nation, as an execrable traffic. To arrest it, to put an end to it, this nation keeps a squadron, at immense cost, on the coast of Africa. Everywhere, in this country, it is safe to speak of this foreign slave-trade, as a most inhuman traffic, opposed alike to the laws of God and of man. The duty to extirpate and destroy it, is admitted even by our DOCTORS OF DIVINITY. In order to put an end to it, some of these last have consented that their colored brethren (nominally free) should leave this country, and establish themselves on the western coast of Africa! It is, however, a notable fact, that, while so much execration is poured out by Americans, upon those engaged in the foreign slave-trade, the men engaged in the slave-trade between the states pass without condemnation, and their business is deemed honorable.

Behold the practical operation of this internal slave-trade, the American slave-trade, sustained by American politics and American religion. Here you will see men and women, reared like swine, for the market. You know what is a swine-drover? I will show you a man-drover. They inhabit all our Southern States. They perambulate the country, and crowd the highways of the nation, with droves of human stock. You will see one of these human flesh jobbers, armed with pistol, whip and bowie-knife, driving a company of a hundred men, women, and children, from the Potomac to the slave market at New Orleans. These wretched people are to be sold singly, or in lots, to suit purchasers. They are food for the cotton-field, and the deadly sugar-mill. Mark the sad procession, as it moves wearily along, and the inhuman wretch who drives them. Hear his savage yells and his blood-chilling oaths, as he hurries on his affrighted captives! There, see the old man, with locks thinned and gray. Cast one glance, if you please, upon that young mother, whose shoulders are bare to the scorching sun, her briny tears falling on the brow of the babe in her arms. See, too, that girl of thirteen, weeping, *yes*! weeping, as she thinks of the mother from whom she has been torn! The drove moves tardily. Heat and sorrow have nearly consumed their strength; suddenly you hear a quick snap, like the discharge of a rifle; the fetters clank, and the chain rattles simultaneously; your ears are saluted with a scream, that seems to have torn its way to the centre of your soul! The crack you heard, was the sound of the slave-whip; the scream you heard was from the woman you saw with the babe. Her speed had faltered under the weight of her child and her chains! that gash on her shoulder tells her to move on. Follow this drove to New Orleans. Attend the auction; see men examined like horses; see the forms of women rudely and brutally exposed to the shocking gaze of American slave-buyers. See this drove sold and separated for ever; and never forget the deep, sad sobs that arose from that scattered multitude. Tell me citizens, WHERE, under the sun, you can witness a spectacle more fiendish and shocking. Yet this is but a glance at the American slave-trade, as it exists, at this moment, in the ruling part of the United States.

I was born amid such sights and scenes. To me the American slave-trade is a terrible reality. When a child, my soul was often pierced with a sense of its horrors. I lived on Philpot Street, Fell's Point Baltimore, and have watched from the wharves, the slave ships in the Basin, anchored from the shore, with their cargoes of human flesh, waiting for favorable winds to waft them down the Chesapeake. There was, at that time, a grand slave mart kept at the head of Pratt Street, by Austin Woldfolk *[sic]*. His agents were sent into every town and county in Maryland, announcing

their arrival, through the papers, and on flaming *"hand-bills,"* headed CASH FOR NEGROES. These men were generally well dressed men, and very captivating in their manners. Ever ready to drink, to treat, and to gamble. The fate of many a slave has depended upon the turn of a single card; and many a child has been snatched from the arms of its mother, by bargains arranged in a state of brutal drunkenness.

The flesh-mongers gather up their victims by dozens, and drive them, chained, to the general depot at Baltimore. When a sufficient number have been collected here, a ship is chartered, for the purpose of conveying the forlorn crew to Mobile, or to New Orleans. From the slave prison to the ship, they are usually driven in the darkness of night; for since the anti-slavery agitation, a certain caution is observed.

In the deep still darkness of midnight, I have been often aroused by the dead heavy footsteps, and the pitious cries of the chained gangs that passed our door. The anguish of my boyish heart was intense; and I was often consoled, when speaking to my mistress in the morning, to hear her say that the custom was very wicked; that she hated to hear the rattle of the chains, and the heart-rending cries. I was glad to find one who sympathised with me in my horror.

Fellow-citizens, this murderous traffic is, to-day, in active operation in this boasted republic. In the solitude of my spirit, I see clouds of dust raised on the highways of the South; I see the bleeding footsteps; I hear the doleful wail of fettered humanity, on the way to the slave-markets, where the victims are to be sold like *horses, sheep,* and *swine,* knocked off to the highest bidder. There I see the tenderest ties ruthlessly broken, to gratify the lust, caprice and rapacity of the buyers and sellers of men. My soul sickens at the sight.

"Is this the land your Fathers loved,
The freedom which they toiled to win?
Is this the earth whereon they moved?
Are these the graves they slumber in?"

But a still more inhuman, disgraceful, and scandalous state of things remains to be presented.

By an act of the American Congress, not yet two years old, slavery has been nationalized in its most horrible and revolting form. By that act, Mason & Dixon's line has been obliterated; New York has become as Virginia; and the power to hold, hunt, and sell men, women and children, as slaves, remains no longer a mere state institution, but is now an institution of the whole United States. The power is co-extensive with the star-spangled banner, and American Christianity. Where these go, may also go the merciless slave-hunter. Where these are, man is not sacred. He is a bird for the sportsman's gun. By that most foul and fiendish of all human decrees, the liberty and person of every man are put in peril. Your broad republican domain is hunting ground for *men*. *Not* for thieves and robbers, enemies of society, merely, but for men guilty of no crime. Your law-makers have commanded all good citizens to engage in this hellish sport. Your President, your Secretary of State, your *lords, nobles*, and ecclesiastics, enforce, as a duty you owe to your free and glorious country, and to your God, that you do this accursed thing. Not fewer than forty Americans, have, within the past two years, been hunted down, and, without a moment's warning, hurried away in chains, and consigned to slavery, and excruciating torture. Some of these have had wives and children, dependent on them for bread; but of this, no account was made. The right of the hunter to his prey, stands superior to the right of marriage, and to *all* rights in this republic, the rights of God included! For black men there are neither law, justice, humanity, nor religion. The Fugitive Slave *Law* makes MERCY TO THEM, A CRIME; and bribes the judge who tries them. An American JUDGE GETS TEN DOLLARS FOR EVERY VICTIM HE CONSIGNS to slavery, and five, when he fails to do so. The oath of any two villains is sufficient, under this hell-black enactment, to send the most pious and exemplary black man into the remorseless jaws of slavery! His own testimony is nothing. He can bring no witnesses for himself. The minister of American justice is bound, by the

law to hear but *one* side; and *that* side, is the side of the oppressor. Let this damning fact be perpetually told. Let it be thundered around the world, that, in tyrant-killing, king-hating, people-loving, democratic, Christian America, the seats of justice are filled with judges, who hold their offices under an open and palpable *bribe*, and are bound, in deciding in the case of a man's liberty, *to hear only his accusers!*

In glaring violation of justice, in shameless disregard of the forms of administering law, in cunning arrangement to entrap the defenceless, and in diabolical intent, this Fugitive Slave Law stands alone in the annals of tyrannical legislation. I doubt if there be another nation on the globe, having the brass and the baseness to put such a law on the statute-book. If any man in this assembly thinks differently from me in this matter, and feels able to disprove my statements, I will gladly confront him at any suitable time and place he may select.

RELIGIOUS LIBERTY

I take this law to be one of the grossest infringements of Christian Liberty, and, if the churches and ministers of our country were not stupidly blind, or most wickedly indifferent, they, too, would so regard it.

At the very moment that they are thanking God for the enjoyment of civil and religious liberty, and for the right to worship God according to the dictates of their own consciences, they are utterly silent in respect to a law which robs religion of its chief significance, and makes it utterly worthless to a world lying in wickedness. Did this law concern the *"mint, anise* and *cummin"*—abridge the right to sing psalms, to partake of the sacrament, or to engage in any of the ceremonies of religion, it would be smitten by the thunder of a thousand pulpits. A general shout would go up from the church, demanding *repeal, repeal, instant repeal!*—And it would go hard with that politician who presumed to solicit the votes of

* Rev. R. R. Raymond.

the people without inscribing this motto on his banner. Further, if this demand were not complied with, another Scotland would be added to the history of religious liberty, and the stern old covenanters would be thrown into the shade. A John Knox would be seen at every church door, and heard from every pulpit, and Fillmore would have no more quarter than was shown by Knox, to the beautiful, but threacherous Queen Mary of Scotland.—The fact that the church of our country, (with fractional exceptions,) does not esteem "the Fugitive Slave Law" as a declaration of war against religious liberty, implies that that church regards religion simply as a form of worship, an empty ceremony, and *not* a vital principle, requiring active benevolence, justice, love and good will towards man. It esteems sacrifice above mercy; psalm-singing above right doing; solemn meetings above practical righteousness. A worship that can be conducted by persons who refuse to give shelter to the houseless, to give bread to the hungry, clothing to the naked, and who enjoin obedience to a law forbidding these acts of mercy, is a curse, not a blessing to mankind. The Bible addresses all such persons as "scribes, pharisees, hypocrites, who pay tithe of *mint, anise,* and *cummin,* and have omitted the weightier matters of the law, judgment, mercy and faith."

THE CHURCH RESPONSIBLE

But the church of this country is not only indifferent to the wrongs of the slave, it actually takes sides with the oppressors. It has made itself the bulwark of American slavery, and the shield of American slave-hunters. Many of its most eloquent Divines, who stand as the very lights of the church, have shamelessly given the sanction of religion, and the bible, to the whole slave system.—They have taught that man may, properly, be a slave; that the relation of master and slave is ordained of God; that to send back an escaped bondman to his master is clearly the duty of all the followers of the Lord Jesus Christ; and this horrible blasphemy is palmed off upon the world for Christianity.

For my part, I would say, welcome infidelity! welcome atheism! welcome anything! in preference to the gospel, *as preached by those Divines!* They convert the very name of religion into an engine of tyranny, and barbarous cruelty, and serve to confirm more infidels, in this age, than all the infidel writings of Thomas Paine, Voltaire, and Bolingbroke, put together, have done! These ministers make religion a cold and flinty-hearted thing, having neither principles of right action, nor bowels of compassion. They strip the love of God of its beauty, and leave the throne of religion a huge, horrible, repulsive form. It is a religion for oppressors, tyrants, man-stealers, and *thugs.* It is not that *"pure and undefiled religion"* which is from above, and which is *"first pure, then peaceable, easy to be entreated,* full of mercy and good fruits, *without partiality, and without hypocrisy."* But a religion which favors the rich against the poor; which exalts the proud above the humble; which divides mankind into two classes, tyrants and slaves; which says to the man in chains, *stay there;* and to the oppressor, *oppress on;* it is a religion which may be professed and enjoyed by all the robbers and enslavers of mankind; it makes God a respecter of persons, denies his fatherhood of the race, and tramples in the dust the great truth of the brotherhood of man. All this we affirm to be true of the popular church, and the popular worship of our land and nation—a religion, a church and a worship which, on the authority of inspired wisdom, we pronounce to be an abomination in the sight of God. In the language of Isaiah, the American church might be well addressed, "Bring no more vain oblations; incense is an abomination unto me: the new moons and Sabbaths, the calling of assemblies, I cannot away with; it is iniquity, even the solemn meeting. Your new moons, and your appointed feasts my soul hateth. They are a trouble to me; I am weary to bear them; and when ye spread forth your hands I will hide mine eyes from you. Yea! when ye make many prayers, I will not hear. YOUR HANDS ARE FULL OF BLOOD; cease to do evil, learn to do well; seek judgment; relieve the oppressed; judge for the fatherless; plead for the widow."

The American church is guilty, when viewed in connection with what it is doing to uphold slavery; but it is superlatively guilty when viewed in connection with its ability to abolish slavery.

The sin of which it is guilty is one of omission as well as of commission. Albert Barnes but uttered what the common sense of every man at all observant of the actual state of the case will receive as truth, when he declared that "There is no power out of the church that could sustain slavery an hour, if it were not sustained in it."

Let the religious press, the pulpit, the Sunday school, the conference meeting, the great ecclesiastical, missionary, bible and tract associations of the land array their immense powers against slavery, and slaveholding; and the whole system of crime and blood would be scattered to the winds, and that they do not do this involves them in the most awful responsibility of which the mind can conceive.

In prosecuting the anti-slavery enterprise, we have been asked to spare the church, to spare the ministry; but *how*, we ask, could such a thing be done? We are met on the threshold of our efforts for the redemption of the slave, by the church and ministry of the country, in battle arrayed against us; and we are compelled to fight or flee. From *what* quarter, I beg to know, has proceeded a fire so deadly upon our ranks, during the last two years, as from the Northern pulpit? As the champions of oppressors, the chosen men of American theology have appeared—men, honored for their so called piety, and their real learning. The LORDS of Buffalo, the SPRINGS of New York, the LATHROPS of Auburn, the COXES and SPENCERS of Brooklyn, the GANNETTS and SHARPS of Boston, the DEWEYS of Washington, and other great religious lights of the land, have, in utter denial of the authority of *Him*, by whom they professed to be called to the ministry, deliberately taught us, against the example of the Hebrews, and against the remonstrance of the Apostles, they teach *that we ought to obey man's law before the law of God.*

My spirit wearies of such blasphemy; and how such men can be supported, as the "standing types and representatives of Jesus Christ," is a mystery which I leave others to penetrate. In speaking of the American church, however, let it be distinctly understood that I mean the *great mass* of the religious organizations of our land. There are exceptions, and I thank God that there are. Noble men may be found, scattered all over these Northern States, of whom Henry Ward Beecher, of Brooklyn, Samuel J. May, of Syracuse, and my esteemed friend* on the platform, are shining examples; and let me say further, that, upon these men lies the duty to inspire our ranks with high religious faith and zeal, and to cheer us on in the great mission of the slave's redemption from his chains.

RELIGION IN ENGLAND AND RELIGION IN AMERICA

One is struck with the difference between the attitude of the American church towards the anti-slavery movement, and that occupied by the churches in England towards a similar movement in that country. There, the church, true to its mission of ameliorating, elevating, and improving the condition of mankind, came forward promptly, bound up the wounds of the West Indian slave, and restored him to his liberty. There, the question of emancipation was a high religious question. It was demanded, in the name of humanity, and according to the law of the living God. The Sharps, the Clarksons, the Wilberforces, the Buxtons, the Burchells and the Knibbs, were alike famous for their piety, and for their philanthropy. The anti-slavery movement *there*, was not an anti-church movement, for the reason that the church took its full share in prosecuting that movement: and the anti-slavery movement in this country will cease to be an anti-church movement, when the church of this country shall assume a favorable, instead of a hostile position towards that movement.

Americans! your republican politics, not less than your republican religion, are flagrantly inconsistent. You boast of your love of liberty, your superior civilization, and your pure Christianity, while the whole political power of the nation, as embodied in the two great political parties, is solemnly pledged to support and perpetuate the enslavement of three millions of your countrymen. You hurl your anathemas at the crowned headed tyrants of Russia and Austria, and pride yourselves on your Democratic institutions, while you yourselves consent to be the mere *tools* and *body-guards* of the tyrants of Virginia and Carolina. You invite to your shores fugitives of oppression from abroad, honor them with banquets, greet them with ovations, cheer them, toast them, salute them, protect them, and pour out your money to them like water; but the fugitives from your own land, you advertise, hunt, arrest, shoot and kill. You glory in your refinement, and your universal education; yet you maintain a system as barbarous and dreadful, as ever stained the character of a nation—a system begun in avarice, supported in pride, and perpetuated in cruelty. You shed tears over fallen Hungary, and make the sad story of her wrongs the theme of your poets, statesmen and orators, till your gallant sons are ready to fly to arms to vindicate her cause against her oppressors; but, in regard to the ten thousand wrongs of the American slave, you would enforce the strictest silence, and would hail him as an enemy of the nation who dares to make those wrongs the subject of public discourse! You are all on fire at the mention of liberty for France or for Ireland; but are as cold as an iceberg at the thought of liberty for the enslaved of America.—You discourse eloquently on the dignity of labor; yet, you sustain a system which, in its very essence, casts a stigma upon labor. You can bare your bosom to the storm of British artillery, to throw off a three-penny tax on tea; and yet wring the last hard earned farthing from the grasp of the black laborers of your country. You profess to believe "that, of one blood, God made all nations of men to dwell on the face of all the earth," and hath commanded all men, everywhere to love one another; yet you notoriously hate, (and glory in your hatred,) all men whose skins are not colored like your own. You declare, before the world, and are understood by the world to declare, that you "*hold these truths to be self evident, that all men are created equal; and are endowed by their Creator with certain inalienable rights; and that, among these are, life, liberty, and the pursuit of happiness*;" and yet, you hold securely, in

a bondage, which according to your own Thomas Jefferson, "*is worse than ages of that which your fathers rose in rebellion to oppose*," *a seventh part* of the inhabitants of your country.

Fellow-citizens! I will not enlarge further on your national inconsistencies. The existence of slavery in this country brands your republicanism as a sham, your humanity as a base pretence, and your Christianity as a lie. It destroys your moral power abroad[;] it corrupts your politicians at home. It saps the foundation of religion; it makes your name a hissing, and a bye-word to a mocking earth. It is the antagonistic force in your government, the only thing that seriously disturbs and endangers your *Union*. It fetters your progress; it is the enemy of improvement, the deadly foe of education; it fosters pride; it breeds insolence; it promotes vice; it shelters crime; it is a curse to the earth that supports it; and yet, you cling to it, as if it were the sheet anchor of all your hopes. Oh! be warned! be warned! a horrible reptile is coiled up in your nation's bosom; the venomous creature is nursing at the tender breast of your youthful republic; *for the love of God, tear away*, and fling from you the hideous monster, and *let the weight of twenty millions, crush and destroy it forever!*

THE CONSTITUTION

But it is answered in reply to all this, that precisely what I have now denounced is, in fact, guaranteed and sanctioned by the Constitution of the United States; that, the right to hold, and to hunt slaves is a part of that Constitution framed by the illustrious Fathers of this Republic.

Then, I dare to affirm, notwithstanding all I have said before, your fathers stooped, basely stooped.

"To palter with us in a double sense:
And keep the word of promise to the ear,
But break it to the heart."

And instead of being the honest men I have before declared them to be, they were the veriest imposters that ever practised on mankind. *This* is the inevitable conclusion, and from it there is no escape; but I differ from those who charge this baseness on the framers of the Constitution of the United States. *It is a slander upon their memory*, at least, so I believe. There is not time now to argue the constitutional question at length; nor have I the ability to discuss it as it ought to be discussed. The subject has been handled with masterly power by Lysander Spooner, Esq., by William Goodell, by Samuel E. Sewall, Esq., and last, though not least, by Gerrit Smith, Esq. These gentlemen have, as I think, fully and clearly vindicated the Constitution from any design to support slavery for an hour.

Fellow-citizens! there is no matter in respect to which, the people of the North have allowed themselves to be so ruinously imposed upon, as that of the pro-slavery character of the Constitution. In *that* instrument I hold there is neither warrant, license, nor sanction of the hateful thing; but interpreted, as it *ought* to be interpreted, the Constitution is a GLORIOUS LIBERTY DOCUMENT. Read its preamble, consider its purposes. Is slavery among them? Is it at the gateway? or is it in the temple? it is neither. While I do not intend to argue this question on the present occasion, let me ask, if it be not somewhat singular that, if the Constitution were intended to be, by its framers and adopters, a slaveholding instrument, why neither *slavery, slaveholding*, nor *slave* can anywhere be found in it. What would be thought of an instrument, drawn up, *legally* drawn up, for the purpose of entitling the city of Rochester to a track of land, in which no mention of land was made? Now, there are certain rules of interpretation, for the proper understanding of all legal instruments. These rules are well established. They are plain, commonsense rules, such as you and I, and all of us, can understand and apply, without having passed years in the study of law. I scout the idea that the question of the constitutionality, or unconstitutionality of slavery, is not a question for the people. I hold that every American citizen has a right to form an opinion of the constitution, and to propagate that opinion, and to use all honorable means to make his opinion the prevailing one. Without this right, the liberty of an

American citizen would be as insecure as that of a Frenchman. Ex-Vice-President Dallas tells us that the constitution is an object to which no American mind can be too attentive, and no American heart too devoted. He further says, the constitution, in its words, is plain and intelligible, and is meant for the home-bred, unsophisticated understandings of our fellow-citizens. Senator Berrien tells us that the Constitution is the fundamental law, that which controls all others. The charter of our liberties, which every citizen has a personal interest in understanding thoroughly. The testimony of Senator Breese, Lewis Cass, and many others that might be named, who are everywhere esteemed as sound lawyers, so regard the constitution. I take it, therefore, that it is not presumption in a private citizen to form an opinion of that instrument.

Now, take the constitution according to its plain reading, and I defy the presentation of a single pro-slavery clause in it. On the other hand it will be found to contain principles and purposes, entirely hostile to the existence of slavery.

I have detained my audience entirely too long already. At some future period I will gladly avail myself of an opportunity to give this subject a full and fair discussion.

Allow me to say, in conclusion, notwithstanding the dark picture I have this day presented, of the state of the nation, I do not despair of this country. There are forces in operation, which must inevitably, work the downfall of slavery. "*The arm of the Lord is not shortened*," and the doom of slavery is certain. I, therefore, leave off where I began, with *hope*. While drawing encouragement from "the Declaration of Independence," the great principles it contains, and the genius of American Institutions, my spirit is also cheered by the obvious tendencies of the age. Nations do not now stand in the same relation to each other that they did ages ago. No nation can now shut itself up, from the surrounding world, and trot round in the same old path of its fathers without interference. The time *was* when such could be done. Long established customs of hurtful character could formerly fence themselves in, and do their evil work with social impunity. Knowledge was then confined and enjoyed by the privileged few, and the multitude walked on in mental darkness. But a change has now come over the affairs of mankind. Walled cities and empires have become unfashionable. The arm of commerce has borne away the gates of the strong city. Intelligence is penetrating the darkest corners of the globe. It makes its pathway over and under the sea, as well as on the earth. Wind, steam, and lightning are its chartered agents. Oceans no longer divide, but link nations together. From Boston to London is now a holiday excursion. Space is comparatively annihilated.—Thoughts expressed on one side of the Atlantic, are distinctly heard on the other.

The far off and almost fabulous Pacific rolls in grandeur at our feet. The Celestial Empire, the mystery of ages, is being solved. The fiat of the Almighty, "*Let there be Light*," has not yet spent its force. No abuse, no outrage whether in taste, sport or avarice, can now hide itself from the all-pervading light. The iron shoe, and crippled foot of China must be seen, in contrast with nature. *Africa must rise and put on her yet unwoven garment. "Ethiopia shall stretch out her hand unto God."* In the fervent aspirations of William Lloyd Garrison, I say, and let every heart join in saying it:

> God speed the year of jubilee
>   The wide world o'er!
> When from their galling chains set free,

> Th' oppress'd shall vilely bend the knee,
> And wear the yoke of tyranny
>   Like brutes no more.
> That year will come, and freedom's reign,
> To man his plundered rights again
>   Restore.
> God speed the day when human blood
>   Shall cease to flow!
> In every clime be understood,
> The claims of human brotherhood,
> And each return for evil, good,
>   Not blow for blow;
> That day will come all feuds to end,
> And change into a faithful friend
>   Each foe.
> God speed the hour, the glorious hour,
>   When none on earth
> Shall exercise a lordly power,
> Nor in a tyrant's presence cower;
> But *all to* manhood's stature tower,
>   By equal birth!
> THAT HOUR WILL COME, to each, to all,
> And from his prison-house, the thrall
>   Go forth.
> Until that year, day, hour, arrive,
> With head, and heart, and hand I'll strive,
> To break the rod, and rend the gyve,
> The spoiler of his prey deprive—
>   So witness Heaven!
> And never from my chosen post,
> Whate'er the peril or the cost,
>   Be driven.

ABRAHAM LINCOLN

This address was delivered on November 19, 1863, at the dedication of the cemetery at Gettysburg, Pennsylvania.

Gettysburg Address

Four score and seven years ago our fathers brought forth on this continent, a new nation, conceived in Liberty, and dedicated to the proposition that all men are created equal.

Now we are engaged in a great civil war, testing whether that nation, or any nation so conceived and so dedicated, can long endure. We are met on a great battle-field of that war. We have come to dedicate a portion of that field, as a final resting place for those who here gave their lives that that nation might live. It is altogether fitting and proper that we should do this.

But, in a larger sense, we can not dedicate—we can not consecrate—we can not hallow—this ground. The brave men, living and dead, who struggled here, have consecrated it, far above our poor power to add or detract. The world will little note, nor long remember what we say here, but it can never forget what they did here. It is for us the living,

rather, to be dedicated here to the unfinished work which they who fought here have thus far so nobly advanced. It is rather for us to be here dedicated to the great task remaining before us—that from these honored dead we take increased devotion to that cause for which they gave the last full measure of devotion—that we here highly resolve that these dead shall not have died in vain—that this nation, under God, shall have a new birth of freedom—and that government of the people, by the people, for the people, shall not perish from the earth.

This address was delivered on March 4, 1865. The following month the Civil War ended, and Lincoln was assassinated.

Second Inaugural Address

Fellow Countrymen:

At this second appearing to take the oath of the presidential office, there is less occasion for an extended address than there was at the first. Then a statement, somewhat in detail, of a course to be pursued, seemed fitting and proper. Now, at the expiration of four years, during which public declarations have been constantly called forth on every point and phase of the great contest which still absorbs the attention, and engrosses the energies of the nation, little that is new could be presented. The progress of our arms, upon which all else chiefly depends, is as well known to the public as to myself; and it is, I trust, reasonably satisfactory and encouraging to all. With high hope for the future, no prediction in regard to it is ventured.

On the occasion corresponding to this four years ago, all thoughts were anxiously directed to an impending civil war. All dreaded it—all sought to avert it. While the inaugural address was being delivered from this place, devoted altogether to *saving* the Union without war, insurgent agents were in the city seeking to *destroy* it without war—seeking to dissolve the Union, and divide effects, by negotiation. Both parties deprecated war; but one of them would *make* war rather than let the nation survive; and the other would *accept* war rather than let it perish. And the war came.

One eighth of the whole population were colored slaves, not distributed generally over the Union, but localized in the Southern part of it. These slaves constituted a peculiar and powerful interest. All knew that this interest was, somehow, the cause of the war. To strengthen, perpetuate, and extend this interest was the object for which the insurgents would rend the Union, even by war; while the government claimed no right to do more than to restrict the territorial enlargement of it. Neither party expected for the war, the magnitude, or the duration, which it has already attained. Neither anticipated that the *cause* of the conflict might cease with, or even before, the conflict itself should cease. Each looked for an easier triumph, and a result less fundamental and astounding. Both read the same Bible, and pray to the same God; and each invokes His aid against the other. It may seem strange that any men should dare to ask a just God's assistance in wringing their bread from the sweat of other men's faces; but let us judge not that we be not judged. The prayers of both could not be answered; that of neither has been answered fully. The Almighty has His own purposes. "Woe unto the world because of offences! for it must needs be that offences come; but woe to that man by whom the offence cometh!" If we shall suppose that

American Slavery is one of those offences which, in the providence of God, must needs come, but which, having continued through His appointed time, He now wills to remove, and that He gives to both North and South, this terrible war, as the woe due to those by whom the offence came, shall we discern therein any departure from those divine attributes which the believers in a Living God always ascribe to Him? Fondly do we hope—fervently do we pray—that this mighty scourge of war may speedily pass away. Yet, if God wills that it continue, until all the wealth piled by the bond-man's two hundred and fifty years of unrequited toil shall be sunk, and until every drop of blood drawn with the lash, shall be paid by another drawn with the sword, as was said three thousand years ago, so still it must be said "the judgments of the Lord, are true and righteous altogether."

With malice toward none; with charity for all; with firmness in the right, as God gives us to see the right, let us strive on to finish the work we are in; to bind up the nation's wounds; to care for him who shall have borne the battle, and for his widow, and his orphan—to do all which may achieve and cherish a just, and a lasting peace, among ourselves, and with all nations.

ELIZABETH CADY STANTON

Elizabeth Cady Stanton (1815–1902), leader of the women's rights movement, delivered this address in 1892 before the Judiciary Committee of the U.S. House of Representatives and then before the Committee on Woman Suffrage of the U.S. Senate.

The Solitude of Self

Mr. Chairman and Gentlemen of the Committee:

We have been speaking before Committees of the Judiciary for the last twenty years, and we have gone over all the arguments in favor of the sixteenth amendment which are familiar to all you gentlemen; therefore, it will not be necessary that I should repeat them again.

The point I wish plainly to bring before you on this occasion is the individuality of each human soul—our Protestant idea, the right of individual conscience and judgment—our republican idea, individual citizenship. In discussing the right of woman, we are to consider, first, what belongs to her as an individual, in a world of her own, the arbiter of her own destiny, an imaginary Robinson Crusoe with her woman Friday on a solitary island.

Her rights under such circumstances are to use all her faculties for her own safety and happiness.

Secondly, if we consider her as a citizen, as a member of a great nation, she must have the same rights as all other members, according to the fundamental principles of our government.

Thirdly, viewed as a woman, an equal factor in civilization, her rights and duties are still the same—individual happiness and development.

Fourthly, it is only the incidental relations of life, such as mother, wife, sister, daughter, which may involve some special duties and training. In the usual discussion in regard to woman's sphere, such men as Herbert Spencer, Frederic Harrison, and Grant Allen uniformly subordinate her rights and duties as an individual, as a citizen, as a woman, to

Reprinted from *The Search for Self-Sovereignty: The Oratory of Elizabeth Cady Stanton*, edited by Beth M. Waggonspack, New York, Greenwood Press, 1987. By permission of the publisher.

the necessities of these incidental relations, some of which a large class of women may never assume. In discussing the sphere of man we do not decide his rights as an individual, as a citizen, as a man, by his duties as a father, a husband, a brother, or a son, relations some of which he may never fill. Moreover, he would be better fitted for these very relations, and whatever special work he might choose to do to earn his bread, by the complete development of all his faculties as an individual.

Just so with woman. The education that will fit her to discharge the duties in the largest sphere of human usefulness, will best fit her for whatever special work she may be compelled to do.

The isolation of every human soul and the necessity of self-dependence must give each individual the right to choose his own surroundings.

The strongest reason for giving woman all the opportunities for higher education, for the full development of her faculties, her forces of mind and body; for giving her the most enlarged freedom of thought and action; a complete emancipation from all forms of bondage, of custom, dependence, superstition; from all the crippling influences of fear; is the solitude and personal responsibility of her own individual life. The strongest reason why we ask for woman a voice in the government under which she lives; in the religion she is asked to believe; equality in social life, where she is the chief factor; a place in the trades and professions, where she may earn her bread, is because of her birthright to self-sovereignty; because, as an individual, she must rely on herself. No matter how much women prefer to lean, to be protected and supported, nor how much men desire to have them do so, they must make the voyage of life alone, and for safety in an emergency they must know something of the laws of navigation. To guide our own craft, we must be captain, pilot, engineer; with chart and compass to stand at the wheel; to watch the wind and waves and know when to take in the sail, and to read the signs in the firmament over all. It matters not whether the solitary voyager is man or woman.

Nature having endowed them equally, leaves them to their own skill and judgment in the hour of danger, and, if not equal to the occasion, alike they perish.

To appreciate the importance of fitting every human soul for independent action, think for a moment of the immeasurable solitude of self. We come into the world alone, unlike all who have gone before us; we leave it alone under circumstances peculiar to ourselves. No mortal ever has been, no mortal ever will be like the soul just launched on the sea of life. There can never again be just such environments as make up the infancy, youth and manhood of this one. Nature never repeats herself, and the possibilities of one human soul will never be found in another. No one has ever found two blades of ribbon grass alike, and no one will ever find two human beings alike. Seeing, then, what must be the infinite diversity in human character, we can in a measure appreciate the loss to a nation when any large class of the people is uneducated and unrepresented in the government. We ask for the complete development of every individual, first, for his own benefit and happiness. In fitting out an army we give each soldier his own knapsack, arms, powder, his blanket, cup, knife, fork and spoon. We provide alike for all their individual necessities, then each man bears his own burden.

Again we ask complete individual development for the general good; for the consensus of the competent on the whole round of human interest; on all questions of national life, and here each man must bear his share of the general burden. It is sad to see how soon friendless children are left to bear their own burdens before they can analyze their feelings; before they can even tell their joys and sorrows, they are thrown on their own resources. The great lesson that nature seems to teach us at all ages is self-dependence, self-protection, self-support. What a touching instance of a child's solitude; of that hunger of heart for love and recognition, in the case of a little girl who helped to dress a Christmas tree for the children of the family in which she served.

On finding there was no present for herself she slipped away in the darkness and spent the night in an open field sitting on a stone, and when found in the morning was weeping as if her heart would break. No mortal will ever know the thought that passed through the mind of the friendless child in the long hours of that cold night, with only the silent stars to keep her company. The mention of her case in the daily papers moved many generous hearts to send her presents, but in the hours of her keenest sufferings she was thrown wholly on herself for consolation.

In youth our most bitter disappointments, our brightest hopes and ambitions are known only to ourselves; even our friendship and love we never fully share with another; there is something of every passion in every situation we conceal. Even so in our triumphs and our defeats.

The successful candidate for Presidency and his opponent each have a solitude peculiarly his own, and good form forbids either to speak of his pleasure or regret. The solitude of the king on his throne and the prisoner in his cell differs in characters and degree, but it is solitude nevertheless.

We ask no sympathy from others in the anxiety and agony of a broken friendship or shattered love. When death sunders our nearest ties, alone we sit in the shadows of our affliction. Alike mid the greatest triumphs and darkest tragedies of life we walk alone. On the divine heights of human attainments, eulogized and worshipped as a hero or a saint, we stand alone. In ignorance, poverty, and vice, as a pauper or criminal, alone we starve or steal; alone we suffer the sneers and rebuffs of our fellows; alone we are hunted and hounded through dark courts and alleys, in by-ways and highways; alone we stand in the judgment seats; alone in the prison cell we lament our crimes and misfortunes; alone we expiate them on the gallows. In hours like these we realize the awful solitude of individual life, its pains, its penalties, its responsibilities; hours in which the youngest and most helpless are thrown on their own resources for guidance and consolation. Seeing then that life must ever be a march and a battle, that each

soldier must be equipped for his own protection, it is the height of cruelty to rob the individual of a single natural right.

To throw obstacles in the way of a complete education, is like putting out the eyes; to deny the rights of property, like cutting off the hands. To deny political equality is to rob the ostracized of all self-respect; of credit in the market place; of recompense in the world of work; of a voice among those who make and administer the law; a choice in the jury before whom they are tried, and in the judge who decides their punishment. Shakespeare's play of Titus and Andronicus [sic] contains a terrible satire on woman's position in the nineteenth century—"Rude men" (the play tells us) "seize the king's daughter, cut out her tongue, cut off her hands, and then bade her go call for water and wash her hands." What a picture of woman's position. Robbed of her natural rights, handicapped by law and custom at every turn, yet compelled to fight her own battles, and in the emergencies of life to fall back on herself for protection.

The girl of sixteen, thrown on the world to support herself, to make her own place in society, to resist the temptations that surround her and maintain a spotless integrity, must do all this by native force or superior education. She does not acquire this power by being trained to trust others and distrust herself. If she wearies of the struggle, finding it hard work to swim upstream, and allows herself to drift with the current, she will find plenty of company, but not one to share her misery in the hour of her deepest humiliation. If she tries to retrieve her position, to conceal the past, her life is hedged about with fears lest willing hands should tear the veil from what she fain would hide. Young and friendless, she knows the bitter solitude of self.

How the little courtesies of life on the surface of society, deemed so important from man towards woman, fade into utter insignificance in view of the deeper tragedies in which she must play her part alone, where no human aid is possible.

The young wife and mother, at the head of some establishment with a kind husband to shield her from the adverse winds of life, with wealth, fortune, and position, has a certain harbor of safety, secure against the ordinary ills of life. But to manage a household, have a desirable influence in society, keep her friends and the affections of her husband, train her children and servants well, she must have a rare common sense, wisdom, diplomacy, and a knowledge of human nature. To do all this she needs the cardinal virtues and the strong points of character that the most successful statesman possesses.

An uneducated woman, trained to dependence, with no resources in herself must make a failure of any position in life. But society says women do not need a knowledge of the world; the liberal training that experience in public life must give, all the advantages of collegiate education; but when for the lack of all this, the woman's happiness is wrecked, alone she bears her humiliation; and the solitude of the weak and the ignorant is indeed pitiful. In the wild chase for the prizes of life they are ground to powder.

In age, when the pleasures of youth are passed, children grown up, married and gone, the hurry and bustle of life in a measure over, when the hands are weary of active service, when the old armchair and the fireside are the chosen resorts, then men and women alike must fall back on their own resources. If they cannot find companionship in books, if they have no interest in the vital questions of the hour, no interest in watching the consummation of reforms, with which they might have been identified, they soon pass into their dotage. The more fully the faculties of the mind are developed and kept in use, the longer the period of vigor and active interest in all around us continues. If from a lifelong participation in public affairs a woman feels responsible for the laws regulating our system of education, the discipline of our jails and prisons, the sanitary conditions of our private homes, public buildings, and thoroughfares, an interest in commerce, finance, our foreign relations, in any or all of these questions, her solitude will at least be respectable, and she will not be driven to gossip or scandal for entertainment.

The chief reason for opening to every soul the doors to the whole round of human duties and pleasures is the individual development thus attained, the resources thus provided under all circumstances to mitigate the solitude that at times must come to everyone. I once asked Prince Krapotkin, the Russian nihilist, how he endured his long years in prison, deprived of books, pen, ink, and paper. "Ah," he said, "I thought out many questions on which I had a deep interest. In the pursuit of an idea I took no note of time. When tired of solving knotty problems I recited all the beautiful passages in prose or verse I had ever learned. I became acquainted with my self and my own resources. I had a world of my own, a vast empire, that no Russian jailor or Czar could invade." Such is the value of liberal thought and broad culture when shut from all human companionship, bringing comfort and sunshine within even the four walls of a prison cell.

As women ofttimes share a similar fate, should they not have all the consolation that the most liberal education can give? Their suffering in the prisons of St. Petersburg; in the long, weary marches to Siberia, and in the mines, working side by side with men, surely call for all the self-support that the most exalted sentiments of heroism can give. When suddenly roused at midnight, with the startling cry of "Fire! Fire" to find the house over their heads in flames, do women wait for men to point the way to safety? And are the men, equally bewildered and half suffocated with smoke, in a position to more than save themselves?

At such times the most timid women have shown a courage and heroism in saving their husbands and children that has surprised everybody. Inasmuch, then, as woman shares equally the joys and sorrows of time and eternity, is it not the height of presumption in man to propose to represent her at the ballot box and the throne of grace, do her voting in the state, her praying in the church, and to assume the position of priest at the family altar.

Nothing strengthens the judgment and quickens the conscience like individual responsibility.

Nothing adds such dignity to character as the recognition of one's self-sovereignty; the right to an equal place, everywhere conceded; a place earned by personal merit, not an artificial attainment by inheritance, wealth, family, and position. Seeing, then that the responsibilities of life rest equally on man and woman, that their destiny is the same, they need the same preparation for time and eternity. The talk of sheltering woman from the fierce storms of life is the sheerest mockery, for they beat on her from every point of the compass, just as they do on man, and with more fatal results, for he has been trained to protect himself, to resist, to conquer. Such are the facts in human experience, the responsibilities of individual sovereignty. Rich and poor, intelligent and ignorant, wise and foolish, virtuous and vicious, man and woman, it is ever the same, each soul must depend wholly on itself.

Whatever the theories may be of woman's dependence on man, in the supreme moments of her life he can not bear her burdens. Alone she goes to the gates of death to give life to every man that is born into the world. No one can share her fears, no one can mitigate her pangs; and if her sorrow is greater than she can bear, alone she passes beyond the gates into the vast unknown.

From the mountain tops of Judea, long ago, a heavenly voice bade His disciples, "Bear ye one another's burdens," but humanity has not yet risen to that point of self-sacrifice, and if ever so willing, how few the burdens are that one soul can bear for another. In the highways of Palestine; in prayer and fasting on the solitary mountain top; in the Garden of Gethsemane; before the judgment seat of Pilate; betrayed by one of His trusted disciples at His last supper; in His agonies on the cross, even Jesus of Nazareth, in these last sad days on earth, felt the awful solitude of self. Deserted by man, in agony he cries, "My God! My God! Why hast Thou forsaken me." And so it ever must be in the conflicting scenes of life, in the long weary march, each one walks alone. We may have many friends, love, kindness, sympathy and charity to smooth our pathway in everyday life, but in the tragedies and triumphs of human experience each mortal stands alone.

But when all artificial trammels are removed, and women are recognized as individuals, responsible for their own environments, thoroughly educated for all positions in life they may be called to fill; with all the resources in themselves that liberal thought and broad culture can give; guided by their own conscience and judgment; trained to self-protection by a healthy development of the muscular system and skill in the use of weapons of defense, and stimulated to self-support by a knowledge of the business world and the pleasure that pecuniary independence must ever give; when women are trained in this way they will, in a measure, be fitted for those years of solitude that come to all, whether prepared or otherwise. As in our extremity we must depend on ourselves, the dictates of wisdom point to complete individual development.

In talking of education how shallow the argument that each class must be educated for the special work it proposes to do, and all those faculties not needed in this special walk must lie dormant and utterly wither for want of use, when perhaps, these will be the very faculties needed in life's greatest emergencies. Some say, "Where is the use of drilling girls in the languages, the sciences, in law, medicine, theology?"

As wives, mothers, housekeepers, cooks, they need a different curriculum from boys who are to fill all positions. The chief cooks in our great hotels and ocean steamers are men. In large cities men run the bakeries; they make our bread, cake and pies. They manage the laundries; they are now considered our best milliners and dressmakers. Because some men fill these departments of usefulness, shall we regulate the curriculum in Harvard and Yale to their present necessities? If not, why this talk in our best colleges of a curriculum for girls who are crowding into the trades and professions; teachers in all our public schools rapidly filling many lucrative and honorable positions in life? They are showing, too, their calmness and courage in the most trying hours of human experience.

You have probably all read in the daily papers of the terrible storm in the Bay of Biscay when a tidal wave made such havoc on the shore, wrecking vessels, unroofing houses and carrying destruction everywhere. Among other buildings the woman's prison was demolished. Those who escaped saw men struggling to reach the shore. They promptly by clasping hands made a chain of themselves and pushed out into the sea, again and again, at the risk of their lives until they had brought six men to shore, carried them to a shelter, and did all in their power for their comfort and protection.

What special school of training could have prepared these women for this sublime moment of their lives? In times like this humanity rises above all college curriculum and recognizes Nature as the greatest of all teachers in the hour of danger and death. Women are already the equals of men in the whole of realm of thought, in art, science, literature, and government. With telescopic vision they explore the starry firmament, and bring back the history of the planetary world. With chart and compass they pilot ships across the mighty deep, and with skillful finger send electric messages around the globe. In galleries of art the beauties of nature and the virtues of humanity are immortalized by them on their canvas and by their inspired touch dull blocks of marble are transformed into angles of light.

In music they speak again the language of Mendelssohn, Beethoven, Chopin, Schumann, and are worthy interpreters of their great thoughts. The poetry and novels of the century are theirs, and they have touched the keynote of reform in religion, politics, and social life. They fill the editor's and professor's chair, and plead at the bar of justice, walk the wards of the hospital, and speak from the pulpit and the platform; such is the type of womanhood that an enlightened public sentiment welcomes today, and such the triumph of the facts of life over the false theories of the past.

Is it, then, consistent to hold the developed woman of this day within the narrow political limits as the dame with the spinning wheel and knitting needle occupied in the past? No! No! Machinery has taken the labors of woman as well as man on its tireless shoulders; the loom and the spinning wheel are but dreams of the past; the pen, the brush, the easel, the chisel, have taken their places, while the hopes and ambitions of women are essentially changed.

We see reason sufficient in the outer conditions of human beings for individual liberty and development, but when we consider the self-dependence of every human soul we see the need of courage, judgment, and the exercise of every faculty of mind and body, strengthened and developed by use, in woman as well as man.

Whatever may be said of man's protecting power in ordinary conditions, mid all the terrible disasters by land and sea, in the supreme moments of danger, alone, woman must ever meet the horrors of the situation; the Angel of Death even makes no royal pathway for her. Man's love and sympathy enter only into the sunshine of our lives. In that solemn solitude of self, that links us with the immeasurable and the eternal, each soul lives alone forever. A recent writer says:

> I remember once, in crossing the Atlantic, to have gone upon the deck of the ship in midnight, when a dense black cloud enveloped the sky, and the great dep was roaring madly under the lashes of demoniac winds. My feelings was not of danger or fear (which is a base surrender of the immortal soul), but of utter desolation and loneliness; a little speck of life shut in by a tremendous darkness. Again I remember to have climbed on the slopes of the Swiss Alps, up beyond the point where vegetation ceases, and the stunted conifers no longer struggle against the unfeeling blasts. Around me lay a huge confusion of rocks, out of which the gigantic ice peaks shot into the measureless blue of the heavens, and again my only feeling was the awful solitude.

And yet, there is a solitude, which each and every one of us has always carried with him, more inaccessible than the ice-cold mountains, more profound than the midnight sea; the solitude of self. Our inner being, which we call ourself, no eye nor touch of man or angel has ever pierced. It is more hidden than the caves of the gnome; the sacred adytum of the oracle; the hidden chamber of eleusinian mystery, for to it only omniscience is permitted to enter.

Such is individual life. Who, I ask you, can take, dare take, on himself the rights, the duties, the responsibilities of another human soul?

JOHN DEWEY

John Dewey (1859–1952), the foremost American philosopher of the first half of the twentieth century, delivered this talk on February 22, 1937, to the National Education Association meeting in New Orleans.

Democracy

Democracy is much broader than a special political form, a method of conducting government, of making laws and carrying on governmental administration by means of popular suffrage and elected officers. It is that of course. But it is something broader and deeper than that.

The political and governmental phase of democracy is a means, the best means so far found, for realizing ends that lie in the wide domain of human relationships and the development of human personality. It is, as we often say, though perhaps without appreciating all that is involved in the saying, a way of life, social and individual. The key-note of democracy as a way of life may be expressed, it seems to me, as the necessity for the participation of every mature human being in formation of the values that regulate the living of men together—which is necessary from the standpoint of both the general social welfare and the full development of human beings as individuals.

Universal suffrage, recurring elections, responsibility of those who are in political power to the voters, and the other factors of democratic government are means that have been found expedient for realizing democracy as the truly human way of living. They are not a final end and a final value. They are to be judged on the basis of their contribution to an end. It is a form of idolatry to erect means into the end which they serve. Democratic political forms are simply the best means that human wit has devised up to a special time in history. But they rest back upon the idea that no man or limited set of men is wise enough or good enough to rule others without their consent; the positive meaning of this statement is that all those who are affected by social institutions must have a

From *The Collected Works of John Dewey, Later Works*, vol. 11. Copyright © 1986 by the Center for Dewey Studies. Reprinted by permission of the publisher, Southern Illinois University Press.

share in producing and managing them. The two facts that each one is influenced in what he does and enjoys and in what he becomes by the institutions under which he lives, and that therefore he shall have, in a democracy, a voice in shaping them, are the passive and active sides of the same fact.

The development of political democracy came about through substitution of the method of mutual consultation and voluntary agreement for the method of subordination of the many to the few enforced from above. Social arrangements which involve fixed subordination are maintained by coercion. The coercion need not be physical. There have existed, for short periods, benevolent despotisms. But coercion of some sort there has been; perhaps economic, certainly psychological and moral. The very fact of exclusion from participation is a subtle form of suppression. It gives individuals no opportunity to reflect and decide upon what is good for them. Others who are supposed to be wiser and who in any case have more power decide the question for them and also decide the methods and means by which subjects may arrive at the enjoyment of what is good for them. This form of coercion and suppression is more subtle and more effective than is overt intimidation and restraint. When it is habitual and embodied in social institutions, it seems the normal and natural state of affairs. The mass usually become unaware that they have a claim to a development of their own powers. Their experience is so restricted that they are not conscious of restriction. It is part of the democratic conception that they as individuals are not the only sufferers, but that the whole social body is deprived of the potential resources that should be at its service. The individuals of the submerged mass may not be very wise. But there is one thing they are wiser about than anybody else can be, and that is where the shoe pinches, the troubles they suffer from.

The foundation of democracy is faith in the capacities of human nature; faith in human intelligence, and in the power of pooled and cooperative experience. It is not belief that these things are complete but that if given a show they will grow and be able to generate progressively the knowledge and wisdom needed to guide collective action. Every autocratic and authoritarian scheme of social action rests on a belief that the needed intelligence is confined to a superior few who because of inherent natural gifts are endowed with the ability and the right to control the conduct of others; laying down principles and rules and directing the ways in which they are carried out. It would be foolish to deny that much can be said for this point of view. It is that which controlled human relations in social groups for much the greater part of human history. The democratic faith has emerged very, very recently in the history of mankind. Even where democracies now exist, men's minds and feelings are still permeated with ideas about leadership imposed from above, ideas that developed in the long early history of mankind. After democratic political institutions were nominally established, beliefs and ways of looking at life and of acting that originated when men and women were externally controlled and subjected to arbitrary power, persisted in the family, the church, business and the school, and experience shows that as long as they persist there, political democracy is not secure.

Belief in equality is an element of the democratic credo. It is not, however, belief in equality of natural endowments. Those who proclaimed the idea of equality did not suppose they were enunciating a psychological doctrine, but a legal and political one. All individuals are entitled to equality of treatment by law and in its administration. Each one is affected equally in quality if not in quantity by the institutions under which he lives and has an equal right to express his judgment, although the weight of his judgment may not be equal in amount when it enters into the pooled result to that of others. In short, each one is equally an individual and entitled to equal opportunity of development of his own capacities, be they large or small in range. Moreover, each has needs of his own, as significant to him as those of others are to them. The very fact of natural and psychological inequality is all the more reason for establishment by law of equality of opportunity, since otherwise the former becomes a means of oppression of the less gifted.

While what we call intelligence be distributed in unequal amounts, it is the democratic faith that it is sufficiently general so that each individual has something to contribute whose value can be assessed only as it enters into the final pooled intelligence constituted by the contributions of all. Every authoritarian scheme, on the contrary assumes that its value may be assessed by some *prior* principle, if not of family and birth or race and color or possession of material wealth, then by the position and rank a person occupies in the existing social scheme. The democratic faith in equality is the faith that each individual shall have the chance and opportunity to contribute whatever he is capable of contributing, and that the value of his contribution be decided by its place and function in the organized total of similar contributions—not on the basis of prior status of any kind whatever.

I have emphasized in what precedes the importance of the effective release of intelligence in connection with personal experience in the democratic way of living. I have done so purposely because democracy is so often and so naturally associated in our minds with freedom of *action*, forgetting the importance of freed intelligence which is necessary to direct and to warrant freedom of action. Unless freedom of individual action has intelligence and informed conviction back of it, its manifestation is almost sure to result in confusion and disorder. The democratic idea of freedom is not the right of each individual to *do* as he pleases, even if it be qualified by adding "provided he does not interfere with the same freedom on the part of others." While the idea is not always, not often enough, expressed in words, the basic freedom is that of freedom of *mind* and of whatever degree of freedom of action and experience is necessary to produce freedom of intelligence. The modes of freedom guaranteed in the Bill of Rights are all of this nature: Freedom of belief and conscience, of expression of opinion, of assembly for discussion and conference, of the press as an organ of communication. They are guaranteed because without them individuals are not free to develop and society is deprived of what they might contribute. . . .

There is some kind of government, of control, wherever affairs that concern a number of persons who act together are engaged in. It is a superficial view that holds government is located in Washington and Albany. There is government in the family, in business, in the church, in every social group. There are regulations, due to custom if not to enactment, that settle how individuals in a group act in connection with one another.

It is a disputed question of theory and practice just how far a democratic political government should go in control of the conditions of action within special groups. At the present time, for example, there are those who think the federal and state governments leave too much freedom of independent action to industrial and financial groups and there are others who think the Government is going altogether too far at the present time. I do not need to discuss this phase of the problem much less to try to settle it. But it must be pointed out that if the methods of regulation and administration in vogue in the conduct of secondary social groups are non-democratic, whether directly or indirectly or both, there is bound to be an unfavorable reaction back into the habits of feeling, thought and action of citizenship in the broadest sense of that word. The way in which any organized social interest is controlled necessarily plays an important part in forming the dispositions and tastes, the attitudes, interests, purposes and desires, of those engaged in carrying on the activities of the group. For illustration, I do not need to do more than point to the moral, emotional, and intellectual effect upon both employers and laborers of the existing industrial system. Just what the effects specifically are is a matter about which we know very little. But I suppose that every one who reflects upon the subject admits that it is impossible that the ways in which activities are carried on for the greater part of the waking hours of the day; and the way in which the shares of individuals are involved in the management of affairs in such a matter as gaining a livelihood and attaining material and social security, can only be a highly important factor in shaping personal dispositions; in short, forming character and intelligence.

In the broad and final sense all institutions are educational in the sense that they operate to form the attitudes, dispositions, abilities, and disabilities that constitute a concrete personality. The principle applies with special force to the school. For it is the main business of the family and the school to influence directly the formation and growth of attitudes and dispositions, emotional, intellectual and moral. Whether this educative process is carried on in a predominantly democratic or non-democratic way becomes therefore a question of transcendent importance not only for education itself but for its final effect upon all the interests and activities of a society that is committed to the democratic way of life. . . .

There are certain corollaries which clarify the meaning of the issue. Absence of participation tends to produce lack of interest and concern on the part of those shut out. The result is a corresponding lack of effective responsibility. Automatically and unconsciously, if not consciously, the feeling develops, "this is none of our affair; it is the business of those at the top; let that particular set of Georges do what needs to be done." The countries in which autocratic government prevails are just those in which there is least public spirit and the greatest indifference to matters of general as distinct from personal concern. . . . Where there is little power, there is correspondingly little sense of positive responsibility—It is enough to do what one is told to do sufficiently well to escape flagrant unfavorable notice. About larger matters a spirit of passivity is engendered. . . .

It still is also true that incapacity to assume the responsibilities involved in having a voice in shaping policies is bred and increased by conditions in which that responsibility is denied. I suppose there has never been an autocrat, big or little, who did not justify his conduct on the ground of the unfitness of his subjects to take part in government. . . . But, as was said earlier, habitual exclusion has the effect of reducing a sense of responsibility for what is done and its consequences. What the argument for democracy implies is that the best way to produce initiative and constructive power is to exercise it. Power, as well as interest, comes by use and practice. . . .

The fundamental beliefs and practices of democracy are now challenged as they never have been before. In some nations they are more than challenged. They are ruthlessly and systematically destroyed. Everywhere there are waves of criticism and doubt as to whether democracy can meet pressing problems of order and security. The causes for the destruction of political democracy in countries where it was nominally established are complex. But of one thing I think we may be sure. Wherever it has fallen it was too exclusively political in nature. It had not become part of the bone and blood of the people in daily conduct of its life. Democratic forms were limited to Parliament, elections, and combats between parties. What is happening proves conclusively, I think, that unless democratic habits of thought and action are part of the fiber of a people, political democracy is insecure. It cannot stand in isolation. It must be buttressed by the presence of democratic methods in all social relationships. The relations that exist in educational institutions are second only in importance in this respect to those which exist in industry and business, perhaps not even to them. . . .

I can think of nothing so important in this country at present as a rethinking of the whole problem of democracy and its implications. Neither the rethinking nor the action it should produce can be brought into being in a day or year. The democratic idea itself demands that the thinking and activity proceed cooperatively.

THE UNIVERSAL DECLARATION OF HUMAN RIGHTS

This statement was adopted by the General Assembly of the United Nations on December 10, 1948.

PREAMBLE

Whereas recognition of the inherent dignity and of the equal and inalienable rights of all members of the human family is the foundation of freedom, justice and peace in the world,

Whereas disregard and contempt for human rights have resulted in barbarous acts which have outraged the conscience of mankind, and the advent of a world in which human beings shall enjoy freedom of speech and belief and freedom from fear and want has been proclaimed as the highest aspiration of the common people,

Whereas it is essential, if man is not to be compelled to have recourse, as a last resort, to rebellion against tyranny and oppression, that human rights should be protected by the rule of law,

Whereas it is essential to promote the development of friendly relations between nations,

Whereas the peoples of the United Nations have in the Charter reaffirmed their faith in fundamental human rights, in the dignity and worth of the human person and in the equal rights of men and women and have determined to promote social progress and better standards of life in larger freedom,

Whereas Member States have pledged themselves to achieve, in co-operation with the United Nations, the promotion of universal respect for and observance of human rights and fundamental freedoms,

Whereas a common understanding of these rights and freedoms is of the greatest importance for the full realization of this pledge,

Now, Therefore THE GENERAL ASSEMBLY proclaims THIS UNIVERSAL DECLARATION OF HUMAN RIGHTS as a common standard of achievement for all peoples and all nations, to the end that every individual and every organ of society, keeping this Declaration constantly in mind, shall strive by teaching and education to promote respect for these rights and freedoms and by progressive measures, national and international, to secure their universal and effective recognition and observance, both among the peoples of Member States themselves and among the peoples of territories under their jurisdiction.

ARTICLE 1

All human beings are born free and equal in dignity and rights. They are endowed with reason and conscience and should act towards one another in a spirit of brotherhood.

ARTICLE 2

Everyone is entitled to all the rights and freedoms set forth in this Declaration, without distinction of any kind, such as race, colour, sex, language, religion, political or other opinion, national or social origin, property, birth or other status. Furthermore, no distinction shall be made on the basis of the political, jurisdictional or international status of the country or territory to which a person belongs, whether it be independent, trust, non-self-governing or under any other limitation of sovereignty.

ARTICLE 3

Everyone has the right to life, liberty and security of person.

ARTICLE 4

No one shall be held in slavery or servitude; slavery and the slave trade shall be prohibited in all their forms.

ARTICLE 5

No one shall be subjected to torture or to cruel, inhuman or degrading treatment or punishment.

ARTICLE 6

Everyone has the right to recognition everywhere as a person before the law.

ARTICLE 7

All are equal before the law and are entitled without any discrimination to equal protection of the law. All are entitled to equal protection against any discrimination in violation of this Declaration and against any incitement to such discrimination.

ARTICLE 8

Everyone has the right to an effective remedy by the competent national tribunals for acts violating the fundamental rights granted him by the constitution or by law.

ARTICLE 9

No one shall be subjected to arbitrary arrest, detention or exile.

ARTICLE 10

Everyone is entitled in full equality to a fair and public hearing by an independent and impartial tribunal, in the determination of his rights and obligations and of any criminal charge against him.

ARTICLE 11

(1) Everyone charged with a penal offence has the right to be presumed innocent until proved guilty according to law in a public trial at which he has had all the guarantees necessary for his defence.

(2) No one shall be held guilty of any penal offence on account of any act or omission which did not constitute a penal offence, under national or international law, at the time when it was committed. Nor shall a heavier penalty be imposed than the one that was applicable at the time the penal offence was committed.

ARTICLE 12

No one shall be subjected to arbitrary interference with his privacy, family, home or correspondence, nor to attacks upon his honour and reputation. Everyone has the right to the protection of the law against such interference or attacks.

ARTICLE 13

(1) Everyone has the right to freedom of movement and residence within the borders of each state.

(2) Everyone has the right to leave any country, including his own, and to return to his country.

ARTICLE 14

(1) Everyone has the right to seek and to enjoy in other countries asylum from persecution.

(2) This right may not be invoked in the case of prosecutions genuinely arising from non-political crimes or from acts contrary to the purposes and principles of the United Nations.

ARTICLE 15

(1) Everyone has the right to a nationality.
(2) No one shall be arbitrarily deprived of his nationality nor denied the right to change his nationality.

ARTICLE 16

(1) Men and women of full age, without any limitation due to race, nationality or religion, have the right to marry and to found a family. They are entitled to equal rights as to marriage, during marriage and at its dissolution.
(2) Marriage shall be entered into only with the free and full consent of the intending spouses.
(3) The family is the natural and fundamental group unit of society and is entitled to protection by society and the State.

ARTICLE 17

(1) Everyone has the right to own property alone as well as in association with others.
(2) No one shall be arbitrarily deprived of his property.

ARTICLE 18

Everyone has the right to freedom of thought, conscience and religion; this right includes freedom to change his religion or belief, and freedom, either alone or in community with others and in public or private, to manifest his religion or belief in teaching, practice, worship and observance.

ARTICLE 19

Everyone has the right to freedom of opinion and expression; this right includes freedom to hold opinions without interference and to seek, receive and impart information and ideas through any media and regardless of frontiers.

ARTICLE 20

(1) Everyone has the right to freedom of peaceful assembly and association.
(2) No one may be compelled to belong to an association.

ARTICLE 21

(1) Everyone has the right to take part in the government of his country, directly or through freely chosen representatives.
(2) Everyone has the right of equal access to public service in his country.
(3) The will of the people shall be the basis of the authority of government; this will shall be expressed in periodic and genuine elections which shall be by universal and equal suffrage and shall be held by secret vote or by equivalent free voting procedures.

ARTICLE 22

Everyone, as a member of society, has the right to social security and is entitled to realization, through national effort and international co-operation and in accordance with the organization and resources of each State, of the economic, social and cultural rights indispensable for his dignity and the free development of his personality.

ARTICLE 23

(1) Everyone has the right to work, to free choice of employment, to just and favourable conditions of work and to protection against unemployment.
(2) Everyone, without any discrimination, has the right to equal pay for equal work.
(3) Everyone who works has the right to just and favourable remuneration ensuring for himself and his family an existence worthy of human dignity, and supplemented, if necessary, by other means of social protection.

(4) Everyone has the right to form and to join trade unions for the protection of his interests.

ARTICLE 24

Everyone has the right to rest and leisure, including reasonable limitation of working hours and periodic holidays with pay.

ARTICLE 25

(1) Everyone has the right to a standard of living adequate for the health and well-being of himself and of his family, including food, clothing, housing and medical care and necessary social services, and the right to security in the event of unemployment, sickness, disability, widowhood, old age or other lack of livelihood in circumstances beyond his control.

(2) Motherhood and childhood are entitled to special care and assistance. All children, whether born in or out of wedlock, shall enjoy the same social protection.

ARTICLE 26

(1) Everyone has the right to education. Education shall be free, at least in the elementary and fundamental stages. Elementary education shall be compulsory. Technical and professional education shall be made generally available and higher education shall be equally accessible to all on the basis of merit.

(2) Education shall be directed to the full development of the human personality and to the strengthening of respect for human rights and fundamental freedoms. It shall promote understanding, tolerance and friendship among all nations, racial or religious groups, and shall further the activities of the United Nations for the maintenance of peace.

(3) Parents have a prior right to choose the kind of education that shall be given to their children.

ARTICLE 27

(1) Everyone has the right freely to participate in the cultural life of the community, to enjoy the arts and to share in scientific advancement and its benefits.

(2) Everyone has the right to the protection of the moral and material interests resulting from any scientific, literary or artistic production of which he is the author.

ARTICLE 28

Everyone is entitled to a social and international order in which the rights and freedoms set forth in this Declaration can be fully realized.

ARTICLE 29

(1) Everyone has duties to the community in which alone the free and full development of his personality is possible.

(2) In the exercise of his rights and freedoms, everyone shall be subject only to such limitations as are determined by law solely for the purpose of securing due recognition and respect for the rights and freedoms of others and of meeting the just requirements of morality, public order and the general welfare in a democratic society.

(3) These rights and freedoms may in no case be exercised contrary to the purposes and principles of the United Nations.

ARTICLE 30

Nothing in this Declaration may be interpreted as implying for any State, group or person any right to engage in any activity or to perform any act aimed at the destruction of any of the rights and freedoms set forth herein.

MARTIN LUTHER KING JR

Martin Luther King Jr. (1929–1968), a Baptist minister and leader of the civil rights movement, wrote this letter in 1963, while serving a jail sentence for participating in a civil rights demonstration. King was awarded the Nobel Peace Prize in 1964. He was assassinated in 1968.

Letter from a Birmingham City Jail

My dear Fellow Clergymen,

While confined here in the Birmingham city jail, I came across your recent statement calling our present activities "unwise and untimely." Seldom, if ever, do I pause to answer criticism of my work and ideas. If I sought to answer all of the criticisms that cross my desk, my secretaries would be engaged in little else in the course of the day, and I would have no time for constructive work. But since I feel that you are men of genuine good will and your criticisms are sincerely set forth, I would like to answer your statement in what I hope will be patient and reasonable terms.

I think I should give the reason for my being in Birmingham, since you have been influenced by the argument of "outsiders coming in." I have the honor of serving as president of the Southern Christian Leadership Conference, an organization operating in every southern state, with headquarters in Atlanta, Georgia. We have some eighty-five affiliate organizations all across the South—one being the Alabama Christian Movement for Human Rights. Whenever necessary and possible we share staff, educational and financial resources with our affiliates. Several months ago our local affiliate here in Birmingham invited us to be on call to engage in a nonviolent direct-action program if such were deemed necessary. We readily consented and when the hour came we lived up to our promises. So I am here, along with several members of my staff, because we were invited here. I am here because I have basic organizational ties here.

Beyond this, I am in Birmingham because injustice is here. Just as the eighth century prophets left their little villages and carried their "thus saith the Lord" far beyond the boundaries of their hometowns; and just as the Apostle Paul left his little village of Tarsus and carried the gospel of Jesus Christ to practically every hamlet and city of the Graeco-Roman world, I too am compelled to carry the gospel of freedom beyond my particular hometown. Like Paul, I must constantly respond to the Macedonian call for aid.

Moreover, I am cognizant of the interrelatedness of all communities and states. I cannot sit idly by in Atlanta and not be concerned about what happens in Birmingham. Injustice anywhere is a threat to justice everywhere. We are caught in an inescapable network of mutuality, tied in a single

From *A Testament of Hope: The Essential Writings of Martin Luther King, Jr.*, edited by James M. Washington. Copyright © 1986 by Coretta Scott King, executrix of the estate of Martin Luther King, Jr. Reprinted by permission of Harper & Row, Publishers, Inc.

garment of destiny. Whatever affects one directly affects all indirectly. Never again can we afford to live with the narrow, provincial "outside agitator" idea. Anyone who lives in the United States can never be considered an outsider anywhere in this country.

You deplore the demonstrations that are presently taking place in Birmingham. But I am sorry that your statement did not express a similar concern for the conditions that brought the demonstrations into being. I am sure that each of you would want to go beyond the superficial social analyst who looks merely at effects, and does not grapple with underlying causes. I would not hesitate to say that it is unfortunate that so-called demonstrations are taking place in Birmingham at this time, but I would say in more emphatic terms that it is even more unfortunate that the white power structure of this city left the Negro community with no other alternative.

In any nonviolent campaign there are four basic steps: (1) collection of the facts to determine whether injustices are alive, (2) negotiation, (3) self-purification, and (4) direct action. We have gone through all of these steps in Birmingham. There can be no gain-saying of the fact that racial injustice engulfs this community.

Birmingham is probably the most thoroughly segregated city in the United States. Its ugly record of police brutality is known in every section of this country. Its unjust treatment of Negroes in the courts is a notorious reality. There have been more unsolved bombings of Negro homes and churches in Birmingham than any city in this nation. These are the hard, brutal and unbelievable facts. On the basis of these conditions Negro leaders sought to negotiate with the city fathers. But the political leaders consistently refused to engage in good faith negotiation.

Then came the opportunity last September to talk with some of the leaders of the economic community. In these negotiating sessions certain promises were made by the merchants—such as the promise to remove the humiliating racial signs from the stores. On the basis of these promises

Rev. Shuttlesworth and the leaders of the Alabama Christian Movement for Human Rights agreed to call a moratorium on any type of demonstrations. As the weeks and months unfolded we realized that we were the victims of a broken promise. The signs remained. Like so many experiences of the past we were confronted with blasted hopes, and the dark shadow of a deep disappointment settled upon us. So we had no alternative except that of preparing for direct action, whereby we would present our very bodies as a means of laying our case before the conscience of the local and national community. We were not unmindful of the difficulties involved. So we decided to go through a process of self-purification. We started having workshops on nonviolence and repeatedly asked ourselves the questions, "Are you able to accept blows without retaliating?" "Are you able to endure the ordeals of jail?" We decided to set our direct-action program around the Easter season, realizing that with the exception of Christmas, this was the largest shopping period of the year. Knowing that a strong economic withdrawal program would be the by-product of direct action, we felt that this was the best time to bring pressure on the merchants for the needed changes. Then it occurred to us that the March election was ahead and so we speedily decided to postpone action until after election day. When we discovered that Mr. Connor was in the run-off, we decided again to postpone action so that the demonstrations could not be used to cloud the issues. At this time we agreed to begin our nonviolent witness the day after the run-off.

This reveals that we did not move irresponsibly into direct action. We too wanted to see Mr. Connor defeated; so we went through postponement after postponement to aid in this community need. After this we felt that direct action could be delayed no longer.

You may well ask, "Why direct action? Why sitins, marches, etc.? Isn't negotiation a better path?" You are exactly right in your call for negotiation. Indeed, this is the purpose of direct action. Nonviolent direct action seeks to create such a crisis and establish such creative tension that a community that has constantly refused to negotiate is forced to confront the issue. It seeks so to dramatize the issue that it can no longer be ignored. I just referred to the creation of tension as a part of the work of the nonviolent resister. This may sound rather shocking. But I must confess that I am not afraid of the word tension. I have earnestly worked and preached against violent tension, but there is a type of constructive nonviolent tension that is necessary for growth. Just as Socrates felt that it was necessary to create a tension in the mind so that individuals could rise from the bondage of myths and half-truths to the unfettered realm of creative analysis and objective appraisal, we must see the need of having nonviolent gadflies to create the kind of tension in society that will help men to rise from the dark depths of prejudice and racism to the majestic heights of understanding and brotherhood. So the purpose of the direct action is to create a situation so crisis-packed that it will inevitably open the door to negotiation. We, therefore, concur with you in your call for negotiation. Too long has our beloved Southland been bogged down in the tragic attempt to live in monologue rather than dialogue.

One of the basic points in your statement is that our acts are untimely. Some have asked, "Why didn't you give the new administration time to act?" The only answer that I can give to this inquiry is that the new administration must be prodded about as much as the outgoing one before it acts. We will be sadly mistaken if we feel that the election of Mr. Boutwell will bring the millennium to Birmingham. While Mr. Boutwell is much more articulate and gentle than Mr. Connor, they are both segregationists, dedicated to the task of maintaining the status quo. The hope I see in Mr. Boutwell is that he will be reasonable enough to see the futility of massive resistance to desegregation. But he will not see this without pressure from the devotees of civil rights. My friends, I must say to you that we have not made a single gain in civil rights without determined legal and nonviolent pressure. History is the long and tragic story of the fact that privileged groups seldom give up their privileges voluntarily. Individuals may see the moral light and voluntarily give up their unjust posture; but as Reinhold Niebuhr has reminded us, groups are more immoral than individuals.

We know through painful experience that freedom is never voluntarily given by the oppressor; it must be demanded by the oppressed. Frankly, I have never yet engaged in a direct action movement that was "well-timed," according to the timetable of those who have not suffered unduly from the disease of segregation. For years now I have heard the words "Wait!" It rings in the ear of every Negro with a piercing familiarity. This "Wait" has almost always meant "Never." It has been a tranquilizing thalidomide, relieving the emotional stress for a moment, only to give birth to an ill-formed infant of frustration. We must come to see with the distinguished jurist of yesterday that "justice too long delayed is justice denied." We have waited for more than 340 years for our constitutional and God-given rights. The nations of Asia and Africa are moving with jetlike speed toward the goal of political independence, and we still creep at horse and buggy pace toward the gaining of a cup of coffee at the lunch counter. I guess it is easy for those who have never felt the stinging darts of segregation to say, "Wait." But when you have seen vicious mobs lynch your mothers and fathers at will and drown your sisters and brothers at whim; when you have seen hate-filled policemen curse, kick, brutalize and even kill your black brothers and sisters with impunity; when you see the vast majority of your twenty million Negro brothers smothering in an airtight cage of poverty in the midst of an affluent society; when you suddenly find your tongue twisted and your speech stammering as you seek to explain to your six-year-old daughter why she can't go to the public amusement park that has just been advertised on television, and see tears welling up in her little eyes when she is told that Funtown is closed to colored children, and see the depressing clouds of inferiority begin to form in her little mental sky, and see her begin to distort her little personality by unconsciously developing a bitterness toward white people; when you have to concoct an answer for a five-year-old son asking in agonizing pathos: "Daddy, why do white people treat colored people so mean?"; when you take a cross-country drive and find it necessary to sleep night after night in the uncomfortable corners of your automobile because no motel will accept you; when you are humiliated day in and day out by nagging signs reading "white" and "colored"; when your first name becomes "nigger" and your middle name becomes "boy" (however old you are) and your last name becomes "John," and when your wife and mother are never given the respected title "Mrs."; when you are harried by day and haunted by night by the fact that you are a Negro, living constantly at tiptoe stance never quite knowing what to expect next, and plagued with inner fears and outer resentments; when you are forever fighting a degenerating sense of "nobodiness"; then you will understand why we find it difficult to wait. There comes a time when the cup of endurance runs over, and men are no longer willing to be plunged into an abyss of injustice where they experience the blackness of corroding despair. I hope, sirs, you can understand our legitimate and unavoidable impatience.

You express a great deal of anxiety over our willingness to break laws. This is certainly a legitimate concern. Since we so diligently urge people to obey the Supreme Court's decision of 1954 outlawing segregation in the public schools, it is rather strange and paradoxical to find us consciously breaking laws. One may well ask, "How can you advocate breaking some laws and obeying others?" The answer is found in the fact that there are two types of laws: there are *just* and there are *unjust* laws. I would agree with Saint Augustine that "An unjust law is no law at all."

Now what is the difference between the two? How does one determine when a law is just or unjust? A just law is a man-made code that squares with the moral law or the law of God. An unjust law is a code that is out of harmony with the moral law. To put it in the terms of Saint Thomas Aquinas, an unjust law is a human law that is not rooted in eternal and natural law. Any law that uplifts human personality is just. Any law that degrades human personality is unjust. All segregation statutes are unjust because segregation distorts the soul and damages the personality. It gives the segregator a false sense of superiority, and the segregated a false sense of inferiority. To use the words of Martin Buber, the great Jewish philosopher, segregation substitutes an "I-it" relationship for the "I-thou" relationship, and ends up relegating persons to the status of things. So segregation is not only politically, economically and sociologically unsound, but it is morally wrong and sinful. Paul Tillich has said that sin is separation. Isn't segregation an existential expression of man's tragic separation, an expression of his awful estangement, his terrible sinfulness? So I can urge men to disobey segregation ordinances because they are morally wrong.

Let us turn to a more concrete example of just and unjust laws. An unjust law is a code that a majority inflicts on a minority that is not binding on itself. This is difference made legal. On the other hand a just law is a code that a majority compels a minority to follow that it is willing to follow itself. This is sameness made legal.

Let me give another explanation. An unjust law is a code inflicted upon a minority which that minority had no part in enacting or creating because they did not have the unhampered right to vote. Who can say that the legislature of Alabama which set up the segregation laws was democratically elected? Throughout the state of Alabama all types of conniving methods are used to prevent Negroes from becoming registered voters and there are some counties without a single Negro registered to vote despite the fact that the Negro constitutes a majority of the population. Can any law set up in such a state be considered democratically structured?

These are just a few examples of unjust and just laws. There are some instances when a law is just on its face and unjust in its application. For instance, I was arrested Friday on a charge of parading without permit. Now there is nothing wrong with an ordinance which requires a permit for a parade, but when the ordinance is used to preserve segregation and to deny citizens the First Amendment privilege of peaceful assembly and peaceful protest, then it becomes unjust.

I hope you can see the distinction I am trying to point out. In no sense do I advocate evading or defying the law as the rabid segregationist would do. This would lead to anarchy. One who breaks an unjust law must do it *openly, lovingly* (not hatefully as the white mothers did in New Orleans when they were seen on television screaming, "nigger, nigger, nigger"), and with a willingness to accept the penalty. I submit that an individual who breaks law that conscience tells him is unjust, and willingly accepts the penalty by staying in jail to arouse the conscience of the community over its injustice, is in reality expressing the very highest respect for law.

Of course, there is nothing new about this kind of civil disobedience. It was seen sublimely in the refusal of Shadrach, Meshach and Abednego to obey the laws of Nebuchadnezzar because a higher moral law was involved. It was practiced superbly by the early Christians who were willing to face hungry lions and the excruciating pain of chopping blocks, before submitting to certain unjust laws of the Roman Empire. To a degree academic freedom is a reality today because Socrates practiced civil disobedience.

We can never forget that everything Hitler did in Germany was "legal" and everything the Hungarian freedom fighters did in Hungary was "illegal." It was "illegal" to aid and comfort a Jew in Hitler's Germany. But I am sure that if I had lived in Germany during that time I would have aided and comforted my Jewish brothers even though it was illegal. If I lived in a Communist country today where certain principles dear to the Christian faith are suppressed, I believe I would openly advocate disobeying these anti-religious laws. I must make two honest confessions to you, my Christian and Jewish brothers. First, I must

confess that over the last few years I have been gravely disappointed with the white moderate. I have almost reached the regrettable conclusion that the Negro's great stumbling block in the stride toward freedom is not the White Citizen's Counciler or the Ku Klux Klanner, but the white moderate who is more devoted to "order" than to justice; who prefers a negative peace which is the absence of tension to a positive peace which is the presence of justice; who constantly says, "I agree with you in the goal you seek, but I can't agree with your methods of direct action"; who paternalistically feels that he can set the timetable for another man's freedom; who lives by the myth of time and who constantly advised the Negro to wait until a "more convenient season." Shallow understanding from people of good will is more frustrating than absolute misunderstanding from people of ill will. Lukewarm acceptance is much more bewildering than outright rejection.

I had hoped that the white moderate would understand that law and order exist for the purpose of establishing justice, and that when they fail to do this they become dangerously structured dams that block the flow of social progress. I had hoped that the white moderate would understand that the present tension of the South is merely a necessary phase of the transition from an obnoxious negative peace, where the Negro passively accepted his unjust plight, to a substance-filled positive peace, where all men will respect the dignity and worth of human personality. Actually, we who engage in nonviolent direct action are not the creators of tension. We merely bring to the surface the hidden tension that is already alive. We bring it out in the open where it can be seen and dealt with. Like a boil that can never be cured as long as it is covered up but must be opened with all its pus-flowing ugliness to the natural medicines of air and light, injustice must likewise be exposed, with all of the tension its exposing creates, to the light of human conscience and the air of national opinion before it can be cured.

In your statement you asserted that our actions, even though peaceful, must be condemned because they precipitate violence. But can this assertion be logically made? Isn't this like condemning the robbed man because his possession of money precipitated the evil act of robbery? Isn't this like condemning Socrates because his unswerving commitment to truth and his philosophical delvings precipitated the misguided popular mind to make him drink the hemlock? Isn't this like condemning Jesus because His unique God-consciousness and never-ceasing devotion to his will precipitated the evil act of crucifixion? We must come to see, as federal courts have consistently affirmed, that it is immoral to urge an individual to withdraw his efforts to gain his basic constitutional rights because the quest precipitates violence. Society must protect the robbed and punish the robber.

I had also hoped that the white moderate would reject the myth of time. I received a letter this morning from a white brother in Texas which said: "All Christians know that the colored people will receive equal rights eventually, but it is possible that you are in too great of a religious hurry. It has taken Christianity almost two thousand years to accomplish what it has. The teachings of Christ take time to come to earth." All that is said here grows out of a tragic misconception of time. It is the strangely irrational notion that there is something in the very flow of time that will inevitably cure all ills. Actually time is neutral. It can be used either destructively or constructively. I am coming to feel that the people of ill will have used time much more effectively than the people of good will. We will have to repent in this generation not merely for the vitriolic words and actions of the bad people, but for the appalling silence of the good people. We must come to see that human progress never rolls in on wheels of inevitability. It comes through the tireless efforts and persistent work of men willing to be co-workers with God, and without this hard work time itself becomes an ally of the forces of social stagnation. We must use time creatively, and forever realize that the time is always ripe to do right. Now is the time to make real the promise of democracy, and transform our pending national elegy into a creative psalm of brotherhood. Now is the time to lift our national policy from the quicksand of racial injustice to the solid rock of human dignity.

You spoke of our activity in Birmingham as extreme. At first I was rather disappointed that fellow clergymen would see my nonviolent efforts as those of the extremist. I started thinking about the fact that I stand in the middle of two opposing forces in the Negro community. One is a force of complacency made up of Negroes who, as a result of long years of oppression, have been so completely drained of self-respect and a sense of "somebodiness" that they have adjusted to segregation, and, of a few Negroes in the middle class who, because of a degree of academic and economic security, and because at points they profit by segregation, have unconsciously become insensitive to the problems of the masses. The other force is one of bitterness and hatred, and comes perilously close to advocating violence. It is expressed in the various black nationalist groups that are springing up over the nation, the largest and best known being Elijah Muhammad's Muslim movement. This movement is nourished by the contemporary frustration over the continued existence of racial discrimination. It is made up of people who have lost faith in America, who have absolutely repudiated Christianity, and who have concluded that the white man is an incurable "devil." I have tried to stand between these two forces, saying that we need not follow the "donothingism" of the complacent or the hatred and despair of the black nationalist. There is the more excellent way of love and nonviolent protest. I'm grateful to God that, through the Negro church, the dimension of nonviolence entered our struggle. If this philosophy had not emerged, I am convinced that by now many streets of the South would be flowing with floods of blood. And I am further convinced that if our white brothers dismiss as "rabble-rousers" and "outside agitators" those of us who are working through the channels of nonviolent direct action and refuse to support our nonviolent efforts, millions of Negroes, out of frustration and despair, will seek solace and security in black nationalist ideologies, a development that will lead inevitably to a frightening racial nightmare.

Oppressed people cannot remain oppressed forever. The urge for freedom will eventually come. This is what happened to the American Negro. Something within has reminded him of his birth-right of freedom; something without has reminded him that he can gain it. Consciously and unconsciously, he has been swept in by what the Germans call the *Zeitgeist*, and with his black brothers of Africa, and his brown and yellow brothers of Asia, South America and the Caribbean, he is moving with a sense of cosmic urgency toward the promised land of racial justice. Recognizing this vital urge that has engulfed the Negro community, one should readily understand public demonstrations. The Negro has many pent-up resentments and latent frustrations. He has to get them out. So let him march sometime; let him have his prayer pilgrimages to the city hall; understand why he must have sit-ins and freedom rides. If his repressed emotions do not come out in these nonviolent ways, they will come out in ominous expressions of violence. This is not a threat; it is a fact of history. So I have not said to my people "get rid of your discontent." But I have tried to say that this normal and healthy discontent can be channelized through the creative outlet of nonviolent direct action. Now this approach is being dismissed as extremist. I must admit that I was initially disappointed in being so categorized.

But as I continued to think about the matter I gradually gained a bit of satisfaction from being considered an extremist. Was not Jesus an extremist in love—"Love your enemies, bless them that curse you, pray for them that despitefully use you." Was not Amos an extremist for justice—"Let justice roll down like waters and righteousness like a mighty stream." Was not Paul an extremist for the gospel of Jesus Christ—"I bear in my body the marks of the Lord Jesus." Was not Martin Luther an extremist—"Here I stand; I can do none other so help me God." Was not John Bunyan an extremist—"I will stay in jail to the end of my days before I make a butchery of my conscience." Was not Abraham Lincoln an extremist—"This nation cannot survive half slave and half free." Was not Thomas Jefferson an extremist—"We hold these truths to be self-evident, that all men are created equal." So the question is not whether we will be extremist but what kind of extremist will we be. Will we be extremists for hate or will we be extremists for love? Will we be extremists for the preservation of injustice—or will we be extremists for the cause of justice? In that dramatic scene on Calvary's hill, three men were crucified. We must not forget that all three were crucified for the same crime—the crime of extremism. Two were extremists for immorality, and thusly fell below their environment. The other, Jesus Christ, was an extremist for love, truth and goodness, and thereby rose above his environment. So, after all, maybe the South, the nation and the world are in dire need of creative extremists.

I had hoped that the white moderate would see this. Maybe I was too optimistic. Maybe I expected too much. I guess I should have realized that few members of a race that has oppressed another race can understand or appreciate the deep groans and passionate yearnings of those that have been oppressed and still fewer have the vision to see that injustice must be rooted out by strong, persistent and determined action. I am thankful, however, that some of our white brothers have grasped the meaning of this social revolution and committed themselves to it. They are still all too small in quantity, but they are big in quality. Some like Ralph McGill, Lillian Smith, Harry Golden and James Dabbs have written about our struggle in eloquent, prophetic and understanding terms. Others have marched with us down nameless streets of the South. They have languished in filthy roach-infested jails, suffering the abuse and brutality of angry policemen who see them as "dirty nigger-lovers." They, unlike so many of their moderate brothers and sisters, have recognized the urgency of the moment and sensed the need for powerful "action" antidotes to combat the disease of segregation.

Let me rush on to mention my other disappointment. I have been so greatly disappointed with the white church and its leadership. Of course, there are some notable exceptions. I am not unmindful of the fact that each of you has taken some significant stands on this issue. I commend you, Rev. Stallings, for your Christian stance on this past Sunday, in welcoming Negroes to your worship service on a non-segregated basis. I commend the Catholic leaders of this state for integrating Springhill College several years ago.

But despite these notable exceptions I must honestly reiterate that I have been disappointed with the church. I do not say that as one of the negative critics who can always find something wrong with the church. I say it as a minister of the gospel, who loves the church; who was nurtured in its bosom; who has been sustained by its spiritual blessings and who will remain true to it as long as the cord of life shall lengthen.

I had the strange feeling when I was suddenly catapulted into the leadership of the bus protest in Montgomery several years ago that we would have the support of the white church. I felt that the white ministers, priests and rabbis of the South would be some of our strongest allies. Instead, some have been outright opponents, refusing to understand the freedom movement and misrepresenting its leaders; all too many others have been more cautious than courageous and have remained silent behind the anesthetizing security of the stained-glass windows.

In spite of my shattered dreams of the past, I came to Birmingham with the hope that the white religious leadership of this community would see the justice of our cause, and with deep moral concern, serve as the channel through which our just grievances would get to the power structure. I had hoped that each of you would understand. But again I have been disappointed. I have heard numerous religious leaders of the South call upon their worshippers to comply with a desegregation decision because it is the *law*, but I have longed to hear white ministers say, "Follow this decree because integration is morally *right* and the Negro is your brother." In the midst of blatant injustices

inflicted upon the Negro, I have watched white churches stand on the sideline and merely mouth pious irrelevancies and sanctimonious trivialities. In the midst of a mighty struggle to rid our nation of racial and economic injustice, I have heard so many ministers say, "Those are social issues with which the gospel has no real concern," and I have watched so many churches commit themselves to a completely otherworldly religion which made a strange distinction between body and soul, the sacred and the secular.

So here we are moving toward the exit of the twentieth century with a religious community largely adjusted to the status quo, standing as a taillight behind other community agencies rather than a headlight leading men to higher levels of justice.

I have traveled the length and breadth of Alabama, Mississippi and all the other southern states. On sweltering summer days and crisp autumn mornings I have looked at her beautiful churches with their lofty spires pointing heavenward. I have beheld the impressive outlay of her massive religious education buildings. Over and over again I have found myself asking: "What kind of people worship here? Who is their God? Where were their voices when the lips of Governor Barnett dripped with words of interposition and nullification? Where were they when Governor Wallace gave the clarion call for defiance and hatred? Where were their voices of support when tired, bruised and weary Negro men and women decided to rise from the dark dungeons of complacency to the bright hills of creative protest?"

Yes, these questions are still in my mind. In deep disappointment, I have wept over the laxity of the church. But be assured that my tears have been tears of love. There can be no deep disappointment where there is not deep love. Yes, I love the church; I love her sacred walls. How could I do otherwise? I am in a rather unique position of being the son, the grandson and the great-grandson of preachers. Yes, I see the church as the body of Christ. But, oh! How we have blemished and scarred that body through social neglect and fear of being nonconformists.

There was a time when the church was very powerful. It was during that period when the early Christians rejoiced when they were deemed worthy to suffer for what they believed. In those days the church was not merely a thermometer that recorded the ideas and principles of popular opinion; it was a thermostat that transformed the mores of society. Wherever the early Christians entered a town the power structure got disturbed and immediately sought to convict them for being "disturbers of the peace" and "outside agitators." But they went on with the conviction that they were "a colony of heaven," and had to obey God rather than man. They were small in number but big in commitment. They were too God-intoxicated to be "astronomically intimidated." They brought an end to such ancient evils as infanticide and gladiatorial contest.

Things are different now. The contemporary church is often a weak, ineffectual voice with an uncertain sound. It is so often the arch-supporter of the status quo. Far from being disturbed by the presence of the church, the power structure of the average community is consoled by the church's silent and often vocal sanction of things as they are.

But the judgment of God is upon the church as never before. If the church of today does not recapture the sacrificial spirit of the early church, it will lose its authentic ring, forfeit the loyalty of millions, and be dismissed as an irrelevant social club with no meaning for the twentieth century. I am meeting young people every day whose disappointment with the church has risen to outright disgust.

Maybe again, I have been too optimistic. Is organized religion too inextricably bound to the status quo to save our nation and the world? Maybe I must turn my faith to the inner spiritual church, the church within the church, as the true *ecclesia* and the hope of the world. But again I am thankful to God that some noble souls from the ranks of organized religion have broken loose from the paralyzing chains of conformity and joined us as active partners in the struggle for freedom. They have left their secure congregations and walked the streets of Albany, Georgia, with us. They have gone through the highways of the South on tortuous rides for freedom. Yes, they have gone to jail with us. Some have been kicked out of their churches, and lost support of their bishops and fellow ministers. But they have gone with the faith that right defeated is stronger than evil triumphant. These men have been the leaven in the lump of the race. Their witness has been the spiritual salt that has preserved the true meaning of the gospel in these troubled times. They have carved a tunnel of hope through the dark mountain of disappointment.

I hope the church as a whole will meet the challenge of this decisive hour. But even if the church does not come to the aid of justice, I have no despair about the future. I have no fear about the outcome of our struggle in Birmingham, even if our motives are presently misunderstood. We will reach the goal of freedom in Birmingham and all over the nation, because the goal of America is freedom. Abused and scorned though we may be, our destiny is tied up with the destiny of America. Before the Pilgrims landed at Plymouth we were here. Before the pen of Jefferson etched across the pages of history the majestic words of the Declaration of Independence, we were here. For more than two centuries our foreparents labored in this country without wages; they made cotton king; and they built the homes of their masters in the midst of brutal injustice and shameful humiliation—and yet out of a bottomless vitality they continued to thrive and develop. If the inexpressible cruelities of slavery could not stop us, the opposition we now face will surely fail. We will win our freedom because the sacred heritage of our nation and the eternal will of God are embodied in our echoing demands.

I must close now. But before closing I am impelled to mention one other point in your statement that troubled me profoundly. You warmly commended the Birmingham police force for keeping "order" and "preventing violence." I don't believe you would have so warmly commended the police force if you had seen its angry violent dogs literally biting six unarmed, nonviolent Negroes.

I don't believe you would so quickly commend the policemen if you would observe their ugly and inhuman treatment of Negroes here in the city jail; if you would watch them push and curse old Negro women and young Negro girls; if you would see them slap and kick old Negro men and young boys; if you will observe them, as they did on two occasions, refuse to give us food because we wanted to sing our grace together. I'm sorry that I can't join you in your praise for the police department.

It is true that they have been rather disciplined in their public handling of the demonstrators. In this sense they have been rather publicly "nonviolent." But for what purpose? To preserve the evil system of segregation. Over the last few years I have consistently preached that nonviolence demands that the means we use must be as pure as the ends we seek. So I have tried to make it clear that it is wrong to use immoral means to attain moral ends. But now I must affirm that it is just as wrong, or even more so, to use moral means to preserve immoral ends. Maybe Mr. Connor and his policemen have been rather publicly nonviolent, as Chief Pritchett was in Albany, Georgia, but they have used the moral means of nonviolence to maintain the immoral end of flagrant racial injustice. T. S. Eliot has said that there is no greater treason than to do the right deed for the wrong reason.

I wish you had commended the Negro sit-inners and demonstrators of Birmingham for their sublime courage, their willingness to suffer and their amazing discipline in the midst of the most inhuman provocation. One day the South will recognize its real heroes. They will be the James Merediths, courageously and with a majestic sense of purpose facing jeering and hostile mobs and the agonizing loneliness that characterizes the life of the pioneer. They will be old, oppressed, battered Negro women, symbolized in a seventy-two-year-old woman of Montgomery, Alabama, who rose up with a sense of dignity and with her people decided not to ride the segregated buses, and responded to one who inquired about her tiredness with ungrammatical profundity: "My feet is tired, but my soul is rested." They will be the young high school and college students, young ministers of the gospel and a host of their elders courageously and nonviolently sitting-in at lunch counters and willingly going to jail for conscience's sake. One day the South will know that when these disinherited children of God sat down at lunch counters they were in reality standing up for the best in the American dream and the most sacred values in our Judeo-Christian heritage, and thusly, carrying our whole nation back to those great walls of democracy which were dug deep by the Founding Fathers in the formulation of the Constitution and the Declaration of Independence.

Never before have I written a letter this long (or should I say a book?). I'm afraid that it is much too long to take your precious time. I can assure you that it would have been much shorter if I had been writing from a comfortable desk, but what else is there to do when you are alone for days in the dull monotony of a narrow jail cell other than write long letters, think strange thoughts, and pray long prayers?

If I have said anything in this letter that is an overstatement of the truth and is indicative of an unreasonable impatience, I beg you to forgive me. If I have said anything in this letter that is an understatement of the truth and is indicative of my having a patience that makes me patient with anything less than brotherhood, I beg God to forgive me.

I hope this letter finds you strong in the faith. I also hope that circumstances will soon make it possible for me to meet each of you, not as an integrationist or a civil rights leader, but as a fellow clergyman and a Christian brother. Let us all hope that the dark clouds of racial prejudice will soon pass away and the deep fog of misunderstanding will be lifted from our fear-drenched communities and in some not too distant tomorrow the radiant stars of love and brotherhood will shine over our great nation with all of their scintillating beauty.

Yours for the cause of Peace and Brotherhood,
Martin Luther King, Jr.